KU-387-265

THE

WRITER'S
HANDBOOK
2002

Barry Turner has worked on both sides of publishing, as an editor and marketing director and as an author. He started his career as a journalist with *The Observer* before moving on to television and radio. He has written over twenty books including *A Place in the Country*, which inspired a television series, and a best selling biography of the actor, Richard Burton.

His recent work includes a radio play, travel articles, serialising books for *The Times*, editing the magazine *Country* and writing a one-man show based on the life of the legendary theatre critic, James Agate. This is his fifteenth year as editor of *The Writer's Handbook* and his fourth as editor of *The Statesman's Yearbook*.

THE
CREATIVE
WRITING
COURSEBOOK

Edited by JULIA BELL & PAUL MAGRS
from the University of East Anglia
Foreword by ANDREW MOTION

Forty Authors Share Advice and Exercises for Fiction and Poetry

A comprehensive guide to improving your creative writing

Edited by Julia Bell and Paul Magrs, teachers at UEA – universally acknowledged to be one of the best places in the world for the teaching of creative writing – this book takes aspiring writers through the key stages of practice, from gathering material to shaping and finishing.

Throughout the book, exercises and activities encourage writers to develop their skills, with the contributors providing a unique and generous pool of information as they share experience and expertise.

The contributors include the late Malcolm Bradbury, Russell Celyn Jones, Patricia Duncker, Nell Dunn, Vicki Feaver, Maureen Freely, Lesley Glaister and David Lodge, among others.

£14.99   Paperback   400 pages   Macmillan

Available from bookshops, or order from
Macmillan Direct on 01256 302699

THE
WRITER'S HANDBOOK
2002

EDITOR

BARRY TURNER

MACMILLAN

First published 1988
This edition published 2001 by
Macmillan
an imprint of Pan Macmillan Ltd
Pan Macmillan, 20 New Wharf Road,
London N1 9RR
Basingstoke and Oxford
Associated companies throughout the world
www.panmacmillan.com

Copyright © 2001 Macmillan Publishers Ltd

All rights reserved. No reproduction, copy or transmission of this publication may
be made without written permission. No paragraph of this publication may be
reproduced, copied or transmitted save with written permission or in accordance
with the provisions of the Copyright, Designs and Patents Act 1988, or under the terms
of any licence permitting limited copying issued by the Copyright Licensing Agency,
90 Tottenham Court Road, London W1P 9HE. Any person who does any
unauthorised act in relation to this publication may be liable to criminal
prosecution and civil claims for damages.

9 8 7 6 5 4 3 2 1

A CIP catalogue record for this book is available from the British Library

ISBN 0 333 905636

Credits

Publisher *Morven Knowles*
Editor *Barry Turner*
Editorial Assistant *Jill Fenner*
Poetry Editor *Peter Finch*
Contributors *Bob G Ritchie*
　　　　　　Gareth Shannon
　　　　　　David Hooper
Tax and Finance Adviser *Ian Spring*
Production *Lee Bekker*

Typeset by Heronwood Press, Medstead, Hants
Printed and bound in Great Britain by Mackays of Chatham plc, Kent

Contents

Learning by Experience

The Writer's Handbook is in its fifteenth edition. Barry Turner looks back on the teenage years.

Optimism ran high in the first edition of *The Writer's Handbook*. Fifteen years ago 'the aspiring author had everything to play for', or so we believed. And with good reason. A refreshing wind of change was blowing across the market place. Better-produced books at affordable prices were being sold more energetically in ever greater numbers. And there was plenty of money around to invest in new talent. Takeover mania, some fifty buy-ups of old established names in less than two years, often achieved at spectacular prices, caused jitters among writers who feared the loss of the cosy editorial chat favoured by the smaller houses. But publication by a conglomerate had its compensations, not least the sales muscle to propel a title into the bestseller lists.

Beyond the book world, the media outlook was no less rosy. We were promised more newspapers and magazines, more hours of television and radio, more of everything. And this had to mean more opportunities for writers.

Well, up to a point. There were contradictory forces that went largely undetected in the mid-eighties. Maybe we should have known that Kingsley Amis was right when he famously argued that 'more means worse'. Instead, *The Writer's Handbook* along with other observers of the literary scene, chose the sanguine view that 'more simply means more, neither better nor worse'. We then stood back in dismay as standards plummeted.

On television, the dedication to pushing audience figures up and costs down led to a plethora of chat shows and panel games and the near disappearance of modern drama. Writers who did best from the multiplicity of channels were adapters of costume classics and the creators of long-running situation comedies and police series. On radio, the expansion of airtime was filled by news, endlessly repeated, with inconsequential discussion. ('Well John, at the end of the day . . .') Movies went for monosyllabic action – audiences were said to get impatient with a script that had a lot of words – while the press favoured bigger headlines and more pictures.

Books were different, as the publishers never ceased to remind us. Every year the output of titles edged upwards so that by the mid-nineties it touched 100,000. But this achievement masked changes in publishing that made life harder for some writers and for newcomers in general. Creeping Americanisation – nowadays we would call it globalisation – was the single biggest influence on publishing economics. Nearly all the conglomerates were transatlantic companies either controlled from New York or with powerful American subsidiaries. Increasingly, a sellable book in the UK meant a book that would also do well in the US. Shrewd writers adapted their style accordingly. At the same time, buying in from the US was a soft option for publishers who paid modestly for titles that had already earned their keep in Barnes and Noble. Of the new titles appearing each year in the UK, at least 15,000 were American imports. The chief impact was on fiction. Claims that we were turning out more novels every year were misleading. Once reprints and American authors were crossed off, output was shown to have changed little in forty years.

It wasn't all bad news. Brave new publishers appeared on the scene. Hodder Headline, Bloomsbury and Orion quickly made their mark but others (Carcanet, Fourth Estate, Granta, Canongate, Serpent's Tail, The X Press) less well known in the general market, were discovering original and exciting talents. The new technology (new then, old-fashioned now) so simplified the printing of books that anyone with modest capital could set up as a publisher. In 1995, Whitakers listed no less than 25,000 small publishers. Most were one-man, indeed, one-book affairs with little prospect of being anything else, but the fact that they were there at all suggested a creative energy that promised well.

Encouraging also was the steady increase in the volume of books sold. The lift-off titles were rarely from the literary establishment but the fact that a screen-obsessed public was ready, even eager, to read was encouraging. Those who lost out were the middle-range authors, those who could list a few titles which earned more on Public Lending Rights than on retail. No one wanted to know them, not the big boys who were obsessed by megasellers nor the newcomers who were looking for fresh talent.

The cries of outrage by the dispossessed were drowned out by the roar of unbridled commerce. Authors with a place on the inside track discovered that book sales were only part of their good fortune. As the century came to an end the book, more than ever before, was the starter for every other medium. Books could be serialised for newspapers, adapted for television, read on radio, made into movies, themed for merchandising and filleted for computer games. The book was the easiest and cheapest way of starting a trend. If the punters took to a book they would take to anything. Publishers and agents became overnight experts in subsidiary rights.

The economics of writing was set to become yet more complex. After the joys of the mobile telephone (fancy being able to spend a journey chatting about cover designs with your editor) came the orgasmic pleasures of the Internet. Suddenly, any writer could find readers, if only former train spotters. But making money from the Net was another matter, as Stephen King and other author entrepreneurs soon discovered. This is not to say that a money-making formula will not be found. It is early days. HarperCollins has just launched the first e-book list. Already we have updates of technical and reference books on Web pages, electronic journals are multiplying and we are well into the age of print-on-demand with books transmitted online and printed when, where and in whatever quantities they are needed. Can it be long before a choice of books on a handy portable screen becomes the commuter's companion?

And best of all, as yet no one has conceived of a way of cutting out the writer. Technology will get ever more surreal but in so far as it depends on words, somebody has to write them. Those with the necessary creative skills have everything going for them. But where have we heard that story before?

UK Publishers

Abacus
See **Little, Brown & Co (UK)**

ABC–Clio Ltd
Old Clarendon Ironworks, 35a Great
Clarendon Street, Oxford OX2 6AT
☎01865 311350 Fax 01865 311358
Email oxford@abc-clio.ltd.uk
Website www.abc-clio.com
Managing Director *Tony Sloggett*
Editorial Director *Dr Robert G. Neville*

Formerly Clio Press Ltd. *Publishes* academic and
general reference works, social sciences and
humanities. Markets, outside North America,
the Web, CD-ROM publications and reference books of the American parent company.
SERIES *World Bibliographical; Clio Montessori.*
   Royalties paid twice-yearly.

Abington Publishing
See **Woodhead Publishing Ltd**

Absolute Classics
See **Oberon Books**

Absolute Press
Scarborough House, 29 James Street West,
Bath BA1 2BT
☎01225 316013 Fax 01225 445836
Email sales@absolutepress.demon.co.uk
Website www.absolutepress.demon.co.uk
Managing/Editorial Director *Jon Croft*

FOUNDED 1979. *Publishes* food and wine-
related subjects as well as travel guides and the
Streetwise Maps series of city maps. About 10
titles a year. *Outlines*, launched in 1997, is a
series of monographs on gay and lesbian creative artists. In 2001 a new gay travel series,
Gay Times Travel Guides, was launched, co-
published with *Gay Times*. No unsolicited mss.
Synopses and ideas for books welcome.
   Royalties paid twice-yearly.

Abson Books London
5 Sidney Square, London E1 2EY
☎020 7790 4737 Fax 020 7790 7346
Email absonbooks@aol.com
Chairman *M.J. Ellison*

FOUNDED 1971 in Bristol. *Publishes* language

glossaries and curiosities. No unsolicited mss;
synopses and ideas for books welcome.
   Royalties paid twice-yearly.

Academy Group Ltd
John Wiley & Sons, 4th Floor, International
House, 7 High Street, Ealing Broadway,
London W5 5DB
☎020 8326 3800 Fax 020 8326 3801
Chairman *John Jarvis*
Commissioning Editor *Maggie Toy*
Approx. Annual Turnover £2 million

FOUNDED 1969. Became part of John Wiley &
Sons, Inc. group in 1997. *Publishes* architecture
and design. Welcomes unsolicited mss, synopses and ideas.
   Royalties paid annually.

Acair Ltd
Unit 7, 7 James Street, Stornoway, Isle of
Lewis, Scotland HS1 2QN
☎01851 703020 Fax 01851 703294
Email acair@sol.co.uk

Specialising in matters pertaining to the
Gaidhealtachd, Acair publishes books in Gaelic
and English on Scottish history, culture and the
Gaelic language. 75% of their children's books
are targeted at primary school usage and are
published exclusively in Gaelic.
   Royalties paid twice-yearly.

Actinic Press
See **Cressrelles Publishing Co. Ltd**

Acumen Publishing Limited
15A Lewins Yard, East Street, Chesham,
Buckinghamshire HP5 1HQ
☎01494 794398 Fax 01494 784850
Email steven.gerrard@acumenpublishing.co.uk
Website www.acumenpublishing.co.uk
Managing Director *Steven Gerrard*

FOUNDED in 1998 as an independent publisher
for the higher education market. *Publishes*
academic books on philosophy, history and
politics. 6 titles in 2000. No unsolicited mss.
Synopses and ideas for books welcome; send
written proposal as per Acumen guidelines.
   Royalties paid annually.

Addison Wesley Longman
See **Pearson Education**

Adelphi
See **David Campbell Publishers Ltd**

Adlard Coles Nautical
See **A.&C. Black (Publishers) Ltd**

African Books Collective
The Jam Factory, 27 Park End Street, Oxford
OX1 1HU
☎01865 726686 Fax 01865 793298
Email abc@dial.pipex.com
Website www.africanbookscollective.com

FOUNDED 1990. Collectively owned by its 17
founder member publishers. Exclusive distribution in N. America, UK, Europe and
Commonwealth countries outside Africa for 54
African participating publishers. Concentration is
on scholarly/academic, literature and children's
books. Mainly concerned with the promotion
and dissemination of African-published material
outside Africa. Supplies African-published books
to African libraries and organisations and *publishes*
resource books on African publishing. TITLES
African Writers' Handbook; *African Publishers
Networking Directory*; *Women in Publishing and the
Book Trade in Africa*.

Age Concern Books
1268 London Road, London SW16 4ER
☎020 8765 7200 Fax 020 8765 7211
Email books@ace.org.uk
Website www.ageconcern.org.uk
Approx. Annual Turnover £400,000

Publishing arm of Age Concern England.
Publishes related non-fiction only. No fiction.
About 18 titles a year. Unsolicited mss, synopses and ideas welcome for new practical
handbooks.

Airlife Publishing Ltd
101 Longden Road, Shrewsbury, Shropshire
SY3 9EB
☎01743 235651 Fax 01743 232944
Email airlife@airlifebooks.com
Website www.airlifebooks.com
Editorial Head *Peter Coles*
Approx. Annual Turnover £3 million

IMPRINTS **Airlife** Specialist aviation titles for
pilots, historians and enthusiasts. Also twentieth
century naval and military history. About 70
titles a year. TITLES *Airlife's World Aircraft; John
'Cat's Eyes' Cunningham; U-boat Tankers; Pilot's
Weather.* **Swan Hill Press** Natural history,
environmental studies, countryside pursuits,
marine and wildlife art. About 35 titles a year.
TITLES *Deer of Britain and Ireland; Geology of
Britain; World of Weather; A Cloud of Sail.*
  Unsolicited mss, synopses and ideas for
books welcome.
  Royalties paid annually; twice-yearly by
arrangement.

Ian Allan Publishing Ltd
Riverdene Business Park, Molesey Road,
Hersham, Surrey KT12 4RG
☎01932 266600 Fax 01932 266601
Email info@ianallanpub.co.uk
Website www.ianallanpub.co.uk
Chairman *David Allan*
Managing Director *Tony Saunders*

Specialist transport publisher – atlases, maps,
railway, aviation, road transport, military, maritime, reference. About 80 titles a year. Send
sample chapter and synopsis with s.a.e. Manages
distribution and sales for third party publishers.
  IMPRINTS **Dial House** Sporting titles;
Midland Publishing (see entry); **OPC**
Railway titles.

J.A. Allen & Co.
An imprint of Robert Hale Ltd, Clerkenwell
House, 45–47 Clerkenwell Green, London
EC1R 0HT
☎020 7251 2661 Fax 020 7490 4958
Email allen@halebooks.com
Publisher *Caroline Burt*
Approx. Annual Turnover £750,000

FOUNDED 1926 as part of J.A. Allen & Co.
(The Horseman's Bookshop) Ltd. Bought by
Robert Hale Ltd in 1999. *Publishes* equine
and equestrian non-fiction. About 20 titles a
year. Mostly commissioned but willing to consider unsolicited mss of technical/instructional
material related to all aspects of horses and
horsemanship.
  Royalties paid twice-yearly.

Allen Lane
See **Penguin UK**

Allison & Busby
Suite 111, Bon Marche Centre, 241 Ferndale
Road, London SW9 8BJ
☎020 7738 7888 Fax 020 7733 4244
Email all@allisonbusby.co.uk
Website www.allisonandbusby.co.uk
Publishing Director *David Shelley*

FOUNDED 1967. *Publishes* literary fiction, crime
fiction, biography and writers' guides. About 40

titles a year. TITLES *Chang & Eng* Darin Strauss; *Get Carter* Ted Lewis; *The Internet Writer's Handbook 2001/2* Karen Scott. Send synopses with two sample chapters, not full mss. No replies without s.a.e.

Authors' Rating With one of the youngest publishing directors in the business (David Shelley is in his mid-20s), the reborn A&B is concentrating on fiction with a youth bias. The *Internet Writer's Handbook* is no relation.

Amber Lane Press Ltd
Cheorl House, Church Street, Charlbury, Oxfordshire OX7 3PR
☎01608 810024 Fax 01608 810024
Email jamberlane@aol.com
Chairman *Brian Clark*
Managing Director/Editorial Head *Judith Scott*

FOUNDED 1979 to publish modern play texts. *Publishes* plays and books on the theatre. About 4 titles a year. TITLES *Oroonoko* 'Biyi Bandele; *Sand Castles* Bob Larbey; *Disposing of the Body* Hugh Whitemore (play texts); *Theatre in a Cool Climate* Vera Gottlieb and Colin Chambers. 'Expressly *not* interested in poetry.' No unsolicited mss. Synopses and ideas welcome.
Royalties paid twice-yearly.

AMCD (Publishers) Ltd
PO Box 182, Altrincham, Cheshire WA15 9UA
☎0161 434 5105 Fax 0161 434 5105
Email j.s.adams@talk21.com
Website www.amcd.co.uk
Managing Director *John Stewart Adams*

FOUNDED 1988. *Publishes* financial directories, books on China, local history, business books and foreign language dictionaries. Took over the Jensen Business Books imprint in 1993 and is well placed in electronic reference after developing its own software. In conjunction with JHC (Technology) Ltd, AMCD offers publishers access to the electronic book market with their reference, dictionary and directory Pop-Up© software packages which can handle most languages. About 5 titles a year. TITLES *Deregulation of the Gold Market in China; Financial Dictionaries – Chinese, Japanese, Russian, Spanish, French; Around Haunted Croydon; Buying and Selling a Shop; Depression Challenges; Handguide to the Placenames of Alderley Edge*. Ideas for business books, children's books and books on European history, China or the Far East welcome in synopsis form (no mss). No poetry, fiction or historical romance. Final mss must be on disk.
Royalties paid twice yearly.

Amsco
See **Omnibus Press**

Andersen Press Ltd
20 Vauxhall Bridge Road, London SW1V 2SA
☎020 7870 8703/8700 Fax 020 7233 6263
Email andersenpress@randomhouse.co.uk
Website www.andersenpress.co.uk
Managing Director/Publisher *Klaus Flugge*
Editorial Director *Janice Thomson*
Editor, Fiction *Audrey Adams*

FOUNDED 1976 by Klaus Flugge and named after Hans Christian Andersen. *Publishes* children's high-quality picture books and fiction. Seventy per cent of the books are sold as co-productions abroad. TITLES *Elmer* David McKee; *One Little Angel* Ruth Brown; *I Want My Potty* Tony Ross; *Badger's Parting Gifts* Susan Varley; *little.com* Ralph Steadman; *Cat in the Manger* Michael Foreman; *Preston Pig Books* Colin McNaughton; *Junk* Melvin Burgess. Unsolicited mss welcome for picture books; synopsis in the first instance for books for young readers up to age 12. No poetry or short stories.
Royalties paid twice-yearly.

The Angel's Share
See **Neil Wilson Publishing Ltd**

Anness Publishing Ltd
Hermes House, 88–89 Blackfriars Road, London SE1 8HA
☎020 7401 2077 Fax 020 7633 9499
Chairman/Managing Director *Paul Anness*
Publisher/Partner *Joanna Lorenz*

FOUNDED 1989. *Publishes* highly illustrated co-edition titles: general non-fiction – cookery, crafts, interior design, gardening, photography, decorating, lifestyle and children's. About 400 titles a year. IMPRINTS **Lorenz Books**; **Aquamarine**; **Hermes House**; **Peony Press**; **Southwater**.

Antique Collectors' Club
5 Church Street, Woodbridge, Suffolk P12 1DS
☎01394 385501 Fax 01394 384434
Email sales@antique-acc.com
Website www.antique-acc.com
Managing Director *Diana Steel*
Director *Mark Eastment*

FOUNDED 1966. Has a five-figure membership spread over the UK and the world. The Club's magazine *Antique Collecting* is sold on a subscription basis (currently £25 *p.a.*) and is published 10 times a year. It is sent free to members who may also buy the Club's books at special pre-publication prices. *Publishes* specialist books on antiques and collecting, the decorative arts, architecture and gardening. The price guide series was introduced in 1968 with the first edition of *The Price Guide to Antique Furniture*. Subject areas include furniture, silver/jewellery, metalwork, glass, textiles, art reference, ceramics, horology. Recent TITLES *Tiffany Silver Flatware* William Hood; *English Country Furniture* David Knell; *Spot the Book Title* Simon Drew; *Irish Botanical Illustrators* Patrick Butler. Unsolicited synopses and ideas for books welcome. No mss.

Royalties paid quarterly as a rule, but can vary.

Anvil Press Poetry Ltd

Neptune House, 70 Royal Hill, London SE10 8RF
☎020 8469 3033 Fax 020 8469 3363
Email anvil@anvilpresspoetry.com
Website www.anvilpresspoetry.com

Editorial Director *Peter Jay*

FOUNDED 1968 to promote English-language and foreign poetry, both classic and contemporary, in translation. English list includes Peter Levi, Dick Davis, Dennis O'Driscoll and Carol Ann Duffy. Translated books include Bei Dao, Celan, Dante, Lalic, Baudelaire, Lorca and Neruda. Preliminary enquiry required for translations. Unsolicited book-length collections of poems are welcome from writers whose work has appeared in poetry magazines. Please enclose adequate return postage.

Authors' Rating With a little help from the Arts Council, Anvil has become one of the foremost publishers of living poets.

Apollos

See **Inter-Varsity Press**

Apple

See **Quarto Publishing** under **UK Packagers**

Appletree Press Ltd

The Old Potato Station, 14 Howard Street South, Belfast BT7 1AP
☎028 9024 3074 Fax 028 9024 6756
Email reception@appletree.ie
Website www.appletree.ie

Managing Director *John Murphy*
Publishing Manager *Paul Harron*

FOUNDED 1974. *Publishes* cookery and other small-format gift books, plus general non-fiction of Irish and Scottish interest. TITLES *Little*

Cookbook series (about 40 titles); *Ireland: The Complete Guide*. No unsolicited mss; send initial letter or synopsis.

Royalties paid twice-yearly in the first year, annually thereafter. For the *Little Cookbook* series, a standard fee is paid.

Aquamarine

See **Anness Publishing Ltd**

Arc Publications

Nanholme Mill, Shaw Wood Road, Todmorden, Lancashire OL14 6DA
☎01706 812338 Fax 01706 818948
Email arc.publications@virgin.net
Website www.arcpublications.co.uk

Publishers *Rosemary Jones, Angela Jarman*
General Editor *Tony Ward*
Associate Editors *John Kinsella (International), David Morley (UK), Jean Boase-Beier (Translations)*

FOUNDED in 1969 to specialise in the publication of contemporary poetry from new and established writers both in the UK and abroad. AUTHORS Miklós Radnóti (Hungary), C.K. Stead (New Zealand), Sarah Day (Australia), Donald Atkinson, Andy Brown, Gail Dendy (South Africa), Mary Jo Salter, Brian Henry (USA), Claude de Burine (France), Cevat Çapan (Turkey). 13 titles a year. Authors submitting material should ensure that it is compatible with the current list, include a history of published works and enclose an s.a.e. if they wish mss to be returned. Electronic submissions are not accepted. IMPRINT **Arc Music** specialises in profiles of contemporary composers (particularly where none have existed hitherto) and symposia which take a 'new approach' to well-visited territory. Composers include Hans Werner Henze, John Corigliano and Haydn. Commissioned work only.

Argentum

See **Aurum Press Ltd**

Aris & Phillips Ltd

Teddington House, Warminster, Wiltshire BA12 8PQ
☎01985 213409 Fax 01985 212910
Email Aris.Phillips@btinternet.com
Website www.arisandphillips.com

Managing/Editorial Director *Adrian Phillips*
Editor, Hispanic Classics *Lucinda Phillips*

FOUNDED 1972 to publish books on Egyptology. A family firm which has remained independent. *Publishes* academic, classical, oriental and hispanic. About 20 titles a year. TITLES *Campo Libre* (series); *Mammals of Ancient Egypt* Osborn; *The Reign of Ramesses IV* A.J. Peden; *The Third Intermediate Period in Egypt (1100–650BC)* K.A. Kitchen. With such a highly specialised list, unsolicited mss and synopses are not particularly welcome, but synopses will be considered.

Royalties paid twice-yearly.

Arms & Armour Press
See **Cassell**

Arnold
See **Hodder Headline Plc**

Arrow
See **Random House Group Ltd**

Artech House
46 Gillingham Street, London SW1V 1AH
☎020 7596 8750 Fax 020 7630 0166
Email jlancashire@artechhouse.co.uk
Website www.artechhouse.com

Managing Director (USA) *William M. Bazzy*
Senior Commissioning Editor *Dr Julie Lancashire*

FOUNDED 1969. European office of Artech House Inc., Boston. *Publishes* electronic engineering, especially telecommunications, computer communications, computing, optoelectronics, signal processing, digital audio and video, intelligent transportation systems and technology management (books, software and videos). 60–70 titles a year. Unsolicited mss and synopses considered.

Royalties paid twice-yearly.

Ashgate Publishing Ltd
Gower House, Croft Road, Aldershot,
Hampshire GU11 3HR
☎01252 331551
Fax 01252 317446 (Ashgate)/
344405 (Gower)/3685954 (Lund Humphries)
Email info@ashgatepub.co.uk
Website www.ashgate.com *and* www.gowerpub.com

Chairman *Nigel Farrow*

FOUNDED 1967. *Publishes* business and professional titles under the **Gower** imprint and humanities, social sciences, law and legal studies under the **Ashgate** imprint. In December 1999 acquired **Lund Humphries**, publisher of art books and exhibition catalogues.

DIVISIONS **Ashgate** *Sarah Markham* Social sciences; *John Smedley* History/Variorum collected studies; *Rachel Lynch* Music and history; *Pamela Edwardes* Art history; *John Hindley* Aviation studies. **Gower** *Jo Burges, Ingmar Folkmans* Business and management; *Jonathan Norman* Training resources; *John Irwin* Law and legal studies. **Lund Humphries** *Lucy Myers*. Access the websites for information on submission of material.

Ashgrove Publishing
55 Richmond Avenue, London N1 0LX
☎020 7713 7540 Fax 020 7837 5061
Email edit@ashgrove.demon.co.uk
Website www.ashgrovepublishing.com

Chairman/Managing Director *Brad Thompson*
Approx. Annual Turnover £75,000

Acquired by Hollydata Publishers in 1999, Ashgrove has been publishing for over twenty years. *Publishes* mind, body, spirit, health, cookery, sports. 5 titles in 2000. No unsolicited mss; approach with letter and outline in the first instance.

Royalties paid annually.

Ashmolean Museum Publications
Ashmolean Museum, Beaumont Street,
Oxford OX1 2PH
☎01865 278009 Fax 01865 278018
Website www.ashmol.ox.ac.uk

Publisher/Editorial Head *Ian Charlton*

The Ashmolean Museum, which is wholly owned by Oxford University, was FOUNDED in 1683. The first publication appeared in 1890 but publishing did not really start in earnest until the 1960s. *Publishes* European and Oriental fine and applied arts, European archaeology and ancient history, Egyptology and numismatics, for both adult and children's markets. About 8 titles a year. No fiction, American/African art, ethnography, modern art or post-medieval history. Most publications are based on and illustrated from the Museum's collections.

IMPRINTS **Ashmoleum Museum Publications**; **Griffith Institute** (Egyptology imprint). Recent TITLES *Glass of Four Millennia; Edward Ardizzone; Chinese Paintings; Tudor England; Corpus of Buyid Coins; Embroideries and Samplers from Islamic Egypt; Jules Flandrin Paintings; Twentieth Century Sculpture*. No unsolicited mss.

Royalties paid annually.

Associated University Presses (AUP)
See **Golden Cockerel Press Ltd**

The Athlone Press
See **The Continuum International Publishing Group Ltd**

Atlantic Europe Publishing Co. Ltd
Greys Court Farm, Greys Court, Nr Henley on Thames, Oxfordshire RG9 4PG
☎01491 628188   Fax 01491 628189
Email info@AtlanticEurope.com
Directors *Dr B.J. Knapp, D.L.R. McCrae*
Websites www.AtlanticEurope.com *and* www.curriculumVisions.com

Closely associated, since 1990, with Earthscape Editions packaging operation. *Publishes* full-colour, highly illustrated children's non-fiction in hardback for international co-editions and text books. Not interested in any other material. Main focus is on National Curriculum titles, especially in the fields of mathematics, science, technology, social history and geography. About 25 titles a year. Unsolicited synopses and ideas for non-fiction curriculum-based books welcome but s.a.e. essential for return of submissions.
Royalties or fees paid depending on circumstance.

AUP (Associated University Presses)
See **Golden Cockerel Press Ltd**

Aurum Press Ltd
25 Bedford Avenue, London WC1B 3AT
☎020 7637 3225   Fax 020 7580 2469
Email editorial@aurumpress.co.uk
Managing Director *Bill McCreadie*
Editorial Director *Piers Burnett*
Approx. Annual Turnover £2.5 million
FOUNDED 1977. Formerly owned by Andrew Lloyd Webber's Really Useful Group, now owned jointly by Piers Burnett, Bill McCreadie and Sheila Murphy, all of whom worked together in the '70s for André Deutsch. Committed to producing high-quality, illustrated/non-illustrated adult non-fiction in the areas of general human interest, art and craft, lifestyle, sport and travel. About 60 titles a year. IMPRINTS **Argentum** Practical photography books; **Jacqui Small** High-quality lifestyle books.
Royalties paid twice-yearly.

AuthorsOnline
Adams Yard, Maidenhead Street, Hertford, Hertfordshire SG14 1DR
☎01992 503151   Fax 01992 535424
Email theeditor@authorsonline.co.uk
Website www.authorsonline.co.uk
Owner *AuthorsOnLine Ltd.*
Managing Director *Gary Lee*
Editor *Richard Fitt*
Approx. Annual Turnover £1 million
FOUNDED 1997. *Publishes* new and reverted rights work in both electronic format via their website and traditional hard-copy. All genre welcome. Also offers a service to help authors self-publish in both formats. Submit mss by post or e-mail. Further information available via the website.

Autumn Publishing Ltd
North Barn, Appledram Barns, Birdham Road, Near Chichester, West Sussex PO20 7EQ
☎01243 531660   Fax 01243 774433
Email autumn@autumnpublishing.co.uk
Managing Director *Campbell Goldsmid*
Editorial Director *Ingrid Goldsmid*
FOUNDED 1976. Publisher of children's puzzle, activity and sticker books. About 50 titles a year. Unsolicited synopses and ideas for books welcome if they come within relevant subject areas.
Payment varies according to contract; generally a flat fee.

Award Publications Limited
1st Floor, 27 Longford Street, London NW1 3DZ
☎020 7388 7800   Fax 020 7388 7887
Email info@awardpublications.co.uk
FOUNDED 1958. *Publishes* children's books, both fiction and reference. 40 titles in 2000. IMPRINT **Horus Editions**. No unsolicited mss, synopses or ideas.

Azure
See **Society for Promoting Christian Knowledge**

Baillière Tindall
See **Harcourt Publishers Limited**

Duncan Baird Publishers
Castle House, 75–76 Wells Street, London W1T 3QH
☎020 7323 2229   Fax 020 7580 5692
Email james@dbairdpub.co.uk
Managing Director *Duncan Baird*
Editorial Director *Bob Saxton*
Approx. Annual Turnover £5 million
FOUNDED in 1992 to publish and package co-editions overseas and went on to launch its

own publishing operation in 1998. *Publishes* illustrated cultural reference, world religions, health, mind, body and spirit, lifestyle, graphic design. 20 titles in 2000. No unsolicited mss. Synopses and ideas welcome; approach in writing in the first instance with s.a.e. No fiction or UK-only subjects.

Royalties paid twice-yearly.

Bantam/Bantam Press
See **Transworld Publishers**

Barefoot Books Ltd
124 Walcot Street, Bath BA1 5BG
☎01225 322400 Fax 01225 322499
Email edit@barefootbooks.com
Website www.barefootbooks.com
Managing Director *Nancy Traversy*
Publisher *Tessa Strickland*
Approx. Annual Turnover £1.2 million

FOUNDED in 1993. *Publishes* high-quality children's picture books, particularly new and traditional stories from a wide range of cultures. 44 titles in 2000. TITLES *The Genius of Leonardo*; *The Gigantic Turnip*; *Tales From Old Ireland*. No unsolicited mss.

Royalties paid twice-yearly.

Authors' Rating Writers of children's books would do well to keep track of Barefoot which, from small beginnings, is building a quality list that must be the envy of bigger publishers.

Barny Books
The Cottage, Hough on the Hill, Near Grantham, Lincolnshire NG32 2BB
☎01400 250246 Fax 01400 250246
Managing Director/Editorial Head *Molly Burkett*
Business Manager *Tom Cann*
Approx. Annual Turnover £10,000

FOUNDED with the aim of encouraging new writers and illustrators. *Publishes* mainly children's books but moving into adult fiction and non-fiction. TITLES *Queen's Royal Lancers* Molly Burkett; *Once Upon a Wartime* (series); *Eric's War* Cathy Ryan; *Melvin's Incredible Journey* Robert Montgomery. Too small a concern to have the staff/resources to deal with unsolicited mss. Writers with strong ideas should approach Molly Burkett by letter in the first instance. Also runs a readership and advisory service for new writers (£10 fee for short stories or illustrations; £25 fee for full-length stories).

Royalties Division of profits 50/50.

Authors' Rating A gutsy small publisher with a sense of fun which appeals to youngsters.

Barrie & Jenkins
See **Random House Group Ltd**

B.T. Batsford Ltd
9 Blenheim Court, Brewery Road, London N7 9NT
☎020 7700 7611 Fax 020 7700 4552
Email info@batsford.com
Website www.batsford.com
Chairman *John Needleman*
Publisher *Roger Huggins*
Approx. Annual Turnover £2 million

FOUNDED in 1843 as a bookseller, and began publishing in 1874. Acquired by the Chrysalis Group Plc in 1999. A world leader in books on chess, arts and craft. *Publishes* non-fiction: archaeology, bridge and chess, cinema, crafts and hobbies, fashion and costume, graphic design and gardening. About 100 titles a year.

Royalties paid twice in first year, annually thereafter.

BBC Worldwide Ltd
80 Wood Lane, London W12 0TT
☎020 8433 2000 Fax 020 8433 3707
Website www.bbcworldwide.com
Editorial Manager *Richard Larkham*
Approx. Annual Turnover £450 million

Publishes TV tie-in and some stand-alone titles, including books which, though linked with BBC television or radio, may not simply be the 'book of the series'. Also TV tie-in titles for children. 90 titles a year. TITLES Gary Rhodes' *New British Classics* and *At the Table*; *A History of Britain* Simon Schama; and autobiographies – Terry Wogan, Steve Redgrave, Esther Rantzen. Unsolicited mss (which come in at the rate of about 20 weekly) are rarely accepted. However, strong ideas well expressed will always be considered, and promising letters stand a chance of further scrutiny.

Royalties paid twice-yearly.

Authors' Rating Aside from OUP which, as a charity, does not pay tax it is hard to think of a publisher starting with a bigger advantage than the BBC. All those TV tie-ins and top celebrities eager to write their biographies! But the major expansion is in video and talking books. The BBC archive is a treasure trove still waiting to be fully explored. But more new titles can be expected now that BBC has bought Cover to Cover, a leading producer of unabridged readings on tape. So far BBC has fought shy of full-length readings. This will now change. All writers, including those not yet broadcasting names, are likely to benefit.

Bedford Square Press
See **NCVO Publications**

Belair
See **Folens Limited**

Belitha Press Ltd
See entry under **UK Packagers**

Ben Gunn
See **SB Publications**

David Bennett Books
See entry under **UK Packagers**

Berg Publishers
150 Cowley Road, Oxford OX4 1JJ
☎01865 245104 Fax 01865 791165
Email enquiry@berg.demon.co.uk
Website www.berg.demon.co.uk

Editorial & Managing Director *Kathryn Earle*
Production Director *Sara Everett*

Publishes scholarly books in the fields of history, fashion, cultural studies, social sciences and humanities. About 52 titles a year plus one journal, *Fashion Theory*. TITLES *The Internet: An Ethnographic Approach* Daniel Miller and Don Slater; *'Don We Now Our Gay Apparel': Gay Men's Dress in the 20th Century* Shaun Cole; *Wild Things: The Material Culture of Everyday Life* Judy Attfield; *Filming Women in the Third Reich* Jo Fox; *Deep Trout: Angling in Popular Culture* William Washabaugh. IMPRINT **Oswald Wolff Books**. No unsolicited mss. Synopses and ideas for books welcome.
Royalties paid annually.

Berkswell Publishing Co. Ltd
PO Box 420, Warminster, Wiltshire BA12 9XB
☎01985 840189 Fax 01985 840243
Email John.Stidolph@btinternet.com

Managing Director *John Stidolph*

FOUNDED 1974. *Publishes* illustrated books, royalty, heritage, country sports, biography, books about Wessex and *The Churchwarden's Yearbook*. No fiction. About 4 titles a year. Unsolicited mss, synopses and ideas for books welcome.
Royalties paid according to contract.

Berlitz Publishing Co. Ltd
Suite 120, 24–25 Nutford Place, London W1H 5YN
☎020 7569 3160 Fax 020 7725 7013
Email publishing@berlitz.co.uk
Website www.berlitz.com

Managing Director *R. Kirkpatrick*

FOUNDED 1970. Part of Berlitz International, which also comprises language instruction and translation divisions. *Publishes* travel and language-learning products only: travel guides, phrasebooks and language courses. SERIES *Pocket Guides; Berlitz Complete Guide to Cruising and Cruise Ships; Phrase Books; Pocket Dictionaries; Business Phrase Books; Self-teach: Rush Hour Commuter Cassettes; Think & Talk; Berlitz Kids.* No unsolicited mss.

BFI Publishing
British Film Institute, 21 Stephen Street, London W1T 1LN
☎020 7255 1444 Fax 020 7636 2516
Website www.bfi.org.uk

Head of Publishing *Andrew Lockett*
Approx. Annual Turnover £600,000

FOUNDED 1982. Part of the **British Film Institute**. *Publishes* academic and general film/television-related books. About 30 titles a year. TITLES *Film Classics* (series); *Modern Classics* (series); *The Cinema Book, revised edition* eds. Pam Cook and Mieke Bernink; *BFI Film & Television Handbook* (annual) Eddie Dyja. Unsolicited synopses and ideas preferred to complete mss.
Royalties paid annually.

BFP Books
Focus House, 497 Green Lanes, London N13 4BP
☎020 8882 3315 Fax 020 8886 5174

Chief Executive *John Tracy*
Commissioning Editor *Stewart Gibson*

FOUNDED 1982. The publishing arm of the Bureau of Freelance Photographers. *Publishes* illustrated books on photography, mainly aspects of freelancing and marketing pictures. No unsolicited mss but ideas welcome.

Big Fish
See **C&B Publishing plc**

Clive Bingley Books
See **Library Association Publishing**

Birlinn Ltd

Unit 8 Canongate Venture, 5 New Street,
Edinburgh EH8 5BH
☎0131 556 6660 Fax 0131 557 6250
Email info@birlinn.co.uk
Website www.birlinn.co.uk

Managing Editor *Hugh Andrew*

FOUNDED 1992. Acquired **John Donald Publishers** in 1999 (see entry). *Publishes* local and military history, Gaelic, humour, Highland history, adventure, Scottish reference, guidebooks and folklore. 80 titles in 2000. No unsolicited mss; synopses and ideas welcome.
  Royalties paid.

Black & White Publishing Ltd

99 Giles Street, Edinburgh EH6 6BZ
☎0131 625 4500 Fax 0131 625 4501
Email mail@blackandwhitepublishing.com
Website www.blackandwhitepublishing.com

Director *Campbell Brown*

FOUNDED 1990. *Publishes* general fiction and non-fiction, including memoirs, sport, cookery, humour and guidebooks. Text only submissions via website or synopsis and sample chapter by post with s.a.e. or return postage.
  Royalties paid twice-yearly.

A.&C. Black (Publishers) Ltd

Alderman House, 37 Soho Square, London
W1D 3QZ
☎020 7758 0200 Fax 020 7758 0222
Email enquiries@acblack.com

Chairman *Nigel Newton*
Managing Director *Jill Coleman*
Approx. Annual Turnover £7.75 million
(Group turnover)

Publishes children's and educational books, including music, for 3–15-year-olds, arts and crafts, ceramics, fishing, ornithology, nautical, reference, sport, theatre and travel. About 125 titles a year. Acquisitions brought the Herbert Press' art, design and general books, Adlard Coles' sailing list and Christopher Helm's and Pica Press's natural history and ornithology lists into A.&C. Black's stable. Bought by **Bloomsbury Publishing** in May 2000.
  IMPRINTS **Adlard Coles Nautical**; **Christopher Helm**; **The Herbert Press**; **Pica Press**. TITLES *New Mermaid* drama series; *Who's Who*; *Writers' & Artists' Yearbook*; *Know the Game* sports series; *Blue Guides* travel series; *Rockets* and *Graffix* children's series. Initial enquiry appreciated before submission of mss.

Royalties Payment varies according to contract.

Authors' Rating After years as a small but hallowed reference and education publisher, A.&C. Black (who were A.&C. exactly?) has jumped to the front ranks by merging with Bloomsbury. The great and the good will soon be able to check their *Who's Who* entry online.

Black Ace Books

PO Box 6557, Forfar DD8 2YS
☎01307 465096 Fax 01307 465494
Website www.blackacebooks.com

Managing Directors *Hunter Steele, Boo Wood*

FOUNDED 1991. *Publishes* new fiction, Scottish and general; some non-fiction including biography, history, philosophy and psychology. 36 titles in print. IMPRINTS **Black Ace Books**, **Black Ace Paperbacks** TITLES *Succeeding at Sex and Scotland, Or the Case of Louis Morel* Hunter Steele; *Spitfire Girls* Carol Gould; *Count Dracula (The Authorized Version)* Hagen Slawkberg; *Caryddwen's Cauldron* Paul Hilton. Completed books only. 'Check out our website first. Then, if appropriate, *send only*: one-page covering letter, one-page synopsis, one full page of text and large s.a.e. If possible, include one-page recommendation from suitable referee such as published author, book reviewer or university teacher of literature. No poetry, children's, cookery, DIY, religion.'
  Royalties paid twice-yearly.

Black Butterfly Children's Books

See **Writers and Readers Ltd**

Black Dagger Crime

See **Chivers Press Ltd**

Black Lace

See **Virgin Books Ltd**

Black Sheep Books

PO Box 538, Hemel Hempstead,
Hertfordshire HP2 5GT
Fax 01442 252848
Email blacksheepbooks@supanet.com
Website www.blacksheepbooks.co.uk

Crime/Thrillers *Jack Crane*
General *Mark Evans*
Children's *Lisa Goode*
Approx. Annual Turnover £100,000

FOUNDED 1996. 'Bridges the gap between conventional publishers and literary agents by producing and promoting introductory publications.' Produces books by new writers in small print runs with a view to placing them with a larger publisher. *Publishes* true crime, crime fiction, thrillers, general fiction and non-fiction, children's. 12 titles in 2002. 'New writers preferred. We are receptive to any exciting material in any genre.' Submissions should be by post with s.a.e. or via the website.

Royalties paid twice-yearly.

Black Spring Press Ltd

Burbage House, 83–85 Curtain Road, London EC2A 3BS

☎020 7613 3066 Fax 020 7613 0028

Email general@dexterhaven.demon.co.uk

Directors *Robert Hastings, Alexander Hastings*

FOUNDED 1986. *Publishes* fiction, literary criticism, biography. About 5 titles a year. TITLES *King Ink 2* Nick Cave; *The Mortdecai Trilogy* Kyril Bonfiglioli; *The Tenant* Roland Topor; *Beautiful Losers* Leonard Cohen; *The Terrible News* collection of Russian short stories by Zamyatin, Babel, Kharms, *et al.* No unsolicited mss.

Royalties paid twice-yearly.

Black Swan

See **Transworld Publishers**

Blackie & Co. Publishers

107–111 Fleet Street, London EC4A 2AB

☎020 7936 9021 Fax 020 7936 9100

Email editors@blackiepublishers.com

Website www.blackiepublishers.com

Editorial Head *Bettina Croft*

Editors *Jill Redgrave, Linda Alexander*

A new company FOUNDED in 1999 which *publishes* literature, crime, fiction and non-fiction, heritage, educational, computers/the Internet, religious, some children's, biographical, scientific/environmental books: popular and academic. About 20–30 titles a year. TITLES *Darkwater Towers* Colin Campbell; *As the Dawn Breaketh* Bernard Hyde-Tingley; *Crossover* Nick Wilson; *Moggworld* Katie Mullens. No unsolicited mss.

Royalties paid annually.

Blackstaff Press Ltd

Blackstaff House, Wildflower Way, Apollo Road, Belfast BT12 6TA

☎028 9066 8074 Fax 028 9066 8207

Email info@blackstaffpress.com

Website www.blackstaffpress.com

Director/Editorial Head *Anne Tannahill*

FOUNDED 1971. *Publishes* mainly, but not exclusively, Irish interest books, fiction, poetry, history, politics, illustrated editions, natural history and humour. About 25 titles a year. Unsolicited mss considered, but preliminary submission of synopsis plus short sample of writing preferred. Return postage *must* be enclosed.

Royalties paid twice-yearly.

Authors' Rating This Belfast publisher is noted for a strong backlist, 'wonderfully well-presented catalogues and promotional material'.

Blackwell Publishers Ltd

108 Cowley Road, Oxford OX4 1JF

☎01865 791100 Fax 01865 791347

Website www.blackwellpublishers.co.uk

Chairman *Nigel Blackwell*

Managing Director *René Olivieri*

Approx. Annual Turnover £23.7 million

FOUNDED 1926. A rapidly expanding Anglo-American company. The focus is on international research journals and undergraduate textbooks in social sciences, business and humanities; computer-aided instruction on PC applications. About 300 titles a year (joint venture with **Polity Press**) and over 250 journals.

DIVISIONS **Books** *Philip Carpenter* **Journals** *Sue Corbett, Claire Andrews*. Unsolicited synopses with specimen chapter and table of contents welcome.

Royalties paid annually US *associates* Blackwell Publishers Inc., Maldon, Massachusetts; InfoSource Inc., Winter Park, Florida.

Authors' Rating Continuing expansion is thanks largely to successful exploitation of the US academic market where Blackwell scores more than half its total sales.

Blackwell Science Ltd

Osney Mead, Oxford OX2 0EL

☎01865 206206 Fax 01865 721205

Website www.blackwell-science.com

Chairman *Nigel Blackwell*

Group Managing Director *Robert Campbell*

Managing Director (UK) *Jon Conibear*

Publishing Directors *Dr Andrew Robinson* (Medicine); *Simon Rallison* (Science); *Dr Jon Walmsley* (Professional)

Approx. Annual Turnover £105 million (Group turnover)

FOUNDED 1939. Rapid growth since the 1970s along with expansion into Europe in the late 1980s. Also owner of Danish academic publisher Munksgaard. *Publishes* medical, professional (including Fishing News Books) and science. About 400 titles a year, plus 350 journals, now available online. TITLES *Diseases of the Liver and*

Biliary System Sherlock; *Essential Immunology* Roitt; *Textbook of Dermatology* Champion. Unsolicited mss and synopses welcome.

Royalties paid annually. *Overseas subsidiaries* in USA, Australia, Japan, Hong Kong, Paris, Berlin and Vienna; editorial offices in London and Edinburgh.

Authors' Rating Blackwell Science's main business is in scientific journals, mostly produced in partnership with learned societies, and medical publishing. Much of the growth is in mainland Europe where Blackwell Science has offshoots in Berlin, Paris and Vienna.

Blake Publishing
3 Bramber Court, 2 Bramber Road, London W14 9PB
☎020 7381 0666 Fax 020 7381 6868
Email words@blake.co.uk
Managing Director *John Blake*
Deputy Managing Director *Rosie Ries*

FOUNDED 1991 and rapidly expanding. Bought the assets of Smith Gryphon Ltd in 1997 when that publishing house went into receivership. *Publishes* mass-market non-fiction. No fiction, children's, specialist or non-commercial. About 60 titles a year. No unsolicited mss; synopses and ideas welcome. Please enclose s.a.e.
Royalties paid twice-yearly.

Authors' Rating Literary folk sniff at Blake – so tabloid, my dear. But there is something refreshing about a publisher who knows a good story when it hits him in the eye. How many of his rivals would have jumped at the chance of bringing out *The Guv'nor*, Lenny McLean's East End gangster autobiography or James Hewitt's account of his affair with Princess Diana? Nearly all of them, of course, but they were too slow off the mark. Blake concedes that most of his authors are acquaintances from his days as a journalist. But if anyone has a big idea for a sports title, he could be interested.

Blandford Press
See **Cassell**

Bloodaxe Books Ltd
Highgreen, Tarset, Northumberland NE48 1RP
☎01434 240500 Fax 01434 240505
Email editor@bloodaxebooks.demon.co.uk
Website www.bloodaxebooks.demon.co.uk
Managing/Editorial Director *Neil Astley*

Publishes poetry, literature and criticism, and related titles by British, Irish, European, Commonwealth and American writers. 95 per cent of the list is poetry. About 40 titles a year. TITLES include three major anthologies, *The Bloodaxe Book of 20th Century Poetry* Edna Longley (ed.); *The New Poetry* Hulse, Kennedy and Morley (eds.); *Sixty Women Poets* Linda France (ed.); *Selected Poems* Jenny Joseph; *Poems* J.H. Prynne; *Poems 1960–2000* Fleur Adcock; recent collections by Selima Hill, Helen Dunmore and Peter Reading. Unsolicited poetry mss welcome; send a sample of no more than 10 poems with s.a.e., 'but if you don't read contemporary poetry, don't bother'. Authors of other material should write in the first instance.
Royalties paid annually.

Authors' Rating Assisted by regional Arts Council funding, Bloodaxe is one of the liveliest and most innovative of poetry publishers with a list that takes in some of the best of the younger poets.

Bloomsbury Publishing Plc
38 Soho Square, London W1D 3HB
☎020 7494 2111 Fax 020 7434 0151
Website www.bloomsburymagazine.com
Chairman/Chief Executive *Nigel Newton*
Publishing Directors *Alexandra Pringle, Liz Calder, Kathy Rooney, Arabella Stein, Sarah Odedina, Jonathan Glasspool*
Approx. Annual Turnover £26 million

FOUNDED 1986 by Nigel Newton, David Reynolds, Alan Wherry and Liz Calder. Over the following years Bloomsbury titles were to appear regularly on *The Sunday Times* bestseller list and many of its authors have gone on to win prestigious literary prizes. In 1991 Nadine Gordimer won the **Nobel Prize for Literature**; Michael Ondaatje's *The English Patient* won the 1992 **Booker Prize**; in 1997 Anne Michaels' *Fugitive Pieces* won both the **Orange Prize for Fiction** and the Guardian Fiction Prize. J.K. Rowling's *Harry Potter and the Philosopher's Stone, Harry Potter and the Chamber of Secrets* and *Harry Potter and the Prisoner of Azkaban* won the **Nestlé Smarties Book Prize** in 1997, 1998 and 1999 respectively. Margaret Atwood's *The Blind Assassin* won the **Booker Prize** in 2000. Published *The Encarta World English Dictionary* in 1999. Acquired **A.&C. Black (Publishers) Ltd** in May 2000.

Publishes literary fiction and non-fiction, including general reference. AUTHORS include J.K. Rowling, Margaret Atwood, T.C. Boyle, Daniel Goleman, David Guterson, John Irving, Jay McInerney, Will Self, Hunter S. Thompson,

Rupert Thomson, Joanna Trollope. Unsolicited mss and synopses welcome; no poetry.

Royalties paid twice-yearly.

Authors' Rating The triumphant march continues. Hardly a week passes without Bloomsbury scoring another victory. The latest – *Harry Potter and the Goblet of Fire* – had the highest ever initial print run, 4.8 million copies. But it is not all J.K. Rowling. Other successes like Margaret Atwood's Booker Prize winner, *The Blind Assassin*, head a strong fiction list. The problem for new writers, of course, is finding a way through the crowd of other hopefuls beseiging the Soho offices. Have a go by all means but don't expect a quick response.

Boatswain Press
See **Kenneth Mason Publications Ltd**

Bobcat
See **Omnibus Press**

Bodley Head
See **Random House Group Ltd**

The Book Guild Ltd
Temple House, 25 High Street, Lewes, East Sussex BN7 2LU
☎01273 472534   Fax 01273 476472
Email info@bookguild.co.uk
Website www.bookguild.co.uk
Chairman *George M. Nissen, CBE*
Managing Director *Carol Biss*

FOUNDED 1982. *Publishes* fiction, human interest, media, children's fiction, academic, natural history, naval and military, biography, art. About 80 titles a year. Expanding mainstream list plus developing the human interest/media genre.

DIVISIONS/TITLES
Media/Entertainment *You Should Have Been in Last Night* Richard Stone. **Human Interest** *Wipe Your Crutch Before You Leave* David Strutt. **Fiction** *Lessons From An Angel* Sarah Dykins. **Photography/Art** *Charles Fairfax Murray* David Elliott. **Travel** *Restless for Morocco* Peter Rogers. **History** *Rudolf Hess and Germany's Reluctant War 1939–41* Alfred Smith. **Natural History** *Unto the Hills* Patrick Coulcher. **Children's** *Eurocats* Street and Naylor.
IMPRINT **Temple House Books** Nonfiction: *The Fitzroy* Sally Fiber; *Colditz, Last Stop* Jack Pringle. Unsolicited mss, ideas and synopses welcome.

Royalties paid twice-yearly.

Authors' Rating Regularly advertises for authors who may be asked to cover their own production costs. But in promoting its services, The Book Guild is more up-front with its clients than the typical vanity publisher who promises the earth and delivers next to nothing.

Border Lines Biographies
See **Seren**

Boulevard Books & The Babel Guides
71 Lytton Road, Oxford OX4 3NY
☎01865 712931   Fax 01865 712931
Email raybabel@dircon.co.uk
Website www.raybabel.dircon.co.uk
Managing Director *Ray Keenoy*

Specialises in contemporary world fiction by young writers in English translation. Existing or forthcoming series of fiction from Brazil, Italy, Latin America, Low Countries, Greece, and elsewhere. The Babel Guides series of popular guides to fiction in translation started in 1995.

DIVISONS
Latin American *Ray Keenoy* TITLE *Hotel Atlantico* J.G. Noll. **Italian** *Fiorenza Conte* TITLE *The Toy Catalogue* Sandra Petrignani. **Brazil** *Dr David Treece* TITLE *From the Heart of Brazil* (anthology). **Low Countries** *Prof. Theo Hermans*. **Greece** *Marina Coriolano-Likourezos*. **Babel Guides to Fiction in Translation** *Ray Keenoy* Series Editor TITLES *Babel Guide to Italian Fiction in Translation*; *Babel Guide to the Fiction of Portugal, Brazil & Africa in Translation*; *Babel Guide to French Fiction in English Translation*; *Babel Guide to Jewish Fiction*; *Babel Guide to Scandinavian Fiction*. Suggestions and proposals for translations of contemporary fiction welcome. Also seeking contributors to forthcoming Babel Guides (all literatures).

Royalties paid annually.

Bounty
See **Octopus Publishing Group**

Bowker
Windsor Court, East Grinstead House,
East Grinstead, West Sussex RH19 1XA
☎01342 336185   Fax 01342 336192
Website www.bowker.co.uk
Group Publishing Director *Gerard Dummett*
Managing Director *Charles Halpin*
Publisher *Geraldine Turpie*

Owned by **Reed Elsevier**, Bowker is part of Reed Business Information in the UK.

Publishes library reference, library science, bibliography, biography, African studies, business and professional directories. Unsolicited mss will not be read. Approach with ideas only.
. *Royalties* paid annually.

Boxtree
See **Macmillan Publishers Ltd**

Marion Boyars Publishers Ltd
24 Lacy Road, London SW15 1NL
☎020 8788 9522 Fax 020 8789 8122
Email marion.boyars@talk21.com
Website www.marionboyars.co.uk
Editor *Julia Silk*
Editor, Non-fiction *Ken Hollings*
FOUNDED 1975, formerly Calder and Boyars. *Publishes* biography and autobiography, economics, fiction, literature and criticism, music, philosophy, poetry, politics and world affairs, psychology, sociology and anthropology, theatre and drama, film and cinema, women's studies. About 30 titles a year. AUTHORS include Georges Bataille, Ingmar Bergman, Heinrich Böll, Hortense Calisher, Jean Cocteau, Clive Collins, Warwick Collins, Carlo Gébler, Julian Green, Ivan Illich, Pauline Kael, Ken Kesey, Kenzaburo Oe, Hubert Selby, Igor Stravinsky, Frederic Tuten, Eudora Welty, Judith Williamson, Tom Wiseman. Unsolicited mss not welcome for fiction or poetry; submissions from agents only. Unsolicited synopses and ideas welcome for non-fiction.
 Royalties paid annually. *Overseas associates* Marion Boyars Publishers Inc., 1489 Lincoln Avenue, Saint Paul, MN 551015, USA.

Boydell & Brewer Ltd
PO Box 9, Woodbridge, Suffolk IP12 3DF
☎01394 411320
Publishes non-fiction only, principally medieval studies. All books commissioned. No unsolicited material.

Bradt Travel Guides
19 High Street, Chalfont St Peter, Buckinghamshire SL9 9QE
☎01753 893444 Fax 01753 892333
Email info@bradt-travelguides.com
Website www.bradt-travelguides.com
Managing Director *Hilary Bradt*
Editorial Head *Tricia Hayne*
Approx. Annual Turnover £400,000
FOUNDED in 1974 by Hilary Bradt. *Specialises* in travel guides to off-beat places. 7 titles in 2000. TITLES *Guide to Ethiopia; Madagascar; Mali; Zanzibar; Cuba*, etc.; *Wildlife Guide to Madagascar; Galapagos; Antarctica; Rail Guides to USA; India; Backpacking Guides; By Road Guides*. No unsolicited mss; synopses and ideas for travel guidebooks (not travelogues) welcome.
 Royalties paid twice-yearly.

Brassey's
9 Blenheim Court, Brewery Road, London N7 9NT
☎020 7700 7611 Fax 020 7700 4552
Website www.brasseys.com
Chairman *John Needleman*
Began life as *Brassey's Naval Annual* in 1886 to become the most important publisher of serious defence-related material in the world. Acquired by the Chrysalis Group Plc in 1999. *Publishes* books and journals on defence, international relations, military history, maritime and aeronautical subjects and defence terminology.
 IMPRINTS **Brassey's; Conway Maritime Press** Naval history and ship modelling; **Putnam Aeronautical Books** Technical and reference.
 Royalties paid annually.

Nicholas Brealey Publishing
36 John Street, London WC1N 2AT
☎020 7430 0224 Fax 020 7404 8311
Website www.nbrealey-books.com
Managing Director *Nicholas Brealey*
FOUNDED 1992. Innovative books for business that address the most critical and interesting issues of the new century – from business to consumer behaviour, from self-help to leadership, from those promoting understanding of global change to cross-cultural culture. Recently acquired the US publisher Intercultural Press, a specialist publisher in the field of crossing cultures. 20 titles a year. TITLES *Shackleton's Way; The Natural Advantage; The Electronic B@zaar; The Soul of the New Consumer; The Power Laws; The 80/20 Principle; Digital Capital; The Dance of Change*. No fiction, poetry or leisure titles. No unsolicited mss; synopses and ideas welcome.
 Royalties paid twice-yearly.

Authors' Rating Looks to be succeeding in breaking away from the usual computer-speak business manuals to publish information and literate texts. Lead titles have a distinct trans-Atlantic feel.

The Breedon Books Publishing Co. Ltd

Breedon House, 3 Parker Centre, Derby
DE21 4SZ
☎01332 384235 Fax 01332 364063
Email anton@breedonpublishing.co.uk

Editorial Director *A.C. Rippon*
Approx. Annual Turnover £1 million

FOUNDED 1983. *Publishes* biography, local history, old photographs, heritage and sport. 35 titles in 2000. Unsolicited mss, synopses and ideas welcome if accompanied by s.a.e. No poetry or fiction.

Royalties paid annually.

Breese Books Ltd

164 Kensington Park Road, London W11 2ER
☎020 7727 9426 Fax 020 7229 3395
Email MBreese999@aol.com

Chairman/Managing Director *Martin Ranicar-Breese*
Websites: www.sherlockholmes.co.uk *and*
www.abracadabra.co.uk

FOUNDED in 1975 to produce specialist conjuring books and then went on to become a leading publisher of Sherlock Holmes pastiches. TITLES *Sherlock Holmes and the Disappearing Prince* Edmund Hastie; *Breese's Guide to Modern First Editions* (produced on a regular basis for book collectors). There is little point in submitting material on any subjects other than the above.

Authors' Rating Having cut back on his publishing programme Martin Breese is offering a Critical Eye Service to advise authors on how to make their work saleable. There are no guarantees of publication and there is a charge but for some, straight practical advice may be useful.

Brepols Publishers

2 Byron Mews, Hampstead, London
NW3 2NQ
☎020 7284 4359 Fax 020 7267 8764

Editorial Director *Johan Van Der Beke*

UK office of the Belgian academic publisher. FOUNDED 1796. *Publishes* scholarly monographs and collections in any field of pre-modern humanities. 100 titles a year. IMPRINT **Harvey Miller Publishers** FOUNDED 1974. *Publishes* academic studies in medieval and Renaissance art history only. 10–12 titles a year. No unsolicited mss; synopses and ideas welcome.

Royalties paid twice-yearly.

Brimax

See **Octopus Publishing Group**

Bristol Classical Press

See **Gerald Duckworth & Co. Ltd**

British Academic Press

See **I.B. Tauris & Co. Ltd**

The British Academy

10 Carlton House Terrace, London
SW1Y 5AH
☎020 7969 5200 Fax 020 7969 5300
Email secretary@britac.ac.uk
Website www.britac.ac.uk

Publications Officer *Janet English*
Publications Assistant *Vicky Baldwin*

FOUNDED 1901. The primary body for promoting scholarship in the humanities, the Academy publishes many series stemming from its own long-standing research projects, or series of lectures and conference proceedings. Main subjects include history, philosophy and archaeology. About 15 titles a year. SERIES *Auctores Britannici Medii Aevi; Early English Church Music; Fontes Historiae Africanae; Records of Social and Economic History.* Proposals for these series are welcome and are forwarded to the relevant project committees. The British Academy is a registered charity and does not publish for profit.

Royalties paid only when titles have covered their costs.

The British Library

96 Euston Road, London NW1 2DB
☎020 7412 7704 Fax 020 7412 7768
Email blpublications@bl.uk

Publishing Manager *David Way*
Approx. Annual Turnover £950,000

FOUNDED 1979 as the publishing arm of The British Library to publish works based on the historic collections and related subjects. *Publishes* bibliographical reference, manuscript studies, illustrated books based on the Library's collections, and book arts. TITLES *The British Library Guide to Calligraphy, Illumination and Heraldry; The British Library Writers' Lives Series; Encyclopedia of Ephemera; Medieval Herbals.* About 50 titles a year. Unsolicited mss, synopses and ideas welcome if related to the history of the book, book arts or bibliography. No fiction or general non-fiction.

Royalties paid annually.

The British Museum Press
46 Bloomsbury Street, London WC1B 3QQ
☎020 7323 1234 Fax 020 7436 7315
Website www.britishmuseum.co.uk
Managing Director *Patrick Wright*
Director of Press and Merchandise *Emma Way*

The book publishing division of The British Museum Company Ltd. FOUNDED 1973 as British Museum Publications Ltd; relaunched 1991 as British Museum Press. *Publishes* ancient history, archaeology, ethnography, art history, exhibition catalogues, guides, children's books, and all official publications of The British Museum. Around 50 titles a year. TITLES *Egypt; Indigo; Sutton Hoo: Burial Ground of Kings?; The Atlantic Celts: Ancient People or Modern Invention?; The Classical Cookbook; How to Read Egyptian Hieroglyphs.* Synopses and ideas for books welcome.
Royalties paid twice-yearly.

Brockhampton Press Ltd
See **Caxton Publishing Group**

Andrew Brodie Publications
PO Box 23, Wellington, Somerset TA21 8YX
☎01823 665345 Fax 01823 665345
Email andrew@andrewbrodie.co.uk
Website www.andrewbrodie.co.uk
Chairman *Andrew Brodie*
Approx. Annual Turnover £250,000

FOUNDED 1992. *Publishes* children's books. 26 titles in 2000. TITLES *Spelling Today* series; *Handwriting Today; Numeracy Today; Homework Today; Spelling for Literacy.* Unsolicited mss, synopses and ideas for books welcome; send a letter in the first instance.
Royalties paid annually.

John Brown Publishing Ltd
The New Boathouse, 136–142 Bramley Road, London W10 6SR
☎020 7565 3000 Fax 020 7565 3055
Chairman/Managing Director *John Brown*

FOUNDED 1987. *Publishes* magazines, including *Gardens Illustrated; Fortean Times; Classic FM; Viz* and adult comic annuals. Does not welcome unsolicited mss.
Royalties paid twice-yearly.

Brown, Son & Ferguson, Ltd
4–10 Darnley Street, Glasgow G41 2SD
☎0141 429 1234 Fax 0141 420 1694
Email info@skipper.co.uk
Website www.skipper.co.uk
Chairman/Joint Managing Director
T. Nigel Brown

FOUNDED 1850. *Specialises* in nautical textbooks, both technical and non-technical. Also Scottish one-act/three-act plays. Unsolicited mss, synopses and ideas for books welcome.
Royalties paid annually.

Bryntirion Press
Bryntirion, Bridgend, Mid-Glamorgan CF31 4DX
☎01656 655886 Fax 01656 665919
Email press@draco.co.uk
Chief Executive *Gerallt Wyn Davies*
Press Manager *Huw Kinsey*
Approx. Annual Turnover £100,000

Owned by the Evangelical Movement of Wales. *Publishes* Christian books in English and Welsh. 1999 TITLES *Christian Handbook; Walk Worthy; From Shore to Shore; Reformation: Yesterday, Today and Tomorrow.* No unsolicited mss; synopses and ideas welcome.
Royalties paid annually.

Bucknell University Press
See **Golden Cockerel Press Ltd**

Burns & Oates
See **The Continuum International Publishing Group Ltd**

Business Books
See **Random House Group Ltd**

Business Education Publishers Ltd
The Solar Building, Duxford International, Sunderland, Tyne & Wear SR3 3XW
☎0191 525 2400 Fax 0191 520 1815
Email info@bepl.com
Website www.bepl.com
Managing Director *Mrs A. Murphy*
Approx. Annual Turnover £400,000

FOUNDED 1981. *Publishes* business education, economics and law for BTEC and GNVQ reading. Currently expanding into further and higher education, computing, community health services, travel and tourism, occasional papers for institutions and local government administration. Unsolicited mss and synopses welcome.
Royalties paid annually.

Buster Books
See **Michael O'Mara Books Ltd**

Butterworth-Heinemann International

See **Reed Educational & Professional Publishing**

Butterworths

See **Reed Elsevier plc**

Butterworths Tolley

Tolley House, 2 Addiscombe Road, Croydon, Surrey CR9 5AF
☎020 8686 9141 Fax 020 8686 3155
Managing Director *Stephen Stout*

Part of Reed Elsevier Legal Division.
 DIVISIONS **Tolley Publishing; Charles Knight Publishing; Payroll Alliance; Butterworths Tax Publications**.

C&B Publishing plc (Collins & Brown)

London House, Great Eastern Wharf, Parkgate Road, London SW11 4NQ
☎020 7924 2575 Fax 020 7924 7725
Email info@cb-publishing.co.uk
Website www.cb-publishing.co.uk
Managing Director *Kate Macphee*
Publishing Director *Colin Ziegler*
Approx. Annual Turnover £25 million

FOUNDED 1989. Acquired by **Chrysalis** in April 2001. *Publishes* illustrated non-fiction. About 250 titles a year. GROUP IMPRINTS Adult Non-fiction: **Collins & Brown** Publisher *Colin Ziegler* Lifestyle and interiors, gardening, health, mind, body and spirit, photography, practical art and craft. **Pavilion Books** (see entry). Children's non-fiction: **Belitha Press** and **David Bennett Books** (see entries under **UK Packagers**); **Big Fish** Publisher *Peter Osborn*. No unsolicited mss; outlines with s.a.e. only.
 Royalties paid twice-yearly.

Authors' Rating After a troubled year which ended with the closure of a direct marketing subsidiary and a writing off of Internet investment, C&B was bought by Chrysalis Group, a 'financially sound partner' to ensure its future as a multimedia publisher.

Cadogan Guides

Network House, 1 Ariel Way, London W12 7SL
☎020 8600 3550 Fax 020 8600 3599
Email cadoganguides@morrispub.co.uk
Editorial Director *Vicki Ingle*

FOUNDED 1982. *Publishes* travel guides. Most titles are commissioned. No unsolicited material.

Calder Publications Ltd

51 The Cut, London SE1 8LF
☎020 7633 0599 Fax 020 7633 0599
Email enquiries@calderpub.demon.co.uk
Website www.calderpublications.com
Chairman/Managing Director/Editorial Head *John Calder*

Formerly John Calder (Publishers) Ltd. A publishing company which has grown around the tastes and contacts of John Calder, the iconoclast of the literary establishment. The list has a reputation for controversial and opinion-forming publications; Samuel Beckett is perhaps the most prestigious name. The list includes all of Beckett's prose and poetry. *Publishes* autobiography, biography, drama, literary fiction, literary criticism, music, opera, poetry, politics, sociology. AUTHORS Antonin Artaud, Marguerite Duras, Martin Esslin, Erich Fried, P.J. Kavanagh, Robert Menasse, Robert Pinget, Luigi Pirandello, Alain Robbe-Grillet, Nathalie Sarraute, L.F. Celine, Eva Figes, Claude Simon, Howard Barker (plays), ENO opera guides. *No new material accepted.*
 Royalties paid annually.

Authors' Rating Known for his patronage of eccentric talents, John Calder is one of the few publishers to carry the flag for the English language 'which is in great danger of disappearing under the American vernacular'.

California University Press

See **University Presses of California, Columbia & Princeton Ltd**

Cambridge University Press

The Edinburgh Building, Shaftesbury Road, Cambridge CB2 2RU
☎01223 312393 Fax 01223 315052
Website www.cambridge.org
Chief Executive *R.J. Mynott*

The oldest printer and publisher in the world with long-established branches in the USA and Australia and more recently established branches in Spain, Africa, South America and East Asia. Winner of The Queen's Award for Export Achievement in 1998. Over the last ten years, Cambridge has opened many new offices around the world. Its books are sold in more than 200 countries. Publications include the Cambridge Histories and Companions, encyclopedias and dictionaries; the **Canto** series;

popular science and scientific and medical reference; major ELT courses; coursebooks for the National Curriculum; Cambridge Reading; and Cambridge Low Price Editions for the developing world. *Publishes* academic/educational and reference books for English-language markets worldwide, at all levels from primary school to postgraduate, together with a list of Spanish titles. Also ELT, Bibles and over 140 academic journals. Over 23,000 authors in 106 different countries and about 1800 new titles a year.

PUBLISHING GROUPS
Bibles *C.J. Wright* **ELT** *C.J.F. Hayes* **Science Publishing** *A.E. Crowden* **Humanities and Social Sciences** *A.M.C. Brown* **Professional Publishing** *R.W.A. Barling* **Education** *A.C. Gilfillan* **Journals** *C. Guettler.* Synopses and ideas for educational, ELT and academic books are welcome (and preferable to the submission of unsolicited mss). No fiction or poetry.
Royalties paid twice-yearly.

Authors' Rating The move towards online academia has accelerated with CUP's linking up with the British Library, LSE, the Smithsonian, the New York Public Library and Columbia University to provide a global Internet library and learning system. The content will be free but income (it is hoped) will come from course participation and advertising.

Camden Press Ltd
46 Colebrooke Row, London N1 8AF
☎020 7226 2061 Fax 020 7226 2418
Chairman *Bob Borzello*
FOUNDED 1985. *Publishes* social issues; all books are launched in connection with major national conferences. DIVISION **Publishing for Change** *Bob Borzello* TITLE *Living with the Legacy of Abuse.* IMPRINT **Mindfield** TITLES *Hate Thy Neighbour: The Race Issue; Therapy on the Couch.* No unsolicited material. Approach by telephone in the first instance.
Royalties paid annually.

Camden Softcover Large Print
See **Chivers Press Ltd**

David Campbell Publishers Ltd
Gloucester Mansions, 140a Shaftesbury Avenue, London WC2H 8HD
☎020 7539 7600 Fax 020 7379 4060
Email books@everyman.uk.com
Website www.everyman.uk.com
Managing Director *David Campbell*
Approx. Annual Turnover £3.5 million

FOUNDED 1990 with acquisition of Everyman's Library (established 1906) bought from J.M. Dent. *Publishes* classics of world literature, pocket poetry anthologies and travel guides. AUTHORS include Bulgakov, Bellow, Borges, Forster, Grass, Mann, Nabokov, Orwell, Rushdie, Updike and Waugh. No unsolicited mss. IMPRINT **Adelphi** Illustrated books.
Royalties paid annually.

Campbell Books
See **Macmillan Publishers Ltd**

Candle Books
See **Angus Hudson Ltd** under **UK Packagers**

Canongate Books Ltd
14 High Street, Edinburgh EH1 1TE
☎0131 557 5111 Fax 0131 557 5211
Email info@canongate.co.uk
Website www.canongate.net
Publisher *Jamie Byng*
Approx. Annual Turnover £2.1 million

FOUNDED 1973. Acquired by US-based publisher **Grove/Atlantic** in October 2000. *Publishes* a wide range of fiction and non-fiction. There is a strong Scottish slant to part of the house. Lead titles in 2000 included Michel Faber's *Under the Skin* and Laura Herd's *Born Free*, both of which were shortlisted for the **Whitbread** first novel award. About 40 titles were planned for 2001.

IMPRINTS
Canongate Classics Adult paperback series dedicated solely to important works of Scottish literature; **Canongate Crime** Paperback series featuring writers from all around the world, includes **Canongate Crime Classics** dedicated to reprinting lost classics of the genre; **Canongate International** Fiction in translation; **Kelpie** Children's paperback fiction series; **Payback Press** Afro-American, Black orientated fiction and non-fiction; music, history, politics, biography and poetry; **Mojo Books** A new imprint in collaboration with Emap's *Mojo* magazine, combining informed, incisive music writing with Canongate's extensive list of existing music titles.
Royalties paid twice-yearly.

Authors' Rating Now under the wing of a US publisher, Canongate has the opportunity to broaden its activities without losing its independence. Grove/Atlantic, though bigger than its Scottish partner, has the same tradition of imaginative publishing. The match promises well for both partners.

Canterbury Press Norwich
See **Hymns Ancient & Modern Ltd**

Canto
See **Cambridge University Press**

Capall Bann Publishing
Freshfields, Chieveley, Berkshire RG20 8TF
☎01635 247050/248711
Fax 01635 247050/248711
Email capallbann1@virgin.biz.com
Website www.capallbann.co.uk
Chairman *Julia Day*
Editorial Head *Jon Day*

FOUNDED 1993 with three titles and now have over 200 in print. Family-owned and -run company which *publishes* British traditions, folklore, computing, boating, animals, alternative healing, environmental, Celtic lore, mind, body and spirit. About 40 titles a year. TITLES *Practical Spirituality; Celtic Lore; Handbook of Fairies; Talking to the Earth; Bruce Roberts' Boatbuilding.* Unsolicited proposals for books welcome. No e-mailed submissions – correspondence only, please. No fiction or poetry.
Royalties paid twice-yearly.

Jonathan Cape Ltd
See **Random House Group Ltd**

Carcanet Press Ltd
4th Floor, Conavon Court, 12–16 Blackfriars Street, Manchester M3 5BQ
☎0161 834 8730 Fax 0161 832 0084
Email pnr@carcanet.u-net.com
Website www.carcanet.co.uk
Chairman *Kate Gavron*
Managing Director/Editorial Director
  Michael Schmidt

In the last thirty years Carcanet has grown from an undergraduate hobby into a substantial venture. Robert Gavron bought the company in 1983 and it has established strong European, Commonwealth and American links. Winner of the **Sunday Times Small Publisher of the Year** award in 2000, it took over the Oxford Poets list from **Oxford University Press** in 1999 which it now publishes as a distinct imprint. *Publishes* poetry, academic, literary biography, fiction in translation and translations. About 60 titles a year, including the *PN Review* (six issues yearly). AUTHORS Homero Aridjis, John Ashbery, Eavan Boland, Joseph

Brodsky, Donald Davie, Natalia Ginzburg, Robert Graves, Elizabeth Jennings, Edwin Morgan, Les Murray, Frederic Raphael, Leonardo Sciascia, Iain Crichton Smith, Pedro Tamen, Charles Tomlinson. Poetry submissions: 6–10 poems with covering letter and return postage if the material is to be sent back.
Royalties paid annually.

Authors' Rating Ever in the forefront of imaginative publishing, Carcanet has taken a step closer to the source of its literary creativity by setting up a postgraduate Writing School at Manchester Metropolitan University. (See entry under **Writers' Courses, Circles and Workshops**.)

Cardiff Academic Press
St Fagans Road, Fairwater, Cardiff CF5 3AE
☎029 2056 0333 Fax 029 2055 4909
Managing Director *R.G. Drake*
Academic publishers.

Carfax Publishing
See **Taylor & Francis Group plc**

Carlton Publishing Group
20 Mortimer Street, London W1T 3JW
☎020 7612 0400 Fax 020 7612 0401
Email enquiries@carltonbooks.co.uk
Website www.carlton.com
Managing Director *Jonathan Goodman*
Publishing Director *Piers Murray Hill*
Approx. Annual Turnover £17 million

FOUNDED 1992. Owned by Carlton Communications, Carlton's books are aimed at the mass market for subjects such as TV tie-ins, lifestyle, computer games, sport, health, New Age, puzzles, popular science and rock'n'roll. *Publishes* illustrated leisure and entertainment. Prime UK customers include the Book Club and WHSmith.

DIVISIONS **Carlton Books**; **André Deutsch** Autobiography, biography, history, military history, humour and the arts; **Granada Media**; **Manchester United Books**. No unsolicited mss; synopses and ideas welcome. No novels, science fiction, poetry or children's fiction.
Royalties paid twice-yearly.

Authors' Rating Linked to the largest programme producer in the ITV network, Carlton Books has built a reputation on co-editions for the international market and television tie-ins. Noted for speed of taking a book from first idea to publication. A boost for the Deutsch list is promised, the aim being to restore this famous imprint to the top end of the quality market.

Carroll & Brown Publishers Limited
20 Lonsdale Road, London NW6 6RD
☎020 7372 0900 Fax 020 7372 0460
Email mail@carrollandbrown.co.uk
Managing Director *Amy Carroll*
Approx. Annual Turnover £3.5 million

FOUNDED in 1989 as a packaging operation and commenced publishing in 2000. *Publishes* practical cookery, health, gardening, lifestyle, mind, body and spirit. TITLES *The Angelic Year; Le Cordon Bleu Wine Essenetials; The First-time Gardener; What's My Future?; Exercise for Strong Bones*. Synopses and ideas for illustrated books welcome; approach in writing in the first instance. No fiction.
Payment Fees or royalties paid.

Frank Cass & Co Ltd
Crown House, 47 Chase Side, Southgate, London N14 5BP
☎020 8920 2100 Fax 020 8447 8548
Email info@frankcass.com
Website www.frankcass.com
Chairman *Frank Cass*
Managing Director *Stewart Cass*
Managing Editor (Books) *Andrew Humphrys*

Publishes books and journals in the fields of politics, international relations, military and security studies, history, Middle East and African studies, economics, development studies. TITLES *Central Asia Meets the Middle East* ed. David Henashin; *In Pursuit of Military Excellence* Shimon Naveh; *Knowing Your Friends* Martin S. Alexander.

DIVISIONS
Woburn Press Educational list TITLES *Her Majesty's Inspectorate of Schools Since 1944* John E. Dunford; *Going Comprehensive in England and Wales* Alan C. Kercknoff. **Vallentine Mitchell/Jewish Chronicle Publications** Books of Jewish interest TITLES *The Library of Holocaust Testimonies* series; *Soldier of Jerusalem* Uzi Narkiss. Unsolicited mss considered but synopsis with covering letter preferred.
Royalties paid annually.

Cassell
Wellington House, 125 Strand, London WC2R 0BB
☎020 7420 5555 Fax 020 7240 7261
Managing Director *John Mitchinson*

FOUNDED 1848 by John Cassell. Bought by Collier Macmillan in 1974, then by CBS Publishing Europe in 1982. Returned to independence in 1986 as Cassell plc. Acquired by the **Orion Publishing Group** in December 1998. *Publishes* general non-fiction, poetry, reference and illustrated.

IMPRINTS
Cassell General Books TITLES *Poems on the Underground; Cordon Bleu Complete Cookery Techniques; Cacti: The Illustrated Dictionary; Shaker.*
    Arms & Armour Press *Ian Drury* TITLES *First World War Sourcebook; Napoleonic Weapons & Warfare; Great Battles of the Royal Navy.*
    Blandford Press TITLES *Celebration of Maritime Art; Spiders of the World; Celtic Art Sourcebook; Make Your Own Electric Guitar.*
    Ward Lock TITLES *Mrs Beeton's Book of Cookery and Household Management; Home & Garden Style; Ward Lock Gardening Encyclopedia.*
No unsolicited mss; synopses with sample chapters considered.

Castle Publications
See **Nottingham University Press**

Kyle Cathie Ltd
122 Arlington Road, London NW1 7HP
☎020 7692 7215 Fax 020 7692 7260
Email general.enquiries@kyle-cathie.com

FOUNDED 1990 to publish and promote 'books we have personal enthusiasm for'. *Publishes* non-fiction: cookery, food and drink, health and beauty, mind, body & spirit, gardening, homes and interiors, reference and occasional books of classic poetry. TITLES *Bob Flowerdew's Organic Bible; Henrietta Green's Farmers' Market Cookbook; Natural Superwoman* Rosamond Richardson; *Spells for Teenage Witches* Marina Baker. About 25 titles a year. No unsolicited mss. 'Synopses and ideas are considered in the fields in which we publish.'
Royalties paid twice-yearly.

Catholic Truth Society (CTS)
40–46 Harleyford Road, London SE11 5AY
☎020 7640 0042 Fax 020 7640 0046
Email f.martin@cts-online.org.uk
Website www.cts-online.org.uk
Chairman *Rt. Rev. Peter Smith*
General Secretary *Fergal Martin*
Approx. Annual Turnover £500,000

FOUNDED originally in 1868 and re-founded in 1884. *Publishes* religious books – Roman

Catholic; a variety of doctrinal, moral, biographical, devotional and liturgical publications, including a large body of Vatican documents and sources. Unsolicited mss, synopses and ideas welcome if appropriate to their list.
Royalties paid annually.

Caucasus World
See **Curzon Press Ltd**

Causeway Press Ltd
PO Box 13, 129 New Court Way, Ormskirk, Lancashire L39 5HP
☎01695 576048 Fax 01695 570714
Chairman/Managing Director
   M. Haralambos
Approx. Annual Turnover £2 million

FOUNDED in 1982. *Publishes* educational textbooks only. 11 titles in 2000. TITLES *Mathematics for AQA; Mathematics for Edexcel; Psychology in Focus; GCSE Business Studies; Media Studies.* Unsolicited mss, synopses and ideas welcome.
Royalties paid annually.

Caxton Publishing Group
20 Bloomsbury Street, London WC1B 3QA
☎020 7636 7171 Fax 020 7636 1922
Email office@caxtonpublishing.com
Website www.caxtonpublishing.com
Chairman *Stephen Hill*
Managing Director *John Maxwell*
Approx. Annual Turnover £4 million

FOUNDED 1999. *Specialises* in reprinting out-of-print works for the 'value' market worldwide and commissioning new general non-fiction publications in reference, cookery, gardening and children's. 200 titles a year.
   DIVISIONS/IMPRINTS **Brockhampton Press Ltd** Children's fiction and non-fiction. **Caxton Editions Ltd** General non-fiction, reference and military. **Knight Paperbacks Ltd** Fiction. No unsolicited mss; synopses and ideas welcome; send letter in the first instance.
Royalties paid twice-yearly.

CBA Publishing
Bowes Morrell House, 111 Walmgate, York YO1 9WA
☎01904 671417 Fax 01904 671384
Website www.britarch.ac.uk
Publications Officer *Jane Thorniley-Walker*
Approx. Annual Turnover £80,000

Publishing arm of the **Council for British Archaeology**. *Publishes* academic archaeology reports, practical handbooks, yearbook, *British Archaeology* (bi-monthly magazine), *Young Archaeologist* (magazine of the Young Archaeologists' Club), monographs, archaeology and education. TITLES *Our Changing Coast; A Survey of the Intertidal Archaeology of Langstone Harbour; Prehistoric Roman and Post-Roman Landscapes of the Great Ouse Valley.*
Royalties not paid.

CBD Research Ltd
Chancery House, 15 Wickham Road, Beckenham, Kent BR3 5JS
☎020 8650 7745 Fax 020 8650 0768
Email cbdresearch@cbdresearch.freeserve.co.uk
Website www.cbdresearch.co.uk
Chairman *G.P. Henderson*
Managing Director *S.P.A. Henderson*
Approx. Annual Turnover £500,000

FOUNDED 1961. *Publishes* directories and other reference guides to sources of information. About 6 titles a year. No fiction.
   IMPRINT **Chancery House Press** Non-fiction of an esoteric/specialist nature for 'serious researchers and the dedicated hobbyist'. Unsolicited mss, synopses and ideas welcome.
Royalties paid quarterly.

Centaur Press
See **Open Gate Press**

Century
See **Random House Group Ltd**

Chadwyck-Healey Ltd
The Quorum, Barnwell Road, Cambridge CB5 8SW
☎01223 215512 Fax 01223 215513
Website www.chadwyck.co.uk
General Manager *Steven Hall*
Approx. Annual Turnover £9.5 million

Part of Bell & Howell. *Publishes* humanities and literary databases on the Web, CD-ROM and microform. Key TITLES include *KnowUK; Literature Online; The English Poetry Database; Periodical Contents Index; KnowEurope.* No unsolicited mss. Synopses and ideas welcome for reference works only.
Royalties paid annually.

Chambers Harrap Publishers Ltd
7 Hopetoun Crescent, Edinburgh EH7 4AY
☎0131 556 5929 Fax 0131 556 5313
Website www.chambersharrap.com
Managing Director *Maurice Shepherd*
Administrator *Stephanie Gloyer*

Publishes dictionaries and reference. The imprint was founded in the early 1800s to publish self-education books, but soon diversified into dictionaries and other reference works. The acquisition of Harrap Publishing Group's core business strengthened its position in the dictionary market, adding bilingual titles, covering almost all the major European languages, to its English-language dictionaries. About 24 titles a year. Send synopsis with accompanying letter rather than completed mss.

Chancery House Press
See **CBD Research Ltd**

Channel 4 Books
See **Macmillan Publishers Ltd**

Geoffrey Chapman
See **The Continuum International Publishing Group Ltd**

Paul Chapman Publishing Ltd
See **Sage Publications Ltd**

Chapman Publishing
4 Broughton Place, Edinburgh EH1 3RX
☎0131 557 2207 Fax 0131 556 9565
Email editor@chapman-pub.co.uk
Website www.chapman-pub.co.uk

Managing Editor *Joy Hendry*

A venture devoted to publishing works by the best of the Scottish writers, both up-and-coming and established, published in *Chapman* magazine, Scotland's leading literary quarterly. Has expanded publishing activities considerably over the last two years and is now publishing a wider range of works though the broad policy stands. *Publishes* poetry, drama, short stories, books of contemporary importance in 20th-century Scotland. About 4 titles a year. TITLES *Gold of Kildonan; Songs of the Grey Coast; Whins* George Gunn; *The Collected Shorter Poems* Tom Scott; *Alien Crop* Janet Paisley; *Good Girls Don't Cry* Margaret Fulton Cook; *Wild Women Series – Wild Women of a Certain Age* Magi Gibson; *Wild Women Anthology*. No unsolicited mss; synopses and ideas for books welcome.
Royalties paid annually.

Chapmans Publishers
See **The Orion Publishing Group Ltd**

Charnwood
See **F.A. Thorpe (Publishing)**

Chartered Institute of Personnel and Development
CIPD House, Camp Road, London SW19 4UX
☎020 8263 3387 Fax 020 8263 3850
Email publish@cipd.co.uk
Website www.cipd.co.uk

Part of CIPD Enterprises Limited. *Publishes* people management and training titles. A list of 200 titles. Unsolicited mss, synopses and ideas welcome.
Royalties paid annually.

Chatham Publishing
See **Gerald Duckworth & Co Ltd**

Chatto & Windus Ltd
See **Random House Group Ltd**

Cherrytree Books
See **Evans Brothers**

Chicken House Publishing
2 Palmer Street, Frome, Somerset BA11 1DS
☎01373 454488 Fax 01373 454499
Email doublecluck.com

Chairman/Managing Director *Barry Cunningham*

New children's publishing house FOUNDED in 2000. *Publishes* books 'that are aimed at real children' – fiction, original picture books, gift books and fun non-fiction. Aiming to publish about 25 titles a year. 'We are always on the lookout for new talent.' Unsolicited material welcome; send letter with synopsis and sample chapters.
Royalties paid twice-yearly.

Child's Play (International) Ltd
Ashworth Road, Bridgemead, Swindon, Wiltshire SN5 7YD
☎01793 616286 Fax 01793 512795
Email allday@childs-play.com
Website www.childs-play.com

Chief Executive *Neil Burden*

FOUNDED in 1972, Child's Play is an independent publisher specialising in learning through play, whole child development, life-skills and values. *Publishes* books, games and A–V materials. TITLES Books: *Big Hungry Bear; There Was an Old Lady; Puzzle Island; Children of the Sun; Ten Beads Tall; Pocket Pals; Sliders; Roly Poly Books; Book Buddies; Mrs Honey's Tree; Big Books and Storysacks;* Games: *Dizzy Bizzy; Safe Places; Arithmetic Lotto.* Unsolicited mss welcome. Send s.a.e. for return or response. Expect to wait two months for a reply.

Royalties Outright or royalty payments are subject to negotiation.

Chimera
See **Pegasus Elliot Mackenzie Publishers**

Chivers Press Ltd
Windsor Bridge Road, Bath BA2 3AX
☎01225 335336 Fax 01225 310771
Email sales@chivers.co.uk
Website www.chivers.co.uk
Managing Director *Julian R. Batson*
Approx. Annual Turnover £9 million

Publishes reprints for libraries mainly, in large-print editions, including biography and autobiography, children's, crime, fiction and spoken word cassettes. No unsolicited material.

IMPRINTS
Chivers Large Print; Gunsmoke Westerns; Galaxy Children's Large Print; Camden Softcover Large Print; Paragon Softcover Large Print; Windsor Large Print; Black Dagger Crime. Chivers Audio Books (see entry under **Audio Books**).
Royalties paid twice-yearly.

Christian Focus Publications
Geanies House, Fearn, Tain, Ross-shire IV20 1TW
☎01862 871011 Fax 01862 871699
Email info@christianfocus.com
Website www.christianfocus.com
Chairman *R.W.M. Mackenzie*
Managing Director *Willie Mackenzie*
Children's Editor *Catherine Mackenzie*
Approx. Annual Turnover £1.2 million

FOUNDED 1979 to produce children's books for the co-edition market. Now a major producer of Christian books. *Publishes* adult and children's books, including some fiction for children but not adults. No poetry. About 80 titles a year. Unsolicited mss, synopses and ideas welcome from Christian writers. Publishes for all English-speaking markets, as well as the UK.

IMPRINTS **Christian Focus** General books; **Mentor** Study books; **Christian Heritage** Classic reprints.
Royalties paid annually.

Christian Heritage
See **Christian Focus Publications**

Chrysalis Books Ltd
10 Blenheim Court, Brewery Road, London N7 9NT
☎020 7700 7611 Fax 020 7700 4552
Email info@batsford.com
Website www.chrysalisbooks.co.uk
Chairman *John Needleman*

The holding company for the book publishing division of the media group, Chrysalis Group Plc, encompassing **Brassey's** (see entry) – incorporating **Conway Maritime Press** and **Putnam Aeronautical Books**; **B.T. Batsford** (see entry); **C&B Publishing plc** (see entry); **Pavilion Books Ltd** (see entry); **Greenwich Editions** (promotional books and gifts); **Ramboro Books** (remainder books); **Robson Books** (see entry); **Salamander Books** (see entry); **ZigZag Children's Books** (illustrated books for 2–15-year-olds).

Authors' Rating When Element (mind, body and spirit books) went down the tube last year, Chrysalis snapped up those titles not bought by HarperCollins. Since this was its seventh acquisition in less than two years, resources are evidently on tap for expansion which should benefit existing imprints such as Robson and Batsford.

Churchill Livingstone
See **Harcourt Publishers Limited**

Cicerone Press
2 Police Square, Milnthorpe, Cumbria LA7 7PY
☎015395 62069 Fax 015395 63417
Email info@cicerone.demon.co.uk
Website www.cicerone.demon.co.uk
Managing/Editorial Director *Jonathan Williams*

FOUNDED 1969. Guidebook publisher for outdoor enthusiasts. About 20 titles a year. No fiction or poetry. TITLES *Walking in the Alps*; *Jordan: Walks, Treks, Caves and Climbs*; *County* and *Long Distance Walking* series of guides. No unsolicited mss; synopses and ideas considered.
Royalties paid twice-yearly.

Cico Books
1st Floor, 32 Great Sutton Street, London EC1V 0NB
☎020 7253 7960 Fax 020 7253 7967
Email mail@cicobooks.co.uk
Managing Director *Mark Collins*
Publisher *Cindy Richards*

FOUNDED in 1999 by Mark Collins and Cindy

Richards (both formerly with Collins & Brown) 'to offer flexibility by being small, selling co-edition rights to overseas publishers'. *Publishes* lifestyle and interiors, mind, body and spirit. About 12 titles a year. No unsolicited mss, synopses or ideas.

Royalties paid twice-yearly.

Claridge Press
Horsell's Farm Cottage, Sunday Hill, Brinkworth, Wiltshire SN15 5AS
☎01666 510272 Fax 01666 510013
Email info@claridgepress.com
Website www.claridgepress.com

Managing Editor *Andrea Downing*

FOUNDED 1987. Developed from the quarterly *Salisbury Review*. *Publishes* current affairs – political, philosophical and sociological – from a right-wing viewpoint. SERIES *Thinkers of our Time*. TITLES *Reviving the Muse: Music After Modernism; Peter Simple's Century; Dignified and Efficient – The British Monarchy in the Twentieth Century*. Unsolicited mss welcome within given subject areas.

Royalties paid according to contract.

Clarion
See **Elliot Right Way Books**

T.&T. Clark
59 George Street, Edinburgh EH2 2LQ
☎0131 225 4703 Fax 0131 220 4260
Email ggreen@tandtclark.co.uk
Website www.tandtclark.co.uk

Managing Director/Editorial Head
Geoffrey Green

FOUNDED 1821. Part of the **Continuum International Publishing Group Ltd**. *Publishes* religion, theology and philosophy for academic and professional markets. About 35 titles a year, including journals. TITLES *Church Dogmatics* Karl Barth; *The Romans Debate* Karl Donfried; *In the Beginning* Joseph Ratzinger. Unsolicited mss, synopses and ideas for books welcome.

Royalties paid annually.

James Clarke & Co.
PO Box 60, Cambridge CB1 2NT
☎01223 350865 Fax 01223 366951
Email publishing@jamesclarke.co.uk
Website www.jamesclarke.co.uk

Managing Director *Adrian Brink*

Parent company of **The Lutterworth Press** (see entry). *Publishes* scholarly and academic works, mainly theological, directory and reference titles. TITLES *Libraries Directory* (book and CD-ROM versions); *Image Government: monar-chical metamorphoses 1649–1702; Milton and the Preaching Arts*. Approach in writing with ideas in the first instance.

Peter Collin Publishing Ltd
32–34 Great Peter Street, London SW1P 2DB
☎020 7222 1155 Fax 020 7222 1551
Email info@pcp.co.uk
Website www.petercollin.com

Chairman *P.H. Collin*

FOUNDED 1985. *Publishes* dictionaries only, including specialised dictionaries in English for students and specialised bilingual dictionaries for translators (French, German, Swedish, Spanish, Greek, Chinese, Hungarian). About 20 titles a year. Synopses and ideas welcome. No unsolicited mss; copy must be supplied on disk.

Royalties paid twice-yearly.

Collins
See **HarperCollins Publishers Ltd**

Collins & Brown
See **C&B Publishing plc**

Colonsay Books
See **House of Lochar**

Colourpoint Books
Unit D5, Ards Business Centre, Jubilee Road, Newtownards, Co. Down BT23 4YH
☎028 9182 0505 Fax 028 9182 1900
Email info@colourpoint.co.uk
Website www.colourpoint.co.uk

Partners *Sheila M. Johnston, Norman Johnston*
Approx. Annual Turnover £200,000

FOUNDED 1993. *Publishes* school textbooks and transport (covering mainland Britain as well as Northern Ireland), plus books of Irish interest. No fiction. 10 titles in 2000. Approach in writing in the first instance; include return postage, please.

Royalties paid twice-yearly.

Columbia University Press
See **University Presses of California, Columbia & Princeton Ltd**

Compendium Publishing Ltd
1st Floor, 43 Frith Street, London W1V 5TE
☎020 7287 4570 Fax 020 7494 0583
Email compendiumpub@aol.com

Managing Director *Alan Greene*
Editorial Director *Simon Forty*

FOUNDED 1996. *Publishes* and packages for

international publishing companies – general non-fiction: history, reference, hobbies, children's, transport and militaria. 25 titles in 2000. IMPRINT **Windrow & Greene** Military books. No unsolicited mss; synopses and ideas preferred.

Royalties paid twice-yearly.

Condor
See **Souvenir Press Ltd**

Condé Nast Books
See **Random House Group Ltd**

Conran Octopus
See **Octopus Publishing Group**

Constable & Robinson Ltd
3 The Lanchesters, 162 Fulham Palace Road, London W6 9ER
☎020 8741 3663 Fax 020 8748 7562
Email enquiries@constablerobinson.com
Website www.constablerobinson.com
Non-Executive Chairman *Benjamin Glazebrook*
Managing Director *Nick Robinson*
Directors *Jan Chamier, Nova Jayne Heath, Adrian Andrews*
Approx. Annual Turnover £5 million

Constable & Co FOUNDED in 1890 by Archibald Constable, a grandson of Walter Scott's publisher. Robinson Publishing Ltd FOUNDED in 1983 by Nick Robinson. In December 1999 Constable and Robinson combined their individual shareholdings into a single company, Constable & Robinson Ltd. IMPRINTS **Constable** (Hardbacks) *Carol O'Brien*, Editorial Director *Publishes* biography and autobiography, crime fiction, general and military history, psychology, travel, climbing, landscape photography and outdoor pursuits guidebooks. **Robinson** (Paperbacks) *Krystyna Green* Senior Commissioning Editor *Publishes* crime, science fiction, *Daily Telegraph* health books, the Mammoth series, psychology, true crime, military history and *Smarties* children's books. Unsolicited sample chapters, synopses and ideas for books welcome. No mss; no e-mail submissions. Enclose return postage.

Authors' Rating The merging of two small but highly regarded independent publishers promises well for authors who enjoy close attention from their editors. The broad scope of the fiction and non-fiction lists suggests a flexible response to book proposals.

Consultants Bureau
See **Kluwer Academic/Plenum Publishers**

Consumers' Association
See **Which? Books/Consumers' Association**

The Continuum International Publishing Group Limited
The Tower Building, 11 York Road, London SE1 7NX
☎020 7922 0880 Fax 020 7922 0881
Website www.continuumbooks.com
Chairman/Managing Director *Philip Sturrock*
Approx. Annual Turnover £10 million

FOUNDED in 1999 by a buy-out of the academic and religious publishing of **Cassell** and the acquisition of Continuum New York. *Publishes* academic, religious and general books. 300 titles in 2000. DIVISIONS **Academic** *Janet Joyce* Textbooks, reference books and monographs in the humanities, social sciences, business and computing studies, education and performing arts. IMPRINTS **Pinter; Leicester University Press; Mansell; Athlone** TITLES *Directory of Publishing; Companion to 20th Century Theatre; Reflective Teaching in the Primary School.* **Religious** *Robin Baird-Smith*
IMPRINTS **Geoffrey Chapman; Mowbray; T.&T. Clark; Burns & Oates** TITLES *Pilgrims in Rome; Jerome Biblical Commentary.* **General Books** *Robin Baird-Smith Publishes* authors such as Christopher Booker, John Bayley and Anthony O'Hear. Unsolicited synopses and ideas within the subject areas listed above welcome; approach in writing in the first instance. *Overseas associate* The Continuum International Publishing Group Inc., New York.

Royalties paid twice-yearly.

Authors' Rating To prove the point that reading is still primarily an intellectual exercise, Continuum is going strongly for books about philosophy and religion. But quality is the hallmark across the entire list.

Conway Maritime Press
See **Brassey's**

Thomas Cook Publishing
PO Box 227, Peterborough PE3 6PU
☎01733 503571 Fax 01733 503596
Managing Director *Kevin Fitzgerald*
Approx. Annual Turnover £1.7 million

Part of the Thomas Cook Group Ltd, publishing

commenced in 1873 with the first issue of Cook's Continental Timetable. *Publishes* guidebooks, maps and timetables. About 20 titles a year. No unsolicited mss; synopses and ideas welcome as long as they are travel-related.

Royalties paid annually.

Leo Cooper
See **Pen & Sword Books Ltd**

Corgi
See **Transworld Publishers**

Cornwall Books
See **Golden Cockerel Press Ltd**

Coronet
See **Hodder Headline Plc**

Countryside Books
2 Highfield Avenue, Newbury, Berkshire RG14 5DS
☎01635 43816   Fax 01635 551004
Email info@countrysidebooks.co.uk
Website www.countrysidebooks.co.uk

Publisher *Nicholas Battle*

FOUNDED 1976. *Publishes* local interest paperbacks on regional subjects, generally by English county. Local history, genealogy, walking and photographic, aviation and military, some transport. Over 300 titles available. Unsolicited mss and synopses welcome but no fiction, poetry, natural history or personal memories.

Royalties paid twice-yearly.

Cressrelles Publishing Co. Ltd
10 Station Road Industrial Estate, Colwall, Malvern, Worcestershire WR13 6RN
☎01684 540154   Fax 01684 540154

Managing Director *Leslie Smith*

Publishes a range of general books, drama and chiropody titles.

IMPRINTS **Actinic Press** Specialises in chiropody; **J. Garnet Miller Ltd** Plays and theatre texts; **Kenyon-Deane** Plays and drama textbooks.

Cromwell Publishers
Suite 87, 405 Kings Road, London SW10 0BB
☎020 7644 3924   Fax 020 7352 2833
Email editorial@cromwellpublishers.co.uk
Website www.cromwellpublishers.co.uk

FOUNDED 1995. *Publishes* fiction and non-fiction in paperback format: memoirs, biography, auto-

biography, religion/inspirational, popular sciences, young children, health. 'May consider some poetry.' No cookery, academic, manuals or erotica. 100 titles to date. No unsolicited mss; send synopsis and one sample chapter with return postage to New Submissions. IMPRINTS **Cromwell Children**; **Cromwell Publishing**.

Royalties paid annually.

Authors' Rating Liable to ask authors to contribute towards costs of publication.

Croom Helm
See **Routledge**

Crossway
See **Inter-Varsity Press**

The Crowood Press Ltd
The Stable Block, Crowood Lane, Ramsbury, Marlborough, Wiltshire SN8 2HR
☎01672 520320   Fax 01672 520280
Email enquiries@crowood.com
Website www.crowood.com

Chairman *John Dennis*
Managing Director *Ken Hathaway*

Publishes sport and leisure titles, including animal and land husbandry, climbing and walking, maritime, country sports, equestrian, fishing and shooting; also chess and bridge, crafts, dogs, gardening, natural history, aviation, military history and motoring. About 70 titles a year. Preliminary letter preferred in all cases.

Royalties paid annually.

James Currey Publishers
73 Botley Road, Oxford OX2 0BS
☎01865 244111   Fax 01865 246454

Chairman *James Currey*
Managing Director/Editorial Director
Douglas H. Johnson

FOUNDED 1985. A specialist publisher. *Publishes* academic paperback books on Africa, the Caribbean and Third World: history, anthropology, economics, sociology, politics and literary criticism. Approach in writing by post with synopsis if material is 'relevant to our needs'.

Royalties paid annually.

Curzon Press Ltd
51a George Street, Richmond, Surrey TW9 1HJ
☎020 8948 4660   Fax 020 8332 6735

Managing Director *Malcolm G. Campbell*

Specialised   scholarly   publishing   house.

Publishes academic/scholarly books on history, languages and linguistics, philosophy, religion and theology, sociology and anthropology, cultural studies and reference, mainly in the context of Asia but also Africa. IMPRINTS **Caucasus World; Japan Library**.

Cygnus Arts
See **Golden Cockerel Press Ltd**

Dalesman Publishing Co. Ltd
Stable Courtyard, Broughton Hall, Skipton, North Yorkshire BD23 3AZ
☎01756 701381 Fax 01756 701326
Email editorial@dalesman.co.uk
Website www.dalesman.co.uk
Editor *Terry Fletcher*

Publishers of *Dalesman, Cumbria and Lake District* and *Peak District* magazines, and regional books covering Yorkshire, the Lake District and the Peak District. Subjects include crafts and hobbies, geography and geology, guidebooks, history and antiquarian, humour, travel and topography. Will consider mss on subjects listed above. About 20 titles a year.
Royalties paid annually.

Terence Dalton Ltd
Water Street, Lavenham, Sudbury, Suffolk CO10 9RN
☎01787 249291 Fax 01787 248267
Website www.lavenhamgroup.co.uk
Director/Editorial Head *Elisabeth Whitehair*
FOUNDED 1967. Part of the Lavenham Group Plc, a family company. *Publishes* non-fiction and currently contract-publishes water and environment books for Chartered UK Institution. No unsolicited mss; send synopsis with two or three sample chapters. Ideas welcome.
Royalties paid annually.

The C.W. Daniel Co. Ltd
1 Church Path, Saffron Walden, Essex CB10 1JP
☎01799 521909 Fax 01799 513462
Email cwdaniel@dial.pipex.com
Website www.cwdaniel.com
Managing Director *Ian Miller*
Approx. Annual Turnover £1 million
FOUNDED in 1902 by a man who knew and was a follower of Tolstoy, the company was taken over by its present directors in 1973. Output increased following the acquisition in 1980 of health and healing titles from the Health Science Press, the purchase of Neville Spearman Publishers' metaphysical list in 1985 and the list of L.N. Fowler in 1998. *Publishes* New Age: alternative healing and metaphysical. About 15 titles a year. No fiction, diet or cookery. Unsolicited synopses and ideas welcome; no unsolicited mss.
Royalties paid annually.

Darf Publishers Ltd
277 West End Lane, London NW6 1QS
☎020 7431 7009 Fax 020 7431 7655
Website www.darfpublishers.co.uk
Chairman/Managing Director *M.B. Fergiani*
Editorial Head *A. Bentaleb*
Approx. Annual Turnover £500,000
FOUNDED 1982 to publish books and reprints on the Middle East, history, theology and travel. *Publishes* geography, history, language, literature, oriental, politics, theology and travel. About 10 titles a year. TITLES *Moslems in Spain; Travels of Ibn Battuta; The Barbary Corsairs; Elementary Arabic; Travels in Syria and the Holy Land.*
Royalties paid annually. *Overseas associates* Dar Al-Fergiani, Cairo, Tripoli and Tunis.

Darton, Longman & Todd Ltd
1 Spencer Court, 140–142 Wandsworth High Street, London SW18 4JJ
☎020 8875 0155 Fax 020 8875 0133
Email mail@darton-longman-todd.co.uk
Editorial Director *Brendan Walsh*
Approx. Annual Turnover £1 million
FOUNDED in 1959. In July 1990 DLT became a common ownership company, owned and run by staff members. A leading ecumenical, predominantly Christian, publisher, with a strong emphasis on spirituality, theology and the ministry and mission of the Church. About 50 titles a year. TITLES *Jerusalem Bible; New Jerusalem Bible; God of Surprises; Audacity to Believe.* Sample material for books on theological or spiritual subjects considered.
Royalties paid twice-yearly.

David & Charles Children's Books
See **Gullane Children's Books**

David & Charles Publishers
Brunel House, Forde Close, Newton Abbot, Devon TQ12 4PU
☎01626 323200 Fax 01626 323317

Email mail@davidandcharles.co.uk
Website www.davidandcharles.co.uk
Managing Director *Budge Wallis*
Approx. Annual Turnover £10 million

FOUNDED 1960 as a specialist company. *Publishes* illustrated non-fiction for international markets, specialising in needlecraft, crafts, art techniques, practical photography, interiors and equestrian. No fiction, poetry or memoirs. About 50 titles a year. TITLES *Stitcher's Bible; Dolls' House Details; Watercolour in a Weekend; Photos That Sell; Enlightened Equitation; The Complete Equine Veterinary Manual.* Unsolicited mss will be considered if return postage is included; synopses and ideas welcome for the subjects listed above.
Royalties paid twice-yearly.

Authors' Rating The name suggests nice young men who sell antiques but D&C was always sturdy Middle England, a publisher that traded in nostalgia for steam engines and trams. After a few rocky years with Reader's Digest, a management buyout started a gradual recovery which has now led to a takeover by F&W Publications, a US company with corresponding strengths in 'how-to' titles and book clubs. A radical shake up followed. The gardening list closed, the children's list was sold and there was more concentration on profitable titles. But for an important if narrower sector of popular non-fiction, the prospects look good.

Christopher Davies Publishers Ltd

PO Box 403, Swansea, West Glamorgan SA1 4YF
☎01792 648825 Fax 01792 648825
Managing Director/Editorial Head
Christopher T. Davies
Approx. Annual Turnover £50,000

FOUNDED 1949 to promote and expand Welsh-language publications. By the 1970s the company was publishing over 50 titles a year but a subsequent drop in Welsh sales led to the establishment of a small English list which has continued. *Publishes* biography, cookery, history, sport and literature of Welsh interest. About 3 titles a year. TITLES *An A–Z of Wales and the Welsh; Ivor Allchurch M.B.E., Biography; Historic Gower; Who's Who in Welsh History.* No unsolicited mss. Synopses and ideas for books welcome.
Royalties paid twice-yearly.

Authors' Rating A favourite for Celtic readers and writers.

Giles de la Mare Publishers Ltd

PO Box 25351, London NW5 1ZT
☎020 7485 2533 Fax 020 7485 2534
Email gilesdelamare@dial.pipex.com
Chairman/Managing Director *Giles de la Mare*
Approx. Annual Turnover £45,000

FOUNDED 1995 and commenced publishing in April 1996. *Publishes* mainly non-fiction, especially art and architecture, biography, history, music. TITLES *Married to the Amadeus* Muriel Nissel; *Venice: An Anthology Guide* Milton Grundy; *History at War* Noble Frankland; *Duchess of Cork Street* Lillian Browse; *Erasmus Darwin* Desmond King-Hall; *Shakespeare and the Prince of Love* Anthony Arlidge; *Flint Architecture of East Anglia* Stephen Hart; *19th Century British Painting* Luke Herrmann. Unsolicited mss, synopses and ideas welcome after initial telephone call.
Royalties paid twice-yearly.

Dean

See **Egmont Books**

Debrett's Peerage Ltd

Brunel House, 55a North Wharf Road, London W2 1XR
☎020 7915 9633 Fax 020 7753 4212
Email people@debretts.co.uk
Website www.debretts.co.uk
Chairman *Christopher Haines*
Commercial Director *Howard Clare*

FOUNDED 1769. The company's main activity (in conjunction with **Macmillan**) is the quinquennial *Debrett's Peerage and Baronetage* (published in 2000) and annual *Debrett's People of Today* (also available on CD-ROM). Debrett's general books are published under licence through **Headline**.
Royalties paid twice-yearly.

Dedalus Ltd

Langford Lodge, St Judith's Lane, Sawtry, Cambridgeshire PE28 5XE
☎01487 832382 Fax 01487 832382
Email DedalusLimited@compuserve.com
Chairman *Juri Gabriel*
Managing Director *Eric Lane*
Approx. Annual Turnover £200,000

FOUNDED 1983. *Publishes* contemporary European fiction and classics and original literary fiction in the fields of magic realism, surrealism, the grotesque and bizarre. 16 titles in 2000. TITLES

The Decadent Traveller; The Arabian Nightmare Robert Irwin; *False Ambassador* Christopher Harris; *The Political Map of the Heart* Pat Gray; *Music in a Foreign Language* Andrew Crumey (winner of the **Saltire Best First Book Award** in 1994). Welcomes submissions for original fiction and books suitable for its list but 'most people sending work in have no idea what kind of books Dedalus publishes and merely waste their efforts'. Particularly interested in intellectually clever and unusual fiction. A letter about the author should always accompany any submission. No replies without s.a.e.

DIVISIONS/IMPRINTS **Original Fiction in Paperback; Contemporary European Fiction 1992–2000; Dedalus European Classics; Empire of the Senses; Bizarre Literary Concept Books**.
Royalties paid annually.

Authors' Rating A small, quality publisher which actually recognises that good books can come from foreign language writers.

University of Delaware
See **Golden Cockerel Press Ltd**

JM Dent
See **The Orion Publishing Group Ltd**

André Deutsch Ltd
See **Carlton Publishing Group**

Dial House
See **Ian Allan Publishing Ltd**

Dinas
See **Y Lolfa Cyf**

Diva Books
Worldwide House, 116/134 Bayham Street, London NW1 0BA
☎020 7482 2576 Fax 020 7284 0329
Website www.prowler.co.uk
Contacts *Gillian Rodgerson, Helen Sandler*

Part of the Millivres–Prowler Group. New lesbian imprint. *Publishes* literary and popular fiction, non-fiction. TITLES *Girl2Girl; Mush; The Comedienne.* 'Rights by negotiation.'

John Donald Publishers Ltd
Unit 8 Canongate Venture, 5 New Street, Edinburgh EH8 5BH
☎0131 556 6660 Fax 0131 557 6250
Managing Director *Hugh Andrew*

Bought by **Birlinn Ltd** in 1999. *Publishes* academic and scholarly, archaeology, architecture, textbooks, guidebooks, local, military and social history. About 20 titles a year. New books are published as an imprint of Birlinn Ltd.
Royalties paid annually.

Donhead Publishing Ltd
Lower Coombe, Donhead St Mary, Shaftesbury, Dorset SP7 9LY
☎01747 828422 Fax 01747 828522
Email jillpearce@donhead.com
Website www.donhead.com
Contact *Jill Pearce*

FOUNDED 1990 to specialise in publishing how-to books for building practitioners; particularly interested in architectural conservation material. *Publishes* building, architecture and heritage only. 6 titles a year. TITLES *Preserving Post-War Heritage; Stone Cleaning; Architecture 1900; Encyclopaedia of Architectural Terms; Gauged Brickwork; Cleaning Historic Buildings; Brickwork; Practical Stone Masonry; Conservation of Timber Buildings; Surveying Historic Buildings; English Heritage Directory of Building Limes; Heritage, Sands and Aggregates; Creative Re-use of Buildings; Journal of Architectural Conservation* (3 issues yearly). Unsolicited mss, synopses and ideas welcome.

Dorling Kindersley Ltd
Part of the Penguin Group, 80 Strand, London WC2R 0RL
☎020 7010 3000 Fax 020 7010 6060
Website www.dk.com
Chief Executive *Anthony Forbes Watson*
Publisher *Christopher Davis*
Approx. Annual Turnover
  UK £29.1 million; US £36.5 million

FOUNDED 1974. Packager and publisher of illustrated non-fiction: cookery, crafts, gardening, health, travel guides, atlases, natural history and children's information and fiction. Launched a US imprint in 1991 and an Australian imprint in 1997. Acquired Henderson Publishing in 1995 and was purchased by Pearson plc for £311 million in 2000.

DIVISIONS
Adult: **Travel/Reference** Publisher *Douglas Amrine*; **General/Lifestyle** Publisher *Valerie Buckingham*. Children's: **Licensing** Publisher *Michael Herridge*; **Reference** Publisher *Miriam Farby*; **PreSchool/Primary** Publisher *Sophie Mitchell*. IMPRINTS **Ladybird; Eyewitness Guides; Eyewitness Travel Guides**. TITLES

BMA Complete Family Health Encyclopedia; *RHS A–Z Encyclopedia of Garden Plants*; *Children's Illustrated Encyclopedia*; *The Way Things Work*. Unsolicited synopses/ideas for books welcome.

Authors' Rating Always in the forefront of imaginative non-fiction publishing, DK got into trouble when it over invested in *Star Wars* and other passing fancies. Enter Pearson or, more precisely, Penguin with a rescue package that has seen DK return to prosperous form. Having closed the Family Learning and CD-ROM divisions, the focus is on 'soft learning' products for the trade and education markets. Most titles are team efforts with writers and illustrators working closely with an in-house editor.

Doubleday
See **Transworld Publishers**

Ashley Drake Publishing Ltd
PO Box 733, Cardiff CF14 2YX
☎029 2056 0343 Fax 029 2056 1631
Email post@ashleydrake.com
Website www.ashleydrake.com
Managing Director *Ashley Drake*
Approx. Annual Turnover £70,000

FOUNDED 1995. *Publishes* academic, trade and Welsh-language books. 20 titles in 1999. No unsolicited mss; synopses and ideas for the Welsh Academic Press and St David's Press imprints welcome. No scientific or computing books.

IMPRINTS
St David's Press Sport, music, cookery and general trade. TITLES *When Pele Broke Our Hearts – Wales and the 1958 World Cup*; *Welsh Names for Children – The Complete Guide*. **Welsh Academic Press** English language academic, scholarly humanities and social sciences. TITLES *The American West*; *The Electoral Handbook of Wales 1900–2001*; *Celtic Radicals* and *Celtic Poetry Library* series. **Gwasg Addysgol Cymru** Welsh-language educational titles. TITLES *Dyddiadur Anne Frank* (*Diary of Anne Frank*). **Y Ddraig Fach** Welsh-language titles for children. Welsh editions of Ladybird/Disney and Ladybird/Dreamworks mini-hardbacks.
Royalties paid annually.

Drake Educational Associates
St Fagans Road, Fairwater, Cardiff CF5 3AE
☎029 2056 0333 Fax 029 2055 4909
Managing Director *R.G. Drake*
Educational publishers.

Dref Wen
28 Church Road, Whitchurch, Cardiff CF14 2EA
☎029 2061 7860 Fax 029 2061 0507
Email gwil_drefwen@btinternet.com
Chairman *R. Boore*
Managing Director *G. Boore*
FOUNDED 1970. *Publishes* Welsh language and bilingual children's books, Welsh and English educational books for Welsh learners. No unsolicited material.
Royalties paid annually.

Dryden Press
See **Harcourt Publishers Limited**

Duck Editions/Duckbacks
See **Gerald Duckworth & Co. Ltd**

Gerald Duckworth & Co. Ltd
61 Frith Street, London W1D 3JL
☎020 7434 4242 Fax 020 7434 4420
Email info@duckworth-publishers.co.uk
Website www.ducknet.co.uk
Publisher/CEO *Thomas J. Hedley*
Editorial Director *Sarah Such*
Approx. Annual Turnover £2 million

FOUNDED 1898 by Gerald Duckworth. Original publishers of Virginia Woolf. Other early authors include Hilaire Belloc, John Galsworthy, D.H. Lawrence and George Orwell. Duckworth is a general trade publisher with eminent authors such as Beryl Bainbridge, D.J. Taylor and John Bayley in addition to a strong academic division.

IMPRINTS/DIVISIONS **Bristol Classical Press** Classical texts and modern languages; **Chatham Publishing** Maritime history; **Duck Editions** Contemporary literary fiction and non-fiction; **Duckworth Academic**; **Duckworth General**; **Duckbacks**. No unsolicited mss; synopses and sample chapters only. Enclose s.a.e. or return postage for response/return.
Royalties paid twice-yearly at first, annually thereafter.

Authors' Rating Once noted for erudition and books by Beryl Bainbridge, Duckworth has reinvented itself as a publisher for the youth market. A new imprint, Duck Editions, offering an intriguing collection of quirkish titles, will attract submissions from way-out authors who find that their work does not fit easily into conventional publishing. Another sign of aggressive expansion is the creation of Drake Films to commission screenplays which may be taken on to production or sold as part of a production package.

Duncan Petersen Publishing Limited

31 Ceylon Road, London W14 0PY
☎020 7371 2356   Fax 020 7371 2507
Directors *Andrew Duncan, Mel Petersen*
FOUNDED 1986. Publisher and packager of childcare, business, antiques, birds, nature, atlases, walking and travel books. IMPRINT **Duncan Petersen** SERIES *Charming Small Hotel Guides; Independent Traveller's Guides; Backroads Driving Guides; On Foot* (city walking guides). Unsolicited synopses and ideas for books welcome.
Fees paid.

Martin Dunitz Ltd

The Livery House, 7–9 Pratt Street, London NW1 0AE
☎020 7482 2202   Fax 020 7267 0159
Website www.dunitz.co.uk
Managing Director *Martin Dunitz*
Production Director *Rosemary Allen*
Journals Manager *Ian Mellor*
Acquired by the **Taylor & Francis Group plc** in 1999. *Publishes* specialist medical and dentistry atlases, texts, pocketbooks, slide atlases and CD-ROMs aimed at an international market. Particular areas of focus are psychiatry, neurology, cardiology, orthopaedics, dermatology, oncology and bone metabolism. The company won the Queen's Award for Export Achievement in 1991. 90–100 titles a year. Unsolicited synopses and ideas welcome but no mss. TITLES *International Journal of Cardiovascular Interventions, International Journal of Psychiatry in Clinical Practice, Journal of Cutaneous Laser Therapy; Amyotrophic Lateral Sclerosis and Other Motor Neuron Disorders.*
Royalties paid twice-yearly.

Eagle/Little Eagle
See **Inter Publishing Ltd**

Earthlight
See **Simon & Schuster UK Limited**

Earthscan Publications
See **Kogan Page Ltd**

Ebury Press
See **Random House Group Ltd**

Economist Books
See **Profile Books**

Edinburgh University Press

22 George Square, Edinburgh EH8 9LF
☎0131 650 4218   Fax 0131 662 0053
Website www.eup.ed.ac.uk
Chairman *David Martin*
Managing Director *Timothy Wright*
Editorial Director *Jackie Jones*
Editor, Polygon *Alison Bowden*
Publishes academic and scholarly books (and journals): gender studies, geography, history – ancient, classical, medieval and modern, Islamic studies, linguistics, literary criticism, media and cultural studies; philosophy, politics, Scottish studies, theology and religious studies. About 100 titles a year.
IMPRINTS
Polygon Fiction and poetry, general trade books, Scottish literary, cultural and oral history; **Polygon@Edinburgh** Scottish politics and culture. No unsolicited mss for EUP titles; mss welcome for Polygon (not poetry) and Polygon@Edinburgh but must be accompanied by s.a.e. for reply/return; letter/synopsis preferred in the first instance.
Royalties paid annually.

Éditions Aubrey Walter

Heretics Books (2000) Ltd, 27 Old Gloucester Street, London WC1N 3XX
Email aubrey@gmppubs.co.uk
Director *Aubrey Walter*
Publishes visual work by gay artists and photographers, usually in the form of a monograph showcasing one artist's work. TITLES *Life and Work of Henry Scott Tuke* Emmanuel Cooper; *The Bear Cult* Chris Nelson; *Paintings* Sadao Hasegawa; *The Erotic Art of Duncan Grant; Nubile Nostalgia* photos by Stephen Garkii. Work may be submitted on disk, transparency, photocopy or photograph.
Payment One-off fee negotiable.

Egmont Books

239 Kensington High Street, London W8 6SA
☎020 7761 3500   Fax 020 7761 3510
Email <firstname>.<lastname>@ecb.egmont.com
Also at: Unit 7, Millbank House, Riverside Park, Bollin Walk, Wilmslow, Cheshire SK9 1BJ
☎01625 543800
Managing Director *Susannah McFarlane*
Fiction *Cally Poplak*

Picture Books *Ramona Reihill*
Learning, Baby and Toddler *Nina Filipek*
(at Wilmslow address)

Part of the Egmont Group (Copenhagen), Egmont Books comprises the original imprints of Heinemann Young Books and Methuen Children's Books (both over 100 years old), and Hamlyn Children's Books. *Publishes* children's picture books, fiction and non-fiction; licensed characters for children. About 350 titles a year.

IMPRINTS **Mammoth** TITLES *The Ghost of Thomas Kempe; The Little Prince; Tintin.* **Heinemann; Methuen** TITLES *Thomas the Tank Engine; Winnie-the-Pooh;* **Dean.** No unsolicited mss. Synopses and ideas welcome; approach in writing with s.a.e.
Royalties paid twice-yearly.

Authors' Rating Taking second place in a recent survey of efficient publishers, Egmont has refined its list to focus more on really strong sellers. The emphasis now is on fiction and picture books. A sturdy back list helps to keep the show on the fast track.

Element Books
See **HarperCollins Publishers Ltd**

11:9
See **Neil Wilson Publishing Ltd**

Edward Elgar Publishing Ltd
Glensanda House, Montpellier Parade, Cheltenham, Gloucestershire GL50 1UA
☎01242 226934 Fax 01242 262111
Email info@e-elgar.co.uk
Website www.e-elgar.co.uk

Chairman *Alex Ryan*
Managing Director *Edward Elgar*

FOUNDED 1986. International publisher in economics, the environment, public policy and social sciences. 207 titles in 2000. TITLES *Who's Who in Economics* (3rd ed.); *Handbook of Environmental and Resource Economics; Who's Who in the Management Sciences.* No unsolicited mss; synopses and ideas in the subject areas listed above welcome. Approach by letter or e-mail; no telephone inquiries.
Royalties paid annually.

Elliot Right Way Books
Kingswood Buildings, Lower Kingswood, Tadworth, Surrey KT20 6TD
☎01737 832202 Fax 01737 830311
Email info@right-way.co.uk

Website www.right-way.co.uk

Managing Directors *A. Clive Elliot, Malcolm G. Elliot*

FOUNDED 1946 by Andrew G. Elliot. *Publishes* paperback how-to and educative titles on an unlimited variety of home reference, indoor and outdoor leisure pursuits, careers and business. Subjects include cookery, DIY, family financial and legal matters, public speaking, weddings, jokes, parenting, etiquette, English skills, driving, fishing, horse riding, drawing, music, puzzles, crosswords and quizzes, job seeking, running your own company.

IMPRINTS
Right Way Instructional paperbacks in B format for the most popular subjects; **Right Way Plus** Larger C format for more specialised subjects; **Clarion** B format for promotional/ultra low-price range. Unsolicited mss, synopses and ideas for books welcome.
Royalties paid annually.

Ellipsis London Ltd
2 Rufus Street, London N1 6PE
☎020 7739 3157 Fax 020 7739 3175
Email <name>@ellipsis.co.uk
Website www.ellipsis.com

Contact *Tom Neville*

FOUNDED 1992. Formerly a subsidiary of Zurich-based Artemis Verlags AG but now an independent publishing house. *Publishes* architecture, unpopular culture and music; contemporary art on CD-ROM. About 30 titles a year. No unsolicited material.
Royalties paid annually.

Aidan Ellis Publishing
Whinfield, Herbert Road, Salcombe, South Devon TQ8 8HN
☎01548 842755 Fax 01548 844356
Email aidan@aepub.demon.co.uk
Website www.demon.co.uk/aepub

Partners/Editorial Heads *Aidan Ellis, Lucinda Ellis*

FOUNDED in 1971. *Specialises* in general trade books and non-fiction. TITLES *Eternity Regained* – final part of Marguerite Yourcenar's autobiographical trilogy; *Reunited! Loved Ones Traced by the Red Cross* Michael Johnstone; *The Royal Gardens in Windsor Great Park* Charles Lyte; *Trees For Your Garden* Roy Lancaster; *Pesca* Ian B. Hart; *Guide du Fromage* Pierre Androuët; *Kenwood* John Carswell. Ideas and synopses welcome (return postage, please).
Royalties paid twice-yearly.

Elm Publications/Training
Seaton House, Kings Ripton, Huntingdon, Cambridgeshire PE28 2NJ
☎01487 773254 Fax 01487 773359
Managing Director *Sheila Ritchie*

FOUNDED 1977. *Publishes* textbooks, teaching aids, educational resources, educational software and languages, in the fields of business and management for adult learners. Books and teaching/training resources are generally commissioned to meet specific business, management and other syllabuses. 'We are actively seeking good training materials for business/management, especially tested and proven.' About 30 titles a year. Ideas are welcome; first approach in writing with outline or by a brief telephone call.
Royalties paid annually.

Elsevier Science Ltd
The Boulevard, Langford Lane, Kidlington, Oxford OX5 1GB
☎01865 843000 Fax 01865 843010
Website www.elsevier.nl
Managing Director *Gavin Howe*

Parent company **Reed Elsevier**, Amsterdam. Now incorporates Pergamon Press. *Publishes* academic and professional reference books, scientific, technical and medical books, journals, CD-ROMs and magazines.
DIVISION **Elsevier and Pergamon** *Barbara Barrett, Peter Desmond, Chris Lloyd, Paul Evans.* Unsolicited mss, synopses and ideas for books welcome.
Royalties paid annually.

Emissary Publishing
PO Box 33, Bicester, Oxfordshire OX26 4ZZ
☎01869 323447 Fax 01869 324096
Editorial Director *Val Miller*

FOUNDED 1992. *Publishes* mainly humorous paperback books; no poetry or children's. Runs a biennial Humorous Novel Competition in memory of the late Peter Pook and publishes the winning novel (s.a.e. for details). No unsolicited mss or synopses.
Royalties paid twice-yearly.

Empiricus Books
See **Janus Publishing Company Ltd**

English Heritage (Publications)
23 Savile Row, London W1S 2ET
☎020 7973 3703 Fax 020 7973 3680
Website www.english-heritage.org.uk

Head of Publications and Design *Val Horsler*
FOUNDED 1984 to publish English Heritage guidebooks and a range of academic material related directly to the work of the organisation. No unsolicited material.

Enitharmon Press
36 St George's Avenue, London N7 0HD
☎020 7607 7194 Fax 020 7607 8694
Email books@enitharmon.demon.co.uk
Director *Stephen Stuart-Smith*

FOUNDED 1967. An independent company with an enterprising editorial policy, Enitharmon has established itself as one of Britain's leading poetry presses. Patron of 'the new and the neglected', Enitharmon prides itself on the success of its collaborations between writers and artists. *Publishes* poetry, literary criticism, fiction, art and photography. TITLES include *The World of Gilbert & George: The Storyboard* Gilbert & George; *Selected Poems* Kevin Crossley-Holland; *The Cat Without E-Mail* Alan Brownjohn; *The Zoo Father* Pascale Petit. No unsolicited mss.
Royalties paid according to contract.

Epworth Press
c/o Methodist Publishing House, 20 Ivatt Way, Peterborough, Cambridgeshire PE3 7PG
☎01733 332202 Fax 01733 331201
Chairman *Dr John A. Newton, CBE*
Editor *Gerald M. Burt*

Publishes Christian books only: philosophy, theology, biblical studies, pastoralia and social concern. No fiction, poetry or children's. A series based on the text of the *Revised Common Lectionary*, entitled *Companion to the RCL*, was launched in 1998 and the two new series *Exploring Methodism* and *Thinking Things Through* continue. About 10 titles a year. TITLES *Groundwork of Christian Spirituality* Gordon S. Wakefield; *Deuteronomy* R.W. Clements; *No Easy Answers* Barbara Baisley. Unsolicited mss considered but write to enquire in the first instance. Authors wishing to have their mss returned must send sufficient postage.
Royalties paid annually.

Essentials
See **How To Books Ltd**

Euromonitor
60–61 Britton Street, London EC1M 5UX
☎020 7251 8024 Fax 020 7608 3149
Website www.euromonitor.com
Chairman *R.N. Senior*

Managing Director *T.J. Fenwick*
Approx. Annual Turnover £9 million

FOUNDED 1972. International business information publisher specialising in library and
professional reference books, market reports,
electronic databases, journals and CD-ROMs.
Publishes business reference, market analysis and
information directories only. About 200 titles a
year.

DIVISIONS **Market Analysis** *T. Kitchen,
S. Holmes*; **Reference Books & Directories**
S. Hunter. TITLES *Credit & Charge Cards: The
International Market*; *Europe in the Year 2000*;
European Marketing Handbook; *European Directory
of Trade and Business Associations*; *World Retail
Directory and Sourcebook*.

Payment is generally by flat fee.

Europa Publications Ltd
See **Taylor & Francis Group plc**

Evans Brothers Ltd
2A Portman Mansions, Chiltern Street,
London W1U 6NR
☎020 7935 7160 Fax 020 7487 0921
Email sales@evansbrothers.co.uk
Website www.evansbooks.co.uk

Managing Director *Stephen Pawley*
International Publishing Director *Brian
Jones*
UK Publisher *Su Swallow*
Approx. Annual Turnover £3.5 million

FOUNDED 1908 by Robert and Edward Evans.
Originally published educational journals,
books for primary schools and teacher education. After rapid expansion into popular fiction and drama, both were sacrificed to a major
programme of educational books for schools in
East and West Africa. A new UK programme
was launched in 1986 followed by the acquisition of Hamish Hamilton's non-fiction list
for children in 1990. Acquired interests in
Cherrytree Books and Zero to Ten in 1999.
Publishes UK children's and educational books,
and educational books for Africa, the
Caribbean and Latin America. About 90 titles a
year.

IMPRINTS **Cherrytree Books** Publisher
Angela Sheehan; **Zero to Ten** (327 High
Street, Slough, Berkshire SL1 1TX) Publisher
Anna McQuinn. Unsolicited mss, synopses and
ideas for books welcome.

Royalties paid annually. *Overseas associates* in
Kenya, Cameroon, Sierra Leone; Evans Bros
(Nigeria Publishers) Ltd.

Everyman
See **The Orion Publishing Group Ltd**

Everyman's Library
See **David Campbell Publishers Ltd**

University of Exeter Press
Reed Hall, Streatham Drive, Exeter, Devon
EX4 4QR
☎01392 263066 Fax 01392 263064
Email uep@exeter.ac.uk
Website www.ex.ac.uk/uep/

Publisher *Simon Baker*

FOUNDED 1956. *Publishes* academic books:
archaeology, classical studies, history, maritime
studies, English literature (especially medieval),
linguistics, European studies, modern languages and literature, film history, performance
studies, Arabic studies and books on Exeter and
the South West. About 30 titles a year.
Proposals welcomed in the above subject areas.

Royalties paid annually.

Exley Publications Ltd
16 Chalk Hill, Watford, Hertfordshire
WD19 4BG
☎01923 248328 Fax 01923 800440
Email editorial@exleypublications.co.uk

Editorial Director *Helen Exley*

FOUNDED 1976. Independent family company.
Publishes giftbooks, quotation anthologies and
humour. All in series only – no individual
titles. About 35 titles a year.

DIVISIONS **Gift Series** TITLES *To a Very Special
Friend/ Daughter/Mother; Golf, Love, Friendship
Quotations*. **Value Series** TITLES *Words on
Courage, Joy, Hope, Peace and Calm, Serenity,
Wisdom*, etc. **Cartoon Series** TITLES *The Fanatics
Guide to Golf, Cats, Dads*, etc. 'Writers needed
who can create personal messages and quotations.
Emotion that's never sugary or sentimental.'

Faber & Faber Ltd
3 Queen Square, London WC1N 3AU
☎020 7465 0045 Fax 020 7465 0034
Website www.faber.co.uk

Chairman/Managing Director *Matthew
Evans*
Approx. Annual Turnover £10 million

Geoffrey Faber founded the company in the
1920s, with T.S. Eliot as an early recruit to the
board. The original list was based on contemporary poetry and plays (the distinguished
backlist includes Eliot, Auden and MacNeice).
Publishes poetry and drama, children's, fiction,

film, music, politics, biography, wine.

DIVISIONS

Fiction Editor-in-Chief *Jon Riley* AUTHORS P.D. James, Peter Carey, Giles Foden, Michael Frayn, Kazuo Ishiguro, Barbara Kingsolver, Milan Kundera, Hanif Kureishi, John Lanchester, John McGahern, Lorrie Moore, Andrew O'Hagan, Jane Smiley; **Children's** *Suzy Jenvey* AUTHORS Terry Deary, Gaye Hicyilmaz, Russell Stannard; **Plays** *Peggy Paterson*; **Film** *Walter Donohue* AUTHORS Samuel Beckett, Alan Bennett, David Hare, Brian Friel, Patrick Marber, Harold Pinter, Tom Stoppard, Woody Allen, John Boorman, Joel and Ethan Coen, John Hodge, Martin Scorsese, Quentin Tarantino; **Music** *Belinda Matthews* AUTHORS Humphrey Burton, John Drummond, Alexander Goehr, Mark Steyn, Elizabeth Wilson; **Poetry** *Paul Keegan* AUTHORS Simon Armitage, Douglas Dunn, Seamus Heaney, Ted Hughes, Tom Paulin; **Non-fiction** *Julian Loose* AUTHORS John Carey, Simon Garfield, Adam Phillips, Jan Morris, Jenny Uglow.
Royalties paid twice-yearly.

Authors' Rating Faber is particularly strong on poetry and the performance arts. A pointer to the future is the poetry database set up as a joint venture with Chadwyck-Healey.

Fairleigh Dickinson University Press
See **Golden Cockerel Press**

Falmer Press
See **Taylor & Francis Group plc**

Farming Press
United Business Media International, Sovereign House, Sovereign Way, Tonbridge, Kent TN9 1RW
☎01732 377539 Fax 01732 377465
Website www.farmingpress.com
Contact *Editorial Dept.*

Owned by United Business & Media Plc. *Publishes* specialist books and videos on farming, agriculture and rural life. About 15 books and videos a year. Synopses and ideas on the subject areas listed above considered; no unsolicited mss.
Royalties paid twice-yearly.

Fernhurst Books
Duke's Path, High Street, Arundel, West Sussex BN18 9AJ
☎01903 882277 Fax 01903 882715
Email sales@fernhurstbooks.co.uk
Website www.fernhurstbooks.co.uk

Chairman/Managing Director *Tim Davison*

FOUNDED 1979. For people who love watersports. *Publishes* practical, highly-illustrated handbooks on sailing and watersports. TITLES *The Skipper's Pocketbook; Championship Laser Racing; Crewing to Win; Yacht Racing; Boat Handling Under Sail & Power; The History of Surfing.* No unsolicited mss; synopses and ideas welcome.
Royalties paid twice-yearly.

Financial Times Management
See **Pearson Education**

Findhorn Press Ltd
The Park, Findhorn, Moray IV36 3TY
☎01309 690582 Fax 01309 690036
Email books@findhorn.org
Website www.findhornpress.com
Directors *Karin Bogliolo, Thierry Bogliolo*
Approx. Annual Turnover £320,000

FOUNDED 1971. *Publishes* mind, body, spirit, New Age and healing. 10 titles in 2000. Unsolicited synopses and ideas welcome if they come within their subject areas. No children's books, fiction or poetry.
Royalties paid twice-yearly.

Firefly Publishing
See **Helter Skelter Publishing**

First & Best in Education Ltd
Unit K, Earlstrees Court, Earlstrees Road, Corby, Northamptonshire NN17 4HH
☎01536 399004 Fax 01536 399012
Email firstbest9@aol.com
Website www.schools.co.uk *and*
  www.firstandbest.co.uk
Publisher *Tony Attwood*
Editor *Anne Cockburn*

Publishers of over 1000 educational books of all types for all ages of children and for parents and teachers. All books are published as being suitable for photocopying and/or as electronic books. 'Looking for new authors of educational books all the time. No fiction, please.' TITLES *Raising Grades Through Study Skills; Parents Survival Guide Series; Business Sponsorship of Secondary Schools; Revision, Study and Exam Techniques Guide.* IMPRINTS **Multi-Sensory Learning** (see entry) and **School Improvement Reports**. In the first instance check the website or send s.a.e. for details of requirements and current projects to *Anne Cockburn*, Editorial Dept. at the address above.
Royalties paid twice-yearly.

Fitzgerald Publishing

89 Ermine Road, Ladywell, London SE13 5JJ
☎020 8690 0597

Managing Editor *Tim Fitzgerald*
General Editor *Andrew Smith*

FOUNDED 1974. *Specialises* in scientific studies of insects and spiders. 1–2 titles a year. TITLES *Keeping Spiders and Insects in Captivity*; *Tarantulas of the USA; Scorpions of Medical Importance* and *Earth Tigers – Tarantulas of Borneo* (TV/video documentary). Unsolicited mss, synopses and ideas for books welcome. Also considers video scripts for video documentaries. New video documentary: *Desert Tarantulas*.

Fitzjames Press

See **Motor Racing Publications**

Fitzroy Dearborn Publishers

310 Regent Street, London W1B 3AX
☎020 7636 6627   Fax 020 7636 6982
Email post@fitzroydearborn.co.uk
Website www.fitzroydearborn.com

Managing Director *Daniel Kirkpatrick*
Publisher *Roda Morrison*
Commissioning Editors *Mark Hawkins-Dady, Anne-Lucie Norton, Gillian Lindsey, Jonathan Dore, Lesley Henderson*

Publishes reference books: the arts, history, literature, business, science and the social sciences. About 50 titles a year. TITLES *Encyclopedia of German Literature; Encyclopedia of Greece and the Hellenic Tradition; Encyclopedia of Literary Translation into English; Reader's Guide to the History of Science; Encyclopedia of Palaeontology.* IMPRINT **Glenlake Business Books**. Unsolicited mss, synopses and ideas welcome for reference books.

Royalties paid twice-yearly. *US associate* Fitzroy Dearborn Publishers, 919 North Michigan Ave., Suite 760, Chicago, IL 60611.

Fitzwarren Publishing

2 Orchard Drive, Aston Clinton, Aylesbury, Buckinghamshire HP22 5HR
☎01296 632627   Fax 01296 630028

Contact *Julie Stretton*

Publishes two or three books a year, mainly layman's handbooks on legal matters. All books published so far have followed a rigid 128-page format. Written approaches and synopses from prospective authors welcome. Authors, although not necessarily legally qualified, are expected to know their subject as well as a lawyer would.

Royalties paid twice-yearly.

Five Star

See **Serpent's Tail**

Flame

See **Hodder Headline Plc**

Flamingo

See **HarperCollins Publishers Ltd**

Flicks Books

29 Bradford Road, Trowbridge, Wiltshire BA14 9AN
☎01225 767728   Fax 01225 760418
Email flicks.books@dial.pipex.com

Publishing Director *Matthew Stevens*

FOUNDED 1986. Devoted solely to publishing books on the cinema and related media. TITLES *Queen of the 'B's: Ida Lupino Behind the Camera* ed. Annette Kuhn; *By Angels Driven: The Films of Derek Jarman* ed. Chris Lippard. Unsolicited mss, synopses and ideas within the subject area are welcome.

Royalties paid annually or twice yearly.

Floris Books

15 Harrison Gardens, Edinburgh EH11 1SH
☎0131 337 2372   Fax 0131 346 7516
Email floris@floris.demon.co.uk

Managing Director *Christian Maclean*
Editors *Christopher Moore, Gale Winskill*
Approx. Annual Turnover £350,000

FOUNDED 1977. *Publishes* books related to the Steiner movement, including The Christian Community, as well as arts & crafts, children's, history, religious, science, social questions and Celtic studies. No unsolicited mss. Synopses and ideas for books welcome.

Royalties paid annually.

Fodor's

See **Random House Group Ltd**

Folens Limited

Apex Business Centre, Boscombe Road, Dunstable, Bedfordshire LU5 4RL
☎01582 478110   Fax 01582 472575
Email folens@folens.com
Website www.folens.com

Chairman *Dirk Folens*
Managing Director *Malcolm Watson*

FOUNDED 1987. Leading educational publisher. About 150 titles a year. IMPRINTS **Folens**; **Belair**. Unsolicited mss, synopses and ideas for educational books welcome.

Royalties paid annually.

For Beginners™
See **Writers and Readers Ltd**

Mary Ford Publications Ltd
See **Michael O'Mara Books Ltd**

W. Foulsham & Co.
The Publishing House, Bennetts Close,
Slough, Berkshire SL1 5AP
☎01753 526769 Fax 01753 535003
Chairman *R.S. Belasco*
Managing Director *B.A.R. Belasco*
Approx. Annual Turnover £2.2 million
FOUNDED 1819 and now one of the few
remaining independent family companies to
survive takeover. *Publishes* non-fiction on most
subjects including lifestyle, travel guides, family
reference, cookery, diet, health, DIY, business,
self improvement, self development, astrology,
dreams, MBS. No fiction. IMPRINT **Quantum**
Mind, body and spirit titles. TITLES *Classic
1000 Cocktails; A Brit's Guide to Orlando and
Walt Disney World 2000.* Unsolicited mss, synopses and ideas welcome. Around 60 titles a
year.
Royalties paid twice-yearly.

Foundery Press
See **Methodist Publishing House**

Fount
See **HarperCollins Publishers Ltd**

Fountain Press
Newpro UK Ltd., Old Sawmills Road,
Faringdon, Oxfordshire SN7 7DS
☎01367 242411 Fax 01367 241124
Email sales@newprouk.co.uk
Publisher *H.M. Ricketts*
Approx. Annual Turnover £800,000
FOUNDED 1923 when it was part of the
Rowntree Trust Social Service. Owned by the
British Electric Traction Group until 1982 when
it was bought out by H.M. Ricketts. Acquired
by Newpro UK Ltd in July 2000. *Publishes*
mainly photography and natural history. About
25 titles a year. TITLES *Photography Yearbook;
Antique and Collectable Cameras; Camera Manual*
(series). Unsolicited mss and synopses welcome.
Royalties paid twice-yearly.

Authors' Rating Highly regarded for production values, Fountain has the reputation for
involving authors in every stage of the publishing process.

Fourth Estate Ltd
77–85 Fulham Palace Road, London W6 8JB
☎020 8741 4414 Fax 020 8307 4466
Email general@4thestate.co.uk
Website www.4thestate.co.uk
Managing Director *Christopher Potter*
Publishing Director *Clive Priddle*
Approx. Annual Turnover £17 million
FOUNDED 1984. Acquired by **HarperCollins**
in July 2000, Fourth Estate has a strong repu-
tation for literary fiction and up-to-the-minute
non-fiction. *Publishes* fiction, popular science,
current affairs, biography, humour, self-help,
travel, reference. About 100 titles a year.
DIVISIONS
**Literary   Fiction/Non-fiction;   General
Fiction/Non-Fiction** TITLES *The Fowler
Family Business* Jonathan Meades; *John Henry
Days* Colson Whitehead; *East of Acre Lane* Alex
Wheatle; *A Year of Wonders* Geraldine Brookes;
Spike Island Philip Hoare; *The Healing Land*
Rupert Isaacson; *England; The Making of the
Myth* Maureen Duffy; *Annie's Box.* Charles
Darwin, his Daugher and Human Evolution
Randal Keynes; *1066 and the Hidden History of
the Bayeaux Tapestry* Andrew Bridgeford. No
unsolicited mss; synopses welcome.
Royalties paid twice-yearly.

Authors' Rating For a time it seemed that
Fourth Estate was bucking the trend. Here was
a small general publisher which managed to
thrive with an unconventional list encompassing not a few sleepers – books by little known
authors that go on to become bestsellers like
Dava Sobel's *Longitude.* But the attempt to
break into the American market proved the
need for a partner with real muscle. Then
along comes HarperCollins with an irresistible
offer not only for the company but for the
founder of Fourth Estate, Victoria Barnsley,
who is now the UK head of HarperCollins.

Free Association Books Ltd
57 Warren Street, London W1P 5PA
☎020 7388 3182 Fax 020 7388 3187
Email fab@fa-b.com
Website www.fa-b.com
Managing Director/Publisher *T.E. Brown*
Publishes psychoanalysis and psychotherapy,
psychology, cultural studies, sexuality and
gender, women's studies, applied social sci-
ences. TITLES *Reaching the Young Autistic Child*
S. Janert; *Judo With Words* B. Berchan;
Psychoanalytic Psychotherapy Trainings – A Guide
R.M. Jones; *A Compendium of Lacanian Terms*

Marks, Murphy and Glowinski. Always send a letter in the first instance accompanied by a book outline.

Royalties paid twice-yearly. *Overseas associates* ISBS, USA; Astam, Australia.

W.H. Freeman

Palgrave, Houndsmill, Basingstoke, Hampshire RG21 6XS
☎01256 329242 Fax 01256 330688
President *Elizabeth Widdicombe* (New York)
Sales & Marketing Director *Margaret Hewinson*

Following integration into the BFW (Bedford, Freeman, Worth) College Group, USA, Freeman now *Publishes* academic educational and textbooks in biochemistry, biology and zoology, chemistry, geography and geology, mathematics and statistics, medical, natural history, neuroscience, palaeontology, physics. Freeman's editorial office is in New York (Basingstoke is a sales and marketing office only) but unsolicited mss can go through Basingstoke. Those which are obviously unsuitable will be sifted out; the rest will be forwarded to New York.

Royalties paid annually.

Samuel French Ltd

52 Fitzroy Street, London W1T 5JR
☎020 7387 9373 Fax 020 7387 2161
Email theatre@samuelfrench-london.co.uk
Website www.samuelfrench-london.co.uk
Chairman *Charles R. Van Nostrand*
Managing Director *Vivien Goodwin*

FOUNDED 1830 with the object of acquiring acting rights and publishing plays. *Publishes* plays only. About 50 titles a year. Unsolicited mss considered only after initial submission of synopsis and specimen scene. Such material should be addressed to the Performing Rights Department.

Royalties paid twice-yearly for books; performing royalties paid monthly, subject to a minimum amount.

Authors' Rating Thrives on the amateur dramatic societies who are forever in need of play texts. Editorial advisers give serious attention to new material but a high proportion of the list is staged before it goes into print. Non-established writers are advised to try one-act plays, much in demand by the amateur dramatic societies but rarely turned out by well-known playwrights.

David Fulton (Publishers) Ltd

Ormond House, 26/27 Boswell Street, London WC1N 3JD
☎020 7405 5606 Fax 020 7831 4840
Email mail@fultonpublishers.co.uk
Website www.fultonpublishers.co.uk
Chairman/Publisher *David Fulton*
Managing Director *David Hill*
Senior Commissioning Editor *Nina Stibbe*
Approx. Annual Turnover £1.8 million

FOUNDED 1987. *Publishes* non-fiction: books for teachers and teacher training at B.Ed and PGCE levels for early years, primary, secondary and virtually all aspects of special education; geography for undergraduates. Currently developing a range of curriculum materials (in book form, packs, on CD-ROM and/or disk) for use by teachers in the classroom. In 1995, David Fulton set up a Fulton Fellowship in Special Education (see entry under **Bursaries, Fellowships and Grants**). About 90 titles a year. No unsolicited mss; synopses and ideas for books welcome.

Royalties paid twice-yearly.

Authors' Rating David Fulton has shown how niche publishing can succeed even in a difficult market. Known chiefly for books on learning difficulties, he gets most of his ideas and authors by going to education conferences.

Gaia Books Ltd

66 Charlotte Street, London W1T 4QE
☎020 7323 4010 Fax 020 7323 0435
Email info@gaiabooks.com
Website www.gaiabooks.co.uk
Also at: 20 High Street, Stroud, Gloucestershire GL5 1AZ
Tel 01453 752985 Fax 01453 752987
Managing Director *Joss Pearson*

FOUNDED 1983. *Publishes* ecology, health, natural living, gardening, interiors, and mind, body & spirit, mainly in practical self-help illustrated reference form for Britain and the international market. About 12 titles a year. TITLES *Healing Drinks; The Feng Shui Kitchen; The Healing Energies of Earth; The Edible Container Garden; Pilates; The Fertility Plan.* Most projects are conceived in-house but outlines and mss with s.a.e. considered. 'From submission of an idea to project go ahead may take up to a year. Authors become involved with the Gaia team in the editorial, design and promotion work needed to create and market a book.'

Gairm Publications

29 Waterloo Street, Glasgow G2 6BZ
☎0141 221 1971 Fax 0141 221 1971
Chairman *Prof. Derick S. Thomson*

FOUNDED 1952 to publish the quarterly Gaelic periodical *Gairm* and soon moved into publishing other Gaelic material. Acquired an old Glasgow Gaelic publishing firm, Alexander MacLaren & Son, in 1970. *Publishes* a wide range of Gaelic and Gaelic-related books: dictionaries, grammars, handbooks, children's, fiction, poetry, biography, music and song. TITLES *The Companion to Gaelic Scotland; Derick Thomson's collection of poems, Meall Garbh/The Rugged Mountain.* Catalogue available.

Galaxy Children's Large Print

See **Chivers Press Ltd**

J. Garnet Miller Ltd

See **Cressrelles Publishing Co. Ltd**

Garnet Publishing Ltd

8 Southern Court, South Street, Reading,
Berkshire RG1 4QS
☎0118 959 7847 Fax 0118 959 7356
Email enquiries@garnet-ithaca.demon.co.uk
Website www.garnet-ithaca.co.uk
Managing Director *Ken Banerji*

FOUNDED 1992 and purchased Ithaca Press in the same year. *Publishes* art, architecture, photography, archive photography, cookery, travel classics, travel, comparative religion, Islamic culture and history, foreign fiction in translation. Core subjects are Middle Eastern but list is rapidly expanding to be more general. About 30 titles a year.

IMPRINTS
Garnet Publishing *Emma Hawker* TITLES *The Story of Islamic Architecture; Traditional Greek Cooking; Jerusalem: Caught in Time* series.
Ithaca Press *Adel Kamal* Specialises in postgraduate academic works on the Middle East, political science and international relations. About 20 titles a year. TITLES *The Making of the Modern Gulf States; The Palestinian Exodus; French Imperialism in Syria; Philby of Arabia.* Unsolicited mss not welcome – write with outline and ideas first plus current c.v.
　Royalties paid twice-yearly. *Sister companies:* All Prints, Beirut; Garnet France, Paris.

Gay Men's Press

PO Box 3220, Brighton, East Sussex BN2 5AU
☎01273 672823 Fax 01273 672159
Website www.prowler.co.uk

Contact *Peter Burton*

Part of the Millivres-Prowler Group. *Publishes* books on gay-related issues: a wide range of fiction from literary to popular. TITLES *The Linguist* Sebastian Beaumont; *The Butterfly Boy* Richard Cawley; *Attrition* Simon Lovat; *Wasted* Aiden Shaw. Work should be submitted on disk. Send synopsis with sample chapters rather than complete mss.
　Royalties negotiable.

Gay Times Books

3 Broadbent Close, 20 Highgate High Street,
London N6 5GG
☎020 8340 7711 Fax 020 8347 7667
Website www.gaytimes.co.uk
Contact *Nick Hilton*

An imprint of the Millivres-Prowler Group. *Publishes* gay non-fiction and an annual fiction anthology. TITLES *Gay Planet; Gay Star Signs; Gay Times Book of Short Stories.* 'Looking for original mss and co-publishing opportunities.'

Gazelle Books

See **Angus Hudson Ltd** under **UK Packagers**

Geddes & Grosset

David Dale House, New Lanark ML11 9DJ
☎01555 665000 Fax 01555 665694
Publishers *Ron Grosset, R. Michael Miller*
Approx. Annual Turnover £2.2 million

FOUNDED 1989. Publisher of children's and reference books. Unsolicited mss, synopses and ideas welcome. No adult fiction.

Stanley Gibbons Publications

5 Parkside, Christchurch Road, Ringwood,
Hampshire BH24 3SH
☎01425 472363 Fax 01425 470247
Website www.stanleygibbons.co.uk
Chairman *P. Fraser*
Editorial Head *D. Aggersberg*
Approx. Annual Turnover £3 million

Long-established force in the philatelic world with over a hundred years in the business. *Publishes* philatelic reference catalogues and handbooks. Approx. 15 titles a year. Reference works relating to other areas of collecting may be considered. TITLES *How to Arrange and Write Up a Stamp Collection; Stanley Gibbons British Commonwealth Stamp Catalogue; Stamps of the World.* Foreign catalogues include Japan and Korea, Portugal and Spain, Germany, Middle East, Balkans, China. Monthly publication

Gibbons Stamp Monthly (see entry under **Magazines**). Unsolicited mss, synopses and ideas welcome.

Royalties by negotiation.

Robert Gibson & Sons Glasgow Limited

17 Fitzroy Place, Glasgow G3 7SF
☎0141 248 5674 Fax 0141 221 8219
Email Robert.GibsonSons@btinternet.com

Chairman/Managing Director
R.G.C. Gibson

FOUNDED 1850 and went public in 1886. *Publishes* educational books only, and has been agent for the Scottish Certificate of Education Examination Board since 1902 which, in 1997, became the Scottish Qualification Authority. About 40 titles a year. Unsolicited mss preferred to synopses/ideas.

Royalties paid annually.

Ginn & Co
See **Reed Educational & Professional Publishing**

Glenlake Business Books
See **Fitzroy Dearborn Publishers**

Golden Cockerel Press Ltd

16 Barter Street, London WC1A 2AH
☎020 7405 7979 Fax 020 7404 3598
Email lindesay@btinternet.com

Directors *Tamar Lindesay, Andrew Lindesay*

FOUNDED 1980 to distribute titles for US-based Associated University Presses Inc., New Jersey. *Publishes* academic titles mostly: art, film, history, literary criticism, music, philosophy, sociology and special interest. About 120 titles a year.

IMPRINTS **AUP: Bucknell University Press**; **University of Delaware**; **Fairleigh Dickinson University Press**; **Lehigh University Press**; **Susquehanna University Press**. Also: **Cygnus Arts** Non-academic books on the arts; **Cornwall Books** Trade hardbacks.

Authors' Rating Very much attuned to American interests with trans-Atlantic spelling and punctuation predominating. Some writers may find the process wearisome but those who persevere win through to a wider market.

Gomer Press

Wind Street, Llandysul, Ceredigion SA44 4QL
☎01559 362371 Fax 01559 363758
Email gwasg@gomer.co.uk

Website www.gomer.co.uk

Chairman/Managing Director *J.H. Lewis*

FOUNDED 1892. *Publishes* adult fiction and non-fiction, children's fiction and educational material in English and Welsh. About 100 titles a year (65 Welsh; 35 English).

IMPRINTS **Gomer Press** *Bethan Mair, Gordon Jones, Francesca Rhyddeich*. **Pont Books** *Mairwen Prys Jones*. No unsolicited mss, synopses or ideas.

Royalties paid twice-yearly.

Gower
See **Ashgate Publishing Ltd**

GPC Books
See **University of Wales Press**

Graham & Trotman
See **Kluwer Law International**

Graham & Whiteside

Tuition House, 5–6 Francis Grove, London SW19 4DT
☎020 8947 1011 Fax 020 8947 1163
Website www.graham-whiteside.com

Sales & Marketing Director *Pauline Murphy*

FOUNDED 1995. Part of the Gale Group. *Publishes* annual directories for the business and professional market with titles dating back to 1975 originally published by Graham & Trotman. 22 annual directories, including: *Major Companies of Europe; Major Companies of the Arab World; Major Companies of the Far East and Australasia.* Proposals for new projects welcome.

Royalties paid annually.

Graham-Cameron Publishing

The Studio, 23 Holt Road, Sheringham, Norfolk NR26 8NB
☎01263 821333 Fax 01263 821334

Editorial Director *Mike Graham-Cameron*
Art Director *Helen Graham-Cameron*

FOUNDED 1984 as a packaging operation. *Publishes* illustrated factual books for children, adults, institutions and business; also biography, education and social history. TITLES *Up From the Country; In All Directions; The Holywell Story; Let's Look at Dairying.* No unsolicited mss.

Royalties paid annually. *Subsidiary company*: Graham-Cameron Illustration (agency).

Granada Media
See **Carlton Publishing Group**

Granta Books

2–3 Hanover Yard, Noel Road, London
N1 8BE
☎020 7704 9776 Fax 020 7354 3469
Website www.granta.com

Publishing Director Neil Belton
Associate Publisher Gail Lynch

FOUNDED 1979. *Publishes* literary fiction and
general non-fiction. About 25 titles a year. No
unsolicited mss; synopses and sample chapters
welcome.
Royalties paid twice-yearly.

Authors' Rating After a brave try at breaking
into general publishing with quality fiction,
Granta has pulled back, cutting its title output
by half and aligning its programme more
closely with the editorial policies of *Granta*
magazine.

W. Green (Scotland)
See **Sweet & Maxwell Ltd**

Green Books

Foxhole, Dartington, Totnes, Devon TQ9 6EB
☎01803 863260 Fax 01803 863843
Email greenbooks@gn.apc.org
Website www.greenbooks.co.uk

Chairman Satish Kumar
Publisher John Elford
Approx. Annual Turnover £200,000

FOUNDED in 1987 with the support of a number of Green organisations. Closely associated
with *Resurgence* magazine. *Publishes* high-quality
books on a wide range of Green issues, including economics, politics and the practical application of Green thinking. No fiction or books
for children. TITLES *Forest Gardening* Robert A.
de J. Hart; *Eco-Renovation* Edward Harland; *The
Growth Illusion* Richard Douthwaite; *The Green
Lanes of England* Valerie Belsey; *The Organic
Directory* ed. Clive Litchfield. No unsolicited
mss. Synopses and ideas welcome.
Royalties paid twice-yearly.

Green Print
See **The Merlin Press Ltd**

Greenhill Books/ Lionel Leventhal Ltd

Park House, 1 Russell Gardens, London
NW11 9NN
☎020 8458 6314 Fax 020 8905 5245
Email LionelLeventhal@compuserve.com
Website www.greenhillbooks.com

Managing Director Lionel Leventhal

FOUNDED 1984 by Lionel Leventhal (ex-**Arms
& Armour Press**). *Publishes* aviation, military
and naval books, and its Napoleonic Library
series. Synopses and ideas for books welcome.
No unsolicited mss.
Royalties paid twice-yearly.

Greenwich Editions
See **Chrysalis Books Ltd**

Gresham Books Ltd

46 Victoria Road, Summertown, Oxfordshire
OX2 7QD
☎01865 513582 Fax 01865 512718
Email greshambks@btinternet.com
Website www.gresham-books.co.uk

Managing Director Paul A. Lewis
Approx. Annual Turnover £300,000

A small specialist publishing house. *Publishes*
hymn and service books for schools and
churches, school histories, also craftbound
choir and orchestral folders and Records of
Achievement. TITLES include music and
melody editions of *Hymns for Church and School*;
The School Hymnal; Praise and Thanksgiving. No
unsolicited material but ideas welcome.

Griffith Institute
See **Ashmolean Museum Publications Ltd**

Grisewood & Dempsey
See **Kingfisher Publications plc**

Grub Street

The Basement, 10 Chivalry Road, London
SW11 1HT
☎020 7924 3966/7738 1008
Fax 020 7738 1009
Email post@grubstreet.co.uk
Website www.grubstreet.co.uk

Managing Director John Davies

FOUNDED 1982. *Publishes* cookery, food and
wine, health, military and aviation history
books. About 20 titles a year. Unsolicited mss
and synopses welcome in the above categories.
Royalties paid twice-yearly.

Guild of Master Craftsman Publications Ltd

166 High Street, Lewes, East Sussex BN7 1XU
☎01273 477374 Fax 01273 478606

Chairman A.E. Phillips
Approx. Annual Turnover £2 million

FOUNDED 1974. Part of G.M.C. Services Ltd.
Publishes woodworking, craft, photography and

gardening books, magazines and videos. 40 titles in 2000. Unsolicited mss, synopses and ideas for books welcome. No fiction.

Royalties paid twice-yearly.

Guinness World Records Ltd

338 Euston Road, London NW1 3BD
☎020 7891 4567 Fax 020 7891 4501
Email info@guinnessrecords.com
Website www.guinnessworldrecords.com

CEO *Stephen Nelson*
Vice-President, Media *Ian Castello-Cortes*
Vice-President, Business Development *Lisa Kennedy*
Approx. Annual Turnover £20 million

FOUNDED in 1954 to publish *The Guinness Book of Records*, published in 35 languages and the highest-selling copyright book in the world. The company is now a multimedia business. Its television shows have gained a global audience of more than 100 million and are shown in over 30 countries. In 2000 the company launched its Web business. In addition to *Guinness World Records* the company publishes the annual industry-standard volume *British Hit Singles*. Contact from prospective researchers, editors and designers welcome.

Authors' Rating As we go to press, this renowned one-title publishing company is up for sale. In fact, Guinness is well and truly a multimedia setup which is likely to atract bids from such as Disney and Time Warner.

Gullane Children's Books

Winchester House, 259–269 Old Marylebone Road, London NW1 5XJ
☎020 7616 7200 Fax 020 7616 7201

Editorial Director *Mandy Suhr*

FOUNDED 1994. Formerly David & Charles Children's Books; acquired by multi-media group, Gullane Entertainment in 2001. *Publishes* board books, novelty books, picture books and gift collections for children of 0–12 years. Unsolicited mss, synopses and ideas welcome.

Royalties paid twice-yearly.

Gunsmoke Westerns

See **Chivers Press Ltd**

Gwasg Addysgol Cymru

See **Ashley Drake Publishing Ltd**

Gwasg Carreg Gwalch

12 Iard Yr Orsaf, Llanrwst, Conwy LL26 0EH
☎01492 642031 Fax 01492 641502
Email books@carreg-gwalch.co.uk

Website www.carreg-gwalch.co.uk

Managing Editor *Myrddin ap Dafydd*

FOUNDED in 1990. *Publishes* Welsh language; English books of Welsh interest – history, folklore, guides and walks. No fiction. 90 titles in 2000. Unsolicited mss, synopses and ideas welcome.

Royalties paid.

Gwasg Prifysgol Cymru

See **University of Wales Press**

Peter Halban Publishers

22 Golden Square, London W1R 3PA
☎020 7437 9300 Fax 020 7437 9512
Email books@halbanpublishers.com
Website www.halbanpublishers.com

Directors *Peter Halban, Martine Halban*

FOUNDED 1986. Independent publisher. *Publishes* biography, autobiography and memoirs, history, philosophy, theology, politics, literature and criticism, Judaica and world affairs. 6–8 titles a year. No unsolicited material. Approach by letter in first instance.

Royalties paid twice-yearly for first two years, thereafter annually in December.

Robert Hale Ltd

Clerkenwell House, 45–47 Clerkenwell Green, London EC1R 0HT
☎020 7251 2661 Fax 020 7490 4958

Chairman/Managing Director *John Hale*

FOUNDED 1936. Family-owned company. *Publishes* adult fiction (but not interested in category crime, romance or science fiction) and non-fiction. No specialist material (education, law, medical or scientific). Acquired **NAG Press Ltd** in 1993 with its list of horological, gemmological, jewellery and metalwork titles and **J.A. Allen & Co.** in 1999 with its extensive list of horse and dog books (see entry). Over 250 titles a year. TITLES Non-fiction: *Gary Cooper* Jeffrey Meyers; *Webley Air Pistols* Gordon Bruce; *Pursuit of Stillwater Trout* Brian Clarke; *Supernatural Peak District* David Clarke; *Travel Writing* Janet Macdonald; *No Defence* Kate Wilhelm; *Illusions* Jean Saunders; *Corkscrew* Donald E. Westlake. Unsolicited mss, synopses and ideas for books welcome.

Royalties paid twice-yearly.

Authors' Rating Smiled upon in a Society of Authors survey on author relations, Robert Hale has carved out a profitable niche for popular non-fiction.

Halsgrove

Halsgrove House, Lower Moor Way,
Tiverton, Devon EX16 6SS
☎01884 243242 Fax 01884 243325
Email sales@halsgrove.com
Website www.halsgrove.com

Joint Managing Directors *Simon Butler,
Steven Pugsley*
Approx. Annual Turnover £2.2 million

FOUNDED in 1990 from defunct Maxwell-
owned publishing group. Grown into the
region's largest publishing and distribution
group, specialising in books, video and audio
tapes. *Publishes* local history, cookery, biography and art, mainly in hardback. 130 titles in
2000. Also established a series of local interest
magazines in southern England. No fiction or
poetry. Unsolicited mss, synopses and ideas for
books of regional interest welcome.
Royalties paid annually.

Hambledon and London

102 Gloucester Avenue, London NW1 8HX
☎020 7586 0817 Fax 020 7586 9970
Email office@hambledon.co.uk

Editorial Director *Martin Sheppard*
Commissioning Director *Tony Morris*

FOUNDED 1980 as The Hambledon Press.
Winner of the **Sunday Times Award for
Small Publishers** in 2001. *Publishes* history and
biography. TITLES *Churchill: A Study in Greatness*
Geoffrey Best; *Old Masters: Great Artists in Old
Age* Thomas Dormandy; *Family Names and
Family History* David Hey; *Dr Johnson's Women*
Norma Clarke. No unsolicited mss; send prelim-
inary letter. Synopses and ideas welcome.
Royalties paid twice-yearly. *Overseas distributor*
New York University Press (USA and Canada).

Hamish Hamilton

See **Penguin UK**

Hamlyn Children's Books

See **Egmont Books**

Hamlyn Octopus

See **Octopus Publishing Group**

Harcourt Publishers Limited

32 Jamestown Road, London NW1 7BY
☎020 7424 4200
Fax 020 7482 2293/7485 4752
Website www.harcourt-international.com

Owned by US parent company. *Publishes* scientific, technical and medical books, college
textbooks, educational & occupational test. No
unsolicited mss.

IMPRINTS **Baillière Tindall**; **Dryden Press**;
Churchill Livingstone; **Holt Rinehart and
Winston**; **Mosby International**; **T. & A.D.
Poyser**; **W.B. Saunders & Co. Ltd.**;
Saunders Scientific Publications.

Authors' Rating After Wiley, the second
fastest growing publisher by turnover of professional and education books.

Harlem River Press

See **Writers and Readers Ltd**

Harlequin Mills & Boon Ltd

Eton House, 18–24 Paradise Road,
Richmond, Surrey TW9 1SR
☎020 8288 2800 Fax 020 8288 2899
Website www.eharlequin.com *or*
www.millsandboon.co.uk

Managing Director *F. Gejrot*
Editorial Director *Karin Stoecker*
Approx. Annual Turnover £25 million

FOUNDED 1908. Owned by the Canadian-
based Torstar Group. *Publishes* romantic fiction
and historical romance. Over 600 titles a year.

IMPRINTS

**Mills & Boon Romance/Mills & Boon
Tender Romance** *Tessa Shapcott, Samantha Bell*
(50–55,000 words) Contemporary romances
with international settings, focusing on hero and
heroine. **Mills & Boon Medical Romance**
Sheila Hodgson (50–55,000 words) Modern medical practice provides a unique background to
love stories. **Mills & Boon Historical
Romance** *Linda Fildew* (75–80,000 words)
Historical romances. **MIRA** *Linda Fildew* (minimum 100,000 words) Individual women's fiction.

Mills & Boon Temptation titles are
acquired through the Canadian office.
Silhouette Desire, **Special Edition**,
Sensation and **Intrigue** imprints are handled
by US-based **Silhouette Books** (see **US
Publishers**). Please send query letter in the
first instance. Tip sheets and guidelines for the
Mills & Boon series available from the website
or Harlequin Mills & Boon Editorial Dept.
(please send s.a.e.).
Royalties paid twice-yearly.

Authors' Rating Having suffered a mid-'90s
fall off in the appeal of soft romances which left
too much to the imagination, Mills & Boon has
trawled for younger writers who are closer to
real life. Competition is tough (M&B has a

network of around 12,000 authors worldwide) and royalties are generally below the trade average. But every title scores six-figure sales. You can't have everything.

Harley Books

Martins, Great Horkesley, Colchester, Essex CO6 4AH
☎01206 271216 Fax 01206 271182
Email harley@keme.co.uk
Managing Director *Basil Harley*

FOUNDED 1983. Natural history publishers specialising in entomological and botanical books. Mostly definitive, high-quality illustrated reference works. TITLES *The Moths and Butterflies of Great Britain and Ireland; Dragonflies of Europe; The Flora of Hampshire; The Liverwort Flora of the British Isles; The Spiders of Great Britain and Ireland.*

Royalties paid twice-yearly in the first year, annually thereafter.

HarperCollins Publishers Ltd

77–85 Fulham Palace Road, London W6 8JB
☎020 8741 7070 Fax 020 8307 4440
Website www.fireandwater.com
Also at: Freepost PO Box, Glasgow G4 0NB
☎ 0141 772 3200 Fax 0141 306 3119
President/CEO (US) *Jane Friedman*
CEO/Publisher *Victoria Barnsley*
Approx. Annual Turnover £200 million

Publisher of high-profile authors like Jeffrey Archer, J.G. Ballard, Fay Weldon, Frank McCourt and John Major. Owned by News Corporation. Since 1991 there has been a period of consolidated focus on key management issues within the HarperCollins empire. This has led to various imprints being phased out in favour of others, among them Grafton and Fontana, which have been merged under the HarperCollins paperback imprint. Acquired Fourth Estate in 2000 and Element Books in 2001. **Booker Prize** and **Pulitzer Prize** winners in 1997.

DIVISIONS

Trade Divisional Managing Director *Adrian Bourne.* Publishing Directors *Nick Sayers* (Fiction); *Michael Fishwick* (Non-fiction); *Susan Watt.* IMPRINTS **Collins Crime**; **Collins Willow** (sport) Publishing Director *Michael Doggart;* **Flamingo** (literary fiction, both hardback and paperback) Publishing Director *Philip Gwyn Jones;* **HarperCollins Audiobooks** (see entry under **Audio Books**); **HarperCollins Entertainment** Publishing Director *Val*

Hudson; **HarperCollins Paperbacks**; **Tolkien**; **Voyager** (science fiction/fantasy) Publishing Director *Jane Johnson.* Over 650 titles a year, hardback and paperback. No longer accepts unsolicited submissions.

Fourth Estate (see entry).

Thorsons Divisional Managing Director *Stephen Bray.* Health, nutrition, business, parenting, popular psychology, positive thinking, self-help, divination, therapy, recovery, feminism, women's issues, mythology, religion, yoga, tarot, personal development, sexual politics, biography, history, popular culture. About 250 titles a year. IMPRINT **Element Books**.

Children's Divisional Managing Director *Kate Harris.* IMPRINTS **Picture Lions**; **HarperCollins Audio** (see entry under **Audio Books**); **Jets** Quality picture books and book and tape sets for under 7s; all categories of fiction for the 6–14 age group; dictionaries for pre-school and primary. About 250 titles a year. No longer accepts unsolicited mss.

Reference Divisional Managing Director *Stephen Bray.* IMPRINTS **HarperCollins**; **Collins New Naturalist Library**; **Collins Gems**; **HC Illustrated**; **Janes** (military); **Times Books**; **Times Atlases** Encyclopedias, guides and handbooks, phrase books and manuals on popular reference, art instruction, illustrated, cookery and wine, crafts, DIY, gardening, military, natural history, pet care, Scottish, pastimes. About 120 titles a year.

Educational Divisional Managing Director *Kate Harris.* Textbook publishing for schools and FE colleges (5–18-year-olds): all subjects for primary education including the **Letterland** imprint and the **Collins Study and Revision Guides**. Strong presence in all major secondary and curriculum areas; sociology, business studies and economics in FE. (Former Holmes McDougall, Unwin Hyman, Mary Glasgow Primary Publications, and part of Harcourt, Brace & Co. educational imprints have been incorporated under Collins Educational.) About 90 titles a year.

Dictionaries Divisional Managing Director *Kate Harris.* IMPRINTS **Collins**; **Collins Cobuild**; **Collins Gem** Includes the *Collins English Dictionary* range with dictionaries and thesauruses, *Collins Bilingual Dictionary* range (French, German, Spanish, Italian, etc.), and the *Cobuild* series of English dictionaries, grammars and EFL books. About 50 titles a year.

Religious Divisional Managing Director *Adrian Bourne.* A broad-based religious publisher across all denominations. IMPRINTS **HarperCollins**; **Fount**; **Marshall Pickering**

Extensive range covering both popular and academic spirituality, music and reference. Marshall Pickering: bibles, missals, prayer books, and hymn books. About 150 titles a year.

HarperCollins Cartographic Divisional Managing Director *Stephen Bray*. The cartographic division and Times Books now joined as one division. IMPRINTS **Collins**; **Collins Longman**; **Nicholson/Ordnance Survey** Maps, atlases and guides (Collins; Collins Longman); leisure maps, educational titles (Collins Longman); London titles (Nicholson); waterway guides (Nicholson/Ordnance Survey); reference and non-fiction. About 30 titles a year.

HarperCollins E Publishing Editorial Director *Leo Hollis* Internet publishing programme launched in February 2001. IMPRINT **PerfectBound** TITLES *Soul Mountain* Gao Xingjian; *Pride Before the Fall: The Trials of Bill Gates and the End of the Microsoft Era* John Heilemann; *Sharpe's Trafalgar* Bernard Cornwell.

Authors' Rating Last year HarperCollins had 30 titles in the *Sunday Times* bestsellers and 57 in the *New York Times* list. But these were bought at a high price. HC has now acquired a new MD in Victoria Barnsley, formerly head of Fourth Estate, who has a track record in finding unknown writers and turning them into profitable names. Expect less chequebook publishing and more excitement of discovering real talent. HC achieved a notable first with the launch of a trade e-book list.

Harrap

See **Chambers Harrap Publishers Ltd**

Harvard University Press

Fitzroy House, 11 Chenies Street, London WC1E 7EY
☎020 7306 0603 Fax 020 7306 0604
Email info@HUP-MITpress.co.uk
Website www.hup.harvard.edu

Director *William Sisler*
General Manager *Ann Sexsmith*

European office of **Harvard University Press**, USA. *Publishes* academic and scholarly works in history, politics, philosophy, economics, literary criticism, psychology, sociology, anthropology, women's studies, biological sciences, classics, history of science, art, music, film, reference. All mss go to the American office: 79 Garden Street, Cambridge, MA 02138 (see entry under **US Publishers**).

The Harvill Press Ltd

2 Aztec Row, Berners Road, London N1 0PW
☎020 7704 8766 Fax 020 7704 8805
Website www.harvill.com

Publisher *Christopher MacLehose*
Editorial Director *Margaret Stead*

FOUNDED in 1946, the Harvill list was bought by Collins in 1959, of which it remained an imprint until returning to its original independent status in early 1995. *Publishes* literature in translation (especially Russian, Italian and French), English literature, quality thrillers, illustrated books and Africana, plus an occasional literature anthology. 90–100 titles in 2000. AUTHORS Mikhail Bulgakov, Raymond Carver, Richard Ford, Jean-Christophe Grange, Peter Høeg, Robert Hughes, Giuseppe T. di Lampedusa, Henning Mankell, Peter Matthiessen, Haruki Murakami, Boris Pasternak, José Saramago, W.G. Sebald, Aleksandr Solzhenitsyn. Synopses and ideas welcome. No educational or technical books.

Royalties paid twice-yearly.

Authors' Rating Strong on translated fiction, the two-way traffic means that Harvill's English language writers tend to do well in Europe. Relations with authors are said to be close and friendly.

Haynes Publishing

Sparkford, Near Yeovil, Somerset BA22 7JJ
☎01963 440635 Fax 01963 440825
Email info@haynes-manuals.co.uk
Website www.haynes.co.uk

Chairman *John H. Haynes, OBE*
Approx. Annual Turnover £28.7 million

FOUNDED in 1960 by John H. Haynes. Family-run business. The mainstay of its programme has been the *Owners' Workshop Manual*, first published in the mid 1960s and still running off the presses today. Indeed the company maintains a strong bias towards motoring and transport titles. Acquired **Sutton Publishing Ltd** in March 2000 (see entry). *Publishes* DIY service and repair manuals for cars, motorbikes and general leisure plus other related topics.

IMPRINT

Haynes *Matthew Minter* Service and repair manuals; *Mark Hughes* Motoring, motor sport, cars, motorcycles, home, DIY and leisure titles. Unsolicited submissions welcome if they come within the subject areas covered.

Royalties paid twice-yearly. *Overseas subsidiaries* Haynes Manuals Inc., California, USA, Editions

Haynes S.A., France, Haynes Publishing Nordiska AB, Sweden.

Authors' Rating There were financial stresses associated with the purchase of Sutton Publishing but if Haynes was to grow further it had to break out of the car manual straitjacket. More leisure titles can be expected.

Hazar Publishing Ltd
147 Chiswick High Road, London W4 2DT
☎020 8742 8578 Fax 020 8994 1407
Email marie@hazarpublishing.com
Website www.hazarpublishing.com
Managing Director *Gregory Hill*
Editorial Head *Marie Clayton*
Approx. Annual Turnover £700,000

FOUNDED 1993, An independent publisher of illustrated books. *Publishes* children's picture books and pop-up books and adult non-fiction on design and architecture. About 15 titles a year.
  Royalties paid twice-yearly.

Hazleton Publishing
3 Richmond Hill, Richmond, Surrey TW10 6RE
☎020 8948 5151 Fax 020 8948 4111
Email info@hazletonpublishing.com
Website www.hazletonpublishing.com
Publisher/Managing Director *R.F. Poulter*

Publisher of the leading Grand Prix annual *Autocourse*, now in its 50th edition. *Publishes* high-quality motor sport titles including annuals. TITLES *Motocourse; Rallycourse*. About 13 titles a year. No unsolicited mss/ synopses and ideas welcome. Interested in all motor sport titles.
  Royalties payment varies.

Headline
See **Hodder Headline Plc**

Heartline Books Limited
PO Box 22598, London W8 7GB
☎020 7376 3930 Fax 020 7376 0999
Email enquiries@heartlinebooks.co.uk
Website www.heartlinebooks.com
Chair *Mary-Jo Wormell*
Managing Director *Robert Williams*
Senior Editor *Sue Curran*

FOUNDED on St Valentine's Day 2001 to *publish* romantic fiction only. TITLES *Beguiled* Kay Gregory; *Soul Whispers* Julia Wild; *Red Hot Lover* Lucy Merritt. 'We are interested in contemporary romantic fiction only (no historical, sagas, etc.).' No unsolicited mss; submit synopsis and three sample chapters initially, addressed to the senior editor, *Sue Curran*.
  Royalties paid twice-yearly.

William Heinemann
See **Random House Group Ltd**

Heinemann Educational
See **Reed Educational & Professional Publishing**

Heinemann Young Books
See **Egmont Books**

Helicon Publishing Ltd
42 Hythe Bridge Street, Oxford OX1 2EP
☎01865 204204 Fax 01865 204205
Email admin@helicon.co.uk
Website www.helicon.co.uk
Managing Director *David Attwooll*
Editorial Director *Hilary McGlynn*
Approx. Annual Turnover £3.5 million

FOUNDED 1992 from the management buy-out of former Random Century's reference division. Led by David Attwooll, the buy-out included the Hutchinson encyclopedia titles and databases, along with other reference titles. Helicon is now a 100% subsidiary of WHSmith. The Helicon list, which is represented by Hodder & Stoughton Educational, is increasing its range of reference titles, particularly in history, science and current affairs and is maintaining its lead in electronic publishing, especially in the area of online licensing, where it has relationships with several key UK and US blue-chip service providers. TITLES *The Hutchinson Encyclopedia*. Electronic: *The Penguin Hutchinson Reference Suite*; *The Hutchinson Encyclopedia of Music*; *The Hutchinson Educational Encyclopedia 2001*; *The Hutchinson Science Reference, Suite*; *The Hutchinson History Reference Suite*.

Christopher Helm Publishers Ltd
See **A.&C. Black (Publishers) Ltd**

Helter Skelter Publishing
4 Denmark Street, London WC2H 8LL
☎020 7836 1151 Fax 020 7240 9880
Email helter@skelter.demon.co.uk
Website www.helterskeltermusic.com
Contact *Sean Body*

FOUNDED 1995. *Publishes* music books only. 10 titles a year. IMPRINTS **Helter Skelter Publishing**; **Firefly Publishing**. Unsolicited mss, synopses and ideas welcome.

Henderson Publishing
See **Dorling Kindersley Ltd**

Ian Henry Publications Ltd
20 Park Drive, Romford, Essex RM1 4LH
☎01708 749119 Fax 01708 736213
Managing Director *Ian Wilkes*
FOUNDED 1976. *Publishes* local history, transport history and Sherlockian pastiches. 8–10 titles a year. TITLES *An Essex Pastoral; Shoebury Story; Sherlock Holmes Book of Magic.* No unsolicited mss. Synopses and ideas for books welcome.
Royalties paid twice-yearly.

The Herbert Press
See **A.&C. Black (Publishers) Ltd**

Hermes House
See **Anness Publishing Ltd**

Nick Hern Books
The Glasshouse, 49a Goldhawk Road,
London W12 8QP
☎020 8749 4953 Fax 020 8746 8746
Email info@nickhernbooks.demon.co.uk
Chairman/Managing Director *Nick Hern*
Approx. Annual Turnover £400,000
FOUNDED 1988. Fully independent since 1992. *Publishes* books on theatre and film: from how-to and biography to plays and screenplays. About 30 titles a year. No unsolicited playscripts. Synopses, ideas and proposals for other theatre material welcome. Not interested in material unrelated to the theatre or cinema.

Hippo
See **Scholastic Ltd**

Historic Military Press
See **SB Publications**

HMSO
See **The Stationery Office Ltd**

Hobsons Publishing
Challenger House, 42 Adler Street, London
E1 1EE
☎020 7958 5000 Fax 020 7958 5001
Website www.hobsons.com
Chairman *Martin Morgan*
Group Managing Director *Christopher Letcher*
Approx. Annual Turnover £17.7 million
FOUNDED 1973. A division of Harmsworth Publishing Ltd, part of the Daily Mail & General Trust. *Publishes* course and career guides, under exclusive licence and royalty agreements for CRAC (Careers Research and Advisory Bureau); computer software; directories and specialist titles for employers, government departments and professional associations. TITLES *Graduate Employment and Training; Degree Course Guides; The Which Degree Series; Which University* (CD-ROM); *The POSTGRAD Series: The Directory of Graduate Studies; The Directory of Further Education.*

Hodder & Stoughton
See **Hodder Headline Plc**

Hodder Headline Plc
338 Euston Road, London NW1 3BH
☎020 7873 6000 Fax 020 7873 6024
Website www.hodderheadline.com
Group Chief Executive *Tim Hely Hutchinson*
Approx. Annual Turnover £93.2 million
Formed in June 1993 through the merger of Headline Book Publishing and Hodder & Stoughton. Headline was formed in 1986 and had grown dramatically, whereas Hodder & Stoughton was 125 years old with a diverse range of publishing. About 2000 titles a year. The company was acquired by the WHSmith Group plc in 1999.
DIVISIONS
Headline Book Publishing Managing Director *Amanda Ridout*. **Non-fiction** Publishing Director *Heather Holden-Brown*; **Fiction** Publishing Director *Jane Morpeth*; **Headline** *Anne Williams*; **Headline Feature** *Bill Massey*; **Review** *Geraldine Cooke*. *Publishes* commercial and literary fiction (hardback and paperback) and popular non-fiction including biography, cinema, countryside, food and wine, popular science, TV tie-ins and sports yearbooks. IMPRINTS **Headline**; **Headline Feature**; **Review**. AUTHORS Catherine Alliott, Ronan Bennett, Raymond Blanc, Martina Cole, Josephine Cox, Lucy Ellmann, John Francome, Ken Hom, Jennifer Johnston, Cathy Kelly, Dean Koontz, James Patterson, Anthony Worrall Thompson.
  Hodder & Stoughton General Managing Director *Martin Neild*, Deputy Managing Director *Sue Fletcher*. **Non-fiction** *Roland Philipps*; **Sceptre** *Carole Welch*; **Fiction** *Carolyn Mays*; **Audio** (See entry under **Audio Books**). *Publishes* commercial and literary fiction; biography, autobiography, history, self-help, humour, travel and other general interest

non-fiction; audio. IMPRINTS **Hodder & Stoughton**; **Lir**; **Coronet**; **Flame**; **New English Library**; **Sceptre**. AUTHORS Dickie Bird, Melvyn Bragg, John le Carré, Justin Cartwright, Alex Ferguson, Charles Frazier, Elizabeth George, Amy Jenkins, Thomas Keneally, Stephen King, Ed McBain, Malcolm Gluck, Rosamunde Pilcher, Mary Stewart.

Hodder & Stoughton Educational Managing Director *Philip Walters*. **Humanities, Tests, Science & Scotland** *Lis Tribe*; **Languages, Business, Psychology, English and Mathematics** *Tim Gregson-Williams*; **Teach Yourself**; **Trade Education** *Jo Osborne*. Textbooks for the primary, secondary, tertiary and further education sectors and for self-improvement. IMPRINT **Hodder & Stoughton Educational**.

Hodder Children's Books Managing Director *Mary Tapissier*. IMPRINTS **Hodder Children's Books**; **Signature**; **Wayland**. AUTHORS Enid Blyton, John Cunliffe, Lucy Daniels, Mick Inkpen, Hilary McKay, Joan Lingard, Jenny Oldfield, Christopher Pike.

Hodder & Stoughton Religious Managing Director *Charles Nettleton*. **Bibles & Liturgical** *Emma Sealey*; **Christian paperbacks** *Judith Longman*. Bibles, commentaries, liturgical works (both printed and software), and a wide range of Christian paperbacks. IMPRINTS **New International Version of the Bible**; **Hodder Christian Books**.

Arnold Managing Director *Richard Stileman*. **Humanities** *Chris Wheeler*; **STM** *Nick Dunton*; **Health Sciences** *Georgina Bentliff*; **Journals** *Mary Attree*. Academic and professional books and journals.

Royalties

Authors' Rating Being owned by WHSmith has not cramped the style of this hugely energetic publisher. Imaginative ideas are given the full treatment including forceful marketing.

Holt Rinehart and Winston
See **Harcourt Publishers Limited**

Honeyglen Publishing Ltd
56 Durrels House, Warwick Gardens, London W14 8QB
☎020 7602 2876 Fax 020 7602 2876
Directors *N.S. Poderegin, J. Poderegin*

FOUNDED 1983. A small publishing house whose output is 'extremely limited'. *Publishes* history, philosophy of history, biography and selective fiction. No children's or science fiction. TITLES *The Soul of India; A Child of the Century* Amaury de Riencourt; *With Duncan Grant in South Turkey* Paul Roche; *Vladimir, The Russian Viking* Vladimir Volkoff; *The Dawning* Milka Bajic-Poderegin; *Quicksand* Louise Hide. Unsolicited mss welcome.

Honno Welsh Women's Press
c/o Theological College, King Street, Aberystwyth, Ceredigion SY23 2LT
☎01970 623150 Fax 01970 623150
Email editor@honno.co.uk
Website www.honno.co.uk
Editor *Gwenllian Dafydd*

FOUNDED in 1986 by a group of women who wanted to create more opportunities for women in publishing. A co-operative operation which *publishes* fiction (adult and teenage) and children's books, all with a Welsh connection. About 6 titles a year. Welcome mss and ideas for books from women only. All material must have a Welsh connection and be sent as hard copy, not by e-mail.
Royalties paid annually.

Horus Editions
See **Award Publications Limited**

House of Lochar
Isle of Colonsay, Argyll PA61 7YR
☎01951 200232 Fax 01951 200232
Email Lochar@colonsay.org.uk
Chairman *Kevin Byrne*
Managing Director *Georgina Hobhouse*
Approx. Annual Turnover £95,000

FOUNDED 1995 on a tiny island, taking advantage of new technology and mains electricity and taking over some 20 titles from Thomas and Lochar. About 10 titles a year. *Publishes* mostly Scottish – history, topography, transport and fiction. IMPRINTS **House of Lochar** TITLES *The Crofter and the Laird; The Clyde in Pictures; Alexander III*. AUTHORS (fiction) Neill Gunn, Naomi Mitchison, Marion Campbell. **Colonsay Books** TITLES *Summer in the Hebrides*. **West Highland Series** Mini walking guides. No poetry or books unrelated to Scotland or Celtic theme. Unsolicited mss, synopses and ideas welcome if relevant to subjects covered.
Royalties paid annually.

House of Stratus
24c Old Burlington Street, London W1X 1RL
☎020 7494 6400 Fax 020 7494 6444
Website www.houseofstratus.com
CEO *David Lane*

Commercial Director *Tim Forrester*

FOUNDED 1999. *Publishes* fiction and non-fiction. Backlist of over 1200 titles including C.P. Snow, Brian Aldiss, Nevil Shute and G.K. Chesterton. About 30 titles annually. Submissions should incorporate a synopsis, sample chapter and author c.v.

Royalties paid twice-yearly. Overseas offices in New York.

How To Books Ltd

3 Newtec Place, Magdalen Road, Oxford OX4 1RE
☎01865 793806 Fax 01865 248780
Email info@howtobooks.co.uk
Website www.howtobooks.co.uk

Publisher/Managing Director *Giles Lewis*

FOUNDED in 1991, How To Books is an independent reference publisher which *publishes* reference books and three popular SERIES. **How To** titles are practical, accessible books that encourage their readers to improve their lives and develop their skills. **Essentials** are handy books explaining specific skills to busy people. **Quick Fix** are fun volumes that present small changes that will make a big difference in life. Subjects covered include business & management, computers & the Net, home & family, career choices & career development, living & working abroad, personal finance, small business & self employment, study & student guides, creative writing. Authors are given guidance in the development of their books.

Human Horizons

See **Souvenir Press Ltd**

Human Science Press

See **Kluwer Academic/Plenum Publishers**

Hunt & Thorpe

See **John Hunt Publishing Ltd**

John Hunt Publishing Ltd

46a West Street, New Alresford, Hampshire SO24 9AU
☎01962 736880 Fax 01962 736881
Email sandra@johnhuntpub.demon.co.uk

Approx. Annual Turnover £1.5 million

Publishes children's and religious titles only – about 25 a year. IMPRINTS **Hunt & Thorpe**; **John Hunt Publishing**; **Arthur James**; **O Books**. Unsolicited material welcome.

C. Hurst & Co.

38 King Street, London WC2E 8JZ
☎020 7240 2666 Fax 020 7240 2667
Email hurst@atlas.co.uk
Website www.hurstpub.co.uk

Chairman/Managing Director *Christopher Hurst*
Editorial Heads *Christopher Hurst, Michael Dwyer*

FOUNDED 1967. An independent company, cultivating a concern for literacy, detail and the visual aspects of the product. *Publishes* contemporary history, politics and social science. About 20 titles a year. TITLES *The Origins of Japanese Trade Supremacy; The Rwanda Crisis – History of a Genocide; Listening People, Speaking Earth: Contemporary Paganism; Yugoslavia's Bloody Collapse; Following Ho Chi Minh – Memoirs of a North Vietnamese Colonel.* No unsolicited mss. Synopses and ideas welcome.

Royalties paid twice in first year, annually thereafter.

Hutchinson

See **Random House Group Ltd**

Hymns Ancient & Modern Ltd

St Mary's Works, St Mary's Plain, Norwich, Norfolk NR3 3BH
☎01603 612914 Fax 01603 624483

Chairman *Very Rev. Dr Henry Chadwick, KBE*
Chief Executive *G.A. Knights*
Publisher, Canterbury Press Norwich *Christine Smith*
Publisher, RMEP *Mary Mears*
Publisher, SCM Press *Alex Wright*
Approx. Annual Turnover £4 million

Publishes hymn books for churches, schools and other institutions. All types of liturgical and general religious books and material for religious and social education. Owns SCM-Canterbury Press Ltd controlling the IMPRINTS **SCM Press** (see entry). **Canterbury Press Norwich** Liturgical and general religious books TITLES *Simple Guide to Common Worship; Leading Intercessions; The Saints of the Anglican Calendar.* **Religious and Moral Education Press (RMEP)** Religious, social and moral books for primary and secondary schools, assembly material and books for teachers and administrators. **G.J. Palmer & Sons Ltd** TITLES *Church Times* (see entry under **Magazines**); *The Sign* and *Home Words* – two monthly nationwide parish magazine inserts. Ideas welcome; no unsolicited mss.

Royalties paid annually.

Icon Books Ltd

Grange Road, Duxford, Cambridge CB2 4QF
☎01763 208008 Fax 01763 208080
Email info@iconbooks.co.uk
Website www.iconbooks.co.uk

Managing Director *Peter Pugh*
Editorial Director *Richard Appignanesi*
Publishing Director *Jeremy Cox*

FOUNDED 1992. SERIES **Introducing** Graphic
introductions to key figures and ideas in the
history of science, philosophy, psychology,
religion and the arts TITLE *Introducing Quantum
Theory*. **Readers' Guides** Student guides to
secondary sources in English literature TITLE
The Poetry of Ted Hughes. **Postmodern
Encounters** Provocative mini-essays exploring a key theme in the work of a major thinker
in psychology, philosophy and science TITLE
Nietzsche and Postmodernism. **Ideas in
Psychoanalysis** Mini-essays on key terms in
psychoanalysis TITLE *Superego*. **Revolutions in
Space** New narrative non-fiction exploring
specific discoveries in the history of science
TITLE *Harvey and the Circulation of the Blood*.

Royalties paid twice yearly. *Overseas associate*
Totem Books, USA, distributed by National
Book Network.

I.M.P. Fiction Ltd

PO Box 14691, London SE1 2ZA
☎020 7357 8007 Fax 020 7357 8068
Email info@impbooks.com
Website www.impbooks.com

Managing Director *Kaye Roach*

FOUNDED 1998. *Publishes* 'innovative new cutting-edge' fiction. No crime or science fiction.
4 titles in 2000. Approach in writing, enclosing
biography, synopsis, first three chapters and
s.a.e. Material will not be returned if postage
and packing not provided.

Royalties paid twice-yearly.

The In Pinn

See **Neil Wilson Publishing Ltd**

Independent Music Press

PO Box 14691, London SE1 2ZA
☎020 7357 8007 Fax 020 7357 8608
Email info@impbooks.com
Website www.impbooks.com

Managing Director *Martin Roach*

FOUNDED 1992. *Publishes* music biography and
youth culture. No jazz or classical. TITLES
include biographies of Travis, Stereophonics,
Oasis, Prodigy and Ian Hunter's *Diary of a Rock*
'n' Roll Star. 4 titles in 2000. Approach in writing, enclosing biography, synopsis, first three
chapters and s.a.e. Material will not be returned
if postage and packing not provided.

Royalties paid twice-yearly.

Independent Voices

See **Souvenir Press Ltd**

The Industrial Society

Robert Hyde House, 48 Bryanston Square,
London W1H 2EA
☎020 7479 2000 Fax 020 7723 7375
Website www.indsoc.co.uk

Head of Publishing *Carl Upsall*
Commissioning Editor *Susannah Lear*
Approx. Annual Turnover (Publishing
    Division) £1.6 million

Industrial Society Publications, which is part of
The Industrial Society ('a registered charity
committed to making work fulfilling'), has been
publishing books for over 20 years. *Specialises* in
business, management, self-development, train-
ing, staff development, human resources – both
books and special reports. TITLES *The Heart
Aroused; Fifty Ways to Personal Development;
Body Talk – Skills of Positive Image; Navigating
Complexity*. SERIES *Your Personal Trainer*.
Unsolicited mss, synopses and ideas welcome.
No fiction or illustrated non-fiction.

Royalties paid twice-yearly.

Informa Pharmaceutical & Healthcare

Mortimer House, 37–41 Mortimer Street,
London W1T 3JH
☎020 7453 2370 Fax 020 7453 2387
Website www.monitorpress.co.uk

Publisher *Zöe Turner*

Part of LLP Professional Publishing, a trading
division of Informa Publishing Group Ltd.
Publishes a range of medical/tax business to
business newsletters, special reports and books
aimed at senior management and professional
practices. 6 newsletter titles a year. Unsolicited
synopses and ideas welcome. Initial approach
in writing.

Inter Publishing Ltd

6–7 Leapale Road, Guildford, Surrey
GU1 4JX
☎01483 306309 Fax 01483 579196
Email eagle_ips@compuserve.com

Managing Director *David Wavre*
Approx. Annual Turnover £500,000

FOUNDED 1990. *Publishes* religious plus some gift and art books. About 24 titles a year. IMPRINTS **Eagle**; **Little Eagle** Christian books for young children. Unsolicited mss, synopses and ideas for books welcome.
Royalties paid twice-yearly.

Inter-Varsity Press

38 De Montfort Street, Leicester LE1 7GP
☎0116 255 1754 Fax 0116 254 2044
Email ivp@uccf.org.uk
Website www.ivpbooks.com
Chairman *Ralph Evershed*
Chief Executive *Frank Entwistle*
FOUNDED mid-'30s as the publishing arm of Universities and Colleges Christian Fellowship, it has expanded to wider Christian markets worldwide. *Publishes* Christian belief and lifestyle, reference and bible commentaries. About 50 titles a year. No secular material or anything which fails to empathise with orthodox Protestant Christianity.
IMPRINTS **IVP**; **Apollos**; **Crossway** TITLES *The Bible Speaks Today; The Care of Creation* Berry; *Matters of Life and Death* Wyatt. No unsolicited mss; synopses and ideas welcome.
Royalties paid twice-yearly.

International Thomson Publishing
See **Thomson Learning**

Internet Handbooks

Unit 5 Dolphin Building, Queen Anne's Battery, Plymouth, Devon PL4 0LP
☎01752 262626 Fax 01752 262641
Email editor@internet-handbooks.co.uk
Website www.internet-handbooks.co.uk
Owner *Internet Handbooks Ltd*
Managing Director *Roger Ferneyhough*
FOUNDED in 1998 by Roger Ferneyhough following his sale of **How To Books** in 1996. *Publishes* practical step-by-step guides to help the reader get the most out of the Internet with the series set to grow to around 30 titles. 50 titles in 2000. TITLES *The Internet for Writers; Where to Find It On the Internet; Marketing Your Business on the Internet; Personal Finance on the Internet.* The Internet Handbooks website offers substantial and free online help on a broad range of topics for all Internet users. Welcomes material for books about the internet; a telephone call or e-mail is advised in the first instance.
Royalties paid annually.

Intrigue
See **Harlequin Mills & Boon Ltd**

Isis Publishing

7 Centremead, Osney Mead, Oxford OX2 0ES
☎01865 250333 Fax 01865 790358
Part of the Ulverscroft Group Ltd. *Publishes* large-print books – fiction and non-fiction – and unabridged audio books. Together with **Soundings** (see entry under **Audio Books**) produce around 4000 titles on audio tape and CD. AUTHORS Catherine Cookson, Stephen King, Terry Pratchett, Willy Russell. No unsolicited mss as Isis undertakes no original publishing.
Royalties paid twice-yearly.

Ithaca Press
See **Garnet Publishing Ltd**

IVP
See **Inter-Varsity Press**

Jacqui Small
See **Aurum Press Ltd**

Arthur James
See **John Hunt Publishing Ltd**

Jane's Information Group

163 Brighton Road, Coulsdon, Surrey CR5 2YH
☎020 8700 3700 Fax 020 8763 1006
Website www.janes.com
Managing Director *Alfred Rolington*
FOUNDED 1898 by Fred T. Jane with the publication of *All The World's Fighting Ships*. Now part of The Thomson Corporation. In recent years management has been focusing on growth opportunities in its core business and in enhancing the performance of initiatives like Jane's information available online and on CD-ROM. *Publishes* magazines and yearbooks on defence, aerospace and transport topics, with details of equipment and systems; plus directories and strategic studies. Also *Jane's Defence Weekly* (see entry under **Magazines**).

DIVISIONS
Magazines TITLES *Jane's Defence Weekly; Jane's International Defense Review; Jane's Airport Review; Jane's Defence Upgrades; Jane's Navy International; Jane's Islamic Affairs Analyst; Jane's Missiles and Rockets.* **Publishing** *Karen Heffer, Fabiana Angelini* TITLES *Defence, Aerospace Yearbooks.* **Security** *John Boatman* TITLES *Jane's Intelligence Review; Foreign Report; Jane's Sentinel* (regional

security assessment); *Police Review.* **Transport** *Alan Condron* TITLES *Transportation Yearbooks;* CD-ROM and electronic development and publication. Unsolicited mss, synopses and ideas for reference/yearbooks welcome.

Royalties paid twice-yearly. *Overseas associates* Jane's Information Group Inc., USA.

Janus Publishing Company Ltd

76 Great Titchfield Street, London W1P 7AF
☎020 7580 7664 Fax 020 7636 5756
Email publisher@januspublishing.co.uk
Managing Director *Sandy Leung*

Publishes fiction, human interest, memoirs, philosophy, mind, body and spirit, religion and theology, social questions, popular science, history, spiritualism and the paranormal, poetry and young adults. About 400 titles in print. IMPRINTS **Janus Books** Subsidy publishing; **Empiricus Books** Non-subsidy publishing. TITLES *The Anarchists in the Spanish Civil War; Nature of the Self; Healing Connections; Politics and Human Nature; Tales of French Corsairs and Revolutions; Child of the Thirties; Napoleon 1813.* Unsolicited mss welcome.

Royalties paid twice-yearly. Agents in the USA, Europe and Asia.

Authors' Rating Authors may be asked to cover their own productions costs but Janus seems to be moving into conventional publishing with its Empiricus imprint.

Japan Library

See **Curzon Press Ltd**

Jarrold Publishing

Whitefriars, Norwich, Norfolk NR3 1TR
☎01603 763300 Fax 01603 662748
Email publishing@jarrold.com
Website www.jarrold-publishing.co.uk
Managing Director *Caroline Jarrold*

Part of Jarrold & Sons Ltd, the printing and publishing company FOUNDED in 1770. *Publishes* UK tourism, travel, leisure, history and calendars. Material tends to be of a high pictorial content. About 30 titles a year. Unsolicited mss, synopses and ideas welcome but before submitting anything, approach in writing to the editorial department.

Royalties paid quarterly.

Jensen Business Books

See **AMCD (Publishers) Ltd**

Jets

See **HarperCollins Publishers Ltd**

Jewish Chronicle Publications

See **Frank Cass & Co Ltd**

Michael Joseph

See **Penguin UK**

Kahn & Averill

9 Harrington Road, London SW7 3ES
☎020 8743 3278 Fax 020 8743 3278
Email kahn@averill23.freeserve.co.uk
Managing Director *Mr M. Kahn*

FOUNDED 1967 to publish children's titles but now specialises in music titles. A small independent publishing house. *Publishes* music and general non-fiction. No unsolicited mss; synopses and ideas for books considered.

Royalties paid twice-yearly.

Karnak House

300 Westbourne Park Road, London W11 1EH
☎020 7243 3620 Fax 020 7243 3620
Email karnakhouse@aol.com
Managing Director *Amon Saba Saakana*

FOUNDED 1979. *Specialises* in African and Caribbean studies. *Publishes* anthropology, education, Egyptology, history, language and linguistics, literary criticism, music, parapsychology, prehistory. No poetry, humour or sport. About 12 titles a year. No unsolicited mss; send introduction or synopsis with one sample chapter. Synopses and ideas welcome.

Royalties paid twice-yearly. *Overseas subsidiaries* The Intef Institute, and Karnak House, Illinois, USA.

Kelpie

See **Canongate Books Ltd**

Kenilworth Press Ltd

Addington, Buckingham, Buckinghamshire MK18 2JR
☎01296 715101 Fax 01296 715148
Email editorial@kenilworthpress.co.uk
Website www.kenilworthpress.co.uk
Chairman/Managing Director *David Blunt*
Approx. Annual Turnover £500,000

FOUNDED in 1989 with the acquisition of Threshhold Books. The UK's principal instructional equestrian publisher, producing the official books of the British Horse Society, the famous *Threshold Picture Guides,* and a range of authoritative titles sold around the world. About 10 titles a year.

IMPRINT **Kenilworth Press** TITLES *British Horse Society Manuals; Dressage with Kyra; A*

Modern Horse Herbal; *For the Good of the Rider*; *No Foot, No Horse*; *Threshold Picture Guides 1–45*. Unsolicited mss, synopses and ideas welcome but only for titles concerned with the care or riding of horses or ponies.

Royalties paid twice-yearly.

Kenyon-Deane

See **Cressrelles Publishing Co. Ltd**

Laurence King

71 Great Russell Street, London WC1B 3BP
☎020 7430 8850 Fax 020 7430 8880
Email enquiries@laurence-king.co.uk
Website www.laurence-king.co.uk

Chairman *Robin Hyman*
Managing Director *Laurence King*

FOUNDED 1991. Publishing imprint of UK packager **Calmann & King Ltd** (see entry under **UK Packagers**). *Publishes* full-colour illustrated books on art history, the decorative arts, carpets and textiles, graphic design, architecture and interior design. Unsolicited material welcome.

Royalties paid twice-yearly.

Kingfisher Publications Plc

New Penderel House, 283–288 High Holborn, London WC1V 7HZ
☎020 7903 9999 Fax 020 7242 4979
Email sales@kingfisherpub.co.uk

Chairman *Bertil Hessel*

Formerly Larousse plc until 1997 when the company name changed to Kingfisher Publications Plc. FOUNDED 1994 when owners, Groupe de la Cité (also publishers of the Larousse dictionaries in France), merged their UK operations of Grisewood & Dempsey and **Chambers Harrap Publishers Ltd** (see entry).

DIVISION
Kingfisher *Ann-Janine Murtagh*, Publishing Director, Fiction; *Gill Denton* Non-fiction. FOUNDED in 1973 by Grisewood & Dempsey Ltd. *Publishes* children's fiction and non-fiction in hardback and paperback: story books, rhymes and picture books, fiction and poetry anthologies, young non-fiction, activity books, general series and reference. No unsolicited mss accepted.

Royalties paid twice-yearly where applicable.

Jessica Kingsley Publishers Ltd

116 Pentonville Road, London N1 9JB
☎020 7833 2307 Fax 020 7837 2917
Email post@jkp.com
Website www.jkp.com

Managing Director *Jessica Kingsley*
Senior Editor *Amy Lankester-Owen*

FOUNDED 1987. Independent publisher of books for professionals and academics on social and behavioural sciences, including special needs, arts therapies, child psychology, psychotherapy (including forensic psychotherapy), practical theology and social work. Over 100 titles a year. 'We are actively publishing and commissioning in autism and Asperger Syndrome. We welcome suggestions for books and proposals from prospective authors. Proposals should consist of an outline of the book, a contents list, assessment of the market, and author's c.v. and should be addressed to Jessica Kingsley. Complete manuscript should not be sent.' No fiction or poetry.

Royalties paid twice-yearly.

Kluwer Academic/ Plenum Publishers

241 Borough High Street, London SE1 1GB
☎020 7940 7490 Fax 020 7940 7495
Email mail@plenum.co.uk
Website www.plenum.co.uk

Managing Director *Dr Ken Derham*
Editor *Joanna Lawrence*

FOUNDED 1966. A division of **Kluwer Academic/Plenum Publishing**, New York. The London office is the editorial base for the company's UK and European operations. *Publishes* postgraduate, professional and research-level scientific, technical and medical textbooks, monographs, conference proceedings and reference books. About 200 titles (worldwide) a year.

IMPRINTS **Consultants Bureau**; **Kluwer Academic/Plenum Publishers**; **Plenum Press**; **Human Science Press**. Proposals for new publications will be considered, and should be sent to the editor.

Royalties paid annually.

Kluwer Law International

Sterling House, 66 Wilton Road, London SW1V 1DE
☎020 7821 1123 Fax 020 7630 5229

Director of Operations *Marcel Nieuwenhuis*

FOUNDED 1995. Parent company: Wolters Kluwer Group. Kluwer Law International consists of three components: the law list of Graham & Trotman, Kluwer Law and Taxation and Martinus Nyhoff. *Publishes* international law. 200 titles a year. Unsolicited synopses and ideas for books on law at an international level welcome.

Royalties paid annually.

Charles Knight Publishing
See **Butterworths Tolley**

Knight Paperbacks Ltd
See **Caxton Publishing Group**

Kogan Page Ltd
120 Pentonville Road, London N1 9JN
☎020 7278 0433 Fax 020 7837 3768/6348
Email kpinfo@kogan-page.co.uk
Website www.kogan-page.co.uk *or*
www.earthscan.co.uk
Managing Director *Philip Kogan*
Approx. Annual Turnover £8 million

FOUNDED 1967 by Philip Kogan to publish *The Industrial Training Yearbook*. In 1992 acquired Earthscan Publications. *Publishes* business and management reference books and monographs, education and careers, marketing, personal finance, personnel, small business, training and industrial relations, transport, plus journals. Further expansion is planned, particularly in the finance and high-tech, EC publications areas, yearbooks and directories, and international business reference. Has initiated a number of electronic publishing projects and provision of EP content. About 280 titles a year.

DIVISIONS
Kogan Page *Pauline Goodwin, Philip Mudd, Peter Chadwick*. **Earthscan Publications** *Jonathan Sinclair Wilson* Has close associations with the International Institute for Environment and Development and with the Worldwide Fund for Nature. *Publishes* Third World issues and their global implications, and general environmental titles, both popular and academic. About 50 titles a year. Unsolicited mss, synopses and ideas for books welcome.
Royalties paid twice-yearly.

Authors' Rating Distribution problems gave Kogan Page a few nasty months but there has been no letup in the publication of books for aspiring professionals and business people.

Ladybird
See **Dorling Kindersley Ltd**

Landmark Publishing Ltd
Waterloo House, 12 Compton, Ashbourne, Derbyshire DE6 1DA
☎01335 347349 Fax 01335 347303
Email landmark@clara.net
Website www.landmarkpublishing.co.uk
Chairman *Mr R. Cork*

Managing Director *Mr C.L.M. Porter*
Approx. Annual Turnover £350,000

FOUNDED in 1996 following the demise of Moorland Publishing. *Publishes* itinerary-based travel guides and industrial history. 36 titles in 2000. No unsolicited mss; telephone in the first instance.
Royalties twice-yearly.

Larousse Plc
See **Kingfisher Publications Plc**

Lawrence & Wishart Ltd
99A Wallis Road, London E9 5LN
☎020 8533 2506 Fax 020 8533 7369
Email lw@l-w-bks.demon.co.uk
Website www.l-w-bks.co.uk
Managing Director/Editor *Sally Davison*

FOUNDED 1936. An independent publisher with a substantial backlist. *Publishes* current affairs, cultural politics, economics, history, politics and education. 15–20 titles a year. TITLES *A New Modernity; Liberty or Death; The Struggle for Democracy in Britain 1780–1830; Rosa Luxemburg: An Intimate Portrait.*
Royalties paid annually, unless by arrangement.

The Learning Institute
Honeycombe House, Bagley, Wedmore, Somerset BS28 4TD
☎01934 713563 Fax 01934 713492
Email courses@inst.org
Website www.inst.org
Managing Director *Kit Sadgrove*

FOUNDED 1994 to publish home-study courses in vocational subjects such as garden design, writing and computing. *Publishes* subjects that show the reader how to work from home, gain a new skill or enter a new career. Interests include self-improvement, interior design, hobbies, parenting, health, careers, music and investment. TITLES *Become a Freelance Photographer; Master the Art of Painting.* Author's guidelines sent on receipt of s.a.e. No unsolicited mss; send synopses and ideas only.
Royalties paid quarterly.

Lehigh University Press
See **Golden Cockerel Press Ltd**

Leicester University Press
See **Continuum International Publishing Group Ltd**

Lennard Associates Ltd

Windmill Cottage, Mackerye End,
Harpenden, Hertfordshire AL5 5DR
☎01582 715866 Fax 01582 715121
Email mailbox@lenqap.demon.co.uk

Chairman/Managing Director *Adrian
Stephenson*

FOUNDED 1979. Publisher of sporting yearbooks,
personality books, and television associated titles.
YEARBOOKS *The Cricketers' Who's Who; RFU
Club Directory; Official PFA Footballers' Factfile;
British Boxing Yearbook; Wooden Spoon Rugby
World.* No unsolicited mss.

IMPRINTS **Lennard Publishing**; **Queen
Anne Press**. Acquired the latter and most of
its assets in 1992.

Payment Both fees and royalties by arrangement.

Letterland

See **HarperCollins Publishers Ltd**

Charles Letts

See **New Holland Publishers (UK) Ltd**

Lionel Leventhal Ltd

See **Greenhill Books**

Dewi Lewis Publishing

8 Broomfield Road, Heaton Moor, Stockport
SK4 4ND
☎0161 442 9450 Fax 0161 442 9450
Email mail@dewilewispublishing.com
Website www.dewilewispublishing.com

Contacts *Dewi Lewis, Caroline Warhurst*
Approx. Annual Turnover £240,000

FOUNDED 1994. *Publishes* fiction, photography
and visual arts. 16 titles in 2000. TITLES *Industry
of Souls* Martin Booth (shortlisted for the 1998
Booker Prize); *Common Sense* Martin Parr;
New York 1954–5 William Klein. Mss in the
above categories are welcome, provided return
postage is enclosed; no synopses or ideas,
please.

Royalties paid twice-yearly.

Lexis-Nexis

See **Reed Elsevier plc**

John Libbey & Co. Ltd

PO Box 276, Eastleigh SO50 5YS
☎023 8065 0208 Fax 023 8065 0259
Email johnlibbey@aol.com
Website www.johnlibbey.com

Chairman/Managing Director *John Libbey*

FOUNDED 1979. *Publishes* medical books and
cinema/animation books and journals. *Specialises* in epilepsy, neurology, nuclear medicine,
nutrition and obesity. Synopses and ideas welcome. *Overseas subsidiary* John Libbey Eurotext
Ltd, France.

Librapharm Ltd

Gemini House, 162 Craven Road, Newbury,
Berkshire RG14 5NR
☎01635 522651 Fax 01635 36294
Website www.librapharm.com

Chairman *Mr M.W. Frost*
Managing Director *Dr P.L. Clarke*
Approx. Annual Turnover £500,000

FOUNDED 1995 as a partial buyout from
Kluwer Academic Publishers (UK) academic
list. *Publishes* medical and scientific books and
periodicals. IMPRINT **Petroc Press**. TITLES
Neighbour: The Inner Consultation; *Moulds:
Emergencies in General Practice*; *Primary Care
Psychiatry* (journal); *Current Medical Research and
Opinion* (journal). Unsolicited mss, synopses
and ideas for medical books welcome.

Royalties paid twice-yearly.

Library Association Publishing

7 Ridgmount Street, London WC1E 7AE
☎020 7255 0590/0505 (text phone)
Fax 020 7255 0591
Email lapublishing@la-hq.org.uk
Website www.la-hq.org.uk/lapublishing

Managing Director *Janet Liebster*

Publishing arm of **The Library Association**.
Publishes library and information science,
monographs, reference, IT training materials
and bibliography aimed at library and information professionals. About 35 titles a year.

IMPRINTS **Library Association Publishing**;
Clive Bingley Books Over 200 titles in print,
including *Walford's Guide to Reference Material* and
AACR2. Unsolicited mss, synopses and ideas
welcome provided material falls firmly within
the company's specialist subject areas.

Royalties paid annually.

Frances Lincoln Ltd

4 Torriano Mews, Torriano Avenue, London,
NW5 2RZ
☎020 7284 4009 Fax 020 7267 5249
Email <firstname>@frances-lincoln.com

Managing Director *John Nicol*

FOUNDED 1977. *Publishes* highly illustrated
non-fiction: gardening, art and interiors, spirituality and healing, health, crafts, children's

picture and information books; and stationery. About 60 titles a year.

DIVISIONS

Adult Non-fiction *Jo Christian* TITLES *Chatsworth* Duchess of Devonshire; *The Gravel Garden* Beth Chatto; **Children's General Fiction and Non-fiction** *Janetta Otter-Barry* TITLES *The Wanderings of Odysseus* Rosemary Sutcliffe, illus. Alan Lee; **Stationery** *Anne Fraser* TITLES *RHS Diary and Address Book*; *National Gallery Diary and Address Book*. Synopses and ideas for books considered.

Royalties paid twice-yearly.

Linden Press
See **Open Gate Press**

Linford Romance/Linford Mystery/Linford Western
See **F.A. Thorpe (Publishing)**

Lion Publishing
Peter's Way, Sandy Lane West, Oxford OX4 5HG
☎01865 747550 Fax 01865 747568
Email enquiry@lion-publishing.co.uk
Website www.lion-publishing.co.uk
Managing Director *Paul Clifford*
Approx. Annual Turnover £6.77 million
FOUNDED 1971. A Christian book publisher, strong on illustrated books for a popular international readership, with rights sold in over 100 languages worldwide. *Publishes* a diverse list with Christian viewpoint the common denominator. All ages, from board books for children to multi-contributor adult reference, educational, paperbacks and colour co-editions and gift books.

DIVISIONS **Adult** *Faith Cummins*; **Children's and Giftlines** *Charlotte Stewart*. Unsolicited mss accepted provided they have a positive Christian viewpoint intended for a wide general and international readership.

Royalties paid twice-yearly.

Authors' Rating After a troubled year in which the religion list was hit by 'enormous competition from general as well as specialist publishers', Lion has refocused its programme to concentrate on illustrated information and reference books.

Lir
See **Hodder Headline Plc**

Little Tiger Press
An imprint of Magi Publications, 1 The Coda Centre, 189 Munster Road, London SW6 6AW
☎020 7385 6333 Fax 020 7385 7333
Email info@littletiger.co.uk
Publisher *Monty Bhatia*
Editor *Linda Jennings*
Approx. Annual Turnover £4 million
Publishes children's picture and novelty books for ages 0–9. No texts over 1200 words. About 24 titles a year. Unsolicited mss, synopses and new ideas welcome, but please telephone first.

Royalties paid annually.

Little, Brown & Co. (UK)
Brettenham House, Lancaster Place, London WC2E 7EN
☎020 7911 8000 Fax 020 7911 8100
Email uk@littlebrown.com
Website www.littlebrown.co.uk
Chief Executive *David Young*
Publisher *Ursula Mackenzie*
Approx. Annual Turnover £36.8 million
FOUNDED 1988. Part of Time-Warner Inc. Began by importing its US parent company's titles and in 1990 launched its own illustrated non-fiction list. Two years later the company took over former Macdonald & Co. *Publishes* hardback and paperback fiction, literary fiction, crime, science fiction and fantasy; and general non-fiction, including illustrated: architecture and design, fine art, photography, biography and autobiography, cinema, gardening, history, humour, travel, crafts and hobbies, reference, cookery, wines and spirits, DIY, guidebooks, natural history and nautical.

IMPRINTS **Abacus** *Richard Beswick* Literary fiction and non-fiction paperbacks; **Orbit** *Tim Holman* Science fiction and fantasy; **Little Brown/ Warner** *Alan Samson, Barbara Boote, Hilary Hale* Mass-market fiction and non-fiction; **X Libris** *Sarah Shrubb* Women's erotica; **Illustrated** *Julia Charles* Hardbacks; **Virago** (see entry). Approach in writing in the first instance. No unsolicited mss.

Royalties paid twice-yearly.

Authors' Rating A quality publisher that manages to cover an impressive range of new writing. Much praised by authors for friendly efficiency.

Liverpool University Press
4 Cambridge Street, Liverpool L69 7ZU
☎0151 794 2233 Fax 0151 794 2235
Website www.liverpool-unipress.co.uk

Managing Director/Editorial Head *Robin Bloxsidge*

LUP's primary activity is the publication of academic and scholarly books and journals but it also has a limited number of trade titles. Although its principal focus is on the arts and social sciences, in which it is active in a wide variety of disciplines, the LUP list includes some STM books. 30–40 titles a year. TITLES *The Musical Work: Reality or Invention?; Demography, State and Society: Irish Migrants to Britain 1921–1971; Merseypride: Essays in Liverpool Exceptionalism; The Eye Book: Eyes and Eye Problems Explained; Ramsey Campbell and Modern Horror Fiction; Public Sculpture of Leicestershire and Rutland; Social Theory after the Holocaust; Crime and the Criminal Justice System.*

Royalties paid annually.

Livewire Books for Teenagers
See **The Women's Press**

Lonely Planet Publications Ltd
10A Spring Place, London NW5 3BH
☎020 7428 4800   Fax 020 7428 4828
Email go@lonelyplanet.co.uk
Website www.lonelyplanet.com
Owner *Lonely Planet (Australia)*
Editorial Head *Katharine Leck*
General Manager *Charlotte Hindle*
Approx. Annual Turnover £30 million

FOUNDED in 1973 by Tony and Maureen Wheeler to document a journey from London across Asia to Australia. Since then, Lonely Planet has grown into a global operation with headquarters in Melbourne and offices in Paris, California and London. *Publishes* travel guidebooks, phrasebooks, travel literature, pictorial books, city maps, regional atlases, diving and snorkelling, walking, cycling, wildlife, healthy, restaurant, pre-departure guidebooks. In 2000 Lonely Planet set up a commercial travel slide library called **Lonely Planet Images** (lpi@lonelyplanet.com.au). No unsolicited mss; synopses and ideas welcome.

Royalties negotiable.

Lorenz Books
See **Anness Publishing Ltd**

Peter Lowe (Eurobook Ltd)
PO Box 52, Wallingford, Oxfordshire OX10 0XU
☎01865 858333   Fax 01865 858263
Email eurobook@compuserve.com
Managing Director *Peter Lowe*

FOUNDED 1968. *Publishes* popular science and illustrated adult non-fiction. No unsolicited mss; synopses and ideas (with s.a.e.) welcome. No adult fiction.

Lund Humphries
See **Ashgate Publishing Ltd**

The Lutterworth Press
PO Box 60, Cambridge CB1 2NT
☎01223 350865   Fax 01223 366951
Email publishing@lutterworth.com
Website www.lutterworth.com
Managing Director *Adrian Brink*

The Lutterworth Press dates back to the 18th century when it was founded by the Religious Tract Society. In the 19th century it was best known for its children's books and magazines, both religious and secular, including *The Boys' Own Paper*. Since 1984 it has been an imprint of **James Clarke & Co** (see entry). *Publishes* religious books for adults and children, adult non-fiction, children's fiction and non-fiction. TITLES *Lutterworth Dictionary of the Bible; Riverside Journey: a portrait of the Derwent; Small Communities in Religious Life: making them work; Never Ones for Theory?: England and the war of ideas.* Approach in writing with ideas in the first instance.

Royalties paid annually.

Macdonald & Co.
See **Little, Brown & Co. (UK)**

McGraw-Hill Publishing Company
McGraw-Hill House, Shoppenhangers Road, Maidenhead, Berkshire SL6 2QL
☎01628 502500   Fax 01628 770224
Email alfred_waller@mcgraw-hill.com
Website www.mcgraw-hill.co.uk
Publishing Director, Europe *Alfred Waller*

FOUNDED 1899. Owned by US parent company. Began publishing in Maidenhead in 1965, having had an office in the UK since 1899. *Publishes* business and economics, accountancy, finance, computer science and business computing for the academic, student and professional markets. Around 50 titles a year. Unsolicited mss, synopses and ideas welcome. See website for author's guide and how to submit new book proposals.

Royalties paid twice-yearly.

Macmillan Publishers Ltd

The Macmillan Building, 4 Crinan Street, London N1 9XW
☎020 7833 4000 Fax 020 7843 4640
Website www.macmillan.com

Chief Executive *Richard Charkin*
Approx. Annual Turnover £300 million (Book Publishing Group)

FOUNDED 1843. Macmillan is one of the largest publishing houses in Britain, publishing approximately 1400 titles a year. In 1995, Verlagsgruppe Georg von Holtzbrinck, a major German publisher, acquired a majority stake in the Macmillan Group. In 1996, Macmillan bought Boxtree, the successful media tie-in publisher and, in 1997, purchased the Heinemann English language teaching list from Reed Elsevier. Unsolicited proposals, synopses and mss are welcome in all divisions of the company (with the exception of Macmillan Children's Books). Authors who wish to send material to Macmillan General Books should note that there is a central submissions procedure in operation. Send a synopsis and the first 3–4 chapters with a covering letter and return postage to the Submissions Editor, Pan Macmillan, 20 New Wharf Road, London N1 9RR.

DIVISIONS
Palgrave Brunel Road, Houndmills, Basingstoke, Hampshire RG21 6XS ☎01256 329242 Fax 01256 3479476 Managing Director *Dominic Knight*. **Academic** *Josie Dixon*; **College**: **Humanities & Social Sciences Division** *Frances Arnold*; **Business, Computer Science & Engineering** *Chris Glennie*; **Professional Business & Management Division** *Stephen Rutt*; **Journals** *David Bull*. *Publishes* textbooks, monographs and journals in academic and professional subjects. Publications in both hard copy and electronic format.
Macmillan Heinemann English Language Teaching Macmillan Oxford, 4 Between Towns Road, Oxford OX4 3PP ☎01865 405700 Fax 01865 405701 Email elt@mhelt.com Website www.mhelt.com Executive Director *Christopher Paterson*; Managing Directors *Mike Esplen, Chris Harrison*; Publishing Directors *Sue Bale, Alison Hubert*. *Publishes* a wide range of ELT titles and educational books for the international education market.
Pan Macmillan 20 New Wharf Road, London N1 9RR ☎020 7014 6000 Fax 020 7014 6001 Managing Director *David North*; Editor-in-Chief (adult imprints) *Peter Straus*;

Publishing Director (Macmillan, Pan, Picador) *Maria Rejt* Publishes under **Macmillan**, **Pan**, **Picador**, **Sidgwick & Jackson**, **Boxtree**, **Channel 4 Books**, **Macmillan Children's Books**, **Campbell Books**.

IMPRINTS
Macmillan (FOUNDED 1843) Publisher *Jeremy Trevathan*, Editorial Directors (fiction) *Imogen Taylor, Peter Lavery*. *Publishes* commercial and literary fiction including genre fiction, crime, thrillers, romantic, sci-fi, fantasy and horror. Editorial Director (non-fiction) *Georgina Morley*. *Publishes* autobiography, biography, business and industry, economics, gift books, history, natural history, travel, philosophy, politics and world affairs, psychology, gardening and cookery, popular science. Editorial Director (reference) *Morven Knowles*. *Publishes* trade reference titles.
Pan (FOUNDED 1947) Publisher *Clare Harington*. *Publishes* fiction: novels, detective fiction, sci-fi, fantasy and horror. Serious non-fiction: history, biography, science. General non-fiction: sports and games, film and theatre, travel, gardening and cookery.
Picador (FOUNDED 1972) Publisher *Peter Straus*, Senior Editorial Director *Ursula Doyle*. *Publishes* literary international fiction and non-fiction.
Sidgwick & Jackson (FOUNDED 1908) Publisher *Gordon Scott Wise*. *Publishes* popular non-fiction in hardback and trade paperback with strong personality or marketable identity, from celebrity and showbusiness to ancient mystery, music and true-life adventure to inspirational and branded books. Also military history list.
Macmillan Audio Books (See entry under **Audio Books**)
Boxtree Publisher *Gordon Scott Wise*. *Publishes* media tie-in titles, including TV, film, music and internet, plus entertainment licences, pop culture, humour and event-related books. TITLES *Dilbert; Father Ted; The Motley Fool; Who Wants to be a Millionaire?; James Bond; Purple Ronnie; Crimewatch; Antiques Roadshow.* **Channel 4 Books** Publisher *Ms Charlie Carman*. *Publishes* TV tie-in titles – books that stand on their own merits and not just the 'book of the series'. About 50 titles a year. TITLES *Friends; Water Colour Challenge; Time Team; Dawson's Creek; Frasier; South Park.*
Macmillan Children's Books (New Wharf Road address) Managing Director *Kate Wilson*; **Fiction**, **Non-Fiction**, **Poetry** *Sarah Davies*; **Picture Books**, **Gift Books** *Alison Green*; **Campbell Books** *Dereen Taylor*.

IMPRINTS **Macmillan**, **Pan**, **Campbell Books**. *Publishes* novels, board books, picture books, non-fiction (illustrated and non-illustrated), poetry and novelty books in paperback and hardback. No unsolicited material.

Macmillan Online Publishing (Crinan Street address) Chief Executive Officer *Ian Jacobs*, Editorial Director *Jane Turner*. *Publishes* works of reference in academic, professional and vocational subjects, online resources. TITLES *The New Grove Dictionary of Music and Musicians* ed. Stanley Sadie; *The Dictionary of Art* ed. Jane Turner.

Royalties paid annually or twice-yearly depending on contract.

Authors' Rating The big change this year has been the rebirth of Palgrave, a famous name from the reference backlist, to become the global name for all academic imprints, including those in the US. At the same time a 50 per cent investment increase is promised for academic publishing, much of which will go online. A new children's list and a new adult imprint are promised later in the year but, as we go to press, details are still under wraps.

Magi Publications
See **Little Tiger Press**

Mainstream Publishing Co. (Edinburgh) Ltd
7 Albany Street, Edinburgh EH1 3UG
☎0131 557 2959 Fax 0131 556 8720
Email editorial@mainstreampublishing.com
Website www.mainstreampublishing.com

Directors *Bill Campbell, Peter MacKenzie*
Approx. Annual Turnover £2.75 million

Publishes art, autobiography/biography, current affairs, health, sport, history, illustrated and fine editions, photography, politics and world affairs, popular paperbacks. Over 80 titles a year. TITLES *Deadly Beat—Inside the Royal Ulster Constabulary* Richard Latham; *Cover-up of Convenience – The Hidden Scandal of Lockerbie* Ian Ferguson and John Ashton; *The South Downs Way* Martin King; *The Bedsers* Alan Hill. Ideas for books considered, but they should be preceded by a letter, synopsis and s.a.e. or return postage.

Royalties paid twice-yearly.

Authors' Rating A Scottish company aiming for a British profile. Keen on finding authors who 'can develop with us'.

Mammoth
See **Egmont Books**

Management Books 2000 Ltd
Cowcombe House, Cowcombe Hill,
Chalford, Gloucestershire GL6 8HP
☎01285 760722 Fax 01285 760708
Email m.b.2000@virgin.net
Website www.mb2000.com

Publisher *Nicholas Dale-Harris*
Approx. Annual Turnover £500,000

FOUNDED 1993 to develop a range of books for executives and managers working in the modern world of business, supplemented with information through other media like seminars, audio and video. *Publishes* business and management and sponsored titles. About 30 titles a year. Unsolicited mss, synopses and ideas for books welcome.

Manchester United Books
See **Carlton Publishing Group**

Manchester University Press
Oxford Road, Manchester M13 9NR
☎0161 275 2310 Fax 0161 274 3346
Email mup@man.ac.uk
Website www.man.ac.uk/mup

Publisher/Chief Executive *David Rodgers*
Approx. Annual Turnover £2 million

FOUNDED 1903. MUP is Britain's third largest university press, with a list marketed and sold worldwide. Remit consists of occasional trade publications but mainly A-level and undergraduate textbooks and research monographs. *Publishes* in six main areas: literature and cultural studies, history and history of art, politics, economics, design, film and media. About 120 titles a year, plus journals.

DIVISIONS **Humanities** *Matthew Frost*; **History/Art History/Religion** *Alison Whittle*; **Politics and Economics** *Tony Mason*. Unsolicited mss welcome.

Royalties paid annually.

George Mann Books
PO Box 22, Maidstone, Kent ME14 1AH
☎01622 759591 Fax 01622 209193

Chairman/Managing Director *George Mann*

FOUNDED 1972, originally as library reprint publishers, but has moved on to other things with the collapse of the library market. *Publishes* original non-fiction and selected reprints. Not considering new fiction for publication. 'Will only consider and respond to authors who, in the present publishing climate, are prepared to support some of the costs of publication. Unsolicited material not accompanied by return postage will neither be read nor returned.'

Royalties paid annually.

Mansell
See **Continuum International Publishing Group Ltd**

Manson Publishing Ltd
73 Corringham Road, London NW11 7DL
☎020 8905 5150 Fax 020 8201 9233
Email manson@man-pub.demon.co.uk
Chairman/Managing Director *Michael Manson*
Approx. Annual Turnover £700,000

FOUNDED 1992. *Publishes* scientific, technical, medical and veterinary. 15 titles in 2000. No unsolicited mss; synopses and ideas will be considered.

Royalties paid twice-yearly.

Marshall Pickering
See **HarperCollins Publishers Ltd**

Marshall Publishing
See **Marshall Editions Ltd** under **UK Packagers**

Marston House
Marston House, Marston Magna, Yeovil, Somerset BA22 8DH
☎01935 851331 Fax 01935 851372
Managing Director/Editorial Head *Anthony Birks-Hay*

FOUNDED 1989. Publishing imprint of book packager Alphabet & Image Ltd. *Publishes* fine art, architecture, ceramics. 4 titles a year.

Royalties paid twice-yearly, or flat fee in lieu of royalties.

Kenneth Mason Publications Ltd
Dudley House, 12 North Street, Emsworth, Hampshire PO10 7DQ
☎01243 377977 Fax 01243 379136
Chairman *Kenneth Mason*
Managing Director *Piers Mason*
Approx. Annual Turnover £500,000

FOUNDED 1958. *Publishes* diet, health, fitness, nutrition and nautical. No fiction. About 15 titles a year. Initial approach by letter with synopsis only. IMPRINTS **Boatswain Press**; **Research Disclosure**.

Royalties paid twice-yearly in first year, annually thereafter.

Kevin Mayhew Publishers
Buxhall, Stowmarket, Suffolk IP14 3BW
☎01449 737978 Fax 01449 737834
Email info@kevinmayhewltd.com
Website www.kevinmayhewltd.com
Chairman *Kevin Mayhew*
Managing Director *Gordon Carter*
Commissioning Editors *Kevin Mayhew, Jonathan Bugden*
Approx. Annual Turnover £4 million

FOUNDED in 1976. One of the leading sacred music and Christian book publishers in the UK. *Publishes* religious titles – liturgy, sacramental, devotional, also children's books and school resources. Unsolicited synopses and mss welcome; telephone prior to sending material, please.

IMPRINT **Palm Tree Press** *Kevin Mayhew* Bible stories, colouring/activity and puzzle books for children.

Royalties paid annually.

Melrose Press Ltd
St Thomas Place, Ely, Cambridgeshire CB7 4GG
☎01353 646600 Fax 01353 646601
Email tradesales@melrosepress.co.uk
Website www.melrosepress.co.uk
Chairman *Richard A. Kay*
Managing Director *Nicholas S. Law*
Approx. Annual Turnover £2 million

FOUNDED 1960. Took on its present name in 1969. *Publishes* biographical who's who reference only (not including *Who's Who*, which is published by **A.&C. Black**).

DIVISION **International Biographical Centre** *Jon Gifford*. TITLES *International Authors and Writers Who's Who; International Who's Who in Music; Who's Who in Asia and the Pacific Nations*.

Mentor
See **Christian Focus Publications**

Mercat Press
53 South Bridge, Edinburgh EH1 1YS
☎0131 622 8252 Fax 0131 557 8149
Email enquiries@jthin.co.uk
Website www.mercatpress.com
Chairman/Managing Director *D. Ainslie Thin*

Editorial Heads *Tom Johnstone, Seán Costello, Camilla James*

FOUNDED 1971 as an adjunct to the large Scottish-based bookselling chain of James Thin. Began by publishing reprints of classic Scottish literature but now produces a wide range of new non-fiction titles. In 1992 the company acquired the bulk of the stock of Aberdeen University Press and the backlist expanded greatly as a result. In 1999 it took over some 60 titles from the Stationery Office's Scottish heritage list. New titles are added regularly. *Publishes* Scottish classics reprints and non-fiction of Scottish interest. This includes walking guides and historical and literary books. TITLES *West Highland Way, Official Guide* Bob Aitken and Roger Smith; *25 Walks* series; *Hell of a Journey* Mike Cawthorne; *Golden City, Scottish Children's Street Games and Songs* James Ritchie; *The Scots Kitchen* F. Marian McNeill. Unsolicited synopses of non-fiction Scottish interest books, preferably with sample chapters, are welcome. No new fiction or poetry.
Royalties paid annually.

The Merlin Press Ltd
PO Box 30705, London WC2E 8QD
☎020 7836 3020 Fax 020 7497 0309
Email info@merlinpress.co.uk
Website www.merlinpress.co.uk
Managing Director *Anthony W. Zurbrugg*
FOUNDED 1956. *Publishes* economics, history, philosophy, left-wing politics. No fiction. IMPRINTS **Merlin Press**; **Green Print**.TITLES *Socialist Register* (annual); *The Essential E.P. Thompson*; *Men and Power*. About 10 titles a year.
Royalties paid twice-yearly.

Methodist Publishing House
20 Ivatt Way, Peterborough, Cambridgeshire PE3 7PG
☎01733 332202 Fax 01733 331201
Website www.mph.org.uk
Chair *Dudley Coates*
Chief Executive *Brian Thornton*
Approx. Annual Turnover £2 million
FOUNDED 1800. Owned by the Methodist Church. *Publishes* a wide range of books, magazines and resources which are sold to Christians in the UK and overseas. 21 titles in 2001. Launching a new bi-monthly magazine *Flame* with a target readership of 35,000. IMPRINTS **Epworth Press** (see entry); **Foundery Press** *Brian Thornton*. Unsolicited

mss, synopses and ideas welcome; send sample chapter and contents with covering letter.
Royalties paid twice-yearly.

Methuen Children's Books
See **Egmont Books**

Methuen Publishing Ltd
215 Vauxhall Bridge Road, London SW1V 1EJ
☎020 7798 1600 Fax 020 7233 9827
Email <name>@methuen.co.uk
Website www.methuen.co.uk
Managing Director *Peter Tummons*
Publishing Director *Max Eilenberg*
FOUNDED 1889. Methuen was owned by Reed International until it was bought by Random House in 1997. Purchased by a management buy-out team in 1998. *Publishes* fiction and non-fiction; drama, film, performing arts, humour. 60 titles in 2000. DIVISIONS **General**; **Drama**; **Film**; **Theatre**. No unsolicited mss; synopses and ideas welcome. Prefers to be approached via agents or a letter of inquiry. No first novels, cookery books, personal memoirs.
Royalties paid twice-yearly.

Michelin Tyre plc
The Edward Hyde Building, 38 Clarendon Road, Watford, Hertfordshire WD1 1SX
☎01923 415000 Fax 01923 415052
Website www.michelin-travel.com
FOUNDED 1900 as a travel publisher. *Publishes* travel guides, maps and atlases, children's I-Spy books. Travel-related synopses and ideas welcome; no mss.

Midland Publishing – An imprint of Ian Allan Publishing Ltd
4 Watling Drive, Hinckley LE10 3EY
☎01455 255490 Fax 01455 255495
Email midlandbooks@compuserve.com
Publisher *N.P. Lewis*
Publishes aviation, military and railways. No wartime memoirs. No unsolicited mss; synopses and ideas welcome.
Royalties paid quarterly.

Milet Publishing Limited
19 North End Parade, London W14 0SJ
☎020 7603 5477 Fax 020 7610 5475
Email info@milet.com
Website www.milet.com
Managing Directors *Sedat Turhan, Patricia Billings*

FOUNDED 1995. *Publishes* children's books–dual language and in English; world literature for adults and language books. Over 200 titles in 2000. DIVISIONS **Children's, English**; **Children's, Dual Language** *Patricia Billings* TITLES *Night and Day; Small World Series.* **World Literature**; **Language Books** *Sedat Turhan* TITLE *The Other Side of the Mountain.* Welcomes synopses and ideas for books. Send proposal, outline or synopsis with sample text and/or artwork, either by post or e-mail. 'We like bold, original stories and artwork, both multicultural and contemporary.'

Royalties paid twice-yearly.

Harvey Miller Publishers
See **Brepols Publishers**

Miller's
See **Octopus Publishing Group**

Mills & Boon
See **Harlequin Mills & Boon Ltd**

Mindfield
See **Camden Press Ltd**

Minerva Press Ltd
6th Floor, Canberra House, 315–317 Regent Street, London W1B 2HS
☎020 7580 4114 Fax 020 7580 9256
Email mail@minerva-press.co.uk
Website www.minerva-press.co.uk
Director of Publications *Sarah Hughes*
FOUNDED in 1992, but the imprint can be traced back to 1792. *Publishes* fiction and non-fiction; memoirs/biography, poetry, religion, philosophy, history and children's. 300 titles in 2000. TITLES *The Lost Grandad* Geoff Steward; *Out of Nazi Germany and Trying to Find My Way* Irene Matthews; *Walking on Water* Nick Corbler. Specialises in new authors. Unsolicited mss, synopses and ideas for books welcome.

Royalties paid twice-yearly. Offices in Miami, New Delhi and Rio de Janeiro, with representation in Australia.

Authors' Rating Liable to ask authors to contribute towards costs of publication.

MIRA
See **Harlequin Mills & Boon Ltd**

Mitchell Beazley
See **Octopus Publishing Group**

Mojo.
See **Canongate Books Ltd**

Monarch Books
Concorde House, Grenville Place, London NW7 3SA
☎020 8959 3668 Fax 020 8959 3678
Email monarch@angushudson.com
Director *Nick Jones*
An imprint of **Angus Hudson Ltd** (see entry under **UK Packagers**). *Publishes* an independent list of Christian books across a wide range of concerns. About 30 titles a year. IMPRINT **Monarch** Upmarket paperback list with Christian basis and strong social concern agenda including psychology, future studies, politics, mission, theology, leadership and spirituality. Unsolicited mss, synopses and ideas welcome. 'Regretfully, no poetry or fiction.'

Mosby International
See **Harcourt Publishers Limited**

Motor Racing Publications
Unit 6, The Pilton Estate, 46 Pitlake, Croydon, Surrey CR0 3RY
☎020 8681 3363 Fax 020 8760 5117
Email mrp.books@virgin.net
Website www.oberon.co.uk/mrp
Chairman/Editorial Head *John Blunsden*
FOUNDED soon after the end of World War II to concentrate on motor-racing titles. Fairly dormant in the mid '60s but was reactivated in 1968 by a new shareholding structure. John Blunsden later acquired a majority share and major expansion followed in the '70s. About 10–12 titles a year. *Publishes* motor-sport history, classic car collection and restoration, road transport, motorcycles, off-road driving and related subjects.

IMPRINTS **Fitzjames Press**; **Motor Racing Publications** No unsolicited mss. Send synopses and ideas in specified subject areas in the first instance.

Royalties paid twice-yearly.

Mowbray
See **The Continuum International Publishing Group Ltd**

Multi-Sensory Learning Ltd
Highgate House, Groom's Lane, Creaton, Northampton NN6 8NN
☎01536 399003 Fax 01604 882812
Email pipattwood@aol.com

Senior Editor *Philippa Attwood*

Publishes materials and books related to dyslexia; the multi-sensory learning course for dyslexic pupils needing literacy skills development, plus numerous other items on assessment, reading, maths, music, etc. for dyslexics. Keen to locate authors able to write materials for dyslexic people and for teachers of dyslexics.

Murdoch Books UK Ltd

Ferry House, 51–57 Lacy Road, London SW15 1PR
☎020 8355 1480 Fax 020 8355 1499
CEO *Robert Oerton*
Publisher *Catie Ziller*
Approx. Annual Turnover £3.6 million

Owned by Australian media group Murdoch Magazines Pty Ltd. *Publishes* full-colour non-fiction: homes and interiors, gardening, cookery, craft, cake decorating and DIY. About 46 titles a year. Synopses and ideas for books welcome; no unsolicited mss.
Royalties paid twice-yearly.

John Murray (Publishers) Ltd

50 Albemarle Street, London W1S 4BD
☎020 7493 4361 Fax 020 7499 1792
Email johnmurray@dial.pipex.com
Website www.johnmurray.co.uk
Chairman *John R. Murray*
Managing Director *Nicholas Perren*

FOUNDED 1768. Independent publisher. *Publishes* general trade books, educational (secondary school and college textbooks) and Success Studybooks.
DIVISIONS **General Books** *Grant McIntyre*; **Educational Books** *Nicholas Perren*. Unsolicited material discouraged.
Royalties paid twice yearly.

Authors' Rating The country's oldest privately owned publisher – the standard bearer for Jane Austen, the Brontës, Byron and Darwin – survives on a quality list, supplemented by schoolbooks which have not been doing too well of late. But who would not cheer for a national institution.

NAG Press Ltd
See **Robert Hale Ltd**

National Trust Publications

36 Queen Anne's Gate, London SW1H 9AS
☎020 7222 9251 Fax 020 7222 5097
Website www.nationaltrust.org.uk/bookshop
Chairman *Charles Nunneley*

Director-General *Fiona Reynolds*
Publisher *Margaret Willes*

Publishing arm of The National Trust, FOUNDED in 1895 by Robert Hunter, Octavia Hill and Hardwicke Rawnsley to protect and conserve places of historic interest and beauty. *Publishes* gardening, cookery, handbooks, social history, architecture, general interest and children's books. TITLES *Literary Trails; The Art of Dress; Flora Domestica; Children of the Great Country Houses; Hadrian's Wall: An Historic Landscape*. No unsolicited material.
Royalties paid twice-yearly.

Nautical Data Ltd

12 North Street, Emsworth, Hampshire PO10 7DQ
☎01243 377977 Fax 01243 379136
Email info@nauticaldata.com
Website www.nauticaldata.com
Managing Director *Piers Mason*
Approx. Annual Turnover £750,000

FOUNDED 1999. Part of **Macmillan Publishers Ltd**. *Publishes* nautical almanacs, pilots and nautical reference. 14 titles in 2000. No unsolicited mss; synopses and ideas welcome. No fiction or non-nautical themes.
Royalties paid twice-yearly.

NCVO Publications

Regent's Wharf, 8 All Saints Street, London N1 9RL
☎020 7713 6161 Fax 020 7713 6300
Website www.ncvo-voc.org.uk
Publications Manager *Maria Kane*
Approx. Annual Turnover £140,000

FOUNDED 1928. Publishing imprint of the National Council for Voluntary Organisations, embracing former Bedford Square Press titles and NCVO's many other publications. The list reflects NCVO's role as the representative body for the voluntary sector. *Publishes* directories, management and trustee development, legal, finance and fundraising titles of primary interest to the voluntary sector. TITLES *The Voluntary Agencies Directory; The Good Trustee Guide; The Good Campaigns Guide; The Good Financial Management Guide; The Good Employment Guide*. No unsolicited mss as all projects are commissioned in-house.
Royalties paid twice-yearly.

Thomas Nelson & Sons Ltd
See **Nelson Thornes Limited**

Nelson Thornes Limited

Delta Place, 27 Bath Road, Cheltenham, Gloucestershire GL53 7Th
☎01242 267100 Fax 01242 221914
Email cservices@nelsonthornes.com
Website www.nelsonthornes.com

Managing Director Oliver Gadsby

FOUNDED in 2000 following the merger of Stanley Thornes (Publishers) Ltd and Thomas Nelson & Sons Ltd. Part of the Wolters Kluwer Group of companies. Educational publisher of printed and electronic product, from pre-school to Higher Education. Unsolicited mss, synopses and ideas for books welcome if appropriate to specialised lists.
Royalties paid annually.

Authors' Rating The merger of Nelson with Stanley Thornes has created the second largest education publisher in the UK (Pearson is the first). The most successful divisions such as health and science are helped by the dominant position in the market held by the parent company, Wolters Kluwer.

New Beacon Books Ltd

76 Stroud Green Road, London N4 3EN
☎020 7272 4889 Fax 020 7281 4662

Chairman John La Rose
Managing Director Sarah White
Approx. Annual Turnover £120,000

FOUNDED 1966. *Publishes* fiction, history, politics, poetry and language, all concerning black people. 1 title in 2000. No unsolicited material.
Royalties paid annually.

New English Library

See **Hodder Headline Plc**

New Holland Publishers (UK) Ltd

Garfield House, 86–88 Edgware Road, London W2 2EA
☎020 7724 7773 Fax 020 7258 1293 (editorial)
Email postmaster@nhpub.co.uk

Managing Director John Beaufoy
Publishing Director Yvonne McFarlane
Approx. Annual Turnover £6 million

FOUNDED 1956. Relaunched in 1987 as a publisher of illustrated books for the international market. In 1993, NH acquired Charles Letts Publishing Division list and four years later the then parent company (New Holland Struik Group, South Africa) acquired Southern Book Publishers, while their sister company (New Holland Australia) acquired the natural history and lifestyle divisions of Reed Australia. With its HQ in London, New Holland Publishers (UK) Ltd has now become the International Publishing Division of Johnnic Communications, one of Africa's leading publishing groups. It also has offices in Australia and New Zealand. *Publishes* non-fiction, practical and inspirational books in categories including cookery and food, crafts, DIY, fishing, gardening, interior design, mind, body and spirit, natural history, indoor and outdoor sports, travel and general books. No unsolicited mss; synopses and ideas welcome.
Royalties paid twice-yearly.

Nexus

See **Virgin Books Ltd**

Nexus Special Interests

Nexus House, Azalea Drive, Swanley, Kent BR8 8HY
☎01322 660070 Fax 01322 667633
Website www.nexusonline.com

Contact Jackie Hollingsworth

Publishes aviation, engineering, leisure and hobbies, modelling, electronics, health, craft, wine and beer making, woodwork. Send synopses rather than completed mss.
Royalties paid twice-yearly.

NFER-Nelson Publishing Co. Ltd

Darville House, 2 Oxford Road East, Windsor, Berkshire SL4 1DF
☎01753 858961 Fax 01753 856830
Website www.nfer-nelson.co.uk

Managing Director Michael Jackson

FOUNDED 1981. Part of Granada Learning Ltd. *Publishes* educational and psychological tests and training materials. Main interest is in educational, clinical and occupational assessment and training material. Unsolicited mss welcome.
Royalties vary according to each contract.

Nia

See **The X Press**

Nicholson

See **HarperCollins Publishers Ltd**

Nightingale Books

See **Pegasus Elliot Mackenzie Publishers**

James Nisbet & Co. Ltd
Pirton Court, Prior's Hill, Pirton, Hitchin,
Hertfordshire SG5 3QA
☎01462 713444 Fax 01462 713444
Chairman *E.M. Mackenzie-Wood*
FOUNDED 1810 as a religious publisher and
expanded into more general areas from around
1850 onwards. The first educational list
appeared in 1926 but the company now concentrates on business studies with the education
largely discontinued. About 5 titles a year. No
fiction, leisure or religion. No unsolicited mss;
synopses and ideas welcome.
Royalties paid twice-yearly.

NMS Publishing Limited
Royal Museum, Chambers Street, Edinburgh
EH1 1JF
☎0131 247 4026 Fax 0131 247 4012
Email ltaylor@nms.ac.uk
Website www.nms.ac.uk
Chairman *Mark Jones*
Director *Lesley A. Taylor*
Approx. Annual Turnover £250,000
FOUNDED 1987 to *publish* non-fiction related
to the National Museums of Scotland collec-
tions: academic and general; children's; archae-
ology, history, decorative arts worldwide, his-
tory of science, technology, natural history and
geology, poetry. 15 titles in 2000. TITLES *Scots'
Lives* series; *Scotland's Past in Action; Scotland's
Crafts; Heaven and Hell and Other Worlds of the
Dead; The Making of the Museum of Scotland;* and
Clarissa Dickson Wright's *Hieland Foodie.* No
unsolicited mss; only interested in synopses and
ideas for books which are genuinely related to
NMS collections and to Scotland in general.
Royalties paid twice-yearly.

No Exit Press
See **Oldcastle Books Ltd**

Nonesuch Press
See **Reinhardt Books Ltd**

Northcote House Publishers Ltd
Horndon House, Horndon, Tavistock, Devon
PL19 9NQ
☎01822 810066 Fax 01822 810034
Managing Director *Brian Hulme*
FOUNDED 1985. *Publishes* a series of literary crit-
ical studies, in association with the British
Council, *Writers and their Work;* education man-
agement, literary criticism, educational dance
and drama. A new series of study aids for A-level

students and undergraduates in the humanities is
in preparation. 20 titles in 2000. 'Well-thought-
out proposals, including contents and sample
chapter(s), with strong marketing arguments
welcome.'
Royalties paid annually.

Nottingham University Press
Manor Farm, Main Street, Thrumpton,
Nottingham NG11 0AX
☎0115 983 1011 Fax 0115 983 1003
Email editor@nup.com
Website www.nup.com
Managing Editor *Dr D.J.A. Cole*
Approx. Annual Turnover £250,000
Initially concentrated on agricultural and food
sciences titles but has now branched into new
areas including engineering, lifesciences, medi-
cine, law and sport. Sports books published
under subsidiary, Castle Publications. TITLES
*Global 2050; Lung Function Tests; Diet,
Lipoproteins and Coronary Heart Disease; Nutrition
of Sows and Boars; Writing and Presenting Scientific
Papers.* **Castle Publications** TITLES *The Mental
Game of Golf; The Natural Sportsman; Rinks to
Arenas, 10 Years of British Ice Hockey; The Cricket
Coach's Guide to Man Management.*
Royalties paid twice-yearly.

O Books
See **John Hunt Publishing Ltd**

Oak
See **Omnibus Press**

Oberon Books
521 Caledonian Road, London N7 9RH
☎020 7607 3637 Fax 020 7607 3629
Email oberon.books@btinternet.com
Website www.oberonbooks.com
Publishing Director *James Hogan*
Managing Director *Charles D. Glanville*
A rapidly expanding company, Oberon *pub-
lishes* play texts (usually in conjunction with a
production) and theatre books. *Specialises* in
contemporary plays and translations of
European classics. IMPRINTS **Oberon Books;
Absolute Classics.** AUTHORS/TRANSLATORS
include Rodney Ackland, Michel Azama, Neil
Bartlett, John Barton, Simon Bent, Steven
Berkoff, Ranjit Bolt, Ken Campbell,
Marguerite Duras, Dario Fo, Jonathan Gems,
Pam Gems, Trevor Griffiths, Sir Peter Hall,
Christopher Hampton, Giles Havergal, Rolf
Hochhuth, Ruth Leon, Henry Livings, Robert
David MacDonald, Kenneth McLeish, Adrian

Mitchell, Sheridan Morley, John Mortimer, Stephen Mulrine, Jimmy Murphy, Meredith Oakes, John Osborne, Stewart Parker, Michael Pennington, David Pownall, Dennis Quilley, Colin Teevan, Reza de Wet, John Whiting, Charles Wood.

Octagon Press Ltd
PO Box 227, London N6 4EW
☎020 8348 9392 Fax 020 8341 5971
Website www.octagonpress.com
Managing Director *George R. Schrager*
Approx. Annual Turnover £100,000
FOUNDED 1972. *Publishes* philosophy, psychology, travel, Eastern religion, translations of Eastern classics and research monographs in series. 4–5 titles a year. Unsolicited material not welcome. Enquiries in writing only.
Royalties paid annually.

Octopus Publishing Group
2–4 Heron Quays, London E14 4JP
☎020 7531 8400 Fax 020 7531 8650
Website www.octopus-publishing.co.uk
Chief Executive *Derek Freeman*
Approx. Annual Turnover £45 million
(Group)
Formed following a management buyout of Reed Consumer Books from Reed Elsevier plc in August 1998.

Conran Octopus
Fax 020 7531 8627
Email info-co@conran-octopus.co.uk
Website www.conran-octopus.co.uk
Managing Director *Caroline Proud* Quality illustrated lifestyle books, particularly interiors, design, cookery, gardening and crafts TITLES *The Essential House Book* Terence Conran; *Fork to Fork* Monty Don; *Passion for Seafood* Gordon Ramsey; *New Retail* Rasshied Din.

Hamlyn Octopus
Email info-ho@hamlyn.co.uk
Website www.hamlyn.co.uk
Managing Director *Alison Goff* Popular non-fiction, particularly cookery, gardening, craft, sport, health, film and music TITLES *Larousse Gastronomique; Hamlyn All Colour Cookbook; Hamlyn Book of Gardening; Hamlyn Book of DIY & Decorating.*

Mitchell Beazley/Miller's
Fax 020 7537 0773
Email info-mb@mitchell-beazley.co.uk
Website www.mitchell-beazley.co.uk
Publisher/Managing Director *Jane Aspden*

Quality illustrated reference books, particularly food and wine, gardening, interior design and architecture, antiques, general reference TITLES *Hugh Johnson's Pocket Wine Book; The New Joy of Sex; Miller's Antiques and Collectibles Price Guides.*

Philip's
Fax 020 7531 8460
Email george.philip@philips-maps.co.uk
Website www.philips-maps.co.uk
Managing Director *John Gaisford* World atlases, globes, astronomy, road atlases, encyclopaedias, thematic reference TITLES *Philip's Atlas of the World; Philip's Modern School Atlas; Philip's Guide to the Stars and Planets; Ordnance Survey Street Atlas; Philip's Navigator Road Atlas; Philip's Millennium Encyclopaedia; Philip's Atlas of World History.*

Brimax
Fax 020 7531 8607
Email brimax@brimax.octopus.co.uk
Managing Director *Des Higgins* Mass-market board and picture books for children, age groups 1–10.

Bounty
Fax 020 7531 8607
Email bountybooksinfo-bp@bountybooks.co.uk
Managing Director *Laura Bamford* Bargain and promotional books. New, repackaged and reissued titles.

Digital Octopus
Fax 020 7537 0479
Managing Director *Ciaran Fenton* Digitally-formatted titles.

Octopus TV
Fax 020 7531 8469
Contact *Nicholas Price* Television programmes from Octopus publications.
Royalties paid twice-yearly/annually, according to contract in all divisions.

Oldcastle Books Ltd
18 Coleswood Road, Harpenden, Hertfordshire AL5 1EQ
☎01582 761264 Fax 01582 761264
Email info@noexit.co.uk
Website www.noexit.co.uk *or*
   www.pocketessentials.com
Managing Director *Ion S. Mills*
FOUNDED 1985. *Publishes* crime/noir fiction, gambling non-fiction and 96pp mini-reference titles on film, ideas, history, music, etc. 50 titles

in 2000. *No unsolicited mss.* Send synopses and ideas. IMPRINTS **No Exit Press** TITLES *Fierce Invalids Home from Hot Climates* Tom Robbins; *Mr Blue* Edward Bunker; **Oldcastle Books** TITLES *The Hand I Played* David Spanier; *Football Betting to Win* Jacques Black; **Pocketessentials** TITLES *Alfred Hitchcock; Vampire Films; Conspiracy Theories.*
Royalties paid twice-yearly.

Oldie Publications
45/46 Poland Street, London W1F 7NA
☎020 7734 2225 Fax 020 7734 2226
Website www.theoldie.co.uk
Chairman *Richard Ingrams*

FOUNDED in 1992. Book publishing arm of *The Oldie* magazine. *Publishes* compilations from the magazine, including cartoon books. TITLES *I Once Met; Dictionary For Our Time; The Fourth Oldie Annual; Jennifer's Diary: By One Fat Lady* Jennifer Paterson. No unsolicited mss; synopses and ideas (with return postage) welcome.

Michael O'Mara Books Ltd
9 Lion Yard, Tremadoc Road, London
SW4 7NQ
☎020 7720 8643 Fax 020 7627 8953
Email <firstname.lastname>@
    michaelomarabooks.com
Website www.mombooks.com
Chairman *Michael O'Mara*
Managing Director *Lesley O'Mara*
Approx. Annual Turnover £5 million

FOUNDED 1985. Independent publisher. *Publishes* general non-fiction, royalty, history, humour, children's novelties, anthologies and reference. TITLES *Diana: Her True Story* Andrew Morton; *Eye of the Storm* Peter Ratcliffe; the 'Little Book' series, including *WAN2TLK?*. IMPRINTS **Mary Ford Publications Ltd** Cake decorating; **Buster Books** Children's. Unsolicited mss, synopses and ideas for books welcome.
Royalties paid twice-yearly.

Authors' Rating From Diana to Monica via Morton. The route to riches may look simple enough but plenty of other publishers have lost their way. With fun titles ideal for the gift market O'Mara is also expanding into homecraft and children's books.

Omnibus Press
Music Sales Ltd, 8–9 Frith Street, London
W1V 5TZ
☎020 7434 0066 Fax 020 7734 2246

Email chris.charlesworth@musicsales.co.uk
Website www.omnibuspress.com
Editorial Head *Chris Charlesworth*

FOUNDED 1971. Independent publisher of music books, rock and pop biographies, song sheets, educational tutors, cassettes, videos and software. IMPRINTS **Amsco; Bobcat; Oak; Omnibus; Wise Publications**. Unsolicited mss, synopses and ideas for books welcome.
Royalties paid twice-yearly.

Oneworld Publications
185 Banbury Road, Oxford OX2 7AR
☎01865 310597 Fax 01865 310598
Email info@oneworld-publications.com
Website www.oneworld-publications.com
Editorial Director *Juliet Mabey*

FOUNDED 1986. *Publishes* adult non-fiction across a range of subjects from world religions and social issues to psychology and philosophy. 30 titles in 1999. A series on world religions was launched in 1994 with authors such as Geoffrey Parrinder, Keith Ward, Klaus Klostermaier and John Hicks. A series of concise encyclopedias has been launched on world religions, a series of short histories of countries was launched in 2000 and a new series on philosophy was planned for 2001. Lead TITLE for 2000: *Rumi – Past and Present, East and West* Franklin Lewis. No unsolicited mss; synopses and ideas welcome, but should be accompanied by s.a.e. for return of material and/or notification of receipt. No autobiographies, fiction, poetry or children's.
Royalties paid annually.

Onlywomen Press Ltd
40 St Lawrence Terrace, London W10 5ST
☎020 8354 0796 Fax 020 8960 2817
Email onlywomen_press@compuserve.com
Website www.onlywomenpress.com
Editorial Director *Lilian Mohin*

FOUNDED 1974. *Publishes* feminist lesbian books only: literary fiction, popular fiction (crime, sci-fi, romance), non-fiction (feminist theory, literary criticism) and poetry. Up to 6 titles a year. Unsolicited mss, synopses and ideas welcome. Submissions should be accompanied by s.a.e. for response and/or return of material as well as a covering letter 'identifying the author and summarising the work enclosed'.

OPC
See **Ian Allan Publishing Ltd**

Open Gate Press (incorporating Centaur Press 1954)

51 Achilles Road, London NW6 1DZ
☎020 7431 4391 Fax 020 7431 5129
Email books@opengatepress.co.uk
Managing Directors *Jeannie Cohen, Elisabeth Petersdorff*

FOUNDED in 1989 to provide a forum for psychoanalytic social and cultural studies. *Publishes* psychoanalysis, philosophy, social sciences, politics, literature, religion, animal rights, environment. SERIES *Psychoanalysis and Society*. Also publishes a journal of psychoanalytic social studies, *New Analysis*. IMPRINTS **Open Gate Press**; **Centaur Press**; **Linden Press**. Since the acquisition of Centaur Press, Open Gate Press is continuing its work, in particular the *Kinship Library* – a series on the philosophy, politics and application of humane education. Synopses and ideas for books and articles welcome.
Royalties paid twice-yearly.

Open University Press

Celtic Court, 22 Ballmoor, Buckingham,
Buckinghamshire MK18 1XW
☎01280 823388 Fax 01280 823233
Email enquiries@openup.co.uk
Website www.openup.co.uk
Managing Director *John Skelton*
Approx. Annual Turnover £3 million

FOUNDED 1977 as an imprint independent of the Open University's course materials. *Publishes* academic and professional books in the fields of education, management, sociology, health studies, politics, psychology, women's studies. No economics or anthropology. Not interested in anything outside the social sciences. About 100 titles a year. No unsolicited mss; enquiries/proposals only.
Royalties paid annually.

Orbit

See **Little, Brown & Co. (UK)**

Orchard Books

See **The Watts Publishing Group Ltd**

The Orion Publishing Group Limited

Orion House, 5 Upper St Martin's Lane,
London WC2H 9EA
☎020 7240 3444 Fax 020 7240 4822
Chairman *Jean-Louis Lisimachio*
Chief Executive *Anthony Cheetham*
Group Managing Director *Peter Roche*

Approx. Annual Turnover £60 million
FOUNDED 1992 by Anthony Cheetham, Rosemary Cheetham and Peter Roche. Incorporates Weidenfeld & Nicolson, JM Dent and Chapmans Publishers. Acquired **Cassell** in 1998 (see entry).

DIVISIONS
Orion Managing Director *Malcolm Edwards* IMPRINTS **Orion** General Publishing Director *Jane Wood* Hardcover fiction/non-fiction; **Orion Media** Publishing Director *Trevor Dolby* Film and TV; **Orion Children's** Managing Director *Judith Elliott* Children's fiction/non-fiction.
  Weidenfeld & Nicolson Managing Director *Ion Trewin* IMPRINTS **Weidenfeld General** Publishing Director *Richard Milbank* General non-fiction, biography and autobiography; **Phoenix House** Publishing Director *Maggie McKernan* Literary fiction.
  Mass Market Managing Director *Susan Lamb* IMPRINTS **Orion**; **Phoenix**; **Phoenix Illustrated**; **Everyman**.

Authors' Rating The objective is clear. Orion wants to be up there with the lead players like HarperCollins, Penguin and Hodder Headline. To do so, turnover has got to increase to £100 million which means taking a much bigger share of the fiction market. Prospective bestseller writers take note. But niche publishing such as history (chiefly under the Weidenfeld imprint) is also likely to grow.

Osprey Publishing Ltd

Elms Court, Chapel Way, Botley, Oxford
OX2 9LP
☎01865 727022 Fax 01865 727017/727019
Email osprey@ospreypublishing.com
Website www.ospreypublishing.com
Managing Director *Jonathan Parker*
Editor, Military/Military History *Jane Penrose*
Editor, Aviation *Tony Holmes*

Publishes illustrated history, military history and aviation from around the world. FOUNDED 1969, Osprey became independent from **Reed Elsevier** in February 1998. 98 titles in 1999.

MILITARY SERIES *Order of Battle; Men-at-Arms; Elite Campaign; New Vanguard; Warrior.* HISTORY SERIES *Landmarks in History; Essentials.* AVIATION SERIES *Aircraft of the Aces; Combat Aircraft; Aviation Pioneers; Aviation Elites.* No unsolicited mss; synopses and ideas welcome.
Royalties paid twice-yearly.

Peter Owen Ltd

73 Kenway Road, London SW5 0RE
☎020 7373 5628/7370 6093
Fax 020 7373 6760
Email admin@peterowen.com
Website www.peterowen.com

Chairman *Peter Owen*
Editorial Director *Antonia Owen*

FOUNDED 1951. *Publishes* biography, general non-fiction, English-language literary fiction and translations, sociology. 'No genre or children's fiction; the company only rarely takes on first novels.' AUTHORS Jane Bowles, Paul Bowles, Shusaku Endo, Anna Kavan, Jean Giono, Anaïs Nin, Jeremy Reed, Peter Vansittart. 35–40 titles a year. Unsolicited synopses welcome for non-fiction material; mss should be preceded by a descriptive letter and synopsis with s.a.e.

Royalties paid twice-yearly. *Overseas associates* worldwide.

Authors' Rating Peter Owen has been described as 'a publisher of the old and idiosyncratic school'. He has seven Nobel prizewinners on his list.

Oxford University Press

Great Clarendon Street, Oxford OX2 6DP
☎01865 556767   Fax 01865 556646
Email enquiry@oup.co.uk
Website www.oup.co.uk

Chief Executive *Henry Reece*
Approx. Annual Turnover £300 million

A department of the university, OUP grew from the university's printing works and developed into a major publishing business in the 19th century. *Publishes* academic books in all categories: student texts, scholarly journals, schoolbooks, ELT material, dictionaries, reference, music, bibles, electronic publishing, as well as paperbacks, general non-fiction and children's books. Around 3000 titles a year.

DIVISIONS
Academic *I.S. Asquith* Academic and college titles in all disciplines; dictionaries and non-lexical reference, trade books, journals and electronic publishing. TITLES *Concise Oxford Dictionary; Birds of the Western Palearctic;* **Educational** *F.E. Clarke* National Curriculum courses and children's literature; **ELT** *P.R. Mothersole* ELT courses and dictionaries. OUP welcomes first-class academic material in the form of proposals or accepted theses.

Royalties paid twice-yearly. *Overseas subsidiaries* Sister company in USA; also branches in Australia, Canada, East Africa, Hong Kong, India, Japan, Pakistan, Singapore, South Africa, Spain. Offices in Argentina, Brazil, France, Germany, Greece, Italy, Taiwan, Thailand, Turkey, Uruguay. Joint companies in Malaysia, Nigeria and Germany.

Authors' Rating Like all good academic publishers, OUP has gone online in a big way. But with the *Oxford English Dictionary* to offer, how could they go wrong? Science, medical, law and economic journals are set to follow. Contributors who look to enhance their modest rewards, please note. Another success story is children's fiction, headed by a new mass market list.

Palgrave

See **Macmillan Publishers Ltd**

Palm Tree Press

See **Kevin Mayhew Publishers**

G.J. Palmer & Sons Ltd

See **Hymns Ancient & Modern Ltd**

Pan

See **Macmillan Publishers Ltd**

Papermac

See **Macmillan Publishers Ltd**

Paragon Press Publishing

Suite 676, 37 Store Street, London WC1W 7QF
☎020 7644 4816
Email editorial@paragonpress-publishing.com
Website www.paragonpress-publishing.com

Managing Editor *Reggie Sharp*

FOUNDED 1998. *Publishes* fiction and non-fiction, books for children's and educational. DIVISIONS **Paragon** Fiction and non-fiction AUTHORS Steve Bruce, Lynne Braithwaite, Hope Dubé, James Lansbury, Richard Mackenzie, J.S. Matthews, Peter Thorp, David Young. **Paragon Children** *Piggles* Brian Charlton; *Stuck at Mr Aberleke's* R. Macdonald; *Wizard Spell* series. **Paragon Education** Ideas always welcome. TITLES *Teach Your Child Maths; Planning for Effective Teaching.* **Paragon Summaries** Factual series for higher and further education. Covers all areas of modern knowledge – literature, history, sciences, film and media. Initial enquiries by e-mail or large s.a.e. for submission guidelines.

Authors' Rating Liable to ask authors to contribute towards costs of publication.

Paragon Softcover Large Print
See **Chivers Press Ltd**

Paternoster Publishing
PO Box 300, Kingstown Broadway, Carlisle, Cumbria CA3 0QS
☎01228 512512 Fax 01228 593388
Website www.paternoster-publishing.com
Publishing Director *Mark Finnie*
Approx. Annual Turnover £2 million
A division of STL Ltd. IMPRINTS:

The Paternoster Press Editorial Controller *Jill Morris* FOUNDED 1936. *Publishes* academic, religion and learned/church/life-related journals. Over 80 titles a year. TITLES *Complete Short Works of J.I. Packer*, *All's Well* R.T. Kendall.

Paternoster Lifestyle Editorial Controller *Nancy Lush* FOUNDED 1966. *Publishes* Christian books on evangelism, discipleship and mission. About 30 titles a year. TITLES *Operation World* Patrick Johnstone; *Window on the World* Jill Johnstone; and many titles by Elisabeth Elliot and A.W. Tozer. Unsolicited mss, synopses and ideas for books welcome.
Royalties paid twice-yearly.

Pavilion Books Ltd
London House, Great Eastern Wharf, Parkgate Road, London SW11 4NQ
☎020 7350 1230 Fax 020 7350 1260
Email <firstname.surname>@pavilionbooks.co.uk
Website www.pavilionbooks.co.uk
Publishing Director *Vivien James*

Acquired by **Chrysalis** in 2001. *Publishes* illustrated books in children's, biography, cookery, gardening, humour, art, interiors, music, sport and travel. Unsolicited mss not welcome. Ideas and synopses for non-fiction titles and children's fiction considered.
Royalties paid twice-yearly.

Payback Press
See **Canongate Books Ltd**

Pearson Education
Edinburgh Gate, Harlow, Essex CM20 2JE
☎01279 623623 Fax 01279 431059
Website www.pearsoned-ema.com
Contracts & Copyrights Department
  Manager *Brenda Gvozdanovic*

FOUNDED in 1998 following the merger of Addison Wesley Longman, Financial Times Management and **Simon & Schuster**'s educational list. *Publishes* for a range of curriculum subjects, including English language teaching for students at primary and secondary school level, college and university, as well as for professionals. All unsolicited mss should be addressed to the Manager, Contracts and Copyrights Department.
Royalties paid twice-yearly. *Overseas associates* worldwide.

Authors' Rating The world's leading education publisher is heavily committed to Internet products for institutions and consumers. Much of the expansion is in the US.

Pegasus Elliot Mackenzie Publishers
Sheraton House, Castle Park, Cambridge CB3 0AX
☎01223 370012 Fax 01223 370040
Email editors@pegasuspublishers.com
Website www.pegasuspublishers.com
Senior Editor *D. W. Stern*
Editor *R. Sabir*

Publishes fiction and non-fiction, general interest, biography, autobiography, children's, history, humour, science fiction, poetry, travel, war, memoirs, crime and erotica, also Internet and E books. IMPRINTS **Vanguard Press**; **Nightingale Books**; **Chimera** TITLES *Virgins are in Short Supply* Kevin Laffan; *I was Branded by Ronnie Kray* Lennie Hamilton; *The Green Berets in Korea* Fred Hayhurst. Unsolicited mss, synopses and ideas considered if accompanied by return postage.
Royalties paid twice-yearly.

Authors' Rating Liable to ask authors to contribute to production costs.

Pen & Sword Books Ltd
47 Church Street, Barnsley, South Yorkshire S70 2AS
☎01226 734734 Fax 01226 734438
Website www.pen-and-sword.co.uk
Chairman *Sir Nicholas Hewitt*
Managing Director *Charles Hewitt*
Imprint Manager *Henry Wilson*

One of the leading military history publishers in the UK. *Publishes* non-fiction only, specialising in naval and aviation history, WW1, WW2, Napoleonic, autobiography and biography. Also publishes *Battleground* series for battlefield tourists. About 100 titles a year. IMPRINTS **Leo Cooper**; **Wharncliffe Publishing** (see entry). Unsolicited synopses and ideas welcome; no unsolicited mss.

Royalties paid twice-yearly. *Associated company* **Wharncliffe Publishing**.

Penguin UK
A Pearson Company, 80 Strand, London WC2R 0RL
☎020 7010 3000 Fax 020 7010 6060
Website www.penguin.co.uk
President *David Wan*
CEO (UK) *Anthony Forbes Watson*
Approx. Annual Turnover £121 million

Owned by Pearson plc. The world's best known book brand and for more than 60 years a leading publisher whose adult and children's lists include fiction, non-fiction, poetry, drama, classics, reference and special interest areas. Reprints and new work.

DIVISIONS
Penguin General Books Managing Director *Helen Fraser* Adult fiction and non-fiction is published in hardback under Michael Joseph, Viking and Hamish Hamilton imprints. Paperbacks come under the Penguin imprint. IMPRINTS **Viking/Penguin** Publisher *Juliet Annan* Publishing Director *Tony Lacey*; **Hamish Hamilton** Publisher *Simon Prosser*; **Michael Joseph/Penguin** Publishing Director *Tom Weldon*. Does not accept unsolicited mss.
  Penguin Press Managing Director *Andrew Rosenheim* Publishing Director *Stuart Proffitt* Academic adult non-fiction, reference, specialist and classics. IMPRINTS **Allen Lane**; **Buildings of England**; **Classics**; **Penguin Books** No unsolicited mss.
  Dorling Kindersley Ltd (see entry).
  Frederick Warne Managing Director *Sally Floyer* Classic children's publishing and merchandising including *Beatrix Potter*™; *Flower Fairies*; *Orlando*. **Ventura** Publisher *Sally Floyer* Producer and packager of *Spot* titles by Eric Hill.
  Ladybird (see **Dorling Kindersley Ltd**).
  Puffin Hardback IMPRINTS **Hamish Hamilton Children's**; **Viking Children's**; Paperback IMPRINT **Puffin** Publishers *Penny Morris* (fiction, poetry and picture books), *Clare Hulton* (media and popular non-fiction). Leading children's paperback list, publishing in virtually all fields including fiction, non-fiction, poetry, picture books, media-related titles. No unsolicited mss; synopses and ideas welcome.
  Penguin Audiobooks (see entry under **Audio Books**).
  Royalties paid twice-yearly. *Overseas associates* worldwide.

Authors' Rating One of the few publishing brand names that is instantly recognisable by book buyers, Penguin has such a huge list, back and front, that its sales performance is seen as a barometer for the rest of the trade. It is encouraging, therefore, that Penguin is determinedly upbeat despite a levelling of the back list market and mixed results in children's publishing. The good news is that the adult imprints – Viking, Hamish Hamilton and Michael Joseph – are all doing well, not least in attracting new authors with bestseller potential.

Peony Press
See **Anness Publishing Ltd**

PerfectBound
See **HarperCollins Publishers Ltd**

Pergamon Press
See **Elsevier Science Ltd**

Persephone Books
28 Great Sutton Street, London EC1V 0DS
☎020 7253 5454 Fax 020 7253 5656
Email sales@persephonebooks.co.uk
Website www.persephonebooks.co.uk
Managing Director *Nicola Beauman*

FOUNDED 1999. *Publishes* reprint fiction and non-fiction, mostly 'by women, for women and about women'. 8 titles a year. TITLES *William – An Englishman* Cicely Hamilton; *Miss Pettigrew Lives For a Day* Winifred Watson; *Good Evening, Mrs Craven* Mollie Downes; *Consequences* E.M. Delafield. No unsolicited material.
  Royalties paid twice-yearly

Petroc Press
See **Librapharm Ltd**

Phaidon Press Limited
Regent's Wharf, All Saints Street, London N1 9PA
☎020 7843 1000 Fax 020 7843 1010
Email <name>@phaidon.com
Website www.phaidon.com
Chairman/Publisher *Richard Schlagman*
Managing Director *Andrew Price*
Deputy Publisher *Amanda Renshaw*
Approx. Annual Turnover £18 million

Publishes quality books on the visual arts, including fine art, art history, architecture, design, photography, decorative arts, music and performing arts. Recently started producing videos. About 100 titles a year.
DIVISIONS/SERIES (with Editorial Heads) **Architecture and Design** *Karen Stein, Vivian*

Constantin-Opolous; **Art and Ideas Series** *Pat Barylski*; **Contemporary Art** *Gilda Williams*; **Photography** *Amanda Renshaw*; **55 Series** *Kendall Clarke*; **Academic** *Bernard Dod*. Unsolicited mss welcome but 'only a small amount of unsolicited material gets published'.

Royalties paid twice-yearly.

Authors' Rating Ah, those seductive art books. The quality of illustrations is superb and since language is a minor barrier to sales, Phaidon is doing well on the Continent with subsidiaries in France and Germany.

Philip's
See **Octopus Publishing Group**

Phillimore & Co. Ltd
Shopwyke Manor Barn, Chichester, West Sussex PO20 6BG
☎01243 787636 Fax 01243 787639
Email bookshop@phillimore.co.uk
Website www.phillimore.co.uk

Chairman *Philip Harris*
Managing Director *Noel Osborne*
Approx. Annual Turnover £1.3 million

FOUNDED in 1897 by W.P.W. Phillimore, Victorian campaigner for local archive conservation in Chancery Lane, London. Became the country's leading publisher of historical source material and local histories. Somewhat dormant in the 1960s, it was revived by Philip Harris in 1968. *Publishes* British local and family history, including histories of institutions, buildings, villages, towns and counties, plus guides to research and writing in these fields. About 70 titles a year. No unsolicited mss; synopses/ideas welcome for local or family histories.

IMPRINT **Phillimore** *Noel Osborne* TITLES *Domesday Book; A History of Essex; Carlisle; The Haberdashers' Company; Channel Island Churches; Bolton Past; Warwickshire Country Houses*.

Royalties paid annually.

Phoenix/Phoenix House/ Phoenix Illustrated
See **The Orion Publishing Group Ltd**

Piatkus Books
5 Windmill Street, London W1P 1HF
☎020 7631 0710 Fax 020 7436 7137
Email info@piatkus.co.uk
Website www.piatkus.co.uk

Managing Director *Judy Piatkus*
Approx. Annual Turnover £5.5 million

FOUNDED 1979 by Judy Piatkus. The company is customer-led and is committed to publishing fiction, both commercial and literary, and non-fiction. *Specialises* in publishing books and authors 'who we feel enthusiastic and committed to as we like to build for long-term success as well as short-term!' *Publishes* fiction, biography and autobiography, health, mind, body and spirit, popular psychology, self-help, history, science, business and management, cookery 'and other books that tempt us'. In 1996 launched a list of mass-market non-fiction and fiction titles. About 175 titles a year (70 of which are fiction).

DIVISIONS
Non-fiction *Gill Bailey* TITLES *Optimum Nutrition Bible* Patrick Holford; *Detox Yourself* Jane Scrivner; *Clear Your Clutter with Feng Shui* Karen Kingston; *10 Day MBA* Steven Silbiger; *Queen* Laura Jackson. **Fiction** *Judy Piatkus* TITLES *Bouncing Back* Zoë Barnes; *Big Trouble* Dave Barry; *Carolina Moon* Nora Roberts; *Three Women* Marge Piercy; *Mind Games* Hilary Norman. Piatkus is expanding its range of books and welcomes synopses and first three chapters.

Royalties paid twice-yearly.

Authors' Rating 'Independent general publishing is alive and well and flourishing at Piatkus Books,' says Judy Piatkus, founder of the company which this year celebrates its 21st birthday. To prove the point Piatkus turned in record results achieved by strong sales across the list rather than for a few high profile titles. Authors praise an editorial team wedded to quality.

Pica Press
See **A.&C. Black (Publishers) Ltd**

Picador
See **Macmillan Publishers Ltd**

Piccadilly Press
5 Castle Road, London NW1 8PR
☎020 7267 4492 Fax 020 7267 4493
Email books@piccadillypress.co.uk
Website www.piccadillypress.co.uk

Publisher/Managing Director *Brenda Gardner*
Approx. Annual Turnover £870,000

FOUNDED 1983. Independent publisher of children's and parental books. 30 titles in 2000. Welcomes approaches from authors 'but we would like them to know the sort of books we do. It is frustrating to get inappropriate material. They should check in their local libraries or bookshops. We will send a catalogue (please enclose s.a.e.)'. No adult or cartoon-type material.

Royalties paid twice-yearly.

Pictorial Presentations
See **Souvenir Press Ltd**

Picture Lions
See **HarperCollins Publishers Ltd**

Pimlico
See **Random House Group Ltd**

Pinter
See **Continuum International Publishing Group Ltd**

Pitkin Unichrome Ltd
Healey House, Dene Road, Andover, Hampshire SP10 2AA
☎01264 409200 Fax 01264 334110
Email guides@pitkin-unichrome.com
Website www.britguides.com

Managing Director *Heather Hook*

Pitkin Guides, FOUNDED in 1947, was part of **Reed Books** from 1988 to March 1998 when it merged with Unichrome. *Publishes* illustrated souvenir guides.

Plenum Publishers/Plenum Press
See **Kluwer Academic/Plenum Publishers**

Pluto Press Ltd
345 Archway Road, London N6 5AA
☎020 8348 2724 Fax 020 8348 9133
Email pluto@plutobks.demon.co.uk
Website www.plutobooks.com

Managing Director *Roger Van Zwanenberg*
Publishing Director *Anne Beech*

FOUNDED 1970. Has developed a reputation for innovatory publishing in the field of non-fiction. *Publishes* academic and scholarly books across a range of subjects including cultural studies, politics and world affairs. About 50–60 titles a year. Key titles for 2000 included Noam Chomsky's latest work and books on the sanctions against Iraq, media propaganda and Che Guevara. Prospective authors are encouraged to consult the website for guidelines on submitting proposals.

Pocketessentials
See **Oldcastle Books Ltd**

Point
See **Scholastic Ltd**

The Policy Press
University of Bristol, 34 Tyndall's Park Road, Bristol BS8 1PY
☎0117 954 6800 Fax 0117 973 7308

Managing Director *Alison Shaw*

The Policy Press is a specialist publisher of policy studies. Material published, in the form of books, reports, practice guides and journals, is taken from research findings and provides critical discussion of policy initiatives and their impact, and also recommendations for policy change. 45–50 titles per year. No unsolicited mss; brief synopses and ideas welcome.

Politico's Publishing
8 Artillery Row, London SW1P 1RZ
☎020 7931 0090 Fax 020 7828 8111
Email publishing@politicos.co.uk
Website www.politicos.co.uk/publishing

Chairman *John Simmons*
Managing Director *Iain Dale*
Publishing Director *Sean Magee*
Approx. Annual Turnover £250,000

FOUNDED 1998. Sister company to Politico's Bookstore in Westminster. *Publishes* political books. 25 titles in 2000. TITLES *In My Own Time* Jeremy Thorpe; *Cherie Blair* Linda McDougall; *Brief Encounters* Gyles Brandreth. Unsolicited mss, synopses and ideas welcome; telephone in the first instance.

Royalties paid annually.

Polity Press
65 Bridge Street, Cambridge CB2 1UR
☎01223 324315 Fax 01223 461385

FOUNDED 1984. All books are published in association with **Blackwell Publishers**. *Publishes* archaeology and anthropology, criminology, economics, feminism, general interest, history, human geography, literature, media and cultural studies, medicine and society, philosophy, politics, psychology, religion and theology, social and political theory, sociology. Unsolicited synopses and ideas for books welcome.

Royalties paid annually.

Polygon/Polygon@Edinburgh
See **Edinburgh University Press**

Pont Books
See **Gomer Press**

Pop Universal
See **Souvenir Press Ltd**

Portland Press Ltd
59 Portland Place, London W1B 1QW
☎020 7580 5530   Fax 020 7323 1136
Email editorial@portlandpress.com
Website www.portlandpress.com
Chairman *Professor A.J. Turner*
Managing Director *Rhonda Oliver*
Managing Editor *Pauline Starley*
Approx. Annual Turnover £2.5 million

FOUNDED 1990 to expand the publishing activities of the Biochemical Society (1911). *Publishes* biochemisty and medicine for graduate, postgraduate and research students. Expanding the list to include schools and general readership. 6 titles in 2000. TITLES *Plant Systematics for the 21st Century; Essays in Biochemistry: Molecular Trafficking; Lifelong Learning Policy and Research*. Unsolicited mss, synopses and ideas welcome. No fiction.
Royalties paid twice-yearly.

T. & A.D. Poyser
See **Harcourt Publishers Limited**

Prestel Publishing Limited
4 Bloomsbury Place, London N1 6LD
☎020 7323 5004   Fax 020 7636 8004
Website www.prestel.com
Chairman *Jürgen Tesch*

FOUNDED 1924. *Publishes* art, architecture, photography, children's and general illustrated books. No fiction. Unsolicited mss, synopses and ideas welcome. Approach by post or email.

Princeton University Press
See **University Presses of California, Columbia & Princeton Ltd**

Prion Books Ltd
Imperial Works, Perren Street, London NW5 3ED
☎020 7482 4248   Fax 020 7482 4203
Managing Director *Barry Winkleman*
Publishing Director *Andrew Goodfellow*

Formerly a packaging operation but began publishing under the Prion imprint in 1987. *Publishes* non-fiction: humour, popular culture, historical and literary reprints, beauty, food and drink, sex, psychology and health. About 40 titles a year. Unsolicited mss, synopses and ideas welcome only with s.a.e.
Royalties paid twice-yearly.

Profile Books
58A Hatton Gardens, London EC1N 8LX
☎020 7404 3001   Fax 020 7404 3003
Email info@profilebooks.co.uk
Website www.profilebooks.co.uk
Managing Director *Andrew Franklin*
Approx. Annual Turnover £2 million

FOUNDED 1996. *Publishes* serious nonfiction including current affairs, history, politics, psychology, cultural criticism, business and management. Winner of the **Sunday Times Small Publisher of the Year Award** 1999/2000. AUTHORS include Alan Bennett, J.M. Coetzee, Francis Fukuyama and Peter Nichols.

IMPRINTS **Profile Books** *Andrew Franklin*; **Economist Books** *Stephen Brough*. No unsolicited mss.
Royalties paid twice-yearly.

Authors' Rating Profile has achieved impressive growth while maintaining author-friendly relations.

Prowler Books/Zipper Books
3 Broadbent Close, 20 Highgate High Street, London N6 5GG
☎020 8340 7711   Fax 020 8347 7667
Website www.prowler.co.uk
Contact *Nick Hilton*

Part of the Millivres-Prowler Group. *Publishes* gay male erotica. TITLES *Overload* ed. David Laurents; *The Initiation* David Keane; *Gladiator School* Ben Elliott. Looking for mss of 60–80,000 words. Rights bought for single printing, non-royalty deals.

Publishing House
Trinity Place, Barnstaple, Devon EX32 9HJ
☎01271 328892   Fax 01271 328768
Email publishinghouse@vernoncoleman.com
Website www.vernoncoleman.com
Managing Director *Vernon Coleman*
Editorial Head *Sue Ward*
Approx. Annual Turnover £750,000

FOUNDED 1989. Self-publisher of fiction, health, humour, animals, politics. Over 50 books published. TITLES *Bodypower; Village Cricket Tour; Alice's Diary; Mrs Caldicot's Cabbage War; How to Publish Your Own Book* all by Vernon Coleman. No submissions.

Puffin
See **Penguin UK**

Pushkin Press Ltd
123 Biddulph Mansions, Elgin Avenue, London W9 1HU
☎020 7266 9136   Fax 020 7266 9136
Email pushkinpressltd@compuserve.com
Website www.pushkinpress.com

Chairman *Melissa Ulfane*
Editorial Head *Diana Di Carcaci*
Contact *Petra Howard-Wuerz*
Approx. Annual Turnover £500,000

Publishes novels, essays and poetry drawn from the best of classic and contemporary European literature.
Royalties paid twice-yearly.

Putnam Aeronautical Books
See **Brassey's**

Quadrille Publishing Ltd
Alhambra House, 27–31 Charing Cross Road, London WC2H 0LS
☎020 7839 7117 Fax 020 7839 7118
Chairman *Sue Thomson*
Managing Director *Alison Cathie*
Publishing Director *Anne Furniss*

FOUNDED in 1994 by four ex-directors of Conran Octopus, with a view to producing a small list of top-quality illustrated books. *Publishes* non-fiction, including cookery, gardening, interior design and decoration, craft, health. 20 titles in 2001. TITLES *Just Desserts* Gordon Ramsay; *Foliage* David Joyce; *Understanding Modern* Andrew Weaving. No unsolicited mss; synopses and ideas for books welcome. No fiction or children's books.
Royalties paid twice-yearly.

Quantum
See **W. Foulsham & Co.**

Quartet Books
27 Goodge Street, London W1T 2LD
☎020 7636 3992 Fax 020 7637 1866
Chairman *Naim Attallah*
Managing Director *Jeremy Beale*
Publishing Director *Stella Kane*
Approx. Annual Turnover £1 million

FOUNDED 1972. Independent publisher. *Publishes* contemporary literary fiction including translations, popular culture, biography, music, history, politics and some photographic books. Unsolicited sample chapters with return postage welcome; no poetry, romance or science fiction. Submissions by disk or email are not accepted.
Royalties paid twice-yearly.

Queen Anne Press
See **Lennard Associates Ltd**

Quick Fix
See **How To Books Ltd**

Quiller Press
46 Lillie Road, London SW6 1TN
☎020 7499 6529 Fax 020 7381 8941
Email greenwood@quiller.conx.co.uk
Managing/Editorial Director *Jeremy Greenwood*

Specialises in sponsored books and publications sold through non-book trade channels as well as bookshops. *Publishes* architecture, biography, business and industry, children's, collecting, cookery, DIY, gardening, guidebooks, humour, reference, sports, travel, wine and spirits. About 10 titles a year. TITLES *Willis Faber Book of Tennis and Rackets* Lord Aberdare; *Mews Style* Sebastian Deckker; *In Vanity Fair* Roy Matthews and Peter Mellini. Most ideas originate in-house – unsolicited mss not welcome unless the author sees some potential for sponsorship or guaranteed sales.
Royalties paid twice-yearly.

Radcliffe Medical Press Ltd
18 Marcham Road, Abingdon, Oxfordshire OX14 1AA
☎01235 528820 Fax 01235 528830
Email contact.us@radcliffemed.com
Website www.radcliffe-oxford.com
Managing Director *Andrew Bax*
Editorial Director *Gillian Nineham*
Approx. Annual Turnover £1.5 million

FOUNDED 1987. Medical publishers which began by specialising in books for general practice and health service management. *Publishes* clinical, management, health policy books, training materials and CD-ROMs. 80 titles in 2000. Unsolicited mss, synopses and ideas welcome. No non-medical or medical books aimed at lay audience.
Royalties paid twice-yearly.

Radcliffe Press
See **I.B. Tauris & Co. Ltd**

Ramboro Books
See **Chrysalis Books Ltd**

The Ramsay Head Press
9 Glenisla Gardens, Edinburgh EH9 2HR
☎0131 662 1915 Fax 0131 662 1915
Email conrad.wilson@genie.co.uk
Managing Director *Conrad Wilson*

FOUNDED 1968 by Norman Wilson, OBE. A small independent family publisher. *Publishes* biography, cookery, Scottish fiction and non-fiction, plus the biannual literary magazine

InScotland. About 3–4 titles a year. TITLES *When It Works It Feels Like Play* Tessa Ransford; *The Happy Land* Howard Denton and Jim C. Wilson. Synopses and ideas for books of Scottish interest welcome.

Royalties paid twice-yearly.

The Random House Group Ltd

Random House, 20 Vauxhall Bridge Road, London SW1V 2SA
☎020 7840 8400 Fax 020 7233 6058
Email enquiries@randomhouse.co.uk
Website www.randomhouse.co.uk
Chief Executive/Chairman *Gail Rebuck*
Deputy Chairman *Simon Master*
Managing Director *Ian Hudson*

Random's increasing focus on trade publishing, both here and in the US, has been well rewarded, with sales continuing to grow over the last year. Random House Group Ltd is the parent company of three separate publishing divisions and of **Transworld** (see entry). The three divisions are: General Books, the Group's largest publishing division; Children's Books, and Ebury Press Special Books. General Books is divided into two operating groups, allowing hardcover editors to see their books through to publication in paperback. The literary imprints Jonathan Cape, Secker & Warburg, Yellow Jersey Press and Chatto & Windus work side by side with paperback imprints Vintage and Pimlico to form one group; trade imprints Century, William Heinemann and Hutchinson go hand-in-hand with Arrow to form the other group.

IMPRINTS
Jonathan Cape Ltd ☎020 7840 8576 Fax 020 7233 6117 Publishing Director *Dan Franklin* Biography and memoirs, current affairs, fiction, history, photography, poetry, politics and travel. IMPRINT **Yellow Jersey**.

Secker & Warburg ☎020 7840 8649 Fax 020 7233 6117 Editorial Director *Geoff Mulligan* Principally literary fiction with some non-fiction.

Chatto & Windus Ltd ☎020 7840 8522 Fax 020 7233 6117 Publishing Director *Alison Samuel* Art, belles-lettres, biography and memoirs, current affairs, essays, fiction, history, poetry, politics, philosophy, translations and travel.

Century (including **Business Books**) ☎020 7840 8555 Fax 020 7233 6127 Publisher *Kate Parkin*, Publishing Director Non-fiction *Mark Booth* General fiction and non-fiction, plus business management, advertising, communication, marketing, selling, investment and financial titles.

William Heinemann ☎020 7840 8400 Fax 020 7233 6127 Publishing Director Fiction *Lynne Drew*, Publishing Director Non-fiction *Ravi Mirchandani* General non-fiction and fiction, especially history, biography, science, crime, thrillers and women's fiction.

Hutchinson ☎020 7840 8564 Fax 020 7233 7870 Publishing Director *Sue Freestone* General fiction and non-fiction including notably belles-lettres, current affairs, politics, travel and history.

Arrow ☎020 7840 8516 Fax 020 7233 6127 Publishing Director *Andy McKillop* Mass-market paperback fiction and non-fiction.

Pimlico ☎020 7840 8630 Fax 020 7233 6117 Publishing Director *Will Sulkin* Large-format quality paperbacks in the fields of history, biography, popular culture and literature.

Vintage ☎020 7840 8531 Fax 020 7233 6127 Publisher *Caroline Michel* Quality paperback fiction and non-fiction. Vintage was founded in 1990 and has been described as one of the 'greatest literary success stories in recent British publishing'.

Children's Books (at Transworld Publishers, 61–63 Uxbridge Road, London W5 5SA ☎020 8579 2652) Managing Director *Philippa Dickinson*, Deputy Managing Director *Gill Evans* IMPRINTS **Hutchinson** Publishing Director *Caroline Roberts*; **Jonathan Cape** Publishing Director *Tom Maschler*; **Bodley Head** Publishing Director *Anne McNeil*; **Red Fox** and **Tellastory** Publishing Director *Pilar Jenkins*.

Ebury Press Special Books ☎020 7840 8400 Fax 020 7840 8406 Managing Director *Amelia Thorpe*, Publisher *Fiona MacIntyre*, Associate Publisher *Julian Shuckburgh* IMPRINTS **Ebury Press**; **Vermilion**; **Rider**; **Barrie & Jenkins**; **Condé Nast Books**; **Fodor's**. Art, antiques, biography, Buddhism, cookery, gardening, health and beauty, homes and interiors, personal development, spirituality, travel and guides, sport, TV tie-ins. About 150 titles a year. Unsolicited mss, synopses and ideas for books welcome.

AtRandom ☎020 7840 8400 Fax 020 7233 6127 Director *Mark McCallum* Original fiction and non-fiction e-book list launched in 2001.

Royalties paid twice-yearly for the most part.

Authors' Rating The first British trade publisher to announce a dedicated e-book list – to be called AtRandom – has to be doing well in other sectors. In fact, it is not that long ago that Random was turning in heavy losses. Less than a decade on, this high-powered publisher has quadrupled turnover and made profits healthy enough to invest in an impressie range of new writers. Synopses and manuscripts may be passed on to freelance readers, but there is reasonable assurance that they are at least read.

Ransom Publishing Ltd

Ransom House, Unit 1, Brook Street, Watlington, Oxfordshire OX49 5PP
☎01491 613711 Fax 01491 613733
Email ransom@ransompublishing.co.uk
Website www.ransom.co.uk

Managing Director *Jenny Ertle*

FOUNDED 1995 by ex-McGraw-Hill publisher. Partnerships formed with, among others, Channel 4 and the ICL. *Publishes* educational and consumer multimedia and study packs. Over 30 CD-ROMs, most with educational support packs. TITLES include *The Little Monsters* series; *Whale of a Tale* series including maths, science, language and geography; *Tom Paint; The Castle Under Siege; The History of the Universe; The History of Life; Rivers* plus natural history CD-ROMs.

Ravette Publishing Limited

Unit 3 Tristar Centre, Star Road, Partridge Green, West Sussex RH13 8RA
☎01403 711443 Fax 01403 711554
Email ravettepub@aol.com

Chairman/Managing Director *Margaret Lamb*
Approx. Annual Turnover £250,000

FOUNDED 1995. A small independent publisher producing a range of best-selling series for both adults and children, including Garfield, Peanuts, BIG, Bret the Vet and The Odd Squad. *Publishes* children's, fiction and humour. 31 titles in 2000. Unsolicited mss, synopses and ideas welcome; approach by post – s.a.e. must be enclosed if reply required.

Royalties paid twice-yearly.

Reader's Digest Association Ltd

11 Westferry Circus, Canary Wharf, London E14 4HE
☎020 7715 8000 Fax 020 7715 8181
Email gbeditorial@readersdigest.co.uk
Website www.readersdigest.co.uk

Managing Director *Andrew Lynam-Smith*
Editorial Head *Cortina Butler*

Publishes gardening, natural history, cookery, history, DIY, travel and word books. About 20 titles a year. TITLES *Family Encyclopedia of World History; Know Your Rights; Yesterday's Britain;* *Foods That Harm, Foods That Heal; Country Walks and Scenic Drives.*

Reaktion Books

79 Farringdon Road, London EC1M 3JU
☎020 7404 9930 Fax 020 7404 9931
Email info@reaktionbooks.co.uk
Website www.reaktionbooks.co.uk

Managing Director *Michael R. Leaman*

FOUNDED in Edinburgh in 1985 and moved to its London location in 1988. *Publishes* art history, architecture, Asian studies, cultural studies, design, film, geography, history, photography and travel writing. About 30 titles a year. TITLES *Bodies Politic: Disease, Death and Doctors in Britain, 1650–1900* Roy Porter; *Eyewitnessing: The Use of Images as Historical Evidence* Peter Burke; *A History of Writing* Steven Roger Fischer; *Romania* Lucian Boia. No unsolicited mss; synopses and ideas welcome.

Royalties paid twice-yearly.

Reardon Publishing

56 Upper Norwood Street, Leckhampton, Cheltenham, Gloucestershire GL53 0DU
☎01242 231800
Website www.reardon.co.uk

Managing Editor *Nicholas Reardon*

FOUNDED in the mid 1970s. Family-run publishing house specialising in local interest and tourism in the Cotswold area. Member of the **Outdoor Writers Guild**. *Publishes* walking and driving guides, and family history for societies. 10 titles a year. TITLES *The Cotswold Way* (video); *The Cotswold Way Map; Cotswold Walkabout; Cotswold Driveabout; The Donnington Way; The Haunted Cotswolds.* Unsolicited mss, synopses and ideas welcome with return postage only. Also distributes for other publishers such as Ordnance Survey. See also **WALKfree Productions Ltd** under **Audio Books**.

Royalties paid twice-yearly.

Red Fox

See **Random House Group Ltd**

William Reed Directories

Broadfield Park, Crawley, West Sussex RH11 9RT
☎01293 613400 Fax 01293 610322
Email directories@william-reed.co.uk
Website www.foodanddrink.co.uk *or* www.on-tap.net *or* www.grocertv.co.uk

Editorial Manager *Sulann Staniford*

William Reed Directories, a division of William Reed Publishing, was ESTABLISHED in

1990. Its portfolio includes 13 titles covering the food, drink, non-food, catering, retail and export industries. The titles are produced as directories, market research reports, exhibition catalogues and electronic publishing.

Reed Educational & Professional Publishing

Halley Court, Jordan Hill, Oxford OX2 8EJ
☎01865 311366 Fax 01865 314641
Website www.repp.co.uk
Chief Executive *John Philbin*

A member of the **Reed Elsevier plc** group, REPP incorporates Heinemann Educational, Ginn and Butterworth-Heinemann in the UK; Greenwood Heinemann and Rigby in the USA; Rigby Heinemann in Australia.

Heinemann Educational Fax 01865 314140 Managing Director *Bob Osborne*, Primary *Paul Shuter*, Secondary *Kay Symons*. Textbooks/literature/other educational resources for primary and secondary school and further education. Mss, synopses and ideas welcome.

Ginn & Co Fax 01865 314189 Managing Director *Paul Shuter*, Editorial Director *Jill Duffy*. Textbook/other educational resources for primary and secondary schools.

Butterworth-Heinemann International Linacre House, Jordan Hill, Oxford OX2 8EJ ☎01865 310366 Fax 01865 314541 Managing Director *Philip Shaw*, Engineering & Technology *Neil Warnock-Smith*, Business *Kathryn Grant*. Books and electronic products across business, technical and open-learning fields for students and professionals.

Royalties paid twice-yearly/annually, according to contract in all divisions.

Reed Elsevier plc

25 Victoria Street, London SW1H 0EX
☎020 7222 8420 Fax 020 7227 5799
Website www.r-e.com

125 Park Avenue, 23rd Floor, New York, NY 10017, USA
☎001 212 309 5498 Fax 001 212 309 5480

Van de Sande Bakhuyzenstraat 4, 1061 AG Amsterdam, The Netherlands
☎00 31 20 515 9341 Fax 00 31 20 683 2617
Chief Executive Officer (UK) *Crispin Davis*

Reed Elsevier plc group is one of the world's leading publishers of scientific, legal, taxation, reference, educational, professional and business materials.

DIVISIONS **Reed Educational & Professional Publishing** (see entry); **Reed**

Elsevier Legal Division; **Elsevier Science** (see entry); **Butterworths** Halsbury House, 35 Chancery Lane, London WC2A 1EL ☎020 7400 2500 Fax 020 7400 2842 *Publishes* legal and accountancy textbooks, journals, law reports, CD-ROMs and online services; **Butterworths Tolleys** (see entry); **Lexis-Nexis**.

Regency House Publishing Limited

3 Mill Lane, Broxbourne, Hertfordshire EN10 7AZ
☎01992 479988 Fax 01992 479966
Email regencyhouse@btinternet.com
Chairman *Brian Trodd*
Managing Director *Nicolette Trodd*
Approx. Annual Turnover £1 million

FOUNDED 1991. Publisher and packager of mass-market non-fiction. No fiction. No unsolicited material.

Royalties paid twice-yearly.

Reinhardt Books Ltd

Flat 2, 43 Onslow Square, London SW7 3LR
☎020 7589 3751
Chairman/Managing Director *Max Reinhardt*
Director *Joan Reinhardt*

FOUNDED in 1887 as H.F.L. (Publishers), it was acquired by Max Reinhardt in 1947, changing its name to the present one in 1987. First publication under the new name was Graham Greene's *The Captain and the Enemy*. Also publishes under the **Nonesuch Press** imprint. AUTHORS include Mitsumasa Anno, Alistair Cooke and Maurice Sendak. New books are no longer considered.

Royalties paid according to contract.

Religious & Moral Educational Press (RMEP)

See **Hymns Ancient & Modern Ltd**

Research Disclosure

See **Kenneth Mason Publications Ltd**

Review

See **Hodder Headline Plc**

Richmond House Publishing Company Ltd

Douglas House, 3 Richmond Buildings, London W1V 5AE
☎020 7437 9556 Fax 020 7287 3463
Email sales@rhpco.co.uk
Website www.rhpco.co.uk

Managing Directors *Gloria Gordon,*
Spencer Block

Publishes directories for the theatre and entertainment industries. TITLES *British Theatre Directory 2001; Artistes and Agents 2001; London Seating Plan Guide.* Synopses and ideas welcome.

Rider
See **Random House Group Ltd**

Right Way Plus
See **Elliot Right Way Books**

Robinson Publishing Ltd
See **Constable & Robinson Ltd**

Robson Books
10 Blenheim Court, Brewery Rod, London
N7 9NT
☎020 7700 7444 Fax 020 7700 4552

Publisher *Jeremy Robson*
Editorial Head *Lorna Russell*

FOUNDED 1973. Part of the Chrysalis Group plc. *Publishes* general non-fiction, including biography, cookery, gardening, guidebooks, health and beauty, humour, travel, sports and games. About 70 titles a year. Unsolicited synopses and ideas for books welcome (s.a.e. essential for reply).
Royalties paid twice-yearly.

RotoVision
Sheridan House, 112/116A Western Road,
Hove, East Sussex BN3 1DD
☎01273 727268 Fax 01273 727269
Website www.rotovision.com

Managing Director *Brian Morris*
Creative Director *Angie Patchell*
Editor-in-Chief *Natalia Price-Cabrera*

FOUNDED 1996. Rapidly-expanding visual arts publishers with a strong emphasis on education and inspiration. *Publishes* graphic design, photography, web design, advertising, film, architecture, practical art, lighting design, interiors, product design, packaging design. 38 titles in 2001. TITLES *Animation: 2D and Beyond* Jane Pilling; *Stage Design* Tony Davis; *No-Copy Advertising* Lazar Dzamic; *Colour for Websites* Molly Holzschlag. No unsolicited mss; written synopses and ideas welcome; no phone calls, please. No academic or fiction.
Flat fee paid.

Round Hall
See **Sweet & Maxwell Ltd**

Roundhouse Publishing Group
Millstone, Limers Lane, Northam, North
Devon EX39 2RG
☎01237 474474 Fax 01237 474774
Email roundhouse.pub@virgin.net

Editorial Head *Alan Goodworth*

ESTABLISHED 1991. *Publishes* cinema and media-related titles. TITLES *Cinema of Oliver Stone; Cinema of Stanley Kubrick; Italian Cinema; Toms, Coons, Mulattoes, Mammies and Bucks.* Represents and distributes a broad range of non-fiction publishing houses throughout the UK and Europe. No unsolicited mss.
Royalties paid twice-yearly.

Routledge
11 New Fetter Lane, London EC4P 4EE
☎020 7583 9855 Fax 020 7842 2298
Website www.routledge.com

Managing Director *Roger Horton*
Publishing Directors *Claire L'Enfant,*
Alan Jarvis, Mary MacInnes
Approx. Annual Turnover £35.5 million
(Group)

Routledge was formed in 1987 through an amalgamation of Routledge & Kegan Paul, Methuen & Co., Tavistock Publications, and Croom Helm. Subsequent acquisitions include the Unwin Hyman academic list from **HarperCollins** (1991), *Who's Who* and historical atlases from **Dent/Orion** (1994), archaeology and ancient history titles from **Batsford** (1996), and the E & FN Spon imprint from ITP Science (1997). In 1998, Routledge became a subsidiary of **Taylor & Francis Group plc** (see entry). *Publishes* academic and professional books and journals in the social sciences, humanities, health sciences and the built environment for the international market. Subjects: addiction, anthropology, archaeology, architecture, Asian studies, biblical studies, the built environment, business and management, civil engineering, classics, heritage, construction, counselling, criminology, development and environment, dictionaries, economics, education, environmental engineering, geography, health, history, Japanese studies, journals, language, leisure studies and leisure management, linguistics, literary criticism, media and culture, Middle East, nursing, philosophy, politics, political economy, psychiatry, psychology, reference, social administration, social studies and sociology, therapy, theatre and performance studies, women's studies. No poetry, fiction, travel or astrology.

About 900 titles a year. Send synopses with sample chapter and c.v. rather than complete mss.

Royalties paid annually and twice-yearly, according to contract.

Ryland Peters and Small Limited
Kirkman House, 12–14 Whitfield Street, London W1T 2RP
☎020 7436 9090 Fax 020 7436 9790
Email info@rps.co.uk
Website www.rylandpeters.com
Managing Director *David Peters*
Publishing Director *Alison Starling*

FOUNDED 1996. *Publishes* highly illustrated lifestyle books aimed at an international market, covering gardening, cookery, interior design. No fiction. No unsolicited mss; synopses and ideas welcome.

Royalties paid twice-yearly.

Sage Publications
6 Bonhill Street, London EC2A 4PU
☎020 7374 0645 Fax 020 7374 8741
Website www.sagepub.co.uk
Managing Director *Stephen Barr*
Editorial Director *Ziyad Marar*

FOUNDED 1971. *Publishes* academic books and journals in humanities and the social sciences. Bought academic and professional books publisher Paul Chapman Publishing Ltd in April 1998.

Royalties paid twice-yearly.

Saint Andrew Press
Department of Communication, Church of Scotland, 121 George Street, Edinburgh EH2 4YN
☎0131 225 5722 Fax 0131 220 3113
Email cofs.standrew@dial.pipex.com
Website www.churchofscotland.org.uk
Head of Publishing *Ann Crawford*
Approx. Annual Turnover £225,000

FOUNDED in 1954 to publish and promote the 17-volume series *The Daily Study Bible New Testament* by Professor William Barclay. Owned by the Church of Scotland Board of Communication. *Publishes* religious, Scottish interest and some children's books. No fiction. 7 titles in 2000. Proposals welcome in synopsis form.

Royalties paid annually.

St David's Press
See **Ashley Drake Publishing Ltd**

St Pauls Publishers
187 Battersea Bridge Road, London SW11 3AS
☎020 7978 4300 Fax 020 7978 4370
Email editions@stpauls.org.uk
Publisher *Andrew Pudussery*

Publishing division of the Society of St Paul. Began publishing in 1914 but activities were fairly limited until around 1948. *Publishes* religious material only: theology, scripture, catechetics, prayer books, children's material and biography. Unsolicited mss, synopses and ideas welcome. About 40 titles a year.

Salamander Books Ltd
8 Blenheim Court, Brewery Road, London N7 9NT
☎020 7700 7799 Fax 020 7700 3918
Email salamander@chrysalisbooks.co.uk
Website www.salamanderbooks.com
Managing Director *David Spence*
Editorial Directors *Charlotte Davies,*
  Will Steeds

FOUNDED 1973. Part of the Chrysalis Group plc. *Publishes* colour illustrated books, mainly on collecting, cookery, interiors, gardening, music, crafts, military, aviation, pet care, sport and transport. About 60 titles a year. No unsolicited mss but synopses and ideas for the above subjects welcome.

Royalties Outright fee paid instead of royalties.

Sangam Books Ltd
57 London Fruit Exchange, Brushfield Street, London E1 6EP
☎020 7377 6399 Fax 020 7375 1230
Email sangambks@aol.com
Executive Director *Anthony de Souza*

Traditionally an educational publisher of school and college level textbooks. Also *publishes* art, India, medicine, science, technology, social sciences, religion, plus some fiction in paperback.

W.B. Saunders & Co. Ltd/ Saunders Scientific Publications
See **Harcourt Publishers Limited**

Savitri Books Ltd
See entry under **UK Packagers**

SB Publications
c/o 19 Grove Road, Seaford, East Sussex BN25 1TP
☎01323 893498 Fax 01323 893860

Email sales@sbpublications.swinternet.co.uk
Website www.sbpublications.swinternet.co.uk
Managing Director *Steve Benz*
FOUNDED 1987. *Specialises* in local history, including themes illustrated by old picture postcards and photographs; also travel, guides (town, walking), maritime history and railways. 25 titles a year.
IMPRINTS **Historic Military Press**; **Ben Gunn** TITLES *Lewes Then and Now*; *Curiosities of East Sussex*; *A Dorset Quiz Book*; *Q – The Biography of Desmond Llewelyn*. Also provides marketing and distribution services for local authors.
Royalties paid annually.

Sceptre
See **Hodder Headline Plc**

Scholastic Ltd
Villiers House, Clarendon Avenue, Leamington Spa, Warwickshire CV32 5PR
☎01926 887799   Fax 01926 883331
Website www.scholastic.co.uk
Chairman *M.R. Robinson*
Managing Director *David Kewley*
Approx. Annual Turnover £50 million
FOUNDED 1964. Owned by US parent company. *Publishes* children's fiction and non-fiction and education for primary schools.
DIVISIONS
Scholastic Children's Books *Richard Scrivener* Commonwealth House, 1–19 New Oxford Street, London WC1A 1NU ☎020 7421 9000 Fax 020 7421 9001 IMPRINTS **Scholastic Press** (hardbacks); **Hippo** (paperbacks); **Point** (paperbacks) TITLES *Horrible Histories*; *Goosebumps*; *Point Horror*.
   Educational Publishing *Anne Peel* (Villiers House address) Professional books and classroom materials for primary teachers, plus magazines such as *Child Education, Junior Education, Junior Focus, Infant Projects, Nursery Education; Literacy Time, Numeracy Time, Art & Design*.
   Red House Book Clubs *Mike Crossley, Victoria Birkett* Cotswold Business Park, Witney, Oxford OX8 5YT ☎01993 893456 Fax 01993 776813 The Book Club group sells to families at home through The Red House Book Club, through Red House School Book Clubs (four different clubs catering for children from 4–15), and through the Red House International Schools Club.
   School Book Fairs *Mike Robinson* The Book Fair Division sells directly to children,

parents and teachers in schools through 27,000 week-long book events held in schools throughout the UK.
Royalties paid twice-yearly.

Authors' Rating Another beneficiary of the Harry Potter phenomenon (via its children's book clubs), Scholastic also leads the intellectual sector of children's publishing with Philip Pullman who, by any literary standards, takes some beating. Fiction for 8 to 12-year-olds is seen as a growth sector. Noted for its author-friendly skills, Scholastic has strengthened its marketing base with the purchase of Grolier, the leading US pre-school book club.

SCM Press
9–17 St Albans Place, London N1 0NX
☎020 7359 8033   Fax 020 7359 0049
Email scmpress@btinternet.com
Website www.scm-canterburypress.co.uk
Publishing Director *Alex Wright*
Approx. Annual Turnover £700,000
Publishes culturally-engaged theology, philosophy of religion, and religious ethics from an interdisciplinary and inter-faith perspective. About 35 titles a year. No unsolicited mss or proposals considered.
Royalties paid annually.

Authors' Rating Leading publisher of religious ideas with well-deserved reputation for fresh thinking. At SCM, 'questioning theology is the norm'.

Scottish Cultural Press/
Scottish Children's Press
See **S.C.P. Publishers Ltd**

S.C.P. Publishers Ltd (trading as Scottish Cultural Press)
Unit 13d, Newbattle Abbey Business Annexe, Newbattle Road, Dalkeith EH22 3LJ
☎0131 660 6366   Fax 0131 660 6414
Email info@scottishbooks.com
Directors *Avril Gray, Brian Pugh*
FOUNDED 1992. *Publishes* Scottish interest titles, including cultural literature, poetry, archaeology, local history. DIVISION **S.C.P. Children's Ltd** (trading as **Scottish Children's Press**) Children's fiction and non-fiction. Unsolicited mss, synopses and ideas welcome provided return postage is included but telephone before sending material, please.
Royalties paid.

Scribner
See **Simon & Schuster UK Limited**

Seafarer Books
102 Redwald Road, Rendlesham,
Woodbridge, Suffolk IP12 2TE
☎01394 420789 Fax 01394 461314
Email info@seafarerbooks.com
Website www.seafarerbooks.com
Sole Proprietor *Patricia M. Eve*

FOUNDED 1968. *Publishes* sailing titles, with an
emphasis on the traditional. AUTHORS Jack
London, Erskine Childers, Adrian Seligman,
Frank Mulville, Bjorn Larsson. No unsolicited
mss; preliminary letter essential before making
any type of submission.
Royalties paid twice-yearly.

Search Press Ltd
Wellwood, North Farm Road, Tunbridge
Wells, Kent TN2 3DR
☎01892 510850 Fax 01892 515903
Email searchpress@searchpress.com
Website www.searchpress.com
Managing Director *Martin de la Bédoyère*
Commissioning Editor *Rosalind Dace*

FOUNDED 1970. *Publishes* full-colour art, craft,
needlecrafts: papermaking and papercrafts, paint-
ing on silk, art techniques, embroidery. TITLES *A
Beginner's Guide to Drawing and Painting in
Watercolour; Batik for Artists and Quilters; Basic
Woodwork; Handmade Clay Crafts*. No unsolicited
mss; synopsis with sample chapter welcome.
Royalties paid annually.

Secker & Warburg
See **Random House Group Ltd**

Sensation
See **Harlequin Mills & Boon Ltd**

Seren
First Floor, 38–40 Nolton Street, Bridgend
CF31 3BN
☎01656 663018 Fax 01656 649226
Email seren@seren.force9.co.uk
Website www.seren-books.com
Chairman *Cary Archard*
Managing Director *Mick Felton*
Approx. Annual Turnover £150,000

FOUNDED 1981 as a specialist poetry publisher
but has now moved into general literary pub-
lishing with an emphasis on Wales. *Publishes*
poetry, fiction, literary criticism, drama, biog-
raphy, art, history and translations of fiction. 25
titles in 1999.
DIVISIONS **Poetry** *Amy Wack* AUTHORS
Owen Sheers, Tony Curtis, Sheenagh Pugh,
Duncan Bush, Deryn Rees-Jones. **Drama**
Amy Wack AUTHORS Edward Thomas, Charles
Way, Lucinda Coxon. **Fiction**, **Art**, **Literary
Criticism**, **History**, **Translations** *Mick Felton*
AUTHORS Christopher Meredith, Leslie
Norris, Richard John Evans.
IMPRINT **Border Lines Biographies**
TITLES *Bruce Chatwin; Dennis Potter; Mary
Webb; Wilfred Owen; Raymond Williams*, etc.
Unsolicited mss, synopses and ideas for books
welcome.
Royalties paid twice yearly.

Serpent's Tail
4 Blackstock Mews, London N4 2BT
☎020 7354 1949 Fax 020 7704 6467
Email info@serpentstail.com
Website www.serpentstail.com
Contact *Ben Cooper*
Approx. Annual Turnover £650,000

FOUNDED 1986. Won the **Sunday Times
Small Publisher of the Year Award** (1989)
and the Ralph Lewis Award for new fiction
(1992). Serpent's Tail has introduced to British
audiences a number of major internationally
known writers. Noted for its strong emphasis on
design and an eye for the unusual. *Publishes* contemporary fiction, contemporary gay fiction and
non-fiction, including works in translation,
crime, popular culture and biography. No
poetry, romance or fantasy. About 40 titles a
year.
IMPRINTS **Serpent's Tail** TITLES *Nineteen
Seventy Seven* David Peace; *Whatever* Michel
Houellebecq; *This is Serbia Calling* Matthew
Collin; *Pornocopia* Laurence O'Toole. **Five
Star** TITLES *Acid Casuals* Nicholas Blincoe;
Always Outnumbered, Always Outgunned Walter
Mosley; *Beneath the Blonde* Stella Duffy. Send
preliminary letter outlining proposal with a
sample chapter and s.a.e. No unsolicited mss.
Prospective authors unfamiliar with Serpent's
Tail are advised to study the list before submit-
ting anything.
Royalties paid annually.

Authors' Rating A publisher noted for originality which means doing what the conglomerates are unwilling or unable to do. An exciting fiction list much praised by its own and
other publishers' authors.

Severn House Publishers

9–15 High Street, Sutton, Surrey SM1 1DF
☎020 8770 3930 Fax 020 8770 3850
Email info@severnhouse.com
Website www.severnhouse.com

Chairman *Edwin Buckhalter*
Editorial *Amanda Stewart*

FOUNDED 1974. A leader in library fiction
publishing. *Publishes* hardback fiction: romance
science fiction, horror, fantasy, crime. About
140 titles a year. No unsolicited material.
Synopses/proposals preferred through *bona fide*
literary agents only.

Royalties paid twice-yearly. *Overseas associate*
Severn House Publishers Inc., New York.

Sheed & Ward Ltd

4 Rickett Street, London SW6 1RU
☎020 7610 2722 Fax 020 7610 3373
Email sheed@breathemail.net
Website www.sheed.co.uk

Managing Director *Martin Redfern*
Approx. Annual Turnover £90,000

FOUNDED 1926. *Publishes* theological and spiritual books for the Roman Catholic market. No
fiction, children's or illustrated books. 3 titles
in 2000. No unsolicited mss; synopses and ideas
welcome. Approach by mail in the first
instance.

Royalties paid annually.

Sheffield Academic Press

Mansion House, 19 Kingfield Road, Sheffield
S11 9AS
☎0114 255 4433 Fax 0114 255 4626
Email admin@sheffac.demon.co.uk
Website www.sheffieldacademicpress.com

Managing Director *Mrs Jean R.K. Allen*
Approx. Annual Turnover £1.5 million

FOUNDED in 1976. Originally known as JSOT
Press. Now the leading academic publisher of
biblical titles. Recently expanded its list to
include archaeology, literary studies, history
and culture, languages, contemporary
European studies, scientific, professional, reference. 110 titles in 2000. Unsolicited mss, synopses and ideas welcome. No fiction.

IMPRINTS **Sheffield Academic Press** *Jean
Allen*; **Subis**.
Royalties paid annually

Sheldon Press

See **Society for Promoting Christian
Knowledge**

Shepheard-Walwyn (Publishers) Ltd

Suite 604, The Chandlery, 50 Westminster
Bridge Road, London SE1 7QY
☎020 7721 7666 Fax 020 7721 7667
Email books@shepheard-walwyn.co.uk
Website www.shepheard-walwyn.co.uk

Managing Director *Anthony Werner*
Approx. Annual Turnover £150,000

FOUNDED 1972. 'We regard books as food for
the mind and want to offer a wholesome diet
of original ideas and fresh approaches to old
subjects.' *Publishes* general non-fiction in three
main areas: Scottish interest; gift books in calligraphy and/or illustrated; history, political
economy, philosophy. About 5 titles a year.
Synopses and ideas for books welcome.

Royalties paid twice-yearly.

The Shetland Times Ltd

Prince Alfred Street, Lerwick, Shetland
ZE1 0EP
☎01595 693622 Fax 01595 694637
Email publishing@shetland-times.co.uk
Website www.shetland-books.co.uk

Managing Director *Robert Wishart*
Publications Manager *Charlotte Black*

FOUNDED 1872 as publishers of the local newspaper. Book publishing followed thereafter
plus publication of monthly magazine, *Shetland
Life*. *Publishes* anything with Shetland connections – local and natural history, music, crafts,
maritime. Prefers material with a Shetland
theme/connection.

Royalties paid annually.

Shire Publications Ltd

Cromwell House, Church Street, Princes
Risborough, Buckinghamshire HP27 9AA
☎01844 344301 Fax 01844 347080
Website www.shirebooks.co.uk

General Manager *Sue Ross*

FOUNDED 1967. *Publishes* original non-fiction
paperbacks. About 25 titles a year. No unsolicited material; send introductory letter with
detailed outline of idea.

Royalties paid annually.

Authors' Rating You don't have to live in the
country to write books for Shire but it helps.
With titles like *Church Fonts, Haunted Inns* and
Discovering Preserved Railways there is a distinct
rural feel to the list. Another way of putting it, to
quote owner John Rotheroe, Shire specialises in
'small books on all manner of obscure subjects'.

Short Books

15 Highbury Terrace, London N5 1UP
☎020 7226 1607 Fax 020 7226 4769
Website www.theshortbookco.com

Contacts *Rebecca Nicolson, Aurea Carpenter*

FOUNDED 1872 in May 2001 by two former journalists, Rebecca Nicolson and Aurea Carpenter, Short Books aims to bridge the gap between publishing and journalism, producing informative, entertaining non-fiction at a conquerable length (approx. 20,000 words). 21 titles in 2001. SERIES Novella-length portraits of the co-stars of history; **Front Lines** Essays, investigations, reportage by authors including Paul Theroux, David Sexton and John Sutherland; **The History Files** Lively biographies of intriguing figures from the past, aimed at children aged 9–12. No poetry or fiction.
Royalties paid twice-yearly.

Sidgwick & Jackson

See **Macmillan Publishers Ltd**

Sigma Press

1 South Oak Lane, Wilmslow, Cheshire
SK9 6AR
☎01625 531035 Fax 01625 536800
Email info@sigma.press
Website www.sigmapress.co.uk

Chairman/Managing Director *Graham Beech*

FOUNDED in 1980 as a publisher of technical books. Sigma Press now publishes mainly in the leisure area. *Publishes* outdoor, local heritage, myths and legends, sports, dance and exercise. Approx. 40 titles in 2000. No unsolicited mss; synopses and ideas welcome.
DIVISION **Sigma Leisure** TITLES *The Coniston Tigers* (biography); *Walking the Wainwrights; Salsa & Merengue Step-by-Step; How to Run a Marathon; Laugh Away the Fat.*
Royalties paid twice-yearly.

Signature

See **Hodder Headline Plc**

Silhouette Desire

See **Harlequin Mills & Boon Ltd**

Simon & Schuster UK Limited

Africa House, 64–78 Kingsway, London
WC2B 6AH
☎020 7316 1900 Fax 020 7316 0331
CEO/Managing Director *Ian Chapman*
Publishers *Suzanne Baboneau* (Fiction), *Helen Gummer* (Non-fiction)

Editorial Director, Scribner *Martin Fletcher*
FOUNDED 1986. Offshoot of the leading American publisher. *Publishes* general fiction, including science fiction under its **Earthlight** imprint (Editor *John Jarrold*) and non-fiction in hardback and paperback. Literary fiction and non-fiction is published in trade paperback under the **Scribner** imprint. No academic or technical material.
Royalties paid twice-yearly.

Authors' Rating With one of the best known American publishing names, Simon & Schuster has long relied on imported titles. But this is set to change. The new editorial team, with a supporting budget, is aiming to give more space to UK writers.

Skoob Books Ltd

11A–15 Sicilian Avenue, Southampton Row,
London WC1A 2QH
☎020 7404 3063 Fax 020 7404 4398
Email books@skoob.com
Website www.skoob.com

Editorial office: 76A Oldfield Road, London
N16 0RS Tel/Fax 020 7275 9811
Managing Director *I.K. Ong*
Editorial *M. Lovell*

Publishes literary guides, cultural studies, esoterica/occult, poetry, new writing from the Orient. No unsolicited mss, synopses or ideas. TITLES *Skoob Directory of Secondhand Bookshops; The Necronomicon* George Hay; *Perspectives on Post-Colonial Literature* D.C.R.A. Goonetilleke; *The Space of City Trees* Arthur Yap.

Smith Gryphon Ltd

See **Blake Publishing**

Colin Smythe Ltd

PO Box 6, Gerrards Cross, Buckinghamshire
SL9 8XA
☎01753 886000 Fax 01753 886469
Email sales@colinsmythe.co.uk
Website www.colinsmythe.co.uk

Managing Director *Colin Smythe*
Approx. Annual Turnover £2.2 million

FOUNDED 1966. *Publishes* Anglo-Irish literature, drama; criticism and history. About 15 titles a year. No unsolicited mss. Also acts as literary agent for a small list of authors including Terry Pratchett.
Royalties paid annually/twice-yearly.

Society for Promoting Christian Knowledge (SPCK)

Holy Trinity Church, Marylebone Road,
London NW1 4DU
☎020 7643 0382 Fax 020 7643 0391
Website www.spck.org.uk

Director of Publishing *Simon Kingston*

FOUNDED 1698, SPCK is the third oldest publisher in the country.
IMPRINTS **SPCK** Editorial Director *Joanna Moriaty* Theology, academic, liturgy, prayer, spirituality, Biblical studies, educational resources, mission, pastoral care, gospel and culture, worldwide. **Sheldon Press** Editor *Liz Marsh* Popular medicine, health, self-help, psychology. **Triangle** Senior Editor *Alison Barr* Popular Christian paperbacks. **Azure** Senior Editor *Alison Barr* General spirituality.
Royalties paid annually.

Authors' Rating Religion with a strong social edge.

Southwater
See **Anness Publishing Ltd**

Souvenir Press Ltd
43 Great Russell Street, London WC1B 3PA
☎020 7580 9307/8 & 7637 5711/2/3
Fax 020 7580 5064

Chairman/Managing Director *Ernest Hecht*

Independent publishing house. FOUNDED 1951. *Publishes* academic and scholarly, animal care and breeding, antiques and collecting, archaeology, autobiography and biography, business and industry, children's, cookery, crafts and hobbies, crime, educational, fiction, gardening, health and beauty, history and antiquarian, humour, illustrated and fine editions, magic and the occult, medical, military, music, natural history, philosophy, poetry, psychology, religious, sociology, sports, theatre and women's studies. About 55 titles a year. Souvenir's Human Horizons series for the disabled and their carers is one of the most pre-eminent in its field and recently celebrated 20 years of publishing for the disabled.
IMPRINTS/SERIES
Condor; **Human Horizons**; **Independent Voices**; **Pictorial Presentations**; **Pop Universal**; **The Story-Tellers**. TITLES *Muhammad Ali: The Birth of a Legend, Miami 1961–1964* Flip Schulke with Matt Schudel; *Zero, The Biography of a Dangerous Idea* Charles Seife; *Searle's Cats* Ronald Searle; *The Art of Napping at Work* Camille and Bill Anthony;

Solutions for Novelists; Secrets of a Master Editor Sol Stein; *Cobra Trap* Peter O'Donnell; *Opium* Barbara Hodgson. Unsolicited mss considered but initial letter of enquiry required.
Royalties paid twice-yearly.

Authors' Rating Amazing isn't it that in these days of mega businesses, a smallish independent publisher can survive and thrive. In his fifty years of running Souvenir, Ernest Hecht has proved time and again that he has an eye for the bestseller – this is, after all, the man who launched Arthur Hailey – but his success owes as much to his love of the outrageous and a quirky sense of fun. Who else would have published a history of bottoms (*The Rear View*) or *Fairy Spells, Seeing and Communicating with the Fairies*?

SPCK
See **Society for Promoting Christian Knowledge**

Special Edition
See **Harlequin Mills & Boon Ltd**

Spectrum
See **F.A. Thorpe (Publishing)**

Spellmount Ltd
The Old Rectory, Staplehurst, Kent
TN12 0AZ
☎01580 893730 Fax 01580 893731
Email enquiries@spellmount.com
Website www.spellmount.com

Managing Director *Jamie Wilson*
Approx. Annual Turnover £400,000

FOUNDED 1983. *Publishes* history and military history. About 30 titles a year. Synopses/ideas for books in these specialist fields welcome, enclosing return postage.
Royalties paid biannually for two years, then annually.

E & FN Spon
See **Routledge**

Springer–Verlag London Limited
Sweetapple House, Catteshall Road,
Godalming, Surrey GU7 3DJ
☎01483 418800 Fax 01483 415144
Email postmaster@svl.co.uk
Website www.springer.co.uk

Managing Director *John Watson*
Editorial Director *Beverley Ford*
Approx. Annual Turnover £5 million

The UK subsidiary of BertelsmannSpringer of Germany. *Publishes* science, technical and medical books and journals. About 150 titles a year, plus journals. Specialises in computing, engineering, medicine, mathematics, statistics, astronomy. All UK published books are sold through Springer's German and US companies as well as in the UK. Not interested in social sciences, fiction or school books but academic and professional science and amateur astronomy mss or synopses welcome.

Royalties paid annually.

Stainer & Bell Ltd

PO Box 110, 23 Gruneisen Road, London N3 1DZ
☎020 8343 3303 Fax 020 8343 3024
Email post@stainer.co.uk
Website www.stainer.co.uk

Managing Directors *Carol Y. Wakefield, Keith M. Wakefield*
Publishing Director *Nicholas Williams*
Approx. Annual Turnover £790,000

FOUNDED 1907 to publish sheet music. *Publishes* music and religious subjects related to hymnody. Unsolicited synopses/ideas for books welcome. Send letter enclosing brief précis.

Royalties paid annually.

Star Kids Limited

10 Greycoat Place, London SW1P 1SB
☎020 7960 6071 Fax 020 7960 6172
Email info@starkids.uk.com
Website www.starkids.uk.com

Managing Director *Richard Carr*

An investment subsidiary of **Egmont Books** FOUNDED IN 2000. *Publishes* children's non-fiction – home learning and educational books. 45 titles in 2000.

Harold Starke Publishers Ltd

Pixey Green, Stradbroke, Near Eye, Suffolk IP21 5NG
☎01379 388334 Fax 01379 388335
Website red@eclat.force9.co.uk

Directors *Harold K. Starke, Naomi Galinski*

Publishes adult non-fiction, medical and reference. No unsolicited mss.

Royalties paid annually.

The Stationery Office Ltd

St Crispins, Duke Street, Norwich, Norfolk NR3 1PD
☎01603 622211 Fax 01603 694313 (Editorial)
Website www.thestationeryoffice.com

Chief Executive *Fred J. Perkins*
Approx. Annual Turnover £250 million

Formerly HMSO, which was FOUNDED 1786. Became part of the private sector in October 1996. 11,000 new titles each year with 50,000 titles in print. Publisher of material sponsored by Parliament, government departments and other official bodies. Also commercial publishing in the following broad categories: business and professional, environment, transport, education and law.

Stevens

See **Sweet & Maxwell Ltd**

STM

See **Hodder Headline Plc**

The Story-Tellers

See **Souvenir Press Ltd**

Straightline Publishing Ltd

29 Main Street, Bothwell, Glasgow G71 8RD
☎01698 853000 Fax 01698 854208

Director *Frank Docherty*
Editors *B. Taylor, P. Bellew*

FOUNDED 1989. *Publishes* magazines and directories – trade and technical – books of local interest. 11 titles in 2000. TITLES *Cabletalk*; *Information Builder*. No unsolicited material.

Royalties paid annually.

Subis

See **Sheffield Academic Press**

Summersdale Publishers

46 West Street, Chichester, West Sussex PO19 1RP
☎01243 771107 Fax 01243 786300
Email enquiries@summersdale.com
Website www.summersdale.com

Directors *Stewart Ferris, Alastair Williams*
Editor *Elizabeth Kershaw*
Approx. Annual Turnover £1 million

FOUNDED 1990. *Publishes* non-fiction: humour, travel literature, self-help, biography, sport, gift books, cookery. 60 titles in 2001. TITLES *Snowball Oranges; Good Vibrations – Coast to Coast by Harley; Trans-Siberia; Espresso with the Headhunters; The World Commuter*. No unsolicited mss; synopses and ideas welcome.

Royalties paid.

Sunshine People Plc

Apsley House, Apsley Road, New Malden, Surrey KT3 3NJ
☎020 8942 8800 Fax 020 8942 7722
Email valerie@sunshine-people.com

Website www.sunshine-people.com
Managing Director *Elisabeth Bataille*
FOUNDED 2000. *Publishes* illustrated children's books in English and French supported by audio cassettes and CD-ROMs; also toys. 7 titles in 2000. TITLES *The Doctor of the Little Forest; Timmy and the Primrose; Two Kings*. No unsolicited material as all work is produced in-house.

Susquehanna University Press
See **Golden Cockerel Press**

Sutton Publishing Ltd
Phoenix Mill, Thrupp, Stroud, Gloucestershire GL5 2BU
☎01453 731114 Fax 01453 731117
Managing Director *Keith Fullman*
Publishing Director *Peter Clifford*
Approx. Annual Turnover £5.5 million
FOUNDED 1978. Acquired by **Haynes Publishing** in March 2000. *Publishes* academic, archaeology, biography, countryside, history, military, regional interest, local history, pocket classics (lesser known novels by classic authors), transport. About 240 titles a year. Send synopses rather than complete mss.
Royalties paid twice-yearly.

Authors' Rating Now part of Haynes Publishing, this imaginative history publisher will almost certainly benefit from stronger marketing and distribution.

Swan Hill Press
See **Airlife Publishing Ltd**

Sweet & Maxwell Ltd
100 Avenue Road, London NW3 3PF
☎020 7393 7000 Fax 020 7393 7010
Email <firstname.lastname>@
  sweetandmaxwell.co.uk
Website www.sweetandmaxwell.co.uk
Managing Director *Wendy Beecham*
FOUNDED 1799. Part of The Thomson Corporation. *Publishes* legal and professional materials in all media, looseleaf works, journals, law reports and on CD-ROM. About 150 book titles a year, with live backlist of over 700 titles, 75 looseleaf services and more than 80 legal periodicals. Not interested in material which is non-legal. The legal and professional list is varied and contains many academic titles, as well as treatises and reference works in the legal and related professional fields.
IMPRINTS **Sweet & Maxwell**; **Sweet & Maxwell Asia**; **Stevens**; **W. Green**

(Scotland); **Round Hall/Sweet & Maxwell (Ireland)** General Manager *Elanor McGarry*. Ideas welcome. Writers with legal/professional projects in mind are advised to contact the company at the earliest possible stage in order to lay the groundwork for best design, production and marketing of a project.
Royalties and fees paid according to contract.

Take That Ltd
PO Box 200, Harrogate, North Yorkshire HG1 2YR
☎01423 507545 Fax 01423 526035
Website www.takethat.co.uk
Chairman/Managing Director *C. Brown*
FOUNDED 1986. Independent publisher of computing, finance and gambling titles (books and magazines). TITLES *Understand Financial Risk in a Day; Complete Beginner's Guide to the Internet; Successful Spread Betting*. About 10 titles a year. Unsolicited synopses for books welcome; 'no s.a.e., no reply'.
Royalties paid twice-yearly.

Tango Books
See **Sadie Fields Productions Ltd** under **UK Packagers**

Taschen
See entry under **European Publishers**

I.B. Tauris & Co. Ltd
6 Salem Road, London W2 4BU
☎020 7243 1225 Fax 020 7243 1226
Website www.ibtauris.com
Chairman/Publisher *Iradj Bagherzade*
Managing Director *Jonathan McDonnell*
FOUNDED 1984. Independent publisher. *Publishes* general non-fiction and academic in the fields of international relations, current affairs, history, politics, cultural, media and film studies, Middle East studies. Joint projects with Cambridge University Centre for Middle Eastern Studies, Institute for Latin American Studies and Institute of Ismaili Studies. *Distributes* The New Press (New York) outside North America. *Represents* **Curzon Press** in the UK. IMPRINTS **Tauris Parke Books** Illustrated books on architecture, travel, design and culture. **Tauris Parke Paperbacks** Trade titles, including art and art history. **British Academic Press** Academic monographs. **Radcliffe Press** Colonial history and biography. Unsolicited synopses and book proposals welcome.
Royalties paid twice-yearly.

Tavistock Publications
See **Routledge**

Taylor & Francis Group plc
11 New Fetter Lane, London EC4P 4EE
☎020 7583 9855　Fax 020 7842 2298
Website www.tandf.co.uk
Chairman *Robert Kiernan*
Chief Executive *Anthony Selvey*
Approx. Annual Turnover £115 million

FOUNDED 1798 with the launch of *Philosophical Magazine* which has been in publication ever since (now a solid state physics journal). The Group is now a public company but with strong academic connections among the major shareholders. **Falmer Press** joined the group in 1979 and it doubled its size in the late '80s with the acquisition of Crane Russak in 1986 and Hemisphere Publishing Co in 1988. In 1995, acquired Lawrence Erlbaum Associates Ltd and Brunner/Mazel in 1997, adding to the growing list of psychology publications. In 1996, UCL Press Ltd was purchased, adding further to its portfolio of publications in science and humanities. In 1997, Garland Publishing Inc., New York, and in 1998 Routledge Publishing Holdings Ltd, including Carfax Publishing and E & FN Spon were acquired. The most recent additions to the Taylor & Francis Group are Europa Publications Ltd, the reference book publisher covering international affairs, politics and economics, and **Martin Dunitz Ltd** (see entry) in 1999. Acquired the international journals division of Scandinavian University Press in 2000, adding over 60 academic journals to a total list of 50. *Publishes* scientific, technical, education titles at university, research and professional levels. About 1700 titles a year. Unsolicited mss, synopses and ideas welcome.

Royalties paid yearly. *Overseas offices* Taylor & Francis Inc., Philadelphia, PA and New York, Hemisphere Publication Services, Singapore, Taylor & Francis AS, Norway and Sweden.

Authors' Rating One of those companies that barely registers with authors until they look at some of the famous imprints that are gathered under the corporate umbrella. Very much into higher education and reference, further expansion is predicted, particularly in the US. Plans are well ahead for making all the titles available in e-book format.

Teach Yourself
See **Hodder Headline Plc**

Telegraph Books
1 Canada Square, Canary Wharf, London E14 5DT
☎020 7538 6826　Fax 020 7538 6064
Website www.booksonline.co.uk
Owner *Telegraph Group Ltd*
Publisher *Susannah Charlton*
Approx. Annual Turnover £3 million

Concentrates on Telegraph branded books in association/collaboration with other publishers. Also runs Telegraph Books Direct, a direct mail, phone-line bookselling service and off-the-page sales for other publishers' books. *Publishes* general non-fiction: journalism, business and law, cookery, education, gardening, wine, guides, sport, puzzles and games. About 50 titles a year. Only interested in books if a Telegraph link exists. No unsolicited material.

Royalties paid twice-yearly.

Tellastory
See **Random House Group Ltd**

Temple House Books
See **The Book Guild Ltd**

Thames and Hudson Ltd
181A High Holborn, London WC1V 7QX
☎020 7845 5000　Fax 020 7845 5050
Email mail@thameshudson.co.uk
Website www.thamesandhudson.com
Managing Director *Thomas Neurath*
Editorial Head *Jamie Camplin*
Approx. Annual Turnover £20 million

Publishes art, archaeology, architecture and design; biography, fashion, garden and landscape design, graphics, history, illustrated and fine editions, mythology, music, photography, popular culture, style, travel and topography. 200 titles a year. SERIES *World of Art; New Horizons; Celtic Design; Hip Hotels; Most Beautiful Villages; Prospects for Tomorrow.* TITLES *Looking Back at Francis Bacon; Sensation; The Shock of the New; Vision: Fifty Years of British Creativity; Colour and Culture; The Book of Kells; The Dalai Lama's Secret Temple; Garden Mania; Fashion Illustration Now; Ancient Egypt: The Great Discoveries; Cybershops.* Send preliminary letter and outline before mss.

Royalties paid twice-yearly.

Authors' Rating Fifty years in the business, Thames and Hudson has a fine record of publishing quality illustrated books on art and design. The World of Art series, a huge range of modestly priced, scholarly books, is probably the best of its kind anywhere in the world.

Financial success rests on producing the sort of books that easily carry over to other languages.

Thomson Learning

Berkshire House, 168–173 High Holborn, London WC1V 7AA
☎020 7497 1422 Fax 020 7497 1426
Email info@itpuk.co.uk
Website www.thomsonlearning.co.uk
CEO (Worldwide) *Bob Christie*
CEO (Thomson Learning EMA) *Jeff Scott*
Publishing Director (Thomson Learning EMA) *Julian Thomas*

FOUNDED 1993. Formerly International Thomson Publishing, part of the Thomson Corporation and as such has offices worldwide with the UK office being reported to by Copenhagen (for Europe), Turkey (Middle East) and South Africa. *Publishes* education. TITLES *Management and Cost Accounting* Drury; *Strategy – Process, Content, Contact* DeWitt and Meyer. Unsolicited material aimed at students is welcome but telephone in the first instance to check out the idea.

Royalties vary according to contract.

Stanley Thornes (Publishers) Ltd
See **Nelson Thornes Limited**

F.A. Thorpe (Publishing)
The Green, Bradgate Road, Anstey, Leicester LE7 7FU
☎0116 236 4325 Fax 0116 234 0205
Chairman *David Thorpe*
Group Chief Executive *Robert Thirlby*
Approx. Annual Turnover £500,000

FOUNDED in 1964 to supply large print books to libraries. Part of the Ulverscroft Group Ltd. *Publishes* fiction and non-fiction large print books. No educational, gardening or books that would not be suitable for large print. 444 titles in 2000. DIVISIONS **Charnwood**; **Ulverscroft**. IMPRINTS **Linford Romance**; **Linford Mystery**; **Linford Western**; **Spectrum**. No unsolicited material.

Thorsons
See **HarperCollins Publishers Ltd**

Times Books
See **HarperCollins Publishers Ltd**

Titan Books
144 Southwark Street, London SE1 0UP
☎020 7620 0200 Fax 020 7620 0032
Email editorial@titanmail.com

Managing Director *Nick Landau*
Editorial Director *Katy Wild*

FOUNDED 1981. Now a leader in the publication of graphic novels and film and television tie-ins. *Publishes* comic books/graphic novels, film and television titles. About 70–80 titles a year.

IMPRINT **Titan Books** TITLES *Batman; Superman; Alien; Star Trek; Star Wars; The Simpsons; The X Files; The Avengers.* No unsolicited fiction or children's books, please. Ideas for film and TV titles considered; send synopsis/outline with sample chapter. No email submissions. Author guidelines available.

Royalties paid twice-yearly.

The Toby Press
PO Box 2455, London W1A 5WY
☎020 7580 5440 Fax 020 7580 5442
Email toby@tobypress.com
Website www.tobypress.com
Chairman *M. Miller*

FOUNDED 1999. *Publishes* fiction only and markets the books directly to readers through its website and the *Toby Press Review*, a quarterly magazine. About 20 titles a year. TITLES *Failing Paris* Samantha Dunn; *Absence* Raymond Tallis; *Cardiofitness* Alessandra Montrucchio. Send first chapters only; 'unsolicited mss will *not* be returned'.

Royalties paid twicie-yearly. *Overseas subsidiary* in the USA.

Tolkien
See **HarperCollins Publishers Ltd**

Tolley Publishing
See **Butterworths Tolley**

Transworld Publishers, A division of the Random House Group Ltd
61–63 Uxbridge Road, London W5 5SA
☎020 8579 2652 Fax 020 8579 5479
Email info@transworld-publishers.co.uk
Website www.booksattransworld.co.uk
Chairman *Mark Barty-King*
Joint Managing Directors *Larry Finlay, Patrick Janson-Smith*
Approx. Annual Turnover £72 million

FOUNDED 1950. A subsidiary of **Random House, Inc.**, New York, which in turn is a wholly-owned subsidiary of Bertelsmann AG, Germany. *Publishes* general fiction and non-fiction, children's books, sports and leisure.

DIVISIONS
Adult Trade *Patrick Janson-Smith* IMPRINTS

Bantam *Francesca Liversidge*; **Bantam Press** *Sally Gaminara*; **Corgi**; **Black Swan** *Bill Scott-Kerr*; **Doubleday** *Marianne Velmans*. AUTHORS Kate Atkinson, Charlotte Bingham, Bill Bryson, Catherine Cookson, Jilly Cooper, Ben Elton, Nicholas Evans, Frederick Forsyth, Robert Goddard, Germaine Greer, Joanne Harris, Stephen Hawking, Anne McCaffrey, Andy McNab, Terry Pratchett, Willy Russell, Gerald Seymour, Danielle Steel, Joanna Trollope, Mary Wesley.

Children's & Young Adult Books *Philippa Dickinson* IMPRINTS **Doubleday** (hardcover); **Picture Corgi**; **Corgi Pups**; **Young Corgi**; **Corgi Yearling**; **Corgi**. AUTHORS Ian Beck, Malorie Blackman, Anthony Browne, Helen Cooper, Peter Dickinson, Dick King-Smith, K.M. Peyton, Terry Pratchett, Philip Pullman, Robert Swindells, Jacqueline Wilson.

Royalties paid twice-yearly. *Overseas associates* Random House Australia Pty Ltd; Random House New Zealand; Random House (Pty) Ltd (South Africa).

Authors' Rating One of the best in the business, an object lesson in making quality pay. For frontlist paperbacks, according to the *Bookseller*, 'no one can touch Transworld'.

Trentham Books Ltd

Westview House, 734 London Road, Stoke on Trent, Staffordshire ST4 5NP
☎01782 745567 Fax 01782 745553
Website www.trentham-books.co.uk
Chairman/Managing Director *Dr John Eggleston*
Editorial Head *Dr Gillian Klein*
Approx. Annual Turnover £1 million

Publishes education (nursery, school and higher), social sciences, intercultural studies and law for professional readers *not* for children and parents. Also academic and professional journals. No fiction, biography or poetry. About 25–30 titles a year. Unsolicited mss, synopses and ideas welcome if relevant to their interests. Material only returned if adequate s.a.e. sent.
Royalties paid annually.

Triangle

See **Society for Promoting Christian Knowledge**

Trident Press Ltd

Empire House, 175 Piccadilly, London W1V 9DB
☎020 7491 8770 Fax 020 7491 8664
Email admin@tridentpress.ie

Website www.tridentpress.com
Managing Director *Peter Vine*
Approx. Annual Turnover £550,000
FOUNDED 1997. *Publishes* TV tie-ins, natural history, travel, geography, underwater/marine life, history, archaeology, culture and fiction. 8 titles in 1999.

DIVISIONS **Fiction/General Publishing** *Paula Vine;* **Natural History** *Peter Vine.* TITLES *Red Sea Sharks; The Elysium Testament; BBC Wildlife Specials; UAE in Focus.* No unsolicited mss; synopses and ideas welcome, particularly TV tie-ins. Approach in writing or *brief* communications by email, fax or telephone.
Royalties paid annually.

Trotman & Co. Ltd

2 The Green, Richmond, Surrey TW9 1PL
☎020 8486 1150 Fax 020 8486 1161
Website www.trotmanpublishing.co.uk
Chairman *Andrew Fiennes Trotman*
Editorial Director *Amanda Williams*
Approx. Annual Turnover £3 million
Publishes general careers books, higher education guides, teaching support material, employment and training resources. About 50 titles a year. TITLES *Degree Course Offers; The Student Book; UCAS/Trotman Complete Guides; Students' Money Matters.* Unsolicited material welcome. Also active in the educational resources market, producing recruitment brochures.
Royalties paid twice-yearly.

20/20

See **The X Press**

UCL Press Ltd

See **Taylor & Francis Group**

Ulverscroft

See **F.A. Thorpe (Publishing)**

University Presses of California, Columbia & Princeton Ltd

1 Oldlands Way, Bognor Regis, West Sussex PO22 9SA
☎01243 842165 Fax 01243 842167
Email lois@upccp.demon.co.uk

Publishes academic titles only. US-based editorial offices. Over 200 titles a year. Enquiries only.

Usborne Publishing Ltd

83–85 Saffron Hill, London EC1N 8RT
☎020 7430 2800 Fax 020 7430 1562
Email mail@usborne.co.uk

Website www.usborne.com

Managing Director *Peter Usborne*
Editorial Director *Jenny Tyler*
Approx. Annual Turnover £14 million

FOUNDED 1973. *Publishes* non-fiction, fiction, computer books, puzzle books and music for children and young adults. Some titles for parents. Up to 100 titles a year. Non-fiction books are written in-house to a specific format and therefore unsolicited mss are not normally welcome. Ideas which may be developed in-house are sometimes considered. Fiction for children may be considered. Keen to hear from new illustrators and designers.
  Royalties paid twice-yearly.

Authors' Rating A children's publisher that thrives on the conviction that learning can be fun. More titles promised but most of these are likely to be developed in-house. The latest idea is Internet-linked reference books.

Vallentine Mitchell
See **Frank Cass & Co Ltd**

Vanguard Press
See **Pegasus Elliot Mackenzie Publishers**

Ventura
See **Penguin UK**

Vermilion
See **Random House Group Ltd**

Verso
6 Meard Street, London W1F 0EG
☎020 7437 3546 Fax 020 7734 0059
Website www.versobooks.com

Chairman *George Galfalvi*
Managing Director *Colin Robinson*
Approx. Annual Turnover £2 million

Formerly New Left Books which grew out of the *New Left Review*. *Publishes* politics, history, sociology, economics, philosophy, cultural studies, feminism. TITLES *The Prophet Armed: Trotsky 1879–1921* Isaac Deutscher; *The Trial of Henry Kissinger* Christopher Hitchens; *Through the Looking Glass: A Dissenter Inside New Labour* Liz Davies; *The Murder of Lumumba* Ludo de Witte; *Rock 'til You Drop* John Strausbaugh; *Close up: Iranian Cinema, Past, Present and Future* Hamid Dabashi; *Hollywood Flatlands: Animation, Critical Theory and the Avant-Garde* Esther Leslie; *The Red Velvet Seat: Women's Writings on the Cinema: The First Fifty Years* Lant and Periz (eds.). No unsolicited mss; synopses and ideas for books welcome.

Royalties paid annually. *Overseas office* in New York.

Authors' Rating Dubbed by the *Bookseller* as 'one of the most successful small independent publishers'.

Viking/Viking Children's
See **Penguin UK**

Vintage
See **Random House Group Ltd**

Virago Press
Little, Brown & Co. (UK), Brettenham House, Lancaster Place, London WC2E 7EN
☎020 7911 8000 Fax 020 7911 8100
Website www.virago.co.uk

Publisher *Lennie Goodings*
Senior Editor *Antonia Hodgson*
Editor, Virago Modern Classics *Jill Foulston*
Approx. Annual Turnover £2.5 million

FOUNDED in 1973 by Carmen Callil, Virago recently passed its quarter century of publishing fiction and non-fiction books of quality by women. *Publishes* approximately 50 new books a year in the areas of autobiography, biography, fiction, history, politics, psychology and women's issues. IMPRINTS **Virago Modern Classics** 20th-century reprints; **Virago Vs** AUTHORS Margaret Atwood, Maya Angelou, Gail Anderson-Dargatz, Nina Bawden, Jennifer Belle, Sarah Dunant, Marilyn French, Gaby Hauptman, Michele Roberts, Natasha Walter, Sarah Waters. Send synopsis and sample chapter and return postage with all unsolicited material.
  Royalties paid twice-yearly.

Virgin Books Ltd
Thames Wharf Studios, Rainville Road, London W6 9HT
☎020 7386 3300 Fax 020 7386 3360
Website www.virgin-books.com

Chairman *Mark Fisher*
Managing Director *K.T. Forster*
Approx. Annual Turnover £10 million

The Virgin Group's book publishing company. *Publishes* non-fiction, reference and large-format illustrated books on entertainment and popular culture, particularly music and books about film, showbiz, sport, biography, autobiography and humour. Launched a series of travel guides in 1999. No poetry, short stories, individual novels, children's books.

DIVISIONS
Non-fiction IMPRINT **Virgin** Editorial Director

Humphrey Price; Music Scout *Stuart Slater*, **Sport** Senior Editor *Jonathan Taylor*, **Illustrated Books** Editor *James Bennett*; **Travel** Editorial Director *Carolyn Thorne*.

Fiction IMPRINTS **Virgin**; **Black Lace** Senior Editor *Kerri Sharp*; **Nexus** Editor *Paul Copperwaite*.

Royalties paid twice-yearly.

Authors' Rating Having pulled out of TV tie-ins and specialist music publishing, Virgin then cut back on its travel list. This leaves mass market music, sport and business and some worried authors. Oh yes, and there is Black Lace, Britain's leading seller of erotic fiction written by women for women. Maybe the rest of the company could learn a few lessons. There are rumours of a possible sale but, as yet, no bidders have made themselves known.

The Vital Spark
See **Neil Wilson Publishing Ltd**

Voyager
See **HarperCollins Publishers Ltd**

University of Wales Press
6 Gwennyth Street, Cathays, Cardiff CF24 4YD
☎029 2023 1919 Fax 029 2023 0908
Email press@press.wales.ac.uk
Website www.wales.ac.uk/press

Director *Susan Jenkins*
Deputy Director *Richard Houdmont*
Approx. Annual Turnover £425,000

FOUNDED 1922. *Publishes* academic and scholarly books in English and Welsh in four core areas: history, Welsh and Celtic Studies, European Studies, religion and philosophy. 60 titles in 2000.
IMPRINTS **GPC Books; Gwasg Prifysgol Cymru; University of Wales Press** TITLES *The Visual Culture of Wales: Industrial Society* Peter Lord; *The Contemporary Challenge of Modernist Theology* Paul Badham; *Editing Women* ed. Anne M. Hutchinson. Unsolicited mss considered.
Royalties paid annually.

Walker Books Ltd
87 Vauxhall Walk, London SE11 5HJ
☎020 7793 0909 Fax 020 7587 1123

Editors *Vanessa Clarke, Caroline Royds, Denise Johnstone-Burt, Mara Bergman*
Approx. Annual Turnover £31.7 million

FOUNDED 1979. *Publishes* illustrated children's books, children's fiction and non-fiction. About 300 titles a year. TITLES *Where's Wally?* Martin Handford; *Five Minutes' Peace* Jill Murphy; *Can't You Sleep, Little Bear?* Martin Waddell & Barbara Firth; *Guess How Much I Love You* Sam McBratney & Anita Jeram; *Stormbreaker* Anthony Horowitz; *MapHead* Lesley Howarth. Unsolicited mss welcome.
Royalties paid twice-yearly.

Authors' Rating Having sorted out its problems in the US, Walker is back on expansionist route. The bad news for UK writers is the plan to originate more books across the Atlantic.

Wallflower Press
16 Chalk Farm Road, Camden Lock, London NW1 8AG
☎020 7485 0110 Fax 020 7485 0116
Email info@wallflowerpress.co.uk
Website www.wallflowerpress.co.uk

Editorial Director *Yoram Allon*
Chief Editor *Del Cullen*
Approx. Annual Turnover £100,000

FOUNDED 1999. *Publishes* academic and popular film studies and related media and cultural studies. 9 titles in 2000. Unsolicited mss, synopses and ideas welcome. No fiction or academic material not related to the arts, humanities and social sciences.
Royalties paid twice-yearly.

Ward Lock
See **Cassell**

Ward Lock Educational Co. Ltd
1 Christopher Road, East Grinstead, West Sussex RH19 3BT
☎01342 318980 Fax 01342 410980
Email wle@lingkee.com

Owner *Ling Kee (UK) Ltd*

FOUNDED 1952. *Publishes* educational books (primary, middle, secondary, teaching manuals) for all subjects, specialising in maths, science, geography, reading and English and currently focusing on Key Stages 1 and 2.

Frederick Warne
See **Penguin UK**

Warner
See **Little, Brown & Co. (UK)**

Franklin Watts
See **The Watts Publishing Group Ltd**

The Watts Publishing Group Ltd
96 Leonard Street, London EC2A 4XD
☎020 7739 2929 Fax 020 7739 6487
Email <gm>@wattspub.co.uk
Managing Director *Marlene Johnson*

Part of Groupe Lagardere. *Publishes* children's
non-fiction, reference, information, gift, fiction, picture and novelty. About 300 titles a
year.
IMPRINTS **Franklin Watts** *Philippa Stewart*
Non-fiction and information; **Orchard Books**
Francesca Dow Fiction, picture and novelty books.
Unsolicited mss, synopsis and ideas for books
welcome.
Royalties paid twice-yearly. *Overseas associates*
in Australia and New Zealand.

Wayland Publishers Ltd
See **Hodder Headline Plc**

Weidenfeld & Nicolson
See **The Orion Publishing Group Ltd**

Welsh Academic Press
See **Ashley Drake Publishing Ltd**

Westzone Publishing Ltd
19 Clifford Street, London W1X 1RH
☎020 7734 6002 Fax 020 7734 6003
Email westzone@westzonepublishing.com
Website www.westzonepublishing.com

Chairman *Gavin Aldred*
Managing Director *Nicholas Kenney*
Editorial Head *Mark Reynolds*
Approx. Annual Turnover £2 million

LAUNCHED in September 2000 with a projected output of 30 titles a year. Cutting-edge
photo-reportage books. 'Takes photography,
culture and contemporary art in a new direction.' Unsolicited mss, synopsis and ideas welcome; approach by letter in the first instance.
No children's or educational books.
Royalties paid quarterly.

Wharncliffe Publishing
47 Church Street, Barnsley, South Yorkshire
S70 2AS
☎01226 734222 Fax 01226 734438
Website www.local-books.com

Chairman *Sir Nicholas Hewitt*
Managing Director *Charles Hewitt*
Imprint Manager *Mike Parsons*

An imprint of **Pen & Sword Books Ltd**.
Wharncliffe is the book and magazine publishing arm of an old-established, independently

owned newspaper publishing and printing
house. *Publishes* local history throughout the
UK, focusing on nostalgia and old photographs. SERIES *Aspects*. No unsolicited mss;
synopsis and ideas welcome.
Royalties paid twice-yearly.

Which? Books/ Consumers' Association
2 Marylebone Road, London NW1 4DF
☎020 7830 6000 Fax 020 7830 7660
Website www.which.net

Director *Sheila McKechnie*
Head of Publishing *Gill Rowley*

FOUNDED 1957. Publishing arm of the
Consumers' Association, a registered charity.
Publishes non-fiction: information, reference
and how-to books on travel, gardening, health,
personal finance, consumer law, food, careers,
crafts, DIY. Titles must offer direct value or
utility to the UK consumer. 25–30 titles a year.
IMPRINT **Which? Books** *Gill Rowley* TITLES
*The Good Food Guide; The Good Skiing and
Snowboarding Guide; The Which? Hotel Guide;
The Which? Wine Guide; Wills and Probate; Be
Your Own Financial Adviser*. No unsolicited mss;
send synopsis and ideas only.
Royalties, if applicable, paid twice-yearly.

J. Whitaker & Sons Ltd
Endeavour House, 189 Shaftesbury Avenue,
London WC2H 8JT
☎020 7420 6000 Fax 020 7836 2909
Website www.whitaker.co.uk

Managing Director *Jonathan Nowell*

FOUNDED in 1858 by bookseller Joseph
Whitaker and remained independent until
acquired by BPI, American subsidiary of the
Dutch group VNU, in 1999. Published
Whitaker's Almanac from 1868 until the title
was sold to the Stationery Office in 1997.
Provides a range of services for the book trade
including the **ISBN Agency**, BookBank,
SourceData and Book Track. *Publishes* biblio-
graphic reference products. TITLES *Whitaker's
Books in Print; Information Age; Directory of
Publishers (The Red Book)*; and the journal of
the book trade, *The Bookseller*.

Whittet Books Ltd
Hill Farm, Stonham Road, Cotton,
Stowmarket, Suffolk IP14 4RQ
☎01449 781877 Fax 01449 781898
Email annabel@whittet.dircon.co.uk

Managing Director *Annabel Whittet*

Publishes natural history, pets, poultry, horses, domestic livestock, rural interest. Unsolicited mss, synopses and ideas for books welcome. *Royalties* paid twice-yearly.

Whurr Publishers Ltd

19B Compton Terrace, London N1 2UN
☎020 7359 5979 Fax 020 7226 5290
Email info@whurr.co.uk
Website www.whurr.co.uk
Chairman/Managing Director *Colin Whurr*
Approx. Annual Turnover £1 million

FOUNDED in 1987. *Publishes* speech and language therapy, nursing, psychology, psychotherapy, audiology, special education including dyslexia, ADHD, autism and Downs syndrome. No fiction and general trade books. 50 titles in 2000. Unsolicited mss, synopses and ideas welcome within their specialist fields only. 'Whurr Publishers believes authors can be best served by a small, specialised company' combining old-fashioned service with the latest publishing technology.
Royalties paid twice-yearly.

Wild Goose Publications

Iona Community, Unit 16, Six Harmony Row, Glasgow G51 3BA
☎0141 440 0985 Fax 0141 440 2338
Email alex.wildgoose@appleonline.net
Website www.iona.books.com
Editorial Head *Sandra Kramer*
Approx. Annual Turnover £200,000

The publications division of the Iona Community was ESTABLISHED in 1985 to publish topical books covering the teachings and ideals of the Community founded in 1938 by Lord Macleod. *Publishes* mind, body and spirit books, religious songbooks, meditations and music. 12 titles in 2000. TITLES *A Wee Worship Book; Protest for Peace; Dandelions and Thistles.* Unsolicited mss, synopses and ideas welcome; approach in writing in the first instance. No fiction.
Royalties paid twice-yearly.

Wiley Europe Ltd

Baffins Lane, Chichester, West Sussex PO19 1UD
☎01243 779777 Fax 01243 775878
Website www.wiley.co.uk
Managing Director *Dr John Jarvis*
Publishing Directors *Mike Davis, Stephen Smith*
Approx. Annual Turnover £57 million

FOUNDED 1807. US parent company. *Publishes* professional, reference trade and text books, scientific, technical and biomedical.

DIVISIONS
Architecture *Maggie Toy*; **Business** *Sarah Stevens*; **Business/Management** *Diane Taylor*; **Chemistry** *Helen McPherson*; **Computing** *Simon Plumtree*; **Earth Sciences** *Sally Wilkinson*; **Engineering** *Jan de Landtsheer*; **Medicine & Life Sciences** *Deborah Reece*; **Finance** *Sally Smith, Samantha Whittaker*; **HR/Marketing** *Claire Plimmer*; **Psychology** *Vivien Ward*; **Structural Engineering, Material Science & Physics** *David Hughes*; **Technology** *Ann-Marie Halligan*. Unsolicited mss welcome, as are synopses and ideas for books.
Royalties paid annually.

Authors' Rating When it comes to scientific, technical and medical books, Wiley is racing ahead. Last year it was the fastest growing professional and educational publisher. Academic authors are attracted by the American connection. Online publishing is set to increase.

Neil Wilson Publishing Ltd

Suite 303a, The Pentagon Centre, 36 Washington Street, Glasgow G3 8AZ
☎0141 221 1117 Fax 0141 221 5363
Email info@nwp.sol.co.uk
Website www.nwp.co.uk
Chairman *Gordon Campbell*
Managing Director/Editorial Director
 Neil Wilson
Approx. Annual Turnover £300,000

FOUNDED 1992. *Publishes* Scottish interest and history, biography, humour and hillwalking, whisky and beer; also cookery and Irish interest. About 10 titles a year. NWP manages the **11:9** fiction imprint for new Scottish writing, launched in 2000, which is financed under the New Directions Lottery fund, distributed by the Scottish Arts Council. In addition, three non-fiction IMPRINTS were launched in 2000: **The In Pinn** Outdoor pursuits; **The Angel's Share** Whisky, drink and food-related subjects; **The Vital Spark** Humour. Unsolicited mss, synopses and ideas welcome. No politics, academic or technical.
Royalties paid twice-yearly.

Philip Wilson Publishers Ltd

7 Deane House, 27 Greenwood Place, London NW5 1LB
☎020 7284 3088 Fax 020 7284 3099
Email pwilson@monoclick.to.uk

Chairman *Philip Wilson*

FOUNDED 1976. *Publishes* art, art history, antiques and collectables. 15 titles in 2000.

Windhorse Publications
11 Park Road, Moseley, Birmingham
B13 8AB
☎0121 449 9191 Fax 0121 449 9191
Email windhorse@compuserve.com
Chairman *Dharmashura*
Editorial Head *Jnanasiddhi*
Approx. Annual Turnover £250,000

FOUNDED 1977. *Publishes* meditation and Buddhism and biographies of Buddhists. Associated with the FWBO, a world-wide Buddhist movement. 10 titles in 2000. TITLES *Tales of Freedom; What is Sangha?; Meditating.* Unsolicited mss, synopses and ideas welcome; approach by letter or email in the first instance.
Royalties paid quarterly.

Windrow & Greene
See **Compendium Publishing Ltd**

Windsor Large Print
See **Chivers Press Ltd**

Wise Publications
See **Omnibus Press**

WIT Press
Ashurst Lodge, Ashurst, Southampton,
Hampshire SO40 7AA
☎023 8029 3223 Fax 023 8029 2853
Email marketing@witpress.com
Website www.witpress.com
Owner *Computational Mechanics International Ltd, Southampton*
Chairman *Professor C.A. Brebbia*
Managing Director/ Editorial Head *Lance Sucharov*

FOUNDED in 1980 as Computational Mechanics Publications to publish engineering analysis titles. Changed to WIT Press to reflect the increased range of publications. *Publishes* scientific and technical, mainly at postgraduate level and above, including architecture, environmental engineering, bioengineering. 50 titles in 2000. TITLES *The Revival of Dresden; Applied Virtual Instrumentation; Seismic Isolation; The Sustainable City: Urban Regeneration and Sustainability.* Unsolicited mss, synopses and ideas welcome; approach by post or email. No non-scientific or technical material or lower level (school- and college-level texts).

Royalties paid annually. *Overseas subsidiary* Computational Mechanics, Inc., Billerica, USA.

Woburn Press
See **Frank Cass & Co Ltd**

Oswald Wolff Books
See **Berg Publishers**

The Women's Press
34 Great Sutton Street, London EC1V 0LQ
☎020 7251 3007 Fax 020 7608 1938
Website www.the-womens-press.com
Managing Director *Elsbeth Lindner*
Approx. Annual Turnover £1 million

Part of the Namara Group. First title published in 1978. *Publishes* women only: quality fiction and non-fiction. Fiction usually has a female protagonist and a woman-centred theme. International writers and subject matter encouraged. Non-fiction: books for and about women generally; gender politics, race politics, disability, feminist theory, health and psychology, literary criticism. About 50 titles a year.

IMPRINTS
Women's Press Classics; **Livewire Books for Teenagers** Fiction and non-fiction series for young adults. Synopses and ideas for books welcome. No mss without previous letter, synopsis and sample material.
Royalties paid twice-yearly.

Authors' Rating Aims to move up the ranks of fiction publishers with at least one lead title each season.

Woodhead Publishing Ltd
Abington Hall, Abington, Cambridge
CB1 6AH
☎01223 891358 Fax 01223 893694
Email wp@woodhead-publishing.com
Website www.woodhead-publishing.com
Chairman *Alan Jessup*
Managing Director *Martin Woodhead*
Approx. Annual Turnover £1.3 million

FOUNDED 1989. *Publishes* engineering, materials technology, finance and investment, food technology, environmental science. TITLES *Welding International* (journal); *Reinforced Plastics Durability; Meat Science 6e; Base Metals Handbook; Foreign Exchange Options.* About 40 titles a year.

DIVISIONS
Woodhead Publishing *Martin Woodhead;*
Abington Publishing (in association with the

Welding Institute) *Patricia Morrison*. Unsolicited material welcome.
Royalties paid annually.

Wordsmill & Tate Publishers
88 Kingsway, Holborn, London WC2B 6AA
☎020 7841 2715 Fax 020 7841 1001
Email <name>@wordsmill.com
Website www.wordsmill.com
Commissioning Editor *Matthew Tate*
Editorial Coordinator *Jane Barrington*

New independent publisher *specialising* in hardback and paperback general fiction and non-fiction, biography, autobiography, memoirs, children's and history. No poetry, erotica or cookery. About 35–40 titles a year. Unsolicited material welcome with return postage. First time authors should send synopsis and sample chapters only.
Royalties paid twice-yearly.

Wordsworth Editions Ltd
Cumberland House, Crib Street, Ware, Hertfordshire SG12 9ET
☎01920 465167 Fax 01920 462267
Email enquiries@wordsworth-editions.com
Editorial Office: 6 London Street, London W2 1HL ☎020 7706 8822 Fax 020 7706 8833
Email laelia.hartnoll@wordsworth-editions.com
Directors *M.C.W. Trayler, E.G. Trayler*
Chief Editor *L.K. Hartnoll*
Approx. Annual Turnover £4 million

FOUNDED 1987. *Publishes* classics of English and world literature, reference books, poetry, children's classics, military history. Recently launched a new series of myth, legend and folklore books. About 75 titles a year. No unsolicited mss.

Writers and Readers Ltd
PO Box 29522, London N1 8FB
☎020 7226 2522 Fax 020 7359 1406
Email begin@writersandreaders.com
Website www.writersandreaders.com
Publisher *Glenn Thompson*

FOUNDED 1974. *Publishes* children's books, black history, documentary and comic books. 5 titles in 2000.
DIVISIONS **For Beginners**™ *Vastiana Belfon* TITLES *Philosophy for Beginners; Brecht for Beginners;* **Black Butterfly Children's Books** *Deborah Dyson* TITLE *Big Friend, Little Friend;* **Harlem River Press** *Deborah Dyson* TITLES *Revolutionary Suicide; Silent Terror.* No unsolicited mss; synopses and ideas welcome; approach by letter in the first instance. No poetry.
Royalties paid annually. *Overseas office* in New York.

X Libris
See **Little Brown & Co. (UK)**

The X Press
6 Hoxton Square, London N1 6NU
☎020 7729 1199 Fax 020 7729 1771
Email vibes@xpress.co.uk
Chairman *Dotun Adebayo*
Managing Director *Steve Pope*

LAUNCHED in 1992 with the cult bestseller *Yardie*, The X Press is the leading publisher of Black-interest fiction in the UK. Also *publishes* general fiction and children's fiction. 28 titles in 2000. IMPRINTS **The X Press** TITLES *Yardie; Baby Father;* **Nia** TITLE *In Search of Satisfaction;* **20/20** TITLE *Curvy Lovebox.* Send mss rather than synopses or ideas (enclose s.a.e.). No poetry.
Royalties paid annually.

Y Ddraig Fach
See **Ashley Drake Publishing Ltd**

Y Lolfa Cyf
Talybont, Ceredigion SY24 5AP
☎01970 832304 Fax 01970 832782
Email ylolfa@ylolfa.com
Website www.ylolfa.com/
Managing Director *Garmon Gruffudd*
General Editor *Lefi Gruffudd*
Approx. Annual Turnover £800,000

FOUNDED 1967. Small company which publishes mainly in Welsh; has its own four-colour printing and binding facilities. *Publishes* Welsh language publications; Celtic language tutors; English language books for the Welsh and Celtic tourist trade; nationalism and music. 33 titles in 2000. Expanding slowly. TITLES *My Kingdom of Books* Richard Booth; *The Welsh Learner's Dictionary* Heini Gruffudd; *The Fight for Welsh Freedom* Gwynfor Evans. Has recently launched the partly author-subsidised **Dinas** imprint for non-mainstream books of Welsh interest in English and Welsh. Write first with synopses or ideas.
Royalties paid twice-yearly.

Yale University Press (London)
23 Pond Street, London NW3 2PN
☎020 7431 4422 Fax 020 7431 3755
Managing Director/Editorial Director
John Nicoll

FOUNDED 1961. Owned by US parent company. *Publishes* academic and humanities. About 200 titles (worldwide) a year. Unsolicited mss and synopses welcome if within specialised subject areas.

Royalties paid annually.

Authors' Rating A publisher with a marvellous talent for turning out scholarly books which also appeal to the general reader. Academic writers who want to reach a wider audience should take note.

Roy Yates Books

Smallfields Cottage, Cox Green, Rudgwick, Horsham, West Sussex RH12 3DE
☎01403 822299 Fax 01403 823012

Chairman/Managing Director *Roy Yates*
Approx. Annual Turnover £120,000

FOUNDED 1990. *Publishes* children's books only. No unsolicited material as books are adaptations of existing popular classics suitable for translation into dual-language format.

Royalties paid quarterly.

Yellow Jersey

See **Random House Group Ltd**

Zastrugi Books

PO Box 2963, Brighton, East Sussex
BN1 6AW
☎01273 566369 Fax 01273 566369/562720

Chairman *Ken Singleton*

FOUNDED 1997. *Publishes* English-language teaching books only. No unsolicited mss; synopses and ideas for books welcome.

Royalties paid twice-yearly.

Zed Books Ltd

7 Cynthia Street, London N1 9JF
☎020 7837 4014 Fax 020 7833 3960
Email hosie@zedbooks.demon.co.uk
Website www.zedbooks.demon.co.uk

Approx. Annual Turnover £1 million

FOUNDED 1976. *Publishes* international and Third World affairs, development studies, women's studies, environmental studies, cultural studies and specific area studies. No fiction, children's or poetry. About 50 titles a year.

DIVISIONS **Development & Environment** *Robert Molteno*; **Women's Studies, Cultural Studies** *Louise Murray*. TITLES *The Development Dictionary* ed. Wolfgang Sachs; *Staying Alive* Vandana Shiva; *The Autobiography of Nawal* Nawal El Saadawi. No unsolicited mss; synopses and ideas welcome though.

Royalties paid annually.

Zero to Ten

See **Evans Brothers Ltd**

ZigZag Children's Books

See **Chrysalis Books Limited**

Aiming for the Top –
How to Write a Bestseller

Barry Turner

If it is true (and it probably is) that everyone has at least one good story in their mental kitbag, it follows that everyone has the potential for creating a bestseller. It helps to be able to string words into sentences, more so if the sentences hold together as a convincing narrative. But don't get hooked up on the question of writing skills at this early stage. It is the idea that counts. If the idea is strong enough, a one-page synopsis and a sample chapter can attract the mega money needed to launch a title into the sales stratosphere. The circumstances and timing have to be right. If a big publisher shows an interest in an idea, it is just possible that an even bigger publisher will want to get in on the act. If buying fever then takes hold, before long the bidders need calculators to count the number of zeros.

When a book idea is signed up for a large sum of money, it is in the interests of the publisher to do his damnedest to make his prediction of a bestseller come true. So, having beguiled an author with a large advance, the publisher goes on to spend vast amounts on marketing. The self-fulfilling prophecy then comes into play. An expensively packaged book has the best chance of becoming a bestseller.

It does not always work. There are many casualties along the way. John Lanchester was backed by Faber to the tune of £300,000 for two novels. When the first, *Mr Phillips*, came out last year, sales were less than 4,000 copies or what you might expect for a talented first-time writer launched on little more than a sales rep's recommendation. Little, Brown paid £250,000 for a novel called *Ladies' Man*. When last heard of, it had sold around 1,500 copies. After an indecently short interval, one young hopeful touted as a six-figure discovery was spotted queuing for her social security.

But the sob stories are the exceptions that prove the rule, as are those rarities, the bestsellers that no one planned for. In publishing a surprise is around every corner. Until recently it was widely assumed that what with computer games and wall-to-wall television, the children's book market had had its day. Then along came Harry Potter. Who would have thought that Stephen Hawking's *A Brief History of Time* would stay in the bestseller list for two years or Dava Sobel's *Longitude* would sell close on a million copies?

It was ever thus. Writing in the 1930s, Cyril Connolly mused on the unforeseen popularity of such books as *Brave New World* and *Goodbye Mr Chips*, which were expected to sell respectably but were never treated as bestsellers, least of all by their creators, before the floodgates opened. Hooked on literary mystique, Connolly tried to explain the phenomenon as a 'chemical combination of illusion and disillusion' which just shows what happens when a critic takes himself too seriously. It makes more sense to ignore the oddballs and to focus on the bestsellers that do seem to fit some sort of pattern.

Take the airport novel. The outlets in the airport shopping malls are among the most profitable in the country. A sample of airport bookshops suggests that close on half the sales are in the category of blockbuster fiction with authors such as John Grisham, Jilly Cooper, Stephen King, Patricia Cornwell, Wilbur Smith and Danielle Steel leading the race to the cash register. Hardly surprising when the customers in most need of diversion are mostly long-haul travellers or tourists heading for the beach. The novels with the strongest appeal offer a rattling good story populated by larger than life characters in exotic locations where they engage in plenty of action laced with sex, intrigue, corruption, treachery, betrayal and more sex. An eye-catching cover and a memorable title are essential features.

Never underestimate the appeal of a good story. It is easy to join with the darlings of the literary pages to sneer at the bestsellers. Anthony Burgess said it all for the elitists when he opined, 'The books that make the most money are those that lack style and subtlety and present a grossly over-simplified picture of life. Such books are poor art, and life is too short to bother with any art that is not the best of its kind.'

Writers on Writing

For a quick guide to the essentials of good writing, refer to masters of the craft. Evelyn Waugh identified three qualities:

- ☐ Lucidity – which can be acquired.
- ☐ Elegance – which you can strive all your life to achieve.
- ☐ Distinctive Voice – for which you can only pray.

To which George Orwell adds six practicalities:

- ☐ Never use a metaphor, simile or other figure of speech which you are used to seeing in print.
- ☐ Never use a long word when a short one will do.
- ☐ If it is possible to cut a word out, always cut it out.
- ☐ Never use the passive where you can use the active.
- ☐ Never use a foreign phrase, a scientific word or a jargon word if you can think of an everyday English equivalent.
- ☐ Break any of these rules sooner than say anything manifestly barbarous.

Orwell's last rule seems to endorse the view of those who hold that there are no rules. This is certainly the view of Hugh Leonard:

Writing is neither profession nor vocation but an incurable illness. Those who give up are not writers and never were. Those who persevere do so not from pluck or determination but because they cannot help it. They are sick and advice is an impudence.

But bestselling is not necessarily bad writing. Dickens, Conan Doyle, Trollope, Greene, Waugh, Wodehouse were all bestsellers in their time and have remained so, albeit buoyed up by exam syllabuses and TV adaptations. Of those featured in recent bestseller list, Sebastian Faulks, Nick Hornby, Minette Walters and Ian Rankin are among those who will long outlive their marketing hype.

Even so, the message for the newcomer is: keep it simple. Don't try too hard to impress the literary editors who, in any case, give more space to contentious books which allow for debate than to books with mass appeal.

A story line should be convertible to a one-paragraph summary. Originality is not the issue. Most plots are a rehash of what has gone before. What is important is the setting. The story must be of the moment. Spy thrillers were all the rage until the end of the Cold War. Then, suddenly, spies were out of fashion. Even writers of the quality of John le Carré had to work hard to reinvent themselves and hold on to their bestseller appeal.

Spot the trends. Peter Mayle scored a direct hit with *A Year in Provence* and its

---

Starting Points

1   Study the market. Read what has made other authors successful. What have they got that you may be missing?

2   Think ahead. Aim at what will interest readers of tomorrow. Many newcomers make the mistake of writing on subjects that were fashionable two years ago.

3   Learn the basics of story telling. Do you have a strong central character, a plot that zips along, is not too complex but keeps up the tension?

4   Write about what interests you. That is not the same as saying write about what you know. Research can compensate for lack of first-hand experience.

5   Think American. The American market is far larger than that of the UK. Also, most of the big publishers are American led. Whatever they say about the UK offshoots having total independence, the editors in London want to impress their masters with titles that have trans-Atlantic appeal.

6   Make it easy for a publisher or agent to make a judgement. All that is needed is a synopsis (two or three pages), sample chapters (in sequence), a letter of introduction saying who you are, what you do and whether you have been published before. Do not send a complete manuscript or add in compliments from friends and family (they are unreliable critics to put it mildly). Be professional. Typing and spelling mistakes suggest a sloppy writer. Single spacing may save paper but it is hell to read or annotate. Never e-mail. Have you seen what a manuscript can do to block up the technological works?

7   Go for it. The challenge is to persuade the movers and shakers in publishing that your idea is brighter than all the other ideas floating about. It is not enough to believe, others have to believe too, the more the merrier. Get out and sell. A retiring personality rarely if ever enters the ranks of bestsellerdom.

sequels because he published during a recession when his middle-class readers dreamed of escaping to an affordable Shangri-la. Mayle was repeating the success of a now forgotten author, Winifred Fortescue, who brought some cheer to the dismal 1930s with *Perfume from Provence* and other similarly wistful titles. Come the next dip in the economy, someone else will make a fortune writing about a far-off place where property is cheap and the good life is to be had on a modest income. New Zealand, perhaps?

Some types of book have a long running appeal. The Aga saga, novels of domestic upheaval in the shires epitomised by *The Rector's Wife* and other Joanna Trollope titles, have been popular for well over a decade and show no signs of losing their staying power.

Bestsellerdom is not limited to fiction. To return to the airport bookshops, recent money spinners have include *Georgiana, Duchess of Devonshire*, *Stalingrad* and Jeremy Paxman's *The English*, confirming the enduring appeal of biography, popular history and the famous name. *The English* would not have done so well if it had been written by Fred Nugget.

If the headlines are to be believed it is nearly always the fiction writers who make the big money. But it is not so. If J.K. Rowling is Britain's highest-paid woman by virtue of her Harry Potter books, the earnings of Delia Smith are not to be sniffed at. Her cookery titles are grossing around £10 million a year.

And what about J.M. Bond. You've heard of him, of course. No? Well, J.M. Bond is a best-selling author if ever there was one; thirty-six titles in print turning over in a good year up to a million in bookshop sales. J.M. Bond is the creator of such titles as *3rd Year Mathematics Assessment Papers*, a sequel to the equally gripping *2nd Year Mathematics Assessment Papers*. He is the living proof that there are many more ways than one of achieving bookshop stardom.

Making It into Film

For the author of a bestseller the money earned from bookshop sales is just the beginning. A hot literary property can be exploited in all sorts of profitable ways – film and TV adaptations, talking books, video, serialisations, book-club editions and computer games.

It is one of the ironies of publishing that while the decline, even the disappearance of the book is widely predicted by the promoters of rival media it is, increasingly, the book which provides them with their inspiration and raw material. The explanation is simple. The publication of a book is a relatively cheap method of testing the market. Think of it from the point of view of a Hollywood studio. The money paid for the film rights to a novel, though often gigantic in publishing terms, is as nothing compared to the cost of creating a screenplay from scratch. And with an original screenplay, who knows how it will turn out? If, on the other hand, a novel becomes a bestseller, it is a fair assumption that it will translate into a successful movie. *Captain Corelli's Mandolin, Chocolat, Angela's Ashes, Fever Pitch, Charlotte Gray, Birdsong* and *Longitude* have all followed this route.

A small army of specialist agents dedicate themselves to persuading producers that those who read the book will want to see the movie. It is not quite as easy as it sounds. For a start, the film and television industry attracts more con artists than an estate agents' convention. 'The only bounced cheques I have ever experienced in more than 30 years of rights selling have been from film or television companies,' says Carole Blake whose agency Blake Friedmann retains a media law firm to check for contractual loopholes. The complexity of the task hardly needs arguing when film contracts run to 50 pages or more.

Producers come in all guises. The independent with a shared desk in Wardour Street may have the backup of a major studio but then again he may simply be taking a chance on hitting the jackpot. An offer may come from an actor in chase of a meaty role or from a scriptwriter short on ideas of his own. As a general rule, an eagerness to produce is in inverse proportion to the capacity to deliver.

For the writer busy with his next masterpiece and innocent of the nefarious practices of media types, professional support is needed. That, or risking losing all. Rod Hall, whose eponymous agency specialises in the sale of film and television rights, claims to know 'most if not all of those hunting for material. We can even track the passing seasons with the progress of bright young things fresh from university to significant film and television producers'. It is more complicated in the States. 'There are just too many people involved. Pretty well every actor or director who is earning over a couple of million a picture now runs their own production company financed by a studio.'

The seven-figure deals that attract press headlines can often mislead. 'Outright payment for a property is very rare,' says Nick Marston of the agents Curtis Brown. In fact, he can think of only one recent example, *The Horse Whisperer*, where substantial money has been paid up front. 'A typical option, attracting an offer of £5,000 to £10,000 will be for twelve or eighteen months and is renewable, though after three years it is likely that the producer will have lost interest.' Moreover, only about one in ten options is exercised. Part of the problem is that it can take up to five years for a producer, director and stars to get their act together. In that time, interest may have shifted to the next hot property.

Even the success stories have their downside. Authors who sell out to the film industry must know that they have surrendered all proprietorial claims. Any resemblance between an original book and the screen adaptation will be entirely coincidental and there is nothing the author can do about it. Tom Clancy, whose box-office hits include *The Hunt for Red October* and *Patriot Games* compares selling film rights to pimping your daughter. A more optimistic view is taken by Nick Hornby whose novel *High Fidelity* hit the screen: 'The way I see it, selling the film rights to a book is a no-lose situation for a writer. Someone gives you money for work you have already done; if the film is bad, you will attract a few more readers, and if it is good (or, failing that, successful), chances are that your readership will increase.'

Add in a sizeable cheque and what more could an author want?

Irish Publishers

International Reply Coupons (IRCs)
For return postage, IRCs are required (*not* UK postage stamps). These are available from post offices: letters, 60 pence; mss according to weight.

An Gúm
Cúirt Fhreidric, Sr. Fhreidric Thuaidh, Baile Átha Cliath 1
☎00 353 1 889 2800 Fax 00 353 1 873 1140
Email gum@educ.irlgov.ie
Senior Editor *Seosamh Ó Murchú*
Editor *Antain Mag Shamhráin*
FOUNDED 1926. Formerly the Irish language publications branch of the Department of Education and Science. Has now become part of the North/South Language Body established under the Good Friday Agreement to provide general reading, textbooks and dictionaries in the Irish language. *Publishes* educational, children's, music, lexicography and general. Little fiction or poetry. About 50 titles a year. Unsolicited mss, synopses and ideas for books welcome. Also welcomes reading copies of first and second level school textbooks with a view to translating them into the Irish language.
Royalties paid annually.

Anvil Books
45 Palmerston Road, Dublin 6
☎00 353 1 497 3628 Fax 00 353 1 496 8263
Managing Director *Rena Dardis*
FOUNDED 1964 with emphasis on Irish history and biography. Expansion of the list followed to include more general interest Irish material and in 1982 The Children's Press was established. *Publishes* Irish history, biography (particularly 1916–22), folklore and children's fiction (for ages 9–14). No adult fiction, poetry, fantasy, short stories or illustrated books for children under 9. About 7 titles a year. 'Because of promotional requirements, only books by Irish-based authors considered and only books of Irish interest.' Send synopsis only with IRCs (no UK stamps); unsolicited mss not returned.
Royalties paid annually.

Ashfield Press
See **Blackhall Publishing**

Attic Press Ltd
c/o Cork University Press, Crawford Business Park, Crosses Green, Cork
☎00 353 21 432 1725
Fax 00 353 21 431 5329
Email s.wilbourne@ucc.ie
Website www.iol.ie/~atticirl/
Publisher *Sara Wilbourne*
FOUNDED 1988. Began life in 1984 as a forum for information on the Irish feminist movement. *Publishes* teenage fiction, and non-fiction (history, women's studies, politics, biography). About 10 titles a year. Does not accept unsolicited proposals in adult fiction.
Royalties paid twice-yearly.

Blackhall Publishing
8 Priory Hall, Stillorgan, Co. Dublin
☎00 353 1 278 5090 Fax 00 353 1 278 4446
Email blackhall@tinet.ie
Website www.blackhallpublishing.com
Managing Director *Gerard O'Connor*
Commissioning Editor *Ruth Garvey*
Publishes business, management and law books. Main subject areas include accounting, finance, management, marketing and law books aimed at both students and professionals in the industry. TITLES *Effective Top Team Management Teams*; *Brandwatching*; *Adwatching*; *Individuals and Enterprise*; *Customer Friendly – Design Guidelines for ECommerce* (available as an e-book). IMPRINTS **Ashfield Press** Irish-interest books, both fiction and non-fiction. TITLES *Music for Middlebrows*; *The Brothers Behan*. **Inns Quay** TITLE *Irish Business Law*. Unsolicited mss and synopses welcome.
Royalties paid annually.

Blackwater Press
c/o Folens Publishers, Hibernian Industrial Estate, Greenhills Road, Tallaght, Dublin 24
☎00 353 1 413 7200 Fax 00 353 1 413 7280
Email john.o'connor@folens.ie
Chief Executive *Dirk Folens*

Managing Director *John O'Connor*

Part of Folens Publishers. *Publishes* political, sports, fiction (*Margaret Burns*) and children's (*Deidre Whelan*). 84 titles in 2000.

Bradshaw Books

Tigh Filí, Thompson House, MacCurtain Street, Cork
☎00 353 21 450 9274
Fax 00 353 21 455 1617
Email admin@cwpc.ie
Website www.tighfili.com
Managing Director *Maire Bradshaw*
Literature Office *Liz Willows*

FOUNDED 1985. *Publishes* poetry, short stories, women's issues, spiritual, children's books. 6 titles in 2000. SERIES *Cork Literary Review; Eurochild; Millennium Poets*. Submit letter, synopsis, sample chapters and s.a.e.
Royalties not generally paid.

Brandon/Mount Eagle

Dingle, Co. Kerry
☎00 353 66 915 1463
Fax 00 353 66 915 1234

Publisher *Steve MacDonogh*
Approx. Annual Turnover £350,000

FOUNDED in 1997. *Publishes* strong Irish fiction and some non-fiction. About 15 titles a year. Not seeking unsolicited mss.

Edmund Burke Publisher

Cloonagashel, 27 Priory Drive, Blackrock, Co. Dublin
☎00 353 1 288 2159 Fax 00 353 1 283 4080
Email deburca@indigo.ie
Website www.deburcararebooks.com

Chairman *Eamonn De Búrca*
Approx. Annual Turnover £250,000

Small family-run business publishing historical and topographical and fine limited-edition books relating to Ireland. TITLES *History of the County of Mayo* Knox; *King Charles II Irish Army List* Dalton; *History of Dun Laoghaire Harbour* De Courcy Ireland; *Great Book of Irish Genealogies* 5 Vols.; *Irish Flower Garden Replanted* Nelson and Walsh; *The Three Candles, a Bibliographical Catalogue* de Búrca. Unsolicited mss welcome. No synopses or ideas.
Royalties paid annually.

Butterworth Ireland Limited

26 Upper Ormond Quay, Dublin 7
☎00 353 1 872 8514 (Law)/8524 (Tax)
Fax 00 353 1 873 1378

Chairman *S. Stout (UK)*
Tax Editor – Managing *Susan Keegan*
Legal Editor – Managing *Louise Leavy*
List Development Editor – Tax *David Hession*
List Development Editor – Law *Ciara Fitzpatrick*

Subsidiary of Butterworth & Co. Publishers, London, (**Reed Elsevier** is the holding company). Leading publisher of Irish law and tax titles. *Publishes* solely law and tax books. 22 titles in 2000. Unsolicited mss, synopses and ideas welcome for titles within the broadest parameters of tax and law.
Royalties paid twice-yearly.

The Children's Press

See **Anvil Books**

The Chronicle of Ireland

PO Box 3847, Foxrock, Dublin 18
☎00 353 1 235 2657 Fax 00 353 1 285 0157
Email natcollom@aol.com
Managing Editor *Harry Walsh*

Publishes the Chronicle of Ireland series, a two-volume annual review of the coverage by the main national media of the political, commercial and social developments in Ireland, North and South. IMPRINT **"G" Gulliver Book**.

Cló Iar-Chonnachta

Indreabhán, Connemara, Galway
☎00 353 91 593307 Fax 00 353 91 593362
Website www.cic.ie
Chairman/Director *Micheál Ó Conghaile*
Editor *Róisín Ní Mhianáin*
Approx. Annual Turnover 250,000

FOUNDED 1985. *Publishes* fiction, poetry, plays and children's, mostly in Irish, including translations. Also publishes cassettes of writers reading from their own works. 12 titles in 2000. TITLES *Sna Fir* Micheál ó Conghaile; *Breandán Ó hEithir, Iomramh Aonair* Liam Mac Con Iomaire; *The Village Sings* Gabriel Fitzmaurice; *Out in the Open* Cathal ó Searcaigh.
Royalties paid annually.

The Columba Press

55A Spruce Avenue, Stillorgan Industrial Park, Blackrock, Co. Dublin
☎00 353 1 294 2556 Fax 00 353 1 294 2564
Email sean@columba.ie (editorial) *or*
info@columba.ie (general)
Website www.columba.ie

Chairman *Neil Kluepfel*
Managing Director *Seán O'Boyle*

Approx. Annual Turnover £800,000

FOUNDED 1985. Small company committed to growth. *Publishes* religious and counselling titles. 30 titles in 2000. (Backlist of 225 titles.) TITLES *Cardinal Thomas Winning: An authorised biography* Vivienne Belton; *Where Three Streams Meet: Celtic Spirituality* Seán Ó Duinn, OSB. Unsolicited ideas and synopses rather than full mss preferred.

Royalties paid twice-yearly.

Cork University Press

Crawford Business Park, Crosses Green, Cork, Co. Cork
☎00 353 21 490 2980   Fax 00 353 21 431 5329
Email corkunip@ucc.ie
Website www.corkuniversitypress.com
Publisher *Sara Wilbourne*
Editor *Caroline Somers*

FOUNDED 1925. Relaunched in 1992, the Press *publishes* academic and some trade titles. 26 titles in 2000. Two journals, *Irish Review* (bi-annual), an interdisciplinary cultural review, and *The Irish Journal of Feminist Studies* (bi-annual), are now part of the list. Unsolicited synopses and ideas welcome for textbooks, academic monographs, belles lettres, illustrated histories and journals.

Royalties paid twice-yearly.

CJ Fallon Limited

Lucan Road, Palmerstown, Dublin 20
☎00 353 1 616 6400   Fax 00 353 1 616 6499
Email editorial@cjfallon.ie
Website www.cjfallon.ie
Owner *Adare Printing Group*
Managing Director *Henry McNicholas*
Editorial Head *Niall White*

FOUNDED 1927. Educational publishers for first and second level schools in Ireland. Unsolicited mss, synopses and ideas welcome; approach in writing in the first instance. No non-educational material considered.

Royalties paid annually.

Flyleaf Press

4 Spencer Villas, Glenageary, Co. Dublin
☎00 353 1 280 6228   Fax 00 353 1 283 1693
Email Flyleaf@indigo.ie
Website www.flyleaf.ie
Managing Director *Dr James Ryan*

FOUNDED 1981 to publish natural history titles. Now concentrating on family history and Irish history as a background to family history. No fiction. TITLES *Irish Records; Longford and its People; Tracing Your Kerry Ancestors; Tracing Your Dublin Ancestors.* Unsolicited mss, synopses and ideas for books welcome.

Royalties paid twice-yearly.

Four Courts Press Ltd

Fumbally Lane, Dublin 8
☎00 353 1 453 4668   Fax 00 353 1 453 4672
Email info@four-courts-press.ie
Website www.four-courts-press.ie
Chairman/Managing Director *Michael Adams*
Director *Martin Healy*

FOUNDED 1972. *Publishes* mainly scholarly books in the humanities. About 60 titles a year. Synopses and ideas for books welcome.

Royalties paid annually.

Gateway

See **Gill & Macmillan**

Gill & Macmillan

10 Hume Avenue, Park West, Dublin 12
☎00 353 1 500 9500   Fax 00 353 1 500 9599
Website www.gillmacmillan.ie
Managing Director *M.H. Gill*
Approx. Annual Turnover £7 million

FOUNDED 1968 when M.H. Gill & Son Ltd and Macmillan Ltd formed a jointly owned publishing company. *Publishes* biography/autobiography, history, current affairs, literary criticism (all mainly of Irish interest), guidebooks, cookery. Also educational textbooks for secondary and tertiary levels. About 100 titles a year. Contacts: *Hubert Mahony* (educational); *Fergal Tobin* (general); *Ailbhe O'Reilly* (tertiary textbooks). IMPRINTS **Newleaf** *Eveleen Coyle* Popular health, psychology, mind, body and spirit; **Gateway** Spirituality, cosmic issues, environment, alternative science. Unsolicited synopses and ideas welcome. Not interested in fiction or poetry.

Royalties paid subject to contract.

Goldcrest

See **Poolbeg Press Ltd**

Inns Quay

See **Blackhall Publishing**

Institute of Public Administration

57–61 Lansdowne Road, Dublin 4
☎00 353 1 269 7011   Fax 00 353 1 269 8644
Email Sales@ipa.ie
Website www.ipa.ie
Chairman *Paddy Donnelly*
Director-General *John Gallagher*

Publisher *Tony McNamara*
Approx. Annual Turnover £600,000

FOUNDED 1957 by a group of public servants, the Institute of Public Administration is the Irish public sector management development agency. The publishing arm of the organisation is one of its major activities. *Publishes* academic and professional books and periodicals: history, law, politics, economics and Irish public administration for students and practitioners. 10 titles and 2 reprints in 2000. TITLES *Administration Yearbook & Diary; Sources of Economic Information; A New Partnership in Education; A Vital National Interest: Ireland in Europe 1973–98*. No unsolicited mss; synopses and ideas welcome. No fiction or children's publishing.
Royalties paid annually.

Irish Academic Press Ltd

44 Northumberland Road, Ballsbridge, Dublin 4
☎00 353 1 668 8244 Fax 00 353 1 660 1610
Email info@iap.ie Website www.iap.ie
Chairman *Frank Cass* (London)
Managing Editor *Linda Longmore*
Approx. Annual Turnover £250,000

FOUNDED 1974. *Publishes* academic monographs and humanities. 17 titles in 2000. Unsolicited mss, synopses and ideas welcome.
Royalties paid annually.

Irish Management Institute

Sandyford Road, Dublin 16
☎00 353 1 207 8400 Fax 00 353 1 295 5150
Email bill.carroll@imi.ie
Website www.imi.ie
Chief Executive *Barry Kenny*
Approx. Annual Turnover £10 million

FOUNDED 1952. The Institute, owned by its members, both corporate and individual, works to improve the practice of management. Offers managers a wide range of management development services. *Publishes* a newsletter, *Management Focus* on a bi-monthly basis, distributed to members. Other publications include periodic economic reports and management research and texts. Mss, synopses and ideas relevant to Irish management practice welcome.
Royalties paid annually.

The Lilliput Press

62–63 Sitric Road, Arbour Hill, Dublin 7
☎00 353 1 671 1647 Fax 00 353 1 671 1233
Email info@lilliputpress.ie
Website www.lilliputpress.ie

Chairman *Kathy Gilfillan*
Managing Director *Antony Farrell*
Approx. Annual Turnover £200,000

FOUNDED 1984. *Publishes* non-fiction: literature, history, autobiography and biography, ecology, essays; criticism; fiction and poetry. About 20 titles a year. TITLES *Ulysses: The Dublin Edition; The Growth Illusion* (ecology); *Gander at the Gate* (autobiography); *Nature in Ireland; Visiting Rwanda; Hugh Lane 1875–1915* (biography); *Malinski* (fiction); *The Aran Islands* (photography). Unsolicited mss, synopses and ideas welcome. No children's or sport titles.
Royalties paid annually.

Marino Books
See **Mercier Press Ltd**

Mercier Press Ltd

5 French Church Street, Cork
☎00 353 21 427 5040
Fax 00 353 21 427 4969
Email books@mercier.ie
Website www.mercier.ie
Also at: 16 Hume Street, Dublin 2
☎00 353 1 661 5299 Fax 00 353 1 661 8583
Email books@marino.ie
Chairman *George Eaton*
Managing Director *John F. Spillane*

FOUNDED 1944. One of Ireland's largest publishers with a list of approx 250 Irish interest titles. IMPRINTS **Mercier Press** *Mary Feehan* Children's, politics, history, mind, body, spirit. **Marino Books** *Jo O'Donoghue* Fiction, current affairs, women's interest. TITLES *The Course of Irish History;* all of John B. Keane's works; *Mortally Wounded; Real Cool; The Celtic Tiger: The Inside Story of Ireland's Boom Economy.* Unsolicited mss, synopses and ideas welcome.
Royalties paid annually.

Mount Eagle
See **Brandon/Mount Eagle**

Newleaf
See **Gill & Macmillan**

The O'Brien Press Ltd

20 Victoria Road, Rathgar, Dublin 6
☎00 353 1 492 3333 Fax 00 353 1 492 2777
Email books@obrien.ie
Website www.obrien.ie
Managing Director/Publisher *Michael O'Brien*
Editorial Director *Íde Ní Laoghaire*

FOUNDED 1974 to publish biography and books

on the environment. Also *publishes* business, adult fiction, crime, popular biography, music and travel. In recent years the company has become a substantial force in children's publishing, concentrating mainly on juvenile novels. No poetry or academic. About 40 titles a year. TITLES *The Black Widow* Niamh O'Connor; *Joey Dunlop, King of the Roads* Stephen Davison; *The Power Game: Fianna Fail Since Lemass* Stephen Collins. Unsolicited mss (with return postage enclosed), synopses and ideas for books welcome.

Royalties paid annually.

Oak Tree Press
Merrion Building, Lower Merrion Street, Dublin 2
☎00 353 1 676 1600   Fax 00 353 1 676 1644
Email oaktreep@iol.ie
Website www.oaktreepress.com
Managing Director *Brian O'Kane*

FOUNDED 1992. Specialist publisher of business and professional books: accounting, finance, management and law, aimed at students and practitioners in Ireland, the UK and USA. About 30 titles a year. TITLES *Being Irish; Coaching for Growth; The Kerry Way; Networking for Success; Greatest Irish Americans of the 20th Century*. Unsolicited mss and synopses welcome; send to *David Givens*, General Manager, at the address above.

Royalties paid twice-yearly.

On Stream Publications Ltd
Cloghroe, Blarney, Co. Cork
☎00 353 21 385798   Fax 00 353 21 385798
Email info@onstream.ie
Website www.onstream.ie
Chairman/Managing Director *Roz Crowley*
Approx. Annual Turnover £200,000

FOUNDED 1992. Formerly Forum Publications. *Publishes* academic, fiction, cookery, wine, general health and fitness, local history, railways, photography and practical guides. About 6 titles a year. TITLES *Keeping Resources Human – A Practical Guide to Retaining Staff; The Book of Scarves: 100 Ideas; Dealing With Chronic Pain; A Pinch of This – Tastes of Home-Cooking*. Synopses and ideas welcome. No children's books.

Royalties paid annually.

Poolbeg Press Ltd
123 Baldoyle Industrial Estate, Baldoyle, Dublin 13
☎00 353 1 832 1477   Fax 00 353 1 832 1430
Email poolbeg@poolbeg.com

Website www.poolbeg.com
Publisher *Paula Campbell*

FOUNDED 1976 to publish the Irish short story and has since diversified to include all areas of fiction (literary and popular), children's fiction and non-fiction, and adult non-fiction: history, biography and topics of public interest. About 70 titles a year. Unsolicited mss, synopses and ideas welcome (mss preferred). No drama.

IMPRINTS **Poolbeg** (paperback and hardback); **Children's Poolbeg**; **Goldcrest**; **Wren**.

Royalties paid twice-yearly.

Real Ireland Design Ltd
27 Beechwood Close, Boghall Road, Bray, Co. Wicklow
☎00 353 1 286 0799   Fax 00 353 1 282 9962
Managing Director *Desmond Leonard*

Producers of calendars, diaries, posters, greetings cards and books, servicing the Irish tourist industry. *Publishes* photography and tourism. About 2 titles a year. No fiction. Unsolicited mss, synopses and ideas welcome.

Royalties paid twice-yearly.

Royal Dublin Society
Science Section, Ballsbridge, Dublin 4
☎00 353 1 668 0866   Fax 00 353 1 660 4014
Email carol.power@rds.ie
Website www.rds.ie
President *Col. W.A. Ringrose*

FOUNDED 1731 for the promotion of agriculture, science and the arts, and throughout its history has published books and journals towards this end. *Publishes* conference proceedings, biology and the history of Irish science. TITLES *Agricultural Development for the 21st Century; The Right Trees in the Right Places; Agriculture & the Environment; Water of Life; Science, Technology & Realism; Science Centres for Ireland; Blueprint for a National Irish Science Centre; Science Education in Crisis*; occasional papers in *Irish Science & Technology* series.

Royalties not generally paid.

Royal Irish Academy
19 Dawson Street, Dublin 2
☎00 353 1 676 2570   Fax 00 353 1 676 2346
Executive Secretary *Patrick Buckley*
Editor of Publications *Rachel McNicholls*
Approx. Annual Turnover (publication sales) £100,000

FOUNDED in 1785, the Academy has been publishing since 1787. Core publications are jour-

nals but more books published in last 14 years. *Publishes* academic, Irish interest and Irish language. About 7 titles a year. Welcomes mss, synopses and ideas of an academic standard.
Royalties paid annually, where applicable.

Salmon Publishing Ltd
Knockeven, Cliffs of Moher, Co. Clare
☎00 353 65 708 1941
Fax 00 353 65 708 1621
Email salpub@iol.ie
Website www.salmonpoetry.com
Managing Director *Jessie Lendennie*
Approx. Annual Turnover £100,000

FOUNDED 1982. *Publishes* contemporary Irish and international poetry. 11 titles in 2000. TITLES *The White Page/An Bhileog Bhán: Twentieth Century Irish Women Poets* ed. Joan McBreen; *The Portable Creative Writing Workshop* Pat Boran; *Story Hunger* Jerah Chadwick; *A Curb in Eden* Joseph Enweiler; *Split the Lark: Selected Poems* R.T. Smith. Query letter before submission of material.
Royalties paid twice-yearly.

Simon & Schuster
See **Town House and Country House**

Sitric Books
62–63 Sitric Road, Arbour Hill, Dublin 7
☎00 353 1 671 1682 Fax 00 353 1 671 1233
Chair *Vivienne Guinness*
Managing Director *Antony Farrell*

FOUNDED 2000. *Publishes* current affairs, biography and fiction. About 5 titles a year. TITLES *Diary of a Teddy Boy; The Beat; Promises to Keep: A woman's medical nightmare and her husband's search for the truth; She Moves Through the Boom.* Unsolicited mss, synopses and ideas welcome. No children's or sports titles.
Royalties paid annually.

Tír Eolas
Newtownlynch, Doorus, Kinvara,
Co. Galway
☎00 353 91 637452 Fax 00 353 91 637452
Publisher/Managing Director *Anne Korff*
Approx. Annual Turnover £50,000

FOUNDED 1987. *Publishes* books and guides on ecology, archaeology, folklore and culture. TITLES *The Shannon Floodlands; Not a Word of a Lie; The Book of Aran; Women of Ireland, A Biographic Dictionary; Kinvara, A Seaport Town on Galway Bay; A Burren Journal; The Shores of Connemara.* Unsolicited mss, synopses and ideas

for books welcome. No specialist scientific and technical, fiction, plays, school textbooks or philosophy.
Royalties paid annually.

Town House and Country House
Trinity House, Charleston Road, Ranelagh, Dublin 6
☎00 353 1 497 2399 Fax 00 353 1 497 0927
Email books@townhouse.ie
Managing Director *Treasa Coady*

FOUNDED 1980. *Publishes* commercial fiction, art and archaeology, biography and environment. About 20 titles a year. TITLES *Love Like Hate Adore* Deirdre Purcell; *Mary, Mary* Julie Parsons; *Now is the Time* Sr. Stanislaus Kennedy; *Wild Wicklow* Richard Nairn and Miriam Crowley. IMPRINT **Simon & Schuster**. Unsolicited mss, synopses and ideas welcome. No children's books.
Royalties paid twice-yearly.

Veritas Publications
7–8 Lower Abbey Street, Dublin 1
☎00 353 1 878 8177 Fax 00 353 1 878 6507
Email publications@veritas.ie
Director *Maura Hyland*

FOUNDED 1969 to supply religious textbooks to schools and later introduced a more general religious list. Part of the Catholic Communications Institute. *Publishes* religious books only. About 30 titles a year. Unsolicited mss, synopses and ideas for books welcome.
Royalties paid annually.

Wolfhound Press
68 Mountjoy Square, Dublin 1
☎00 353 1 874 0354 Fax 00 353 1 872 0207
Website www.wolfhound.ie *or*
www.drumshee.com
Managing Director *Seamus Cashman*

FOUNDED 1974. Member of **Clé** - the Irish Book Publishers Association. *Publishes* art, biography, children's, fiction, general non-fiction, history, photography, literature, literary studies, audio and gift books. About 30 titles a year (mainly Irish interest). TITLES *Famine; Celtic Fury; Talking to God; Eye Witness Bloody Sunday; Father Brown's Titanic Album.* Unsolicited mss (with synopses and s.a.e.) and ideas welcome but by post only.
Royalties paid annually.

Wren
See **Poolbeg Press Ltd**

Irish Literary Agents

The Book Bureau Literary Agency
1st Floor, 4 Great Strand Street, Dublin 1
☎00 353 1 667 0528   Fax 00 353 1 661 1973
Contact *Geraldine Nichol*

Handles mainstream adult and literary fiction. 'Strong editorial support before submission to publishers.' Send preliminary letter, synopsis and first five chapters; return postage/IRCs essential. *Commission* Home 10%; Overseas 20%. Works with foreign associates.

The Lisa Richards Agency
46 Upper Baggot Street, Dublin 4
☎00 353 1 660 3534   Fax 00 353 1 660 3545
Email fogrady@eircom.net
Contact *Faith O'Grady*

FOUNDED 1998. *Handles* commercial and literary fiction, thrillers, non-fiction, children's books; TV, film, radio and theatre scripts. No science fiction. Approach with 3–4 chapters and a synopsis of the rest. No reading fee. CLIENTS Colm Keena, Pauline McLynn, David O'Doherty, S. O'Donovan, Martin Malone.

Commission Home 10%; UK 15%; US & Translation 20%. *Overseas associate* **The Marsh Agency** for translation rights.

Jonathan Williams Literary Agency
Ferrybank House, 6 Park Road, Dun Laoghaire, Co. Dublin
☎00 353 1 280 3482   Fax 00 353 1 280 3482
Contact *Jonathan Williams*

FOUNDED 1980. *Handles* general trade books: fiction, auto/biography, travel, politics, history, music, literature and criticism, gardening, cookery, sport and leisure, humour, reference, social questions, photography. Some poetry, business and children's, but less of a speciality. No plays, science fiction, mind, body and spirit, computer books, theology, multimedia, motoring, aviation. No reading fee unless 'the author wants a very fast opinion'. Initial approach by phone or letter. *Commission* Home 10%; US 15%; Translation 15%. *Overseas associates* Borderline Literary Agency, Italy; Lora Fountain Agency, France; Jan Michael, The Netherlands.

Taking Off: A Writer's Diary

Bob G. Ritchie

January

Hope this year starts as well as last year ended. In November the *Guardian* bought my article. Only the utmost self-control stopped me screaming in the street. It prompted a flurry of half-baked ideas for yet more articles, most of which I fortunately kept to myself. Predictably, the few I allowed to see the light of day were speedily turned down. Quite what possessed me to think of myself as a feature writer I've no idea.

When I finally decided to make a serious attempt at becoming a full-time writer I knew exactly what I wanted to write and why. Thirty-five years ago my sister died and I had to exorcise her ghost. So I start the new year in earnest by resuming the radio play I've been writing based on her life. Feel very pleased with the idea of it being played out entirely in the head of a middle-aged British businessman trapped beneath the rubble of the Kobe earthquake and show it to a couple of friends who profess themselves 'very moved'.

Two days after I send the final script to the BBC I read in Shaun McLaughlin's *Writing for Radio* '. . . often the reason for writing is a form of personal catharsis and therapy, but . . . many of these plays do very little to inform or to heal the listener . . .' With a sinking heart I realise exactly what I got wrong. Immediately feel like calling the BBC and asking for the play back.

February

Decide radio drama is not for me. Write five short stories in as many days and run them past a few friends and acquaintances, an exercise that ends with them all in complete disagreement. In desperation I send the most romantic to a women's magazine. It comes back within a couple of weeks with the suggestion that I send for their contributor guidelines.

Personally I prefer the one about a couple whose abortive participation in a TV game show ends in murder, but being so obviously written to be read aloud I can see it sitting at the BBC for the next six months. I'm also fond of the one inspired by a photo taken from Bobby Kennedy's funeral train, but by the time it's finished, it runs to over 10,000 words. Who publishes stories that long?

I decide the short story exercise was exactly that: an exercise.

A little scene pops into my head while sitting in a traffic jam. School gate with lots of children being collected by their mothers; suddenly Ferrari screeches to a halt and out stumbles a beautiful blonde in sunglasses; mothers and children gape; she calls to two of the children but they don't recognise her; she tears off her sunglasses and blonde wig: 'It's me, mum!' Her children tumble into the car and it roars off. Feels like a scene from a TV caper. Why is she in disguise? Where did she get the car? Why is she in such a hurry?

Resume The Novel. Something I've been working on spasmodically for the last two or three years. A friend e-mails me after reading the first draft: 'have some good news and some bad: I think you have something here, but it needs completely rewriting', and suggests I expand the last thirty pages to more than a hundred and move the main revelation from the end of the book to the middle. Oh, is that all?

March

Receive a cheque for £200 from the *Guardian*, almost five months after publication. Reminds me of Robert Benchley's definition of a freelance writer: someone who is paid per piece or per word or perhaps. Still, at least it's something to put on the tax return.

Getting thoroughly into The Novel. My social life is fast disappearing. The Novel is set in both England and the US and I could definitely do with an English English–US English dictionary, but am amazed to discover such a thing doesn't seem to exist. The best I can find is a USA phrasebook produced by Lonely Planet, which tells me among other useful stuff that chewed fine with breath is a hamburger with onions. I start my own list and make a note to tell OUP there's a gap in the market.

Continue to accumulate other reference books including, from my late father's library, a classical dictionary dated 1834 which tells me the world was created in 4004BC and that the festival of the goddess Anaitis was concluded by 'scenes of the greatest lasciviousness and intemperance'. Bit like *Emmerdale*, then. Just in case I end up writing for *Casualty*, I also acquire a medical dictionary, which Celia Brayfield's *How to Write a Bestseller* insists is essential. However, though these tomes now line up before me like a Hadrian's Wall of knowledge keeping out the pagan hordes of ignorance, I confess I use them little. I am not, after all, trying to write documentaries. If I need a choral society to exist in a suburb of Boston I'll make one up. It's enough that it's a reasonable assumption; I'm not going to spend half a day trying to find out what the real one's called.

Radio play comes back – predictably – and with no more than the standard rejection letter. Doesn't hurt too much. That's the advantage of a long gap between submission and response: you move on.

April

Finally become a serious writer: I delete the games from my computer.

Take a break from The Novel; with only two weeks to the deadline I decide to enter the BBC Talent competition and blow the dust off the first draft for a sitcom pilot I wrote three years ago. On a first read through I actually laugh out loud two or three times, which must be a good sign. But by the tenth rewrite I fail to find a single line even faintly amusing. Maybe I've lost my sense of humour.

Back to The Novel, but keep getting distracted by ideas for other novels, as if there's some sort of unstoppable cancerous reproductive process going on inside my brain. Sometimes they come almost as fully formed stories, sometimes merely as snatches of dialogue, scenes, vague images. Dutifully I scribble them into my ideas file. It depresses me that the vast majority will never be used. I only hope that when the time comes I can pick out the ones 'with legs', as they say in Hollywood.

May

Complete the final draft of The Novel. I go over and over the first chapter, then send it and a synopsis to the few publishers I think will be interested. Spend two days on the covering letter, trying to make my writing experience sound more substantial than it really is without actually lying. Then go out and get thoroughly pissed. Feel as if I have been living down a mine for the last four months.

June

Decide that the woman in the Ferrari has inadvertently run off with the proceeds of a bank robbery.

Have clever idea for another radio play. Man comes up with completely incontrovertible proof of the existence of God. Twist is that God doesn't want to be considered merely a fact of life, like the sun coming up; he'd much rather be believed in and worshipped. So he suppresses the proof. Feel certain this will appeal enormously to typical fifty-five-year-old female afternoon Radio 4 listener.

First rejections of The Novel arrive. Most are standard letters, a few more encouraging. Overall opinion seems to be against the story itself rather than the way I tell it. One publisher rejects it on the grounds that they only accept books of a minimum length. An odd criterion. James Thurber said writers are of two kinds, the takers out and the putters in. Always worried I was one of the latter. Now panic I'm too much of the former. I cheer myself up by focusing on the occasional flattering words and ignoring the rest: 'impressive story', 'very well written', 'an authentic feeling', 'cleverly executed', 'entirely promising'. But sometimes feel it would be less cruel to be told straight out to take up accountancy.

Keep coming across stories in the press about twenty-five-year-old girls getting six figure advances for novels about twenty-five-year-old girls. I console myself with the thought that publishing is subject to fashion just like everything else. Publishers always know exactly what they want, something entirely original yet exactly the same as last year's hit. In other words just what William Goldman said of Hollywood: no one knows anything.

July

A publisher likes The Novel! Aren't publishers wonderful? And it's one of the big ones! Only a handwritten note on a compliments slip asking to see the rest of it, but quite enough to persuade me to spend the entire day calling friends and casually dropping it into the conversation.

The next morning – nursing a hangover – I start reading it through to check for typos and realise within a couple of hours that it is truly, heart-sinkingly, mind-numbingly dreadful. Feel close to tears. I've spent months on it, almost shut myself away from human contact. Can't face yet another rewrite.

August
Continue rewriting The Novel.

September
The sit com comes back. I'd forgotten all about it. Got a long letter from BBC Talent explaining how it had passed two selection stages and reached the final ninety scripts out of over five thousand and would I please send them anything else I write? I call the BBC for more feedback and have a nice chat with a charming lady who promises to send me their readers' comments. I decide to rewrite it anyway and try the independent TV production companies. Maybe sit com is what I'm good at.

Radio play about God comes back, but also with encouraging words. They 'really enjoyed' it, I demonstrate 'a sound sense of the demands of the medium, a dry sense of humour and a good command of old-fashioned storytelling'. No, maybe radio is the place for me.

Finish major rewrite of first half of The Novel and decide to await response to that before embarking on the rest. Send it off. Frankly, glad to see the back of it.

October
Realise that the story of the woman in the Ferrari is Cinderella. Also realise that Cinderella isn't about how even the poorest of us can find wealth and happiness, it's about the benefits of a good makeover. The Ferrari is her coach, the bloke driving it her fairy godmother. I also manage to work in a nervous breakdown, a bank robbery, an unfaithful husband, two precocious schoolboys, a case of mistaken identity, a car chase and – as recommended in *Shakespeare in Love* – a dog.

November
Continue 'Makeover' (working title for Cinderella) – with William Smethurst's *Writing for Television* beside me. Reminds me that when I was merely dabbling in writing I was too proud – or stupid – to admit that writing is a skill to be learnt like any other. I thought I could somehow just 'do it'. No longer, thank goodness. Now feel I'm learning all the time.

The Novel comes back: 'not convincing enough'. Know exactly what they mean. Unfortunately before I can put it in the file marked 'Not to be Opened until after my Death', another publisher expresses interest in seeing the full manuscript. Decide to put off decision till the new year. Secretly feel that I'm just not ready to write a good novel yet.

December
A small success – though not an actual sale – but enough to justify a small celebratory drink. A friend gives me a copy of *Writer's Market* (F&W Publications,

1507 Dana Ave., Cincinnati, Ohio 45207), the US equivalent of *The Writer's Handbook*, and among some excellent articles for first-time writers is one on how to write good 'query letters'. The advice seems so sound I immediately put it into practice in a proposal to an editor. And he likes it! Seems just the right lesson to take into the new year: advice works.

On TV David Renwick says that something like *One Foot in the Grave* happens to a writer only once in a lifetime, if he's lucky. It's somehow reassuring to know that even the most successful don't have it all their own way.

Then I have the most blindingly brilliant idea for a radio play, so brilliant in fact that I write the 45 minute script in five days. This is the one. Absolutely.

Postscript

2001: so far the usual mix of good days and bad months. I have a story published in *The Erotic Review* and they'd love to have a look at any others. Thanks to this hand-book's editor I now contribute a fortnightly column to WritersServices.com. Struggling to keep to around 500 words, I'm reminded of Henry James' apology for the length of a letter: 'if I'd had more time I'd have made it shorter'.

The Novel is rejected by publisher no. 2 but is now on publisher no. 3. I'm about to start rewrite no. 9. Now no longer a simple love story but a lurid tale of transexuality, megalomania, rape and multiple murder. How did that happen? Five-day radio play is rejected – but encouragingly. Likewise my TV sitcom pilot set in an intensive care unit, whose humour one reader satisfyingly describes as 'sick'. The Makeover idea, my 21st century take on Cinderella, interests half a dozen TV production companies enough to ask to see the full script. And now I'm just polishing my *Casualty* entry for this year's BBC Talent competition. In the evenings I watch *ER* and call it work.

*After successful careers writing about IT and co-directing an internet services company, Bob Ritchie is now trying to make a living as a creative writer. He has had short stories published in various high-street magazines and contributes a regular column about the ups and downs of the writer's life to WritersServices.com (see **Useful Websites at a Glance**).*

Audio Books

Abbey Home Entertainment Group Ltd
See **Just Entertainment**

BBC Spoken Word
Woodlands, 80 Wood Lane, London
W12 0TT
☎020 8433 2230 Fax 020 8433 3851

Owner *BBC Worldwide Ltd*
Publisher *Jan Paterson*

BBC Spoken Word consists of the following IMPRINTS: **BBC Cover to Cover** Email email@covertocover.co.uk Editorial Director *Helen Nicoll* Unabridged readings of adult and children's fiction. AUTHORS include Charles Dickens, Jane Austen, Thomas Hardy, Anthony Trollope, Dick King-Smith, Jacqueline Wilson, Anne Fine, J.K. Rowling and A.A. Milne. Unsolicited work not accepted. **BBC Radio Collection and BBC Radio 4 Books** Email radio.collection@bbc.co.uk Editorial Director *Mary Kalemkerian* ESTABLISHED 1988. BBC Radio Collection releases material associated with BBC Radio and Television. *Publishes* fiction and drama, non-fiction, poetry, children's and sound effects. TITLES *BBC Radio Shakespeare; Alan Bennett; This Sceptred Isle; Hancock; Steptoe; Round The Horne; Agatha Christie; Sherlock Holmes.* Almost all releases sourced from BBC Radio and Television. Unsolicited work not accepted.

Canongate Audio
See **Canongate Books** under **UK Publishers**

Cavalcade Story Cassettes
See **Chivers Audio Books**

Chivers Audio Books
Windsor Bridge Road, Bath BA2 3AX
☎01225 335336 Fax 01225 310771
Website www.chivers.co.uk

Managing Director *Julian Batson*

Part of **Chivers Press Limited**. *Publishes* a wide range of titles on both cassette and CD. Primarily for the library and direct mail markets. Fiction, autobiography, non-fiction, children's and crime. 260 titles to be published in 2001. TITLES *The Brethren* John Grisham; *When We Were Orphans* Kazuo Ishiguro; *The Clematis Tree* Ann Widdecombe; *The Amber Spyglass* Philip Pullman.

IMPRINTS **Chivers Audio Books, Chivers Children's Audio Books, Cavalcade Story Cassettes**.

Chrome Dreams
12 Seaforth Avenue, New Malden, Surrey
KT3 6JP
☎020 8715 9781 Fax 020 8241 1426
Email ob@chromedreams.co.uk
Website www.chromedreams.co.uk

Managing Director *Rob Johnstone*

FOUNDED 1998. A small record and music management company producing audio-biographies of current rock and pop artists and legendary performers on CD. Planning to move into book publishing shortly. 64 titles in 2000. Ideas for biographies welcome.

Corgi Audio
Transworld Publishers, A division of the Random House Group Ltd, 61–63 Uxbridge Road, London W5 5SA
☎020 8579 2652 Fax 020 8231 6666

Joint Managing Directors *Larry Finlay, Patrick Janson-Smith*

Publishes fiction, autobiography, children's and humour. TITLES *Discworld Series* Terry Pratchett; *Down Under* Bill Bryson and other travel writing; *A Kentish Lad* Frank Muir; *The Horse Whisperer* Nicholas Evans.

Cover To Cover
See **BBC Spoken Word**

CSA Telltapes Ltd
101 Chamberlayne Road, London
NW10 3ND
☎020 8960 8466 Fax 020 8968 0804
Email michelle@csatelltapes.demon.co.uk
Website www.csatelltapes.demon.co.uk

Managing Director *Clive Stanhope*

FOUNDED 1989. *Publishes* fiction, children's,

short stories, poetry, travel, biographies. Over 100 titles to-date. Tends to favour quality/classic/nostalgic/timeless literature for the 30+ age group. TITLES *Carry on Jeeves* P.G. Wodehouse; *Alfie* Bill Naughton; *The Third Man* Graham Greene; *Hideous Kinky* Esther Freud; *Room at the Top* John Braine; *Midwich Cuckoos* John Wyndham; *How Proust Can Change Your Life* Alain de Botton; *Classic Stories of the Old and New Testaments*.

CYP Children's Audio

The Fairway, Bush Fair, Harlow, Essex CM18 6LY
☎01279 444707 Fax 01279 445570
Email enquiries@cypmusic.co.uk
Website www.kidsmusic.co.uk
Joint Managing Directors *Mike Kitson, Paul Thorp*
FOUNDED 1978. *Publishes* children's material for those under 10 years of age; educational, entertainment, licensed characters (*Mr Men; Little Miss*). Ideas for cassettes welcome.

Faber.Penguin Audiobooks

80 Strand, London WC2R 0RL
☎020 7010 3000 Fax 020 7010 6060
Email audio@penguin.co.uk
Website www.penguin.co.uk
3 Queen Square, London WC1N 3AU
☎020 7465 0045 Fax 020 7465 0108
Head of Audio Publishing *Anna Archer*
(at Strand address)
Publishing Director *Joanna Mackle*
(at Queen Square address)

A joint venture between **Penguin Books** and **Faber & Faber**. *Publishes* 25–30 titles per year, drawing on the strength of Faber's authors. AUTHORS include Ted Hughes, Philip Larkin, Garrison Keillor, Sylvia Plath, T.S. Eliot, Wendy Cope, William Golding, Seamus Heaney, Paul Muldoon.

Halsgrove

See entry under **UK Publishers**

HarperCollins AudioBooks

77–85 Fulham Palace Road, London W6 8JB
☎020 8741 7070
Fax 020 8307 4517 (adult)/8307 4291 (child)
The HarperCollins audio list was launched in the late eighties.

ADULT
Managing Director *Adrian Bourne*, **Publisher** *Rosalie George Publishes* a wide range including popular and classic fiction, non-fiction, Shakespeare and poetry. 60 titles in 2000. TITLES *'Tis* Frank McCourt; *The Blind Assassin* Margaret Atwood; *The Wrong Boy* Willy Russell; *Iris: A Memoir* John Bayley; *Black Notice* Patricia Cornwell; *Inconceivable* Ben Elton; *John Major: The Autobiography*; *Losing My Virginity* Richard Branson.

CHILDREN'S DIVISION
Publishing Director *Gail Penston*, **Senior Editors** *Stella Paskins*, *Gillie Russell* (fiction) *Publishes* picture books/cassettes and story books/cassettes as well as single and double tapes for children aged 2–13 years. Fiction, songs, early learning, poetry etc. 60 titles in 2000. AUTHORS C.S. Lewis, Roald Dahl, Enid Blyton, Robin Jarvis, Colin and Jacqui Hawkins, Ian Whybrow, Lynne Reid Banks, Robert Westall, Jean Ure, Nick Butterworth, Judith Kerr.

Hodder Headline Audio Books

338 Euston Road, London NW1 3BH
☎020 7873 6000 Fax 020 7873 6024
Website www.hodder.co.uk
Publisher *Rupert Lancaster*
LAUNCHED in 1994 with 50 titles. A strong list, especially for theatre, vintage radio, film tie-ins, poetry plus fiction and non-fiction. Approx 200 titles in 2000. AUTHORS Louis de Bernières, Dickie Bird, John LeCarré, Alex Ferguson, Stephen King, Ellis Peters, Rosamunde Pilcher, Terry Waite, Mary Wesley.

Isis Audio Books

See **Isis Publishing** under **UK Publishers**

Just Entertainment

13 Blenheim Terrace, St John's Wood, London NW8 0EH
☎020 7625 3600 Fax 020 7625 3100
Managing Director *Anne Miles*
Formerly Abbey Home Entertainment Group Ltd, instigators in the development of the spoken word. With over 20 years' experience in recording, marketing and distribution of audio, book and cassette, their catalogue includes major children's story characters such as *Thomas the Tank Engine, Postman Pat* and *Winnie the Pooh*. Specialises in children's audio cassettes. TITLES *Macdonald's Farm*, in conjunction with GMTV; *Baby Bright* in conjunction with Great Ormond Street Hospital; *Watership Down*.

Ladybird Books Ltd

Ground Floor, 39 Stoney Street, Nottingham
NG1 1LX
☎0115 948 6900 Fax 0115 948 6901
Publisher *Sophie Mitchell*

Part of **Dorling Kindersley Ltd**. Only *publishes* recordings of titles which appear on the Ladybird book list. TITLES *The Railway Children; Gulliver's Travels; Little Red Riding Hood; Puss in Boots; Farmyard Stories for Under Fives.*

Laughing Stock Productions

81 Charlotte Street, London W1P 1LB
☎020 7637 7943 Fax 020 7436 1646
Managing Director *Colin Collino*

FOUNDED 1991. Issues a wide range of comedy cassettes from family humour to alternative comedy. 12–16 titles per year. TITLES *Red Dwarf; Shirley Valentine* (read by Willy Russell); *Rory Bremner; Peter Cook Anthology; Sean Hughes; John Bird and John Fortune; Eddie Izzard.*

Macmillan Audio Books

20 New Wharf Road, London N1 9RR
☎020 7843 2650 Fax 020 7843 2651
Email a.muirden@macmillan.co.uk
Website www.macmillan.co.uk
Owner *Macmillan Publishers Ltd*
Manager *Alison Muirden*

FOUNDED 1995. *Publishes* adult fiction, non-fiction and autobiography, focusing mainly on lead book titles and releasing audio simultaneously with hard or paperback publication. About 40 titles a year. AUTHORS Wilbur Smith, Ken Follett, Colin Dexter, Clare Francis, Minette Walters, Michael Ondaatje, Helen Fielding, Elizabeth Jane Howard, Martin Cruz Smith, James Herbert, Janet Evanovich, Niall Williams, Lynda La Plante, Julie Parsons, Rennie Airth, V.S. Naipaul.

Mr Punch Productions

139 Kensington High Street, London
W8 6SU
☎020 7368 0088 Fax 020 7368 0051
Email editor@mrpunch.com
Managing Director *Stewart Richards*

FOUNDED 1995. Independent producer of audio books – drama and non-fiction. Over 70 titles with SERIES including *Classic Journals; Hollywood Playhouse*, Oscar-winning films specially adapted for the radio and performed by many of the original stars; *Variety Bandbox,* archive variety radio; *Classic Radio Drama; Great British Trials*, dramatised versions of original trial transcripts. TITLES *Wisdens; The Letters & Journals of Lord Nelson; Wonderful Life; Rebecca; Scott of the Antarctic; Tales From the Old Testament.* 'Always interested in non-fiction ideas that are suitable for performing in the first person (single- or multi-voice production).'

Naxos AudioBooks

18 High Street, Welwyn, Hertfordshire
AL6 9EQ
☎01438 717808 Fax 01438 717809
Email Naxos_Audiobooks@compuserve.com
Website www.naxosaudiobooks.com
Owner *HNH International, Hong Kong/Nicolas Soames*
Managing Director *Nicolas Soames*

FOUNDED 1994. Part of Naxos, the classical budget CD company. *Publishes* classic and modern fiction, non-fiction, children's and junior classics, drama and poetry. TITLES *Paradise Lost* Milton; *Ulysses* Joyce; *Kim* Kipling; *Decline and Fall of the Roman Empire* Gibbon.

Penguin Audiobooks

80 Strand, London WC2R 0RL
☎020 7010 3000 Fax 020 7010 6060
Email audio@penguin.co.uk
Website www.penguin.co.uk
Head of Audio Publishing *Anna Archer*

Launched in November 1993 and has rapidly expanded since then to reflect the diversity of Penguin Books' list. *Publishes* mostly fiction, both classical and contemporary, non-fiction, autobiography and an increasing range of children's titles under the **Puffin Audiobooks** imprint. Approx. 70 titles a year. Contemporary AUTHORS include: Dick Francis, Barbara Vine, Anne Fine, Gillian Cross, John Mortimer, Roald Dahl, Tom Clancy, Sue Townsend, Philip Ridley, Nick Hornby.

Puffin Audiobooks

See **Penguin Audiobooks**

Random House Audiobooks

20 Vauxhall Bridge Road, London
SW1V 2SA
☎020 7840 8400 Fax 020 7233 6127
Owner *Random House Group Ltd.*
Managing Director *Kate Parkin*
Manager *Victoria Williams*

The audiobooks division of Random House

started early in 1991. Acquired the Reed Audio list in 1997. *Publishes* fiction, non-fiction and self help. 23 titles in 2000. AUTHORS include John Grisham, Stephen Fry, Charles Handy, Patricia Cornwell, Michael Crichton and Ruth Rendell.

CHILDREN'S DIVISION IMPRINT **Tellastory** AUTHORS include Jane Hissey, Shirley Hughes, David McKee and Michael Palin.

Rickshaw Productions

64 Fields Court, Warwick CV34 5HP
☎0780 3553214 Fax 01926 402490
Email rickprod@aol.com
Website www.rickshaw-audiobooks.com

Executive Producer *Ms L.J. Fairgrieve*

FOUNDED 1998. *Publishes* adult fiction, specialising in Eastern and Far Eastern literature, both classic and modern (in English translation). Also looking for unpublished writers of any genre apart from poetry. TITLES *Chinese Classic Stories* (read by Martin Jarvis); *Chinese Women's Stories* (Miriam Margolyes); *The Carved Pipe/The Tall Woman and Her Short Husband* (Elizabeth Lindsay); *The Halfway-House Hotel* by Richard James (Peter Mimmack). Ideas for new stories welcome.

Simon & Schuster Audio

Africa House, 64–78 Kingsway, London WC2B 6AH
☎020 7316 1900 Fax 020 7316 0332
Email rumana.haider@simonandschuster.co.uk

Audio Manager *Rumana Haider*

Simon & Schuster Audio began by distributing their American parent company's audio products. Moved on to repackaging products specifically for the UK market and in 1994 became more firmly established in this market with a huge rise in turnover. *Publishes* adult fiction, self help, business, Star Trek and Alien Voices titles. TITLES *Animal Instincts* Alan Titchmarsh; *The Time Machine* H.G. Wells; *Popcorn* Ben Elton; *The 7 Habits of Highly Successful People* Stephen R. Covey; *Deja Dead* Kathy Reichs; *Lethal Seduction* Jackie Collins; *Ramses* Christian Jacq; *Rhinoceros* Colin Forbes.

Smith/Doorstop Cassettes

The Poetry Business, The Studio, Byram Arcade, Huddersfield, West Yorkshire HD1 1ND
☎01484 434840 Fax 01484 426566
Email edit@poetrybusiness.co.uk
Website www.poetrybusiness.co.uk

Co-directors *Peter Sansom, Janet Fisher*

Publishes poetry, read and introduced by the writer. AUTHORS Simon Armitage, Sujata Bhatt, Carol Ann Duffy, Les Murray, Ian McMillan.

Soundings

Isis House, Kings Drive, Whitley Bay, Tyne & Wear NE26 2JT
☎0191 253 4155 Fax 0191 251 0662
Website www.isis-publishing.co.uk

FOUNDED in 1982. Part of the Ulverscroft Group Ltd. *Publishes* fiction and non-fiction; crime, romance. About 190 titles a year. AUTHORS include Angus McVicar, Barbara Cartland, Catherine Cookson, Olivia Manning, Derek Tangye, Lyn Andrews, Susan Sallis, Mary Jane Staples, Alexander Fullerton, Patrick O'Brian, Pamela Oldfield.

Tellastory

See **Random House Audiobooks**

WALKfree Productions Ltd

Reardon Publishing, 56 Upper Norwood Street, Leckhampton, Cheltenham, Gloucestershire GL53 0DU
☎01242 231800
Website www.reardon.co.uk

Publishing/Sales Director *Nicholas Reardon*

FOUNDED 1996. In association with the Ordnance Survey, produces *WALKfree Audio-Guides* which 'cultivate a new form of country walking experience in the countryside'. The audio tape is accompanied by a 16-page guide book containing an Ordnance Survey Travelmaster map extract plus outline route maps. Each guide also offers advice on convenient places for refreshment and local contacts. TITLES *The Cotswolds; Peak District; Hadrian's Wall*.

Through the Popularity Barrier
Poetry in 2002

Peter Finch

Has poetry broken through the popularity barrier? You'd think so from the coverage that the Poet Laureate gets in our national press, from the fact that singing superstar Robbie Williams writes a bit, and so does Paul McCartney, and that even Tony Blair now quotes verse at TUC conferences. Poetry has a currency today that it appears not to have had in a long time. It's not odd, any more, to be a poet. But that's the surface. Sales do not bear this universality out. Do you see *Poetry Review* among the hundreds of magazines at WHSmith's? Do you find *Acumen* on the racks at airports? When was the last time you spotted someone reading *PN Review* on the underground? Poetry's reputation as the mind candy of the new millennium far outstrips its true performance.

'A poem is concentrated, a closed fist', said Sylvia Plath and maybe there lies the root of poetry's problem. Popularity implies acceptance across a wide public front and the punters, it seems, need things fast and in their faces. Contemporary poetry may shine like fashionable chrome but it's a hard thing to take in without dedicating a bit of time. And even then you may not get the whole thing. 'A poem must leave a little mystery in the world,' says Don Patterson, and that's obviously too much for many.

The Irish poet Eavan Boland believes that poetry today has totally lost the faith of its audience. By throwing away form and rhyme back in Pound's day at the advent of Modernism poetry began its long slow slide towards marginalisation. The public, apparently, does not want verse and especially that which concentrates on condensation and literary tricks at the expense of recognisable and memorably presented meaning. 'Any comparison between the currency of poetry today and that of a hundred years ago shows a staggering loss of purpose and centrality,' says Boland. Bearing this out, national poetry sales appear to make up only a measly two per cent of the total book market. For the land that gave us Tennyson, Byron, Milton, Wordsworth, Pope and Shakespeare that's pathetic.

Poetry books sell in miserably small numbers – under 300 copies for a volume from a lesser-known; hardly more than a thousand for someone most of us have actually heard of. There are exceptions, naturally. Everyone wanted to read the final instalment of the long-running Ted Hughes–Sylvia Plath saga, and *Birthday Letters* sold brilliantly. So did Heaney's translations. 'If the author of *Beowulf* had known more than a thousand years ago that a translation of his epic tale was now topping the bestseller lists I think he'd have been more than a little surprised,' remarked Poetry Society director Christina Patterson. But for most of the poetry world it's the poets themselves who make up the market. A large and stable non-practising audience simply does not exist; poetry, it seems, is not a spectator sport.

But should that devalue it? Certainly not. There are probably more poets writing today than there have ever been in the history of our nations. A back of the envelope calculation works out at one poet for every twenty thousand head of population. And most of these brave bards fancy their chances at publication. Who can blame them? On the surface poetry is everywhere. Mimi Khalvati is resident poet at the Royal Mail, Wendy Cope at the law firm of Lovell, White and Durrant. Carol Ann Duffy has acquired herself poetry's largest ever development grant – £75,000 – from the National Endowment for Science, Technology and Arts (NESTA). The Poet Laureate, Andrew Motion, has turned out to be the most talented, public-minded and genuinely useful post-holder in decades. Single-handedly Motion has focused media attention on poetry, increased profile, developed opportunity, while, most importantly, maintaining standard. The job matters again. The Nation's Favourite poems get displayed on radio and TV. Lottery money via the now thoroughly renovated Poetry Society has spent two years putting poetry into places one previously just couldn't imagine it going – gas platforms, railway companies, chip shops, Marks and Spencers. Official arts policy is to broaden the base and enable everyone to participate. The *Poetry on the Underground* scheme, which displays a mix of classic and contemporary poetry on the world's most travelled metro and sells shedloads of anthologies on the back of it, is being imitated, first in the north-east and, more recently, in Devon, with a local *Poetry on the Buses* scheme run by Green Books. There are more and more grants being made available for poetry periodicals and small publishing programmes. No flood but a steady increase on the doleful support poetry has received down the years.

Do you join in? If you imagine that what's eating you is some god-sent unique talent with which you simply have to put pen to paper in order to bang the stanzas out then, probably, best not. Among poetry's thousands there are too many already who think that verse is simple stuff. Poetry may *pack*, but to do that successfully it needs work. It is undeniable that some poems will emerge fully formed, virtually whole as they are. But those are very much the exceptions. Most work trickles out slowly – an idea, an image, a flash of a notion of how the thing might go. Then comes the hard stuff. The plan, the writes and rewrites, the cuts and changes, the hash and rehash. If your poetry isn't going through this kind of process then the chances are that it won't amount to too much. Poetry shouldn't be easy material which comes out of its creators like toothpaste. It should emerge with ponder, with doubt and with difficulty all around. Is what you have on the sheet before you a poem? Does it amount to anything new, anything startling, anything splendid, a different, entrancing, engaging way of looking at the world? Ask yourselves these questions. Scratch the thing out. Redo it. Throw away more than you keep. Learn to kill your babies. Keep only that which really rocks. Do that. Then read on.

What should you read?

The way in is first to discover what poetry actually is. To do this means putting time in at the bookshop and at the library. Be as open and catholic as you can in your selection. Ensure you check out the whole scene – the past, the present, mainstream English literature along with work in translation, the poets you find you like as well as those you find difficult. Appreciation will not come without effort. Stay the course.

Ask at your booksellers for their recommendations. Check Waterstone's or Blackwell's, who both carry some stock. A few years back Waterstone's brought out their own *Waterstone's Guide to Poetry Books* edited by Nick Rennison which provided a decent map. Most shops these days carry a basic stock, but if you need more then get hold of the Poetry Library's current list of shops with a specific interest in poetry. Enquire at your local library. Start with a recent anthology of contemporary verse. You'll be spoilt for choice here, the new millennium has rushed a whole crop of century-definers into print. To get a broad view of what's going on, not only should you read Edna Longley's *Bloodaxe Book of Twentieth Century Poetry*, Simon Armitage and Robert Crawford's Penguin *British and Irish Poetry Since the War,* Sean O'Brien's *The Firebox* (Picador), Michael Schmidt's *The Harvill Book of Twentieth-Century Poetry In English* (Harvill), Hulse, Kennedy and Morley's Bloodaxe *The New Poetry*, Peter Forbes' *Scanning The Century* (Viking), and Ian Sinclair's *Conductors of Chaos* (Picador), but also Richard Caddel and Peter Quartermain's *Other: British and Irish Poetry since 1970* (Wesleyan), Sarah-Jane Lovett's *Oral* (Sceptre), Lemn Sissay's *The Fire People – A Collection of Contemporary Black British Poets* (Payback Press), Jeni Couzyn's *The Bloodaxe Book of Contemporary Women Poets*, Tony Frazer's *A State Of Independence* (Stride), *Poems For the Millennium Volume Two: From Postwar to Millennium* edited by Jerome Rothenberg and Pierre Joris (California), and *Postmodern American Poetry*, a really splendid selection edited by Paul Hoover (Norton). This last title might be harder to find but will be worth the effort. Fill in with a standard overview of poetry in English since Chaucer. Ted Hughes and Seamus Heaney's two Faber anthologies *The Rattle Bag* and *The School Bag* are good scatter guns. For a more balanced historical view try Christopher Ricks' *The Oxford Book of English Verse*, Paul Keegan's *New Penguin Book of English Verse*, Helen Gardner's *New Oxford Book of English Verse*, the great *Norton Anthology of Poetry* or long-term standby *Palgrave's Golden Treasury* (OUP).

Progress to the literary magazine. Write off to a number of the magazine addresses which follow this article and ask the price of sample copies. Enquire about subscriptions. Expect to pay something but it shouldn't break the bank. It is important that poets read not only to familiarise themselves with what is currently fashionable and to increase their own facility for self-criticism, but to help support the activity in which they wish to participate. Buy – this is vital for little mags, it is the only way in which they are going to survive.

OK, I'm well read. What next?

Are you personally convinced that your work is ready? If you are uncertain, then most likely that will be the view of everyone else. Check your text for glips and blips. Rework it. Root out any clichés or archaic poetry expressions such as O, doeth, bewilld'd and the like. Drop any of what Peter Sansom calls 'spirit of the age' poetry words. Do without shards, lozenges, lambent patina, and stippled seagulls. If you work with rhyme attempt to avoid the obvious. Check that any metre you may be using actually works. Try not to clank. If by this time your writing still sounds OK, then go ahead.

The Internet and World Wide Web

The Internet is not a diversion. For the poet, or for that rare beast, the non-contributing poetry consumer, the Web has now moved into high focus. No longer a simple extension of conventional print, it is now an actual substitute which you ignore at your peril. Growth over the past few years has been nothing short of enormous. Poetry on the Web has gone from nothing to everything in four years. With the advent of free access (although not yet free phone calls) and complimentary Web space an increasing number of poetry enthusiasts and publishers have set up sites. Some have abandoned conventional print to operate solely online; others have launched without ever having known ink and paper. Cyberspace – the place where it all happens – is a mirror of the conventional world. The electronic replicates the real. Here are online books, magazines, historical and contemporary archives, reference works, creative tools, discussion forums and news round-ups. Many dedicate themselves entirely to poetry.

Journals
Online magazines range from those which mirror their print-based cousins (and in some cases are simply direct copies) to completely innovative, interactive compilations which mix sound and action with the text. The Web is no static place. It provides movement, video, sound and user-defined typeface along with actual text. Some mags (e-zines, online journals) offer playable recordings of their poets performing, others give space for readers to add criticism. More and more are opening chat rooms and forums where readers can exchange views. The difference between online and print-based magazines becomes more apparent when you discover that what you get when you visit is not simply an enhanced version of the current issue but access to the entire back catalogue. All searchable, storable and, best of all, free.

Geography dissolves online. America is no further and no more costly to access than Britain. One of the great mags, John Tranter's *Jacket*, is based in Australia. It's just as easy to read as George Simmers' UK *Snakeskin*, Ethan Paquan's *Slope* or Rick Lupert's Los Angeles *Poetry Super Highway*. In fact, half the time, the user has no idea precisely where the site being accessed is physically based. Place ceases to matter, language takes over. Online journals can range from the terrible to the terrific. For my money the aforementioned *Jacket*, *Perihelion*, the very flashy UK newcomer *Boomerang*, where Neil Rollinson has managed to attract contributions from many highly reputable poets, Rupert Loydell's revived *Stride*, and Jennifer Ley's *Riding The Meridian* are some of the world's best. Not all is in English, either. For an experience of the Welsh strict metres have a look at *Cartref Cynghanedd ar y We* (The Home of Cynghanedd on the Web).

How do you contribute? As with all poetry ventures, read first. Will you fit in? If you think so then send your poems by e-mail, included in the body of the text or as an attached ASCII (Text Only) file, no s.a.e. needed. More than likely you'll get an instant answer. No more waiting around for six weeks before your poems return, rejected and dog-eared. Online can be lightning fast.

Cyberspace is huge. Some of the sites which list online journals, such as *Peter Howard's Poetry Contacts*, seems to go on for days. Starting your own mag is easy – frictionless, Bill Gates calls it – and size presents little difficulty. On the Web it is easy to put up more, so in terms of quality of content that often means less. Not only are the UK's computer literate newbies up there but America, Canada, Japan, South America and Australia's too.

Competitions

Naturally there is an online variant to the more traditional send five pounds and your best work contests. Many of these canvass entries from the unconnected and offer Web publication as the prize. For some poets this will no doubt be sufficient reward. Others accept online entries and chose their winners by asking readers to vote – again online. The selling point for these competitions is judged to be the enormous audience supposedly sitting around out there in front of their screens. The potential certainly is large – four or five hundred million users already connected and with more joining every day. Yet how many actually bother to access poetry remains debatable. The Web counters which publicly log visitors to sites are notoriously untrustworthy but even if most of them only tell half truths they are still recording a pretty large number of readers.

Books

If you tire of contributing to the websites of others then why not start your own? A whole collection of verse online will present relatively little difficulty. Most Internet Service Providers (ISPs) offer an amount of free Web space to users or, if you can put up with the adverts, you can claim a home for nothing at somewhere like Geocities. Building your own *Home Page* is certainly not beyond anyone capable of using a word processor. Many ISPs also provide free page creation software. If you'd like to see the kind of thing that's possible have a look at the site of poet Matthew Francis, or for something more graphically challenging, Neil Rollinson's dark creation. You might also care to look at my own, *The Peter Finch Archive*. If you are reticent get a fan to set up a site devoted to your works. This has happened to David Gascoyne, to J.H. Prynne, Maya Angelou, Ivor Cutler, Benjamin Zephaniah and others. Most of us, however, seem to like the idea of self-build. If you have a recording of yourself doing your stuff then get one jump ahead. Put that up there too.

Hypertext

Naturally the Web has developed its own verse forms. Most of these straddle the boundaries between verse, sound and image, much in the way that concrete poetry did fifty years ago. Many critics dismiss the new work as simply moving graphic art but protagonists see the world very differently. In the launch for its *Artszone*, the all-embracing BBC website chose to feature four excellent hypertext poets (including Peter Howard and Robert Kendall). But hypertext poetry is better experienced than reported. *Webartery* will give you links to some of the leading practitioners.

Groups

To reduce the poet's traditional feeling of isolation the Net presents a number of opportunities. World-wide poets, once they've got over the stunning breadth of Net facilities, are usually hard to shut up. E-mail provides one vehicle. Here bands of poets circulate their work, their criticisms and their views of world literature. Join a group (no cost, just ask) and you'll find a daily delivery of e-mails in your inbox. Some groups are moderated, which means that contributions are filtered by a controlling individual, although most are free-for-alls. Discussion can range from the moronic to the stimulating. *The British and Irish Poets Group* established by Ric Caddel and *Poetryetc*, an outgrowth of the list begun by John Kinsella, are two worth trying.

A variant on e-mail discussion groups is Usenet Newsgroups. Newsgroups run through their own dedicated software (provided by your ISP as part of your subscription, and usually your e-mail program) and are open to contributions from anyone anywhere. Articles are delivered to your screen for consumption. If you want to contribute then type it up and it's done. The principal poetry newsgroups, *rec.arts.poems* and *alt.arts.poetry.comments*, offer pretty varied fare. By their world-wide nature they tend to be American dominated and standards of contribution are not always that high. But they are places where you can get an instant reaction to your latest poem. There are also masterclasses out there with established poets offering online advice. The BBC, Chadwyck-Healey and the Poetry Society are some of the organisations which have offered virtual residencies with well-known bards.

Tools and resources

The Net offers a multitude of these. There are online spellcheckers, thesauri, an anagram creator, Shakespeare and Bible concordances, a rhyming dictionary. The archives of universities (particularly in America) offer the great poetry of the past in comprehensive quantity. Download facsimile editions of *The Germ* (the first ever poetry magazine, from 1850) or hear Seamus Heaney recite. Read the complete works of Blake, find out what powered the Beat generation, discover how Hardy worked, check the roots of modern verse. You can find not only the texts themselves but entire critical apparatuses, historical contexts, biographies, bibliographies, portraits, shoe sizes and names of lovers for most of the greats. You can access information on poetry readings or check at the British Council for data on literature festivals. For a glimpse at the broader picture check UNESCO's huge World Poetry Directory. Students revel in posting their dissertations. Archives want their knowledge made available to the everyone. Interested in a particular style? Haiku? Visual poetry? Traditional forms? They've all got their sites.

E-commerce

Shopping on the Net is now the preferred method for buying specialist material. The big Internet bookshops – bol.com and Amazon – both offer the hunter for that difficult to obtain poetry title searchable lists. Buying online is generally safe and swift although as with all mail order only as perfect as the van that brings the package to your door. The UK *Poetry Book Society*, which acts as a poetry book club (see **Organisations of Interest to Poets**), is also taking advantage of Internet sales.

How to find them

Use the search engine. The big ones – Yahoo, Google, HotBot, Excite, AltaVista – can return enormous lists in response to keying in the word *poetry*. I got 149,529 results out of AltaVista. Much easier is to log on to one of a number of poetry resource sites which run clickable lists of relevant pages. The UK Poetry Society, The Poetry Library and the *Poetry Review*'s 'Web watcher', Peter Howard's home page, are worth consulting. Ted Slade's *Poetry Kit* provides a large amount of poetry information, competition lists, resources and a whole raft of self-help articles. And for a good world-wide look try *Pif Magazine*.

Where next?

New ideas arrive all the time. *trAce*, the major online writing project set up at Nottingham-Trent University with support from the Arts Council, is signposting many of the ways Net writing can go. At the BBC website you can create your own works on screen using a virtual form of magnetic poetry more usually seen on the fronts of fridges. Peter Howard's site runs a number of online poetry generators. The user keys in basic vocab and the Java script does the rest. On the other hand you may prefer to use your own creative engines. Log on now.

Some Web addresses for poets

Annedd y Cynganeddwyr   www.cynghanedd.com
BBC   www.bbc.co.uk

Boomerang	www.boomeranguk.com/
British Poets e-mail list	www.jiscmail.ac.uk/lists/british-poets.html
Chadwyck-Healey	lion.chadwyck.co.uk
Electronic Poetry Centre	wings.buffalo.edu/epc
Matthew Francis	www.7greenhill.freeserve.co.uk/
Jacket (magazine)	www.jacket.zip.com.au
John Kinsella	freespace.virgin.net/reality street
The Opening Line (workshops)	www.openingline.co.uk
Perihelion (magazine)	webdelsol.com/Perihelion
Peter Finch Archive	www.peterfinch.co.uk
Peter Howard's Poetry Page	www.hphoward.demon.co.uk/poetry/
Pif Magazine	pifmagazine.com/2001/03/
Poetry Book Society	www.poetrybooks.co.uk
Poetry Kit (magazine)	www.poetrykit.org/
Poetryetc e-mail list	www.jiscmail.ac.uk/lists/poetryetc.html
The Poetry Library	www.poetrylibrary.org.uk
The Poetry Society (UK)	www.poetrysoc.com/index.htm
Riding The Meridian (magazine)	www.heelstone.com/meridian/
Slope (magazine)	www.slope.org
Snakeskin (magazine)	homepages.nildram.co.uk/~simmers/
Stride	www.stridemagazine.co.uk
Trace	trace.ntu.ac.uk/
Webartery	www.webartery.com
World Poetry Directory	www.unesco.org

Commercial publishers

Despite the obvious possibilities of making something from poetry in the traditional hard copy commercial market place the number of those conglomerate publishers involved is actually pretty limited. Where once there was a multitude of mainstream poetry imprints there are now only three or four. Poetry is increasingly seen today as the quality line which enhances a publisher's list. It is rarely there to make profit but more often to impart class and fashion to the list. Despite a decade or more of poetry booms the stuff is still basically a commercial risk. Compared to other lines slim volumes are slow sellers. Their editors are almost always part-time or have other jobs within the company and are never allowed to publish what they would really like.

The obvious exception to this approach is long-term market leader and envy of the whole business **Faber & Faber**. Here editor Paul Kegan and Jane Feaver preside over a list which continues to be as important to the firm as when T.S. Eliot inaugurated it more than seventy years ago. The best poetry does transcend the limits of the traditional market, they believe. This is the imprint most poets would like to join. The greats of the twentieth century are here – Pound, Eliot,

Plath, Hughes, Larkin. Seamus Heaney made half a million in sales when he won the Nobel Prize. Wendy Cope regularly sells into five figures. The imprint is built on distinctively designed class and on the roster of contemporary poets are some of the best we have – Simon Armitage, Derek Walcott, Don Paterson, Glyn Maxwell, Andrew Motion, Jo Shapcott, Hugo Williams, Paul Muldoon, Douglas Dunn. The press publish up to sixty poetry titles each year and have been vigorously relaunching and rebranding themselves to 're-emphasise the predominance of Faber Poetry' (as if they needed to). Kegan will read all manuscripts submitted. Send a brief covering letter and a sample of your writing (10–20 poems) not forgetting s.a.e. if you think this is where you'll fit in. (The Faber website is at www.faber.co.uk)

Oxford University Press was once a serious rival to Faber with an eclectic list of moderns, post-moderns and classics. But that's the past. Oxford has now abandoned contemporary verse in favour of its backlist and historical erudition.

The commercial editor most admired for his taste is still **Cape**'s Robin Robertson. His list is by no means all things to all people. Peter Redgrove, Matthew Sweeney, Anne Carson, John Burnside, Sharon Olds and Michael Longley are typical. Roberston, himself a fine poet, produces four to five titles annually – all books, no anthologies and with a number sourced from the other side of the Atlantic. The care taken in their production is obvious. Check them out, these books look worth the money. Worth trying? Yes, but potential contributors should never waste anyone's time by not looking at the list first. Poetry at fellow Random House press, **Chatto & Windus**, is now in the hands of Rebecca Carter. Some of the imprint's old vigour is now seeping back with an output of two or three titles a year including Alan Jenkins, Fred D'Aguiar and Kate Clanchy. But unless supported by a strong recommendation from an established fellow practitioner Carter does not want to see unsolicited manuscripts.

Both Chatto and Cape preview examples from their lists in the poem for the day section of the Random House website (www.randomhouse.co.uk).

The **Harvill Press** runs one of the smaller commercial poetry lists, publishing one or two new titles annually. Central are the works of Paul Durcan and the late Raymond Carver. They also publish Michael Schmidt's fine anthology *The Harvill Book of Twentieth Century Poetry In English*. They'll look at new manuscripts but chances are slim. New writers would be better off starting elsewhere.

Among the other commercial houses activity appears to be limited to nominal titles, anthologies or backlist obligations. **BBC Worldwide** churns and churns out Nation's Favourites. **Bloomsbury** reprints poetry classics and work for children (including Benjamin Zephaniah and Adrian Henri) along with the occasional popular adult title from the likes of Anne Michaels. **Cassell** anthologises the poems from the London Underground (which sell so well you'd think they'd be encouraged to try something else). **Virgin** sells shedloads of Robbie Williams. **Souvenir** anthologises cats and dogs. **Dent** recycles Rimbaud and Irish humanism. **Granta** does Blake Morrison. **HarperCollins** centres on humour. **Hodder & Stoughton** collects the inspirational and the Christian. **Methuen** sticks with

John Hegley. **Orion** has R.S. Thomas, Ben Okri and the Illustrated Poetry Please. **Boxtree** presents Purple Ronnie. Some specialist interests are dealt with at **Lion** (Christian verse), **Saqi** (Arab) and **Windhorse** (Buddhist) – but it isn't a lot.

The smaller operators

Not all commercial publishing is vast and conglomerate. A few independents still exist and on their lists poetry occasionally occurs. **Canongate Books** (now part of the American literary publisher **Grove**) publishes Anna Akhmatova and Alan Spence's Scottish haiku. Northern Ireland general publisher **Blackstaff Press** brings out one or two poetry titles annually, including Frank Ormsby's *The Hip Flask: Short Poems from Ireland*. Welsh family firm **Gwasg Gomer** produces tidy editions of Gillian Clarke, Janet Dube, Nigel Jenkins and others. Former *Sunday Times* Small Publisher of the Year, **Polygon** (which is an imprint of **Edinburgh University Press**), continues to mix Gaelic with English as part of its 'poetry for the new generation' policy. Jackie Jones and Robert Crawford are editors. The press has at least half a dozen poets on the list including Donny O'Rourke, Roddy Gorman, Liz Lochhead and W.N. Herbert. They also publish *Pocket Books*, a series which mixes poetry with photography. Check their *The Dream State: The New Scottish Poets*. Send in if you are part of the Scottish renaissance. Others in the field include **Wolfhound**, **Sigma**, and **Y Lolfa.**

Universities

With the collapse of **OUP**'s contemporary interest activity among UK presses is sparse. Reprints and literary studies at **Cambridge**, the same at **Manchester**. At the **University of Wales Press**, which publishes a splendid series of collected works from Welsh poets, you need to be dead. American university presses such as Nebraska, **Harvard**, **Chicago**, **Michigan**, Ohio, **Yale**, Duke, Northeastern, **Iowa**, **Syracuse** and **California** along with **W.W. Norton** do an increasing amount of verse but exclusively by Americans. No chances there.

Women

There were days when **Virago** was out front here but no longer. Becoming part of **Little, Brown** clearly means becoming less partisan. The press more or less only publishes poetry from novelists already elsewhere on their lists – Margaret Atwood, Michele Roberts, Maya Angelou. There are no plans for expansion. At **The Women's Press**, Virago's traditional competitor, the situation is much the same – original good intentions gone to be replaced by keeping Alice Walker in print. The **Onlywomen Press**, however, has kept its interest. Lilian Mohin tries to publish two poetry titles annually. Judith Barrington, Minnie Bruce Pratt, Jackie Kay, U.A. Fanthorpe and Rosie Bailey are typical. Generally, however, women poets are better served by the poetry specialists. More of them anon.

The mass-market paperback

The popular end is where many poets imagine the best starting place to be. Paperback houses were founded to publish inexpensive reprints of hard-covered originals and, despite years of innovation and market posturing, to a large extent still fulfil this role. Being neither cheap nor (in sales terms) that popular, poetry does not really fit in. Among the carousels at airports you do not see it. Check the empires of **Arrow**, **Bantam**, **Corgi**, **Headline** and **Mills & Boon**. If you discount the inspirational, you won't find a book of verse between them. **Vintage**, to its credit, publishes the occasional anthology and runs reprints of Iain Sinclair but he is also a successful novelist. Elsewhere nothing, although there are two exceptions. At **Penguin**, where things are always different, poetry has a significant role. With its unfailing commercial ear the company has correctly assessed the market for contemporary and traditional verse and systematically and successfully filled it. Reprinting important volumes pioneered by less commercial poetry presses, originating historic and thematic anthologies, reviving classic authors and producing a multitude of translations en route, Penguin continues to provide an almost unrivalled introduction to the world of verse. But appearances aside, this is most certainly no place for the beginner. 'We publish almost no new or unknown poets. In fact we publish very little new poetry beyond a small circle of established poets. We concentrate on selecteds and general anthologies,' publishing director Tony Lacey told me. The company focuses on sure sellers such as James Fenton, Geoffrey Hill, Tony Harrison and Roger McGough. The main thrust remains the re-packaging of selecteds from proven bards such as Simon Armitage, Carol Ann Duffy, U.A. Fanthorpe and Dannie Abse, a good range of modern poets in translation along with larger sets from the likes of William Empson, Allen Ginsberg and John Ashbery. The *Penguin Modern Poets'* second series of loosely connected trios has thirteen volumes and represents an excellent cross-section of British and Irish contemporary verse. The company's poetry overview anthologies, the Simon Armitage and Robert Crawford edited *British and Irish Poetry Since the War*, Peter Forbes' *Scanning the Century*, and Paul Keegan's *New Penguin Book of English Poetry* are musts. Despite these obvious winners Lacey sees the whole market for verse as small, despite the hype. (Penguin online is at www.penguin.com)

Penguin's nearest rival, **Picador**, the literary imprint from **Pan Macmillan**, is exhibiting considerable vigour and is now widely regarded as one of the country's leading poetry publishers. Under the commanding eye of successful and non-metropolitan poet Don Paterson it has moved into high gear, putting out a stream of successful collections both from new poets such as Robin Robertson, Paul Farley and Colette Bryce and from established names such as Carol Ann Duffy, Kathleen Jamie, Kate Clanchy, Michael Donaghy and Sean O'Brien, not forgetting the bestselling American poet Billy Collins. With its reliable content Picador is turning itself into a UK reference point. Paterson will bring out at least six new titles annually as well as an anthology. Recent examples include Sean O'Brien's critically acclaimed *The Firebox* and Carol Ann Duffy's anthology of love poems *Hand in Hand*. Worth trying here? 'Certainly: ten poems better than a full-length MS, but establish some track record in the reputable journals first,' advises Paterson.

The specialists

Despite commercial disparagement, poetry is nonetheless readily available. But where? With the specialist independents. These are the small army of semi-commercial operations scattered across the country. They are run by genuine poetry enthusiasts whose prime concern starts not with money but with the furtherance of their art. Begun as classic small presses which soon outgrew the restraints of back-bedroom offices and under-the-stairs warehousing, they are now a real force on the poetry scene. You can find them in Waterstone's, you can see them in Blackwell's and at Ottakar's. Most receive grant aid, without which their publishing programmes would be sunk. They are models of what poetry publishing should be – active, involving, alert and exciting. They promote their lists through readings, tours, websites and broadcasts and they involve their authors in the production and sales of their books. Never before have new poets been faced with so many publishing opportunities. And if there is any criticism then this is it. Too many books jamming the market. Just how does the reader see through the flood? By reputation, I guess. Two have emerged well ahead of the pack – **Carcanet** and **Bloodaxe**. Along with **Faber** these two now dominate British poetry publishing.

Taking them alphabetically the first of these is Neil Astley's acclaimed **Bloodaxe Books**. Publishing forty titles annually, the press brings out more poetry books than any other British imprint. Picking up poets dropped by the commercial operators, discovering new ones and selling on to the world's anthologists, this is certainly one of poetry's best proving grounds. Based in Northumberland and begun in Newcastle in the late 1970s, the press is unhindered by a past catalogue of classical wonders or an overly regional concern. It relentlessly pursues the new. Astley presents the complete service from thematic anthologies, world greats and selecteds to slim volumes by total newcomers. The press has its own range of excellent handbooks to the scene including *Getting Into Poetry* and *Writing Poems* along with an increasing range of critical volumes. Best poetry sellers are their anthologies: Linda France's *Sixty Women Poets*, Jeni Couzyn's *Contemporary Women Poets*, their decade-framing anthology *The New*

Poetry. With commendable concern to stay ahead Bloodaxe has produced Edna Longley's great *Bloodaxe Book of Twentieth Century Poetry* and Herbert and Hollis' *Strong Words*, an important collection of manifestos and poetics. Bloodaxe relishes the chance to publish work from outside the standard English mainstream – Ireland, Scotland, and Wales are all well represented, as are more traditional UK outsiders such as J.H. Prynne. They also give prominence to major American, European and Commonwealth poets including a number in bilingual editions. There is a multimedia thrust – a series of poets on cassette (including a revival of the British Council's recordings of contemporary poets), and a revamped Bloodaxe website (www.bloodaxebooks.demon.co.uk). Bloodaxe will not go rusty with age. Newcomers are advised to send a sample rather than a full collection. 'If you don't read contemporary poetry we are unlikely to be interested in your work,' comments Astley. A simple way to taste the imprint's range is to try their two house anthologies, *Poetry With An Edge* and *New Blood*.

The second, **Carcanet Press**, has been the consistent recipient of critical accolades. Publishing four Nobel Prize-winning authors and four Pulitzers helps. Although it is no longer exclusively a publisher of verse, putting out fiction, criticism, lives and letters, the press still gives poetry pre-eminence. It has over 600 titles in print, reps in forty-two countries and a programme that brings out forty to sixty poetry and poetry-related titles annually. Managing director Michael Schmidt agrees with Auden's observation that most people who read verse read it for some reason other than the poetry. He fights the tide with his own mainstream journal, *PN Review*. Carcanet has a policy of serious quality. 'I am strongly aware of the anti-modernist slant in a lot of poetry publishing, and publish to balance this,' he comments. 'Most submissions we receive come from people ignorant of the list to which they are submitting. Nothing is more disheartening than to receive a telephone call asking whether Carcanet publishes poetry.' The press has a four-part editorial programme: to publish new writing, to dust down substantial but neglected figures of this and earlier centuries, to encourage the translation of poetry, and to publish poets' prose and work relating to modern poetry. Typical of their list are Ian Macmillan, John Ashbery, Gillian Clarke, Paula Meehan, Edwin Morgan, Les Murray, Sophie Hannah, Miles Champion, Eavan Boland, and bestseller Elizabeth Jennings. Carcanet has an air of purpose about it. 'We avoid the Technicolor and pyrotechnic media razzmatazz,' says Schmidt. Have a look at their website (www.carcanet.co.uk), which is complete with links to the standard online booksellers. New poets are welcome to submit but check both your own past performance as well Carcanet's style before you go ahead. Schmidt's *New Poetries* anthologies give an idea where his taste is going next.

Production standards among other specialists can be equally as good as Carcanet and Bloodaxe although annual output (and as a consequence opportunity for the new poet) is substantially less.

Anvil Press Poetry, founded by Peter Jay in 1968, remains committed to Jay's original ideal of independent, alternative publishing. Over thirty years later, Anvil still publishes its earliest poets – such as Gavin Bantock, Anthony Howell and Harry Guest – although Jay is careful to avoid cliques. The best of new English language poets are constantly sought, and a sampler of these is found in this year's *Anvil New Poets 3* anthology. In addition, Anvil has won a deserved reputation for publishing the best of poetry in translation from around the world – poets such as Tagore, Seferis, Bei Dao, Lorca, Hikmet. Producing around a dozen titles a year, Anvil give particular attention to typographical detail, jacket design and quality of binding, making each publication exceptionally attractive. Anvil's bestselling poet is Carol Ann Duffy, with editions of works by Rimbaud, Baudelaire, Lorca and Dante continuing to sell steadily. A recent success among Anvil's contemporary poets was Dennis O'Driscoll's *Weather Permitting*, which won a Lannan award. For those who wish to familiarize themselves with the flavour of the Anvil list, Jay's acclaimed anthology *The Spaces of Hope* gives a perfect starting point.

Enitharmon Press represents quality, cares about presentation and operates 'at the unfashionable end' of the poetry publishing spectrum. Its books, often concerned with the process of bringing together word and image, are produced to the highest of standards. Enitharmon has little interest in fashion. The press is, as Anne Stevenson put it, 'dedicated to a poetry of the human spirit in an age of rampant commercialism'. Owner Stephen Stuart-Smith continues a policy of publishing between eight and twelve volumes annually by new, established and unjustly neglected poets. Typical of the list are Pascale Petit, Myra Schneider, Vernon Scannell, Kevin Crossley-Holland and Anthony Thwaite. The press has seen a surge in interest in the anthology, bringing out volumes covering women's views of their parents, *The Exeter Riddles* and *Tying the Song,* a first from The Poetry School. 'It seems unlikely that many new names will be added to the list, as Enitharmon is the only major poetry publisher in Britain which receives no regular subsidy' – which is a pity. We need more from publishers like Stuart-Smith.

Seren Books is a Welsh-based literary house publishing novels, art books, short fiction, biographies and critical texts. Started by Cary Archard as an offshoot of the magazine *Poetry Wales*, the imprint still maintains a solid interest in verse, publishing at least six new single author volumes annually. In receipt of Arts Council of Wales sponsorship, the bias towards work from Wales and the border regions is both admirable and inevitable. Poetry editor Amy Wack reads *everything* submitted but admits that she has only ever accepted one unsolicited manuscript in her entire tenure. Poets should read more, she told me. Editions are quality productions with plenty of attention paid to design inside and out. Typical recent poets include Forward winner Sheenagh Pugh, Deryn Rees-Jones, Paul Henry, Robert Minhinnick and Tony Curtis. Their major bestseller is Dannie Abse's *Twentieth Century Anglo-Welsh Poetry*. A good press sampler is their anthology *Oxygen – New Poets from Wales*. They have also published their own guide to the scene, *The Poetry Business*.

Tony Ward's **Arc Publications**, based in Lancashire, publishes a dozen poetry titles annually. 'We publish work that we believe important, innovative, and of outstanding quality,' Ward told me. The imprint has David Morley and John

Kinsella on the board and maintains a backlist approaching a hundred titles. Ivor Cutler, John Kinsella and W.N. Herbert are top sellers. The press publishes *Visible Poets,* a parallel text series aimed at bringing significant foreign poets to the attention of English audiences. (The Arc website is at www.arcpublications.co.uk) Prospective poets should not expect a quick response (allow up to four months, no submissions by e-mail) and should most certainly familiarise themselves with the Arc list before sending. 'We do not wish to put writers off or dampen enthusiasm, but we have never yet accepted an unpublished author,' is the official line. You have been warned.

Ward has an excellent reputation as a printer to the poetry press community and does a splendid job also for David Tipton's **Redbeck Press**. Tipton, who came up the pamphlet route used by many a small press, has now driven Redbeck into the top echelon in terms of volume of output (ten or so new titles annually), range of contributors − everything from Nick Toczek's performance pieces to Gavin Bantock's floating world − and quality of production. His star title of recent times has been Debjani Chatterjee's 200-page *Redbeck Anthology of British South Asian Poetry*. Other Redbeck poets include John Freeman, Jim Burns, Barry Tebb, Kim Taplin, Jenny Swann and Alan Dent. Non-centralist to the core.

Rupert Loydell's **Stride** has gathered a good reputation for catholic taste and running risks. After thirty-three issues in hard copy his eponymous magazine is now available again on the Web (www.stridemagazine.co.uk). Based in the south-west, output is eight books annually. The backlist runs to more than 200 titles ranging from the totally unknown to the famous. Stride almost perfectly fills the gap between the avant garde and the user-friendly. No one else is operating here. 'Our books are as likely to discuss free jazz, techno music or drug culture as marvel at the effect of sunlight on water, question ideas of belief or explore the intricacies of languages and the visual arts; as likely to use collage and cut-up as reinvent the sonnet; more likely to challenge and excite than send you to sleep' is the official line. The arrival of an American editor, Ethan Paquin, emphasises Stride's international interests. The press runs individual collections, criticism, and interviews, along with a range of excellent, alternative anthologies. Stride responds to submissions swiftly, invariably within three weeks and often within three days. Successes include Robert Lax, Charles Wright, Peter Redgrove, Robert Sheppard and their series of interviews on poetics, *Binary Myths*. Check Stride's anthology *Ladder To the Next Floor* for a sampler of how the press got where it is or look at their website (www.madbear.demon.co.uk/stride/).

Peterloo Poets, based in Cornwall, represents poetry without frills, without fuss and most definitely without the avant garde. Run by Harry Chambers, the press aims to publish quality work by new and neglected poets, some of them late starters (although if you have been flogging your stuff around the circuit for years and got nowhere then Chambers is unlikely to be your saviour); to co-publish with reputable presses abroad; and to establish a Peterloo list of succeeding volumes by a core of poets of proven worth. Heaney described Chambers as one of the 'great hearers and hearteners of the work being done in British and

Irish poetry'. Peterloo, which represents a stable centre for many people's idea of what poetry is, runs an active backlist of nearly 200 titles. Bestsellers include U.A. Fanthorpe, John Mole, Elma Mitchell, John Whitworth, and Dana Gioia. Recent additions include Wayne Burrows and Tim Cunningham. Peterloo, now in its twenty-fifth year, runs its own poetry competition (£2000 first prize – see entry under **Prizes**) and insists that prospective contributors to the press have had at least six poems in reputable magazines. Send a full manuscript accompanied by a stamped envelope large enough to carry it back to you. Chambers currently takes a couple of months to reply and is full to 2003.

Michael Hulse has begun **Leviathan**, along with its spin-off journal *Leviathan Quarterly*, with high production standards. His assembled editorial team includes John Kinsella and Anne Michaels. He has plans for six or so titles annually of British and American work alongside classics and poetry from India, Canada, Cuba, Italy and the Netherlands. On the stocks so far are Kit Wright, Jackie Wills, Roger Finch, Giles Goodland and Stephanos Papadopoulous. Co-publication with Rattapallax in New York boosts the imprint. In difficult times this is a brave venture.

There are other presses with less prodigious outputs but whose editions are still up there with the best of them. In Northumberland Margaret and Peter Lewis's **Flambard Press** has maintained its stature. Begun in 1991 it now publishes around five titles annually in the Bloodaxe style. With aid from Northern Arts the press is interested in new and neglected poets, especially from the North and the borders, along with proposals for books in translation. Gerard Benson, Joolz and Amanda White are typical poets. Gladys Mary Coles has developed her **Headland Publications** into a regular Peterloo clone. Her interest centres on north-west England and north Wales: Brian Wake, Alison Chisholm, and Anne Born top the list. Ken Edwards' **Reality Street Editions** specialises in 'linguistically innovative writing by women and men on both sides of the Atlantic'. Publishing a small number of single-author volumes, translations, ground-breaking anthologies along with a series of four-poet showcases, the press takes the new poetry seriously although offers little scope for the newcomer. Typical authors include Barbara Guest, Cris Cheek and Denise Riley. The press has also published book/CD packages and runs an excellent website (www.freespace.virgin.net/reality.street). Nicholas Johnson's **Etruscan Books** carries the flame for UK avant-garde poetry and performance with an excellent series of readers, chapbooks and multi-contributor volumes along with a first-class anthology of contemporary material, *Foil*. If anyone is pushing the edge out then Johnson is. Output is backed up by extensive poetry tours and festival appearances. Poets include Bob Cobbing, Tom Leonard, Tom Raworth, Sean Rafferty, Maggie O'Sullivan, Bill Griffiths and Tom Pickard.

Paul Beasley's **57 Productions** represents performance poetry heartland and, realising that most of his material works better on audio, has concentrated on editions on cassette and CD. All the biggies are here: Adrian Mitchell, Zephaniah, Jackie Kay, Lemn Sissay, Joolz, Linton Kwesi Johnson, and, amazingly, Gillian Clarke. Check their *Hearsay, Performance poems plus* anthology cassette and book.

At the self-styled poetry capital of Britain, no other place than Huddersfield, Janet Fisher and Peter Sansom run **Smith/Doorstop**, the poetry imprint of their enterprising **Poetry Business** (see **Organisations of Interest to Poets**). The press produces some excellent-looking full-length collections. Dorothy Nimmo, Martin Stannard, Paul Mills, Carcanet Press MD Michael Schmidt, and Michael Laskey are typical authors.

Jessie Lendennie runs **Salmon Publishing** from the Cliffs of Moher, Co. Clare, with connections at Spruce Island, Alaska, where they are planning a North American poetry centre and writers' retreat. The press publishes some of the best designed titles in the West. An Irish connection is pretty useful when trying here, although Salmon does look at material from further afield. Typical poets include Adrienne Rich, Rita Ann Higgins, Marvin Bell, Linda McCarriston, James Simmons and Mary O'Malley. Their anthology of contemporary Irish women poets, *The White Page*, is a terrific achievement. Recent titles include a *Selected and New Poems* from fantasy/science fiction writer Ray Bradbury (his first to be published outside the US) and *The Chair: Conversations with Poets from the North of Ireland* by John Brown. Salmon has an excellent website (www.salmonpoetry.com). And if the poetry is not flowing you can book in to a Salmon Creative Writing Workshop (£100 for the weekend) or spend a week or two as one of their Writers' Place residents.

Peepal Tree is the largest independent publisher of Caribbean, South Asian and black British poetry. Founded in 1986, it now produces around eight poetry titles annually. Typical poets include Kwame Dawes, Marcia Douglas, Cyril Dabydeen and Stewart Brown. Editors Jeremy Poynting and Hannah Banister read over 1,000 submissions annually and are not known for their speedy responses. Send five or six examples of your work along with a biographical note and wait. You can get a Peepal Tree catalogue and news updates by e-mail (hannah@peepal.demon.co.uk).

Elsewhere Lewis Davies's prose outfit, **Parthian Books**, has appointed Richard Gwyn as poetry editor and is putting out fine editions of Ifor Thomas, Patrick Jones and a new anthology of young Welsh contemporaries. **Blackwater Press** in Leicester has a growing list of new and established poets including Kate Foley, Ian Parks, David H.W. Grubb and Robert Hamberger.

As technology continues to make life easier for publishers it becomes harder to draw the line between the poetry specialists and the classic small presses. Maybe by now such a division does not exist at all.

The traditional outlets

Poetry has a place in our national press but traditionally a small one. The *Independent* runs a daily poem (and doesn't pay), so does the *Express* (which does). The *Guardian* features verse from time to time as do some of the serious Sunday heavies. The *Times Literary Supplement* gives over considerable space on a regular basis but it does have its favourites. The *London Review of Books* shows a similar interest although neither appear very keen to use unsolicited work from the mailbox. Among other journals the situation is fluid. Poetry gets in when someone on the staff shows an interest. Check your targets along the shelves at WHSmith's. Local newspapers and freesheets occasionally devote pages to contributions from readers, mostly dire doggerel and largely unpaid, although it *is* publication. If your paper doesn't do this, try sending in. Much of this might sound quite reassuring for the poet but the truth is that were poetry to cease to exist overnight, then these publications would continue to operate without a flicker. Who, other than the poets, would notice?

The regional anthologies

Running in parallel with the high-ground literary approach of much of the poetry world are empires largely unknown to the taste-makers and ignored by the critics. The biggest, Ian and Tracy Walton's **Forward Press** in Peterborough, now turns over a million and a half annually, has almost 5,000 titles in print, and reckons to account for around ten per cent of all verse published in the UK. Depressed with 'twenty years of not being able to enjoy poetry' because it was inevitably obscure, the couple have moved from back kitchen to three-storey office block in the service of 480,000 active British verse scribblers. 'A high proportion of the thousands of letters we receive tell us that many people find poetry over-complex and difficult to understand' runs one of their brochures. For more than a decade, since it was founded, Forward Press has enthusiastically promoted an 'accessible, sincere poetry which everyone can relate to'. The higher realms are not for them. Publishing under a number of imprints including **Poetry Now**, **Anchor Books** and **Triumph House**, the operation receives thousands of contributions annually. Poets are sourced through free editorial copy in regional newspapers. The contributors flow in their hundreds. 'It is a bit like amateur dramatics,' Ian told me, 'anyone can take part.'

Forward's outstanding success is built on its approachability. The Waltons and their team of exclusively young editors include as many as 160 poems in each anthology. Submissions under thirty lines are preferred. Costs are kept down by using in-house printing equipment – a Ryobi digital press – coupled to serviceable bindings. If you want to see your work in print, and for most contributors this is the whole raison d'être for writing, then you have to buy a copy. For many poets this will be their first appearance in book form and chances are they will purchase more than a single copy. This is not a traditional vanity operation. No one is actually being ripped off nor are the publishers raking in exorbitant profits. Page for page their titles are not much more expensive than those of Cape or Faber and are cheaper than the output of some little presses. However, distribution is patchy – not that many Forward titles make the shelves of our national chains, although efforts have been made. As for many of the small presses, interested parties are encouraged to buy direct. Forward's critics claim that quality is being neglected in exchange for quantity. Dumb down your criteria for inclusion, cram the poems in, sell more copies. Undoubtedly the genuine literary achievement of appearing in one of Forward's books is questionable. But in mitigation it must be said that for some writers this will be their much needed beginning (check Angela Macnab and Sally Spedding) but for others the only success they are ever going to get.

Forward's much criticised royalty payment scheme has been replaced with the Forward Press Top 100 Awards, which offer a total of £10,000 to the best of the poets published annually in their many anthologies.

In addition to their schools and regional collections Forward runs four magazines, *Poetry Now, Scribbler!* and *Wordsmith* (for young writers) and *Triumph Herald* (which specialises in Christian verse), a print and design service for self-publishers, and **Spotlight** – a series which showcases a dozen new poets a time. Their **Writers' Bookshop** imprint publishes a most useful series of guides to the publishing scenes in Britain, America and Australia including subject and genre guides, directories and handbooks. Forward offers the complete poetry life. If *Season's Delight, Poetic Bond, Happy Days, Cleansing Thoughts* and *Portraits of Life* sound like your scene send for the group's newsletters (Remus House, Coltsfoot Drive, Woodston, Peterborough PE2 9JX), ring them (01733 890099), check their website (www.forwardpress.co.uk) or e-mail your request (aja@forwardpress.co.uk). You'll find no dubious accommodation address dealing here but, on the other hand, few literary giants either.

Envious of Forward's success at catching the hearts and minds of most of the UK's poetry hobbyists, a good number of rival empire builders have risen in their wake. Regional poetry anthologies, Best of Britain collections, compendiums of English, Scottish, Irish and Welsh verse abound. Contributions are sourced through notices on library walls, local freesheets, local radio and through direct mail. These operations vary from the glossy to a number of pathetically produced and, one hopes, short-lived, incarnations based in the non-metropolitan sticks. No actual rip-off occurs and contributors get in whether they purchase or not. But if you want to see your work then you must buy and the books can cost upwards of £20. Before agreeing to contribute check the press's output. Do not submit blindly, research their backlist. It is what Faber would demand of you. The rule applies to the whole poetry scene.

The small press and the little magazine

Hobbyist publishing ventures have been with us for quite a long time. And today it's easier than ever to get your own small mag into the market place or to bring out your own book. Technologically literate poets are everywhere. Publishing has been stripped of its mystery. Access to decent printers and the computers that drive them are commonplace. Desk-top publishing and word processing software make it so easy to do. Disposable income has gone up. Poets in growing numbers are able and willing to establish competent one-person publishing operations, turning out neat, professional-looking titles on a considerable scale.

These are the small presses and little magazines. They sell to new and generally non-traditional markets, rarely finding space on bookshop shelves where they are regarded as unshiftable nuisances. Professional distribution remains the age-old problem and, using conventional routes, is probably now utterly unsolvable. However, the answer is around the corner. As publication shifts into cyberspace the difficulties of hard-copy distribution will fall away. But for now small mags still go hand-to-hand among friends, at slams, readings, concerts, creative writing classes, literary functions, and via subscriptions, and are liberally exchanged among all those concerned. The network is large. The question remains: is anyone out there not directly concerned with the business of poetry actually reading it? But that is another story.

Statistically, the small presses and the little magazines are the largest publishers of new poetry both in terms of range and circulation. They operate in a bewildering blur of shapes and sizes everywhere from Brighton to Birmingham and Aberystwyth to Aberdeen. Have a look at Derrick Woolf's fine *Poetry Quarterly Review* (Coleridge Cottage, Nether Stowey, Somerset TA5 1NQ) which carries regular reviews, or Andy Cox's broad ranging *Zene* (5 Martins Lane, Witcham, Ely, Cambridgeshire CB6 2LB; www.tta-press.freewire.co.uk). There is also an excellent, browsable small magazine information website at Daniel Trent's *Little Magazines* (www.little-magazines.co.uk), which exhibits flair and information in equal measure.

This country's best poetry magazines all began as classic littles. Between them *PN Review*, *Ambit*, *Outposts*, *Orbis*, *Poetry Review*, *Rialto*, *Acumen*, *Staple*, *Terrible Work*, *The North*, *Smiths Knoll*, *Envoi* and *Stand* do not come up to even half the circulation of journals like *Shooting Times* and *Practical Fishkeeping* – which says a lot about the way society values its poetry. Nonetheless, taken as a group, they will get to almost everyone who matters. They represent poetry as a whole. Read these and you will get some idea of where the cutting edge is. In the second division in terms of kudos lie the regional or genre specialists such as *HU* (Irish poetry), *The New Welsh Review*, *Poetry Wales*, *Poetry Ireland*, *The Stinging Fly* (Dublin's literary magazine), *Psycopoetica* (psychologically based poetry), *Krax* (humorous verse), *Writing Women*, *Christian Poetry Review*, *Snapshots Haiku Magazine* and *Time Haiku*. All these magazines are well produced, sometimes with the help of grants, and all represent a specific point of view. In Wales there is *Barddas* for poets using the strict metres and in Scotland *Lallans* for poets working in Lowland Scots. The vast majority of small magazines, however, owe no allegiance and range: from quality general round ups like *Billy Liar*, *Tears In The Fence*, *Arete*, *Obsessed With Pipework* and *Seam* (small enough to slide up your sleeve), and annuals, such as the excellent *Tabla*, to irregulars like *The Yellow Crane* (interesting new poems), *Konfluence* (tracking creative Ley lines), *Breathe* (helps keep poetry alive), *Multi Storey* (if you feel like you're on the edge), *The Red Wheelbarrow* (so much depends), *The Interpreter's House* (the best prose and verse that the editor can get) and *Skald* (general poetry). Some like *The Penniless Press* are for the poor of pocket and the rich of mind, *Fire* goes for the rambling and otherwise unpublishable while *The News That Stays News* is a private affair. If you can't find a magazine that suits you and your style then you can't be writing poetry. On the other hand if you are really sure you are then start your own.

Among the small presses there is a similar range. **Equipage**, **Writers Forum**, **Prest Roots Press**, **West House Books** and **Shearsman Books** keep the modernist tradition right there at the front; **Rockingham Press**, with its four or five titles annually, stays safe, solid and conventional; **Odyssey**, the side-line of *Poetry Quarterly Review*, based at the aptly named Coleridge Cottage in Somerset, mixes the mainstream with the wobbling edge; **Door-to-Everywhere** produces the smallest of folded sheets; **Dangaroo** has Third World and ethnic concerns. **The Collective** works the Welsh marches; **Shoestring Press** under the control of John Lucas publishes the pamphlets most admire. **Iron**, **Pikestaff Pamphlets** and **Flarestack Publishing** do sterling work. **Y Lolfa** publishes unofficial bards. For the new writer these kinds of presses are the obvious place to try first. Indeed it is where many have. Who put out T.S. Eliot's first? A small publisher. Dannie Abse, Peter Redgrove, James Fenton and Dylan Thomas, the same. R.S. Thomas, Ezra Pound and Edgar Allen Poe didn't even go that far – they published themselves.

Poetry for children

The thing to remember here is that children rarely buy poetry for themselves, nor are there poetry magazines aimed at them. On the other hand there are a great number of children's poets out there – Duffy, McGough, Henri and Patten would be much lesser authors if they'd ignored the under-eighteens. The schools system regularly pays poets to read to their classes and teach their children. Macmillan, Faber, Penguin, Walker and a few other publishers run specialist children's poetry lists. The market switches between the traditional and the hilarious – *Whizz Bang Orang-Utan* compiled by John Foster is a typical title. If you have appropriate work send in a few samples marked for the attention of the children's poetry editor. But do not imagine this market to be easy nor a place where you can unload your adult failures. Kids do not suffer fools gladly. For more information check with the Poetry Society, which publishes a number of 'poetry in schools' checklists along with a handbook.

Cash

Despite a small number of very high value awards (£75,000 plus) made by various government agencies to the select few, a lot of writers new to the business are surprised to learn that their poetry will not make them much money. For most, being a poet is not really much of an occupation. You get better wages delivering papers. There will be the odd £10 from the better heeled magazine, perhaps even as much as £60 or so from those periodicals lucky enough to be in receipt of a grant, but generally it will be free copies of the issues concerned, thank you letters and little more. Those with collections published by a subsidised, specialist publisher can expect a couple of hundred as an advance on royalties. Those using the small presses can look forward to a handful of complimentary copies. On the Internet published poets usually get nothing at all. The truth is that poetry itself is under-valued. You can earn money writing about it, reviewing it, lecturing on it, teach-ing it or, certainly, by giving public performances (£100 standard here, £1,000 or more if you are Roger McGough, much more if you are Seamus Heaney). In fact, most things in the poetry business will earn better money than the verse itself. This isn't capitalism, this is art.

Readings

Since the great Beat Generation Albert Hall reading of 1964, there has been an ever-expanding phenomenon of poets on platforms, reading or reciting their stuff to an audience that can be anywhere between raptly attentive and fast asleep. Jaci Stephen, writing in the *Daily Mirror*, reckoned readings to be like jazz. 'Both involve a small group of people making a lot of noise, and then, just when you think it's all over, it carries on.' But I believe there can be a magic in the spoken poem. Not everything, certainly. But when it's good it can be sublime. Yet for some writers the whole thing has devolved so far as to become a branch of the entertainment industry or, in the case of poetry slams (see **Competitions**, below), an opportunity to show off in front of friends. Whichever way you view it, it is certainly an integral part of the business and one in which the beginner is going to need to engage sooner or later. Begin by attending and see how others manage. Watch out for local events advertised at your local library or ring your local arts board. Poets with heavy reputations can often turn out to be lousy per-formers while many an amateur can really shake it down. Don't expect to catch every image as you listen. Readings are not places for total comprehension but more for glancing blows. Treat it as fun and it will be. If you are trying things yourself for the first time, make sure you've brought your books along to sell, stand upright, drop the shoulders, gaze at a spot at the back of the hall and blow.

Music

Poetry has made many inroads into the music business. There was a time when this meant Spike Milligan standing up and spouting in front of a jazz band or middle-of-the-road brass run behind John Betjeman reciting but no longer. There are quite a number of poets now working with musicians, starting bands or using pre-recorded backing tracks. The advent of rap and hip-hop and the ready use of the speech sample as a component part of dancefloor beats has turned the public ear. Dub poets – such as Linton Kwesi Johnson – have long used reggae as a backdrop for their words and the likes of Americans Sonja Sohn, Saul Williams and Dana Bryant have been softening up the cool crowd with their funk-backed hooks. This is certainly a non-traditional approach well away from poetry's conventional involvement with literature and with books. Check the clubs (and the events mounted by *Apples & Snakes* in London) to hear more and expect what you find to be nothing like what you expected.

Competitions and awards

Poetry competitions have been the vogue for decades now with the most unlikely organisations sponsoring them. The notion here is that anonymity ensures fairness. Entries are made under pseudonyms, so that if your name does happen to be Andrew Motion then this won't help you much. Results seem to bear this out too. The big competitions run biennially by the **Arvon Foundation** with the help of commercial sponsors, the **Academi**'s *Cardiff International* and the **Poetry Society**'s *National* attract an enormous entry and usually throw up quite a number of complete unknowns among the winners. And why do people bother? Cash prizes can be large – thousands of pounds – but it costs at least a few quid a poem to enter, and often much more than that. If it is cash you want, then the Lottery scratchcards are a better bet. And there has been a trend for winners to come from places like Cape Girardeau, Missouri and Tibooburra, Australia. The odds are getting longer. Who won the last Arvon? I don't remember. But if you do fancy a try then it is a pretty innocent activity. You tie up a poem for a few months and you spend a few pounds. Winners' tips include reading the work of the judges to see how they do it, submitting non-controversial middle-of-the-road smiling things, and doing this just before the closing date so you won't have to wait too long. Try two or three of your best. Huge wodges are costly and will only convince the judges of your insecurity. Have a look at *The Ring Of Words* (Sutton Publishing), an excellent historical anthology of Arvon winners and runners-up. For contests to enter watch the small mags, write to your regional arts board, check out *The New Writer* (one of the best listings around), *Poetry London*, *Writer's News* or the listings in *Orbis* magazine, look on the notice board at your local library, or write for the regularly updated list from the **Poetry Library** in London (see **Organisations of Interest to Poets**).

Combining both competition and reading is the Poetry Slam. Here all-comers are given the opportunity to strut their stuff for around three closely timed minutes before a usually not all that literary crowd. Points are awarded much in the style found in ice skating. You get them for a combination of performance and audience reaction. Scatology and street-wise crowd pleasing are more likely to get you through the rounds than closely honed work. The events, which involve much shouting, can be a lot of fun.

Poetry Awards are slightly different. These are usually made for published books, and convention generally requires your publisher to make the nomination rather than you. These glittering prizes are increasingly going up in value. Both the annual T.S. Eliot and Forward Prizes are now worth £10,000 a time, with the poetry section of the Whitbread Book Award not far behind. To win one of these your book needs to be pretty hot.

Radio and TV

After a highly successful five-year run of polling the nation for their favourite poems BBC TV this year allowed National Poetry Day to slide back to radio. TV coverage for poetry has always been scant. It is so hard to make verse visually appealing. Some producers have tried, notably Peter Symes at BBC2. Symes' approach is to avoid the poem illustrated and to concentrate instead on documentary-style collaborations between commissioned poet and film-maker. He's done well with Tony Harrison. He also makes poetry documentaries; one last year covered Ian Macmillan's creative workshops for prostitutes. Film-maker Brian Hill has produced a number of collaborations with Simon Armitage for Channel Four (including the splendid *Drinking for England*). Digital TV, however, with its almost insatiable appetite for material, is potentially a much better market. At BBC Knowledge they have already tried televised poetry slams. Poetry can also occasionally be found ladled between the music on MTV but inevitably by the media-promoted bards.

Most poetry on air actually sticks with radio. Last National Poetry Day saw Poet Laureate Andrew Motion commission new sonnets from some of the UK's best (including Fred D'Aguiar, Kathleen Jamie, Carol Ann Duffy and George Szirtes) and have these scattered through the Radio 4 schedules. Sue Roberts is the editor/producer of *Fine Lines* from Manchester, which features pairs of poets in discussion. Sue is keen to offer drama with poetry and had several successes including *Room of Leaves* by Amanda Dalton. Sara Davies at Bristol looks after Radio 4's regular long-running Sunday 4.30 strand with *Poetry Please* (a listeners' request show which uses only published material). Fiona Mclean produces poetry for Radio 3 including new translations of Piers Plowman and a series of Poetry Proms featuring the work of a range of writers including some from the first poet resident at the proms, Jo Shapcott. Radio 1 puts poetry into some of its evening slots, showcasing poets who have high street-cred. Independent radio is trying verse as fillers.

Poetry on radio is a large but difficult market. The BBC are pretty definite about having no remit to use 'unpublished or amateur verse'. Programme ideas should always be directed to a programme making department at the BBC rather than to Radio 4 or Radio 3. If you are determined to put your verse on air then local and regional radio offer better possibilities. Try sending in self-produced readings on cassette (if you are any good at it) or topical poetry which regional magazine programmes could readily use. Don't expect to be paid much.

Starting up

Probably the best place will be locally. Find out through the library or the nearest arts board which writers' groups gather in your area and attend. There you will meet others of a like mind, encounter whatever locally produced magazines there might be and get a little direct feedback on your work. 'How am I doing?' is a big question for the emerging poet and although criticism is not all that hard to come by, do not expect it from all sources. Magazine editors, for example, will rarely have the time to offer advice. It is also reasonable to be suspicious of that offered by friends and relations – they will no doubt be only trying to please. Writers' groups present the best chance for poets to engage in honest mutual criticism. But if you'd prefer a more detached, written analysis of your efforts and are willing to pay a small sum, then you could apply to *Prescription*, the service operated nationally by the Poetry Society (22 Betterton Street, London WC2H 9BU), to the service run by the Arts Council of Wales (see **Arts Councils and Regional Arts Boards**) or to those run on an area basis by your local arts board. There are also a number of non-subsidised critical services which you will find advertised in writers' magazines.

Read; if it's all a mystery to you, try Tony Curtis' *How to Study Modern Poetry* (Macmillan), Matthew Sweeney and John Hartley Williams' *Teach Yourself Writing Poetry*, Peter Sansom's excellent *Writing Poems* (Bloodaxe) or my own *The Poetry Business* (Seren). How real poets actually work can be discovered by reading C.B. McCully's the *Poet's Voice and Craft* (Carcanet) or *How Poets Work* (Seren). After all this, if you still think it's appropriate, try sending in.

How to do it

- Increase your chances of acceptance by following simple, standard procedure.
- Type or print on a single side of the paper, A4 size, single-spacing with double between stanzas, exactly as you'd wish your poem to appear when printed.
- Give the poem a title, clip multi-page works together, include your name and address at the foot of the final sheet. Avoid files, plastic covers, stiffeners and fancy clips of any sort.
- Keep a copy, make a record of what you send where and when, leave a space to note reaction.
- Send in small batches – six is a good number – with a brief covering letter saying who you are. Leave justification, apology and explanation for your writers' group.
- Include a self-addressed, stamped envelope of sufficient size for reply and/or return of your work.
- Be prepared to wait some weeks for a response. Don't pester. Be patient. Most magazines will reply in the end.
- Never send the same poem to two places at the same time (and this includes e-zine vs. hard copy: the jury is still out on whether or not the inclusion of

a poem on your own personal website actually counts as publication). If you've entered the poem for a competition then make sure you never simultaneously send it elsewhere.

■ Send your best. Work which fails to fully satisfy even the author is unlikely to impress anyone else.

Where?

Try the list that follows. This is by no means the whole UK small press scene, only those where potential contributors might stand a chance. Even here do not expect unrelenting positive responses: magazines get overstocked, editors change, addresses shift, policy alters, operators run out of steam. Be prepared to hunt around and for a lot of your work to come back. You can help improve things by buying copies. Send in an s.a.e. asking how much. The total market is vast and if you want to go further than the *Writer's Handbook* listings then you could consult the following: the *Small Press Guide*, which only covers journals (Writers' Bookshop, Remus House, Coltsfoot Drive, Woodston, Peterborough PE2 9JX), *Light's List of Literary Magazines*, which contains both UK and US addresses (John Light, Photon Press, The Lighthouse, 37 The Meadows, Berwick upon Tweed, Northumberland TD15 1NY), the Internet directory at *Little Magazines* (see The Small Press and Little Magazine, above) or Len Fulton's *Directory of Poetry Publishers* (Dustbooks) – the main American directory.

Scams and cons

With poetry overpopulated by participants it is not surprising that the con artist should make an appearance. There are plenty of people out there taking money off beginner writers and offering very little in return. The traditional vanity anthology, once the staple of the trickster, is now in retreat following a number of successful campaigns. Nonetheless variations and embellishments on the approach resurface steadily. These include offers to put your poetry to music setting you off on the road to stardom, readings of your verse by actors with deep voices to help you break into the local radio market (there isn't one) and further requests for cash to have entries on you appear in leather-bound directories of world poets. Everyone appears, including your uncle. There are bogus competitions where entry fees bear no relation to final prize money (or such prize money turns out never to be forthcoming) and the advertised 'publication of winners in anthology form' often means shelling out more for what will turn out to be a badly printed abomination crammed full of weak work. Poets should look very carefully at anything which offers framed certificates, scrolls or engraved wall hangings. They should also be wary of suggestions that they have come high in the State of Florida's Laureateship Contest (or some such like) and have been awarded a calligraphed testimonial. Presentation usually occurs at a three-day festival held in one of the state's most expensive hotels. To get your bit of paper you need to stay for all three days and it is you who has to settle the bill. If you try your luck at a no-entry-fee, advertised in the Sunday papers international competition don't be too surprised to find you've made it through round one – that happens to everyone. The scam starts with round two when they start to ask you for money.

How do you spot the tricksters? They change their names and addresses at will. They bill themselves as Foundations, Societies, Libraries, National Associations, Guilds. They sound so plausible. If you have the slightest suspicion then check with the Poetry Society (see **Organisations of Interest to Poets**). In the poetry world genuine advertisements for contributions are rare. And if anyone asks you for money then forget it. It is not the way things should be done.

The next step

Once you have placed a few poems you may like to consider publishing a booklet. There are as many small presses around as there are magazines. Start with the upmarket professionals by all means – Jonathan Cape, Faber & Faber – but be prepared for compromise. The specialists and the small presses are swifter and more open to new work.

If all else fails you could do it yourself. Blake did, so did Walt Whitman. Modern technology puts the process within the reach of us all and if you can put up a shelf, there is a fair chance you will be able to produce a book to go on it. Read my *How to Publish Yourself* (Allison & Busby). Remember that publishing the book may be as hard as writing it but marketing and selling it is quite something else. Check Alison Baverstock's *How To Market Books* (Kogan Page) if you really want to get ahead.

The listings

None of the lists of addresses that follow in **Poetry Presses** and **Poetry Magazines** are exhaustive. Publishers come and go with amazing frequency. There will always be the brand-new press on the look-out for talent and the projected magazine desperate for contributions. For up to the minute information check with some of the **Organisations of Interest to Poets** (see page 169).

Poetry has a huge market. It pays to keep your ear to the ground. The magazines and presses listed here have all been active during the past eighteen months and most (although be warned, *not all*) have indicated a willingness to look at new work. Those with a positive uninterest in receiving unsolicited work have been excluded. In all cases check before sending. Ask to see a catalogue or a sample copy. Good luck.

Poetry Presses

The presses listed here have all been active during the past 18 months and most have indicated a willingness to look at new work. Those with no interest in receiving unsolicited work have been excluded. In all cases check before sending. Ask to see a catalogue or a sample copy.

Anchor Books
Remus House, Coltsfoot Drive, Woodston, Peterborough PE2 9JX
☎01733 898102 Fax 01733 313524
Email anchorbooks@forwardpress.co.uk
Website www.forwardpress-co.uk

Contact *Steve Twelvetree*

An imprint of the **Forward Press** group.

Anvil Press Poetry Ltd
Neptune House, 70 Royal Hill, London SE10 8RF
☎020 8469 3033 Fax 020 8469 3363
Email anvil@anvilpresspoetry.com

Contact *Peter Jay*

Contemporary British poetry and poetry in translation. See entry under **UK Publishers**.

Arc Publications
Nanholme Mill, Shaw Wood Road, Todmorden, Lancs OL14 6DA
☎01706 812338 Fax 01706 818948
Email arc.publications@virgin.net
Website www.arcpublications.co.uk

Contact *Tony Ward*

Contemporary poetry from new and established writers both in the UK and abroad. See entry under **UK Publishers**.

ASLS – Association for Scottish Literary Studies
Dept of Scottish History, 9 University Gardens, Glasgow G12 8QH
☎0141 330 5309 Fax 0141 330 5309

To promote the study, teaching and writing of the languages of Scotland. See entry under **Professional Associations**.

Aural Images
5 Hamilton Street, Astley Bridge, Bolton, Lancs BL1 6RJ
Contacts *Susan & Alan White*

Poetry, youth arts workshops.

Bad Press
43 Kingsdown House, Amhurst Road, London E8 2AS
☎00 33 235 403326 Fax 00 33 235 403326
Email boxall@badpress.com
Website www.badpress.com

Contact *Philip Boxall*

100pp biannual, publishing new fiction, poetry and graphics.

BB Books
Spring Bank, Longsight Road, Copster Green, Blackburn, Lancs BB1 9EU
Contact *Dave Cunliffe*

Post-Beat poetics and counterculture theoretic. Iconoclastic rants and anarchic psychocultural tracts. See also **Global Tapestry Journal**.

Big Little Poem Books
3 Park Avenue, Melton Mowbray, Leics LE13 0JB
☎01664 850228 Fax 01664 850228

Contact *Robert Richardson*

Contemporary approaches to the lyric and epigram.

Blackwater Press
PO Box 5115, Leicester LE2 8ZD

Contemporary poetry from new and established writers.

Blade Press
Maynrys, Glen Chass, Port St Mary, Isle Of Man IM9 5PN
Contact *Jane Holland*

Bloodaxe Books
Highgreen, Tarset, Northumberland NE48 1RP
☎01434 240500 Fax 01434 240505
Email editor@bloodaxebooks.demon.uk
Website www.bloodaxebooks.demon.co.uk

Contact *Neil Astley*

Britain's leading publisher of new poetry . See entry under **UK Publishers**.

Cherry On The Top Press

29 Vickers Road, Firth Park, Sheffield S5
6UY
☎0114 244 1202 Fax 0114 244 1202
Email dgk-cvk@email.msn.com

Contact *David Kennedy*

The Collective

Penlanlas Farm, Llantilio Pertholey, Y-fenni,
Gwent NP7 7HN
☎01873 856350 Fax 01873 859487
Email john.jones6@which.net
Website www.welshwriters.com

Contact *John Jones*

Non-profit promoter and publisher of contemporary poetry.

Community of Artists and Poets Press

Sydenham House, 44 Cromwell Road,
Whitstable, Kent CT5 1NN
☎01227 281806
Website www.artistspress.co.uk

Contact *Philip Bennetta*

Dedicated to making artists books, hand-sewn
poetry pamphlets, with online gallery & magazine.

Corbie Press

57 Murray Street, Montrose, Angus
DD10 8JZ
☎01674 672625

Contact *Neil Mathers*

Scottish & European literature, art, philosophy,
some poetry. See also **Epoch Magazine**.

Creative Energy Publications

363 Holmsdale Road, London SE25 6PN
☎020 8653 7660

Contact *Ted Smith-Orr*

Pamphlets of football/sport poetry.

Diamond Twig

5 Bentinck Road, Newcastle upon Tyne
NE4 6UT
☎0191 273 5326
Email diamond.twig@virgin.net

Dionysia Press

20a Mongomery Street, Edinburgh EH7 5JS
☎0131 478 0927 Fax 0131 478 2572

Contact *Denise Smith*

Collections of poetry, words, translations. See
also **Understanding** magazine.

Door – To – Everywhere

3 Park Avenue, Melton Mowbray, Leics
LE13 0JB
Contact *Robert Richardson*

Poem card series.

Enitharmon Press

36 St George's Avenue, London N7 0HD
☎020 7607 7194 Fax 020 7607 8694
Email books@enitharmon.demon.co.uk

Contact *Stephen Stuart-Smith*

Poetry and criticism. See entry under **UK
Publishers**.

Equipage

Jesus College, Cambridge CB5 8BL
Contact *Rod Mengham*

Erran Publishing

43 Willow Road, Carlton, Notts NG4 3BH
Email erranpublishing@hotmail.com
Website www.poetichours.homestead.com
Contact *Nick Clark*

Non-profit supprter of third world charities.

Etruscan Books

28 Fowler's Court, Fore Street, Buckfast,
Devon TQ11 0AA
☎01364 643128 Fax 01364 643054

Contact *Nicholas Johnson*

Modernist, sound, visual poetry, Gaelic, lyric
poetry, US/UK poets.

Everyman Press

53 West Vale, Neston, Cheshire CH64 9SE
Contact *Elizabeth Boyd*

See also **Eclipse** magazine.

Feather Books

PO Box 438, Shrewsbury, Shropshire
SY3 0WN
☎01743 872177 Fax 01743 872177
Email john@waddysweb.free.uk
Website www.waddysweb.com

Contact *Rev. J. Waddington-Feather*

Quarterly magazine of Christian poetry and
prayers. See entry under **Small Presses**.

Flambard

Stable Cottage, East Fourstones, Hexham,
Northumberland NE47 5DX
☎01434 674360 Fax 01434 674178
Email admin@signature-books.co.uk
Website www.flambardpress.co.uk

Contact *Peter Elfed Lewis*

Concentrates on poetry but also publishes fiction, expecially crime and mystery.

Flarestack Publishing

Redditch Library, 15 Market Place, Redditch
B98 8AR
☎01527 63291 Fax 01527 68571
Email flare.stack@virgin.net

Contact *Charles Johnson*

Considers first collections for A5 stapled pamphlet publication. See also **Obsessed With Pipework** magazine.

Four Quarters Press

7 The Towers, Stevenage, Herts SG1 1HE

Green Books

Foxhole, Dartington, Totnes, Devon TQ9 6EB
☎01803 863260 Fax 01803 863843
Email greenboooks@gn.apc.org
Website www.greenbooks.co.uk/books

Poetry on the buses scheme.

Green Fire Press

76 Station Park, Lower Largo, Fife KY8 6DW

Grendon House

8 Laxay, Lochs, Isle of Lewis HS2 9PJ
☎01851 830418 Fax 01851 830412
Email grendon.house@virginnet.co.uk
Website
treespace.virginnet.co.uk/grendon.house

Contact *Francis T. Lewis*

Poetry in small collections. See also **Cpr International** magazine.

Halfcrown Publishers

198 Victoria Avenue, Kingston upon Hull
HU5 3DY

Headland Publications

Ty Coch, Galltegfa, Ruthin, Denbighshire
LL15 2AR
☎0151 625 9128 Fax 0151 625 9128

Contact *Gladys Mary Coles*

Fine editions of poetry; anthologies.

Hippopotamus Press

22 Whitewell Road, Frome, Somerset
BA11 4EL
☎01373 466653 Fax 01373 466653

Contact *Roland John*

First collections of verse from those with a track record in the magazines. See also **Outposts** magazine.

Honno Welsh Women's Press

Editorial Office, c/o Theological College, King Street, Aberystwyth, Ceredigion SY23 2LT
☎01970 623150 Fax 01970 626765
Email editor@honno.co.uk
Website www.honno.co.uk

Contact *Gwenllian Dafydd*

The Welsh women's press – novels, childrens fiction, short stories, poetry and autobiographical anthologies. See entry under **UK Publishers**.

Hub Editions

Longholm, East Bank, Wingland, Sutton Bridge, Spalding, Lincolnshire PE12 9YS

Contact *Colin Blundell*

Poetry, experimental writing, challenges to the status quo, high-class hand-made perfect bound products.

I★d Books

Connah's Quay Library, Wepre Drive, Connah's Quay, Deeside, Flintshire
☎0161 226 3419

Contact *Clive Hopwood*

Poetry, fiction, local history.

Intimacy Books

15 Waterlow Road, Maidstone, Kent
ME14 2TR

Contact *Adam McKeown*

Communication experienced as nakedness (Laure). See also **Intimacy** magazine.

Katabasis

10 St Martin's Close, London NW1 0HR
☎020 7485 3830 Fax 020 7485 3830
Email katabasispress@netscapeonline.co.uk
Website www.katabasis.co.uk

Contact *Dinah Livingstone*

Down-to-earth and utopian poetry and prose from home and abroad – English and Latin American.

The King's England Press

21 Commercial Road, Goldthorpe, Rotherham, S. Yorks S63 9BL
Email enquiries@kingsengland.demon.co.uk
Website www.kingsengland.demon.co.uk

Contact *Steve Rudd*

Children's books including poetry.

Kite Books

16 Fane Close, Stamford, Lincs PE9 1HG
☎01780 754193

Contact *Kevin Troop*

Kite modern poetry series includes two poets per book. See also **The Third Half** magazine.

Lapwing Publications
1 Ballysillan Drive, Belfast BT14 8HQ
☎028 9087 5134 Fax 028 9087 5134

Contacts *Dennis & Rene Greig*

Small first collections in pamphlet format

Leafe Press
1 Leafe Close, Chilwell, Nottingham NG9 6NR

Leviathan
Market House, Market Place, Deddington, Oxford OX15 0SE
☎01869 338240 Fax 01869 338310
Email leviathanmh@hotmail.com

Contact *Michael Hulse*

See also **Leviathan Quarterly** magazine.

Little Big Words Poetry Press
62 Willowhale Green, Bognor Regis, West Sussex PO21 4LW
☎07930 269061

Contact *Paul D. Nicklin*

See also **Viztex Publications**.

Llwynywll Press
2 Llyn Y Grant Terrace, Cardiff CF23 9EW
Contact *Andrew Belsey*

Lomond Press
4 White Craigs, Kinnesswood, Kinross KY13 7JN
Contact *R.L. Cook*

Malfunction Press
Rose Cottage, 3 Tram Lane, Buckley, Flintshire CH7 3JB
☎01244 543820
Email rosecot@presford.freeserve.co.uk

Contact *Peter E. Presford*

Dedicated to mainly sci-fi & fantasy.

Mariscat Press
3 Mariscat Road, Glasgow G41 4ND
☎0141 423 7291
Email davidmcmenemy@compuserve.com

Contact *Hamish Whyte*

Currently publishing only poetry pamphlets.

Mudfog Press
11 Limes Road, Linthorpe, Middlesborough TS5 6RQ

☎01642 864428 Fax 01642 264955
Email cleveland.arts@onyxnet.co.uk

Contact *Andy Croft & Others*

The best new writers from Teesside.

Mynah Poets
13 Belvedere, Balby, Doncaster DN4 9DU
Email mynahpoets@trotcat.freeserve.co.uk
Contact *Mick Blakesley*

Lo-tech, well-designed pamphlets – quirky intelligent material – no avantgardists.

New Hope International
20 Werneth Avenue, Gee Cross, Hyde, Cheshire SK14 5NL
Email newhope@iname.com
Website www.nhi.clara.net/online.htm
Contact *Gerald England*

Poetry booklet publisher. See also **Aabye** magazine.

Oasis Books
12 Stevenage Road, Fulham, London SW6 6ES
☎020 7736 5059

Contact *Ian Robinson*

Pamphlets of poetry and prose. See also **Oasis** magazine.

The Old Stile Press
Catchmays Court, Llandogo, Nr Monmouth, Monmouthshire NP25 4TN
☎01291 689226
Email oldstile@dircon.co.uk

Contacts *Frances & Nicholas McDowell*

Fine, hand printed books with text and images.

The One Time Press
Model Farm, Linstead Magna, Halesworth, Suffolk IP19 0DT
☎01986 785422

Contact *Peter Wells*

Poetry of the forties in limited editions. Illustrated.

Original Plus
11 Heatherton Park, Bradford on Tone, Taunton, Somerset TA4 1EV
☎01823 461725
Email smithsssj@aol.com
Website members.aol.com/smithsssj/index.html

Contact *Sam Smith*

Requires something extra – another language or markedly original. See also **The Journal** magazine.

Othername Press
14 Rosebank, Rawtenstall, Rossendale
BB4 7RD
Poetry and surrealism.

Oversteps Books
Oversteps, Froude Road, Salcombe, S. Devon
TQ8 8LH
☎01548 843713   Fax 01548 843713

Paradise Press
80 College Road, Isleworth, Middlesex
TW7 5DS
Contact *Roy Heaps*
The gay authors self-publishing society.

Partners In Poetry
289 Elmwood Avenue, Feltham, Middlesex
TW13 7QB
☎0777 9193676
Contact *Ian Deal*
Competitions and poetry pamphlets.

Peepal Tree Press Ltd
17 King's Avenue, Leeds, W. Yorks LS6 1QS
☎0113 245 1703   Fax 0113 246 8368
Email hannah@peepal.demon.co.uk
Contact *Jeremy Poynting*
Best in Caribbean and south Asian writing from
around the world. See under **Small Presses**.

Peterloo Poets
The Old Chapel, Sand Lane, Calstock,
Cornwall PL18 9QX
☎01822 8333473
Email poets@peterloo.fsnet.co.uk
Contact *Harry Chambers*
Contemporary English poetry.

The Phlebas Press
21 Overton Gardens, Mannamead, Plymouth,
Devon PL3 5BX

Picture Poems
114 Broadway, Herne Bay, Kent CT6 8HA
☎01227 360525
Email picturepoems@hbaykent.freeserve.co.uk
Contact *Barbara Dordi*
Publishers of original artwork with poetry/
prose. See also **Equinox** magazine.

Pigasus Press
13 Hazely Combe, Arreton, Isle Of Wight
PO30 3AJ
☎01983 865668

Email pigasus.press@virgin.net
Contact *Tony Lee*
Science fiction poetry in irregular themed
anthologies. See also **The Zone** magazine.

Pikestaff Press
Ellon House, Harpford, Sidmouth, Devon
EX10 0NH
☎01395 568941
Contact *Robert Roberts*
Contemporary English poets, mainly pamphlets.

Poems in the Waiting Room
PO Box 488, Richmond TW9 4SW
Email leelda@globalnet.co.uk
Contact *Michael Lee*
Pamphlets for medical waiting rooms.

The Poetry Business
The Studio, Byram Arcade, Huddersfield, W.
Yorks HD1 1ND
☎01484 434840   Fax 01484 426566
Email edit@poetrybusiness.co.uk
Website www.poetrybusiness.co.uk
Contacts *Peter Sansom & Janet Fisher*

Poetry Monthly Press
39 Cavendish Road, Long Eaton, Nottingham
NG10 4HY
☎0115 946 1267
Email martinholroyd@compuserve.com
Website ourworld.compuserve.com/home-
page/martinholroyd
Contact *Martin Holroyd*
See also **Poetry Monthly** magazine.

Poetry Now
Remus House, Coltsfoot Drive, Woodston,
Peterborough PE2 9JX
☎01733 898101   Fax 01733 313524
Email poetrynow@forwardpress.co.uk
Website www.forwardpress.co.uk
Contact *Heather Killingray*
Lively, personal and contemporary, also deals
with womenswords. See also **Poetry Now**
magazine.

Poetry Now Young Writers
Remus House, Coltsfoot Drive, Woodston,
Peterborough PE2 9JX
☎01733 890066   Fax 01733 313524
Email forward_press@compuserve.com
Website www.forwardpress.co.uk
Contact *Andrew Head*

Publishers of children's poetry. See also **Scribbler!** magazine.

Poetry Today

Remus House, Coltsfoot Drive, Woodston, Peterborough PE2 9JX
☎01733 890099 Fax 01733 313524
Email forward_press@compuserve.com
Website www.forwardpress.co.uk

Part of the **Forward Press** group.

Poets Anonymous

70 Aveling Close, Purley, Surrey CR8 4DW
Email poets@poetsanon.org.uk
Website www.poetsanon.org.uk
Contact *Peter L. Evans*

Anthologies & collections of predominately south London poets. See also **Poetic Licence** magazine.

Polygon

Edinburgh Univ. Press, 22 George Square, Edinburgh EH8 9LF
☎0131 650 4213 Fax 0131 650 4218
Email polygon@eup.ed.ac.uk
Website www.eup.ed.ac.uk
Contact *Alison Bowden*

Prize-winning independent literary publisher specialising in new fiction & poetry. See entry under **UK Publishers**.

Prest Roots Press

34 Alpine Court, Lower Ladyes Hills, Kenilworth CV8 2GP
Contact *P.E. Larkin*

O'erweening poetry.

Puddle Press

2b Hamilton Court, Taunton, Somerset TA1 2PA
Contact *Geoff Sawers*

Experimental poetry.

QQ Press

York House, 15 Argyle Terrace, Rothsay, Isle of Bute PA20 0BD
Contact *Alan Carter*

Poetry. See also **Quantum Leap** magazine.

Raunchland Publications

18 Canon Lynch Court, Dunfermline, Fife KY12 8AU
Email raunchland@hotmail.com
Website website.lineone.net/~johningay/
  raunchland.htm

Contact *John Mingay*

Limited edition poetry/graphics booklets.

Reality Street Editions

4 Howard Court, Peckham Rye, London SE15 3PH
☎020 7639 7297
Email reality.street@virgin.net
Website freespace.virgin.net/reality.street
Contact *Ken Edwards*

New poetry from Britain, Europe and America.

Red Candle Press

9 Milner Road, Wisbech, Cambs PE13 2LR
'Traditionalist poetry is our great interest.' See also **Candelabrum Poetry Magazine**.

Redbeck Press

24 Aireville Road, Frizinghall, Bradford BD9 4HH
☎01274 498135
Contact *David Tipton*

Contemporary poetry and some short fiction.

Rialto Publications

PO Box 309, Aylsham, Norwich, Norfolk NR11 6LN
Contact *Michael Mackmin*

Poetry. See also **The Rialto** magazine.

Rive Gauche Publishing

69 Lower Redland Road, Bristol BS6 6SP
☎0117 974 5106
Contact *P.V.T. West*

Poetry by women writing and performing in Bristol.

Route

School Lane, Glasshoughton, Castleford WF10 4QH

British south Asian writers.

Rump Booklets

63 Dixon Lane, Wortley, Leeds, W. Yorks LS12 4RR
Contact *Andy Robson*

Light-hearted, contemporary poetry, short fiction & graphics. See also **Krax** magazine.

Searle Publishing

6 Bramerton Lodge, Easthill Lane, Bramerton, Norwich, Norfolk NR14 7EQ
Contact *David Searle*

Run by writers for writers.

Seren
First Floor, 38–40 Nolton Street, Bridgend
CF31 3BN
☎01656 663018 Fax 01656 649226
Email seren@seren.force9.co.uk
Website www.seren-books.com
Contact *Mick Felton*

Poetry, fiction, lit crit, biography, essays. See under **UK Publishers** and **Poetry Wales** magazine.

Shoestring Press
19 Devonshire Avenue, Beeston, Nottingham
NG9 1BS
☎0115 925 1827
Contact *John Lucas*

Poetry & fiction.

Sixties Press
89 Connaught Road, Sutton, Surrey SM1 3RJ
Contact *Barry Tebb*

The work of Barrry Tebb and others. See also **Poetry Now Newsletter**.

Stride Publications
11 Sylvan Road, Exeter, Devon EX4 6EW
Email editor@stridebooks.co.uk
Website www.stridebooks.co.uk
Contact *Rupert Loydell*

Poetry, fiction, essays and interviews.

Summer Palace Press
Cladnagerach, Kilbeg, Kilcar, Co Donegal
Republic of Ireland
☎00 353 733 8448 Fax 00 353 733 8448
Contacts *Kate & John Newman*

Poetry collections.

Survivors' Poetry Scotland
4 C3 Templeton Centre, Templeton Street, Glasgow G40 1DA
☎ 0141 556 4554 Fax 0141 400 8442
Email sps@spscot.co.uk
Website www.spscot.co.uk

For survivors of the mental health system. See entry under **Organisations of Interest to Poets**.

Tabla
Dept of English, University of Bristol, Bristol
BS8 1TB Fax 0117 928 8860
Email stephen.james@bristol.ac.uk
Website www.bristol.ac.uk/tabla
Contact *Dr Stephen James*

Publisher of the annual *Tabla Book of New Verse*.

Thumbscrew Press
PO Box 657, Oxford OX2 6PH
Email tim.kendall@bristol.ac.uk
Website www.bristol.ac.uk/thumbscrew
Contact *Tim Kendall*

Pamphlets by new and established poets. See also **Thumbscrew** magazine.

Touched Press
4 Varley House, County Street, London
SE1 6AL
☎020 7403 5451 Fax 020 7403 5446
Email touchedpress@aol.com
Contact *Armorel Weston*

Triumph House
Remus House, Coltsfoot Drive, Woodston, Peterborough PE2 9JX
☎01733 898102 Fax 01733 313524
Email triumphhouse@forwardpress.co.uk
Website www.forwardpress.co.uk
Contact *Steve Twelvetree*

A Christian poetry imprint publishing many anthologies annually. See also **Triumph Herald** magazine.

Two Rivers Press
35–39 London Street, Reading, Berkshire
RG1 4PS
Contact *Peter Hay*

A cooperative which welcomes artists, writers, designers and anyone who can change a light-bulb. See also **The Waterlog** magazine.

United Press Ltd
1 Yorke Street, Burnley, Lancs BB11 1HD
☎01282 459533 Fax 01282 412679
Email mail@upltd.co.uk
Website www.upltd.co.uk
Contact *Peter Quinn*

Publishes poetry & prose including national poetry anthology.

Vennel Press
8 Richmond Road, Staines, Middlesex
TW18 2AB
Email vennel@hotmail.com
Website
www.indigogroup.co.uk/llpp/vennel.html
Contact *Richard Price*

Modern Scottish poetry; poetry in translation; poetry that takes its bearings from modernism.

Viztex Publications

62 Willowhale Green, Bognor Regis,
West Sussex PO21 4LW
☎07930 269061

Contact *Paul D. Nicklin*

See also **Little Big Words Poetry Press**.

Waldean Press

17 London Road, Tetbury, Gloucestershire
GL8 8HR

The best contemporary poetry in quality pamphlets.

Wanda Publications

Word And Action, 75 High Street,
Wimborne, Dorset BH21 1HS
☎01202 889669
Email wanda@wordandaction.com

Poetry, stories, local history and world of instant theatre. See also **South** magazine.

West House Books

16a Priory Road, Nether Edge, Sheffield
S7 1LW
Email alan@nethedge.demon.co.uk
Contact *Alan Halsey*

Writers Forum

89a Petherton Road, London N5 2QT
☎020 7226 2657

Contact *Bob Cobbing*

Innovative language and visual poetries. See also **And** magazine.

Writers' Own Publications

121 Highbury Grove, Clapham, Bedford
MK41 6DU
☎01234 294785

Contact *Mrs E.M. Pickering*

Yorkshire Art Circus Ltd

School Lane, Glass Houghton, Castleford,
West Yorkshire WF10 4QH
☎01977 550401

Community publisher. See entry under **Small Presses**.

Zum Zum Books

Goshem, Bunlight, Drumnadrochit,
Inverness-shire IV63 6AX
☎01456 450402

Contact *Neil Oram*

Wild, brilliant, deep, sensous, philosophical poetry.

Poetry Magazines

The magazines listed here have all been active during the past 18 months and most are willing to look at new work. In all cases check before sending. Ask to see a catalogue or a sample copy.

Aabye
20 Werneth Avenue, Gee Cross, Hyde, Cheshire SK14 5NL
Website www.nhi.clara.net/nhihome.htm

Contact *Gerald England*

Contemporary international poetry journal open to all genres. See also **New Hope International** press.

Acumen
6 The Mount, Higher Furzeham, Brixham, Devon TQ5 8QY
☎01803 851098 Fax 01803 851098

Contact *Patricia Oxley*

Good poetry, intelligent articles and wide-ranging reviews. See also **The Long Poem Group Newsletter**.

Advance
Hilton House, 39 Long John Hill, Norwich, Norfolk NR1 2JP
☎01603 449845 Fax 01603 449845

Contact *Michael K. Moore*

Contemporary poetry. For all who want to climb up the poetry listings.

The Affectionate Punch
35 Brundage Road, Manchester M22 0BY

Contact *Andrew Tutty*

Biannual journal of well-presented poetry (40 lines max) and fiction (1500 words max).

Agenda
5 Cranbourne Court, Albert Bridge Road, London SW11 4PE
☎020 7228 0700 Fax 020 7228 0700

Contact *William Cookson*

Quarterly poetry magazine, founded 1959.

And
89a Petherton Road, London N5 2QT
☎020 7226 2657

Contacts *Bob Cobbing & Adrian Clarke*

Visual and linguistically innovative poetries. See also **Writers Forum** press.

Areopagus
101 Maytree Close, Winchester SO22 4JF
Fax 0870 1346384
Website www.churchnet.org.uk/areopagus/index.html

Contact *Julian Barritt*

A Christian based arena for creative writers.

Arete
8 New College Lane, Oxford OX1 3BN
☎01865 289193 Fax 01895 289194
Email craig.raine@new.ox.ac.uk
Website www.aretemagazine.com

Contact *Craig Raine*

Fiction, poetry, reportage, reviews.

As Well As
69 Orchard Croft, Harlow, Essex CM20 3BG

Contact *John Steer*

Awen
38 Pierrot Steps, 71 Kursaal Way, Southend on Sea, Essex SS1 2UY

Contact *David John Tyrer*

Poetry and vignette-length fiction of any style/genre. See also **Garbaj** and **Monomyth** magazines.

Banipal
PO Box 22300, London W13 8ZQ
☎020 8568 9747 Fax 020 8568 8509
Website www.banipal.com

Contact *Margaret Obank*

Modern Arab literature.

A Bard Hair Day
289 Elmwood Avenue, Feltham, Middlesex TW13 7QB
☎0777 919 3676
Website partners_writing_group.homestead.com

Contact *Ian Deal*

General poetry and short story magazine. See also **Seventh Sense** magazine and **The Word Life Journal**.

Billy Liar
7/8 Trinity Chare, Quayside, Newcastle upon Tyne NE1 3DF
☎0191 296 6787 Fax 0191 296 6787
Contacts *Paul Summers & Others*
State of the nation through fiction, journalism, poetry, visual art and reviews.

The Black Rose
56 Marlescroft Way, Loughton, Essex IG10 3NA Fax 020 8508 1757
Website www.expage.com/blackrosepoetry
Contact *Bonita Hall*
Bi-monthly poetry magazine, all styles considered, new poets welcome.

The Blighter
PO Box 29557, London N1 1TZ
Contact *Les*

Borderlines
Nant Y Brithyll, Llangynyw, Welshpool, Powys SY21 0JS
☎01938 810263
Contacts *Dave Bingham & Kevin Bamford*
Open poetry mag published by the Anglo-Welsh Poetry Society.

Braquemard
20 Terry Street, Hull HU3 1UD
Website www.braquemard.fsnet.co.uk
Contact *David Allenby*
Forty pages of excellent poetry, prose & artwork.

Breakfast All Day
See **Bad Press**

Breathe Poetry Magazine
2 Grimshoe Road, Downham Market, Norfolk PE38 9RA
Website www.zyworld.com/sharonsweet
Contact *Sharon Sweet*
Contemporary British poetry.

Brittle Star
83 Barretts Grove, London N16 8AP

The Brobdignagian Times
96 Albert Road, Cork, Republic of Ireland
Contact *Giovanni Malito*
Poetry, very short fiction, cover art.

Buzzwords
Calvers Farm, Thelveton, Diss, Norfolk IP21 4NG
Email zoeking@calversfarm.fsnet.co.uk
Website www.buzzwordsmagazine.co.uk
Contact *Zoe King*
Poetry, short fiction, mixing new with the established.

C P R Internations (formerly Christian Poetry Review)
Grendon House, 8 Laxay, Lochs, Isle Of Lewis H52 9PJ
☎01851 830418 Fax 01851 830412
Website www.planet-scotland.com
Contact *Frances T. Lewis*
Aims to provide a platform for new and established poets who also happen to be Christian.

Cadenza
PO Box 1768, Rugby CV21 4ZA
Contact *Jo Good*
Poetry and prose.

Candelabrum Poetry Magazine
9 Milner Road, Wisbech, Cambs PE13 2LR
Contact *Leonard McCarthy*
Twice-yearly poetry mostly traditional. See also **Red Candle Press**.

Cannon Fodder
11 Cholmley Villas, Portsmouth Road, Thames Ditton, Surrey KT7 0XU

Chapman
4 Broughton Place, Edinburgh, Scotland EH1 3RX
☎0131 557 2207 Fax 0131 556 9565
Website www.chapman-pub.co.uk
Contact *Joy M. Hendry*
The best in Scottish and international writing, well-established writers & the up-and-coming. See entries under **UK Publishers** and **Magazines**.

Coffee House, The
Charnwood Arts, Loughborough, Leics LE11 3DU
☎01509 822558 Fax 01509 822559
Website www.cuttlefish.com/
Contact *Deborah Tyler-Bennett*
Poetry, short prose & visual art, featuring new and familiar local and international voices.

Connections
13 Wave Crest, Whitstable, Kent CT5 1EH
Contact *Narissa Knights*

Poetry, short stories, articles, news and reviews from new & established writers.

Connections
165 Domonic Drive, New Eltham, London SE9 3LE

Contact *Jeanne Conn*

Cpr International
Grendon House, 8 Laxay, Lochs, Isle Of Lewis HS2 9PJ
☎01851 830418 Fax 01851 830412
Website treespace.virginnet.co.uk/
    grendon.house

Contact *Francis T. Lewis*

Poetry and reviews – the shorter poem preferred. See also **Grendon House** press.

Current Accounts
16–18 Mill Lane, Horwich, Bolton, Lancs BL6 6AT

Poetry, short fiction, articles – magazine of the Bank Street Writers' Group.

Cyphers
3 Selskar Terrace, Ranelagh, Dublin 6, Republic of Ireland Fax 00 353 1 497 8866

Contact *Eilean Ní Chuilleanain*

Irish literary magazine: poetry, prose, reviews.

The Dark Horse
31 Melville Street, Top Flat Left, Pollokshields, Glasgow G41 2JL

Contact *Gerry Cambridge*

Poetry.

David Jones Journal, The
The David Jones Society, 48 Sylvan Way, Sketty, Swansea SA2 9JB
☎01792 206144 Fax 01792 205305

Contact *Anne Price-Owen*

Articles, poetry, information, reviews and inspired works.

Deliberately Thirsty
Argyll Publishing, Glenaruel, Argyll PA22 3AE
Website www.deliberatelythirsty.co

Contact *Sean Bradley*

New poetry, fiction & drama.

The Devil
247 Gray's Inn Road, London WC1X 8JR
☎020 8994 7767

Contact *Stephen Plaice*

Prose, poetry, fiction, reviews, major interviews. (Formerly The Printer's Devil.)

Dial 174
21 Mill Road, Watlington, King's Lynn, Norfolk PE33 0HH
☎01553 811949

Contact *Joseph Hemmings*

Poetry, short storie, articles, travelogues, artwork, etc.

Dream Catcher
14 Garth Terrace, York YO30 6DU
☎01904 628138 Fax 01904 628138
Website www.openingline.co.uk/magazines/
    dreamcatcher

Contact *Paul Sutherland*

Poetry, prose, b&w photographs, from national & international contributors .

Eastern Rainbow
17 Farrow Road, Whaplode Drove, Spalding, Lincs PE12 0TS
☎01406 330242
Website www.lineone.net/~peaceandfreedom/

Contact *Paul Rance*

Focuses on 20th century culture via poetry, prose & art .

Eclipse
53 West Vale, Neston, Cheshire CH64 9SE

Contact *Elizabeth Boyd*

Bi-monthly poetry mag – all types and styles welcome. See also **Everyman Press**.

Edinburgh Review
22a George Square, Edinburgh EH8 9LF
☎0131 650 6207 Fax 0131 662 0553
Website www.eup.edd.ac.uk/

Contact *Alex Thomson*

Twice-yearly literature and ideas magazine. See entry under **Magazines**.

Envoi
44 Rudyard Road, Biddulph Moor, Stoke-on-Trent ST8 7JN

Contact *Roger Elkin*

Poetry, sequences, features, reviews, competitions.

Epoch Magazine
57 Murray Street, Montrose, Angus DD10 8JZ
☎01674 672625

Contact *Neil Mathers*

Scottish & European literature, art, philosophy, some poetry. See also **Corbie Press**.

Equinox
114 Broadway, Herne Bay, Kent CT6 8HA
☎01227 360525

Contact *Barbara Dordi*

Journal of contemporary poetry illustrated with original artwork. See also **Picture Poems** press.

Fan the Flames
c/o Brikhouse C S, The Barns, Sheepcote Lane, Silver End, Witham, Essex
Website www.fantheflames.co.uk

Contact *Emma Reed*

Poetry & prose quarterly, distributed throughout the UK.

Fife Lines
67 Dunlin Avenue, Collydean, Glenrothes KY7 6TD

Contact *Ian Nimmo White*

Profiling the work of established and new poets.

Fire
Field Cottage, Old Whitehill, Tackley, Kidlington, Oxon OX5 3AB
☎01869 331300
Website www.poetical.org

Contact *Jeremy Hilton*

Poetry: alternative, unfashionable, experimental, spiritual, demotic; occasional experimental prose.

First Time
The Snoring Cat, 136 Harold Road, Hastings, East Sussex TN35 5NN

Contact *Josephine Austin*

New poets.

Flaming Arrows
County Sligo V E C, Riverside, Sligo, Republic of Ireland
☎00 353 71 45844

Contact *Leo Regan*

Stories, poetry, contemplative, metaphysical, spiritual themes grounded in senses.

Gairm
15 Struan Road, Glasgow G44 3AT
☎0141 221 1971

Contact *Derick Thomson*

All Gaelic literary quarterly. See also **Gairm Publications** under **UK Publishers**.

Garbaj
38 Pierrot Steps, 71 Kursaal Way, Southend on Sea, Essex SS1 2UY

Contact *David John Tyrer*

Humourous/non-pc poetry, vignette-length fiction, fake news, etc. See also **Awen** and **Monomyth** magazines.

Gargoyle
152 Harringay Road, London N15 3HL
☎020 8292 3632   Fax 020 8292 3632
Email admin@gargoyle.uk.com

Contact *Maja Prausnitz*

New poets, artists and fiction writers. See entry under **Magazines**.

Gentle Reader Poetry
8 Heol Pen Y Bryn, Penyrheol, Caerphilly CF83 2JX
☎029 2088 6369

Contact *Lynne E. Jones*

Annual poetry anthology. Welomes new poets. Prefers simple poems not too profound.

Global Tapestry Journal
Spring Bank, Longsight Road, Copster Green, Blackburn, Lancs BB1 9EU
☎01254 249128

Contact *Dave Cunliffe*

Global Bohemia, post-Beat and counterculture orientation. See also **BB Books**.

Green Queen
BM Box 5700, London WC1N 3XX

Contact *Elsa Wallace*

Occasional magazine, Green issues, lesbian & gay fiction, articles, poetry.

How Do I Love Thee?
1 Blue Ball Corner, Water Lane, Winchester, Hants SO23 0ER
Website freespace.virgin.net/poetry.life/

Contact *Adrian Bishop*

The magazine for love poetry.

HQ Poetry Magazine (Haiku Quarterly)
39 Exmouth Street, Swindon, Wiltshire SN1 3PU
☎01793 523927
Website www.dspace.dial.pipex.com/town/
   park/yaw74/HQ.htm

Contact *Kevin Bailey*

General poetry mag with slight bias towards impeistic/haikuesque work.

HU – The Honest Ulsterman
49 Main Street, Greyabbey, Co Down
BT22 2NF

Contact *Tom Clyde*

Ireland's premier journal for new poems, prose, articles.

Inclement
White Rose House, 8 Newmarket Road, Fordham, Ely, Cambs CB7 5LL

Contact *Michelle Foster*

All forms and styles of poetry.

Interchange
Dept of English, U W A, Penglais, Aberystwyth, Ceredigion SY23 3DY
Fax 01970 622530
Website www.aber.ac.uk/~engwww/

Poetry, reviews and articles from Wales and the rest of the world.

The Interpreter's House
10 Farrell Road, Wootton, Bedfordsire
MK43 9DU

Contact *Merryn Williams*

Poems and stories up to 2500 words; new and established writers.

Intimacy
15 Waterlow Road, Maidstone, Kent
ME14 2TR
☎01622 670419

Contact *Adam McKeown*

Communication experienced as nakedness (Laure).

Iota
67 Hady Crescent, Chestefield, Derbyshire
S41 0EB
☎01246 276532

Contact *David Holliday*

Poetry and reviews. Iota, having no particular hobby-horses, poets are free to ride their own.

Island
Stable Cottage, Lydale, Edinbane, Isle Of Skye
IV51 9PX

Contact *Robert Ford*

New poetry inspired by nature and human relationships with the earth.

The Journal
11 Heatherton Park, Bradford on Tone, Taunton, Somerset TA4 1EV
☎01823 461725

Contact *Sam Smith*

Poems in translation alongside poetry written in English. See also **Original Plus** press.

Juju
39 Walnut Street, Belfast BT7 1EN

Contact *Patrick Sanders*

Twice-yearly poetry magazine looking at the unusual lurking behind the everyday.

Konfluence
Bath House, Bath Road, Nailsworth, Glos
GL6 0JB
☎01453 835896   Fax 01453 8355587

Contact *Mark Floyer*

Good quality crafted poetry – West Country bias but no regional/generic exclusivity.

Krax
63 Dixon Lane, Wortley, Leeds, W. Yorks
LS12 4RR

Contact *Andy Robson*

Light-hearted, contemporary poetry, short fiction & graphics. See also **Rump Booklets**.

Lallans
Scots Language Society, A K Bell Library, York Place, Perth PH2 8AP
☎01738 440199

Contact *John Law*

The literary magazine for writing in Scots.

Lateral Moves
5 Hamilton Street, Astley Bridge, Bolton, Lancs BL1 6RJ

Contacts *Nick Britton & Alan White*

Poems, stories, articles, humour, listings, letters, interviews, how-tos, quotes, artwork, reviews, jokes.

Leviathan Quarterly
Market House, Market Place, Deddington, Oxford OX15 0SE
☎01869 338240   Fax 01869 338310
Email leviathanmh@hotmail.com

Contacts *Michael Hulse & John Kinsella*

See also **Leviathan** press.

Lexikon
PO Box 754, Stoke On Trent ST1 4BU
☎01782 205060 Fax 01782 285331
Website www.lexicon-publishing.co.uk
Contact *Francis Anderson*

Links
Bude Haven, 18 Frankfield Rise, Tunbridge
Wells, Kent TN2 5LF
Contact *Bill Headdon*
Poetry magazine committed to quality writing
& reviews.

The Long Poem Group Newsletter
6 The Mount, Higher Furzeham, Brixham,
South Devon TQ5 8QY
☎01803 851098 Fax 01803 851098
Website www.bath.ac.uk/~exxdgdc
Contact *William Oxley*
Newsletter of the Long Poem Group.

Magma
43 Keslake Road, London NW6 6DH
Website www.champignon.net/magma
Contact *David Boll*
New poetry plus poetry reviews and inter-
views.

Magpie's Nest
176 Stoney Lane, Sparkhill, Birmingham
B12 8AN
Contact *Bel Saini*
Poetry & short fiction on an unusual theme.

Markings
77 High Street, Kirkcudbright DG6 4JW
☎01557 331557 Fax 01557 331557
Contacts *John Hudson & Anne Darling*
Poetry, stories, art & criticism focusing on
Scotland and abroad.

Merseyside Arts Magazine
PO Box 21, Liverpool L19 3RX
Contact *Bernard F. Spencer*
Data on local activity.

Metre
Dept of English, Trinity College, Dublin 2,
Republic of Ireland
Contact *David Wheatley*
A magazine of international poetry & critical
prose.

Monomyth
38 Pierrot Steps, 71 Kursaal Way, Southend
on Sea, Essex SS1 2UY
Contact *D.J. Tyler*
Poetry, prose & articles; all genres, styles and
lengths considered. New writers welcome. See
also **Awen** and **Garbaj** magazines.

Moonstone
C.h., Unit 2, Commercial Courtyard, Settle,
N. Yorks BD24 9RH
Contact *Talitha Clare*
Pantheistic/ecological poetry.

MPT –
Modern Poetry in Translation
School of Humanities, Strand, London
WC2R 2LS
☎020 7848 2360 Fax 020 7848 2145
Website www.kcl.ac.uk/mpt
Contact *Daniel Weissbort*
Poems from everywhere translated into English.

Multi – Storey
PO Box 62, Levenshulme, Manchester
M19 1TH
Website www.multistorey.co.uk
Contact *Finella Davenport*
Biannual literary magazine.

Never Bury Poetry
Bracken Clock, Troutbeck Close, Hawkshaw,
Bury, Lancs BL8 4LJ
☎01204 884080
Website www.nbpoetry.care4free.net
Contact *Jean Tarry*
Quarterly founded 1989. International reputa-
tion. Each issue has a different theme.

New Horizon
64 Arcacia Avenue, Huyton, Liverpool L36 5TP
☎0151 489 5179
Website www.fswo.com/newhorizon
Contact *Soumyen Maitra*
Poems & short stories from new and established writers.

New Soup Dragon
Dept 40, 255 Wilmslow Road, Rusholme,
Manchester M14 5LW
Contact *Suzanne Whalen*
Contemporary poetry particularly from women.

New Welsh Review
Chapter Arts Centre, Market Road, Canton, Cardiff CF5 1QE
☎029 2066 5529 Fax 029 2066 5529

Contact *Robin Reeves*

Wales's leading literary quarterly in English: articles, poems, etc.

The North
The Studio, Byram Arcade, Huddersfield, W. Yorks HD1 1ND
☎01484 434840 Fax 01484 426566
Website www.poetrybusiness.co.uk

Contacts *Peter Sansom & Janet Fisher*

Contemporary poetry and graphics, extensive reviews.

Northwords
The Stable, Long Road, Avoch, Rosshire IV9 8QR
☎01381 621561

Contact *Angus Dunn*

Poetry, short fiction and reviews, focusing on the North.

Oasis
12 Stevenage Road, Fulham, London SW6 6ES
☎020 7736 5059

Contact *Ian Robinson*

Poetry, short fiction, essays, reviews, etc. See also **Oasis Books** press.

Obsessed With Pipework
Redditch Library, 15 Market Place, Redditch B98 8AR
☎01527 63291 Fax 01527 68571

Contact *Charles Johnson*

Open quarterly; 'poetry to surprise and delight with a high-wire aspect'. See also **Flarestack Publishing** press.

Orbis
27 Valley View, Primrose, Jarrow, Tyne & Wear NE32 5QT
☎0191 489 7055 Fax 0191 430 1297

Contact *Mike Shields*

An independent international quarterly of poetry & prose with many reader-friendly features.

Other Poetry
29 Western Hill, Durham DH1 4RL

Contacts *Michael Standen & Others*

Poems, reviews and interviews.

Outposts
22 Whitewell Road, Frome, Somerset BA11 4EL
☎01373 466653 Fax 01373 466653

Contact *Roland John*

Longest surviving independent poetry magazine in the UK. See also **Hippopotamus Press**.

Page 84
P E F Productions, 196 High Street, London N22 8HH
Website www.84spythere.freehosting.net

Panda
46 First Avenue, Clase, Swansea SA6 7LL

Contact *Esmond Jones*

Poetry and prose.

Peace and Freedom
17 Farrow Road, Whaplode Drove, Spalding, Lincs PE12 0TS
☎01406 330242
Website www.lineone.net/~peaceandfreedom/

Contact *Paul Rance*

Poetry/prose/art mag – humanitarian, environment.

Peer Poetry
26 (wh) Arlington House, Bath BA1 1QN
☎01225 445298

Contact *Paul Amphlett*

80-page poetry biannual – publishes winners' collections – s.a.e. for details.

Penniless Press, The
100 Waterloo Road, Ashton, Preston, Lancs PR2 1EP
☎01772 736421

Contact *Alan Dent*

Quarterly for the poor pocket & the rich mind. Poetry, fiction, essays.

Pennine Ink Magazine
The Gallery, Mid-Pennine Arts, Yorke Street, Burnley, Lancs BB11 1HD

Contact *Joan McEvoy*

Poetry and prose reflecting traditional and modern trends.

Planet
P O Box 44, Aberystwyth SY23 3ZZ
☎01970 611255 Fax 01970 611197
Website www.planetmagazine.org.uk

Contact *John Barnie*

The Welsh Internationalist – current affairs, arts, environment.

Planet Prozak

31a Waldron Avenue, Brierley Hill, Dudley DY5 3RU Fax 01384 835819

Website www.planetprozak.freeserve.co.uk

Contact *Stephen E. Bennion*

Short fiction, poetry & humour; sci-fi, fantasy, gothic horror & the bizarre.

PN Review

4th Floor, Conavon Court, 12–16 Blackfriars Street, Manchester M3 5BQ

☎0161 834 8730 Fax 0161 832 0084

Website www.carcanet.co.uk

Contact *Michael Schmidt*

See **Carcanet Press** under **UK Publishers**.

Poet Tree

289 Elmwood Avenue, Feltham, Middlesex TW13 7QB

☎0181 751 8652

Website partners_writing_group.homestead.com

Contact *Ian Deal*

General poetry and short story magazine. See also **Seventh Sense** and **The Word Life Journal**.

Poetic Hours

See **Erran Publishing** press

Poetic Licence

70 Aveling Close, Purley, Surrey CR8 4DW

Website www.poetsanon.org.uk

Contact *Peter L. Evans*

Original unpublished poems and drawings. See also **Poets Anonymous** press.

Poetry Can Bulletin

Unit 11, Kuumba Project, Hepburn Road, Bristol BS2 8UD

☎0117 942 6976 Fax 0117 944 1478

Website www.poetrycan.demon.co.uk

Contact *Lesley Rose*

News, reviews, opportunities and info about poetry activity in Bristol, Bath and beyond.

The Poetry Church

Feather Books, PO Box 438, Shrewsbury, Shrops SY3 0WN

☎01743 872177 Fax 01743 872177

Website www.waddysweb.com

Contact *Rev. J. Waddington-Feather*

Quarterly magazine of Christian poetry and prayers. See **Feather Books** under **Small Presses**.

Poetry File

Arts Advisor, Arts & Media, 5 Belmont Street, Shrewsbury SY1 1TE

☎01743 243755 Fax 01743 344773

Contact *Neil Rathmell*

Poems for children (5–16), two editions per year.

Poetry Ireland Review/ Eigse Eireann

Bermingham Tower, Upper Yard, Dublin 2, Republic of Ireland

☎00 353 1 671 4632 Fax 00 353 1 671 4634

Website www.poetryireland.ie

Contact *Niamh Morris*

Quarterly journal of poetry and reviews.

Poetry Life

1 Blue Bell Corner, Water Lane, Winchester, Hampshire S023 0ER

Website freespace.virgin.net/poetry.life/

Contact *Adrian Bishop*

News, reviews, articles, interviews & comment. See also **How Do I Love Thee?** magazine.

Poetry London

1a Jewel Road, London E17 4QU

Website www.poetrylondon.co.uk

Contact *Pascale Petit*

Poetry, listings, information. (Formerly *Poetry London Newsletter*.)

Poetry Monthly

39 Cavendish Road, Long Eaton, Nottingham NG10 4HY

☎0115 9461267

Email martinholroyd@compuserve.com

Website ourworld.compuserve.com/ homepage/martinholroyd

Contact *Martin Holroyd*

Wellcrafted, dynamic, fresh & individual poems. See also **Poetry Monthly Press**.

Poetry Nottingham International

71 Saxton Avenue, Heanor, Derbyshire DE75 7PZ

Contacts *Cathy Grindrod & Others*

Poetry, articles, letters, features, reviews, 48–56 pages, quarterly.

Poetry Now

Remus House, Coltsfoot Drive, Woodston, Peterborough PE2 9JX
☎01733 898101 Fax 01733 313524
Website www.forwardpress.co.uk

Contact *Rebecca Mee*

Incorporating *Rhyme Arrival* magazine – communicating across the barriers. See also **Poetry Now** press.

Poetry Now Newsletter

89 Connaught Road, Sutton, Surrey S
M1 3RJ

Contact *Barry Tebb*

The work of Barrry Tebb and others. See also **Sixties Press**.

The Poetry of People

Sub Verse, PO Box 71, Northolt UB5 4YY
☎020 8864 9851
Website www.btinternet.com/~elle.finn/
    SubVerse.htm

Contact *Elle Finn*

Poetry Review

Poetry Society, 22 Betterton Street, London WC2H 9BX
☎020 7420 9883 Fax 020 7240 4818
Website www.poetrysoc.com

Contact *Peter Forbes*

A quarterly forum on the state of poetry.

Poetry Salzburg

12 Dartmouth Avenue, Bath BA2 1AT
Contacts *Fred Beake & Others*

Poetry magazine, formerly *The Poet's Voice*. Published with the University of Salzburg.

Poetry Scotland

3 Spittal Street, Edinburgh EH3 9DY
☎0131 229 7252

Contact *Sally Evans*

All-poetry broadsheet with Scottish emphasis.

Poetry Wales

1st & 2nd Floors, 38–40 Nolton Street, Bridgend CF31 3BN
☎01656 663018 Fax 01656 649226
Website www.seren-books.com

Contact *Robert Minhinnick*

Focuses on new & established poets from Wales plus translations, articles, reviews. See also **Seren** under **UK Publishers**.

Power

80 Three Firs Way, Burghfield Common, Reading, Berks RG7 3QJ

PQR – Poetry Quarterly Review

Coleridge Cottage, Nether Stowey, Somerset TA5 1NQ
☎01278 732662

Contact *Derrick Woolf*

In-depth reviews of mainstream/small-press poetry.

Presence

12 Grovehall Ave, Leeds, W. Yorks LS11 7EX
Website members.netscapeonline.co.uk/
    haikupresence

Contact *Martin Lucas*

Haiku, senryu, tanka, renku & related poetry in English.

Pretext

School of English & American Studies, University of East Anglia, Norwich, Norfolk NR4 7TJ
☎01603 592689
Email julian.jackson@uea.ac.uk
Website www.penaninc.co.uk

Contacts *Julia Bell & Paul Magrs*

New fiction and poetry – essays on the world of writing.

Prop

31 Central Avenue, Farnworth, Bolton, Lancs BL4 0AU
☎01204 707428

Contacts *Steven Blythe & Chris Hart*

Poetry, short fiction plus related essays, reviews & interviews.

Pulsar

34 Lineacre Close, Grange Park, Swindon, Wilts SN5 6DA
☎01793 875941 Fax 01793 875941
Website www.btinternet.com/~pulsarpoetry

Contact *David Pike*

Hard hitting/inspirational poetry – quarterly.

Purple Patch

25 Griffiths Road, West Bromwich B71 2EH

Contact *Geoff Stevens*

Poetry mag founded 1976 – includes reviews & gossip column.

Quantum Leap
York House, 15 Argyle Terrace, Rothsay, Isle of Bute PA20 0BD

Contact *Alan Carter*

User-friendly magazine – encourages new writers – all types of poetry. See also **QQ Press**.

The Quarterly Muse
5 Grosvenor Close, Great Sankey, Warrington, Cheshire WA5 1XQ
☎01925 574476

Contact *Jane Reid*

Inspiring, friendly publication with quarterly theme.

Quid
Gonville & Caius College, Cambridge CB2 1TA

Contact *Keston Sutherland*

Rain Dog
PO Box 68, Manchester M19 2XD
Email rd-poetry@yahoo.com
Website www.page27.co.uk/jan/ps

Contact *Jan Whalen*

Biannual. Original contemporary poetry, sequences, reviews. Poetry by women particularly welcome.

The Reader
The English Dept., University of Liverpool, Liverpool L69 7ZR
Email readers@thereader.co.uk
Website www.thereader.co.uk

Contact *Jane Davis*

A magazine about writing worth reading. See entry under **Magazines**.

The Rialto
Mackmin, PO Box 309, Aylsham, Norwich, Norfolk NR11 6LN

Contact *Michael Mackmin*

'Simply the best' – Carol Ann Duffy. See also **Rialto Publications**.

Rising
80 Cazenove Road, Stoke Newington, London N16 6AA
Website www.saltpetre.com

Contact *Tim Wells*

The readers' wives of poetry mags.

Roundyhouse
PO Box 433, Swansea SA1 6WX

Contacts *Sally Roberts Jones & Others*

The poetry scene in Wales and beyond.

The Rue Bella
2f1, 15 Warrender Park Terrace, Edinburgh EH19 1EG
Website www.rubella.co.uk

Poetry – new writers.

Salt: International Journal of Poetry and Poetics
Churchill College, Cambridge CB3 0DS

Contact *John Kinsella*

Saltburn Scene
Glenside Cottage, Glenside Terrace, Saltburn, Cleveland

Contact *Mark Beevers*

Science, rock music, poetry, folk & fairy lore, history local & otherwise.

Scribbler!
Remus House, Coltsfoot Drive, Woodston, Peterborough PE2 9JX
☎01733 890066   Fax 01733 313524
Website www.forwardpress.co.uk

Contact *Lynsey Hawkins*

Publishers of children's poetry. See also **Poetry Now Young Writers** press.

Seam
PO Box 3684, Danbury, Chelmsford, Essex CM3 4GP

Contact *Maggie Freeman*

New poetry by established and new poets.

Seventh Sense
289 Elmwood Avenue, Feltham, Middlesex TW13 7QB
☎0777 9193676
Website partners_writing_group.homestead.com

Contact *Ian Deal*

Dedicated to the ongoing spiritual quest. See also **A Bard Hair Day** and **The Word Life Journal**.

The Shop: A Magazine Of Poetry
The Rectory, Toormore, Goleen, Co Cork Republic of Ireland

Contact *John Wakeman*

International but with emphasis on Irish poetry.

Skald

2 Greenfield Terrace, Hill Street, Menai
Bridge, Ynys Mon LL59 5AY
☎01248 716343

Contact *Zoe Skoulding*

Poetry and artwork, English & Welsh.

Skinklin Star

9 University Gardens, University Of Glasgow,
Glasgow G12 8QH
Website www.arts.gla.ac.uk/skinklin-star

Contact *Matt Ewart*

A2 full-colour broadsheet of the best poets in
Scotland.

Smiths Knoll

49 Church Road, Little Glemham,
Woodbridge, Suffolk IP13 0BJ

Contacts *Roy Blackman & Michael Laskey*

Clear, honest, well-crafted poems.

Smoke

The Windows Project, 1st Floor, Liver
House, Liverpool L1 4HY
☎0151 709 3688

Contact *Dave Ward*

Poetry, graphics, short prose – 24pp – biannual.

South

Wanda Publications, c/o Word and Action
(Dorset), 75 High Street, Wimborne, Dorset
BH21 1HS
☎01202 889669
Email wanda@wordandaction.com

Contact *Anne Jennings*

Poetry for the Southern Counties.

Stand

School Of English, University Of Leeds,
Leeds, W. Yorks LS2 9JT
☎ 0113 233 4794 Fax 0113 233 4791
Email stand@english.novel.leeds.ac.uk
Website saturn.vcu.edu/~dlatane/stand.html

Quarterly magazine of poetry, fiction, reviews
and cultural criticism.

Staple New Writing

Padley Rise, Nether Padley, Grindleford
Hope Valley, Derbys S32 2HE
☎ 01433 631949

Contact *Ann Atkinson*

Mainstream poetry & fiction magazine, established 1982: not a closed shop.

The Stinging Fly

PO Box 6016, Dublin 8, Republic of Ireland
Website www.stingingfly.org

Contact *Declan Meade*

Dublin's literary magazine. New Irish and
international writing. Poetry and short fiction.

Superfluity

Scribbled Publications, PO Box 6234,
Nottingham NG2 5EX

Contact *Peter Larkin*

Tartarus Press

Coverley House, Carlton, Leyburn, N. Yorks
DL8 4AY
☎01969 640399 Fax 01969 640399

Contact *Raymond Russell*

Publishes Arthur Machen & related decadent
and mystical writers.

Tears In The Fence

38 Hod View, Stourpaine, Nr Blandford
Forum, Dorset DT11 8TN
☎01258 456803 Fax 01258 454026
Website www.wanderingdog.co.uk

Contact *David Caddy*

A magazine looking for the unusual, perceptive, risk-taking, lived and visionary literature.

Temenos Academy Review

14 Gloucester Gate, London NW1 4HG
☎01233 813663

10th Muse

33 Hartington Road, Southampton, Hants
SO214 OEW

Contact *Andrew Jordan*

Poetry, prose and graphics, ideally combining
lyricism and the pastoral with experimental
techniques.

The Text

The Word Hoard, Kirklees Media Centre,
Huddersfield, W. Yorks HD1 1RL
☎01484 452070 Fax 01484 455049

Contact *Keith Jafrate*

Loose-leaf magazine for fiction, experimental
writing, & long poems.

The Third Half

16 Fane Close, Stamford, Lincs PE9 1HG
☎01780 754193

Contact *Kevin Troop*

Looking for a good script – do you have one? See also **Kite Books** press.

Thumbscrew
PO Box 657, Oxford OX2 6PH
Website www.bristol.ac.uk/thumbscrew

Contact *Tim Kendall*

International journal of poetry and poetry criticism. See also **Thumbscrew Press**.

Time Haiku
Kings Head Hill, London E4 7JG

Contact *Dr Erica Facey*

Haiku magazine aimed at experts and beginners.

Tremblestone
Corporation Building, 10f How Street, The Barbican, Plymouth PL4 0DB

Contact *Kenny Knight*

Triumph Herald
Remus House, Coltsfoot Drive, Woodston, Peterborough PE2 9JX
☎01733 898102 Fax 01733 313524
Website www.forwardpress.co.uk

Contact *Steve Twelvetree*

A Christian writers magazine with poetry, stories and articles written by subscribers. See also **Triumph House** press.

Under Surveillance
107 Southover Street, Brighton, East Sussex BN2 2UA

Contact *Eddie Harriman*

Poetry.

Understanding
20a Mongomery Street, Edinburgh EH7 5JS
☎0131 478 0927 Fax 0131 478 2572

Contact *Denise Smith*

Poetry and fiction. See also **Dionysia Press**.

The Unruly Sun
The Rising Arts Centre, 30 Silver Street, Reading, Berks RG1 2ST
Contacts *Jennifer Hoskins & Others*

Upstart!
19 Cawarden, Stantonbury, Milton Keynes MK14 6AH
☎01908 317535

Contact *Carol Barac*

Literary magazine.

Urthona
3 Coral Park, Henley Road, Cambridge CB1 3EA
☎01223 566567 Fax 01223 566568
Website www.urthona.com

Contact *Shantigarbha*

Art & Buddhism. Builds bridges between Buddhism and Western culture.

Wasafiri
Dept of English and Drama, Queen Mary & Westfield College, Mile End Road, London E1 4NS
☎020 7882 3120 Fax 020 7882 3357
Email wasafiri@qmw.ac.uk
Website www.english.qmw.ac.uk/wasafiri

Contact *Susheila Nasta*

Literary journal of African, Asian, Caribbean & black British writing. See entry under **Magazines**.

The Waterlog
35–39 London Street, Reading, Berks RG1 4PS

Contact *Peter Hay*

The best innovative new writing with art & lavish illustration. See also **Two Rivers Press**.

The Word Hoard
Kirklees Media Centre, 7 Northumberland Street, Huddersfield, W. Yorks HD2 2NY
☎01484 452070 Fax 01482 455049
Website www.openingline.co.uk

News of the arts development cooperative including some poetry.

The Word Life Journal
289 Elmwood Avenue, Feltham, Middlesex TW13 7QB
☎0777 919 3676
Website partners_writing_group.homestead.com

Contact *Ian Deal*

Poetry magazine dedicated to the ongoing romantic renaissance. See also **A Bard Hair Day** and **Seventh Sense** magazines.

Write Here! Right Now!
115 High Street, Belton, Nr Doncaster, S. Yorks DN9 1NR
☎0114 275 8115
Website www.spiderco.co.uk

Contact *Rachael J. Webb*

A bi-monthly magazine for amateur writers (poetry & prose).

Writers' Cauldron

PO Box 241, Oakengates, Shropshire TF2 9XZ
☎01952 277872
Website www.writers.brew.clar.net/club

Contact *Amanda Gillies*

Magazine for new writers and rhyming poets with news, competitions, reviews.

The Yellow Crane

20 Princes Court, The Walk, Roath, Cardiff CF2 3AU

Contact *Jonathan Brookes*

Interesting new poems from South Wales and beyond.

Zine-on-a-CD

35 Kearsley Road, Sheffield S2 4TE
Website www.andysav.free-online.co.uk/zine.htm

Contact *Andrew Savage*

Poetry, music, reviews, interviews & short stories.

The Zone

13 Hazely Combe, Arreton, Isle Of Wight PO30 3AJ
Website freespace.virgin.net/pigasus.press/index.htm

Contact *Tony Lee*

Mag of SF stories, articles, reviews and verse.

Organisations of Interest to Poets

A survey of some of the societies, groups and other bodies which may be of interest to practising poets. Organisations not listed should send details to the Editor for inclusion in future editions.

Academi – The Welsh National Literature Promotion Agency
3rd Floor, Mount Stuart House, Mount Stuart Square, Cardiff Bay, Cardiff CF10 5FQ
☎029 2047 2266 Fax 029 2049 2930
Email post@academi.org
Website www.academi.org

North West Wales Office: Ty Newydd, Llanystumdwy, Cricieth, Gwynedd LL52 0LW
West Wales Office: Dylan Thomas Centre, Somerset Place, Swansea SA1 1RR

Chief Executive *Peter Finch*

The writers' organisation of Wales with special responsibility for literary activity, writers' residencies, writers on tour, festivals, writers' groups, readings, tours, exchanges and other development work. **Yr Academi Gymreig/The Welsh Academy** won the 1998 Arts Council of Wales franchise for Wales–wide literature development. It has offices in Cardiff and fieldworkers based in North West, North East and West Wales. *Publishes* the Lottery-funded *Encyclopedia of Wales*, the Welsh-medium literary magazine *Taliesin*, the *Academi English-Welsh Dictionary*, co-publisher of *The New Welsh Review* along with a number of other projects. The Academi sponsors a range of annual contests including the prestigious **Cardiff International Poetry Competition**. Publishes *A470* a bi-monthly literary information magazine.

Alternative Press Collection
See **The Little Magazine Collection**

Apples & Snakes
Battersea Arts Centre, Lavender Hill, London SW11 5TN
☎020 7924 3410 Fax 020 7924 3763
Email apples@snakes.demon.co.uk

Contacts *Maja Prausnitz, Nicky Crabb*

Set up in 1982 as a platform for poetry which would be popular, relevant, a cross-cultural activity and accessible to the widest possible range of people. Operates a successful poetry in education scheme. Presents fortnightly shows at the Battersea Arts Centre and occasionally around London and the UK.

Arts Councils and Regional Arts Boards
For a full list of addresses see **Arts Councils and Regional Arts Boards** on page 556.

The Arvon Foundation
See entry under **Writers' Courses, Circles and Workshops**

Association of Small Press Poets
7 Pincott Place, London SE4 2ER
☎020 7277 8831 Fax 08707 403511
Email info@smallpresspoets.co.uk
Website www.smallpresspoets.co.uk

Coordinator *Ruth Booth*

Association of poets wishing to increase the sales of their work. *Publishes The Big Poetry Catalogue* as a sales tool, *Appraisal* newsletter and offers various competitions, appraisal services and discounts on Robooth Publications, the ASPP coordinator's own press. Membership charges, on a sliding scale, start at £18.

The British Haiku Society
Sinodun, Shalford, Braintree, Essex CM7 5HN
☎01371 851097
Website www.britishhaikusociety.org

General Secretary *David Cobb*

FORMED in 1990. Promotes the appreciation and writing within the British Isles of haiku, senyru, tanka, haibun and renga by way of tutorials, workshops, exchange of poems, critical comment and information. The Society runs a haiku library and administers the annual James W. Hackett Award and the prestigious **Sasakawa** prize. *Publishes The Haiku Kit* teaching pack and the quarterly journal, *Blithe Spirit*.

The Eight Hand Gang

5 Cross Farm, Station Road, Padgate,
Warrington WA2 0QG
Secretary *John F. Haines*

An association of SF poets. *Publishes Handshake*,
a single-sheet newsletter of SF poetry and
information available free in exchange for an
s.a.e.

The Football Poets

Clevedon, Coronation Road, Rodborough,
Stroud, Gloucestershire GL5 3SB
☎01453 752168
Email stuart.butler@ic24.net
Website www.footballpoets.net

The Stroud Football Poets exist to promote
writing about football worldwide. Formed by
Dennis Gould and Stuart Butler in 1995 the
organisation runs football poetry readings and
performances of plays. Their website is a fast
and entertaining mix of literature and soccer.
Performance bookings and membership enquiries should be directed to Crispin Thomas
(crispin@ctmuk.freeserve.co.uk).

The Little Magazine Collection, Poetry Store and Alternative Press Collections

The Library, University College London,
Gower Street, London WC1E 6BT
☎020 7679 7796 Fax 020 7679 7727
Contact *John Allen*

Housed at University College London Library,
these are the fruits of Geoffrey Soar and David
Miller's interest in UK and US alternative publishing, with a strong emphasis on poetry. The
Little Magazines Collection runs to over 3600
titles mainly in the more experimental and
avant-garde areas. The Poetry Store consists of
over 12,200 small press items, mainly from the
'60s onwards, again with some stress on experimental work. In addition, there are reprints of
classic earlier little magazines, from Symbolism
through to the present.

Anyone who is interested can consult the
collections, and it helps if you have some idea
of what you want to see. Bring evidence of
identity for a smooth ride. The collections can
be accessed by visiting the Manuscripts and
Rare Books Room at University College at the
address above between 10.00 am and 5.00 pm
on weekdays. Most items are available on
inter-library loans.

The Northern Poetry Library

Central Library, The Willows, Morpeth,
Northumberland NE61 1TA
☎01670 534524/534514 Fax 01670 534513
Email amenities@northumberland.gov.uk

Membership available to everyone in Cleveland,
Cumbria, Durham, Northumberland and Tyne
and Wear. Associate membership available for
all outside the region. Over 15,000 books and
magazines for loan including virtually all poetry
published in the UK since 1968. Postal lending
available too.

The Poet's House/Teach na hÉigse

Clonbarra, Falcarragh, Co. Donegal, Republic
of Ireland
☎00 353 74 65470 Fax 00 353 74 65471
Email phouse@iol.ie
Director *Janice Fitzpatrick Simmons*

Set in the heart of Donegal Gaeltacht, the centre offers a year-long residential MA aong with
three ten-day summer courses (to apply send
three poems). During each session there are
three resident and six visiting poets. Recent
poets have included Peter Sirr, Paul Durcan,
Michael Longley, Menna Elfyn, Frank Ormsby
and Medbh McGuckian.

The Poetry Book Society

Book House, 45 East Hill, London
SW18 2QZ
☎020 8870 8403 Fax 020 8877 1615
Website www.poetrybooks.co.uk
Director *Clare Brown*

For readers, writers, students and teachers of
poetry. FOUNDED in 1953 by T.S. Eliot and
funded by the Arts Council, the PBS is a unique
membership organisation and book club providing up-to-date and comprehensive information about poetry from publishers in the UK
and Ireland. Members receive the quarterly *PBS
Bulletin* packed with articles by poets, poems,
news, listings and access to discounts of at least
25% off featured titles. These range from modern
classics to contemporary works. The transactional website has over 1000 titles available at
discount to members. There are three membership packages – two of which include a number
of new books specially selected by the Society's
panel of experts – along with, at both primary
and secondary levels, a special package for teachers. Subscriptions start at £10. The PBS also runs
the annual **T.S. Eliot Prize** for the best collection of new poetry.

The Poetry Business

The Studio, Byram Arcade, Westgate,
Huddersfield, West Yorkshire HD1 1ND
☎01484 434840 Fax 01484 426566
Email edit@poetrybusiness.co.uk
Website www.poetrybusiness.co.uk
Administrators *Peter Sansom, Janet Fisher*

FOUNDED in 1986, the Business *publishes The
North* magazine and books, pamphlets and cassettes under the **Smith/Doorstop** imprint. It
runs an annual competition and organises
monthly writing Saturdays. Send an s.a.e. for full
details.

Poetry Can

Unit 11, Kuumba Project, 20–22 Hepburn
Road, Bristol BS2 8UD
☎0117 942 6976 Fax 0117 944 1478
Email hester@poetrycan.demon.co.uk
Website www.poetrycan.demon.co.uk
Coordinator *Hester Cockcroft*

FOUNDED in 1995, Poetry Can is a poetry
development agency working across the Bristol
and Bath area. It organises events and projects,
supports the creative and professional development of poets and *publishes* a bi-monthly
bulletin of poetry news and activity.

Poetry Ireland/Eigse Eireann

Bermingham Tower, Upper Yard, Dublin
Castle, Dublin, Republic of Ireland
☎00 353 1 6714632 Fax 00 353 1 6714634
Email poetry@iol.ie
Website www.poetryireland.ie
General Manager *Joseph Woods*

The national organisation for poetry in Ireland,
with its four core activities being readings, publications, education and an information and
resource service. Organises readings by Irish and
international poets countrywide. Through its
website, telephone, post and public enquiries,
Poetry Ireland operates as a clearing house for
everything pertaining to poetry in Ireland.
Operates the Writers in Schools scheme.

Publishes Poetry Ireland News, a bi-monthly
newsletter containing information on events,
competitions and opportunities. *Poetry Ireland
Review* is published quarterly and is the journal of
record for poetry in Ireland; current editor: *Biddy
Jenkinson*. The organisation also produces occasional publications, most recently, *Watching the
River Flow, a Century in Irish Poetry*. As a member
of the International Translation Network, it has
produced 12 dual-language titles by foreign
poets.

The Poetry Library

Royal Festival Hall, Level 5, London
SE1 8XX
☎020 7921 0943/0664 Fax 020 7921 0939
Email poetrylibrary@rfh.org.uk
Website www.poetrylibrary.org.uk
Librarian *Mary Enright*

FOUNDED by the Arts Council in 1953. A collection of 45,000 titles of modern poetry since
1912, from Georgian to Rap, representing all
English-speaking countries and including
translations into English by contemporary
poets. Two copies of each title are held, one
for loan and one for reference. A wide range of
poetry magazines and ephemera from all over
the world are kept along with casettes, records
and videos for consultation, with many available for loan. There is also a children's poetry
section with a teacher's resource collection.

An information service compiles lists of
poetry magazines, competitions, publishers,
groups and workshops which are available
from the Library on receipt of a large s.a.e. or
from the website. It also has a noticeboard for
lost quotations, through which it tries to identify lines or fragments of poetry which have
been sent in by other readers.

General enquiry service available. Membership is free but proof of identity and address are
essential to join. Open 11.00 am to 8.00 pm,
Tuesday to Sunday. The Library's website is
one of the best poetry resources on the Net.

Beside the Library is *The Voice Box*, a performance space especially for literature. For details
of current programme ring 020 7921 0971.

Poetry London

1a Jewel Road, London E17 4QU
Email editors@plondon.demon.co.uk
Website www.poetrylondon.co.uk
Contacts *Anna Robinson* (listings), *Pascale Petit*
(poetry editor), *Scott Verner* (reviews),
Peter Daniels Lucziwski (production)

Published three times a year, *Poetry London*
includes poetry by new and established writers,
reviews of recent collections and anthologies,
features on issues relating to poetry, and an
encyclopædic listings section of virtually everything to do with poetry in the capital and the
South East. The magazine also carries a limited
coverage of events elsewhere.

The Poetry School

1a Jewel Road, London E17 4QU
☎020 8985 0090/8223 0401
Coordinator *Mimi Khalvati*

Funded by the London Arts Board the School offers a core programme of tuition in reading and writing poetry through a series of workshops, courses, masterclasses and seminars. Tutors include Graham Fawcett, Alison Fell, Roddy Lumsden, Carole Satyamurti, Stephen Knight and others. The School also provides a forum for practitioners to share experiences, develop skills and extend appreciation of the traditional and innovative aspects of their art.

The Poetry Society
22 Betterton Street, London WC2H 9BX
☎020 7240 9880 Fax 020 7240 4818
Email info@poetrysoc.com
Website www.poetrysoc.com
Chair *Judith Palmer*
Director *Christina Patterson*

FOUNDED in 1909, which ought to make it venerable, the Society exists to help poets and poetry thrive in Britain. In the past decade it has undergone a renaissance, reaching out from its Covent Garden base to promote the national health of poetry in a range of imaginative ways. Membership costs £32 for individuals. *Poetry News* membership is £15. Current activities include:

- Quarterly, recently redesigned magazine of new verse, views and criticism, *Poetry Review*, edited by Peter Forbes.
- Quarterly newsletter, *Poetry News*.
- Promotions, events and cooperation with Britain's many literature festivals, poetry venues and poetry publishers.
- Competitions and awards, including the annual **National Poetry Competition** in association with BT (£5000 first prize).
- A manuscript diagnosis service, *The Poetry Prescription*, which gives detailed reports on submissions. Reduced rates for members.
- Seminars, fact sheets, training courses, ideas packs.
- Provides information and advice, publishes books, posters and resources for schools and libraries. Education membership costs £45/£25 and includes *The Young Poetry Pack*, *The Poetry Book For Primary Schools* and *Jumpstart Poetry For Secondary Schools*, colourful poetry posters for Keystages 1, 2, 3 and 4. Many of Britain's most popular poets – including Michael Rosen, Roger McGough and Jackie Kay – contribute, offering advice and inspiration. (The Society's education website is at www.poetryclass.net)
- The Poetry Café serving snacks and drink to members, friends and guests, part of The Poetry Place, a venue for many poetry activities – readings, poetry clinics, workshops and poetry launches. This space is available for bookings.

Recent projects include *Poetry Places*, a national programme of residencies, placements and projects.

Poetry Store
See **The Little Magazine Collection**

Point
Halsesteenweg 31–22, B–9402 Ninove, Belgium
☎00 32 54 32 4748 Fax 00 32 54 32 4660
Email elpoeta@point-editions.com
Website www.point-editions.com
Director *Germain Droogenbroodt*

FOUNDED as Poetry International in 1984, Point is based in Belgium. A multilingual publisher of contemporary verse from *established* poets, the organisation has brought out more than 60 titles in at least eight languages, including English. Editions run the original work alongside a verse translation into Dutch made in cooperation with the poet. The organisation's website is highly developed and features much English language verse. Point also co-organises an annual international poetry festival.

Regional Arts Boards
See **Arts Councils and Regional Arts Boards**

Scottish Poetry Library
5 Crichton's Close, Canongate, Edinburgh EH8 8DT
☎0131 557 2876
Email inquiries@spl.org.uk
Website www.spl.org.uk
Librarian *Robyn Marsack*

A comprehensive reference and lending collection of work by Scottish poets in Gaelic, Scots and English, plus the work of British and international poets. Stock includes books, tapes, videos, news cuttings and magazines. Borrowing is free to all. Services include a postal lending scheme, for which there is a small fee, a mobile library which can visit schools and other centres by arrangement, exhibitions, bibliographies, publications, information and promotion in the field of poetry. Also available is an online catalogue and computer index to poetry and poetry periodicals. The membership scheme costs £20 annually.

Members receive a newsletter and other benefits and support the library.

Survivors' Poetry

Diorama Arts Centre, 34 Osnaburgh Street, London NW1 3ND
☎020 7916 5317 Fax 020 7916 0830
Email survivors@survivorspoetry.org.uk

A unique national literature organisation promoting poetry by survivors of mental distress through workshops, readings and performances to audiences all over the UK. It was FOUNDED in 1991 by four poets with first-hand experience of the mental health system. Survivors' community outreach work provides training and performance workshops and publishing projects. A survivor may be defined as a person with a current or past experience of psychiatric hospitals; a recipient of ECT, tranquillisers or other medication; a user of counselling and therapy services; a survivor of sexual abuse or child abuse; anyone who has empathy with the experience of survivors.

Survivors' Poetry Scotland

4C4 Templeton Centre, 62 Templeton Street, Glasgow G40 1DA
☎0141 556 4554 Fax 0141 400 8442
Email sps@spscot.co.uk
Website www.spscot.co.uk

Project Manager *Chris Ballance*
Administrator *Wallace MacBain*
Managing Editor *Gerry Loose*

Promotes poetry by suvivors of mental distress through a poetry magazine, *Nomad*, which appears three times a year; writing workshops (four a week in Glasgow); and monthly performance evenings. SPS has set up groups in Dumfries, Edinburgh, Dundee and Aberdeen.

Tŷ Newydd

Llanystumdwy, Criccieth, Gwynedd LL52 0LW
☎01766 522811 Fax 01766 523095
Email tynewydd@dial.pipex.com
Website www.academi.org

Director *Sally Baker*

Run by the Taliesin Trust, an independent, Arvon-style residential writers centre established in the one-time home of Lloyd George in North Wales. The programme (in both Welsh and English) has a regular poetry content. (See also **Writers' Courses, Circles and Workshops**.) Fees start at £100 for weekends and £310 for week-long courses. Among the many tutors to-date have been: Gillian Clarke, U.A. Fanthorpe, Roger McGough, Carol Ann Duffy, Liz Lochhead, Peter Finch and Paul Henry. Send for the centre's descriptive leaflets and a copy of its newsletter.

Small Presses

Aard Press

c/o Aardverx, 31 Mountearl Gardens, London SW16 2NL

Managing Editors *D. Jarvis, Dawn Redwood*

FOUNDED 1971. *Publishes* artists' bookworks, experimental/visual poetry, 'zines, eonist literature, topographics, ephemera and international mail-art documentation. Very small editions. No unsolicited material or proposals.
Royalties not paid. No sale-or-return deals.

Abbey Press

Abbey Grammar School, Courtenay Hill, Newry, Co. Down BT34 2ED
☎028 3026 3142 Fax 028 3026 2514

Also at: 12 The Pines, Jordanstown, Newtonabbey, Co. Antrim BT37 0SE
☎028 9086 0230

Editor *Adrian Rice*
Administrator *Mel McMahon*

FOUNDED in 1997, Abbey Press is a fast growing literary publisher with a strong poetry list. Also *publishes* biography, memoirs, fiction, history, politics, Irish language and academic. Lists currently full.

AK Press/AKA Books

PO Box 12766, Edinburgh EH8 9YE
☎0131 555 5165 Fax 0131 555 5215
Email ak@akedin.demon.co.uk
Website www.akuk.com

Managing Editor *Alexis McKay*

AK Press grew out of the activities of AK Distribution which distributes a wide range of radical (anarchist, feminist, etc.) literature (books, pamphlets, periodicals, magazines), both fiction and non-fiction. *Publishes* politics, history, situationist work, occasional fiction in both book and pamphlet form. About 12 titles a year. Proposals and synopses welcome if they fall within AK's specific areas of interest.
Royalties paid.

Akros Publications

33 Lady Nairn Avenue, Kirkcaldy, Fife KY1 2AW
☎01592 651522

Publisher *Duncan Glen*

FOUNDED 1965. *Publishes* poetry collections, pamphlets and anthologies; literary essays and studies; travel books with a literary slant; local histories and memoirs. About 10 titles a year. Ideas for books welcome; no unsolicited mss.
Royalties paid twice-yearly.

The Alembic Press

Hyde Farm House, Marcham, Abingdon, Oxon OX13 6NX
☎01865 391391 Fax 01865 391322
Email AlembicPrs@aol.com
Website members.aol.com/alembicprs/

Owner *Claire Bolton*

FOUNDED 1976. Publisher of hand-produced books by traditional letterpress methods. Short print-runs. *Publishes* bibliography, book arts and printing, miniatures and occasional poetry. Book design and production service to like-minded authors wishing to publish in this manner. No unsolicited mss.

Allardyce, Barnett, Publishers

14 Mount Street, Lewes, East Sussex BN7 1HL
☎01273 479393 Fax 01273 479393
Website www.abar.net

Publisher *Fiona Allardyce*
Managing Editor *Anthony Barnett*

FOUNDED 1981. *Publishes* art, literature and music. About 3 titles a year. IMPRINT **Allardyce Book**. Unsolicited mss and synopses cannot be considered.

Anglo-Saxon Books

Frithgarth, Thetford Forest Park, Hockwold cum Wilton, Norfolk IP26 4NQ
☎01842 828430 Fax 01842 828332
Email tony@asbooks.co.uk
Website www.asbooks.co.uk

Managing Editor *Tony Linsell*

FOUNDED 1990 to promote a greater awareness of and interest in early English history and culture. Originally concentrated on Old English texts but now also publishes less academic, more popular titles. Seeking titles for all periods of English history. *Publishes* English history, culture, language and society. About 5–10 titles a year. Unsolicited synopses welcome but return postage necessary.

Royalties paid at standard rate.

Athelney

1 Providence Street, King's Lynn, Norfolk PE30 5ET   Fax 01842 828332

Managing Editor *John Cooper*

FOUNDED 2000. *Publishes* nationalism in general; English nationalism in particular. Unsolicited outlines/contents page/first chapter welcome. Please enclose return postage.

Royalties – standard rate.

AVERT

AIDS Education and Research Trust, 4 Brighton Road, Horsham, West Sussex RH13 5BA

☎01403 210202   Fax 01403 211001

Email info@avert.org

Website www.avert.org

Managing Editor *Annabel Kanabus*

Publishing arm of the AIDS Education and Research Trust, a national registered charity established 1986. *Publishes* books and leaflets about HIV infection and AIDS. About 3 titles a year. Unsolicited mss, synopses and ideas welcome.

Royalties paid accordingly.

M.&M. Baldwin

24 High Street, Cleobury Mortimer, Kidderminster DY14 8BY

☎01299 270110   Fax 01299 270110

Email mb@mbaldwin.free-online.co.uk

Managing Editor *Dr Mark Baldwin*

FOUNDED 1978. *Publishes* local interest/history, WW2 codebreaking and inland waterways books. Up to 5 titles a year. Unsolicited mss, synopses and ideas for books welcome (not general fiction).

Royalties paid.

Bardon Enterprises

6 Winter Road, Southsea, Hampshire PO4 9BT

☎023 9287 4900   Fax 023 9287 4900

Email info@bardon-enterprises.co.uk

Website www.bardon-enterprises.co.uk

Managing Director *W.B. Henshaw*

FOUNDED 1996. *Publishes* music, art, biography, poetry, academic books and sheet music. 22 titles in 2000 plus 42 pieces of music.

Unsolicited mss, synopses and ideas welcome. No pictorial books. 'Cost free publishing.'

Bards Original Publishing

Studio 1, 9 The Mount, Burtons' St Leonards, East Sussex TN38 0HR

☎01424 201029   Fax 01424 201029

Email bards.original@ukgateway.net

Managing Editor *Tony Gill*

FOUNDED 1999. *Publishes* books on cricket, including fiction. *Specialises* in cricket club histories from club level to national teams. 1 title in 2000. Welcomes unsolicited mss, synopses and ideas for books. Initial approach by telephone.

Royalties paid.

BB Books

See under **Poetry Presses**

The Better Book Company

Warblington Lodge, The Gardens, Warblington, Near Havant, Hampshire PO9 2XH

☎023 9248 1160   Fax 023 9249 2819

Managing Editor *James Jude Garvey*

FOUNDED 1996. *Publishes* fiction, histories, memoirs, poetry, religious, scientific, company histories. 30 titles in 2001. Offers a complete editorial, design, printing and marketing service to self-publishing authors in all genre. A free booklet, *A Complete Guide to Self-Publishing*' is available on request.

Between the Lines

9 Woodstock Road, London N4 3ET

☎020 8374 5526   Fax 020 8374 5736

Email btluk@aol.com

Website www.interviews–with–poets.com

Editorial Board *Peter Dale, Ian Hamilton, Philip Hoy, J.D. McClatchy*

FOUNDED 1998. *Publishes* extended interviews with leading contemporary poets. By the end of 2001, the eight volumes published (featuring W.D. Snodgrass, Michael Hamburger, Anthony Thwaite, Anthony Hecht, Donald Hall, Thom Gunn, Richard Wilbur, Seamus Heaney) will have been joined by five more (Donald Justice, Paul Muldoon, Ian Hamilton, Charles Simic, Hans Magnus Enzensberger). Each volume features a career sketch, a primary and secondary bibliography, a representative selection of quotations from the poets' critics and reviewers, an uncollected poem and a photograph.

The Bewildered Publishing Company Ltd

Argoed Hall, Tregaron, Ceredigion SY25 6JR
☎01974 298070   Fax 01974 298708
Email argoed.hall@btinternet.com

Publisher *John Wilson*

FOUNDED in 1999 'to provide a direct route to the book market for authors with an unconventional approach to writing and publishing'. *Publishes* humorous paperbacks. 3 titles in 2000. No unsolicited material; initial inquiry by telephone, e-mail or letter.

Royalties not paid.

Black Cat Books
See **Neil Miller Publications**

BlackAmber Books Ltd

PO Box 10812, London SW7 4ZG
☎020 7373 3178   Fax 020 7373 3178
Email information@blackamber.com
Website www.blackamber.com

Publisher *Rosemarie Hudson*

FOUNDED 1998. Home of 'the best writing emanating from the vibrant, mostly young, immigrant-descended population'. A collection point for British and European Black and Asian literature. 'Gives an outlet for the creative voice of European racial minorities, demonstrating their strengths and place in a multi-cultural world.'

The Book Castle

12 Church Street, Dunstable, Bedfordshire LU5 4RU
☎01582 605670   Fax 01582 662431
Email bc@book-castle.busclub.net
Website www.book-castle.co.uk

Managing Editor *Paul Bowes*

FOUNDED 1986. *Publishes* non-fiction of local interest (Bedfordshire, Hertfordshire, Buckinghamshire, Oxfordshire, Northamptonshire, the Chilterns). 6+ titles a year. About 70 titles in print. Unsolicited mss, synopses and ideas for books welcome.

Royalties paid.

Book-in-Hand Ltd

20 Shepherds Hill, London N6 5AH
☎020 8341 7650   Fax 020 8341 7650
Email books@book-in-hand.demon.co.uk

Contact *Ann Kritzinger*

Print production service for self-publishers. Includes design and editing advice to give customers a greater chance of selling in the open market.

Bookmarque Publishing

26 Cotswold Close, Minster Lovell, Oxfordshire OX8 5SX
☎01993 775179

Managing Editor *John Rose*

FOUNDED 1987. Publishing business with aim of filling gaps in motoring history of which it is said 'there are many'. *Publishes* motoring history, motor sport and 'general' titles. About 8 titles a year. All design and typesetting of books done in-house. Unsolicited mss and synopses welcome on transport titles. S.a.e. required for reply or return of material or for advice on publishing your work.

Royalties paid.

Brantwood Books

PO Box 144, Orpington, Kent BR6 6LZ
☎01689 833117   Fax 01689 833117
Website www.planxty.com/brantwood

Publisher *Philip Turner*

FOUNDED 1997. *Publishes* highly illustrated, limited edition print runs of specialist cinema titles, ranging from Russian cinema architecture to 32-page illustrated guides to British, North American and worldwide cinema circuit histories. DIVISIONS **Brantwood Books** and **Outline Publications** UK/US cinema circuit and film studio histories; **Brantwood Biographical** Biographies of movie moguls, producers and directors; **Brantwood Miniature Life** Series of outline biographies of popular movie stars; **Brantwood Technical** Screen, film and camera/projection topics. Consideration given to ideas which can be adapted to a 32-page format; initial approach in writing, please.

Brilliant Publications

The Old School Yard, Leighton Road, Northall, Dunstable, Bedfordshire LU6 2HA
☎01525 222844   Fax 01525 221250
Email sales@brilliantpublications.co.uk
Website www.brilliantpublications.co.uk

Publisher *Priscilla Hannaford*

FOUNDED 1993. *Publishes* resource books for teachers, parents and others working with 0–13-year-olds. 10–15 titles a year. SERIES *How to Dazzle at ...* (9–13-year-olds with special needs); *How to be Brilliant at ...* (7–11-year-olds); *How to Sparkle at ...* (5–7-year-olds); *Activities* (3–5-year-olds). Submit synopsis and sample pages in the first instance. No children's books. Potential authors are strongly advised to look at the format of existing books before submitting synopses.

Royalties paid twice-yearly.

Business Innovations Research

Tregeraint House, Zennor, St Ives, Cornwall
TR26 3DB
☎01736 797061 Fax 01736 797061
Email great-ideas@ukgateway.net
Website www.great-ideas.com
Managing Director *John T. Wilson*

Publishes business books and newsletters, home study courses, and guidebooks. Production service available to self-publishers.

Charlewood Press

7 Weavers Place, Chandlers Ford, Eastleigh, Hampshire SO53 1TU
☎023 8026 1192
Email gponting@clara.net
Website www.home.clara.net/gponting/
    index-page11.html
Managing Editors *Gerald Ponting,*
    Anthony Light

FOUNDED 1987. Publishes local history books on the Fordingbridge area, researched and written by the two partners, and leaflets on local walks. No unsolicited mss.
    Royalties not paid.

The Cheverell Press

Great Cheverell Mill, Devizes, Wiltshire
SN10 5UP
☎01380 816877 Fax 01380 816878
Managing Editor *Sarah de Larrinaga*

Publishes careers, media and performing arts. No fiction. IMPRINTS **The Cheverell Press**; **First Hand Books**. Currently using researchers/ writers on a fee basis, rather than royalties. No unsolicited mss. Started as a self–publisher and has produced a self–publishers information pack. Write for details.

Chrysalis Press

7 Lower Ladyes Hills, Kenilworth, Warwickshire CV8 2GN
☎01926 855223 Fax 01926 856611
Managing Editor *Brian Boyd*

FOUNDED 1994. *Publishes* fiction, literary criticism and biography. No unsolicited mss.
    Royalties paid.

CK Publishing

151 Brookfield Road, Cheadle, Cheshire
SK8 1EY
☎0161 491 6074
Email editor@ckpublishing.co.uk
Website www.ckpublishing.co.uk
Managing Editor *Calum Kerr*

Publishes novels and poetry collections; also *Writer's Muse,* a bi-monthly creative writing magazine featuring short stories, poetry, reviews, articles, biography, etc. Unsolicited mss welcome; no synopses or ideas. S.a.e. essential.
    Royalties paid for book collections. No payment for *Writer's Muse* magazine – free copies.

Clinamen Press Ltd

Enterprise House, Whitworth Street West, Manchester M1 5WG
☎0161 237 3355 Fax 0161 237 3727
Email bstebbing@clinamen.net
Website www.clinamen.net

FOUNDED 1998. *Publishes* philosophy, literary criticism and art theory. No unsolicited mss; two sample chapters with covering letter welcome. See also **the-phone-book.com** under **Electronic Publishers & Other Services**.

CNP Publications

The Roseland Institute, Gorran, St Austell, Cornwall
☎01726 843501 Fax 01726 843501
Email trelispen@care4free.net
Managing Editor *Dr James Whetter*

FOUNDED 1975. *Publishes* quarterly journal *The Cornish Banner/An Baner Kernewek;* also poetry, booklets of Celtic design, political essays, Cornish history. 1–2 titles a year. Cornish history published under the **Lyfrow Trelyspen** imprint. Unsolicited mss, synopses and ideas welcome.
    Royalties not paid.

Codex Books

PO Box 148, Hove, East Sussex BN3 3DQ
☎01273 728000 Fax 01273 205502
Email codex@codexbooks.co.uk
Website www.codexbooks.co.uk
Managing Editor *Hayley Ann*

FOUNDED 1994. *Publishes* 'cutting edge fiction', journalism and non-fiction. Includes cyber punk, pulp, experimental fiction, gay fiction and music-related titles. AUTHORS Billy Childish, Stewart Home, Mark Manning (aka Zodiac Mindwarp) and Jeff Noon. Prefers to receive sample (approx. 50pp) with brief synopsis and author info.
    Royalties paid.

Columbia Publishing Wales Limited

Glen More, 6 Cwrt y Camden, Brecon, Powys LD3 7RR
☎01874 625270 Fax 01874 625270
Email dafydd@columbiapublishing.co.uk

Website www.columbiapublishing.co.uk

Managing Editor *Dafydd Gittins*

FOUNDED 2000. *Publishes* fiction and non-fiction – books, film and music (mainly pop and rock). Subjects suitable for film or television. 2 titles in 2000. No unsolicited mss. Synopses and ideas welcome; approach by letter or e-mail in the first instance.

Royalties paid.

Copperfield Books

Hillbrook House, Lyncombe Vale Road, Bath BA2 4LS

☎01225 442835 Fax 01225 319755

Email sales@www.darcybook.com

Website www.darcybook.com

Managing Director *John Brushfield*

Publishes paperback fiction and general non-fiction. No unsolicited mss; 'we only commission books to our own specification'.

Corvus Books

See **ignotus press**

The Cosmic Elk

68 Elsham Crescent, Lincoln LN6 3YS

☎01522 820922

Email cosmicelk@zoom.co.uk *or* cosmicelk@hotmail.com *or* heather.hobden@ntlworld.com

Contact *Heather Hobden*

FOUNDED in 1988 to publish *John Harrison and the Problem of Longitude* (now in its 7th edition). Continues to publish easily updated card and comb bound booklets on science and history, with associated products such as the John Harrison tea towel. Also web pages. 'New work always welcome on science or history topics suited to format. Please e-mail first to discuss.'

Crescent Moon Publishing and Joe's Press

PO Box 393, Maidstone, Kent ME14 5XU

Email info@crescentmoon.org.uk

Website www.crescentmoon.org.uk

Managing Editor *Jeremy Robinson*

FOUNDED 1988 to publish critical studies of figures such as D.H. Lawrence, Thomas Hardy, André Gide, Walt Disney, Rilke, Leonardo da Vinci, Mark Rothko, C.P. Cavafy and Hélène Cixous. *Publishes* literature, criticism, media, art, feminism, painting, poetry, travel, guidebooks, cinema and some fiction. Literary magazine, *Passion*, launched February 1994. Quarterly. *Pagan America*, twice-yearly anthology of

American poetry. About 15–20 titles per year. Do not send whole mss. Unsolicited synopses and ideas welcome but approach in writing first and send an s.a.e.

Royalties negotiable.

Crossbridge Books

345 Old Birmingham Road, Bromsgrove B60 1NX

☎0121 447 7897 Fax 0121 445 1063

Email Mohr_Books@compuserve.com

Website www.mohrbooks.co.uk

Managing Director *Eileen Mohr*

FOUNDED 1995. *Publishes* Christian books for adults and children. 1–2 titles a year including Trevor Dearing's latest books. No unsolicited mss; telephone in the first instance. No New Age or books not biblically Christian. IMPRINT **Mohr Books**.

Royalties paid twice-yearly.

Crown House Publishing

Crown Buildings, Bancyfelin, Carmarthen SA33 5ND

☎01267 211345 Fax 01267 211882

Website www.crownhouse.co.uk

Editorial Director *David Bowman*

Publishing Director *Bridget Shine*

FOUNDED 1998. *Publishes* titles in the areas of psychology, Neuro-Linguistic Programming (NLP), personal growth, stress management, business, health and hypnosis. The aim of our list is to both demystify the latest psychological advances, particularly in the fields of NLP and hypnosis, and provide professional therapists, consultants and trainers with books detailing the latest cutting-edge developments in their field. Approx. 20 titles a year.

Royalties paid twice-yearly.

Day Books

3 Park Street, Charlbury, Oxfordshire OX7 3PS

☎01608 811196 Fax 01608 811196

Email diaries@day-books.com

Website www.day-books.com

Managing Editor *James Sanderson*

FOUNDED in 1997 to *publish* a series of great diaries from around the world, one of the most recent being *Inside Stalin's Russia*. Unsolicited mss, synopses and ideas welcome. Include return postage if return of material is required.

Dionysia Press Ltd

See under **Poetry Presses**

The Dragonby Press
15 High Street, Dragonby, Scunthorpe, North Lincolnshire DN15 0BE
☎01724 840645
Email rah.williams@virgin.net
Website freespace.virgin.net/rah.williams/
Managing Editor *Richard Williams*

FOUNDED 1987 to publish affordable bibliography for reader, collector and dealer. About 3 titles a year. Unsolicited mss, synopses and ideas welcome for bibliographical projects only.
Royalties paid.

Dramatic Lines
PO Box 201, Twickenham TW2 5RQ
☎020 8296 9502 Fax 020 8296 9503
Email mail@dramaticlinespublishers.co.uk
Website www.dramaticlinespublishers.co.uk
Managing Editor *John Nicholas*

FOUNDED to promote drama for young people. Publications with a wide variety of theatrical applications including classroom use and school assemblies, drama examinations, auditions, festivals and theatre group performance. Unsolicited drama related mss, proposals and synopses welcome.
Royalties paid.

Education Now Publishing Cooperative Ltd
113 Arundel Drive, Bramcote Hills, Nottingham NG9 3FQ
☎0115 925 7261 Fax 0115 925 7261
Website www.gn.apc.org/edheretics
Managing Editors *Dr Roland Meighan, Philip Toogood*

A non-profit research and writing group set up in reaction to 'the totalitarian tendencies of the 1988 Education Act'. Its aim is to widen the terms of the debate about education and its choices. *Publishes* reports on positive educational initiatives such as flexi-schooling, mini-schooling, small schooling, home-based education and democratic schooling. 4–5 titles a year. No unsolicited mss or ideas. Enquiries only.
Royalties generally not paid.

Educational Heretics Press
113 Arundel Drive, Bramcote Hills, Nottingham NG9 3FQ
☎0115 925 7261 Fax 0115 925 7261
Website www.gn.apc.org/edheretics
Directors *Janet & Roland Meighan*

Non-profit venture which aims to question the dogmas of schooling in particular and educa-tion in general, and establish the logistics of the next learning system. No unsolicited material. Enquiries only.
Royalties not paid but under review.

EKO Publishing
Nant Yr Hafod Cottage, Llandegla, Wrexham, Denbighshire LL11 3BG
☎01978 790442
Managing Editor *Brian W. Burnett*

FOUNDED 1996 to publish modern, lively books and magazines in and about Esperanto. Unsolicited mss, synopses and ideas welcome.
Royalties paid.

Enable Enterprises
PO Box 1974, Coventry CV3 1YG
☎0800 358 8484 Fax 0870 133 2447
Email writers@enableenterprises.net
Website www.enableenterprises.net
Contact *Simon Stevens*

Enable Enterprises provides a wide range of accessibilty and disability services including publications on relevant issues. It welcomes unsolicited material related to accessibility and disability issues.

Fand Music Press
The Barony, 16 Sandringham Road, Petersfield, Hampshire GU32 2AA
☎01730 267341 Fax 01730 267341
Email fandmusicpress@printed-music.com
Website www.printed-music.com/fandmusicpress
Managing Editor *Peter Thompson*

FOUNDED in 1989 as a sheet music publisher, Fand Music Press has expanded its range to include CD recordings and books on music. Recently started publishing poetry and short stories. 10 titles in 2000. No unsolicited mss. Write with ideas in the first instance.

Feasac Press
See **ignotus press**

Feather Books
PO Box 438, Shrewsbury, Shropshire SY3 0WN
☎01743 872177 Fax 01743 872177
Email john@waddysweb.freeuk.com
Website www.waddysweb.com
Managing Director *Rev. John Waddington-Feather*
Directors *David Grundy, Tony Reavill*

FOUNDED 1980 to publish writers' group work.

All material has a strong Christian ethos. *Publishes* poetry (mainly, but not exclusively, religious); Christian mystery novels (the Revd. D.I. Blake Hartley series); Christian children's novels; seasonal poetry collections and *The Poetry Church* magazine. 20 titles a year. Produces poetry, drama and music CD/cassettes. No unsolicited mss, synopses or ideas. All correspondence to include s.a.e., please.

Fern House

19 High Street, Haddenham, Ely,
Cambridgeshire CB6 3XA
☎01353 740222 Fax 01353 741987
Email info@fernhouse.com
Website www.fernhouse.com
Managing Editor *Rodney Dale*

FOUNDED 1995. *Publishes* non-fiction with a bias towards biography, reference and technology. 4 titles in 2000. Unsolicited synopses and ideas welcome 'but please study the website first to avoid wasting time'.
Royalties paid.

First Hand Books

See **The Cheverell Press**

Five Leaves Publications

PO Box 81, Nottingham NG5 4ER
☎0115 969 3597
Email fiveleaf01@surfaid.org
Website www.fiveleaves.co.uk

Contact *Ross Bradshaw*

FOUNDED 1995 (taking over the publishing programme of Mushroom Bookshop), producing 6–8 titles a year. *Publishes* fiction, poetry, politics and Jewish interest. Publisher of several books by Michael Rosen. Titles normally commissioned.
Royalties and fees paid.

Forth Naturalist & Historian

University of Stirling, Stirling FK9 4LA
☎01259 215091 Fax 01786 464994
Email lindsay.corbett@stir.ac.uk
Website www.stir.ac.uk/departments/
  natural sciences/

Also at: 30 Dunmar Drive, Alloa,
Clackmannanshire FK10 2EH
Honorary Secretary *Lindsay Corbett*

FOUNDED 1975 by the collaboration of Stirling University members and the Central Regional Council to promote interests and publications on central Scotland. Aims to provide a 'valuable local studies educational resource for mid-Scotland schools, libraries and people'. Runs an annual symposium: Man and the Landscape ('Conserving Biodiversity and Heritage' in 2000). *Publishes* naturalist, historical and environmental studies and maps, including 1890s maps 25" to the mile – 24 of Central Scotland areas/places with historical notes. Over 20 selected papers from the annual *The Forth Naturalist & Historian* (Vol. 23 in 2000) are published in pamphlet form. Welcomes papers, mss and ideas relevant to central Scotland.
Royalties not paid.

Frontier Publishing

Windetts, Kirstead, Norfolk NR15 1EG
☎01508 558174 Fax 01508 550194
Website www.frontierpublishing.co.uk

Managing Editor *John Black*

FOUNDED 1983. *Publishes* travel, photography and literature. 2–3 titles a year. No unsolicited mss; synopses and ideas welcome.
Royalties paid.

Galactic Central Publications

Imladris, 25A Copgrove Road, Leeds, West Yorkshire LS8 2SP
Email philsp@compuserve.com
Website www.philsp.cwc.net
Managing Editor *Phil Stephensen-Payne*

FOUNDED 1982 in the US. *Publishes* science fiction bibliographies. About 4 titles a year. All new publications originate in the UK. Unsolicited mss, synopses and ideas welcome.

The Gargoyle's Head

Chatham House, Gosshill Road, Chislehurst, Kent BR7 5NS
☎020 8467 8475 Fax 020 8295 1967

Managing Editor *Jennie Gray*

FOUNDED 1990. *Publishes* a six-monthly magazine and newsletter plus books and supplements on Gothic and macabre subjects. History, literary criticism, reprints of forgotten texts, biography, architecture, art, etc., usually with a gloomy and black-hued flavour. About 4 titles a year. Synopses and ideas welcome.
Flat fee paid.

Geological Society Publishing House

Unit 7, Brassmill Enterprise Centre, Brassmill Lane, Bath BA1 3JN
☎01225 445046 Fax 01225 442836
Website bookshop.geolsoc.org.uk

Managing Editor *Mike Collins*

Publishing arm of the Geological Society

which was founded in 1807. *Publishes* undergraduate and postgraduate texts in the earth sciences. 25 titles a year. Unsolicited mss, synopses and ideas welcome.

Royalties not paid.

Gilnoc Publications Ltd
PO Box 61, Lingfield, Surrey RH7 6FE
☎01342 892682
Email charles@gilnoc.co.uk
Website www.gilnoc.co.uk

FOUNDED by self-publishing author Charles J. Ayling. Published three titles in the first year, one children's book and two with strong gospel themes. 'Would be happy to consider similar titles.' Contact by letter, marked 'New Works', with brief description.

Glosa Education Organisation
PO Box 18, Richmond, Surrey TW9 2GE
Managing Editor *Wendy Ashby*

FOUNDED 1981. *Publishes* textbooks, dictionaries and translations for the teaching, speaking and promotion of Glosa (an international, auxiliary language); also a newsletter and journal. Rapid growth in the last couple of years. In 1994 launched *Sko-Glosa*, a publication for and by younger students of Glosa to be distributed to schools in different countries. Also in 1994 published several fairy stories and activity pages for school children who are learning Glosa in school. Unsolicited mss and ideas for Glosa books welcome.

Grant Books
The Coach House, New Road, Cutnall Green, Droitwich, Worcestershire WR9 0PQ
☎01299 851588 Fax 01299 851446
Email golf@grantbooks.co.uk
Website www.grantbooks.co.uk

Managing Editor *H.R.J. Grant*

FOUNDED 1978. *Publishes* golf-related titles only: course architecture, history, biography, etc., but no instructional material. New titles and old, plus limited editions. About 6 titles a year. Unsolicited mss, synopses and ideas welcome.

Royalties paid.

Great Northern Publishing
PO Box 202, Scarborough, North Yorkshire YO11 3GE
☎01723 581329 Fax 01723 581329
Email books@greatnorthernpublishing.co.uk
Website www.greatnorthernpublishing.co.uk

Senior Editor *Diane Crowther*

FOUNDED in 1999, originally as a journal/

newsletter and general publisher and also as a self-publishing venture. Offers full publishing service, including advice on marketing and sales to first-time authors as well as museums, charities, groups and businesses. *Publishes* fiction and non-fiction in most genres; no romantic, religious, political or feminist books. 3 titles in 2000. Now runs Internet-based bookshop stocking selected titles alongside its own. No unsolicited mss; send letter in the first instance.

Royalties paid twice-yearly.

Grevatt & Grevatt
9 Rectory Drive, Newcastle upon Tyne NE3 1XT
Chairman/Editorial Head *Dr S.Y. Killingley*

FOUNDED 1981. Alternative publisher of works not normally commercially viable. Three books have appeared with financial backing from professional bodies. *Publishes* academic titles and conference reports, particularly language, linguistics and religious studies. Some poetry also. No unsolicited mss. Synopses and ideas should be accompanied by s.a.e. Offers typesetting, editing and other services; s.a.e. with enquiries.

Royalties paid annually (after first 500 copies).

GRM Publications
PO Box 213, Leeds LS6 4YQ
☎0113 275 2456 Fax 0113 275 2456
Managing Editors *Graham Wade, Elizabeth Wade*

FOUNDED 1996. Publishes monographs on classical music and musicians.

GSSE
11 Malford Grove, Gilwern, Abergavenny, Monmouthshire NP7 0RN
☎01873 830872
Email GSSE@zoo.co.uk
Owner/Manager *David P. Bosworth*

Publishes newsletters (main publication, *OLS News*) and booklets describing classroom practice (at all levels of education and training). Ideas welcome – particularly from practising teachers, lecturers and trainers describing how they use technology in their teaching.

Royalties paid by arrangement.

The Guerrilla Press
B.M. Betelguise, London WC1N 3XX
Website www.geocities.com/CapitolHill/6743
Managing Editor *Tim Telsa*

FOUNDED in 1997 'to challenge the authority of

psychiatric care'. *Publishes* political – mainly work of an anarchist nature – 'that would be ignored by most publishers'. About 10 titles a year. Unsolicited mss, synopses and ideas welcome; send letter with description of proposed ms plus return postage.
Royalties not paid.

Happy House
3b Castledown Avenue, Hastings, East Sussex TN34 3RJ
☎01424 434778
FOUNDED 1992 as a self-publishing venture for a Dave Arnold/Martin Honeysett collaboration of poetry and cartoons.

Haunted Library
Flat 1, 36 Hamilton Street, Hoole, Chester, Cheshire CH2 3JQ
☎01244 313685   Fax 01244 313685
Email pardos@globalnet.co.uk
Website www.users.globalnet.co.uk/~pardos/GS.html
Managing Editor *Rosemary Pardoe*
FOUNDED 1979. *Publishes* a twice-yearly ghost story magazine in the antiquarian tradition of M.R. James. The magazine features stories, news and articles. No unsolicited mss.
Royalties not paid.

Headpress
40 Rossall Avenue, Radcliffe, Manchester M26 1JD
☎0161 796 1935   Fax 0161 796 1935
Email david.headpress@zen.co.uk
Website www.headpress.com
Managing Editor *David Kerekes*
FOUNDED 1991. *Publishes Headpress* journal, devoted to the strange and esoteric, and books on film, popular and underground culture. No fiction or poetry. Unsolicited material welcome; send letter in the first instance.

Heart of Albion Press
2 Cross Hill Close, Wymeswold, Loughborough, Leicestershire LE12 6UJ
☎01509 880725
Email albion@indigogroup.co.uk
Website www.indigogroup.co.uk/albion/
Managing Editor *R.N. Trubshaw*
FOUNDED 1990 to publish books and booklets on the East Midlands area. *Publishes* mostly local history. Future publications on CD-ROM only. No unsolicited mss.
Royalties negotiable.

Hermitage Press
77 Old Tiverton Road, Exeter, Devon EX4 6NG
☎01392 683617   Fax 01392 683617
Managing Editor *John Evans*
FOUNDED 2000. *Publishes* books about books, nature conservation, spiritual path, history, biography. No unsolicited mss; send synopses and ideas by post or fax.
Royalties paid.

Hilmarton Manor Press
Calne, Wiltshire SN11 8SB
☎01249 760208   Fax 01249 760379
Email hilmartonpress@lineone.net
Chairman/Managing Director *Charles Baile de Laperriere*
Publishes fine art reference only.
Royalties paid.

Horseshoe Publications
PO Box 37, Kingsley, Frodsham, Cheshire WA6 8DR
☎01928 787477 (Afternoons and evenings)
Managing Editor *John C. Hibbert*
FOUNDED in 1994, initially to publish work of Cheshire writers. Poetry, short stories and own writing. Shared cost publishing considered in certain circumstances. Reading fee on full mss £25. Unsolicited mss, synopses and ideas in the realm of commercial fiction welcome. S.a.e. for return.

ignotus press
BCM-Writer, 27 Old Gloucester Street, London WC1N 3XX
☎01530 831916   Fax 01530 831916
Email ignotuspress@hotmail.com
Publisher *Suzanne Ruthven*
Specialises in full length esoteric non-fiction and fiction relating to all traditions although writers are advised to send s.a.e. for authors' guidelines before submitting material for consideration. 'All mss are checked for accuracy and knowledge of subject by specialists who will reject New Age idealism, fantasy, mind, body & spirit'. Also *publishes Alphard* (formerly *Comhairle*). The articles and features published in the quarterly magazine illustrate the range of material sought by any of the ignotus press imprints. Free sample back issues available – send 2x1st class stamps.
IMPRINTS **Corvus Books** *Christine Sempers* A5 booklets and spiral-bound workbooks on a world-wide range of esoteric and mysteries

techniques. **Feasac Press** *Frances Denton* The cultural aspects of esoteria, i.e. history, anthopology, psychology and sociology of the different traditions, including art and craft, short fiction and poetry.

Royalties paid.

Inner Sanctum Publications

75 Greenleaf Gardens, Polegate, East Sussex BN26 6PQ

☎01323 484058

Email books@ethericrealms.com

Website www.ethericrealms.com

Managing Editor *Mary Hession*

FOUNDED in 1999 to *publish* spiritual books. Unsolicited mss, synopses and ideas welcome; approach in writing in the first instance.

Royalties not paid.

Intellect Books

PO Box 862, Bristol BS99 1DE

☎0117 955 6811 Fax 0117 955 6811

Email info@intellectbooks.com

Website www.intellectbooks.com

Chairman *Masoud Yazdani*

Managing Director *Robin Beecroft*

A multidisciplinary publisher for both individual and institutional readers. Tracks newest developments in digital creative media – art, film, television, theatre design, etc. – and examines distinct theories in education, language, gender study and international culture through scholarly articles. Also publishes in AI, computer science and human-computer interaction in books, journals and website.

Royalties paid.

Iolo

38 Chaucer Road, Bedford MK40 2AJ

☎01234 301718 Fax 01234 270175

Managing Director *Dedwydd Jones*

Publishes Welsh theatre-related material and campaigns for a Welsh National Theatre. Ideas on Welsh themes welcome; approach in writing.

Irishpulp

'The Book Capital', PO Box 23, Hay-on-Wye, Herefordshire HR3 5YF

☎0870 401 4245 Fax 0870 401 4245

Email irishpulp@irishpulp.com

Website www.irishpulp.com

Managing Editor *Sean Fox*

FOUNDED 1999. *Specialises* in promoting Irish writers with a 'cathartic writing style' on themes

such as the Irish conflict and emigration. *Publishes* novels, short stories, poems and memoirs. 1 title in 2000. 'New, unpublished authors particularly welcome.' Send letter, synopsis, sample chapters (no more than 200 words) and s.a.e.

Royalties paid.

Ivy Publications

72 Hyperion House, Somers Road, London SW2 1HZ

☎020 8671 6872 Fax 020 8671 3391

Proprietor *Ian Bruton-Simmonds*

FOUNDED 1989. *Publishes* educational, science, fiction, philosophy, children's, travel, literary criticism, history, film scripts. No unsolicited mss; send two pages, one from the beginning and one from the body of the book, together with synopsis (one paragraph) and s.a.e. No cookery, gardening or science fiction.

Royalties paid annually.

JAC Publications

28 Bellomonte Crescent, Drayton, Norwich, Norfolk NR8 6EJ

☎01603 861339

Managing Editor *John James Vasco*

Publishes World War II Luftwaffe history only. Unsolicited mss welcome. No synopses or ideas.

Royalties paid.

The Jupiter Press

Oracle House, 1–3 Gospel End Road, Sedgley, Dudley, West Midlands DY3 3LT

☎01902 665477 Fax 01902 678655

Managing Editor *Gordon Drury*

FOUNDED 1995. Looking for niche market and information publications, particularly sport orientated (golf and soccer), also quiz, puzzles and games content. Also interested in clairvoyance, esoteric subjects. Synopses and ideas for books welcome.

Royalties paid.

Katabasis

See under **Poetry Presses**

Kittiwake

3 Glantwymyn Village Workshops, Nr. Machynlleth, Montgomeryshire SY20 8LY

☎01650 511314 Fax 01650 511602/

eFax: 0870 132 7404

Email david@perrocarto.co.uk

Website perrocarto.co.uk

Managing Editor *David Perrott*

FOUNDED 1986. *Publishes* guidebooks only, with an emphasis on careful design/production. Unsolicited mss, synopses and ideas for guidebooks welcome. Specialist research, writing, cartographic and electronic publishing services available.

Royalties paid.

Libri Publications Ltd

Suite 296, 37 Store Street, London WC1E 7QF
☎020 7627 3748 Fax 020 7627 3748
Email libri@annal.dircon.co.uk

Managing Editor *Anna Lethbridge*

FOUNDED 1998. *Publishes* scholarly but accessible archaeology, especially that of Egypt, the Middle East and Mediterranean area; also biography. 1 title in 2000. No unsolicited mss; synopses and ideas are welcome with s.a.e. but e-mail inquiry preferred in the first instance.

Royalties paid twice-yearly.

The Lindsey Press

Unitarian Headquarters, 1–6 Essex Street, Strand, London WC2R 3HY
☎020 7240 2384 Fax 020 7240 3089
Email ga@unitarian.org.uk

Convenor *Kate Taylor*

ESTABLISHED at the end of the 18th century as a vehicle for disseminating liberal religion. Adopted the name of The Lindsey Press at the beginning of the 20th century (after Theophilus Lindsey, the great Unitarian Theologian). *Publishes* books reflecting liberal religious thought or Unitarian denominational history. Also worship material: hymn books, collections of prayers, etc. No unsolicited mss; synopses and ideas welcome.

Royalties not paid.

Logaston Press

Logaston, Woonton, Almeley, Herefordshire HR3 6QH
☎01544 327344

Managing Editors *Andy Johnson, Ron Shoesmith*

FOUNDED 1985. *Publishes* guides, archaeology, social history, rural issues and local history for Wales, the Welsh Border and West Midlands. 8–10 titles a year. Unsolicited mss, synopses and ideas welcome. Return postage appreciated.

Royalties paid.

Luath Press Ltd

543/2 Castlehill, The Royal Mile, Edinburgh EH1 2ND
☎0131 225 4326 Fax 0131 225 4324
Email gavin.macdougall@luath.co.uk

Website www.luath.co.uk

Managing Editor *G.H. MacDougall*

FOUNDED 1981. *Publishes* mainly books with a Scottish connection. Current list includes guide books, walking and outdoor, history, folklore, politics and global issues, cartoons, fiction, poetry, biography, food and drink, environment, music and dance, sport and *On the Trail* SERIES. About 20–30 titles a year. Unsolicited mss, synopses and ideas welcome; 'committed to publishing well-written books worth reading'.

Royalties paid.

Lyfrow Trelyspen

See **CNP Publications**

Madison Publishing Ltd

Fairway House, 27 Comyn Road, London SW11 1QB
☎07770 873399 Fax 020 7585 0079

Managing Director *Nathan Andrew Iyer*

FOUNDED 1995. *Publishes* British fiction. No unsolicited mss. Synopses (no more than 2pp) and ideas welcome.

Marine Day Publishers

64 Cotterill Road, Surbiton, Surrey KT6 7UN
☎020 8399 7625

Managing Editor *Anthony G. Durrant*

FOUNDED 1990. Part of The Marine Press Ltd. *Publishes* local history.

Royalties not paid.

Matching Press

1 Watermans End, Matching Green, Harlow, Essex CM17 0RQ
☎01279 731308

Publisher *Patrick Streeter*

FOUNDED 1993. *Publishes* biography, autobiography, social history and fiction. Enquiries welcome.

Royalties paid.

Maypole Editions

22 Mayfair Avenue, Ilford, Essex IG1 3DQ
☎020 8252 3937

Contact *Barry Taylor*

Publisher of plays and poetry in the main. 2–3 titles a year. Unsolicited mss welcome provided return postage is included. Poetry always welcome for collected anthologies and should be approximately 30 lines of tight verse, broadly covering social concerns, ethnic minority issues, feminist incident, romance generally, travel and lyric rhyming verse. No politics except evenly comparative. The biannual collected anthology is designed as a small press platform for first-time poets who might not otherwise get into print, and a permanent showcase for those already published who want to break into the mainstream. Catalogue £1, plus A5 s.a.e. 'Please be patient when sending work because of the huge volume of submissions.' Exempt Charity Status.

Meadow Books
22 Church Meadow, Milton under Wychwood, Chipping Norton, Oxfordshire OX7 6JG
☎01993 831338

Managing Director *C. O'Neill*

FOUNDED 1990. Published *A Picture of Health* and *More Pictures of Health*.

Mercia Cinema Society
19 Pinder's Grove, Wakefield, West Yorkshire WF1 4AH
☎01924 372748
Email mervyn.gould@virgin.net

Managing Editor *Brian Hornsey*

FOUNDED 1980 to foster research into the history of picture houses. *Publishes* books and booklets on the subject, including cinema circuits and chains. Books are often tied in with specific geographical areas. Unsolicited mss, synopses and ideas.
Royalties not paid.

Meridian Books
40 Hadzor Road, Oldbury, West Midlands B68 9LA
☎0121 429 4397

Managing Editor *Peter Groves*

FOUNDED 1985 as a small home-based enterprise following the acquisition of titles from Tetradon Publications Ltd. *Publishes* walking and regional guides. 4–5 titles a year. Unsolicited mss, synopses and ideas welcome if relevant. Send s.a.e. if mss to be returned.
Royalties paid.

Mermaid Turbulence
Annaghmaconway, Cloone, Leitrim, Republic of Ireland
☎00 353 78 36134 Fax 00 353 78 36134

Managing Director *Mari-Aymone Djeribi*

FOUNDED in 1993 with the first issue of *element* – an international literary journal. *Publishes* essays, fiction, poetry, cookery, children's and artists' books. 7 titles in 2001. Unsolicited mss,

synopses and ideas welcome. No pulp fiction. Approach in writing, enclosing s.a.e.
Royalties paid annually.

Merton Priory Press Ltd
67 Merthyr Road, Whitchurch, Cardiff CF14 1DD
☎029 2052 1956 Fax 029 2062 3599
Email merton@dircon.co.uk

Managing Director *Philip Riden*

FOUNDED 1993. *Publishes* academic and mid-market history, especially local, industrial and transport history; also memoirs and autobiographies. About 6 titles a year. Full catalogue available.
Royalties paid twice-yearly.

Neil Miller Publications
Mount Cottage, Grange Road, Saint Michael's, Tenterden, Kent TN30 6EE

Managing Editor *Neil Miller*

FOUNDED 1994. *Publishes* short tales with a twist, comedy, suspense, mystery, fantasy, science fiction, horror and the bizarre under the **Black Cat Books** imprint. Also *publishes* paperbacks: classics, rare tales, tales of the unexpected. New authors always welcome. Evaluation and critique service available for large mss. 'We seek short story writers, in any genre. No unsolicited/unrequested mss, please. In the first instance, send £7.75 and large 45-pence s.a.e. for author's package, which includes free book listing hundreds of possible publication outlets for new authors, or our latest novel; please state preference. We have published 170 new authors since 1994. We will help and advise on anything well written and researched. Now accepting novels and short poems.'

Millers Dale Publications
7 Weavers Place, Chandlers Ford, Eastleigh, Hampshire SO53 1TU
☎023 8026 1192
Email gponting@clara.net
Website www.home.clara.net/gponting/index-page10.html

Managing Editor *Gerald Ponting*

FOUNDED 1990. *Publishes* books on local history related to central Hampshire. Also books related to slide presentations by Gerald Ponting. Ideas for local history books on Hampshire considered.

Minority Rights Group
379 Brixton Road, London SW9 7DE
☎020 7978 9498 Fax 020 7738 6265
Email minority.rights@mrgmail.org

Website www.minorityrights.org
Deputy Head of Communications *Angela Warren*

FOUNDED in the late 1960s, MRG works to raise awareness of minority issues worldwide. *Publishes* books, reports and educational material on minority rights. 8–10 titles a year.

Mohr Books
See **Crossbridge Books**

Morton Publishing
PO Box 23, Gosport, Hampshire PO12 2XD
Managing Editor *Nik Morton*

FOUNDED 1994. *Publishes* fiction – genre novellas (eg crime, science fiction, fantasy, horror, western), max. 20,000 words; short story anthologies – max. 4000 words per story. Unsolicited synopses and ideas for books welcome; enclose s.a.e. Also offers literary agent service of guidance and advice (fees on application)
Royalties paid annually.

Need2Know
Remus House, Coltsfoot Drive, Woodston, Peterborough PE2 9JX
☎01733 898103 Fax 01733 313524
Email andrew@forwardpress.co.uk
Website www.forwardpress.co.uk
Managing Editor *Andrew Head*

FOUNDED 1995 'to fill a gap in the market for self-help books'. Need2Know is an imprint of Forward Press (see under **Poetry Presses**). *Publishes* contemporary health and lifestyle issues. Mss, synopses and ideas for books welcome with return postage. It is important to ensure the project fits in with the series and that the subject is not already covered. For further information and an author brief, call *Andrew Head.*
Payment Advance plus 15% royalties.

Nimbus Press
18 Guilford Road, Leicester LE2 2RB
☎0116 270 6318 Fax 0116 270 6318
Email clifford.sharp@nimbuspress.co.uk
Website www.nimbuspress.co.uk
Managing Editor *Clifford Sharp*
Assistant Editor *Justin Moulder*

FOUNDED in 1991 to encourage churches to use drama in worship. *Publishes* Christian drama, humour, Christian apologetics, etc. Plays of no more than 30 minutes' length and suitable for church drama groups welcome. About 4–5 titles a year.
Royalties paid.

Northern Lights
Cumbria County Council, Cultural Services, Arroyo Block, The Castle, Carlisle, Cumbria CA3 8UR
☎01228 607306 Fax 01228 67299
Email susan.tranter@cumbriacc.gov.uk
Managing Editor *Susan Tranter*

FOUNDED in 2000 to publish 'the best new poetry, short fiction and theatre writing from Cumbria'. *Publishes* 4 pamphlets a year – poetry and fiction. Welcomes mss, synopses and ideas from previously unpublished writers in Cumbria. Send letter in the first instance.
Royalties not paid.

Norvik Press Ltd
School of Language, Linguistics & Translation Studies, University of East Anglia, Norwich, Norfolk NR4 7TJ
☎01603 593356 Fax 01603 250599
Email norvik.press@uea.ac.uk
Website www.uea.ac.uk/llt/norvik_press
Managing Editors *Janet Garton, Michael Robinson*

Small academic press. *Publishes* the journal *Scandinavica* and books related to Scandinavian literature. About 4 titles a year. Interested in synopses and ideas for books within its *Literary History and Criticism* series. No unsolicited mss.
Royalties paid.

The Nostalgia Collection
Silver Link Publishing Ltd, The Trundle, Ringstead Road, Great Addington, Kettering, Northamptonshire NN14 4BW
☎01536 330588 Fax 01536 330588
Email sales@nostalgiacollection.com
Website www.nostalgiacollection.com
Managing Editor *Peter Townsend*

FOUNDED 1985 in Lancashire, changed hands in 1990 and now based in Northamptonshire. Small independent company specialising in nostalgia titles including illustrated books on towns and cities, villages and rural life, rivers and inland waterways, industrial heritage, railways, trams, ships and other transport subjects. *Publishes* postwar nostalgia on all aspects of social history under the **Past and Present Publishing** imprint.
Fees paid.

Novel Publishing
PO Box 6105, Leighton Buzzard LU7 9YT
☎01296 661119 Fax 01296 668442
Email writeon@novelpublishing.com
Website www.novelpublishing.com

Managing Editor *Liz Jeannet*

FOUNDED 1999. *Publishes* fiction. 'All genres of exciting new fiction considered but must have real literary quality.' 1 title in 2000. Unsolicited mss, synopses and ideas welcome; send letter or e-mail in the first instance.

Payment No advance, royalties only.

Nyala Publishing

4 Christian Fields, London SW16 3JZ
☎020 8764 6292
Fax 020 8764 6292/0115 981 9418
Email nyala.publish@geo-group.demon.co.uk
Editorial Head *J.F.J. Douglas*

FOUNDED 1996. Publishing arm of Geo Group. *Publishes* biography, travel and general non-fiction. No unsolicited mss; synopses and ideas considered. Also offers a wide range of printing and publishing services. 'Quality low-cost printing a speciality.'

Royalties paid twice-yearly.

Orpheus Publishing House

4 Dunsborough Park, Ripley Green, Ripley, Guildford, Surrey GU23 6AL
☎01483 225777 Fax 01483 225776
Email orpheuspubl.ho@btinternet.com
Managing Editor *J.S. Gordon*

FOUNDED 1996. *Publishes* 'well-researched and properly argued' books in the fields of occult science, esotericism and comparative philosophy/religion. 'Keen to encourage good (but sensible) new authors.' In the first instance, send maximum three-page synopsis with s.a.e.

Royalties by agreement.

Outline Publications

See **Brantwood Books**

Palladour Books

Hirwaun House, Aberporth, Nr. Cardigan, Ceredigion SA43 2EU
☎01239 811658 Fax 01239 811658
Email palladour@powellj33.freeserve.co.uk
Managing Editors *Jeremy Powell, Anne Powell*

FOUNDED 1986. Started with a twice-yearly issue of catalogues on the literature and poetry of World War I. Occasional catalogues on World War II poetry have also been issued. No unsolicited mss.

Royalties not paid.

Panacea Press Limited

86 North Gate, Prince Albert Road, London NW8 7EJ

☎020 7722 8464 Fax 020 7586 8187
Managing Editor *Erwin Brecher*

FOUNDED as a self-publisher but now open for non-fiction from other authors. Material of academic value considered provided it commands a wide general market. No unsolicited mss; synopses and ideas welcome. Approach by fax or letter. No telephone calls.

Royalties paid annually.

Paradise Press

See **Gay Authors Workshop** under **Writers' Courses, Circles and Workshops**

Parapress Ltd

5 Bentham Hill House, Stockland Green Road, Tunbridge Wells, Kent TN3 0TJ
☎01892 512118 Fax 01892 512118
Email e.imlay.parapress@virgin.net
Managing Editor *Elizabeth Imlay*
Production and Promotion *James Ewing*

FOUNDED 1993. *Publishes* animals, autobiography, biography, history, literary criticism, military and naval, music, self-help, sports. Some self-publishing. About 6 titles a year.

Parthian

53 Colum Road, Cardiff CF10 3EF
☎029 2034 1314 Fax 029 2034 1314
Email parthianbooks@yahoo.co.uk
Website www.parthianbooks.co.uk
Chairman *Gillian Griffiths*
Publisher *Richard Davies*

FOUNDED 1993. *Publishes* contemporary Welsh fiction, drama and poetry in English, also translations of Welsh language fiction. No unsolicited mss; synopses with sample chapters and ideas welcome.

Royalties paid annually.

Partnership Publishing Ltd

56 Market Street, Wellington, Telford, Shropshire TF1 1DT
☎01952 415334 Fax 01952 406762
Email info@publish.uk.ws
Managing Director *Steve Rooney*

Publisher of *Bus and Coach Professional; Professional Recovery; MOT Professional; Oakengates & District News; Wellington News.* Offers full magazine publication services, including design and production, editorial and advertising sales service.

Past and Present Publishing

See **The Nostalgia Collection**

Paupers' Press

27 Melbourne Road, West Bridgford,
Nottingham NG2 5DJ
☎0115 981 5063   Fax 0115 981 5063
Email stan2727uk@aol.com
Website members.aol.com/stan2727uk/
   pauper.htm

Managing Editor *Colin Stanley*

FOUNDED 1983. *Publishes* extended essays in
booklet form (about 15,000 words) on literary
criticism and philosophy. About 6 titles a year.
Limited hardback editions of bestselling titles.
No unsolicited mss but synopses and ideas for
books welcome.
   Royalties paid.

Peepal Tree Press Ltd

17 King's Avenue, Leeds, West Yorkshire LS6
1QS
☎0113 245 1703   Fax 0113 245 9616
Email hannah@peepal.demon.co.uk

Managing Editor *Jeremy Poynting*

FOUNDED 1985. *Publishes* fiction, poetry, drama
and academic studies. *Specialises* in Caribbean,
Black British and south Asian writing. About 18
titles a year. In-house printing and finishing facilities. AUTHORS include **Forward Poetry Prize**
winner Kwame Dawes. 'Please send an A5 s.a.e.
with a 38p stamp for a copy of our submission
guidelines.' Write or 'phone for a free catalogue.
   Royalties paid.

The Penniless Press

100 Waterloo Road, Ashton, Preston,
Lancashire PR2 1EP

Editor *Alan Dent*

Publishes quarterly magazine with literary,
philosophical, artistic and political content,
including reviews of poetry, fiction, non-fiction and drama. Prose of up to 3000 words
welcome. No mss returned without s.a.e.
   Payment Free copy of magazine.

Pipers' Ash Ltd

'Pipers' Ash', Church Road, Christian
Malford, Chippenham, Wiltshire SN15 4BW
☎01249 720563   Fax 0870 0568916
Email pipersash@supamasu.com
Website www.supamasu.com

Managing Editor *Mr A. Tyson*

FOUNDED 1976 to publish technical manuals for
computer-controlled systems. Later broadened
the company's publishing activities to include
individual collections of contemporary short stories, science fiction short stories, poetry, short

novels, local histories, children's fiction, philosophy, biographies, translations and general non-
fiction. 18 titles a year. Synopses and ideas welcome; 'new authors with potential will be
actively encouraged'. Offices in New Zealand
and Australia.
   Royalties paid annually.

Planet

PO Box 44, Aberystwyth, Ceredigion
SY23 5ZZ
☎01970 611255   Fax 01970 611197
Email planet.enquiries@planetmagazine.org.uk
Website www.planetmagazine.org.uk

Managing Editor *John Barnie*

FOUNDED 1985 as publisher of the arts and current affairs magazine *Planet: The Welsh Internationalist* and branched out into book publishing
in 1995. All books so far have been commissioned. Unsolicited synopses and ideas welcome.
   Royalties paid.

Playwrights Publishing Co.

70 Nottingham Road, Burton Joyce,
Nottinghamshire NG14 5AL
☎0115 931 3356
Email playwrightspublishingco@yahoo.co.uk
Website geocities.com/playwrightspublishingco

Managing Editors *Liz Breeze, Tony Breeze*

FOUNDED 1990. *Publishes* one-act and full-
length plays. Unsolicited scripts welcome. No
synopses or ideas. Reading fees: £15 one act;
£30 full length.
   Royalties paid.

Pomegranate Press

Dolphin House, 51 St Nicholas Lane, Lewes,
Sussex BN7 2JZ
☎01273 470100   Fax 01273 470100
Email sussexbooks@compuserve.com
Website ourworld.compuserve.com/
   homepages/sussexbooks

Managing Editor *David Arscott*

FOUNDED in 1992 by writer/broadcaster David
Arscott, who also administers the **Sussex Book
Club**. *Specialises* in books about Sussex. IMPRINT
Pomegranate Practicals How-to books.
   Royalties paid twice-yearly.

David Porteous Editions

PO Box 5, Chudleigh, Newton Abbot,
Devon TQ13 0YZ
☎01626 853310   Fax 01626 853663
Email editorial@davidporteous.com
Website www.davidporteous.com

Publisher *David Porteous*

FOUNDED 1992 to produce high quality colour illustrated books on hobbies and leisure for the UK and international markets. *Publishes* crafts, hobbies, art techniques and needlecrafts. No poetry or fiction. 3–4 titles a year. Unsolicited mss, synopses and ideas welcome if return postage included.
  Royalties paid twice-yearly.

Power Publications
1 Clayford Avenue, Ferndown, Dorset BH22 9PQ
☎01202 875223 Fax 01202 875223
Email powerpublications@powerpublicatons. co.uk
Contact *Mike Power*

FOUNDED 1989. *Publishes* local interest, pub walk guides and mountain bike guides. 2–3 titles a year. Unsolicited mss/synopses/ideas welcome.
  Royalties paid.

Praxis Books
Crossways Cottage, Walterstone, Herefordshire HR2 0DX
☎01873 890695
Email 100543.3270@compuserve.com
Website www.rebeccatope.com
Proprietor *Rebecca Smith*

FOUNDED 1992. *Publishes* reissues of Victorian fiction, memoirs, diaries and general interest. 17 titles to date. Unsolicited mss accepted with s.a.e. No fiction, children's or humour. Editing service available. Flexible funding negotiable. 'I am most likely to accept work with a clearly identifiable market.'

Primrose Hill Press Ltd
58 Carey Street, London WC2A 2JB
☎020 7405 7484 Fax 020 7405 7459
Email info@primrosehillpress.co.uk
Managing Director *Brian H.W. Hill*

FOUNDED in 1997, having taken over the stock and projects in progress of Silent Books Ltd. *Publishes* general art titles, wood engraving, poetry and books for the gift market, 'all high quality productions'. No fiction. About 12 titles a year. Unsolicited mss, synopses and ideas welcome.

QED of York
1 Straylands Grove, York YO31 1EB
☎01904 424242 Fax 01904 424381
Email qed@enterprise.net
Managing Editor *John Bibby*

Publishes and distributes resource guides and learning aids, including laminated posters, for mathematics and science. Synopses (3pp) and ideas for books welcome. QED arranges publicity for other small presses and has many contacts overseas. Provides publishing services for other publishers and arranges exhibitions at Frankfurt, LIBF, educational conferences (storage, display stands, crates, etc. available for loan).
  Royalties by agreement.

QueenSpark Books
49 Grand Parade, Brighton, East Sussex BN2 2QA
☎01273 571710 Fax 01273 571710

A community writing and publishing group run mainly by volunteers who work together to write and produce books. Since the early 1970s they have published 70 titles, mainly local autobiographies. Writing workshops and groups held on a regular basis. New members welcome.

Redstone Press
7A St Lawrence Terrace, London W10 5SU
☎020 7352 1594 Fax 020 7352 8749
Email redstone.press@virgin.net
Website jrothenstein@redstonepress.co.uk
Managing Editor *Julian Rothenstein*

FOUNDED 1987. *Publishes* art and literature. About 5 titles a year. No unsolicited mss; synopses and ideas welcome but familiarity with Redstone's list advised in the first instance.
  Royalties paid.

The Riverside Press
PO Box 388A, Surbiton, Surrey KT7 0ZT
☎020 8339 0945 Fax 020 8339 0945
Email ed@good-writing-matters.com
Website www.good-writing-matters.com
Managing Editor *Michael Russell*

FOUNDED 1998 to publish short-run titles from new writers. Mainly fiction but also special interest non-fiction. Editorial support service provided. No unsolicited mss. Send synopses/ideas and three chapters only with covering letter.
  Royalties paid.

The Robinswood Press
30 South Avenue, Stourbridge, West Midlands DY8 3XY
☎01384 397475 Fax 01384.440443
Email robinswoodpress@cwcom.net
Website www.robinswood.co.uk
Managing Editor *Christopher J. Marshall*

FOUNDED 1985. *Publishes* education, particularly teacher resources, SEN. Also collaborative publishing, e.g. with Camphill Foundation and Birmingham Royal Ballet. 12–15 titles a year. Unsolicited mss, synopses and ideas welcome.
Royalties paid.

Romer Publications
PO Box 10120, NL–1001 EC Amsterdam, The Netherlands
☎00 31 20 676 9442 Fax 00 31 20 676 9442
Email harrymelkman@hotmail.com
Managing Editor *Hubert de Brouwer*
FOUNDED 1986. *Publishes* critical reflection on origins and legitimacy of established institutions; law and history. Unsolicited mss, synopses and ideas within the areas covered welcome.
Royalties paid.

Route
See **Yorkshire Art Circus Ltd**

SAKS Publications
PO Box 33504, London, E9 7YE
☎020 8985 9419 Fax 020 8985 9419
Email hotspotwriters@compuserve.com
Publisher *Kadija George*
FOUNDED 1996. *Publishes* anthologies and short story collections by writers of Black African descent. No unsolicited mss.

Scottish Cultural Press/ Scottish Children's Press
Unit 13d, Newbattle Abbey Business Annexe, Newbattle Road, Dalkeith EH22 3LJ
☎0131 660 6366 (Cultural Press)/4757 (Children's Press) Fax 0131 660 6414
Email info@scottishbooks.com
Website www.scottishbooks.com
Editor (Cultural Press) *Brian Pugh*
Editor (Children's Press) *Avril Gray*
FOUNDED 1992. Began publishing in 1993. *Publishes* Scottish interest titles, including cultural, literature, poetry, archaeology, local history, children's fiction and non-fiction. No unsolicited mss; prospective authors should telephone before sending material and a copy of submission guidelines for the relevant company will be sent to them.
Royalties paid.

Serif
47 Strahan Road, London E3 5DA
☎020 8981 3990 Fax 020 8981 3990
Managing Editor *Stephen Hayward*

FOUNDED 1993. *Publishes* cookery, Irish and African studies and modern history; no fiction. Ideas and synopses welcome; no unsolicited mss.
Royalties paid.

Sherlock Publications
6 Bramham Moor, Hill Head, Fareham, Hampshire PO14 3RU
☎01329 667325
Email sherlock.publications@btinternet.com
Managing Editor *Philip Weller*
FOUNDED to supply publishing support to a number of Sherlock Holmes societes. *Publishes* Sherlock Holmes and other Conan Doyle studies only. About 14 titles a year. No unsolicited mss; synopses and ideas welcome.
Royalties not paid.

Sickle Moon Books
3 Inglebert Street, London EC1R 1XR
☎020 7713 8277 Fax 020 7713 8277
Email info@sicklemoon.co.uk *or* barnaby@inglebert.demon.co.uk
Partners *Rose Baring, Barnaby Rogerson*
FOUNDED in 2000 by two travel writers to publish books on travel literature. 4 titles in 2000. No unsolicited mss; synopses and ideas for travel books welcome. Approach by mail.
Royalties paid annually.

Spacelink Books
115 Hollybush Lane, Hampton, Middlesex TW12 2QY
☎020 8979 3148
Website spacelink.50megs.com
Managing Director *Lionel Beer*
FOUNDED 1986. Named after a UFO magazine published in the 1960/70s. *Publishes* non-fiction titles connected with UFOs, Fortean phenomena and paranormal events. No unsolicited mss; send synopses and ideas. Publishers of *TEMS News* for the Travel and Earth Mysteries Society. Distributors of a wide range of related titles and magazines.
Royalties and fees paid according to contract.

Stenlake Publishing
Ochiltree Sawmill, The Lade, Ochiltree, Ayrshire KA18 2NX
☎01290 423114 Fax 01290 423114
Email david@stenlake.co.uk
Website www.stenlake.co.uk

Publishes local history, railways, shipping, aviation and industrial. 38 titles in 2000. Unsolicited mss, synopses and ideas welcome if accompanied by s.a.e. Freelance writers with experience in above fields also sought for specific commissions.

Royalties or fixed fee paid.

Stone Flower Limited
PO Box 1513, Ilford IG1 3QU
Managing Editor *L.G. Norman*

FOUNDED 1989. *Publishes* biography, law, humour and general fiction. Currently developing a new-style series of legal and general textbooks. Will consider mss, synopses and ideas only if sent with s.a.e. or IRC. Approach in writing in the first instance.

Stride
11 Sylvan Road, Exeter, Devon EX4 6EW
Email editor@stridebooks.co.uk
Website www.stridebooks.co.uk
Managing Editor *Rupert Loydell*

FOUNDED in 1982 as a magazine and booklet series. Since the mid-1980s, the press has published paperback editions of imaginative new writing. *Publishes* poetry, experimental fiction, criticism, reviews, interviews, arts (particularly experimental music). 12 titles in 2000. Unsolicited mss preferred to synopses. Ideas for future books welcome. Approach in writing only (with s.a.e.).

Royalties sometimes paid; free copies usually.

Studymates Ltd
PO Box 2, Bishops Lydgard, Somerset TA4 3YE
☎01823 432002 Fax 01823 430047
Email info@studymates.co.uk
Website www.studymates.co.uk
Managing Editor *Graham Lawlor, MA*

FOUNDED 1998 as part of International Briefings Ltd and taken over by education broadcaster Graham Lawlor in August 2000. *Publishes* self-help guides of 20,000–30,000 words, not necessarily for academic qualifications. 14 titles planned for 2001. Titles already commissioned include a guide for parents supporting their children to read. Authors wishing to submit proposals must follow the format set out in the author kit on the website. Material not in the correct format will be rejected.

Tamarind Ltd
PO Box 52, Northwood, Middlesex HA6 1UN
☎020 8866 8808 Fax 020 8866 5627
Email TamrindLTD@aol.com

Managing Editor *Verna Wilkins*

FOUNDED 1987 to publish picture books which give Black children a high, unselfconscious, positive profile. Won Gold Award for Best Product, Nursery & Creche Exhibition, 1994; featured BBC TV Words and Pictures: *Time to Get Up, Dave and the Tooth Fairy*; Book of the Month, Junior Education: *Profile of Benjamin Zephaniah* 1999. All titles sold into both trade and educational markets. Age range: 2–12.

Tarquin Publications
Stradbroke, Diss, Norfolk IP21 5JP
☎01379 384218 Fax 01379 384289
Email enquiries@tarquin-books.demon.co.uk
Website www.tarquin-books.demon.co.uk
Managing Editor *Gerald Jenkins*

FOUNDED 1970 as a hobby which gradually grew and now *publishes* mathematical, cut-out models, teaching and pop-up books. Other topics covered if they involve some kind of paper cutting or pop-up scenes. 9 titles in 2001. No unsolicited mss; letter with 1–2 page synopses welcome.

Royalties paid.

Tartarus Press
Coverley House, Carlton-in-Coverdale, Leyburn, North Yorkshire DL8 4AY
☎01969 640399 Fax 01969 640399
Email tartarus@pavilion.co.uk
Website freepages.pavilion.net/users/tartarus
Proprietor *Raymond Russell*
Editor *Rosalie Parker*

FOUNDED 1987. *Publishes* fiction, short stories, reprinted classic supernatural fiction and reference books. About 12 titles a year. 'Please do not send submissions. We cater to a small, collectable market; we solicit the fiction we publish.'

T.C.L. Publications
8 Hywel Way, Pembroke SA71 4EF
☎01646 685637
Managing Editor *Duncan Haws*

FOUNDED 1966 as Travel Creatours Limited (TCL). *Publishes* nautical books only – the *Merchant Fleet* series (40 vols.). 3 titles in 2000. Unsolicited mss welcome, 'provided they are in our standard format and subject matters'.

Royalties paid.

TESANA Multimedia
180 Newbridge Street, Newcastle upon Tyne NE1 2TE
☎0191 232 6189 Fax 0191 232 6190

Email pentaxion@pentaxion.force9.co.uk

Director *Rick Anderson*

Specialises in the development of multimedia CD-ROM and Web-based material tailored to requirements. 'We will discuss and advise on project proposals and ideas, evaluate option choices and, if required, handle project management. Ideas welcome. No unsolicited mss.

Trafford Publishing

Suite 6E, 2333 Government Street, Victoria, British Columbia, Canada V8T 4P4
☎001 250 383 6864 Fax 001 250 383 6804
Email editorial@trafford.com
Website www.trafford.com

Managing Editor *Bruce Batchelor*

FOUNDED 1995. A self-publishing venture offering 'on-demand publishing ... serving authors from 16 countries'. Books are usually published and publicised within 6 to 8 weeks. Package price is US$950. All genres welcome. Preferred approach by e-mail.

Royalties paid.

Tuckwell Press Ltd

The Mill House, Phantassie, East Linton, East Lothian EH40 3DG
☎01620 860164 Fax 01620 860164
Email tuckwellpress@sol.co.uk
Website www.tuckwellpress.co.uk

Managing Director *John Tuckwell*

FOUNDED 1995. *Publishes* history, archaeology, literature, ethnology, biography, architecture, gardening history, genealogy, palaeography, with a bias towards Scottish and academic texts, also north of England. 120 titles in print. No unsolicited mss but synopses and ideas welcome if relevant to subjects covered.

Royalties paid annually.

Tuesday Morning Publishing

PO Box 12608, London SE14 6ZR
☎020 8244 0000 Fax 020 8244 1000
Email tuesdaymorning@cwcom.net

Managing Editor *David Lee*

FOUNDED 1998. *Publishes* fiction, aimed mostly at a youth orientated readership. Books with film potential most welcome. 8–12 titles in 2001. Prefers introductory phone call or e-mail before submission of material. 'Authors should be tenacious self-publicists who do not think that making a book successful stops when they write "The End".'

Payment on negotiable profit-share basis.

Veritam

Pilgrims, Redway, Porlock, Minehead, Somerset TA24 8QF
☎01643 862637
Email neil.trickett@virgin.net

Managing Editor *Neil Trickett*

FOUNDED 1998. *Publishes* fiction with a strong philosophical/literary thrust. Also non-fiction with 'uncompromising efforts to find reality'. No unsolicited mss; synopses and ideas considered. Approach in writing in the first instance.

Royalties paid 'where appropriate'.

Wakefield Historical Publications

19 Pinder's Grove, Wakefield, West Yorkshire WF1 4AH
☎01924 372748
Email kate@airtime.co.uk

Managing Editor *Kate Taylor*

FOUNDED 1977 by the Wakefield Historical Society to publish well-researched, scholarly works of regional (namely West Riding) historical significance. 1–2 titles a year. Unsolicited mss, synopses and ideas for books welcome.

Royalties not paid.

Whittles Publishing

Roseleigh House, Latheronwheel, Caithness KW5 6DW
☎01593 741240 Fax 01593 741360
Email whittl@globalnet.co.uk
Website www.users.globalnet.co.uk/~whittl

Managing Editor *Dr Keith Whittles*

FOUNDED 1986 to offer freelance commissioning and consulting. Started publishing a few years ago in the field of civil engineering and surveying. Also general books with a marine/Scottish theme. 6 titles in 2000. Unsolicited mss, synopses and ideas welcome on appropriate themes.

Royalties paid annually.

Witan Books & Publishing Services

Cherry Tree House, 8 Nelson Crescent, Cotes Heath, via Stafford ST21 6ST
☎01782 791673

Managing Editor *Jeff Kent*

FOUNDED in 1980 for self-publishing and commenced publishing other writers in 1991. *Publishes* general books, including biography, education, environment, geography, history, politics, popular music and sport. 2 titles in 2001. Witan Publishing Services, which began as an offshoot to help writers get their work into print, offers guidance, editing, proofreading, etc.

Unsolicited mss, synopses and ideas welcome (include s.a.e.).

Royalties paid.

Woodstock Books

Ilkley Road, Otley, West Yorkshire LS21 3JP
☎01943 467958 Fax 01943 850057
Email woodstock@smith-settle.co.uk
Editorial office: The School House, South Newington, Banbury, Oxfordshire OX15 4JJ
Managing Director *Ken Smith*
Editorial Director *James Price*

FOUNDED1989. *Publishes* literary reprints only. Main series: *Revolution and Romanticism, 1789–1834; Hibernia: Literature and Nation in Victorian Ireland; Decadents, Symbolists, Anti-Decadents: Poetry of the 1890s.*

The Worple Press

12 Havelock Road, Tonbridge, Kent TN9 1JE
☎01732 367466 Fax 01732 352057
Email theworpleco.@aol.com
Managing Editors *Peter Carpenter, Amanda Knight*

FOUNDED 1997. Independent publisher specialising in poetry, art and alternative titles. 4 titles in 2000. No unsolicited mss. Write or phone for catalogue and flyers.

Royalties paid.

Writers' Bookshop

Remus House, Coltsfoot Drive, Woodston, Peterborough PE2 9JX
☎01733 898103 Fax 01733 313524
Email andrew@forwardpress.com
Website www.forwardpress.com
Managing Editor *Kerrie Pateman*

Writers' Bookshop is an imprint of Forward Press (see under **Poetry Presses**). *Publishes* writers' aids in the form of directories and how-to guides. Best-known annual title is the *Small Press Guide*. For further information and an author brief, call *Andrew Head*.

Payment Advance plus 15% royalties.

Xavier Music Ltd

PO Box 17, Abergavenny NP8 1XA
☎01874 730897 Fax 01874 730897
Email xavier@so-strong.com
Website www.so-strong.com
Managing Editor *Peter Lloyd*

Opened the books division in 1993 to publish poetry, prose and theatre works by Labi Siffre. *Publishes* poetry and one-act plays. No unsolicited material.

Royalties not paid.

Yorkshire Art Circus Ltd

School Lane, Glasshoughton, Castleford, West Yorkshire WF10 4QH
☎01977 603028 Fax 01977 603028
Email nicole@route-online.com
Website www.route-online.com
Books Coordinator *Ian Daley*

FOUNDED 1986. *Publishes* contemporary fiction (novels and short stories) and local interest (Yorkshire and Humberside) under their **Route** imprint. No local history, children's, autobiography, poetry, reference or nostalgia. Unsolicited mss discouraged; authors should send for fact sheet first. Write or ring for free catalogue.

Royalties paid.

Electronic Publishing and Other Services

ABCtales
PO Box 34203, London NW5 1FX
☎020 7209 2607 Fax 020 7209 2594
Email mail@abctales.com
Website www.abctales.com

Owner *Burgeon Creative Ideas Ltd*
Editor *Diana Bird*

FOUNDED by A. John Bird, MBE, co-founder of the *Big Issue* magazine, Tony Cook and Gordon Roddick. ABCtales is a free website and monthly print magazine dedicated to publishing and developing new writing. Content is predominantly short stories and poetry but includes interviews and lifestyle features, photo essays, reviews (games, websites, film, music), competitions and a children's section – youngABCtales. Anyone can upload creative writing to the website; the best work is selected for paid publication in the print magazine.

AtRandom
See **The Random House Group Ltd** under **UK Publishers**

Authors OnLine
See entry under **UK Publishers**

Book Affairs Ltd
74 Lee Road, Perivale, Middlesex UB6 7DB
Email enquiries@BookAffairs.com
Website www.BookAffairs.com

Directors *Rohail Ahmad, Samar Ahmad*

FOUNDED 1999. Website for new authors; fiction only. Material is vetted initially for literary quality then complete manuscripts are made available on the website. Readers can download and read the books and submit reviews, in particular their opinion as to whether the book should be published or not. Reader-approved books are then submitted to publishers for consideration. See website for details.

Book4Publishing
46 Listley Street, Bridgnorth, Shropshire WV16 4AW
☎01746 761298
Email enquiries@book4publishing.com
Website www.book4publishing.com

Managing Director *Mark Horton-Oliver*

FOUNDED 2000. *Specialises* in helping new and unpublished authors gain recognition for their work by displaying synopses and up to 5000 words on the Book4Publishing website. Publishers and agents are contacted, giving a brief description of the work, and invited to view the mss on screen. Authors are charged a one-off fee for registering and promoting their work. Mss, synopses and ideas welcome; Initial enquiries by e-mail or post. Planning to move into e-publishing in 2002.

Chameleon HH Publishing
The Quarry House, East End, Witney, Oxfordshire OX8 6QA
☎01993 880223 Fax 01993 880236
Email marion@chameleonhh.co.uk &
david@chameleonhh.co.uk
Website www.chameleonhh.co.uk

Directors *David Hall, Marion Hazzledine*

FOUNDED 1997. CD-ROM and Web publishers on behalf of commercial publishers, institutes, associations and government bodies. Also, **E- and I-Commerce** – welcomes unsolicited mss for electronic publishing from self-publishers. Consulting and advice on CD-ROM and Web publishing.

Claritybooks.com
Colt Farm, Bromley Green Road, Ashford, Kent TN26 2EQ
Email editor@claritybooks.com
Website www.claritybooks.com

Publishes in a copyright protected, encrypted electronic format designed to be readable on multiple devices. Will consider all fiction and non-fiction categories from literary to genre, whether full length, novella or short stories. Special interest in professional/business 'how-to' books, good health/beauty/relationship guides, computing instruction. Children's books (including illustrated), especially structured readers, fiction for all ages. Educational study guides, tie-ins with current exam syllabi. Humour, particularly observational/commentary on modern sexual politics, working life and times. Travel guides, both UK and abroad; travel photography, restaurant and hotel guides. Unsolicited submissions welcome. Send synopsis stating the target market and first three chapters – in paper form only, double-spaced. S.a.e. required for return of material. E-mail submissions/attachments will not be read. Enquiries by e-mail.

Context Limited

Grand Union House, 20 Kentish Town Road, London NW1 9NR
☎020 7267 8989 Fax 020 7267 1133
Email postmaster@context.co.uk
Website www.context.co.uk

FOUNDED 1986. Electronic publisher of UK and European legal and offical information on CD-ROM, online and the Internet. TITLE *JUSTIS Cartoons* CD-ROM, developed jointly with the **Centre for the Study of Cartoons and Caricature** at the University of Kent (see entry under **Library Services**), contains over 18,000 political cartoons published in British newspapers from 1912 to 1990. No unsolicited mailshots; enquiries only.

ePublish Scotland

236 Magdala Terrace, Galashiels, Selkirkshire TD1 2HT
☎01896 752109
Email info@epublish-scotland.com
Website www.epublish-scotland.com

Managing Director *John Brewer*

FOUNDED 1999. *Publishes* in electronic format with an emphasis on educational material. 'We wish to expand our range of products and encourage other authors to consider distributing their work through us.' Welcomes synopses and ideas; approach by e-mail in the first instance.

Fledgling Press Limited

7 Lennox Street, Edinburgh EH4 1QB
☎0131 332 6867
Email info@fledglingpress.co.uk
Website www.fledglingpress.co.uk

Director *Zander Wedderburn*

FOUNDED 2000. Internet publisher, aiming to be 'a launching pad for new authors taking flight. Special interest in authentic writing about the human condition, including autobiography, diaries, poetry and fictionalised variations on these.' Also academic and management writing, especially in the areas of shiftwork and working time. Send mss and other details by e-mail from the website or by post. Currently no fee for mounting selected work. Links into short-run book production.
Royalties 50%, paid quarterly.

HarperCollins E Publishing

See **HarperCollins Publishers Ltd** under **UK Publishers**

Macmillan Online Publishing

See **Macmillan Publishers Ltd** under **UK Publishers**

New Authors Showcase

Rivendell, Kingsgate, Torquay, Devon TQ2 8QA
☎01803 326617
Email james@newauthors.org.uk
Website www.newauthors.org.uk

Contact *Barrie E. James*

FOUNDED 1997. A Internet site for new writers and poets to display their work to publishers. No unsolicited mss. First approach should be by sending s.a.e.

NewNovelPublishing.com

Henleaze Business Centre, Henleaze House, Hartbury Road, Henleaze, Bristol BS9 4PN
Website www.newnovelpublishing.com

Internet publishing service for new authors of fiction. No submissions by e-mail. Send synopsis and first fifteen pages together with reading fee of £15 and s.a.e. See website for submission details.

NoSpine.com

25c Fonthill Road, London N4 3HY
☎020 7281 8326 Fax 0870 052 6882
Email info@nospine.com
Website www.nospine.com

Managing Director *Andrew Gardner*

An electronic self-publishing venture 'designed by authors for authors'. NoSpine accepts electronic mss and arranges sales and distribution in return for a commission on each sale. Authors retain complete control over their work, full copyright, and set their own sale prices of which they retain 80%. 'We are not a vanity publisher, nor a subsidy publisher. No author ever pays us a penny: in effect we are a writers' cooperative.' All new submissions are refereed by the founding authors to screen out unacceptable or illegal material.

Online Originals

Priory Cottage, Wordsworth Place, London NW5 4HG
☎020 7267 4244
Email editor@onlineoriginals.com
Website www.onlineoriginals.com

Managing Editor *David Gettman*

Commissioning Editor *Dr Christopher Macann*

Publishes book-length works on the Internet only. Acquires global electronic rights (including print-on-demand and digital reading) in literary fiction, intellectual non-fiction, drama, fiction for young readers (ages 8–16). No poetry, fantasy, how-to, self-help, picture books, cookery, hobbies, crafts or local interest. 40 titles in 2000. TITLES *The Seed of Joy* William Amos; *Eden Park* Craig Filleyh; *Quintet* Frederick Forsyth. Unsolicited mss, synopses and ideas for books welcome. *All* communications are by e-mail and authors must have Internet access. Submissions or enquiries on paper or diskette will be discarded. Guidelines available from the e-mail address above.

Royalties paid annually (50% royalties on standard price of £6 or $9).

Reardon and Rawes

56 Upper Norwood Street, Leckhampton, Cheltenham, Gloucestershire GL53 0DU
☎01242 231800
Website www.reardon.co.uk

Editor *Nicholas Reardon*

FOUNDED 1996. *Publishes* re-issues of out-of-print titles in electronic/multimedia format. Non-fiction historical titles only. TITLES *Picture of Bristol – A Guide* Rev. John Evans; *Proverbs and Family Mottoes* J.A. Mair; *Wessex to Essex* Rosemary Barham. Unsolicited mss welcome.

Royalties not paid

Self Publishing

See entry under **Useful Websites at a Glance**.

Steel Caves

56 Canon Road, Bromley, Kent BR1 2SP
Email bob@21bg.co.uk
Website www.steelcaves.com

Publications Director *Bob Campbell*

FOUNDED 1998. Bi-weekly online magazine. Also offers editorial and research services. *Specialises* in science fiction, fantasy and horror. Unsolicited mss welcome, 'preferably a small selection of your writing'. See website for submission guidelines.

Storyteller-UK
Website www.storyteller.org.uk

Storyteller-UK consists of two monthly online magazines: *The Friendly Spirit* contains short stories, poetry and children's stories of a 'warm, sympathetic and at times nostalgic' nature; *The Wanton Spirit*, in contrast, is 'risqué, erotic and realistic'. Submissions on any subject, especially from female writers, are welcome. Wordage for both magazines is from 3500 to 5000 total. See guidelines for authors for further information. Submissions by e-mail only.

Storywise

Email submissions@storywise.co.uk
Website www.storywise.co.uk

Non-profit-making fiction website for writers 'who have not managed, or don't wish to have their work published in the traditional format'. Submission information available via e-mail.

the-phone-book.com

Enterprise House, Whitworth Street West, Manchester M1 5WG
☎0161 237 3355 Fax 0161 237 3727
Email editor@the-phone-book.com
Website www.the-phone-book.com

FOUNDED 2001. *Publishes* ultra-short fiction of less than 150 words online to website and wap site.

Triple Hitter

See entry under **Useful Websites at a Glance**.

WritersServices

See entry under **Useful Websites at a Glance**.

www.sparemanjoe.co.uk

65 Sycamore Avenue, Newport, Gwent NP19 9AJ
Email a.p.pumford@ntlworld.com
Website www.sparemanjoe.co.uk
Proprietor *Joe Pumford*

Established to promote the works of writers living within the NP19 cachment area in south Wales. The service is free for a period of one month, the site being updated monthly but anyone wishing to keep their work online beyond a month will be charged £1 per week for a minimum of 24 weeks. For writers outside the NP19 area a fee of £30 plus £1 per week rental, minimum 50 weeks, is payable in advance. Maximum free space available: up to 2000 words; rented space: 100,000 words. Initial contact by post; no e-mails. 'We aim to encourage new writers and writers' groups. We will publish your group's collections in electronic book form for a negotiable fee.'

Critical Clauses

Publishing contracts are getting longer and more complex.
Gareth Shannon offers a quick guide to getting the best deal.

Few things can be more exciting and more nerve-racking for an author than to receive that first contract from a publisher. At first glance, it is the headline-grabbing advance – or sometimes the lack of it – that seems most important, but canny authors and agents have realised that it pays to read the small print.

For example, what proportion of the advance will be due on signature? Ideally one third (or more if you can present a good case) with the remaining two-thirds due on delivery and publication respectively. If you have a contract for several books, will all of the advance money be added together and sit against future royalties from all books, or will each book be separately accounted for against its portion of the advance?

Much is written about royalties and what you can expect. In addition to *The Writer's Handbook* both the Society of Authors and the Writers' Guild have a helpful advisory service for members which can be used to gauge the fairness of an offer. Royalties – like the advance – are usually the first items to be agreed, even before there is sight of a contract, so find out as much as you can before saying 'yes'. The rest of the contract follows the agent-publisher boilerplate, if there is one, with exceptional items held open for negotiation. This second stage of the negotiation tends to deal mostly with subsidiary rights.

If you are represented by an agent, the details are not usually contentious since the agent will make sure that they are weighted in the author's favour. If there is no agent involved, it is likely that you can improve a contract significantly with some research and a little negotiation. No serious publisher is going to withdraw an offer to publish if you do not say 'yes' by return. Indeed, everyone expects that there will have to be some movement between an opening offer and the terms of a final signed contract. What is needed is an understanding of what it is reasonable to ask for and what makes a changed offer worth accepting.

Before looking at some of the major subsidiary rights deals it is worth stating an obvious truism that 'no two books are perceived equally'. One book hits its target market without any great effort on the part of publisher or author while another is declared out of print and appears now and then in one of those 'What I wish I had published' columns in the trade press, but which no one seems eager to reissue despite singing its praises. Yet another title appeals to the US market and the right to publish it there is sold for a small fortune, but many others, despite everyone's best efforts, slip further down the list of available titles at each passing book fair. What follows is a few guiding principles to deals which may, in the right circumstances, be relevant to your book.

Serial rights

For the right book, serialisation in a national newspaper can be one of the most lucrative rights to be exercised. Serialisation of extracts prior to the book's publication (first serial rights) is more lucrative than serialisation after publication (second serial rights). Obviously the book must strike some chord with the newspaper – either from a similarity in philosophy, or because its subject would be of more than passing interest to its readers. Most agents jealously guard these rights but when they are controlled by the publisher the following splits in revenue are typical: first serial rights may be divided as high as 90:10 in the author's favour, while second serial rights are usually 75:25. The days of the political memoir and its accompanying big money newspaper serial deal may have passed but there is still a sale to targeted markets both in the UK and overseas. Fees can range from a few hundred pounds to a hundred thousand plus. Anything that throws new light on people or events in the news will command higher fees.

US rights

This has always been seen as the most important market for many books, yet there is still no easy route to achieving success in the US. In an ideal world, the US publisher will pay an advance and royalty to the UK publisher which is then shared with the author. A successful author – if not represented by an agent – might receive 85 per cent of this income, while a less well-known writer might receive around 60 per cent. Often, though, this is not the whole story. One publishing firm might have a successful track record of selling rights in the US and offer no more than 75 per cent of these proceeds to its authors. On the other hand, a newly formed company with no obvious connections might happily offer 85 per cent though with no realistic chance that these rights will be sold. If pressed to grant these rights to a publisher, there is nothing to be lost by asking about its experience in the US market. But don't forget that 60 or 75 per cent of something is better than holding on to the rights and then not exploiting them.

There are other deals where printed copies are sold to a US publisher at a fixed price. Under this type of arrangement, a book priced at £18 in the UK might be sold for around £5 with consequently little return for the publisher or the author. These situations are very similar to the co-edition market for illustrated books. Why do it then? It is not the first choice but it is a way to present books to the US market and to try to build up recognition of both publisher and author. The author can expect 7½ to 10 per cent of the publisher's income from this type of deal, the sums varying according to whether bound or unbound copies are sold.

Translation rights

A large market in Spanish- and German-speaking countries for rights to works in English is frequently overlooked by authors. Deals tend to be on an advance and royalty basis, though small companies in emerging markets might try for a flat fee. An author can expect 75 to 80 per cent of any proceeds. Some agents and publishers use local agents for translation deals which means more commission deducted from any sums due to the author. Working alone, translation can be a leap of faith for an author who has no knowledge of overseas publishers, but a little research on the company's website, or a query to a local online writers' discussion group can pay dividends.

Electronic verbatim text rights

The current theory is that this will one day be a lucrative source of income but events so far have not borne this out. Most publishers now expect to be granted some form of electronic text rights when they acquire a book and it pays to find out how near they are to exploiting these rights. There is little point in either an author or publisher controlling rights which they are not capable of fully exploiting.

Only a few years ago, it looked as though content providers (authors and publishers) would be able to license their works to websites and make a small fortune from such sales. Today, this idea seems to have vanished as most Internet sites do not require any payment and the received wisdom is that this so-called 'free distribution' model is here to stay. Not everyone agrees though, and sites such as that of the *Wall Street Journal* are still charging users to access areas of the site. If anything the recent downturn in fortunes of this new economy might persuade site owners that a combination of free and paid access is the only way to survive. Then there are the large portal sites such as Yahoo! or BTInternet which can only survive by offering users content on a wide variety of subjects. Many of these portal sites will not pay for using others' content, while others expect the publisher to pay to make the material available. The argument is that it is a form of marketing for the publisher and there should be money available in a marketing budget for this showcasing. In these cases, there is precious little return for authors unless it is from increased book sales, although there should be the chance of commissions from content teams attached to a site. These content teams are the editorial hub of a website and are responsible for writing and commissioning the content that appears on it. Many of these teams have newspaper or magazine backgrounds so will be used to newspaper or magazine fee scales and writers should price their work accordingly. This market may be static at present but as sites are redesigned and new ones form it is likely that it will take off again. Those writers who have bothered to keep up to date with such developments will be in a good position to be first in with their work.

*Gareth Shannon is a director of **Roger Palmer Limited Media Contracts**. Previously he was Rights Manager at IPC Media Ltd, the magazine publisher, which he joined after five years as Assistant General Secretary at the Society of Authors.*

For further research investigate the websites of some of the US talent unions, e.g. www. nwu.org or www.asja.org. The Society of Authors' quarterly journal The Author *often analyses current issues in authors' contracts, supplementing the material contained in its* Quick Guide *series of booklets. Though written from the point of view of a publisher's rights department, Lynette Owen's book* Selling Rights *(second ed., Blueprint, 1994) contains a wealth of background information that helps to put offered terms into economic perspective.*

Useful Websites at a Glance

Academi (Welsh Academy/Yr Academi Gymreig)
www.academi.org
News of events, publications and funding for Welsh-based literary events. (See entry under **Professional Associations and Societies**.)

Alliance of Literary Societies
www.sndc.demon.co.uk/als.htm
Details of societies and events. (See entry under **Professional Associations and Societies**.)

Amazon Bookshop
www.amazon.co.uk
Access to more than 1.5 million UK published titles. A wide range of online shopping, including books, music and videos.

Ancestry
www.ancestry.com/
Family history information – databases, articles and other sources of genealogical data.

The Arts Council of England
www.artscouncil.org.uk
Includes information on applying for funding, publications and the National Lottery. (See entry under **Arts Councils and Regional Arts Boards**.)

Arvon Foundation
www.arvonfoundation.org
Information on the three Arvon centres in the UK. (See entry under **Writers' Courses, Circles and Workshops**.)

Association for Scottish Literary Studies
www.asls.org.uk
The educational charity promoting the languages and literature of Scotland. (See entry under **Professional Associations and Societies**.)

Association of Authors' Agents (AAA)
www.agentssoc.co.uk
UK agents' organisation including list of current members. (See entry under **Professional Associations and Societies**.)

Association of Authors' Representatives (AAR)
www.aar-online.org
US agents' organisation including list of current members. (See entry under **Professional Associations and Societies**.)

Authors' Licensing and Copyright Society (ALCS)
www.alcs.co.uk
Details of membership, news, publications, legal issues and rights, plus links to related sites. (See entry under **Professional Associations and Societies**.)

Author–Publisher Network
www.author.co.uk
Services for writers, information network, newsletter and online magazine. (See entry under **Professional Associations and Societies**.)

BBC
www.bbc.co.uk
Access to all BBC departments and services.

bibliofind
www.bibliofind.com
Over 20 million second-hand and rare books, periodicals and ephemera for sale online.

BOL
www.bol.com
Internet shopping, including books and music; a database of over 1.5 million titles.

Book Trust
www.booktrust.org.uk
Book information service, guide to prizes and awards, links to other book organisations, factsheets for writers. (See entry under **Professional Associations and Societies**.)

British Association of Picture Libraries and Agencies (BAPLA)
www.bapla.org.uk
Free telephone referrals available from the BAPLA database through this website. (See entry under **Professional Associations and Societies**.)

British Centre for Literary Translation
www.literarytranslation.com
A joint Web site with the British Council containing workshops by leading translators, contacts and networks, and listings of translation conferences, seminars and events. (See

entry under **Professional Associations and Societies**.)

British Council
www.britishcouncil.org
Information on the Council's English Language services, education programmes, science and health links, and information exchange. (See entry under **Professional Associations and Societies**.)

British Film Institute (bfi)
www.bfi.org.uk
Information on the services offered by the Institute. (See entry under **Professional Associations and Societies**.)

British Library
www.bl.uk
Reader service enquiries, access to main catalogues, information on collections, links to the various Reading Rooms and exhibitions. (See related entries under **Libraries**.)

Children's Writing Resource Center
www.write4kids.com
US website for children's writers, whether published or beginners. Includes special reports, advice, chat links, news on the latest bestsellers and links to related sites.

Complete Works of William Shakespeare
the-tech.mit.edu/Shakespeare/works.html
Access to the text of the complete works with search facility, quotations and discussion pages.

Copyright Advice and Anti-Piracy Hotline
www.copyright-info.org
Copyright advice and information. (See entry under **Professional Associations and Societies**.)

Copyright Licensing Agency Ltd (CLA)
www.cla.co.uk
Copyright information, customer support and information on CLA services. (See entry under **Professional Associations and Societies**.)

Crime Writers' Association (CWA)
www.thecwa.co.uk
Website of the professional crime writers' association. (See entry under **Professional Associations and Societies**.)

The Eclectic Writer
www.eclectics.com/writing/writing.html
US website offering a selection of articles on advice for writers on topics such as 'Proper Manuscript Format', 'Electronic Publishing', 'How to Write a Synopsis' and 'Motivation'. Also a Character Chart for fiction writers and an online discussion board.

Electronic Telegraph
www.telegraph.co.uk
The Daily Telegraph online – one of the first UK national newspapers to establish itself on the web.

Encyclopaedia Britannica
www.eb.com
A subscription gives access to the entire *Encyclopaedia Britannica* database as well as Merriam-Webster's *Collegiate Dictionary* and the *Britannica Book of the Year*. (A 30-day free trial is available.) EB online also gives links to more than 130,000 sites selected, rated and reviewed by Britannica editors.

The English Association
www.le.ac.uk/engassoc
News, publications, conference and membership information. (See entry under **Professional Associations and Societies**.)

Federation of Worker Writers and Community Publishers (FWWCP)
www.fwwcp.mcmail.com
Links to members of the FWWCP, the Federation magazine, information on membership. (See entry under **Professional Associations and Societies**.)

Film Angel
www.filmangel.co.uk
Established in 2000 by **Hammerwood Films** to create a shop window for writers and would-be film angels alike. Writers submit a short synopsis which can be displayed for a pre-determined period, for a fee, while would-be angels are invited to finance a production of their choice.

Financial Times
www.ft.com
Financial Times online.

Guide to Grammar and Style
www.andromeda.rutgers.edu/~jlynch/Writing/
A guide to grammar and style which is organised alphabetically, plus articles and links to other grammatical reference sites.

Great Books Online
www.bartleby.com
An ever-expanding list of great books published online for reference, free of charge.

The Guardian
www.guardian.co.uk
Website of *The Guardian* and *The Observer* newspapers online.

Hansard
www.parliament.the-stationery-office.co.uk/pa/cm/cmhansrd.htm
The official record of debates and written answers in the House of Commons. The transcript of each day's business appears at noon on the following weekday.

House of Commons Research Library
www.parliament.uk/commons/lib/research/rpintro.htm
Gives access to the text of research reports prepared for MPs on a wide range of current issues.

HTML Writers Guild
www.hwg.org
US organisation offering resources, support, representation and education for web authors. (See entry under **Professional Associations and Societies**.)

The Independent
www.independent.co.uk
The *Independent* newspaper online.

Ingenta
www.ingenta.com
Established in 1998, Ingenta is the largest online academic research service in the UK. Formed through a public/private partnership with the University of Bath, the site offers 'free searching of millions of academic and professional articles from thousands of journals online'.

Institute of Linguists
www.iol.org.uk
Discussion forum, news on regional societies, job opportunities, 'Find a Linguist' service, and *The Linguist* magazine. (See entry under **Professional Associations and Societies**.)

Institute of Translation and Interpreting (ITI)
www.iti.org.uk
Web site of the professional association of translators and interpreters, with the ITI Directory, publications, training and membership information. (See entry under **Professional Associations and Societies**.)

Internet Bookshop
www.bookshop.co.uk
Online bookshop with 1.4 million UK and US titles.

Internet Classics Archive
classics.mit.edu
Includes 441 works of classical literature by 59 different authors. Mostly Greek and Roman works with some Chinese and Persian. All are in English translation

Journalism UK
www.journalismuk.co.uk
A website for UK-based journalists who write for text-based publications. Includes links to newspapers, magazines, e-zines, news sources plus information on jobs, training and organisations.

JustBooks
www.jstbooks.co.uk
Second-hand and antiquarian online bookshop with 1.3 million titles offered by nearly 300 booksellers.

The Library Association
www.la-hq.org.uk
The professional body for librarians and information managers. (See entry under **Professional Associations and Societies**.)

The Mirror
www.mirror.co.uk
The Mirror newspaper online.

Mr William Shakespeare and the Internet
daphne.palomar.edu/Shakespeare
Guide to scholarly Shakespeare resources on the Internet.

National Union of Journalists (NUJ)
www.gn.apc.org/media
Represents those journalists who work in all sectors of publishing, print and broadcasting. (See entry under **Professional Associations and Societies**.)

Novel Advice Newsletter
www.noveladvice.com
A free US journal aimed at the fiction writer; full text of current and past issues online.

PEN
www.pen.org.uk
Web site of the English Centre of International PEN. News of events, membership details. (See entry under **Professional Associations and Societies**.)

Poets and Writers Online
www.pw.org
A US site containing publishing advice, a directory of writers, online bookstore, literary links, news, articles on aspects of writing, grants and awards.

Producers Alliance for Cinema and Television (PACT)
www.pact.co.uk
Publications, jobs in the industry, production companies, membership details. (See entry under **Professional Associations and Societies**.)

The Publisher
www.thepublisher.co.uk
New website for publishers, launched at the London Book Fair in March 2001. Contains directories, e-services, information resources and news.

Publishers Association
www.publishers.org.uk
Information about the Association and careers in publishing, also 'Getting Published' pages. (See entry under **Professional Associations and Societies**.)

Pure Fiction
www.purefiction.com
Described as 'the website for anybody who loves to read – or aspires to write – bestselling fiction'. Contains book reviews, writing advice, a writers showcase and an online bookshop.

Royal Society of Literature
www.rslit.org
Information on lectures, discussions and readings; membership details and prizes. (See entry under **Professional Associations and Societies**.)

Science Fiction Foundation Collection
www.liv.ac.uk/~sawyer/sffchome.html
The research library of the Science Fiction Foundation, based at the University of Liverpool. Includes links to the Foundation, the John Wyndham archive, the Foundation's journal and other SF collections and associations. (See entry under **Library Services**.)

Scottish Arts Council
www.sac.org.uk
Information on funding and events; 'Image of the Month' and 'Poem of the Month'. (See entry under **Arts Councils and Regional Arts Boards**.)

Scottish Book Trust
www.scottishbooktrust.com
Information on the Trust's activities and a link to its Book Information Service. (See entry under **Professional Associations and Societies**.)

Scottish Library Association
www.slainte.org.uk
Links to various services and major Scottish websites and information on people, organisations, libraries, events and resources of Scottish interest. (See entry under **Professional Associations and Societies**.)

Scottish Publishers Association
www.scottishbooks.org
Links to members' websites; information on activities and publications. (See entry under **Professional Associations and Societies**.)

Screenwriters and Playwrights Home Page
www.teleport.com/~cdeemer/scrwriter.html
A website maintained by US screenwriter Charles Deemer. Links to a discussion forum and 'Screenwright', an electronic screenwriting course.

Screenwriters Online
screenwriter.com/insider/news.html
Described as the 'only professional screenwriter's site run by major screenwriters who get their scripts and screenplays made into movies'. Contains screenplay analysis, expert articles and *The Insider Report*.

Self Publishing
www.SelfPublishing.co.uk
Set up to allow writers to advertise their books on the Internet. Mostly of appeal to self-published authors but open to everyone by publishing a 'taster' of one chapter of a novel or equivalent for other books.

Society of Authors
www.writers.org.uk/society
Includes FAQs for new writers, diary of events, membership details, links to publishers' and other societies' Web sites. (See entry under **Professional Associations and Societies**.)

Society of Freelance Editors and Proofreaders (SFEP)
www.sfep.org.uk
Basic information about the Society. (See under **Professional Associations and Societies**.)

Society of Indexers
www.socind.demon.co.uk
Indexing information for publishers and authors, 'Electronic Indexers Available' pages. Membership information. (See entry under **Professional Associations and Societies**.)

South Bank Centre, London
www.sbc.org.uk
Links to the Royal Festival Hall, the Hayward Gallery and Poetry Library; news of literature events.

The *Sun*
www.the-sun.co.uk
Website of the *Sun* newspaper.

The Times
www.the-times.co.uk
Website of *The Times* newspaper.

trAce Online Writing Community
www.trace.ntu.ac.uk
Based at Nottingham Trent University, trAce is an online centre for writers and readers worldwide to share and critique their work, discuss favourite books and talk. Also holds occasional (live) conferences and workshops. Links to a wide range of useful sites for writers.

Triple Hitter
www.tripplehitter.net
Website dedicated to 'aiding aspiring writers in obtaining their big break' by showcasing their work free of charge. Includes various interviews, links and helpful hints.

The Arts Council of Wales
www.ccc-acw.org.uk
Information on publications, council meetings, the arts in Wales. Links to other arts websites. (See entry under **Arts Councils and Regional Arts Boards**.)

The Web Writer
www.geocities.com/Athens/Parthenon/ 8390/TOC.htm
A site for writers who want to write for publication on the web. A wide range of information and advice includes getting online, choosing a computer, saving money on your PC, dealing with Windows, software information, researching online, how to build a website, being a writer, website issues.

Welsh Academy – see **Academi**

Welsh Books Council (Cyngor Llyfrau Cymru)
www.cllc.org.uk *and* www.gwales.com
Information about books from Wales, editorial and design services, 'Wales Book Day'. (See entry under **Professional Associations and Societies**.)

Writers Guild of Great Britain
www.writers.org.uk/guild
A wide range of information including rates of pay, articles on topics such as copyright, news, writers' resources and industry regulations. (See entry under **Professional Associations and Societies**.)

Writers, Artists and their Copyright Holders (WATCH)
www.watch-file.com
Database of copyright holders in the UK and North America. (See entry under **Professional Associations and Societies**.)

Writernet
www.writernet.org.uk
Formerly the New Playwrights Trust. Information, advice and guidance for writers on all aspects of the live and recorded performance.

WritersNet
www.writers.net
A directory of writers, editors, publishers and literary agents.

Writersservices
www.writersservices.com
Established in March 2000 by Chris Holifield, deputy managing director and publisher at Cassell. Offers factsheets, book reviews, advice, links and other resources for writers including editorial services, contract vetting and self-publishing. (Enquiries: info@writersservices.com)

WWWebster Dictionary/WWWebster Thesaurus
www.m-w.com/home.htm
Merriam-Webster Online. Includes a search facility for words in the *Webster Dictionary* or *Webster Thesaurus*; word games, 'Word of the Day' and Language Info Zone.

UK Packagers

Aladdin Books Ltd
28 Percy Street, London W1P 0LD
☎020 7323 3319 Fax 020 7323 4829
Email aladdin2@dircon.co.uk
Managing Director *Charles Nicholas*
Approx. Annual Turnover £3.5 million

FOUNDED in 1979 as a packaging company but with joint publishing ventures in the UK and USA. *Commissions* children's fully illustrated, non-fiction reference books. 40 titles in 1999. IMPRINTS **Aladdin Books** *Bibby Whittaker* Children's reference; **Nicholas Enterprises** *Charles Nicholas* Adult non-fiction; **The Learning Factory** *Charles Nicholas* Early learning concepts 0–4 years. TITLES *Encyclopedia of Awesome Dinosaurs; The Atlas of Animals.* Will consider synopses and ideas for children's non-fiction with international sales potential only. No fiction.

Fees usually paid instead of royalties.

The Albion Press Ltd
Spring Hill, Idbury, Oxfordshire OX7 6RU
☎01993 831094 Fax 01993 831982
Chairman/Managing Director *Emma Bradford*

FOUNDED 1984. *Commissions* illustrated trade titles, particularly children's. About 4 titles a year. TITLES *From a Distance* Jane Ray and Julie Gold; *The Little Mermaid and other Fairy Stories* Isabelle Brent. Unsolicited synopses and ideas for books not welcome.

Royalties paid; fees paid for introductions and partial contributions.

Alphabet & Image Ltd
See **Marston House** under **UK Publishers**

Amber Books Ltd
Bradleys Close, 74–77 White Lion Street, London N1 9PF
☎020 7520 7600 Fax 020 7520 7606/7
Email name@amberbooks.co.uk
Managing Director *Stasz Gnych*
Editorial Head *Sally Harper*

FOUNDED 1989. *Commissions* military, aviation, transport, sport, combat, survival and fitness, naval history, crime and general reference. 40–50 titles in 2000. No fiction, cookery, gardening or lifestyle. IMPRINT **Brown Books**. No unsolicited material.

Fees paid.

Archival Facsimiles Limited
The Old Bakery, 52 Crown Street, Banham, Norwich, Norfolk NR16 2HW
☎01953 887277 Fax 01953 888361
Email erskpres@aol.com
Website www.erskine-press.com
Chief Executive *Crispin de Boos*

FOUNDED 1986. Specialist private publishers for individuals and organisations. Produces scholarly reprints and limited editions for academic/business organisations in Europe and the USA, ranging from leather-bound folios of period print reproductions to small illustrated booklets. Under the **Erskine Press** imprint publishes books on Antarctic exploration, general interest autobiographies and medical related 'Patient's Guides' (*Hip & Knee Replacement*; *Chronic Fatigue Syndrome*). No unsolicited mss. Ideas welcome.

Royalties paid twice-yearly.

AS Publishing
73 Montpelier Rise, London NW11 9DU
☎020 8458 3552 Fax 020 8458 0618
Managing Director *Angela Sheehan*

FOUNDED 1987. *Commissions* children's illustrated non-fiction. No unsolicited synopses or ideas for books, but approaches welcome from experienced authors, editors and illustrators in this field.

Fees paid.

BCS Publishing Ltd
2nd Floor, Temple Court, 109 Oxford Road, Cowley, Oxford OX4 2ER
☎01865 770099 Fax 01865 770050
Managing Director *Steve McCurdy*
Approx. Annual Turnover £200,000

Commissions general interest non-fiction for the international co-edition market.

Belitha Press Ltd
London House, Great Eastern Wharf, Parkgate Road, London SW11 4NQ
☎020 7978 6330 Fax 020 7223 4936
Managing Director *Peter Osborn*

Publishing Director *Chester Fisher*

FOUNDED 1980. *Commissions* children's non-fiction in all curriculum areas. About 125 titles a year. All titles are expected to sell in at least four co-editions. TITLES *World Cities; The Other Half of History; Life in Victorian Times; Our Earth; Future Tech; Speedy Machines; Building Works; Looking at Animals.* IMPRINT **Big Fish** *Chester Fisher* Children's interactive non-fiction. TITLES *Quiz Master; Internet Action; Amazing Magic.* No unsolicited mss. Synopses and ideas for books welcome from experienced children's writers.

Bender Richardson White

PO Box 266, Uxbridge, Middlesex UB9 5BD
☎01895 832444 Fax 01895 835213
Email brw@brw.co.uk

Partners *Lionel Bender, Kim Richardson, Ben White*

FOUNDED 1990 to produce illustrated non-fiction for children aged 7–14 for publishers in the UK and abroad. 40 titles in 2000. Unsolicited material not welcome.
Fees paid.

David Bennett Books Ltd

London House, Great Eastern Wharf, Parkgate Road, London SW11 4NQ
☎020 7738 0314 Fax 020 7223 4936
Website www.db-books.co.uk

Managing Editor *Helen Mortimer*
Creative Director *Val Pidgeon*

FOUNDED 1989. Part of **C&B Publishing plc**. Producer of children's books: picture and novelty books, interactive and board books, baby gifts and non-fiction for babies and toddlers. Synopses and ideas for books welcome. Unsolicited mss may not be returned. No fiction or poetry.
Payment Both fees and royalties.

Big Fish

See **Belitha Press Ltd**

Book Packaging and Marketing

3 Murswell Lane, Silverstone, Towcester, Northamptonshire NN12 8UT
☎01327 858380 Fax 01327 858380
Email martin@marixevans.freeserve.co.uk

Contact *Martin F. Marix Evans*

FOUNDED 1989. Essentially a project management service, handling books demanding close designer/editor teamwork or complicated multi-contributor administration, for publishers, business 'or anyone who needs one'. Mainly illustrated adult non-fiction including military, travel, historical, home reference and coffee-table books. No fiction or poetry. 5–8 titles a year. Proposals considered but rarely come to fruition; most books are bespoke by publishers. Additional writers are sometimes required for projects in development. TITLES *The Fall of France 1940; Contemporary Photographers,* 3rd ed.; *Encyclopedia of the Boer War; The Battles of the Somme 1916–18; The Military Heritage of Britain and Ireland; Passchendale and the Battle of Ypres; American Voices of World War I.*
Payment Authors contract direct with client publishers; fees paid on first print usually and royalties on reprint but this depends on publisher.

Breslich & Foss Ltd

20 Wells Mews, London W1T 3HQ
☎020 7580 8774 Fax 020 7580 8784
Email sales@breslichfoss.com

Directors *Paula Breslich, K.B. Dunning*
Approx. Annual Turnover £1 million

Packagers of non-fiction titles only, including art, children's, crafts, gardening and health. Unsolicited mss welcome but synopses preferred. Include s.a.e. with all submissions.
Royalties paid twice-yearly.

Brown Books

See **Amber Books Ltd**

Brown Wells and Jacobs Ltd

Forresters Hall, 25–27 Westow Street, London SE19 3RY
☎020 8771 5115 Fax 020 8771 9994
Email postmaster@popking.demon.co.uk
Website www.bwj.org

Managing Director *Graham Brown*

FOUNDED 1979. *Commissions* non-fiction, novelty, pre-school and first readers, natural history and science. About 40 titles a year. Unsolicited synopses and ideas for books welcome.
Fees paid.

Calmann & King Ltd

71 Great Russell Street, London WC1B 3BP
☎020 7430 8850 Fax 020 7430 8880
Email enquiries@calmann-king.co.uk
Website www.calmann-king.com

Chairman *Robin Hyman*
Managing Director *Laurence King*

FOUNDED 1976. *Commissions* books on art, the decorative arts, design, architecture, graphic design, carpets and textiles. About 40 titles a year. Unsolicited synopses and ideas for books welcome.

Royalties paid twice-yearly.

Cameron Books (Production) Ltd

PO Box 1, Moffat, Dumfriesshire DG10 9SU
☎01683 220808 Fax 01683 220012
Email info@cameronbooks.co.uk
Website www.cameronbooks.co.uk

Directors *Ian A. Cameron, Jill Hollis*
Approx. Annual Turnover £400,000

Commissions contemporary art, film, design, collectors' reference, natural history, social history, decorative arts, architecture, gardening and cookery. About 6 titles a year. Unsolicited synopses and ideas for books welcome.

Payment varies with each contract.

Chancerel International Publishers Ltd

120 Long Acre, London WC2E 9ST
☎020 7240 2811 Fax 020 7836 4186
Email chancerel@chancerel.com
Website www.chancerel.com

Managing Director *W.D.B. Prowse*

FOUNDED 1976. *Commissions* and *publishes* language-teaching materials in English, German, French, Spanish, Italian and Japanese. Language teachers/writers often required as authors/consultants, especially native speakers other than English.

Payment generally by flat fee but royalties sometimes.

Roger Coote Publishing

Gissing's Farm, Fressingfield, Eye, Suffolk IP21 5SH
☎01379 588044 Fax 01379 588055
Email rgc@ndirect.co.uk

Director *Roger Goddard-Coote*

FOUNDED 1993. Packager of children's and adult non-fiction for trade, school and library markets. About 40 titles a year. No fiction. Include s.a.e. for return.

Fees paid; no royalties.

Diagram Visual Information Ltd

195 Kentish Town Road, London NW5 2JU
☎020 7482 3633 Fax 020 7482 4932
Email diagramviz@aol.com

Managing Director *Bruce Robertson*

FOUNDED 1967. Producer of library, school, academic and trade reference books. About 10 titles a year. Unsolicited synopses and ideas for books welcome.

Fees paid; no payment for sample material/submissions for consideration.

Direct Image Publishing

Beckside, Lindale, Grange over Sands, Cumbria LA11 6NA
☎015395 33443 Fax 015395 35794
Email elaine@directimageprod.demon.co.uk
Website www.directimageprod.co.uk

Co-Directors *Chris Ware, Elaine Ware*

A sub-division of Direct Image Productions Ltd. FOUNDED in 1992 to support video training programmes. Two key areas: outdoor education; complimentary therapies. Builds training programmes and publishes teachers' resource material, usually as part of a video and book package. No unsolicited mss; approach with letter and outline of idea in first instance.

Payment One-off fee.

Duncan Petersen Publishing Limited

See entry under **UK Publishers**

Eddison Sadd Editions

St Chad's House, 148 King's Cross Road, London WC1X 9DH
☎020 7837 1968 Fax 020 7837 2025
Email reception@eddisonsadd.co.uk

Managing Director *Nick Eddison*
Editorial Director *Ian Jackson*
Approx. Annual Turnover £3.5 million

FOUNDED 1982. Produces a wide range of popular illustrated non-fiction – mind, body, spirit and complementary therapies are particular strengths – with books published in 25 countries. Ideas and synopses are welcome but titles must have international appeal.

Royalties paid twice yearly; flat fees paid when appropriate.

Erskine Press

See **Archival Facsimiles Limited**

Expert Publications Ltd

Sloe House, Halstead, Essex CO9 1PA
☎01787 474744 Fax 01787 474700
Email expert@lineone.net

Chairman *Dr. D.G. Hessayon*

FOUNDED 1993. Produces the *Expert* series of books by Dr. D.G. Hessayon. Currently 18 titles in the series, including *The NEW Flower Expert; The Evergreen Expert; The Vegetable &*

Herb Expert; The Flowering Shrub Expert; The Container Expert. No unsolicited material.

Haldane Mason Ltd

59 Chepstow Road, London W2 5BP
☎020 7792 2123 Fax 020 7221 3965
Email haldane.mason@dial.pipex.com

FOUNDED 1994. *Commissions* adult and children's illustrated non-fiction and young children's fiction. Adult list consists mainly of mind, body and spirit; children's age range 0–11. 30 titles in 2000. Unsolicited synopses and ideas welcome; approach in writing in the first instance. No adult fiction. *Fees* paid.

Angus Hudson Ltd

Concorde House, Grenville Place, Mill Hill, London NW7 3SA
☎020 8959 3668 Fax 020 8959 3678
Email coed@angushudson.com

Managing Director *Nicholas Jones*
Approx. Annual Turnover £3.5 million

FOUNDED 1977. Management buyout from Maxwell Communications in 1989. Leading packager of religious co-editions. *Commissions* Christian books for all ages and co-editioning throughout the world. About 150 titles a year. Publishes under **Candle Books**; **Gazelle Books** and **Monarch Books** (see entry under **UK Publishers**) imprints. Prototype dummies complete with illustrations welcome for consideration. Synopses for text books welcome; no unsolicited mss, please.
Royalties paid.

The Learning Factory

See **Aladdin Books Ltd**

Lexus Ltd

13 Newton Terrace, Glasgow G3 7PJ
☎0141 221 5266 Fax 0141 226 3139
Email pt@lexus.win-uk.net

Managing/Editorial Director *P.M. Terrell*

FOUNDED 1980. Compiles bilingual reference, language and phrase books. About 10 titles a year. TITLES *Rough Guide Phrasebooks; Collins Italian Concise Dictionary; Harrap Study Aids; Hugo's Phrase Books; Harrap Shorter French Dictionary* (revised); *Impact Specialist Bilingual Glossaries; Oxford Student's Japanese Learner.* No unsolicited material. Books are mostly commissioned. Freelance contributors employed for a wide range of languages.
Payment generally flat fee.

Lionheart Books

10 Chelmsford Square, London NW10 3AR
☎020 8459 0453 Fax 020 8451 3681

Senior Partner *Lionel Bender*
Partner *Madeleine Samuel*
Approx. Annual Turnover £250,000

A design/editorial packaging team. Titles are primarily commissioned from publishers. Highly illustrated non-fiction for children aged 8–14, mostly natural history, history and general science. About 20 titles a year.
Payment generally flat fee.

Market House Books Ltd

2 Market House, Market Square, Aylesbury, Buckinghamshire HP20 1TN
☎01296 484911 Fax 01296 437073
Website www.mhbref.com

Directors *Dr Alan Isaacs, Dr John Daintith, Peter Sapsed*

FOUNDED 1970. Formerly Laurence Urdang Associates. *Commissions* dictionaries, encyclopedias and reference. About 15 titles a year. TITLES *Brewer's 20th Century Phrase and Fable; Oxford Dictionary for Science Writers and Editors; Oxford Dictionary of Accounting; Bloomsbury Thesaurus; Larousse Thematica* (6 volume encyclopedia); *Collins English Dictionary; The Macmillan Encyclopedia; Grolier Bibliographical Encyclopedia of Scientists* (10 vols); *Oxford Paperback Encyclopedia; Oxford International Business Dictionary; Penguin Biographical Dictionary of Women; Penguin Shakespeare Dictionary; Penguin Dictionary of Plant Sciences; Oxford Dictionary of Medicines; New Penguin Dictionary of the Theatre.* Unsolicited material not welcome as most books are compiled in-house.
Fees paid.

Marshall Editions Ltd

The Orangery, 161 New Bond Street, London W1S 2UF
☎020 7291 8222 Fax 020 7291 8233
Website www.marshalleditions.com

Publisher *Barbara Anderson Marshall*
Editorial Director (adult titles) *Ellen Dupont*
Editorial Director (children's) *Linda Cole*

FOUNDED 1977. *Commissions* non-fiction, including health, gardening, lifestyle, self-improvement, leisure, popular science and visual information for children. Also Marshall Publishing which *publishes* business training, education and consumer reference titles.

Monkey Puzzle Media Ltd
Gissing's Farm, Fressingfield, Eye, Suffolk
IP21 5SH
☎01379 588044 Fax 01379 588055
Email rgc@ndirect.co.uk
Chairman/Managing Director *Roger
Goddard-Coote*
Editorial Director *Alex Edmonds*
FOUNDED 1998. Packager of adult and children's
non-fiction for trade, school, library and mass
markets. About 60 titles a year. No fiction or
textbooks. Synopses and ideas welcome. Include
s.a.e. for return.
Fees paid; no royalties.

Mike Moran Productions Ltd
33 Warner Road, Ware, Hertfordshire
SG12 9JL
☎01920 466003 Fax 01920 466003
Email mmoran@frankcass.com
Website www.mikemoranphotography.co.uk
Chairman/Managing Director
Mike Moran
Packager and publisher. TITLES *MM Publisher
Database; MM Printer Database* (available in UK,
European and international editions).

Nicholas Enterprises
See **Aladdin Books Ltd**

Orpheus Books Limited
2 Church Green, Witney, Oxfordshire
OX28 4AW
☎01993 774949 Fax 01993 700330
Email info@orpheusbooks.com
Chairman *Nicholas Harris*
FOUNDED 1993. *Commissions* children's non-
fiction. 8 titles in 2001. No unsolicited material.
Fees paid.

Playne Books Limited
Chapel House, Trefin, Haverfordwest,
Pembrokeshire SA62 5AU
☎01348 837073 Fax 01348 837063
Director *Gill Davies*
Design & Production *David Playne*
FOUNDED 1987. *Commissions* early learning titles
for young children – fun ideas with an educa-
tional slant and novelty books. Also highly illus-
trated and practical books on any subject.
Synopses and ideas by prior arrangement only.
Royalties paid 'on payment from publishers'.
Fees sometimes paid instead of royalties.

Mathew Price Ltd
The Old Glove Factory, Bristol Road,
Sherborne, Dorset DT9 4HP
☎01935 816010 Fax 01935 816310
Email mathewp@mathewprice.com
Chairman/Managing Director *Mathew Price*
Approx. Annual Turnover £1 million
Commissions full-colour novelty picture books
and fiction for young children plus children's
non-fiction for all ages.
Fees sometimes paid instead of royalties.

Quarto Publishing
The Old Brewery, 6 Blundell Street, London
N7 9BH
☎020 7700 6700 Fax 020 7700 4191
Website www.quarto.com
Chairman *Laurence Orbach*
FOUNDED 1976. Britain's largest book packager.
Commissions illustrated non-fiction, including
painting, graphic design, visual arts, history,
cookery, gardening, crafts. *Publishes* under the
Apple imprint. Unsolicited synopses/ideas for
books welcome.
Payment Flat fees paid.

Reader's Digest Children's Publishing Ltd
King's Court, Parsonage Lane, Bath BA1 1ER
☎01225 463401 Fax 01225 460942
Email jill.eade@readersdigest.co.uk
Website www.childrens-books.com
Commercial Director *Paul E. Stuart*
Part of the Reader's Digest Group. *Commissions*
children's projects in novelty or interactive for-
mats – acetate, pop-up, toy add-ons. Also reli-
gious list. About 60 titles a year. No unsolicited
material; all editorial matters dealt with by New
York office (see entry under **US Publishers**).
Royalties or flat fee according to contract.

Regency House Publishing Limited
See entry under **UK Publishers**

Sadie Fields Productions Ltd
4C/D West Point, 36–37 Warple Way,
London W3 0RG
☎020 8746 1171 Fax 020 8746 1170
Email sheri@tangobooks.co.uk
Directors *David Fielder, Sheri Safran*
FOUNDED 1981. Children's books with international co-edition potential: pop-ups, three-
dimensional, novelty, picture and board books,

1500 words maximum. About 30 titles a year. Approach with preliminary letter and sample material in the first instance. *Publishes* in the UK under the **Tango Books** imprint.

Royalties based on a per-copy-sold rate and paid in stages.

Salariya Book Company Ltd

25 Marlborough Place, Brighton, East Sussex BN1 1UB
☎01273 603306 Fax 01273 693857
Email salariya@salariya.com
Managing Director *David Salariya*

FOUNDED 1989. Children's information books – fiction, history, art, music, science, architecture, education and picture books.

Payment by arrangement.

Savitri Books Ltd

115J Cleveland Street, London W1P 5PN
☎020 7436 9932 Fax 020 7580 6330
Managing Director *Mrinalini S. Srivastava*
Approx. Annual Turnover £200,000

FOUNDED 1983 and since 1998, Savitri Books has also become a publisher in its own right (textile crafts). Keen to work 'very closely with authors/illustrators and try to establish long-term relationships with them, doing more books with the same team of people'. *Commissions* illustrated non-fiction, crafts, New Age and nature. About 7 titles a year. Unsolicited synopses and ideas for books 'very welcome'.

Sheldrake Press

188 Cavendish Road, London SW12 0DA
☎020 8675 1767 Fax 020 8675 7736
Email mail@sheldrakepress.demon.co.uk
Website www.sheldrakepress.demon.co.uk
Publisher *Simon Rigge*
Approx. Annual Turnover £250,000

Commissions illustrated non-fiction: history, travel, style, cookery and stationery. TITLES *The Victorian House Book; The Shorter Mrs Beeton; The Power of Steam; The Railway Heritage of Britain; Wild Britain; Wild France; Wild Spain; Wild Italy; Wild Ireland; Amsterdam: Portrait of a City* and Kate Greenaway stationery books. Synopses and ideas for books welcome, but not interested in fiction.

Fees or royalties paid.

Stonecastle Graphics Ltd/ Touchstone

Old Chapel Studio, Plain Road, Marden, Tonbridge, Kent TN12 9LS
☎01622 832590 Fax 01622 832592
Email touchstone@touchstone.ndirect.co.uk
Website www.touchstonedesign.co.uk
Partner *Paul Turner*
Partner/Editorial Head *Sue Pressley*
Approx. Annual Turnover £300,000

FOUNDED 1976. Formed additional design/ packaging partnership, Touchstone, in 1983. *Commissions* illustrated non-fiction general books – motoring, health, sport, leisure, home interest and popular culture. 20 titles in 2000. TITLES *Pregnancy – A Week-by-Week Guide; Popular Freshwater Tropical Fish; Tracing Your Ancestors; Entertaining in Style; The History of British Bikes.* Unsolicited synopses and ideas for books welcome.

Fees paid.

Templar Publishing

Pippbrook Mill, London Road, Dorking, Surrey RH4 1JE
☎01306 876361 Fax 01306 889097
Email editorial@templarco.co.uk
Website www.templarco.co.uk
Managing Director/Editorial Head
 Amanda Wood
Approx. Annual Turnover £8 million

FOUNDED 1981. A division of The Templar Company plc. · *Commissions* novelty and gift books, picture books and children's illustrated non-fiction. 100 titles a year. Synopses and ideas for books welcome.

Royalties by arrangement.

Toucan Books Ltd

Fourth Floor, 32–38 Saffron Hill, London EC1N 8FH
☎020 7404 8181 Fax 020 7404 8282
Managing Director *Robert Sackville-West*
Approx. Annual Turnover £1,600,000

FOUNDED 1985. *Specialises* in international co-editions and fee-based editorial, design and production services to film. *Commissions* illustrated non-fiction only. About 20 titles a year. TITLES *The Eventful Century; The Earth, Its Wonders, Its Secrets; Leith's Cookery Bible; Charles II; The Complete Photography Course; Journeys into the Past* series; *People and Places.* Unsolicited synopses and ideas for books welcome. No fiction or non-illustrated titles. Change of address expected late 2001.

Royalties paid twice-yearly; fees paid in addition to or instead of royalties.

Touchstone

See **Stonecastle Graphics Ltd**

Webb & Bower (Publishers) Ltd

9 Duke Street, Dartmouth, Devon TQ6 9PY
☎01803 835525 Fax 01803 835552

Managing Director *Richard Webb*

FOUNDED 1975. *Specialises* in licensing illustrated non-fiction books from its portfolio of 350 titles.
Royalties paid twice-yearly.

David West Children's Books

7 Princeton Court, 55 Felsham Road, Putney, London SW15 1AZ
☎020 8780 3836 Fax 020 8780 9313
Email dww@btinternet.com

FOUNDED 1992. *Commissions* children's illustrated reference books. No fiction or adult books. 35 titles in 2000. Unsolicited ideas and synopses welcome; approach in writing in the first instance.
Fees and royalties paid annually.

Windrow & Greene

See **Compendium Publishing Ltd** under
UK Publishers

Wordwright Publishing

8 St Johns Road, Saxmundham, Suffolk
IP17 1BE
☎01728 604204 Fax 01728 604029
Email wordwright@clara.co.uk

Contact *Charles Perkins*

FOUNDED by ex-editorial people 'so good writing always has a chance with us'. *Commissions* illustrated non-fiction: social history and commment, military history, women's issues, sport. *Specialises* in military and social history, natural history, science, art, cookery, and gardening. About 6–8 titles a year. Unsolicited synopses/ideas (a paragraph or so) welcome for illustrated non-fiction.
Payment usually fees but royalties (twice-yearly) paid for sales above a specified number of copies.

Working Partners Ltd

1 Albion Place, London W6 0QT
☎020 8748 7477 Fax 020 8748 7450
Email enquiries@workingpartnersltd.co.uk

Contacts *Ben Baglio, Rod Ritchie*

Specialises in children's mass-market series fiction books. Creators of *Animal Ark; Puppy Patrol; Dolphin Diaries; Heartland; Sheltie; Survive!* No unsolicited mss. Welcomes approaches from interested authors. Contact *Deborah Smith*, Editorial Director.
Payment Both fees and royalties by arrangement.

Zöe Books Ltd

15 Worthy Lane, Winchester, Hampshire
SO23 7AB
☎01962 851318
Email enquiries@zoebooks.co.uk
Website www.zoebooks.co.uk

Managing Director *Imogen Dawson*

FOUNDED 1990. *Specialises* in full-colour information and reference books for schools and libraries worldwide. *Publishes* about 30 titles a year. Does *not* publish picture books or fiction. No freelance work available.
Fees paid.

Book Clubs

David Arscott's Sussex Book Club
Dolphin House, 51 St Nicholas Lane, Lewes,
Sussex BN7 2JZ
☎01273 470100 Fax 01273 470100
Email sussexbooks@compuserve.com
Website www.ourworld.compuserve.com/
    homepages/sussexbooks

FOUNDED January 1998. *Specialises* in books
about the county of Sussex. Represents all the
major publishers of Sussex books and offers a
wide range of titles. Free membership without
obligation to buy.

Artists' Choice
PO Box 3, Huntingdon, Cambridgeshire
PE28 0QX
☎01832 710201 Fax 01832 710488

Specialises in books for the amateur artist at all
levels of ability.

BCA (Book Club Associates)
Greater London House, Hampstead Road,
London NW1 7TZ
☎020 7760 6500 Fax 020 7760 6901

With two million members, BCA is Britain's
largest book club organisation. Consists of 31
book clubs, catering for general and specific
interests. These include: Ancient & Medieval
History Book Club, The Arts Guild, The Book
Club of Ireland, Books For Children, The
Christian Book Club, Discovery, The English
Book Club, Ergo, Escape (female fiction), The
Travel Book Club, Fantasy and Science Fiction,
History Guild, Home Software World, The
Literary Guild, Military and Aviation Book
Society, Mind, Body & Spirit, Mystery and
Thriller Club, Quality Paperbacks Direct,
Railway Book Club, World Books, Mango,
Taste, Escape (travel) and Computer Books
Direct.

Bibliophile Books
5 Thomas Road, London E14 7BN
☎020 7515 9222 Fax 020 7538 4115
Email orders@bibliophilebooks.com
Website www.bibliophilebooks.com

New books covering a wide range of subjects
at discount prices. Write, phone or fax for free
catalogue 10 times a year.

Cygnus Books
PO Box 15, Llandeilo, Carmarthenshire
SA19 6YX
☎01550 777701 Fax 01550 777569
Email enquiries@cygnus-books.co.uk
Website www.cygnus-books.co.uk

'Books for your next step in spirituality and complementary health care.' See website for over
1000 hand-picked titles. Publishes *The Cygnus
Review* magazine which features 50–60 reviews
on new mind, body and spirit titles each month.

The Folio Society
44 Eagle Street, London WC1R 4FS
☎020 7400 4222 Fax 020 7400 4242

Fine editions of classic fiction, history and
memoirs; also some children's classics.

Letterbox Library
71–73 Allen Road, London N16 8RY
☎020 7503 4801 Fax 020 7503 4800

Children's book cooperative. Hard and softcover, non-sexist and multi-cultural books for
children from one to teenage.

Poetry Book Society
See entry under **Organisations of Interest to
Poets**

Readers Union Ltd
Brunel House, Forde Close, Newton Abbot,
Devon TQ12 2DW
☎01626 323200 Fax 01626 323318

Has ten book clubs, all dealing with specific
interests: Country Review, The Craft Club,
Craftsman Society, Equestrian Society, The
Gardeners Society, Life Matters, Needlecrafts
with Cross Stitch, Focal Point, Ramblers &
Climbers Society, Today's Family.

Red House Book Clubs
See **Scholastic Ltd** under **UK Publishers**

The Women's Press Book Club
The Women's Press, 34 Great Sutton Street,
London EC1V 0LQ
☎020 7251 3007 Fax 020 7608 1938
Email judith@the-womens-press.com
Website www.the-womens-press.com

'Best women writers from more than 70 publishers.' Fiction, biography and autobiography; popular mind, body and spirit; health and self-help; also a collection of women's studies, social issues and current affairs.

Writers' News Book Society
PO Box 6058, Nairn IV12 4WB
☎01667 453351 Fax 01667 452365
Specialises in books for writers.

Chandler Tells How

Raymond Chandler was one of the great novelists of the twentieth century. Forget the plots; his style was wonderfully succinct, clear and compelling. He was also a perceptive and witty commentator on the literary scene. *The Chandler Papers* (edited by Tom Hiney and Frank McShane) contains a wealth of advice for anyone contemplating a writing career. Older hands may learn a thing or two as well.

When I open a book and see writing like 'her appearance was indeed shocking'; 'I felt the first stab of remorse'; 'rich full-bodied beauty' etc. I get the impression that I am reading a dead language, that awful petrified mandarin English which no one can get away with except perhaps Maugham, and not always he.

Funny thing civilization. It promises so much and all it delivers is mass production of shoddy merchandise and shoddy people.

My experience with trying to help people to write has been limited but extremely intensive. I have done everything from giving would-be writers money to live on to plotting and rewriting their stories for them, and so far I have found it to be all waste. The people whom God or nature intended to be writers find their own answers, and those who have to ask are impossible to help. They are merely people who want to be writers.

Most writers have the egotism of actors with none of the good looks or charm.

I HATE PUBLICITY. It is nearly always dishonest and quite always stupid. I don't think it means anything at all. You don't get any until you are 'copy' and what you get makes you hate yourself.

Why do women write such ordinary books? Their observation of everyday life is splendid, but they never seem to develop any color . . .

That feeling you get in English books and so seldom in ours that the country with all its small details is a part of their lives and that they love it. We are so rootless here. I've lived half my life in California and made what use of it I could, but I could leave it forever without a pang.

Publishers may apologize to authors and to other publishers and to other writers. But with agents it is enough that you let them live.

Talking of agents, when I opened the morning paper one morning last week I saw that it had finally happened: somebody shot one. It was probably for the wrong reasons, but at least it was a step in the right direction.

The trouble with most English mystery writers, however well known in their world, is that they can't turn a corner. About halfway through a book they start fooling around with alibis, analysing bits and pieces of evidence and so on. The story dies on them. The great fault of American mystery writers, on the other hand, is a lack of texture, a sort of naiveté which probably comes from them not being very well educated or well read.

A writer has nothing to trade but his life. Most are frustrated bastards with unhappy domestic lives.

Taken from The Chandler Papers*, published by Hamish Hamilton (ISBN: 0241140366; £20.00) and reprinted with the kind permission of The Estate· of Raymond Chandler.*

UK Agents

★ = Members of the **Association of Authors' Agents**

Abbey Agency Literary Services

26 Stamford Avenue, Royston, Hertfordshire
SG8 7DD
☎01763 220947
Email admin@abbeyagency.com

Contact *Elizabeth Baker*

FOUNDED 1999. *Handles* general fiction and
non-fiction; crime, fantasy, suspense, horror,
biography, historical, military, humour and erotica. Submissions welcome from minority groups
and new writers. No children's books, short
stories or science fiction. Initial approach: synopsis and two sample chapters. Please include
return postage. Reading fee may be charged for
full mss. CLIENTS Gavin Miller (US), Derek Fox,
Mike Vardy, Kay Gillespie. *Commission* Home
10%; US 20%.

Sheila Ableman Literary Agency

122 Arlington Road, London NW1 7HP
☎020 7485 3409 Fax 020 7485 3409
Email sheila@ableman.freeserve.co.uk

Contact *Sheila Ableman*

FOUNDED 1999. *Handles* non-fiction including
history, science, biography and autobiography.
Specialises in TV tie-ins and celebrity ghost writing. No poetry, children's, cookery, gardening
or sport. Unsolicited mss welcome. Approach in
writing with publishing history, c.v., synopsis,
three chapters and s.a.e. for return. No reading
fee. *Commission* Home 15%; US & Translation
20%.

The Agency (London) Ltd★

24 Pottery Lane, Holland Park, London
W11 4LZ
☎020 7727 1346 Fax 020 7727 9037
Email info@theagency.co.uk

Contacts *Stephen Durbridge, Leah Schmidt,*
Sebastian Born, Julia Kreitman, Bethan Evans,
Hilary Delamere, Katie Haines, Wendy Gresser

FOUNDED 1995. *Handles* children's fiction, TV,
film, theatre, radio scripts. No adult fiction or
non-fiction. Send letter with s.a.e. No reading
fee. CLIENTS include William Boyd, Andrew
Davies, Jimmy McGovern, Lucy Gannon.
Commission Home 10%; US various.

Gillon Aitken Associates Ltd★

29 Fernshaw Road, London SW10 0TG
☎020 7351 7561 Fax 020 7376 3594

Contacts *Gillon Aitken, Clare Alexander*

FOUNDED 1977. *Handles* fiction and non-fiction.
No plays or scripts unless by existing clients.
Send preliminary letter, with synopsis and return
postage, in the first instance. No reading fee.
CLIENTS include Pat Barker, John Cornwell,
Linda Davies, Sarah Dunant, Sebastian Faulks,
Niall Fergusson, Helen Fielding, Germaine
Greer, Susan Howatch, Candia McWilliam, V.S.
Naipaul, Jonathan Raban, Piers Paul Read,
Gillian Slovo, Colin Thubron, A.N. Wilson.
Commission Home 10%; US 15%; Translation
20%.

Michael Alcock Management★

96 Farringdon Road, London EC1R 3EA
☎020 7837 8137 Fax 020 7837 8787
Email alcockmgt@cs.com

Contacts *Michael Alcock, Cathy Fischgrund*

FOUNDED 1997. *Handles* general non-fiction
including current affairs, biography and memoirs, history, lifestyle, health and personal development; some literary and commercial mainstream fiction. No unsolicited mss; approach by
letter in the first instance giving details of writing
and other media experience, plus synopsis and
s.a.e. (for fiction send first two chapters as well).
No reading fee. CLIENTS include Tamsin
Blanchard, James Burke, Tom Dixon, Philip
Dunn, Kevin Gould, Mark Griffiths, Joanna
Hall, Lisa Hilton, Kathryn Marsden, Lynne
Robinson, Barnaby Rogerson, Ruby & Millie.
Commission Home 15%; US and Translation
20%.

Jacintha Alexander Associates

See **Lucas Alexander Whitley**

Darley Anderson Literary, TV & Film Agency★

Estelle House, 11 Eustace Road, London
SW6 1JB
☎020 7385 6652 Fax 020 7386 9689
Email darley.anderson@virgin.net

Contacts *Darley Anderson, Kerith Biggs* (crime/foreign rights), *Elizabeth Wright* (women's fiction/love stories/'tear-jerkers'), *Michelle Hockley* (non-fiction), *Carrie Neilson* (children's books/TV)

Run by an ex-publisher with a sympathetic touch and a knack for spotting and encouraging talent who is known to have negotiated over £1,000,000 in advances and a Hollywood film deal for one first-time novelist and a £350,000 UK advance for another first-time novelist. *Handles* commercial fiction and non-fiction; children's fiction; also selected scripts for film and TV. No academic books or poetry. *Special interests* Fiction: all types of thrillers and young male fiction. All types of American and Irish novels, women's fiction including contemporary, sagas, tear-jerkers, women in jeopardy. Also crime/ mystery (American/hard-boiled/cosy/historical), horror and comedy. Non-fiction: celebrity autobiographies, biographies, 'true life' women in jeopardy, relevatory history and science, popular psychology, self-improvement, diet, health, beauty and fashion, humour/cartoons, gardening, cookery, inspirational and religious. Send letter and outline with first three chapters; return postage/s.a.e. essential. CLIENTS Richard Asplin, Anne Baker, Catherine Barry, Paul Carson, Caroline Carver, Lee Child, Martina Cole, John Connolly, Joseph Corvo, Martina Devlin, Rose Doyle, Joan Jonker, Frank Lean, Carole Matthews, Lesley Pearse, Allan Pease, Adrian Plass, Mary Ryan, Fred Secombe, Rebecca Shaw, Peter Sheridan, Linda Taylor. *Commission* Home 15%; US 20%; Translation 20–25%; TV/Film/Radio 20%. *Overseas associates* APA Talent and Literary Agency (LA/Hollywood); Liza Dawson Associates (New York); and leading foreign agents throughout the world.

Anubis Literary Agency

79 Charles Gardner Road, Leamington Spa, Warwickshire CV31 3BG
☎01926 832644 Fax 01926 311607

Contacts *Steve Calcutt, Maggie Heavey*

FOUNDED 1994. *Handles* mainstream adult fiction, especially science fiction, fantasy, horror, crime and women's. Also literary fiction. Scripts for film and TV. No children's books, poetry, short stories, journalism, academic or non-fiction. No unsolicited mss; send a covering letter and brief (one-page) synopsis (s.a.e. essential). No telephone calls. No reading fee. CLIENTS include Lesley Asquith, Georgie Hale, Tim Lebbon, Adam Roberts, Steve Saville,

Zoe Sharp. *Commission* Home 15%; US & Translation 20%.

Arcadia Agency

4 Lonsdale Drive, Oakwood EN2 7LH
☎020 8363 6423/0780 1721976
Email foula@church44.freeserve.co.uk

Contacts *Athina F. Churchill, Alex Spyro*

FOUNDED 1999. *Handles* general fiction and some non-fiction. *Specialises* in crime, fantasy, horror, romantic and historical novels, science fiction, children's and general interest. Non-fiction: autobiography, archaeology, spirituality, travel, women's issues, economic and world issues, fitness/diet, some specialist educational textbooks (business studies related and accountancy) and research theses. No gardening, sport, short stories or poetry. CLIENTS include Mim Gibney, J. Murrow, Katie Mullins. New writers welcome. Initial contact by letter or e-mail. Synopsis with three specimen chapters preferred; enclose return postage. *Commission* Home 10%; US & Translation 20%.

Author Literary Agents

53 Talbot Road, Highgate, London N6 4QX
☎020 8341 0442/07989 318245 (mobile)
Fax 020 8341 0442
Email agile@authors.co.uk

Contact *John Havergal*

New writing, illustration and other creative work 'targeting profitable fiction and non-fiction audiences' considered. No unsolicited submissions. S.a.e. and first chapter (only) writing sample or work sample initially. *Commission* Writing: Home 15%; Non-UK & Translation 25%; Illustration & other non-writing media: Publishing 25%; Non-Publishing 33.34% (plus VAT).

Black C.A.T. Literary Agents

Queen Adelaide Farm, Queen Adelaide, Ely, Cambridgeshire CB7 4TZ
☎01353 663013 Fax 01353 663013

Contacts *Vanessa Carter-James, John Charles, Roland Frederick*

FOUNDED 1999. *Handles* women's issues, biography, autobiography, media, theatre, plays/scripts, current affairs, health, education, adventure, European matters, fiction and non-fiction. No erotica. No reading fee. 'Helps the unknown author to achieve publication.' CLIENTS D. Barrie, Bernard Hyde-Tingley, J.H. Miller. Send synopsis with three specimen chapters and return postage. *Commission* Home 10%; US 20%.

Blake Friedmann
Literary Agency Ltd★

122 Arlington Road, London NW1 7HP
☎020 7284 0408 Fax 020 7284 0442
Email <firstname>@blakefriedmann.co.uk
Website www.blakefriedmann.co.uk

Contacts *Carole Blake* (books), *Julian Friedmann* (film/TV), *Conrad Williams* (original scripts/radio), *Isobel Dixon* (books)

FOUNDED 1977. *Handles* all kinds of fiction from genre to literary; a varied range of specialised and general non-fiction, plus scripts for TV, radio and film. No poetry, juvenile, science fiction or short stories (unless from existing clients). *Special interests* commercial women's fiction, literary fiction, upmarket non-fiction. Unsolicited mss welcome but initial letter with synopsis and first two chapters preferred. Letters should contain as much information as possible on previous writing experience, aims for the future, etc. No reading fee. CLIENTS include Ted Allbeury, Jane Asher, Joanna Briscoe, Elizabeth Chadwick, Teresa Crane, Barbara Erskine, Maeve Haran, John Harvey, Ken Hom, Paul Johnston, Glenn Meade, Lawrence Norfolk, Joseph O'Connor, Michael Ridpath, Tim Sebastian. *Commission* Books: Home 15%; US & Translation 20%. Radio/TV/Film: 15%. *Overseas associates* throughout Europe, Asia and the US.

David Bolt Associates

12 Heath Drive, Send, Surrey GU23 7EP
☎01483 721118 Fax 01483 721118

Contact *David Bolt*

FOUNDED 1983. *Handles* fiction and general non-fiction. No books for small children or verse (except in special circumstances). No scripts. *Special interests* fiction, African writers, biography, history, military, theology. Preliminary letter with s.a.e. essential. Reading fee for unpublished writers. Terms on application. CLIENTS include Chinua Achebe, David Bret, Joseph Rhymer, Colin Wilson. *Commission* Home 10%; US & Translation 19%.

Book Affairs Ltd

See entry under **Electronic Publishing and Other Services**

BookBlast Ltd

PO Box 20184, London W10 5AU
☎020 8968 3089 Fax 020 8932 4087

Contact *Address material to the Company*

HANDLES traditional and underground fiction and non-fiction. No unsolicited mss. No submissions on disk, by fax or e-mail. Preliminary letter, synopsis, biographical information and s.a.e. essential, also names of agents and publishers previously contacted. *Commission* Home 12%; US & Translation 20%; TV & Radio 15%; Film 20%.

Alan Brodie Representation Ltd (incorporating **Michael Imison Playwrights Ltd**)

211 Piccadilly, London W1V 9LD
☎020 7917 2871 Fax 020 7917 2872
Email info@alanbrodie.com

Contacts *Alan Brodie, Sarah McNair*

FOUNDED 1989. *Handles* theatre, film and TV scripts. No books. Preliminary letter plus professional recommendation and c.v. essential. No reading fee but s.a.e. required. *Commission* Home 10%; Overseas 15%.

Rosemary Bromley
Literary Agency

Avington, Near Winchester, Hampshire
SO21 1DB
☎01962 779656 Fax 01962 779656
Email juvenilia@clam.co.uk

Contact *Rosemary Bromley*

FOUNDED 1981. *Handles* non-fiction. Also scripts for TV and radio. No poetry or short stories. *Special interests* natural history, leisure, biography and cookery. No unsolicited mss. No fax enquiries. Send preliminary letter with full details. Enquiries unaccompanied by return postage will not be answered. CLIENTS Elisabeth Beresford, Linda Birch, Gwen Cherrell, Teresa Collard, Estate of Fanny Cradock, Glenn Hamilton, Cathy Hopkins, Keith West, Ron Wilson, John Wingate. *Commission* Home 10%; US 15%; Translation 20%.

Felicity Bryan★

2A North Parade, Banbury Road, Oxford
OX2 6LX
☎01865 513816 Fax 01865 310055

Contact *Felicity Bryan*

FOUNDED 1988. *Handles* fiction of various types and non-fiction with emphasis on history, biography, science and current affairs. No scripts for TV, radio or theatre. No crafts, how-to, science fiction or light romance. No unsolicited mss. Best approach by letter. No reading fee. CLIENTS include Karen Armstrong, Humphrey Carpenter, John Charmley, Liza Cody, Artemis Cooper, Angela Huth, Diarmaid MacCulloch,

Sue MacGregor, James Naughtie, John Julius Norwich, Iain Pears, Rosamunde Pilcher, Matt Ridley, Miriam Stoppard, Roy Strong, John Sulston. *Commission* Home 10%; US & Translation 20%. *Overseas associates* Andrew Nurnberg, Europe; several agencies in US.

Peter Bryant (Writers)

94 Adelaide Avenue, London SE4 1YR
☎020 8691 9085 Fax 020 8692 9107

Contact *Peter Bryant*

FOUNDED 1980. *Special interests* animation, children's fiction and TV sitcoms. Also *handles* drama scripts for theatre, radio, film and TV. No reading fee for these categories but return postage essential for all submissions. CLIENTS include Isabelle Amyes, Geoffrey Beevers, Andrew Brenner, Jimmy Hibbert, Penny Lloyd, Allan Plenderleith, Ruth Silvestre, Peter Symonds, George Tarry. *Commission* 10%. *Overseas associate* Hartmann & Stauffacher, Germany.

Brie Burkeman★

14 Neville Court, Abbey Road, London NW8 9DD
☎0709 223 9113 Fax 0709 223 9111
Email brie.burkeman@mail.com

Contact *Brie Burkeman*

FOUNDED 2000. *Handles* commercial and literary full-length fiction and non-fiction. Film, TV, theatre scripts. No academic, text, poetry, short stories, musicals or short films. No reading fee. Preliminary letter preferred. Return postage essential. Also independent film and TV consultant to literary agents. *Commission* Home 15%; Overseas 20%.

Juliet Burton Literary Agency

2 Clifton Avenue, London W12 9DR
☎020 8762 0148 Fax 020 8743 8765

Contact *Juliet Burton*

FOUNDED 1999. *Handles* fiction and non-fiction. *Special interests* crime and women's fiction. No plays, film scripts, articles, poetry or academic material. No reading fee. Approach in writing in the first instance; send synopsis and two sample chapters with s.a.e. No unsolicited mss. *Commission* Home 10%; US & Translation 20%.

Campbell Thomson & McLaughlin Ltd★

1 King's Mews, London WC1N 2JA
☎020 7242 0958 Fax 020 7242 2408

Contacts *John McLaughlin, Charlotte Bruton*

FOUNDED 1931. *Handles* fiction and general non-fiction, excluding children's. No plays, film/TV scripts, articles, short stories or poetry. No unsolicited mss or synopses. Preliminary letter with s.a.e. essential. No reading fee. *Overseas associates* Fox Chase Agency, Pennsylvania; Raines & Raines, New York.

Capel & Land Ltd★

29 Wardour Street, London W1D 6PS
☎020 7734 2414 Fax 020 7734 8101
Email robert@capelland.co.uk

Contact *Georgina Capel*

FOUNDED 2000. *Handles* fiction and non-fiction. Also film, TV, theatre and radio scripts. No children's or illustrated books. Send sample chapters and synopsis with covering letter in the first instance. No reading fee. CLIENTS Kunal Basu, Julie Burchill, Andrew Greig, Andrew Roberts, Lucy Wadham. *Commission* Home, US & Translation 15%.

Casarotto Ramsay and Associates Ltd

National House, 60–66 Wardour Street, London W1V 3HP
☎020 7287 4450 Fax 020 7287 9128
Email agents@casarotto.uk.com

Film/TV/Radio *Jenne Casarotto, Tracey Smith, Charlotte Kelly, Jodi Shields, Alison Bond*
Stage *Tom Erhardt, Mel Kenyon*
(**Books** *Handled by* **Lutyens and Rubinstein**)

Took over the agency responsibilities of Margaret Ramsay Ltd in 1992, incorporating a strong client list, with names like Alan Ayckbourn, Caryl Churchill, Willy Russell and Muriel Spark. *Handles* scripts for TV, theatre, film and radio. No unsolicited material without preliminary letter. CLIENTS include J.G. Ballard, Edward Bond, Simon Callow, David Hare, Terry Jones, Neil Jordan, Willy Russell. *Commission* Home 10%; US & Translation 20%. *Overseas associates* worldwide.

Celia Catchpole

56 Gilpin Avenue, London SW14 8QY
☎020 8255 7200 Fax 020 8288 0653

Contact *Celia Catchpole*

FOUNDED 1996. *Handles* children's books – artists and writers. No TV, film, radio or theatre scripts. No poetry. No unsolicited mss. *Commission* Home 10% (writers) 15% (artists); US & Translation 20%. Works with associate agents abroad.

Chapman & Vincent

The Mount, Sun Hill, Royston, Hertfordshire
SG8 9AT
☎01763 245005   Fax 01763 243033

Contacts *Jennifer Chapman, Gilly Vincent*

A small agency whose clients come mainly from personal recommendation. The agency aims to look after only a small number of predominantly non-fiction writers and is not actively seeking clients but happy to consider really original work. Does not handle poetry, children's books or genre fiction. Please do not telephone or submit by fax. Write with two sample chapters and enclose s.a.e. CLIENTS include George Carter, Leslie Geddes-Brown, Sara George, Rowley Leigh, John Miller, Dorit Peleg. *Commission* Home 15%; US & Europe 20%.

Mic Cheetham Literary Agency

11–12 Dover Street, London W1S 4LJ
☎020 7495 2002   Fax 020 7495 5777

Contact *Mic Cheetham*

ESTABLISHED 1994. *Handles* general and literary fiction, crime and science fiction, and some specific non-fiction. No film/TV scripts apart from existing clients. No children's, illustrated books or poetry. No unsolicited mss. Approach in writing with publishing history, first two chapters and return postage. No reading fee. CLIENTS include Iain Banks, Carol Birch, Anita Burgh, Laurie Graham, Toby Litt, Ken MacLeod, China Miéville, Antony Sher. *Commission* Home 10%; US & Translation 20%. Works with **The Marsh Agency** for all translation rights.

Judith Chilcote Agency★

8 Wentworth Mansions, Keats Grove, London
NW3 2RL
☎020 7794 3717   Fax 020 7794 7431

Contact *Judith Chilcote*

FOUNDED 1990. *Handles* commercial fiction, TV tie-ins, health and nutrition, sport, cinema, self-help, popular psychology, biography and autobiography, cookery and current affairs. No academic, science fiction, children's, short stories, film scripts or poetry. No approaches by e-mail. Send letter with c.v., synopsis, three chapters and s.a.e. for return. No reading fee. *Commission* Home 15%; Overseas 20–25%.

Teresa Chris Literary Agency

43 Musard Road, London W6 8NR
☎020 7386 0633

Contact *Teresa Chris*

FOUNDED 1989. *Handles* crime, general, women's, commercial and literary fiction, and non-fiction: history, biography, health, cookery, lifestyle, sport and fitness, gardening, etc. *Specialises* in crime fiction and commercial women's fiction. No scripts. Film and TV rights handled by co-agent. No poetry, short stories, fantasy, science fiction or horror. Unsolicited mss welcome. Send query letter with first two chapters plus two-page synopsis (*s.a.e. essential*) in first instance. No reading fee. CLIENTS include Stephen Booth, Susan Clark, Tamara McKinley, Marguerite Patten, Danuta Reah, Kate Tremayne. *Commission* Home 10%; US 15%; Translation 20%. *Overseas associates* Thompson & Chris Literary Agency, USA; representatives in most other countries.

Mary Clemmey Literary Agency★

6 Dunollie Road, London NW5 2XP
☎020 7267 1290   Fax 020 7267 1290

Contact *Mary Clemmey*

FOUNDED 1992. *Handles* fiction and non-fiction – high-quality work with an international market. No science fiction, fantasy or children's books. TV, film, radio and theatre scripts from existing clients only. No unsolicited mss. Approach by letter only giving a description of the work in the first instance. S.a.e. essential. No reading fee. CLIENTS include Paul Gilroy, Sheila Kitzinger, Ray Shell, Elaine Showalter, Prof. David Wiggins; US & Canadian clients: The Bukowski Agency, **Frederick Hill Associates**, Lynn C. Franklin Associates Ltd, The Miller Agency, Roslyn Targ Literary Agency Inc. *Commission* Home 10%; US & Translation 20%. *Overseas Associate* Elaine Markson Literary Agency, New York.

Jonathan Clowes Ltd★

10 Iron Bridge House, Bridge Approach,
London NW1 8BD
☎020 7722 7674   Fax 020 7722 7677

Contacts *Ann Evans, Isobel Creed,*
Lisa Whadcock

FOUNDED 1960. Pronounced 'clewes'. Now one of the biggest fish in the pond, and not really for the untried unless they are true high-flyers. Fiction and non-fiction, plus scripts. No textbooks or children's. *Special interests* situation comedy, film and television rights. No unsolicited mss; authors come by recommendation or by successful follow-ups to preliminary letters. CLIENTS include David Bellamy, Len Deighton, Elizabeth Jane Howard, Doris Lessing, David Nobbs, Gillian White and the estate of Kingsley Amis. *Commission* Home & US 15%; Translation

19%. *Overseas associates* **Andrew Nurnberg Associates**; Sane Töregard Agency.

Elspeth Cochrane
Personal Management

14/2 Second Floor, South Bank Commercial Centre, 140 Battersea Park Road, London SW11 4NB

☎020 7622 0314 Fax 020 7622 5815

Email elspeth@elspethcochrane.co.uk

Contact *Elspeth Cochrane*

FOUNDED 1960. *Handles* fiction, non-fiction, biographies, screenplays. Subjects have included Richard Burton, Marlon Brando, Sean Connery, Clint Eastwood, Lord Olivier. Also scripts for all media, with special interest in drama. No unsolicited mss. Preliminary letter, synopsis and s.a.e. is essential in the first instance. CLIENTS include Royce Ryton, Robert Tanitch. *Commission* 12½% ('but this can change; the percentage is negotiable, as is the sum paid to the writer').

Rosica Colin Ltd

1 Clareville Grove Mews, London SW7 5AH

☎020 7370 1080 Fax 020 7244 6441

Contact *Joanna Marston*

FOUNDED 1949. *Handles* all full-length mss, plus theatre, film, television and sound broadcasting but few new writers being accepted. Preliminary letter with return postage essential; writers should outline their writing credits and whether their mss have previously been submitted elsewhere. May take 3–4 months to consider full mss; synopsis preferred in the first instance. No reading fee. *Commission* Home 10%; US 15%; Translation 20%.

Conville & Walsh Limited★

118–120 Wardour Street, London W1V 3LA

☎020 7287 3030 Fax 020 7287 4545

Email <firstname>@convilleandwalsh.com

Directors *Clare Conville, Patrick Walsh* (book rights), *Sam North* (film/TV rights)

ESTABLISHED in 2000 by Clare Conville (ex-**A. P. Watt**) and Patrick Walsh (ex-**Christopher Little Literary Agency**). *Handles* literary and commercial fiction plus serious, narrative and non-fiction. Clare Conville also represents many successful children's authors. Particularly interested in first novelists. CLIENTS Jez Alborough, Tom Burningham, Kate Cann, Tom Conran, Michael Cordy, Professor John Emsley, Steve Erikson, Katy Gardner, Christopher Hart, Dermot Healy, Jamie Holland, Tom Holland, Sebastian Horsley, David Huggins, Viven Kelly,

Guy Kennaway, P.J. Lynch, Hector Macdonald, Harland Miller, Jacqui Murhall, Rebecca Ray, Patrick Redmond, Candace Robb, Nicky Singer, Simon Singh, Doron Swade, Adam Wishart, Isabel Wolff and the estate of Francis Bacon. *Commission* Home 15%; US & Translation 20%.

Jane Conway-Gordon★

1 Old Compton Street, London W1D 5JA

☎020 7494 0148 Fax 020 7287 9264

Contact *Jane Conway-Gordon*

FOUNDED 1982. Works in association with **Andrew Mann Ltd**. *Handles* fiction and general non-fiction. No poetry or science fiction. Unsolicited mss welcome; preliminary letter and return postage essential. No reading fee. *Commission* Home 15%; US & Translation 20%. *Overseas associates* **McIntosh & Otis, Inc.**, New York; plus agencies throughout Europe and Japan.

Rupert Crew Ltd★

1A King's Mews, London WC1N 2JA

☎020 7242 8586 Fax 020 7831 7914

Email *(correspondence only)* rupertcrew@ compuserve.com

Contacts *Doreen Montgomery, Caroline Montgomery*

FOUNDED 1927. International representation, handling volume and subsidiary rights in fiction and non-fiction properties. No plays or poetry, journalism or short stories. Preliminary letter and return postage essential. No reading fee. *Commission* Home 15%; Elsewhere 20%.

Curtis Brown Group Ltd★

Haymarket House, 28/29 Haymarket, London SW1Y 4SP

☎020 7396 6600 Fax 020 7396 0110

Email cb@curtisbrown.co.uk

Also at: 37 Queensferry Street, Edinburgh EH2 4QS

☎0131 225 1286/1288 Fax 0131 225 1290

Chairman *Paul Scherer*

Group Managing Director *Jonathan Lloyd*

Directors *Mark Collingbourne* (Finance), *Fiona Inglis* (MD, Australia)

Books, London *Jonathan Lloyd, Jane Bradish-Ellames, Anna Davis, Jonny Geller, Hannah Griffiths, Ali Gunn, Camilla Hornby, Anthea Morton-Saner, Peter Robinson, Vivienne Schuster, Mike Shaw, Elizabeth Stevens*

Books, Edinburgh *Giles Gordon*

Foreign Rights *Diana Mackay, Carol Jackson, Kate Cooper*

Film/TV/Theatre *Nick Marston* (MD,
　Media Division), *Ben Hall, Peter Murphy,*
　Philip Patterson
Presenters *Sue Freathy, Julian Beynon*
Talent *Sue Latimer* (MD, Talent Division),
　Amanda Scott

Long-established literary agency, whose first sales
were made in 1899. Merged with John
Farquharson, forming the Curtis Brown Group
Ltd in 1989. Also represents directors, designers,
presenters and actors. *Handles* a wide range of
subjects including fiction, general non-fiction,
children's books and associated rights (including
multimedia) as well as film, theatre, TV and radio
scripts. Outline for non-fiction and short synopsis for fiction with two or three sample chapters
and autobiographical note. No reading fee.
Return postage essential. *Commission* Home
10%; US & Translation 20%. *Overseas associates* in
Australia, Canada and the US.

Judy Daish Associates Ltd

2 St Charles Place, London W10 6EG
☎020 8964 8811　Fax 020 8964 8966

Contacts *Judy Daish, Sara Stroud,*
　Deborah Harwood

FOUNDED 1978. Theatrical literary agent.
Handles scripts for film, TV, theatre and radio.
No books. Preliminary letter essential. No
unsolicited mss.

Caroline Davidson
Literary Agency

5 Queen Anne's Gardens, London W4 1TU
☎020 8995 5768　Fax 020 8994 2770

Contact *Caroline Davidson*

FOUNDED 1988. *Handles* fiction and non-
fiction, including archaeology, architecture,
art, astronomy, biography, cookery, crafts,
design, fitness, gardening, health, history,
medicine, music, natural history, reference, science, self-help and how-to, TV tie-ins. Many
highly illustrated books. Finished, polished first
novels positively welcomed. No occult, short
stories, children's, plays or poetry. Writers
should send an initial letter giving details of the
project, including the first 50 pages of their
novel if a fiction writer, together with c.v. and
return postage. Submissions without the latter
are not considered or returned. CLIENTS Susan
Aldridge, Peter Barham, Nigel Barlow, Anna
Beer, Amy Brown, Stuart Clark, Andrew
Dalby, Emma Donoghue, Robert Feather,
Anna Grayson, Anissa Helou, Paul Hillyard,
Tom Jaine, Huon Mallalieu, Simon Nolan,
Diane Purkiss, Roland Vernon. *Commission*

US, Home, Commonwealth, Translation
12½%; occasionally more (20%) if sub-agents
are involved.

Merric Davidson Literary Agency

12 Priors Heath, Goudhurst, Cranbrook, Kent
TN17 2RE
☎01580 212041　Fax 01580 212041
Email mdla@msn.com

Contacts *Merric Davidson, Wendy Suffield*

FOUNDED 1990. *Handles* fiction, general non-
fiction and children's books. No scripts. No
academic, short stories or articles. Particularly
keen on contemporary fiction. No unsolicited
mss. Send preliminary letter with synopsis and
biographical details. S.a.e. essential for
response. No reading fee. CLIENTS include
Valerie Blumenthal, Alys Clare, Francesca
Clementis, Murray Davies, Harold Elletson,
Alison Habens, Frankie Park, Mark Pepper,
Luke Sutherland. *Commission* Home 10%; US
15%; Translation 20%.

Felix de Wolfe

Garden Offices, 51 Maida Vale, London
W9 1SD
☎020 7289 5770　Fax 020 7289 5731

Contact *Felix de Wolfe*

FOUNDED 1938. *Handles* quality fiction only,
and scripts. No non-fiction or children's. No
unsolicited mss. No reading fee. CLIENTS
include Jan Butlin, Robert Cogo-Fawcett,
Carolina Giammetta, Brian Glover, Sheila
Goff, John Kershaw, Bill MacIlwraith, Angus
Mackay, Gerard McLarnon, Braham Murray,
Julian Slade, Malcolm Taylor, David
Thompson, Paul Todd, Dolores Walshe.
Commission Home 12½%; US 20%.

Dorian Literary Agency (DLA)

Upper Thornehill, 27 Church Road, St
Marychurch, Torquay, Devon TQ1 4QY
☎01803 312095　Fax 01803 312095

Contact *Dorothy Lumley*

FOUNDED 1986. *Handles* mainstream and commercial full-length adult fiction; specialities are
women's (including contemporary and sagas),
crime and thrillers; horror, science fiction and
fantasy. Also, limited non-fiction: primarily
self-help and media-related subjects. No
poetry, children's, theatrical scripts, short
stories, academic or technical. Introductory letter with synopsis/outline and first chapter
(with return postage) only, please. Equiries or
submissions by fax or e-mail not acceptable.

No reading fee. CLIENTS include Gillian Bradshaw, Stephen Jones, Brian Lumley, Amy Myers, Dee Williams. *Commission* Home 10%; US 15%; Translation 20–25%. Works with agents in most countries for translation.

Toby Eady Associates Ltd

9 Orme Court, London W2 4RL
☎020 7792 0092 Fax 020 7792 0879
Email toby@tobyeady.demon.co.uk *or*
  jessica@tobyeady.demon.co.uk
Website www.tobyeadyassociates.co.uk
Contacts *Toby Eady, Jessica Woollard*

Handles fiction, and non-fiction. Approach by personal recommendation. No film/TV scripts or poetry. *Special interests* China, Middle East, Africa, India. CLIENTS INCLUDE Jung Chang, Fadia Faqir, Liu Hong, Ma Jian, David Landau, Kenan Makiya, Nuha Al Radi, Lin Ping, Amir Taheri, Annie Wang, Xinran Xue, Bernard Cornwell, Mark Burnell, John Carey, Kuki Gallmann, Francesca Marciano, Shyama Perera, Fiammetta Rocco, Ann Wroe. *Commission* Home 10–15%; Elsewhere 20%. *Overseas associates* USA: Ed Breslin; France: La Nouvelle Agence; Germany: Mohrbooks; Holland: Jan Michael; Scandinavia, Italy, Spain: Rosie Buckman; China: Joanne Wang.

Eddison Pearson Ltd

3rd Floor, 22 Upper Grosvenor Street,
London W1X 9PB
☎020 7629 2414 Fax 020 7629 7181
Email box1@eddisonpearson.com
Contact *Clare Pearson*

FOUNDED 1995. *Handles* children's books, literary fiction and non-fiction, contemporary fiction, poetry for the literary market. Please enquire in writing, enclosing s.a.e. E-mail enquiries also welcome. No unsolicited mss; send a brief sample of work in the first instance. No reading fee. *Commission* Home 10%; US & Translation 15%.

Edwards Fuglewicz★

49 Great Ormond Street, London
WC1N 3HZ
☎020 7405 6725 Fax 020 7405 6726
Contacts *Ros Edwards, Helenka Fuglewicz*

FOUNDED 1996. *Handles* fiction (literary and commercial; not science fiction, horror or fantasy); non-fiction: biography, history, popular culture. No scripts. Unsolicited mss welcome; approach in writing in the first instance with covering letter giving brief c.v., up to three

chapters and a synopsis (enclose s.a.e. for return of mss); disks and e-mail submissions not acceptable. No reading fee. *Commission* Home 10%; US & Translation 20%.

Faith Evans Associates★

27 Park Avenue North, London N8 7RU
☎020 8340 9920 Fax 020 8340 9910
Contact *Faith Evans*

FOUNDED 1987. Small agency. *Handles* fiction and non-fiction. New clients by personal recommendation only; no unsolicited mss or phone calls, please. CLIENTS include Melissa Benn, Madeleine Bourdouxhe, Eleanor Bron, Carolyn Cassady, Caroline Conran, Helen Falconer, Midge Gillies, Ed Glinert, Helena Kennedy, Cleo Laine, Seumas Milne, Tom Paulin, Christine Purkis, Sheila Rowbotham, Lorna Sage, Hwee Hwee Tan, Marion Urch, Harriet Walter, Elizabeth Wilson, Andrea Weiss. *Commission* Home 15%; US & Translation 20%. *Overseas associates* worldwide.

Lisa Eveleigh Literary Agency★

3rd Floor, 11/12 Dover Street, London
W1S 4LJ
☎020 7399 2801 Fax 020 7399 2803
Email eveleigh@dial.pipex.com
Contact *Lisa Eveleigh*

FOUNDED 1996. *Handles* literary and commercial fiction and non-fiction. No scripts, science fiction or historical fiction. No reading fee. CLIENTS include Christina Balit, Philip Casey, Paul Heiney, Lisa Kopper, Irma Kurtz, Margaret Leroy, Libby Purves, Grace Wynne-Jones. *Commission* Home 10%; US & Translation 20%. *Associates* Translation: **Gillon Aitken Associates Ltd**; US: Anderson Grinberg Literary Management.

John Farquharson★

See **Curtis Brown Group Ltd**

Film Rights Ltd

See **Laurence Fitch Ltd**

Laurence Fitch Ltd

Southbank Commercial Centre, 140 Battersea Park Road, London SW11 4NB
☎020 7720 6000
Email information@laurencefitch.com
Website www.laurencefitch.com
Contact *Brendan Davis*

FOUNDED 1952, incorporating the London Play Company (1922) and in association with Film

Rights Ltd (1932). *Handles* children's and horror books, scripts for theatre, film, TV and radio only. No unsolicited mss. Send synopsis with sample scene(s) in the first instance. No reading fee. CLIENTS include Carlo Ardito, Hindi Brooks, John Chapman & Ray Cooney, John Graham, Glyn Robbins, Gene Stone, the estate of Dodie Smith, Edward Taylor. *Commission* UK 10%; Overseas 15%. *Overseas associates* worldwide.

Jill Foster Ltd
9 Barb Mews, Brook Green, London W6 7PA
☎020 7602 1263 Fax 020 7602 9336
Email agents@jfl.uninet.co.uk
Contacts *Jill Foster, Alison Finch, Simone Bassi, Simon Williamson*

FOUNDED 1976. *Handles* scripts for TV, drama and comedy. No fiction, short stories or poetry. No unsolicited mss; approach by letter in the first instance. No reading fee. CLIENTS include Colin Bostock-Smith, Ian Brown, Jan Etherington and Gavin Petrie, Phil Ford, Rob Gittins, Jenny Lecoat, Peter Tilbury, Susan Wilkins. *Commission* Home 12½%; Books, US & Translation 15%.

Fox & Howard Literary Agency
4 Bramerton Street, London SW3 5JX
☎020 7352 8691 Fax 020 7352 8691
Contacts *Chelsey Fox, Charlotte Howard*

FOUNDED 1992. A small agency, specialising in non-fiction, that prides itself on 'working closely with its authors'. *Handles* biography, history and popular culture, reference, business, gardening, mind, body and spirit, self-help, health. No unsolicited mss; send letter, synopsis and sample chapter with s.a.e. for response. No reading fee. CLIENTS Sarah Bartlett, Simon Collin, Professor Bruce King, Tony Clayton Lea, Marion Shoard, Maryon Stewart, Jane Struthers. *Commission* Home 10–15%; US & Translation 20%.

French's
78 Loudoun Road, London NW8 0NA
☎020 7483 4269 Fax 020 7722 0754
Contact *Mark Taylor*

FOUNDED 1973. *Handles* fiction and non-fiction; and scripts for all media, especially novels and screenplays. No religious or medical books. No unsolicited mss. 'For unpublished authors we offer a reading service at £65 per ms, exclusive of postage.' Interested authors should write in the first instance. *Commission* Home 10%.

Futerman, Rose & Associates★
17 Deanhill Road, London SW14 7DQ
☎020 8286 4860 Fax 020 8286 4861
Email GRose17@aol.com
Website www.futermanrose.co.uk
Contact *Guy Rose*

FOUNDED 1984. *Handles* scripts for film, TV and theatre. Commercial fiction and non-fiction with film potential; biography and show business. Send preliminary letter with a brief resumé, detailed synopsis and s.a.e. CLIENTS include Kevan Barker, Alexandra Connor, Diana Douglas Darrid, Iain Duncan Smith, Lee Dunne, Kingsley Fielding, Russell Warren Howe, Ronnie Kirkwood, Sue Lenier, Angela Meredith, Gordon Thomas, Judy Upton, Simon Woodham. *Commission* Literature: Home 12½%; Overseas: 17½%. Drama/Screenplays: Home 15%; Overseas 20%. *Overseas associates* worldwide.

Jüri Gabriel
35 Camberwell Grove, London SE5 8JA
☎020 7703 6186 Fax 020 7703 6186
Contact *Jüri Gabriel*

Handles quality fiction, non-fiction and (almost exclusively for existing clients) film, TV and radio rights/scripts. Jüri Gabriel worked in television, wrote books for 20 years and is chairman of **Dedalus** publishers. No short stories, articles, verse or books for children. Unsolicited mss ('two-page synopsis and three sample chapters in first instance, please') welcome if accompanied by return postage and letter giving sufficient information about author's writing experience, aims, etc. CLIENTS include Nigel Cawthorne, Diana Constance, Miriam Dunne, Pat Gray, Duncan Green, James Hawes, Robert Irwin, Mike Jay, David Madsen, Richard Mankiewicz, David Miller, Prof. Cedric Mims, John Outram, Dr Stefan Szymanski, Frances Treanor, Dr Terence White, Dr Robert Youngson. *Commission* Home 10%; US & Translation 20%.

Eric Glass Ltd
28 Berkeley Square, London W1X 6HD
☎020 7629 7162 Fax 020 7499 6780
Contact *Janet Glass*

FOUNDED 1934. *Handles* fiction, non-fiction and scripts for publication or production in all media. No poetry, short stories or children's works. No unsolicited mss. No reading fee. CLIENTS include Marc Camoletti, Charles Dyer and the estates of Rodney Ackland, Jean Cocteau, Philip King, Robin Maugham,

Beverley Nichols, Jack Popplewell, Jean-Paul Sartre, Arthur Schnitzler. *Commission* Home 10%; US & Translation 20%. *Overseas associates* in the US, Australia, France, Germany, Greece, Holland, Italy, Japan, Poland, Scandinavia, South Africa, Spain.

David Godwin Associates
55 Monmouth Street, London WC2H 9DG
☎020 7240 9992 Fax 020 7395 6110
Contacts *David Godwin, Penny Jones*
FOUNDED 1996. *Handles* literary and general fiction, non-fiction, biography. No scripts, science fiction or children's. No reading fee. Send covering letter with first three chapters. *Commission* Home 10%; Overseas 20%.

Annette Green Authors' Agent
6 Montem Street, London N4 3BE
☎020 7281 0009 Fax 020 7686 5884
Email agreen@literaryagency.freeserve.co.uk
Contact *Address material to the Company*
FOUNDED 1998. *Handles* literary and general fiction and non-fiction, upmarket popular culture, biography and memoirs. No dramatic scripts, poetry, or children's. Preliminary letter and s.a.e. essential. No reading fee. CLIENTS include Nick Barlay, Bill Broady, Justin Hill, Max Kinnings, Maria McCann, Ian Marchant, Owen Sheers, Elizabeth Woodcraft. *Commission* Home 15%; US & Translation 20%.

Christine Green Authors' Agent★
40 Doughty Street, London WC1N 2LF
☎020 7831 4956 Fax 020 7405 3935
Contact *Christine Green*
FOUNDED 1984. *Handles* fiction (general and literary) and general non-fiction. No scripts, poetry or children's. No unsolicited mss; initial letter and synopsis preferred. No reading fee but return postage essential. *Commission* Home 10%; US & Translation 20%.

Louise Greenberg★
The End House, Church Crescent, London N3 1BG
☎020 8349 1179 Fax 020 8343 4559
Email louisegreenberg@msn.com
Contact *Louise Greenberg*
FOUNDED 1997. *Handles* literary fiction and non-fiction. No poetry, health or sport. No reading fee. Unsolicited mss welcome but send letter in first instance; s.a.e. essential. *Commission* Home 10%; US 15%; Translation 20%. *Dramatic associate* **Micheline Steinberg Playwrights**.

Greene & Heaton Ltd★
37 Goldhawk Road, London W12 8QQ
☎020 8749 0315 Fax 020 8749 0318
Contacts *Carol Heaton, Judith Murray, Antony Topping*
A small agency with a varied list of clients. *Handles* fiction (no science fiction, fantasy or children's books) and general non-fiction. No original scripts for theatre, film or TV. No reply to unsolicited submissions without s.a.e. and/or return postage. CLIENTS include Mark Barrowcliffe, Geraldine Bedell, Bill Bryson, Jan Dalley, Marcus du Sautoy, Colin Forbes, Michael Frayn, P.D. James, Mary Morrissy, William Shawcross, Sarah Waters. *Commission* Home 10%; US & Translation 20%.

Gregory & Radice Authors' Agents★
3 Barb Mews, London W6 7PA
☎020 7610 4676 Fax 020 7610 4686
Email info@gregoryradice.co.uk
Website www.gregoryradice.co.uk
Contact *Jane Gregory*
Editorial *Suzanne Amphlet, Lisanne Radice* (consultant)
Rights *Jane Barlow*
FOUNDED 1987. *Handles* all kinds of fiction and general non-fiction. *Special interest* fiction – literary, commercial, crime, suspense and thrillers. 'We are particularly interested in books which will also sell to publishers abroad.' No original plays, film or TV scripts (only published books are sold to film and TV). No science fiction, fantasy, poetry, academic or children's books. No reading fee. Editorial advice given to own authors. No unsolicited mss; send a preliminary letter with c.v., synopsis, first three chapters and future writing plans (plus return postage). Short submissions by fax or e-mail. *Commission* Home 20%; US, Translation, Radio/TV/Film 20%. Is well represented throughout Europe, Asia and US.

David Grossman Literary Agency Ltd
118b Holland Park Avenue, London W11 4UA
☎020 7221 2770 Fax 020 7221 1445
Contact *Material should be addressed to the Submissions Dept.*
FOUNDED 1976. *Handles* full-length fiction and general non-fiction – good writing of all kinds and anything healthily controversial. No verse or technical books for students. No original screenplays or teleplays (only works existing in volume

form are sold for performance rights). Generally works with published writers of fiction only but 'truly original, well-written novels from beginners' will be considered. Best approach by preliminary letter giving full description of the work and, in the case of fiction, with the first 50 pages. All material must be accompanied by return postage. No approaches or submissions by fax or e-mail. No unsolicited mss. No reading fee. *Commission* Rates vary for different markets. *Overseas associates* throughout Europe, Asia, Brazil and the US.

The Rod Hall Agency Limited

7 Goodge Place, London W1T 4SF
☎020 7637 0706 Fax 020 7637 0807
Email office@rodhallagency.com
Website www.rodhallagency.com

Contacts *Rod Hall, Clare Barker, Charlotte Mann*

FOUNDED 1997. *Handles* drama for film, TV and theatre. Does not represent writers of episodes for TV series where the format is provided but represents originators of series. No stage musicals. CLIENTS include Simon Beaufoy (*The Full Monty*), Jeremy Brock (*Mrs Brown*), Lee Hall (*Billy Elliot*), Liz Lochhead (*Perfect Days*), Martin McDonagh (*The Beauty Queen of Leenane*). Introductory letter required with brief description of the work to be considered together with c.v. No reading fee. *Commission* Home 10%; US 15%; Translation 20%.

Margaret Hanbury
Literary Agency*

27 Walcot Square, London SE11 4UB
☎020 7735 7680 Fax 020 7793 0316
Email maggie@mhanbury.demon.co.uk

Contact *Margaret Hanbury*

Personally run agency representing quality fiction and non-fiction. No plays, scripts, poetry, children's books, fantasy, horror. No unsolicited approaches at present. *Commission* Home 15%; Overseas 20%.

Roger Hancock Ltd

4 Water Lane, London NW1 8NZ
☎020 7267 4418 Fax 020 7267 0705
Email hancockltd@aol.com

Contact *Material should be addressed to the Company*

FOUNDED 1961. *Special interests* drama and light entertainment. Scripts only. No books. Unsolicited mss not welcome. Initial phone call required. No reading fee. *Commission* 10%.

Antony Harwood Limited

109 Riverbank House, 1 Putney Bridge Approach, London SW6 3JD
☎020 7384 9209 Fax 020 7384 9206
Email mail@antonyharwood.com

Contacts *Antony Harwood, James Macdonald Lockhart*

FOUNDED 2000. *Handles* fiction and non-fiction. Send letter and synopsis with return postage in the first instance. No reading fee. CLIENTS Alan Hollinghurst, A.L. Kennedy, Tim Parks, Douglas Kennedy, Chris Manby, Peter F. Hamilton. *Commission* Home 10%; US 15%; Translation 20%.

A.M. Heath & Co. Ltd★

79 St Martin's Lane, London WC2N 4RE
☎020 7836 4271 Fax 020 7497 2561

Contacts *Bill Hamilton, Sara Fisher, Sarah Molloy, Victoria Hobbs*

FOUNDED 1919. *Handles* fiction, general non-fiction and children's. No dramatic scripts, poetry or short stories. Preliminary letter and synopsis essential. No reading fee. CLIENTS Joan Aiken, Christopher Andrew, Bella Bathurst, Anita Brookner, Helen Cresswell, Patricia Duncker, Geoff Dyer, Katie Fforde, Lesley Glaister, Graham Hancock, Hilary Mantel, Hilary Norman, Susan Price, John Sutherland, Adam Thorpe, Barbara Trapido. *Commission* Home 10–15%; US & Translation 20%; Film & TV 15%. *Overseas associates* in the US, Europe, South America, Japan and the Far East.

Rupert Heath Literary Agency

The Beeches, Furzedown Lane, Amport, Hampshire SP11 8BW
☎01264 773583 Fax 01264 771142
Email rupheath@hotmail.com

Contact *Rupert Heath*

FOUNDED 2000. *Handles* literary and general fiction and non-fiction, including history, biography and autobiography, current affairs, popular science, the arts and some popular culture. No scripts, short stories, poetry or children's. Approach with e-mail or letter (synopsis, sample champter and s.a.e.). No reading fee. *Commission* Home 15%; US & Translation 20%. *Overseas associates* worldwide.

David Higham Associates Ltd★

5–8 Lower John Street, Golden Square, London W1F 9HA
☎020 7437 7888 Fax 020 7437 1072

Scripts *Nicky Lund, Georgina Ruffhead, Gemma Hirst*
Books *Anthony Goff, Bruce Hunter, Jacqueline Korn, Caroline Walsh, Daniela Bernardelle*

FOUNDED 1935. *Handles* fiction and general non-fiction: biography, history, current affairs, etc. Also scripts. Preliminary letter with synopsis essential in first instance. No reading fee. CLIENTS include John le Carré, Stephen Fry, Jane Green, James Herbert, Jeremy Paxman. *Commission* Home 10%; US & Translation 20%.

Vanessa Holt Ltd★

59 Crescent Road, Leigh-on-Sea, Essex SS9 2PF
☎01702 473787 Fax 01702 471890
Email vanessa@holtlimited.freeserve.co.uk

Contact *Vanessa Holt*

FOUNDED 1989. *Handles* general fiction, non-fiction and non-illustrated children's books. No scripts, poetry, academic or technical. *Specialises* in crime fiction, commercial and literary fiction, and particularly interested in books with potential for sales abroad and/or to TV. No unsolicited mss. Approach by letter in first instance; s.a.e. essential. No reading fee. *Commission* Home 15%; US & Translation 20%; Radio/TV/Film 15%. Represented in all foreign markets.

Kate Hordern Literary Agency

18 Mortimer Road, Clifton, Bristol BS8 4EY
☎0117 923 9368 Fax 0117 973 1941
Email katehordern@compuserve.com

Contact *Kate Hordern*

FOUNDED 1999. *Handles* quality literary and commercial fiction including women's, suspense and genre fiction; also general non-fiction including history, cultural history, popular science. No children's books. Approach in writing in the first instance with details of project. Synopsis required for fiction; proposal/chapter breakdown for non-fiction. Sample chapters on request only. S.a.e. essential. No reading fee. CLIENTS Richard Bassett, Frances Chapman, Jeff Dawson, Paul Grieve. *Commission* Home 15%; US & Translation 20%. *Overseas associates* Carmen Balcells Agency, Spain; Synopsis Agency, Russia and various agencies in Asia.

Valerie Hoskins Associates

20 Charlotte Street, London W1T 2NA
☎020 7637 4490 Fax 020 7637 4493
Email vha@vhassociates.co.uk

Contacts *Valerie Hoskins, Rebecca Watson*

FOUNDED 1983. *Handles* scripts for film, TV and radio. *Special interests* feature films, animation and TV. No unsolicited scripts; preliminary letter of introduction essential. No reading fee. *Commission* Home 12½%; US 20% (maximum).

Tanja Howarth Literary Agency★

19 New Row, London WC2N 4LA
☎020 7240 5553/7240 6696
Fax 020 7379 0969
Email tanja.howarth@virgin.net

Contact *Tanja Howarth*

FOUNDED 1970. Interested in taking on both fiction and non-fiction from British writers. No children's books, plays or poetry, but all other subjects considered providing the treatment is intelligent. *No unsolicited mss.* Preliminary letter preferred. No reading fee. Also an established agent for foreign literature, particularly from the German language. *Commission* Home 15%; Translation 20%.

ICM

Oxford House, 76 Oxford Street, London W1D 1BS
☎020 7636 6565 Fax 020 7323 0101

Contacts *Greg Hunt, Cathy King, Hugo Young, Michael McCoy, Sue Rodgers, Jessica Sykes*

FOUNDED 1973. *Handles* film, TV and theatre scripts. No books. No unsolicited mss. Preliminary letter essential. No reading fee. *Commission* 10%. *Overseas associates* ICM, New York/Los Angeles.

IMG Literary UK

The Pier House, Strand on the Green, Chiswick, London W4 3NN
☎020 8233 5000 Fax 020 8233 5001

IMG Literary US, 825 Seventh Avenue, Ninth Floor, New York, NY 10009
☎001 212 489 5400 Fax 001 212 246 1118

Chairman *Mark H. McCormack*
Agents *Sarah Wooldridge (UK), Mark Reiter, David McCormick, Carolyn Krupp, Lisa Queen, Susan Reed (US), Fumiko Matsuki (Japan)*

Handles celebrity books, sports-related books, commercial fiction, non-fiction and how-to business books. No theatre, children's, poetry or academic books. *Commission* Home & US 20%; Elsewhere 25%.

Michael Imison Playwrights Ltd

See **Alan Brodie Representation Ltd**

Intercontinental Literary Agency★

33 Bedford Street, London WC2E 9ED
☎020 7379 6611 Fax 020 7379 6790
Email ila@ila-agency.co.uk

Contacts *Anthony Guest Gornall, Nicki Kennedy*

FOUNDED 1965. *Handles* translation rights only for, among others, the authors of **Peters Fraser & Dunlop**, London; **Lucas Alexander Whitley**, London; Harold Matson Co. Inc., New York.

International Scripts

1A Kidbrooke Park Road, Blackheath,
London SE3 0LR
☎020 8319 8666 Fax 020 8319 0801

Contacts *Bob Tanner, Pat Hornsey, Jill Lawson*

FOUNDED 1979 by Bob Tanner. *Handles* most types of books (non-fiction and fiction) and scripts for most media. No poetry, articles or short stories. Preliminary letter plus s.a.e. required. CLIENTS include Jane Adams, Zita Adamson, Simon Clark, Cory Daniells, Paul Devereux, Ed Gorman, Peter Haining, Julie Harris, Robert A. Heinlein, Anna Jacobs, Richard Laymon, Nick Oldham, Mary Ryan, John and Anne Spencer, Janet Woods, **Barrons** (USA), Masquerade Books (USA). *Commission* Home 15%; US & Translation 20%. *Overseas associates* include Ralph Vicinanza, USA; Thomas Schlück, Germany; Eliane Benisti, France.

Jankow & Nesbit (UK) Ltd

29 Adam & Eve Mews, London W8 6UG
☎020 7376 2733 Fax 020 7376 2915
Email queries@janklow.co.uk

Contact *Tif Loehnis*

FOUNDED 2000. *Handles* fiction and non-fiction; commercial and literary. No unsolicited mss. Send full outline (non-fiction), synopsis and three sample chapters (fiction) plus informative covering letter and return postage. US and foreign rights handled by **Janklow & Nesbit Associates** in New York.

John Johnson
(Authors' Agent) Limited★

Clerkenwell House, 45/47 Clerkenwell Green, London EC1R 0HT
☎020 7251 0125 Fax 020 7251 2172
Email johnjohnson@btinternet.com

Contacts *Andrew Hewson, Margaret Hewson, Elizabeth Fairbairn*

FOUNDED 1956. *Handles* general fiction and non-fiction. No science fiction, technical or academic material. Scripts from existing clients only. No unsolicited mss; send a preliminary letter and s.a.e. in the first instance. No reading fee. *Commission* Home 10%; US 15–20%; Translation 20%.

Jane Judd Literary Agency★

18 Belitha Villas, London N1 1PD
☎020 7607 0273 Fax 020 7607 0623

Contact *Jane Judd*

FOUNDED 1986. *Handles* general fiction and non-fiction: women's fiction, crime, thrillers, literary fiction, humour, biography, investigative journalism, health, women's interests and travel. 'Looking for good contemporary women's fiction but not Mills & Boon-type.' No scripts, academic, gardening or DIY. Approach with letter, including synopsis, first chapter and return postage. Initial telephone call helpful in the case of non-fiction. CLIENTS include Patrick Anthony, the John Brunner estate, Andy Dougan, Jill Mansell, Jonathon Porritt, Rosie Rushton, Manda Scott. *Commission* Home 10%; US & Translation 20%.

Juvenilia

Avington, Near Winchester, Hampshire
SO21 1DB
☎01962 779656 Fax 01962 779656
Email juvenilia@clara.co.uk

Contact *Rosemary Bromley*

FOUNDED 1973. *Handles* young/teen fiction and picture books; non-fiction and scripts for TV and radio. No poetry or short stories unless part of a collection or picture book material. No unsolicited mss. Send preliminary letter with full details of work and biographical outline in first instance. Preliminary letters unaccompanied by return postage will not be answered. No enquiries by phone or fax. CLIENTS include Paul Aston, Elisabeth Beresford, Linda Birch, Denis Bond, Terry Deary, Steve Donald, Ann Evans, Gaye Hicyilmaz, Tom Holt, Tony Maddox, Phil McMylor, Elizabeth Pewsey, Saviour Pirotta, Eira Reeves, Kelvin Reynolds, James Riordan, Peter Riley, Malcolm Rose, Cathy Simpson, Margaret Stuart Barry, Keith West. *Commission* Home 10%; US 15%; Translation 20%.

Tamar Karet

56 Priory Road, London N8 7EX
☎020 8340 6460
Email tamar@btinternet.com

Contact *Tamar Karet*

New agency started in 2001 by publisher with particular experience of fiction, social affairs and illustrated books. *Specialises* in fiction, travel, leisure, health, cookery, biography, history, social affairs and politics. No academic, poetry, science fiction, horror, militaria or scripts. No unsolicited mss; send synopsis and sample with s.a.e. *Commission* Home 15%; US & Translation 20%.

Michelle Kass Associates★
36–38 Glasshouse Street, London W1B 5DL
☎020 7439 1624 Fax 020 7734 3394
Contacts *Michelle Kass, Sarah Spedding*

FOUNDED 1991. *Handles* literary fiction and film primarily. Approach with telephone call/explanatory letter in the first instance. No reading fee. *Commission* Home 10%; US & Translation 15–20%.

Frances Kelly★
111 Clifton Road, Kingston upon Thames, Surrey KT2 6PL
☎020 8549 7830 Fax 020 8547 0051
Contact *Frances Kelly*

FOUNDED 1978. *Handles* non-fiction, including illustrated: biography, history, art, self-help, food & wine, complementary medicine and therapies, finance and business books; and academic non-fiction in all disciplines. No scripts except for existing clients. No unsolicited mss. Approach by letter with brief description of work or synopsis, together with c.v. and return postage. *Commission* Home 10%; US & Translation 20%.

Paul Kiernan
PO Box 120, London SW3 4LU
☎020 7352 5562 Fax 020 7351 5986
Contact *Paul Kiernan*

FOUNDED 1990. *Handles* fiction and non-fiction, including autobiography and biography, plus specialist writers like cookery or gardening. Also scripts for TV, film, radio and theatre (TV and film scripts from book-writing clients only). No unsolicited mss. Preferred approach is by letter or personal introduction. Letters should include synopsis and brief biography. No reading fee. CLIENTS include K. Banta, Lord Chalfont, Ambassador Walter J.P. Curley, Sir Paul Fox. *Commission* Home 15%; US 20%.

Knight Features
20 Crescent Grove, London SW4 7AH
☎020 7622 1467 Fax 020 7622 1522
Contacts *Peter Knight, Gaby Martin, Ann King-Hall, Andrew Knight*

FOUNDED 1985. *Handles* motor sports, cartoon books, puzzles, business, history, factual and biographical material. No poetry, science fiction or cookery. No unsolicited mss. Send letter accompanied by c.v. and s.a.e. with synopsis of proposed work. CLIENTS include David Kerr Cameron, Frank Dickens, Christopher Hilton, Gray Jolliffe, Angus McGill, Chris Maslanka, Barbara Minto. *Commission* dependent upon authors and territories. *Overseas associates* United Media, US; Auspac Media, Australia.

Labour and Management Limited
Milton House, Milton Street, Waltham Abbey, Essex EN9 1EZ
☎01992 711511/614527
Fax 01992 711511/614527
Email TriciaSumner@email.msn.com
Contact *Tricia Sumner*

FOUNDED 1995. *Specialises* in literary fiction, theatre, TV, radio and film. *Special interests* in multicultural, gay, feminist and anti-establishment writing. No new authors taken on except by recommendation. No unsolicited mss. CLIENTS include Marion Baraitser, Kathleen Kiirik Bryson, John R. Gordon, Barry Grossman, Sophia Kingshill, Angela Lanyon, Roland Moore, Catherine Muschamp. *Commission* Home 12½%; Overseas 20%.

Cat Ledger Literary Agency★
33 Percy Street, London W1P 9FG
☎020 7436 5030 Fax 020 7631 4273
Contact *Cat Ledger*

FOUNDED 1996. *Handles* non-fiction: popular culture – film, music, sport, travel, humour, biography, politics; investigative journalism; fiction (non-genre). No scripts. No children's, poetry, fantasy, science fiction, romance. No unsolicited mss; approach with preliminary letter, synopsis and s.a.e. No reading fee. *Commission* Home 10%; US & Translation 20%.

Barbara Levy Literary Agency★
64 Greenhill, Hampstead High Street, London NW3 5TZ
☎020 7435 9046 Fax 020 7431 2063
Contacts *Barbara Levy, John Selby*

FOUNDED 1986. *Handles* general fiction, non-fiction, and film and TV rights. No unsolicited mss. Send detailed preliminary letter in the first instance. No reading fee. *Commission* Home 10%; US 20%; Translation by arrangement, in conjunction with **The Marsh Agency**. *US associate* Arcadia Ltd, New York.

Limelight Management★
33 Newman Street, London W1P 3PD
☎020 7637 2529 Fax 020 7637 2538
Email limelight.management@virgin.net

Contacts *Fiona Lindsay, Linda Shanks*

FOUNDED 1991. *Handles* general non-fiction and fiction books; cookery, gardening, antiques, interior design, wine, art and crafts and health. No TV, film, radio or theatre. Not interested in science fiction, short stories, plays, children's. *Specialises* in illustrated books. Unsolicited mss welcome; send preliminary letter (s.a.e. essential). No reading fee. *Commission* Home 15%; US & Translation 20%.

Litopia® Corporation Ltd
186 Bickenhall Mansions, Bickenhall Street, London W1V 6BX
☎020 7224 1748 Fax 020 7224 1802
Email info@litopia.com
Website www.litopia.com

Managing Director *Peter Cox*

FOUNDED in 1993 by author Peter Cox to manage a restricted number of clients. 'We are prepared to consider any author, known or unknown, with major international potential.' Sells directly to key overseas markets with particular emphasis on the USA. 'Litopia personnel visit New York once a month.' No radio or theatre scripts. No unsolicited mss; prospective clients must follow the submissions procedure as explained on Litopia's website. No reading fee. CLIENTS Peggy Brusseau, Brian Clegg, John Collis, Senator Orrin Hatch, Commodore Scott Jones, USN, Jeffrey Kottler, Dorree Lynn, Michael J. Nelson, Michelle Paver, Tom Stevenson. *Commission* by negotiation.

The Christopher Little Literary Agency★
10 Eel Brook Studios, 125 Moore Park Road, London SW6 4PS
☎020 7736 4455 Fax 020 7736 4490
Email <firstname>@christopherlittle.net

Contacts *Christopher Little, Jeanine Berigliano, Kellee Nunley*

FOUNDED 1979. *Handles* commercial and literary full-length fiction and non-fiction. No poetry, plays, science fiction, fantasy, textbooks, illustrated children's or short stories. Film scripts for established clients only. No unsolicited submissions. *Commission* Home 15%; US, Canada, Translation, Audio, Motion Picture 20%.

London Independent Books
26 Chalcot Crescent, London NW1 8YD
☎020 7706 0486 Fax 020 7724 3122

Proprietor *Carolyn Whitaker*

FOUNDED 1971. A self-styled 'small and idiosyncratic' agency. *Handles* fiction and non-fiction reflecting the tastes of the proprietors. All subjects considered (except computer books and young children's), providing the treatment is strong and saleable. Scripts handled only if by existing clients. *Special interests* boats, travel, travelogues, commercial fiction. No unsolicited mss; letter, synopsis and first two chapters with return postage the best approach. No reading fee. *Commission* Home 15%; US & Translation 20%.

The Andrew Lownie Literary Agency★
17 Sutherland Street, London SW1V 4JU
☎020 7828 1274 Fax 020 7828 7608
Email lownie@globalnet.co.uk
Website www.andrewlownie.co.uk

Contact *Andrew Lownie*

FOUNDED 1988. *Specialises* in non-fiction, especially history, biography, current affairs, military history, UFOs, reference and packaging celebrities and journalists for the book market. No poetry, short stories or science fiction. Formerly a journalist, publisher and himself the author of 12 non-fiction books, Andrew Lownie's CLIENTS include Theo Aronson, Ken Bates, Juliet Barker, the Marquess of Bath, Guy Bellamy, the Joyce Cary estate, Jonathan Fryer, Timothy Good, Gloria Hunniford, Leo McKinstry, Patrick MacNee, Norma Major, Sir John Mills, Nick Pope, John Rae, Richard Rudgley, Desmond Seward, Jeremy Thorpe, Alan Whicker, Lawrence James, editors of the *Oxford Classical Dictionary* and *Cambridge Guide to Literature in English*. Approach with letter, synopsis, sample chapter and s.a.e. Translation rights handled by **The Marsh Agency**. *Commission* Worldwide 15%.

Lucas Alexander Whitley★
(incorporating **Jacintha Alexander Associates**)
14 Vernon Street, London W14 0RJ
☎020 7471 7900 Fax 020 7471 7910
Email <firstname>@lawagency.co.uk

Contacts *Mark Lucas, Julian Alexander, Araminta Whitley, Annabel Hardman, Celia Hayley, Lucinda Cook, Peta Nightingale, Rowan Routh, Matthew Lawrence*

FOUNDED 1996. *Handles* full-length commercial

and literary fiction and non-fiction. No plays, poetry, textbooks, children's books or fantasy. Film and TV scripts handled for established clients only. Unsolicited mss considered; send brief covering letter, short synopsis and two sample chapters. S.a.e. essential. No e-mailed submissions. *Commission* Home 15%; US & Translation 20%. *Overseas associates* worldwide.

Lutyens and Rubinstein★
231 Westbourne Park Road, London W11 1EB
☎020 7792 4855 Fax 020 7792 4833

Partners *Sarah Lutyens, Felicity Rubinstein*
Submissions *Susannah Godman*

FOUNDED 1993. *Handles* adult fiction and non-fiction books. No TV, film, radio or theatre scripts. Unsolicited mss accepted; send introductory letter, c.v., two chapters and return postage for all material submitted. No reading fee. *Commission* Home 15%; US & Translation 20%.

Duncan McAra
28 Beresford Gardens, Edinburgh EH5 3ES
☎0131 552 1558 Fax 0131 552 1558

Contact *Duncan McAra*

FOUNDED 1988. *Handles* fiction (literary fiction) and non-fiction, including art, architecture, archaeology, biography, military, travel and books of Scottish interest. Preliminary letter, synopsis and sample chapter (including return postage) essential. No reading fee. *Commission* Home 10%; Overseas 20%.

Bill McLean
Personal Management Ltd
23B Deodar Road, London SW15 2NP
☎020 8789 8191

Contact *Bill McLean*

FOUNDED 1972. *Handles* scripts for all media. No books. No unsolicited mss. Phone call or introductory letter essential. No reading fee. CLIENTS include Dwynwen Berry, Graham Carlisle, Jeff Dodds, Jane Galletly, Patrick Jones, Lynn Robertson Hay, Tony Jordan, Bill Lyons, Annie Marshall, John Maynard, Michael McStay, Les Miller, Ian Rowlands, Jeffrey Segal, Ronnie Smith, Barry Thomas, Frank Vickery, Mark Wheatley. *Commission* Home 10%.

McLean and Slora Agency
20A Eildon Street, Edinburgh EH3 5JU
☎0131 556 3368 Fax 0131 624 4029

Contact *Barbara McLean*

FOUNDED 1996. *Handles* literary fiction; some non-fiction including biography. *Specialises* in

books of Scottish interest. No science fiction, cookery, children's books, poetry or scripts. No unsolicited mss. Send preliminary letter, synopsis, sample chapter(s); s.a.e. essential. No initial reading fee. CLIENTS Tom Bryan, John Herdman, Ruari McLean. *Commission* Home 10%; US & Translation 20%.

Eunice McMullen
Children's Literary Agent Ltd
38 Clewer Hill Road, Windsor, Berkshire SL4 4BW
☎01753 830348 Fax 01753 833459

Contact *Eunice McMullen*

FOUNDED 1992. *Handles* all types of children's material in particular picture books. Has 'an excellent' list of picture book authors and illustrators. Authors with track record in this area only. *No unsolicited scripts.* CLIENTS include Wayne Anderson, Reg Cartwright, Jason Cockcroft, Ross Collins, Siobhan Dodds, Richard Fowler, Charles Fuge, Susie Jenkin-Pearce, Angela McAllister, David Melling, Graham Oakley, Sue Porter, Carol Thompson, Susan Winter, David Wood. *Commission* Home 10%; US 15%; Translation 20%.

Andrew Mann Ltd★
1 Old Compton Street, London W1V 5PH
☎020 7734 4751 Fax 020 7287 9264
Email manscript@compuserve.com

Contacts *Anne Dewe, Tina Betts*

FOUNDED 1975. *Handles* fiction, general non-fiction and film, TV, theatre, radio scripts. No unsolicited mss. Preliminary letter, synopsis and s.a.e. essential. No reading fee. *Commission* Home 15%; US & Translation 20%. *Overseas associates* various.

Manuscript ReSearch
PO Box 33, Bicester, Oxfordshire OX26 4ZZ
☎01869 323447 Fax 01869 324096

Contact *Graham Jenkins*

FOUNDED 1988. Principally *handles* scripts suitable for film/TV outlets. Will only consider book submissions from established clients. Preferred first approach from new contacts is by letter with brief outline and s.a.e. *Commission* Home 10%; Overseas 20%.

Marjacq Scripts Ltd
34 Devonshire Place, London W1G 6JW
☎020 7935 9499 Fax 020 7935 9115
Email enquiries@marjacq.com
Website www.marjacq.com

Contact *Mark Hayward*

HANDLES general fiction and non-fiction, and screenplays. Special interest in crime, sagas and science fiction. No poetry, children's books or plays. Send synopsis and three chapters; will suggest revision for promising mss. No reading fee. *Commission* Home 10%; Overseas 20%.

The Marsh Agency★
11/12 Dover Street, London W1S 4LJ
☎020 7399 2800 Fax 020 7399 2801
Email enquiries@marsh-agency.co.uk
Website www.marsh-agency.co.uk

Contacts *Paul Marsh*

FOUNDED 1994. International rights specialists selling English and foreign language writing. No TV, film, radio or theatre. No unsolicited mss. CLIENTS include several British and American agencies and publishers, and some individual authors.

Martinez Literary Agency
60 Oakwood Avenue, Southgate, London N14 6QL
☎020 8886 5829

Contacts *Mary Martinez, Francoise Budd*

FOUNDED 1988. *Handles* high-quality fiction, children's books, arts and crafts, interior design, alternative health/complementary medicine, autobiography, biography, popular music, sport and memorabilia books. Not accepting any new writers. *Commission* Home 15%; US, Overseas & Translation 20%; Performance Rights 20%.

MBA Literary Agents Ltd★
62 Grafton Way, London W1T 5DW
☎020 7387 2076 Fax 020 7387 2042
Email agent@mbalit.co.uk

Contacts *Diana Tyler, John Richard Parker, Meg Davis, Laura Longrigg, David Riding*

FOUNDED 1971. *Handles* fiction and non-fiction, TV, film, radio and theatre scripts. No poetry. Works in conjunction with agents in most countries. Also UK representative for **Writers House, Inc**, the Donald Maass Agency and the JABberwocky Agency. No unsolicited mss. CLIENTS include Campbell Armstrong, A.L. Barker, estate of Harry Bowling, Jeffrey Caine, Glenn Chandler, Andrew Cowan, Patricia Finney, Maggie Furey, Sue Gee, Joanna Hines, the estate of B.S. Johnson, Robert Jones, Paul J. McAuley, Anne McCaffrey, Susan Oudot, Sir Roger Penrose, Anne Perry, Gervase Phinn, Christopher Russell, Jim Shields, Iain Sinclair,

Mark Wallington, Patrick Wilde, Paul Wilson, Valerie Windsor. *Commission* Home 15%; Overseas 20%; Theatre/TV/Radio 10%; Film 10–20%.

Midland Exposure
4 Victoria Court, Oadby, Leicestershire LE2 4AF
☎0116 271 8332 Fax 0116 281 2188
Email partners@midlandexposure.co.uk
Website www.midlandexposure.co.uk

Partners *Cari Crook, Lesley Gleeson*

FOUNDED 1996. *Handles* short fiction for magazines only. *Specialises* in women's, teenage and children's magazine fiction. No books. 'Keen to encourage new writers.' Unsolicited mss welcome. Please ring for current reading fee. *Commission* Home 15–25%; US 20%.

Christy Moore Ltd
See **Sheil Land Associates Ltd**

William Morris Agency (UK) Ltd★
52/53 Poland Street, London W1F 7LX
☎020 7534 6800 Fax 020 7534 6900

Television *Holly Pye*
Books *Stephanie Cabot, Eugenie Furniss*

FOUNDED 1965. Worldwide theatrical and literary agency with offices in New York, Beverly Hills and Nashville and associates in Sydney. *Handles* TV scripts, fiction and general non-fiction. No unsolicited film, TV or stage material *at all*. Mss for books with preliminary letter. No reading fee. *Commission* TV & UK Books 10%; US Books & Translation 20%.

Michael Motley Ltd
The Old Vicarage, Tredington, Tewkesbury, Gloucestershire GL20 7BP
☎01684 276390 Fax 01684 297355

Contact *Michael Motley*

FOUNDED 1973. *Handles* only full-length mss (i.e. 60,000+). No short stories or journalism. No science fiction, horror, poetry or original dramatic material. New clients by referral only. No unsolicited mss. No reading fee. *Commission* Home 10%; US 15%; Translation 20%. *Overseas associates* in all publishing centres.

Judith Murdoch Literary Agency★
19 Chalcot Square, London NW1 8UA
☎020 7722 4197

Contact *Judith Murdoch*

FOUNDED 1993. *Handles* full-length fiction only.

No thrillers, science fiction/fantasy, children's, poetry or short stories. No unsolicited mss; approach in writing only enclosing first two chapters and brief synopsis. Return postage/s.a.e. essential. No reading fee. Translation rights handled by **The Marsh Agency**. *Commission* Home 15%; US & Translation 20%.

The Narrow Road Company
182 Brighton Road, Coulsdon, Surrey CR5 2NF
☎020 8763 9895 Fax 020 8763 9329
Email narrowroad@freeuk.com
Contacts *Richard Ireson, Andrea Hood*
FOUNDED 1986. Part of the Narrow Road Group. Theatrical literary agency. *Handles* scripts for TV, theatre, film and radio. No novels or poetry. No unsolicited mss; approach by letter with c.v. and one-page synopsis. Interested in writers with some experience and original ideas. CLIENTS include David Halliwell, Sheila Kelley, Deepak Verma, Alex Lowe.

William Neill-Hall Ltd
Old Oak Cottage, Ropewalk, Mount Hawke, Truro, Cornwall TR4 8DW
☎01209 891427 Fax 01209 891427
Email wneill-hall@msn.com
Contact *William Neill-Hall*
FOUNDED 1995. *Handles* general non-fiction, religion. No TV, film, theatre or radio scripts; no fiction or poetry. *Specialises* in religion, sport, history and current affairs. No unsolicited mss. Approach by phone or letter. Enclose return postage. No reading fee. CLIENTS Mary Batchelor, Archbishop of Canterbury (George Carey), Richard Foster, Juliet Janvrin, Jennifer Rees Larcombe, Peter Owen-Jones, David Pytches, Mary Pytches, Philip Yancey. *Commission* Home 10%; US 15%; Translation 20%.

New Authors Showcase
See entry under **Electronic Publishing and Other Services**

The Maggie Noach Literary Agency★
22 Dorville Crescent, London W6 0HJ
☎020 8748 2926 Fax 020 8748 8057
Email m-noach@dircon.co.uk
Contact *Maggie Noach*
FOUNDED 1982. Pronounced 'no-ack'. *Handles* a wide range of well-written books including general non-fiction, especially biography, com-mercial fiction and non-illustrated children's books for ages 7–12. No scientific, academic or specialist non-fiction. No poetry, plays, short stories or books for the very young. Recom-mended for promising young writers but *very* few new clients taken on as it is considered vital to give individual attention to each author's work. Unsolicited mss not welcome. Approach by letter (*not by telephone or e-mail*), giving a brief description of the book and enclosing a few sam-ple pages. Return postage essential. No reading fee. *Commission* Home 15%; US & Translation 20%.

Andrew Nurnberg Associates Ltd★
Clerkenwell House, 45–47 Clerkenwell Green, London EC1R 0HT
☎020 7417 8800 Fax 020 7417 8812
Email all@nurnberg.co.uk
Directors *Andrew Nurnberg, Sarah Nundy, D. Roger Seaton, Vicky Mark*
Associate Director *Anna Chodakowska*
FOUNDED in the mid-1970s. *Specialises* in foreign rights, representing leading authors and agents. Branches in Moscow, Bucharest, Budapest, Prague, Sofia, Warsaw and Riga. *Commission* Home 15%; US & Translation 20%.

Alexandra Nye
44 Braemar Avenue, Dunblane, Perthshire FK15 9EB
☎01786 825114
Contact *Alexandra Nye*
FOUNDED 1991. *Handles* fiction and topical non-fiction. *Special interests* literary fiction and history. Unsolicited mss welcome (s.a.e. essen-tial for return). Preliminary approach by letter, with synopsis, preferred. Reading fee for sup-ply of detailed report. CLIENTS include Dr Tom Gallagher, Harry Mehta, Robin Jenkins. *Commission* Home 10%; US 20%; Translation 15%.

David O'Leary Literary Agents
10 Lansdowne Court, Lansdowne Rise, London W11 2NR
☎020 7229 1623 Fax 020 7727 9624
Email d.o'leary@virgin.net
Contact *David O'Leary*
FOUNDED 1988. *Handles* fiction, both popular and literary, and non-fiction. Areas of interest include thrillers, history, popular science, Russia and Ireland (history and fiction). No poetry or science fiction. No unsolicited mss but happy to discuss a proposal. Ring or write in the first

instance. No reading fee. CLIENTS include David Crackanthorpe, James Kennedy, Nick Kochan, Jim Lusby, Derek Malcolm, Ken Russell. *Commission* Home 10%; US 10%. *Overseas associates* Lennart Sane, Scandinavia/Spain/South America; Tuttle Mori, Japan.

Deborah Owen Ltd★
78 Narrow Street, Limehouse, London E14 8BP
☎020 7987 5119/5441 Fax 020 7538 4004
Contacts *Deborah Owen*
FOUNDED 1971. Small agency specialising in representing authors direct around the world. *Handles* international fiction and non-fiction (books which can be translated into a number of languages). No scripts, poetry, science fiction, children's or short stories. No unsolicited mss. No new authors at present. CLIENTS include Penelope Farmer, Amos Oz and Delia Smith. *Commission* Home 10%; US & Translation 15%.

Owen Robinson Literary Agents
20 Tolbury Mill, Bruton, Somerset BA10 0DY
☎01749 812008 Fax 01749 812008
Email jpr@owenrobinson.netlineuk.net (enquiries only)
Contact *Justin Robinson*
FOUNDED 1998. *Handles* fiction and non-fiction. No plays, film scripts, poetry or short stories. No reading fee (ms appraisal, copy editing and wordprocessing available on request). No unsolicited mss. Approach in writing with s.a.e. in the first instance; send synopsis and three sample chapters subsequently. CLIENTS include Michael Holt, Valerie Kershaw, Roger Nichols, Alistair Owen, Ann Taylor. *Commission* Home 10%; US & Translation 15–20%. Works with agents overseas.

Mark Paterson & Associates★
10 Brook Street, Wivenhoe, Colchester, Essex CO7 9DS
☎01206 825433 Fax 01206 822990
Email info@mark.paterson.co.uk
Website www.markpaterson.co.uk
Contacts *Mark Paterson, Mary Swinney, Penny Tyndale-Hardy*
FOUNDED 1961. World rights representatives of authors and publishers handling many subjects, with specialisation in psychoanalysis and psychotherapy. CLIENTS range from Balint, Bion, Casement and Ferenczi, through to Freud and Winnicott; plus Hugh Brogan, Peter Moss and the estates of Sir Arthur Evans, Hugh Schonfield and Dorothy Richardson. No fiction, scripts, poetry, children's, articles, short stories or 'unsaleable mediocrity'. No unsolicited mss, but preliminary letter and synopsis with s.a.e. welcome. *Commission* 20% (including sub-agent's commission).

John Pawsey
60 High Street, Tarring, Worthing, West Sussex BN14 7NR
☎01903 205167 Fax 01903 205167
Contact *John Pawsey*
FOUNDED 1981. Experience in the publishing business has helped to attract some top names here, but the door remains open for bright, new talent. *Handles* non-fiction: biography, politics, current affairs, show business, gardening, travel, sport, business and music; and fiction. Will consider any well-written novel except science fiction, fantasy and horror. *Special interests* sport, current affairs and popular fiction. No drama scripts, poetry, short stories, journalism or academic. Preliminary letter with s.a.e. essential. No reading fee. CLIENTS include Jenny Bond, Dr David Lewis, David Rayvern Allen, Patricia Hall, Elwyn Hartley Edwards, Peter Hobday, Jon Silverman. *Commission* Home 10–15%; US & Translation 19%. *Overseas associates* in the US, Japan, South America and throughout Europe.

Maggie Pearlstine Associates Ltd★
31 Ashley Gardens, Ambrosden Avenue, London SW1P 1QE
☎020 7828 4212 Fax 020 7834 5546
Email post@pearlstine.co.uk
Contact *Maggie Pearlstine*
FOUNDED 1989. Small, selective agency. *Handles* general non-fiction and fiction. *Special interest:* history, current affairs, biography and health. No children's, poetry, horror, science fiction, short stories or scripts. Seldom takes on new authors. Prospective clients should write an explanatory letter and enclose s.a.e. and the first chapter only. No submissions accepted by fax, e-mail or from abroad. No reading fee. CLIENTS Debbie Beckerman, John Biffen, Matthew Baylis, Kate Bingham, Menzies Campbell, Kim Fletcher, Dr Frank Furedi, Uri Geller, Roy Hattersley, Rachel Holmes, Prof Lisa Jardine, Charles Kennedy, Mark Leonard, Alex Parsons, Claire Macdonald, Dr Raj Persaud, Prof Lesley Regan, Hugo Rifkind, Jackie Rowley, Henrietta Spencer-Churchill,

Alan Stewart, Jack Straw, Prof Robert Winston, Shaun Woodward. Translation rights handled by **Gillon Aitken Associates Ltd**. *Commission* Home 12½% (fiction), 10% (non-fiction); US & Translation 20%; TV, Film & Journalism 20%.

Peters Fraser & Dunlop Group Ltd
See **PFD**

PFD★
Drury House, 34–43 Russell Street, London WC2B 5HA
☎020 7344 1000
Fax 020 7836 9539/7836 9541
Email postmaster@pfd.co.uk
Website www.pfd.co.uk

Joint Chairmen *Anthony Jones, Tim Corrie*
Managing Director *Anthony Baring*
Books *Caroline Dawnay, Michael Sissons, Pat Kavanagh, Charles Walker, Rosemary Canter, Robert Kirby, Simon Trewin, James Gill*
Serial *Pat Kavanagh, Carol MacArthur*
Film/TV *Anthony Jones, Tim Corrie, Norman North, Charles Walker, Vanessa Jones, St. John Donald, Rosemary Scoular, Natasha Galloway, Jago Irwin, Louisa Thompson*
Actors *Maureen Vincent, Ginette Chalmers, Dallas Smith, Lindy King, Ruth Young, Lucy Brazier, Chris Harris*
Theatre *Kenneth Ewing, St John Donald, Nicki Stoddart, Rosie Cobbe*
Children's *Rosemary Canter*
Multimedia *Rosemary Scoular*

FOUNDED 1988 as a result of the merger of A. D. Peters & Co. Ltd and Fraser & Dunlop, and was later joined by the June Hall Literary Agency. *Handles* all sorts of books including fiction and children's, plus scripts for film, theatre, radio and TV material. Prospective clients should write 'a full letter, with an account of what he/she has done and wants to do and enclose, when possible, a detailed out-line and sample chapters'. Screenplays and TV scripts should be addressed to the 'Film & Script Dept.' Enclose s.a.e. No reading fee. CLIENTS include Julian Barnes, Alan Bennett, Alain de Botton, A.S. Byatt, estate of C.S. Forester, Nicci Gerrard, Robert Harris, Nick Hornby, Clive James, Russell Miller, estate of Nancy Mitford, John Mortimer, Andrew Motion, Douglas Reeman, Ruth Rendell, Anthony Sampson, Gerald Seymour, Tom Stoppard, Emma Thompson, Joanna Trollope, estate of Evelyn Waugh. *Commission* Home 10%; US & Translation 20%.

Charles Pick Consultancy Ltd★
3/3 Bryanston Place, London W1H 2DE
☎020 7402 8043 Fax 020 7724 5990
Email martincpick@cs.com

Contacts *Martin Pick, Sandra Sljivic*

FOUNDED 1985. *Handles* Fiction and non-fiction general books. Deals only with scripts by existing clients. No unsolicited mss. Pefers an approach to be made on the recommendation of someone qualified in their field. Send letter with a short description/synopsis. *Commission* Home 15%; US & Translation 20%; Film 20%.

Laurence Pollinger Limited★
9 Staple Inn, London WC1V 7QH
☎020 7404 0342 Fax 020 7242 5737
Email laurencepollinger@compuserve.com
Website www.laurencepollinger.com

Managing Director *Gerald J. Pollinger*
Adult List *Lorella Belli*
Children's List *Lesley Hadcroft*
Permissions/Foreign Rights *Heather Chalcroft*

FOUNDED 1958. A successor of Pearn, Pollinger & Higham. *Handles* all types of general trade adult and children's fiction and non-fiction books; some screenwriting, electronic media and illustrators/photographers. CLIENTS include Michael Coleman, Michael Cox, Vera Chapman, Allan Frewin Jones, Philip Gross, Gene Kemp, Adrienne Kennaway, Alan McDonald, Gary Paulsen, Nicholas Rhea and Sue Welford. Also the estates of H.E. Bates, Louis Bromfield, Erskine Caldwell, D.H. Lawrence, John Masters, Alan Moorehead, W. Heath Robinson, William Saroyan and other notables. Unsolicited material considered if pre-ceded by letter. *Commission* Home 15%; Translation 20%. Overseas and media associates.

Shelley Power Literary Agency Ltd★
13 rue du Pré Saint Gervais, 75019 Paris, France
☎00 33 1 42 38 36 49
Fax 00 33 1 40 40 70 08
Email shelley.power@wanadoo.fr

Contact *Shelley Power*

FOUNDED 1976. Shelley Power works between London and Paris. This is an English agency with London-based administration/accounts office and the editorial office in Paris. *Handles* general commercial fiction, quality fiction, business books, self-help, true crime, investigative exposés, film and entertainment. No scripts, short stories, children's or poetry. Preliminary letter with brief outline of project (plus return postage as from UK or France) essential. 'We do not consider submissions by e-mail.' No reading fee. *Commission* Home 10%; US & Translation 19%.

PVA Management Limited

Hallow Park, Worcester WR2 6PG
☎01905 640663 Fax 01905 641842
Email books@pva.co.uk
Managing Director *Paul Vaughan*

FOUNDED 1978. *Handles* non-fiction only. Please send synopsis and sample chapters together with return postage. *Commission* 15%.

Radala & Associates

17 Avenue Mansions, Finchley Road, London NW3 7AX
☎020 7794 4495 Fax 020 7431 7636
Contacts *Richard Gollner, Neil Hornick, Anna Swan, Andy Marino*

FOUNDED 1970. *Handles* quality fiction, non-fiction, drama, performing and popular arts, psychotherapy. Also provides editorial services, initiates in-house projects and can recommend independent professional readers if unable to read or comment on submissions. No poetry or screenplays. Prospective clients should send a short letter plus synopsis (maximum 2pp), first two chapters (double-spaced, numbered pages) and s.a.e. for return. *Commission* Home 10%; US 15–20%; Translation 20%. *Overseas associates* **Writers House, Inc.** (Al Zuckerman), New York; plus agents throughout Europe.

Rogers, Coleridge & White Ltd★

20 Powis Mews, London W11 1JN
☎020 7221 3717 Fax 020 7229 9084
Contacts *Deborah Rogers, Gill Coleridge, Patricia White, David Miller, Laurence Laluyaux*
Foreign Rights *Ann Warnford-Davis, Laurence Laluyaux*

FOUNDED 1967. *Handles* fiction, non-fiction and children's books. No poetry, plays or technical books. No unsolicited mss, please and no submissions by fax or e-mail. Rights representative in UK and translation for several New York agents. *Commission* Home 10%; US 15%; Translation 20%. *Overseas associate* ICM, New York.

Frederick Rosschild Security

PO Box 155, Great Yarmouth, Norfolk NR31 8GY
Contact *Frederick Rosschild*
FOUNDED 1994. *Handles* all types of fiction and non-fiction. Adult and children's books. Full-length novels, sagas and short stories. No plays or poetry. *Specialises* in debut writers. Unsolicited mss welcome but initial contact should be by letter enclosing A5 envelope and £1 of loose stamps to cover p&p of information booklet. No telephone calls. *Commission* Home 12%; Foreign 24%. Translations from French and German into English (UK), and English (US) into English (UK) by negotiation.

Hilary Rubinstein Books

32 Ladbroke Grove, London W11 3BQ
☎020 7792 4282 Fax 020 7221 5291
Email hrubinstein@beeb.net
Contact *Hilary Rubinstein*

FOUNDED 1992. *Handles* fiction and non-fiction. No poetry or drama. Approach in writing in the first instance. No reading fee but return postage, please. CLIENTS Lucy Irvine, Eric Lomax, Donna Williams. *Commission* Home 10%; US & Translation 20%. *Overseas associates* **Ellen Levine Literary Agency** New York; **Andrew Nurnberg Associates** (European rights).

Uli Rushby-Smith Literary Agency

72 Plimsoll Road, London N4 2EE
☎020 7354 2718 Fax 020 7354 2718
Contact *Uli Rushby-Smith*

FOUNDED 1993. *Handles* fiction and non-fiction, commercial and literary, both adult and children's. Film and TV rights handled in conjunction with a sub-agent. No plays or poetry. Approach with an outline, two or three sample chapters and explanatory letter in the first instance (s.a.e. essential). No reading fee. *Commission* Home 10%; US & Translation 20%. Represents UK rights for **Curtis Brown**, New York (children's) and 2.13.61 in the USA, Penguin (Canada), Penguin South Africa, the Alice Toledo Agency (NL) and Columbia University Press.

The Saddler Literary Agency

9 Curzon Road, London W5 1NE
☎020 8998 4868 Fax 020 8998 8851
Email john@saddler.fsnet.co.uk
Contact *John Saddler*

FOUNDED March 2001. John Saddler has been senior editor of **Black Swan**, an editorial director of **Fourth Estate**, publishing director of **Flamingo** and, until 2000, was publisher of Anchor Books, the literary imprint of

Transworld Publishers. *Handles* fiction and non-fiction. Send preliminary letter with synopsis and return postage in the first instance. No reading fee. *Commission* Home 10%; US & Translation 20%.

Rosemary Sandberg Ltd
6 Bayley Street, London WC1B 3HB
☎020 7304 4110 Fax 020 7304 4109
Email rosemary@sandberg.demon.co.uk
Contact *Rosemary Sandberg*

FOUNDED 1991. In association with **Ed Victor Ltd**. *Handles* children's picture books and novels. *Specialises* in children's writers and illustrators. No unsolicited mss as client list is currently full. *Commission* 10%.

The Sayle Agency★
11 Jubilee Place, London SW3 3TD
☎020 7823 3883 Fax 020 7823 3363
Email info@thesayleagency.co.uk
Website www.thesayleagency.co.uk
Books *Rachel Calder*
Film/TV *Jane Villiers, Matthew Bates*

Handles fiction, crime and general. Non-fiction: current affairs, social issues, travel, biographies, historical; TV and film scripts. No plays, poetry, children's, textbooks, science fiction, fantasy, horror or musicals. No unsolicited mss. Preliminary letter essential, including a brief biographical note and (for books) a synopsis and two or three sample chapters; (for scripts) an outline and sample pages. Return postage essential. No reading fee. CLIENTS Books: Stephen Amidon, Pete Davies, Margaret Forster, Georgina Hammick, Andy Kershaw, Phillip Knightley, Rory MacLean, Denise Mina, Ann Oakley, Kate Pullinger, Ronald Searle, Gitta Sereny, William Styron, Chris Wallace, Mary Wesley. Drama: William Corlett, Shelagh Delaney, Marc Evans, John Forte, Stuart Hepburn, David Hilton, Chris Monger, Sue Townsend. *Commission* Home 10%; US & Translation 20%. *Overseas associates* Elaine Markson Literary Agency and Darhansoff & Verrill, USA; translation rights handled by **The Marsh Agency**.

Seifert Dench Associates
24 D'Arblay Street, London W1F 8EH
☎020 7437 4551 Fax 020 7439 1355
Website www.seifert-dench.co.uk
Contacts *Linda Seifert, Elizabeth Dench, Michelle Arnold*

FOUNDED 1972. *Handles* scripts for TV and film. Unsolicited mss will be read, but a letter with

sample of work and c.v. (plus s.a.e.) is preferred. CLIENTS include Peter Chelsom, Tony Grisoni, Stephen Volk. *Commission* Home 10–15%. *Overseas associates* include: William Morris/Sanford Gross and C.A.A., Los Angeles.

The Sharland Organisation Ltd
The Manor House, Manor Street, Raunds, Northamptonshire NN9 6JW
☎01933 626600 Fax 01933 624860
Email tsoshar@aol.com
Contacts *Mike Sharland, Alice Sharland*

FOUNDED 1988. *Specialises* in national and international film and TV negotiations. Also negotiates multimedia, interactive TV deals and computer game contracts. *Handles* scripts for film, TV, radio and theatre; also non-fiction. Markets books for film and handles stage, radio, film and TV rights for authors. No scientific, technical or poetry. No unsolicited mss. Preliminary enquiry by letter or phone essential. *Commission* Home 15%; US & Translation 20%. *Overseas associates* various.

Vincent Shaw Associates Ltd
20 Jay Mews, Kensington Gore, London SW7 2EP
☎020 7581 8215 Fax 020 7225 1079
Email vincentshaw@clara.net
Contact *Vincent Shaw*

FOUNDED 1954. *Handles* TV, radio, film and theatre scripts. Unsolicited mss welcome. Approach in writing enclosing s.a.e. No phone calls. *Commission* Home 10%; US & Translation by negotiation. *Overseas associate* Herman Chessid, New York.

Sheil Land Associates Ltd★ (incorporating Richard Scott Simon Ltd 1971 and Christy Moore Ltd 1912)
43 Doughty Street, London WC1N 2LF
☎020 7405 9351 Fax 020 7831 2127
Email info@sheilland.co.uk
Agents, UK & US *Sonia Land, Luigi Bonomi, Sam Boyce, Vivien Green, Amanda Preston*
Film/Theatrical/TV *John Rush, Roland Baggot*
Foreign *Amelia Cummins*

FOUNDED 1962. *Handles* full-length general, commercial and literary fiction and non-fiction, including: social politics, history, military history, gardening, thrillers, crime, romance, fantasy, drama, biography, travel, cookery and humour, UK and foreign estates. Also theatre, film, radio and TV scripts. Welcomes approaches from new clients either to start or to develop their careers. Preliminary letter with s.a.e. essential. No reading fee. CLIENTS include Peter Ackroyd, John Blashford-Snell, Steve Ballesteros, Melvyn Bragg, Stephanie Calman, Catherine Cookson Estate, Anna del Conte, Seamus Deane, Alan Drury, Erik Durschmied, Alan Garner, Bonnie Greer, Susan Hill, Richard Holmes, HRH The Prince of Wales, John Humphries, Charlotte Lamb, James Long, Richard Mabey, Colin McDowell, Van Morrison, Patrick O'Brian Estate, Esther Rantzen, Pam Rhodes, Jean Rhys Estate, Martin Riley, Colin Shindler, Tom Sharpe, Brian Sykes, Jeffrey Tayler, Alan Titchmarsh, Rose Tremain, John Wilsher, Paul Wilson. *Commission* Home 15%; US & Translation 20%. *Overseas associates* Georges Borchardt, Inc. (Richard Scott Simon). UK representatives for Farrar, Straus & Giroux, Inc. US film and TV representation: CAA, APA, and others.

Caroline Sheldon Literary Agency★

71 Hillgate Place, London W8 7SS
☎020 7727 9102

Contact *Caroline Sheldon*

FOUNDED 1985. *Handles* adult fiction, in particular women's, both commercial and literary novels. Also full-length children's fiction. No TV/film scripts unless by book-writing clients. Send letter with all relevant details of ambitions and four chapters of proposed book (enclose large s.a.e.). No reading fee. *Commission* Home 10%; US & Translation 20%.

Jeffrey Simmons

10 Lowndes Square, London SW1X 9HA
☎020 7235 8852 Fax 020 7235 9733

Contact *Jeffrey Simmons*

FOUNDED 1978. *Handles* biography and autobiography, cinema and theatre, fiction (both quality and commercial), history, law and crime, politics and world affairs, parapsychology and sport (but not exclusively). No science fiction/fantasy, children's books, cookery, crafts, hobbies or gardening. Film scripts handled only if by book-writing clients. *Special interests* personality books of all sorts and fiction from young writers (i.e. under 40) with a future. Writers become clients by personal introduction or by letter, enclosing a synopsis if possible, a brief biography, a note of any previously published books, plus a list of any publishers and agents who have already seen the mss. *Commission* Home 10–15%; US & Foreign 15%.

Richard Scott Simon Ltd
See **Sheil Land Associates Ltd**

Robert Smith Literary Agency★

12 Bridge Wharf, 156 Caledonian Road, London N1 9UU
☎020 7278 2444 Fax 020 7833 5680
Email robertsmith.literaryagency@virgin.net

Contact *Robert Smith*

FOUNDED 1997. *Handles* non-fiction; biography, health and nutrition, cookery, lifestyle, showbusiness and true crime. No scripts, fiction, poetry, academic or children's books. No unsolicited mss. Send a letter and synopsis in the first instance. No reading fee. CLIENTS Neil and Christine Hamilton, James Haspiel, Christine Keeler, Luisa Moore, Norman Parker, Mike Reid, Christopher Warwick. *Commission* Home 15%; US & Translation 20%. *Overseas associates* Frédérique Poretta Literary Agency (France); Thomas Schlück Literary Agency (Germany).

Elaine Steel

110 Gloucester Avenue, London NW1 8HX
☎020 8348 0918 Fax 020 8341 9807
Email ecmsteel@aol.com

Contact *Elaine Steel*

FOUNDED 1986. *Handles* scripts, screenplays and books. No technical or academic. Initial phone call preferred. CLIENTS include Les Blair, Anna Campion, Michael Eaton, Brian Keenan, Troy Kennedy Martin, Rob Ritchie, Ben Steiner. *Commission* Home 10%; US & Translation 20%.

Abner Stein★

10 Roland Gardens, London SW7 3PH
☎020 7373 0456 Fax 020 7370 6316

Contact *Abner Stein*

FOUNDED 1971. Mainly represents US agents and authors but *handles* some full-length fiction and general non-fiction. No scientific, technical, etc. No scripts. Send letter and outline in the first instance rather than unsolicited mss. *Commission* Home 10%; US & Translation 20%.

Micheline Steinberg Playwrights

409 Triumph House, 187–191 Regent Street, London W1R 7WF
☎020 7287 4383 Fax 020 7287 4384
Email steinplays@aol.com

Contacts *Micheline Steinberg, Ginny Sennett*

FOUNDED 1988. *Specialises* in plays for stage, TV, radio and film. Best approach by preliminary letter (with s.a.e.). Dramatic associate for **Laurence Pollinger Limited**. *Commission* Home 10%; Elsewhere 15%.

Shirley Stewart Literary Agency

36 Brand Street, Greenwich, London SE10 8SR
☎020 8853 1381 Fax 020 8305 2175

Director *Shirley Stewart*

FOUNDED 1993. *Handles* literary fiction and non-fiction. No scripts, children's, science fiction, fantasy or poetry. Will consider unsolicited material; send letter with two or three sample chapters in the first instance. S.a.e. essential. Submissions by fax or on disk not accepted. No reading fee. *Commission* Home 10%; US & Translation 20%. *Overseas associate* **Curtis Brown Ltd**, New York.

The Susijn Agency

820 Harrow Road, London NW10 5JU
☎020 8968 7435 Fax 020 8354 0415
Email info@thesusijnagency.com
Website www.thesusijnagency.com

Contact *Laura Susijn*

FOUNDED April 1998. *Specialises* in selling rights worldwide in literary fiction and non-fiction. Preliminary letter, synopsis and first two chapters preferred. No reading fee. Also represents non-English language authors and publishers for UK, US and translation rights worldwide. *Commission* Home 15%; US & Translation 15–20%.

J.M. Thurley Management

30 Cambridge Road, Teddington, Middlesex TW11 8DR
☎020 8977 3176 Fax 020 8943 2678
Email JMThurley@aol.com

Contact *Jon Thurley*

FOUNDED 1976. *Handles* full-length fiction, non-fiction, TV and films. Particularly interested in strong commercial and literary fiction. Will provide creative and editorial assistance to promising writers. No unsolicited mss; approach by letter in the first instance with synopsis and first three chapters plus return postage. No reading fee. *Commission* Home 15%; US & Translation 15%.

Lavinia Trevor Agency★

The Glasshouse, 49A Goldhawk Road, London W12 8QP
☎020 8749 8481 Fax 020 8749 7377

Contact *Lavinia Trevor*

FOUNDED 1993. *Handles* general fiction and non-fiction, including popular science. No poetry, academic, technical or children's books. No TV, film, radio, theatre scripts. Approach with a preliminary letter, a brief autobiography and first 50–100 typewritten pages. S.a.e. essential. No reading fee. *Commission* rate by agreement with author.

Jane Turnbull★

13 Wendell Road, London W12 9RS
☎020 8743 9580 Fax 020 8749 6079
Email agents@cwcom.net

Contact *Jane Turnbull*

FOUNDED 1986. *Handles* fiction and non-fiction. No science fiction, sagas or romantic fiction. *Specialises* in biography, history, current affairs, health and diet. No unsolicited mss. Approach with letter in the first instance. No reading fee. Translation rights handled by **Gillon Aitken Associates Ltd**. *Commission* Home 10%; US & Foreign 20%.

Ed Victor Ltd★

6 Bayley Street, Bedford Square, London WC1B 3HB
☎020 7304 4100 Fax 020 7304 4111

Contacts *Ed Victor, Graham Greene, Maggie Phillips, Sophie Hicks, Lizzy Kremer*

FOUNDED 1976. *Handles* a broad range of material but leans towards the more commercial ends of the fiction and non-fiction spectrums. No scripts, no academic. Takes on very few new writers. After trying his hand at book publishing and literary magazines, Ed Victor, an ebullient American, found his true vocation. Strong opinions, very pushy and works hard for those whose intelligence he respects. Loves nothing more than a good title auction. CLIENTS include Douglas Adams, Frederick Forsyth, Josephine Hart, Jack Higgins, Erica Jong, Kathy Lette, Erich Segal, Lisa St Aubin de Terán and the estates of Raymond Chandler, Dame Iris Murdoch, Sir Stephen Spender and Irving Wallace. *Commission* Home 15%; US 15%; Translation 20%.

Walker Associates

31 Agar Grove, London NW1 9UG
☎020 7813 9352 Fax 020 7813 9352

Contacts *Michael Walker, John Hastings, Alison Butler*

FOUNDED 1999. *Handles* contemporary fiction. *Specialises* in psychological thrillers/horror and humour. No drama, poetry, short stories or children's fiction. No reading fee. Unsolicited mss welcome. Prospective clients should send preliminary letter including brief c.v., synopsis and first three chapters; s.a.e. essential for return. *Commission* Home 10%; US & Translation 20%.

Cecily Ware Literary Agents
19C John Spencer Square, London N1 2LZ
☎020 7359 3787 Fax 020 7226 9828

Contacts *Cecily Ware, Gilly Schuster, Warren Sherman*

FOUNDED 1972. Primarily a film and TV script agency representing work in all areas: drama, children's, series/serials, adaptations, comedies, etc. No unsolicited mss or phone calls. Approach in writing only. No reading fee. *Commission* Home 10%; US 10–20% by arrangement.

Warner Chappell Plays Ltd
See **Josef Weinberger Plays**

Watson, Little Ltd★
Capo Di Monte, Windmill Hill, London NW3 6RJ
☎020 7431 0770 Fax 020 7431 7225
Email sz@watlit.demon.co.uk

Contacts *Sheila Watson, Mandy Little, Sugra Zaman*

Handles fiction and non-fiction. *Special interests* history, popular science, psychology, self-help and business books. No scripts. Not interested in authors who wish to be purely academic writers. Send preliminary ('intelligent') letter with synopsis. *Commission* Home 15%; US 24%; Translation 19%. *Overseas associates* worldwide.

A.P. Watt Ltd★
20 John Street, London WC1N 2DR
☎020 7405 6774 Fax 020 7831 2154
Email apw@apwatt.co.uk
Website www.apwatt.co.uk

Directors *Caradoc King, Linda Shaughnessy, Derek Johns, Joanna Frank, Georgia Garrett, Nick Harris* (Associate)

FOUNDED 1875. The oldest-established literary agency in the world. *Handles* full-length type-scripts, including children's books, screenplays for film and TV, and plays. No poetry, academic or specialist works. No unsolicited mss accepted. CLIENTS include Trezza Azzopardi, Quentin Blake, Marika Cobbold, Helen Dunmore, Nicholas Evans, Giles Foden, Janice Galloway, Martin Gilbert, Nadine Gordimer, Linda Grant, Colin and Jacqui Hawkins, Michael Holroyd, Michael Ignatieff, Mick Jackson, Philip Kerr, John Lanchester, Alison Lurie, Jan Morris, Andrew O'Hagan, Zadie Smith, Graham Swift, Colm Toibin and the estates of Wodehouse, Graves and Maugham. *Commission* Home 10%; US & Translation 20%.

Josef Weinberger Plays
12–14 Mortimer Street, London W1T 3JJ
☎020 7580 2827 Fax 020 7436 9616
Email general.info@jwmail.co.uk
Website www.josef-weinberger.com

Contact *Michael Callahan*

Formerly Warner Chappell Plays, Josef Weinberger is now both agent and publisher of scripts for the theatre. No unsolicited mss; introductory letter essential. No reading fee. CLIENTS include Ray Cooney, John Godber, Peter Gordon, Debbie Isitt, Arthur Miller, Sam Shepard, John Steinbeck. *Overseas representatives* in the US, Canada, Australia, New Zealand, India, South Africa and Zimbabwe.

John Welch, Literary Consultant & Agent
Milton House, Milton, Cambridge CB4 6AD
☎01223 860641 Fax 01223 440575

Contact *John Welch*

FOUNDED 1992. *Handles* military history, aviation, history, biography and sport. No fiction, poetry, children's books or scripts for radio, TV, film or theatre. Already has a full hand of authors so no new authors being considered at present. CLIENTS include Alexander Baron, Michael Calvert, Timothy Jenkins, Norman Scarfe, Peter Trew, David Wragg. *Commission* Home 10%.

White Flag
☎01792 539266
Email chrisbevan@w-f-la.com
Website www.w-f-la.com

Contact *Christopher E. Bevan*

FOUNDED 2001. *Handles* film screenplays only (no restriction on type). No unsolicited mss; access the website for submission guidelines. No reading fee. *Commission* Home & US 20%.

Dinah Wiener Ltd★
12 Cornwall Grove, Chiswick, London W4 2LB
☎020 8994 6011 Fax 020 8994 6044

Contact *Dinah Wiener*

FOUNDED 1985. *Handles* fiction and general non-fiction: auto/biography, popular science, cookery. No scripts, children's or poetry.

Approach with preliminary letter in first instance, giving full but brief c.v. of past work and future plans. Mss submitted must include s.a.e. and be typed in double-spacing. CLIENTS include T.J. Armstrong, Valerie-Anne Baglietto, Malcolm Billings, Alison Brodie, Hugh Brune, Guy Burt, Victoria Corby, David Deutsch, Robin Gardiner, Jenny Hobbs, Mark Jeffery, Tania Kindersley, Daniel Snowman, Peta Tayler, Rachel Trethewey, Marcia Willett. *Commission* Home 15%; US & Translation 20%.

Michael Woodward Creations Ltd

Parlington Hall, Aberford, West Yorkshire LS25 3EG
☎0113 281 3913   Fax 0113 281 3911
Email art@mwc.uk.com

Contacts *Michael Woodward, Janet Woodward*

FOUNDED 1979. International licensing company with own in-house studio. Worldwide representation for artists and illustrators. Current properties include *Rambling Ted, Teddy Tum Tum, Railway Children, Kit 'n' Kin, Bad Taste Bears, Robots in Big Boots*. New artists should forward full-concept synopses with sample illustrations. Scripts or stories not accepted without illustration/design or concept mock-ups. No standard commission rate; varies according to contract.

The Wylie Agency (UK) Ltd

4–8 Rodney Street, London N1 9JH
☎020 7843 2150   Fax 020 7843 2151
Email mail@wylieagency.co.uk

Handles fiction and non-fiction. No scripts or children's books. Approach in writing with three sample chapters, synopsis and s.a.e./return postage. No reading fee. *Commission* Home 10%; USA 15%; Translation 20%.

Zebra Agency

Broadland House, 1 Broadland, Shevington, Lancashire WN6 8DH
☎0794 958 4758
Email admin@zebraagency.co.uk
Website www.zebraagency.co.uk

Contacts *Dee Jones, Cara Wooi*

FOUNDED 1997. *Handles* non-fiction and general fiction including crime, suspense and drama, murder, mysteries, adventure, thrillers, horror and science fiction. Also scripts for TV, radio, film and theatre. No reading fee. Editorial advice given to new authors. No unsolicited mss; send preliminary letter giving publishing history and brief c.v., with synopsis and first three chapters (plus return postage). No phone calls or submissions by fax or e-mail. *Commission* Home 10%; US & Translation 20%.

National Newspapers

Departmental e-mail addresses are too numerous to include in this listing. They can be obtained from the newspaper's main switchboard or the department in question

Business a.m.
40 Torphichen Street, Edinburgh EH3 8JB
☎0131 330 0000 Fax 0131 330 0003
Email info@businessam.co.uk
Website www.businessam.co.uk
Owner *Bonnier Group (Sweden)*
Editor *John Penman*
Circulation 13,008

Subscription tabloid, launched in September 2000, aimed at the Scottish business community. Published Monday to Friday, the paper covers commerce, industry, finance and politics 'through Scottish eyes'. Includes *Investor* and *Business p.m.* sections.
  Deputy Editor *Paul Stokes*

Daily Express
Ludgate House, 245 Blackfriars Road, London SE1 9UX
☎020 7928 8000 Fax 020 7620 1654
Website www.expressnewspapers.co.uk
Owner *Northern & Shell Media/Richard Desmond*
Editor *Chris Williams*
Circulation 938,890

Under new owner Richard Desmond, publisher of *OK!* magazine, the paper features a large amount of celebrity coverage. The general rule of thumb is to approach in writing with an idea; all departments are prepared to look at an outline without commitment. Ideas welcome but already receives many which are 'too numerous to count'.
  News Editor *David Leigh*
  Diary Editor *John McEntee (William Hickey)*
  Features Editor *Heather O'Connor*
  City Editor *Stephen Kahn*
  Political Editor *Patrick O'Flynn*
  Sports Editor *Chris Baldock*
  Planning Editor (News Desk) should be circulated with copies of official reports, press releases, etc., to ensure news desk cover at all times.

OK! Express: Tuesday showbiz supplement.

Saturday magazine **Editor** *Martin Smith*
  Payment negotiable.

Daily Mail
Northcliffe House, 2 Derry Street, Kensington, London W8 5TT
☎020 7938 6000 Fax 020 7937 4463
Owner *Associated Newspapers/Lord Rothermere*
Editor *Paul Dacre*
Circulation 2.45 million

In-house feature writers and regular columnists provide much of the material. Photo-stories and crusading features often appear; it's essential to hit the right note to be a successful *Mail* writer. Close scrutiny of the paper is strongly advised. Not a good bet for the unseasoned. Accepts news on savings, building societies, insurance, unit trusts, legal rights and tax.
  News Editor *Tony Gallagher*
  City Editor *Alex Brummer*
  'Money Mail' Editor *Tony Hazell*
  Political Editor *David Hughes*
  Education Editor *Tony Halpin*
  Diary Editor *Nigel Dempster*
  Features Editor *Veronica Wadley*
  Literary Editor *Jane Mays*
  Sports Editor (Deputy) *Graham Hunter*
  Femail *Lisa Collins*

Weekend: Saturday supplement **Editor** *Heather McGlone*

Daily Record
One Central Quay, Glasgow G3 8DA
☎0141 248 7000 Fax 0141 242 3340
Website www.record-mail.co.uk
Owner *Trinity Mirror plc*
Circulation 600,285
Editor-in-Chief *Peter Cox*

Mass-market Scottish tabloid. Freelance material is generally welcome.
  News Editor *Tom Hamilton*
  Features Editor *Laura Collins*
  Business Editor *Colin Calder*
  Education *Euan McColm*
  Political Editor *Paul Sinclair*
  Sports Editor *Gordon Waddell*
  Women's Page *Jill Main*
  Magazine Editor *Angela Dewar*

Daily Sport

19 Great Ancoats Street, Manchester M60 4BT
☎0161 236 4466 Fax 0161 236 4535
Website www.dailysport.co.uk
Owner *Sport Newspapers Ltd*
Editor David Beevers
Circulation 235,000

Tabloid catering for young male readership. Unsolicited material welcome; send to News Editor.

News Editor *Pam McVitie*
Sports Editor *Marc Smith*

Daily Star

Ludgate House, 245 Blackfriars Road, London SE1 9UX
☎020 7928 8000 Fax 020 7922 7960
Website www.megastar.co.uk
Owner *Richard Desmond*
Editor *Peter Hill*
Circulation 588,727

Competes with *The Sun* for off-the-wall news and features. Freelance opportunities available.

Deputy Editor *Hugh Whittow*
Features Editor *Dawn Neesom*
Sports Editor *Jim Mansell*

The Daily Telegraph

1 Canada Square, Canary Wharf, London E14 5DT
☎020 7538 5000 Fax 020 7513 2506
Website www.telegraph.co.uk
Owner *Conrad Black*
Editor *Charles Moore*
Circulation 1.02 million

Unsolicited mss not generally welcome – 'all are carefully read and considered, but only about one in a thousand is accepted for publication'. As they receive about 20 weekly, this means about one a year. Contenders should approach the paper in writing, making clear their authority for writing on that subject. No fiction.

News Editor *Richard Spencer* Tip-offs or news reports from *bona fide* journalists. Must phone the news desk in first instance. Maximum 200 words. *Payment* minimum £40 (tip).

Arts Editor *Sarah Crompton*
City Editor *Neil Collins*
Political Editor *George Jones*
Diary Editor *Sam Leith* Always interested in diary pieces; contact *Peterborough* (Diary column).
Education *John Clare*
Environment *Charles Clover*
Features Editor *Richard Preston* Most ma-

terial supplied by commission from established contributors. New writers are tried out by arrangement with the features editor. Approach in writing. Maximum 1500 words.

Literary Editor *Kate Summerscale*
Sports Editor *David Welch* Occasional opportunities for specialised items.
Style Editor *Rachel Forder*
Wellbeing Editor *Vicky Rands*
Payment by arrangement.

Daily Telegraph Weekend: Saturday colour supplement. **Editor** *Rachel Simhon*.

Financial Times

1 Southwark Bridge, London SE1 9HL
☎020 7873 3000 Fax 020 7873 3076
Email <firstname>.<lastname>@ft.com
Website www.ft.com
Owner *Pearson*
Editor *Richard Lambert*
Circulation 482,086

FOUNDED 1888. UK and international coverage of business, finance, politics, technology, management, marketing and the arts. All feature ideas must be discussed with the department's editor in advance. Not snowed under with unsolicited contributions – they get less than any other national newspaper. Approach by e-mail with ideas in the first instance.

News Editor *William Lewis*
Features Editor *John Gapper*
Arts Editor *Peter Aspden*
Financial Editor *Jane Fuller*
Literary Editor *Jan Dalley*
Diary Editor *Sonny Tucker*
Education *Jim Kelly*
Environment *Vanessa Houlder*
Political Editor *Brian Groom*
Small Businesses *Katherine Campbell*
Sports Editor *David Owen*

Weekend FT and **the business**. **Editor** *Julia Cuthbertson*

How to Spend It Monthly magazine. **Editor** *Gillian de Bono*

The Guardian

119 Farringdon Road, London EC1R 3ER
☎020 7278 2332 Fax 020 7837 2114
Website www.guardian.co.uk
Owner *The Scott Trust*
Editor *Alan Rusbridger*
Circulation 401,665

Of all the nationals *The Guardian* probably offers the greatest opportunities for freelance writers, if only because it has the greatest number of specialised pages which use freelance work. But mss must be directed at a specific slot.

News Editor *Clare Margetson* No opportunities except in those regions where there is presently no local contact for news stories.

Arts Editor *Dan Glaister*

Literary Editor *Claire Armitstead*

Executive Financial Editor *Paul Murphy*

Managing Editor, City *Steve Bosfield*

On Line *Vic Keegan* Science, computing and technology. A good part of Thursday's paper, almost all written by freelancers. Expertise essential – but not a trade page; written for 'the interested man in the street' and from the user's point of view. Computing/communications (Internet) articles should be addressed to *Jack Schofield*; science articles to *Tim Radford*. Mss on disk or by e-mail (neil.mcintosh@guardian.co.uk).

Diary Editor *Matthew Norman*

Education Editor *Will Woodward* Expert pieces on modern education welcome.

Environment *John Vidal*

Features Editor *Ian Katz* Receives up to 50 unsolicited mss a day; these are passed on to relevant page editors.

Guardian Society *David Brindle* Focuses on social change – the forces affecting us, from environment to government policies. Top journalists and outside commentators.

Media Editor *Janine Gibson* Nine pages a week, plus 'New Media'. Outside contributions are considered. All aspects of modern media, advertising and PR. Background insight important. Best approach is by e-mail (janine.gibson@guardian.co.uk)

Political Editor *Mike White*

Sports Editor *Ben Clissitt*

Women's Page *Libby Brooks* Runs three days a week. Unsolicited ideas used if they show an appreciation of the page in question. Maximum 800–1000 words. Write, e-mail (libby.brooks@guardian.co.uk) or fax on 020 7239 9935.

*The **Guardian Weekend*** glossy Saturday issue. **Editor** *Katharine Viner*. *The **Guide*** *Tim Lusher*.

The Herald (Glasgow)

200 Renfield Street, Glasgow G2 3PR
☎0141 302 7000 Fax 0141 302 7070
Website www.theherald.co.uk

Owner *S.M.G.*

Editor *Mark Douglas-Home*

Circulation 101,079

The oldest national newspaper in the English-speaking world, The Herald, which dropped its 'Glasgow' prefix in February 1992, was bought by Scottish Television in 1996. Lively, quality, national Scottish daily broadsheet. Approach with ideas in writing or by phone in first instance.

News Editor *Bill McDowall*

Arts Editor *Keith Bruce*

Business Editor *Robert Powell*

Diary *Tom Shields*

Education *Liz Buie*

Sports Editor *Iain Scott*

Herald Magazine *Cate Devine*

The Independent

Independent House, 191 Marsh Wall, London E14 9RS
☎020 7005 2000 Fax 020 7005 2999
Website www.independent.co.uk

Owner *Independent Newspapers*

Editor *Simon Kelner*

Circulation 226,007

FOUNDED October 1986. *The Independent* and *The Independent on Sunday* were acquired by Irish tycoon Tony O'Reilly's Independent Newspapers from Mirror Group Newspapers in March 1998. Particularly strong on its arts/media coverage, with a high proportion of feature material. Theoretically, opportunities for freelancers are good. However, unsolicited mss are not welcome; most pieces originate in-house or from known and trusted outsiders. Ideas should be submitted in writing.

News Editor *Jason Burt*

Features *Laurence Earle*

Arts Editor *Ian Irvine*

Business Editor *Jeremy Warner*

Education *Richard Garner*

Environment *Michael McCarthy*

Literary Editor *Boyd Tonkin*

Political Editor *Andrew Grice*

Sports Editor *Paul Newman*

Travel Editor *Jeremy Atiyah*

The Independent Magazine: Saturday supplement. **Editor** *Andrew Tuck*.

The Information **Editor** *Nick Coleman*.

Independent on Sunday

Independent House, 191 Marsh Wall, London E14 9RS
☎020 7005 2000 Fax 020 7005 2999
Website www.independent.co.uk/sindy/ sindy.html

Owner *Independent Newspapers*

Editor *Tristan Davies*

Circulation 250,514

FOUNDED 1986. Regular columnists contribute most material but feature opportunites exist. Approach with ideas in first instance.

News Editor *David Randall*
Focus Editor *Simon O'Hagan*
Culture Editor *Marcus Field*
Comment Editor *Catherine Pepinster*
Business Editor *Jason Nissé*
Education Editor *Judith Judd*
Literary Editor *Suzi Feay*
Environment *Geoffrey Lean*
Political Editor *Colin Brown*
Sports Editor *Neil Morton*
Travel Editor *Oliver Bennett*
Review supplement. **Editor** *Richard Askwith.*

International Herald Tribune

6 bis, rue des Graviers, 92521 Neuilly, Paris, France
☎0033 1 4143 9300 Fax 0033 1 4143 9338
Email iht@iht.com
Website www.iht.com

Executive Editor *David Ignatius*
Managing Editor *Walter Wells*
Deputy Editors *Katherine Knorr,*
Charles Mitchelmore
Circulation 225,000

Published in France, Monday to Saturday, and circulated in Europe, the Middle East, North Africa, the Far East and the USA. General news, business and financial, arts and leisure. Uses regular freelance contributors. Contributor policy can be found on the website at: www.iht.com/contributor.htm

The Mail on Sunday

Northcliffe House, 2 Derry Street, Kensington, London W8 5TS
☎020 7938 6000 Fax 020 7937 3829

Owner *Associated Newspapers/Lord Rothermere*
Editor *Peter Wright*
Circulation 2.39 million

Sunday paper with a high proportion of newsy features and articles. Experience and judgement required to break into its band of regular feature writers.

News Editor *Paul Field*
Financial Editor *Alex Brummer*
Business Editor *Ruth Sunderland*
Diary Editor *Nigel Dempster*
Features Editor/Women's Page *Sian James*
Books *Marilyn Warnick*
Political Editor *Simon Walters*
Sports Editor *To be appointed*
Night & Day Editor *Christena Appleyard*
Review Editor *Jim Gillespie*

You – The Mail on Sunday Magazine: colour supplement. Many feature articles, supplied entirely by freelance writers. **Acting Editor** *Sue Peart* . **Features Editor** *Catherine Fenton*

The Mirror

1 Canada Square, Canary Wharf, London E14 5AP
☎020 7293 3000 Fax 020 7293 3409
Website www.mirror.co.uk

Owner *Trinity Mirror plc*
Editor *Piers Morgan*
Circulation 2.22 million

No freelance opportunities for the inexperienced, but strong writers who understand what the tabloid market demands are always needed.

News Editor *Conor Hanna*
Features Editor *Mark Thomas*
Political Editor *James Hardy*
Business Editor *Clinton Manning*
Education Editor *Dorothy Lepkowska*
Showbusiness Diary Editor *Kevin O'Sullivan*
Sports Editor *Des Kelly*

Morning Star

1st Floor, Cape House, 787 Commercial Road, London E14 7HG
☎020 7538 5181 Fax 020 7538 5125
Email morsta@geo2.poptel.org.uk

Owner *Peoples Press Printing Society*
Editor *John Haylett*
Circulation 9,000

Not to be confused with the *Daily Star*, the *Morning Star* is the farthest left national daily. Those with a penchant for a Marxist reading of events and ideas can try their luck, though feature space is as competitive here as in the other nationals.

News Editor *Ian Morrison*
Features & Arts Editor *Kevin Russell*
Political Editor *Mike Ambrose*
Foreign Editor *Brian Denny*
Sports Editor *Alex Reid*

News of the World

1 Virginia Street, London E98 1NW
☎020 7782 1000 Fax 020 7583 9504
Website www.newsoftheworld.co.uk

Owner *News International plc/Rupert Murdoch*
Editor *Rebekah Wade*
Circulation 4.04 million

Highest circulation Sunday paper. Freelance contributions welcome. News and features editors welcome tips and ideas.

Assistant Editor (News) *Phil Taylor*
Assistant Editor (Features) *Gary Thompson*
Business/City Editor *Peter Prendergast*
Political/Environment Editor *Ian Kirby*
Sports Editor *Mike Dunn*

Sunday Magazine: colour supplement. **Editor** *Judy McGuire*. Showbiz interviews and strong human-interest features make up most of the content, but there are no strict rules about what is 'interesting'. Unsolicited mss and ideas welcome.

The Observer

119 Farringdon Road, London EC1R 3ER
☎020 7278 2332 Fax 020 7713 4250
Email editor@observer.co.uk
Website www.observer.co.uk

Owner *Guardian Newspapers Ltd*
Editor *Roger Alton*
Circulation 450,410

FOUNDED 1791. Acquired by Guardian Newspapers from Lonrho in May 1993. Occupies the middle ground of Sunday newspaper politics. Unsolicited material is not generally welcome, 'except from distinguished, established writers'. Receives far too many unsolicited offerings already. No news, fiction or special page opportunities. The newspaper runs annual competitions which change from year to year. Details are advertised in the newspaper.

Executive Editor, News *Andy Malone*
Features Editor *Gaby Wood*
Arts Editor *Jane Ferguson*
Review Editor *Lisa O'Kelly*
Comment Editor *Mike Holland*
Literary Editor *Robert McCrum*
City Editor *Paul Farrelly*
Science Editor *Robin McKie*
Education Correspondent *Tracy McVeigh*
Environment Editor *Anthony Browne*
Literary Editor *Robert McCrum*
Sports Editor *Brian Oliver*

Life: arts and lifestyle supplement. **Editor** *Allan Jenkins*.

The Observer Sport Montly: glossy magazine supplement launched in 2000. **Editor** *Matthew Tench*.

The Observer Food Monthly: launched summer 2001. **Editor** *Lucy Cavendish*.

Scotland on Sunday

108 Holyrood Road, Edinburgh EH8 8AS
☎0131 620 8620 Fax 0131 620 8491
Website www.scotsman.com

Owner *Scotsman Publications Ltd*
Editor *Margot Wilson*
Circulation 97,547

Scotland's top-selling quality broadsheet. Welcomes ideas rather than finished articles.

News Editor *Sebastian Hamilton*
Features Editor *Vicky Allan*

Scotland on Sunday Magazine: colour supplement. **Editor** *Vicky Allan*. Features on personalities, etc.

The Scotsman

108 Holyrood Road, Edinburgh EH8 8AS
☎0131 620 8620 Fax 0131 620 8616 (Editorial)
Website www.scotsman.com

Owner *Scotsman Publications Ltd*
Editor *Rebecca Hardy*
Circulation 88,873

Scotland's national newspaper. Many unsolicited mss come in, and stand a good chance of being read, although a small army of regulars supply much of the feature material not written in-house.

News Editor *David Lee*
Business Editor *Ian Watson*
Education *Seonag MacKinnon*
Features Editor *Charlotte Ross*
Book Reviews *David Robinson*

The Sun

1 Virginia Street, London E1 9BD
☎020 7782 4000 Fax 020 7782 4108
Email <firstname>.<lastname>@the-sun.co.uk
Website www.the-sun.co.uk

Owner *News International plc/Rupert Murdoch*
Editor *David Yelland*
Circulation 3.49 million

Highest circulation daily with a populist outlook; very keen on gossip, pop stars, TV soap, scandals and exposés of all kinds. No room for non-professional feature writers; 'investigative journalism' of a certain hue is always in demand, however.

News Editor *Sue Thompson*
Features Editor *Sam Carlisle*
Deputy Editor, Sports *Ted Chadwick*
Woman's Editor *Vicki Grimshaw*
Fashion Editor *Catherine Westwood*

Sunday Business

3 Waterhouse Square, Holborn Bars,
142 Holborn, London EC1N 2NP
☎020 7961 0000 Fax 020 7961 0102
Website www.sundaybusiness.co.uk

Owner *Press Holdings*

Editor *Nils Pratley*
Circulation 55,586

LAUNCHED April 1996 and 'relaunched' February 1998. National newspaper dedicated to business, finance and politics.
News Editor *Dominic O'Connell*
Features Editor *Topaz Amoore*
City Editor *Richard Wachman*

BusinessandPleasure magazine. **Editor** *Topaz Amoore.*

Sunday Express

Ludgate House, 245 Blackfriars Road, London SE1 9UX
☎020 7928 8000 Fax 020 7620 1654
Website www.expressnewspapers.co.uk
Owner *Northern & Shell Media/Richard Desmond*
Editor *Martin Townsend*
Circulation 1.01 million

The general rule of thumb is to approach in writing with an idea; all departments are prepared to look at an outline without commitment. Ideas welcome but already receives many which are 'too numerous to count'.
News Editor *David Dillon*
Features Editor *To be appointed*
Business Editor *Richard Phillips*
Political Editor *Julia Hartley-Brewer*
Sports Editor *To be appointed*

S: Sunday supplement on celebrities, homes, food and health. **Editor** *To be appointed.* No unsolicited mss. All contributions are commissioned. Ideas in writing only. *Enjoy*: Sunday showbiz and travel supplement.
Payment negotiable.

Sunday Herald

200 Renfield Street, Glasgow G2 3PR
☎0141 302 7800 Fax 0141 302 7809
Email editor@sundayherald.com
Website www.sundayherald.com
Owner *S.M.G.*
Editor *Andrew Jaspan*
Circulation 54,316

Also at: 10 George Street, Edinburgh EH2 2DU ☎0131 200 8100 Fax 0131 200 8088

LAUNCHED February 1999. Scottish seven-section broadsheet.
Deputy Editor *Richard Walker*
News Editor *David Milne*
Political Editor *Douglas Fraser*
Sports Editor *David Dick*
Entertainment Editor *Barry Didcock*
Magazine Editor *Kathleen Morgan*

Sunday Mail

One Central Quay, Glasgow G3 8DA
☎0141 309 3000 Fax 0141 309 3587
Website www.record-mail.co.uk
Owner *Trinity Mirror plc*
Editor *Allan Rennie*
Circulation 716,126

Popular Scottish Sunday tabloid.
News Editor *Jim Wilson*
Features Editor *Susie Cormack*

Seven Days: weekly supplement. **Editor** *Liz Steele.*

Sunday Mirror

1 Canada Square, Canary Wharf, London E14 5AP
☎020 7293 3000 Fax 020 7293 3939
Website www.sundaymirror.co.uk
Owner *Trinity Mirror*
Editor *Tina Weaver*
Circulation 1.84 million

In general terms contributions are welcome, though the paper patiently points out it has more time for those who have taken the trouble to study the market. Initial contact in writing preferred, except for live news situations. No fiction.
News Editor *tba* The news desk is very much in the market for tip-offs and inside information. Contributors would be expected to work with staff writers on news stories. Approach by telephone or fax in the first instance.
Finance *Anna Day*
Features Editor *Jane Johnson* 'Anyone who has obviously studied the market will be dealt with constructively and courteously.' Cherishes its record as a breeding ground for new talent.
Sports Editor *Steve McKenlay*

Personal: colour supplement. **Editor** *Kate Bravery.*

Sunday People

1 Canada Square, Canary Wharf, London E14 5AP
☎020 7293 3000 Fax 020 7293 3517
Website www.people.co.uk
Owner *Trinity Mirror plc*
Editor *Neil Wallis*
Circulation 1.4 million

Slightly up-market version of *The News of the World*. Keen on exposés and big-name gossip. Interested in ideas for investigative articles. Phone in first instance.
News Editor *James Weatherup*
Features Editor *Alison Phillips*

Political Editor *Nigel Nelson*
Sports Editor *Lee Clayton*
Travel Editor *Richard Allen*

The People Magazine. **Editor** *Amanda Cable.*
Approach by phone with ideas in first instance.

Sunday Post

2 Albert Square, Dundee DD1 9QJ
☎01382 223131 Fax 01382 201064
Email post@dcthomson.co.uk
Website www.sundaypost.com

Owner *D.C. Thomson & Co. Ltd*
Editor *David Pollington*
Circulation 700,000

Contributions should be addressed to the editor.

Sunday Post Magazine: monthly colour supplement. **Editor** *Maggie Dun.*

Sunday Sport

19 Great Ancoats Street, Manchester
M60 4BT
☎0161 236 4466 Fax 0161 236 4535
Website www.sundaysport.co.uk

Owner *David Sullivan*
Editor *Mark Harris*
Circulation 185,593

FOUNDED 1986. Sunday tabloid catering for a particular sector of the male 15–35 readership. As concerned with 'glamour' (for which, read: 'page 3') as with human interest, news, features and sport. Unsolicited mss are welcome; receives about 90 a week. Approach should be made by phone in the case of news and sports items, by letter for features. All material should be addressed to the news editor.

Assistant Editor, News *Simon Dean* Offbeat news, human interest, preferably with photographs.

Features Editor *Sarah Stephens* Regular items: glamour, showbiz and television, as well as general interest.

Sports Editor *Marc Smith* Hard-hitting sports stories on major soccer clubs and their personalities, plus leading clubs/people in other sports. Strong quotations to back up the news angle essential.

Payment negotiable and on publication.

Sunday Telegraph

1 Canada Square, Canary Wharf, London
E14 5DT
☎020 7538 5000 Fax 020 7538 6242
Website www.telegraph.co.uk

Owner *Conrad Black*
Editor *Dominic Lawson*

Circulation 809,615

Right-of-centre quality Sunday paper which, although traditionally formal, has pepped up its image to attract a younger readership. Unsolicited material from untried writers is rarely used. Contact with idea and details of track record.

News Editor *Chris Boffey*
Features Editor *Sandy Mitchell*
City Editor *Neil Bennett*
Political Editor *Joe Murphy*
Education Editor *Martin Bentham*
Arts Editor *Anna Murphy*
Environment Editor *David Harrison*
Literary Editor *Miriam Gross*
Diary Editor *Adam Helliker*
Sports Editor *Jon Ryan*

Sunday Telegraph Magazine **Editor** *Lucy Tuck*

The Sunday Times

1 Pennington Street, London E98 1ST
☎020 7782 5000 Fax 020 7782 5658
Website www.sunday-times.co.uk

Owner *News International plc/Rupert Murdoch*
Editor *John Witherow*
Circulation 1.4 million

FOUNDED 1820. Tendency to be anti-establishment, with a strong crusading investigative tradition. Approach the relevant editor with an idea in writing. Close scrutiny of the style of each section of the paper is strongly advised before sending mss. No fiction. All fees by negotiation.

News Editor *Charles Hymas* Opportunities are very rare.

News Review Editor *Sarah Baxter* Submissions are always welcome, but the paper commissions its own, uses staff writers or works with literary agents, by and large. The features sections where most opportunities exist are *Style* and *The Culture*.

Culture Editor *Helen Hawkins*
Business Editor *Rory Godson*
City Editor *Kirstie Hamilton*
Education Editor *Judith O'Reilly*
Science/Environment *Jonathan Leake*
Literary Editor *Caroline Gascoigne*
Sports Editor *Alex Butler*
Style Editor *Robert Johnston*

Sunday Times Magazine: colour supplement. **Editor** *Robin Morgan.* No unsolicited material. Write with ideas in first instance.

The Times

1 Pennington Street, London E98 1TT
☎020 7782 5000 Fax 020 7488 3242
Website www.thetimes.co.uk

Owner *News International plc/Rupert Murdoch*
Editor *Peter Stothard*
Circulation 711,365

Generally right (though features can range in tone from diehard to libertarian). *The Times* receives a great many unsolicited offerings. Writers with feature ideas should approach by letter in the first instance. No fiction.

Deputy Editor *Ben Preston*
News Editor *John Wellman*
Features Editor *Anne Barrowclough*
Associate Editor *Brian MacArthur*

City/Financial Editor *Patience Wheatcroft*
Diary Editor *Giles Coren*
Arts Editor *Sarah Vine*
Education *John O'Leary*
Literary Editor *Erica Wagner*
Political Editor *Phil Webster*
Sports Editor *David Chappell*

***Weekend Times* Editor** *Jane Wheatley*

The Times Magazine: Saturday supplement.
Editor *Gill Morgan*

Times 2 Editor *Sandra Parsons*

Freelance Rates – Newspapers

Freelance rates vary enormously. The following minimum rates, set by the **National Union of Journalists**, should be treated as guidelines. The NUJ has no power to enforce minimum rates on newspapers that do not recognise the Union. It is up to freelancers to negotiate the best deal they can.

National newspapers

(Including *The Herald, Sunday Herald, Daily Record, Sunday Mail, The Scotsman, Scotland on Sunday, Evening Standard*)

Features (including reviews, obituaries, etc) Broadsheet rates start at under £220 per 1000 words and as low as £100 in Scotland, but sums of over £500 are common. Tabloids often pay considerably more than broadsheets though items are usually shorter.

News News may be paid for per 1000 words or by the day. When payment is by the word, the minimum should be £230 per 1000 words or pro rata. (Applies to all areas of news reporting, including sport.)

Day Rates A low minimum of £125. Accept day rates only if required to be in the office for the day.

Exclusives These can command very high fees, depending on how much the newspaper wants the story. A prominent position for the piece should command £550 or more. A guaranteed minimum of at least £280 should be negotiated in case it appears further down the page in a shorter form.

Colour Supplements Higher rates of payment should apply.

Crosswords 15 × 15 squares and under: at least £120; 15 × 15 squares and over: at least £150.

Regional & provincial newspapers (England & Wales)

According to the NUJ, freelance rates in many papers in this area (especially in provincials) have remained static over the last few years – 'a fact that makes individual negotiation all the more important, and which makes positive recommendations impossible'. The 'lineage' system (payment per line of text published – usually four words) is common in provincials, at around £2–3 per ten lines, and 20–30 pence per line thereafter, for both news and features. 'Payment on dailies and Sundays is still way below acceptable levels.'

Crosswords At least £70.

Regional Newspapers

Regional Newspapers are listed in alphabetical order under town. Thus the *Evening Standard* appears under 'L' for London; the *Lancashire Evening Post* under 'P' for Preston.

Aberdeen

Evening Express (Aberdeen)
PO Box 43, Lang Stracht, Mastrick, Aberdeen
AB15 6DF
☎01224 690222 Fax 01224 344106
Email d.martin@ajl.co.uk

Owner *Northcliffe Newspapers Group Ltd*
Editor *Donald Martin*
Circulation 68,191

Circulates in Aberdeen and the Grampian region. Local, national and international news and pictures, sport. Family platforms include *What's On, Counter* (consumer news), *Eating Out Guide, Family Days Out*. Unsolicited mss welcome 'if on a controlled basis'.
  News Editor *Richard Prest* Freelance news contributors welcome.
  Payment £30–60.

The Press and Journal
PO Box 43, Lang Stracht, Mastrick, Aberdeen
AB15 6DF
☎01224 690222 Fax 01224 663575

Owner *Northcliffe Newspapers Group Ltd*
Editor *Derek Tucker*
Circulation 104,548

Circulates in Aberdeen, Grampians, Highlands, Tayside, Orkney, Shetland and the Western Isles. A well-established regional daily which is said to receive more unsolicited mss a week than the *Sunday Mirror*. Unsolicited mss are nevertheless welcome; approach in writing with ideas. No fiction.
  News Editor *Fiona McWhirr* Wide variety of hard or off-beat news and features relating especially, but not exclusively, to the North of Scotland.
  Sports Editor *Jim Dolan*
  Women's Page *Susan Mansfield*
  Payment by arrangement.

Barrow -in-Furness

North West Evening Mail
Abbey Road, Barrow in Furness, Cumbria
LA14 5QS
☎01229 821835 Fax 01229 840164
Email news@nwemail.co.uk
Website www.nwemail.co.uk

Owner *CN Group Ltd*
Editor *Sara Hadwin*
Circulation 20,815

All editorial material should be addressed to the editor.
  Assistant Editor (Production) *Bill Myers*
  Sports Editor *Leo Clarke*

Basildon

Evening Echo
Newspaper House, Chester Hall Lane, Basildon, Essex SS14 3BL
☎01268 522792 Fax 01268 282884

Owner *Newsquest Media Group (a Gannett company)*
Editor *Martin McNeill*
Circulation 47,000

Relies almost entirely on staff and regular outside contributors, but will very occasionally consider material sent on spec. Approach the editor in writing with ideas. Although the paper is Basildon-based, its largest circulation is in the Southend area.

Bath

The Bath Chronicle
Windsor House, Windsor Bridge Road, Bath
BA2 3AU
☎01225 322322 Fax 01225 322291

Owner *BUP Plc*
Editor *David Gledhill*
Circulation 17,501

Local news and features especially welcomed.
  Deputy Editor *John McCready*
  News Editor *Paul Wiltshire*

Features Editor *Matt Mills*
Sports Editor *Neville Smith*

Belfast

Belfast News Letter
46–56 Boucher Crescent, Belfast BT12 6QY
☎028 9068 0000 Fax 028 9066 4412

Owner *Century Newspapers Ltd*
Editor *Geoff Martin*
Circulation 33,853

Weekly supplements: *Farming Life* ; *Business News Letter*; *Female Times*; *The Guide*; *Sports Ulster*; *City Limits*.
Deputy Editor *Mike Chapman*
News Editors *Ric Clark, Steven Moore*
Features Editor *Geoff Hill*
Sports Editor *Brian Millar*
Fashion & Lifestyle/Property Editor
  Sandra Chapman
Business Editor *Adrienne McGill*
Agricultural Editor *David McCoy*

Belfast Telegraph
Royal Avenue, Belfast BT1 1EB
☎028 9026 4000 Fax 028 9055 4506/4540

Owner *Independent News & Media (UK)*
Editor *Edmund Curran*
Circulation 121,015

Weekly business, property and recruitment supplements.
Deputy Editor *Jim Flanagan*
News Editor *Paul Connolly*
Features Editor *John Caruth*
Sports Editor *John Laverty*
Business Editor *Nigel Tilson*

The Irish News
113/117 Donegall Street, Belfast BT1 2GE
☎028 9032 2226 Fax 028 9033 7505

Owner *Irish News Ltd*
Editor *Noel Doran*
Circulation 51,677

All material to appropriate editor (phone to check), or to the news desk.
Head of Content *Fiona McGarry*
Arts Editor *Tim Brannigan*
Sports Editor *Thomas Hawkins*
Women's Page *Ann Molloy*

Sunday Life
124–144 Royal Avenue, Belfast BT1 1EB
☎028 9033 1133 Fax 028 9055 4507

Owner *Independent News & Media (UK)*
Circulation 96,612

Editor/General Manager *Martin Lindsay*
  Deputy Editor *Dave Culbert*
  Features Editor *Sue Corbett*
  Sports Editor *Jim Gracey*

Birmingham

Birmingham Evening Mail
28 Colmore Circus, Queensway, Birmingham B4 6AX
☎0121 236 3366 Fax 0121 233 0271

Owner *Trinity Mirror Plc*
Editor *Roger Borrell*
Circulation 138,828

Freelance contributions are welcome, particularly topics of interest to the West Midlands and Women's Page pieces offering original and lively comment.
News Editor *Steve Dyson*
Features Editor *Carol Cole*
Women's Page *Diane Parkes*

Birmingham Post
28 Colmore Circus, Queensway, Birmingham B4 6AX
☎0121 236 3366 Fax 0121 625 1105

Owner *Trinity Mirror Plc*
Publisher *Dan Mason*
Circulation 21,833

One of the country's leading regional newspapers. Freelance contributions are welcome. Topics of interest to the West Midlands and pieces offering lively, original comment are particularly welcome.
News Editor *Chris Russon*
Features Editor *Lisa Piddington*

Sunday Mercury (Birmingham)
28 Colmore Circus, Queensway, Birmingham B4 6AZ
☎0121 236 3366 Fax 0121 234 5877

Owner *Trinity Mirror Plc*
Editor *David Brookes*
Circulation 110,501
  Assistant Editor (News & Features)
    Bernard Cole
  Assistant Editor (Sport) *Lee Gibson*

Blackburn

Lancashire Evening Telegraph
Newspaper House, High Street, Blackburn, Lancashire BB1 1HT
☎01254 678678 Fax 01254 680429
Website www.thisislancashire.co.uk

Owner *Newsquest Media Group Ltd (a Gannett company)*
Editor *Kevin Young*
Circulation 43,919

News stories and feature material with an East Lancashire flavour (a local angle, or written by local people) welcome. Approach in writing with an idea in the first instance. No fiction.
   News/Features/Women's Page Editor *Andrew Turner*

Blackpool
The Gazette (Blackpool)
PO Box 20, Avroe House, Avroe Crescent, Blackpool, Lancashire FY4 2DP
☎01253 400888 Fax 01253 361870

Owner *RIM*
Managing Director/Editor-in-Chief *Philip Welsh*
Circulation 40,002
Associate Editor *Neil Hepburn*

Unsolicited mss welcome in theory. Approach in writing with an idea. Supplements: *The Result* (sport, Monday); *Eve* (women, Tuesday); *Wheels* (motoring, Wednesday); *Property* (Thursday); *Big Weekend* (entertainment, Friday); *Sevendays* (entertainment & leisure, Saturday).
   Sports Editor *Jonathan Lee*

Bolton
Bolton Evening News
Newspaper House, Churchgate, Bolton, Lancashire BL1 1DE
☎01204 522345 Fax 01204 365068
Email ben_editorial@newsquest.co.uk
Website www.thisislancashire.co.uk

Owner *Newsquest Media Group Ltd (a Gannett company)*
Editor *Steve Hughes*
Circulation 42,035

Business, children's page, travel, local services, motoring, fashion and cookery.
   News Editor *Lyn Ashwell*
   Features Editor/Women's Page *Angela Kelly*

Bournemouth
Daily Echo
Richmond Hill, Bournemouth, Dorset BH2 6HH
☎01202 554601 Fax 01202 292115

Owner *Newsquest Media Group Ltd (a Gannett company)*

Editor *Neal Butterworth*
Circulation 45,090

FOUNDED 1900. Has a strong features content and invites specialist articles, particularly on unusual and contemporary subjects but only with a local angle. Supplements: business, education, homes and gardens, motoring, what's on, *Weekender*. Regular features on weddings, property, books, local history, green issues, the Channel coast. All editorial material should be addressed to the **News Editor** *Andy Martin*.
   Payment on publication.

Bradford
Telegraph & Argus (Bradford)
Hall Ings, Bradford, West Yorkshire BD1 1JR
☎01274 729511 Fax 01274 723634
Website www.thisisbradford.co.uk

Owner *Newsquest Media Group Ltd (a Gannett company)*
Editor *Perry Austin-Clarke*
Circulation 51,838

No unsolicited mss – approach in writing with samples of work. No fiction.
   Assistant Editor (News & Features) *Damian Bates* Local features and general interest. Showbiz pieces. 600–1000 words (maximum 1500).
   Sports Editor *Alan Birkinshaw*

Brighton
Evening Argus
Argus House, Crowhurst Road, Hollingbury, Brighton, East Sussex BN1 8AR
☎01273 544544 Fax 01273 505703
Email simonb@argus-btn.co.uk
Website www.thisisbrighton.co.uk

Owner *Newsquest (Sussex) Ltd*

Editor-in-Chief *Simon Bradshaw*
Circulation 50,285
   News Editor *Rebecca Stephens*
   Sports Editor *Chris Giles*

Bristol
Evening Post
Temple Way, Bristol BS99 7HD
☎0117 934 3000 Fax 0117 934 3575
Email mail@epost.co.uk
Website www.epost.co.uk

Owner *Bristol United Press plc*
Editor *Mike Lowe*
Circulation 79,346

News Editor *Kevan Blackadder*
  Features Editor *Bill Davis*
  Sports Editor *Chris Bartlett*

Western Daily Press
Temple Way, Bristol BS99 7HD
☎0117 934 3000 Fax 0117 934 3574
Email WDEditor *or* WDNews *or*
WDFeats@bepp.co.uk
Website www.westpress.co.uk

Owner *Bristol Evening Post & Press Ltd*
Editor *Terry Manners*
Circulation 52,373

  Sports Editor *Bill Beckett*
  Women's Page *Lynda Cleasby*

Burton upon Trent
Burton Mail
65–68 High Street, Burton upon Trent,
Staffordshire DE14 1LE
☎01283 512345 Fax 01283 515351
Email editorial@burtonmail.co.uk

Owner *Burton Daily Mail Ltd*
Editor *To be appointed*
Circulation 18,456

Fashion, health, wildlife, environment, nostal-
gia, financial/money (Monday); consumer,
motoring (Tuesday); women's world, rock
(Wednesday); property (Thursday); motoring,
farming, what's on (Friday); what's on, leisure
(Saturday).
  News/Features Editor *Andrew Parker*
  Sports Editor *Rex Page*
  Women's Page *Bill Pritchard*

Cambridge
Cambridge Evening News
Winship Road, Milton, Cambridge CB4 6PP
☎01223 434434 Fax 01223 434415

Owner *Cambridge Newspapers Ltd*
Editor *Colin Grant*
Circulation 41,563

News Editor *Helen Montgomery*
  Business Editor *Jenny Chapman*
  Sports Editor *To be appointed*

Cardiff
South Wales Echo
Thomson House, Havelock Street, Cardiff
CF10 1XR
☎029 2022 3333 Fax 029 2058 3624
Website www.icwales.com

Owner *Trinity Mirror Plc*
Editor *Robin Fletcher*
Circulation 75,959

Circulates in South and Mid Glamorgan and
Gwent.
  Head of News & Design *Nick Machin*
  Head of Features & Development *Neil*
    Cammies
  Head of Sport *Carl Difford*

Wales on Sunday
Thomson House, Havelock Street, Cardiff
CF10 1XR
☎029 2022 3333 Fax 029 2025 8725

Owner *Trinity Mirror plc*
Editor *Alan Edmunds*
Circulation 62,286

LAUNCHED 1989. Tabloid with sports supple-
ment. Does not welcome unsolicited mss.
  News Editor *Ceri Gould*
  Features/Women's Page *Mike Smith*
  Sports Editor *Paul Abbandonato*

The Western Mail
Thomson House, Havelock Street, Cardiff
CF10 1XR
☎029 2022 3333 Fax 029 2058 3652
Email nfowler@wme.co.uk
Website www.icwales.com

Owner *Trinity Mirror Plc*
Editor *Neil Fowler*
Circulation 64,172

Circulates in Cardiff, Merthyr Tydfil,
Newport, Swansea and towns and villages
throughout Wales. Mss welcome if of a topical
nature, and preferably of Welsh interest. No
short stories or travel. Approach in writing to
the editor. 'Usual subjects already well cov-
ered, e.g. motoring, travel, books, gardening.
We look for the unusual.' Maximum 1000
words. Opportunities also on women's page.
Supplements: Saturday Magazine; Education;
Welsh Homes; Country and Farming;
Business; Sport; Motoring.
  Deputy Editor *Alastair Milburn*
  Head of Content *Lee Wenham*
  Sports Editor *Philip Blanche*

Carlisle
News & Star
Newspaper House, Dalston Road, Carlisle,
Cumbria CA2 5UA
☎01228 612600 Fax 01228 612601

Owner *Cumbrian Newspaper Group Ltd*

Editor *Keith Sutton*
Circulation 25,375

> **Assistant Editor** *Nick Turner*
> **Deputy Editor** *Steve Johnston*
> **Sports Editor** *Mike Gardner*
> **Women's Page** *Jane Loughran*

Chatham

Kent Today

395 High Street, Chatham, Kent ME4 4PQ
☎01634 830600 Fax 01634 829484

Owner *Kent Messenger Group*
Editor *Bob Diamond*
Circulation 21,567

Business Editor *Trevor Sturgess*
> **Community Editor** *David Jones*
> **Sports Editor** *Mike Rees*

Cheltenham

Gloucestershire Echo

1 Clarence Parade, Cheltenham,
Gloucestershire GL50 3NY
☎01242 271900 Fax 01242 271848

Owner *Northcliffe Newspapers Group Ltd*
Editor *Anita Syvret*
Circulation 25,426

All material, other than news, should be
addressed to the editor.
> **News Editor** *Owen Jones*

Chester

Chronicle Newspapers (Chester & North Wales)

Chronicle House, Commonhall Street,
Chester CH1 2BJ
☎01244 340151 Fax 01244 340165
Email elangton@chron8.demon.co.uk
Website www.cheshirenews.co.uk

Owner *Trinity Mirror Plc*
Editor-in-Chief *Eric Langton*

All unsolicited feature material will be considered.

Colchester

Evening Gazette (Colchester)

Oriel House, 43–44 North Hill, Colchester,
Essex CO1 1TZ
☎01206 506000 Fax 01206 508274
Email newsdesk@thisisessex.co.uk
Website www.thisisessex.co.uk

Owner *Newsquest (Essex)*
Editor *Irene Kettle*
Circulation 28,206

Monday–Friday daily newspaper servicing
north and mid-Essex including Colchester,
Harwich, Clacton, Braintree, Witham, Maldon
and Chelmsford. Unsolicited mss not generally
used. Relies heavily on regular contributors.
> **Features Editor** *Iris Clapp*

Coventry

Coventry Evening Telegraph

Corporation Street, Coventry CV1 1FP
☎024 7663 3633 Fax 024 7655 0869
Email editorial@go2coventry.co.uk
Website www.IcCoventry.co.uk

Owner *Trinity Mirror Plc*
Editor *Alan Kirby*
Circulation 82,417

Unsolicited mss are read, but few are published.
Approach in writing with an idea. No fiction. All
unsolicited material should be addressed to the
editor. Maximum 600 words for features.
> **News Editor** *John West*
> **Features Editor** *Steve Chilton*
> **Sports Editor** *Roger Draper*
> **Women's Page** *Barbara Argument*
> *Payment* negotiable.

Darlington

The Northern Echo

Priestgate, Darlington, Co. Durham
DL1 1NF
☎01325 381313 Fax 01325 380539
Email echo@nen.co.uk
Website www.thisisthenortheast.co.uk

Owner *Newsquest (North East) Ltd (a Gannett company)*
Editor *Peter Barron*
Circulation 70,358

FOUNDED 1870. Freelance pieces welcome but
telephone first to discuss submission.
> **News Editor** *Nigel Burton* Interested in
reports involving the North-East or North
Yorkshire. Preferably phoned in.
> **Features Editor** *Jenny Needham* Background
pieces to topical news stories relevant to the area.
Must be arranged with the features editor before
submission of any material.
> **Business Editor** *Jonathan Jones*
> **Sports Editor** *Nick Loughlin*
> *Payment* and length by arrangement.

Derby

Derby Evening Telegraph

Northcliffe House, Meadow Road, Derby
DE1 2DW
☎01332 291111   Fax 01332 253027

Owner *Northcliffe Newspapers Group Ltd*
Acting Editor *Mike Norton*
Circulation 60,691

Weekly business supplement.
  News Editor *Andy Wright*
  Features Editor/Women's Page *Nigel Poulson*
  Sports Editor *Steve Nicholson*
  Motoring Editor *Bob Maddox*

Doncaster

The Doncaster Star

40 Duke Street, Doncaster, South Yorkshire
DN1 3EA
☎01302 344001   Fax 01302 768340
Email graham.walker@rim.co.uk

Owner *Sheffield Newspapers Ltd*
Editor/News Editor *Graham Walker*
Circulation 9,716

All editorial material to be addressed to the editor.
  Sports Editor *Steve Hossack*
  Women's Page *Jane Stapleton*

Dundee

The Courier and Advertiser

80 Kingsway East, Dundee DD4 8SL
☎01382 223131   Fax 01382 454590
Email courier@dcthomson.co.uk
Website www.thecourier.co.uk

Owner *D.C. Thomson & Co. Ltd*
Editor *Adrian Arthur*
Circulation 92,775

Circulates in East Central Scotland. Features occasionally accepted on a wide range of subjects, particularly local/Scottish interest – including finance, insurance, agriculture, motoring, modern homes, lifestyle and fitness. Maximum length, 500 words.
  News Editor *Arliss Rhind*
  Features Editor/Women's Page *Shona Lorimer*
  Sports Editor *Graham Dey*

Evening Telegraph

80 Kingsway East, Dundee DD4 8SL
☎01382 223131   Fax 01382 454590

Owner *D.C. Thomson & Co. Ltd*

Editor *Alan Proctor*
Circulation 30,290

Circulates in Tayside, Dundee and Fife. All material should be addressed to the editor.

East Anglia

East Anglian Daily Times

See under ***Ipswich***

Eastern Daily Press

See under ***Norwich***

Edinburgh

Evening News

108 Holyrood Road, Edinburgh EH1 1YT
☎0131 620 8620   Fax 0131 620 8696
Website www.edinburghnews.com

Owner *European Press Holdings Ltd*
Editor *John C. McLellan*
Circulation 90,000

FOUNDED 1873. Circulates in Edinburgh, Fife, Central and Lothian. Coverage includes: entertainment, gardening, motoring, shopping, fashion, health and lifestyle, showbusiness. Occasional platform pieces, features of topical and/or local interest. Unsolicited feature material welcome. Approach the appropriate editor in writing.
  Associate Editor (News) *David Lee*
  Associate Editor (Features) *Helen Martin*
  Sports Editor *Martin Dempster*
  Payment NUJ/house rates.

Exeter

Express & Echo

Heron Road, Sowton, Exeter, Devon
EX2 7NF
☎01392 442211
Fax 01392 442294/442287 (editorial)
Email echonews@westcountrypublications.
  co.uk
Website www.thisisexeter.co.uk

Owner *Westcountry Publications Limited*
Editor *Steve Hall*
Circulation 30,978

Weekly supplements: *Business Week; Property Echo; Wheels; Weekend Echo.*
  Content/Features Editor/Women's Page *Sue Kemp*
  Sports Editor *Simon Mills*

Glasgow

Evening Times

200 Renfield Street, Glasgow G2 3PR
☎0141 302 7000 Fax 0141 302 6677
Email TimesEditorial@scottishmedia.com

Owner *S.M.G.*
Editor *Charles McGhee*
Circulation 110,585

Circulates in Glasgow and the west of Scotland.
Supplements: *Job Search; Home Front; Woman; Times Out* (leisure); *Times Out Weekend Extra.*
   News Editor *Graeme Smith*
   Features Editor *Russell Kyle*
   Sports Editor *David Stirling*
   Women's Editor *Agnes Stevenson*

The Herald (Glasgow)

See **National Newspapers**

Gloucester

The Citizen

St John's Lane, Gloucester GL1 2AY
☎01452 424442
Fax 01452 420664 (Editorial)

Owner *Northcliffe Newspapers Group Ltd*
Editor *Spencer Feeney*
Circulation 34,813

All editorial material to be addressed to the **News Editor** *Gavin Curry*.

Gloucestershire Echo

See under *Cheltenham*

Greenock

Greenock Telegraph

2 Crawfurd Street, Greenock PA15 1LH
☎01475 726511 Fax 01475 783734

Owner *Clyde & Forth Press Ltd*
Editor *Stewart Peterson*
Circulation 19,872

Circulates in Greenock, Port Glasgow, Gourock, Kilmacolm, Langbank, Bridge of Weir, Inverkip, Wemyss Bay, Skelmorlie, Largs. Unsolicited mss considered 'if they relate to the newspaper's general interests'. No fiction. All material to be addressed to the editor.

Grimsby

Grimsby Telegraph

80 Cleethorpe Road, Grimsby, N.E. Lincs DN31 3EH
☎01472 360360 Fax 01472 372257

Email newsdesk@grimsbytelegraph.co.uk

Owner *Northcliffe Newspapers Group Ltd*
Editor *Peter Moore*
Circulation 71,167

Sister paper of the *Scunthorpe Evening Telegraph.* Unsolicited mss generally welcome. Approach in writing. No fiction. Weekly supplement: *Business Telegraph.* All material to be addressed to the **News Editor** *S.P. Richards.* Particularly welcomes hard news stories – approach in haste by telephone.
   Special Publications Editor *B. Farnsworth*

Guernsey

Guernsey Press & Star

Braye Road, Vale, Guernsey, Channel Islands GY1 3BW
☎01481 240240 Fax 01481 240235
Email newsroom@guernsey-press.com
Website www.guernsey-press.com

Owner *Guiton Group*
Editor *Richard Digard*
Circulation 16,000

Special pages include children's and women's interest, gardening and fashion.
   News Editor *James Falla*
   Sports Editor *Rob Batiste*
   Women's Page *Jackie Chappell*

Halifax

Evening Courier

PO Box 19, King Cross Street, Halifax, West Yorkshire HX1 2SF
☎01422 260200 Fax 01422 260341

Owner *Johnston Press Plc*
Editor *Edward Riley*
Circulation 29,000

   News Editor *John Kenealy*
   Features Editor *William Marshall*
   Sports Editor *Ian Rushworth*
   Women's Page *Diane Crabtree*

Hartlepool

Hartlepool Mail

New Clarence House, Wesley Square, Hartlepool TS24 8BX
☎01429 274441 Fax 01429 869024
Email post@hartmail.demon.co.uk
Website www.hartlepoolmail.co.uk

Owner *Johnston Press Plc*
Editor *Harry Blackwood*
Circulation 23,614

News Editor *Gavin Ledwith*
Features Editor *Bernice Saltzer*
Sports Editor *Roy Kelly*

Huddersfield

Huddersfield Daily Examiner
Queen Street South, Huddersfield, West
Yorkshire HD1 2TD
☎01484 430000 Fax 01484 437789

Owner *Trinity Mirror Plc*
Editor *John Williams*
Circulation 35,218

Home improvement, home heating, weddings,
dining out, motoring, fashion, services to trade
and industry.
  Deputy Editor *John Bird*
  News Editor *Neil Atkinson*
  Features Editor *Andrew Flynn*
  Sports Editor *John Gledhill*
  Women's Page *Hilarie Stelfox*

Hull

Hull Daily Mail
Blundell's Corner, Beverley Road, Hull, East
Yorkshire HU3 1XS
☎01482 327111 Fax 01482 584353
Website www.thisishull.co.uk

Owner *Northcliffe Newspapers Group Ltd*
Editor *John Meehan*
Circulation 85,000

Content Editor *Paul Hartley*
  Features Editors *Lucy Smith*, *Matt
  Stephenson*

Ipswich

East Anglian Daily Times
Press House, 30 Lower Brook Street, Ipswich,
Suffolk IP4 1AN
☎01473 230023 Fax 01473 211391
Email EADT@ecng.co.uk
Website www.suffolk.now.co.uk

Owner *Eastern Counties Newspapers Group Ltd*
Editor *Terry Hunt*
Circulation 46,008

FOUNDED 1874. Unsolicited mss generally not
welcome; three or four received a week and
almost none are used. Approach in writing in the
first instance. No fiction. Supplements: Young
Readers' section (Monday); Business (Tuesday);
Job Quest (Wednesday); Property (Thursday);
Motoring (Friday); Magazine (Saturday).
  News Editor *Mark Hindle* Hard news stories
involving East Anglia (Suffolk, Essex particularly)

or individuals resident in the area are always of
interest.
  Features *Julian Forbes* Mostly in-house, but
will occasionally buy in when the subject is of
strong Suffolk/East Anglian interest. Photo
features preferred (extra payment). Special ad-
vertisement features are regularly run. Some
opportunities here. Maximum 1000 words.
  Sports Editor *Nick Garnham*
  Women's Page *Victoria Hawkins*

Evening Star
30 Lower Brook Street, Ipswich, Suffolk
IP4 1AN
☎01473 230023 Fax 01473 225296

Owner *Eastern Counties Newspaper Group*
Editor *Nigel Pickover*
Circulation 30,391

  Deputy Editor (News) *Russell Cook*
  Sports Editor *Mike Horne*

Jersey

Jersey Evening Post
PO Box 582, Jersey, Channel Islands JE4 8XQ
☎01534 611611 Fax 01534 611622
Email editorial@jerseyeveningpost.com
Website www.thisisjersey.com

Owner *Jersey Evening Post Ltd*
Editor *Chris Bright*
Circulation 23,081

Special pages: gardening, motoring, property,
boating, technology, young person's (16–25),
women, food and drink, personal finance, rock
reviews, health, business.
  News Editor *Sue Le Ruez*
  Features Editor *Richard Pedley*
  Sports Editor *Ron Felton*

Kent

Kent Messenger
See under **Maidstone**

Kent Today
See under **Chatham**

Kettering

Evening Telegraph
Newspaper House, Ise Park, Rothwell Road,
Kettering, Northamptonshire NN16 8GA
☎01536 506100 Fax 01536 506195
Email etnewsdesk@northantsnews.co.uk
Website www.northantsnews.com

Owner *Johnston Press Plc*

Managing Editor *Lee Bearton*
Circulation 33,346

Northamptonshire Business Guide (weekly); *Guide* supplement (Thursday/Saturday), featuring TV, gardening, videos, films, eating out; and an occasional supplement, *Home & Garden*.
News Editor *Nick Tite*
Sports Editor *Ian Davidson*

Lancashire
Lancashire Evening Post
See under **Preston**

Lancashire Evening Telegraph
See under **Blackburn**

Leamington Spa
Leamington Spa Courier
32 Hamilton Terrace, Leamington Spa, Warwickshire CV32 4LY
☎01926 888222 Fax 01926 451690
Email editorial@leamingtoncourier.co.uk
Website www.leamingtononline.co.uk
Owner *Central Counties Newspapers*
Editor *Martin Lawson*
Circulation 13,410

One of the Leamington Spa Courier Series which also includes the *Warwick Courier* and *Kenilworth Weekly News*. Unsolicited feature articles considered, particularly matter with a local angle. Telephone with idea first.
News Editor *Richard Parker*

Leeds
Yorkshire Evening Post
Wellington Street, Leeds, West Yorkshire LS1 1RF
☎0113 243 2701 Fax 0113 238 8536
Email eped@ypn.co.uk
Owner *Regional Independent Media*
Editor *Neil Hodgkinson*
Circulation 100,596

Evening sister of the *Yorkshire Post*.
News Editor *David Helliwell*
Features Editor *Anne Pickles*
Sports Editor *Martin Rose*
Women's Page *Jayne Dawson*

Yorkshire Post
Wellington Street, Leeds, West Yorkshire LS1 1RF
☎0113 243 2701 Fax 0113 238 8537
Owner *Regional Independent Media*

Editor *Tony Watson*
Circulation 75,836

A serious-minded, quality regional daily with a generally conservative outlook. Three or four unsolicited mss arrive each day; all will be considered but initial approach in writing preferred. All submissions should be addressed to the editor. No fiction, poetry or family histories.
Head of Content *John Furbisher*
Features Editor *Mick Hickling* Open to suggestions in all fields (though ordinarily commissioned from specialist writers).
Sports Editor *Bill Bridge*
Women's Page *Jill Armstrong*

Leicester
Leicester Mercury
St George Street, Leicester LE1 9FQ
☎0116 251 2512 Fax 0116 253 0645
Website www.thisisleicestershire.co.uk
Owner *Northcliffe Newspapers Group Ltd*
Editor *Nick Carter*
Circulation 111,630
Head of News *Richard Bettsworth*
Features Editor *Alex Dawon*

Lincoln
Lincolnshire Echo
Brayford Wharf East, Lincoln LN5 7AT
☎01522 820000 Fax 01522 804493
Email editorecho@lincolnshireecho.co.uk
Owner *Northcliffe Newspapers Group Ltd*
Editor *Michael Sassi*
Circulation 29,206

Best buys, holidays, motoring, dial-a-service, restaurants, sport, leisure, home improvement, record reviews, gardening corner, stars. All editorial material to be addressed to the editor.

Liverpool
Daily Post
PO Box 48, Old Hall Street, Liverpool L69 3EB
☎0151 227 2000 Fax 0151 236 4682
Email online@day-post.u-net.com
Owner *Trinity Mirror Plc*
Editor *Alastair Machray*
Circulation 72,776

Unsolicited mss welcome. Receives about six a day. Approach in writing with an idea. No fiction. Local, national/international news, current affairs, profiles – with pictures. Maximum 800–1000 words.

Features Editor *Jane Haase*
News Editor *Andrew Edwards*
Sports Editor *Richard Williamson*
Women's Page *Margaret Kitchen*

Liverpool Echo

PO Box 48, Old Hall Street, Liverpool L69 3EB
☎0151 227 2000   Fax 0151 236 4682

Owner *Liverpool Daily Post & Echo Ltd*
Editor *Mark Dickinson*
Circulation 157,999

One of the country's major regional dailies. Unsolicited mss welcome; initial approach with ideas in writing preferred.

News Editor *Andrew Edwards*
Features Editor *Jane Wolstenholme*
Sports Editor *Ken Rogers*
Women's Editor *Susan Lee*

London

Evening Standard

Northcliffe House, 2 Derry Street, London W8 5EE
☎020 7938 6000   Fax 020 7937 2648
Website www.thisislondon.com

Owner *Associated Newspapers/Lord Rothermere*
Editor *Max Hastings*
Circulation 435,778

Long-established evening paper, serving Londoners with both news and feature material. Genuine opportunities for London-based features. Produces a weekly colour supplement, *ES The Evening Standard Magazine*, a weekly listings magazine *Hot Tickets* and regular weekly supplements: *Just the Job* (Monday), *Homes & Property* (Wednesday), and *ES Wheels* (Friday).

Deputy Editor *Andrew Bordiss*
Associate Editor (Features) *Nicola Jeal*
News Editor *Ian Walker*
Features Editor *Bernice Davison*
Sports Editor *Simon Greenberg*
Editor, *ES* *Mimi Spencer*
Editor, *Hot Tickets* *Mark Booker*

Maidstone

Kent Messenger

6 & 7 Middle Row, Maidstone, Kent ME14 1TG
☎01622 695666   Fax 01622 757227
Email kentmessenger@thekmgroup.co.uk
Website www.kentonline.co.uk

Owner *Kent Messenger Group*
Associate Director, Editorial *Simon Irwin*
Circulation 48,425

Very little freelance work is commissioned.

Manchester

Manchester Evening News

164 Deansgate, Manchester M60 2RD
☎0161 832 7200   Fax 0161 834 3814
Website www.manchesteronline.co.uk

Owner *Manchester Evening News Ltd*
Editor *Paul Horrocks*
Circulation 173,446

One of the country's major regional dailies. Initial approach in writing preferred. No fiction. *Personal Finance* (Mon); *Health* (Tues); *Homes & Property* (Wed); *Small Business* (Thurs); *Lifestyle* (Fri/Sat); *Holidays* (Sat).

News Editor *Steve Panter*
Features Editor *Maggie Henfield* Regional news features, personality pieces and showbiz profiles considered. Maximum 1200 words.
Sports Editor *Peter Spencer*
Women's Page *Diane Cooke*
Payment based on house agreement rates.

Middlesbrough

Evening Gazette

Borough Road, Middlesbrough, Cleveland TS1 3AZ
☎01642 234242   Fax 01642 249843

Owner *Trinity International Holdings plc*
Editor *Paul Robertson*
Circulation 69,000

Special pages: business, motoring, home, computing.

News Editor *Chris Styles*
Features Editor/Women's Page *Kathryn Armstrong*
Business *Helen Logan*
Sports Editor *Allan Boughey*
Councils *Sandy McKenzie*
Education *Julie Martin*
Consumer *Michelle Ruane*
Health *Mike Blackburn*

Mold

Evening Leader

Mold Business Park, Wrexham Road, Mold, Clwyd CH7 1XY
☎01352 707707   Fax 01352 752180

Owner *North Wales Newspapers*
Editor *Reg Herbert*

Circulation 30,976

Circulates in Wrexham, Flintshire, Rhyl, Deeside and Chester. Special pages/features: motoring, travel, arts, women's, children's, photography, local housing, information and news for the disabled, music and entertainment.

News Editors *Joanne Shone, Nick Bourne*
Features Editor/Women's Page *Debra Greenhouse*
Sports Editor *Allister Syme*

Newcastle upon Tyne
Evening Chronicle
Thomson House, Groat Market, Newcastle upon Tyne, Tyne and Wear NE1 1ED
☎0191 232 7500 Fax 0191 232 2256
Website www.evening-chronicle.co.uk

Owner *Trinity Mirror Plc*
Editor *Alison Hastings*
Circulation 107,346

Receives a lot of unsolicited material, much of which is not used. Family issues, gardening, pop, fashion, cooking, consumer, films and entertainment guide, home improvements, motoring, property, angling, sport and holidays. Approach in writing with ideas.

News Editor *Mick Smith*
Features Limited opportunities due to full-time feature staff. Maximum 1000 words.
Sports Editor *Paul New*
Women's Interests *Kay Jordan*

The Journal
Thomson House, Groat Market, Newcastle upon Tyne, Tyne & Wear NE1 1ED
☎0191 232 7500
Fax 0191 232 2256/201 6044
Email jnl.newsdesk@ncjmedia.co.uk
Website www.the-journal.co.uk

Owner *Trinity Mirror Plc*
Editor *Gerard Henderson*
Circulation 51,936

Daily platforms include farming and business. Monthly full-colour business supplement: *The Journal Northern Business Magazine*.

Deputy Editor *Anne Edwards*
Sports Editor *Kevin Dinsdale*
Arts & Entertainment Editor *David Whetstone*
Environment Editor *Tony Henderson*
Business Editor *Peter Jackson*

Sunday Sun
Thomson House, Groat Market, Newcastle upon Tyne, Tyne & Wear NE1 1ED

☎0191 201 6330 Fax 0191 230 0238
Email peter.montellier@ncjmedia.co.uk

Owner *Trinity Mirror Plc*
Editor *Peter Montellier*
Circulation 100,382

All material should be addressed to the appropriate editor (phone to check), or to the editor.

Sports Editor *Dylan Younger*

Newport
South Wales Argus
Cardiff Road, Maesglas, Newport, Gwent NP9 1QW
☎01633 810000 Fax 01633 777202

Owner *Newsquest*
Editor *Gerry Keighley*
Circulation 30,644

Circulates in Newport, Gwent and surrounding areas.

News Editor *Nicole Garnon*
Sports Editor *Carson Wishart*

Northampton
Chronicle and Echo
Upper Mounts, Northampton NN1 3HR
☎01604 467000 Fax 01604 467190

Owner *Northamptonshire Newspapers*
Editor *Mark Edwards*
Circulation 27,778

Unsolicited mss are 'not necessarily unwelcome but opportunities to use them are rare'. Approach in writing with an idea. No fiction. Supplements: *Sports Chronicle* (Monday); *Property Week* (Wednesday); *What's On Guide* (Thursday); *Weekend Motors* (Friday).

News Editor *Richard Edmondson*
Features Editor/Women's Page *Jessica Pilkington*
Sports Editor *Steve Pitts*

Northern Ireland
Belfast News Letter
See under *Belfast*

Belfast Telegraph
See under *Belfast*

The Irish News
See under *Belfast*

Sunday Life
See under *Belfast*

Norwich

Eastern Daily Press
Prospect House, Rouen Road, Norwich,
Norfolk NR1 1RE
☎01603 628311   Fax 01603 612930
Website www.ecn.co.uk
Owner *Eastern Counties Newspapers*
Editor *Peter Franzen*
Circulation 76,579

Most pieces by commission only. Supplements:
what's on (daily); motoring, business, property
pages, women's interests, agriculture (all
weekly); employment (twice-weekly); arts focus
(monthly); plus horse and rider, boating, golf and
wildlife; Saturday full colour magazine.
  News Editor *Paul Durrant*
  Features Editor *David Macaulay*
  Sports Editor *David Thorpe*
  Magazine Editor *Peter Waters*

Evening News
Prospect House, Rouen Road, Norwich,
Norfolk NR1 1RE
☎01603 628311   Fax 01603 219060
Email david.bourn@ecng.co.uk
Website www.ecn.co.uk
Owner *Eastern Counties Newspapers Group Ltd*
Editor *David Bourn*
Circulation 36,458

Includes special pages on local property,
motoring, children's page, pop, fashion, arts,
entertainments and TV, gardening, local music
scene, home and family.
  Assistant Editor *Sheree Elston*
  Deputy Editor *Roy Strowger*
    (roy.strowger@ecng.co.uk)
  Features Editor *Derek James*

Nottingham

Evening Post Nottingham
Castle Wharf House, Nottingham NG1 7EU
☎0115 948 2000   Fax 0115 964 4032
Owner *Northcliffe Newspapers Group Ltd*
Editor *Graham Glen*
Circulation 97,000

Unsolicited mss occasionally used. Good local
interest only. Maximum 800 words. No fiction. Send ideas in writing. Supplements:
motoring, business, holidays and travel supplements; financial, employment and consumer
pages.
  News Editor *Claire Lumley*
  Deputy Editor *Jon Grubb*
  Sports Editor *Tim Walters*

Oldham

Evening Chronicle
PO Box 47, Union Street, Oldham,
Lancashire OL1 1EQ
☎0161 633 2121   Fax 0161 652 2111
Email oec@compuserve.com
Owner *Hirst Kidd & Rennie Ltd*
Editor *Jim Williams*
Circulation 32,206

Motoring, food and wine, women's page, busi-
ness page.
  News Editor *Mike Attenborough*
  Women's Page *Janice Barker*

Oxford

Oxford Mail
Osney Mead, Oxford OX2 0EJ
☎01865 425262   Fax 01865 425554
Owner *Newsquest (Oxfordshire) Ltd*
Editor *Jim McClure*
Circulation 35,000

Unsolicited mss are considered but a great many
unsuitable offerings are received. Approach in
writing with an idea, rather than by phone. No
fiction. All fees negotiable.

Paisley

Paisley Daily Express
14 New Street, Paisley PA1 1YA
☎0141 887 7911   Fax 0141 887 6254
Email pde@s-un.co.uk
Owner *Scottish & Universal Newspapers Ltd*
Editor *Norman Macdonald*
Circulation 9,067

Circulates in Paisley, Linwood, Renfrew, Johnstone, Elderslie, Neilston and Barrhead. Unsolicited mss welcome only if of genuine local
interest. The paper does not commission work,
and will consider submitted material. Maximum
1000–1500 words. All submissions to the editor.
  News Editor *Anne Dalrymple*
  Sports Reporters *Michelle Evans, Matt
    Vallance*

Plymouth

Evening Herald
17 Brest Road, Derriford Business Park,
Derriford, Plymouth, Devon PL6 5AA
☎01752 765500   Fax 01752 765527
Email news@westcountrypublications.co.uk
Website www.thisisplymouth.co.uk
Owner *Northcliffe Newspapers Group Ltd*

Editor *Alan Qualtrough*
Circulation 53,626

All editorial material to be addressed to the editor or the **News Editor** *Bill Martin*.

Sunday Independent
Burrington Way, Plymouth, Devon PL5 3LN
☎01752 206600 Fax 01752 206164

Owner *Newscom Plc*
Editor *Nikki Rowlands*
Circulation 38,958

Tabloid Sunday covering the whole of the West Country from Bristol to Weymouth and Land's End. News stories/tips, news features. All editorial should be addressed to the editor. *Payment* by arrangement.

Western Morning News
17 Brest Road, Derriford Business Park, Derriford, Plymouth, Devon PL6 5AA
☎01752 765500 Fax 01752 765535

Owner *Northcliffe Newspapers Group Ltd*
Editor *Barrie Williams*
Circulation 53,050

Unsolicited mss welcome, but must be of topical and local interest and addressed to the **News Editor**, *Claire Jardine*.
   Sports Editor *Rick Cowdery*

Portsmouth
The News
The News Centre, Hilsea, Portsmouth, Hampshire PO2 9SX
☎023 9266 4488 Fax 023 9267 3363
Email newsdesk@thenews.co.uk
Website www.thenews.co.uk

Owner *Portsmouth Printing & Publishing Ltd*
Editor *Mike Gilson*
Circulation 73,161

Unsolicited mss not generally accepted. Approach by letter.
   News Editor *Mary Acheson*
   Features Editor *John Millard* General subjects of S.E. Hants interest. Maximum 600 words. No fiction.
   Sports Editor *Colin Channon* Sports background features. Maximum 600 words.

Preston
Lancashire Evening Post
Olivers Place, Eastway, Fulwood, Preston, Lancashire PR2 9ZA
☎01772 254841 Fax 01772 880173

Website www.lep.co.uk
Owner *Regional Independent Media*
Editor *Roger Borrell*
Circulation 48,831

Unsolicited mss are not generally welcome; many are received and not used. All ideas in writing to the editor.

Reading
Reading Evening Post
8 Tessa Road, Reading, Berkshire RG1 8NS
☎0118 918 3000 Fax 0118 959 9363
Email editorial@reading-epost.co.uk
Owner *Guardian Media Group*
Editor *Andy Murrill*
Circulation 23,802

Unsolicited mss welcome; one or two received every day. Fiction rarely used. Interested in local news features, human interest, well-researched investigations. Special sections include holidays & travel (Monday); food page; children's page (Tuesday); style page (Wednesday); business (Wednesday & Friday); motoring and motorcycling; gardening; rock music (Friday).

Scarborough
Scarborough Evening News
17–23 Aberdeen Walk, Scarborough, North Yorkshire YO11 1BB
☎01723 363636 Fax 01723 383825
Email editor@scarborough-news.demon.co.uk
Website www.scarboroughveningnews.co.uk
Owner *Yorkshire Regional Newspapers Ltd*
Editor *David Penman*
Circulation 17,154

Special pages include property (Monday); motoring (Tuesday/Friday).
   News Editor *Neil Pickford*
   Motoring *Dennis Sissons*
   Sports Editor *Charles Place*
   All other material should be addressed to the editor.

Scotland
Daily Record (Glasgow)
See **National Newspapers**

Scotland on Sunday (Edinburgh)
See **National Newspapers**

The Scotsman (Edinburgh)
See **National Newspapers**

Sunday Herald (Glasgow)
See **National Newspapers**

Sunday Mail (Glasgow)
See **National Newspapers**

Sunday Post (Dundee)
See **National Newspapers**

Scunthorpe
Scunthorpe Evening Telegraph
Doncaster Road, Scunthorpe, N.E. Lincs
DN15 7RQ
☎01724 273273 Fax 01724 273101

Owner *Northcliffe Newspapers Group Ltd*
Editor *Michelle Lalor*
Circulation 24,292

All correspondence should go to the **News Editor** *Lisa Wheaton*.

Sheffield
The Star
York Street, Sheffield, South Yorkshire S1 1PU
☎0114 276 7676 Fax 0114 272 5978

Owner *Sheffield Newspapers Ltd*
Editor *Peter Charlton*
Circulation 102,749

Unsolicited mss not welcome, unless topical and local.
    News Editor *Bob Westerdale* Contributions only accepted from freelance news reporters if they relate to the area.
    Features Editor *Jim Collins* Very rarely requires outside features, unless on specialised subject.
    Sports Editor *Martin Smith*
    Women's Page *Jo Davison*
    Payment negotiable.

Shropshire
Shropshire Star
See under *Telford*

South Shields
Gazette
Chapter Row, South Shields, Tyne & Wear
NE33 1BL
☎0191 455 4661 Fax 0191 456 8270
Website www.shields-gazette.co.uk

Owner *Northeast Press Ltd*
Editor *Rob Lawson*
Circulation 23,332

News Editor *Gary Welford*
Sports Editor *John Cornforth*
Women's Page *Joy Yates*

Southampton
The Southern Daily Echo
Newspaper House, Test Lane, Redbridge, Southampton, Hampshire SO16 9JX
☎023 8042 4777 Fax 023 8042 4770

Owner *Newscom Plc*
Editor *Ian Murray*
Circulation 60,343

Unsolicited mss 'tolerated'. Approach the editor in writing with strong ideas; staff supply almost all the material.

Stoke-on-Trent
The Sentinel/Sentinel Sunday
Sentinel House, Etruria, Stoke on Trent, Staffordshire ST1 5SS
☎01782 602525 Fax 01782 280781
(Sentinel)/201167 (Sentinel Sunday)
Website www.thisisstaffordshire.co.uk

Owner *Staffordshire Sentinel Newspapers Ltd*
Editor *Sean Dooley*
Circulation 90,368 (Sentinel)

Weekly sports final supplement. All material should be sent to the **Head of Content** *Michael Wood*.

Sunderland
Sunderland Echo
Echo House, Pennywell, Sunderland, Tyne & Wear SR4 9ER
☎0191 501 5800 Fax 0191 534 4861
Email andrew@northeast-press.co.uk

Owner *Johnston Press Plc*
Group Editorial Director *Andrew Smith*
Circulation 57,703

All editorial material to be addressed to the **News Editor** *Patrick Lavelle* (echo.news@ northeast-press.co.uk).

Swansea
South Wales Evening Post
Adelaide Street, Swansea, West Glamorgan SA1 1QT
☎01792 510000 Fax 01792 514697
Email postbox@swwp.co.uk
Website www.thisissouthwales.co.uk

Owner *Northcliffe Newspapers Group Ltd*

Editor *George Edwards*
Circulation 66,576

Circulates throughout south west Wales.
News Editor *Jonathan Isaacs*
Features Editor *Andy Pearson*
Sports Editor *David Evans*

Swindon
Evening Advertiser
100 Victoria Road, Swindon, Wiltshire
SN1 3BE
☎01793 528144 Fax 01793 542434
Email editor@newswilts.co.uk
Website www.thisiswiltshire.co.uk

Owner *Newsquest (Wiltshire) Ltd*
Editor *Simon O'Neill*
Circulation 26,343

Copy and ideas invited. 'All material must be
strongly related or relevant to the town of
Swindon or the county of Wiltshire.' Little
scope for freelance work. Fees vary depending
on material.
Deputy Editor *Pauline Leighton*
News Editor *Mark Drew*
Sports Editor *Matt Reeder*

Telford
Shropshire Star
Ketley, Telford, Shropshire TF1 5HU
☎01952 242424 Fax 01952 254605
Owner *Shropshire Newspapers Ltd*
Editor *Adrian Faber*
Circulation 89,619

No unsolicited mss; approach the editor with
ideas in writing in the first instance. No news
or fiction.
News Editor *Sarah-Jane Smith*
Head of Supplements *Sharon Walters*
Limited opportunities; uses mostly in-house or
syndicated material. Maximum 1200 words.
Sports Editor *Alun Owen*

Torquay
Herald Express
Harmsworth House, Barton Hill Road,
Torquay, Devon TQ2 8JN
☎01803 676000 Fax 01803 676299/676228
Email editor@thisissouthdevon.co.uk
Website www.thisissouthdevon.co.uk

Owner *Northcliffe Newspapers Group Ltd*
Editor *B. Hanrahan*
Circulation 30,174

Drive scene, property guide, *What's On Now* –
leisure guide, Monday sports, special pages, rail
trail, Saturday surgery, nature and conservation
column. Supplements: *Gardening* (quarterly);
Visitors Guide and *Antiques & Collectables* (fortnightly); *Devon Days Out* (every Saturday in
summer and at Easter and May Bank Holidays).
Unsolicited mss generally not welcome. All
editorial material should be addressed to the
editor in writing.

Wales
South Wales Argus
See under *Newport*

South Wales Echo
See under *Cardiff*

South Wales Evening Post
See under *Swansea*

Wales on Sunday
See under *Cardiff*

West of England
Western Mail
See under *Cardiff*

Express & Echo
See under *Exeter*

Western Daily Press
See under *Bristol*

Western Morning News
See under *Plymouth*

Weymouth
Dorset Evening Echo
Fleet House, Hampshire Road, Granby
Industrial Estate, Weymouth, Dorset
DT4 9XD
☎01305 830930 Fax 01305 830956
Owner *Newsquest Media Group Ltd (a Gannett
company)*
Editor *David Murdock*
Circulation 20,430

Farming, by-gone days, films, arts, showbiz,
brides, children's page, motoring, property,
weekend leisure and entertainment including
computers and gardening.
News Editor *Paul Thomas*
Sports Editor *Paul Baker*

Wolverhampton

Express & Star
Queen Street, Wolverhampton, West
Midlands WV1 1ES
☎01902 313131 Fax 01902 319721
Owner *Midlands News Association*
Editor *Warren Wilson*
Circulation 182,146

> **Deputy Editor** *Richard Ewels*
> **News Editor** *John Bray*
> **Features Editor** *Jim Walsh*
> **Sports Editor** *Steve Gordos*
> **Women's Page** *Shirley Tart*

Worcester

Evening News
Berrow's House, Hylton Road, Worcester
WR2 5JX
☎01905 748200 Fax 01905 748009
Owner *Newsquest (Midlands South) Ltd*
Editor *Stewart Gilbert*
Circulation 23,102

Local events (Tuesday); jobs/careers (Wednesday); property (Thursday); showbiz/what's on, motoring/Pulse pop page (Friday); holidays/what's on (Saturday).

> **News Editor** *Tina Faulkner*
> **Features Editor/Women's Page** *Mark Higgitt*
> **Sports Editor** *Paul Ricketts*

York

Evening Press
PO Box 29, 76–86 Walmgate, York
YO1 9YN
☎01904 653051 Fax 01904 612853
Email editor@ycp.co.uk
Website www.thisisyork.co.uk
Owner *Newsquest Media Group (a Gannett company)*
Editor *Elizabeth Page*
Circulation 42,074

Unsolicited mss not generally welcome, unless submitted by journalists of proven ability. *Business Press Pages* (Tuesday); *Property Press* (Thursday); *Friday Night Fever* – what's on (Friday); *8 Days* TV supplement (Saturday).

> **News Editor** *Fran Clee*
> **Picture Editor** *Martin Oates*
> **Sports Editor** *Martin Jarred*
> *Payment* negotiable.

Yorkshire

Yorkshire Evening Post
See under *Leeds*

Yorkshire Post
See under *Leeds*

Magazines

ABCtales

See entry under **Electronic Publishing and Other Services**

Abraxas

57 Eastbourne Road, St Austell, Cornwall PL25 4SU
☎01726 64975 Fax 01726 64975
Email palnew7@hotmail.com
Website www.abrax7.stormloader.com

Owner *Paul Newman*
Editors *Paul Newman, Pamela Smith-Rawnsley*

FOUNDED 1991. QUARTERLY incorporating the *Colin Wilson Newsletter*. Unsolicited mss welcome after a study of the magazine – initial approach by phone or letter preferred.

Features Essays, translations and reviews. Welcomes provocative, lively articles on little-known literary figures and new slants on psychology, existentialism and ideas. Maximum length 2000 words. *Payment* nominal if at all.

Fiction One story per issue. Maximum 2000 words. Favours compact, obsessional stories.

Poetry Double-page spread – slight penchant for the surreal but open to most styles. *Payment* free copy of magazine.

Acclaim

See **The New Writer**

Accountancy

40 Bernard Street, London WC1N 1LD
☎020 7833 3291 Fax 020 7833 2085

Owner *Institute of Chartered Accountants in England and Wales*
Editor *Brian Singleton-Green*
Circulation 62,657

FOUNDED 1889. MONTHLY. Written ideas welcome.

Features *Brian Singleton-Green* Accounting/tax/business–related articles of high technical content aimed at professional/managerial readers. Maximum 2000 words. *Payment* by arrangement.

Accountancy Age

32–34 Broadwick Street, London W1A 2HG
☎020 7316 9000/Features: 020 7316 9611
Fax 020 7316 9250
Email accountancy_age@vnu.co.uk
Website www.accountancyage.com

Owner *VNU Business Publications*
Editor *Damian Wild*
News Editor *Chris Quick* (020 7316 9233)
Circulation 77,697

FOUNDED 1969. WEEKLY. Unsolicited mss welcome. Ideas may be suggested in writing provided they are clearly thought out.

Features *Liz Loxton* Topics right across the accountancy, business and financial world. Maximum 2000 words.
Payment negotiable.

Ace Tennis Magazine

9–11 North End Road, London W14 8ST
☎020 7605 8000 Fax 020 7602 2323
Email Dominic.Bliss@acemag.co.uk

Owner *Tennis GB*
Editor *Dominic Bliss*
Circulation 45,000

FOUNDED 1996. MONTHLY specialist tennis magazine. News (250 words max.) and features (2000 words max.). No unsolicited mss; send feature synopses by fax in the first instance. No tournament reports.
Payment £150–200 per 1000 words.

Active Life

Lexicon, 1st Floor, 1–5 Clerkenwell Road, London EC1M 5PA
☎020 7253 5775 Fax 020 7253 5676
Email activelife@lexicon–uk.com
Website www.activelifemag.co,

Owner *Lexicon Editorial Group Services*
Editor *Helene Hodge*

FOUNDED 1990. BI-MONTHLY magazine aimed at over 50s. General consumer interests including travel, finance, property, leisure. Opportunities for freelancers in all departments, including fiction. Approach in writing with synopsis of ideas. Authors' notes available on receipt of s.a.e.

Acumen

See under **Poetry Magazines**

Aeroplane

IPC Media Ltd., King's Reach Tower, Stamford Street, London SE1 9LS
☎020 7261 5849 Fax 020 7261 5269

Email aeroplane_monthly@ipcmedia.com
Owner *IPC Country & Leisure Media Ltd*
Editor Michael Oakey
Circulation 34,575

FOUNDED 1973. MONTHLY. Historic aviation and aircraft preservation from its beginnings to the 1960s. No post-1960 aircraft types; no poetry. Will consider news items and features written with authoritative knowledge of the subject, illustrated with good quality photographs.
   News *Tony Harsmworth* Maximum 500 words.
   Features *Michael Oakey* Maximum 3000 words. *Payment* £60 per 1000 words; £10–40 per picture used. Approach by letter in the first instance.

African Affairs
Dept of Historical & Cultural Studies, Goldsmiths College, University of London, New Cross, London SE14 6NW
☎020 7919 7486 Fax 020 7919 7398
Email afraf@compuserve.com
Owner *Royal African Society*
Editors *David Killingray, Stephen Ellis*
Circulation 2250

FOUNDED 1901. QUARTERLY learned journal publishing articles on recent political, social and economic developments in sub-Saharan countries. Also included are historical studies that illuminate current events in the continent. Unsolicited mss welcome. Maximum 8000 words. *No payment.*

Air International
PO Box 100, Stamford, Lincolnshire PE9 1XQ
☎01780 755131 Fax 01780 757261
Email malcolm_english@keymags.co.uk
Owner *Key Publishing Ltd*
Editor *Malcolm English*

FOUNDED 1971. MONTHLY. Civil and military aircraft magazine. Unsolicited mss welcome but initial approach by phone or in writing preferred.

Air Pictorial
HPC, Drury Lane, St Leonards on Sea, East Sussex TN38 9BJ
☎01424 720477 Fax 01424 443693
Email editor@airpictorial.com
Owner *Hastings Printing Company*
Editor *Barry C. Wheeler*
Circulation 21,000

FOUNDED 1939. MONTHLY review of aviation for those interested in military, commercial and business aircraft and equipment – old and new.

Will consider articles on military and civil aircraft, airports, air forces, current and historical subjects. No fiction. **Features** 'New writers always welcome and if the copy is not good enough it is returned with guidance attached.' Maximum 5000 words. **News** Items are always considered from new sources. Maximum 300 words. *Payment* negotiable.

AirForces Monthly
PO Box 100, Stamford, Lincolnshire PE9 1XQ
☎01780 755131 Fax 01780 757261
Email edafm@keymags.co.uk
Owner *Key Publishing Ltd*
Editor *Alan Warnes*
Circulation 24,749

FOUNDED 1988. MONTHLY. Modern military aircraft magazine. Unsolicited mss welcome but initial approach by phone or in writing preferred.

Alphard
See **ignotus press** under **Small Presses**

Amateur Gardening
Westover House, West Quay Road, Poole, Dorset BH15 1JG
☎01202 440840 Fax 01202 440860
Owner *IPC Media Ltd*
Editor *Adrian Bishop*
Circulation 55,417

FOUNDED 1884. WEEKLY. New contributions are welcome especially if they are topical and informative. All articles/news items should be supported by colour pictures (which may or may not be supplied by the author).
   Features Topical and practical gardening articles. Maximum 1000 words.
   News Compiled and edited in-house generally but all stories welcomed.
   Payment negotiable.

Amateur Photographer
IPC Media Ltd., King's Reach Tower, Stamford Street, London SE1 9LS
☎020 7261 5100/0870 444 5000 (switchboard) Fax 020 7261 5404
Email amateurphotographer@ipcmedia.com
Website www.amateurphotographer.com
Owner *IPC Media Ltd*
Editor *Garry Coward-Williams*
Circulation 30,578

FOUNDED 1884. WEEKLY. For the competent amateur with a technical interest. Freelancers are used but writers should be aware that there is ordinarily no use for words without pictures.

Amateur Stage

Hampden House, 2 Weymouth Street,
London W1W 5BT
☎020 7636 4343 Fax 020 7636 2323
Email cvtheatre@aol.com

Owner *Platform Publications Ltd*
Editor *Charles Vance*

Some opportunity here for outside contributions. Topics of interest include amateur premières, technical developments within the amateur forum and items relating to landmarks or anniversaries in the history of amateur societies. Approach in writing only (include s.a.e. for return of mss).
No payment.

Animal Action

Causeway, Horsham, West Sussex RH12 1HG
☎01403 264181 Fax 01403 241048
Email publications@rspca.org.uk
Website www.rspca.org.uk

Owner *RSPCA*
Editor *Michaela Miller*
Circulation 80,000

BI-MONTHLY. RSPCA youth membership magazine. Articles (pet care, etc.) are written in-house. Good-quality animal photographs welcome.

Animal Prints

Worthing Animal Aid, PO Box 4065,
Worthing, West Sussex BN11 3JL
☎01903 877144 Fax 01903 877144
Email WorthingAnimalAid@btinternet.com

Owner *Worthing Animal Aid*
Editor *Lilian Taylor*
Circulation 400

FOUNDED 1999. QUARTERLY magazine that aims to advance the animal movement. Welcomes contributions that are well researched, subtly thought provoking and have the potential for stimulating discussion. Approach in writing. *Payment* Complimentary copies of relevant issue.

The Antique Dealer and Collectors' Guide

PO Box 805, Greenwich, London SE10 8TD
☎020 8691 4820 Fax 020 8691 2489
Email antiquedealercollectorsguide@
  ukbusiness.com
Website www.antiquecollectorsguide.co.uk

Owner *Statuscourt Ltd*
Publisher *Philip Bartlam*
Circulation 12,500

FOUNDED 1946. TEN ISSUES YEARLY. Covers all aspects of the antiques and fine art worlds. Unsolicited mss welcome.

Features Practical but readable articles on the history, design, authenticity, restoration and market aspects of antiques and fine art. Maximum 2000 words. *Payment* £76 per 1000 words.

News Items on events, sales, museums, exhibitions, antique fairs and markets. Maximum 300 words.

Antique Interiors International

162 Packington Street, Islington, London
N1 8RA
☎020 7359 6011 Fax 020 7226 3780

Owner *Antique Publications*
Editor-in-Chief *Alistair Hicks*
Circulation 22,000

FOUNDED 1986. QUARTERLY. Amusing coverage of antiques, art and interiors. Unsolicited mss not welcome. Approach by phone or in writing in the first instance. Interested in freelance contributions on international art news items.

Antiques & Art Independent

PO Box 1945, Comely Bank, Edinburgh
EH4 1AB
☎07000 765263 Fax 0131 332 4481
Email antiquesnews@hotmail.com
Website www.antiquesnews.co.uk

Owner *Gallery UK Ltd*
Publisher/Editor *Tony Keniston*
Circulation 21,000

FOUNDED 1997. BI-MONTHLY. Up-to-date information for the British antiques and art trade, circulated to dealers and collectors throughout the UK. News, photographs, gossip and controversial views on all aspects of the fine art and antiques world welcome. Articles on antiques and fine arts themselves are not featured. Approach in writing with ideas.

Apollo Magazine

1 Castle Lane, London SW1E 6DR
☎020 7233 6640 Fax 020 7630 7791
Email editorial@apollomag.com

Owner *Paul Z. Josefowitz*
Editor *David Ekserdjian*

FOUNDED 1925. MONTHLY. Specialist articles on art and antiques, exhibition and book reviews, exhibition diary, information on dealers and auction houses. Unsolicited mss welcome. Interested in specialist, usually new research in fine arts, architecture and antiques. Not interested in crafts or practical art, photography or art after 1945.

Aquarist & Pondkeeper

TRMG, Winchester Court, 1 Forum Place,
Hatfield, Hertfordshire AL10 0RN
☎01707 273999　Fax 01707 269333
Email aandpeditor@btinternet.com

Owner *TRMG*
Editor *Derek Lambert*
Circulation 20,000

FOUNDED 1924. MONTHLY. Covers all aspects of aquarium and pondkeeping: conservation, herpetology (study of reptiles and amphibians), news, reviews and aquatic plant culture. Unsolicited mss welcome. Ideas should be submitted in writing first.

Features Good opportunities for writers on any of the above topics or related areas. 1500–3000 words, plus illustrations. **News** Very few opportunities.

Architects' Journal

151 Rosebery Avenue, London EC1R 4GB
☎020 7505 6700　Fax 020 7505 6701
Website www.ajplus.co.uk

Owner *EMAP Construct*
Editor *Isabel Allen*
Circulation 18,000

WEEKLY trade magazine dealing with all aspects of the industry. No unsolicited mss. Approach in writing with ideas.

Architectural Design

John Wiley & Sons, 4th Floor, International House, Ealing Broadway Centre, London W5 5DB
☎020 8326 3800　Fax 020 8326 3801

Owner *John Wiley & Sons Ltd*
Executive Editor *Maggie Toy*
Editor *Helen Castle*
Senior Production Editor *Mariangela Palazzi-Williams*
Circulation 5,000

FOUNDED 1930. BI-MONTHLY. Sold as a book as well as a journal, *AD* charts theoretical and topical developments in architecture. Format consists of 112pp, the first part dedicated to a theme compiled by a specially commissioned guest-editor; the back section (AD+) carries series and more current one-off articles. Unsolicited mss not welcome generally, though journalistic contributions will be considered for the back section.

The Architectural Review

151 Rosebery Avenue, London EC1R 4GB
☎020 7505 6725　Fax 020 7505 6701
Website www.arplus.com

Owner *EMAP Construct*
Editor *Peter Davey*
Circulation 22,700

MONTHLY professional magazine dealing with architecture and all aspects of design. No unsolicited mss. Approach in writing with ideas.

Arena

Block A, 2nd Floor, Exmouth House, Pine Street, London EC1R 0JH
☎020 7689 9999　Fax 020 7689 0901

Owner *Emap élan East*
Editor *Mark Ellen*
Circulation 37,080

Style and general interest magazine for men. Intelligent feature articles and profiles.

Features Fashion, lifestyle, film, television, politics, business, music, media, design, art, architecture and sport.

Art & Design

Villiers House, Clarendon Avenue, Leamington Spa, Warwickshire CV32 5PR
☎01926 887799　Fax 01926 883331

Owner *Scholastic Ltd*
Editor *Sian Morgan*
Circulation 12,000

FOUNDED 1936. MONTHLY aimed at a specialist market – the needs of primary school teachers, art coordinators and pupils. Ideas and synopses considered for commission.

Features The majority of contributors are primary school teachers with good art and craft skills and familiar with the curriculum.

News Handled by in-house staff. No opportunities.

Art Monthly

Suite 17, 26 Charing Cross Road, London WC2H 0DG
☎020 7240 0389　Fax 020 7497 0726
Email info@artmonthly.co.uk
Website www.artmonthly.co.uk

Owner *Brittania Art Publications*
Editor *Patricia Bickers*
Circulation 6000

FOUNDED 1976. TEN ISSUES YEARLY. News and features of relevance to those interested in modern and contemporary visual art. Unsolicited mss welcome. Contributions should be addressed to the deputy editor, accompanied by s.a.e.

Features Always commissioned. Interviews and articles of up to 1500 words on art theory, individual artists, contemporary art history and issues affecting the arts (e.g. funding and arts education). Exhibition reviews of 750–1000 words; book reviews of 750–1000 words.

News Brief reports (250–300 words) on art issues.

Payment negotiable.

The Art Newspaper

70 South Lambeth Road, London SW8 1RL
☎020 7735 3331 Fax 020 7735 3332
Email feedback@theartnewspaper.com
Website www.theartnewspaper.com

Owner *Umberto Allemandi & Co. Publishing*
Editor *Anna Somers Cocks*
Circulation 22,000

FOUNDED 1990. ELEVEN ISSUES YEARLY. Tabloid format with hard news on the international art market, news, museums, exhibitions, archaeology, conservation, books and current debate topics. Length 250–2000 words. No unsolicited mss. Approach with ideas in writing. Commissions only.

Payment £120 per 1000 words.

The Artist

Caxton House, 63–65 High Street, Tenterden, Kent TN30 6BD
☎0158076 3673 Fax 0158076 5411
Website www.theartistmagazine.co.uk

Owner/Editor *Sally Bulgin*
Circulation 19,000

FOUNDED 1931. MONTHLY. Art journalists, artists, art tutors and writers with a good knowledge of art materials are invited to write to the editor with ideas for practical and informative features about art, materials, techniques and artists.

Artscene

Dean Clough Industrial Park, Halifax, West Yorkshire HX3 5AX
☎01422 322527 Fax 01422 322518
Email artscene@btconnect.com

Owner *Yorkshire and Humberside Arts*
Editor *Victor Allen*
Circulation 25,000

FOUNDED 1973. MONTHLY. Listings magazine for Yorkshire and Humberside. No unsolicited mss. Approach by phone with ideas.

Features Profiles of artists (all media) and associated venues/organisers of events of interest. Topical relevance vital. Maximum length 1500 words. *Payment* £100 per 1000 words.

News Artscene strives to bring journalistic values to arts coverage – all arts 'scoops' in the region are of interest. Maximum length 500 words. *Payment* £100 per 1000 words.

Asian Times

Unit 2, 65 Whitechapel Road, London E1 1DU
☎020 7650 2000 Fax 020 7650 2001
Website www.ethnicmedia.co.uk

Owner *Ethnic Media Group*
Editor *Emenike Pio*
Circulation 33,000

FOUNDED 1983. WEEKLY community paper for the Asian community in Britain. Interested in relevant general, local and international issues. Approach in writing with ideas for submission.

Athletics Weekly

83 Park Road, Peterborough, Cambridgeshire PE1 2TN
☎01733 898440 Fax 01733 898441
Email results@athletics-weekly.co.uk
Website www.athleticsweekly.com

Owner *Descartes Publishing*
Editor *Nigel Walsh*
Circulation 20,000

FOUNDED 1945. WEEKLY. Covers track and field, road, fell, cross-country, race walking, athletic features and sports politics.

News *Jason Henderson* Maximum 400 words.
Features *Tony Ward* Maximum 2000 words. Approach in writing.

Payment negotiable.

Attitude

Ludgate House, 245 Blackfriars Road, London SE1 9UX
☎020 7928 8000 Fax 020 7922 7600
Email attitude@express.co.uk

Owner *Northern & Shell plc*
Editor *Adam Mattera*
Circulation 50,000

FOUNDED 1994. MONTHLY. Style magazine aimed primarily, but not exclusively, at gay men. Celebrity, fashion and cultural coverage. Brief summaries of proposed features, together with details of previously published work, should be sent by post or fax only. 'It sounds obvious, but anyone wanting to contribute to the magazine should read it first.'

The Author

84 Drayton Gardens, London SW10 9SB
☎020 7373 6642

Owner *The Society of Authors*
Editor *Derek Parker*
Manager *Kate Pool*
Circulation 8,500

FOUNDED 1890. QUARTERLY journal of the

Society of Authors. Most articles are commissioned.

Auto Express
30 Cleveland Street, London W1P 5FF
☎020 7907 6200 Fax 020 7907 6234
Email editorial@autoexpress.co.uk
Website www.autoexpress.co.uk
Owner *Dennis Publishing*
Editor *David Johns*
Circulation 95,000

FOUNDED 1989. WEEKLY consumer motoring title with news, drives, tests, investigations, etc. **Features** *Lydia Aydon* Welcomes ideas. No fully-written articles – features will be commissioned if appropriate and good enough. Maximum 2000 words. *Payment £300 per 1000 words*. **News** *Richard Yarrow* News stories and tip-offs welcome. Fillers, 150 words max.; leads, 300 words. Approach by e-mail.

Autocar
60 Waldegrave Road, Teddington, Middlesex TW11 8LG
☎020 8943 5630 Fax 020 8267 5759
Email autocar@haynet.com
Owner *Haymarket Magazines Ltd*
Editor *Rob Aherne*
Circulation 77,403

FOUNDED 1895. WEEKLY. All news stories, features, interviews, scoops, ideas, tip-offs and photographs welcome.
News *Phil McNamara*
Payment negotiable.

B Magazine
17–18 Berners Street, London W1T 3LN
☎020 7664 6470 Fax 020 7070 3401
Email letters@bmagazine.co.uk
Owner *Attic Futura*
Editor *Gina Johnson*
Circulation 216,620

MONTHLY women's fashion and beauty magazine aimed at women in their twenties. Will consider real-life stories, emotional issues and celebrity features. Ideas for features should be sent to *Catherine McDonnoll*. No short stories or opinion pieces. Approach in writing.

Baby Magazine
WVIP, 53–79 Highgate Road, London NW5 1TW
☎020 7331 1000 Fax 020 7331 1225
Email jackie.gutherie@wvip.co.uk
Owner *WVIP*
Editor *Jackie Gutherie*

Circulation 79,000

MONTHLY. For parents-to-be and parents of children up to two years old. No unsolicited mss.
Features Send synopsis of feature with covering letter in the first instance. Unsolicited material is not returned.

Baby's Best Buys
WVIP, 53–79 Highgate Road, London NW5 1TW
☎020 7331 1000 Fax 020 7331 1241
Email dan.bromage@wvip.co.uk
Owner *WVIP*
Editor *Dan Bromage*

QUARTERLY. Comprehensive product testing for parenting equipment and maternity wear.

Back Brain Recluse (BBR)
PO Box 625, Sheffield S1 3GY
Website www.bbr-online.com/backbrainrecluse
Owner/Editor *Chris Reed*

Welcomes proposals for future volumes in the BBR sequence – novels, non-fiction works or new media projects (no short stories). Expects to publish no more than two titles per year. Include the following when submitting your proposal: a brief summary of the project, including a short description of relevant features, with a brief synopsis for novels. Give an outline of the key differences between this title and others already available. Selling features: reasons why this title can be expected to be more successful than similar titles and any interesting extra information to provide a feel for this work. Include reviews of previously published work, endorsements by well-known writers, etc. Give details of your ideal back cover blurb.

The Badminton Times
PO Box 36, Brecon LD3 0WD
☎01874 754033
Editor *Mr R. Richardson*

FOUNDED 1980. QUARTERLY. Events, players, fashion and footwear, rackets, facilities, technique and tactics.

Balance
Diabetes UK, 10 Queen Anne Street, London W1G 9LH
☎020 7323 1531 Fax 020 7636 5762
Email balance@diabetes.org.uk
Owner *British Diabetic Association*
Editor *Martin Cullen*

Circulation 200,000

FOUNDED 1935. BI-MONTHLY. Unsolicited mss are not accepted. Writers may submit a brief proposal in writing. Only topics relevant to diabetes will be considered.

Features Medical, diet and lifestyle features written by people with diabetes or with an interest and expert knowledge in the field. General features are mostly based on experience or personal observation. Maximum 1500 words. *Payment* NUJ rates.

News Short pieces about activities relating to diabetes and the lifestyle of diabetics. Maximum 150 words.

The Banker
149 Tottenham Court Road, London
W1P 9LL
☎020 7896 2507 Fax 020 7896 2586
Website www.thebanker.com

Owner *Financial Times Business*
Editor *Stephen Timewell*
Circulation 24,000

FOUNDED 1926. MONTHLY. News and features on banking, finance and capital markets worldwide and technology.

BBC Gardeners' World Magazine
Woodlands, 80 Wood Lane, London
W12 0TT
☎020 8433 3959 Fax 020 8433 3986
Email gwletters@bbc.co.uk
Website www.gardenersworld.com

Owner *BBC Worldwide Publishing Ltd*
Editor *Adam Pasco*
Circulation 310,770

FOUNDED 1991. MONTHLY. Gardening advice, ideas and inspiration. No unsolicited mss. Approach by phone or in writing with ideas – interested in features about exceptional small gardens. Also interested in any exciting new gardens showing good design and planting ideas. 'The magazine aims to be the first to bring news of new trends and developments, and always welcomes ideas from contributors.'

BBC Good Food
Woodlands, 80 Wood Lane, London
W12 0TT
☎020 8433 2000 Fax 020 8433 3931
Website www.bbcworldwide.com

Owner *BBC Worldwide Ltd*
Editor *Orlando Murrin*
Circulation 301,413

FOUNDED 1989. MONTHLY food and drink

magazine with television and radio links. No unsolicited mss.

BBC Good Homes Magazine
Woodlands, 80 Wood Lane, London
W12 0TT
☎020 8433 2391 Fax 020 8433 2691
Website www.bbcgoodhomes.com

Owner *BBC Worldwide Ltd*
Editor *Julie Savill*
Circulation 133,220

FOUNDED 1998. MONTHLY. Interiors, gardening, property, home shopping. No non-homes related features, fiction or puzzles. **Features** *Gill Smith* Readers' homes; property features from specialists. Approach by letter with cuttings.

BBC History Magazine
Room A1004, Woodlands, 80 Wood Lane, London W12 0TT
☎020 8433 2433 Fax 020 8433 3292
Email bbchistory@galleon.co.uk
Website www.bbcworldwide.com/historymag

Owner *BBC Worldwide Publishing Ltd*
Editor *Greg Neale*
Circulation 50,000

FOUNDED 2000. MONTHLY. General news and features on British and international history, with books and CD reviews, listings of history events, TV and radio history programmes and regular features for those interested in history and current affairs. Will consider submissions from academic or otherwise expert historians/archaeologists. Ideas for regular features are welcome. Also publishes cartoons, a monthly quiz and crossword. 'We cannot guarantee to acknowledge all unsolicited mss.' **Features** should be pegged to anniversaries or forthcoming books/TV programmes, etc. 750–3000 words. **News** 400–500 words. Send short letter or e-mail with synopsis, giving appropriate sources, pegs for publication dates, etc. *Payment* negotiable.

BBC Homes & Antiques
Woodlands, 80 Wood Lane, London
W12 0TT
☎020 8433 3490 Fax 020 8433 3867
Website www.bbcworldwide.com/antiques

Owner *BBC Worldwide Publishing Ltd*
Editor *Judith Hall*
Circulation 176,455

FOUNDED 1993. MONTHLY traditional home interest magazine with a strong bias towards antiques and collectables. Opportunities for freelancers are limited; most features are commissioned from regular stable of contributors.

No fiction, health and beauty, fashion or general showbusiness. Approach with ideas by phone or in writing.

Features *Caroline Wheater* At-home features: inspirational houses – people-led items. Pieces commissioned on recce shots and cuttings. Guidelines available on request. Celebrity features: 'at homes or favourite things' – send cuttings of relevant work published. Maximum 1500 words.

Special Pages Regular feature – 'Memories'. Maximum 800 words.

Payment negotiable.

BBC Music Magazine

Room A1004, Woodlands, 80 Wood Lane, London W12 0TT
☎020 8433 2000 Fax 020 8433 3292
Email music.magazine@bbc.co.uk
Website www.bbcmusicmagazine.com
Owner *BBC Worldwide Publishing Ltd*
Editor *Helen Wallace*
Circulation 121,046 (worldwide)

FOUNDED 1992. MONTHLY. All areas of classical music. Not interested in unsolicited material. Approach with ideas only, by fax.

BBC Top Gear Magazine

Woodlands, 80 Wood Lane, London W12 0TT
☎020 8433 3716 Fax 020 8433 3754
Website www.topgear.com
Owner *BBC Worldwide Publishing Ltd*
Editor *Kevin Blick*
Circulation 184,000

FOUNDED 1993. MONTHLY companion magazine to the popular TV series. No unsolicited material as most features are commissioned.

BBC Wildlife Magazine

Broadcasting House, Whiteladies Road, Bristol BS8 2LR
☎0117 973 8402 Fax 0117 946 7075
Email wildlife.magazine@bbc.co.uk
Owner *BBC Worldwide Publishing Ltd*
Editor *Rosamund Kidman Cox*
Circulation 60,135

FOUNDED 1963 (formerly *Wildlife*, née *Animals*). MONTHLY. Unsolicited mss generally not welcome.

Features Most features commissioned from writers with expert knowledge of wildlife or conservation subjects. Maximum 3500 words. *Payment* £200–450.

News Most news stories commissioned from known freelancers. Maximum 800 words. *Payment* £80–120

Bee World

18 North Road, Cardiff CF10 3DT
☎029 2037 2409 Fax 029 2066 5522
Email mail@ibra.org
Website www.ibra.org.uk
Owner *International Bee Research Association*
Editor *Dr P.A. Munn*
Circulation 1700

FOUNDED 1919. QUARTERLY. High-quality factual journal, including peer-reviewed articles, with international readership. Features on apicultural science and technology. Unsolicited mss welcome but authors should write to the editor for guidelines before submitting material.

Bella

H. Bauer Publishing, Academic House, 24–28 Oval Road, London NW1 7DT
☎020 7241 8000 Fax 020 7241 8056
Owner *H. Bauer Publishing*
Editor-in-Chief *Jackie Highe*
Circulation 532,668

FOUNDED 1987. WEEKLY. Women's magazine specialising in real-life, human interest stories.

Features *Sue Ricketts* Contributions welcome for some sections of the magazine: readers' letters, 'Blush with Bella' and 'Bella Rat'.

Fiction *Linda O'Byrne* Maximum 1200–2000 words. Send s.a.e. for guidelines.

Best

197 Marsh Wall, London E14 9SG
☎020 7519 5500 Fax 020 7519 5516
Owner *National Magazine Company*
Editor *Louise Court*
Circulation 431,352

FOUNDED 1987. WEEKLY women's magazine. Multiple features, news, short stories on all topics of interest to women. Important for would-be contributors to study the magazine's style which differs from many other women's weeklies. Approach in writing with s.a.e.

Features Maximum 1500 words. No unsolicited mss.

Fiction Short story slot; unsolicited mss accepted. Maximum 1000 words. Send s.a.e. for guidelines.

Payment negotiable.

Best of British

Ian Beacham Publishing, Bank Chambers, 27a Market Place, Market Deeping, Lincolnshire PE6 8EA
☎01778 342814
Email beacham@british.fsbusiness.co.uk

Website www.best-of-british.com
Owner *Ian Beacham Publishing*
Editor *Peter Kelly*
Editor-in-Chief *Ian Beacham*

FOUNDED 1994. MONTHLY magazine celebrating all things British, both past and present. Emphasis on nostalgia – memories from the 1940s, 1950s and 1960s. Study of the magazine is advised in the first instance. All preliminary approaches should be made in writing.

Best Solutions
38 Broad Street, Earls Barton,
Northamptonshire NN6 0ND
☎01635 522488 Fax 01635 522212
Website www.bestsolutions.co.uk
Owner *Grahame White*
Editor *Geoff Ellis*
Circulation 300,000

FOUNDED 1996. QUARTERLY business to business consultancy magazine. No unsolicited mss. 'Interested in articles (1000 words) for heads of substantial consultancy practices.' Approach in writing.

The Big Issue
236–240 Pentonville Road, London N1 9JY
☎020 7526 3200 Fax 020 7526 3201
Editor-in-Chief *A. John Bird*
Editor *Matthew Collin*
Deputy Editor *Adam Macqueen*
Circulation 253,785

FOUNDED 1991. WEEKLY. An award-winning campaigning and street-wise general interest magazine sold in London, the Midlands, the North East and South of England. Separate regional editions sold in Manchester, Scotland, Wales, the South West and Ireland.
Features *Adam Macqueen* Interviews, campaigns, comment, opinion and social issues reflecting a varied and informed audience. Balance includes social issues but mixed with arts and cultural features. Freelance writers used each week – commissioned from a variety of contributors. Best approach is to fax or post synopses to features editor with examples of work in the first instance. Maximum 1500 words. *Payment* £160 for 1000 words.
News *Gibby Zobel* Hard-hitting exclusive stories with emphasis on social injustice aimed at national leaders.
Arts *Tina Jackson* Interested in comment, interviews and analysis ideas. Reviews written in-house. Send synopses to arts editor.

Bird Life Magazine
RSPB, The Lodge, Sandy, Bedfordshire SG19 2DL
☎01767 680551 Fax 01767 683262
Email derek.niemann@rspb.org.uk
Owner *Royal Society for the Protection of Birds*
Editor *Derek Niemann*
Circulation 90,000

FOUNDED 1965. BI-MONTHLY. Bird, wildlife and nature conservation for 8–12-year-olds (RSPB Wildlife Explorer members). No unsolicited mss. No 'captive/animal welfare' articles.
Features *Derek Niemann* Unsolicited material rarely used.
News *Derek Niemann* News releases welcome. Approach in writing in the first instance.

Birds
RSPB, The Lodge, Sandy, Bedfordshire SG19 2DL
☎01767 680551 Fax 01767 683262
Email birds.editor@rspb.org.uk
Owner *Royal Society for the Protection of Birds*
Editor *R.A. Hume*
Circulation 585,000

QUARTERLY magazine which covers not only wild birds but also wildlife and related conservation topics. No interest in features on pet birds or 'rescued' sick/injured/orphaned ones. Content refers mostly to RSPB work so opportunities for freelance work on other subjects are limited. Phone to discuss.

Birdwatch
3D/F Leroy House, 436 Essex Road, London N1 3QP
☎020 7704 9495 Fax 020 7704 2767
Website www.birdwatch.co.uk
Owner *Solo Publishing*
Editor *Dominic Mitchell*
Circulation 15,000

FOUNDED 1992. MONTHLY magazine featuring illustrated articles on all aspects of birds and birdwatching, especially in Britain. No unsolicited mss. Approach in writing with synopsis of 100 words maximum. Annual **Birdwatch Bird Book of the Year** award (see entry under **Prizes**).
Features *Dominic Mitchell* Unusual angles/ personal accounts, if well-written. Articles of an educative or practical nature suited to the readership. Maximum 2000 words.
Fiction *Dominic Mitchell* Very little opportunity although occasional short story published. Maximum 1500 words.

News *David Mairs* Very rarely use external material.
Payment £40 per 1000 words.

Bizarre
John Brown Publishing, The New Boathouse, 136–142 Bramley Road, London W10 6SR
☎020 7565 3000 Fax 020 7565 3055
Email bizarre@johnbrown.co.uk
Website www.bizarremag.com
Owner *John Brown Publishing*
Editor *Joe Gardiner*
Circulation 119,057

FOUNDED 1997. MONTHLY magazine featuring amazing stories and images from around the world. No fiction, poetry, illustrations, short snippets.

Features *Joe Gardiner* Particularly interested in global stories and celebrity interviews. Maximum 2500 words. Approach in writing
Payment £200 per 1000 words.

Black Beauty & Hair
Hawker Consumer Publications Ltd, 13 Park House, 140 Battersea Park Road, London SW11 4NB
☎020 7720 2108 Fax 020 7498 3023
Email info@blackbeauty.co.uk
Website www.blackbeauty.co.uk
Owner *Hawker Consumer Publications Ltd*
Editor *Irene Shelley*
Circulation 21,719

BI-MONTHLY with one annual special: *The Hairstyle Book* in October; and a *Bridal Supplement* in the April/May issue. Black hair and beauty magazine with emphasis on authoritative articles relating to hair, beauty, fashion, health and lifestyle. Unsolicited contributions welcome.

Features Beauty and fashion pieces welcome from writers with a sound knowledge of the Afro-Caribbean beauty scene plus bridal features. Minimum 1000 words.
Payment £100 per 1000 words.

Bliss Magazine
Endeavour House, 189 Shaftesbury Avenue, London WC2H 8JG
☎020 7208 3478 Fax 020 7208 3591
Email christina.reeves@ecm.emap.com
Owner *EMAP élan*
Editor *Liz Nice*
Circulation 300,191

FOUNDED 1995. MONTHLY teenage lifestyle magazine for girls. No unsolicited mss; 'call the deputy editor with an idea and then send it in.'

News *Katie Masters* Worldwide teenage news. Maximum 200 words. *Payment* £50–100.

Features *Lisa Smasarski* Real life teenage stories with subjects willing to be photographed. Reports on teenage issues. Maximum 2000 words. *Payment* £350.

The Book Collector
PO Box 12426, London W11 3GW
☎020 7792 3492 Fax 020 7792 3492
Email info@thebookcollector.co.uk
Website www.thebookcollector.co.uk
Owner *The Collector Ltd*
Editor *Nicolas J. Barker*

FOUNDED 1950. QUARTERLY magazine on bibliography and the history of books, book-collecting, libraries and the book trade.

The Book Directory
'Ambleside', 52 Heaton Street, Brampton, Chesterfield, Derbyshire S40 3AQ
☎01246 230408
Owner/Editor *Ron Mihaly*
Circulation 2500 (quarterly)

FOUNDED 1997. QUARTERLY. Carries articles of a bibliographical nature, quarterly list of book fairs, auction news, for sale/wanted ads. Unsolicited mss and ideas welcome – but write first, please. Maximum 2000 words.
Payment Commissions: £15 per 1000 words.

Book World Magazine
2 Caversham Street, London SW3 4AH
☎020 7351 4995 Fax 020 7351 4995
Owner *Christchurch Publishers Ltd*
Editor *James Hughes*
Circulation 5500

FOUNDED 1980. MONTHLY news and reviews for serious book collectors, librarians, antiquarian and other booksellers. No unsolicited mss. Interested in material relevant to literature, art and book collecting. Send letter in the first instance.

Bookdealer
Suite F22, Park Hall Estate, 40 Martell Road, West Dulwich, London SE21 8EN
☎020 8761 5570 Fax 020 8761 5570
Editor *Barry Shaw*

WEEKLY trade paper which acts almost exclusively as a platform for people wishing to buy or sell rare/out-of-print books. Twelve-page editorial only; occasional articles and book reviews by regular freelance writers.

Books

39 Store Street, London WC1F 7DB
☎020 7692 2900 Fax 020 7419 2111

Editor *Liz Thomson*
Circulation 100,000

Formerly *Books and Bookmen*. Free consumer magazine dealing chiefly with features about authors and reviews of books. Carries few commissioned pieces.
Payment negotiable.

The Bookseller

Endeavour House, 5th Floor, 189 Shaftesbury Avenue, London WC2H 8TJ
☎020 7420 6006 Fax 020 7420 6103
Website www.theBookseller.com

Owner *J. Whitaker & Sons Ltd*
Editor *Nicholas Clee*

Trade journal of the publishing and book trade – the essential guide to what is being done to whom. Trade news and features, including special features, company news, publishing trends, etc. Unsolicited mss rarely used as most writing is either done in-house or commissioned from experts within the trade. Approach in writing first.
Features *Jenny Bell*
News *Ms Danuta Kean*

Boxing Monthly

40 Morpeth Road, London E9 7LD
☎020 8986 4141 Fax 020 8986 4145
Email bm@boxing-monthly.demon.co.uk
Website www.boxing-monthly.co.uk

Owner *Topwave Ltd*
Editor *Glyn Leach*
Circulation 30,000

FOUNDED 1989. MONTHLY. International coverage of professional boxing; previews, reports and interviews. Unsolicited material welcome. Interested in small hall shows and grass-roots knowledge. No big fight reports. Approach in writing in the first instance.

Boyz

72 Holloway Road, London N7 8NZ
☎020 7296 6230 Fax 020 7296 0026
Email hudson@boyz.co.uk

Editor *David Hudson*
Circulation 55,000

FOUNDED 1994. WEEKLY entertainment and features magazine aimed at a gay readership covering clubs, fashion, TV, films, music, theatre, celebrities and the UK gay scene in general. Unsolicited mss are looked at but not often used.

Brides

Vogue House, Hanover Square, London W1S 1JU
☎020 7499 9080 Fax 020 7460 6369

Owner *Condé Nast Publications Ltd*
Editor *Sandra Boler*
Circulation 64,620

BI-MONTHLY. Much of the magazine is produced in-house, but a good, relevant feature on cakes, jewellery, music, flowers, etc. is always welcome. Maximum 1000 words. Prospective contributors should telephone with an idea in the first instance.

British Birds

The Banks, Mountfield, Robertsbridge, East Sussex TN32 5JY
☎01580 882039 Fax 01580 882038
Email editor@britishbirds.co.uk

Editor *Dr R. Riddington*
Circulation 8,000

FOUNDED 1907. MONTHLY ornithological journal. Features annual *Reports on Rare Birds in Great Britain*, bird news from official national correspondents throughout Europe and sponsored competitions for Bird Photograph of the Year, Bird Illustrator of the Year and Young Ornithologists of the Year. Unsolicited mss welcome from ornithologists only.
Features Well-researched, original material relating to Western Palearctic birds welcome. Maximum 6000 words.
News *Bob Scott/Wendy Dickson* Items ranging from conservation to humour. Maximum 200 words.
Payment only for photographs, drawings and paintings.

British Chess Magazine

The Chess Shop, 44 Baker Street, London W1U 7RT
☎020 7486 8222 Fax 020 7486 3355
Email bcmchess@compuserve.com
Website www.bcmchess.co.uk

Director/Editor *John Saunders*

FOUNDED 1881. MONTHLY. Emphasis on tournaments, the history of chess and chess-related literature. Approach in writing with ideas. Unsolicited mss not welcome unless from qualified chess experts and players.

British Medical Journal

BMA House, Tavistock Square, London WC1H 9JR
☎020 7387 4499 Fax 020 7383 6418
Email editor@bmj.com

Website www.bmj.com
Owner *British Medical Association*
Editor *Professor Richard Smith*

One of the world's leading general medical journals.

British Philatelic Bulletin
Royal Mail National, Gavrelle House,
2–14 Bunhill Row, London EC1Y 8HQ
☎020 7847 3321   Fax 020 7847 3359

Owner *Royal Mail*
Editor *John Holman*
Circulation 30,000

FOUNDED 1963. MONTHLY bulletin giving details of forthcoming British stamps, features on older stamps and postal history, and book reviews. Welcomes photographs of interesting, unusual or historic letter boxes.

Features Articles on all aspects of British philately. Maximum 1500 words.

News Reports on exhibitions and philatelic events. Maximum 500 words. Approach in writing in the first instance.

Payment £45 per 1000 words.

British Railway Modelling
The Maltings, West Street, Bourne,
Lincolnshire PE10 9PH
☎01778 391176   Fax 01778 393668
Email davidb@warnersgroup.co.uk
Website www.brmodelling.com

Owner *Warners Group Publications Plc*
Managing Editor *David Brown*
Deputy Editor *John Emerson*
Circulation 18,347

FOUNDED 1993. MONTHLY. A general magazine for the practising modeller. No unsolicited mss but ideas are welcome. Interested in features on quality models, from individual items to complete layouts. Approach in writing.

Features Articles on practical elements of the hobby, e.g. locomotive construction, kit conversions, etc. Layout features and articles on individual items which represent high standards of the railway modelling art. Maximum length 6000 words (single feature). *Payment* up to £60 per published page.

News News and reviews containing the model railway trade, new products, etc. Maximum length 1000 words. *Payment* up to £60 per published page.

Broadcast
33-39 Bowling Green Lane, London
EC1R 0DA
☎020 7505 8014   Fax 020 7505 8050

Owner *EMAP Communications*
Editor *Lucy Rouse*
Circulation 14,297

FOUNDED 1960. WEEKLY. Opportunities for freelance contributions. Write to the relevant editor in the first instance.

Features *Katy Elliott* Any broadcasting issue. Maximum 1500 words.

News *Colin Robertson* Broadcasting news. Maximum 350 words.

Payment £200 per 1000 words.

Brownie
17–19 Buckingham Palace Road, London
SW1W 0PT
☎020 7834 6242   Fax 020 7828 5791
Email MarionT@guides.org.uk
Website www.guides.org.uk

Owner *The Guide Association*
Editor *Marion Thompson*
Circulation 20–21,000

FOUNDED 1962. MONTHLY. Aimed at Brownie members aged 7–10.

Articles Crafts and simple make-it-yourself items using inexpensive or scrap materials.

Fiction Brownie content an advantage. No adventures involving unaccompanied children in dangerous situations – day or night. Maximum 800 words.

Payment £50 per 1000 words pro rata.

Bukowski Journal
PO Box 11271, Wood Green, London
N22 8BF
Email bukzine@aol.com
Website www.bukzine.co.uk
Owner/Editor *Rikki Hollywood*
Circulation 1000

FOUNDED 1999 to promote the work of American barfly and author, Charles Bukowski. 'A platform for lovers and haters of his work.' Welcomes provocative, lively articles, essays, illustrations on Bukowski or like-minded souls such as Robert Crumb, Dan Fante, etc. Approach by e-mail or letter. *Payment* Free copy of journal.

The Burlington Magazine
14–16 Duke's Road, London WC1H 9SZ
☎020 7388 1228   Fax 020 7388 1230
Email editorial@burlington.org.uk
Website www.burlington.org.uk

Owner *The Burlington Magazine Publications Ltd*
Editor *Caroline Elam*

FOUNDED 1903. MONTHLY. Unsolicited contributions welcome on the subject of art history provided they are previously unpublished. All preliminary approaches should be made in writing.

Exhibition Reviews Usually commissioned, but occasionally unsolicited reviews are published if appropriate. Maximum 1000 words.

Articles Maximum 4500 words. *Payment* £100 (maximum).

Shorter Notices Maximum 2000 words. *Payment* £50 (maximum).

Bus and Coach Professional
56 Market Street, Wellington, Telford, Shropshire TF1 1DT
☎01952 415334 Fax 01952 406762
Email editorial@busandcoach.com
Website www.busandcoach.com

Editorial Director *Steve Rooney*

MONTHLY magazine for executives and senior managers in the bus and coach industry. 'Strong on news and features. Some opportunities for well-written freelance material if relevant to our requirement. Phone or e-mail before submission.'

Business Brief
PO Box 582, Five Oaks, St Saviour, Jersey JE4 8XQ
☎01534 611600 Fax 01534 611610
Email mspeditorial@msppublishing.com

Owner *MSP Publishing*
Editor *Peter Body*
Circulation 6,000

FOUNDED 1989. MONTHLY magazine covering business developments in the Channel Islands and how they affect the local market. Styles itself as the magazine for business people rather than just a magazine about business. Interested in business-orientated articles only – 800 words maximum. Approach the editor by telephone initially.

Payment £8.50 per 100 words.

Business Life
Haymarket House, 1 Oxendon Street, London SW1Y 4EE
☎020 7925 2544 Fax 020 7976 1088

Owner *Premier Media Partners*
Editor *Alex Finer*
Circulation 193,000

TEN ISSUES YEARLY including two double issues. Glossy business travel magazine distributed on European airline routes. Unsolicited mss not welcome. Few opportunities for freelancers. Approach with ideas in writing only.

Business Traveller
Condor House, 5–14 St Paul's Churchyard, London EC4N 8BE
☎020 7778 0000 Fax 020 7778 0022
Website www.businesstraveller.com

Owner *Perry Publications*
Editor-in-Chief *Julia Brookes*
Circulation 42,000

MONTHLY. Consumer publication. Opportunities exist for freelance writers but unsolicited contributions tend to be about leisure travel rather than business travel. Would-be contributors are advised to study the magazine or the website first. Approach in writing with ideas.

Payment varies.

Camcorder User
WVIP, 53–79 Highgate Road, London NW5 1TW
☎020 7331 1000 Fax 020 7331 1242
Email camusermail@yahoo.co.uk

Owner *WVIP*
Editor *Robert Hull*
Circulation 21,797

FOUNDED 1988. MONTHLY magazine dedicated to camcorders, with features on creative technique, shooting advice, new equipment, accessory round-ups and interesting applications on location. Unsolicited mss, illustrations and pictures welcome. *Payment* negotiable.

Campaign
22 Bute Gardens, London W6 7HN
☎020 8267 4683 Fax 020 8267 4914
Website www.campaignlive.com

Owner *Haymarket Publishing Ltd*
Editor *Caroline Marshall*
Circulation 17,700

FOUNDED 1968. WEEKLY. Lively magazine serving the advertising and related industries. Freelance contributors are best advised to write in the first instance.

Features Articles of 1500–2000 words.

News Relevant news stories of up to 320 words.

Payment negotiable.

Camping and Caravanning
Greenfields House, Westwood Way, Coventry, Warwickshire CV4 8JH
☎024 7669 4995 Fax 024 7669 4886

Owner *Camping and Caravanning Club*
Editor *Nick Harding*
Circulation 154,058

FOUNDED 1901. MONTHLY. Interested in journalists with camping and caravanning knowledge. Write with ideas for features in the first instance.

Features Outdoor pieces in general, plus items on specific regions of Britain. Maximum 1200 words. Illustrations to support text essential.

Camping Magazine

5 Sun Street, Lewes, East Sussex BN7 2QB
☎01273 477421   Fax 01273 477421

Owner *Warners Group Publications*
Editor *John Lloyd*

FOUNDED 1961. MONTHLY magazine with features on camping. Aims to reflect this enjoyment by encouraging readers to appreciate the outdoors and to pursue an active camping holiday, whether as a family in a frame tent or as a lightweight backpacker. Articles that have the flavour of the camping lifestyle without being necessarily expeditionary or arduous are always welcome. Study of the magazine is advised in the first instance. Ideas welcome. Contact editor by phone before sending mss.

Payment negotiable.

Canal and Riverboat

PO Box 618, Norwich, Norfolk NR7 0QT
☎01603 708930   Fax 01603 708934
Email bluefoxfilms@netscapeonline.co.uk
Website www.canalandriverboat.com

Owner *A.E. Morgan Publications Ltd*
Editor *Chris Cattrall*
Circulation 26,000

Covers all aspects of waterways, narrow boats and cruisers. Contributions welcome. Make initial approach in writing.

Features Waterways, narrow boats and motor cruisers, cruising reports, practical advice, etc. Unusual ideas and personal comments are particularly welcome. Maximum 2000 words. Articles should be supplied in PC Windows format disk. *Payment* around £50 per page.

News Items of up to 300 words welcome on the Inland Waterways System, plus photographs if possible. *Payment* £15.

Car Mechanics

Kelsey Publishing Ltd, PO Box 13, Westerham, Kent TN16 3WT
☎01959 541444   Fax 01959 541400
Email carmechanics@kelsey.co.uk

Owner *Kelsey Publishing*
Editor *Peter Simpson*
Circulation 35,000

MONTHLY. Practical guide to maintenance and repair of post–1978 cars for DIY and the motor trade. Unsolicited mss, with good-quality colour prints or transparencies, 'at sender's risk'. Ideas preferred. Initial approach by letter or phone welcome and strongly recommended, 'but please read a recent copy first for style'.

Features Good, technical, entertaining and well-researched material welcome, especially anything presenting complex matters clearly and simply.

Payment by arrangement ('but generous for the right material').

Caravan Life

Warners Group Publications plc, The Maltings, West Street, Bourne, Lincolnshire PH10 9PH
☎01778 391165   Fax 01778 425437
Email caravanlife@warnersgroup.co.uk

Editor *Michael Le Caplain*
Circulation 16,119

FOUNDED 1987. Magazine for experienced caravanners and enthusiasts providing practical and useful information and product evaluation. Opportunities for caravanning, relevant touring and travel material with good-quality colour photographs.

Caravan Magazine

IPC Media Ltd., Focus House, Dingwall Avenue, Croydon, Surrey CR9 2TA
☎020 8774 0600   Fax 020 8774 0939
Website www.linkhouse.co.uk/caravan.html

Owner *IPC Media Ltd*
Editor *Rob McCabe*
Circulation 17,744

FOUNDED 1933. MONTHLY. Unsolicited mss welcome. Approach in writing with ideas. All correspondence should go direct to the editor.

Features Touring with strong caravan bias, technical/DIY features and how-to section. Maximum 1500 words.

Payment by arrangement.

Caribbean Times

Unit 2, 65 Whitechapel Road, London E1 1DU
☎020 7650 2000   Fax 020 7650 2001
Website www.ethnicmedia.co.uk

Owner *Ethnic Media Group*
Editor *Ron Shillingford*
Circulation 22,500

FOUNDED 1981. WEEKLY community paper for the African and Caribbean communities in Britain. Interested in general, local and international issues relevant to these communities. Approach in writing with ideas for submission.

Carmarthenshire Life

Swan House Publishing, Swan House, Bridge Street, Newcastle Emlyn, Carmarthenshire SA38 9DX
☎01239 710632   Fax 01239 710632
Email davidfielding@themail.co.uk
Owner *Swan House Publishing*
Editor *David Fielding*

FOUNDED 1995. BI-MONTHLY county magazine with articles on local history, issues, characters, off-beat stories with good colour or b&w photographs. No country diaries, short stories or poems. Most articles are commissioned from known freelancers but 'always prepared to consider ideas from new writers'. No mss. Send cuttings of previous work (published or not) and synopsis to the editor.

Cat World

Avalon Court, Star Road, Partridge Green, West Sussex RH13 8RY
☎01403 711511   Fax 01403 711521
Email editor@catworld.co.uk
Website www.catworld.co.uk
Owner *Ashdown Publishing Ltd*
Editor *Judy Trewin*
Circulation 20,000

FOUNDED 1981. MONTHLY. Unsolicited mss welcome but initial approach in writing preferred.
  Features Lively, first-hand experience features on every aspect of the cat. Breeding features and veterinary articles by acknowledged experts only. Preferred length 750 or 1700 words. Accompanying pictures should be good quality and sharp.
  News Short, concise, factual or humorous items concerning cats. Maximum 100 words.
  Submissions on disk (MS Word) if possible, with accompanying hard copy and s.a.e. for return or by e-mail.

Catholic Gazette

The Chase Centre, 114 West Heath Road, London NW3 7TX
☎020 8458 3316   Fax 020 8905 5780
Email catholic.gazette@cms.org.uk
Website www.cms.org.uk/gazette
Owner *Catholic Missionary Society*
Editor *Peter Wilson*
Circulation 1600

FOUNDED 1910. MONTHLY. Covers the work of the Catholic Missionary Society – evangelisation, scripture and prayer features. Interested in items on what is going on in the Catholic Church in England and Wales. Maximum

2000 words for features with *payment* of £15 for first page and £10 thereafter. 'Rear Light' – personal comment page: maximum 400 words. *Payment* £15. Approach in writing.

The Catholic Herald

Lamb's Passage, Bunhill Row, London EC1Y 8TQ
☎020 7588 3101   Fax 020 7256 9728
Email catholic@atlas.co.uk
Website www.catholicherald.co.uk
Editor *Dr William Oddie*
Deputy Editor *Luke Coppen*
  Literary Editor *Damian Thompson*
Circulation 22,000

WEEKLY. Interested mainly in straight Catholic issues but also in general humanitarian matters, social policies, the Third World, the arts and books.
  Payment by arrangement.

CCC Magazine

IPC Focus Network, Focus House, Dingwall Avenue, Croydon, Surrey CR9 2TA
☎020 8774 0946   Fax 020 8774 0935
Owner *IPC Media Ltd*
Editor *Steve Kirk*
Circulation 25,045

FOUNDED 1963. MONTHLY. Unsolicited mss welcome but prospective contributors are advised to make initial contact in writing.
  Features Technical articles on current motorsport and unusual sport-orientated road cars. Length by arrangement.
  Payment negotiable.

Celebrity Looks

Endeavour House, 189 Shaftesbury Avenue, London WC2H 8JG
☎020 7437 9011   Fax 020 7208 3586
Owner *EMAP élan Publications*
Editor *Margi Conklin*
Circulation 132,032

MONTHLY celebrity-led magazine for young women aged 16–24, with fashion, beauty and hair, as well as general interest features, interviews, giveaways, etc. Freelance writers are occasionally used in all areas of the magazine. Contact the editor with ideas.
  Payment varies.

Challenge

50 Loxwood Avenue, Worthing, West Sussex BN14 7RA
☎01903 824174   Fax 01903 824376
Owner *Challenge Support*

Editor *Donald Banks*
Circulation 70,000

FOUNDED 1958. MONTHLY Christian newspaper which welcomes contributions. No fiction. Send for sample copy of writers' guidelines in the first instance.

News Items of up to 500 words (preferably with pictures) 'showing God at work', and human interest photo stories. 'Churchy' items not wanted. Stories of professional sportsmen and musicians who are Christians always wanted but check first to see if their story has already been used.

Women's Page Relevant items of interest welcome.

Payment negotiable.

Chapman

4 Broughton Place, Edinburgh EH1 3RX
☎0131 557 2207 Fax 0131 556 9565
Email editor@chapman-pub.co.uk
Website www.chapman-pub.co.uk

Owner/Editor *Joy Hendry*
Circulation 2000

FOUNDED 1970. QUARTERLY. Scotland's quality literary magazine. Features poetry, short works of fiction, criticism, reviews and articles on theatre, politics, language and the arts. Unsolicited material welcome if accompanied by s.a.e. Approach in writing unless discussion is needed. Priority is given to full-time writers.

Features Topics of literary interest, especially Scottish literature, theatre, culture or politics. Maximum 5000 words.

Fiction Short stories, occasionally novel extracts if self-contained. Maximum 6000 words. *Payment* by negotiation.

Special Pages Poetry, both UK and non-UK in translation (mainly, but not necessarily, European). *Payment* by negotiation.

Chat

IPC Media Ltd., King's Reach Tower, Stamford Street, London SE1 9LS
☎020 7261 6565 Fax 020 7261 6534
Website www.ipc.media.co.uk/pubs/chat.htm

Owner *IPC Connect Ltd*
Editor *Keith Kendrick*
Circulation 469,769

FOUNDED 1985. WEEKLY general interest women's magazine. Unsolicited mss considered; approach in writing with ideas. Not interested in contributors 'who have never bothered to read *Chat* and therefore don't know what type of magazine it is'.

Features *June Smith-Sheppard* Human interest and humour. Maximum 1000 words. *Payment* up to £600 maximum.

Fiction *Olwen Rice* Maximum 800 words.

Cheshire Life

2nd Floor, Oyston Mill, Strand Road, Preston, Lancashire PR1 8UR
☎01772 722022 Fax 01772 736496
Website www.cheshirelife.co.uk

Owner *Life Magazines*
Editor *Patrick O'Neill*
Circulation 15,000

FOUNDED 1934. MONTHLY. Homes, gardens, personalities, business, farming, conservation, property, heritage, books, fashion, arts, science – anything which has a Cheshire connection.

Child Education

Scholastic Ltd, Villiers House, Clarendon Avenue, Leamington Spa, Warwickshire CV32 5PR
☎01926 887799 Fax 01926 883331
Website www.scholastic.co.uk

Owner *Scholastic Ltd*
Editor *Jeremy Sugden*
Circulation 45,000

FOUNDED 1923. MONTHLY magazine aimed at teachers of children aged 4–7 years. Practical articles from teachers about education for this age group are welcome. Maximum 900 words. Approach in writing with synopsis.

Choice

Kings Chambers, 39–41 Priestgate, Peterborough, Cambridgeshire PE1 1FR
☎01733 555123 Fax 01733 427500
Email choice.bayardpresse@talk21.com

Owner *Bayard Presse (UK) Ltd*
Editor *Sue Dobson*
Circulation 100,000

MONTHLY full-colour, lively and informative magazine for people aged 50 plus which helps them get the most out of their lives, time and money after full-time work.

Features Real-life stories, hobbies, interesting (older) people, British heritage and countryside, involving activities for active bodies and minds, health, relationships, book/entertainment reviews. Unsolicited mss read (s.a.e. for return of material); write with ideas and copies of cuttings if new contributor. No phone calls, please.

Rights/Money All items affecting the magazine's readership are written by experts. Areas of interest include pensions, state benefits, health, finance, property, legal.

Payment by arrangement.

Christian Herald

Christian Media Centre, 96 Dominion Road, Worthing, West Sussex BN14 8JP
☎01903 821082 Fax 01903 821081
Email news@christianherald.org.uk
Website www.christianherald.org.uk

Owner *Christian Media Centre Ltd*
Editor *Russ Bravo*
Circulation 15,000

WEEKLY. Evangelical, inter-denominational Christian newspaper aimed at committed Christians. News, bible-based comment and incisive features. No poetry. Contributors' guidelines available.
Payment Christian Media rates.

Church Music Quarterly

Cleveland Lodge, Westhumble, Dorking, Surrey RH5 6BW
☎01306 872800 Fax 01306 887260
Email ejones@rscm.com
Website www.rscm.com

Owner *Royal School of Church Music*
Editor *Esther Jones*
Circulation 17,000

QUARTERLY. Contributions welcome. Telephone in the first instance.
Features Articles on church music or related subjects considered. Maximum 2000 words.
Payment £60 per page.

Church of England Newspaper

20–26 Brunswick Place, London N1 6DZ
☎020 7216 6400 Fax 020 7216 6410
Website www.cen@parlicom.com

Owner *Parliamentary Communications Ltd*
Editor *Colin Blakely*
Circulation 9,500

FOUNDED 1828. WEEKLY. Almost all material is commissioned but unsolicited mss are considered.
Features *Jonathan Wynne-Jones* Preliminary enquiry essential. Maximum 1200 words.
News *Claire Shelley* Items must be sent promptly and should have a church/Christian relevance. Maximum 200–400 words.
Payment negotiable.

Church Times

33 Upper Street, London N1 0PN
☎020 7359 4570 Fax 020 7226 3073
Email news@churchtimes.co.uk *or*
features@churchtimes.co.uk
Website www.churchtimes.co.uk

Owner *Hymns Ancient & Modern*
Editor *Paul Handley*
Circulation 35,701

FOUNDED 1863. WEEKLY. Unsolicited mss considered.
Features *Prudence Fay* Articles and pictures (any format) on religious topics. Maximum 1600 words. *Payment* £100 per 1000 words.
News *Helen Saxbee* Occasional reports (commissions only) and up-to-date photographs.
Payment by arrangement.

Classic Bike

EMAP Automotive, Media House, Lynchwood, Peterborough Business Park, Peterborough, Cambridgeshire PE2 6EA
☎01733 467000 Fax 01733 468466
Email classic.bike@econ.emap.com

Owner *EMAP Active Ltd*
Editor *Brian Crichton*
Circulation 50,000

FOUNDED 1978. MONTHLY. Mainly pre-1972 classic motorcycles with a heavy bias to British marques. Approach in writing.
News Genuine news with good illustrations, if possible, suitable for a global audience. Maximum 400 words.
Features British motorcycle industry inside stories, technical features 'that can be understood by all', German, Spanish and French machine features, people. Maximum 2000 words.
Special Pages How-to features, oddball machines, stunning pictures, features with a fresh slant.
Payment £100–125 per 1000 words, plus pictures.

Classic Boat

Focus House, Dingwall Avenue, Croydon, Surrey CR9 2TA
☎020 8744 0603 Fax 020 8744 0943
Email cb@ipcmedia.com
Website www.classicboat.co.uk

Owner *IPC Media Ltd*
Editor *Dan Houston*
Circulation 16,264

FOUNDED 1987. MONTHLY. Traditional boats and classic yachts, old and new; maritime history. Unsolicited mss, particularly if supported by good photos, are welcome. Sail and power boat pieces considered. Approach in writing with ideas. Interested in well-researched stories on all nautical matters. News reports welcome. Contributor's notes available (s.a.e.).
Features Boatbuilding, boat history and

design, events, yachts and working boats. Material must be well-informed and supported where possible by good-quality or historic photos. Maximum 3000 words. Classic is defined by excellence of design and construction – the boat need not be old and wooden! *Payment* £75–100 per published page.

News New boats, restorations, events, boatbuilders, etc. Maximum 500 words. *Payment* according to merit.

Classic Cars

Media House, Peterborough Business Park, Lynchwood, Peterborough PE2 6EA
☎01733 468219 Fax 01733 468228
Owner *EMAP Automotive Ltd*
Editor *Mark Walton*
International Editor *Robert Coucher*
Circulation 86,177

FOUNDED 1973. THIRTEEN ISSUES YEARLY. International classic car magazine containing entertaining and informative articles about classic cars, events and associated personalities. Contributions welcome.

Classical Guitar

1 & 2 Vance Court, Trans Britannia Enterprise Park, Blaydon on Tyne NE21 5NH
☎0191 414 9000 Fax 0191 414 9001
Email classicalguitar@ashleymark.co.uk
Website www.ashleymark.co.uk
Owner *Ashley Mark Publishing Co.*
Editor *Colin Cooper*

FOUNDED 1982. MONTHLY.

Features *Colin Cooper* Usually written by staff writers. Maximum 1500 words. *Payment* by arrangement.

News *Thérèse Wassily Saba* Small paragraphs and festival concert reports welcome. *No payment*.

Reviews *Tim Panting* Concert reviews of up to 250 words usually written by staff reviewers.

Classical Music

241 Shaftesbury Avenue, London WC2H 8TF
☎020 7333 1742 Fax 020 7333 1769
Email classical.music@rhinegold.co.uk
Website www.rhinegold.co.uk
Owner *Rhinegold Publishing Ltd*
Editor *Keith Clarke*

FOUNDED 1976. FORTNIGHTLY. A specialist magazine using precisely targeted news and feature articles aimed at the music business. Most material is commissioned but professionally written unsolicited mss are occasionally published. Freelance contributors may approach in writing

with an idea but should familiarise themselves beforehand with the style and market of the magazine.
Payment negotiable.

Classics

Berwick House, 8–10 Knoll Rise, Orpington, Kent BR6 0PS
☎01689 887200 Fax 01689 838844
Email classics@splpublishing.co.uk
Owner *SPL Publishing Ltd*
Editor *Andrew Charman*

FOUNDED 1997. MONTHLY how-to magazine for classic car owners, featuring everything from repairing and restoring to buying, selling and enjoying all types of cars from the '50s to '80s. Includes vehicle comparison tests, price guide, practical advice and technical know-how from experts and owners, plus hundreds of readers' free ads.

Features Illustrated features on classic car maintenance, repair and restoration with strong technical content and emphasis on DIY.

News All classic car related news stories and topical photos.

Climber

Warners Group Publications plc, West Street, Bourne, Lincolnshire PE10 9PH
☎01778 391117
Owner *Warners Group Publications plc*
Editor *Bernard Newman*

FOUNDED 1962. MONTHLY. Unsolicited mss welcome (they receive about ten a day). Ideas welcome.

Features Freelance features (accompanied by photographs) are accepted on climbing and mountaineering in the UK and abroad, but the standard of writing must be extremely high. Maximum 2000 words. *Payment* negotiable.

News No freelance opportunities as all items are handled in-house.

Club International

2 Archer Street, London W1D 7AW
☎020 7292 8000 Fax 020 7734 5030
Email club@pr-org.co.uk
Owner *Paul Raymond*
Editor *Robert Swift*
Circulation 180,000

FOUNDED 1972. MONTHLY. Features and short humorous items aimed at young male readership aged 18–30.

Features Maximum 1000 words.
Shorts 200–750 words.
Payment negotiable.

Coin News

Token Publishing Ltd, Orchard House,
Duchy Road, Heathpark, Honiton, Devon
EX14 1YD
☎01404 46972 Fax 01404 44788
Email info@coin-news.com
Website www.coin-news.com
Owners *J.W. Mussell, Carol Hartman*
Editor *J.W. Mussell*
Circulation 10,000
FOUNDED 1964. MONTHLY. Contributions welcome. Approach by phone in the first instance.
   Features Opportunity exists for well-informed authors 'who know the subject and do their homework'. Maximum 2500 words.
   Payment £20 per 1000 words.

Community News

Bridge House, Blackden Lane, Goostrey,
Cheshire CW4 8PZ
☎01477 534440/533403 Fax 01477 535756
Email scoop2001@aol.com
Owner *Hill Bros. (Leek) Ltd*
Editor *John Williams*
Circulation 28,000
FOUNDED 1981. Formerly *Town and Country Post*. MONTHLY. Local news and features on Cheshire. Very little freelance material is used. No unsolicited mss. Approach by telephone in the first instance.

Company

National Magazine House, 72 Broadwick
Street, London W1V 2BP
☎020 7439 5000 Fax 020 7439 5117
Owner *National Magazine Co. Ltd*
Editor *Sam Baker*
Circulation 260,646
MONTHLY. Glossy women's magazine appealing to the independent and intelligent young woman. A good market for freelancers: 'We look for great newsy features relevant to young British women'. Keen to encourage bright, new, young talent, but uncommissioned material is rarely accepted. Feature outlines are the only sensible approach in the first instance. Maximum 1500–2000 words. Features to *Celia Duncan*, Features Editor.
   Payment £250 per 1000 words.

Compass Sport

Ballencrieff Cottage, Ballencrieff Toll,
Bathgate, West Lothian EH48 4LD
☎01506 632728 Fax 01506 635444
Email pages@clara.net
Website home.clara.net/pages
Owner *Pages Editorial & Publishing Services*
Editor *Suse Coon*
BI-MONTHLY orienteering magazine covering all disciplines of the sport including mountain marathons, mountain bike O, ski O and trail O. Includes profiles and articles on relevant topics, with subsections on fixtures, junior news and mountain marathons which are compiled by sub-editors. Letters, puzzles and competition. Phone or e-mail to discuss content and timing.
   Payment by arrangement.

Computer Arts Special

30 Monmouth Street, Bath BA1 2BW
☎01225 442244 Fax 01225 732361
Email deborah.jones@futurenet.co.uk
Website www.computerarts.co.uk
Owner *The Future Network*
Editor *Deborah Jones*
FOUNDED 1999. MONTHLY. The world of computer arts – 3D, web design, photoshop, digital video. No unsolicited mss. Interested in tutorials, profiles, tips, software and hardware reviews. Approach by post or e-mail.

Computer Weekly

Quadrant House, The Quadrant, Sutton,
Surrey SM2 5AS
☎020 8652 3122 Fax 020 8652 8979
Email computer.weekly@rbi.co.uk
Owner *Reed Business Information*
Editor *Karl Schneider*
Circulation 143,000
FOUNDED 1966. Freelance contributions welcome.
   Features *Mark Lewis* Always looking for good new writers with specialised industry knowledge. Previews and show features on industry events welcome. Maximum 1500 words.
   News Some openings for regional or foreign news items. Maximum 300 words.
   Payment Up to £50 for stories/tips.

Computing, The IT Newspaper

32–34 Broadwick Street, London W1A 2HG
☎020 7316 9000 Fax 020 7316 9160
Email computing@vnu.co.uk
Website www.vnu.com
Owner *VNU Business Publications Ltd*
Editor *Douglas Hayward*
Deputy Editor *Chris Middleton*
Circulation 135,000
FOUNDED 1973. WEEKLY newspaper for IT professionals.
   Features Editor *Sally Whittle*

News *Mike Gubbins*
Unsolicited technical articles welcome. Please enclose s.a.e. for return.
Payment negotiable.

Condé Nast Traveller

Vogue House, Hanover Square, London W1S 1JU
☎020 7499 9080 Fax 020 7493 3758
Email traveller@condenast.co.uk
Website www.cntraveller.co.uk

Owner *Condé Nast Publications*
Editor *Sarah Miller*
Circulation 76,163

FOUNDED 1997. MONTHLY travel magazine. Proposals rather than completed mss preferred. Approach in writing in the first instance. No unsolicited photographs. 'The magazine has a no freebie policy and no writing can be accepted on the basis of a press or paid-for trip.'

Conservative Heartland

WRAP Communications Ltd, The Fire Station, 170 Tabernacle Street, London EC2A 4SD
☎020 7300 7340 Fax 020 7300 7341
Email info@wrapcom.com
Website www.wrapcom.com

Owner *Wrap Communications/The Conservative Party*
Editor *Roger Wilsher*
Circulation 260,000

FOUNDED 1999. THREE ISSUES YEARLY. Conservative Party magazine. Lifestyle articles, political comment and information. No unsolicited material; approach by telephone or e-mail with idea in the first instance.

Features Ideas for stories about relevant political issues ('not necessarily the most obvious') with human interest angle. Maximum 1000 words. *Payment* £250 per 1000 words.

News Stories about Party initiatives in constituences and regions. Maximum 300 words. *Payment* £75 per 300 words.

Contemporary Review

PO Box 1242, Oxford OX1 4FJ
☎01865 201529 Fax 01865 201529
Email editorial@contemporaryreview.co.uk

Owner *Contemporary Review Co. Ltd*
Editor *Dr Richard Mullen*

FOUNDED 1866. MONTHLY. Covers international affairs and politics, literature and the arts, history and religion. No fiction. Maximum 3000 words.

Literary Editor *Dr James Munson* Monthly

book section with reviews which are always commissioned.
Payment £5 per page.

Cosmopolitan

National Magazine House, 72 Broadwick Street, London W1V 2BP
☎020 7439 5000 Fax 020 7439 5016

Owner *National Magazine Co. Ltd*
Editor *Lorraine Candy*
Circulation 460,086

MONTHLY. Designed to appeal to the mid-twenties, modern-minded female. Popular mix of articles, with emphasis on relationships and careers, and hard news. No fiction. Will rarely use unsolicited mss but always on the look-out for 'new writers with original and relevant ideas and a strong voice'. Send short synopsis of idea. All would-be writers should be familiar with the magazine.
Payment about £250 per 1000 words.

Cotswold Life

Treaford House, 54 Lansdown Road, Cheltenham, Gloucestershire GL51 6QB
☎01242 255334 Fax 01242 255116
Email info@cotswoldlife.co.uk

Owner *Loyalty & Conquest Communications Ltd*
Managing Editor *David MacDonald*
Circulation 10,000

FOUNDED 1968. MONTHLY. News and features on life in the Cotswolds. Contributions welcome.

Features Interesting places and people, reminiscences of Cotswold life in years gone by, and historical features on any aspect of Cotswold life. Approach in writing in the first instance. Maximum 1500–2000 words.
Payment by negotiation after publication.

Counselling at Work

Association for Counselling at Work, Eastlands Court, St Peter's Road, Rugby, Warwickshire CV21 3QP
☎0131 667 0110
Email sula@cwcom.net

Owner *British Association for Counselling and Psychotherapy*
Editor *Ian Macwhinnie*
Circulation 1600

FOUNDED 1993. QUARTERLY official journal of the Association for Counselling at Work, a division of B.A.C. Looking for well-researched articles (500–1600 words) about *any* aspect of workplace counselling. Mss from those employed as counsellors or in welfare posts are particularly welcome. Photographs accepted. No fiction or poetry. Send A4 s.a.e. for writer's guidelines and sample copy of the journal. *No payment.*

Country Homes and Interiors
IPC Media Ltd., King's Reach Tower, Stamford Street, London SE1 9LS
☎020 7261 6451 Fax 020 7261 6895
Owner *IPC Media Ltd*
Editor *Deborah Barker*
Circulation 95,063

FOUNDED 1986. MONTHLY. The best approach for prospective contributors is with an idea in writing as unsolicited mss are not welcome.

Features *Jean Carr* Monthly personality interviews of interest to an intelligent, affluent readership (women and men), aged 25–44. Maximum 1200 words.

Houses *Arabella St John Parker* Country-style homes with excellent design ideas. Length 1000 words.

Payment negotiable.

Country Life
IPC Media Ltd., King's Reach Tower, Stamford Street, London SE1 9LS
☎020 7261 7058 Fax 020 7261 5139
Website www.countrylife.co.uk
Owner *IPC Media Ltd*
Editor *Clive Aslet*
Circulation 45,649

ESTABLISHED 1897. WEEKLY. *Country Life* features articles which relate to architecture, countryside, wildlife, rural events, sports, arts, exhibitions, current events, property and news articles of interest to town and country dwellers. Strong informed material rather than amateur enthusiasm. 'We regret we cannot be liable for the safe custody or return of any solicited or unsolicited materials.'

Payment variable, depending on word length and picture size.

Country Living
National Magazine House, 72 Broadwick Street, London W1V 2BP
☎020 7439 5000 Fax 020 7439 5093
Website www.countryliving.co.uk
Owner *National Magazine Co. Ltd*
Editor *Susy Smith*
Circulation 160,162

Magazine aimed at country dwellers and town dwellers who love the countryside. Covers people, conservation, wildlife, houses (gardens and interiors) and country businesses. No unsolicited mss. *Payment* negotiable.

Country Smallholding
Broad Leys Publishing Company, Buriton House, Station Road, Newport, Saffron Walden, Essex CB11 3PL
☎01799 540922 Fax 01799 541367
Website www.countrysmallholding.com
Editor *Elaine Nichols*
Owners *D. and K. Thear*
Circulation 21,000

FOUNDED 1975. MONTHLY journal dealing with practical country living. Unsolicited mss welcome; around 30 received each week. Articles should be detailed and practical, based on first-hand knowledge and experience of smallholding.

Country Sports
The Old Town Hall 367 Kennington Road, London SE1 4PT
☎020 7582 5432 Fax 020 7793 8484
Owner *Countryside Alliance*
Editor *Graham Downing*
Circulation 60,000

FOUNDED 1996. QUARTERLY magazine on country sports and conservation issues. No unsolicited mss.

Country Walking
Apex House, Oundle Road, Peterborough, Cambridgeshire PE2 9NP
☎01733 898100 Fax 01733 465070
Owner *EMAP Plc*
Editor *Nicola Dela-Croix*
Circulation 54,163

FOUNDED 1987. MONTHLY magazine containing walks, features related to walking and things you see, country crafts, history, nature, photography, etc., plus pull-out walks guide containing 25+ routes every month. Very few unsolicited mss accepted. An original approach to subjects welcomed. Not interested in book or gear reviews, news cuttings or poor-quality pictures. Approach by letter or e-mail with ideas.

Features *Emma Kendall* Send synopsis.

Special Pages 'Down your way' section walks. Accurately and recently researched walk and fact file. Points of interest along the way and pictures to illustrate. Please contact for guidelines (unsolicited submissions not often accepted for this section).

Payment not negotiable.

The Countryman
Stable Courtyard, Broughton Hall, Skipton, North Yorkshire BD23 3AZ
☎01756 701381
Owner *Countryman Publishing Ltd*

Editor *David Wheeler*
Circulation 25,825

FOUNDED 1927. MONTHLY. Unsolicited mss with s.a.e. welcome; about 120 received each week. Contributors are strongly advised to study the magazine's content and character in the first instance. Articles supplied with top quality illustrations (colour transparencies, archive b&w prints and line drawings) are far more likely to be used. Maximum article length 1500 words.

The Countryman's Weekly (incorporating **Gamekeeper and Sporting Dog**)

Yelverton, Devon PL20 7PE
☎01822 855281 Fax 01822 855372
Email countrymansweekly@
  countryside-inter.net

Publisher *Vic Gardner*
Features Editor *Kelly Gardner*

FOUNDED 1895. WEEKLY. Unsolicited material welcome.
  Features On any country sports topic. Maximum 1000 words.
  Payment rates available on request.

County

PO Box 2486, Cane End, Reading, Berkshire RG4 6YJ
☎0118 972 4800 Fax 0118 972 4900

Owners *Mr and Mrs Watts*
Editor *Mrs Ashlyn Watts*
Circulation 50,000

FOUNDED 1986. QUARTERLY lifestyle magazine featuring homes, interiors, gardening, fashion and beauty, motoring, leisure and dining. Welcomes unsolicited mss. All initial approaches should be made in writing.

The Cricketer International

Third Street, Langton Green, Tunbridge Wells, Kent TN3 0EN
☎01892 862551 Fax 01892 863755
Email editorial@cricketer.co.uk
Website www.cricketer.com

Owner *Ben G. Brocklehurst*
Editor *Peter Perchard*
Circulation 40,000

FOUNDED 1921. MONTHLY. Unsolicited mss considered. Ideas in writing only. No initial discussions by phone. All correspondence should be addressed to the editor.

Crimewave

5 Martins Lane, Witcham, Ely, Cambridgeshire CB6 2LB
☎01353 777931
Email ttapress@aol.com
Website www.tta-press.freewire.co.uk

Owner *TTA Press*
Editor *Andy Cox*

FOUNDED 1998. QUARTERLY B5 colour magazine of crime fiction. 'The UK's only magazine specialising in crime short stories, publishing the very best from across the spectrum.' Every issue contains stories by authors who are household names in the crime fiction world but room is found for lesser known and unknown writers. *Taking Care of Frank* by Antony Mann, from Crimewave 2, won the **CWA/Macallan Short Story Dagger** award in 1999. Submissions welcome (not via e-mail) with appropriate return postage. Potential contributors are advised to study the magazine. Contracts exchanged upon acceptance. *Payment* on publication.

Cumbria and Lake District Magazine

Stable Courtyard, Broughton Hall, Skipton, North Yorkshire BD23 3AZ
☎01756 701381 Fax 01756 701326
Email editorial@dalesman.co.uk
Website www.dalesman.co.uk

Owner *Dalesman Publishing Co. Ltd*
Editor *Terry Fletcher*
Circulation 17,000

FOUNDED 1951. MONTHLY. County magazine of strong regional and countryside interest, focusing on the Lake District. Unsolicited mss welcome. Maximum 1500 words. Approach in writing or by phone with feature ideas.

Cycle Sport

IPC Media Ltd., Focus House, Dingwall Avenue, Croydon CR9 2TA
☎020 8774 0828 Fax 020 8686 0947

Owner *IPC Media Ltd*
Editor *Luke Edwardes-Evans*
Circulation 20,667

FOUNDED 1993. MONTHLY magazine dedicated to professional cycle racing. Unsolicited ideas for features welcome.

Cycling Weekly

IPC Media Ltd, Focus House, Dingwall Avenue, Croydon, Surrey CR9 2TA
☎020 8774 0811 Fax 020 8774 0952

Owner *IPC Media Ltd*

Editor *Robert Garbutt*
Circulation 30,657

FOUNDED 1891. WEEKLY. All aspects of cycle sport covered. Unsolicited mss and ideas for features welcome. Approach in writing with ideas. Fiction rarely used.

Features Cycle racing, technical material and related areas. Maximum 2000 words. Most work commissioned but interested in seeing new work. *Payment* around £60–120 per 1000 words (quality permitting).

News Short news pieces, local news, etc. Maximum 300 words. *Payment* £15 per story.

The Dalesman

Stable Courtyard, Broughton Hall, Skipton, North Yorkshire BD23 3AZ
☎01756 701381 Fax 01756 701326
Email editorial@dalesman.co.uk

Owner *Dalesman Publishing Co. Ltd*
Editor *Terry Fletcher*
Circulation 52,787

FOUNDED 1939. Now the biggest-selling regional publication of its kind in the country. MONTHLY magazine with articles of specific Yorkshire interest. Unsolicited mss welcome; receives approximately ten per day. Initial approach in writing or by phone. Maximum 1500 words.

Payment negotiable.

Dance Theatre Journal

Laban Centre London, Laurie Grove, London SE14 6NH
☎020 8692 4070 Fax 020 8694 8749
Email dtj@laban.co.uk
Website www.dantheatrejournal.co.uk

Owner *Laban Centre London*
Editor *Ian Bramley*
Circulation 2000

FOUNDED 1982. QUARTERLY. Interested in features on every aspect of the contemporary dance scene, particularly issues such as the funding policy for dance, critical assessments of choreographers' work and the latest developments in the various schools of contemporary dance. Unsolicited mss welcome. Length 1000–3000 words.

Payment varies 'according to age and experience'.

The Dancing Times

Clerkenwell House, 45–47 Clerkenwell Green, London EC1R 0EB
☎020 7250 3006 Fax 020 7253 6679
Email DT@dancing-times.co.uk

Owner *The Dancing Times Ltd*
Editor *Mary Clarke*

FOUNDED 1910. MONTHLY. Freelance suggestions welcome from specialist dance writers and photographers only. Approach in writing.

Darkness Rising

117 Birchanger Lane, Birchanger, Hertfordshire CM23 5QF
Email michael@micksims.force9.co.uk
Website www.maynard-sims.com
Editors *Mick Sims, Len Maynard*

QUARTERLY anthology of supernatural stories and novellas of any length. Ghost stories, horror, psychological, traditional and modern. New writers and rare fiction from the past. Prefers hard copy submissions or e-mail with Word file attachment. Enclose s.a.e. for any enquiries requiring a response. Full details and guidelines on the website. *Payment* Free copy of relevant issue.

Darts World

28 Arrol Road, Beckenham, Kent BR3 4PA
☎020 8650 6580 Fax 020 8654 4343

Owner *World Magazines Ltd*
Editor *A.J. Wood*
Circulation 24,500

Features Single articles or series on technique and instruction. Maximum 1200 words.

Fiction Short stories with darts theme. Maximum 1000 words.

News Tournament reports and general or personality news required. Maximum 800 words.

Payment negotiable.

Dateline Magazine

Pollet House, St Peter Port, Guernsey GY1 1WF
☎0870 766262 Fax 01481 735353
Email magazine@dateline.co.uk

Owner *Columbus Group plc*
Editor *Nicky Boult*
Circulation 7,000

FOUNDED 1976. MONTHLY magazine for single people. Unsolicited mss welcome.

Features Anything of interest to, or directly concerning, single people. Maximum 2500 words.

News Items required at least six weeks ahead. Maximum 2500 words.

Payment from £45 per 1000 words; £10 per illustration/picture used.

Day by Day

Woolacombe House, 141 Woolacombe Road, Blackheath, London SE3 8QP
☎020 8856 6249

Owner *Loverseed Press*
Editor *Patrick Richards*
Circulation 24,000

FOUNDED 1963. MONTHLY. News commentary and digest of national and international affairs, with reviews of the arts (books, plays, art exhibitions, films, opera, musicals) and county cricket and Test reports among regular slots. Unsolicited mss welcome (s.a.e. essential). Approach in writing with ideas. Contributors are advised to study the magazine in the first instance. (Specimen copy 95p.) UK subscription: £11.60.

News *Ronald Mallone* Interested in themes connected with non-violence and social justice only. Maximum 600 words.

Features No scope for freelance contributions here.

Fiction Very rarely published.

Poems *Michael Gibson* Short poems in line with editorial principles considered. Maximum 20 lines.

Payment negotiable.

Dazed & Confused

112 Old Street, London EC1V 1BD
☎020 7336 0766 Fax 020 7336 0966
Email dazed@confused.co.uk
Website www.confused.co.uk

Owner *Waddell Ltd*
Editor *Rachel Newsome*
Circulation 80,000

FOUNDED 1992. MONTHLY. Cutting edge fashion, music, art interviews and features. No unsolicited material. Approach in writing with ideas in the first instance.

Dead Things Magazine

15 Glazebrook Street, Warrington, Cheshire WA1 3AT
Email letters@deadthings.co.uk
Website www.deadthings.co.uk
Owner/Editor *D. Cowdall*

FOUNDED 1999. QUARTERLY magazine dedicated to horror fiction with the emphasis on horror humour. Short stories plus articles, interviews and competitions. No poetry. Submissions of up to 5000 words; 'send without query; needed all year round. Request our guidelines or see them on the website.' Approach by e-mail or post.

Decanter

First Floor, Broadway House, 2–6 Fulham Broadway, London SW6 5UE
☎020 7610 3929 Fax 020 7381 5282
Email editorial@decantermagazine.com
Website www.decanter.com

Editor *Amy Wislocki*
Circulation 35,000

FOUNDED 1975. Glossy wines and spirits magazine. Unsolicited material welcome but an advance telephone call or faxed outline appreciated. No fiction.

News/Features All items and articles should concern wines, spirits, food and related subjects.

Derbyshire Life and Countryside

Heritage House, Lodge Lane, Derby DE1 3HE
☎01332 347087 Fax 01332 290688

Owner *B.C. Wood*
Editor *Vivienne Irish*
Circulation 11,948

FOUNDED 1931. MONTHLY county magazine for Derbyshire. Unsolicited mss and photographs of Derbyshire welcome, but written approach with ideas preferred.

Descent

51 Timbers Square, Cardiff CF24 3SH
☎029 2048 6557 Fax 029 2048 6557
Email descent@wildplaces.co.uk

Owner *Wild Places Publishing*
Editor *Chris Howes*
Assistant Editor *Judith Calford*

FOUNDED 1969. BI-MONTHLY magazine for cavers and mine enthusiasts. Submissions welcome from freelance contributors who can write accurately and knowledgeably on any aspect of caves, mines or underground structures.

Features General interest articles of under 1000 words welcome, as well as short foreign news reports, especially if supported by photographs/illustrations. Suitable topics include exploration (particularly British, both historical and modern), expeditions, equipment, techniques and regional British news. Maximum 2000 words.

Payment on publication according to page area filled.

Desire

1 Fentiman Road, London SW8 1LD
☎020 7820 8844 Fax 020 7627 5808

Owner *Moondance Media Ltd*
Editor *Ian Jackson*

FOUNDED 1994. SIX ISSUES YEARLY. Britain's first erotic magazine for both women and men, celebrating sex and sensuality with a mix of articles, columns, features, reviews, interviews, fantasy and poetry (1000–2500 words).

For sample copy of magazine plus contributors' guidelines and rates, please enclose 4x first class stamps.

Director

116 Pall Mall, London SW1Y 5ED
☎020 7766 8950 Fax 020 7766 8840
Email director-ed@iod.co.uk

Editor *Joanna Higgins*
Circulation 50,000

1991 Business Magazine of the Year. Published by Director Publications Ltd. for members of the Institute of Directors. Wide range of features from political and business profiles and management thinking to employment and financial issues. Also book reviews. Regular contributors used. Send letter with synopsis/published samples rather than unsolicited mss. Strictly no 'lifestyle' writing.

Payment negotiable.

Disability Now

6 Market Road, London N7 9PW
☎020 7619 7323 Fax 020 7619 7331
Email editor@disabilitynow.org.uk
Website www.disabilitynow.org.uk

Publisher *Scope* (Formerly The Spastics Society)
Editor *Mary Wilkinson*
Circulation 24,526

FOUNDED 1984. Leading MONTHLY newspaper for disabled people in the UK – people with a wide range of physical disabilities, as well as their families, carers and relevant professionals. Freelance contributions welcome. No fiction. Approach in writing.

Features Covering new initiatives and services, personal experiences and general issues of interest to a wide national readership. Maximum 1200 words. Disabled contributors welcome.

News Maximum 300 words.

Special Pages Possible openings for cartoonists.

Payment by arrangement.

Disabled Motorist

DDMC, Cottingham Way, Thrapston, Northamptonshire NN14 4PL
☎01832 734724 Fax 01832 733816
Email ddme@ukonline.co.uk
Website www.ukonline.co.uk/ddmc

Owner *Disabled Drivers' Motor Club*

Editor *Lesley Browne*
Circulation 14,500+

BI-MONTHLY publication of the Disabled Drivers' Motor Club, an organisation which aims to promote and protect the interests and welfare of disabled people and help and encourage them in gaining increased mobility. Various discounts available for members; membership costs £10 p.a. (single), £15 (joint). The magazine includes information for members plus members' letters. Approach in writing with ideas. Unsolicited mss welcome.

Diva, lesbian life and style

Worldwide House, 116–134 Bayham Street, London NW1 0BA
☎020 7482 2576 Fax 020 7284 0329
Email diva@gaytimes.co.uk
Website www.prowler.co.uk

Owner *Millivres Prowler Group*
Editor *Gillian Rodgerson*

FOUNDED 1994. MONTHLY journal of lesbian news and culture. Welcomes news, features, short fiction and photographs. No poetry. Contact the news editor with news items and *Gillian Rodgerson* with features, fiction and photographs. Approach in writing in the first instance.

Dog World

Somerfield House, Wotton Road, Ashford, Kent TN23 6LW
☎01233 621877 Fax 01233 645669

Owner *Dog World Ltd*
Editor *Simon Parsons*
Circulation 26,228

FOUNDED 1902. WEEKLY newspaper for people who are seriously interested in pedigree dogs. Unsolicited mss occasionally considered but initial approach in writing preferred.

Features Well-researched historical items or items of unusual interest concerning dogs. Maximum 1000 words. Photographs of unusual 'doggy' situations occasionally of interest. *Payment* up to £50; photos £15.

News Freelance reports welcome on court cases and local government issues involving dogs.

Eastern Eye

Unit 2, 65 Whitechapel Road, London E1 1DU
☎020 7650 2000 Fax 020 7650 2001
Website www.ethnicmedia.co.uk

Owner *Ethnic Media Group*
Editor *Mujib Islam*
Circulation 40,000

FOUNDED 1989. WEEKLY community paper for the Asian community in Britain. Interested in relevant general, local and international issues. Approach in writing with ideas for submission.

The Ecologist

Unit 18, Chelsea Wharf, 15 Lots Road, London SW10 0QJ
☎020 7351 3578   Fax 020 7351 3617
Email sally@theecologist.org
Website www.theecologist.org

Owner *Ecosystems Ltd*
Editor *Zac Goldsmith*
Managing Editor *Malcolm Tait*
Circulation 20,000

FOUNDED 1970. MONTHLY. Unsolicited mss welcome but best approach is a brief (one-side, A4) proposal to the editor, outlining experience and background and summarising suggested article. Writers should study the magazine for style before submission.

Features Radical approach to political, economic, social and environmental issues, with an emphasis on rethinking the basic assumptions that underpin modern society. Articles of between 500 and 3000 words.

Payment £150 per 1000 words.

The Economist

25 St James's Street, London SW1A 1HG
☎020 7830 7000   Fax 020 7839 2968
Website www.economist.com

Owner *Pearson/individual shareholders*
Editor *Bill Emmott*
Circulation 722,984

FOUNDED 1843. WEEKLY. Worldwide circulation. Approaches should be made in writing to the editor. No unsolicited mss.

The Edge

65 Guinness Buildings, Fulham Palace Road, London W6 8BD
☎020 7460 9444
Email theedgemagazine@cwcom.net
Website www.theedgemagazine.cwc.net

Editor *Graham Evans*

BI-MONTHLY. Looking for feature writers and reviewers: film (non-Hollywood/arts/mainstream), popular culture/books. Imaginative fiction also required: modern SF/horror/urban fiction. Sample copy £2.95 (post-free, cheques payable to 'The Edge'). Writers' guidelines available for s.a.e.

Payment negotiable; fiction: £30 per 1000 words; non-fiction: £50–200 per piece.

Edinburgh Review

22A Buccleuch Place, Edinburgh
☎0131 651 1415
Email edinburgh.review@ed.ac.uk

Publisher *Centre for the History of Ideas in Scotland*
Circulation 750

FOUNDED 1969. THREE ISSUES YEARLY. Articles and fiction on Scottish and international literary, cultural and philosophical themes. Unsolicited contributions are welcome (1600 are received each year), but prospective contributors are strongly advised to study the magazine first. Allow up to six months for a reply.

Features Interest will be shown in accessible articles on philosophy and its relationship to literature or visual art.

Fiction Scottish and international. Maximum 6000 words.

Electrical Times

Quadrant House, The Quadrant, Sutton, Surrey SM2 5AS
☎020 8652 3115   Fax 020 8652 8951

Owner *Reed Business Information*
Editor *Paul Doughty*
Circulation 12,900

FOUNDED 1891. MONTHLY. Aimed at electrical contractors, designers and installers. Unsolicited mss welcome but initial approach preferred.

Elle

Endeavour House, 189 Shaftesbury Avenue, London WC2H 8JG
☎020 7437 9011   Fax 020 7208 3599

Owner *EMAP élan Publications*
Editor *Fiona McIntosh*
Features Director *Lisa Grainger*
Commissioning Editor *Neil McLennan*
Deputy Editor *Rachel Loos*
Circulation 224,355

FOUNDED 1985. MONTHLY fashion glossy. Prospective contributors should approach the relevant editor in writing in the first instance, including cuttings.

Features Maximum 2000 words.

First Word Short articles on current/cultural events, fashion and beauty. Maximum 500 words.

Payment about £250 per 1000 words.

Empire

7th Floor, 189 Shaftesbury Avenue, London WC2H 8JG
☎020 7859 8450   Fax 020 7859 8613
Website www.empireonline.co.uk

Owner *EMAP élan Network*
Editor *Emma Cochrane*
Circulation 165,778

FOUNDED 1989. Launched at the Cannes Film Festival. MONTHLY guide to the movies which aims to cover the world of films in a 'comprehensive, adult, intelligent and witty package'. Although most of *Empire* is devoted to films and the people behind them, it also looks at the developments and technology behind television and video plus music, multimedia and books. Wide selection of in-depth features and stories on all the main releases of the month, and reviews of over 100 films and videos. Contributions welcome but approach in writing first.
Features Behind-the-scenes features on films, humorous and factual features.
Payment by agreement.

The Engineer
50 Poland Street, London W1S 7AX
☎020 7970 4106 Fax 020 7970 4189
Website www.e4engineering.com
Owner *Centaur Communications*
Editor *Paul Carslake*
Circulation 38,000

FOUNDED 1856. WEEKLY news magazine for the UK manufacturing industry.
Features Most outside contributions are commissioned but good ideas are always welcome. Maximum 2000 words.
News Scope for specialist regional freelancers, and for tip-offs. Maximum 500 words.
Technology Technology news from specialists, and tip-offs. Maximum 500 words.
Payment by arrangement.

The English Garden
Romsey Publishing Ltd, Glen House, Stag Place, London SW1E 5AQ
☎020 7233 9191 Fax 020 7630 8084
Email editorial@theenglishgarden.co.uk
Owner *Romsey Publishing Ltd*
Editor *Vanessa Berridge*
Circulation 103,845

FOUNDED 1996. MONTHLY. Features on beautiful gardens with practical ideas on design and planting. No unsolicited mss.
Features *Julia Watson* Maximum 1000–1200 words. Approach in writing in the first instance; send synopsis of 150 words with strong design and planting ideas, or sets of photographs of interesting gardens. 'No stately home or estate gardens with teams of gardeners.'

English Nature Magazine
English Nature, Northminster House, Peterborough, Cambridgeshire PE1 1UA
☎01733 455191 Fax 01733 455436
Email gordon.leel@english-nature.org.uk
Website www.english-nature.org.uk
Owner *English Nature*
Editor *Gordon Leel*
Circulation 16,000

FOUNDED 1992. BI-MONTHLY magazine which explains the work of English Nature, the government adviser on wildlife and conservation policies. No unsolicited material.

The Erotic Review
EPS, 4th Floor, 1 Maddox Street, London W1S 2PZ
☎020 7437 8887 Fax 020 7437 3528
Email editrice@eroticreview.org
Website www.eroticreview.org
Owner *Erotic Print Society*
Editor *Rowan Pelling*
Circulation 30,000

FOUNDED 1997. MONTHLY erotic literary magazine containing articles, humour, fiction, poetry and art work. Unsolicited material welcome. No pornography. Approach in writing in the first instance enclosing a brief sample of work and s.a.e.
Features Esoteric, humorous or real-life experiences. Maximum 2000 words. *Payment* £40–100. **Fiction** Erotic short stories. Maximum 2000 words. *Payment* £50–100.

ES (Evening Standard magazine)
See entry under **Regional Newspapers**

Esquire
National Magazine House, 72 Broadwick Street, London W1V 2BP
☎020 7439 5000 Fax 020 7312 3920
Owner *National Magazine Co. Ltd*
Editor *Peter Howarth*
Circulation 100,482

FOUNDED 1991. MONTHLY. Quality men's general interest magazine. No unsolicited mss or short stories.

Essentials
IPC Media Ltd., King's Reach Tower, Stamford Street, London SE1 9LS
☎020 7261 6970 Fax 020 7261 5262
Owner *IPC Media Ltd*
Editor *Karen Livermore*
Circulation 234,727

FOUNDED 1988. MONTHLY women's interest magazine. Unsolicited mss (not originals) welcome if accompanied by s.a.e. Initial approach in writing preferred. Prospective contributors should study the magazine thoroughly before submitting anything. No fiction.

Features Maximum 2000 words (double-spaced on A4).

Payment negotiable, but minimum £100 per 1000 words.

Essex Countryside
G13 Dugard House, Peartree Road, Stanway, Colchester, Essex CO3 5JX
☎01206 571348 Fax 01206 366982
Email susan.king@ecng.co.uk
Owner *Market Link Publishing Ltd*
Editor *Susan King*
Circulation 17,000

FOUNDED 1952. MONTHLY. Unsolicited material of Essex interest welcome. No general interest material.

Features Countryside, culture and crafts in Essex. Maximum 1500 words.

Payment £40.

The Essex Magazine
See **The Journal Magazines**

Eve
BBC Worldwide, Room AG200, 80 Wood Lane, London W12 0TT
☎020 8433 3700 Fax 020 8433 3359
Email eve@bbc.co.uk
Website www.allabouteve.co.uk
Owner *BBC Worldwide Publishing Ltd*
Editor *Gill Hudson*
Features Editor *Victoria Woodhall*
Circulation 150,000

FOUNDED 2000. MONTHLY. Wide-ranging general interest – aimed at the intelligent 30+ woman. No unsolicited material. Send introductory letter, *recent* writings and outlines for ideas.

Eventing
See **Horse and Hound**

Evergreen
PO Box 52, Cheltenham, Gloucestershire GL50 1YQ
☎01242 537900 Fax 01242 537901
Editor *R. Faiers*
Circulation 75,000

FOUNDED 1985. QUARTERLY magazine featuring articles and poems about Britain. Unsolicited contributions welcome.

Features Britain's natural beauty, towns and villages, nostalgia, wildlife, traditions, odd customs, legends, folklore, crafts, etc. Length 250–2000 words.

Payment £15 per 1000 words; poems £4.

Executive Woman
2 Chantry Place, Harrow, Middlesex HA3 6NY
☎020 8420 1210 Fax 020 8420 1691
Email info@execwoman.com
Website www.execwoman.com
Owner *Saleworld*
Editor *Angela Giveon*
Circulation 85,000

FOUNDED 1987. BI-MONTHLY magazine for female executives in the corporate field and female entrepreneurs.

Features New and interesting business issues and 'Women to Watch'. Health and conferencing, profiles, technology, beauty, fashion, training and arts items. 600–1200 words.

Legal/Financial Opportunities for lawyers/accountants to write on issues in their field. Maximum 600 words.

Payment negotiable.

The Face
2nd Floor, Block A, Exmouth House, Pine Street, London EC1R 0JL
☎020 7689 9999 Fax 020 7689 0300
Owner *EMAP élan*
Editor *Johnny Davis*
Fashion Director *Katie Grand*
Circulation 66,364

FOUNDED 1980. Magazine of the style generation, concerned with who's what and what's cool. Profiles, interviews and stories. No fiction. Acquaintance with the 'voice' of *The Face* is essential before sending mss on spec.

Features *Alex Needham* New contributors should write to the features editor with their ideas. Maximum 3000 words. *Payment* £250 per 1000 words.

Diary No news stories.

Family Circle
IPC Media Ltd., King's Reach Tower, Stamford Street, London SE1 9LS
☎020 7261 5000 Fax 020 7261 5929
Email rebecca.holloway@ipcmedia.com
Owner *IPC Media Ltd*
Editor *Gillian Carter*
Circulation 203,159

FOUNDED 1964. MONTHLY. Little scope for freelancers as most material is produced in-house. Unsolicited material is rarely used, but it is considered. Prospective contributors are best advised to send written ideas to the relevant editor.

Features *Emma Burstall*
Style *Amanda Cooke*
Food and Wine *Corolla Weymouth*
Home *Lucy Searle*
Payment by arrangement.

Family Tree Magazine

61 Great Whyte, Ramsey, Huntingdon, Cambridgeshire PE26 1HJ
☎01487 814050 Fax 01487 711361
Email family-tree-magazine@mcmail.com
Website www.family-tree.co.uk

Owner *ABM Publishing Ltd*
Editor *Sue Fearn*
Circulation 39,000

FOUNDED 1984. MONTHLY. News and features on matters of genealogy. Not interested in own family histories. Approach in writing with ideas. All material should be addressed to *Sue Fearn*.

Features Any genealogically related subject. Maximum 2400 words. No puzzles or fictional articles.

Payment £35 per 1000 words (news and features).

Fancy Fowl

TP Publications, Barn Acre House, Saxtead Green, Suffolk IP13 9QJ
☎01728 685832 Fax 01728 685842
Email ff@prestige.typo.co.uk

Owner *TP Publications*
Editor *Liz Fairbrother*
Circulation 3000

FOUNDED 1979. MONTHLY. Devoted entirely to poultry, waterfowl, turkeys, geese, pea fowl, etc. – management, breeding, rearing and exhibition. Outside contributions of knowledgeable, technical poultry-related articles and news welcome. Maximum 1000 words. Approach by letter. *Payment* negotiable.

Farmers Weekly

Quadrant House, Sutton, Surrey SM2 5AS
☎020 8652 4911 Fax 020 8652 4005
Email farmers.weekly@rbi.co.uk
Website www.fwi.co.uk

Owner *Reed Business Information*
Editor *Stephen Howe*
Circulation 98,268

WEEKLY. 1996 Business Magazine of the Year. For practising farmers. Unsolicited mss considered.

Features A wide range of material relating to farmers' problems and interests: specific sections on arable and livestock farming, farm life, practical and general interest, machinery and business.

News General farming news.
Payment negotiable.

Farming News

Sovereign House, Sovereign Way, Tonbridge, Kent TN9 1RW
☎01732 364422 Fax 01732 377675
Website www.farmgate.co.uk

Owner *United Business Media International*
Editor *Jim van den Bos*
Circulation 66,000

News of direct concern to farmers and the agricultural supply trade.

Fast Car

Berwick House, 8–10 Knoll Rise, Orpington, Kent BR6 0PS
☎01689 887200 Fax 01689 838844
Email fastcar@splpublishing.co.uk

Owner *SPL Publishing Ltd*
Editor *Steve Chalmers*
Circulation 102,537

FOUNDED 1987. THIRTEEN ISSUES YEARLY. Lad's magazine about perfomance tuning and modifying cars. Covers all aspects of this youth culture including the latest street styles and music. Features cars and their owners, product tests and in-car entertainment. Also includes a free reader ads section.

Features Innovative ideas in line with the above and in the *Fast Car* writing style. Generally four pages in length. No Kit-car features, race reports or road test reports of standard cars. Copy should be as concise as possible. *Payment* negotiable.

News Any item in line with the above.

FHM

2nd Floor, The Network Building, 97 Tottenham Court Road, London W1T 4TP
☎020 7504 6000 Fax 020 7504 6300
Website www.fhm.co.uk

Owner *EMAP élan Network Ltd*
Editor *Anthony Noguera*
Circulation 716,679

FOUNDED in 1986 as a free fashion magazine, FHM evolved to become more male oriented but without much public acclaim until EMAP bought the title in 1994. Since then it has become the best-selling men's magazine in the UK covering all areas of men's lifestyle.

Published MONTHLY. Unsolicited mss welcome; send to the deputy editor. Call before sending any photographic material.

The Field

IPC Media Ltd., King's Reach Tower, Stamford Street, London SE1 9LS
☎020 7261 5198 Fax 020 7261 5358
Email lucy_higginson@ipc.co.uk
Website www.thefield.co.uk

Owner *IPC Media Ltd*
Editor *Jonathan Young*
Circulation 33,379

FOUNDED 1853. MONTHLY magazine for those who are serious about the British countryside and its pleasures. Unsolicited mss (and transparencies) welcome but initial approach should be made in writing.

Features Exceptional work on any subject concerning the countryside. Most work tends to be commissioned.
Payment varies.

Film and Video Maker

594A Bolton Road, Pendlebury, Swinton, Manchester M27 4ET
☎0161 794 8282 Fax 0161 793 9696

Owner *Film Maker Publications Ltd*
Editor *Mrs Liz Donlan*
Circulation 2400

FOUNDED in the 1930s. BI-MONTHLY magazine of the Institute of Amateur Cinematographers. Reports, news and views of the Institute. Unsolicited mss welcome but all contributions are unpaid.

Film Review

Visual Imagination Ltd, 9 Blades Court, Deodar Road, London SW15 2NU
☎020 8875 1520 Fax 020 8875 1588
Website www.visimag.com

Owner *Visual Imagination Ltd*
Editor *Neil Corry*
Circulation 50,000

MONTHLY. Reviews, profiles, interviews and special reports on films. Unsolicited material considered.
Payment negotiable.

Fine Food Digest

PO Box 1525, Gillingham, Dorset SP8 5TA
☎01963 371271 Fax 01963 371270
Email bobfarrand@btinternet.com

Owner/Editor *Robert Farrand*
Circulation 4200

FOUNDED 1980. SIX ISSUES YEARLY. Serves the speciality food retail trade. Small budget for freelance material.

First Down

175 Tottenham Court Road, London W1T 7NU
☎020 7323 1988 Fax 020 7637 0862
Email firstdown@indmags.co.uk
Website www.first-down.co.uk

Owner *Independent Magazines (UK) Ltd*
Editor *Keith Webster*
Circulation 15,000

FOUNDED 1986. WEEKLY American football tabloid paper. Features and news. Welcomes contributions; approach in writing.

Fishing News

21 John Street, London WC1N 2BP
☎020 7505 3523 Fax 020 7831 9362
Website www.fishingnews.co.uk

Owner *Informa Group Plc*
Editor *Tim Oliver*
Circulation 13,000

FOUNDED 1913. WEEKLY. All aspects of the commercial fishing industry in the UK and Ireland. No unsolicited mss; telephone inquiry in the first instance. Maximum 600 words for news and 1500 words for features. *Payment* £100 per 1000 words.

Flight International

Quadrant House, The Quadrant, Sutton, Surrey SM2 5AS
☎020 8652 3882 Fax 020 8652 3840
Email flight.international@rbi.co.uk
Website www.flightinternational.com

Owner *Reed Business Information*
Editor *Carol Reed*
Circulation 65,000

FOUNDED 1909. WEEKLY. International trade magazine for the aerospace industry, including civil, military and space. Unsolicited mss considered. Commissions preferred - phone with ideas and follow up with letter. E-mail, modem and disk submissions encouraged.

Features *Carol Reed* Technically informed articles and pieces on specific geographical areas with international appeal. Analytical, in-depth coverage required, preferably supported by interviews. Maximum 1800 words.

News *Andrew Chuter* Opportunities exist for news pieces from particular geographical areas on specific technical developments. Maximum 350 words.
Payment NUJ rates.

Flora International

The Fishing Lodge Studio, 77 Bulbridge Road, Wilton, Salisbury, Wiltshire SP2 0LE
☎01722 743207 Fax 01722 743207

Publisher/Editor *Maureen Foster*
Circulation 16,000

FOUNDED 1974. BI-MONTHLY magazine for flower arrangers and florists. Unsolicited mss welcome. Approach in writing with ideas. Not interested in general gardening articles.

Features Fully illustrated, preferably with b&w photos or illustrations/colour transparencies. Flower arranging, flower gardens and flowers. Floristry items written with practical knowledge and well illustrated are particularly welcome. Maximum 1000 words.

Profiles/Reviews Personality profiles and book reviews.

Payment £50 per 1000 words plus additional payment for suitable photographs.

FlyPast

PO Box 100, Stamford, Lincolnshire PE9 1XQ
☎01780 755131 Fax 01780 757261
Email flypast@keymags.demon.co.uk

Owner *Key Publishing Ltd*
Editor *Ken Ellis*
Circulation 50,577

FOUNDED 1981. MONTHLY. Historic aviation and aviation heritage, mainly military, Second World War period up to c.1970. Unsolicited mss welcome.

Focus

See **British Science Fiction Association** under **Professional Associations**

Focus

National Magazine House, 72 Broadwick Street, London W1V 2BP
☎020 7519 5682 Fax 020 7512 5515
Email sally.palmer@natmags.co.uk

Owner *National Magazine Co. Ltd*
Editor *Nick Smith*
Features Editor *Emma Bayley*
News Editor *Ali MacArthur*
Circulation 55,976

FOUNDED 1996. MONTHLY. Popular science, technology and adventure. Welcomes *relevant* summaries of original ideas. Material should be sent by post.

For Women

Fantasy Publications, 4 Selsdon Way, London E14 9EL
☎020 7308 5090 Fax 020 7308 5075

Email ecoldwell@nasnet.co.uk

Editor *Liz Beresford*
Circulation 60,000

FOUNDED 1992. SIX-WEEKLY magazine of erotic and sex interest for women – health and sex, erotic fiction and erotic photography. No homes and gardens articles. Approach in writing in the first instance. Send e-mail or s.a.e. for submission guidelines.

Features Relationships and sex. Maximum 2500 words. *Payment* £100 per 1000 words.

Fiction *Elizabeth Coldwell* Erotic short stories. Maximum 3000 words. *Payment* £150 total.

Fortean Times: The Journal of Strange Phenomena

PO Box 2409, London NW5 4NP
☎020 8552 5466 Fax 020 7485 5002
Email sieveking@forteantimes.com
Website www.forteantimes.com

Owners/Editors *Bob Rickard/Paul Sieveking*
Circulation 35,000

FOUNDED 1973. MONTHLY. Accounts of strange phenomena and experiences, curiosities, mysteries, prodigies and portents. Unsolicited mss welcome. Approach in writing with ideas. No fiction, poetry, rehashes or politics.

Features Well-researched and referenced material on current or historical mysteries, or first-hand accounts of oddities. Maximum 3000 words, preferably with good relevant photos/ illustrations.

News Concise copy with full source references essential.

Payment negotiable.

Foundation: The International Review of Science Fiction

c/o Dept. of History, University of Reading, Whiteknights, Reading, Berkshire RG6 6AA
☎0118 926 3047 Fax 0118 931 6440
Email e.f.james@reading.ac.uk

Owner *Science Fiction Foundation (reg. Charity 1041052)*
Editor *Professor Edward James*

THRICE-YEARLY publication devoted to the critical study of science fiction.

Payment None.

France Magazine

Dormer House, Digbeth Street, Stow-on-the-Wold, Gloucestershire GL54 1BN
☎01451 833210 Fax 01451 833234
Email editorial@francemag.com
Website www.francemag.com

Owner *Centralhaven*
Editor *Philip Faiers*
Circulation 61,000

FOUNDED 1989. BI-MONTHLY magazine containing all things of interest to Francophiles – in English. Approach in writing in the first instance.

Freelance Market News

Sevendale House, 7 Dale Street, Manchester M1 1JB
☎0161 228 2362, ext 210 Fax 0161 228 3533
Email fmn@writersbureau.com

Editor *Angela Cox*

MONTHLY. News and information on the freelance writers' market, both inland and overseas. Includes market information, competitions, seminars, courses, overseas openings, etc. Short articles (700 words maximum). Unsolicited contributions welcome.
Payment £35 per 1000 words.

The Freelance

See **National Union of Journalists** under **Professional Associations and Societies**

The Friendly Spirit

See **Storyteller–UK** under **Electronic Publishing and Other Services**

FT Expat

4th Floor, 149 Tottenham Court Road, London W1P 9LL
☎020 7896 2000 Fax 020 7896 2229
Email expat.letters@ft.com
Website www.FTExpat.com

Owner *Financial Times Business*
Managing Editor *Hugh Fasken*
Circulation 50,000

FOUNDED January 2001. MONTHLY magazine aimed at British and non-British expatriates and international investors. Unsolicited mss considered, if suitable to the interests of the readership.
Features Up to 1200 words on finance, property, employment opportunities and other topics likely to appeal to readership, such as living conditions in countries with substantial expatriate populations.
Payment negotiable.

Garden Answers (incorporating Practical Gardening)

Apex House, Oundle Road, Peterborough, Cambridgeshire PE2 9NP
☎01733 898100 Fax 01733 466857

Owner *EMAP Active Ltd*
Editor *Gail Major*

Circulation 192,000

FOUNDED 1982. MONTHLY. 'It is unlikely that unsolicited manuscripts will be used, as articles are usually commissioned and must be in the magazine style.' Prospective contributors should approach the editor in writing. Interested in hearing from gardening writers on any subject, whether flowers, fruit, vegetables, houseplants or greenhouse gardening.

Garden News

Bretton Court, Bretton, Peterborough, Cambridgeshire PE3 8DZ
☎01733 264666 Fax 01733 282695

Owner *EMAP Active Publications Ltd*
Editor *Sarah Page*
Circulation 75,000

FOUNDED 1958. Britain's biggest-selling, full-colour gardening WEEKLY. News and advice on growing flowers, fruit and vegetables, plus colourful features on all aspects of gardening especially for the committed gardener. News and features welcome, especially if accompanied by top-quality photos or illustrations. Contact the editor before submitting any material.

The Garden, Journal of the Royal Horticultural Society

Bretton Court, Bretton Centre, Peterborough, Cambridgeshire PE3 8DZ
☎01733 282666 Fax 01733 282655
Email thegarden@rhs.org.uk
Website www.rhs.org.uk

Owner *The Royal Horticultural Society*
Editor *Ian Hodgson*
Circulation 273,387

FOUNDED 1866. MONTHLY journal of the Royal Horticultural Society. Covers all aspects of the art, science and practice of horticulture and garden making. 'Articles must have depth and substance'; approach by letter with a synopsis in the first instance. Maximum 2500 words.

Gardens Illustrated

BBC Worldwide, Woodlands, 80 Wood Lane, London W12 0TT
☎020 8433 1353 Fax 020 8433 2680
Website www.gardensillustrated.com

Owner *BBC Worldwide Publishing Ltd*
Editor *Rosie Atkins*
Circulation 40,880

FOUNDED 1993. TEN ISSUES YEARLY. 'Britain's fastest growing garden magazine' with a world-wide readership. The focus is on garden design, with a strong international flavour. Unsolicited mss are rarely used and it is best that prospective contributors approach the editor with ideas in writing, supported by photographs.

Gardens Made Easy

SPL, Berwick House, 8–10 Knoll Rise, Orpington, Kent BR6 0PS
☎01689 887200 Fax 01689 876438
Email gardens@splpublishing.co.uk
Owner *SPL Publishing Ltd*
Editor *Andrée Frieze*
LAUNCHED April 2000. Aimed at 30–55-year-olds 'who have been inspired by the recent boom in gardening' and want to improve the look of their own gardens.

Gargoyle UK

152 Harringay Road, London N15 3HL
☎020 8889 6320 Fax 020 8292 3632
Email admin@gargoyle.uk.com
Website www.gargoyle.uk.com
Owner/Editor *Maja Prausnitz*
Assistant Editors *Sandra Tharumalingam,*
  Jared Hendrickson
Circulation 5000

FOUNDED 1976. BIANNUAL literary magazine dedicated to championing work by new poets, artists and fiction writers alongside the more established. Formerly one publication – *Gargoyle Magazine* – compiled on two continents, *Gargoyle UK* has now set up shop alone, though still closely linked to *Gargoyle Magazine*. Unsolicited mss welcome, though some knowledge of *Gargoyle* is recommended before submission.
Payment One copy of relevant issue.

Gay Times

Worldwide House, 116–134 Bayham Street, London NW1 0BA
☎020 7482 2576 Fax 020 7284 0329
Website www.prowler.co.uk
Owner *Millivres Prowler Group*
Editor *Colin Richardson*
Circulation 65,000

Covers all aspects of gay life, plus general interest likely to appeal to the gay community, art reviews and news. Regular freelance writers used.
Payment negotiable.

Gibbons Stamp Monthly

Stanley Gibbons, 5 Parkside, Christchurch Road, Ringwood, Hampshire BH24 3SH
☎01425 472363 Fax 01425 470247
Email gsm@stanleygibbons.co.uk
Website www.stanleygibbons.co.uk

Owner *Stanley Gibbons Ltd*
Editor *Hugh Jefferies*
Circulation 22,000
FOUNDED 1890. MONTHLY. News and features. Unsolicited mss welcome. Make initial approach in writing or by telephone to avoid disappointment.
  Features *Hugh Jefferies* Unsolicited material of specialised nature and general stamp features welcome. Maximum 3000 words but longer pieces can be serialised. *Payment* £30–50 per 1000 words.
  News *Michael Briggs* Any philatelic news item. Maximum 500 words. *No payment.*

Girl About Town

Independent House, 191 Marsh Wall, London E14 9RS
☎020 7005 5550 Fax 020 7005 0222
Website www.londoncareers.net
Owner *Independent Magazines*
Editor-in-Chief *Bill Williamson*
News/Style Pages *Dee Pilgrim*
Circulation 85,000
FOUNDED 1972. Free WEEKLY magazine for women aged 18 to 35. Unsolicited mss may be considered. No fiction.
  Features Standards are 'exacting'. Commissions only. Some chance of unknown writers being commissioned. Maximum 1500 words. *Payment* negotiable.

Gliding and Motorgliding International

281 Queen Edith's Way, Cambridge CB1 9NH
☎01223 247725 Fax 01223 413793
Email bryce.smith@virgin.net
Website www.glidingmagazine.com
Owner *Soaring Society of America*
Editor *Gillian Bryce-Smith*
FOUNDED November 1998 for international gliding and motorgliding enthusiasts. Few opportunities for freelance writers. Now on the Internet as the first gliding magazine to be electronic only. *No payment.*

Golf Monthly

IPC Media Ltd., King's Reach Tower, Stamford Street, London SE1 9LS
☎020 7261 7237 Fax 020 7261 7240
Email jane_carter@ipc.media.com
Owner *IPC Media Ltd*
Editor *Jane Carter*
Circulation 73,589
FOUNDED 1911. MONTHLY. Player profiles,

golf instruction, general golf features and columns. Not interested in instruction material from outside contributors. Unsolicited mss welcome. Approach in writing with ideas.

Features Maximum 1500–2000 words.
Payment by arrangement.

Golf Weekly

Bretton Court, Bretton, Peterborough, Cambridgeshire PE3 8DZ
☎01733 264666   Fax 01733 465221
Email simon.caney@ecm.emap.com

Owner *EMAP Active Ltd*
Editor *Simon Caney*
Circulation 20,000

FOUNDED 1890. WEEKLY. Unsolicited material welcome from full-time journalists only. 'Always looking for photographic and written news contributions.' For features, approach in writing in first instance; for news, fax or phone.

Features Maximum 1500 words.
News Maximum 300 words.
Payment negotiable.

Golf World

Bushfield House, Orton, Peterborough, Cambridgeshire PE2 5UW
☎01733 237111   Fax 01733 288025
Website www.golferworld.co.uk

Owner *EMAP Active Ltd*
Editor *Steve Prentice*
Circulation 70,000

FOUNDED 1962. MONTHLY. No unsolicited mss. Approach in writing with ideas.

Good Holiday Magazine

3A High Street, Esher, Surrey KT10 9RP
☎01372 468140   Fax 01372 470765
Email jh@goodholidayideas.com
Website www.goodholidayideas.com

Editor *John Hill*
Circulation 100,000

FOUNDED 1985. QUARTERLY aimed at better-off holiday-makers rather than travellers. Worldwide destinations including Europe and domestic. No unsolicited material. Consult journalist guidelines on the website in the first instance.
Payment negotiable.

Good Housekeeping

National Magazine House, 72 Broadwick Street, London W1V 2BP
☎020 7439 5000   Fax 020 7439 5591
Website www.natmags.co.uk

Owner *National Magazine Co. Ltd*

Editor-in-Chief *Lindsay Nicholson*
Circulation 404,476

FOUNDED 1922. MONTHLY glossy. No unsolicited mss. Write with ideas in the first instance to the appropriate editor.

Features *Kerry Fowler* Most work is commissioned but original ideas are always welcome. No ideas are discussed on the telephone. Send short synopsis, plus relevant cuttings, showing previous examples of work published. No unsolicited mss.

Entertainment *Judy Yorke* Reviews and previews on film, television, theatre and art.

Health *Julie Powell*. Submission guidelines as for Features; no unsolicited mss.

Good Motoring

Station Road, Forest Row, East Sussex RH18 5EN
☎01342 825676   Fax 01342 824847
Email gem@gemrecovery.org.uk
Website www.roadsafety.org.uk

Owner *Guild of Experienced Motorists*
Editor *Derek Hainge*
Circulation 52,000

FOUNDED 1932. QUARTERLY motoring, road safety and travel magazine. Occasional general features. 1500 words maximum. Prospective contributors should approach in writing only.

Good Ski Guide

145–147 Ewell Road, Surbiton, Surrey KT6 6AW
☎020 8399 0022   Fax 020 8786 2951
Email info@goodskiguide.com
Website www.goodskiguide.com

Owner *Profile Media Group*
Editor *Owen Jones*
Circulation 50,000

FOUNDED 1976. FIVE ISSUES YEARLY. Unsolicited mss welcome from writers with a knowledge of skiing and ski resorts. Prospective contributors are best advised to make initial contact in writing as ideas and work need to be seen before any discussion can take place.
Payment negotiable.

The Goodlife Magazine

165A Finborough Road, London SW10 9AP
☎020 7373 7282   Fax 020 7373 3215
Email goodlife@btinternet.com

Owner/Editor *Eileen Spence-Moncrieff*
Circulation 37,502

FOUNDED 1988. Features on fashion, interiors,

restaurants, theatre, social scene, health and beauty. No unsolicited mss.

GQ
Vogue House, Hanover Square, London W1R 0AD
☎020 7499 9080 Fax 020 7495 1679
Website www.gq-magazine.co.uk
Owner *Condé Nast Publications Ltd*
Editor *Dylan Jones*
Circulation 140,112

FOUNDED 1988. MONTHLY. Men's style magazine. No unsolicited material. Write or fax with an idea in the first instance.

Granta
2–3 Hanover Yard, Noel Road, London N1 8BE
☎020 7704 9776 Fax 020 7704 0474
Website www.granta.com
Editor *Ian Jack*
Deputy Editors *Liz Jobey, Sophie Harrison*

QUARTERLY magazine of new writing, including fiction, memoirs, reportage and photography published in paperback book form. Highbrow, diverse and contemporary, with a thematic approach. Unsolicited mss (including fiction) considered. A lot of material is commissioned. Vital to read the magazine first to appreciate its very particular fusion of cultural and political interests. No reviews or news articles. No poetry. Access the website for submission guidelines.
Payment negotiable.

The Great Outdoors
See **TGO**

Guardian Weekend
See under **National Newspapers (The Guardian)**

Guiding Magazine
17–19 Buckingham Palace Road, London SW1W 0PT
☎020 7834 6242 Fax 020 7828 5791
Website www.guides.org.uk
Owner *The Guide Association*
Editor *Jan Clampett*
Circulation 28,000

FOUNDED 1914. MONTHLY. Unsolicited mss welcome provided topics relate to the Movement and/or women's role in society. Ideas in writing appreciated in first instance. No nostalgic, 'when I was a Guide', pieces, please.

Activity Ideas Interesting, contemporary ideas and instructions for activities for girls aged 5 to 18+ to do during unit meetings – crafts, games (indoor/outdoor), etc.
Features Topics that can be useful in the Guide programme. 650–1200 words.
News Guide activities. Maximum 100–150 words.
Payment £70 per 1000 words.

Hair
IPC Media Ltd., King's Reach Tower, Stamford Street, London SE1 9LS
☎020 7261 6975 Fax 020 7261 7382
Owner *IPC Media Ltd*
Editor *Kate Barlow*
Circulation 170,194

FOUNDED 1977. BI-MONTHLY hair and beauty magazine. No unsolicited mss, but always interested in good photographs. Approach with ideas in writing.
Features Fashion pieces on hair trends and styling advice. Maximum 1000 words.
Payment negotiable.

Hair Style
WVIP, 53–79 Highgate Road, London NW5 1TW
☎020 7331 1265 Fax 020 7331 1108
Owner *WVIP*
Editor *Georgina Hersey*

FOUNDED 1998. BI-MONTHLY. Welcomes informative features on beauty, hair and fashion, aimed at women aged 25–45. 1200–2000 words.
Payment approximately £225 per feature, depending on length. Also, celebrity 'style' features and interviews. No fiction. Approach in writing in the first instance.

Hairflair
Hairflair Magazines Ltd, Freebournes House, Freebournes Road, Witham, Essex CM8 3US
☎01376 534547 Fax 01376 534546
Owner *Hairflair Magazines Ltd*
Editor *Ruth Page*
Circulation 60,000

FOUNDED 1982. BI-MONTHLY. Original and interesting hair and beauty-related features written in a young, lively style to appeal to a readership aged 16–35 years. Unsolicited mss not welcome, although freelancers are used.
Features Hair and beauty. Maximum 2000 words.
Payment negotiable.

Harpers & Queen

National Magazine House, 72 Broadwick Street, London W1V 2BP
☎020 7439 5000 Fax 020 7439 5506

Owner *National Magazine Co. Ltd*
Editor *Lucy Yeomans*
Circulation 87,495

MONTHLY. Up-market glossy combining the stylish and the streetwise. Approach in writing (not phone) with ideas.

Features *Harriet Green* Ideas only in the first instance.

News Snippets welcome if very original. *Payment* negotiable.

Health & Efficiency

Burlington Court, Carlisle Street, Goole, East Yorkshire DN14 5EG
☎01405 769712/764206 Fax 01405 763815
Email newfreedom@btinternet.com
Website www.healthandefficiency.co.uk

Owner *New Freedom Publications Ltd*
Editor *Mark Nisbet*
Circulation 15,000

FOUNDED 1898. MONTHLY naturist lifestyle magazine. **Features** Will consider short features on social nudism, longer features on nudist holidays and nudist philosophy. 90% of every issue is by freelance contributors. 1000–1500 words. *Payment* £125–150. **News** 'We are always on the lookout for national and international nudist news stories.' 250–500 words. *Payment* £30–50. No soft porn, 'sexy' stories or sleazy photographs. Approach by post, e-mail or telephone.

Health & Fitness Magazine

WVIP, 53–79 Highgate Road, London NW5 1TW
☎020 7331 1184 Fax 020 7331 1273
Website www.hfonline.co.uk

Owner *WVIP*
Editor *Mary Comber*
Circulation 65,000

FOUNDED 1983. MONTHLY. Will consider ideas; approach in writing in the first instance.

Health Education

The Health Education Unit, Research and Graduate School of Education, University of Southampton, Southampton SO17 1BJ
☎023 8059 3707
Email skw@soton.ac.uk

Owner *MCB University Press*
Editor *Dr Katherine Weare*
Circulation 2000

FOUNDED 1992. SIX ISSUES YEARLY. Health education journal with an emphasis on schools and young people. Professional readership.

Heat

Mappin House, 4 Winsley Street, London W1W 8HF
☎020 7436 1515 Fax 020 7817 8847
Website www.heatmagazine.co.uk

Owner *EMAP élan Network*
Editor *Mark Frith*
Circulation 172,311

FOUNDED January 1999. WEEKLY entertainment magazine dealing with TV, film and radio information, fashion and features, with an emphasis on celebrity interviews and news. Targets 18- to 40-year-old readership, male and female. Articles written both in-house and by trusted freelancers. No unsolicited mss.

Hello!

Wellington House, 69–71 Upper Ground, London SE1 9PQ
☎020 7667 8700 Fax 020 7667 8716

Owner *Hola!* (Spain)
Editor-in-Chief *Philip Hall*
Circulation 502,679

WEEKLY. Owned by a Madrid-based publishing family, *Hello!* has grown faster than any other British magazine since its launch here in 1988 and continues to grow despite the recession. The magazine is printed in Madrid, with editorial offices both there and in London. Major colour features plus regular news pages. Although much of the material is provided by regulars, good proposals do stand a chance. Approach with ideas in the first instance. No unsolicited mss.

Features Interested in celebrity-based features, with a newsy angle, and exclusive interviews from generally unapproachable personalities. *Payment* by arrangement.

Here's Health

Greater London House, Hampstead Road, London NW1 7EJ
☎020 7874 0200 Fax 020 7347 1897

Owner *EMAP Esprit*
Editor *Colette Harris*
Circulation 37,502

FOUNDED 1956. MONTHLY. Full-colour magazine dealing with alternative medicine, nutrition, natural health, wholefoods, supplements, organics and the environment. Prospective contributors should bear in mind that this is a specialist magazine with a pronounced bias

towards alternative/complementary medicine, using expert contributors on the whole.
Payment negotiable.

Heritage

Glen House, Stag Place, London
SW1E 5AQ
☎020 7233 9191 Fax 020 7630 8084
Email editorial@heritagemagazine.co.uk

Owner *Bulldog Magazines*
Editor *James Marchington*
Circulation 73,000

FOUNDED 1984. BI-MONTHLY. Interested in complete packages of written features with high-quality transparencies – words or pictures on their own also accepted. Not interested in poetry, fiction, nostalgia or non-British themes. Approach in writing with ideas.

Features British villages, tours, towns, castles, gardens, traditions, crafts, historical themes and people. Maximum length 1200 words. *Payment* approx. £100 per 1000 words.

News Small pieces – usually picture stories in Diary section. Limited use. Maximum length 100–150 words. *Payment* £20.

Heritage Scotland

28 Charlotte Square, Edinburgh EH2 4ET
☎0131 243 9300 Fax 0131 243 9589

Owner *National Trust for Scotland*
Editor *Ian Gardner*
Circulation 138,878

FOUNDED 1983. QUARTERLY magazine containing heritage/conservation features. No unsolicited mss.

Hi-Fi News

Focus House, Dingwall Avenue, Croydon, Surrey CR9 2TA
☎020 8774 0846 Fax 020 8774 0940
Email hi-finews@ipcmedia.com

Owner *IPC Media Ltd*
Editor *Steve Harris*
Circulation 18,207

FOUNDED 1956. MONTHLY. Write in the first instance with suggestions based on knowledge of the magazine's style and subject. All articles must be written from an informed technical or enthusiast viewpoint.
Payment negotiable, according to technical content.

High Life

Haymarket House, 1 Oxendon Street, London SW1Y 4EE
☎020 7925 2544 Fax 020 7321 2942
Email high_life@premiermp.com
Website www.premiermp.com

Owner *Premier Media Partners*
Editor *Mark Jones*
Circulation 231,696

FOUNDED 1973. MONTHLY glossy. British Airways in-flight magazine. Almost all the content is commissioned. No unsolicited mss. Few opportunities for freelancers.

History Today

20 Old Compton Street, London W1D 4TW
☎020 7534 8000 Fax 020 7534 8008
Email p.furtado@historytoday.com
Website www.historytoday.com

Owner *History Today Trust for the Advancement of Education*
Editor *Peter Furtado*
Circulation 29,269

FOUNDED 1951. MONTHLY. General history and archaeology worldwide, history behind the headlines. Serious submissions only; no 'jokey' material. Approach by post or e-mail.

Home

SPL, Berwick House, 8–10 Knoll Rise, Orpington, Kent BR6 0PS
☎01689 887200 Fax 01689 896847
Email ksleeman@splpublishing.co.uk

Owner *Highbury House Communications*
Editor *Sarah Giles*

MONTHLY magazine with ideas, information and inspiration for the home. Features include style, design, home products, gardens and cookery. Synopses and ideas welcome; approach in writing. No health and lifestyle articles.

Home & Country

104 New Kings Road, London SW6 4LY
☎020 7731 5777 Fax 020 7736 4061

Owner *National Federation of Women's Institutes*
Editor *Susan Seager*
Circulation 55,000

FOUNDED 1919. MONTHLY. Official full-colour journal of the Federation of Women's Institutes, containing articles on a wide range of subjects of interest to women. Strong environmental country slant with crafts and cookery plus gardening appearing every month. Unsolicited mss, photos and illustrations welcome.
Payment by arrangement.

Home & Family

Mary Sumner House, 24 Tufton Street, London SW1P 3RB
☎020 7222 5533 Fax 020 7222 1591

Owner *MU Enterprises Ltd*
Editor *Jill Worth*
Circulation 70,000

FOUNDED 1976. QUARTERLY. Unsolicited mss considered. No fiction or poetry. Features on family life, social problems, marriage, Christian faith, etc. Maximum 1000 words.
Payment 'modest'.

Homes & Gardens

IPC Media Ltd., King's Reach Tower, Stamford Street, London SE1 9LS
☎020 7261 5000 Fax 020 7261 6247

Owner *IPC Media Ltd*
Editor *Matthew Line*
Circulation 165,595

FOUNDED 1919. MONTHLY. Almost all published articles are specially commissioned. No fiction or poetry. Best to approach in writing with an idea, enclosing snapshots if appropriate.

Homes & Ideas

IPC Media Ltd., King's Reach Tower, Stamford Street, London SE1 9LS
☎020 7261 7494 Fax 020 7261 7495

Owner *IPC Media Ltd*
Editor *Sharon Parsons*
Circulation 122,830

FOUNDED 1993. MONTHLY magazine for homeowners looking for new styles and decorating techniques. No unsolicited mss; all work is commissioned.

Horse and Hound

IPC Media Ltd., King's Reach Tower, Stamford Street, London SE1 9LS
☎020 7261 6315 Fax 020 7261 5429
Email jenny_sims@ipc.co.uk

Owner *IPC Media Ltd*
Editor *Arnold Garvey*
Circulation 67,108

FOUNDED 1884. WEEKLY. The oldest equestrian magazine on the market. Contains regular veterinary advice and instructional articles, as well as authoritative news and comment on fox hunting, international and national showjumping, horse trials, dressage, driving and endurance riding. Also weekly racing and point-to-points, breeding reports and articles. Regular books and art reviews, and humorous articles and cartoons

are frequently published. Plenty of opportunities for freelancers. Unsolicited contributions welcome.

Also publishes a sister monthly publication, *Eventing*, which covers the sport of horse trials comprehensively.
Payment NUJ rates.

Horse and Rider

Haslemere House, Lower Street, Haslemere, Surrey GU27 2PE
☎01428 651551 Fax 01428 654108
Email djm@djmurphy.co.uk
Website www.horseandridermagazine.co.uk

Owner *D.J. Murphy (Publishers) Ltd*
Editor *Alison Bridge*
Assistant Editor *Danielle Pascoe*
Circulation 46,000

FOUNDED 1949. MONTHLY. Adult readership, largely horse-owning. News and instructional features, which make up the bulk of the magazine, are almost all commissioned. New contributors and unsolicited mss are occasionally used. Approach the editor in writing with ideas.

Hotline

John Brown Contract Publishing, The New Boathouse, 136–142 Bramley Road, London W10 6SR
☎020 7565 3000 Fax 020 7565 3060
Email info@johnbrown.co.uk
Website www.johnbrowncontract.com

Editor *Siân Phillips*
Circulation 4 million (readership)

FOUNDED 1997. QUARTERLY on-board magazine for Virgin trains. Lifestyle and news-based features. No unsolicited material.

House & Garden

Vogue House, Hanover Square, London W1S 1JU
☎020 7499 9080 Fax 020 7629 2907
Website www.condenast.co.uk

Owner *Condé Nast Publications Ltd*
Editor *Susan Crewe*
Circulation 150,152

FOUNDED 1947. MONTHLY. Most feature material is produced in-house but occasional specialist features are commissioned from qualified freelancers, mainly for the interiors, wine and food sections and travel.

Features *Liz Elliot* Suggestions for features, preferably in the form of brief outlines of proposed subjects, will be considered.

House Beautiful

Jubilee House, 197 Marsh Wall, London E14
9SG
☎020 7519 5500 Fax 020 7519 5518
Owner *National Magazine Co. Ltd*
Editor *Libby Norman*
Circulation 200,083

FOUNDED 1989. MONTHLY. Lively magazine offering sound, practical information and plenty of inspiration for those who want to make the most of where they live. Over 100 pages of easy-reading editorial. Regular features about decoration, DIY and home finance. Approach in writing with synopses or ideas in the first instance.

i-D Magazine

124 Tabernacle Street, London EC2A 4SA
☎020 7490 9710 Fax 020 7251 2225
Email editor@i-dmagazine.co.uk
Website www.i-dmagazine.co.uk
Owner *Levelprint*
Editor *Avril Mair*
Circulation 55,000

FOUNDED 1980. MONTHLY lifestyle magazine for both sexes with a fashion bias. International. Very hip. Does not accept unsolicited contributions but welcomes new ideas from the fields of fashion, music, clubs, art, film, technology, books, sport, etc. No fiction or poetry. 'We are always looking for freelance non-fiction writers with new or unusual ideas.' A different theme each issue – past themes include Green politics, taste, films, sex, love and loud dance music – means it is advisable to discuss feature ideas in the first instance.

Ideal Home

IPC Media Ltd., King's Reach Tower,
Stamford Street, London SE1 9LS
☎020 7261 6505 Fax 020 7261 6697
Owner *IPC Media Ltd*
Editorial Director *Isobel McKenzie-Price*
Circulation 229,728

FOUNDED 1920. MONTHLY glossy. Unsolicited feature articles are welcome if appropriate to the magazine. Prospective contributors wishing to submit ideas should do so in writing to the editor. No fiction.

Features Furnishing and decoration of houses, kitchens or bathrooms; interior design, soft furnishings, furniture and home improvements, lifestyle, travel, etc. Length to be discussed with editor.

Payment negotiable.

The Illustrated London News

20 Upper Ground, London SE1 9PF
☎020 7805 5562 Fax 020 7805 5911
Website www.ilng.co.uk
Owner *James Sherwood*
Editor *Alison Booth*
Circulation 47,547

FOUNDED 1842. BIANNUAL: Christmas and Summer issues, plus the occasional special issue to coincide with particular events. Although the *ILN* covers issues concerning the whole of the UK, its emphasis remains on the capital and its life. Travel, wine, restaurants, events, cultural and current affairs are all covered. There are few opportunities for freelancers but all unsolicited mss are read (receives about five a week). The best approach is with an idea in writing. Particularly interested in articles relating to events and developments in contemporary London, and about people working in the capital. All features are illustrated, so ideas with picture opportunities are particularly welcome.

Image Magazine

Upper Mounts, Northampton NN1 3HR
☎01604 467000 Fax 01604 467190
Email image@northantsnews.co.uk
Owner *Northamptonshire Newspapers Ltd*
Editor *Ruth Supple*
Circulation 12,000

FOUNDED 1905. MONTHLY general interest regional magazine. No unsolicited mss. Approach by phone or in writing with ideas. No fiction.

Features Local issues, personalities, businesses, etc., of Northamptonshire, Bedfordshire, Buckinghamshire interest. Maximum 500 words. *Payment* negotiable.

News No hard news as such, just monthly diary column.

Other Regulars on motoring, fashion, beauty, lifestyle, travel and horoscopes. Maximum 500 words.

In Britain

Glen House, Stag Place, London SW1E 5AQ
☎020 7233 9191 Fax 020 7630 8084
Email in_britain@romseypublishing.com
Editor *Andrea Spain*
Circulation 40,000

FOUNDED in the 1930s. BI-MONTHLY. Travel magazine of the British Tourist Authority. Articles vary from 700 to 1500 words. Not much opportunity for unsolicited work – approach (by e-mail, if possible) with ideas and samples. Words and picture packages preferred (good quality transparencies only).

In Style
Brettenham House, Lancaster Place, London WC2E 7TL
☎020 7322 1510 Fax 020 7322 1511

Owner *Time Warner/AOL*
Editor *Dee Nolan*
Features Editor *Vanessa Friedman*
News Editor *Polly Williams*
Fashion Editor *Paula Reed*

LAUNCHED March 2001. MONTHLY. UK edition of US fashion, beauty, celebrity and lifestyle magazine. Unsolicited material welcome; send by e-mail to individual editors.

Independent Magazine
See under **National Newspapers (The Independent)**

Inspirations For Your Home
Elme House, 133 Long Acre, London WC2E 9AW
☎020 7836 0519 Fax 020 7497 2364

Owner *GE Publishing Ltd*
Editor *Karen Stylianides*
Circulation 97,058

Homes and interiors with practical hands-on approach – decorating, design, house features, makeovers, creative living and gardens. Will consider unsolicited synopses on these subjects.

Insurance Age
69–77 Paul Street, London EC2A 4LQ
☎020 7553 1668 Fax 020 7553 1151
Website www.insuranceage.com

Owner *Informa*
Editor *Karen Woolfson*
Circulation 20,000

FOUNDED 1979. MONTHLY publication circulated to insurance brokers. Covers general insurance (*not* life and pensions). No unsolicited mss. Interested in exclusive stories linked to the insurance broker market; no hi-tech or IT information material.
  News *Luke Satchell* Maximum 400 words.
  Features *Jane Bernstein* Maximum 800 words. *Payment* negotiable.

Interzone: Science Fiction & Fantasy
217 Preston Drove, Brighton, East Sussex BN1 6FL
☎01273 504710

Website www.sfsite.com/interzone
Owner/Editor *David Pringle*
Circulation 10,000

FOUNDED 1982. MONTHLY magazine of science fiction and fantasy. Unsolicited mss are welcome 'from writers who have a knowledge of the magazine and its contents'. S.a.e. essential for return.
  Fiction 2000–6000 words. *Payment* £30 per 1000 words.
  Features Book/film reviews, interviews with writers and occasional short articles. Length by arrangement. *Payment* negotiable.

Investors Chronicle
Maple House, 149 Tottenham Court Road, London W1P 9LL
☎020 7896 2525 Fax 020 7896 2054
Email ceri.jones@ft.com
Website www.investorschronicle.co.uk

Owner *Pearson*
Editor *Ceri Jones*
Commissioning Editor *Richard Andersen*
Circulation 75,000

FOUNDED 1860. WEEKLY. Opportunities for freelance contributors in the survey section only. All approaches should be made in writing. Over forty surveys are published each year on a wide variety of subjects, generally with a financial, business or investment emphasis. Copies of survey list and synopses of individual surveys are obtainable from the surveys editor.
  Payment negotiable.

J17
Endeavour House, 189 Shaftesbury Avenue, London WC2H 8JG
☎020 7208 3408 Fax 020 7208 3590

Owner *EMAP élan Publications*
Editor *Sophie Wilson*
Circulation 200,330

FOUNDED 1983. MONTHLY. News, articles and quizzes of interest to girls aged 13–17. Ideas are sought in all areas. Prospective contributors should send ideas to the deputy editor.
  Beauty *Lara Williamson*
  Features/News *Annabel Brog*
  Payment by arrangement.

Jane's Defence Weekly
Sentinel House, 163 Brighton Road, Coulsdon, Surrey CR5 2YH
☎020 8700 3700 Fax 020 8763 1007
Email jdw@janes.co.uk
Website www.janes.com

Owner *Jane's*
Editor *Clifford Beal*
Circulation 25,492

FOUNDED 1984. WEEKLY. No unsolicited mss. Approach in writing with ideas in the first instance.

Features Current defence topics (politics, strategy, equipment, industry) of worldwide interest. No history pieces. Maximum 2000 words.

Jazz Journal International

3 & 3A Forest Road, Loughton, Essex IG10 1DR
☎020 8532 0456/0678 Fax 020 8532 0440

Owner *Jazz Journal Ltd*
Editor-in-Chief *Eddie Cook*
Circulation 9,000+

FOUNDED 1948. MONTHLY. A specialised jazz magazine, for record collectors, principally using expert contributors whose work is known to the editor. Unsolicited mss not welcome, with the exception of news material (for which no payment is made). It is not a gig guide, nor a free reference source for students.

Jersey Now

PO Box 582, Five Oaks, St Saviour, Jersey, Channel Islands JE4 8XQ
☎01534 611743 Fax 01534 611610
Email mspeditorial@msppublishing.com

Owner *MSP Publishing*
Managing Editor *Peter Body*

Circulation 24,000

FOUNDED 1987. QUARTERLY lifestyle magazine for Jersey covering homes, gardens, the arts, Jersey heritage, motoring, boating, fashion and technology. Upmarket glossy aimed at an informed and discerning readership. Interested in Jersey-orientated articles only – 1200 words maximum. Approach the deputy editor initially. *Payment* negotiable.

Jewish Chronicle

25 Furnival Street, London EC4A 1JT
☎020 7415 1500 Fax 020 7405 9040
Email jconline@jchron.co.uk

Owner *Kessler Foundation*
Editor *Edward J. Temko*
Circulation 50,000

WEEKLY. Unsolicited mss welcome if 'the specific interests of our readership are borne in mind by writers'. Approach in writing, except for urgent current news items. No fiction.

Maximum 1500 words for all material.
Features *Gerald Jacobs*
Leisure/Lifestyle *Alan Montague*
Home News *Barry Toberman*
Foreign News *Jenni Frazer*
Supplements *Angela Kiverstein*
Payment negotiable.

Jewish Quarterly

PO Box 2078, London W1A 1JR
☎020 7629 5004 Fax 020 7629 5110

Publisher *Jewish Literary Trust Ltd*
Editor *Matthew Reisz*

FOUNDED 1953. QUARTERLY illustrated magazine featuring Jewish literature and fiction, politics, art, music, film, poetry, history, dance, community, autobiography, Hebrew, Yiddish, Israel and the Middle East, Judaism, interviews, Zionism, philosophy and holocaust studies. Features a major books and arts section. Unsolicited mss welcome but letter or phone call preferred in first instance.

Jewish Telegraph

Jewish Telegraph Group of Newspapers, 11 Park Hill, Bury Old Road, Prestwich, Manchester M25 0HH
☎0161 740 9321 Fax 0161 740 9325
Email editor@jewishtelegraph.com
Website www.jewishtelegraph.com

Editor *Paul Harris*
Circulation 16,000

FOUNDED 1950. WEEKLY publication with local, national and international news and features. (Separate editions published for Manchester, Leeds, Liverpool and Glasgow.) Unsolicited features on Jewish humour and history welcome.

The Journal Magazines (Norfolk, Suffolk, Cambridgeshire)/ The Essex Magazine

The Old County School, Northgate Street, Bury St Edmunds, Suffolk IP33 1HP
☎01284 701190 Fax 01284 701680

Owner *Acorn Magazines Ltd*
Editor *Pippa Bastin*
Circulation 12,000 each

FOUNDED 1990. MONTHLY magazines covering items of local interest – history, people, conservation, business, places, food and wine, fashion, homes and sport.

Features 750–1250 words maximum, plus pictures. Approach the deputy editor by phone with ideas in the first instance.

Just Seventeen
See **J17**

Kent Life
Datateam Publishing Ltd, London Road,
Maidstone, Kent ME15 8LY
☎01622 687031   Fax 01622 757646

Publisher *Datateam Publishing Ltd*
Editor *Ian Trevett*
Circulation 10,000

FOUNDED 1962. MONTHLY. Strong Kent interest plus fashion, food, books, gardening, wildlife, motoring, property, sport, interiors with local links. Unsolicited mss welcome. Interested in anything with a genuine Kent connection. No fiction or non-Kentish subjects. Approach in writing with ideas. Maximum length 1500 words. *Payment* negotiable.

The Lady
39–40 Bedford Street, London WC2E 9ER
☎020 7379 4717   Fax 020 7836 4620

Editor *Arline Usden*
Circulation 42,505

FOUNDED 1885. WEEKLY. Unsolicited mss are accepted provided they are not on the subject of politics or religion, or on topics covered by staff writers, i.e. fashion and beauty, health, cookery, household, gardening, finance and shopping.
Features Well-researched pieces on British and foreign travel, historical subjects or events; interviews and profiles and other general interest topics. Maximum 1200 words for illustrated two-page articles; 900 words for one-page features; 430 words for first-person 'Viewpoint' pieces. All material should be addressed to the editor. Photographs supporting features may be supplied as colour transparencies or b&w prints. Telephone enquiries about features are not encouraged.

Lakeland Walker
Messrs Warners, Manor Lane, Bourne,
Lincolnshire
☎01778 391000

Contact *John Greenwood*

FOUNDED 1996. BI-MONTHLY. News and features relating to the Lake District and walking in the area – wildlife, local history, places to visit, local transport. Maximum 1000–1500 words. Unsolicited material welcome.

Land Rover World
Focus House, Dingwall Avenue, Croydon,
Surrey CR9 2TA
☎020 8686 2599   Fax 020 8774 0937

Owner *IPC Media Ltd*
Editor *John Carroll*
Circulation 30,000

FOUNDED 1994. MONTHLY. Incorporates *Practical Land Rover World* and *Classic Land Rover World*. Unsolicited material welcome, especially if supported by high-quality illustrations.
Features All articles with a Land Rover theme of interest. Potential contributors are strongly advised to examine previous issues before starting work.
Payment negotiable.

Lexikon
PO Box 754, Stoke-on-Trent, Staffordshire
ST1 4BU
☎01782 205060   Fax 01782 285331
Email enquiries@lexikon-publishing.co.uk
Website www.lexikon-publishing.co.uk

Senior Editor *Francis Anderson*
Poetry Editor *Alan Barrett*
Children's Editor *Roger Bradley*
Submissions email: submissions@
   lexikon-publishing.co.uk

'Sharp, discerning prose, giving writers in the UK and abroad the opportunity to share their work and exchange new ideas.' Poetry, short stories, critical articles, book reviews plus regular competitions with cash prizes. 2000 words maximum for short stories; 60 lines maximum for poetry. Please enclose A4 s.a.e. with all submissions. Subscription (UK): £10 for 4 issues (annual); £15 (2 years). Call for overseas rates. Available in A4 print, on disk, online and (for the blind and visually impaired only) on audiocassette. *Payment* by arrangement.

Lexikon Online Newsletter
PO Box 754, Stoke-on-Trent, Staffordshire
ST1 4BU
☎01782 205060
Email lexikon-subscribe@listbot.com
Website www.lexikon-publishing.co.uk

Editor *Francis Anderson*

Online free newsletter providing news and information to writers, editors and publishers. Includes top literary news stories from around the world, reviews, special features, market news and current competitions. Submissions welcome; non-fiction only. For free subscription, apply by e-mail.

Life&Soul Magazine
PO Box 119, Chipping Norton OX7 6GR
☎01993 832578   Fax 01993 832578

Email editor@lifeandsoul.com
Website www.lifeandsoul.com
Publisher *Karma Publishing Ltd*
Editor *Roy Stemman*
Circulation 3000

QUARTERLY. The only magazine in the world dealing with all aspects of reincarnation – from people who claim to recall their past lives spontaneously to those who have been regressed. It also examines other evidence for immortality, including near-death experiences and spirit communication.

Lincolnshire Life

County Life Ltd, PO Box 81, Lincoln LN1 1HD
☎01522 527127 Fax 01522 560035
Email editorial@lincolnshirelife.co.uk
Website www.lincolnshirelife.co.uk

Publisher *A.L. Robinson*
Executive Editor *Judy Theobald*
Circulation 10,000

FOUNDED 1961. MONTHLY county magazine featuring geographically relevant articles on local culture, history, personalities, etc. Maximum 1000–1500 words. Contributions supported by three or four good-quality photographs are always welcome. Approach in writing.
Payment varies.

The List

14 High Street, Edinburgh EH1 1TE
☎0131 558 1191 Fax 0131 557 8500
Email editor@list.co.uk
Website www.list.co.uk

Owner *The List Ltd*
Publisher *Robin Hodge*
Editor *Mark Fisher*
Circulation 17,500

FOUNDED 1985. FORTNIGHTLY. Events guide covering Glasgow and Edinburgh. Interviews and profiles of people working in film, theatre, music and the arts. Maximum 1200 words. No unsolicited mss. Phone with ideas. News material tends to be handled in-house.
Payment £100.

Literary Review

44 Lexington Street, London W1R 3LH
☎020 7437 9392 Fax 020 7734 1844
Email litrev@dircon.co.uk
Website www.litreview.com

Owner *Namara Group*
Editor *Nancy Sladek*
Circulation 15,000

FOUNDED 1979. MONTHLY. Publishes book reviews (commissioned), features and articles on literary subjects. Prospective contributors are best advised to contact the editor in writing. Unsolicited mss not welcome. Runs a monthly competition, the Literary Review Grand Poetry Competition, on a given theme. Open to subscribers only. Details published in the magazine.
Payment varies.

Living France

Picture House Publishing, 9 High Street, Olney, Buckinghamshire MK46 4EB
☎01234 713203 Fax 01234 711507
Email livingfrance@easynet.co.uk
Website www.livingfrance.com

Publisher *Trevor Yorke*
Editor *Lucy-Jane Cypher*

FOUNDED 1989. MONTHLY. A Francophile magazine catering for those with a passion for France, French culture and lifestyle. Editorial covers all aspects of holidaying, living and working in France. Property section for those owning or wishing to buy a property in France. No unsolicited mss; approach in writing with an idea.

Loaded

IPC Media Ltd., King's Reach Tower, Stamford Street, London SE1 9LS
☎020 7261 5562 Fax 020 7261 5557
Email simon_guirao@ipc.co.uk
Website www.uploaded.com

Owner *IPC Media Ltd*
Editor *Keith Kendrick*
Circulation 351,353

FOUNDED 1994. MONTHLY men's lifestyle magazine featuring music, sport, sex, humour, travel, fashion, hard news and popular culture. Will consider material which comes into these categories; approach in writing in the first instance. No fiction, poetry or articles on relationships.

Logos

5 Beechwood Drive, Marlow, Buckinghamshire SL7 2DH
☎01628 477577 Fax 01628 477577
Email logos-marlow@dial.pipex.com
Website www.osi.hu/cpd/logos.html

Owner *Whurr Publishers Ltd*
Editor *Gordon Graham*
Associate Editor *Betty Graham*

FOUNDED 1990. QUARTERLY. Aims to 'deal in depth with issues which unite, divide, excite and concern the world of books', with an international perspective. Each issue contains 6–8 articles of between 3500–7000 words. 'Logos is a professional forum, not a scholarly journal.' Suggestions and ideas for contributions are welcome, and should be addressed to the editor. 'Guidelines for Contributors' available. Contributors write from their experience as authors, publishers, booksellers, librarians, etc.

No payment.

London Hotel Magazine

165A Finborough Road, London SW10 9AP
☎020 7373 7282 Fax 020 7373 3215

Owner/Editor *Eileen Spence-Moncrieff*

FOUNDED 1995. Features on antiques, fashion, galleries, events and attractions, restaurants, social pages, theatre directories, business. Circulated to 107 major hotels.

London Review of Books

28 Little Russell Street, London WC1A 2HN
☎020 7209 1101 Fax 020 7209 1102
Email edit@lrb.co.uk
Website www.lrb.co.uk

Owner *LRB Ltd*
Editor *Mary-Kay Wilmers*
Circulation 37,778

FOUNDED 1979. FORTNIGHTLY. Reviews, essays and articles on political, literary, cultural and scientific subjects. Also poetry. Unsolicited contributions welcome (approximately 50 received each week). No pieces under 2000 words. Contact the editor in writing. Please include s.a.e.

Payment £150 per 1000 words; poems, £75.

Looking Good

Upper Mounts, Northampton NN1 3HR
☎01604 467000 Fax 01604 476190

Owner *Northamptonshire Newspapers Ltd*
Editor *Ruth Supple*
Circulation 6000

FOUNDED 1984. QUARTERLY county lifestyle magazine of Northamptonshire. Contributions occasionally considered but majority of work is done in-house.

Machine Knitting Monthly

PO Box 1479, Maidenhead, Berkshire SL6 8YX
☎01628 783080 Fax 01628 633250
Email rpa@surf3.net

Owner *RPA Publishing Ltd*
Editor *Anne Smith*

FOUNDED 1986. MONTHLY. Unsolicited mss considered 'as long as they are applicable to this specialist publication. We have our own regular contributors each month but we're always willing to look at new ideas from other writers.' Approach in writing in first instance.

Management Today

174 Hammersmith Road, London W6 7JP
☎020 7413 4566
Email management.today@haynet.com

Owner *Haymarket Business Publications Ltd*
Editor-in-Chief *Rufus Olins*
Circulation 97,976

General business topics and features. Ideas welcome. Send brief synopsis to the editor.
Payment about £330 per 1000 words.

marie claire

2 Hatfields, London SE1 9PG
☎020 7261 5240 Fax 020 7261 5277

Owner *European Magazines Ltd*
Circulation 400,543

FOUNDED 1988. MONTHLY. An intelligent glossy magazine for women, with strong international features and fashion. No unsolicited mss. Approach with ideas in writing. No fiction.

Features *Katie Agnew* Detailed proposals for feature ideas should be accompanied by samples of previous work.

Market Newsletter

Focus House, 497 Green Lanes, London N13 4BP
☎020 8882 3315 Fax 020 8886 5174
Email info@thebfp.com

Owner *Bureau of Freelance Photographers*
Editor *John Tracy*
Deputy Editor *Stewart Gibson*
Circulation 7,000

FOUNDED 1965. MONTHLY. Circulated to members of the Bureau of Freelance Photographers (annual membership fee: £45 UK; £60 Overseas). News of current markets – magazines, books, cards, calendars, etc. – and the type of submissions (mainly photographs) they are currently looking for. Includes details of new magazine launches, publication revamps, etc. Also profiles of particular markets and photographers. Limited scope for non-members to contribute.

Marketing Week

12–26 Lexington Street, London W1R 4HQ
☎020 7970 4000 Fax 020 7970 6721
Email mw.editorial@chiron.co.uk
Website www.marketing-week.co.uk

Owner *Centaur Communications*

Editor *Stuart Smith*
Circulation 40,986

WEEKLY trade magazine of the marketing industry. Features on all aspects of the business, written in a newsy and up-to-the-minute style. Approach with ideas in the first instance.
Features *Joanne Flack*
Payment negotiable.

Match

Bretton Court, Bretton, Peterborough, Cambridgeshire PE3 8DZ
☎01733 260333 Fax 01733 465206
Website www.matchfacts.co.uk
Owner *EMAP Active Ltd*
Editor *Chris Hunt*
Circulation 105,385

FOUNDED 1979. WEEKLY. The UK's biggest-selling football magazine aimed at 10–15-year-olds. Most material is generated in-house by a strong news and features team. Some freelance material used if suitable. No submissions without prior consultation with editor, either by phone or in writing. Work experience placements often given to trainee journalists and students; the majority of staff are recruited through this route.
Features/News Good and original material is always considered. Maximum 500 words.
Payment negotiable.

Matrix

See **British Science Fiction Association** under **Professional Associations**

Maxim

19 Bolsover Street, London W1P 7HJ
☎020 7917 3912 Fax 020 7917 7663
Owner *Dennis Publishing*
Editor *Tom Loxley*
Circulation 328,463

ESTABLISHED 1995. MONTHLY glossy men's lifestyle magazine featuring sex, travel, health, finance, motoring and fashion. No fiction or poetry. Approach in writing in the first instance, sending outlines of ideas only together with examples of published work. Some scope for first-person accounts.

Mayfair

2 Archer Street, Piccadilly Circus, London W1D 7AW
☎020 7292 8000 Fax 020 7734 5030
Email mayfair@pr-org.co.uk
Owner *Paul Raymond Publications*
Editor *Steve Shields*

Circulation 331,760

FOUNDED 1966. THIRTEEN ISSUES YEARLY. Unsolicited material accepted if pertinent to the magazine and if accompanied by suitable illustrative material. 'We will *only* publish work if we can illustrate it.' Interested in features and humour aimed at men aged 18–80. For style, length, etc., writers are advised to study the magazine. 'No more romantic fiction, we beseech you!'

Mayfair Times

102 Mount Street, London W1X 5HF
☎020 7629 3378 Fax 020 7629 9303
Owner *Mayfair Times Ltd*
Editor *Stephen Goringe*
Circulation 20,000

FOUNDED 1985. MONTHLY. Features on Mayfair of interest to both residential and commercial readers. Unsolicited mss welcome.

Medal News

1 Orchard House, Duchy Road, Heathpark, Honiton, Devon EX14 1YD
☎01404 46972 Fax 01404 44788
Email info@medal-news.com
Website www.medal-news.com
Owners *J.W. Mussell, Carol Hartman*
Editor *J.W. Mussell*
Circulation 5000

FOUNDED 1989. MONTHLY. Unsolicited material welcome but initial approach by phone or in writing preferred.
Features 'Opportunities exist for well-informed authors who know the subject and do their homework.' Maximum 2500 words.
Payment £20 per 1000 words.

Media Week

Quantum House, 19 Scarbrook Road, Croydon, Surrey CR9 1LX
☎020 8565 4323 Fax 020 8565 4394
Email weeked@qpp.co.uk
Website www.mediaweek.co.uk
Owner *Quantam*
Editor *Patrick Barrett*
Circulation 22,000

FOUNDED 1986. WEEKLY trade magazine. UK and international coverage on all aspects of commercial media. No unsolicited mss. Approach in writing with ideas.

Melody Maker

See **New Musical Express**

Men's Health

7–10 Chandos Street, London W1G 9AD
☎020 7291 6000 Fax 020 7291 6053
Website www.menshealth.co.uk

Owner *Rodale Press*
Editor *Simon Geller*
Circulation 235,851

FOUNDED 1994. MONTHLY men's healthy lifestyle magazine covering health, fitness, nutrition, stress and sex issues. No unsolicited mss; will consider ideas and synopses tailored to men's health. No fiction, celebrities, sportsmen or extreme sports. Approach in writing in the first instance.

MiniWorld Magazine

Focus House, Dingwall Avenue, Croydon, Surrey CR9 2TA
☎020 8686 2599 Fax 020 8774 0937
Email miniworld@ipc.co.uk
Website www.miniworld.co.uk

Owner *IPC Automotive*
Editor *Monty Watkins*
Circulation 37,122

FOUNDED 1991. MONTHLY car magazine devoted to the Mini. Unsolicited material welcome but prospective contributors are advised to contact the editor.
  Features Maintenance, tuning, restoration, technical advice, classified, sport, readers' cars and social history of this cult car.
  Payment negotiable.

Mizz

IPC Media Ltd., King's Reach Tower, Stamford Street, London SE1 9LS
☎020 7261 6319 Fax 020 7261 6032

Owner *IPC Magazines Ltd*
Executive Editor *Lucie Tobin*
Circulation 163,672

FOUNDED 1985. FORTNIGHTLY magazine for the 10–14-year-old girl. All material should be addressed to the features editor.
  Features *Chloe Thompson/Leslie Sinoway* 'We have a full features team and thus do not accept freelance features.'
  Fiction Maximum 1000 words.

Mojo

Mappin House, 4 Winsley Street, London W1W 8HF
☎020 7436 1515 Fax 020 7312 8296
Email mojo@ecm.emap.com

Owner *EMAP-Metro*
Editor *Paul Trynka*

Circulation 84,010

FOUNDED 1993. MONTHLY magazine containing features, reviews and news stories about rock music and its influences. Receives about five mss per day. No poetry, think-pieces on dead rock stars or similar fan worship.
  Features Amateur writers discouraged except as providers of source material, contacts, etc. *Payment* negotiable.
  News All verifiable, relevant stories considered. *Payment* approx. £150 per 1000 words.
  Reviews Write to Reviews Editor with relevant specimen material. *Payment* approx. £150 per 1000 words.

Moneywise

RD Publications Ltd, 11 Westferry Circus, Canary Wharf, London E14 4HE
☎020 7715 8465 Fax 020 7715 8725
Website www.moneywise.co.uk

Owner *Reader's Digest Association*
Editor *David Ellis*
Circulation 105,000

FOUNDED 1990. MONTHLY. Unsolicited mss with s.a.e. welcome but initial approach in writing preferred.

More!

Endeavour House, 189 Shaftesbury Avenue, London WC2H 8JG
☎020 7208 3165 Fax 020 7208 3595
Email more.letters@ecm.emap.com

Owner *EMAP élan Publications*
Editor *Marina Gask*
Features Director *Steve King*
Editorial Enquiries *Emi Howe*
Circulation 305,344

FOUNDED 1988. FORTNIGHTLY women's magazine aimed at the working woman aged 18–24. Features on sex and relationships plus news. Most items are commissioned; approach features director with idea. Prospective contributors are strongly advised to study the magazine's style before submitting anything.

Mother and Baby

Greater London House, Hampstead Road, London NW1 7EJ
☎020 7874 0200

Owner *EMAP Esprit*
Editor *Dani Zur*
Circulation 83,000

FOUNDED 1956. MONTHLY. Welcomes suggestions for feature ideas about pregnancy, newborn basics, practical babycare, baby development and childcare subjects. Approaches may be made by telephone or in writing to the **Features Editor** *Una Rice.*

Motor Boat & Yachting

IPC Country & Leisure Media Limited, King's Reach Tower, Stamford Street, London SE1 9LS
☎020 7261 5333 Fax 020 7261 5419
Email mby@ipcmedia.com
Website www.mby.com

Owner *IPC Media Ltd*
Editor *Alan Harper*
Circulation 19,736

FOUNDED 1904. MONTHLY for those interested in motor boats and motor cruising.

Features *Alan Harper* Cruising features and practical features especially welcome. Illustrations/photographs (mostly colour) are just as important as text. Maximum 3000 words. *Payment* from £100 per 1000 words or by arrangement.

News *Tom Isitt* Factual pieces. Maximum 200 words. *Payment* up to £50 per item.

Motorcaravan Motorhome Monthly (MMM)

PO Box 44, Totnes, Devon TQ9 5XB
Owner *Sanglier Publications Ltd*
Editor *Mike Jago*
Circulation 27,260

FOUNDED 1966. MONTHLY. 'There's no money in motorcaravan journalism but for those wishing to cut their first teeth...' Unsolicited mss welcome if relevant, but ideas in writing preferred in first instance.

Features Caravan site reports. Maximum 500 words.

Travel Motorcaravanning trips (home and overseas). Maximum 2000 words.

News Short news items for miscellaneous pages. Maximum 200 words.

Fiction Must be motorcaravan-related and include artwork/photos if possible. Maximum 2000 words.

Special pages DIY – modifications to motorcaravans. Maximum 1500 words.

Owner Reports Contributions welcome from motorcaravan owners. Contact the editor for requirements. Maximum 2000 words.

Payment varies.

Ms London

Independent House, 191 Marsh Wall, London E14 9RS
☎020 7005 5959 Fax 020 7005 5999

Website www.londoncareers.net
Owner *Independent Magazines*
Editor-in-Chief *Bill Williamson*
Circulation 85,000

FOUNDED 1968. WEEKLY. Aimed at working women in London, aged 18–35. No unsolicited mss.

Features Content is varied and topical, ranging from celebrity interviews to news issues, fashion, health, careers, relationships and home-buying. Approach in writing only with ideas in the first instance, enclosing sample of published writing. Material should be London-angled, sharp or humorous and fairly sophisticated in content. Maximum 1500 words. *Payment* about £130 per 1000 words on publication.

News Handled in-house but follow-up feature ideas welcome.

Mslexia (For Women Who Write)

PO Box 656, Newcastle upon Tyne NE99 2XD
☎0191 261 6656 Fax 0191 261 6636
Email postbag@mslexia.demon.co.uk
Website www.mslexia.co.uk

Owner *Mslexia Publications Limited*
Editor *Debbie Taylor*
Circulation 8000

FOUNDED 1997. QUARTERLY. Articles, advice, reviews, interviews, events for women writers plus new poetry and prose. Will consider fiction, poetry, features and letters but contributors *must* send for guidelines first.

Multi-Storey

PO Box 62, Levenshulme, Manchester M19 1TH
Email stuff@multistorey.co.uk
Website www.multistorey.co.uk

Editors *Finella Davenport, Gary Parkinson, Bill Jones,*
Web Editor *Mark Sullivan*

FOUNDED 1999. Themed BIANNUAL literary and arts magazine. Short stories, poetry, book reviews as well as interviews with high profile writers and artists. 'Contact us in the first instance for guidelines or visit our website. E-mail or post; always enclose s.a.e. if sending via snail mail.' **News** Maximum 500 words; **Features** Maximum 1500 words; **Fiction** Maximum 4000 words; **Poetry** Maximum 40 lines.

Music Week

8 Montague Close, London SE1 9UR
☎020 7940 8500 Fax 020 7407 7094

Owner *United Business Media International*
Editor *Ajax Scott*

Circulation 13,900

Britain's only WEEKLY music business magazine. No unsolicited mss. Approach in writing with ideas.

Features Analysis of specific music business events and trends.

News Music industry news only.

Musical Opinion

2 Princes Road, St Leonards on Sea, East Sussex TN37 6EL
☎01424 715167 Fax 01424 712214
Email musical-opinion@cwcom.net
Website www.musicalopinion.com
Owner *Musical Opinion Ltd*
Editor *Denby Richards*
Circulation 5000

FOUNDED 1877. QUARTERLY with four free supplements in intervening months. Classical music content, with topical features on music, musicians, festivals, etc., and reviews (concerts, festivals, opera, ballet, jazz, CDs, CD-ROMs, videos, books and printed music). International readership. No unsolicited mss; commissions only. Ideas always welcome though; approach by phone or fax, giving telephone number. It should be noted that topical material has to be submitted six months prior to events. Not interested in review material, which is already handled by the magazine's own regular team of contributors.

Payment negotiable.

My Weekly

80 Kingsway East, Dundee DD4 8SL
☎01382 223131 Fax 01382 452491
Email myweekly@dcthomson.co.uk
Owner *D.C. Thomson & Co. Ltd*
Editor *Harrison Watson*
Circulation 318,294

A traditional women's WEEKLY. D.C. Thomson has long had a policy of encouragement and help to new writers of promise. Ideas welcome. Approach in writing.

Features Particularly interested in human interest pieces (1000–1500 words) which by their very nature appeal to all age groups.

Fiction Three stories a week, ranging in content from the emotional to the off-beat and unexpected. 1000–4000 words. Also serials.

Payment negotiable.

The National Trust Magazine

36 Queen Anne's Gate, London SW1H 9AS
☎020 7222 9251 Fax 020 7222 5097
Email enquiries@ntrust.org.uk
Owner *The National Trust*
Editor *Gaynor Aaltonen*
Circulation 1.38 million

FOUNDED 1968. THREE ISSUES YEARLY. Conservation of historic houses, coast and countryside in England, Northern Ireland and Wales. No unsolicited mss. Approach in writing with ideas.

Natural World

Victory House, 14 Leicester Place, London WC2H 7QH
☎020 7306 0304 Fax 020 7306 0314
Owner *River Publishing Ltd*
Editor *Trevor Lawson*
Circulation 178,000

FOUNDED 1981. THREE ISSUES YEARLY. Unsolicited mss are not accepted. Ideas in writing preferred. No poetry.

Features Popular but accurate articles on British wildlife and the countryside, and only projects associated with the local wildlife trusts. Maximum 1500 words.

News Interested in national wildlife conservation issues involving local nature conservation or wildlife trusts. Maximum 300 words.

Payment negotiable.

The Naturalist

c/o University of Bradford, Bradford, West Yorkshire BD7 1DP
☎01274 234212 Fax 01274 234231
Email m.r.d.seaward@bradford.ac.uk
Owner *Yorkshire Naturalists' Union*
Editor *Prof. M.R.D. Seaward*
Circulation 5000

FOUNDED 1875. QUARTERLY. Natural history, biological and environmental sciences for a professional and amateur readership. Unsolicited mss and b&w illustrations welcome. Particularly interested in material – scientific papers – relating to the north of England. *No payment.*

Nature

The Macmillan Building, 4–6 Crinan Street, London N1 9XW
☎020 7833 4000 Fax 020 7843 4596
Email nature@nature.com
Website www.nature.com
Owner *Macmillan Magazines Ltd*
Editor *Philip Campbell*
Circulation 61,000

Covers all fields of science, with articles and news on science policy only. Little scope for freelance writers.

Needlecraft

30 Monmouth Street, Bath BA1 2BW
☎01225 442244 Fax 01225 732398
Email jenny.dixon@futurenet.co.uk
Owner *Future Publishing*
Editor *Jenny Dixon*
Circulation 23,500

FOUNDED 1991. MONTHLY. Needlework projects with full instructions covering cross stitch, needlepoint, embroidery, patchwork, quilting and lace. Will consider ideas or sketches for projects covering any of the magazine's topics. Initial approaches should be made in writing.

Features on the needlecraft theme. Discuss ideas before sending complete mss. Maximum 1000 words.

Technical pages on 'how to' stitch, use different threads, etc. Only suitable for experienced writers.

Payment negotiable.

New Beacon

224 Great Portland Street, London W1W 5AA
☎020 7388 1266 Fax 020 7388 0945
Website www.rnib.org.uk
Owner *Royal National Institute for the Blind*
Editor *Ann Lee*
Circulation 6000

FOUNDED 1917. MONTHLY (except August). Published in print, braille and on tape and disk. Unsolicited mss welcome. Approach with ideas in writing. Personal experiences by writers who have a sight difficulties (partial sight or blindness), and authoritative items by professionals or volunteers working in the field of sight difficulties welcome. Maximum 1500 words.

Payment negotiable.

New Humanist

Bradlaugh House, 47 Theobald's Road, London WC1X 8SP
☎020 7430 1371 Fax 020 7430 1271
Email jim.herrick@rationalist.org.uk
Owner *Rationalist Press Association*
Editor *Jim Herrick*
Circulation 5000

FOUNDED 1885. QUARTERLY. Unsolicited mss welcome. No fiction.

Features Articles with a humanist perspective welcome in the following fields: religion (critical), humanism, human rights, philosophy, current events, literature, history and science. 2000 words. *Payment* nominal, but negotiable.

Book Reviews 750–1000 words, by arrangement with the editor.

New Impact

Anser House, Courtyard Offices, 3 High Street, Marlow, Buckinghamshire SL7 1AX
☎01628 475570 Fax 01628 475570
Email curious@anserhouse.co.uk
Website www.anserhouse.co.uk
Owner *D.E. Sihera*
Editor *Elaine Sihera*
Features Editor *Mary Howe Clements*
Circulation 10,000

FOUNDED 1993. BI-MONTHLY. Celebrates diversity, enterprise and achievement from a minority ethnic perspective. Unsolicited mss welcome. Interested in training, arts, features, personal achievement, small business features, profiles of personalities especially for a multicultural audience. Promotes the British Diversity Awards each November and the Windrush Awards each June, the Register of Diversity Managers among employers and the Annual Diversity UK Guide.

News Local training/business features – some opportunities. Maximum length 250 words. *Payment* negotiable.

Features Original, interesting pieces with a deliberate multicultural/diversity focus. Personal/professional successes and achievements welcome. Maximum length 1000 words. *Payment* negotiable.

Fiction Short stories, poems – especially from minority writers. Not interested in romantic/sexual narratives. Maximum length 1500 words. *Payment* negotiable.

Special Pages Interviews with personalities – especially Asian, African Caribbean. Maximum length 1200 words. *Payment* negotiable.

New Internationalist

55 Rectory Road, Oxford OX4 1BW
☎01865 728181 Fax 01865 793152
Email ni@newint.org
Website www.newint.org/
Owner *New Internationalist Trust*
Co-Editors *Vanessa Baird, Chris Brazier, David Ransom,*
Circulation 70,000

Radical and broadly leftist in approach, but unaligned. Concerned with world poverty and global issues of peace and politics, feminism and environmentalism, with emphasis on the Third World. Difficult to use unsolicited material as they work to a theme each month and features are commissioned by the editor on that basis. The way in is to send examples of published or unpublished work; writers of interest are taken up.

New Musical Express

IPC Media Ltd., King's Reach Tower,
Stamford Street, London SE1 9LS
☎020 7261 6472 Fax 020 7261 5185
Website www.nme.com
Owner *IPC Media Ltd*
Editor *Ben Knowles*
Circulation 70,003

Britain's best-selling musical WEEKLY. Now
incorporates *Melody Maker*. Freelancers used,
but always for reviews in the first instance.
Specialisation in areas of music (or film, which
is also covered) is a help.
    Reviews: Books/Film *Victoria Segal* **LPs**
John Robinson **Live** *Arwa Haider*. Send in examples of work, either published or specially written samples.

New Nation

Unit 2, 65 Whitechapel Road, London
E1 1DU
☎020 7650 2000 Fax 020 7650 2001
Website www.ethnicmedia.co.uk
Owner *Ethnic Media Group*
Editor *Michael Eboda*
Circulation 30,000

FOUNDED 1996. WEEKLY community paper for
the Black community in Britain. Interested in
relevant general, local and international issues.
Approach in writing with ideas for submission.

New Scientist

1st Floor, 151 Wardour Street, London
W1F 8WE
☎020 7331 2701 Fax 020 7331 2772
Website www.newscientist.com
Owner *Reed Business Information Ltd*
Editor-in-Chief *Dr Alun Anderson*
Editor *Jeremy Webb*
Circulation 135,000

FOUNDED 1956. WEEKLY. No unsolicited mss.
Approach with ideas – one A4-page synopsis –
by fax.
    Features Commissions only, but good ideas
welcome. Maximum 3500 words.
    News *Daniel Clery* Mostly commissions, but
ideas for specialist news welcome. Maximum
1000 words.
    Reviews *Maggie McDonald* Reviews are
commissioned.
    Forum *Richard Fifield* Unsolicited material
welcome if of general/humorous interest and
related to science. Maximum 1000 words.
    Payment negotiable.

The New Shetlander

11 Mounthooly Street, Lerwick, Shetland
ZE1 0BJ
☎01595 693816 Fax 01595 696787
Email shetland@zetnet.co.uk
Owner *Shetland Council of Social Service*
Editors *Alex Cluness, John Hunter*
Circulation 1900

FOUNDED 1947. QUARTERLY literary magazine
containing short stories, essays, poetry, historical articles, literary criticism, political comment, arts and books. The magazine has two
editors and an editorial committee who all look
at submitted material. Interested in considering
short stories, poetry, historical articles with a
northern Scottish or Scandinavian flavour, literary pieces and articles on Shetland. As a
rough guide, items should be between 1000
and 2000 words although longer mss are considered. Initial approach in writing, please.
    Payment Complimentary copy.

New Statesman

Victoria Station House, 191 Victoria Street,
London SW1E 5NE
☎020 7828 1232 Fax 020 7828 1881
Website www.newstatesman.co.uk
Publisher *Spencer Neal*
Editor *Peter Wilby*
Deputy Editor *Cristina Odone*
Circulation 26,000

WEEKLY magazine, the result of a merger
(1988) of *New Statesman* and *New Society*.
Coverage of news, book reviews, arts, current
affairs, politics and social reportage. Unsolicited
contributions with s.a.e. will be considered.
No short stories.
    Books *Jason Cowley*
    Arts *Frances Stonor Saunders*

New Theatre Quarterly

Oldstairs, Kingsdown, Deal, Kent CT14 8ES
☎01304 373448
Email simontrussler@lineone.net
Website www.uk.cambridge.org
Publisher *Cambridge University Press*
Editors *Clive Barker, Simon Trussler*

FOUNDED 1985 (originally launched in 1971 as
Theatre Quarterly). Articles, interviews, documentation and reference material covering all
aspects of live theatre. Recommend preliminary e-mail enquiry before sending contributions. No theatre reviews or anecdotal material.

New Welsh Review

Chapter Arts Centre, Market Road, Cardiff
CF5 1QE
☎029 2066 5529 Fax 029 2066 5529
Email nwr@welshnet.co.uk
Owner *New Welsh Review Ltd*
Editor *Robin Reeves*
Circulation 900

FOUNDED 1988. QUARTERLY Welsh literary
magazine in the English language. Welcomes
material of literary and cultural interest to Welsh
readers and those with an interest in Wales.
Approach in writing in the first instance.

Features Maximum 3000 words. *Payment*
£25 per 1000 words.

Fiction Maximum 5000 words. *Payment*
£40–80 average.

News Maximum 400 words. *Payment*
£10–30.

New Woman

Endeavour House, 189 Shaftesbury Avenue,
London WC2H 8JG
☎020 7437 9011 Fax 020 7208 3585
Website www.newwomanonline.co.uk
Owner *Hachette/EMAP élan Ltd*
Editor *Sara Cremer*
Circulation 281,828

MONTHLY women's interest magazine. Winner
of the PPA 'Magazine of the Year' award in
1998. Aimed at women aged 25–35. An
'entertaining, informative and intelligent' read.
Main topics of interest include men, sex, love,
health, careers, beauty and fashion. Uses mainly
established freelancers but unsolicited ideas
submitted in synopsis form will be considered.
Welcomes ideas from male writers for humorous 'men's opinion' pieces.

Features/News *Lauren Libbert* Articles must
be original and look at subjects or issues from a
new or unusual perspective.

The New Writer

PO Box 60, Cranbrook, Kent TN17 2ZR
☎01580 212626 Fax 01580 212041
Email editor@thenewwriter.com
Website www.thenewwriter.com
Publisher *Merric Davidson*
Editor *Suzanne Ruthven*
Poetry Editor *Abi Hughes-Edwards*

FOUNDED 1996. Published MONTHLY following the merger between *Acclaim* and *Quartos*
magazines. TNW continues to offer practical
'nuts and bolts' advice on poetry and prose but
with the emphasis on *forward-looking* articles

and features on all aspects of the written word
that demonstrate the writer's grasp of contemporary writing and current editorial/publishing
policies. Plenty of news, views, competitions,
reviews and regional gossip in the Newsletter
section; writers' guidelines available with s.a.e.

Features Unsolicited mss welcome. Interested in lively, original articles on writing in its
broadest sense. Approach with ideas in writing in
the first instance. No material is returned unless
accompanied by s.a.e. *Payment* £20 per 1000
words.

Fiction Publishes short-listed entries from
guest writers and subscriber-only submissions.
Payment £10 per story.

Poetry Unsolicited poetry welcome. Both
short and long unpublished poems, providing
they are original and interesting. *Payment* £3
per poem.

New Writing Scotland

Association for Scottish Literary Studies, c/o
Department of Scottish History, 9 University
Gardens, University of Glasgow G12 8QH
☎0141 330 5309 Fax 0141 330 5309
Email d.jones@scothist.arts.gla.ac.uk
Website www.asls.org.uk

Contact *Duncan Jones*

ANNUAL anthology of contemporary poetry and
prose in English, Gaelic and Scots, produced by
the **Association for Scottish Literary Studies**
(see entry under **Professional Associations
and Societies**). Will consider poetry, drama,
short fiction or other creative prose but not full-
length plays or novels, though self-contained
extracts are acceptable. Contributors should be
Scottish by birth or upbringing, or resident in
Scotland. Maximum length of 3500 words is
suggested. Send no more than two short stories
and six poems. Submissions should be accompanied by two s.a.e.s (one for receipt, the other
for return of mss). Mss, which must be sent by
31 January, should be typed, double-spaced, on
one side of the paper only with the sheets
secured at top left-hand corner. Mark with your
name and address and, for prose, an approximate
word count.

newBOOKS.mag

guisemarketing, 15 Scots Drive, Wokingham,
Berkshire RG41 3XF
☎0118 962 9528
Email guypringle@waitrose.com
Owner/Editor *Guy Pringle*
Circulation 5000

FOUNDED 2000. BI-MONTHLY. Contains extracts

from six new books per issue with 500 free copies of each title to be claimed. Supported by articles about the book industry. Aimed at reading groups. Unsolicited contributions welcome; approach by e-mail. Maximum length 800 words plus pictures.

Newcastle Life
See **North East Times**

19
IPC Media Ltd., King's Reach Tower, Stamford Street, London SE1 9LS
☎020 7261 6410 Fax 020 7261 7634

Owner *IPC Media Ltd*
Editor *Samantha Warwick*
Circulation 133,890

FOUNDED 1968. MONTHLY women's magazine aimed at 18–25-year-olds. Aims for a 50/50 balance between fashion/lifestyle aspects and newsier, meatier material, e.g. women in prison, boys, abortion, etc. 40% of the magazine's feature material is commissioned, ordinarily from established freelancers. 'But we're always keen to see bold, original, vigorous writing from people just starting out.'
    Features Approach in writing with ideas.

North East Times
Tattler House, Beech Avenue, Fawdon, Newcastle upon Tyne NE3 4RN
☎0191 284 4495 Fax 0191 285 9606
Email northeasttimes@onyxnet.co.uk

Owner *Chris Robinson (Publishing) Ltd*
Editor *Chris Robinson*
Circulation 10,000

MONTHLY county magazine incorporating *Newcastle Life*. No unsolicited mss. Approach with ideas in writing. Not interested in any material that is not applicable to ABC1 readers.

The North
See **Poetry Magazines**

Now
IPC Media Ltd., King's Reach Tower, Stamford Street, London SE1 9LS
☎020 7261 6274

Owner *IPC Media Ltd*
Editor *Jane Ennis*
Circulation 475,571

FOUNDED 1996. WEEKLY magazine of celebrity gossip, news and topical features aimed at the working woman. Unlikely to use freelance contributions due to specialist content – e.g. exclusive showbiz interviews – but ideas will be considered. Approach in writing; no faxes.

Nursing Times
Greater London House, Hampstead Road, London NW1 7EJ
☎020 7874 0500 Fax 020 7874 0505

Owner *EMAP Healthcare*
Editor *Tricia Reid*
Circulation 58,785

A large proportion of *Nursing Times'* feature content is from unsolicited contributions sent on spec. Pieces on all aspects of nursing and health care, both practical and theoretical, written in a lively and contemporary way, are welcome. Commissions also.
    Payment varies/NUJ rates apply to commissioned material from union members only.

OK! Magazine
Ludgate House, 245 Blackfriars Road, London SE1 9UX
☎020 7928 8000 Fax 020 7579 4607

Owner *Northern & Shell Media/Richard Desmond*
Editor *Nic McCarthy*
Circulation 586,176

FOUNDED 1996. WEEKLY celebrity-based magazine. Welcomes interviews and pictures on well known personalities, and ideas for general features. Approach by phone or fax in the first instance.

The Oldie
45–46 Poland Street, London W1F 7NA
☎020 7734 2225 Fax 020 7734 2226
Email theoldie@theoldie.co.uk
Website www.theoldie.co.uk

Owner *Oldie Publications Ltd*
Editor *Richard Ingrams*
Circulation 30,000

FOUNDED 1992. MONTHLY general interest magazine with a strong humorous slant for the older person. Submissions welcome; enclose s.a.e. No poetry.

OLS (Open Learning Systems) News
11 Malford Grove, Gilwern, Abergavenny, Monmouthshire NP7 0RN
☎01873 830872
Email GSSE@zoo.co.uk

Owner/Editor *David P. Bosworth*
Circulation 300

FOUNDED 1980. QUARTERLY dealing with the

application of open, flexible, distance learning and supported self-study at all educational/training levels. Interested in open-access learning and the application of educational technology to learning situations. Case studies particularly welcome. Not interested in theory of education alone, the emphasis is strictly on applied policies and trends.

Features Learning programmes (how they are organised); student/learner-eye views of educational and training programmes with an open-access approach. Sections on teleworking and lifelong learning. Approach the editor by e-mail or in writing.

No payment for 'news' items. Focus items will negotiate.

On the Ball
The Design Works, William Street, Gateshead, Tyne and Wear NE10 0JP
☎0191 420 8383 Fax 0191 420 4950
Editor *Jennifer O'Neill*
Circulation 30,000

FOUNDED 1996. MONTHLY. The only magazine for women football players. Contributions welcome.

Features *Jennifer O'Neill* International reports, player and team profiles, diet, health and fitness, tactics, training advice, play improvement, fundraising. 1500 words maximum.

News *Wilf Frith* Match reports, team news, transfers, injuries, results and fixtures. 600 words maximum.

Payment negotiable.

Opera
36 Black Lion Lane, London W6 9BE
☎020 8563 8893 Fax 020 8563 8635
Email editor@operamag.clara.co.uk
Website www.opera.co.uk
Owner *Opera Magazine Ltd*
Editor *John Allison*
Circulation 11,500

FOUNDED 1950. MONTHLY review of the current opera scene. Almost all articles are commissioned and unsolicited mss are not welcome. All approaches should be made in writing.

Opera Now
241 Shaftesbury Avenue, London WC2H 8TF
☎020 7333 1740 Fax 020 7333 1769
Email opera.now@rhinegold.co.uk
Publisher *Rhinegold Publishing Ltd*
  Editor-in-Chief *Ashutosh Khandekar*
  Deputy Editor *Antonia Couling*
  Assistant Editor *Matthew Peacock*

FOUNDED 1989. BI-MONTHLY. News, features and reviews aimed at those involved as well as those interested in opera. No unsolicited mss. All work is commissioned. Approach with ideas in writing.

Orbis
See **Poetry Magazines**

Organic Gardening
PO Box 29, Minehead, Somerset TA24 6YY
☎01984 641212 Fax 01984 641212
Email organic.gardening@virgin.net
Editor *Gaby Bartai Bevan*
Circulation 20,000

FOUNDED 1988. MONTHLY. Articles and features on all aspects of gardening based on organic methods. Unsolicited material welcome; 800–2000 words for features and 100–300 for news items. Prefers 'hands-on' accounts of projects, problems, challenges and how they are dealt with. Approach in writing.

Payment by arrangement.

Organics Today
Elim Centre, Lancaster Road, Shrewsbury, Shropshire SY1 3LE
☎01743 440512 Fax 01743 461441
Email org@prestige-typo.co.uk
Owner *Organic Farmers and Growers*
Contact *Editorial Board*
Circulation 2000

FOUNDED 2000. QUARTERLY magazine of the Organic Farmers and Growers Ltd. Features on matters relating to organic farming, processing and growing. Livestock, arable and organic enterprises. 500–2500 words. News, especially parliamentary, welcome. Send outline of ideas in writing.

Payment negotiable.

OS (Office Secretary) Magazine
Brookmead House, Thorney Leys Business Park, Witney, Oxfordshire OX8 7GE
☎01993 894500 Fax 01993 778884
Owner *Peebles Media Group*
Editor *Emma Smith*
Circulation 50,000

FOUNDED 1986. BI-MONTHLY. Features articles of interest to secretaries and personal assistants aged 25–60. No unsolicited mss.

Features Informative pieces on technology and practices, office and employment-related topics. Length 1000 words.

Payment by negotiation.

Outcast
72 New Bond Street, London W1S 1RR
☎0870 345 0444   Fax 0870 345 0445
Email mail@outcastmagazine.co.uk
Website www.outcastmagazine.co.uk
Owner *Outcast Publishing Ltd*
Editor *Chris Morris*
Circulation 40,000

FOUNDED 1999. MONTHLY current affairs magazine aimed at the lesbian, gay and bisexual communities. Focuses on news, politics and debate. Freelance contributions welcome.

News *Jake Sawyer* news@outcastmagazine.co.uk
Features *Emma Butcher* emma@outcastmagazine.co.uk
Arts/Reviews *David Leddy* david@outcastmagazine.co.uk
Payment nominal.

Palmtop Magazine
Palmtop Publications, PO Box 188, Bicester, Oxfordshire OX6 0GP
☎01869 249287   Fax 01869 246043
Email editor@palmtop.co.uk
Website www.palmtop.co.uk
Owners *Mr S. Clack, Miss R.A. Rolfe*
Editor *Mr S. Clack*
Circulation 12,000

FOUNDED 1994. BI-MONTHLY users' magazine for Psion hand-held computers. No unsolicited mss; approach by telephone or e-mail in the first instance.

PC Format
Future Publishing, 30 Monmouth Street, Bath BA1 2BW
☎01225 442244   Fax 01225 732275
Email pcfmail@futurenet.co.uk
Website www.futurenet.co.uk
Owner *Future Publishing*
Editor *Dan Hutchinson*
Circulation 110,227

FOUNDED 1991. FOUR-WEEKLY magazine covering everything for the consumer PC – games, hardware, Internet creativity. Welcomes feature ideas in the first instance; approach by telephone or in writing.

Peakland Walker
33 Park Road, Bakewell, Derbyshire DE45 1AX
☎01629 812034   Fax 01629 812034
Email rolysmith@compuserve.com
Owner *Warners Group Publications*

Editor *Roly Smith*

FOUNDED 1997. QUARTERLY. Predominantly walking, natural history and heritage, serving the Peak District National Park and surrounding area. Unsolicited material considered but telephone first. Maximum 1200 words.

Pembrokeshire Life
Swan House Publishing, Bridge Street, Newcastle Emlyn, Carmarthenshire SA38 9DX
☎01239 710632   Fax 01239 710632
Email davidfielding@themail.co.uk
Owner *Swan House Publishing*
Editor *David Fielding*

FOUNDED 1989. MONTHLY county magazine with articles on local history, issues, characters, off-beat stories with good colour or b&w photographs. No country diaries, short stories, poems. Most articles are commissioned from known freelancers but 'always prepared to consider ideas from new writers'. No mss. Send cuttings of previous work (published or not) and synopsis to the editor.

People Management
Personnel Publications Limited, 17 Britton Street, London EC1M 5TP
☎020 7880 6200   Fax 020 7336 7635
Email editorial@peoplemanagement.co.uk
Website www.peoplemanagement.co.uk
Editor *Steve Crabb*
Circulation 105,000

FORTNIGHTLY magazine on human resources, industrial relations, employment issues, etc. Welcomes submissions but apply for 'Guidelines for Contributors' in the first instance; approach in writing. **Features** *Jane Pickard* **News** *Eila Rana* **Law at Work** *Jill Evans*.

The People's Friend
80 Kingsway East, Dundee DD4 8SL
☎01382 462276/223131   Fax 01382 452491
Email peoplesfriend@dcthomson.co.uk
Owner *D.C. Thomson & Co. Ltd*
Editor *Sinclair Matheson*
Circulation 399,339

The *Friend* is basically a fiction magazine, with two serials and several short stories each week. FOUNDED in 1869, it has always prided itself on providing 'a good read for all the family'. All stories should be about ordinary, identifiable characters with the kind of problems the average reader can understand and sympathise with. 'We look for the romantic and emotional developments of characters, rather than an over-complicated or contrived plot. We regularly use period serials and, occasionally, mystery/adventure.' Guidelines on request with s.a.e.

Short Stories Can vary in length from 1000 words or less to as many as 4000.

Serials Long-run serials of 10–15 instalments or more preferred. Occasionally shorter.

Articles Short fillers welcome.

Payment on acceptance.

Period Living & Traditional Homes

Endeavour House, 189 Shaftesbury Avenue, London WC2H 8JG
☎020 7208 3507 Fax 020 7208 3597

Owner *EMAP élan Ltd*
Editor *Garry Mason*
Circulation 86,098

FOUNDED 1992. Formed from the merger of *Period Living* and *Traditional Homes*. Covers interior decoration in a period style, period house profiles, traditional crafts, renovation of period properties.

Features *Pamela Shipkey*
Payment varies according to length/type of article.

Personal

See under **National Newspapers (Sunday Mirror)**

Personal Finance

Arnold House, 36–41 Holywell Lane, London EC2A 3SF
☎020 7827 5454 Fax 020 7827 0567

Owner *Charterhouse Communications plc*
Editor *Martin Fagan*
Circulation 50,000

ESTABLISHED 1994. MONTHLY finance magazine.

Features All issues relating to personal finance, particularly investment, insurance, banking, mortgages, savings, borrowing, health care and pensions. No corporate articles or personnel issues. Write to the editor with ideas in the first instance. No unsolicited mss. *Payment* £200 per 1000 words.

News All items written in-house.

The Philosopher

Centre for Lifelong Learning, Newcastle University, Newcastle upon Tyne NE1 7RU
Website www.philsoc.freeserve.co.uk

Owner *The Philosophical Society*
Editor *Martin Cohen*

FOUNDED 1913. BIANNUAL journal of the Philosophical Society of Great Britain with an international readership made up of members, libraries and specialist booksellers. Wide range of interests, but leaning towards articles that present philosophical investigation which is relevant to the individual and to society in our modern era. Accessible to the non-specialist. Will consider articles and book reviews. Notes for Contributors available; send s.a.e. or see website.

As well as short philosophical papers, will accept:

News about lectures, conventions, philosophy groups. Ethical issues in the news. Maximum 1000 words.

Reviews of philosophy books (maximum 600 words); discussion articles of individual philosophers and their published works (maximum 2000 words).

Miscellaneous items, including graphics, of philosophical interest and/or merit.

Payment free copies.

Piano

241 Shaftesbury Avenue, London WC2H 8EH
☎020 7333 1724 Fax 020 7333 1769
Email pianomagazine@mail.com
Website www.rhinegold.co.uk

Owner *Rhinegold Publishing*
Editor *Jeremy Siepmann*
Deputy Editor *Matthew Peacock*
Circulation 11,000

FOUNDED 1993. BI-MONTHLY magazine containing features, profiles, technical information, news, reviews of interest to those with a serious amateur or professional concern with pianos or their playing. No unsolicited material. Approach with ideas in writing only.

Picture Postcard Monthly

15 Debdale Lane, Keyworth, Nottingham NG12 5HT
☎0115 937 4079 Fax 0115 937 6197
Email reflections@argonet.co.uk
Website www.postcardcollecting.co.uk

Owners *Brian & Mary Lund*
Editor *Brian Lund*
Circulation 4000

FOUNDED 1978. MONTHLY. News, views, clubs, diary of fairs, sales, auctions, and well-researched postcard-related articles. Might be interested in general articles supported by postcards. Unsolicited mss welcome. Approach by phone or in writing with ideas.

Pilot

The Clock House, 28 Old Town, Clapham, London SW4 0LB
☎020 7498 2506 Fax 020 7498 6920
Email pilotmagazine@compuserve.com
Website www.pilotweb.co.uk
Publisher *Market Link Publishing Ltd*
Editor *Philip Whiteman*
Circulation 27,370

FOUNDED 1968. MONTHLY magazine for private plane pilots. No staff writers; the entire magazine is written by freelancers – mostly regulars. Unsolicited mss welcome but ideas in writing preferred. Perusal of any issue of the magazine will reveal the type of material bought. 700 words of 'Advice to would-be contributors' sent on receipt of s.a.e. (mark envelope 'Advice').

Features *James Gilbert* Many articles are unsolicited personal experiences/travel accounts from pilots of private planes; good photo coverage is very important. Maximum 5000 words. *Payment* £100–700 (first rights). Photos £30–120 each.

News *Mike Jerram* Contributions need to be as short as possible. See *Pilot Notes* and *Old-Timers* in the magazine.

Pink Paper

72 Holloway Road, London N7 8NZ
☎020 7296 6210 Fax 020 7957 0046
Email editorial@pinkpaper.co.uk
Owner *Chronos Group*
Editor *Justin Webb*
Circulation 55,079

FOUNDED 1987. WEEKLY. Only national newspaper for lesbians and gay men covering politics, social issues, health, the arts and all areas of concern to lesbian/gay people. Unsolicited mss welcome. Initial approach by post with an idea preferred. Interested in profiles, reviews, in-depth features and short news pieces.

News Maximum 300 words.
Payment by arrangement.

Planet: The Welsh Internationalist

See **Planet** under **Small Presses**

PN Review

See under **Poetry Magazines**

Poetry Ireland Review

See under **Poetry Magazines**

Poetry Review

See under **Poetry Magazines**

Poetry Scotland

See under **Poetry Magazines**

Poetry Wales

See under **Poetry Magazines**

Ponies Today

TP Publications Ltd, Barn Acre House, Saxtead Green, Suffolk IP13 9QJ
☎01728 685832 Fax 01728 685842
Email trevor@prestige.typo.co.uk
Owner *TP Publications*
Editor *Charlotte Jarvis*

FOUNDED 1998. FIVE ISSUES YEARLY. Magazine for adults who ride, show, breed, exhibit and drive ponies, with the emphasis on native ponies. **Features** All topics relating to ponies covered with the slant on ponies not horses. Length 500–1500 words; photos welcome. **News** Show news and native pony news. Send for free sample copy; phone/write with ideas.

Payment negotiable but modest.

Pony

D.J. Murphy (Publishers) Ltd, Haslemere House, Lower Street, Haslemere, Surrey GU27 2PE
☎01428 651551 Fax 01428 653888
Email pony@djmurphy.co.uk (text only)
Website www.ponymag.com
Owner *D.J. Murphy (Publishers) Ltd*
Editor *Janet Rising*
Assistant Editor *Sarah Lee*
Circulation 32,309

FOUNDED 1948. Lively MONTHLY aimed at 10–16-year-olds. News, instruction on riding, stable management, veterinary care, interviews. Approach in writing with an idea.

Features welcome. Maximum 900 words.

News Written in-house. Photographs and illustrations (serious/cartoon) welcome.

Payment £65 per 1000 words.

Popular Crafts

Nexus House, Azalea Drive, Swanley, Kent BR8 8HU
☎01322 660070 Fax 01322 616319
Website www.popularcrafts.com
Owner *Nexus Special Interests*
Editor *Debbie Moss*
Circulation 32,000

FOUNDED 1980. MONTHLY. Covers crafts of all kinds. Freelance contributions welcome – copy needs to be lively and interesting. Approach in writing with an outline of idea and photographs.

Features Project-based under the following headings: Homecraft; Needlecraft; Popular Craft; Kidscraft; News and Columns. Any craft-related material including projects to make, with full instructions/patterns supplied in all cases; profiles of crafts people and news of craft group activities or successes by individual persons; articles on collecting crafts; personal experiences and anecdotes.

Payment on publication.

PR Week
174 Hammersmith Road, London W6 7JP
☎020 7413 4520 Fax 020 8267 4509
Website www.prweek.com

Owner *Haymarket Business Publications Ltd*
Editor *Kate Nicholas*
Circulation 17,000

FOUNDED 1984. WEEKLY. Contributions accepted from experienced journalists. Approach in writing with an idea.

Features *Ben Bold*
News *David McCormack*
Payment negotiable.

Practical Boat Owner
Westover House, West Quay Road, Poole, Dorset BH15 1JG
☎01202 440820 Fax 01202 440860
Website www.pbo.co.uk

Owner *IPC Media Ltd*
Editor *Rodger Witt*
Circulation 52,800

FOUNDED 1967. MONTHLY magazine of practical information for cruising boat owners. Receives about 1500 mss per year. Interested in hard facts about gear, equipment, pilotage and renovation, etc. from experienced yachtsmen.

Features Technical articles about maintenance, restoration, modifications to cruising boats, power and sail up to 45ft, or reader reports on gear and equipment. European pilotage articles and cruising guides. Approach in writing with synopsis in the first instance.

Payment negotiable.

Practical Caravan
60 Waldegrave Road, Teddington, Middlesex TW11 8LG
☎020 8267 5629 Fax 020 8267 5725
Email practical.caravan@haynet.com
Website www.practicalcaravan.com

Owner *Haymarket Magazines Ltd*
Editor *Carl Rodgerson*
Circulation 47,037

FOUNDED 1967. MONTHLY. Contains caravan reviews, travel features, investigations, products, park reviews. Unsolicited mss welcome on travel relevant only to caravanning/touring vans. No motorcaravan or static van stories. Approach with ideas by phone or letter.

Features Must refer to caravanning, towing. Written in friendly, chatty manner. Features with pictures/transparencies welcome but not essential. Maximum length 2000 words.

Payment negotiable.

Practical Fishkeeping
Apex House, Oundle Road, Peterborough, Cambridgeshire PE2 9NP
☎01733 898100 Fax 01733 898487
Email steve.windsor@ecm.emap.com

Owner *EMAP Apex Publications Ltd*
Managing Editor *Steve Windsor*
Circulation 30,000

MONTHLY. Practical articles on all aspects of fishkeeping. Unsolicited mss welcome. Approach in writing with ideas. Quality photographs of fish always welcome. No fiction or verse.

Practical Gardening
See **Garden Answers**

Practical Parenting
IPC Media Ltd., King's Reach Tower, Stamford Street, London SE1 9LS
☎020 7261 5058 Fax 020 7261 6542

Owner *IPC Media Ltd*
Editor-in-Chief *Jayne Marsden*
Circulation 57,386

FOUNDED 1987. MONTHLY. Practical advice on pregnancy, birth, babycare and childcare up to five years. Submit ideas in writing with synopsis or send mss on spec. Interested in feature articles of up to 3000 words in length, and in readers' experiences/personal viewpoint pieces of between 750–1000 words. All material must be written for the magazine's specifically targeted audience and in-house style.

Payment negotiable.

Practical Photography
Apex House, Oundle Road, Peterborough, Cambridgeshire PE2 9NP
☎01733 898100 Fax 01733 466843
Email practical.photography@ecm.emap.com

Owner *EMAP Active Publications Ltd*
Editor *William Cheung*
Circulation 77,654

THIRTEEN ISSUES YEARLY All types of photography, particularly technique-orientated pictures. No unsolicited mss. Preliminary approach may be made by telephone. Always interested in new ideas.

Features Anything relevant to the world of photography, but not 'the sort of feature produced by staff writers'. Features on technology and humour are two areas worth exploring. Bear in mind that there is a three-month lead-in time. Maximum 2000 words.

News Only 'hot' news applicable to a monthly magazine. Maximum 400 words.

Payment varies.

Practical Wireless

Arrowsmith Court, Station Approach, Broadstone, Dorset BH18 8PW
☎01202 659910 Fax 01202 659950
Email <name>@pwpublishing.ltd.uk
Website www.pwpublishing.ltd.uk
Owner *P.W. Publishing*
Editor *Rob Mannion*
Circulation 27,000

FOUNDED 1932. MONTHLY. News and features relating to amateur radio, radio construction and radio communications. Unsolicited mss welcome. Author's guidelines available (send s.a.e.). Approach by phone with ideas in the first instance. Copy should be supported where possible by artwork, either illustrations, diagrams or photographs.

Payment £54–70 per page.

Practical Woodworking

Nexus Media, Nexus House, Azalea Drive, Swanley, Kent BR8 8HU
☎01322 660070 Fax 01332 616319
Email practical.woodworking@
  nexusmedia.com
Owner *Nexus Media Ltd*
Editor *Mark Chisholm*

FOUNDED 1965. MONTHLY. Contains articles relating to woodworking – projects, techniques, new products, tips, letters, etc. Unsolicited mss welcome. No fiction. Approach with ideas in writing or by phone.

Features Projects, techniques, etc. *Payment* £60–75 per published page.

Prediction

Focus House, Dingwall Avenue, Croydon, Surrey CR9 2TA
☎020 8774 0600 Fax 020 8774 0939
Owner *IPC Media Ltd*
Editor *Jo Logan*
Circulation 35,000

FOUNDED 1936. MONTHLY. Covering astrology and occult-related topics. Unsolicited material

in these areas welcome (about 200–300 mss received every year). Writers' guidelines available on request.

Astrology Pieces should be practical and of general interest. Charts and astro data should accompany them, especially if profiles.

Features Articles on mysteries of the earth, alternative medicine, psychical/occult experiences and phenomena are considered.

News & Views Items of interest to readership welcome. Maximum 300 words.

Pregnancy Magazine

WVIP, 53–79 Highgate Road, London NW5 1TW
☎020 7331 1000 Fax 020 7331 1241
Email dan.bromage@wvip.co.uk
Owner *WVIP*
Editor *Dan Bromage*

BI-MONTHLY magazine for mothers-to-be, giving them the facts they need for successful pregnancy and birth.

Press Gazette

Quantum House, 19 Scarbrook Road, Croydon, Surrey CR9 1LX
☎020 8565 4200 Fax 020 8565 4395
Email pged@qpp.co.uk
Owner *Quantum*
Editor *Philippa Kennedy*
Deputy Editor *Jon Slattery*
Circulation 9,500

WEEKLY magazine for all journalists – in regional and national newspapers, magazines, broadcasting, and online – containing news, features and analysis of all areas of journalism, print and broadcasting. Unsolicited mss welcome; interested in profiles of magazines, broadcasting companies and news agencies, personality profiles, technical and current affairs relating to the world of journalism. Approach with ideas by phone, e-mail, fax or in writing.

Pride

Hamilton House, 55 Battersea Bridge Road, London SW11 3AX
☎020 7228 3110 Fax 020 7228 3129
Website www.urbancity.com
Owner *Carl Cushnie Junior*
Editor *To be appointed*
Circulation 36,000

FOUNDED 1991. MONTHLY lifestyle magazine for Black women with features, beauty, arts and fashion. No unsolicited material; approach in writing with ideas.

Features Issues pertaining to the Black community. 'Ideas and solicited mss are welcomed from new freelancers.' Maximum 2000 words. *Payment* £200. **Fiction** Publishes the occasional short story. Unsolicited mss welcome. Maximum 3000 words. *No payment.* **Beauty** Freelancers used for short features. Maximum 1000 words. *Payment* 15 pence per word.

Prima
197 Marsh Wall, London E14 9SG
☎020 7519 5500 Fax 020 7519 5514
Owner *National Magazine Company*
Editor *Maire Fahey*
Circulation 395,164
FOUNDED 1986. MONTHLY women's magazine.
Features Coordinator *Verity Watkins* Mostly practical and written by specialists, or commissioned from known freelancers. Unsolicited mss not welcome.

Private Eye
6 Carlisle Street, London W1D 3BN
☎020 7437 4017 Fax 020 7437 0705
Email strobes@private-eye.co.uk
Owner *Pressdram*
Editor *Ian Hislop*
Circulation 174,656
FOUNDED 1961. FORTNIGHTLY satirical and investigative magazine. Prospective contributors are best advised to approach the editor in writing. News stories and feature ideas are always welcome, as are cartoons. All jokes written in-house. *Payment* in all cases is 'not great', and length of piece varies as appropriate.

Prospect
4 Bedford Square, London WC1B 3RD
☎020 7255 1281 Fax 020 7255 1279
Email editorial@prospect-magazine.co.uk *or* publishing@prospect-magazine.co.uk
Website www.prospect-magazine.co.uk
Owner *Prospect Publishing Limited*
Editor *David Goodhart*
Circulation 20,000
FOUNDED 1995. MONTHLY. Essays, reviews and research on current/international affairs and cultural issues. No news features. Unsolicited contributions welcome, although more useful to approach in writing with ideas in the first instance.

Psychic News
The Coach House, Stansted Hall, Stansted, Essex CM24 8UD
☎01279 817050 Fax 01279 817051
Website www.snu.org.uk

Owner *Psychic Press 1995 Ltd*
Editor *Lyn Guest de Swarte*
Circulation 40,000
FOUNDED 1932. *Psychic News* is the world's only WEEKLY spiritualist newspaper. It covers subjects such as psychic research, hauntings, ghosts, poltergeists, spiritual healing, survival after death, and paranormal gifts. Unsolicited material considered.

Publishing News
39 Store Street, London WC1E 7DB
☎020 7692 2900 Fax 020 7419 2111
Email mailbox@publishingnews.co.uk
Website www.publishingnews.co.uk
Editor *Rodney Burbeck*
WEEKLY newspaper of the book trade. Hardback and paperback reviews and extensive listings of new paperbacks and hardbacks. Interviews with leading personalities in the trade, authors, agents and features on specialist book areas.

Punch
Trevor House, 100 Brompton Road, London SW3 1ER
☎020 7225 6716 Fax 020 7225 6766
Email edit@punch.co.uk
Website www.punch.co.uk
Owner *Liberty Publishing*
Editor *Richard Brass*
FOUNDED in 1841 and RELAUNCHED in 1996. BI-WEEKLY investigative and gossip magazine. Ideas are welcome; 'phone in the first instance.
Payment negotiable.

Q
Mappin House, 4 Winsley Street, London W1W 8HF
☎020 7436 1515 Fax 020 7312 8247
Website www.qonline.co.uk
Owner *EMAP Metro Publications*
Editor *John McKie*
Circulation 204,014
FOUNDED 1986. MONTHLY. Glossy aimed at educated popular music enthusiasts of all ages. Few opportunities for freelance writers. Unsolicited mss are strongly discouraged. Prospective contributors should approach in writing only.

Quartos Magazine
See **The New Writer**

QWF Magazine
PO Box 1768, Rugby CV21 4ZA
☎01788 334302 Fax 01788 334702
Email jo@qwfmagazine.co.uk

Website www.qwfmagazine.co.uk

Editor *Jo Good*

BI-MONTHLY small press magazine. FOUNDED in 1994, as a showcase for the best in women's short story writing – original and thought-provoking. Only considers stories that are previously unpublished and of less than 4000 words; articles must be less than 1000 words and of interest to the writer. Include covering letter, s.a.e. and brief biography with mss. Also runs script appraisal service and regular short story competitions. For further information and detailed guidelines for contributors, contact the editor at the address above or access the website.

Racing Post (incorporating The Sporting Life)

1 Canada Square, Canary Wharf, London E14 5AP

☎020 7293 3000 Fax 020 7293 3758

Email editor@racingpost.co.uk

Website www.racingpost.co.uk

Owner *Trinity Mirror Plc*

Editor *Alan Byrne*

FOUNDED 1986. DAILY horse racing paper with some general sport. In 1998, following an agreement between the owners of *The Sporting Life* and the *Racing Post*, the two papers merged.

Radio Times

80 Wood Lane, London W12 0TT

☎020 8433 3400 Fax 020 8433 3160

Email radio.times@bbc.co.uk

Website www.radiotimes.com

Owner *BBC Worldwide Limited*

Editor *To be appointed*

Deputy Editor *Liz Vercoe*

Circulation 1.26 million

WEEKLY. UK's leading broadcast listings magazine. The majority of material is provided by freelance and retained writers, but the topicality of the pieces means close consultation with editors is essential. Very unlikely to use unsolicited material. Detailed BBC, ITV, Channel 4, Channel 5 and satellite television and radio listings are accompanied by feature material relevant to the week's output.

Payment by arrangement.

RAIL

Apex House, Oundle Road, Peterborough, Cambridgeshire PE2 9NP

☎01733 898100 Fax 01733 466859

Owner *EMAP Active Ltd*

Managing Editor *Nigel Harris*

Circulation 33,811

FOUNDED 1981. FORTNIGHTLY magazine dedicated to modern railway. News and features, and topical newsworthy events. Unsolicited mss welcome. Approach by phone with ideas. Not interested in personal journey reminiscences. No fiction.

Features By arrangement with the editor. All modern railway British subjects considered. Maximum 2000 words. *Payment* varies/negotiable.

News Any news item welcome. Maximum 500 words. *Payment* varies (up to £100 per 1000 words).

Railway Gazette International

Quadrant House, Sutton, Surrey SM2 5AS

☎020 8652 8608 Fax 020 8652 3738

Website www.railwaygazette.com

Owner *Reed Business Information*

Editor *Murray Hughes*

FOUNDED 1835. MONTHLY magazine written for senior railway managers and engineers worldwide. 'No material for railway enthusiast publications.' Telephone to discuss ideas in the first instance.

The Railway Magazine

IPC Media Ltd., King's Reach Tower, Stamford Street, London SE1 9LS

☎020 7261 5533/5821 Fax 020 7261 5269

Email railway@ipcmedia.com

Website www.ipcmedia.com

Owner *IPC Media Ltd*

Editor *Nick Pigott*

Circulation 33,132

FOUNDED 1897. MONTHLY. Articles, photos and short news stories of a topical nature, covering modern railways, steam preservation and railway history, welcome. Maximum 2000 words, with sketch maps of routes, etc., where appropriate. Unsolicited mss welcome. No poetry.

Payment negotiable.

The Rambler

2nd Floor, Camelford House, 87–90 Albert Embankment, London SE1 7TW

☎020 7339 8500 Fax 020 7339 8501

Email ramblers@london.ramblers.org.uk

Owner *Ramblers' Association*

Editor *Christopher Sparrow*

Circulation 130,000

QUARTERLY. Official magazine of the Ramblers' Association, available to members only. Unsolicited mss welcome. S.a.e. required for return.

Features Freelance features are invited on any aspect of walking in Britain. Length 450–650 words, preferably with good photographs. No general travel articles.

Reader's Digest

11 Westferry Circus, Canary Wharf, London E14 4HE
☎020 7715 8000 Fax 020 7715 8716
Website www.readersdigest.co.uk
Owner *Reader's Digest Association Ltd*
Editor-in-Chief *Russell Twisk*
Circulation 1.1 million

In theory, a good market for general interest features of around 2500 words. However, 'a tiny proportion' comes from freelance writers, all of which are specially commissioned. Toughening up its image with a move into investigative journalism. Opportunities exist for short humorous contributions to regular features – 'Life's Like That', 'Humour in Uniform'. Issues a helpful booklet called 'Writing for Reader's Digest', available by post at £4.50.
Payment up to £200.

The Reader

English Department, University of Liverpool, Liverpool L69 7ZR
Email readers@thereader.co.uk
Website www.thereader.co.uk
Editor *Jane Davis*
Circulation 1200

FOUNDED 1997. BIANNUAL. Poetry, short fiction, literary articles and essays, thought, reviews, recommendations. Contributions from internationally lauded and new voices. Welcomes articles/essays about reading, maximum 2000 words. *Payment* up to £50. Recommendations for good reading, maximum 1000 words. *Payment* £30 approx. Short stories, maximum 2500 words. *Payment* £50 approx. No theoretical style literary discourses. Approach in writing.

Record Collector

43–45 St Mary's Road, Ealing, London W5 5RQ
☎020 8579 1082 Fax 020 8566 2024
Email editor@rcmag.demon.co.uk
Managing Editor *Johnny Dean*
Editor *Andy Davis*

FOUNDED 1979. MONTHLY. Detailed, well-researched articles welcome on any aspect of record collecting or any collectable artist in the field of popular music (1950s–1990s), with com-plete discographies where appropriate. Unsolicited mss welcome. Approach with ideas by phone.
Payment negotiable.

Red

Endeavour House, 189 Shaftesbury Avenue, London WC2H 8JG
☎020 7208 3358 Fax 020 7208 3218
Email alison.williams@ecm.emap.com
Website www.redmagazine.co.uk
Owner *EMAP élan Publications*
Editor *Trish Halpin*
Circulation 155,083

FOUNDED 1998. MONTHLY magazine aimed at the 30-something woman. Will consider material sent in 'on spec' but tends to rely on regular contributors.

Report

ATL, 7 Northumberland Street, London WC2N 5DA
☎020 7930 6441 Fax 020 7925 0529
Owner *Association of Teachers and Lecturers*
Editor *Heather Pinnell*
Circulation 160,000

FOUNDED 1978. EIGHT ISSUES YEARLY during academic terms. Contributions welcome. All submissions should go directly to the editor. Articles should be no more than 800 words and must be of practical interest to the classroom teacher and F.E. lecturers.

Right Now!

PO Box 2085, London W1A 5SX
☎020 8692 7099 Fax 020 8692 7099
Email rightnow@compuserve.com
Website www.right-now.org
Owner *Right Now! Press Ltd*
Editor *Derek Turner*
Circulation 2800

FOUNDED 1993. QUARTERLY right-wing conservative commentary. Welcomes well-documented disputations, news stories and features about British heritage ('the more politically incorrect, the better!'). No fiction or poems. Initial approach in writing.
No payment.

Rugby News

175 Tottenham Court Road, London W1T 7NU
☎020 7323 1944 Fax 020 7323 1943
Website www.rugbynews.net
Owner *Independent Magazines Ltd*

Editor *Graeme Gillespie*
Circulation 44,000

FOUNDED 1987. Contains news, views and features on the UK and the world rugby scene, with special emphasis on clubs, schools, fitness and coaching. Welcomes unsolicited material.

Rugby World

IPC Media Ltd., 23rd Floor, King's Reach Tower, Stamford Street, London SE1 9LS
☎020 7261 6830 Fax 020 7261 5419
Website www.rugbyworld.com
Owner *IPC Media Ltd*
Editor *Paul Morgan*
Circulation 38,500

FOUNDED 1960. MONTHLY. Features of special rugby interest only. Unsolicited contributions welcome but s.a.e. essential for return of material. Prior approach by phone or in writing preferred.

Runner's World

7–10 Chandos Street, London W1M 0AD
☎020 7291 6000 Fax 020 7291 6080
Email rwedit@rodale.co.uk
Website www.runnersworld.co.uk
Owner *Rodale Press*
Editor *Steven Seaton*
Circulation 52,860

FOUNDED 1979. MONTHLY magazine giving practical advice on all areas of distance running including products and training, travel features, news and cross-training advice. Personal running-related articles, famous people who run or off-beat travel articles are welcome. No elite athlete or training articles. Approach with ideas in writing in the first instance.

Running Fitness

2nd Floor, Arcade Chambers, Westgate Arcade, Peterborough, Cambridgeshire PE1 1PY
☎01733 347559 Fax 01733 891378
Owner *Kelsey Publishing*
Editor *Paul Larkins*
Circulation 26,000

FOUNDED 1985. MONTHLY. Instructional articles on running, fitness, and lifestyle, plus running-related activities and health.
Features Specialist knowledge an advantage. Opportunities are wide, but approach with ideas in first instance.
News Opportunities for people stories, especially if backed up by photographs.

Sable

PO Box 33504, London E9 7YE
☎020 8985 9419 Fax 020 8985 9419
Email hotspotwriters@compuserve.com
Owner *S.AK.S. Publications*
Managing Editor *Kadija George*

FOUNDED 2001. QUARTERLY litmag available through direct mail, online and specialist bookshops. Reviews and feature articles for writers of colour and readers interested in ethnically diverse literature. Five new writers in poetry, prose and work in translation per issue. Request submission details. Synopses and ideas welcome in 'Classic Review' and 'Expressions' sections.

Safeway Magazine

Redwood Publishing, 7 Saint Martin's Place, London WC2N 4HA
☎020 7747 0788 Fax 020 7747 0799
Editor *Julie Barton-Breck*
Circulation 1.8 million

FOUNDED 1996. MONTHLY in-store magazine covering food and recipes, beauty, health, family life and ABC cardholder products. Regular freelancers are employed and although outside material is rarely used ideas will be considered for beauty, health, family life and humorous columns. Approach in writing in the first instance.

Saga Magazine

The Saga Building, Middelburg Square, Folkestone, Kent CT20 1AZ
☎01303 771523 Fax 01303 776699
Website www.saga.co.uk
Owner *Saga Publishing Ltd*
Editor *Paul Bach*
Circulation 1.08 million

FOUNDED 1984. MONTHLY. 'Saga Magazine sets out to celebrate the role of older people in society. It reflects their achievements, promotes their skills, protects their interests, and campaigns on their behalf. A warm personal approach, addressing the readership in an up-beat and positive manner, required.' It has a hard core of celebrated commentators/writers (e.g. Clement Freud, Keith Waterhouse) as regular contributors. Articles mostly commissioned or written in-house but exclusive celebrity interviews welcome if appropriate/relevant. Length 1000–1200 words (maximum 1600).

Sailing Today

30 Monmouth Street, Bath BA1 2BW
☎01225 442244 Fax 01225 822793
Email sailingtoday@futurenet.co.uk

Owner *Future Publishing*
Editor *John Kendall*
Deputy Editor *Rupert Holmes*
Development Editor *Keith Colwell*

FOUNDED 1997. MONTHLY practical magazine for cruising sailors. *Sailing Today* covers owning and buying a boat, equipment and products for sailing and is about improving readers' skills, boat maintenance and product tests. Most articles are commissioned but will consider practical features and cruise stories with photos. Approach by telephone or in writing in the first instance.

Sailing with Spirit

4 South View, Nether Heyford, Northampton NN7 3NH
☎01327 342566
Email tigger@gn.apc.org
Website www.onlinehealing.org/sws/
Editor *Keith Beasley*
Circulation 2000

FOUNDED 1996. QUARTERLY holistic magazine for Northamptonshire. Contributors must have local connections and expertise or first-hand experience in matters spiritual, organic or 'green'.

Sainsbury's The Magazine

20 Upper Ground, London SE1 9PD
☎020 7633 0266 Fax 020 7401 9423
Owner *New Crane Publishing*
Editor *Sue Robinson*
Consultant Food Editor *Delia Smith*
Circulation 364,235

FOUNDED 1993. MONTHLY featuring a main core of food and cookery with features, health, beauty, fashion, home, gardening and news. No unsolicited mss. Approach in writing with ideas only in the first instance.

The Salisbury Review

33 Canonbury Park South, London N1 2JW
☎020 7226 7791 Fax 020 7354 0383
Email salisbury-review@easynet.co.uk
Website easyweb.easynet.co.uk/~salisbury-review
Editor *A.D. Harvey*
Managing Editor *Merrie Cave*
Consulting Editor *Roger Scruton*
Circulation 1700

FOUNDED 1982. QUARTERLY magazine of conservative thought. Editorials and features from a right-wing viewpoint. Unsolicited material welcome.

Features Maximum 4000 words.
Reviews Maximum 1000 words.
No payment.

Scotland on Sunday Magazine

See under **National Newspapers (Scotland on Sunday)**

The Scots Magazine

D.C. Thomson & Co., 2 Albert Square, Dundee DD1 9QJ
☎01382 223131 Fax 01382 322214
Email scotsmagazine@dcthomson.co.uk
Website www.scotsmagazine.com
Owner *D.C. Thomson & Co. Ltd*
Editor *John Methven*
Circulation 60,000

FOUNDED 1739. MONTHLY. Covers a wide field of Scottish interests ranging from personalities to wildlife, climbing, reminiscence, history and folklore. Outside contributions welcome; 'staff delighted to discuss in advance by letter'.

The Scottish Farmer

SMG Magazines, 200 Renfield Street, Glasgow G2 3PR
☎0141 302 7700 Fax 0141 302 7799
Email info@calmags.co.uk *or* farmer@calmags.co.uk
Owner *SMG Magazines*
Editor *Alasdair Fletcher*
Circulation 22,000

FOUNDED 1893. WEEKLY. Farmer's magazine covering most aspects of Scottish agriculture. Unsolicited mss welcome. Approach with ideas in writing.

Features *Alasdair Fletcher* Technical articles on agriculture or farming units. 1000–2000 words.

News *John Duckworth* Factual news about farming developments, political, personal and technological. Maximum 800 words.

Weekend Family Pages Rural and craft topics.

Scottish Field

Special Publications, Royston House, Caroline Park, Edinburgh EH5 1QJ
☎0131 551 2942 Fax 0131 551 2938
Email editor@scottishfield.co.uk
Owner *Oban Times*
Editor *Archie Mackenzie*

FOUNDED 1903. MONTHLY. Scotland's quality lifestyle magazine. Unsolicited mss welcome but writers should study the magazine first.

Features Articles of general interest on Scotland and Scots abroad with good photographs or, preferably, colour slides. Approx 1000 words.

Payment negotiable.

Scottish Golfer

Scottish Golf, Gateway East, Technology Park, Dundee DD2 1SW
☎01382 429064 Fax 01382 429001

Owner *Scottish Golf Union*
Editor *Martin Vousden*
Circulation 40,000

FOUNDED mid-1980s. MONTHLY. Features and results, in particular the men's events. No unsolicited mss. Approach in writing with ideas.

Scottish Home & Country

42A Heriot Row, Edinburgh EH3 6ES
☎0131 225 1724 Fax 0131 225 8129
Email magazine@swri.demon.co.uk

Owner *Scottish Women's Rural Institutes*
Editor *Airlie Fleming*
Circulation 12,000

FOUNDED 1924. MONTHLY. Scottish or rural-related issues. Unsolicited mss welcome but reading time may be from 1–2 months. Commissions are rare and tend to go to established contributors only.

Scottish Rugby Magazine

First Press Publishing, 1 Central Quay, Glasgow G3 8DA
☎0141 309 1400 Fax 0141 248 1099
Email editor@scottishrugby.co.uk

Senior Editor *Alex Macleod*
Circulation 19,200

FOUNDED 1990. MONTHLY. Features, club profiles, etc. Approach in writing with ideas.

Scouting Magazine

Gilwell House, Gilwell Park, Chingford, London E4 7QW
☎020 8433 7100 Fax 020 8433 7103

Owner *The Scout Association*
Editor *Anna Sorensen Thomson*
Circulation 20,000

MONTHLY magazine for adults connected to or interested in the Scout Movement. Interested in Scouting-related submissions only.

Payment by negotiation.

Screen

Gilmorehill Centre for Theatre, Film and Television, University of Glasgow, Glasgow G12 8QQ
☎0141 330 5035 Fax 0141 330 3515
Email screen@arts.gla.ac.uk

Publisher *Oxford University Press*
Editors *Annette Kuhn, John Caughie, Simon Frith, Karen Lury, Jackie Stacey*
Editorial Assistant *Caroline Beven*
Circulation 1200

QUARTERLY refereed academic journal of film and television studies for a readership ranging from undergraduates to screen studies academics and media professionals. There are no specific qualifications for acceptance of articles. Straightforward film reviews are not normally published. Check the magazine's style and market in the first instance.

Screen International

33–39 Bowling Green Lane, London EC1R 0DA
☎020 7505 8056 Fax 020 7505 8117
Website www.screendaily.com

Owner *EMAP Communications*
Managing Editor *Leo Barraclough*

International trade paper of the film, video and television industries. Expert freelance writers are occasionally used in all areas. No unsolicited mss. Approach with ideas in writing.

Features *Louise Tutt*
Payment negotiable on NUJ basis.

Sea Breezes

Units 28–30, Spring Valley Industrial Estate, Braddan, Isle of Man IM2 2QS
☎01624 626018 Fax 01624 661655

Owner *Print Centres*
Editor *Captain A.C. Douglas*
Circulation 15,000

FOUNDED 1919. MONTHLY. Covers virtually everything relating to ships and seamen. Unsolicited mss welcome; they should be thoroughly researched and accompanied by relevant photographs. No fiction, poetry, or anything which 'smacks of the romance of the sea'.

Features Factual tales of ships, seamen and the sea, Royal or Merchant Navy, sail or power, nautical history, shipping company histories, epic voyages, etc. Length 1000–4000 words. 'The most readily acceptable work will be that which shows it is clearly the result of first-hand experience or the product of extensive and accurate research.'

Payment £14 per page (about 800 words).

She Magazine

National Magazine House, 72 Broadwick Street, London W1V 2BP
☎020 7439 5000 Fax 020 7312 3981

Owner *National Magazine Co. Ltd*
Editor *Alison Pylkkanen*
Circulation 213,216

Glossy MONTHLY for the thirtysomething woman, addressing her needs as an individual, a partner and a parent. Talks to its readers in an intelligent, humorous and sympathetic way. Features should be about 1500 words long. Approach with ideas in writing. No unsolicited material.
Payment NUJ rates.

Ships Monthly

IPC Country & Leisure Media Ltd, 222 Branston Road, Burton-upon-Trent, Staffordshire DE14 3BT
☎01283 542721 Fax 01283 546436
Email ShipsMonthly@compuserve.com
Owner *IPC Country & Leisure Media Ltd*
Editor *Iain Wakefield*
Circulation 22,000

FOUNDED 1966. MONTHLY A4 format magazine for ship enthusiasts. News, photographs and illustrated articles on all kinds of ships – mercantile and naval, sail and steam, past and present. No yachting. Most articles are commissioned; prospective contributors should telephone in the first instance.

Shoot Magazine

IPC Media Ltd., King's Reach Tower, Stamford Street, London SE1 9LS
☎020 7261 6287 Fax 020 7261 6019
Owner *IPC Media Ltd*
Editor *Colin Mitchell*
Circulation 50,303

FOUNDED 1969. MONTHLY football magazine. No unsolicited mss. Present ideas for news, features or colour photo-features to the editor by letter.
   Features Hard-hitting, topical and off-beat.
   News Items welcome, especially exclusive gossip and transfer speculation.
   Payment negotiable.

Shooting Times & Country Magazine

IPC Media Ltd., King's Reach Tower, Stamford Street, London SE1 9LS
☎020 7261 6180 Fax 020 7261 7179
Owner *IPC Media Ltd*
Editor *Julian Murray-Evans*
Circulation 27,435

FOUNDED 1882. WEEKLY. Covers shooting, fish-

ing and related countryside topics. Unsolicited mss considered.
   Payment negotiable.

Shout Magazine

D.C. Thomson & Co., Albert Square, Dundee, Tayside DD1 9QJ
☎01382 223131 Fax 01382 200880
Email shout@dcthomson.co.uk
Owner *D.C. Thomson Publishers*
Editor *Maria T. Welch*
Circulation 123,360

FOUNDED 1993. FORTNIGHTLY Pop music, soap features, emotional, beauty, fashion, quizzes. Welcomes ideas for fiction, horoscope features and quizzes. Queries by telephone welcome.
   Features *Lesley Macpherson* Write with ideas. Maximum 1500 words. *Payment* varies.
   Fiction *Maria Welch* Supernatural/spooky stories welcome. Max. 1500 words. *Payment* £100.

Shout!

PO Box YR46, Leeds, West Yorkshire LS9 6XG
☎0113 248 5700 Fax 0113 295 6097
Email shoutmag@cwcom.net
Website www.shoutmag.demon.co.uk
Owner/Editor *Mark Michalowski*
Circulation 7000

FOUNDED 1995. MONTHLY lesbian/gay and bisexual news, views, arts and scene for Yorkshire; lgb health and politics. Interested in reviews of Yorkshire lgb events, happenings, news, analysis – 300 to maximum 1000 words. No fiction, fashion or items with no reasonable relevance to Yorkshire and the north.
   Payment £40 per 1000 words.

Shropshire Magazine

77 Wyle Cop, Shrewsbury, Shropshire SY1 1UT
☎01743 362175
Owner *Shropshire Newspapers Ltd*
Editor *Keith Parker*

FOUNDED 1950. MONTHLY. Unsolicited mss welcome but ideas in writing preferred.
   Features Personalities, topical items, historical (e.g. family) of Shropshire; also general interest: homes, weddings, antiques, etc. Maximum 1000 words.
   Payment negotiable 'but modest'.

Sight & Sound

British Film Institute, 21 Stephen Street, London W1T 1LN
☎020 7255 1444 Fax 020 7436 2327

Website www.bfi.org.uk/s&s/
Owner *British Film Institute*
Editor *Nick James*

FOUNDED 1932. MONTHLY. Topical and critical articles on international cinema, with regular columns from the USA and Europe. Length 1000–5000 words. Relevant photographs appreciated. Also book, film and video release reviews. Unsolicited material welcome. Approach in writing with ideas.
Payment by arrangement.

The Sign
See **Hymns Ancient & Modern Ltd** under **UK Publishers**

Ski and Board
The White House, 57–63 Church Road, Wimbledon, London SW19 5SB
☎020 8410 2000 Fax 020 8410 2001
Email s&b@skiclub.co.uk
Website www.skiclub.co.uk
Owner *Ski Club of Great Britain*
Editor *Gill Williams*
Circulation 18,698

FOUNDED 1903. FOUR ISSUES YEARLY. Features from established ski/snowboard writers only.

The Skier and Snowboarder Magazine
Mountain Marketing Ltd., PO Box 386, Sevenoaks, Kent TN13 1AQ
☎01732 779268 Fax 01732 779266
Email skierandsnowboarder@hotmail.com
Owner *Mountain Marketing Ltd*
Editor *Frank Baldwin*
Circulation 20,000

Official magazine to the World Ski and Snowboard Association, UK. SEASONAL. From July to May. FIVE ISSUES YEARLY. Outside contributions welcome.
   Features Various topics covered, including race reports, resort reports, fashion, equipment update, dry slope, school news, new products, health and safety. Crisp, tight, informative copy of 800 words or less preferred.
   News All aspects of skiing news covered.
   Payment negotiable.

Slimming
Greater London House, Hampstead Road, London NW1 7EJ
☎020 7874 0200 Fax 020 7347 1863
Owner *EMAP Esprit*
Editor *Alison Hall*

Circulation 106,029

FOUNDED 1969. ELEVEN ISSUES YEARLY. Leading magazine about slimming, diet and health. Opportunities for freelance contributions on general health (diet-related); psychology related to health and fitness; celebrity interviews. It is best to approach with an idea in writing.
   Payment negotiable.

Smallholder
Hook House, Wimblington March, Cambridgeshire PE15 0QL
☎01326 213333 Fax 01326 213333
Email hock.house@virgin.net
Website www.smallholder.co.uk
Owner *Newsquest*
Editor *Liz Wright*
Circulation 20,000

FOUNDED 1982. MONTHLY. Outside contributions welcome. Send for sample magazine and editorial schedule before submitting anything. Follow up with samples of work to the editor so that style can be assessed for suitability. No poetry or humorous but unfocused personal tales.
   Features New writers always welcome, but must have high level of technical expertise – 'not textbook stuff'. Illustrations and photos welcomed and paid for. Length 750–1500 words.
   News All agricultural and rural news welcome. Length 200–500 words.
   Payment negotiable ('but modest').

Smash Hits
Mappin House, Winsley Street, London W1W 8HF
☎020 7436 1515 Fax 020 7636 5792
Website www.smashhits.net
Owner *EMAP Metro Publications*
Editor *Emma Jones*
Circulation 221,622

FOUNDED 1979. FORTNIGHTLY. Top of the mid-teen market. Unsolicited mss are not accepted, but prospective contributors may approach in writing with ideas.

Snooker Scene
Cavalier House, 202 Hagley Road, Edgbaston, Birmingham B16 9PQ
☎0121 454 2931 Fax 0121 452 1822
Owner *Everton's News Agency*
Editor *Clive Everton*
Circulation 16,000

FOUNDED 1971. MONTHLY. No unsolicited mss. Approach in writing with an idea.

Somerset Magazine

23 Market Street, Crewkerne, Somerset
TA18 7JU
☎01460 270000 Fax 01460 270022
Owner *Community Media Ltd*
Circulation 9000

FOUNDED 1991. MONTHLY magazine with features on any subject of interest (historical, geographical, arts, crafts) to people living in Somerset. Length 1000–1500 words, preferably with illustrations. Unsolicited mss welcome but initial approach in writing preferred.
Payment negotiable.

The Spectator

56 Doughty Street, London WC1N 2LL
☎020 7405 1706 Fax 020 7242 0603
Email editor@spectator.co.uk
Website www.spectator.co.uk
Owner *The Spectator (1828) Ltd*
Editor *Boris Johnson*
Managing Editor *Stuart Reid*
Circulation 56,705

FOUNDED 1828. WEEKLY political and literary magazine. Prospective contributors should write in the first instance to the relevant editor. Unsolicited mss welcome, but no 'follow up' phone calls, please.
Books *Mark Amory*
Payment nominal.

The Sporting Life

See **Racing Post**

Springboard – Writing To Succeed

144 Alexandra Road, Great Wakering, Essex
SS3 0GW
☎01702 216247
Owner/Editor *Sandra Lieberman*
Circulation 200

FOUNDED 1990. QUARTERLY. *Springboard* is not a market for writers but a forum from which they can find encouragement and help. Provides articles, news, market information, competition/folio news directed at helping writers to achieve success. Free to subscribers: a copy of *The Curate's Egg* – a collection of poetry submitted.

The Squash Times

PO Box 36, Brecon LD3 0WD
☎01874 754033
Editor *Mr R. Richardson*
FOUNDED 1980. QUARTERLY. Events, players, news, fashion and footwear, rackets, facilities, technique and tactics.

Staffordshire Life

The Publishing Centre, Derby Street, Stafford
ST16 2DT
☎01785 257700 Fax 01785 253287
Email editor@staffordshirelife.co.uk
Owner *The Staffordshire Newsletter*
Editor *Philip Thurlow-Craig*
Circulation 20,000

FOUNDED 1982. ELEVEN ISSUES YEARLY. Full-colour county magazine devoted to Staffordshire, its surroundings and people. Contributions welcome. Approach in writing with ideas.
Features Maximum 1200 words.
Fashion Copy must be supported by photographs.
Payment NUJ rates.

The Stage (incorporating **Television Today**)

47 Bermondsey Street, London SE1 3XT
☎020 7403 1818 Fax 020 7357 9287
Email info@thestage.co.uk
Website www.thestage.co.uk
Owner *The Stage Newspaper Ltd*
Editor *Brian Attwood*
Circulation 41,500

FOUNDED 1880. WEEKLY. No unsolicited mss. Prospective contributors should write with ideas in the first instance.
Features Preference for middle-market, tabloid-style articles. 'Puff pieces', PR plugs and extended production notes will not be considered. Maximum 800 words.
News News stories from outside London are always welcome. Maximum 300 words.
Payment £100 per 1000 words.

Stamp Magazine

Focus House, Dingwall Avenue, Croydon
CR9 2TA
☎020 8774 0772 Fax 020 8781 6044
Email stampmagazine@ipcmedia.com
Owner *IPC Media Ltd*
Editor *Steve Fairclough*
Circulation 12,000

FOUNDED 1934. MONTHLY news and features on the world of stamp collecting from the past to the present day. Interested in articles by experts on particular countries or themes such as subject matter illustrated on stamps – dogs, politics, etc. Approach in writing.

News *David Stanford* News of latest stamp issues or industry news. Maximum 500 words.

Features *Steve Fairclough* Any features welcome on famous stamps, rarities, postmarks, postal history, exhibitions, postcards, personal collections, auctions. Must be illustrated with colour images ('we can arrange for photography of original stamps'). Maximum 2500 words, or 5000 for 2-part expert piece.

Payment negotiable.

Stand Magazine
See under **Poetry Magazines**

Staple New Writing
See under **Poetry Magazines**

The Strad
7 St. John's Road, Harrow, Middlesex HA1 2EE
☎020 8863 2020 Fax 020 8863 2444
Email thestrad@orpheuspublications.com
Website www.thestrad.com

Owner *Orpheus Publications Ltd*
Editor *Joanna Pieters*
Circulation 17,500

FOUNDED 1890. MONTHLY for classical string musicians, makers and enthusiasts. Unsolicited mss accepted occasionally 'though acknowledgement/return not guaranteed'.

Features Profiles of string players, teachers, luthiers and musical instruments, also relevant research. Maximum 2000 words.

Reviews *Naomi Sadler, Peter Quantrill.*

Payment £110 per 1000 words.

Suffolk and Norfolk Life
Barn Acre House, Saxtead Green, Suffolk IP13 9QJ
☎01728 685832 Fax 01728 685842

Owner *Today Magazines Ltd*
Editor *Kevin Davis*
Circulation 17,000

FOUNDED 1989. MONTHLY. General interest, local stories, historical, personalities, wine, travel, food. Unsolicited mss welcome. Approach by phone or in writing with ideas. Not interested in anything which does not relate specifically to East Anglia.

Features *Kevin Davis* Maximum 1500 words, with photos.

News *Kevin Davis* Maximum 1000 words, with photos.

Special Pages *William Locks* Study the magazine for guidelines. Maximum 1500 words.

Payment £25 (news); £30 (other).

Sugar Magazine
17 Berners Street, London W1T 3LN
☎020 7664 6440 Fax 020 7703 3409

Editor *Jennifer Stringer*
Editorial Director *Lysanne Currie*
Circulation 422,179

FOUNDED 1994. MONTHLY. Everything that might interest the teenage girl. No unsolicited mss. Will consider ideas or contacts for real-life features. No fiction. Approach in writing in the first instance.

Sunday Post Magazine
See under **National Newspapers (Sunday Post, Dundee)**

Sunday Times Magazine
See under **National Newspapers (The Sunday Times)**

Superbike Magazine
Focus House, Dingwall Avenue, Croydon, Surrey CR9 2TA
☎020 8686 2599 Fax 020 8774 0936

Publisher *Keith Foster*
Editor *Kenny Pryde*
Circulation 70,483

FOUNDED 1977. MONTHLY. Dedicated to all that is best and most exciting in the world of high-performance motorcycling. Unsolicited mss, synopses and ideas welcome.

Surrey County
Datateam Publishing Ltd, London Road, Maidstone, Kent ME15 8LY
☎01622 687031 Fax 01622 757646

Owner *Datateam Publishing Ltd*
Editor *Ian Trevett*
Circulation 10,000

FOUNDED 1970. MONTHLY. Strong Surrey interest plus fashion, food, books, gardening wildlife, motoring, property, sport, interiors with local links. Unsolicited mss welcome. Interested in anything with a genuine Surrey connection. No fiction or non-Surrey subjects. Approach in writing with ideas. Maximum length 1500 words. *Payment* negotiable.

Sussex Life
Baskerville Place, 28 Teville Road, Worthing, West Sussex BN11 1UG
☎01903 218719 Fax 01903 820193
Email ian@sussexlife.co.uk
Website www.sussexlife.com

Owner *Sussex Life Ltd*

Editor *Trudi Linscer*
Circulation 70,000

FOUNDED 1965. MONTHLY. Sussex and general interest magazine. Regular supplements on education, fashion, homes and gardens. Interested in investigative, journalistic pieces relevant to the area and celebrity profiles. Unsolicited mss, synopses and ideas in writing welcome. Minimum 500 words.
Payment £15 per 500 words and picture.

Swimming Times
41 Granby Street, Loughborough,
Leicestershire LE11 3DU
☎01509 632207 Fax 01509 632213
Owner *Amateur Swimming Association*
Editor *P. Hassall*
Circulation 20,000

FOUNDED 1923. MONTHLY about competitive swimming and associated subjects. Unsolicited mss welcome.
Features Technical articles on swimming, water polo, diving or synchronised swimming. Length and payment negotiable.

The Tablet
1 King Street Cloisters, Clifton Walk, London W6 0QZ
☎020 8748 8484 Fax 020 8748 1550
Email thetablet@tablet.co.uk
Owner *The Tablet Publishing Co Ltd*
Editor *John Wilkins*
Circulation 21,285

FOUNDED 1840. WEEKLY. Quality international Roman Catholic magazine featuring articles – political, social, cultural, theological or spiritual – of interest to concerned Christian laity and clergy. Unsolicited material welcome (1500 words) if relevant to magazine's style and market. All approaches should be made in writing.
Payment from about £75.

Take a Break
Academic House, 24–28 Oval Road, London NW1 7DT
☎020 7241 8000 Fax 020 7241 8052
Email tab.features@bauer.co.uk
Owner *H. Bauer Publishing Ltd*
Editor *John Dale*
Circulation 1.14 million

FOUNDED 1990. WEEKLY. True-life feature magazine. Approach with ideas in writing.
News/Features Always on the look-out

for good, true-life stories. Maximum 1200 words. *Payment* negotiable.
Fiction Sharp, succinct stories which are well told and often with a twist at the end. All categories, provided it is relevant to the magazine's style and market. Maximum 1000 words. *Payment* negotiable.

Tatler
Vogue House, Hanover Square, London W1S 1JU
☎020 7499 9080 Fax 020 7409 0451
Website www.tatler.co.uk
Owner *Condé Nast Publications Ltd*
Editor *Geordie Greig*
Circulation 82,071

Up-market glossy from the Condé Nast stable. New writers should send in copies of either published work or unpublished material; writers of promise will be taken up. The magazine works largely on a commission basis: they are unlikely to publish unsolicited features, but will ask writers to work to specific projects.
Features *Giles Kime*

Telegraph Magazine
See under **National Newspapers (The Daily Telegraph)**

The Tennis Times
PO Box 36, Brecon LD3 0WD
☎01874 754033
Editor *Mr R. Richardson*

FOUNDED 1980. QUARTERLY. Events, players, news, fashion and footwear, rackets, facilities, technique and tactics.

TGO (The Great Outdoors)
SMG Magazines, 200 Renfield Street, Glasgow G2 3PR
☎0141 302 7700 Fax 0141 302 7799
Email tgo@calmags.co.uk
Owner *SMG Ltd*
Editor *Cameron McNeish*
Circulation 22,000

FOUNDED 1978. MONTHLY. Deals with walking, backpacking and wild country topics. Unsolicited mss are welcome.
Features Well-written and illustrated items on relevant topics. Maximum 2500 words. Colour photographs only, please.
News Short topical items (or photographs). Maximum 300 words.
Payment £200–300 for features; £10–20 for news.

that's life!
Academic House, 24–28 Oval Road, London
NW1 7DT
☎020 7241 8000   Fax 020 7241 8008

Owner *H. Bauer Publishing Ltd*
Editor *Christabel Smith*
Circulation 569,804

FOUNDED 1995. WEEKLY. True-life stories, puzzles, health, homes, parenting, cookery and fun.
Features *Don Smith* Maximum 1600 words. *Payment* £650.
Fiction *Emma Fabian* 1200 words. *Payment* £200–300.

Theologia Cambrensis
Church in Wales Centre, 39 Cathedral Place, Cardiff CF11 9XF
☎029 2023 1638   Fax 029 2023 8835

Owner *The Church in Wales*
Editor *Rev. Gareth Williams*

FOUNDED 1988. THREE ISSUES YEARLY. Concerned exclusively with theology and news of theological interest. Includes religious poetry, letters and book reviews (provided they have a scholarly bias). No secular material. Unsolicited mss welcome. Approach in writing with ideas.

The Third Alternative
5 Martins Lane, Witcham, Ely,
Cambridgeshire CB6 2LB
☎01353 777931
Email ttapress@aol.com
Website www.tta-press.freewire.co.uk

Owner *TTA Press*
Editor *Andy Cox*

FOUNDED 1993. Quarterly A4 colour magazine of horror, fantasy, science fiction and cross-genre fiction, plus interviews, profiles, comment, cinema and artwork. Publishes talented newcomers alongside famous authors. Unsolicited mss welcome if accompanied by s.a.e. or e-mail address for overseas submissions (no length restriction, but no novels or serialisations). Queries and letters welcome via e-mail but submissions as hard copy only. Potential contributors are advised to study the magazine. Contracts are exchanged upon acceptance; payment is upon publication. Winner of several British Fantasy Awards. The magazine is supported by **Eastern Arts** and the **Arts Council of England**.

This England
PO Box 52, Cheltenham, Gloucestershire GL50 1YQ
☎01242 537900   Fax 01242 537901

Owner *This England Ltd*

Editor *Roy Faiers*
Circulation 200,000

FOUNDED 1968. QUARTERLY, with a strong overseas readership. Celebration of England and all things English: famous people, natural beauty, towns and villages, history, traditions, customs and legends, crafts, etc. Generally a rural basis, with the 'Forgetmenots' section publishing readers' recollections and nostalgia. Up to one hundred unsolicited pieces received each week. Unsolicited mss/ideas welcome. Length 250–2000 words.
Payment £25 per 1000 words.

Time
Brettenham House, Lancaster Place, London WC2E 7TL
☎020 7499 4080   Fax 020 7322 1259
Website www.timeeurope.com

Owner *Time Warner, Inc.*
Editors (Europe, Middle East, Africa) *Ann Morrison, Donald Morrison*
Circulation 5.46 million

FOUNDED 1923. WEEKLY current affairs and news magazine. There are few opportunities for freelancers on *Time* as almost all the magazine's content is written by staff members from various bureaux around the world. No unsolicited mss.

Time Out
Universal House, 251 Tottenham Court Road, London W1T 7AB
☎020 7813 3000   Fax 020 7813 6001
Website www.timeout.com

Publisher *Tony Elliott*
Editor *Laura Lee Davies*
Circulation 98,839

FOUNDED 1968. WEEKLY magazine of news and entertainment in London.
Features *Jessica Cargill Thompson* 'Usually written by staff writers or commissioned, but it's always worth submitting an idea by post if particularly apt to the magazine.' 1000–2000 words.
News *Ruth Bloomfield* Despite having a permanent team of staff news writers, sometimes willing to accept contributions from new journalists 'should their material be relevant to the issue'.
Payment £164 per 1000 words.

The Times Educational Supplement
Admiral House, 66–68 East Smithfield, London E1W 1BX
☎020 7782 3000   Fax 020 7782 3200
Email editor@tes.co.uk *or* copy@tes.co.uk

Website www.tes.co.uk
Owner *News International*
Editor *Bob Doe*
Circulation 134,752
FOUNDED 1910. WEEKLY. New contributors are welcome and should fax ideas on one sheet of A4 for news, features or reviews.

Opinion *Jeremy Sutcliffe* 'Platform': a weekly slot for a well-informed and cogently argued viewpoint. Maximum 1200 words. 'Another Voice': a shorter comment on an issue of the day by non-education professionals. Maximum 700 words.

School Management *Neil Levis/* **Governors** *Karen Thornton* Weekly pages on practical issues for school governors and managers. Maximum 800 words.

Research Focus *David Budge*

Further Education *Ian Nash* Includes post-16 education and training in colleges, work and the wider community. Aimed at everyone from teachers/lecturers to leaders and opinion formers in lifelong learning. News, features, comment and opinion on all aspects of college life welcome. Length from 350 words (news) to 1000 maximum (features).

Friday A weekly magazine with *The TES* which includes:

Features *Sarah Bayliss* Unsolicited features are rarely accepted but ideas are welcome accompanied by cuttings and/or c.v. Length from 1000–2000 words.

Arts and Books *Heather Neill*
Resources *Yolanda Brooks*
Curriculum Materials *Mary Cruickshank*

Talkback *Jill Craven* Short, first person pieces, maximum 650 words, are welcome for consideration. Humour from teachers is encouraged, especially for the 'Thank God it's Friday' column.

You and Your Job *Jill Craven*

Online (Computers in Education) *Merlin John* A magazine devoted to information and communications technology appearing with *The TES* nine times a year.

Curriculum Specials *Joyce Arnold* New termly magazines for subject teachers appearing with *The TES*. Subjects covered: science and technology (includes food, textiles, graphics), mathematics, English, music and arts, modern languages, humanities and special needs. Articles should relate to current educational practice. Age range covered is primary to sixth form. Maximum 600–800 words.

Special Issues Occasional pull-out magazine on topics including school management (*Neil Levis*), first appointments (*Jill Craven*), business links (*Ian Nash*), school visits –*Going Places* – (*Yolanda Brooks*).

Primary *Diane Hofkins* A monthly A4 glossy magazine published separately from *The TES*. Articles should aim to help teachers think about their work or provide ideas for teaching. Length no more than 1000 words. It is advisable to send in a proposal before submitting a completed article.

The Times Educational Supplement Scotland

Scott House, 10 South St Andrew Street, Edinburgh EH2 2AZ
☎0131 557 1133 Fax 0131 558 1155
Email scoted@tes.co.uk
Website www.tes.co.uk
Owner *TSL Education Ltd*
Editor *Neil Munro*
Circulation 9000
FOUNDED 1965. WEEKLY. Unsolicited mss welcome.

Features Articles on education in Scotland. Maximum 1000 words.

News Items on education in Scotland. Maximum 600 words.

The Times Higher Education Supplement

Admiral House, 66–68 East Smithfield, London E1W 1BX
☎020 7782 3000 Fax 020 7782 3300
Email editor@thes.co.uk
Website www.thes.co.uk
Owner *News International*
Editor *Auriol Stevens*
Circulation 28,300
FOUNDED 1971. WEEKLY. Unsolicited mss are welcome but most articles and *all* book reviews are commissioned. 'In most cases it is better to write, but in the case of news stories it is all right to phone.'

Books *Andrew Robinson*

Features *Mandy Garner* Most articles are commissioned from academics in higher education.

News *Mary Cook* Freelance opportunities very occasionally.

Science *Steve Farrar*
Science Books *Andrew Robinson*
Foreign *David Jobbins*
Payment by negotiation.

The Times Literary Supplement

Admiral House, 66–68 East Smithfield,
London E1W 1BX
☎020 7782 3000 Fax 020 7782 3100
Website www.the-tls.co.uk

Owner *TSL Education Ltd*
Editor *Ferdinand Mount*
Circulation 35,000

FOUNDED 1902. WEEKLY review of literature.
Contributors should approach in writing and
be familiar with the general level of writing in
the *TLS*.

Literary Discoveries *Alan Jenkins*
Poems *Mick Imlah*
News *Ferdinand Mount* News stories and
general articles concerned with literature, publishing and new intellectual developments anywhere in the world. Length by arrangement.
Payment by arrangement.

Titbits

2 Caversham Street, London SW3 4AH
☎020 7351 4995 Fax 020 7351 4995

Owner *Sport Newspapers Ltd*
Editor *James Hughes*
Circulation 150,000

FOUNDED 1895. MONTHLY. Consumer magazine for men covering show business and general interests. Unsolicited mss and ideas in writing welcome. Maximum 3000 words. News,
features, particularly photofeatures (colour),
and fiction.
Payment negotiable.

Today's Golfer

Bretton Court, Bretton, Peterborough,
Cambridgeshire PE3 8DZ
☎01733 264666 Fax 01733 465248

Owner *EMAP Active Ltd*
Editor *Neil Pope*
Deputy Editor *John McKenzie*
Circulation 83,844

FOUNDED 1988. MONTHLY. Golf instruction,
features, player profiles and news. Most features
written in-house but unsolicited mss will be
considered. Approach in writing with ideas.
Not interested in instruction material from
outside contributors.
Features/News *Kevin Brown* Opinion,
player profiles and general golf-related features.

Top of the Pops Magazine

Room A1136, Woodlands, 80 Wood Lane,
London W12 0TT
☎020 8433 3910 Fax 020 8433 2694
Website www.beeb.com/totp

Owner *BBC Worldwide Publishing*
Editor *Corinna Shaffer*
Circulation 305,122

FOUNDED 1995. MONTHLY teenage pop music
magazine with a lighthearted and humorous
approach. No unsolicited material apart from
pop star interviews.

Total Film

99 Baker Street, London W1U 6FP
☎020 7317 2600 Fax 020 7317 1123
Email totalfilm@futurenet.co.uk
Website www.totalfilm.com

Owner *Future Publishing*
Editor *Matt Mueller*
Circulation 77,000

FOUNDED 1997. MONTHLY reviews-based
movie magazine. Interested in ideas for features,
not necessarily tied in to specific releases, and
humour items. No reviews or interviews with
celebrities/directors. Approach by post or e-mail.

Total Football

30 Monmouth Street, Bath BA1 2BW
☎01225 442244 Fax 01225 732248
Email gary.tipp@futurenet.co.uk

Owner *Future Publishing*
Editor *Gary Tipp*
Circulation 25,177

FOUNDED 1995. MONTHLY. News, features and
reviews covering all aspects of domestic and
international football. Contributions welcome.
Features *Alex Murphy* New and interesting
angles; particularly, funny pieces and fan-based
articles. 2000 words maximum. *Payment* negotiable.
News *Alex Murphy* Unusual stories from all
areas of the game. 500 words maximum.
Payment £75 per 500 words.

Traditional Woodworking

The Well House, High Street, Burton on
Trent, Staffordshire DE14 1JQ
☎01283 742950 Fax 01283 742966

Owner *Waterways World*
Editor *Alan Kidd*

FOUNDED 1988. MONTHLY. Features workshop
projects, techniques, reviews of the latest woodworking tools and equipment, general articles on
woodworking and furniture making. Supplements: *Powertools Quarterly* and *Powertools Guide*.
Features Technical features and furniture
projects welcome. The latter must include drawings and cutting lists. A photograph of the piece
is required before commissioning. Approach in
writing in the first instance. *Payment* negotiable.

Trail

Bretton Court, Bretton, Peterborough,
Cambridgeshire PE3 8DZ
☎01733 264666 Fax 01733 282654
Website www.trailmag.com

Owner *EMAP Active Publishing Ltd*
Editor *Ed Kenyon*
Circulation 36,450

FOUNDED 1990. MONTHLY. Gear reports,
where to walk and practical advice for the hill-
walker and long distance walker. Inspirational
reads on people and outdoor/walking issues.
Health, fitness and injury prevention for high
level walkers and outdoor lovers. Approach by
phone or in writing in the first instance.

Features *Guy Procter* Very limited requirement for overseas articles, 'written to our style'.
Ask for guidelines. Maximum 2000 words.

Limited requirement for guided walks articles. Specialist writers only. Ask for guidelines.
750–2000 words (depending on subject).

Payment £80 per 1000 words.

Traveller

45–49 Brompton Road, London SW3 1DE
☎020 7589 0500 Fax 020 7581 1357
Email traveller@wexas.com
Website www.traveller.org.uk

Owner *Wexas International*
Editor *Jonathan Lorie*
Circulation 35,359

FOUNDED 1970. QUARTERLY.

Features High quality, personal narratives
of remarkable journeys. Articles should be off-
beat, adventurous, authentic. No mainstream
destinations. For guidelines, see website.
Articles must be accompanied by professional
quality, original slides. Freelance articles considered. Maximum 1600 words.

Payment £150 per 1000 words.

Trout Fisherman

EMAP Active Ltd, Bushfield House,
Orton Centre, Peterborough, Cambridgeshire
PE2 5UW
☎01733 237111 Fax 01733 465658

Owner *EMAP Active Ltd*
Editor *Andrew James*
Circulation 42,220

FOUNDED 1977. MONTHLY instructive magazine on trout fishing. Most of the articles are
commissioned, but unsolicited mss and quality
colour transparencies welcome.

Features Maximum 2500 words.
Payment varies.

TVTimes

IPC Media Ltd., King's Reach Tower,
Stamford Street, London SE1 9LS
☎020 7261 7000 Fax 020 7261 7777

Owner *IPC Media Ltd*
Editor *Peter Genower*
Circulation 689,137

FOUNDED 1955. WEEKLY magazine of listings
and features serving the viewers of independent
television, BBC, satellite and radio. Almost no
freelance contributions used, except where the
writer is known and trusted by the magazine.
No unsolicited contributions.

Ulster Tatler

39 Boucher Road, Belfast BT12 6UT
☎028 9068 1371 Fax 028 9038 1915
Email ulstertat@aol.com
Website www.ulstertatler.com

Owner/Editor *Richard Sherry*
Circulation 15,000

FOUNDED 1965. MONTHLY. Articles of local
interest and social functions appealing to
Northern Ireland's ABC1 population. Welcomes unsolicited material; approach by phone
or in writing in the first instance.

Features *Noreen Dorman* Maximum 1500
words.
Fiction *Richard Sherry* Maximum 3000
words.

The Universe

St James's Buildings, Oxford Street,
Manchester M1 6FP
☎0161 236 8856 Fax 0161 236 8530
Website www.the-universe.net

Owner *Gabriel Communications Ltd*
Editor *Joe Kelly*
Circulation 60,000

Occasional use of new writers, but a substantial
network of regular contributors already exists.
Interested in a very wide range of material: all
subjects which might bear on Christian life.
Fiction not normally accepted.

Payment negotiable.

Vector

See **British Science Fiction Association**
under **Professional Associations**

The Vegan

Donald Watson House, 7 Battle Road, St
Leonards on Sea, East Sussex TN37 7AA
☎01424 427393 Fax 01424 717064
Email terry@vegansociety.com

Website www.vegansociety.com
Owner *Vegan Society*
Editor *Terry Bevis*
Circulation 5000

FOUNDED 1944. QUARTERLY. Deals with the ecological, ethical and health aspects of veganism. Unsolicited mss welcome. Maximum 2000 words.
Payment negotiable.

Verbatim The Language Quarterly

PO Box 156, Chearsley, Aylesbury, Buckinghamshire HP18 0DQ
☎01844 208474
Email verbatim.uk@tesco.net
Website www.verbatimmag.com
Owner *Word, Inc.*
Editor *Erin McKean*

FOUNDED in 1974 by Laurence Urdang. QUARTERLY journal devoted to what is amusing, interesting and engaging about the English language and languages in general. Will consider unsolicited material but write for writer's guidelines in the first instance. For a sample copy of the magazine, send 50p (stamp or IRC).
Payment ranges from £20–300, 'depending on length, wit and other merit'.

Vogue

Vogue House, Hanover Square, London W1S 1JU
☎020 7499 9080 Fax 020 7493 1345
Website www.vogue.co.uk
Owner *Condé Nast Publications Ltd*
Editor *Alexandra Shulman*
Circulation 202,694

Condé Nast Magazines tend to use known writers and commission what's needed, rather than using unsolicited mss. Contacts are useful.
Features *Laura Tennant* Upmarket general interest rather than 'women's'. Good proportion of highbrow art and literary articles, as well as travel, gardens, food, home interest and reviews.

The Voice Newspaper

234–244 Stockwell Road, London SW9 9SP
☎020 7737 7377 Fax 020 7274 8994
Email mike.best@the-voice.co.uk
Website www.voice-online.co.uk
Owner *Val McCalla*
Editor-in-Chief *Mike Best*
Circulation 40,000

FOUNDED 1982. WEEKLY newspaper for the Afro Caribbean community. News, features, arts, reviews and special pull-out of jobs and sport. Open to ideas for features, news and arts items; approach in writing.
Payment negotiable.

voiceofshooting.com

BASC, Marford Mill, Rossett, Wrexham, Clwyd LL12 0HL
☎01244 573000 Fax 01244 573001
Owner *The British Association for Shooting and Conservation (BASC)*
Editor *Jeffrey Olstead*
Circulation 120,000

SIX ISSUES PER YEAR. Good articles and stories on shooting, conservation and related areas may be considered although most material is produced in-house. Maximum 1500 words.
Payment negotiable.

Voyager

Mediamark Publishing International, 11 Kingsway, London WC2B 6PH
☎020 7212 9000 Fax 020 7212 9001
Email info@mediamark.co.uk
Owner *Mediamark/bmi british midland*
Editor *Howard Rombough*
Circulation 54,191

TEN ISSUES PER YEAR. In-flight magazine of bmi british midland. Lifestyle features and profiles, plus British Midland information. No unsolicited mss. Approach in writing with ideas in the first instance. No destination travel articles.

The Wanton Spirit

See **Storyteller-UK** under **Electronic Publishing and Other Services**

The War Cry

101 Newington Causeway, London SE1 6BN
☎020 7367 4900 Fax 020 7367 4710
Email warcry@salvationarmy.org.uk
Website www.salvationarmy.org.uk/warcry
Owner *The Salvation Army*
Editor *Major Nigel Bovey*
Circulation 80,000

FOUNDED 1879. WEEKLY magazine containing Christian comments on current issues. Unsolicited mss welcome if appropriate to contents. No fiction or poetry. Approach by phone with ideas.
News relating to Christian Church or social issues. Maximum length 500 words. *Payment* £20 per article.
Features Magazine-style articles of interest to the 'man/woman-in-the-street'. Maximum length 500 words. *Payment* £20 per article.

Wasafiri

Dept of English & Drama, Queen Mary and
Westfield College, Mile End Road, London
E1 4NS
☎020 7882 3120   Fax 020 7882 3357
Email wasafiri@qmw.ac.uk
Website www.english.qmw.ac.uk/wasafiri
Editor *Susheila Nasta*
Managing Editor *Richard Dyer*
Reviews Editor *Paola Marchionni*

BI-ANNUAL literary journal of African, Asian,
Black British and Caribbean culture. Short
stories, poetry, reviews, interviews, criticism and
cross cultural debate, film and literature.
Illustrations in b&w. Send double-spaced mss, in
duplicate, with s.a.e. *Payment* negotiable.

The Water Gardener

Winchester Court, 1 Forum Place, Hatfield,
Hertfordshire AL10 0RN
☎01707 273999   Fax 01707 276555
Email watergardener@trmg.co.uk
Website www.trmg.co.uk
Owner *TRMG*
Publisher *Susie Muir*
Circulation 23,568

FOUNDED 1994. MONTHLY. Everything relevant
to water gardening. Will consider photonews
items and features on aspects of the subject; write
with idea in the first instance. Maximum 2000
words. *Payment* by negotiation.

Waterways World

The Well House, High Street, Burton on
Trent, Staffordshire DE14 1JQ
☎01283 742950   Fax 01283 742957
Email wwedit@the-wellhouse.com
Owner *Waterways World Ltd*
Editor *Hugh Potter*
Circulation 22,408

FOUNDED 1972. MONTHLY magazine for inland
waterway enthusiasts. Unsolicited mss welcome,
provided the writer has a good knowledge of the
subject. No fiction.
  Features *Hugh Potter* Articles (preferably
illustrated) are published on all aspects of inland
waterways in Britain and abroad, including
recreational and commercial boating on rivers
and canals.
  News *Chris Daniels* Maximum 500 words.
Payment £37 per 1000 words.

Waymark

IPROW, PO Box 78, Skipton, North
Yorkshire BD23 4UP

Email comms@iprow.co.uk
Website www.iprow.co.uk
Editor *Clare Denby*
Circulation 1000

FOUNDED 1986. THREE ISSUES YEARLY. Journal
of the Institute of Public Rights of Way Officers.
Glossy, spot colour magazine for countryside
access managers in England and Wales, employed throughout the public and private sectors.
Available to non-members by subscription.
Read by politicians, landowners, environmental
lobbyists and countryside access users.
  News Most produced in-house but some
opportunities for original/off-beat items.
Maximum 500 words.
  Features Ideas welcome on any topic
broadly relating to the British countryside and
public access to it. Controversial, thought provoking pieces readily considered. Maximum
1750 words.
  Special Pages Cartoons or brief humorous
items on an access or countryside/environ-
mental theme welcome. Send ideas in writing
with s.a.e. initially.
  Payment negotiable, up to £35.

Wedding and Home

IPC Media Ltd., King's Reach Tower,
Stamford Street, London SE1 9LS
☎020 7261 7471   Fax 020 7261 7459
Email weddingandhome@ipcmedia.com
Owner *IPC Media Ltd*
Editor *Christine Hayes*
Circulation 56,386

FOUNDED 1985. BI-MONTHLY offering ideas and
inspiration for women planning their wedding.
Most features are written in-house or commissioned from known freelancers. Unsolicited mss
are not welcome, but approaches may be made
in writing.

Weekly News

D.C. Thomson & Co. Ltd., Albert Square,
Dundee DD1 9QJ
☎01382 223131   Fax 01382 201390
Owner *D.C. Thomson & Co. Ltd*
Editor *David Hishmurgh*
Circulation 206,302

FOUNDED 1855. WEEKLY. Newsy, family-
orientated magazine designed to appeal to the
busy housewife. 'We get a lot of unsolicited
stuff and there is great loss of life among them.'
Usually commissions, but writers of promise
will be taken up. Series include showbiz, royals
and television. No fiction.
  Payment negotiable.

West Lothian Life

Ballencrieff Cottage, Ballencrieff Toll,
Bathgate, West Lothian EH48 4LD
☎01506 632728 Fax 01506 635444
Email pages@clara.net
Website home.clara.net/pages

Owner *Pages Editorial & Publishing Services*
Editor *Susan Coon*

QUARTERLY county magazine for people who
live, work or have an interest in West Lothian.
Includes three or four major features (1500
words) on successful people, businesses or initiatives. A local walk takes up the centre spread.
Regular articles by experts on collectables, property, interior design, cookery and local gardening, plus news items, letters and a competition.
Freelance writers used exclusively for main features. Phone first to discuss content and timing.

Payment by arrangement.

What Car?

60 Waldegrave Road, Teddington, Middlesex
TW11 8LG
☎020 8267 5688 Fax 020 8267 5750
Email whatcar@haynet.com
Website www.whatcar.co.uk

Owner *Haymarket Motoring Publications Ltd*
Editor *Steve Fowler*
Circulation 153,164

MONTHLY. The car buyer's bible, *What Car?*
concentrates on road test comparisons of new
cars, news and buying advice on used cars, as
well as a strong consumer section. Some scope
for freelancers. Testing is only offered to the
few, and general articles on aspects of driving
are only accepted from writers known and
trusted by the magazine. No unsolicited mss.

Payment negotiable.

What Hi-Fi? Sound & Vision

38–42 Hampton Road, Teddington,
Middlesex TW11 0JE
☎020 8943 5000 Fax 020 8267 5019
Website www.whathifi.com

Owner *Haymarket Magazines Ltd*
Publishing Director *Kevin Costello*
  Editor *Andy Clough*
Circulation 75,000

FOUNDED 1976. MONTHLY. Features on hi-fi
and new technology. No unsolicited contributions. Prior consultation with the editor essential.

Features General or more specific on hi-fi
and new technology pertinent to the consumer
electronics market.

Reviews Specific product reviews. All
material is now generated by in-house staff.
Freelance writing no longer accepted.

What Investment

Arnold House, 36–41 Holywell Lane, London
EC2A 3SF
☎020 7827 5454 Fax 020 7827 0567

Owner *Charterhouse Communications*
Editor *Sally Wright*
Circulation 37,000

FOUNDED 1983. MONTHLY. Features articles
on a variety of savings and investment matters.
All approaches should be made in writing.

Features Length 1200–1500 words (maximum 2000).

Payment NUJ rates minimum.

What Mortgage

Arnold House, 36–41 Holywell Lane, London
EC2A 3SF
☎020 7827 5454 Fax 020 7827 0567
Website www.themoneypages.com

Owner *Charterhouse Communications*
Deputy Editor *Tamsin Hemsley*
Circulation 25,000

FOUNDED 1982. MONTHLY magazine on property purchase and finance. No unsolicited
material; prospective contributors may make
initial contact with ideas either by telephone or
in writing.

Features Up to 1500 words on related topics are considered. Particularly welcome are
new angles, ideas or specialities relevant to
mortgages.

Payment £175 per 1000 words.

What Satellite TV

WVIP, 53–79 Highgate Road, London
NW5 1TW
☎020 7331 1000 Fax 020 7331 1241
Email wvwhatsat@wvip.co.uk
Website www.wotsat.com

Owner *WVIP*
Editor *Geoff Bains*
Circulation 65,000

FOUNDED 1986. MONTHLY including news,
technical information, equipment tests, programme background, listings. Contributions
welcome – phone first.

Features *Geoff Bains* Unusual installations
and users. In-depth guides to popular/cult
shows. Technical tutorials.

News *Alex Lane* Industry and programming.
250 words maximum.

What's New in Building

City Reach, 5 Greenwich View Place,
Millharbour, London E14 9NN
☎020 7861 6309 Fax 020 7861 6241

Owner *United Business Media International*
Editor *Mark Pennington*
Circulation 31,496

MONTHLY. Specialist magazine covering new products for building. Unsolicited mss not generally welcome. The only freelance work available is rewriting press release material. This is offered on a monthly basis of 25–50 items of about 150 words each.
Payment £5.25 per item.

What's On in London

180–182 Pentonville Road, London N1 9LB
☎020 7278 4393 Fax 020 7837 5838
Email whatson@globalnet.co.uk
Website www.whatsoninlondon.co.uk

Owner *E.G. Shaw*
Editor *Michael Darvell*
Circulation 40,000

FOUNDED 1935. WEEKLY entertainment-based guide and information magazine. Features, listings and reviews. Always interested in well-thought-out and well-presented mss. Articles should have London/Home Counties connection, except during the summer when they can be of much wider tourist/historic interest, relating to unusual traditions and events. Approach the editor by telephone in the first instance.
Features *Graham Hassell*
Art *Rosanna Negrotti*
Cinema *Jason Cairo*
Pop Music *John Coleman*
Classical Music *Michael Darvell*
Theatre *Oliver Jones*
Events *John Coleman*
Payment by arrangement.

Wine

Quest Magazines Ltd., 6–14 Underwood Street, London N1 7JQ
☎020 7549 2572 Fax 020 7549 2550
Email wine@wilmington.co.uk
Website www.connectingdrinks.com

Owner *Wilmington Publishing*
Editor *Chris Losh*
Circulation 35,000

FOUNDED 1983. MONTHLY. No unsolicited mss.
News/Features Wine, spirits, cigars, food and food/wine-related travel stories. Prospective contributors should approach in writing.

Wisden Cricket Monthly

c/o The New Boathouse, 136–142 Bramley Road, London W10 6SR
☎020 7565 3000 Fax 020 7565 3077
Email wisden@johnbrown.co.uk

Owner *Wisden Cricket Magazines Ltd*
Editor *Stephen Fay*
Circulation 20,000

FOUNDED 1979. MONTHLY. Very few uncommissioned articles are used, but would-be contributors are not discouraged. Approach in writing. *Payment* varies.

Woman

IPC Connect Ltd, King's Reach Tower, Stamford Street, London SE1 9LS
☎020 7261 5000 Fax 020 7261 5997

Owner *IPC Media Ltd*
Editor *Carole Russell*
Circulation 636,528

FOUNDED 1937. WEEKLY. Long-running, popular women's magazine which boasts a readership of over 2.5 million. No unsolicited mss. Most work commissioned. Approach with ideas in writing.
Features *Liz Jarvis* Maximum 1250 words.
Books *Carole Russell*

Woman and Home

IPC Media Ltd., King's Reach Tower, Stamford Street, London SE1 9LS
☎020 7261 5176 Fax 020 7261 7346

Owner *IPC Media Ltd*
Editor *Sue James*
Circulation 269,401

FOUNDED 1926. MONTHLY. No unsolicited mss. Prospective contributors are advised to write with ideas, including photocopies of other published work or details of magazines to which they have contributed. S.a.e. essential for return of material. Most freelance work is specially commissioned.

Woman's Journal

IPC Media Ltd., King's Reach Tower, Stamford Street, London SE1 9LS
☎020 7261 6652 Fax 020 7261 7061

Owner *IPC Media Ltd*
Editor *Elsa McAlonan*
Circulation 113,719

FOUNDED 1927. MONTHLY. Original feature ideas on 30+ women and their lives welcome, with samples of previous work. Major features are generally commissioned.
Payment negotiable.

Woman's Own

IPC Media Ltd., King's Reach Tower, Stamford Street, London SE1 9LS
☎020 7261 5500 Fax 020 7261 5346

Owner *IPC Media Ltd*
Editor *Ms Terry Tavner*
Circulation 553,701

FOUNDED 1932. WEEKLY. Prospective contributors should contact the features editor *in writing* in the first instance before making a submission. No unsolicited fiction.

Woman's Realm

Merged with *Woman's Weekly* in 2001.

Woman's Weekly

IPC Media Ltd., King's Reach Tower, Stamford Street, London SE1 9LS
☎020 7261 6131 Fax 020 7261 6322

Owner *IPC Media Ltd*
Editor *Gilly Sinclair*
Deputy Editor *Geoffrey Palmer*
Circulation 469,162

FOUNDED 1911. Mass-market women's WEEKLY.

Features Inspiring, positive human interest stories, especially first-hand experiences, of up to 1200 words. Freelancers used regularly but tend to be experienced magazine journalists. Synopses and ideas should be submitted in writing.

Fiction *Gaynor Davies* Short stories 1000–2500 words; serials 12,000–30,000 words. Guidelines for serials: 'a strong emotional theme with a conflict not resolved until the end'; short stories should have warmth and originality.

Women's Health

WVIP, 53–79 Highgate Road, London NW5 1TW
☎020 7331 1000 Fax 020 7331 1108
Email womens.health@wvip.co.uk

Owner *WVIP*
Editor *Tracey Smith*
Circulation 100,000

FOUNDED 1998. MONTHLY lifestyle magazine with a health twist, taking an irreverant approach. Aimed at ABC1 women of 25–39. No unsolicited mss. Interested in ideas for items with an unconventional angle on fitness, fashion and beauty plus alternative health and food. Approach in writing or by e-mail in the first instance.

Woodworker

Nexus House, Azalea Drive, Swanley, Kent BR8 8HU
☎01322 660070 Fax 01322 616319
Website www.getwoodworking.com

Owner *Nexus Special Interests*
Editor *Mark Ramuz*
Circulation 45,000

FOUNDED 1901. MONTHLY. Contributions welcome; approach with ideas in writing.

Features Articles on woodworking with good photo support appreciated. Maximum 2000 words. *Payment £40–60 per page.*

News Stories and photos (b&w) welcome. Maximum 300 words. *Payment £10–25 per story.*

World Fishing

Nexus House, Swanley, Kent BR8 8HY
☎01322 660070 Fax 01322 616324

Owner *Nexus Media Ltd*
Editor *Adrian Tatum*
Circulation 4800

FOUNDED 1952. MONTHLY. Unsolicited mss welcome; approach by phone or in writing with an idea.

News/Features of a technical or commercial nature relating to the commercial fishing and fish processing industries worldwide. Maximum 1000 words.

Payment by arrangement.

The World of Embroidery

PO Box 42B, East Molesley, Surrey KT8 9BB
☎020 8943 1229 Fax 020 8977 9882
Email magsmag@compuserve.com
Website www.embroiderersguild.com

Owner *Embroiderers' Guild*
Editor *Polly Leonard*
Circulation 14,500

FOUNDED 1933. BI-MONTHLY. Features articles on embroidery techniques, historical and foreign embroidery, and contemporary artists' work with illustrations. Also reviews. Unsolicited mss welcome. Maximum 1000 words.

Payment negotiable.

The World of Interiors

Vogue House, Hanover Square, London W1S 1JU
☎020 7499 9080 Fax 020 7493 4013
Email interiors@condenast.co.uk
Website www.worldofinteriors.co.uk

Owner *Condé Nast Publications Ltd*

Editor-in-Chief *Rupert Thomas*
Circulation 65,183

FOUNDED 1981. MONTHLY. Best approach by fax or letter with an idea, preferably with reference snaps or guidebooks.

Features *Sarah Howell* Most feature material is commissioned. 'Subjects tend to be found by us, but we are delighted to receive suggestions of interiors, archives, little-known museums, collections, etc. unpublished elsewhere, and would love to find new writers.'

World Soccer

IPC Media Ltd., King's Reach Tower, Stamford Street, London SE1 9LS
☎020 7261 5737 Fax 020 7261 7474
Website www.worldsoccer.com

Owner *IPC Media Ltd*
Editor *Gavin Hamilton*
Circulation 56,032

FOUNDED 1960. MONTHLY. Unsolicited material welcome but initial approach by phone or in writing preferred. News and features on world soccer.

World Wide Writers

PO Box 3229, Bournemouth, Dorset BH1 1ZS
☎01202 716043 Fax 01202 740995
Email writintl@globalnet.co.uk
Website www.users.globalnet.co.uk/~writintl

Owner *Writers International Ltd*
Editor *Frederick E. Smith*

FOUNDED 1996. QUARTERLY. Welcomes short stories which must be original and not previously published or broadcast. Length 2500–5000 words.

Writers' Forum

PO Box 3229, Bournemouth, Dorset BH1 1ZS
☎01202 716043 Fax 01202 740995
Email writintl@globalnet.co.uk
Website www.users.globalnet.co.uk/~writintl

Owner *Writers International Ltd*
Editor *John Jenkins*
Circulation 25,000

FOUNDED 1993. BI-MONTHLY magazine covering all aspects of the craft of writing. Well written articles welcome. Write to the editor in the first instance.

Writers' News/Writing Magazine

PO Box 168, Wellington Street, Leeds, West Yorkshire LS1 1RF
☎0113 238 8333 Fax 0113 238 8330

Owner *Yorkshire Post Newspapers*
Editor *Derek Hudson*
Circulation 21,500(WN)/45,000(WM)

FOUNDED 1989. MONTHLY/BI-MONTHLY magazines containing news and advice for writers. *Writers' News* is exclusive to mail-order members who also receive *Writing Magazine* which is available on newsstands. No poetry or general items on 'how to become a writer'. Receive 1000 mss each year. Approach in writing.

News Exclusive news stories of interest to writers. Maximum 350 words.

Features How-to articles of interest to professional writers. Maximum 1500 words.

Yachting Monthly

IPC Media Ltd., King's Reach Tower, Stamford Street, London SE1 9LS
☎020 7261 6040 Fax 020 7261 7555
Website www.yachtingmonthly.com

Owner *IPC Media Ltd*
Editor *Sarah Norbury*
Deputy Editor *Paul Gelder*
Circulation 37,083

FOUNDED 1906. MONTHLY magazine for yachting enthusiasts. Unsolicited mss welcome, but many are received and not used. Prospective contributors should make initial contact in writing.

Features A wide range of features concerned with maritime subjects and cruising under sail; well-researched and innovative material always welcome, especially if accompanied by colour transparencies. Maximum 2750 words.

Payment £90–110 per 1000 words.

Yachting World

IPC Media Ltd., King's Reach Tower, Stamford Street, London SE1 9LS
☎020 7261 6800 Fax 020 7261 6818
Email yachting_world@ipcmedia.com
Website www.yachting-world.com

Owner *IPC Media Ltd*
Editor *Andrew Bray*
Circulation 34,316

FOUNDED 1894. MONTHLY with international coverage of yacht racing, cruising and yachting events. Will consider well researched and written sailing stories. Preliminary approaches should be by phone for news stories and in writing for features.

Payment by arrangement.

You & Your Wedding

Silver House, 31–35 Beak Street, London
W1R 3LD
☎020 7440 3838 (Editorial)
Fax 020 7287 8655

Owner *NatMags Specialist Media (AIM) Ltd*
Editor *Carole Hamilton*
Circulation 62,145

FOUNDED 1985. BI-MONTHLY. Anything relating to weddings, setting up home, and honeymoons. No unsolicited mss. Ideas may be submitted in writing only, especially travel features. No phone calls.

You – The Mail on Sunday Magazine

See under **National Newspapers (The Mail on Sunday)**

Young Writer

Glebe House, Weobley, Hereford HR4 8SD
☎01544 318901 Fax 01544 318901
Email editor@youngwriter.org
Website www.youngwriter.org

Editor *Kate Jones*

Describing itself as 'The Magazine for Children with Something to Say', *Young Writer* is issued three times a year, at the back-to-school times of September, January and April. A forum for young people's writing – fiction and non-fiction, prose and poetry – the magazine is an introduction to independent writing for young writers aged 5–18.

Payment from £20 to £100 for freelance commissioned articles (these can be from adult writers).

Your Cat Magazine

Roebuck House, 33 Broad Street, Stamford,
Lincolnshire PE9 1RB
☎01780 766199 Fax 01780 766416
Website www.yourcat.co.uk

Owner *Bourne Publishing Group*
Editor *Sue Parslow*

FOUNDED 1994. MONTHLY magazine giving practical information on the care of cats and kittens, pedigree and non-pedigree, plus a wide range of general interest items on cats. Will consider 'true life' cat stories (maximum 900 words) and quality fiction. Send synopsis in the first instance. 'No articles written as though by a cat.'

Your Dog Magazine

Roebuck House, 33 Broad Street, Stamford,
Lincolnshire PE9 1RB
☎01780 766199 Fax 01780 766416
Email sarahbpgroup@talk21.com

Owner *BPG (Stamford) Ltd*
Editor *Sarah Wright*
Circulation 26,000

FOUNDED 1995. MONTHLY. Practical advice for pet dog owners. Will consider practical features and some personal experiences (no highly emotive pieces or fiction). Telephone in the first instance.

News Maximum 300–400 words.
Features Maximum 2500 words; limited opportunities.
Payment negotiable.

Your Garden Magazine

IPC Media Ltd., Westover House, West Quay Road, Poole, Dorset BH15 1JG
☎01202 440870 Fax 01202 440860
Email yourgarden@ipc.co.uk

Owner *IPC Media Ltd*
Editor *Adrienne Wild*
Circulation 41,377

FOUNDED 1993. MONTHLY full colour glossy for all gardeners. Welcomes good, solid gardening advice that is well written and fun. Receives approx 50 mss per month but only five per cent are accepted. Always approach in writing in the first instance.

Features Good leisure gardening and inspiration features, preferably with a new slant. Small gardens only. Maximum 800 words. Photographs welcome.
Payment negotiable – all rights preferred.

Your Horse

Bretton Court, Bretton, Peterborough,
Cambridgeshire PE3 8DZ
☎01733 264666 Fax 01733 465200

Owner *EMAP Active Ltd*
Editor *Amanda Stevenson*
Circulation 61,000

For people who live, breath and have fun around horses. Most writing produced in-house but well-targeted articles will always be considered.

Your Life

IPC Media Ltd., King's Reach Tower, Stamford Street, London SE1 9LS
☎020 7261 5000 Fax 020 7261 7678

Owner *IPC Media Ltd*

Editor *Mary Frances*

LAUNCHED April 2001. WEEKLY magazine 'grown-up' (35+) woman. A mix of topical features, fashion, beauty and travel. Interested in topical stories; approach by fax or post with a synopsis in the first instance. No real-life stories or fiction.

Features/News Editor *Caroline Jowett*
Travel Editor *Jane Lofthouse-Smith*
Health *Gill Cox*
Fashion *Sally Ann Carroll*
Practicals *Christine Parsons*
Food *Mari Williams*
Well-being *Viv Fennimore*

Yours Magazine

Homenene House, Orton Centre, Peterborough, Cambridgeshire PE2 5UW
☎01733 237111 Fax 01733 288129

Owner *EMAP Esprit*
Editor *Christine Moss*
Circulation 335,229

FOUNDED 1973. MONTHLY plus four seasonal specials. Aimed at a readership aged 55 and over.

Features Best approach by letter with outline in first instance. Maximum 1000 words.

News Short, newsy items of interest to readership welcome. Length 300–500 words.

Fiction One or two short stories used in each issue.

Payment negotiable.

Zest

National Magazine House, 72 Broadwick Street, London W1V 2BP
☎020 7439 5000 Fax 020 7312 3750

Email zest.mail@natmags.co.uk
Website www.zest.co.uk

Owner *National Magazine Company*
Editor *Eve Cameron*
Features Editor *Rebecca Franks*

FOUNDED 1994. MONTHLY. Health, beauty, fitness, nutrition and general well-being. No unsolicited mss. Prefers ideas in synopsis form; approach in writing.

ZINE

5 Martins Lane, Witcham, Ely, Cambridgeshire CB6 2LB
☎01353 777931
Email ttapress@aol.com
Website www.tta-press.freewire.co.uk

Owner *TTA Press*
Editor *Andy Cox*

FOUNDED 1994. BI-MONTHLY. Features detailed contributors' guidelines of international small press and semi-professional publications, plus varied articles, news, views, reviews and interviews.

Features Unsolicited articles welcome on any aspect of small press publishing: market information, writing, editing, illustrating, interviews and reviews. All genres. Submissions should include adequate return postage. 'Please study the magazine: this will greatly enhance your chances of acceptance.'

The Zone

See entry under **Poetry Magazines**

Freelance Rates – Magazines

Freelance rates vary enormously. The following minimum rates, set by the **National Union of Journalists**, should be treated as guidelines. The NUJ has no power to enforce minimum rates on journals that do not recognise the Union. It is up to freelancers to negotiate the best deal they can.

Examples of NUJ categories for magazines:

Group A (large circulation, well-known titles with over £8000 per page of advertising) *Cosmopolitan, Hello!, marie claire, New Scientist, Radio Times, Woman, Woman's Own.*

Group B (consumer magazines with between £5000 and £8000 per page of advertising) *The Face, Time Out, Moneywise.*

Group C (special interest/large-circulation trade magazines with between £2500 and £5000 per page of advertising) *Accountancy Age, Architect's Journal.*

Group D (less than £2000 per page of advertising or carry no advertising) *Big Issue.*

The following figures are the minimum rates which should be paid by magazines in the above groups for first use only:

Features (per 1000 words)

Group A	£450
Group B	£325
Group C	£250
Group D	£180

Cartoons (b&w)

	Group A	Group B & C	Group D
Minimum fee	£110	£90	£70
Feature strip (up to 4 frames)	£135	£120	£110

For colour, charge at least double these rates.

Crosswords

	Group A	Group B & C	Group D
15 × 15 squares and under	£170	£95	£90
Over 15 × 15 squares	£220	£150	£100

News Agencies

Associated Press Limited
12 Norwich Street, London EC4A 1BP
☎020 7353 1515
Fax 020 7353 8118 (Newsdesk)

Material is either generated in-house or by regulars. Hires the occasional stringer. No unsolicited mss.

Dow Jones Newswires
10 Fleet Place, London EC4M 7QN
☎020 7842 9900 Fax 020 7842 9361

A real-time financial and business newswire operated by Dow Jones & Co., publishers of *The Wall Street Journal*. No unsolicited material.

National News Press and Photo Agency
109 Clifton Street, London EC2A 4LD
☎020 7684 3000 Fax 020 7684 3030

All press releases welcome. Most work is ordered or commissioned. Coverage includes courts, tribunals, conferences, general news, etc. – words and pictures – as well as PR.

Press Association Ltd
292 Vauxhall Bridge Road, London
SW1V 1AE
☎020 7963 7000/7107 (Newsdesk)
Fax 020 7963 7192 (Newsdesk)
Email newsdesk@pa.press.net
Website www.pressassociation.press.net

No unsolicited material. Most items are produced in-house though occasional outsiders may be used. A phone call to discuss specific material may lead somewhere 'but this is rare'.

Reuters
85 Fleet Street, London EC4P 4AJ
☎020 7250 1122

No unsolicited mss.

Solo Syndication Ltd
17–18 Hayward's Place, Clerkenwell, London
EC1R 0EQ
☎020 7566 0360 Fax 020 7566 0388

FOUNDED 1978. *Specialises* in worldwide newspaper syndication of photos, features and cartoons. Professional contributors only.

South Yorkshire Sport
6 Sharman Walk, Apperknowle, Sheffield,
South Yorkshire S18 4BJ
☎01246 414767/07970 284848 (mobile)
Fax 01246 414767
Email Nicksport1@aol.com

Provides written/broadcast coverage of sport in the South Yorkshire area.

Space Press NA
Bridge House, Blackden Lane, Goostrey,
Cheshire CW4 8PZ
☎01477 533403/534440 Fax 01477 535756
Email Scoop2001@aol.com
Website www.CountylifeOnline.com

FOUNDED 1972. Press and picture agency covering Cheshire and the North West, North Midlands, including Knutsford, Macclesfield, Congleton, Crewe and Nantwich, Wilmslow, Alderley Edge, serving national, regional and local press, TV and radio. A member of the National Association of Press Agencies (NAPA).

Television and Radio

BBC TV and Radio

Website www.bbc.co.uk
Director-General *Greg Dyke*

The new structure of the BBC includes the creation of four programming divisions: Drama, Entertainment and Children's; Factual and Learning; News; and Sport. Music Production has moved into the Radio Division but also produces classical music programmes for television. A New Media division develops the BBC's interactive television and online activities.

TELEVISION
BBC Television Centre, Wood Lane, London W12 7RJ ☎020 8743 8000
Director, Television *Mark Thompson*
Controller, BBC1 *Lorraine Heggessey*
Controller, BBC2 *Jane Root*

RADIO
Broadcasting House, Portland Place, London W1A 1AA ☎020 7580 4468
Director of Radio & Music *Jenny Abramsky*
Controller, Radio 1 *Andy Parfitt*
Controller, Radio 2 *James Moir*
Controller, Radio 3 *Roger Wright*
Controller, Radio 4 *Helen Boaden*
Controller, Radio 5 Live *Bob Shennan*

Radio 1 is the popular music-based station; Radio 2 broadcasts popular light entertainment with celebrity presenters; Radio 3 is devoted to classical and contemporary music; Radio 4 is the main news and current affairs station while broadcasting a wide range of other programmes such as consumer matters, wildlife, science, gardening, etc. It also produces the bulk of drama, comedy, serials and readings. Radio 5 Live is the 24-hour news and sport station.

Drama, Entertainment and Children's Division

Director *Alan Yentob*

The BBC New Writing Initiative finds and nurtures new writing talent for Film, TV, Radio and Online, working across BBC Drama, Entertainment and Children's programmes. Runs targeted schemes and workshops linked directly to production and accepts and assesses unsolicited scripts for film, single TV dramas and radio drama. To be considered for one of the schemes run by the New Writing Initiative please send a sample full length drama script to: BBC writers room, Room 222, BBC Broadcasting House, Portland Place, London W1A 1AA. For guidelines on unsolicited scripts please send a large s.a.e. to *Jessica Dromgoole*, **New Writing Coordinator**, BBC Drama, Entertainment and Children's Programmes at the address above.

DRAMA
Controller, Innovation & Factual Drama
 Susan Spindler
Controller, Drama Commissioning
 Jane Tranter
Head of Continuing Drama *Mal Young*
Head of Films *David Thompson*
Head of Development, Serials *Sarah Brown*
Head of Development, Serials *Serena Cullen*
Head of Development, Films *Tracey Scoffield*
Head of Radio Drama *Gordon House*
Executive Producer *Jeremy Mortimer*
Executive Producer *David Hunter*
Executive Producer (Manchester) *Sue Roberts*
Executive Producer (Birmingham)/
 Editor, The Archers *Vanessa Whitburn*
Executive Producer (World Service
 Drama) *Marion Nancarrow*

ENTERTAINMENT
Controller, BBC Entertainment *Doug*
 Whitelaw
Acting Head of Light Entertainment,
 Television *Jonathan Glazier*
Head of Comedy, Television *Geoffrey Perkins*
Head of Comedy Entertainment,
 Television *Jon Plowman*
Producer *Bill Dare*
Editor, Radio Entertainment *John Pidgeon*
Producer, The News Huddlines *Carol Smith*

Programmes produced range from *Shooting Stars* and *Jonathan Creek* on television to *Just a Minute*; *I'm Sorry I Haven't a Clue* and *The News Quiz* on Radio 4. Virtually every comic talent in Britain got their first break writing one-liners for topical comedy weeklies like Radio 2's *The News Huddlines* (currently paying about £10 for a 'quickie' – one- or two-liners). Ideas welcome; fax to Carol Smith on 020 7765 1242. Non-commissioned writers are welcome to attend an open meeting held in the main reception at Broadcasting House, Portland Place, London W1, every Tuesday at 12.45 pm, where ideas can be discussed with the production team of *The News Huddlines*. Over the past 18 months six new writers have been commissioned as a result of these open meetings. See **The Writers Room** for information on Sketch Pad – online comedy writing competitions.

CBBC (Children's BBC)

Controller, CBBC *J. Nigel Pickard*
Head of Programmes *Dorothy Prior*
Head of Acquisitions *Theresa Plummer-Andrews*
Executive Producer,
  CBBC Drama *Elaine Sperber*
Head of Entertainment *Chris Bellinger*
Executive Producer,
  CBBC News and Factual *Roy Milani*
Editor, Blue Peter *Steve Hocking*
Executive Producer,
  CBBC Pre-school *Clare Elstow*
Executive Producer,
  CBBC Education *Sue Nott*
Creative Director, Children's
  Programmes, Scotland *Claire Mundell*

Factual and Learning Division

Joint Directors *Michael Stevenson,*
  Glenwyn Benson

Adult Learning and Children's Education

Head of Adult Learning *Fiona Chesterton*
Head of Education Production *Marilyn Wheatcroft*
Radio Production *Graham Ellis*
Head of Interactive *Liz Cleaver*

BBC Milton Keynes

Walton Hall, Milton Keynes, MK7 6BH
☎01908 655588 Fax 01908 655300

Head of Production *Chris Palmer*

Television and radio production of schools and college programmes, language courses, education for adults, plus multimedia and audiovisual material in partnership with the Open University. The Learning Zone broadcasts education, training and information programmes on BBC2 from midnight during the week.

Specialist Factual– Arts

Creative Director *Franny Moyle*

Television, radio and World Service produc-

tion of arts programmes such as *Omnibus*; *Arena*; *Review*; *Night Waves* and *Meridian*.

Specialist Factual– Documentaries

Controller, Documentaries *Jeremy Gibson*

Programmes include *Watchdog*; *Crimewatch* and *Paddington Green*.

Specialist Factual– Science

Head of Science *Glenwyn Benson*

Produces programmes such as *Animal Hospital* and *Tomorrow's World* for television and radio.

Leisure and Factual Entertainment

Controller *Anne Morrison*
Head of Production *Steve Wallis*

Covers consumer affairs, major national events and informal education, producing television and radio progammes such as *You and Yours*; *Holiday* and *Woman's Hour*.

News Division

Website www.bbc.co.uk/news

BBC News is the world's largest newsgathering organisation, with 2000 journalists, 250 specialist correspondents and 57 bureaux around the world. There are four specialist units: world affairs; economics and business; politics; and social affairs. BBC News serves: BBC1, BBC2, BBC Choice, Radios 1, 2, 3, 4 and 5 Live, BBC News 24, BBC Parliament, BBC World, BBC World Service, News Online, Ceefax.

Director, News *Richard Sambrook*
Assistant Director, News *Mark Damazer*
Head of Business Programmes & Current
  Affairs *Peter Horrocks*
Head of Newsgathering *Adrian Van Klaveran*
Head of New Media *Richard Deverell*
Head of Political Programmes *Fran Unsworth*
Head of Radio News *Stephen Mitchell*
Head of TV News *Roger Mosey*
Deputy Head of TV News *Rachel Attwell*

Television:

Editor, 1 o'clock News *Chris Rybczynski*
Editor, 6 o'clock News *Jay Hunt*
Editor, 10 o'clock News *Mark Popescu*
Editor, Newsnight *Sian Kevill*
Editor, Breakfast News *Richard Porter*
Editor, Breakfast With Frost *Barney Jones*
Editor, World Service News Programmes
  John Morrison

Radio:

Editor, Today *Rod Liddle*

Editor, The World at One/World This Weekend/PM/Broadcasting House *Kevin Marsh*
Managing Editor, Five Live News Programmes *Bill Rogers*
Editors, The World Tonight *Pru Keely, Jenni Russell*

CEEFAX
Room 7013, BBC Television Centre, Wood Lane, London W12 7RJ ☎020 8576 1801
Editor, Ceefax *Paul Brannan*

SUBTITLING
Room 1468, BBC White City, Wood Lane, London W12 7RJ
☎020 8752 7054/0141 339 8844 ext. 2128
A rapidly expanding service available via Ceefax page 888. Units based in both London and Glasgow.

Sport Division

Director, Sport *Peter Salmon*
Executive Editor, Football *Niall Sloane*

Sports news and commentaries across television and Radios 1, 4 and 5 Live, with the majority of output on Radio 5 Live. Regular programmes include *Sportsnight*; *Sports News*; *Sport on Five* and *Littlejohn* (presented by Richard Littlejohn).

BBC Religion

New Broadcasting House, Oxford Road, Manchester M60 1SJ
☎0161 200 2020 Fax 0161 244 3183
Creative Director, Religion *Hugh Faupel*
Creative Director, Documentaries *Ruth Pitt*

Regular programmes for television include *Heaven & Earth; Songs of Praise; Everyman; Heart of the Matter*. Radio output includes *Good Morning Sunday; Sunday Half Hour; Choral Evensong; The Brains Trust; The Daily Service*.

BBC Talent

Website www.bbc.co.uk/talent
Now in its second year, the BBC's search for new talent covers a wide range of areas including TV and radio presenters, filmmakers, sitcom and drama writers, stand-up comedians, actors and singers. For 2001 entry details the BBC Talent brochure is available from post offices, Odeon and ABC Cinemas, McDonalds restaurants or BBC Radio and Regional TV centres; or access the website or see Ceefax page 155.

BBC World Service

PO Box 76, Bush House, Strand, London WC2B 4PH
☎020 7240 3456 Fax 020 7557 1900
Website www.bbc.co.uk/worldservice

Director *Mark Byford*
Director, World Service News & Programme Commissioning *Bob Jobbins*
Head of News *Caroline Howie*

The World Service broadcasts in English and 42 other languages. The English service is round-the-clock, with news and current affairs as the main component. With over 153 million listeners, excluding countries where research is not possible, it reaches a bigger audience than its five closest competitors combined. The World Service is increasingly available throughout the world on local FM stations, via satellite and online as well as through short-wave frequencies. Coverage includes world business, politics, people/events/opinions, development issues, the international scene, developments in science and technology, sport, religion, music, drama, the arts. BBC World Service broadcasting is financed by a grant-in-aid voted by Parliament amounting to £177.6 million for 2001/2002.

The Writers Room

BBC Online/Writers Room, Room 104, Centre House, 56 Wood Lane, London W12 0TT
☎020 8576 8449
Email tim.jokl@bbc.co.uk
Website www.bbc.co.uk/writersroom

Online advice for new writers wishing to break into writing comedy and drama for for television and radio. Advice from professional writers and producers in the form of master classes, Q&As and pratical suggestions. The site is updated weekly and includes news and information plus a forum for writers to share views and discuss current output. Regular writing competitions at the Sketch Pad site at: www.bbc.co.uk/entertainment/sketchpad/

BBC Regional Television

BBC Northern Ireland

Broadcasting House, Ormeau Avenue, Belfast BT2 8HQ ☎028 9033 8000
Website www.bbc.co.uk/northernireland

Controller *Anna Carragher*
Head of Broadcasting *Tim Cooke*

Head of News & Current Affairs
Andrew Colman
Head of Drama *Robert Cooper*
Chief Producer, Sport *Terry Smyth*
Chief Producer, Music & Arts *David Byers*
Chief Producer, Youth & Community
Fedelma Harkin
Head of Factual and Learning *Bruce Batten*
Editor, Learning *Kieran Hegarty*
Editor, Popular Factual *Clare McGin*
Head of Entertainment and Events
Mike Edgar
Editor, TV Current Affairs *Jeremy Adams*
Editor, Political Programmes *Lena Ferguson*
Editor, TV News *Angelina Fusco*
Chief Producer, Religion *Bert Tosh*
Editor, Text Services *Eddie Fleming*

Regular television programmes include *Newsline 6.30; Hearts and Minds* and *Country Times*. Radio stations: BBC Radio Foyle and BBC Radio Ulster (see entries).

BBC Scotland

Broadcasting House, Queen Margaret Drive, Glasgow G12 8DG
☎0141 338 2000
Website www.bbc.co.uk/scotland

Controller *John McCormick*
Head of Network Programmes
Colin Cameron
Head of Drama Television *Barbara McKissack*
Head of Comedy and Entertainment
Mike Bolland
Executive Editor New Media *Julie Adair*
Head of Programmes, Scotland
Ken MacQuarrie
Head of Gaelic *Donalda MacKinnon*
Head of News and Current Affairs
Blair Jenkins
Head of Sport *Neil Fraser*
Head of North *Andrew Jones*
Commissioning Editor, Television
Ewan Angus

Headquarters of BBC Scotland with centres in Aberdeen, Dundee, Edinburgh and Inverness. Regular programmes include *Reporting Scotland* and *Sportscene* on television and *Good Morning Scotland* and *Fred Macaulay* on radio.

Aberdeen

Broadcasting House, Beechgrove Terrace, Aberdeen AB9 2ZT ☎01224 625233

News, plus some features, including the regular *Beechgrove Garden*. Second TV centre, also with regular radio broadcasting.

Dundee

Nethergate Centre, 66 Nethergate, Dundee DD1 4ER ☎01382 202481
News base only; contributors' studio.

Edinburgh

Broadcasting House, Queen Street, Edinburgh EH2 1JF ☎0131 225 3131

Religious, arts and science programming base. Bi-media news operation.

Inverness

7 Culduthel Road, Inverness 1V2 4AD
☎01463 720720

News features for Radio Scotland. HQ for Radio Nan Gaidheal, the Gaelic radio service serving most of Scotland (**Editor** *Ishbel MacLennan*).

BBC Wales

Broadcasting House, Llandaff, Cardiff CF5 2YQ
☎029 2032 2000 Fax 029 2055 2973
Website www.bbc.co.uk/wales

Controller *Menna Richards*
Head of Programmes (Welsh Language)
Keith Jones
Head of Programmes (English Language)
Clare Hudson
Head of News & Current Affairs *Aled Eurig*
Head of Drama *Matthew Robinson*
Series Editor, Pobol y Cwm *Terry Dyddgen-Jones*

Headquarters of BBC Wales, with regional centres in Bangor, Aberystwyth, Carmarthen, Wrexham and Swansea. BBC Wales television produces up to 12 hours of English language programmes a week, 12 hours in Welsh for transmission on **S4C** and an increasing number of hours on network services. Regular programmes include *Wales Today; Wales on Saturday* and *Pobol y Cwm* (Welsh-language soap) on television and *Good Morning Wales; Good Evening Wales; Post Cyntaf* and *Post Prynhawn* on radio.

Bangor

Broadcasting House, Meirion Road, Bangor, Gwynedd LL57 2BY
☎01248 370880 Fax 01248 351443
Head of Centre *Marian Wyn Jones*

BBC Asian Network

BBC Pebble Mill, Epic House, Charles Street, Leicester LE1 3SH
☎0116 251 6688 Fax 0116 253 2004
Email asian.network@bbc.co.uk
Website www.bbc.co.uk/asiannetwork

Managing Editor *Vijay Sharma*

Commenced broadcasting in November 1996. Broadcasts to a Midlands audience during the day and nationwide coverage in the evening. Programmes in English, Bengali, Gujerati, Hindi, Punjabi and Urdu.

BBC Birmingham
Pebble Mill Road, Birmingham B5 7QQ
☎0121 432 8888   Fax 0121 432 8847

Head of Regional and Local Programmes
   Roy Roberts
Output Editor *Charles Watkins*

Home of the Pebble Mill Studio. Output for the network includes: TV – *Doctors; Going For a Song; Countryfile; Top Gear; Dalziel and Pascoe; Call My Bluff; Gardener's World; Real Rooms*. Radio – *The Archers; Shake, Rattle and Roll; Farming Today; Jazz Notes; Late Night Currie; Ramblings With Clare Balding*.

   BBC Birmingham serves opt-out stations in Nottingham and Norwich:

BBC East Midlands (Nottingham)
East Midlands Broadcasting Centre, London Road, Nottingham NG2 4UU
☎0115 955 0500

Head of Regional and Local Programmes
   Alison Ford
Output Editor *Liz Howell*

BBC East (Norwich)
St Catherine's Close, All Saint's Green, Norwich, Norfolk NR1 3ND
☎01603 619331

Head of Regional and Local Programmes
   David Holdsworth
Output Editor *Tim Bishop*

BBC Bristol
Broadcasting House, Whiteladies Road, Bristol BS8 2LR
☎0117 973 2211

**Creative Director, Factual Entertainment
   & Leisure** *Andy Batten-Foster*
**Creative Director, Factual Entertainment
   & Leisure** *Mark Hill*
**Executive Senior Producer, Specialist
   Factual** *Michael Poole*
Head of Natural History Unit *Keith Scholey*

BBC Bristol is the home of the BBC's Natural History Unit, producing programmes such as *Wildlife on One; The Natural World; Cousins; Bill Oddie Goes Wild; Andes to Amazon* and *The Really Wild Show* for BBC1 and BBC2. It also

produces natural history programmes for Radio 4 and Radio 5 Live. The Features department produces a wide range of television programmes, including *999; Antiques Roadshow; Louis Theroux; Barking Mad; The Curious Gardeners; Bargain Hunt; Vets in Practice; War Walks* and *Under the Sun* in addition to radio programmes specialising in history, travel, literature and human interest features for Radio 4.

BBC London
35 Marylebone High Street, London W1M 4AA
☎020 7224 2424

Executive Editor *Jane Mote* (BBC London
   Live and Newsroom South East)
Editor, Newsgathering *Sandy Smith*

BBC North/BBC North West/
BBC North East & Cumbria
The regional centres at Leeds, Manchester and Newcastle make their own programmes on a bi-media approach, each centre having its own head of regional and local programmes.

BBC North (Leeds)
Broadcasting Centre, Woodhouse Lane, Leeds, West Yorkshire LS2 9PX
☎0113 244 1188

Head of Regional and Local Programmes
   Colin Philpott
Editor, Newsgathering *Jake Fowler*
Editor, Look North *Kate Watkins*
Producer, North of Westminster *Rod Jones*
Producer, Close Up North *Ian Cundall*
Producers, Look North *Denise Wallace,
   Nicola Swards*

BBC North West (Manchester)
New Broadcasting House, Oxford Road, Manchester M60 1SJ
☎0161 200 2020

Head of Regional and Local Programmes
   Martin Brooks
Editor, Newsgathering *Barbara Metcalf*
Producers, Northwest Tonight *Tamsin
   O'Brien, Jim Clark*
Producer, Close Up North *Deborah van
   Bishop*
Producer, Northwestminster *Liam Fogarty*

**BBC North East & Cumbria
(Newcastle upon Tyne)**
Broadcasting Centre, Barrack Road, Newcastle Upon Tyne NE99 2NE
☎0191 232 1313

Head of Regional and Local Programmes
Olwyn Hocking
Editor, Newsgathering *Andrew Hartley*
Producers, Look North *Iain Williams,
Andrew Lambert*
Producer, North of Westminster
Michael Wild
Producers, Close Up North *Dave Morrison,
Michael Wild*

BBC South East (Tunbridge Wells)

The Great Hall, Mount Pleasant, Tunbridge
Wells, Kent TN1 1QQ
☎01892 670000

Head of Regional and Local Programmes
Laura Ellis (Responsible for BBC South East
[TV], BBC Radio Kent and BBC Southern
Counties Radio)
Editor, Newsgathering *Rod Beards*
**Executive Producer,
First Sight** *Dippy Chaudhary*

BBC West/BBC South/ BBC South West

The three regional television stations, BBC
West, BBC South and BBC South West produce the nightly news magazine programmes,
as well as regular 30-minute local current affairs
programmes and parliamentary programmes.
Each of the regions operates a comprehensive
local radio service as well as a range of correspondents specialising in subjects like health,
education, business, local government, home
affairs and the environment.

BBC West (Bristol)
Broadcasting House, Whiteladies Road,
Bristol BS8 2LR
☎0117 973 2211

Head of Regional and Local Programmes
Andrew Wilson (Responsible for BBC West
[TV], BBC Radio Bristol, BBC Somerset
Sound, BBC Radio Gloucestershire and
BBC Wiltshire Sound)
Output Editors *Jane Kinghorn, Stephanie
Marshall*
Series Producer, Close Up West *James
MacAlpine*

BBC South (Southampton)
Broadcasting House, Havelock Road,
Southampton, Hampshire SO14 7PU
☎023 8022 6201

Head of Regional and Local Programmes
Eve Turner (Responsible for BBC South
[TV], BBC Radio Berkshire, BBC Radio
Oxford and BBC Radio Solent)
Output Editor *Cathy Burnett*
Series Producer, Southern Eye *Peter Pitt*

BBC South West (Plymouth)
Broadcasting House, Seymour Road,
Mannamead, Plymouth, Devon PL3 5BD
☎01752 229201

Head of Regional and Local Programmes
Leo Devine (Responsible for BBC South
West [TV], BBC Radio Devon, BBC
Radio Cornwall, BBC Radio Guernsey and
BBC Radio Jersey)
Output Editor *Roger Clark*
Editor, Current Affairs *Simon Willis*

BBC Local Radio

Room 2761, Broadcasting House, London
W1A 1AA
☎020 7580 4468
Website www.bbc.co/england

There are 39 local BBC radio stations in England
transmitting on FM and medium wave. These
present local news, information and entertainment to local audiences and reflect the life of the
communities they serve. Each has its own newsroom which supplies local bulletins and national
news service. Many have specialist producers. A
comprehensive list of programmes for each is
unavailable and would soon be out of date. For
general information on programming, contact
the relevant station direct.

BBC Radio Berkshire

PO Box 104.4, Reading, Berkshire
RG94 8FH
☎0645 311444 Fax 0645 311555
Website www.bbc.co.uk/radioberkshire

Editor *Phil Ashworth*

Restored to its original name in 2000 having
been merged with BBC Radio Oxford in 1995
to create BBC Thames Valley.

BBC Radio Bristol

PO Box 194, Bristol BS99 7QT
☎0117 974 1111 Fax 0117 973 2549
Email radio.bristol@bbc.co.uk
Website www.bbc.co.uk/radiobristol

Managing Editor *Jenny Lacey*

Wide range of feature material used.

BBC Radio Cambridgeshire

PO Box 96, 104 Hills Road, Cambridge
CB2 1LD
☎01223 259696 Fax 01223 460832
Email cambs@bbc.co.uk
Website www.bbc.co.uk/radiocambridgeshire
Editor *Andrew Wilson*

Commenced broadcasting in May 1982. Short stories are broadcast occasionally.

BBC Radio Cleveland

PO Box 95FM, Broadcasting House,
Newport Road, Middlesbrough, Cleveland
TS1 5DG
☎01642 225211 Fax 01642 211356
Email radio.cleveland@bbc.co.uk
Website www.bbc.co.uk/radiocleveland
Managing Editor *Andrew Glover*

Material used is mainly local to Teesside, Co. Durham and North Yorkshire, and is almost exclusively news and current affairs.

BBC Radio Cornwall

Phoenix Wharf, Truro, Cornwall TR1 1UA
☎01872 275421 Fax 01872 275045
Email radio.cornwall@bbc.co.uk
Website www.bbc.co.uk/radiocornwall
Editor *Pauline Causey*

On air from 1983 serving Cornwall and the Isles of Scilly. Broadcasts 117 hours of local programmes weekly including news, phone-ins and specialist music. Chris Blount's afternoon programme includes interviews with local authors and arts-related features on Cornish themes.

BBC Coventry and Warwickshire

Holt Court, 1 Greyfriars Road, Coventry
CV1 2WR
☎024 7686 0086 Fax 024 7657 0100
Email coventry.warwickshire@bbc.co.uk
Website www.bbc.co.uk/coventrywarwickshire
Managing Editor *Keith Beech*

Commenced broadcasting in January 1990 as CWR. News, current affairs, public service information and community involvement, relevant to its broadcast area: Coventry and Warwickshire. Occasionally uses the work of local writers, though cannot handle large volumes of unsolicited material. Any material commissioned will need to be strong in local interest and properly geared to broadcasting.

BBC Radio Cumbria

Annetwell Street, Carlisle, Cumbria CA3 8BB
☎01228 592444 Fax 01228 511195
Email radio.cumbria@bbc.co.uk
Website www.bbc.co.uk/radiocumbria
Editor *Nigel Dyson*

Occasional opportunities for plays and short stories are advertised on-air. No outlet for literary material with the exception of *Write Now*, a weekly 30-minute local writing programme broadcast on Sundays at 5.30 pm.

BBC Radio Cymru

Broadcasting House, Llandaff, Cardiff CF5 2YQ
☎029 2032 2000 Fax 029 2055 5960
Email radio.cymru@bbc.co.uk
Website www.bbc.co.uk/cymru
Editor *Aled Glynne Davies*
Editor, Radio Cymru News *Rhian Gibson*

Welsh and English-language programmes, including *Post Cyntaf*, *Chwaraeon* and *Gang Bangor*.

BBC Radio Derby

PO Box 104.5, Derby DE1 3HL
☎01332 361111 Fax 01332 290794
Email radio.derby@bbc.co.uk
Website www.bbc.co.uk/radioderby
Managing Editor *Mike Bettison*

News and information (the backbone of the station's output), local sports coverage, daily magazine and phone-ins, minority interest, Asian and African Caribbean weekly programmes.

BBC Radio Devon

PO Box 1034, Broadcasting House,
Seymour Road, Mannamead, Plymouth,
Devon PL3 5YQ
☎01752 260323 Fax 01752 234599
Email radio.devon@bbc.co.uk
Website www.bbc.co.uk/radiodevon
Also at: Walnut Gardens, St David's Hill,
Exeter, Devon EX4 4DB
☎01392 215651
Managing Editor *John Lilley*
Head of Programmes *Matthew Price*
Head of News *Sarah Solftley*

On air since 1983. Short stories – up to 1000 words from local authors only – used weekly on the Sunday afternoon show (5.05 pm–6.05 pm). Contact *Elaine McFadyen*.

BBC Essex

198 New London Road, Chelmsford, Essex
CM2 9XB
☎01245 616000 Fax 01245 492983
Email essex@bbc.co.uk

Website www.bbc.co.uk/essex

Editor *Margaret Hyde*

Broadcasts local and regional programmes for 20 hours every day aimed at a mature audience. Programmes are a mix of news, interviews, expert contributors, phone-ins, sport and special interest such as gardening. *Write On* is an annual short story competition open to local writers.

BBC Radio Foyle

8 Northland Road, Londonderry BT48 7JD
☎028 7126 2244 Fax 028 7137 8666
Website www.bbc.co.uk/northernireland

Managing Editor *Ana Leddy*
News Producers *Eimear O'Callaghan, Paul McFadden*
Arts/Book Reviews *Colum Arbuckle*
Features *Michael Bradley*

Radio Foyle broadcasts about seven hours of original material a day, seven days a week to the north west of Northern Ireland. Other programmes are transmitted simultaneously with Radio Ulster. The output ranges from news, sport, and current affairs to live music recordings and arts reviews.

BBC Radio Gloucestershire

London Road, Gloucester GL1 1SW
☎01452 308585 Fax 01452 306541
Email radio.gloucestershire@bbc.co.uk
Website www.bbc.co.uk/radiogloucestershire

Managing Editor *Bob Lloyd-Smith*

News and information covering the large variety of interests and concerns in Gloucestershire. Leisure, sport and music, plus African Caribbean and Asian interests. Regular book reviews and interviews with local authors.

BBC GLR

See **BBC London Live**

BBC GMR

PO Box 951, Oxford Road, Manchester M60 1SD
☎0161 200 2000 Fax 0161 236 5804
Email gmr@bbc.co.uk
Website www.bbc.co.uk/gmr

Managing Editor *Karen Hannah*
News Editor *Angela Clarke*
Programmes Editor *Lawrence Mann*

On air from 1970, originally as Radio Manchester. Became BBC GMR in 1988. One of the largest of the BBC local radio stations, broadcasting news, current affairs, phone-ins, help, advice and sport.

BBC Radio Guernsey

Commerce House, Les Banques, St Peter Port, Guernsey, Channel Islands GY1 2HS
☎01481 728977 Fax 01481 713557
Email radio.guernsey@bbc.co.uk
Website www.bbc.co.uk/radioguernsey

Managing Editor *Robert Wallace*

Opened with its sister station, BBC Radio Jersey, in March 1982. Broadcasts 65 hours of local programming a week.

BBC Hereford & Worcester

Hylton Road, Worcester WR2 5WW
☎01905 748485 Fax 01905 748006
Email bbchw@bbc.co.uk
Website www.bbc.co.uk/herefordworcester

Also at: 43 Broad Street, Hereford HR4 9HH
☎01432 355252 Fax 01432 356446

Managing Editor *James Coghill*

Holds competitions on an occasional basis for short stories, plays or dramatised documentaries with a local flavour.

BBC Radio Humberside

9 Chapel Street, Hull, North Humberside HU1 3NU
☎01482 323232 Fax 01482 621403
Email radio.humberside@bbc.co.uk
Website www.bbc.co.uk/radiohumberside

Editor *Helen Thomas*

On air since 1971. Occasionally broadcasts short stories by local writers and holds competitions for local amateur authors and playwrights.

BBC Radio Jersey

18 Parade Road, St Helier, Jersey, Channel Islands JE2 3PL
☎01534 870000 Fax 01534 732569
Email james.filleul@bbc.co.uk
Website www.bbc.co.uk/radiojersey

Managing Editor *Denzil Dudley*
Senior Producer *James Filleul*

Local news, current affairs and community items.

BBC Radio Kent

The Great Hall, Mount Pleasant Road, Tunbridge Wells, Kent TN1 1QQ
☎01892 670000 Fax 01634 830573
Email radio.kent@bbc.co.uk
Website www.bbc.co.uk/radiokent

Managing Editor *Steve Tabchini*

Occasional commissions are made for local interest documentaries and other one-off programmes.

BBC Radio Lancashire

Darwen Street, Blackburn, Lancashire BB2 2EA
☎01254 262411 Fax 01254 680821
Email radio.lancashire@bbc.co.uk
Website www.bbc.co.uk/radiolancashire

Editor *Steve Taylor*

Journalism-based radio station, interested in interviews with local writers. Contact *Jacquie Williams* for *A Lancashire Afternoon*, 2.00 pm to 4.00 pm Monday to Friday.

BBC Radio Leeds

Broadcasting House, Woodhouse Lane, Leeds, West Yorkshire LS2 9PN
☎0113 244 2131 Fax 0113 242 0652
Email radio.leeds@bbc.co.uk
Website www.bbc.co.uk/radioleeds

Managing Editor *Ashley Peatfield*

One of the country's biggest local radio stations, BBC Radio Leeds was also one of the first, coming on air in the 1960s as something of an experimental venture. The station is 'all talk', with a comprehensive news, sport and information service as the backbone of its daily output. BBC Radio Leeds has been a regular finalist for the title of Sony Regional Station of the Year. Has also won two Gold Sonys for best presentation.

BBC Radio Leicester

Epic House, Charles Street, Leicester LE1 3SH
☎0116 251 6688 Fax 0116 251 1463
Email radio.leicester@bbc.co.uk
Website www.bbc.co.uk/radioleicester

Editor *Liam McCarthy*

The first local station in Britain. Occasional interviews with local authors.

BBC Radio Lincolnshire

PO Box 219, Newport, Lincoln LN1 3XY
☎01522 511411 Fax 01522 511726
Email radio.lincolnshire@bbc.co.uk
Website www.bbc.co.uk/radiolincolnshire

Managing Editor *Charlie Partridge*

Unsolicited material considered only if locally relevant. Maximum 1000 words: straight narrative preferred, ideally with a topical content.

BBC London Live 94.9FM

PO Box 94.9, London WC2B 4QH
☎020 7224 2424 Fax 020 7208 9210
Email londonlive@bbc.co.uk
Website www.bbc.co.uk/londonlive

Editor *David Robey*

Formerly Greater London Radio (GLR), launched in 1988, London Live broadcasts news, information, travel bulletins, sport and music to Greater London and the Home Counties. Dotun Adebayo's *Word for Word* explores and celebrates poetry, the spoken word and song lyrics every Sunday between 1.00 pm and 3.00 pm.

BBC Radio Manchester

See **BBC GMR**

BBC Radio Merseyside

55 Paradise Street, Liverpool L1 3BP
☎0151 708 5500 Fax 0151 794 0988
Email radio.merseyside@bbc.co.uk
Website www.bbc.co.uk/radiomerseyside

Editor *Mick Ord*

Write Now, a weekly 25-minute regional writers' programme, is produced at Radio Merseyside and also broadcast on BBC Radio Cumbria. Short stories (maximum 1200 words), plus poetry and features on writing. Contact *Jenny Collins* by post at the address above.

BBC Radio Newcastle

Broadcasting Centre, Barrack Road, Newcastle upon Tyne NE99 1RN
☎0191 232 4141
Email radio.newcastle@bbc.co.uk
Website www.bbc.co.uk/radionewcastle

Editor *Sarah Drummond*
Senior Producer (Programmes) *Jon Harle*

Commenced broadcasting in January 1971. The BBC's eighth biggest local radio station in England, Radio Newcastle reaches an audience of 229,000.

BBC Radio Norfolk

Norfolk Tower, Surrey Street, Norwich, Norfolk NR1 3PA
☎01603 617411 Fax 01603 633692
Email norfolk@bbc.co.uk
Website www.bbc.co.uk/radionorfolk

Editor *David Clayton*

Good local ideas and material welcome for features/documentaries, but must relate directly to Norfolk.

BBC Radio Northampton

Broadcasting House, Abington Street, Northampton NN1 2BH
☎01604 239100 Fax 01604 230709
Email northampton@bbc.co.uk
Website www.bbc.co.uk/radionorthampton

Managing Editor *David Clargo*

Books of local interest are regularly featured. Authors and poets are interviewed on merit.

Poems and short stories are reviewed occasionally, but not broadcast. Runs regular competitions for local writers.

BBC Radio Nottingham
London Road, Nottingham NG2 4UU
☎0115 955 0500 Fax 0115 902 1983
Email radio.nottingham@bbc.co.uk
Website www.bbc.co.uk/radionottingham

Editor *Kate Squire*

Rarely broadcasts scripted pieces of any kind but interviews with authors form a regular part of the station's output.

BBC Radio Oxford
PO Box 95.2, Oxford OX2 7YL
☎0645 311444 Fax 0645 311555
Website www.bbc.co.uk/radiooxford/
    index.shtml

Managing Editor *Phil Ashworth*

Restored to its original name in 2000 having been merged with BBC Radio Berkshire in 1995 to create BBC Thames Valley. No opportunities at present as the outlet for short stories has been discontinued for the time being though the station frequently carries interviews with authors and offers books as prizes.

BBC Radio Scotland (Dumfries)
Elmbank, Lover's Walk, Dumfries DG1 1NZ
☎01387 268008 Fax 01387 252568
Email dumfries@bbc.co.uk

Senior Producer *Willie Johnston*

Previously Radio Solway. The station mainly outputs news bulletins (four daily) although changes have seen the station become more of a production centre with programmes being made for Radio Scotland as well as BBC Radio 2 and 5 Live. Freelancers of a high standard, familiar with Radio Scotland, should contact the producer.

BBC Radio Scotland (Orkney)
Castle Street, Kirkwall, Orkney KW15 1DF
☎01856 873939 Fax 01856 872908

Senior Producer *John Fergusson*

Regular programmes include *Around Orkney* (weekday news programme) and *Bruck* (magazine programme).

BBC Radio Scotland (Selkirk)
Municipal Buildings, High Street, Selkirk TD7 4JX
☎01750 21884 Fax 01750 22400

Contact *Ninian Reid*

Formerly BBC Radio Tweed. Local news bulletins.

BBC Radio Sheffield
Shoreham Street, Sheffield S1 4RS
☎0114 273 1177 Fax 0114 279 6699
Email radio.sheffield@bbc.co.uk
Website www.bbc.co.uk/radiosheffield

Station Editor *Gary Keown*
Programmes Editor *Jeremy Buxton*
News Editor *David Holmes*

Writer interviews, writing-related topics and readings on the Rony Robinson show, Thursdays between 11.10 am and 11.30 am.

BBC Radio Shetland
Pitt Lane, Lerwick, Shetland ZE1 0DW
☎01595 694747 Fax 01595 694307

Senior Producer *Richard Whitaker*

Regular programmes include *Good Evening Shetland*. An occasional books programme highlights the activities of local writers and writers' groups.

BBC Radio Shropshire
2–4 Boscobel Drive, Shrewsbury, Shropshire SY1 3TT
☎01743 248484 Fax 01743 237018
Email radio.shropshire@bbc.co.uk
Website www.bbc.co.uk/radioshropshire

Editor *Tony Fish*

On air since 1985. Unsolicited literary material very rarely used, and then only if locally relevant.

BBC Radio Solent
Broadcasting House, Havelock Road, Southampton, Hampshire SO14 7PW
☎023 8063 1311 Fax 023 8033 9648
Email radio.solent@bbc.co.uk
Website www.bbc.co.uk/radiosolent

Managing Editor *Chris Van Schaick*

Broadcasting since 1970.

BBC Somerset Sound
14 Paul Street, Taunton, Somerset TA1 3PF
☎01823 252437 Fax 01823 332539
Email richard.austin@bbc.co.uk
Website www.bbc.co.uk/radiobristol/somerset/

Editor *Jenny Lacey*

Informal, speech-based programming, with strong news and current affairs output and regular local-interest features, including local writing. Poetry and short stories on the *Adam Thomas Programme*.

BBC Southern Counties Radio

Broadcasting Centre, Guildford, Surrey
GU2 5AP
☎01483 306306 Fax 01483 304952
Email southern.counties.radio@bbc.co.uk
Website www.bbc.co.uk/southerncounties

Also at: 1 Marlborough Place, Brighton,
East Sussex BN1 1TU

Managing Editor *Mike Hapgood*

Formerly known as BBC Radio Sussex and
Surrey. Regular programmes include three
individual breakfast shows: *Breakfast Live in
Brighton with JoAnne Good/in Surrey with Dickie
Dodd/in Sussex with John Radford.*

BBC Radio Stoke

Cheapside, Hanley, Stoke on Trent,
Staffordshire ST1 1JJ
☎01782 208080 Fax 01782 289115
Email radio.stoke@bbc.co.uk
Website www.bbc.co.uk/radiostoke

Managing Editor *Mark Hurrell*

On air since 1968, one of the first eight 'experimental' BBC stations. Emphasis on news, current affairs and local topics. Music represents one
fifth of total output. Unsolicited material of local
interest is welcome – send to *Barbara Adams.*

BBC Radio Suffolk

Broadcasting House, St Matthew's Street,
Ipswich, Suffolk IP1 3EP
☎01473 250000 Fax 01473 210887
Email suffolk@bbc.co.uk
Website www.bbc.co.uk/radiosuffolk

Managing Editor *David Peel*

Strongly speech-based, dealing with news, current affairs, community issues, the arts, agriculture, commerce, travel, sport and leisure.
Programmes sometimes carry interviews with
writers.

BBC Thames Valley

See **BBC Radio Berkshire**and **BBC Radio
Oxford**

BBC Three Counties Radio

PO Box 3CR, Luton, Bedfordshire LU1 5XL
☎01582 637400 Fax 01582 401467
Email 3cr@bbc.co.uk
Website www.bbc.co.uk/threecounties

Managing Editor *Mark Norman*

Encourages freelance contributions from the
community across a wide range of output, including interview and feature material. Interested in
local history topics (five minutes maximum).

BBC Radio Ulster

Broadcasting House, Ormeau Avenue, Belfast
BT2 8HQ
☎028 9033 8000 Fax 028 9033 8800

Head of Broadcasting *Tim Cooke*
Head of Production *Paul Evans*

Programmes broadcast from 6.30 am to midnight weekdays and from 6.55 am to midnight at
weekends. Radio Ulster has won seven Sony
awards in recent years. Programmes include:
*Good Morning Ulster; John Bennett; Gerry Anderson;
Talk Back; Just Jones; Evening Extra; On Your
Behalf; Your Place and Mine* and *Across the Line.*

BBC Radio Wales

Broadcasting House, Llandaff, Cardiff CF5 2YQ
☎029 2032 2000 Fax 029 2032 2674
Email radio.wales@bbc.co.uk
Website www.bbc.co.uk/wales/radio

Editor *Julie Barton*
Editor, Radio Wales News *Geoff Williams*

Broadcasts regular news bulletins Monday to
Friday and until lunchtime on Saturday. Pro-
grammes include *Good Morning Wales; Wales at
One; Adam Walton* and *Kevin Hughes.*

BBC Wiltshire Sound

Broadcasting House, Prospect Place, Swindon,
Wiltshire SN1 3RW
☎01793 513626 Fax 01793 513650
Email wiltshire.sound@bbc.co.uk
Website www.bbc.co.uk/wiltshiresound

Editor *Tony Wargon*

Regular programmes include: *Shirley Ludford's
Mid-Morning Show* (reviews and author interviews).

BBC Radio WM

PO Box 206, Birmingham B5 7SD
☎0121 432 2000 Fax 0121 472 3174
Email radio.wm@bbc.co.uk
Website www.bbc.co.uk/radiowm

Managing Editor *Keith Beech*

News, current affairs and entertainment station.

BBC Radio York

20 Bootham Row, York YO30 7BR
☎01904 641351 Fax 01904 610937
Email radio.york@bbc.co.uk
Website www.bbc.co.uk/radioyork

Editor *Barrie Stephenson*
Senior Broadcast Journalist *William Jenkyns*

A regular outlet for short stories of up to 10 minutes' duration. They must be locally written or
based (i.e. North Yorkshire).

Independent Television

Anglia Television
Anglia House, Norwich, Norfolk NR1 3JG
☎01603 615151   Fax 01603 761245
Email angliatv@angliatv.co.uk
Website www.anglia.tv.co.uk

Managing Director *Graham Creelman*
Director of Programmes *Malcolm Allsop*
Controller of News *Guy Adams*

Anglia Television is a major producer of pro-grammes for the ITV network, including *Trisha, Sunday Morning* and *Survival*. Network dramas for 1999 included: *Where the Heart Is* and *Touching Evil*.

Border Television plc
Television Centre, Durranhill, Carlisle, Cumbria CA1 3NT
☎01228 525101   Fax 01228 541384
Website www.border-tv.com

Chairman *James Graham OBE*
Director of Programmes *Neil Robinson*

Border's programming concentrates on docu-mentaries rather than drama. Most scripts are supplied in-house but occasionally there are commissions. Apart from notes, writers should not submit written work until their ideas have been fully discussed.

Carlton Television (London Region)
101 St Martin's Lane, London WC2N 4AZ
☎020 7240 4000   Fax 020 7240 4171
Website www.carlton.com

Deputy Chief Executive,
  Carlton Media Group *Nigel Walmsley*
Chief Executive, Carlton Channels
  Clive Jones
Director of Programmes,
  Carlton Productions *Steve Hewlett*

Carlton Television holds four of the 15 regional ITV licences: Carlton – the weekday broadcaster for the London region; Carlton Central Region – covering the east, west and south Midlands; and Carlton West Country Region, HTV Wales and HTV West – covering the south west of England. Network drama includes *Where the Heart Is; Perfect* and *The Hunt*. See also **Carlton Productions** under **Film, TV and Video Production Companies**.

Carlton Broadcasting, Carlton Central Region
Gas Street, Birmingham B1 2JP
☎0121 643 9898 Fax 0121 634 4240
Website www.carlton.com/central

Managing Director,
  Carlton Broadcasting *Ian Squires*

Regular regional programmes include *Central Weekend* and *Asian Eye*.

Carlton Broadcasting, Carlton West Country Region
Langage Science Park, Western Wood Way, Plymouth, Devon PL7 5BG
☎01752 333333 Fax 01752 333444
Website www.carlton.com/westcountry

Managing Director *Mark Haskell*
Director of Programmes *Jane McCloskey*
Director of News & Current Affairs *Brad Higgins*

Came on air in January 1993. News, current affairs, documentary and religious program-ming.

HTV Wales
The TV Centre, Culverhouse Cross, Cardiff CF5 6XJ
☎029 2059 0590 Fax 029 2059 7183
Website www.htvwales.co.uk

Controller/Director of Programmes
  Elis Owen

HTV West
Television Centre, Bath Road, Bristol BS4 3HG
☎0117 972 2722 Fax 0117 972 2400
Website www.htvwest.co.uk

Managing Director *Jeremy Payne*
Controller, HTV West & Director of Regional Programmes *Sandra Jones*

Channel 4
124 Horseferry Road, London SW1P 2TX
☎020 7396 4444 Fax 020 7306 8356
Website www.channel4.com

Director of Programmes *Tim Gardam*
Deputy Director of Programmes *Karen Brown*
Head of Film *Paul Webster*
Head of Entertainment *Danielle Lux*

COMMISSIONING EDITORS
Independent Film & Video *Adam Barker*
Arts *Janet Lee*
Head of Drama and Animation *Tessa Ross*

Head of Comedy *Caroline Leddy*
Documentaries *Peter Dale*
News, Current Affairs & Business
  David Lloyd
Sport *David Kerr*
Multicultural Programmes *Yasmin Anwar*
Religion & Features *Janice Hadlow*
Controller of Acquisition *June Dromgoole*

Channel 4 started broadcasting as a national channel in November 1982. It enjoys unique status as the world's only major public service broadcaster funded entirely by its own commercial activities. All programmes are commissioned from independent production companies and are broadcast across the whole of the UK except those parts of Wales covered by S4C. Its FilmFour channel, launched in November 1998, is a premium pay-TV channel featuring modern independent cinema. A second digital channel, E4 was launched in January 2001, broadcasting a range of programmes similar to Channel 4.

Channel 5

22 Long Acre, London WC2E 9LY
☎020 7550 5555 Fax 020 7550 5554
Website www.channel5.co.uk

Chief Executive *Dawn Airey*
Director of Programmes *Kevin Lygo*
Controller of Children's Programmes
  Nick Wilson
Senior Programme Controller
  Michael Attwell
Senior Programme Controller *Chris Shaw*
Controller of Drama *Corinne Hollingworth*

Channel 5 Broadcasting Ltd won the franchise for Britain's third commercial terrestrial television station in 1995 and came on air at the end of March 1997. Regular programmes include *Family Affairs* (Monday to Friday soap opera) and *Open House* (Gloria Hunniford's daytime magazine show), plus documentaries, drama, films, children's programmes, sport and entertainment.

Channel Television

The Television Centre, La Pouquelaye,
St Helier, Jersey, Channel Islands JE1 3ZD
☎01534 816816 Fax 01534 816817
Website www.channeltv.co.uk

Also at: Television House, Bulwer Avenue,
St Sampsons, Guernsey, Channel Islands
GY2 4LA
☎01481 41888 Fax 01481 41878
Managing Director *Michael Lucas*

Director of Programmes *Karen Rankine*
Director of Sales *Gordon De Ste Croix*
Director of Transmission & Resources
  Kevin Banner

Channel Television is the Independent Television broadcaster to the Channel Islands, serving 143,000 residents, most of whom live on the main islands, Jersey, Guernsey, Alderney and Sark. The station has a weekly reach of more than 94% with local programmes (in the region of six hours each week) at the heart of the ITV service to the islands.

GMTV

The London Television Centre, Upper Ground, London SE1 9TT
☎020 7827 7000 Fax 020 7827 7249
Email talk2us@gmtv.co.uk
Website www.gmtv.co.uk

Managing Director *Christopher Stoddart*
Director of Programmes *Peter McHugh*
Managing Editor *John Scammell*
Executive Producer *Martin Frizell*

Winner of the national breakfast television franchise. Jointly owned by Scottish Media Group, Carlton Communications, Walt Disney Company and Granada Group. GMTV took over from TV-AM on 1 January 1993, with live programming from 6.00 am to 9.25 am. Regular news headlines, current affairs, topical features, showbiz and lifestyle, sports and business, quizzes and competitions, travel and weather reports. Launched its digital service, GMTV2, in January 1999, with daily broadcasts from 6.00 am to 9.25 am. News reports, travel, health and lifestyle features, some simulcast with GMTV1. Children's programming on Saturdays.

Grampian Television Limited

Queen's Cross, Aberdeen AB15 4XJ
☎01224 846846 Fax 01224 846800
Website www.grampiantv.co.uk

Managing Director *Derrick Thomson*
Head of News and Current Affairs
  Henry Eagles

Extensive regional news and reports including farming, fishing and sports, interviews and leisure features, various light entertainment, Gaelic and religious programmes, and live coverage of the Scottish political, economic and industrial scene. Serves the area stretching from Fife to Shetland. Regular programmes include *North Tonight; Scotland's Larder* and *Grampian Midweek*.

Granada Television

Quay Street, Manchester M60 9EA
☎0161 832 7211   Fax 0161 953 0283
Website www.granadamedia.com

Director of Programmes *Grant Mansfield*
Controller of Production *Claire Poyser*
**Director of Channel Programming,
   GTP/Controller of Lifestyle
   Programmes, GTV** *James Hunt*
Controller of Drama and Comedy *Andy
   Harries*
**Controller of Current Affairs and
   Features** *Jeff Anderson*
**Controller of Documentaries, History
   and Science** *Bill Jones*
Controller of Entertainment *Duncan Gray*

Opportunities for freelance writers are not great but mss from professional writers will be considered. All mss should be addressed to the head of scripts. Regular programmes include *Coronation Street; World in Action* and *This Morning*.

HTV Wales/ HTV West

See **Carlton Television**

ITN (Independent Television News Ltd)

200 Gray's Inn Road, London
WC1X 8XZ
☎020 7833 3000   Fax 020 7430 4868
Email contact@itn.co.uk
Website www.itn.co.uk

Chief Executive *Stewart Purvis*
Editor-in-Chief *Richard Tait*
Editor, ITN News for ITV *Nigel Dacre*
Editor, Channel 4 News *Jim Gray*
Editor, Channel 5 News *Gary Rogers*

Provider of the main national and international news for ITV, Channel 4 and Channel 5 and radio news for IRN. Programmes on ITV: *Lunchtime News; Evening News; News at Ten*, plus regular news summaries, and three programmes a day at weekends. Programmes on Channel 4 include the in-depth news analysis programmes *Channel 4 News* and *The Big Breakfast News*. Programmes on Channel 5: *5 News Early; 5 News at Noon; 5 News* plus regular updates. ITN also provides *World News For Public Television* and has operating control of *Euronews*, Europe's only pan-European broadcaster. Since August 2000, ITN broadcasts in its own right on ITN News Channel, a 24-hour news service available for television, video, audio and text format.

LWT (London Weekend Television)

The London Television Centre, Upper Ground, London SE1 9LT
☎020 7620 1620
Website www.lwt.co.uk

Chairman *Charles Allen*
Managing Director *Lindsay Charlton*
Director of Programmes *Marcus Plantin*
Director of Production *Tamara Howe*
Controller of Entertainment & Comedy
   Nigel Lythgoe
Controller of Drama *Michele Buck*
Controller of Arts *Melvyn Bragg*
Controller of Factual Programmes *Jim Allen*

Makers of current affairs, entertainment and drama series such as *Blind Date; Surprise Surprise; The Knock; London's Burning* also *The South Bank Show* and *Jonathan Dimbleby*. Provides a large proportion of ITV's drama and light entertainment, and also for BSkyB and Channel 4.

Meridian Broadcasting

Television Centre, Southampton, Hampshire SO14 0PZ
☎023 8022 2555   Fax 023 8033 5050
Email viewerliaison@meridiantv.com
Website www.meridian.tv.co.uk

Managing Director *Mary McAnally*
Controller of Broadcasting *Keith Razey*
Director of News Strategy *Jim Raven*

Meridian's studios in Southampton provide a base for network and regional productions. Regular regional programmes include the award-winning news service, *Meridian Tonight; Countryways* and *Grass Roots*.

S4C

Parc Ty Glas, Llanishen, Cardiff CF14 5DU
☎029 2074 7444   Fax 029 2075 4444
Email s4c@s4c.co.uk
Website www.s4c.co.uk

Chief Executive *Huw Jones*
Director of Programmes *Huw Eirug*

The Welsh 4th Channel, established by the Broadcasting Act 1980, is responsible for a schedule of Welsh and English programmes on the Fourth Channel in Wales. Known as S4C, the analogue service is made up of about 30 hours per week of Welsh language programmes and more than 85 hours of English language output from Channel 4. S4C digital broadcasts in Welsh exclusively for 80 hours per week. Ten hours a week of the Welsh programmes are provided by the BBC; the remainder are purchased from HTV and independent producers. Drama, comedy and documentary are all part of S4C's programming.

Scottish Television Ltd

200 Renfield Street, Glasgow G2 3PR
☎0141 300 3000 Fax 0141 300 3030
Website www.stv.co.uk

Managing Director, Scottish TV
 Sandy Ross
Head of Features & Entertainment
 Agnes Wilkie
Senior News Producer *Paul McKinney*
**Head of Sport & General Factual
 Programmes** *Denis Mooney*
Senior Producer of Regional Drama
 Mark Grindle

Scottish Television produces 16.5 hours of television a week for the central Scotland region. This is made up of news, current affairs and sport, and a wide-ranging portfolio of other programmes ranging from entertainment, documentary and religion to regional drama such as *High Road* and *New Found Land*. The company is always interested in new ideas and proposals.

Teletext Ltd

101 Farm Lane, Fulham, London SW6 1QJ
☎020 7386 5000 Fax 020 7386 5002
Website www.teletext.co.uk

Managing Director *Mike Stewart*
Editor-in-Chief *John Sage*

On 1 January 1993, Teletext Ltd took over the electronic publishing service for both ITV and Channel 4. Transmits a wide range of news pages and features, including current affairs, sport, TV listings, weather, travel, holidays, finance, games, competitions, etc. Also broadcasts on digital terrestrial (Channel 9), digital cable TV and the Web and mobile services.

Tyne Tees Television

Television Centre, Newcastle upon Tyne
NE1 2AL
☎0191 261 0181 Fax 0191 261 2302
Email tyne.tees@granadamedia.com
Website www.granadamedia.com

Managing Director *Margaret Fay*
Director of Broadcasting *Graeme Thompson*
Head of Network Features *Malcolm Wright*
Editor, Current Affairs and Features
 Jane Bolesworth
Managing Editor, News *Graham Marples*
Head of Young People's Programmes
 Lesley Oakden

Head of Regional Affairs *Norma Hope*
Head of Sport *Roger Tames*

Programming covers religion, politics, news and current affairs, regional documentaries, business, entertainment, sport and arts. Regular programmes include *North East Tonight with Mike Neville* and *Around the House* (politics).

UTV (Ulster Television)

Havelock House, Ormeau Road, Belfast
BT7 1EB
☎028 9032 8122 Fax 028 9024 6695
Website www.utvinternet.com

Director of Programming *Alan Bremner*
Head of News & Current Affairs
 Rob Morrison

Regular programmes on news and current affairs, politics, sport, education, music, light entertainment, arts, health and local culture.

Yorkshire Television

The Television Centre, Leeds, West Yorkshire
LS3 1JS
☎0113 243 8283 Fax 0113 244 5107
Website www.granadamedia.com

London office: Global House, 96–108 Great Suffolk Street, London SE1 0BE
☎020 7578 4304 Fax 020 7578 4320

Chairman *Charles Allen*
Managing Director *Richard Gregory*
**Director of Programmes, Yorkshire Tyne
 Tees Productions** *John Whiston*
**Controller of Drama, Yorkshire Tyne
 Tees Productions** *Keith Richardson*
Controller of Drama, YTV *Carolyn Reynolds*
**Controller of Comedy Drama and Drama
 Features** *David Reynolds*
Controller of Factual Programmes
 Chris Bryer
Head of News & Current Affairs
 Clare Morrow
**Deputy Controller of Children's, Granada
 Media Group** *Patrick Titley*

Part of Granada Media Group. Drama series, situation comedies, film productions and long-running series like *Emmerdale* and *Heartbeat*. Always looking for strong writing in these areas, but prefers to find it through an agent. Documentary/current affairs material tends to be supplied by producers; opportunities in these areas are rare but adaptations of published work as a documentary subject are considered. In theory, opportunity exists within series, episode material. Best approach is through a good agent.

Cable and Satellite Television

Artsworld
80 Silverthorne Road, London SW8 2DG
☎020 7819 1160 Fax 020 7819 1161
Email tv@artsworld.com
Website www.artsworld.com
Chairman *Sir Jeremy Isaacs*
Channel Director *Richard Melman*

Satellite arts channel, launched in November 2000. Broadcasts from 7.00 pm to midnight (repeated from 2.00 pm to 7.00 pm the following day) via BSkyB.

Asianet
PO Box 38, Greenford, Middlesex UB6 7SP
☎020 8566 9000 Fax 020 8810 5555
Website www.asianet-tv.com
Chief Executive *Dr Banad Viswanath*
Managing Director *Deepak Viswanath*

Broadcasting since September 1994, Asianet transmits entertainment to the Asian community 24 hours a day in English, Hindi, Gujarati, Punjabi, Bengali, Tamil and Urdu.

British Sky Broadcasting Ltd (BSkyB)
6 Centaurs Business Park, Grant Way, Isleworth, Middlesex TW7 5QD
☎020 7705 3000 Fax 020 7705 3030
Website www.sky.com

Chief Executive *Tony Ball*
Chief Operating Officer *Richard Freudenstein*
Managing Director, Sky Sports *Vic Wakeling*
Director of Broadcasting & Production *Mark Sharman*
Head of Sky News *Nick Pollard*

Launched in 1989, British Sky Broadcasting offers over 200 channels delivering sports, movies, entertainment and news to nearly ten million homes throughout the UK and Eire. Sky digital, launched in 1998, broadcasts over 200 channels to more than five million homes. In 1999 BSkyB launched two revolutionary interactive TV services – Open... and Sky Sports Active – and Sky News Active in June 2000.

Wholly-owned Sky Channels:
Sky Premier
Blockbusting action, comedy and romance, featuring recent box office hits.

Sky MovieMax
Contemporary hit movies, embracing all genres, from Hollywood's major studios.

Sky Cinema
Classic and popular movies from 70 years of cinema, including seasons and retrospectives.

Sky News
Award winning 24-hours news service with hourly bulletins and expert comment.

Sky One
The most frequently watched Sky channel with the accent on family entertainment.

Sky Sports 1/Sky Sports 2/Sky Sports 3/Skysports.comTV/Sky Sports Extra
Over 30,000 hours of sport are broadcast every year across the five Sky Sports channels. Sky Sports 1, 2 and 3 are devoted to live events, support programmes and in-depth sports coverage seven days a week. Two further channels are available on Sky digital: SkySports.comTV provides sports news and the latest results and information 24 hours a day; Sky Sports Extra carries additional sports programming including the award-winning live interactive coverage.

Sky Travel
Magazine shows and documentaries.

.tv
Entertaining, informative and educational programming for experts and beginners.

Joint Ventures:
National Geographic; Nickelodeon; Nick Jr; The History Channel; Paramount; QVC; MUTV; Music Choice Europe; [.tv]; Granada Breeze; Granada Men & Motors; Granada Plus; Sky Travel; Sky News Australia.

CNBC
10 Fleet Place, London EC4M 7QS
☎020 7653 9300 Fax 020 7653 9333
Email feedback@cnbceurope.com
Website www.cnbceurope.com
President *Rick Cotton*

A service of NBC and Dow Jones. 24-hour business and financial news service. Programmes include *Business Centre Europe; European Market Watch; Today's Business Europe; Squawk Box.*

Cable News Network International
CNN House, 19–22 Rathbone Place, London W1P 1DF
☎020 7637 6700 Fax 020 7637 6910
Website www.cnn.com

London Bureau Chief *Tom Mintier*
Vice President & Managing Editor for
   Europe/Middle East/Africa *Tony Maddox*

LAUNCHED in 1985 as the international sister network to CNN. Wholly-owned subsidiary of Time Warner Inc. Distributes 24-hour news to more than 151 million households in more than 212 countries and territories. Eight hours of programmes are originated and produced daily in London: *World News; World Business Today; World Business Tonight; Inside Europe; Hotspots*, plus 20 business news updates.

MTV Networks Europe

180 Oxford Street, London W1N 0DS
☎020 7284 7777 Fax 020 7284 7788
Website www.mtv.co.uk

President & Chief Executive *Brent Hansen*

ESTABLISHED 1987. Europe's 24-hour music and youth entertainment channel, available on cable, via satellite and digitally. Transmitted from London in English across Europe.

NBC Europe

Unit 1/1, Harbour Yard, Chelsea Harbour, London SW10 0XD
☎020 7352 9205 Fax 020 7352 9628

Chairman *Patrick Cox*
Director of Programming *Bernhard Bertram*

24-hour European broad-based news, information and entertainment service in English, with additional programmes in German and advertisements in English and German.

Travel (Landmark Travel Channel)

66 Newman Street, London W1P 3LA
☎020 7636 5401 Fax 020 7636 6424
Website www.travelchannel.co.uk

Launched in February 1994. Broadcasts programmes and information on the world of travel. Destinations reports, lifestyle programmes plus food and drink, sport and leisure pursuits. Transmits from 7.00 am to 1.00 am throughout Europe and Africa.

National Commercial Radio

Classic FM

7 Swallow Place, London W1R 7AA
☎020 7343 9000 Fax 020 7344 2700
Website www.classicfm.com

Chief Executive *Ralph Bernard*
Managing Director/Programme
   Controller *Roger Lewis*

Managing Editor *Darren Henley*

Classic FM, Britain's largest national commercial radio station, started broadcasting in September 1992. Plays accessible classical music 24 hours a day and broadcasts news, weather, travel, business information, political/celebrity/general interest talks, features and interviews. Classic has gone well beyond its expectations, attracting six million listeners a week. Winner of the 'Station of the Year' Sony Award in April 2000.

Digital One

7 Swallow Place, London W1R 7AA
☎020 7288 4600
Email info@digitalone.co.uk
Website www.ukdigitalradio.com

The UK's only national commercial digital radio network. Backed by radio group GWR and cable supplier ntl, Digital One began broadcasting on 15 November 1999. Channels include **Classic FM**, **Virgin Radio** and **Oneword**.

ITN Radio News Channel (Digital)

200 Gray's Inn Road, London WC1X 8XZ
☎020 7833 3000
Website www.itn.co.uk

Chief Editor *Nicholas Wheeler*
Editor *Steve Holt*

Rolling news on digital, 18-hours a day.

Oneword

Landseer House, 19 Charing Cross Road, London WC2H 0ES
☎020 7976 3030 Fax 020 7930 9460
Website www.oneword.co.uk

Managing Director *Ben Budworth*
Head of Programmes *Paul Kent*

The first commercial radio station dedicated solely to the transmission of plays, books, comedy and reviews for those who are 'looking for a break from unrelenting music on the radio'. Broadcasts between 6.00 am and midnight daily on the Digital One network in the UK, on Sky Digital (Channel 942) in Europe and worldwide on the Internet. Programmes include *Between the Lines*, a twice-daily conversation by Paul Blezard with different authors.

TalkSport

PO Box 1089, London SE1 8WQ
☎020 7959 7800
Website www.talksport.net

Head of Sport *Mike Parry*

Commenced broadcasting in February 1995 as Talk Radio UK. Re-launched January 2000 as

TalkSport, the UK's first sports radio station. Broadcasts 24 hours a day. News items can be e-mailed to *Mike Parry* via the website.

Virgin Radio
1 Golden Square, London W1F 9DJ
☎020 7434 1215 Fax 020 7494 1055
Website www.virginradio.co.uk

Chief Executive *John Pearson*
Programme Director *Paul Jackson*

'Ten great songs in a row every hour, all day.' Bought by Chris Evans' Ginger Media Group in December 1997 and acquired by the Scottish Media Group in March 2000.

Independent Local Radio

96.3 Aire FM/Magic 828
51 Burley Road, Leeds, West Yorkshire LS3 1LR
☎0113 283 5500 Fax 0113 283 5501
Website www.airefm.com

Programme Director *Mike Bawden*

Music-based programming. 96.3 Aire FM caters for the 15–34–year–old listener while Magic 828 aims at the 25–44 age group with easy favourites.

Beacon FM/Classic Gold Digital WABC
267 Tettenhall Road, Wolverhampton, West Midlands WV6 0DE
☎01902 461383 Fax 01902 461299
Website www.beaconfm.com

Programme Director *Steve Martin*

Part of the GWR Group plc. No outlets for unsolicited literary material at present.

Big AM
See **Signal One**

Radio Borders
Tweedside Park, Tweedbank, Galashiels TD1 3TD
☎01896 759444 Fax 01896 759494
Website www.radioborders.co.uk

Programme Controller *Danny Gallagher*
Head of News *Angeline McConville*

Music-based station with local and national news.

Breeze
See **Essex FM**

BRMB-FM 96.4/1152 Capital Gold
Nine Brindley Place, 4 Oozells Square, Birmingham B1 2DJ
☎0121 245 5000 Fax 0121 245 5245
Website www.brmb.co.uk

Programme Controller *Adam Bridge*
News Editor *Kevin Pashby*

Music-based stations; no outlets for writers. Part of Capital Radio Plc.

Broadland 102/Classic Gold Digital Amber
47–49 Colegate, Norwich, Norfolk NR3 1DB
☎01603 630621
Fax 01603 630892 (newsroom)
Website www.koko.com

Programme Controller *Dave Brown*

Part of GWR Group plc. Popular music programmes and local news only.

1152 Capital Gold
See **BRMB-FM 96.4**

Capital Radio
30 Leicester Square, London WC2H 7LA
☎020 7766 6000 Fax 020 7766 6100
Website www.capitalfm.com

Group Programme Director *Richard Park*

Began in October 1973 as the country's second commercial radio station (the first, LBC, was launched a week earlier). Europe's largest commercial radio station. Main outlet is entertainment news bulletins, Mon–Thurs at 7.30 pm, called *Entertainment Capital*, covering pop music, films, TV and London events. The vast majority of material is generated in-house.

107.5 CAT FM
Regent Arcade, Cheltenham, Gloucestershire GL50 1JZ
☎01242 699555 Fax 01242 699666
Website www.catfmonline.co.uk

Programme Controller *Ian Timms*

Music-based programmes, broadcasting 24 hours a day.

Central FM Ltd
201–203 High Street, Falkirk FK1 1DU
☎01324 611164 Fax 01324 611168
Website www.centralfm.co.uk

Managing Director *Lewis Carnie*
Programme Controller *Tom Bell*

Broadcasts music, sport and local news to Central Scotland, 24 hours a day.

Century Radio

Century House, PO Box 100, Church Street, Gateshead NE8 2YY

☎0191 477 6666 Fax 0191 477 5660

Programme Controller *Gordon Davidson*

Music, talk, news and interviews, 24 hours a day.

CFM

PO Box 964, Carlisle, Cumbria CA1 3NG

☎01228 818964 Fax 01228 819444

Email studio@cfmradio.com

Programme Controller *Simon Monk*
Head of Commercial Production *Peter White*
News Editor *Bill Macdonald*

Music, news and information station.

Channel 103 FM

6 Tunnell Street, St Helier, Jersey, Channel Islands JE2 4LU

☎01534 888103 Fax 01534 887799

Website www.channel103.com

Station Manager *Richard Johnson*

Music programmes, 24 hours a day.

Chiltern FM/
Classic Gold Digital

Chiltern Road, Dunstable, Bedfordshire LU6 1HQ

☎01582 676200

Fax 01582 676241 (newsroom)

Website www.koko.com

Programme Controller, FM *Trevor James*
Programme Controller, Classic Gold Digital *Don Douglas*

Part of the GWR Group plc. Music-based programmes, broadcasting 24 hours a day.

Classic Gold Digital – Breeze 1521

See **Mercury FM 102.7**

Classic Gold Digital 1332

See **102.7 Hereward FM**

Classic Gold Digital 1359

See **Mercia FM**

Classic Gold Digital 1557

See **Northants 96**

Classic Gold Digital 774

See **Severn Sound FM**

Classic Gold Digital Amber

See **Broadland 102**

Classic Gold Digital WABC

See **Beacon Radio**

Classic Gold GEM AM

See **96 TRENT FM**

Radio Clyde/Clyde 1 FM/
Clyde 2 AM

Clydebank Business Park, Clydebank G81 2RX

☎0141 565 2200 Fax 0141 565 2265

Website www.clydeonline.co.uk

Managing Director *Paul Cooney*

Programmes usually originate in-house or by commission. All documentary material is made in-house. Good local news items always considered. There are three book programmes presented by Alex Dickson each week on Clyde 2 at 10.00 pm – 10.30 pm: *Authors* (Monday) features author interviews while *Hardback Bookcase* (Tuesday) and *Paperback Bookcase* (Wednesday) review latest titles.

Cool FM

See **Downtown Radio**

Downtown Radio/Cool FM

Newtownards, Co. Down, Northern Ireland BT23 4ES

☎028 9181 5555 Fax 028 9181 5252

Email programmes@downtown.co.uk

Website www.downtown.co.uk

Managing Director *John Rosborough*

Downtown Radio first ran a highly successful short story competition in 1988, attracting over 400 stories. The competition is now an annual event and writers living within the station's transmission area are asked to submit material during the winter and early spring. The competition is promoted in association with Eason Shops. For further information, write to *Derek Ray* at the station.

Essex FM/Breeze

Radio House, Clifftown Road, Southend on Sea, Essex SS1 1SX

☎01702 333711 Fax 01702 345224

Programme Director *Jeff O'Brien*

Music-based stations. Part of the GWR Group plc. No real opportunities for writers' work as such, but will occasionally interview local authors of published books. Contact *Tracey Cooper*, Head of News.

Forth AM/Forth FM

Forth House, Forth Street, Edinburgh EH1 3LF
☎0131 475 1226 (AM)/1221 (FM)
Fax 0131 475 1221
Email scott.wilson@fortham.co.uk *or*
david.bain@forthfm.co.uk
Website www.forthonline.co.uk

Head of Forth AM *Scott Wilson*
Head of Forth FM *David Bain*
News Editor *Paul Robertson*

News stories welcome from freelancers. Music-based programming.

FOX FM

Brush House, Pony Road, Cowley, Oxford
OX4 2XR
☎01865 871000 Fax 01865 871037 (news)

Managing Director *Lyn Long*
Head of News *Antony Masters*

Owned by Capital Radio Plc. Music programmes. No outlet for creative writing.

Galaxy 101

Millennium House, 26 Baldwin Street, Bristol
BS1 1SE
☎0117 901 0101 Fax 0117 901 4666
Email newsdesk@galaxy101.co.uk
Website www.galaxy101.co.uk

Programme Controller *Tristan Bolitho*

Dance music, 24 hours a day. Occasionally features books about local places. Contact the Programme Controller in the first instance.

Galaxy 102.2

See **100.7 Heart FM**

Gemini Radio FM/Classic Gold

Hawthorn House, Exeter Business Park,
Exeter, Devon EX1 3QS
☎01392 444444 Fax 01392 444433

Programme Controller (FM) *Kevin Kane*
Programme Controller (AM) *Colin Slade*

Part of Orchard Media Group. No outlets for writers.

GWR FM (West)

PO Box 2000, The Watershed, Bristol
BS99 7SN
☎0117 984 3200 Fax 0117 984 3202
Website www.gwrfm.musicradio.com

Programme Controller, GWR FM (West)
Paul Andrew

Very few opportunities. Almost all material originates in-house. Part of the GWR Group plc.

Hallam FM/Magic AM

Radio House, 900 Herries Road, Sheffield
S6 1RH
☎0114 285 3333 Fax 0114 285 3159
Website www.hallamfm.co.uk

Programme Director *Anthony Gay*

Music, news and features, 24 hours a day.

100.7 Heart FM/Galaxy 102.2

1 The Square, 111 Broad Street, Birmingham
B15 1AS
☎0121 695 0000 Fax 0121 695 0055
Email mail@heartfm.co.uk *or*
mail@galaxy1022.co.uk
Website www.heartfm.co.uk

Managing Director *Paul Fairburn*
Programme Director,
 Heart FM *Alan Carruthers*
Programme Director, Galaxy *Neil Greenslade*

Heart FM commenced broadcasting music, regional news and information in September 1994. Galaxy broadcasts today's dance and soul, news and information.

102.7 Hereward FM/Classic Gold Digital 1332

PO Box 225, Queensgate Centre,
Peterborough, Cambridgeshire PE1 1XJ
☎01733 460460 Fax 01733 281445
Website www.koko.com

Programme Controller *Paul Green*

Part of GWR Group plc. Not usually any openings offered to writers as all material is compiled and presented by in-house staff.

FM 103 Horizon

Broadcast Centre, Crownhill, Milton Keynes,
Buckinghamshire MK8 0AB
☎01908 269111 Fax 01908 564893
Website www.koko.com

Programme Controller *Trevor Marshall*

Part of the GWR Group plc. Music and news.

Invicta FM/Capital Gold

PO Box 100, Whitstable, Kent CT5 3YR
☎01227 772004 Fax 01227 774450
Website www.invictafm.com

Programme Controller *Mike Osborne*

Music-based station, serving listeners in Kent.
Part of Capital Radio Plc.

Island FM

12 Westerbrook, St Sampsons, Guernsey,
Channel Islands GY2 4QQ

☎01481 242000 Fax 01481 249676
Website www.islandfm.guernsey.net
Managing Director *Kevin Stewart*
Music-based programming.

Isle of Wight Radio
Dodnor Park, Newport, Isle of Wight
PO30 5XE
☎01983 822557 Fax 01983 821690
Email mail@iwradio.co.uk
Website www.iwradio.co.uk
Managing Director *Andy Shier*
Programme Manager *Stuart McGinley*

Part of the Local Radio Company, Isle of
Wight Radio is the island's only radio station
broadcasting local news, music and general
entertainment. .

ITN News Direct 97.3 FM/
LBC 1152 AM
200 Gray's Inn Road, London WC1X 8XZ
☎020 7333 0030 (News Direct)/
020 7973 1152 (LBC)
Fax 020 7312 8470 (News Direct)/
020 8565 (LBC)
Email editor@lbc.co.uk *(LBC editorial queries)*
Website www.newsdirect.co.uk *and*
www.lbc.co.uk
Chief Editor, ITN Radio *Nicholas Wheeler*
Editor, ITN News Direct/LBC *Stuart*
    Thomas
ITN News Direct 97.3 FM – 24-hour rolling
news station; LBC 1152 AM – news, views and
information for London.

Key 103
See **Piccadilly 1152**

LBC 1152 AM
See **ITN News Direct 97.3 FM**

105.4 FM Leicester Sound
Granville House, Granville Road, Leicester
LE1 7RW
☎0116 256 1300 Fax 0116 256 1305
Website www.koko.com
Managing Director *Chris Hughes*

Part of GWR Group plc. Predominantly a music
station. Very occasionally, unsolicited material of
local interest – 'targeted at our particular audience' – may be broadcast.

Magic 1152AM
See **Metro Radio**

Magic 1161
See **Viking FM**

Magic 1548
See **Radio City Ltd**

Magic 828
See **96.3 Aire FM**

Magic AM
See **Hallam FM**

Marcher Gold
Marcher Sound Ltd., The Studios, Mold
Road, Wrexham LL11 4AF
☎01978 752202 Fax 01978 759701
Website www.marchergold.co.uk
Programme Controller *Graham Ledger*

Occasional features and advisory programmes.
Hour-long Welsh language broadcasts are aired
weekdays at 6.00 pm.

Medway's Mercury FM
Berkeley House, 186 High Street, Rochester,
Kent ME1 1EY
☎01634 841111 Fax 01634 841122
Website www.koko.com
Managing Director *John Hirst*
Programme Director *Steve Joy*

A wide range of music programming plus news,
views and local interest. Part of the GWR Group
plc.

Mercia FM/
Classic Gold Digital 1359
Mercia Sound Ltd., Hertford Place, Coventry
CV1 3TT
☎024 7686 8200 Fax 024 7686 8202
Managing Director *Carlton Dale*
Programme Controller *Louis Clark*
Music-based station.

Mercury FM 102.7/Classic Gold
Digital – Breeze 1521
The Stanley Centre, Kelvin Way, Manor
Royal, Crawley, West Sussex RH10 2SE
☎01293 519161 Fax 01293 560927
Website www.mercuryfm.co.uk
Programme Controller *Simon Osborne*

Mercury FM plays contemporary music targeting 15–34 years. Breeze 1521 AM plays hits
from the '60s to '90s, targeting 35 years-plus.
Both services carry local, national and international news.

Metro Radio/Magic 1152AM
Swalwell, Newcastle upon Tyne NE99 1BB
☎0191 420 0971 (Metro)/420 3040 (Magic)
Fax 520191 488 0933
Website www.clickmetroradio.com

Programme Director *Tony McKenzie*

Very few opportunities for writers, but phone-in programmes may interview relevant authors.

Minster FM
PO Box 123, Dunnington, York
YO1 5ZX
☎01904 488888 Fax 01904 488811
Website www.minsterfm.co.uk

Managing Director *Lynn Bell*

Music, local news and sport.

Moray Firth Radio
PO Box 271, Scorguie Place, Inverness
IV3 8UJ
☎01463 224433 Fax 01463 243224
Email gerry.robinson@mfr.co.uk

**Managing Director/Programme
  Controller** *Gary Robinson*
Programme Organiser *Ray Atkinson*
Book Reviews *May Marshall*

Book reviews every Sunday morning at 7.00 am–8.00 am.

News Direct 97.3 FM
See **ITN News Direct 97.3 FM**

Northants 96/
Classic Gold Digital 1557
19–21 St Edmunds Road, Northampton
NN1 5DY
☎01604 795600 Fax 01604 795601
Email reception@northants96.musicradio.com
Website www.koko.com

Programme Controller *Mark Jeeves*

Music and news, 24 hours a day. Part of the GWR Group plc.

NorthSound Radio
45 King's Gate, Aberdeen AB15 4EL
☎01224 337000 Fax 01224 400003
Website www.northsound.co.uk

Managing Director *Rod Webster*
Station Director *Gerry Burke*

Features and music programmes 24 hours a day including, mid-morning (9.00 am – midday), *Northsound 2* feature programme.

Ocean Radio
Radio House, Whittle Avenue, Segensworth West, Fareham, Hampshire PO15 5SH
☎01489 589911 Fax 01489 589453
Email info@oceanradio.co.uk
Website www.oceanradiofm.com

Programme Controller *Mark Sadler*
Head of News *Jane Dancer*

Music-based programming only. Part of Capital Radio Plc.

Orchard FM
Haygrove House, Shoreditch, Taunton, Somerset TA3 7BT
☎01823 338448 Fax 01823 321611
Email news@orchardfm.co.uk
Website www.orchardfm.co.uk

Programme Director *Steve Bulley*
News Team *Darren Bevan, Nicola Maxey*.

Music-based programming only.

Piccadilly 1152/Key 103
Castle Quay, Castlefield, Manchester
M15 4PR
☎0161 288 5000 Fax 0161 288 5001

Programme Director *Andrew Robson*

Music-based programming.

Plymouth Sound Radio
Earl's Acre, Alma Road, Plymouth, Devon
PL3 4HX
☎01752 227272 Fax 01752 275605
Website www.koko.com

Programme Controller *Peter Greig*

Music-based station. No outlets for writers. Part of the GWR Group plc.

Premier Radio
Glen House, Stag Place, London
SW1E 5AG
☎020 7316 1300 Fax 020 7233 6706
Email premier@premier.org.uk
Website www.premier.org.uk

Managing Director *Peter Kerridge*

Broadcasts programmes that reflect the beliefs and values of the Christian faith, 24 hours a day.

Q103FM
PO Box 103, Vision Park, Chivers Way, Histon, Cambridge CB4 9WW
☎01223 235255 Fax 01223 235161
Website www.koko.com

Managing Director *Lynda Couch-Smith*

Part of GWR Group plc. Music and news.

96.3 QFM

PO Box 96.3, Paisley PA1 2LG
☎0141 887 9630 Fax 0141 887 0963
Email sales@q-fm.demon.co.uk

Station Director *Gus MacKenzie*
Programme Controller *Dougie Jackson*

Music-based programming plus local information and news. Part of the Wireless Group.

Radio City Ltd/Magic 1548

Radio City Tower, St John's Beacon, 1
Houghton Street, Liverpool L1 1RL
☎0151 472 6800 Fax 0151 472 6821
Website www.radiocity967.com

Managing Director *Sean Marley*
Programme Director *Richard Maddock*

Opportunities for writers are very few and far between as this is predominantly a music station.

Red Dragon FM/Capital Gold

Atlantic Wharf, Cardiff CF10 4DJ
☎029 2066 2066 Fax 029 2066n2060
Website www.reddragonfm.co.uk

Programme Controller *Andy Johnson*
News Editor *Andrew Jones*

Acquired by Capital Radio in 1998. Music-based programming only.

Red Rose Radio

PO Box 301, St Paul's Square, Preston,
Lancashire PR1 1YE
☎01772 556301 Fax 01772 201917
Website www.redrose.demon.co.uk

Programme Director *Mike Bawden*

Music-based station. No outlets for writers.

Sabras Radio

Radio House, 63 Melton Road, Leicester
LE4 6PN
☎0116 261 0666 Fax 0116 266 7776
Email don@sabrasradio.com
Website www.sabrasradio.com

Programme Controller *Don Kotak*

Programmes for the Asian community, broadcasting 24 hours a day.

SCOT FM

Number 1 Albert Quay, Leith, Edinburgh
EH6 7DN
☎0131 554 6677 Fax 0131 625 8401
Website www.scot-fm.com

Managing Director *Mick Hall*
Programme Director *Jay Crawford*

On air since September 1994. Broadcasts music and conversation to the central Scottish region.

Severn Sound FM/ Classic Gold Digital 774

Bridge Studios, Eastgate Centre, Gloucester
GL1 1SS
☎01452 313200 Fax 01452 313213
Website www.koko.com

Managing Director *Neil Cooper*

Part of the GWR Group plc. Music and news.

SGR FM 97.1/96.4

Alpha Business Park, Whitehouse Road,
Ipswich, Suffolk IP1 5LT
☎01473 461000
Fax 01473 241111 (newsdesk)
Website www.sgrfm.co.uk

Managing Director *Mike Stewart*
Programme Controller *Mark Pryke*

Music-based programming.

Signal One/Big AM

Stoke Road, Shelton, Stoke on Trent,
Staffordshire ST4 2SR
☎01782 441300 Fax 01782 441301
Website www.signalone.co.uk

Programme Controller (Signal One)
    Mark Franklin
Programme Controller (Big AM)
    Mark Chivers

Music-based station. No outlets for writers. Part of the Wireless Group.

Southern FM

PO Box 2000, Brighton, East Sussex
BN41 2SS
☎01273 430111 Fax 01273 430098
Website www.southernfm.com

Programme Controller *Tony Aldridge*
News Manager *Laurence King*

Music, news, entertainment and competitions. Part of Capital Radio Plc.

Spectrum Radio

204–206 Queenstown Road, Battersea,
London SW8 3NR
☎020 7627 4433 Fax 020 7627 3409
Email enquiries@spectrumradio.net
Website www.spectrumradio.net

Managing Director *Paul Hogan*

Programmes for a broad spectrum of ethnic groups in London.

Spire FM

City Hall Studios, Malthouse Lane, Salisbury,
Wiltshire SP2 7QQ
☎01722 416644 Fax 01722 416688
Website www.spirefm.co.uk

Station Director *Gary Haberfield*

Music, news current affairs, quizzes and sport.
Won the Sony Award for the best local radio
station in 1994 and 1996.

Sun FM 103.4

PO Box 1034, Sunderland, Tyne & Wear
SR5 2YL
☎0191 548 1034 Fax 0191 548 7171
Website www.sun-fm.com

Managing Director *Brian Lister*
Programme Controller *Simon Grundy*

Music-based programmes only.

Sunrise Radio (Yorkshire)

Sunrise House, 30 Chapel Street, Bradford,
West Yorkshire BD1 5DN
☎01274 735043 Fax 01274 728534

**Programme Controller, Chief Executive
& Chairman** *Usha Parmar*

Programmes for the Asian community in
Bradford.

Sunshine 855

South Shropshire Communications Ltd.,
Sunshine House, Waterside, Ludlow,
Shropshire SY8 1PE
☎01584 873795 Fax 01584 875900
Website www.sunshine855.co.uk

Operations Director *Austin Powell*

Music, news and information, broadcast 24
hours a day.

Swansea Sound 1170 MW

See **The Wave FM**

Tay FM/Radio Tay AM

Radio Tay Ltd., PO Box 123, Dundee
DD1 9UF
☎01382 200800 Fax 01382 423252
Email tayfm@radiotay.co.uk *and*
tayam@radiotay.co.uk

Managing Director/Programme Director
Ally Ballingall

Wholly-owned subsidiary of Scottish Radio
Holdings. Carries a 20-minute book pro-
gramme every Sunday evening, presented by
Mabel Adams. Short stories and book reviews

of local interest are welcome. Send to the programme director.

107.8FM Thames Radio

Brentham House, 45c High Street,
Hampton Wick, Kingston upon Thames,
Surrey KT1 4DG
☎020 8288 1300 Fax 020 8288 1312
Website www.thamesradio.co.uk

Station Manager *Julia Kent*
Programme Controller *Mark Walker*

Music-based programmes of current hits and
classic pop.

96 Trent FM/
Classic Gold GEM AM

29–31 Castlegate, Nottingham NG1 7AP
☎0115 952 7000 Fax 0115 912 9302
Email admin@trentfm.musicradio.com

Managing Director *Chris Hughes*

Part of the GWR Group plc.

2CR-FM/Classic Gold 828

5–7 Southcote Road, Bournemouth, Dorset
BH1 3LR
☎01202 259259 Fax 01202 255244
Email info@2crfm.co.uk
Website www.2crfm.co.uk

Programme Controller *Craig Morris*

Wholly-owned subsidiary of the GWR Group
plc. Serves Dorset and Hampshire. All reviews/
topicality/press releases to the Programme
Controller, 2CR-FM at the address above.

2-Ten FM/Classic Gold Digital

PO Box 2020, Reading, Berkshire
RG31 7FG
☎0118 945 4400
Fax 0118 928 8513 (admin)/8809 (news)
Website www.2-tenfm.co.uk

Programme Controller *Tim Parker*

A subsidiary of the GWR Group plc. Music-
based programming.

Viking FM/Magic 1161

Commercial Road, Hull, North Humberside
HU1 2SG
☎01482 325141 Fax 01482 587067
Website www.clickviking.com

Managing Director *Sue Timson*
Programme Controller *Stuart Baldwin*
News Co-ordinator *Jamie York*

Music-based programming. Part of the EMAP
Group.

The Wave FM/
Swansea Sound 1170 MW

Victoria Road, Gowerton, Swansea SA4 3AB
☎01792 511964 (FM)/511170 (MW)
Fax 01792 511965 (FM)/511171 (MW)
Email admin@thewave.co.uk *or*
admin@swanseasound.co.uk
Website www.the wave.co.uk *or*
swanseasound.co.uk

Station and Programme Director
Andy Griffiths
News Editor *Simon Thompson*

Music-based programming on FM while
Swansea Sound is interested in a wide variety
of material, though news items must be of local
relevance. An explanatory letter, in the first
instance, is advisable.

Wessex FM

Radio House, Trinity Street, Dorchester,
Dorset DT1 1DJ
☎01305 250333 Fax 01305 250052
   Website www.wessexfm.co.uk

Programme Manager *Stewart Smith*

Music, local news, information and features.
These include reviews of theatre, cinema, videos,
local music.

West Sound AM/West FM

Radio House, 54 Holmston Road, Ayr
KA7 3BE
☎01292 283662
Fax 01292 283665/262607 (news)

Website www.west-sound.co.uk *or*
www.westfm.co.uk

Programme Controller *Alan Toomey*

Music-based broadcasting.

102.4 Wish FM

Orrell Road, Wigan WN5 8HJ
☎01942 761024 Fax 01942 777694
Website www.wishfm.net

Programme Controller *John Evington*

Music-based programming plus news and
sport. Part of the Wireless Group.

Wyvern FM

5–6 Barbourne Terrace, Worcester WR1 3JZ
☎01905 612212/746644 (newsroom)
Fax 01905 746637
Website www.koko.com

Managing Director *Neil Cooper*
Programme Controller *Sasha French*

Part of the GWR Group plc. Music-based programming.

Radio XL 1296 AM

KMS House, Bradford Street, Birmingham
B12 0JD
☎0121 753 5353 Fax 0121 753 3111

Station Manager *Barry Curtis*

Asian broadcasting for the West Midlands, 24
hours a day. Broadcasts *Love Express* featuring
love stories and poems. Writers should send
material to *Priya Kular* (email: priya@radioxl.net).

Freelance Rates – Broadcasting

Freelance rates vary enormously. The following minimum rates should be treated as guidelines. Most work can command higher fees from employers. It is up to freelancers to negotiate the best deal they can.

BBC Guidelines for Freelance Minimum Rates

BBC – Published Material
(negotiated by the **Publishers Association** and the **Society of Authors**)

Domestic Radio

Plays/prose (per minute)	£13.24
Prose for dramatisation (per minute)	£10.32
Poems (per half-minute)	£13.24
Prose translation (per minute)	£8.83

World Service Radio (English)

Plays/prose (per minute)	£6.63
Prose for dramatisation (per minute)	£5.17
Poems (per half-minute)	£6.63
Prose translation (per minute)	£4.42

Television

Prose (per minute)	£20.04
Poems (per half-minute)	£23.27

BBC Radio Drama
(negotiated by the **Society of Authors** and the **Writers' Guild**)
A beginner in radio drama should receive at least £43.85 per minute for an original drama script. For an established writer – one who has three or more plays to his credit – the minimum rate per minute is £66.74.

An attendance payment of £39.26 per production is paid to established writers. The rate per script for *The Archers* is £677.

Daily Serial minimum rates:
1) Where the storyline, characters, format, etc. are provided, the minimum fee is £539;
2) Where the overall format and structure are provided but the writer provides the storyline, some characters, etc. the minimum fee is £714. (All fees cover one origination and one repeat.)

BBC Interviews and Talks
Currently under negotiaition but previous rates stood at:
Interviews of up to 5 minutes (for the interviewer): £50; *5 to 8 minutes*: £55; *8 to 10*

minutes: £66.50. *Linked interviews*: 1 interview £8; 2 interviews £107. *Illustrated talks*: £16 per minute.

Features/documentaries
Currently under negotiation but previous rates stood at: up to 7 minutes, £178.50; £25.50 per minute thereafter.

Independent Radio

For details of the **NUJ/CRCA** (Commercial Radio Companies Association) agreement on recommended rates, contact the NUJ Broadcasting Office (see **Professional Associations**).

Research
TV organisations which hire freelancers to research programme items should pay on a day rate which reflects the value of the work and the importance of the programme concerned.

Presentation
In all broadcast media, presenters command higher fees than news journalists. There is considerable variation in what is paid for presenting programmes and videos, according to their audience and importance. Day rates with television companies are usually about £140–160 a day.

Television Drama

For a 60-minute teleplay, the BBC will pay an established writer £7410 and a beginner £4703. The corresponding figures for ITV are £9245 for the established writer and £6568 for a writer new to television but with a solid reputation in other literary areas. ITV also has a 'beginner' category with a payment of £6296 for a 60-minute teleplay.

Day rates for attendance at read-throughs and rehearsals is £67 for the BBC and £74.40 for ITV.

(*NB* ITV rates currently under negotiation)

Feature Films

The **Writers' Guild** and **PACT** agreement of 1992 (still being re-negotiated) allows for a minimum guaranteed payment to the writer of £31,200 on a feature film with a budget in excess of £2 million; £19,000 on a budget from £750,000 to £2 million; £14,000 on a budget below £750,000. However, many in the industry pay rates which take inflation into account and negotiate a royalty provision for uses instead of fixed percentage payments.

Film, TV and Video Production Companies

Aardman
Gas Ferry Road, Bristol BS1 6UN
☎0117 984 8485 Fax 0117 984 8486
Website www.aardman.com

Head of Script Development *Mike Cooper*
Development Executive (Shorts & Series)
Helen Brunsdon

FOUNDED 1972. Award-winning animation studio producing films, television series, videos, commercials and new media properties. OUTPUT includes: *Rex the Runt; Morph Files; Creature Comforts; Wallace and Gromit; Angry Kid; Chicken Run.* No unsolicited submissions.

Absolutely Productions Ltd
8th Floor, Alhambra House, 27–31 Charing Cross Road, London WC2H 0AU
☎020 7930 3113 Fax 020 7930 4114
Email info@absolutely-uk.com
Website www.absolutely-uk.com

Executive Producer *Miles Bullough*

TV and film production company specialising in comedy and entertainment. OUTPUT *Absolutely* series 1–4 (Ch4); *mr don and mr george* (Ch4); *Squawkietalkie* (comedy wildlife programme for Ch4); *The Preventers* (ITV); *Scotland v England* (Ch4); *Barry Welsh is Coming* (HTV); *The Jack Docherty Show* (Ch5); *The Morwenna Banks Show* (Ch5); *Stressed Eric* (BBC2); *Armstrong & Miller* (Paramount/Ch4); *The Creatives* (BBC2); *Trigger Happy* (Ch4); *The Announcement* (Dakota Entertainment).

Abstract Images
117 Willoughby House, Barbican, London EC2Y 8BL
☎020 7638 5123
Email productions@abstract-images.co.uk

Contact *Howard Ross*

Television documentary and drama programming. Also theatre productions. OUTPUT includes *Balm in Gilead* (drama); *Road* (drama); *Bent* (drama); *God: For & Against* (documentary); *This Is a Man* (drama/doc). Encourages new writers; send synopsis in the first instance.

Acacia Productions Ltd
80 Weston Park, London N8 9Tb
☎020 8341 9392 Fax 020 8341 4879
Email acacia@dial.pipex.com
Website www.acaciaproductions.co.uk

Contact *J. Edward Milner*

Producer of television and video documentaries; also news reports, corporates and programmes for educational charities. No unsolicited mss. OUTPUT includes a documentary series in association with TVE, London and NHK, Japan entitled *Last Plant Standing; A Farm in Uganda; Montserrat: Under the Volcano; Spirit of Trees* (8 progs.); *Vietnam: After the Fire.*

Acrobat Television
107 Wellington Road North, Stockport, Cheshire SK4 2LP
☎0161 477 9090 Fax 0161 477 9191
Email info@acrobat-tv.co.uk

Contacts *David Hill, Annie Broom*

Corporate video producer. OUTPUT includes instructional video for the British Association of Ski Instructors; corporate videos for Neilson Sailing, Hepworth Building Products, The Simon Group and First Choice Ski. No unsolicited mss.

Action Time Ltd
1 Heathcock Court, 415 Strand, London WC2R 0NS
☎020 7836 0505 Fax 020 7836 1515

Joint Managing Directors *Stephen Leahy, Trish Kinane*

Major producer and licenser of TV quiz and game entertainment shows such as *Catchphrase; Wipeout; The Mole, Chance of a Lifetime.* Action Time co-produces in Europe, USA and Australia.

Alomo Productions
1 Stephen Street, London W1T 1AL
☎020 7691 6531 Fax 020 7691 6081
Website www.pearsontv.com

A Pearson Television Group company, part of the RTL Group. Major producer of television drama and comedy. OUTPUT *Starting Out; Dirty Work; Goodnight Sweetheart; Birds of a Feather; Love Hurts; The New Statesman; Grown Ups; Unfinished Business; Cry Wolf.* Scripts not welcome unless via agents but new writing is encouraged.

Anglo-Caribbean Productions

1a Gambole Road, Tooting Broadway, London SW17 0QJ
☎07970 715080 Fax 020 8801 7592
Email jasonyoung72@yahoo.com
Website www.anglocaribbean.plus.com

Producer *Jason Young*

Feature films and television serials. OUTPUT *To See Ourselves; The North Londoners; The House of Hope; The Black Englishman; The Young Professionals.* Material must be of an inter-racial nature in order to develop the profile of Black English characters. All scripts via agents only.

Anglo/Fortunato Films Ltd

170 Popes Lane, London W5 4NJ
☎020 8932 7676 Fax 020 8932 7491

Contact *Luciano Celentino*

Film, television and video producer of action comedy and psych-thriller drama. No unsolicited mss.

Antelope (UK) Ltd

29b Montague Street, London WC1B 5BW
☎020 7209 0099 Fax 020 7209 0098
Website www.antelope.co.uk

Managing Director *Mick Csáky*
Head of Production *Justin Johnson*

Film, television and video productions for drama, documentary and corporate material. OUTPUT *Cyberspace* (ITV); *Brunch* (Ch5); *The Pier* (weekly arts and entertainment programme); *Placido Domingo* (ITV); *Baden Powell – The Boy Man; Howard Hughes – The Naked Emperor* (Ch4 'Secret Lives' series); *Hiroshima.* No unsolicited mss – 'we are not reading any new material at present'.

Apex Television Production & Facilities Ltd

Button End Studios, Harston, Cambridge CB2 5NX
☎01223 872900 Fax 01223 873092

Contact *Bernard Mulhern*

Video producer: corporate drama, documentary, commercials and production for a wide range of international companies. Many drama-based training programmes and current-affairs orienta-

ted TV work. No scripts. All work is commissioned against a particular project.

Arena Films Ltd

2 Pelham Road, London SW19 1SX
☎020 8543 3990 Fax 020 8540 3992

Producer *David Conroy*

Film and TV drama. Scripts with some sort of European connection or tie-in particularly welcome.

Argus Video Productions

52 Church Street, Briston, Melton Constable, Norfolk NR24 2LE
☎01263 861152

Contact *Siri Taylor*

Producer of corporate, documentary and educational videos. OUTPUT includes *View & Do* series on leisure and hobby interests; *The Chainsaw Safety* and *Relaxation* series; and *Moving Postcard Series on East Anglia.* No unsolicited mss.

Ariel Productions Ltd

11 Albion Gate, Hyde Park Place, London W2 2LF
☎020 7262 7726 Fax 020 7262 7726

Producer *Otto Plaschkes*

Feature film and television producer. OUTPUT includes *Georgy Girl; Hopscotch; In Celebration; Butley; Doggin' Around.* Encourages new writers through involvement with the **National Film and Television School** and Screen Laboratory. No unsolicited mss.

Arlington Productions Limited

Pinewood Studios, Iver Heath, Buckinghamshire SL0 0NH
☎01753 651700 Fax 01753 656050

Television producer. Specialises in popular international drama, with *occasional* forays into other areas. 'We have an enviable reputation for encouraging new writers but only accept unsolicited submissions via agents.'

The Ashford Entertainment Corporation Ltd

182 Brighton Road, Coulsdon, Surrey CR5 2NF
☎020 8645 0667 Fax 020 8763 2558
Email info@ashford-entertainment.co.uk
Website www.ashford-entertainment.co.uk

Managing Director *Frazer Ashford*
Head of Production *Georgina Huxstep*

FOUNDED in 1996 by award-winning film and

TV producer Frazer Ashford whose credits include *Great Little Trains* (Mainline Television for Westcountry/Ch4, starring the late Willie Rushton); *Street Life* and *Make Yourself at Home* (both for WTV). Produces theatrical films and television – drama, lifestyle and documentaries. Happy to receive ideas for documentaries but submit a one-page synopsis only in the first instance, enclosing s.a.e. 'Be patient, allow up to four weeks for a reply. Be precise with the idea; specific details rather than vague thoughts. Attach a back-up sheet with credentials and supporting evidence, ie, can you ensure that your idea is feasible?'

Assembly Film and Television Ltd

Riverside Studios, Crisp Road, London W6 9RL
☎020 8237 1075 Fax 020 8237 1071
Email judithmurrell@riversidestudios.co.uk
Contacts *William Burdett-Coutts, Judith Murrell*

Television documentary producer. OUTPUT includes the Prudential Awards for the Arts; the London Comedy Festival; Ch4's Black Season, *In Exile: Sitcom* and *Black Books: Sitcom*. Welcomes unsolicited mss. 'We are always interested in looking at new writers.'

Avalon Films

1 Rook's Farm Road, Yelland, Barnstaple, Devon EX31 3EQ
☎01271 860294 Fax 01271 860294
Email producers.avalonfilms@aol.com
Website www.avalonfilms.homstead.com
Joint Managing Directors *Robin Price, Andrew Vincent*
Director of Research & Development *Dennis Price*
Head of Creative Affairs *Teresa Collard*

Production company now specialising in horror/sci-fi/psychological thriller feature films and television drama (period and contemporary). 'We work with a regular team of writers but are still keen to encourage new talent. We help new writers refine their skills and can sometimes place work for them with other production companies. Unsolicited screenplays are given serious consideration.' OUTPUT Feature films, 2001: *Hellborn; The Devil & All His Works; U570; The Silent Vulcan; Satan's Skin of Shining Armour.* TV: *The Heritage Murders; The Cage of Eagles; The Dark World of; Wilkie Collins.*

Bazal

See **Endemol Entertainment UK plc**

Beckmann Productions Ltd

Meadow Court, West Street, Ramsey, Isle of Man IM8 1AE
☎01624 816585 Fax 01624 816589
Email beckmann@enterprise.net
Website www.beckmanngroup.co.uk
Contacts *Stuart Semark, Michael Souter*

Isle of Man-based company. Video and television documentary. OUTPUT *Practical Guide to Europe* (travel series); *Maestro* (12-part series on classical composers); *Ivory Orphans; Ages in History.*

Paul Berriff Productions Ltd

Cedar House, 53 Heads Lane, Hessle, East Yorkshire HU13 0JH
☎01482 641158 Fax 01482 649692
Email pberriff@aol.com
Contact *Paul Berriff*

Television documentary. OUTPUT *Rescue* (13-part documentary for ITV); *M25: The Magic Roundabout* ('First Tuesday'); *Animal Squad Undercover* (Ch4); *Evidence of Abuse* (BBC1 'Inside Story'); *Lessons of Darkness* (BBC2 'Fine Cut'); *The Nick* (Ch4 series); *Confrontation on E Wing* (BBC 'Everyman'); *Astronauts* (Ch4 series); *Streets of Fire* (Ch4 series); *Passport Control* ('Cutting Edge').

Black Coral Productions Ltd

2nd Floor, 241 High Street, London E17 7BH
☎020 8520 2830 Fax 020 8520 2358
Email bcp@coralmedia.co.uk
Website www.m4media.net
Contact *Lazell Daley*

Producer of drama and documentary film and television. Committed to the development of new writing with a particular interest in short and feature-length dramas. Offers a script consultancy service for which a fee is payable. Runs courses – see **Blaze the Trail** under **Writers' Courses, Circles and Workshops**.

Blackwatch Productions Limited

752–756 Argyle Street, Anderston, Glasgow G3 8UJ
☎0141 222 2640/2641 Fax 0141 222 2646
Email info@blackwatchtv.com
Company Director *Nicola Black*
Director *Paul Gallagher*
Research & Development Officer *Heidi Proven*

Film, television, video producer of drama and documentary programmes. OUTPUT incudes *Lightbox* (film drama) and, for Ch4: *Mirrorball* (music video series); *Documentary Lab* (documentary series); *Carry On Darkly* (documentary); *Post Mortem* (drama–doc series). Does not welcome unsolicited mss.

Blue Heaven Productions Ltd
116 Great Portland Street, London W1W 6PJ
☎020 7436 5552 Fax 020 7436 0888

Contact *Christine Benson*

Film and television drama and occasional documentary. OUTPUT *The Ruth Rendell Mysteries; Crime Story: Dear Roy, Love Gillian; Ready When You Are / Screen Challenge* (three series for Meridian Regional); *The Man who Made Husbands Jealous* (Anglia Television Entertainment/Blue Heaven). Scripts considered but treatments or ideas preferred in the first instance. New writing encouraged.

British Lion Screen Entertainment Ltd
Pinewood Studios, Iver, Buckinghamshire SL0 0NH
☎01753 651700 Fax 01753 656391

Chief Executive *Peter R. E. Snell*

Film production. OUTPUT has included *A Man for All Seasons; Treasure Island; A Prayer for the Dying; Lady Jane; The Crucifer of Blood; Death Train.* No unsolicited mss. Send synopses only.

Bronco Films Ltd
The Producers Centre, 61 Holland Street, Glasgow G2 4NJ
☎0141 287 6817 Fax 0141 287 6815
Email broncofilm@btinternet.com

Contact *Peter Broughan*

Film, television and video drama. OUTPUT includes *Rob Roy* (feature film) and *Young Person's Guide to Becoming a Rock Star* (TV series). No unsolicited mss.

Buccaneer Films
5 Rainbow Court, Oxhey, Hertfordshire WD19 4RP
☎01923 254000/07740 902095 (mobile)
Fax 01923 254000

Contact *Michael Gosling*

Corporate video production and still photography specialists in education and sport. No unsolicited mss.

Can Television & Marketing
Smitham House, 127 Brighton Road, Coulsdon, Surrey CR5 2NJ
☎020 8763 9444 Fax 020 8668 0130

Email can.tv@Talk21.com

Contact *Philip Saben*

Television and video producer of corporate programmes and commercials for clients such as London Electricity and NatWest. No unsolicited mss.

Caravel Film Techniques Ltd
The Great Barn Studios, Cippenham Lane, Slough, Berkshire SL1 5AU
☎01753 534828 Fax 01753 571383
Email Ajjcaraveltv.aol.com
Website www.caravelstudios.com

Contact *Anita See*

Film, video and TV: documentary, commercials and corporate. OUTPUT Promos for commercial TV, documentaries for BBC & ITV, sales and training material for corporate blue chip companies. No unsolicited scripts. Prepared to review mostly serious new writing.

Carlton Productions
35–38 Portman Square, London W1H 6NU
☎020 7486 6688 Fax 020 7486 1132
Website www.carltontv.com

Director of Programmes *Steve Hewlett*
Director of Drama & Co-production
  Jonathan Powell
Controller of Entertainment *Mark Wells*
Controller of Factual Programmes *Polly Bide*
Controller of Comedy *Nick Symons*

Makers of independently produced TV drama for ITV. OUTPUT *She's Out; Kavanagh QC; Morse; Boon; Gone to the Dogs; The Guilty; Tanamera; Soldier, Soldier; Seekers; Sharpe; Peak Practice; Cadfael; Faith.* 'We try to use new writers on established long-running series.' Scripts welcome from experienced writers and agents only.

Carnival (Films & Theatre) Ltd
12 Raddington Road, Ladbroke Grove, London W10 5TG
☎020 8968 0968 Fax 020 8968 0155
Email info@carnival-films.co.uk
Website www.carnival-films.co.uk

Contact *Brian Eastman*

Film, TV and theatre producer. OUTPUT Film: *The Mill on the Floss* (BBC); *Firelight* (Hollywood Pictures/Wind Dancer Productions); *Up on the Roof* (Rank/Granada); *Shadowlands* (Savoy/Spelling); *In Hitler's Shadow* (Home Box Office); *Under Suspicion* (Columbia/Rank/LWT). Television: *As If* (Ch4/Columbia); *Lucy Sullivan is Getting Married* (ITV); *The Tenth Kingdom*

(Sky/NBC); *Agatha Christie's Poirot* (ITV/LWT/
A&E); *Every Woman Knows a Secret* and *Oktober*
(both for ITV Network Centre); *The Fragile
Heart* (Ch4); *Crime Traveller* (BBC); *Bugs 1–4*
(BBC); *Anna Lee* (LWT); *All Or Nothing At All*
(LWT); *Head Over Heels* (Carlton); *Jeeves &
Wooster* I–IV (Granada); *Traffik* (Ch4); *Forever
Green 1–3* (LWT); *Porterhouse Blue* (Ch4); *Blott
on the Landscape* (BBC). Theatre: *What a
Performance; Juno & the Paycock; Murder is Easy;
Misery; Ghost Train; Map of the Heart;
Shadowlands; Up on the Roof.*

Cartwn Cymru
Ben Jenkins Court, 19A High Street, Llandaf,
Cardiff CF5 2DY
☎029 2057 5999 Fax 029 2057 5919
Email production@cartwn-
cymru.demon.co.uk

Contact *Naomi Jones*

Animation production company. OUTPUT
Toucan 'Tecs (YTV/S4C); *Funnybones* (S4C/
BBC); *Turandot: Operavox* (S4C/BBC);
Testament: The Bible in Animation (BBC2/S4C);
The Miracle Maker (S4C/BBC/British Screen/
Icon Entertainment International); *Faeries*
(HIT Entertainment plc for CITV).

Celador
39 Long Acre, London WC2E 9LJ
☎020 7240 8101 Fax 020 7497 9541
Email tvhits@celador.co.uk

Head of Entertainment *Colman Hutchinson*
Head of Comedy *Mike Whitehill*

Producer of TV and radio comedy and light
entertainment. OUTPUT *Who Wants to be a
Millionaire; Winning Lines; Commercial Breakdown;
Jasper Carrott – Back to the Front.* 'We are interested in original non-derivative sitcom scripts
and entertainment formats. Some broadcast
experience would be helpful. But as a relatively
small company our script-reading capacity is
limited.'

Celtic Films Ltd
Room 21, Ground Floor, Government
Buildings, Bromyard Avenue, London
W3 7XH
☎020 8740 6880 Fax 020 8740 9755
Email celticfilms@aol.com

Contact *Stuart Sutherland*

Film and television drama producer. OUTPUT
includes 14 feature-length *Sharpe* TV films for
Carlton and *A Life for a Life – The True Story of
Stefan Kiszko* TV film for ITV. Supports new
writing and welcomes unsolicited mss.

Central Office of Information Film & Video
Hercules Road, London SE1 7DU
☎020 7261 8667 Fax 020 7261 8776
Email graison@coi.gov.uk

Contact *Geoff Raison*

Film, video and TV: drama, documentary,
commercials, corporate and public information
films. OUTPUT includes government commercials and corporate information. No scripts.
New writing commissioned as required.

Chameleon Television Ltd
Television House, 104 Kirkstall Road, Leeds,
West Yorkshire LS3 1JS
☎0113 244 4486 Fax 0113 243 1267
Email allen@chameleontv.com

Contacts *Allen Jewhurst, Kevin Sim, Anna Hall*

Film and television drama and documentary
producer. OUTPUT includes *The Reckoning*
(USA/Ch4); *Dunblane* (ITV); *Foul Play* (Ch5);
St Hildas and *Rules of the Game* (both for Ch4);
Divorces From Hell, New Voices and *Shipman* (all
for ITV). Scripts not welcome unless via agents
but new writing is encouraged.

Channel X Communications Ltd
22 Stephenson Way, London NW1 2HD
☎020 7387 3874 Fax 020 7387 0738
Email mail@channelx.co.uk
Website www.channelx.co.uk

Contact *Alan Marke*

FOUNDED 1986 by Jonathan Ross and Alan
Marke to develop Ross's first series *The Last
Resort.* Now producing comedy series and docu-
mentary. Actively developing narrative comedy
and game shows. OUTPUT *Unpleasant World of
Penn & Teller; XYZ; Jo Brand – Through The
Cakehole; Sean's Show; The Smell of Reeves &
Mortimer; Fantastic Facts; One for the Road; Funny
Business; Shooting Stars; Barking; Food Fight;
Johnny Vaughan Meets Madonna; Families at War;
Leftfield; The Cooler; All Back to Mine* (Series 1 &
2); *Celebrities ... the truth; Comedy Cafe; Head to
Toe; Tales of Uplift; Moral Improvement.*

Chatsworth Television Limited
97–99 Dean Street, London W1D 3TE
☎020 7734 4302 Fax 020 7437 3301
Email television@chatsworth-tv.co.uk
Website www.chatsworth-tv.co.uk

Managing Director *Malcolm Heyworth*

Drama, factual and entertainment television producer. Interested in contemporary and factually
based series.

The Children's Film & Television Foundation Ltd

The John Maxwell Building, Elstree Film & TV Studios, Shenley Road, Borehamwood, Hertfordshire WD6 1JG
☎020 8953 0844 Fax 020 8207 0860
Email annahome@cftf.onyxnet.co.uk

Chief Executive *Anna Home*

Involved in the development and co-production of films for children and the family, both for the theatric market and for TV.

Cinécosse

Riversfield Studios, Ellon, Aberdeenshire AB41 9EY
☎01358 722150 Fax 01358 720053
Email admin@cinecosse.co.uk
Website www.cinecosse.co.uk

Contact *Graeme Mowat*

Television and video documentary and corporate productions. OUTPUT includes *Scotland's Larder* (Scottish/Grampian TV); safety and training videos for industry; tourism promotional and sales information. All scripts are commissioned; no unsolicited material.

Cinema Verity Productions Ltd

11 Addison Avenue, London W11 4QS
☎020 7460 2777 Fax 020 7371 3329

Contact *Verity Lambert*

Leading television drama producer whose credits include *She's Out* by Lynda la Plante; *Class Act* by Michael Aitkens; *May to December* (BBC series); *Running Late* by Simon Gray (Screen 1); *The Cazalet Chronicle* by Elizabeth Jane Howard (adapt. Douglas Livingstone; BBC). No unsolicited mss.

Circus Films

See **Elstree (Production) Co. Ltd.**

Claverdon Films Ltd

28 Narrow Street, London E14 8DQ
☎020 7702 8700 Fax 020 7702 8701

Contacts *Tony Palmer, Michela Antonello*

Film and TV: drama and documentary. OUTPUT *Menuhin; Maria Callas; Testimony; In From the Cold; Pushkin; England, My England* (by John Osborne); *Kipling*. Unsolicited material is read, but please send a written outline first.

Cleveland Productions

5 Rainbow Court, Oxhey, Near Watford, Hertfordshire WD19 4RP
☎01923 254000/07740 902095 (mobile)
Fax 01923 254000

Contact *Michael Gosling*

Communications in sound and vision A/V production and still photography specialists in education and sport. No unsolicited mss.

Collingwood & Convergence Productions Ltd

10–14 Crown Street, Acton, London W3 8SB
☎020 8993 3666 Fax 020 8993 9595
Email info@crownstreet.co.uk

Producers *Christopher O'Hare, Terence Clegg, Tony Collingwood*
Head of Development *Helen Stroud*

Film and TV. Convergence Productions produces live action, drama documentaries; Tony Collingwood Productions specialises in children's animation. OUTPUT **Convergence**: *Theo* (film drama series); *Plastic Fantastic* (UK cosmetic surgery techniques, Ch5) and *David Starkey's Henry VIII* (Ch4 historical documentary). **Collingwood**: *RARG* (award-winning animated film); *Captain Zed and the Zee Zone* (ITV); *Daisy-Head Mayzie* (Dr Seuss animated series for Turner Network and Hanna-Barbera); *Animal Stories* (animated poems, ITV network). Unsolicited mss not welcome 'as a general rule as we do not have the capacity to process the sheer weight of submissions this creates. We therefore tend to review material from individuals recommended to us through personal contact with agents or other industry professionals. We like to encourage new writing and have worked with new writers but our ability to do so is limited by our capacity for development. We can usually only consider taking on one project each year, as development/finance takes several years to put in place.'

Convergence Productions Ltd

See **Collingwood & Convergence Productions Ltd**

Cosgrove Hall Films

8 Albany Road, Chorlton–cum–Hardy, Manchester M21 0AW
☎0161 882 2500 Fax 0161 882 2555
Email animation@chf.co.uk

Contacts *Mark Hall, Iain Pelling*

Children's animation producer; film video and television. OUTPUT includes *Noddy* and *Rotten Ralph* (both for BBC); *Lavender Castle* by Gerry Anderson; *The Fox Busters; Animal Shelf; Rocky & the Dodos*; Alison Uttley's *Little Grey Rabbit* (all for children's ITV); Terry Pratchett's

Discworld (Ch4). 'We try to select writers on a project-by-project basis.' Hosted the **Writers' Guild** workshop in 1998.

Creative Channel Ltd
Channel TV, Television Centre, St Helier, Jersey, Channel Islands JE1 3ZD
☎01534 816873 Fax 01534 816889
Email creative@channeltv.co.uk
Website www.channeltv.co.uk
Senior Producer *David Evans*

Part of the Channel Television Group. Producer of TV commercials and corporate material: information, promotional, sales, training and events coverage. CD and DVD production; promotional videos for all types of businesses in the Channel Islands and throughout Europe; plus over 300 commercials a year. No unsolicited mss; new writing/scripts commissioned as required. Interested in hearing from local writers resident in the Channel Islands.

Creative Film Makers Ltd
Pottery Lane House, 34A Pottery Lane, London W11 4LZ
☎020 7229 5131 Fax 020 7229 4999
Contacts *Michael Seligman, Nicholas Seligman*

Corporate and sports documentaries, commercials and television programmes. OUTPUT *The World's Greatest Golfers*, plus various corporate and sports programmes for clients like Nestlé, Benson & Hedges, Wimpey, Bouygues. 'Always open to suggestions but have hardly ever received unsolicited material of any value.' Keen nevertheless to encourage new writers.

The Creative Partnership
13 Bateman Street, London W1D 3AF
☎020 7439 7762
Email sally@thecreativepartnership.co.uk
Website www.thecreativepartnership.co.uk
Contacts *Christopher Fowler, Jim Sturgeon*

'Europe's largest "one-stop shop" for advertising and marketing campaigns for the film and television industries.' Clients include most major and independent film companies. No scripts. 'We train new writers in-house, and find them from submitted c.v.s. All applicants must have previous commercial writing experience.'

Cricket Ltd
Medius House, 63–69 New Oxford Street, London WC1A 1EA
☎020 7845 0300 Fax 020 7845 0303
Email team@cricket-ltd.co.uk
Website www.cricket-ltd.co.uk

Head of Production (Film & Video)
Jonathan Freer

Film and video, live events and conferences, print and design. 'Communications solutions for business clients wishing to influence targeted external and internal audiences.'

Cromdale Films Ltd
12 St Paul's Road, London N1 2QN
☎020 7226 0178
Contact *Ian Lloyd*

Film, video and TV: drama and documentary. OUTPUT *The Face of Darkness* (feature film); *Drift to Dawn* (rock music drama); *The Overdue Treatment* (documentary); *Russia, The Last Red Summer* (documentary). Initial phone call advised before submission of scripts.

Crown Business Communications Ltd
United House, 9 Pembridge Road, London W11 3JY
☎020 7727 7272 Fax 020 7727 9940
Email clarkea@crownbc.com
Website www.crownbc.com
Contact *Alex Clarke*

Leading producer of moving image, live, design, on-/off-line communications for major corporate clients. 'Always interested in talented writers, especially with a sector journalism or Internet experience.'

Cutting Edge Productions Ltd
27 Erpingham Road, Putney, London SW15 1BE
☎020 8780 1476 Fax 020 8780 0102
Email norridge@globalnet.co.uk
Contact *Julian Norridge*

Corporate and documentary video and television. OUTPUT includes US series on evangelicalism, 'Dispatches' on US tobacco and government videos. 'We commission all our writing to order but are open to ideas.'

Cwmni'r Castell Ltd
10 Garth Road, Colwyn Bay, Conwy LL29 8AF
☎01492 512349 Fax 01492 514235
Email castell@enterprise.net
Contact *Elwyn Vaughan Williams*

Television light entertainment and corporate video producer. OUTPUT includes four series with Welsh comedians and *Bob yn Ddau* ('Two by Two') – a daily quiz. Welcomes material from new comedy writers.

Dakota Films Ltd

12A Newburgh Street, London W1F 7RR
☎020 7287 4329 Fax 020 7287 2303
Email info@dakota-films.demon.co.uk
Managing Director *Jonathan Olsberg*

Film and television drama. Feature films include: *Let Him Have It; Othello; Me Without You: 45wpm*. Currently developing a slate of 12 feature film and TV projects, including John Sayles' *Fade to Black*, and a number of projects by new writers. Interested in working with and encouraging new talent but does not consider unsolicited material.

Dareks Production House

58 Wickham Road, Beckenham, Kent
BR3 6RQ
☎020 8658 2012 Fax 020 8325 0629
Email dareks@dircon.co.uk
Contact *David Crossman*

Independent producer of corporate and broadcast television. 'We are interested in *short* (10–15 minute) narrative scripts – initial synopsis by e-mail, please.'

Devlin Morris Productions Ltd

97b West Bow, Edinburgh EH1 2JP
☎0131 226 7728 Fax 0131 226 6668
Email contact@devlinmorris-prod.sol.co.uk
Contacts *Morris Paton, Vivien Devlin*

Independent media production house encompassing international arts and travel writing as well as a range of drama, radio, film and television projects.

Direct Image Productions Ltd

See **Direct Image Publishing** under **UK Packagers**

Diverse Production Limited

Gorleston Street, London W14 8XS
☎020 7603 4567 Fax 020 7603 2148
Website www.diverse.co.uk
Contacts *Roy Ackerman, Narinder Minhas*

Broadcast television production with experience in popular prime-time formats, strong documentaries (one-offs and series), investigative journalism, science, business and history films, travel series, arts and music, talk shows, schools and education. OUTPUT includes *Secret Lives; Omnibus; Cutting Edge; Equinox; Modern Times; Dispatches; Without Walls; Panorama; The Big Idea; Empires and Emperors* and the *Little Picture Show*.

DMS Films Ltd

369 Burnt Oak Broadway, Edgware,
Middlesex HA8 5XZ
☎020 8951 6060 Fax 020 8951 6050
Email danny@argonaut.com
Producer *Daniel San*

Film drama producer. OUTPUT includes *Understanding Jane; Hard Edge; Strangers*. Welcomes unsolicited screenplays.

Double-Band Films

Crescent Arts Centre, 2–4 University Road,
Belfast BT7 1NH
☎028 9024 3331 Fax 028 9023 6980
Email info@doublebandfilms.com
Website www.doublebandfilms.com
Contacts *Michael Hewitt, Dermot Lavery*

Documentary and drama programmes for film and television. Has specialised in documentary production for the past eleven years. OUTPUT *Escobar's Own Goal* and *Kicking the Habit* (both for Ch4); *Still Life* (short drama film). Currently working on a documentary about George Best for Ch4.

Dragon Pictures

23 Golden Square, London W1R 3PA
☎020 7734 6303 Fax 020 7734 6202
Email info@dragonpictures.net
Contacts *Katie Goodson, Lucy Guard*

Feature films, including *Welcome to Sarajevo; Gridlock'd; The Debt Collector; Splendor; A Texas Funeral; Some Voices; Very Annie-Mary*. Likes to encourage young talent but cannot consider unsolicited mss.

Drake A-V Video Ltd

89 St Fagans Road, Fairwater, Cardiff CF5 3AE
☎029 2056 0333 Fax 029 2055 4909
Website www.drakegroup.co.uk
Contact *Ian Lewis*

Corporate A-V film and video, mostly promotional, training or educational. Scripts in these fields welcome. Other work includes interactive multimedia and CD-ROM production.

The Drama House Ltd

Coach Road Cottage, Little Saxham, Suffolk
IP29 5LE
☎01284 810521 Fax 01284 811425
Email jack@dramahouse.co.uk
Website www.drama.house.co.uk
Contact *Jack Emery*

Film and television producer. OUTPUT *Little White Lies* (BBC1); *Breaking the Code* (BBC1);

Witness Against Hitler (BBC1); *Suffer the Little Children* (BBC2). Send two-page synopsis only. All synopses read and returned if accompanied by s.a.e. Interested especially in new writers.

Charles Dunstan Communications Ltd

42 Wolseley Gardens, London W4 3LS
☎020 8994 2328 Fax 020 8994 2328

Contact *Charles Dunstan*

Producer of film, video and TV for documentary and corporate material. OUTPUT *Renewable Energy* for broadcast worldwide in *Inside Britain* series; National Power Annual Report video *The Electric Environment*. No unsolicited scripts.

Ealing Films Limited

Beaumont House, 8 Beaumont Road, Poole, Dorset BH13 7JJ
☎01202 706379 Fax 01202 706944
Email anita@ealingfilms.freeserve.co.uk *or* eben.foggitt@talk21.com

Managing Director *Eben Foggitt*
Head of Development *Anita Simpkins*

Film and television drama producer. Unsolicited mss welcome; 'we encourage new writers'.

Ecosse Films

12 Quayside Lodge, Watermeadow Lane, London SW6 2UZ
☎020 7371 0290 Fax 020 7736 3436
Email info@ecossefilms.com
Website www.ecossefilms.com

Contact *Paula Howarth*

Producer of feature films and television drama such as *Mrs Brown* and *Monarch of the Glen*. Submissions through agents only; 'we need to deal with agents as we are too small to be inundated with unsolicited mss.'

Eden Productions Ltd

24 Belsize Lane, London NW3 5AB
☎020 7435 3242 Fax 020 7794 1519
Email jancis@cix.co.uk *or* nlander@cix.co.uk

Contacts *Nicholas Lander, Jancis Robinson*

Producer of *Jancis Robinson's Wine Course; Vintners' Tales with Jancis Robinson; Taste with Jancis Robinson* and wine training videos for British Airways. No unsolicited mss.

Edinburgh Film Productions

Traquair House, Innerleithen, Peeblesshire EH44 6PP
☎01896 831188

Contact *R. Crichton*

Film, TV drama and documentary. OUTPUT *Sara; Moonacre; Torch; Silent Mouse; The Curious Case of Santa Claus; The Stamp of Greatness*. No unsolicited scripts at present.

Elstree (Production) Co. Ltd

Shepperton Studios, Studios Road, Shepperton, Middlesex TW17 0QD
☎01932 572680/1 Fax 01932 572682
Website www.elsprod.com

Contact *Greg Smith*

Produces feature films and TV drama. OUTPUT *Othello* (BBC); *Great Expectations* (Disney Channel); *Porgy & Bess* (with Trevor Nunn); *Old Curiosity Shop* (Disney Channel/RHI); *London Suite* (NBC/Hallmark); *Animal Farm* and *David Copperfield* (both for Hallmark/TNT). Co-owner of Circus Films with Trevor Nunn for feature film projects.

Endemol Entertainment UK plc

46/47 Bedford Square, London WC1B 3DP
☎020 7462 9000 Fax 020 7462 9001

Chief Executive *Tom Barnicoat*
Creative Director *Peter Bazalgette*
Managing Director, Initial *Tim Hincks*
Managing Director, Bazal *Nikki Cheetham*
Managing Director, Gem *Lucas Church*

Owned by Spanish telecoms and media company, Telefonica, Endemol Entertainment UK plc is one of Britain's largest television production groups producing over 1000 hours of programmes for all the UK's terrestrial networks as well as for satellite and cable. It has two programming divisions: Bazal, specialising in factual entertainment such as *Big Brother* and Initial, specialising in music, live event and entertainment programming. Gem handles full exploitation of rights and brands.

Excalibur Productions

Slack Top Farm, Heptonstall, West Yorkshire HX7 7HA
☎01422 843871 Fax 01422 843871

Contact *Jay Jones*

Most recent productions are medical documentaries such as an investigation into diabetes control sponsored by Bayer Diagnostics, collaborative literary and cultural projects such as *The Boys From Savoy* with David Glass, and corporates for clients such as South Yorkshire Supertram and Datacolor International. Interested in ideas, scripts and possible joint development for broadcast, sell-through and experimental arts.

Extreme International Limited
The Coach House, Ashford Lodge, Halstead, Essex CO9 2RR
☎01787 479000 Fax 01787 479111
Email xtreme@xtremeinternational.com
Website www.xtremeinternational.com

Contact *Alistair Gosling*

Film, television and video; drama and documentary. Unsolicited mss welcome.

Fairline Productions Ltd
15 Royal Terrace, Glasgow G3 7NY
☎0141 331 0077 Fax 0141 331 0066
Email fairprods@aol.com

Contact *Charlene Cruickshank*

Television and video producer of documentary and corporate programmes and commercials. OUTPUT includes *Hooked*, a 15-part angling series (Discovery Channel) plus training and instructional videos for Forbo-Nairn Ltd, Royal Bank of Scotland, and Health & Safety Executive. No unsolicited scripts.

Farnham Film Company Ltd
34 Burnt Hill Road, Lower Bourne, Farnham, Surrey GU10 3LZ
☎01252 710313 Fax 01252 725855
Website www.farnfilm.com

Contact *Ian Lewis*

Television and film: children's drama and documentaries. Unsolicited mss usually welcome but prefers a letter to be sent in the first instance. Check website for current requirements.

Farrant Partnership
429 Liverpool Road, London N7 8PR
☎020 7700 4647 Fax 020 7697 0224
Email farrant.stern@dial.pipex.com

Contact *James Farrant*

Corporate video productions.

Feelgood Fiction
49 Goldhawk Road, London W12 8QP
☎020 8746 2535 Fax 020 8740 6177
Email feelgood@feelgoodfiction.co.uk

Contact *Laurence Bowen*

Producer of film and TV drama. Recent OUTPUT: *Badger*, Series 1&2; *The Hello Girls; Stone, Scissors, Paper; Dual Balls* and *Painted Angels*.

Festival Film and Television Ltd
Festival House, Tranquil Passage, Blackheath, London SE3 0BJ
☎020 8297 9999 Fax 020 8297 1155
Email raymarshall@festivalfilm.com

Contact *Ray Marshall*

Specialises in television drama. In the last nine years has produced 15 Catherine Cookson mini-series for ITV, the latest of which was *A Dinner of Herbs*. Looking primarily for commercial TV projects; will also consider feature films and children's drama. Prefers submissions through an agent. Unsolicited work must be professionally presented or it will be returned unread.

Film and General Productions Ltd
4 Bradbrook House, Studio Place, London SW1X 8EL
☎020 7235 4495 Fax 020 7245 9853

Contacts *Clive Parsons, Davina Belling*

Film and television drama. Feature films include *True Blue* and *Tea with Mussolini*. Also *Seesaw* (ITV drama), *The Greatest Store in the World* (family drama, BBC) and *The Queen's Nose* (children's series, BBC). Interested in considering new writing but subject to prior telephone conversation.

The Firedog Motion Picture Corporation Ltd
182 Brighton Road, Coulsdon, Surrey CR5 2NF
☎020 8660 8663 Fax 020 8763 2558
Email info@firedogfilms.co.uk
Website www.firedogfilms.co.uk

Managing Director *Frazer Ashford*

Owned by the **Ashford Entertainment Corporation Ltd**. 'Happy to see film/drama ideas.' In the first instance, authors should send a one-page synopsis, their writing c.v. and a brief history/submission history of the project to-date.

Firehouse Productions
42 Glasshouse Street, London W1R 5RH
☎020 7439 2220 Fax 020 7439 2210
Email postie@hellofirehouse.com
Website www.hellofirehouse.com

Contacts *Julie-anne Edwards, Gavin Knight*

Corporate films and websites, commercials and pop promos. OUTPUT includes work for De Beers; BT; www.yeovalley.co.uk and Sky Open commercials.

First Creative Ltd
Belgrave Court, Caxton Road, Fulwood, Preston, Lancashire PR2 9PL
☎01772 651555 Fax 01772 651777
Email mail@firstcreative.com

Contact *M. Mulvihill*

Video productions for documentary, corporate and multimedia material. Unsolicited scripts welcome. Open to new writing.

Fitting Images Ltd

The Studio, Henry VII Cottage, Pyrford Road, Pyrford Green, Woking, Surrey GU22 8UX

☎01932 343214 Fax 01932 343184

Email sue@fittingimages.co.uk

Managing Director *Sue Fleetwood*

Promotional, training, medical/pharmaceutical; contacts from experienced writers of drama and comedy welcome. 'We are also interested in broadcast projects.'

Flashback Television Limited

11 Bowling Green Lane, London EC1R 0BD

☎020 7490 8996 Fax 020 7490 5610

Email mailbox@flashbacktv.com

Website www.flashbacktv.com

Contact *Timothy Ball*

Producer of documentaries and factual entertainment such as *Lost Gardens* (Ch4) and *Battle Stations* (A&E).

Flick Media

15 Golden Square, London W1F 9JG

☎020 7734 7979 Fax 020 7287 9495

Website www.flickmedia.co.uk

Contact *John Deery*

Producer of film drama, including *Conspiracy of Silence* and *County Kilburn* (comedy–drama TV series). No unsolicited scripts.

Flicks Films Ltd

101 Wardour Street, London W1F 0UG

☎020 7734 4892 Fax 020 7287 2307

Website www.flicksfilms.com

Managing Director/Producer *Terry Ward*

Film and video: children's animated series and specials. OUTPUT *The Mr Men; Little Miss; Bananaman; The Pondles; Nellie the Elephant; See How They Work With Dig and Dug; Timbuctoo.* Scripts specific to their needs will be considered. 'Always willing to read relevant material.'

Focus Films Ltd

The Rotunda Studios, Rear of 116–118 Finchley Road, London NW3 5HT

☎020 7435 9004 Fax 020 7431 3562

Email focus@pupix.demon.co.uk

Contacts *David Pupkewitz, Lisa Nicholson, Malcolm Kohll (Head of Development)*

Film and TV producer. OUTPUT *The 51st State* (feature film); *Secret Society* (comedy drama feature film); *Crimetime* (feature thriller); *Diary of a Sane Man; Othello.* Projects in development include *Mutant; 90 Minutes; Barry.* No unsolicited scripts.

Mark Forstater Productions Ltd

27 Lonsdale Road, London NW6 6RA

☎020 7624 1123 Fax 020 7624 1124

Contact *Mark Forstater*

Active in the selection, development and production of material for film and TV. OUTPUT *Monty Python and the Holy Grail; The Odd Job; The Grass is Singing; Xtro; Forbidden; Separation; The Fantasist; Shalom Joan Collins; The Silent Touch; Grushko; The Wolves of Willoughby Chase; Between the Devil and the Deep Blue Sea; Doing Rude Things.* No unsolicited scripts.

Friday Productions Ltd

23a St. Leonards Terrace, London SW3 4QG

☎020 7730 0608 Fax 020 7730 0608

Contact *Georgina Abrahams*

Film and TV production for drama material. OUTPUT *Goggle Eyes; Harnessing Peacocks; The December Rose.*

Full Moon Productions

rue Fenelon, Salignac Eyvigues, Perigord 24590, France

☎00 33 553 29 94 06

Email fullmoonproductions@worldonline.fr

Website www.mandy.com/ home.cfm?c=fmp001

Contact *Barry C. Paton*

Documentary and corporate videos. 'We are keen to explore drama production.' No unsolicited scripts; initial contact should be by letter. 'Interested in creative/commercial (i.e. broadcast) ideas that are new and innovative.'

Gabriela Productions Limited

51 Goldsmith Avenue, London W3 6HR

☎020 8993 3158 Fax 020 8993 8216

Email only4contact@yahoo.com

Contact *W. Starecki*

Film and television drama and documentary productions, including *Blooming Youth* and *Dog Eat Dog* for Ch4 and *Spider's Web* for Polish TV. Welcomes unsolicited mss.

Gaia Communications

Sanctuary House, 35 Harding Avenue, Eastbourne, East Sussex BN22 8PL

☎01323 734809/727183 Fax 01323 734809

Email mail@gaiacommunications.co.uk
Website www.gaiacommunications.co.uk
Producer *Robert Armstrong*
Script Editor *Loni Webb*
ESTABLISHED 1987. Video and TV corporate and documentary. OUTPUT *Discovering* (south east regional tourist and local knowledge series); *Holistic* (therapies and general information). 'Submissions must relate to our field of production; synopsis only on first contact.'

Gala International Ltd
25 Stamford Brook Road, London W6 0XJ
☎020 8741 4200 Fax 020 8741 2323
Producer *David Lindsay*

TV commercials, promos, film and TV documentaries.

John Gau Productions
15 St Albans Mansion, Kensington Court Place, London W8 5QH
☎020 7938 1398 Fax 020 7938 1429
Email johngau@hotmail.com
Contact *John Gau*

Documentaries and series for TV, plus corporate video. OUTPUT includes *The Great Sell-Off*; *Reaching for the Skies*; *The Power and The Glory*; *The Team – A Season With McLaren* (all for BBC2); *Korea* series (BBC1); *Voyager* (Central); *The Great Outdoors*; *The Triumph of the Nerds*; *Glory of the Geeks*; *Civil War – England's Fight For Freedom* (all for Ch4); *Lights, Camera, Action!: A Century of the Cinema* (ITV network). Open to ideas from writers.

Noel Gay Television
Shepperton Studios, Studios Road, Shepperton, Middlesex TW17 0QD
☎01932 572569 Fax 01932 572172
Contact *Anne Mensah*

The association with Noel Gay (agency/management, film production and music publishing) makes this one of the most securely financed independents in the business. OUTPUT: *Hububb* – Series 2 & 3 (BBC); *I-Camcorder* (Ch4); *Frank Stubbs Promotes* (Carlton/ITV); *10%ers* – Series 2 (Carlton/ITV); *Call Up the Stars* (BBC1); *Smeg Outs* (BBC video); *Les Bubb* (BBC Scotland); *Red Dwarf* – Series 8; *Making of Red Dwarf* (BBC video); *Dave Allen* (ITV); *Windrush* (BBC2). Joint ventures and companies include a partnership with Odyssey, a leading Indian commercials, film and TV producer, and the Noel Gay Motion Picture Company, whose credits include *Virtual Sexuality*; *Trainspotting* (with Ch4 and Figment Films), and

Killer Tongue, a co-production with Iberoamericana. Other associate NGTV companies are Grant Naylor Productions, Rose Bay Film Productions (see entry) and Pepper Productions. NGTV is willing to accept unsolicited material from writers but 1–2-page treatments only. No scripts, please.

Global Vision Network (GVN) Ltd
Millennium Studios, Elstree Way, Borehamwood, Hertfordshire WD6 1SF
☎020 8236 1330 Fax 020 8236 1331
Email info@gvn.co.uk
Website www.gvn.co.uk
Company Manager *Alex Prior*

Film, TV and video production: documentary, corporate and children's computer-generated imagery. OUTPUT includes educational and science programming and now moving into mainstream entertainment and film. 'Keen to encourage and develop new material and writers; telephone or e-mail first.'

GMT Productions Ltd
The Old Courthouse, 26A Church Street, Bishop's Stortford, Hertfordshire CM23 2LY
☎01279 501622 Fax 01279 501644
Email patrick.wallis@virgin.net
Contacts *Patrick Wallis, Barney Broom*

Film, television and video: drama, documentary, corporate and commercials. No unsolicited mss.

Goldcrest Films International Ltd
65–66 Dean Street, London W1D 4PL
☎020 7437 8696 Fax 020 7437 4448
Email mailbox@goldcrest-post.co.uk
Chairman *John Quested*
Contact *Abigail Walsh*

FOUNDED in the late '70s. Formerly part of the Brent Walker Leisure Group but independent since 1990 following management buy-out led by John Quested. The company's core activities are film production, post-production facilities and worldwide distribution. Scripts via agents only.

The Good Film Company
2nd Floor, 14–15 D'Arblay Street, London W1V 3FP
☎020 7734 1331 Fax 020 7734 2997
Email productions@goodfilms.co.uk
Website www.goodfilms.co.uk
Contact *Yanina Barry*

Commercials and pop videos. CLIENTS include

Hugo Boss, Cadbury's, Wella, National Express Coaches, Camel Cigarettes, Tunisian Tourist Board. *No* unsolicited mss.

Granada Film

4th Floor, 48 Leicester Square, London WC2H 7FB
☎020 7389 8555 Fax 020 7930 8499
Head of Film *Pippa Cross*

Films and TV films. OUTPUT *Essex Boys*; *House of Mirth*; *Longitude*; *My Left Foot*; *Jack & Sarah*; *Misadventures of Margaret*; *Girls Night*; *Rogue Trader*. No unsolicited scripts. Supportive of new writing but often hard to offer real help as Granada are developing mainstream commercial projects which usually requires some status in talent areas.

Granite Film & Television Productions Ltd

Vigilant House, 120 Wilton Road, London SW1V 1JZ
☎020 7808 7230 Fax 020 7808 7231
Contact *Simon Welfare*

Producer of television documentary programmes such as *Nicholas & Alexandra*; *Victoria & Albert* and *Arthur C. Clarke's Mysterious Universe*. No unsolicited mss.

Green Umbrella Ltd

The Production House, 147a St Michael's Hill, Bristol BS2 8DB
☎0117 973 1729 Fax 0117 946 7432
Email postmaster@umbrella.co.uk
Website www.umbrella.co.uk

Television documentary maker and children's drama producer. OUTPUT includes episodes for *The Natural World*, *Wildlife on One* and original series such as *Living Europe* and *Triumph of Life*. Unsolicited treatments relating to natural history and science subjects are welcome.

Greenwich Films Ltd

Studio 2B1, The Old Seager Distillery, Brookmill Road, London SE8 4FT
☎020 8694 2211 Fax 020 8694 2971
Contact *Liza Brown, Development Dept.*

Film, television and video: drama. 'We welcome new writers, though as a small outfit we prefer to meet them through personal contacts as we do not have the resources to deal with too many enquiries. No unsolicited mss, just outlines, please.'

Hammer Film Productions Ltd

92 New Cavendish Street, London W1M 7FA
☎020 7637 2322 Fax 020 7323 2307
Contact *Terry Ilott*

Television and feature films. Due to reorganisation of the company, unable to consider material until futher notice. Please do not send unsolicited scripts or treatments.

Hammerwood Film Productions

110 Trafalgar Road, Portslade, East Sussex BN41 1GS
☎01273 277333 Fax 01273 705451
Email filmangels@freenetname.co.uk
Website www.filmangel.co.uk
Contacts *Ralph Harvey, Petra Ginman*

Film, video and TV drama. OUTPUT *Boadicea – Queen of Death* (film; co-production with Pan-European Film Productions and Mirabilis Films); *Boadicea – A Celtic Tragedy* (TV series). In pre-production: *Road to Nirvana* (Ealing-style comedy); *The Black Egg* (witchcraft in 17th century England); *The Ghosthunter*; *A Symphony of Spies* (true stories of WW2 espionage and resistance required). 'Authors are recommended to access www.filmangel.co.uk (see **Useful Websites at a Glance**).'

Hartswood Films Ltd

Twickenham Studios, The Barons, St Margarets, Middlesex TW1 2AW
☎020 8607 8736 Fax 020 8607 8744
Email films.tv@hartswood.co.uk
Contact *Elaine Cameron*

Film and TV production for drama, comedy and documentary. OUTPUT *Men Behaving Badly* (BBC); *Is It Legal?* (Ch4); *Wonderful You* (ITV); *Border Cafe* (BBC1); *Coupling* (BBC).

Hat Trick Productions Ltd

10 Livonia Street, London W1V 3PH
☎020 7434 2451 Fax 020 7287 9791
Website www.hattrick.com
Contact *Denise O'Donoghue*

Television programmes. OUTPUT includes *Clive Anderson All Talk*; *Small Potatoes*; *The Wilsons*; *The Peter Principle*; *Whatever You Want*; *Confessions*; *Drop the Dead Donkey*; *Father Ted*; *Game On*; *Have I Got News For You*; *If I Ruled the World*; *Room 101*; *Whose Line Is It Anyway?*; *Clive Anderson Talks Bank*; *Dicing with Debt*. The company's drama output includes: *A Very Open Prison*; *Boyz Unlimited*; *Crossing the Floor*; *Eleven Men Against Eleven*; *Gobble*; *Lord of Misrule*; *Mr*

White Goes to Westminster; Underworld; Sex 'n' Death. Films: *The Suicidal Dog; Sleeping Dictionary*.

Head to Head Communication Ltd

The Hook, Plane Tree Crescent, Feltham, Middlesex TW13 7AQ
☎020 8893 7766 Fax 020 8893 2777
Email amanda@hthc.co.uk

Contact *Amanda Anderson*

Producer of business and corporate communication programmes and events.

Healthcare Productions Limited

Unit 1.04 Bridge House, Three Mills, Three Mill Lane, London E3 3DU
☎020 8980 9444 Fax 020 8980 1901
Email penny@healthcareprod.co.uk
Website www.healthcareproductions.co.uk

Contact *Penny Webb*

Television and video: documentary and drama. Produces training and educational material, in text, video and CD-ROM, mostly health-related, social care issues, law and marriage:

Jim Henson Productions Ltd

30 Oval Road, Camden, London NW1 7DE
☎020 7428 4000 Fax 020 7428 4001
Website www.henson.com *and*
  www.muppets.com

Contacts *Angus Fletcher, Sophie Finston*

Feature films and TV: family entertainment and children's. OUTPUT *Gulliver's Travels; Buddy; Muppet Treasure Island; The Muppet Christmas Carol; Muppets From Space; The Dark Crystal; Labyrinth; The Witches* (films); *Dinosaurs* (ABC); *Muppet Tonight* (BBC/Sky); *The Muppet Show* (ITV); *The Storyteller* (Ch4/BBC); *Dr Seuss; The Secret Life of Toys* (BBC); *The Animal Show* (BBC); *Mopatop's Shop* (ITV); *Brats of the Lost Nebula* (WB); *Farscape* (Sci-Fi/USA/BBC); *Bear in the Big Blue House* (Disney Channel/Ch5); *Jim Henson's Construction Site* (ITV); *The Hoobs* (Ch4); *Jack and the Beanstalk: The Untold Story* (CBS); *Telling Stories with Tomie de Paola* and *Donna's Day* (both for Odyssey); *The Fearing Mind* (Fox). Scripts via agents only.

Heritage Theatre Ltd

8 Clanricarde Gardens, London W2 4NA
☎020 7243 2750 Fax 020 7792 8584
Email mars.prod@virgin.net
Website www.heritagetheatre.com

Contact *Robert Marshall*

Video recordings of successful stage plays, sold to the public in VHS and DVD format. 'It is possible to negotiate agreements before the production is staged.'

John Holloway

51 Daybrook Road, Wimbledon, London SW19 3DJ
☎020 8542 7721 Fax 020 8542 7721
Email jhvp@btinternet.com

Contact *John Holloway*

Corporate video. CLIENTS include the Post Office, IBM, British Gas, Freemans, Eastern Electricity, Customs & Excise.

Holmes Associates

38–42 Whitfield Street, London W1T 2RH
☎020 7813 4333 Fax 020 7637 9024

Contact *Andrew Holmes*

Prolific originator, producer and packager of documentary, drama and music television and films. See also **Open Road Films**. OUTPUT has included *Prometheus* (Ch4 'Film on 4'); *The Shadow of Hiroshima* (Ch4 'Witness'); *The House of Bernarda Alba* (Ch4/WNET/Amaya); *Piece of Cake* (LWT); *The Cormorant* (BBC/Screen 2); *John Gielgud Looks Back; Rock Steady; Well Being; Signals; Ideal Home?* (all Ch4); *Timeline* (with MPT, TVE Spain & TRT Turkey); *Seven Canticles of St Francis* (BBC2). Unsolicited drama/film scripts will be considered but may take some time for response.

Hourglass Pictures Ltd

117 Merton Road, Wimbledon, London SW19 1ED
☎020 8540 8786 Fax 020 8542 6598
Email pictures@hourglass.co.uk
Website www.hourglass.co.uk

Director *Martin Chilcott*

Film and video: documentary, drama and commercials. OUTPUT includes television science documentaries and educational programming. Also health and social issues for the World Health Organization and product information for pharmaceutical companies. Open to new writing.

Icon Films

4 West End, Somerset Street, Bristol BS2 8NE
☎0117 924 8535 Fax 0117 942 0386
Email info@iconfilms.co.uk
Website www.iconfilms.co.uk

Contact *Harry Marshall*

Film and TV documentaries. OUTPUT *The Elephant Men* (WNET/Ch4); *The Living Edens –*

Bhutan, The Last Shangri La (ABC/Kane); *Joanna Lumley in the Kingdom of the Thunder Dragon* (BBC); *Lost Civilisations – Tibet* (Time Life for NBC). Specialises in documentaries. Open-minded to new filmmakers. Proposals welcome.

Ideal Image Ltd
Cherrywood House, Crawley Down Road, Felbridge, Surrey RH19 2PP
☎01342 300566 Fax 01342 312566

Contact *Alan Frost*

Producer of documentary and drama for film, video, TV and corporate clients. OUTPUT *Just Another Friday* (corporate drama); *Living in a Box; The Future for Rupert*. No unsolicited scripts.

Imari Entertainment Ltd
PO Box 158, Beaconsfield, Buckinghamshire HP9 1AY
☎01494 677147 Fax 01494 677147
Email info@imari-entertainment.com

Contacts *Jonathan Fowke, David Farey*

TV and video producer, covering all areas of drama and documentary. Also partner company, Imari Multi-media. Unsolicited mss welcome.

Initial
See **Endemol Entertainment UK plc**

Isis Productions
106 Hammersmith Grove, London W6 7HB
☎020 8748 3042 Fax 020 8748 3046
Email isis@isis-productions.com

Directors *Nick de Grunwald, Jamie Rugge-Price*
Production Coordinator *Catriona Lawless*

Formed in 1991, Isis Productions focuses on the production of music and documentary programmes, and co-produces children's programmes under its Rocking Horse banner. OUTPUT *England's Other Elizabeth – Elizabeth Taylor* (BBC 'Omnibus'); *UB40* (ITV 'South Bank Show'); *Fabulous* (BSkyB); *Ivy's Genes* (human genome project, Ch4); *Classic Albums* (international series on the making of the greatest records in rock history, including films on Grateful Dead, Stevie Wonder, Jimi Hendrix, The Band); *Energize!* (kids-in-sport magazine series, Westcountry TV); *Behind the Reporting Line* (behind-the-scenes look at foreign news gathering with Foreign Editor John Simpson, BBC2); *Dido and Aeneas* (film of Purcell's opera, BBC2/Thirteen WNET/ZDF-Arte/NVC Arts); *The Making of Sgt Pepper* (60-min film, Buena Vista International/LWT – winner of Grand Prix at MIDEM).

JAM Pictures and Jane Walmsley Productions
8 Hanover Street, London W1R 9HF
☎020 7290 2676 Fax 020 7290 2677
Email producers@jampix.com

Contacts *Jane Walmsley, Michael Braham*

JAM Pictures was FOUNDED in 1996 to produce drama for film, TV and stage. Projects include: *Son of Pocahontas* (TV film, ABC); *Breakthrough* (feature co-production with Viacom Productions, Inc.); *One More Kiss* (feature, directed by Vadim Jean); *Bad Blood* (UK theatre tour); *Chalet Girls* (ITV sitcom). Jane Walmsley Productions, formed in 1985 by TV producer, writer and broadcaster, Jane Walmsley, has completed award-winning documentaries and features such as *Hot House People* (Ch4). No unsolicited mss. 'Letters can be sent to us, asking if we wish to see mss; we are very interested in quality material.'

KEO Films.Com Ltd
Studio 2B, 151–157 City Road, London EC1V 1JH
☎020 7490 3580 Fax 020 7490 8419
Email keo@keofilms.com
Website www.keofilms.com

Contact *Alethea Palmer*

Television documentaries and factual entertainment. OUTPUT includes BBC's 'QED': *The Maggot Mogul* and *Sleeping it Off*; plus *A Cook on the Wild Side; TV Dinners; Beast of the Amazon* ('Ends of the Earth' series); *Big Snake; Escape to River Cottage; Return to River Cottage; The Real Deal; Ayia Napa, Fantasy Island* and *Shadow People*, all for Ch4. No unsolicited mss.

King Rollo Films Ltd
Dolphin Court, High Street, Honiton, Devon EX14 1HT
☎01404 45218 Fax 01404 45328
Email admin@kingrollofilms.co.uk

Contact *Clive Juster*

Film, video and TV: children's animated series. OUTPUT *Surprise, Surprise; It's My Birthday; Badger's Bring Something Party; How Many Days to My Birthday?; The Trouble With Jack; Bear's Birthday; Elephant Pie; Good Night, Sleep Tight; Go to Sleep; Get into Bed; I'm not Sleepy; Good Night Everyone; Little Princess Bedtime; Bedtime Story; Dad, I Can't Sleep; Spot and His Grandparents Visit the Carnival; Spot's Magical Christmas; Maisy; Philipp; Jakob; Elmer; Spot's Nautical Adventures; Maisy's ABC.* Generally works from existing published material 'although there will always be the odd exception'. Proposals in the first instance. No scripts.

Kingfisher Television Productions Ltd

Carlton Studios, Lenton Lane, Nottingham NG7 2NA
☎0115 964 5262 Fax 0115 964 5263

Contact *Tony Francis*

Broadcast television production.

Kismet Film Company

25 Old Compton Street, London W1D 5JX
☎020 7734 0099 Fax 020 7734 1222
Email kismetfilms@dial.pipex.com

Producer *Michele Camarda*
Head of Development *Nicole Stott*
Development Assistant *Asha Radwan*

Feature films. OUTPUT includes *Photographing Fairies; This Year's Love; Wonderland* and *Born Romantic*. Kismet has recently been forced to decide that it cannot accept unsolicited material. Involved in workshops such as PAL Writer's Workshop, **Equinoxe Screenwriting Workshops** and North by Northwest.

Elene Kostas

37 Colewell Road, London SE22 8QP
Email E9COOOL@aol.com
Contact *Elene Kostas*

Screenwriter and producer of features, series and serials.

Kudos Productions Limited

65 Great Portland Street, London W1N 5DH
☎020 7580 8686 Fax 020 7580 8787
Email reception@kudosproductions.co.uk

Head of Development *Howard Burch*
Head of Drama *Jane Featherstone*

Film and television; drama and documentaries such as *Among Giants* (feature); *The Magician's House* (BBC1 series) and *Psychos* (Ch4 series); *Confidence Lab* (BBC2 series). No unsolicited mss.

Lagan Pictures Ltd

21 Tullaghbrow, Tullaghgarley, Ballymena, Co Antrim BT42 2LY
☎028 2563 9479/077 9852 8797
Fax 028 2563 9479

Producer/Director *Stephen Butcher*
Producer *Alison Grundle*

Film, video and TV: drama, documentary and corporate. OUTPUT *A Force Under Fire* (Ulster TV). In development: *Into the Bright Light of*

Day (drama-doc); *The £10 Float* (feature film); *The Centre* (drama series). 'We are always interested in hearing from writers originating from or based in Northern Ireland or anyone with, preferably unstereotypical, projects relevant to Northern Ireland. We do not have the resources to deal with unsolicited mss, so please phone or write with a brief treatment/synopsis in the first instance.'

Landseer Film and Television Productions Ltd

140 Royal College Street, London NW1 0TA
☎020 7485 7333 Fax 020 7485 7573
Email mail@landseerfilms.com
Website www.landseerfilms.com

Directors *Derek Bailey, Ken Howard, Ross MacGibbon*

Film and video production: documentary, drama, music and arts. OUTPUT *Should Accidentally Fall* (BBC/Arts Council); *Nobody's Fool* ('South Bank Show' on Danny Kaye for LWT); *Gounod's Faust* (Ch4); *Swinger* (BBC2/Arts Council); *Auld Lang Syne* (BBC Scotland); *Nureyev Unzipped* (Ch4); *Retying the Knot – The Incredible String Band* (BBC Scotland); *Benjamin Zander* ('The Works', BBC2); *Zeffirelli* ('The South Bank Show', LWT); *The Judas Tree* (Ch4); *Death of a Legend – Frank Sinatra* ('South Bank Show' special); *Petula Clark* ('South Bank Show'); *Routes of Rock* (Carlton); *See You in Court* (BBC); *Bing Crosby* ('South Bank Show'); *Ballet Boyz* and *4Dance* (both for Ch4).

Lilyville Screen Entertainment Ltd

7 Lilyville Road, London SW6 5DP
☎020 7371 5940 Fax 020 7736 9431
Email tonycash@msn.com

Contact *Tony Cash*

Drama and documentaries for TV. OUTPUT *Poetry in Motion* (series for Ch4); 'South Bank Show': *Ben Elton* and *Vanessa Redgrave*; *Musique Enquête* (drama-based French language series, Ch4); *Landscape and Memory* (arts documentary series for the BBC); Jonathan Miller's production of the *St Matthew Passion* for the BBC; major documentary on the BeeGees for the 'South Bank Show'. Scripts with an obvious application to TV may be considered. Interested in new writing for documentary programmes.

Little Dancer Ltd

Avonway, Naseby Road, London SE19 3JJ
☎020 8653 9343 Fax 020 8286 1722

Contacts *Robert Smith, Sue Townsend*

Television and cinema, both shorts and full-length features.

London Broadcast Ltd

MWB Business Exchange, 77 Oxford Street, London W1R 1RB
☎020 7659 2000 Fax 020 7659 2100
Website www.londonbroadcast.com

Chairman *Eric Peters*
Head of Development & Programming
Michael Jacobs

Television and radio producer specialising in light entertainment, especially the talk show format. Producer of the St Patrick's Day Concert for worldwide television distribution. Also operates a training school for radio and television. Always on the lookout for new talent. Format ideas should be sent to Head of Programming.

London Scientific Films Ltd

Suckling's Yard, Church Street, Ware, Hertfordshire SG12 9EN
☎01920 486602 Fax 01920 462206
Email lsf@compuserve.com

Contact *Mike Cockburn*

Film and video documentary and corporate programming. No unsolicited mss.

Lucida Productions

Studio 1A, 14 Havelock Walk, London SE23 3HG
☎020 8699 5070 Fax 020 8699 5359

Contact *Paul Joyce*

Television and cinema: arts, adventure, current affairs, documentary, drama and music. OUTPUT has included *Motion and Emotion: The Films of Wim Wenders; Dirk Bogarde – By Myself; Sam Peckinpah – Man of Iron; Kris Kristofferson – Pilgrim; Wild One: Marlon Brando; Stanley Kubrick: 'The Invisible Man'; 2001: the Making of a Myth* (Ch4). Currently in development for documentary and drama projects.

Main Communications

Southgate Chambers, 37–39 Southgate Street, Winchester, Hampshire SO23 9EH
☎01962 870680 Fax 01962 870699
Email main@main.co.uk
Website www.main.co.uk

Contact *Eben Wilson*

Multimedia marketing, communications, electronic and publishing company for film, video and TV: drama, documentary and commercials. OUTPUT includes marketing communica-

tions, educational, professional and managerial distance learning, documentary programmes for broadcast TV and children's material. Interested in proposals for television programmes, interactive multimedia and business information texts and programming.

Malone Gill Productions Ltd

27 Campden Hill Road, London W8 7DX
☎020 7937 0557 Fax 020 7376 1727
Email malonegill@cs.com

Contact *Georgina Denison*

Mainly documentary but also some drama. OUTPUT includes *The Face of Russia* (PBS); *Vermeer* ('South Bank Show'); *Highlanders* (ITV); *Storm Chasers; Nature Perfected;* and *The Feast of Christmas* (all for Ch4); *The Buried Mirror: Reflections on Spain and the New World* by Carlos Fuentes (BBC2/Discovery Channel). Approach by letter with proposal in the first instance.

Mike Mansfield Television Ltd

41–42 Berners Street, London W1P 3AA
☎020 7580 2581 Fax 020 7580 2582
Email mikemantv@aol.com

Contact *Mr Hilary McLaren*

Television for BBC, ITV, Ch4 and Ch5. OUTPUT includes *Viva Diva!* (Shirley Bassey music special) and *Jean Michel Jarre Pyramids New Year*.

Bill Mason Films Ltd

Orchard House, Dell Quay, Chichester, West Sussex PO20 7EE
☎01243 783558
Email bill.mason@argonet.co.uk

Contact *Bill Mason*

Film and video: documentaries only. OUTPUT *Racing Mercedes; The History of Motor Racing; The History of the Motor Car.* No need for outside writing; all material is written in-house. The emphasis is on automotive history.

Maverick Television

The Custard Factory, Gibb Street, Birmingham B9 4AA
☎0121 771 1812 Fax 0121 771 1550
Email maverick@mavericktv.co.uk
Website www.mavericktv.co.uk

Contact *Clare Welch*

FOUNDED 1994. High quality and innovative DVC programming in both documentary and drama. Expanding into light entertainment and more popular drama. OUTPUT includes *Trade*

Secrets (BBC2); *Picture This: Accidental Hero* (BBC2); *Motherless Daughters*, *Highland Bollywood: Black Bag*; *Health Alert: My Teenage Menopause* and *Embarrassing Illnesses* (all for Ch4); *Long Haul* (Scottish Screen/STV).

Maya Vision International Ltd

43 New Oxford Street, London WC1A 1BH
☎020 7836 1113 Fax 020 7836 5169
Website www.mayavisionint.com

Contact *John Cranmer*

Film and TV: drama and documentary. OUTPUT *Saddam's Killing Fields* (for 'Viewpoint', Central TV); *3 Steps to Heaven* and *A Bit of Scarlet* (feature films for BFI/Ch4); *A Place in the Sun* and *North of Vortex* (drama for Ch4/Arts Council); *The Real History Show* (Ch4); *In the Footsteps of Alexander the Great* (BBC2 documentary); *Hitler's Search for the Holy Grail* (Ch4 documentary); *Conquistadors* (BBC2 documentary). No unsolicited material; commissions only.

MBP TV

Saucelands Barn, Coolham, Horsham, West Sussex RH13 8QG
☎01403 741620 Fax 01403 741647
Email info@mbptv.com
Website www.mbptv.com

Contact *Phil Jennings*

Maker of film and video specialising in programmes covering equestrianism and the countryside. No unsolicited scripts, but always looking for new writers who are fully acquainted with the subject.

MedSci Healthcare Communications

Stoke Grange, Fir Tree Avenue, Stoke Poges, Buckinghamshire SL2 4NN
☎01753 516644 Fax 01753 516965
Email kerry@medsci.co.uk
Website www.medsci.co.uk

Contacts *Peter Fogarty, Kerry Williams, Louise Simmonds*

Training programmes, interactive CD-based training, websites and medical video programmes for the pharmaceutical industry.

Melendez Films

Suite 501, Triumph House, 189–191 Regent Street, London W1B 4JY
☎020 7434 0220 Fax 020 7434 3131

Contacts *Steven Melendez, Graeme Spurway*

Independent producer working with TV stations. Animated films aimed mainly at a family audience, produced largely for the American market, and prime-time network broadcasting. Also develops and produces feature films (eight so far). OUTPUT has included *Peanuts* (TV specials); *The Lion, the Witch and the Wardrobe; Babar the Elephant* (TV specials); *Dick Deadeye or Duty Done*, a rock musical based on Gilbert & Sullivan operettas. Synopses only, please. Enclose s.a.e. for return.

Mendoza Productions

75 Wigmore Street, London W1H 9LH
☎020 7935 4674 Fax 020 7935 4417
Email dnm@mendoza.demon.com

Contacts *Wynn Wheldon, Debby Mendoza, John Hayes*

Commercials, title sequences (e.g. Alan Bleasdale's *G.B.H.*); party political broadcasts. Currently in pre-production on a feature-length comedy film. Unsolicited mss welcome but 'comedies only, please'. Material will not be returned without s.a.e. Involved with the **Screenwriters' Workshop**.

Mersey Television Company Ltd

Campus Manor, Childwall Abbey Road, Liverpool L16 0JP
☎0151 722 9122 Fax 0151 722 1969

Chairman *Prof. Phil Redmond*

The best known of the independents in the north of England. Makers of television drama. OUTPUT *Brookside; Hollyoaks* (both for Ch4).

Moonstone Films Ltd

5 Linkenhold Mansions, Stamford Brook Avenue, London W6 0YA
☎020 8846 8511 Fax 0870 4017171
Email moonstonefilms@fsmail.net

Contact *Tony Stark*

Television: current affairs, science and history documentaries. OUTPUT *Arafat's Authority*, a critical look at the Palestinian authority in the West Bank and Gaza for the BBC. Unsolicited mss welcome.

MW Entertainments Ltd

48 Dean Street, London W1D 5BF
☎020 7734 7707 Fax 020 7734 7727
Email development@michaelwhite.co.uk

Contact *Michael White*

High-output company whose credits include *Widow's Peak; White Mischief; Nuns on the Run* (co-production with HandMade Films Ltd); *The Comic Strip Series*. Also theatre projects, including *Notre-Dame de Paris; Fame; Me and*

Mamie O'Rourke; She Loves Me; Crazy for You.
Contributions are passed by Michael White to
a script reader for consideration. Please send
film or theatre treatment/synopsis only.

Newgate Company

13 Dafford Street, Larkhall, Bath, Somerset
BA1 6SW
☎01225 318335

Contact *Jo Anderson*

A commonwealth of established actors, directors and playwrights, Newgate originally concerned itself solely with theatre writing (at the
Bush, Stratford, Roundhouse, etc.). However,
in the course of development, several productions fed into a list of ongoing drama for BBC
TV/Ch4. Looking to develop this co-production strand for film, television and radio projects with other 'Indies'.

Northlight Productions Ltd

The Media Village, Grampian Television,
Queen's Cross, Aberdeen AB15 4XJ
☎01224 646460 Fax 01224 646450
Email tv@northlight.co.uk
Website www.northlight.co.uk

Contact *Robert Sproul-Cran*

Film, video and TV: drama, documentary and
corporate work. OUTPUT ranges from high-
end corporate fund-raising videos to *Thicker
Than Water*, a drama series currently in development; *Equinox: Lethal Seas* (documentary on
whirlpools for Ch4/Discovery); two schools'
series for Ch4 including *Chez Mimi*, 5-part
drama sitcom in French. Scripts welcome. Has
links with EAVE (European Audio-Visual
Entrepreneurs) and Media.

Novus Communications Ltd

Spratton Lodge, Spratton, Northamptonshire
NN6 8LD
☎01604 821195 Fax 01604 821651
Email barrie@novus.ltd.uk
Website www.novus.ltd.uk

Contact *Barrie Goulding*

Documentary video producers. OUTPUT *Police
Stop!* (reality programming); *Caught in the Act*
(CCTV documentary); *The Seriously Funny
Guide to Weddings* (starring Roy Barraclough
and Nerys Hughes) and corporate videos for
Ford and Barclays Bank. 'Always interested in
new writing; telephone or e-mail first.'

Octopus TV

See **Octopus Publishing Group** under
UK Publishers

Omnivision

Pinewood Studios, Iver Heath,
Buckinghamshire SL0 0NH
☎01753 656329 Fax 01753 631146
Email info@omnivision.co.uk
Website www.omnivision.co.uk

Contacts *Christopher Morris, Steve Rowsell*

TV and video producers of documentary, corporate, news and sport programming. Also
equipment and facilities hire. Interested in
ideas; approach by letter or e-mail.

ONCommunications

5 East St Helen Street, Abingdon, Oxford
OX14 5EG
☎01235 537400 Fax 01235 530581
Email ON@oncomms-tv.co.uk
Website www.oncomms-tv.co.uk

Contact *Mrs Sharon Frost*

An independent production company FOUNDED
in 1985 to produce high-quality factual programming, including science, current affairs,
authored documentaries for television, as well as
for corporate and heritage markets.

Open Media

The Mews Studio, 8 Addison Bridge Place,
London W14 8XP
Email contact@openmedia.co.uk

Contact *Araminta Phillips*

Broadcast television: OUTPUT *After Dark; The
Secret Cabaret; James Randi Psychic Investigator;
Opinions; Is This Your Life?; Don't Quote Me;
Brave New World; The Talking Show; Natural
Causes; Equinox; Dispatches.*

Open Road Films

38–42 Whitfield Street, London W1T 2RH
☎020 7813 4333 Fax 020 7637 9024

Contact *Andrew Holmes*

New company, formed by **Holmes Associates**
to produce low budget feature films. OUTPUT
Chunky Monkey.

Orlando TV Productions

Up-the-Steps, Little Tew, Chipping Norton,
Oxfordshire OX7 4JB
☎01608 683218 Fax 01608 683364
Email orlando.tv@btinternet.com

Contact *Mike Tomlinson*

Producer of TV documentaries, with science
subjects as a specialisation. OUTPUT includes programmes for *Horizon* and *QED* (BBC).
Approaches by established writers/journalists to
discuss proposals for collaboration are welcome.

Orpheus Productions

6 Amyand Park Gardens, Twickenham,
Middlesex TW1 3HS
☎020 8892 3172 Fax 020 8892 4821
Email richardtaylor@orpheus100.demon.co.uk

Contact *Richard Taylor*

Television documentaries and corporate work.
OUTPUT has included programmes for BBC
Current Affairs, Music and Arts, and the African-
Caribbean Unit as well as documentaries for the
Shell Film Unit and Video Arts. Unsolicited
scripts are welcomed with caution. 'We have a
preference for visually stirring documentaries
with quality writing of the more personal and
idiosyncratic kind, not straight reportage.'

Outcast Production

1 Lewin Road, London SW14 8DR
☎020 8878 9486
Email xifle@bluecarrots.com

Contact *Andreas Wisniewski*

Low-budget feature films. No unsolicited mss;
send synopsis or treatment only. 'We are actively
searching for and encouraging new writing.'

Ovation Productions

One Prince of Wales Passage, 117 Hampstead
Road, London NW1 3EF
☎020 7387 2342 Fax 020 7380 0404

Contact *John Plews*

Corporate video and conference scripts. Unsolicited mss not welcome. 'We talk to new writers
from time to time.' Ovation also runs the fringe
theatre, 'Upstairs at the Gatehouse' in Highgate,
north London, and welcomes new plays.

Oxford Scientific Films Ltd

Lower Road, Long Hanborough, Oxfordshire
OX8 8LL
☎01993 881881 Fax 01993 882808
Email enquiries@osf.uk.com
Website www.osf.uk.com

Commercials Division: 45–49 Mortimer
Street, London W1N 7TD
☎020 7323 0061 Fax 020 7323 0161

Chief Executive *Claire Birks*
Directors *Sean Morris, Nicholas Unsworth,*
   Suzanne Aitzetmuller

Established media company with specialist
knowledge and expertise in award-winning natural history films and science-based programmes.
Film, video and TV: documentaries, TV commercials, multimedia, and educational films.
Scripts welcome. Operates an extensive stills and
film footage library specialising in wildlife and
special effects (see eunder **Picture Libraries**).

Pace Productions Ltd

12 The Green, Newport Pagnell,
Buckinghamshire MK16 0JW
☎01908 618767
Email chris@paceproductions.com
Website www.paceproductions.com

Contact *Chris Pettit*

Film and video: corporate and commercials.

Paladin Pictures Ltd

22 Ashchurch Grove, London W12 9BT
☎020 8740 1811 Fax 020 8740 7220

Contact *Clive Syddall*

Film and television: drama and documentary
programmes such as *Plague Wars* (mini series on
biological warfare, BBC1); *Travels With My
Tutu* with Deborah Bull (BBC2); *Wallace
Simpson – The Demonised Duchess* (Ch4's 'Secret
History'). No unsolicited mss; 'send a letter
with one-page outline of the book to see if we
are interested.' Specialises in working with
non-fiction writers before their books are published to enable TV tie-in.

Barry Palin Associates Ltd

Unit 10 Princeton Court, 55 Felsham Road,
London SW15 1AZ
☎020 8394 5660 Fax 020 8785 0440
Email mail@barrypalinassociates.com

Contact *Barry Palin*

Film, video and TV production for drama, documentary, commercials and corporate material.
OUTPUT *Harmfulness of Tobacco* Anton Chekhov
short story – BAFTA Best Short Film Award-
winner (Ch4); Corporate: Philip Morris, York
International, Republic Bank of New York.

Panther Pictures Ltd

350A Fulham Road, London SW10 9UH
☎07976 256610 Fax 020 7351 1574
Website www.pantherpictures.co.uk

Contact *Robert Sutton*

Feature films, including *Inside/Out*, a US/
UK/Canada/France co-production.

Paper Moon Productions

Wychwood House, Burchetts Green Lane,
Littlewick Green, Nr. Maidenhead, Berkshire
SL6 3QW
☎01628 829819 Fax 01628 825949
Email david@paper-moon.co.uk

Contact *David Haggas*

Television and video: medical and health education documentaries. OUTPUT includes *Shamans and Science*, a medical documentary examining the balance between drugs discovered in nature and those synthesised in laboratories. Unsolicited scripts welcome. Interested in new writing 'from people who really understand television programme-making'.

Parallax Pictures Ltd
7 Denmark Street, London WC2H 8LS
☎020 7836 1478 Fax 020 7497 8062

Contact *Sally Hibbin*

Feature films/television drama. OUTPUT *Riff-Raff; Bad Behaviour; Raining Stones; Ladybird, Ladybird; I.D.; Land and Freedom; The Englishman Who Went up a Hill But Came Down a Mountain; Bliss; Jump the Gun; Carla's Song; The Governess; My Name Is Joe; Stand and Deliver; Dockers; Hold Back the Night; Bread and Roses; Princesa; The Navigators.*

Passion Pictures
25–27 Riding House Street, London W1W 7DU
☎020 7323 9933 Fax 020 7323 9030
Email info@passion-pictures.com

Managing Director *Andrew Ruhemann*

Television commercials: Dairylea, Levi's and, for the BBC, the 3-minute *Future Generations.* Unsolicited mss welcome.

Pathé Pictures
14–17 Kent House, Market Place, London W1N 8AR
☎020 7323 5151 Fax 020 7631 3568

Head of Development *Matthew Gannon*
Development Executive *Richard Warlow*
Development Assistant *Lucy Ryan*

Produces 4–6 theatrical feature films each year. 'We are pleased to consider all material that has representation from an agent or production company.'

PBF Motion Pictures
The Little Pickenhanger, Tuckey Grove, Ripley, Surrey GU23 6JG
☎01483 225179 Fax 01483 224118
Email peter@pbf.co.uk

Contact *Peter B. Fairbrass*

Film, video and TV: drama, documentary, commercials and corporate. Also televised chess series and chess videos. OUTPUT *Grandmaster Chess; Glue Sniffing; RN Special Services; Nightfrights* (night-time TV chiller series). CLIENTS include

GEC-Marconi, Coca Cola, MoD, Marks & Spencer, various government departments, British Consulate. No scripts; send one-page synopsis only in the first instance. 'Good scripts which relate to current projects will be followed up, otherwise not, as PBF do not have the time to reply to proposals which do not interest them. Only good writing stands a chance.'

Pearson Television Ltd
1 Stephen Street, London W1T 1AL
☎020 7691 6000 Fax 020 7691 6100
Website www.pearsontv.com

Chief Executive *Richard Eyre*
Chief Executive, UK Production *Alan Boyd*
Head of Entertainment *Richard Holloway*
Head of Comedy *Tony Charles*

Pearson Television is the global production and content arm of the RTL Group, Europe's largest TV and radio company, formed following the merger of Pearson Television and CLT-UFA. Acquired Thames Television in 1993 (producer of *The Bill*) and Grundy Worldwide (*Neighbours*) in 1995. Further acquisitions were Witzend Productions (*Lovejoy*) and **Alomo Productions** (see entry) in 1996 and **TalkBack Productions** (see entry) in 2000. PTV currently has more than 160 programmes in production in over 40 countries across six continents, with library sales to over 100 countries.

Pelicula Films
59 Holland Street, Glasgow G2 4NJ
☎0141 287 9522 Fax 0141 287 9504

Contact *Mike Alexander*

Television producer. Makers of drama documentaries and music programmes for the BBC and Ch4. OUTPUT *As an Eilean (From the Island); The Trans-Atlantic Sessions 1 & 2; Nanci Griffith, Other Voices 2; Follow the Moonstone.*

Penumbra Productions Ltd
80 Brondesbury Road, London NW6 6RX
☎020 7328 4550 Fax 020 7328 3844
Email nazpenumbra@compuserve.com

Contact *H.O. Nazareth*

Film, video, TV and radio: drama, documentary and information videos on health, housing, arts and political documentaries. OUTPUT includes *Fugitive Pieces* (Radio 3 play); *Stories My Country Told Me* (BBC2, 'Arena'); *Repomen* (Ch4, 'Cutting Edge'). Send synopses only, preferably by e-mail. Keen to assist in the development of new writing but only interested in social issue-based material.

Photoplay Productions Ltd
21 Princess Road, London NW1 8JR
☎020 7722 2500 Fax 020 7722 6662
Email photoplay@compuserve.com

Contact *Patrick Stanbury*

Documentaries for film, television and video plus restoration of silent films and their theatrical presentation. OUTPUT includes *Cinema Europe: The Other Hollywood; Universal Horror; D.W. Griffith: Father of Film* and the 'Channel 4 Silents' series of silent film restoration, including *The Wedding March, The Iron Mask* and *Lon Chaney, Man of 1000 Faces.* In production: *Chaplin and the Great Dictator.* No unsolicited mss; 'we tend to create and write all our own programmes.'

Picardy Media Group
1 Park Circus, Glasgow G3 6AX
☎0141 333 1200 Fax 0141 332 6002
Email jr@picardy.co.uk
Website www.picardy.co.uk

Senior Producer *John Rocchiccioli*

Television and video: arts documentaries, training and promotional videos, education projects, multi-media productions, and TV and cinema commercials. Unsolicited mss welcome; 'keen to encourage new writing.'

Picture Palace Films Ltd
13 Egbert Street, London NW1 8LJ
☎020 7586 8763 Fax 020 7586 9048
Email info@picturepalace.com
Website www.picturepalace.com

Contact *Malcolm Craddock*

FOUNDED 1971. Leading independent producer of TV drama. OUTPUT *Rebel Heart* (BBC Northern Ireland); *Extremely Dangerous* (ITV for Northwestone Films); *A Life for A Life* (ITV); *Sharpe's Rifles* (Carlton TV); *Little Napoleons* (comedy drama, Ch4); *The Orchid House* (drama serial, Ch4); plus episodes of *Eurocops; Tandoori Nights; 4 Minutes; When Love Dies; Ping Pong* (feature film). Material will only be considered if submitted through an agent.

Phil Pilley Productions
Ferryside, Felix Lane, Shepperton, Middlesex TW17 8NG
☎01932 702916 Fax 01932 702916
Email pilley@tinyworld.co.uk

Programmes for TV and video, mainly sports. Now specialising in sporting history books, particularly golf.

Planet 24 Productions Ltd
195 Marsh Wall, London E14 9SG
☎020 7345 2424 Fax 020 7345 9400
Email info@planet24.co.uk
Website www.planet24.com

Managing Director *Mary Durkan*

Television producer of light and factual entertainment, comedy, music, features and computer animation. Wholly owned subsidiary of Carlton Communications plc. OUTPUT TV: *The Big Breakfast; The Word; The Messiah* (live recording); *Hotel Babylon; Gaytime TV; Delicious; Extra Time, Nothing But the Truth; Watercolour Challenge; Andi Meets ...; Richard Whiteley Unbriefed; The Richard Blackwood Show; A Family of My Own.*

Plantagenet Films Limited
Ard-Daraich Studio B, Ardgour, Nr Fort William, Inverness-shire PH33 7AB
☎01855 841348 Fax 01855 841348
Email plantagenetfilms@aol.com

Contact *Norrie Maclaren*

Film and television: documentary and drama programming such as *Dig* (gardening series for Ch4); various 'Dispatches' for Ch4 and 'Omnibus' for BBC. Keen to encourage and promote new writing; unsolicited mss welcome.

Platinum Film & TV Production Ltd
1b Murray Street, London NW1 9RE
☎020 7916 9091 Fax 020 7916 5238
Email inquiries@platinumtv.co.uk

Contact *Terry Kelleher*

Television documentaries, including drama-documentary. OUTPUT *South Africa's Black Economy* (Ch4); *Murder at the Farm* (Thames TV); *The Biggest Robbery in the World* (major investigative true-crime drama-documentary for Carlton TV); *Dead Line* (original drama by Chilean-exiled writer, Ariel Dorfman, for Ch4). Scripts and format treatments welcome.

Portman Productions
Hampton House, 20 Albert Embankment, London SE1 7TJ
☎020 7840 5030 Fax 020 7840 5040
Website www.prime-ent.plc.uk

Television drama. OUTPUT includes: *Gravy Train* and *Gravy Train Goes East*; *Downwardly Mobile*; *Famous Five Series*; *Rebecca*; *Coming Home*; *Nancherro.* Synopses in the first instance, please.

Portobello Pictures
14–15 D'Arblay Street, London W1V 3FP
☎020 7379 5566 Fax 020 7379 5599
Email edwhitmore@portobellopictures.com

Contacts *Ed Whitmore, Tom Hooper*

Film drama, including Jan Sverak's *Dark Blue World* and *Kolya*; Jez Butterworth's *Birthday Girl* and *Mojo*; Tim Roth's *The War Zone*, plus BBC1's *Dalziel & Pascoe* (series 1–3).

Premiere Productions Ltd
3 Colville Place, London W1T 2BH
☎020 7255 1650

Contact *Henrietta Fudakowski*

Film and television. Currently looking for feature film or TV drama scripts, with a preference for stories with humour. No horror or sci fi. Return postage and list of credits essential. Please phone before submitting material.

Gavin Prime Television
Christmas House, 213 Chester Road, Castle Bromwich, Solihull, West Midlands B36 0ET
☎0121 749 7147

Contact *Gavin Prime*

Film and television: comedy, entertainment and animation. No unsolicited mss.

Prospect Pictures
13 Wandsworth Plain, London SW18 1ET
☎020 7636 1234 Fax 020 7636 1236

Contact *Tony McAvoy*

Drama, documentary and corporate video and TV.

Renaissance Films
34–35 Berwick Street, London W1V 3RF
☎020 7287 5190 Fax 020 7287 5191
Website www.renaissance-films.com

Co-Managing Directors *Stephen Evans, Angus Finney*
Director of Development *Caroline Wood*

Feature films: *The Luzhin Defense; The Wings of the Dove; The Madness of King George* (as Close Call Films); *Twelfth Night; Much Ado About Nothing; Peter's Friends; Henry V.* No unsolicited mss.

Renaissance Vision
256 Fakenham Road, Taverham, Norwich, Norfolk NR8 6QW
☎01603 260280 Fax 01603 864857

Contact *B. Gardner*

Video: full range of corporate work (training, sales, promotional, etc.). Producers of educational and special-interest video publications. Willing to consider good ideas and proposals.

Richmond Films & Television Ltd
PO Box 33154, London NW3 4AZ
☎020 7722 6464 Fax 020 7722 6232
Email mail@richmondfilms.com

Contact *Development Executive*

Film and TV: drama and comedy. OUTPUT *Press Gang; The Lodge; The Office; Wavelength; Privates.* '*No unsolicited scripts.* We will accept *two pages only* consisting of a brief treatment of your project (either screenplay or TV series) which includes its genre and its demographics. Please tell us also where the project has been submitted previously and what response you have had. *Your two pages will not be returned.*'

Rocking Horse
See **Isis Productions**

Rose Bay Film Productions
13 Austin Friars, London EC2N 2JX
☎020 7670 1609 Fax 020 8357 0845
Email info@rosebay.co.uk

Contacts *Matthew Steiner, Simon Usiskin*

Formats and TV production: entertainment and comedy. Unsolicited scripts (with s.a.e.) welcome.

Brenda Rowe Productions
42 Wellington Park, Clifton, Bristol BS8 2UW
☎0117 973 0390 Fax 0117 973 8254
Email brenda@roweprod.demon.co.uk

Contact *Brenda Rowe*

Produces observational, investigative, current affairs TV documentaries, and training and promotional videos for business organisations. Open to new work; unsolicited mss welcome.

RS Productions
47 Laet Street, Newcastle upon Tyne NE29 6NN
☎0191 259 1183/4/0771 0064632 (Mobile)
Fax 0191 259 1184
Email enquiries@rsproductions
Website www.rsproductions.co.uk

Contact *Mark Lavender*

Feature films, television and new media: drama, documentary and corporates. Documentaries include: *Shooting the Albatross* and *Moving Mountains* (both for ITV) and *Park Life* (BBC). Encourages new writers and directors;

unsolicited mss welcome with one-page synopsis and s.a.e. for return.

Sands Films
119 Rotherhithe Street, London SE16 4NF
☎020 7231 2209 Fax 020 7231 2119
Website www.sandsfilms.co.uk

Contacts *Richard Goodwin, Christine Edzard, Olivia Stockman*

Film and TV drama. OUTPUT *Little Dorrit; The Fool; As You Like It; A Dangerous Man; The Long Day Closes; A Passage to India; The Kiss; Swan Princess; Berlioz; The Nutcracker; Seven Years in Tibet; The Children's Midsummer Night's Dream.* No unsolicited scripts.

Scala Productions Ltd
15 Frith Street, London W1V 5TS
☎020 7734 7060 Fax 020 7437 3248
Email scalaprods@aol.com

Contacts *Nik Powell, Rachel Wood*

Production company set up by ex-Palace Productions Nik Powell and Stephen Woolley, who have an impressive list of credits including *Company of Wolves; Absolute Beginners; Mona Lisa; Scandal; Crying Game; Backbeat; Hollow Reed; Neon Bible.* Productions include: *24:7; Little Voice; Divorcing Jack; Welcome to Woop Woop; The Lost Son; The Last Yellow; Fanny and Elvis; The Last September; Five Seconds to Spare; Wild About Harry; Last Orders; Boswell for the Defence; A Passionate Woman.* In development: *St Agnes' Stand; Jonathan Wild; Mort; Wise Children; Money; Brian Jones Project; Shang A Lang; A Single Shot; Black and White.*

Scope Productions Ltd
Keppie House, 147 Blythswood Street, Glasgow G2 4EN
☎0141 332 7720 Fax 0141 332 1049
Website www.scopeproductions.co.uk

TV Commercials *Sharon Fullarton*
Corporate *Bill Gordon*

Corporate film and video; broadcast documentaries and sport; TV commercials. Unsolicited, realistic scripts/ideas welcome.

Screen First Ltd
The Studios, Funnells Farm, Down Street, Nutley, East Sussex TN22 3LG
☎01825 712034 Fax 01825 713511
Email info@screenfirst.co.uk

Contacts *M. Thomas, P. Madden*

Television dramas, documentaries, arts and animation programmes. Developing major drama series, feature films, animated specials and series. No unsolicited scripts.

Screen Ventures Ltd
49 Goodge Street, London W1T 1TE
☎020 7580 7448 Fax 020 7631 1265
Email sales@screenventures.com

Contacts *Christopher Mould, Naima Mould*

Film and TV sales and production: documentary, music videos and drama. OUTPUT *Life and Limb* (health documentary, Discovery Health Channel); *Pavement Aristocrats* (SABC); *Woodstock Diary; Vanessa Redgrave* (LWT 'South Bank Show'); *Mojo Working; Burma: Dying for Democracy* (Ch4); *Genet* (LWT 'South Bank Show'); *Dani Dares* (Ch4 series on strong women); *Pagad* (Ch4 news report).

Screenhouse Productions Ltd
378 Meanwood Road, Leeds, West Yorkshire LS7 2JF
☎0113 239 2292 Fax 0113 239 2293
Email info@screenhouse.co.uk
Website www.screenhouse.co.uk/screenhouse

Contacts *Paul Bader, Barbara Govan*

Television documentary producer. OUTPUT includes six series of *Local Heroes*, factual programmes about the greats of science; two series of *Hart-Davis on History*, a magazine series about local history and how to become involved in historical research (both for BBC2); two history series for BBC Knowledge, *History Quest* and *History Fix.* Contact with one-page outline of idea in the first instance.

September Films
Glen House, 22 Glenthorne Road, Hammersmith, London W6 0NG
☎020 8563 9393 Fax 020 8741 7214
Email september@septemberfilms.com
Website www.septemberfilms.com

Head of Production *Elaine Day*
Head of Development *Elaine Gallagher*

Film and television drama and documentary programming. OUTPUT includes *Breathtaking* (feature film, Sky Pictures/IAC); *The Final Day* (ITV/Pearson); *Eddie Irvine – the Inside Track* (Ch4/Pearson); *Geri's World Walkabout* (BBC/Target); *The Lookalikes Agency; Soap Secrets; Snobs* (all for ITV/Meridian); *Reconstruction* (BSkyB). 'We are interested in developing a small number of projects with new writing talent.' Unsolicited mss welcome, 'in most instances'.

Serendipity Picture Company
Media Centre, Emma-Chris Way,
Abbeywood Park, Bristol BS34 7JU
☎0117 906 6541 Fax 0117 906 6542
Email tony@serendipitypictures.com

Contacts *Tony Yeadon, Nick Dance*

Television and video; corporate and documentary programming. Encourages new writing and will consider scripts.

Seventh House Films
1 Hall Farm Place, Bawburgh, Norwich,
Norfolk NR9 3LW
☎01603 749068 Fax 01603 749069
Email caflo.dunn@virgin.net

Contacts *Clive Dunn, Angela Rule*

Documentary for film, video and TV on subjects ranging from arts to history and science to social affairs. OUTPUT *The Last Fling* (life for a paralysed jump-jockey); *Dark Miracle* (an investigation into a near nuclear disaster in East Anglia); *A Pleasant Terror* (life and ghosts of M.R. James); *Piano Pieces* (musical excursion exploring different aspects of the piano); *Rockin' the Boat* (memories of pirate radio); *White Knuckles* (on the road with a travelling funfair); *King Romance* (life of Henry Rider Haggard); *A Drift of Angels* (three women and the price of art); *Bare Heaven* (the life and fiction of L.P. Hartley); *A Swell of the Soil* (life of Alfred Munnings); *Light Out of the Sky* (the art and life of Edward Seago). 'We welcome programme proposals with a view to collaborative co-production. Always interested in original and refreshing expressions for visual media.'

Sianco Cyf
7 Ffordd Segontiwm, Caernarfon, Gwynedd
LL55 2LL
☎01286 673436/0831 726111 (Mobile)
Fax 01286 677616
Email sian@treannedd.demon.co.uk

Contact *Siân Teifi*

Children's, youth and education programmes and children's drama.

SilentSound Films Ltd
Cambridge Court, Cambridge Road, Frinton on Sea, Essex CO13 9HN
☎01255 676381 Fax 01255 676381
Email thj@silentsoundfilms.co.uk
Website www.silentsoundfilms.co.uk *or*
www.londonfoodfilmfiesta.co.uk

Contact *Timothy Foster*

Active in European film co-production with mainstream connections in the USA. Special interest in developing new projects for live orchestral accompaniment. Also film musicals and documentaries on the arts. No unsolicited material.

Siriol Productions
3 Mount Stuart Square, Butetown, Cardiff
CF1 6RW
☎029 2048 8400 Fax 029 2048 5962
Email siriol@baynet.co.uk

Contact *Andrew Offiler*

Animated series, mainly for children. OUTPUT includes *Meeow; Hilltop Hospital; The Hurricanes; Tales of the Toothfairies; Billy the Cat; The Blobs*, as well as the feature films, *Under Milkwood* and *The Princess and the Goblin*. Write with ideas and sample script in the first instance.

Skyline Productions
10 Scotland Street, Edinburgh EH3 6PS
☎0131 557 4580 Fax 0131 556 4377
Email leslie@skyline.uk.com

Producer/Writer *Leslie Hills*

Film and television drama and documentary. Encourages new writers but telephone first before sending material.

SMG TV Productions Ltd
116 New Oxford Street, London WC1A 1HH
☎020 7663 2300

Managing Director *Jagdip Jagpal*
Head of Drama *Eric Coulter*
Executive Producer for Drama *Judy Counihan*
Head of Development for Drama *Kumari Sulgado*
Head of Development and Children's *Elizabeth Partyka*
Head of Factual Programming *Helen Alexander*

SMG TV Productions Ltd makes programmes for the national television networks, including ITV, Ch4 and Sky. Specialises in drama, factual entertainment and children's programming. OUTPUT includes *Taggart; Rebus; Take Me; TFI Friday; Remembering Lockerbie; The Priory; How2.*

Specific Films
25 Rathbone Street, London W1T 1NQ
☎020 7580 7476 Fax 020 7494 2676
Email specificfilms@compuserve.com

Contacts *Michael Hamlyn*

FOUNDED 1991. OUTPUT includes *Mr Reliable* (feature film co-produced by PolyGram and the

AFFC); *The Adventures of Priscilla, Queen of the Desert*, co-produced with Latent Image (Australia) and financed by PolyGram and AFFC; *U2 Rattle and Hum*, full-length feature – part concert film/part cinema verité documentary; *Paws* (executive producer); *The Last Seduction 2* (Polygram); and numerous pop promos for major international artists.

Spectel Productions Ltd
1 Trethorns Court, Ludgvan, Penzance, Cornwall TR20 8HE
☎01736 740989 Fax 01736 740989
Email Davidwebster@email.msn.com

Contact *David Webster*

Film and video: documentary and corporate; also video publishing. No unsolicited scripts.

Spellbound Productions Ltd
90 Cowdenbeath Path, Islington, London N1 0LG
☎020 7713 8066 Fax 020 7713 8067
Email phspellbound@hotmail.com

Contact *Paul Harris*

Specialises in feature films for cinema and drama for television. Keen to support and encourage new writing. Material will only be considered if in correct screenplay format and accompanied by s.a.e.

Spice Factory
81 The Promenade, Brighton, East Sussex BN10 8LS
☎01273 585275 Fax 01273 585304
Email info@spicefactory.co.uk

Contacts *Michael Cowan, Jason Piette*

Film and TV drama producers. OUTPUT *Pilgrim* (starring Ray Liotta); *New Blood* (Nick Moran and John Hurt); *Sabotage* (David Suchet and Stephen Fry); *Heist/211* (Stephen Dorff and Natasha Henstrige). 'Always open to commercial scripts. We have worked with new writers such as Alberto Sciamma, Jonathan Newman and Jeremy Warding.' Is associated with North By Northwest Media Business School.

'Spoken' Image Ltd
8 Hewitt Street, Manchester M15 4GB
☎0161 236 7522 Fax 0161 236 0020
Email multimedia@spoken-image.com

Contacts *Geoff Allman, Steve Foster, Phil Griffin*

Film, video and TV production for documentary and corporate material. Specialises in high-quality brochures and reports, CD-ROMs, exhibitions, conferences, film and video production for broadcast, industry and commerce.

Stirling Film & TV Productions Limited
137 University Street, Belfast BT7 1HP
☎028 9033 3848 Fax 028 9043 8644
Email anne@stirlingtelevision.co.uk

Contact *Anne Stirling*

Producers of broadcast and corporate programming – documentary, sport, entertainment and magazine programmes.

Storm Film Productions Ltd
32–34 Great Marlborough Street, London W1F 7JB
☎020 7439 1616 Fax 020 7439 4477
Email sophie.storm@btclick.com

Contact *Nic Auerbach*

Producer of commercials for clients such as British Airways and Shell. Unsolicited mss welcome.

Straight Forward Film & Television Productions Ltd
Ground Floor, Crescent House, 14 High Street, Holywood, Co. Down BT18 9AZ
☎028 9042 6298 Fax 028 9042 3384
Email enquiries@sforward.prestel.co.uk

Contacts *John Nicholson, Ian Kennedy*

Northern Ireland-based production company specialising in documentary, feature and lifestyle series for both regional and network transmission. OUTPUT includes *We Shall Overcome* (winner of. Best Documentary at 1999 Celtic Television Festival for BBC); *Conquering the Normans* (Ch4 Learning – history of Normans in Ireland); *Gift of the Gab* (Ch4 Learning – contemporary Irish writing); *Fire School* (BBC NI – training of a team of fire-fighters); *Fish Out of Water* (BBC NI – job swaps north and south of the Irish border); *Just Jones* (BBC Radio Ulster daily show); *Sportsweek* (BBC Radio Ulster); *School Challenge* (3rd series, BBC NI); *World Indoor Bowls* (BBC NI).

Strawberry Productions Ltd
36 Priory Avenue, London W4 1TY
☎020 8994 4494 Fax 020 8742 7675

Contact *John Black*

Film, video and TV: drama and documentary; corporate and video publishing.

Sunset + Vine Productions Ltd
30 Sackville Street, London W1S 3DY
☎020 7478 7300 Fax 020 7478 7403

Sports, children's and music programmes for television. No unsolicited mss. 'We hire freelancers only upon receipt of a commission.'

Sweetheart Films
15 Quennel Mansions, Weir Road, London SW12 0NQ
☎020 8673 3855

Producer *Karel Bata*

Low-to-medium-budget feature films. No unsolicited mss; 'an introductory letter with, perhaps, a treatment and short extract would certainly receive consideration. We are constantly on the look-out for talent. Tip: study your craft!'

Table Top Productions
1 The Orchard, Chiswick, London W4 1JZ
☎020 8742 0507 Fax 020 8742 0507
Email alvin@tabletopproductions.com

Contact *Alvin Rakoff*

TV and film. OUTPUT *Paradise Postponed* (TV mini-series); *A Voyage Round My Father; The First Olympics 1896; Dirty Tricks; A Dance to the Music of Time.* No unsolicited mss. Also Dancetime Ltd.

Talisman Films Limited
5 Addison Place, London W11 4RJ
☎020 7603 7474 Fax 020 7602 7422
Email email@talismanfilms.com

Contact *Richard Jackson*

Drama for film and TV: developing the full range of drama – TV series, serials and single films, as well as theatric features. 'We will only consider material submitted via literary agents.' Interested in supporting and encouraging new writing.

TalkBack Productions
20–21 Newman Street, London W1T 1PG
☎020 7861 8000 Fax 020 7861 8001
Email <firstname>.<surname>@talkback.co.uk

Managing Director *Peter Fincham*
Deputy Managing Director *Sally Debonnaire*

TalkBack Productions is a **Pearson Television** company (see entry). Specialises in comedy, comedy drama and drama; also feature lifestyle programmes. OUTPUT *Smith and Jones; Murder Most Horrid; The Day Today; Knowing Me Knowing You with Alan Patridge; In Search of Happiness; They Think It's All Over; Never Mind the Buzzcocks; Brass Eye; House Doctor; She's Gotta Have It; Grand Designs; Sword of Honour; Land of Plenty; Shooting the Past; 11 o'clock Show; Smack the Pony; Big Train; Los Dos Bros.*

Tandem TV & Film Ltd
10 Bargrove Avenue, Hemel Hempstead, Hertfordshire HP1 1QP
☎01442 261576 Fax 01442 219250
Email info@tandemtv.com
Website www.tandemtv.com

Contact *Barbara Page*

Produces training videos, especially health and safety; construction and civil engineering documentaries; drama-doc life stories for satellite television; Christian church and charity documentary, training and promotional programmes. Welcomes unsolicited mss.

Telemagination Ltd
Regency House, 1–4 Warwick Street, London W1R 5WA
☎020 7434 1551 Fax 020 7434 3344
Email mail@tmation.co.uk
Website www.telemagination.co.uk

Contact *Marion Edwards*

Producer of television animation. OUTPUT includes *The Animals of Farthing Wood; Noah's Island; The Last Polar Bears.* No unsolicited material.

Televideo Productions
The Riverside, Furnival Road, Sheffield, South Yorkshire S4 7YA
☎0114 249 1500 Fax 0114 249 1505
Email gking@televideo.co.uk
Website www.televideo.co.uk

Contact *Graham King*

Video and television: TV news and sports coverage, documentary and corporate work; sell-through videos (distributed on own label). OUTPUT includes *The Premier Collection* (football club videos); varied sports coverage for cable, satellite and terrestrial broadcasters plus a wide range of corporate work from drama-based material to documentary.

Teliesyn
Chapter Arts Centre, Market Road, Canton, Cardiff CF5 1QE
☎029 2030 0876 Fax 029 2030 0877
Email tv@teliesyn.demon.co.uk
Website www.teliesyn.co.uk

Contact *Chris Davies*

Film and video: produces drama, documentary, music and social action in English and Welsh.

Celtic Film Festival, BAFTA Cymru, Grierson and Indie award winner. OUTPUT *Llafur Cariad* (epic drama, S4C); *How Red Was My Valley* (documentary series on the Labour Party, BBC2W); *Suckerfish* (35mm short); *Navida Nuestra* (Christmas mass from Argentina, S4C); *Subway Cops and the Mole Kings* (Ch4). Will consider unsolicited mss only if accompanied by synopsis and c.v. Encourages new writing wherever possible, in close association with a producer.

Tern Television Productions Ltd
73 Crown Street, Aberdeen AB11 6EX
☎01224 211123 Fax 01224 211199
Email office@terntv.com
Website www.terntv.com

Contacts *David Strachan, Gwyneth Hardy*

Broadcast, television and corporate video productions. Specialises in factual entertainment. Currently developing drama. Unsolicited mss welcome.

Thames Television
See **Pearson Television Ltd**

Theatre of Comedy Company
See **Theatre Producers**

Tiger Aspect Productions Ltd
5 Soho Square, London W1D 3QA
☎020 7434 0672 Fax 020 7287 1448
Email general@tigeraspect.co.uk
Website www.tigeraspect.co.uk

Contact *Charles Brand*

Television producer for comedy, drama, documentary and entertainment. OUTPUT *Births, Marriages & Deaths; Kid in the Corner; Country House; Gimme Gimme Gimme; Harry Enfield & Chums; Howard Goodalls' Big Bangs; Playing the Field I, II & III; Streetmate I & II; Let Them Eat Cake; The Vicar of Dibley.* Only considers material submitted via an agent or from writers with a known track record.

Tonfedd
Hen Ysgol Aberpwll, Y Felinheli, Bangor, Gwynedd LL56 4JS
☎01248 671167 Fax 01248 671172
Email sharon@ff-eryri.demon.co.uk

Contact *Hefin Elis*

Light entertainment and music.

Touch Productions Ltd
The Malt House Studios, Donhead St Mary, Dorset SP7 9DN
☎01747 828030 Fax 01747 828004

Email touch.productions@virgin.net

Contacts *Erica Wolfe-Murray, Malcolm Brinkworth*

Television documentaries such as *Simon Weston V; Flying Soldiers; Siege Doctors* (all for BBC); *The Good Life; The Surgery; Coast of Dreams; A French Affair; Watching the Detectives; Brown Babies* (all for Ch4); *Bionic Woman* (BBC1, 'QED'); *Dreamtown; Fame School* (both for Meridian). A new drama section based on real-life storieis begins in 2001. Unsolicited mss welcome.

Transatlantic Films Production and Distribution Company
Studio One, 3 Brackenbury Road, London W6 0BE
☎020 8735 0505 Fax 020 8735 0605
Email mail@transatlanticfilms.com
Website www.transatlanticfilms.com

Executive Producer *Revel Guest*

Producer of TV documentaries. OUTPUT *Horse Tales* (Discovery Channel); *History's Turning Points* (The Learning Channel); *Greek Fire* (Ch4); *Four American Composers* (Ch4); *The Horse in Sport* (Ch4); *A Year in the Life of Placido Domingo.* No unsolicited scripts. Interested in new writers to write 'the book of the series', e.g. for *Greek Fire* and *The Horse in Sport*, but not usually drama script writers.

TV Choice Ltd
22 Charing Cross Road, London WC2H 0HR
☎020 7379 0873 Fax 020 7379 0263
Email 101367.2325@compuserve.com
Website ourworld.compuserve.com/ homepages/tvchoice

Contact *Norman Thomas*

Produces a range of educational videos for schools and colleges on subjects such as history, geography, business studies and economics. No unsolicited mss; send proposals only.

Twentieth Century Fox Film Co
Twentieth Century House, 31–32 Soho Square, London W1D 3AD
☎020 7437 7766 Fax 020 7734 3187
Website www.fox.co.uk

London office of the American giant.

Two Four Productions Limited
Quay West Studios, Old Newnham, Plymouth, Devon PL7 5BH
☎01752 333900 Fax 01752 344224
Email enq@twofour.co.uk
Website www.twofour.co.uk

Managing Director *Charles Wace*
Director of Broadcasting *Jill Lourie*

Specialises in factual and leisure programming for network and regional television; corporate presentations for national/international business and charities; and special interest videos for retail/mail order.

Tyburn Film Productions Limited

Pinewood Studios, Iver Heath,
Buckinghamshire SL0 0NH
☎01753 651700 Fax 01753 656050

Feature films. Subsidiary of **Arlington Productions Limited**. No unsolicited submissions.

UBA Ltd

21 Alderville Road, London SW6 2EE
☎01984 623619 Fax 01984 623733
Email TobeShaw@aol.com

Contacts *Peter Shaw, Joanna Shaw*

Feature films and TV for an international market. OUTPUT *Windprints; The Lonely Passion of Judith Hearne* (co-production with HandMade Films Ltd); *Taffin; Castaway; Turtle Diary; Sweeney Todd; Keep the Aspidistra Flying*. In development: *Kinder Garden; Rebel Magic; No Man's Land*. Prepared to commission new writing whether adapted from another medium or based on a short outline/treatment. Concerned with the quality of the script (*Turtle Diary* was written by Harold Pinter) and breadth of appeal. 'Exploitation material' not welcome.

United Film and Television Productions

London Television Centre, Upper Ground,
London SE1 9LT
☎020 7620 1620

Controller of Drama *Michele Buck*

Television drama. OUTPUT *Hornblower; Walking on the Moon* by Martin Sadofski (drama-doc); *Touching Evil* (series III); *Where the Heart Is* (series III).

United Media Ltd

68 Berwick Street, London W1V 3PE
☎020 7287 2396 Fax 020 7287 2398
Email umedia@globalnet.co.uk

Contact *L. Patterson*

Film, video and TV: drama. OUTPUT *To the Lighthouse* (TV movie with BBC); *Jamaica Inn* (HTV mini-series); *The Krays* (feature film with Fugitive/Rank). Will only accept scripts if submitted by an agent or lawyer.

Vanson Productions

PO Box 16926, London SW18 3ZP
☎020 8874 4241 Fax 020 8874 3600
Email vansonproductions@btclick.com

Contact *Yvette Vanson*

OUTPUT *The Murder of Stephen Lawrence* by Paul Greengrass (a film with Granada for ITV; BAFTA 2000 Best Single Drama); *Doomwatch* by John Howlett and Ian McDonald (science drama with **Working Title Films** for Ch5). In development, amongst others, *Undercover Man* by Julian Bond; *Guts & Glitter* by Joanna Leigh; *Cowboys & Angels* by Ian McDonald. Features, *The Fanmaker* by Alex Williams, developed with British Screen; *Algeria* by Greg Dinner. 'No sitcoms; always ring before sending on spec.'

Vera Productions

66–68 Margaret Street, London W1W 8SR
☎020 7436 6116 Fax 020 7436 6117

Contact *Rachel Sutherland*

Produces television comedy such as *Alistair McGowan's Big Impression*; *Rory Bremner* and *Mark Thomas*.

Video Enterprises

12 Barbers Wood Road, High Wycombe,
Buckinghamshire HP12 4EP
☎01494 534144/0831 875216 (Mobile)
Fax 01494 534144
Email maurice@vident.u-net.com
Website www.vident.u-net.com

Contact *Maurice R. Fleisher*

Video and TV, mainly corporate: business and industrial training, promotional material and conferences. No unsolicited material 'but always ready to try out good new writers'.

Brian Waddell Productions Ltd

Strand Studios, 5/7 Shore Road, Holywood,
Co. Down BT18 9HX
☎028 9042 7646 Fax 028 9042 7922
Email bwpl@globalgateway.co.uk

Contacts *Brian Waddell*

Producer of a wide range of television programmes in leisure activities, the arts, music, children's, comedy, travel/adventure and documentaries. Currently developing several film and drama projects.

Wall to Wall Television

8–9 Spring Place, London NW5 3ER
☎020 7485 7424 Fax 020 7267 5292
Website www.walltowall.co.uk

Chief Executive *Alex Graham*

Factual and drama programming. OUTPUT includes *A Rather English Marriage; Glasgow Kiss; Sex, Chips & Rock 'n' Roll; The 1940s House; Body Story and Neanderthal*. Drama ideas welcomed through established agents.

Jane Walmsley Productions
See **JAM Pictures**

The Walnut Partnership
Crown House, Armley Road, Leeds, West Yorkshire LS12 2EJ
☎08707 427070   Fax 08707 427080
Email mail@walnutpartnership.co.uk
Website www.walnutpartnership.co.uk

Contact *Geoff Penn*

A multi-service production company specialising in business communication using video, live events and new media solutions. Clients include HSBC, Yorkshire Electricity, Clydesdale and Yorkshire Banks.

Walsh Bros. Limited
4 The Heights, London SE7 8JH
☎020 8858 5870/8854 5557
Fax 020 8858 6870

Producer/Director *John Walsh*
Producer/Head of Finance *David Walsh, ACA*
Producer/Head of Development *Maura Walsh*

Award-winning producer of drama documentaries and feature films. OUTPUT *Monarch* (feature film on the events on the eve of the death of King Henry VIII); *Trex* (factual series shooting in China, Mexico, Vancouver and Alaska); *Nu Model Armi* (documentary); *Boyz & Girlz*, (documentary series); *Cowboyz & Cowgirlz* (US sequel to the first hit series); *Ray Harryhausen* (profile of the work of Hollywood special effects legend); *The Comedy Store* (behind-the-scenes view of the birthplace of alternative comedy); *The Sceptic & The Psychic; The Sleeper* and *A State of Mind* (film dramas).

Warner Sisters Film & TV Ltd
The Cottage, Pall Mall Deposit, 124 Barlby Road, London W10 6BL
☎020 8960 3550   Fax 020 8960 3880
Email Sisters@WarnerCine.com

Chief Executives *Lavinia Warner, Jane Wellesley, Anne-Marie Casey, Dorothy Viljoen*

FOUNDED 1984. Drama and comedy. TV and feature films. OUTPUT includes *Selling Hitler; Rides; Life's a Gas; She-Play; A Village Affair; Dangerous Lady; Dressing for Breakfast; The Spy*

that Caught a Cold; The Bite; Jilting Joe; The Jump; Lady Audley's Secret; Do or Die. Developing a wide range of projects including *Mad Mary* (feature film).

Paul Weiland Film Company
14 Newburgh Street, London W1F 7RT
☎020 7287 6900   Fax 020 7434 0146
Email action@paulweiland.com

Contact *Mary Francis*

Television commercials and pop promos.

Western Eye Business Television
Easton Business Centre, Felix Road, Easton, Bristol BS5 0HE
☎0117 941 5854   Fax 0117 941 5851

Contact *Jayne Cotton*

Corporate video production for Royal Mail, Re-Solv, NACAB, Water Aid, BT. Looking for experienced writers in the above field.

Michael White Productions Ltd
See **MW Entertainments Ltd**

Windrush Productions Ltd
7 Woodlands Road, Moseley, Birmingham B13 4EH
☎0121 449 6439/07977 059378 (Mobile)
Fax 0121 449 6439
Email beboyyaa@hotmail.com

Contacts *Pogus Caesar, Shawn Caesar*

Television documentaries, including a multicultural series for Carlton TV (*Xpress and Respect*); *The A-Force* (BBC); *I'm Black in Britain* (Central TV); *Drumbeat* (Carlton). Also produces *Windrush E. Smith Show* (comedy) and Pogus Caesar's *Off the Hook* for BBC Radio Pebble Mill. Produces pop promos/corporate videos for a range of clients. Encourages new writing, especially from the regions. 'We try to seek scripts from writers interested in developing new Black fiction/comedy.'

WitzEnd Productions
See **Pearson Television Ltd**

Working Title Films Ltd
Oxford House, 76 Oxford Street, London W1D 1BS
☎020 7307 3000   Fax 020 7307 3001/2/3

Co-Chairmen (Films) *Tim Bevan, Eric Fellner*
Head of Development (Films) *Debra Hayward*
Development Executive (Films) *Chris Clark*
Television *Simon Wright*

Feature films, TV drama; also family/children's

entertainment and TV comedy. OUTPUT Films: *Notting Hill; Elizabeth; Hi Lo Country; Plunkett & Macleane; Bean; The Borrowers; The Matchmaker; Fargo; Dead Man Walking; French Kiss; Four Weddings and a Funeral; The Hudsucker Proxy; The Tall Guy; A World Apart; Wish You Were Here; My Beautiful Laundrette.* Television: *More Tales of the City; Lano and Woodley; The Borrowers I & II; Armisted Maupin's Tales of the City; News Hounds; Echoes; Randall & Hopkirk Deceased; Doomwatch.* No unsolicited mss at present, but keen to encourage new writing nevertheless via New Writers Scheme - contact *Dan Shepherd.*

Worldview Pictures

Unit 10, Cameron House, 12 Castlehaven Road, London NW1 8QW
☎020 7916 4696 Fax 020 7916 1091
Email anyone@worldviewpictures.co.uk
Contacts *Stephen Trombley, Bruce Eadie*

Documentaries and series for television, plus theatrical. OUTPUT *A Death in the Family; Project X* (Discovery); *War and Civilization* (The Learning Channel); *Nuremberg* (Discovery/Ch4); *Raising Hell: The Life of A.J. Bannister; The Execution Protocol* (both for Discovery/BBC/France 2); *Drancy: A Concentration Camp in Paris; The Lynchburg Story* (both for Discovery/Ch4/France 2); *99% Woman* (France 2).

Worthwhile Productions Ltd

16 Biddulph Road, London W6 1JB
☎020 7266 9166 Fax 020 7266 9166
Contact *Jeremy Wootliff*

Feature films, video; documentary, corporate and commercials. Unsolicited mss welcome.

Wortman Productions UK

48 Chiswick Staithe, London W4 3TP
☎020 8994 8886/07976 805976 (Mobile)
Producer *Neville Wortman*

Film, video and TV production for drama, documentary, commercials and corporate material. OUTPUT *House in the Country* John Julius Norwich (ITV series); *Ellington* (jazz series); *Celebration Theatre Company for the Young — The Winter's Tale; Copland's Century* (documentary on Aaron Copland); *Florence Nightingale* (film drama in development). Open to new writing but preferably from agents; single page outline and couple of pages of dialogue.

WOT Images

Suite 3, 44 Mortimer Street, London W1N 7DG
☎020 7323 5901
Contacts *Jackie Thomas, Nick Fleming*

Television and video drama plus a film in development. Welcomes unsolicited mss.

W.O.W. Productions

26A Fordwych Road, London NW2 3TG
☎020 8830 5978 Fax 020 8830 5978
Email wow@dircon.co.uk
Contacts *Carl Schonfeld, Dom Rotheroe*

Film and television drama and documentary programming. OUTPUT includes *A Sarajevo Diary* (documentary) and *My Brother Tom* (feature).

The Writers Studio – a division of Screen Production Associates Ltd

☎020 7267 9953 Fax 020 7267 9953
Email enquiries@screenpro.co.uk
Contacts *Piers Jackson, Nicholas McInerny*

Feature films. OUTPUT *The 4th Man; The Truth Game; Black Badge; The Case; Mothball City; Club Le Monde.* No unsolicited mss. Send preliminary letter outlining project (only movie screenplays) and c.v.

Yoda Productions Ltd

Brooklands Cottage, Guildford Road, Westcott, Dorking, Surrey RH4 3LB
☎01306 886916 Fax 0870 2842772
Email gail@yodaproductions.co.uk
Contact *Gail Lowe*

Medical, scientific, technical marketing and promotional, training videos and multimedia. No unsolicited mss.

Zenith Entertainment Plc

43–45 Dorset Street, London W1H 4AB
☎020 7224 2440 Fax 020 7224 3194
Email general@zenith-entertainment.co.uk
Head of Drama Development *Judith Hackett*

Feature films and TV drama. OUTPUT Films: Todd Haynes' *Velvet Goldmine; Wisdom of Crocodiles*; Nicole Holofcener's *Walking and Talking.* Television: *Hamish Macbeth; Rhodes; Bodyguards; The Uninvited; Bomber; 2000 Acres of Sky.* No unsolicited scripts.

Theatre Producers

Actors Touring Company

Alford House, Aveline Street, London
SE11 5DQ
☎020 7735 8311
Fax 020 7735 1031 attn. ATC
Email atc@cwcom.net

Artistic Director *Gordon Anderson*

'Actors Touring Company takes old stories and works with living writers to produce new theatre.' Collaborations with writers are based on adaptation and/or translation work and unsolicited mss will only be considered in this category. 'We endeavour to read mss but do not have the resources to do so quickly.' As a small-scale company, all plays must have a cast of six or less.

Almeida Theatre Company

Almeida at King's Cross, Omega Place, off Caledonian Road, London N1 9DR
☎020 7226 7432 Fax 020 7704 9581
Website www.almeida.co.uk

Artistic Directors *Ian McDiarmid, Jonathan Kent*

FOUNDED 1980. Now in its twelfth year as a full-time producing theatre, presenting a year-round theatre and music programme in which international writers, composers, performers, directors and designers are invited to work with British artists on challenging new and classical works. Previous productions: *Galileo; Moonlight; The School for Wives; Hamlet; Who's Afraid of Virginia Woolf; Ivanov; The Government Inspector; Naked; The Judas Kiss; The Iceman Cometh; The Jew of Malta; Celebration; The Room; Richard II; Coriolanus; Lulu.* No unsolicited mss: 'our producing programme is very limited and linked to individual directors and actors'.

Alternative Theatre Company Ltd

Bush Theatre, Shepherds Bush Green, London W12 8QD
☎020 7602 3703 Fax 020 7602 7614
Email thebush@dircon.co.uk

Literary Manager *Tim Fountain*

FOUNDED 1972. Trading as The Bush Theatre. Produces nine new plays a year (principally British) including up to three visiting companies also producing new work: 'we are a writer's theatre'. Previous productions: *Kiss of the Spiderwoman* Manuel Puig; *Raping the Gold* Lucy Gannon; *The Wexford Trilogy* Billy Roche; *Love and Understanding* Joe Penhall; *This Limetree Bower* Conor McPherson; *Discopigs* Enda Walsh; *The Pitchfork Disney* Philip Ridley; *Caravan* Helen Blakeman; *Beautiful Thing* Jonathan Harvey; *Killer Joe* Tracy Letts; *Shang-a-Lang* Catherine Johnson; *Howie the Rookie* Mark O'Rowe. Scripts are read by a team of associates, then discussed with the management, a process which takes about four months. The theatre offers a small number of commissions, recommissions to ensure further drafts on promising plays, and a guarantee against royalties so writers are not financially penalised even though the plays are produced in a small house. Writers should send scripts with small s.a.e. for acknowledgement and large s.a.e. for return of script.

Yvonne Arnaud Theatre

Millbrook, Guildford, Surrey GU1 3UX
☎01483 440077 Fax 01483 564071

Contact *James Barber*

Credits include: *The Caretaker* Harold Pinter; *Alarms and Excursions* Michael Frayn; *Tom and Clem* Stephen Churchett; *Life Support* Simon Gray; *Equally Divided* Ronald Harwood; *Comic Potential* Alan Ayckbourn; *The Prisoner of Second Avenue* Neil Simon; *A Passionate Woman* Kay Mellor; *Indian Ink* Tom Stoppard; *Home* David Storey; *Cellmates* Simon Gray; *Letter of Resignation* Hugh Whitemore; *Quartet* Ronald Harwood.

Birmingham Repertory Theatre

Centenary Square, Broad Street, Birmingham B1 2EP
☎0121 245 2000 Fax 0121 245 2100
Website www.birmingham-rep.co.uk

Literary Manager *Ben Payne*
Literary Officer *Caroline Jester*

The Birmingham Repertory Theatre aims to provide a platform for the best work from new writers from both within and beyond the West Midlands region along with a programme which also includes classics and 'discovery' plays. The Rep is committed to a policy of integrated casting and to the production of new work which reflects the diversity of contemporary experience. The commissioning of new plays takes place across the full range of the theatre's activities: in the Main House, The Door (which is a dedicated new writing space) and on tour to community venues in the region. 'Writers are advised that the Rep is very unlikely to produce an unsolicited script. We usually assess unsolicited submissions on the basis of whether it indicates a writer with whom the theatre may be interested in working. The theatre runs a programme of writers' attachments every year in addition to its commissioning policy and maintains close links with *Stagecoach* (the regional writers' training agency) and the **MA in Playwriting Studies** at the University of Birmingham.' For more information contact the Literary Officer.

Black Theatre Co-op
See **Nitro**

Bootleg Theatre Company
23 Burgess Green, Bishopdown, Salisbury, Wiltshire SP1 3El
☎01722 421476
Email colin@thebootlegtheatrecompany.fsnet.co.uk
Contact *Colin Burden*

FOUNDED 1984. Tries to encompass as wide an audience as possible and has a tendency towards plays with socially relevant themes. A good bet for new writing since unsolicited mss are very welcome. 'Our policy is to produce new and/or rarely seen plays and anything received is given the most serious consideration.' Actively seeks to obtain grants to commission new writers for the company. Productions include: *Clubland* by Giles, Harris, Suthers and Mordell; *Rainy Night in Soho* Stephen Giles; *The Truth About Blokes*; *Hanging Hanratty* by Michael Burnham.

Borderline Theatre
Darlington New Church, North Harbour Street, Ayr KA8 8AA
☎01292 281010 Fax 01292 263825
Email <name>@borderlinetheatre.co.uk
Website www.borderlinetheatre.co.uk
Producer *Eddie Jackson*

FOUNDED 1974. Borderline is one of Scotland's leading touring companies. Committed to new writing, it tours an innovative programme of new plays and radical adaptations/translations of classic texts in an accessible and entertaining style. Tours to main-house theatres and small venues throughout Scotland. Productions include the world premières of *The Angels' Share* by Chris Dolan; *The Prince and the Pilot* Anita Sullivan. Previous writers have included Dario Fo, Liz Lochhead and John Byrne. Borderline is also committed to commissioning and touring new plays for young people. Send synopsis with cast size in the first instance.

Bristol Old Vic Theatre Company
(Theatre Royal, New Vic Studio & Basement)
Theatre Royal, King Street, Bristol BS1 4ED
☎0117 949 3993 Fax 0117 949 3996
Email the.bristol.old.vic@cableinet.co.uk

Bristol Old Vic is committed to the commissioning and production of new writing in the Theatre Royal (650 seats). Plays must have enough popular appeal to attract an audience of significant size. In the New Vic Studio (150 seats) up to four plays a year are produced. The theatre will read and report on unsolicited scripts, and asks for a fee of £15 per script to cover the payments to readers. 'We also seek to attract emerging talent to the Basement, a profit-share venue (50 seats) committed to producing one-act plays. Plays for the Basement will be read free of charge although no report can be provided.' In all cases if return of script is required, please supply s.a.e.

Bush Theatre
See **Alternative Theatre Company Ltd**

Carnival (Films & Theatre) Ltd
See entry under **Film, TV and Video Production Companies**

Guy Chapman Productions Ltd
1–2 Henrietta Street, London WC2E 8PS
☎020 7379 7474 Fax 020 7379 8484
Email guy@g-c-a.co.uk
Contacts *Guy Chapman*

Performs to young audiences with innovative, experimental theatre. Productions include: *Shopping and Fucking*; *Love Upon the Throne*; *Crave*; *Disco Pigs*.

Chester Gateway Theatre Trust Ltd
Hamilton Place, Chester, Cheshire CH1 2BH
☎01244 344238 Fax 01244 317277
Website www.gateway-theatre.org
Artistic Director *Deborah Shaw*

FOUNDED 1968. 440-seater, fairly intimate auditorium. Committed to producing at least one new play a year along with a balanced pro-gramme of classics, contemporary plays, Christmas adaptations and re-discoveries (e.g. Noël Coward's *The Young Idea*). Recent pre-mières by Keith Waterhouse, Mick Martin, Dino Aristidou. Also busy Education and Access Department which occasionally commissions work. Writers' group meets fortnightly.

Citizens Theatre

Gorbals, Glasgow G5 9DS
☎0141 429 5561 Fax 0141 429 7374
Email info@citz.co.uk
Website www.citz.co.uk
Artistic Director *Giles Havergal*

No formal new play policy. The theatre has a play reader but opportunities to do new work are limited.

Clwyd Theatr Cymru

Mold, Flintshire CH7 1YA
☎01352 756331 Fax 01352 758323
Email drama@celtic.co.uk
Website www.clwyd-theatr-cymru.co.uk
Literary Manager *William James*

Theatre of the Year 1998–99 (Barclays/TMA), Clwyd Theatr Cymru produces a season of plays each year performed by a core ensemble, along with tours throughout Wales (in English and Welsh). Plays are a mix of classics, revivals, con-temporary drama. Recent new writing includes: *The Journey of Mary Kelly* Siân Evans; *Rape of the Fair Country, Hosts of Rebecca* and *Song of the Earth* all adapt. Manon Eames; *The Changelings* Gregg Cullen; *Celf* by Yasmina Reza; *Damwain a Hap* by Dario Fo, both translated by Manon Eames; *Flora's War/Rhyfel Flora* and *Word for Word/Gair am Air* by Tim Baker. Plays by Welsh writers or with Welsh themes will be considered.

Michael Codron Plays Ltd

Aldwych Theatre Offices, Aldwych, London WC2B 4DF
☎020 7240 8291 Fax 020 7240 8467
General Manager *Paul O'Leary*

Michael Codron Plays Ltd manages the Aldwych Theatre in London's West End. The plays it produces don't necessarily go into the Aldwych but always tend to be big-time West End fare. Previous productions: *Copenhagen; The Invention of Love; Hapgood; Uncle Vanya; The Sneeze; Rise and Fall of Little Voice; Arcadia; Dead Funny*. No particular rule of thumb on subject matter or treatment. The acid test is whether 'something appeals to Michael'. Straight plays rather than musicals.

Colchester Mercury Theatre Limited

Balkerne Gate, Colchester, Essex CO1 1PT
☎01206 577006 Fax 01206 769607
Email mercury.theatre@virgin.net
Artistic Producer *Gregory Floy*
Associate Director *Adrian Stokes*

Producing theatre with a wide-ranging audi-ence. Unsolicited scripts welcome. The theatre has a free playwright's group for adults with a serious commitment to writing plays.

The Coliseum, Oldham

Fairbottom Street, Oldham, Lancashire OL1 3SW
☎0161 624 1731 Fax 0161 624 5318
Chief Executive *Kenneth Alan Taylor*

The policy of the Coliseum is to present high quality work that is unashamedly 'popular'. Has a special interest in new work that has a Northern flavour, however this does not rule out other plays. Unsolicited scripts are all read but will only be returned if a s.a.e. is included.

Contact Theatre Company

Oxford Road, Manchester M15 6JA
☎0161 274 3434 Fax 0161 274 0640
Email info@contact-theatre.org.uk
Artistic Director *John E. McGrath*

FOUNDED 1972. Plays to a young audience (up to 30). New productions have included: *Rupert Street Lonely Hearts Club* Jonathan Harvey; *Tell Me* Matthew Dunster; *Unsuitable Girls* Dolly Dhingra (all world premières). Contact the company for detailed guidelines for writers.

Crucible Theatre

55 Norfolk Street, Sheffield S1 1DA
☎0114 249 5999 Fax 0114 249 6003
Associate Director *Michael Grandage*

'Most of the new work we present will be the result of commissions or a prolonged exchange of ideas and script development with writers in whom we have expressed an interest. However, we are interested in all new work and offer a free script reading service for unsolicited scripts. NB We do not offer readers' reports. Please ring or send s.a.e. for full details of script reading service.'

Cwmni Theatr Gwynedd

Deiniol Road, Bangor, Gwynedd LL57 2TL
☎01248 351707 Fax 01248 351915
Email theatr@globalnet.co.uk
Contact *Artistic Director*

FOUNDED 1984. A mainstream company, performing in major theatres on the Welsh circuit. Welsh-language work only at present. Classic Welsh plays, translations of European repertoire and new work, including adaptations from novels. New Welsh work always welcome; works in English considered if appropriate for translation (i.e. dealing with issues relevant to Wales). 'We are keen to discuss projects with established writers and offer commissions where possible.'

Derby Playhouse
Eagle Centre, Derby DE1 2NF
☎01332 363271 Fax 01332 547200
Website www.derbyplayhouse.demon.co.uk
Artistic Director *Mark Clements*

Derby Playhouse is interested in new work and has produced several world premières over the last year. 'We have a discrete commissioning budget but already have several projects under way. Due to the amount of scripts we receive, we now ask writers to send a letter accompanied by a synopsis of the play, a résumé of writing experience and any ten pages of the script they wish to submit. We will then determine whether we think it is suitable for the Playhouse, in which case we will ask for a full script.' Writers are welcome to send details of rehearsed readings and productions as an alternative means of introducing the theatre to their work.

Druid Theatre Company
Chapel Lane, Galway, Republic of Ireland
☎00 353 91 568660 Fax 00 353 91 563109
Email info@druidtheatre.com
Website www.druidtheatre.com
Contact *Literary Manager*

FOUNDED 1975. Based in Galway and playing nationally and internationally, the company operates a major programme for the development of new writing. While focusing on Irish work, the company also accepts unsolicited material from outside Ireland.

The Dukes Playhouse Ltd
Moor Lane, Lancaster LA1 1QE
☎01524 67461 Fax 01524 846817
Chief Executive *Amanda Belcham*
Artistic Director *Ian Hastings*

FOUNDED 1971. The only producing house in Lancashire. Wide target market for cinema and theatre. Plays in a 320-seater end-on auditorium and in a 174-seater in-the-round studio. In the summer months open-air promenade performances are held in Williamson Park. Also, community based Youth Arts Centre.

Dundee Repertory Theatre
Tay Square, Dundee DD1 1PB
☎01382 227684 Fax 01382 228609
Email hglen@dundeereptheatre.co.uk
Website www.dundeereptheatre.co.uk
Artistic Director *Hamish Glen*

FOUNDED 1939. Plays to a varied audience. Translations and adaptations of classics, and new local plays. Most new work is commissioned. Interested in contemporary plays in translation and in new Scottish writing. No scripts except by prior arrangement.

Eastern Angles Theatre Company
Sir John Mills Theatre, Gatacre Road, Ipswich, Suffolk IP1 2LQ
☎01473 218202 Fax 01473 250954
Email admin@eastsernangles.co.uk
Website www.easternangles.co.uk
Artistic Director *Ivan Cutting*
General Manager *Jill Streatfeild*

FOUNDED 1982. Plays to a rural audience for the most part. New work only: some commissioned, some devised by the company, some researched documentaries. Unsolicited mss welcome from regional writers. 'We are always keen to develop and produce new writing, especially that which is germane to a rural area.'

Edinburgh Royal Lyceum Theatre
See **Royal Lyceum Theatre Company**

English Stage Company Ltd
See **Royal Court Theatre**

English Touring Theatre
New Century Building, Hill Street, Crewe CW1 2BX
☎01270 501800 Fax 01270 501888
Email admin@englishtouringtheatre.co.uk
Website www.englishtouringtheatre.co.uk
Artistic Director *Stephen Unwin*

(NB the company was due to relocate later in 2001.) FOUNDED 1993. National touring company visiting middle-scale receiving houses and arts centres throughout England. Mostly mainstream. Largely classical programme, but with increasing interest to tour one modern English play per year. Strong commitment to Education and Community Outreach work. No unsolicited mss.

Robert Fox Ltd

6 Beauchamp Place, London SW3 1NG
☎020 7584 6855 Fax 020 7225 1638
Email rf@robertfoxltd.com

Contact *Robert Fox*

Producer and co-producer of work suitable for West End production. Previous productions: *Another Country; Chess; Lettice and Lovage; Burn This; When She Danced; The Ride Down Mount Morgan; The Importance of Being Earnest; The Seagull; Goosepimples; Vita & Virginia; The Weekend; Three Tall Women; Skylight; Who's Afraid of Virginia Woolf; Masterclass; A Delicate Balance; Amy's View; Closer; The Lady in the Van; The Caretaker.* Scripts, while usually by established playwrights, are always read.

Gate Theatre Company Ltd

11 Pembridge Road, London W11 3HQ
☎020 7229 5387 Fax 020 7221 6055

Acting Literary Manager *Kate Wild*

FOUNDED 1979. Plays to a mixed, London-wide audience, depending on production. Aims to produce British premières of plays which originate from abroad and translations of neglected classics. Works mainly with translators. Recent productions: *Cuckoos* by Guiseppe Manfridi; *The Three Birds* by Joanna Laurens. Positively encourages writers from abroad to send in scripts or translations. Most unsolicited scripts are read but it is extremely unlikely that new British, Irish or North American plays will have any future at the theatre due to emphasis on plays translated from foreign languages. The Gate does not welcome primary anglophone material and will not read these plays. Always enclose s.a.e. if play needs returning.

Graeae Theatre Company

Hampstead Town Hall, 213 Haverstock Hill, London NW3 4QP
☎020 7681 4755 Fax 020 7681 4756
Email info@graeae.org
Website www.graeae.dircon.co.uk
Minicom 020 7267 3167

Artistic Director *Jenny Sealey*
Executive Producer *Hetty Shand*

Europe's premier theatre company of disabled people, the company tours nationally and internationally with innovative theatre productions highlighting both historical and contemporary disabled experience. Graeae also runs Forum Theatre and educational programmes available to schools, youth clubs and day centres nationally, provides vocational training in theatre arts (including playwriting). Unsolicited scripts – from disabled writers – welcome. New work examining disability issues is commissioned.

Hampstead Theatre

Swiss Cottage Centre, Avenue Road, London NW3 3EX
☎020 7722 9224 Fax 020 7722 3860
Website www.hampstead-theatre.co.uk

Literary Manager *Ben Jancovich*

A brand new Hampstead Theatre is due to open in the autumn of 2002. The building will be an intimate space with a flexible stage and an auditorium capable of expanding to seat 325 (double the current capacity). The artistic policy will continue to be the production of British and international new plays and the development of important young writers. 'We are looking for writers who recognise the power of theatre and who have a story to tell. All plays are read and discussed. We give feedback to all writers with potential.' Writers produced at Hampstead include: Michael Frayn, Roy Williams, Shelagh Stephenson, Simon Block, Philip Ridley, Frank McGuinness, Rona Munro and Brad Fraser.

Harrogate Theatre Company

Oxford Street, Harrogate, North Yorkshire HG1 1QF
☎01423 502710 Fax 01423 563205
Email staff.name@harrogatetheatre.demon.co.uk

Artistic Director *Rob Swain*

Produces four to five productions a year on the main stage, one of which may be a new play but is most likely to be commissioned. Annual mainstage Youth Theatre production may also be commissioned. From August 2001 there will be a Writer in Residence for one year. Over the next two years it is planned to workshop and read new plays by local writers and possibly stage them in the sudio. Unsolicited scripts from outside Yorkshire are unlikely to receive a production or workshop. Please write with a brief synopsis initially.

Heritage Theatre Ltd

See entry under **Film, TV and Video Production Companies**

The Hiss & Boo Company Ltd

1 Nyes Hill, Wineham Lane, Bolney, West Sussex RH17 5SD Fax 01444 882057
Email hissboo@msn.com
Website www.hissboo.co.uk

Contact *Ian Liston*

Particularly interested in new thrillers, comedy thrillers, comedy and melodrama – must be commercial full-length plays. Also interested in plays/plays with music for children. No one-acts. Previous productions: *The Shakespeare Revue; Come Rain Come Shine; Sleighrider; Beauty and the Beast; An Ideal Husband; Mr Men's Magical Island; Mr Men and the Space Pirates; Nunsense; Corpse!; Groucho: A Life in Revue; See How They Run; Christmas Cat and the Pudding Pirates; Pinocchio* and traditional pantos written by Roy Hudd for the company. 'We are keen on revue-type shows and compilation shows but *not* tribute-type performances.' No unsolicited scripts; no telephone calls. Send synopsis and introductory letter in the first instance.

Hull Truck Theatre Company

Spring Street, Hull HU2 8RW
☎01482 224800 Fax 01482 581182

Executive Director *Joanne Gower*

John Godber, of *Teechers, Bouncers, Up 'n' Under* fame, the artistic director of this high-profile Northern company since 1984, has very much dominated the scene in the past with his own successful plays. The emphasis is still on new writing but Godber's work continues to be toured extensively. Most new plays are commissioned. Previous productions: *Dead Fish* Gordon Steel; *Off Out* and *Fish and Leather* both by Gill Adams; *Happy Families* John Godber. The company receives a large number of unsolicited scripts but cannot guarantee a quick response. Bear in mind the artistic policy of Hull Truck, which is 'accessibility and popularity'. In general they are not interested in musicals, or in plays with casts of more than eight.

Stephen Joseph Theatre

Westborough, Scarborough, North Yorkshire YO11 1JW
☎01723 370540 Fax 01723 360506

Artistic Director *Alan Ayckbourn*
Literary Manager *Laura Harvey*

A two-auditoria complex housing a 165-seat end stage theatre/cinema (the McCarthy) and a 400-seat theatre-in-the-round (the Round). Positive policy on new work. For obvious reasons, Alan Ayckbourn's work features quite strongly but a new writing programme ensures plays from other sources are actively encouraged. Also runs a lunchtime season of one-act plays each summer. Writers are advised however that the SJT is very unlikely to produce an unsolicited script – synopses are preferred. Recent commissions and past productions include: *A Listening Heaven* and *Clockwatching* Torben Betts; *Larkin with Women* Ben Brown; *Amaretti Angels* Sarah Phelps; *Something Blue* Gill Adams; *House and Garden* Alan Ayckbourn; *Neville's Island* Tim Firth. 'Writers are welcome to send details of rehearsed readings and productions as an alternative means of introducing the theatre to their work.' Submit to *Laura Harvey* enclosing an s.a.e. for return of mss.

Bill Kenwright Ltd

BKL House, 106 Harrow Road, London W2 1RR
☎020 7446 6200 Fax 020 7446 6222

Contact *Bill Kenwright*

Presents both revivals and new shows for West End and touring theatres. Although new work tends to be by established playwrights, this does not preclude or prejudice new plays from new playwrights. Scripts should be addressed to Bill Kenwright with a covering letter and s.a.e. 'We have enormous amounts of scripts sent to us although we very rarely produce unsolicited work. Scripts are read systematically. Please do not phone; the return of your script or contact with you will take place in time.'

Komedia

Gardner Street, North Lane, Brighton, East Sussex BN1 1UN
☎01273 647101 Fax 01273 647102
Email admin@komedia.co.uk
Website www.komedia.dircon.co.uk

Contact *David Lavender*

FOUNDED in 1994, Komedia promotes, produces and presents new work. Mss of new plays welcome.

Leeds Playhouse

See **West Yorkshire Playhouse**

Leicester Haymarket Theatre

Belgrave Gate, Leicester LE1 3YQ
☎0116 253 0021 Fax 0116 251 3310
Website www.leicesterhaymarkettheatre.org

Artistic Director *Paul Kerryson*

'We aim for a balanced programme of original and established works.' Recent productions include: *A Little Night Music; Rent; East is East; Single Spies; The Crucible; The Wizard of Oz; Sunday in the Park with George*. An Asian initiative has been set up to promote Asian work and Asian practitioners. There is also a full studio season and programme of activity for the outreach and education department, including youth theatre and community tours.

Library Theatre Company

St Peter's Square, Manchester M2 5PD
☎0161 234 1913 Fax 0161 228 6481
Email ltc@libraries.manchester.gov.uk
Website www.libtheatreco.org.uk
Artistic Director *Christopher Honer*

Produces new and contemporary work, as well as occasional classics. No unsolicited mss. Send outline of the nature of the script first. Encourages new writing through the commissioning of new plays and through a programme of rehearsed readings to help writers' development.

Live Theatre Company

7/8 Trinity Chare, Newcastle upon Tyne NE1 3DF
☎0191 261 2694 Fax 0191 232 2224
Email info@live.org.uk
Website www.live.org.uk
Artistic Director *Max Roberts*
Executive Director *Jim Beirne*

FOUNDED 1973. Produces shows at its refurbished 200-seat venue, and also tours regionally and nationally. Company policy is to produce work that is rooted in the culture of the region, particularly for those who do not normally get involved in the arts. The company is particularly interested in promoting new writing. As well as full-scale productions the company organises workshops, rehearsed readings and other new writing activities. The company also enjoys a close relationship with **New Writing North**. Productions include: *Up and Running* Phil Woods; *Buffalo Girls* by Karin Young; *Two* Jim Cartwright; *Cabaret*, and an ambitious cycle of plays – *Twelve Tales of Tyneside* – which involved 12 writers; *Falling Together* Tom Hadaway; *Cooking With Elvis* Lee Hall; *Bones* Peter Straughan; *Laughter When We're Dead* Sean O'Brien and *ne1*.

London Bubble Theatre Company

3–5 Elephant Lane, London SE16 4JD
☎020 7237 4434 Fax 020 7231 2366
Email peth@londonbubble.org.uk
Website www.londonbubble.org.uk
Artistic Director *Jonathan Petherbridge*

Produces workshops, plays and events for a mixed audience of theatregoers and non-theatregoers, wide-ranging in terms of age, culture and class. Previous productions: *Gilgamesh; Sleeping Beauty; Growing People*. Unsolicited mss are received but 'our reading service is extremely limited and there can be a considerable wait before we can give a response'. Commissions approximately one new project a year, often inspired by a promenade site, specific community of interest or workshop group.

Lyric Theatre Hammersmith

King Street, London W6 0QL
☎020 8741 0824 Fax 020 8741 5965
Email enquiries@lyric.co.uk
Website www.lyric.co.uk
Artistic Director *Neil Bartlett*
Executive Director *Simon Mellor*

The main theatre stages an eclectic programme of new and revived classics with a particular interest in music theatre. Interested in developing projects with writers, translators and adaptors. The Lyric does not accept unsolicited scripts. No longer able to produce in its 110-seat studio owing to reduced funding but the venue continues to host work, including new, by some of the best touring companies in the country.

MAC – The Centre for Birmingham

Cannon Hill Park, Birmingham B12 9QH
☎0121 440 4221 Fax 0121 446 4372
Email enquiries@mac-birmingham.org.uk
Website www.birminghamarts.org.uk/
    organisations/mac.html
Director *Dorothy Wilson*

Home of the Geese Theatre Company, Sampad South Asian Arts, Stan's Café Theatre Company and a host of other arts/performance-related organisations based in Birmingham. Details on Geese available from the Centre.

Cameron Mackintosh

1 Bedford Square, London WC1B 3RA
☎020 7637 8866 Fax 020 7436 2683

Musical producer. Productions include *Oliver!; Little Shop of Horrors; Side by Side by Sondheim; Cats; Les Misérables; Phantom of the Opera; Miss Saigon*.

Man in the Moon Theatre Ltd

392 Kings Road, Chelsea, London SW3 5UZ
☎020 7351 5701 Fax 020 7351 1873
Email manmoon@netcomuk.co.uk
Executive Director *Leigh Shine*
Literary Manager *Nick Eisen*
General Manager *John Down*

FOUNDED 1982. Fringe theatre. In 1996,

awarded the Guinness Ingenuity Award for creativity and innovation. Often tries to fit new plays into seasons such as 'Nationalism' and 'Family Values' and very keen to do rehearsed readings. Particularly keen to consider plays which challenge the relationship between performer and audience, also satires, comedies, musicals. Telephone *Nick Eisen* to discuss projects.

Manchester Library Theatre
See **Library Theatre Company**

Midland Arts Centre
See **MAC – The Centre for Birmingham**

New Vic Theatre
Etruria Road, Newcastle under Lyme, Staffordshire ST5 0JG
☎01782 717954 Fax 01782 712885
Artistic Director *Gwenda Hughes*

The New Vic is a purpose-built theatre-in-the-round. Plays to a fairly broad-based audience which tends to vary from one production to another. A high proportion are not regular theatre-goers and new writing has been one of the main ways of contacting new audiences. Synopses preferred to unsolicited scripts.

Newpalm Productions
26 Cavendish Avenue, London N3 3QN
☎020 8349 0802 Fax 020 8346 8257
Contact *Phil Compton*

Rarely produces new plays (*As Is* by William M. Hoffman, which came from Broadway to the Half Moon Theatre, was an exception to this). National tours of productions such as *Peter Pan (The Musical); Noises Off, Seven Brides for Seven Brothers* and *Rebecca*, at regional repertory theatres, are more typical examples of Newpalm's work. Unsolicited mss, both plays and musicals, are, however, welcome; scripts are preferable to synopses.

Nitro
6 Brewery Road, London N7 9NH
☎020 7609 1331 Fax 020 7609 1221
Email btc@dircon.co.uk
Artistic Director *Felix Cross*

FOUNDED 1978. Formerly Black Theatre Co-op. Plays to a mixed audience, approximately 65% female. Usually tours nationally twice a year. 'Committed in the first instance to new writing by Black British writers and work which relates to the Black culture and experi-ence throughout the Diaspora, although anything considered.' Unsolicited mss welcome.

Northcott Theatre
Stocker Road, Exeter, Devon EX4 4QB
☎01392 223999 Fax 01392 223996
Website www.ex.ac.uk/northcott
Artistic Director *Ben Crocker*

FOUNDED 1967. The Northcott is the South-west's principal subsidised repertory theatre, situated on the University of Exeter campus. Describes its audience as 'geographically diverse, with a core audience of AB1s (40–60 age range)'. Continually looking to broaden the base of its audience profile, targeting younger and/or non-mainstream theatregoers. Aims to develop, promote and produce quality new writing which reflects the life of the region and addresses the audience it serves. Generally works on a commission basis but occasionally options existing new work. Unsolicited mss welcome – current turnaround on script-reading service approximately three months and no mss can be returned unless a correct value s.a.e. is included with the original submission.

Northern Stage
Newcastle Playhouse, Barras Bridge, Newcastle upon Tyne NE1 7RH
☎0191 232 3366 Fax 0191 261 8093
Email directors@northernstage.com
Website www.northernstage.com
Artistic Director *Alan Lyddiard*

A contemporary performance company whose trademarks are a strongly visual and physical style, international influences, appeal to young people and strongly linked programmes of community work. As likely to produce devised work as conventional new writing. Before submitting unsolicited scripts, please contact *Brenda Gray*, PA to the Directors.

Norwich Puppet Theatre
St James, Whitefriars, Norwich, Norfolk NR3 1TN
☎01603 615564 Fax 01603 617578
Email norpuppet@hotmail.com
Website www.geocities.com/norwichpuppets
Artistic Director *Luis Boy*
General Manager *Ian Woods*

Plays to a young audience (aged 3–12) but developing shows for adult audiences interested in puppetry. All year round programme plus tours to schools and arts venues. Unsolicited mss welcome if relevant.

Nottingham Playhouse

Nottingham Theatre Trust, Wellington
Circus, Nottingham NG1 5AF
☎0115 947 4361 Fax 0115 947 5759

Artistic Director *Giles Croft*

Aims to make innovation popular, and present
the best of world theatre, working closely with
the communities of Nottingham and
Nottinghamshire. Unsolicited mss will be read.
It normally takes about six months, however,
and 'we have never yet produced an unsolicited script. All our plays have to achieve a
minimum of 60 per cent audiences in a 732-
seat theatre. We have no studio.'

Nottingham Playhouse Roundabout Theatre in Education

Wellington Circus, Nottingham NG1 5AF
☎0115 947 4361 Fax 0115 953 9055
Email andrewb@nottinghamplayhouse.co.uk
Website www.roundabout.org.uk

Contact *Andrew Breakwell*

FOUNDED 1973. Theatre-in-Education company
of the **Nottingham Playhouse**. Plays to a
young audience aged 5–18 years of age. Some
programmes are devised or adapted in-house,
many are commissioned. 'We are committed to
the encouragement of new writing as and when
resources permit. With other major producers in
the East Midlands we will share the resources of
the regional dramaturgy from early 2001. See
website for philosophy and play details. Please
make contact before submitting scripts.'

N.T.C. Touring Theatre Company

The Playhouse, Bondgate Without, Alnwick,
Northumberland NE66 1PQ
☎01665 602586 Fax 01665 605837
Email admin@ntc-touringtheatre.co.uk
Website www.ntc-touringtheatre.co.uk

Contact *Gillian Hambleton*
Administrator *Anna Flood*

FOUNDED 1978. Formerly Northumberland
Theatre Company. A Northern Arts revenue
funded organisation. Predominantly rural, small-
scale touring company, playing to village halls
and community centres throughout the
Northern region, the Scottish Borders and countrywide. Productions range from established classics to new work and popular comedies, but
must be appropriate to their audience. Unsolicited scripts welcome but are unlikely to be produced. All scripts are read and returned with
constructive criticism within six months. Writers
whose style is of interest may then be commis-

sioned. The company encourages new writing
and commissions when possible. Financial con-
straints restrict casting to a *maximum* of five.

Nuffield Theatre

University Road, Southampton, Hampshire
SO17 1TR
☎023 8031 5500 Fax 023 8031 5511

Artistic Director *Patrick Sandford*
Script Executive *John Burgess*

Well known as a good bet for new playwrights,
the Nuffield gets an awful lot of scripts. They
do a couple of new main stage plays every season. Previous productions: *Exchange* by Yuri
Trifonov (trans. Michael Frayn) which transferred to the Vaudeville Theatre; *The Floating
Light Bulb* Woody Allen (British première);
new plays by Claire Luckham: *Dogspot; The
Dramatic Attitudes of Miss Fanny Kemble;* and by
Claire Tomalin: *The Winter Wife*. Open-
minded about subject and style, producing
musicals as well as straight plays. Also opportunities for some small-scale fringe work. Scripts
preferred to synopses in the case of writers new
to theatre. All will, eventually, be read 'but
please be patient. We do not have a large team
of paid readers. We read everything ourselves.'

Octagon Theatre Trust Ltd

Howell Croft South, Bolton, Lancashire
BL1 1SB
☎01204 529407 Fax 01204 380110

Executive Director *John Blackmore*

FOUNDED 1967. The Octagon Theatre has pur-
sued a dynamic policy of commissioning new
plays in recent years. These have been by both
established writers such as Paul Abbott, Tom
Elliott, Henry Livings and Les Smith as well as
new and emerging writers through partnerships
with organisations such as **North West
Playwrights** and the national new writing company **Paines Plough**. Whilst there is no pre-
scriptive 'house style' at the Octagon, the theatre
is nevertheless keen to encourage the development of writers from the North West region,
telling stories that will resonate with the local
audience. Unfortunately, the theatre does not
have a resident literary manager or readers and is
therefore unable to read and respond to unsolicited scripts.

Orange Tree Theatre

1 Clarence Street, Richmond, Surrey TW9 2SA
☎020 8940 0141 Fax 020 8332 0369

Artistic Director *Sam Walters*

One of those theatre venues just out of London

which are good for new writing, both full-scale productions and rehearsed readings. Productions from September 2000: *Arms and the Man* George Bernard Shaw; *The Captain's Tiger* Athol Fugard; *Wild Wild Women* Michael Raymond and Nola York; *The Daugher-in-Law* D.H. Lawrence; *Clockwatching* Torben Betts. Unsolicited mss are read, but patience (and s.a.e.) required.

Out of Joint

20–24 Eden Grove, London N7 8EA
☎020 7609 0207 Fax 020 7609 0203
Email ojo@outofjoint.co.uk

Director *Max Stafford-Clark*
Producer *Graham Cowley*
Literary Manager *Lee White*

FOUNDED 1993. Award-winning theatre company with new writing central to its policy. Produces new plays which reflect society and its concerns, placing an emphasis on education activity to attract young audiences. Welcomes unsolicited mss. Productions include: *Blue Heart* Caryl Churchill; *Our Lady of Sligo* and *The Steward of Christendom* Sebastian Barry; *Shopping and Fucking* and *Some Explicit Polaroids* Mark Ravenhill; *Rita, Sue and Bob Too* Andrea Dunbar; *A State Affair* Robin Soans.

Oxford Stage Company

131 High Street, Oxford OX1 4DH
☎01865 723238 Fax 01865 790625
Website www.oxfordstage.co.uk

Artistic Director *Dominic Dromgoole*

A middle-scale touring company producing established and new plays. At least one new play or new adaptation a year. Due to forthcoming projects not considering unsolicited scripts at present.

Paines Plough

4th Floor, 43 Aldwych, London
WC2B 4DN
☎020 7240 4533 Fax 020 7240 4534
Email office@painesplough.com

Artistic Director *Vicky Featherstone*
Literary Associate *Lucy Morrison*

Tours new plays nationally. Works with writers to develop their skills and voices through workshops, rehearsed readings and playwriting projects. Provides a supportive environment for commissioned writers to push themselves and challenge their craft. Will consider unsolicited material from UK writers (please send s.a.e. for return of script).

Palace Theatre, Watford

Clarendon Road, Watford, Hertfordshire
WD1 1JZ
☎01923 235455 Fax 01923 819664

Artistic Director *Lawrence Till*

An important part of artistic and cultural policy is the active commissioning of new plays. Previous productions: *Diplomatic Wives* Louise Page; *Over A Barrel* Stephen Bill; *The Marriage of Figaro*; *The Barber of Seville* (adapt. Ranjit Bolt); *The Baby* Jon Canter; *Borders of Paradise* Sharman Macdonald; *Elton John's Glasses* David Farr (winner of the 1997 Writers' Guild Best Regional Play award); *The Talented Mr Ripley* Phyllis Nagy; *The Dark* Jonathan Holloway; *The Late Middle Classes* Simon Gray; *Morning Glory* Sarah Daniels; *The True-Life Legend of Mata Hari* Diane Samuels. Also supports local writers with workshops, play readings and script development.

Perth Repertory Theatre Ltd

185 High Street, Perth PH1 5UW
☎01738 472700 Fax 01738 624576
Email theatre@perth.org.uk
Website www.perth.org.uk/perth/theatre.htm

Artistic Director *Michael Winter*
General Manager *Paul Hackett*

FOUNDED 1935. Combination of one- to four-weekly repertoire of plays and musicals, incoming tours and studio productions. Unsolicited mss are read when time permits, but the timetable for return of scripts is lengthy. New plays staged by the company are usually commissioned under the SAC scheme.

Plymouth Theatre Royal

See **Theatre Royal**

Polka Theatre for Children

240 The Broadway, Wimbledon, London
SW19 1SB
☎020 8545 8320 Fax 020 8545 8365
Email info@polkatheatre.com
Website www.polkatheatre.com

Artistic Director *Vicky Ireland*
Administrator *Stephen Midlane*

FOUNDED in 1967 and moved into its Wimbledon base in 1979. Leading children's theatre committed to commissioning and producing new plays. Programmes are planned two years ahead and at least three new plays are commissioned each year. 'Because of our specialist needs and fixed budgets, all our scripts are commissioned from established writers with whom we work very closely. Writers are selected via recommendation and previous work. We do not perform unsolicited scripts. Potential new writers' work is read and discussed on a regular basis; thus we constantly add to our pool of interesting and interested writers.'

Praxis Theatre Company Ltd

24 Wykeham Road, London NW4 2SU
☎020 8203 1916 Fax 020 8203 1916
Email praxisco@globalnet.co.uk
Website www.users.globalnet.co.uk/~praxisco
Artistic Director *Sharon Kennet*

FOUNDED 1993. Performs to a mixed European audience, 'crossing the divide between text-based theatre and visual theatre'. No unsolicited mss. Previous productions and films: *Seed*; *My Brother Whom I Love*; *The Sacred Penman*.

Queen's Theatre, Hornchurch

Billet Lane, Hornchurch, Essex RM11 1QT
☎01708 456118 Fax 01708 452348
Email info@queens-theatre.co.uk
Artistic Director *Bob Carlton*

The Queen's Theatre is a 500-seat producing theatre in the London Borough of Havering and within the M25. ESTABLISHED in 1953, the theatre has been located in its present building since 1975 and produces up to nine in-house productions per year, including pantomime. The Queen's has re-established a permanent core company of actor/musicians under the artistic leadership of Bob Carlton. Aims to produce distinctive and accessible performances in an identifiable house style focused upon actor/musician shows but, in addition, embraces straight plays, classics and comedies. 'New play/musical submissions are welcome and will be read and given a report.' Each year there is a large-scale community play commissioned from a local writer culminating in a summer event beside the theatre. A new writers' group has been established, led currently by David Eldridge. Enquiries about joining should be directed to the education manager.

The Really Useful Group Ltd

22 Tower Street, London WC2H 9NS
☎020 7240 0880 Fax 020 7240 1204
Website www.reallyuseful.com

Commercial/West End theatre producers whose output has included *Jesus Christ Superstar*; *Sunset Boulevard*; *Joseph and the Amazing Technicolor Dreamcoat*; *Cats*; *Phantom of the Opera*; *Starlight Express*; *Daisy Pulls It Off*; *Lend Me a Tenor*; *Arturo Ui*; *The Beautiful Game*; *Whistle Down the Wind*; *Aspects of Love*.

Red Ladder Theatre Company

3 St Peter's Buildings, York Street, Leeds, West Yorkshire LS9 8AJ
☎0113 245 5311 Fax 0113 245 5351
Email wendy@redladder.co.uk
Artistic Director/Literary Manager *Wendy Harris*
Administrator *Janis Smyth*

FOUNDED 1968. Commissioning company touring 2–3 shows a year with a strong commitment to new work and new writers. Aimed at an audience of young people aged between 14–25 years who have little or no access to theatre. Performances held in youth clubs and similar venues where young people choose to meet. Recent productions: *After the End of the World* Mike Kenny; *Picture Me* Noël Greig. The company has scripts in development with Chris O'Connell and Andrea Earl. While unsolicited scripts are not discouraged, the company is particularly keen to enter into a dialogue with writers with regard to creating new work for young people.

Red Shift Theatre Company

TRG2 Trowbray House, 108 Weston Street, London SE1 3QB
☎020 7378 9787 Fax 020 7378 9789
Email rstc@dircon.co.uk
Website www.rstc.dircon.co.uk
Contact *Jonathan Holloway, Artistic Director*
Administrator *Jess Lammin*

FOUNDED 1982. Small-scale touring company which plays to a theatre-literate audience. Unlikely to produce an unsolicited script as most work is commissioned. Welcomes contact with writers – 'we try to see their work' – and receipt of c.v.s and treatments. Occasionally runs workshops bringing new scripts, writers and actors together. These can develop links with a reservoir of writers who may feed the company. Interested in new plays with subject matter which is accessible to a broad audience and concerns issues of importance; also new translations and adaptations. 2000–2001 productions: *Nicholas Nickleby* and *The Love Child*.

Ridiculusmus

1B6C Edenderry Industrial Estate, 326 Crumlin Road, Belfast BT14 7EE
Email Ridiculusmus@yahoo.com
Website www.ridiculusmus.com
Artistic Directors *Jon Hough, David Woods*

FOUNDED 1992. Touring company which plays to a wide range of audiences. Productions have included adaptations of *Three Men In a Boat*; *The*

Third Policeman; At Swim Two Birds and original work: *The Exhibitionists*; *Yes, Yes, Yes* and *Say Nothing*. Unsolicited scripts not welcome.

Royal Court Theatre/ English Stage Company Ltd

Sloane Square, London SW1W 8AS
☎020 7565 5050 Fax 020 7565 5002
(Literary office)
Website www.royalcourttheatre.com
Literary Manager *Graham Whybrow*

The English Stage Company was founded by George Devine in 1956 to put on new plays. John Osborne, John Arden, Arnold Wesker, Edward Bond, Caryl Churchill, Howard Barker and Michael Hastings are all writers this theatre has discovered. Christopher Hampton and David Hare have worked here in the literary department. 'The aim of the Royal Court is to develop and perform the best in new writing for the theatre, encouraging writers from all sections of society to address the problems and possibilities of our times.'

Royal Exchange Theatre Company

St Ann's Square, Manchester M2 7DH
☎0161 833 9333 Fax 0161 832 0881
Website www.royalexchange.co.uk
Literary Manager *Sarah Frankcom*

FOUNDED 1976. The Royal Exchange has developed a new writing policy which it finds is attracting a younger audience to the theatre. The company has produced new plays by Shelagh Stephenson, Brad Fraser, Simon Burke, Jim Cartwright, Peter Barnes and Alex Finlayson. Also English and foreign classics, modern classics, adaptations and new musicals. The Royal Exchange receives 500–2000 scripts a year. These are read by Sarah Frankcom and a team of experienced readers. Only a tiny percentage is suitable, but a number of plays are commissioned each year.

Royal Lyceum Theatre Company

Grindlay Street, Edinburgh EH3 9AX
☎0131 248 4800 Fax 0131 228 3955
Artistic Director *Kenny Ireland*
Administration Manager *Ruth Butterworth*
Administration Director *Sadie McKinlay*

FOUNDED 1965. Repertory theatre which plays to a mixed urban Scottish audience. Produces classic, contemporary and new plays. Would like to stage more new plays, especially Scottish. No full-time literary staff to provide reports on submitted scripts.

Royal National Theatre

South Bank, London SE1 9PX
☎020 7452 3333 Fax 020 7452 3350
Website www.nt-online.org
Literary Manager *Jack Bradley*

The majority of the National's new plays come about as a result of direct commission or from existing contacts with playwrights. There is no quota for new work, though so far more than a third of plays presented have been the work of living playwrights. Writers new to the theatre would need to be of exceptional talent to be successful with a script here, though the Royal National Theatre Studio helps a limited number of playwrights, through readings, workshops and discussions. In some cases a new play is presented for a shorter-than-usual run in the Cottesloe Theatre. Scripts considered (send s.a.e).

Royal Shakespeare Company

Dramaturgy, Barbican Centre, London EC2Y 8BQ
☎020 7382 2303 Fax 020 7382 2320
Website www.rsc.org.uk/
Artistic Director *Adrian Noble*
Dramaturgy *Simon Reade*

The RSC is a classical theatre company based in Stratford upon Avon, bringing its repertoire into London at the Barbican Theatre for six months of the year, and with a residency in Newcastle. It also tours extensively – nationally and internationally. As well as Shakespeare, English classics and foreign classics in translation, new plays counterpoint the RSC's repertory, especially those which celebrate language. 'The dramaturgy department is proactive rather than reactive and seeks out the plays and playwrights it wishes to commission. It will read all translations of classic foreign works submitted, or of contemporary works where the original writer and/or translator is known. It is unable to read unsolicited work from less established writers. It can only return scripts if an s.a.e. is enclosed with submission.'

7:84 Theatre Company Scotland

333 Woodlands Road, Glasgow G3 6NG
☎0141 334 6686 Fax 0141 334 3369
Email 7.84-theatre@btinternet.com
Artistic Director *Gordon Laird*
General Manager *Tessa Rennie*

FOUNDED 1973. One of Scotland's foremost touring theatre companies committed to producing work that addresses current social, cultural and political issues. Recent productions include commissions by Scottish playwrights such as Peter Arnott (*A Little Rain*); Stephen Greenhorn (*Dissent*); David Greig (*Caledonia Dreaming*) and the Scottish premières of Tony Kushner's *Angels in America* and Athol Fugard's *Valley Song*. 'The company is committed to a new writing policy that encourages and develops writers at every level of experience, to get new voices and strong messages on to the stage.' Although happy to read unsolicited scripts, 'it would be impossible to respond in detail to everything that we receive ... we simply do not have the resources to make this possible'. New writing development has always been central to 7:84's core activity and has included Summer Schools and the 7:84 Writers Group. The company continues to be committed to this work and its development.

Shared Experience Theatre

The Soho Laundry, 9 Dufours Place, London W1F 7SJ
☎020 7434 9248 Fax 020 7287 8763
Email admin@setheatre.co.uk
Joint Artistic Directors *Nancy Meckler, Polly Teale*

FOUNDED 1975. Varied audience depending on venue, since this is a touring company. Recent productions have included: *The Birthday Party* Harold Pinter; *Sweet Sessions* Paul Godfrey; *Anna Karenina* (adapt. Helen Edmundson); *Trilby & Svengali* (adapt. David Fielder); *Mill on the Floss* (adapt. Helen Edmundson); *The Danube* Maria Irene Fornes; *Desire Under the Elms* Eugene O'Neill; *War and Peace* (adapt. Helen Edmundson); *The Tempest* William Shakespeare; *Jane Eyre* (adapt. Polly Teale); *I Am Yours* Judith Thompson; *The House of Bernarda Alba* (trans. Rona Munro); *Mother Courage* (trans. Lee Hall); *A Doll's House* (trans. Michael Meyer). No unsolicited mss. Primarily not a new writing company but 'we are interested in innovative new scripts'.

Sherman Theatre Company

Senghennydd Road, Cardiff CF24 4YE
☎029 2064 6901 Fax 029 2064 6902
Artistic Director *Phil Clark*

FOUNDED 1973. Theatre for Young People, with main house and studio. Encourages new writing; has produced 86 new plays in the last ten years. Previous productions include plays by Frank Vickery (*Pullin the Wool*); Helen Griffin (*Flesh and Blood*); Patrick Jones (*Everything Must*

Go); Terry Deary (*Horrible Histories Crackers Christmas*); Mike Kenny (*Puff the Magic Dragon*); Brendan Murray (*Something Beginning With ...*); Roger Williams (*Pop*); Arnold Wesker (*Break, My Heart*). The company has presented four seasons of six new plays live on stage and broadcast on BBC Radio Wales, and four series of one-act lunchtime plays on stage and then filmed for HTV Wales. Priority will be given to Wales-based writers.

Show of Strength

74 Chessel Street, Bedminster, Bristol BS3 3DN
☎0117 902 0235 Fax 0117 902 0196
Email anna@showofstrength.freeserve.co.uk
Artistic Director *Sheila Hannon*

FOUNDED 1986. Plays to an informal, younger than average audience. Aims to stage at least one new play each season with a preference for work from Bristol and the South West. Will read unsolicited scripts but a lack of funding means they are unable to provide written reports. Interested in full-length stage plays; 'we are undeterred by large casts'. OUTPUT *A Busy Day* Fanny Burney; *A Man and Some Women* Githa Sowerby; *Blue Murder* Peter Nichols and *Rough Music* James Wilson (both world premières). Also, three rehearsed readings of new work each season.

Snap People's Theatre Trust

45/47 South Street, Bishop's Stortford, Hertfordshire CM23 3JG
☎01279 461607 Fax 01279 506694
Contacts *Andy Graham, David Padgett*

FOUNDED 1979. Plays to young people (5–11; 12–19), and to the thirty-something-plus age group. Classic adaptations and new writing. Writers should make contact in advance of sending material. New writing is encouraged and should involve, be written for or by young people. 'Projects should reflect the writer's own beliefs, be thought-provoking, challenging and accessible. The writer should be able to work with designers, directors and musicians in the early stages to develop the text and work alongside other disciplines.'

Soho Theatre Company

21 Dean Street, London W1D 3NE
☎020 7287 5060 Fax 020 7287 5061
Email writer@sohotheatre.com
Website www.sohotheatre.com
Artistic Director *Abigail Morris*
Literary Manager *Paul Sirett*

Dedicated to new writing, the company has an

extensive research and development programme consisting of a free script-reading service, workshops and readings. Also runs many courses for new writers. The company produces around four plays a year. Previous productions include: *Office* Shan Khan, winner of the 2000 Verity Bargate Award; *Angels and Saints* Jessica Townsend, joint winner of the 1998 Peggy Ramsay Award; *Jump Mr Malinoff Jump* Toby Whithouse, winner of the 1998 Verity Bargate Award; *Gabriel* Moira Buffini, winner of the 1996 LWT Award; *Be My Baby* Amanda Whittington; *Kindertransporte* Diane Samuels. Runs the **Verity Bargate Award**, a biennial competition (see entry under **Prizes**).

Sphinx Theatre Company
25 Short Street, London SE1 8LJ
☎020 7401 9993 Fax 020 7401 9995
Email sphinxtheatre@demon.co.uk
Artistic Director *Sue Parrish*
General Manager *Amanda Rigali*

FOUNDED 1973. Tours new plays by women nationally to small and mid-scale venues. Synopses and ideas are welcome.

The Steam Industry
Finborough Theatre, 118 Finborough Road, London SW10 9ED
☎020 7244 7439 Fax 020 7835 1853
Website www.steamindustry.itgo.com *or* www.finboroughtheatre.itgo.com
Artistic Director *Phil Willmott*
Director, Finborough Theatre *Neil McPherson*

Since June 1994, the Finborough Theatre has been a base for The Steam Industry who produce in and out of the building. Their output is diverse and prolific and includes a high percentage of new writing alongside radical adaptations of classics and musicals. The space is also available for a number of hires per year and the hire fee is sometimes negotiable to encourage innovative work. Unsolicited scripts are no longer welcome. The company has developed new work by writers such as Chris Lee, Anthony Neilson, Naomi Wallace, Conor McPherson, Tony Marchant, Diane Samuels and Mark Ravenhill.

Swan Theatre
The Moors, Worcester WR1 3EF
☎01905 726969 Fax 01905 723738
Website www.worcesterswantheatre.co.uk
Artistic Director *Jenny Stephens*

Repertory company producing a wide range of plays to a mixed audience coming largely from the City of Worcester and the county of Hereford and Worcester. A writing group meets at the theatre. Unsolicited scripts are discouraged.

Swansea Little Theatre Ltd
Dylan Thomas Theatre, Maritime Quarter, Gloucester Place, Swansea, West Glamorgan SA1 1TY
☎01792 473238
Contact *Annalie Williams (Chair, Artistic Committee)*

A wide variety of plays, from pantomime to the classics. New writing encouraged. New plays considered by the Artistic Committee.

Talawa Theatre Company Ltd
23/25 Great Sutton Street, London EC1V 0DN
☎020 7251 6644 Fax 020 7251 5969
Email hq@talawa.com
Website www.talawa.com
Administrator *Suzannah Bedford*

FOUNDED 1985. 'Aims to provide high quality productions that reflect the significant creative role that Black theatre plays within the national and international arena and also to enlarge theatre audiences from the Black community.' Previous productions include all-Black performances of *The Importance of Being Earnest* and *Antony and Cleopatra*; plus Jamaican pantomime *Arawak Gold; The Gods Are Not to Blame; The Road* Wole Soyinka; *Beef, No Chicken* Derek Walcott; *Flying West* Pearl Cleage; *Othello* William Shakespeare. Seeks to provide a platform for new work from up and coming Black British writers. Send synopsis in the first instance. Runs a black script development project. Talawa is funded by the **London Arts Board** (for three years).

Theatre Absolute
57–61 Corporation Street, Coventry CV1 1GQ
☎024 7625 7380 Fax 024 7655 0680
Email julia@theatreabsolute.demon.co.uk
Website www.theatreabsolute.demon.co.uk
Artistic Director/Writer *Chris O'Connell*
Producer *Julia Negus*

FOUNDED 1992. An independent theatre company which commissions, produces and tours new plays which are based on a strong narrative text and aimed at audiences aged 15 and upwards. Productions include: *Big Burger Chronicles; She's Electric; Car*, winner of an Edinburgh Fringe First Award 1999 and a *Time*

Out Live Award – Best New Play on the London Fringe 1999. Alongside the Belgrade Theatre, the company also runs The Writing House, a script development scheme.

Theatre of Comedy Company
210 Shaftesbury Avenue, London WC2H 8DP
☎020 7379 3345 Fax 020 7836 8181
Email info@toc.dltentertainment.co.uk
Chief Executive *Richard Porter*
Creative Director *Keith Murray*

FOUNDED 1983 to produce new work as well as classics and revivals. Interested in strong comedy in the widest sense – Chekhov comes under the definition as does farce. Also has a light entertainment division, developing new scripts for television, namely situation comedy and series.

Theatre Royal, Plymouth
Royal Parade, Plymouth, Devon PL1 2TR
☎01752 668282 Fax 01752 225892
Email d.prescott@theatreroyal.demon.co.uk
Artistic Director *Simon Stokes*
Artistic Associate *David Prescott*

Stages small-, middle- and large-scale drama including musicals and music theatre. Commissions and produces new plays. Unsolicited scripts are read and responded to.

Theatre Royal Stratford East
Gerry Raffles Square, London E15 1BN
☎020 8534 7374 Fax 020 8534 8381
Email jperies@stratfordeast.com
Website www.stratfordeast.com
New Writing Manager *James Peries*

Lively East London theatre, catering for a very mixed audience, both local and London-wide. Produces plays, musicals, youth theatre and local community plays/events, all of which is new work. Special interest in Asian and Black British work. New initiatives include developing contemporary British musicals. Unsolicited scripts which are fully completed and have never been produced are welcome. After refurbishment, the theatre re-opens in the autumn of 2001.

Theatre Royal Windsor
Windsor, Berkshire SL4 1PS
☎01753 863444 Fax 01753 831673
Email info@theatreroyalwindsor.co.uk
Website www.kenwright.com
Executive Producer *Bill Kenwright*
Executive Director *Mark Piper*

Plays to a middle-class, West End-type audi-

ence. Produces thirteen plays a year and 'would be disappointed to do fewer than two new plays in a year; always hope to do half a dozen'. Modern classics, thrillers, comedy and farce. Only interested in scripts along these lines.

Theatre Workshop Edinburgh
34 Hamilton Place, Edinburgh EH3 5AX
☎0131 225 7942 Fax 0131 220 0112
Artistic Director *Robert Rae*

First ever professional producing theatre to fully integrate disabled actors into all its productions. Plays to a young, broad-based audience with many pieces targeted towards particular groups or communities. OUTPUT has included *D.A.R.E.* Particularly interested in issues-based work for children, youth and minority groups. Frequently engages writers for collaborative work and devised projects. Commissions a significant amount of new writing for a wide range of contexts, from large-scale community plays to small-scale professional productions. Favours writers based in Scotland, producing material relevant to a contemporary Scottish audience.

Tiebreak Touring Theatre
Heartsease High School, Marryat Road, Norwich, Norfolk NR7 9DF
☎01603 435209 Fax 01603 435184
Email tie.break@virgin.net
Website freespace.virgin.net/tie.break
Artistic Director *David Farmer*

FOUNDED 1981. Specialises in high-quality theatre for children and young people, touring schools, youth centres, museums and festivals. Productions: *Suitcase Full of Stories; Flint People; Intake/Outake; Fast Eddy; Breaking the Rules; George Speaks; Frog and Toad; Love Bites; Singing in the Rainforest; Boadicea – The Movie; Dinosaurs on Ice; The Invisible Boy; My Friend Willy; The Ugly Duckling; Almost Human.* New writing encouraged. Interested in low-budget, small-cast material only. School, educational and socially relevant material of special interest. 'Scripts welcome but please ring first to discuss any potential submission.'

The Torch Theatre
St Peter's Road, Milford Haven, Pembrokeshire SA73 2BU
☎01646 694192 Fax 01646 698919
Email torchtheatre@cwcom.net
Website www.torchtheatre.org
Artistic Director *Peter Doran*

FOUNDED 1976. Plays to a mixed audience hard to attract to new work on the whole.

Committed to new work but financing has become somewhat prohibitive. Small-cast pieces with broad appeal welcome. Previous productions: *Frankie and Tommy; School for Wives; Tess of the d'Urbervilles*. The repertoire runs from Ayckbourn to Friel. Scripts sometimes welcome.

Traverse Theatre

Cambridge Street, Edinburgh EH1 2ED
☎0131 228 3223 Fax 0131 229 8443
Email john@traverse.co.uk
Website www.traverse.co.uk
Artistic Director *Philip Howard*
Literary Director *John Tiffany*
International Literary Associate *Katherine Mendelsohn*
Literary Development Office *Hannah Rye*
Literary Assistant *Pauline Diamond*

The Traverse is Scotland's new writing theatre, with a particular commitment to producing new Scottish plays. However, it also has a strong international programme of work in translation and visiting companies. Previous productions: *King of the Fields* Stuart Paterson; *The Speculator* David Greig; *The Juju Girl* Aileen Ritchie; *Perfect Days* Liz Lochhead. Unsolicited scripts accepted only after an initial phone call or letter to *Pauline Diamond*, Literary Assistant.

Trestle Theatre Company

Birch Centre, Hill End Lane, St Albans, Hertfordshire AL4 0RA
☎01727 850950 Fax 01727 855558
Website www.trestle.org.uk (under construction)
Artistic Director *Toby Wilsher*

FOUNDED 1981. Physical, mask touring theatre company. Usually devised work but will be looking to work with writers to create new writing for physical/visual theatre. No unsolicited scripts.

Tricycle Theatre

269 Kilburn High Road, London NW6 7JR
☎020 7372 6611 Fax 020 7328 0795
Website www.tricycle.co.uk
Artistic Director *Nicolas Kent*

FOUNDED 1980. Plays to a very mixed audience, in terms of both culture and class. Previous productions: *Pecong* Steve Carter; *A Love Song for Ulster* Bill Morrison; *Three Hotels* Jon Robin Baitz; *Nuremberg* adapt. from transcripts of the trials by Richard Norton-Taylor; *Srebrenica* adapt. Nicolas Kent; *The Stephen Lawrence Enquiry – The Colour of Justice* adapt. from the enquiry transcripts by Richard

Norton-Taylor; *Wine in the Wilderness* Alice Childress; *Water* Winsome Pinnock. New writing welcome from women and ethnic minorities (particularly Black, Asian and Irish). Looks for a strong narrative drive with popular appeal, not 'studio' plays. Can only return scripts if postage coupons or s.a.e. are enclosed with original submission.

Tron Theatre Company

63 Trongate, Glasgow G1 5HB
☎0141 552 3748 Fax 0141 552 6657
Email neil@tron.co.uk
Website www.tron.co.uk
Administrative Director *Neil Murray*

FOUNDED 1981. Plays to a broad cross-section of Glasgow and beyond, including international tours. Recent productions: *Our Bad Magnet* Douglas Maxwell; *Further Than the Furthest Thing* Zinnie Harris (co-production with the **Royal National Theatre**). Interested in ambitious plays by UK and international writers. No unsolicited mss.

Unicorn Theatre for Children

St Mark's Studios, Chillingworth Road, London N7 8QJ
☎020 7700 0702 Fax 020 7700 3870
Email <name>@unicorntheatre.com
Website www.unicorntheatre.com
Artistic Director *Tony Graham*

FOUNDED 1947 as a touring company, and was resident at the Arts Theatre from 1967 until April 1999. Produces seasons at The Pleasance theatre in north London, a summer show at Regent Park's Open Air Theatre, and tours both nationally and internationally. Plays to children, aged 4–12, their teachers and families. New work in 2000: *Tom's Garden* adapt. by David Wood; *Alice: an Adventure in Wonderland* by Charles Way; *Stardust* by Pomme Clayton; *Firebird* by Susanna Steele. Commissions for 2001 with Michael Rosen, Charles Way and Shahrukh Husein. Plans to build Unicorn Children's Centre with two auditoria in central London in 2003.

Upstairs at the Gatehouse

See **Ovation Productions** under **Film, TV and Video Production Companies**

Charles Vance Productions

Hampden House, 2 Weymouth Street, London W1N 3FD
☎020 7636 4343 Fax 020 7636 2323
Email cvtheatre@aol.com

Contact *Charles Vance*

In the market for medium-scale touring productions and summer-season plays. Hardly any new work and no commissions but writing of promise stands a good chance of being passed on to someone who might be interested in it. Occasional try-outs for new work in the Sidmouth repertory theatre. Send s.a.e. for return of mss.

Warehouse Theatre

62 Dingwall Road, Croydon CR0 2NF
☎020 8681 1257 Fax 020 8688 6699
Email warehous@dircon.co.uk
Website www.warehousetheatre.co.uk
Artistic Director *Ted Craig*

South London's new writing theatre (adjacent to East Croydon railway station) seats 100–120 and produces up to six new plays a year. Also co-produces with, and hosts, selected touring companies who share the theatre's commitment to new work. Continually building upon a tradition of discovering and nurturing new writers, with activities including a monthly writers' workshop and the annual **International Playwriting Festival**. Also hosts youth theatre workshops and Saturday morning children's theatre. Previous productions: *Iona Rain* by Peter Moffat and *Fat Janet is Dead* by Simon Smith (both past winners of the International Playwriting Festival); *The Blue Garden* Peter Moffat; *Coming Up* James Martin Charlton and M. G. 'Monk' Lewis; *The Castle Spectre* edited by Phil Willmott; *Dick Barton Special Agent* and *Dick Barton and the Curse of the Pharaoh's Tomb* Phil Willmott. Unsolicited scripts welcome but it is more advisable to submit plays through the theatre's International Playwriting Festival.

Watford Palace Theatre

See **Palace Theatre**

West Yorkshire Playhouse

Playhouse Square, Leeds, West Yorkshire
LS2 7UP
☎0113 213 7800 Fax 0113 213 7250
Website www.wyp.co.uk

Committed to programming new writing as part of its overall policy. Before sending an unsolicited script please phone or write. The Playhouse does readings and workshops on new plays with writers from all over Britain and also has strong links with local writers and Yorkshire Playwrights. Premières include: *A Passionate Woman* Kay Mellor; *Fathers Day* Maureen Lawrence; *The Beatification of Area Boy* Wole Soyinka; *The Winter Guest* Sharman Macdonald; *You'll Have Had Your Hole* Irvine Welsh.

Whirligig Theatre

14 Belvedere Drive, Wimbledon, London
SW19 7BY
☎020 8947 1732 Fax 020 8879 7648
Email whirligig-theatre@virgin.net
Contact *David Wood*

One play a year in major theatre venues, usually a musical for primary school audiences and weekend family groups. Interested in scripts which exploit the theatrical nature of children's tastes. Previous productions: *The See-Saw Tree; The Selfish Shellfish; The Gingerbread Man; The Old Man of Lochnagar; The Ideal Gnome Expedition; Save the Human; Dreams of Anne Frank; Babe, the Sheep-Pig.*

Michael White Productions Ltd

See **MW Entertainments Ltd** under **Film, TV and Video Production Companies**

White Bear Theatre Club

138 Kennington Park Road, London SE11 4DJ
Administration: 3 Dante Road, Kennington, London SE11 4RB
☎ 020 7793 9193 Fax 020 7793 9193
Contact *Michael Kingsbury*
Administrator *Julia Parr*

FOUNDED 1988. OUTPUT primarily new work for an audience aged 20–35. Unsolicited scripts welcome, particularly new work with a keen eye on contemporary issues, though not agit-prop. *Absolution* by Robert Sherwood was nominated by the Writers' Guild for 'Best Fringe Play' and *Spin* by the same author was the *Time Out* Critics' Choice in 2000. The Writers' Guild, sponsored by the Mackintosh Foundation, is leading writer workshops and readings throughout the year.

Windsor Theatre Royal

See **Theatre Royal Windsor**

The Young Vic

66 The Cut, London SE1 8LZ
☎020 7633 0133 Fax 020 7928 1585
Email info@youngvic.org
Website www.youngvic.org
Artistic Director *David Lan*

FOUNDED 1970. The Young Vic is a theatre for everyone but, above all, for younger artists and audiences. Produces revivals of classics – old and new – as well as annual events that embrace both young people and adults. The main house is one of London's most exciting spaces and seats up to 450. A smaller, flexible space, the Young Vic Studio, seats 80 and is used for research, experiment and performance. Each main house production is accompanied by an extensive programme of Teaching Participation and Research aimed at local schools and colleges. Under the Funded Ticket Scheme 10% of the audience see productions for nothing or very little.

Freelance Rates –
Subsidised Repertory Theatres
(excluding Scotland)

The following minimum rates were negotiated by the **Writers' Guild** and Theatrical Management Association and are set out under the TMA/Writers Agreement.

Theatres are graded by a 'middle range salary level' (MRSL), worked out by dividing the 'total basic salaries' paid by the total number of 'actor weeks' in the year.

	MRSL 1	*MRSL 2*	*MRSL 3*
Commissioned Play			
Commission payment	£3,364	£2,752	£2,141
Delivery payment	£1,530	£1,223	£1,223
Acceptance payment	£1,530	£1,223	£1,223
Non-Commissioned Play			
Delivery payment	£4,895	£3,975	£3,363
Acceptance payment	£1,530	£1,223	£1,223
Rehearsal Attendance	£45.14	£39.60	£36.50

Options

UK (excluding West End)	£1,908
West End/USA	£3,182
Rest of the World	
(English speaking productions)	£2,545

Festivals

Aberystwyth Rich Text Literature Festival

Aberystwyth Arts Centre, Penglais,
Aberystwyth SY23 3DE
☎01970 622889/622883
Email lla@aber.ac.uk

FOUNDED 2000. Annual weekend festival held
in November. Previous guest writers have
included Robin Young, John Stoddart and
Menna Elfyn.

Aldeburgh Poetry Festival

Reading Room Yard, The Street, Brockdish,
Diss, Norfolk IP21 4JZ
☎01379 668345 Fax 01379 668844
Email aldeburghpoetry.trust@virgin.net
Website freespace.virgin.net/aldeburghpoetry.
trust

Festival Director *Naomi Jaffa*

Now in its fourteenth year, an annual international festival of contemporary poetry held on
the first weekend of November in Aldeburgh,
attracting large audiences. Regular features
include a four-week residency leading up to
the festival, poetry readings, children's event,
workshops, public masterclass, lecture, performance spot and the festival prize for the year's
best first collection (see entry under **Prizes**).

Arundel Festival

The Arundel Festival Society Ltd, The Mary
Gate, Arundel, West Sussex BN18 9AT
☎01903 883690/Textphone: 01903 889900
Fax 01903 884243
Email arundel.festival@argonet.co.uk
Website www.argonet.co.uk/arundel.festival

Festival Administrator *Josephine Paxton*

Annual ten-day summer festival (24th August
to 2nd September in 2001). Events include
small-scale theatre, open-air theatre in Arundel
Castle, concerts with internationally known
artists, jazz, visual arts and active fringe.

Aspects Literature Festival

North Down Borough Council, Tower
House, 34 Quay Street, Bangor BT20 5ED
☎028 9127 8032 Fax 028 9146 7744

Festival Director *Kenneth Irvine*

Administrator *Paula Clamp*

FOUNDED 1992. 'Ireland's Premier Literary
Festival' is held at the end of September
(26th–30th in 2001) and celebrates the richness
and diversity of living Irish writers with occasional special features on past generations. It
draws upon all disciplines – fiction (of all
types), poetry, theatre, non-fiction, cinema,
song-writing, etc. It also includes a day of writing for young readers and sends writers to visit
local schools during the festival. Highlights of
recent festivals include appearances by Bernard
MacLaverty, Marion Keyes, Alice Taylor,
Frank Delaney, Seamus Heaney, Brian
Keenan, Fergal Keane.

Bath Fringe Festival

The Bell, 103 Walcot Street, Bath BA1 5BW
☎01225 480079 Fax 01225 480079

Chair *John Wood*

FOUNDED 1981. Complementing the international music festival, the Fringe presents theatre, poetry, jazz, blues, comedy, cabaret, street
performance and more in venues, parks and
streets of Bath during late May and early June.

Bath Literature Festival

5 Broad Street, Bath BA1 5LJ
☎01225 462231 Fax 01225 445551

Festival Director *Nicola Bennett*

FOUNDED 1995. Annual festival (2nd to 10th
March in 2002). Wide range of debates, per-
formances, storytelling, author discussions and
workshops. Previous guests: Andrew Motion,
Jonathan Miller, Tony Parsons, Beryl
Bainbridge, Clive James and Sebastian Faulks.

Belfast Festival at Queen's

Festival House, 25 College Gardens, Belfast
BT9 6BS
☎028 9066 7687 Fax 028 9066 3733
Email festival@qub.ac.uk
Website www.belfastfestival.com

Director *Stella Hall*

FOUNDED 1964. Annual three-week festival held
in the autumn (26th October to 11th November
in 2001). Organised by Queen's University in
association with the **Arts Council of Northern**

Ireland, the festival covers a wide variety of events, including literature. Programme available in September.

Between the Lines – Belfast Literary Festival

Crescent Arts Centre, 2–4 University Road, Belfast BT7 1NH
☎028 9024 2338 Fax 028 9024 6748
Email info@crescentarts.org
Website www.crescentarts.org

Festival Coordinator *Jo Baker*

FOUNDED 1998. Annual 7–10-day international event held in March. Features readings, workshops, open platforms, quizzes and performance. All genres covered: playwriting, prose, poetry, screenwriting, etc. and special events for children. Previous guests include David Lodge, Lemn Sissay, Sheila O'Flanagan, Matthew Sweeney, Medbh McGuckian, Conor O'Callaghan, Merlin Holland, Ciaran Carson. Telephone to join free mailing list.

Beyond the Border International Storytelling Festival

St Donats Arts Centre, St Donats Castle, Vale of Glamorgan CF61 1WF
☎01446 799100 Fax 01446 799101
Email info@beyondtheborder.com
Website www.beyondtheborder.com

Festival Directors *David Ambrose, Ben Haggarty*

FOUNDED 1993. Annual event held over the first full weekend in July when storytellers from around the world gather in the grounds of a medieval cliff-top castle. Features formal and informal story sessions, ballad singing, story-walks, folk and world music, dance and a full programme of events for children.

Book Now!

Langholm Lodge, 146 Petersham Road, Richmond, Surrey TW10 6UX
☎020 8831 6138 Fax 020 8894 7568
Email n.cutting@richmond.gov.uk
Website www.richmond.gov.uk/leisure

Director *Nigel Cutting*

FOUNDED 1992. Annual festival which runs throughout the month of November, administered by the Arts Section of Richmond Council. Principal focus is on poetry and serious fiction, but events also cover biography, writing for theatre, children's writing. Programme includes readings, discussions, workshops, debates, exhibitions, schools events. Writers to appear at past festivals include A.S. Byatt, Penelope Lively, Benjamin Zephaniah, Roger McGough, Rose Tremain, John Mortimer, P.D. James and P.J. O'Rourke.

Bradford Festival

The Wool Exchange, Hustlergate, Bradford, West Yorkshire BD1 1RE
☎01274 309199 Fax 01274 724213
Email info@bradfordfestival.yorks.com
Website www.bradfordfestival.yorks.com

Directors *Mark Fielding, Allan Brack*

FOUNDED 1987. 22nd June to 7th July in 2001. Includes the Literature Festival coordinated by Bradford Libraries' Reader to Reader Project; contact *Tom Palmer* (☎01274 754096; e-mail tom.palmer@bradford.gov.uk).

Brighton Festival

Festival Office, 12a Pavilion Buildings, Castle Square, Brighton, East Sussex BN1 1EE
☎01273 700747 Fax 01273 707505
Email info@brighton-festival.org.uk
Website www.brighton-festival.org.uk

Contact *General Manager*

FOUNDED 1967. For 24 days every May, Brighton hosts England's largest mixed arts festival. Music, dance, theatre, film, opera, literature, comedy and exhibitions. Literary enquiries will be passed to the literature officer. Deadline October for following May.

Bristol Poetry Festival

The Poetry Can, Unit 11, 20–22 Hepburn Road, Bristol BS2 8UD
☎0117 942 6976 Fax 0117 944 1478
Email festival@poetrycan.demon.co.uk
Website www.poetrycan.demon.co.uk

Festival Director *Hester Cockcroft*

FOUNDED 1996. Annual festival taking place across the city every October. A celebration of the best in contemporary poetry, from readings and performances to cabaret and multimedia. Local, national and international poetry is showcased and explored in all its manifestations, with events for everyone including performances and workshops, competitions and commissions, public poetry interventions, community work and cross art form and digital projects. Telephone for further details.

Broadstairs Dickens Festival

10 Eastern Esplanade, Broadstairs, Kent CT10 1DR
☎01843 865265
Website www.broadstairs.gov.uk/ DickensFestivel.html

Organiser *Sylvia Hawkes*

FOUNDED 1937 to commemorate the 100th anniversary of Charles Dickens' first visit to Broadstairs in 1837, which he continued to visit until 1859. The Festival lasts for nine days in June and events include an opening gala concert, a parade, a performance of a Dickens play (*The Old Curiosity Shop* in 2001), duels, melodramas, Dickens readings, a Victorian cricket match, Victorian sea bathing, talks, music hall, three-day Victorian country fair. Costumed Dickensian ladies in crinolines with top-hatted escorts promenade during the week.

Canterbury Festival
Christ Church Gate, The Precincts, Canterbury, Kent CT1 2EE
☎01227 452853 Fax 01227 781830
Email info@canterburyfestival.co.uk
Festival Director *Mark Deller*

FOUNDED 1984. Annual two-week festival held in October (12th to 26th in 2002). A mixed programme of events including talks by visiting authors, readings and storytelling, walks, concerts in the cathedral, jazz, masterclasses, drama, visual arts, opera, film, cabaret and dance.

The Cheltenham Festival of Literature
Town Hall, Imperial Square, Cheltenham, Gloucestershire GL50 1QA
☎01242 263494 Fax 01242 256457
Email sarahsm@cheltenham.gov.uk
Website www.cheltenhamfestivals.co.uk
Festival Director *Sarah Smyth*

FOUNDED 1949. Annual festival held in October. The first purely literary festival of its kind, this festival has over the past decade developed from an essentially local event into the largest and most popular in Europe. A wide range of events including talks and lectures, poetry readings, novelists in conversation, exhibitions, discussions and a large bookshop.

Chester Literature Festival
8 Abbey Square, Chester CH1 2HU
☎01244 319985 Fax 01244 341200
Chairman *John Elsley*

FOUNDED 1989. Annual festival always held in early October (5th to 20th in 2002). Events include international and nationally known writers, as well as events by local literary groups. There is a Literary Lunch, events for children, workshops, competitions, etc. Free mailing list.

City Voice – a festival for readers and writers
Leeds Word Arena, Central Library, Calverley Street, Leeds, West Yorkshire LS1 3TB
☎0113 224 3887 Fax 0113 247 8287
Email sean.burn@leeds.gov.uk
Website www.leeds.gov.uk/wordarena
Festival Director *Sean Burn*

FOUNDED in 1997 by the Leeds **Word Arena** and Leeds Library & Information Services, City Voice focuses on new writing and reading and is held at the beginning of June. Strongly, but not exclusively, features commissioned new writing by Leeds-based writers. Previous events have included a commissioned sculpture based on readings, workshops for writing tutors and open spots in libraries. Visiting authors to-date include Jean Binta Breeze, Patricia Duncker and Courttia Newland. Call to join free mailing list.

Dartington Literary Festival
See **Ways With Words**

Dorchester Festival
Dorchester Arts Centre, School Lane, The Grove, Dorchester, Dorset DT1 1XR
☎01305 266926 Fax 01305 266926
Contact *Artistic Director*

FOUNDED 1996. A biennial four-day festival over early May Bank Holiday weekend (next to be held in 2002) which includes performing, media and visual arts, with associated educational and community projects in the three weeks around the Festival. Includes a wide range of events, in many venues, for all age groups, including some literature and poetry.

The Daphne du Maurier Festival of Arts & Literature
Literary Centre, 5 South Street, Fowey, Cornwall PL23 1AR
☎01726 77477

Annual festival, held over ten days in May. Guests at the 2001 Festival included Angela Lambert, Rabbi Lionel Blue, John Julius Norwich, Barbara Erskine, Willy Russell and Nigel Planer.

Dublin Writers' Festival
Dublin Corporation Arts Office, 20 Parnell Square, Dublin 1, Republic of Ireland
☎00 353 1 872 2816
Fax 00 44 870 137 8797
Email info@dublinwritersfestival.com
Website www.dublinwritersfestival.com

Programme Director *Pat Boran*

Annual festival held in mid-June, including Bloomsday. Features readings, public interviews and discussions, along with a poetry slam and beginners' workshops. Major Irish and international poets and writers.

Dumfries and Galloway Arts Festival

Gracefield Arts Centre, 28 Edinburgh Road, Dumfries DG1 1JQ
☎01387 260447 Fax 01387 260447
Email dgartsfestival@ukgateway.net

Festival Organiser *Rory MacKail*

FOUNDED 1980. Annual week-long festival held at the end of May with a variety of events including classical and folk music, theatre, dance, literary events and exhibitions.

Durham Literary Festival

Durham City Arts, Byland Lodge, Hawthorn Terrace, Durham City DH1 4TD
☎0191 301 8245 Fax 0191 301 8821
Website www.durhamcityarts.demon.co.uk

Festival Coordinator *Alison Lister*

FOUNDED 1989. Annual 2–3-week festival held in June at various locations in the city. Workshops, plus performances, cabaret, and other events.

Edinburgh International Book Festival

Scottish Book Centre, 137 Dundee Street, Edinburgh EH11 1BG
☎0131 228 5444 Fax 0131 228 4333
Email admin@edbookfest.co.uk
Website www.edbookfest.co.uk

Director *Catherine Lockerbie*

FOUNDED 1983. Europe's largest and liveliest public book event, now taking place on an annual basis. Held during the first fortnight of the Edinburgh International Festival, it presents an extensive programme for both adults and children including discussions, readings, lectures, demonstrations and workshops.

Exeter Festival

Festival Office, Civic Centre, Exeter, Devon EX1 1JN
☎01392 265200 Fax 01392 265366
Website www.exeter.gov.uk/festival

Festival Organiser *Lesley Maynard*

FOUNDED 1980. Annual two-week summer festival with a variety of events including concerts, theatre, dance and exhibitions.

Fife Festival of Authors

Fife Council Libraries – Central Area, Libraries HQ, East Fergus Place, Kirkcaldy, Fife KY1 1XT
☎01592 412930
Email david.spalding@fife.gov.uk

Contact *David Spalding*

FOUNDED 1996. Annual festival running in March/April for adults and children. Aims to bring the best of modern writing to the public as well as stimulate and foster creative writing within the local communities. Author readings, poetry events, writing workshops, literary competitions and dramatic presentations feature in the programme. The 2000 Festival, called 'Killing Time', was devoted to crime fiction and included Ian Rankin, Val McDermid, Christopher Brookmyre and eight other popular crime fiction writers.

Grayshott and Hindhead Literary Festival

19 Kay Crescent, Hadley, Hampshire GU35 8AH
☎01428 712892

Festival Organiser *Joe Smith*

FOUNDED 1995. Annual festival which runs over a weekend in mid-September (15th/16th in 2001). The programme features a mix of workshops, lectures and presentations covering classic and contemporary literature and poetry, comedy, creative and script writing. Previous guests include: Deborah Moggach, Roger McGough, U.A. Fanthorpe, Michael Nicholson, Simon Brett.

Greenwich & Docklands Festivals

6 College Approach, London SE10 9HY
☎020 8305 1818 Fax 020 8305 1188
Email info@festival.org
Website www.festival.org

Director *Bradley Hemmings*

Greenwich & Docklands Festivals (GDF) is an arts development and festival production organisation working across east London in the boroughs of Greenwich, Tower Hamlets and Newham. GDF covers the International Festival, London's largest multi-arts festival in July which, in 2000, attracted 55,000 people; First Night, a celebration of New Year's Eve through the arts; and various training and education projects, including work with young people, a disability arts initiative and a refugee video project, which takes place during the year.

Guildford Book Festival

c/o Arts Office, University of Surrey,
Guildford, Surrey GU2 5XH
☎01483 879167 Fax 01483 300803
Website www.guildford.org.uk

Book Festival Director *Glenis Pycraft*

FOUNDED 1990. Held annually, during
October/November. Two-week festival
which includes workshops, poetry performances, children's events, competitions, literary lunches and teas. The festival's appeal lies in
its diversity and its aim is to involve, instruct
and entertain all who care about literature and
to encourage in children a love of reading. In
2000, guest authors included John Mortimer,
Prof. Susan Greenfield, Miranda Seymour,
Robert Goddard, Michael Dobbs, Kathy Lette,
Ned Sherrin, Janet Evanovich, Martin Jarvis,
John Hegley and John Suchet.

Hallam Literature Festival and Book Fair

School of Cultural Studies, Sheffield Hallam
University, 32 Colegiate Crescent Campus,
Sheffield S10 2BP
☎0114 225 2228 Fax 0114 225 4403

Festival Coordinator *E.A. Markham*

FOUNDED 1997. The second festival, held in
1999, featured critics and literary journalists
reflecting the range of the university's Creative
Writing programme, book launches, stage
readings of new plays, poetry readings, discussions on the short story and televised debates
between writers. The next festival is to be held
at Easter, 2002.

Haringey Literature Festival

Haringey Arts Council, The Chocolate
Factory, Clarendon Road, London N22 6XJ
☎020 8365 7500 Fax 020 8365 8686
Email captainino.hac@teleregion.co.uk

Festival Organiser *Dana Captainino*

FOUNDED 1995. Annual festival which runs
from March to October. The programme is a
mixture of poetry and literature in the form of
readings, discussions, workshops and masterclasses. Writers who have appeared at past festivals include: Diran Adebayo, Peter Lovesey,
Michael Donaghy, Anna Pavord, Louis de
Bernières, Nick Hornby, Blake Morrison,
Bernice Rubens, James Kelman, Jean Binta
Breeze, Beryl Bainbridge and Deborah
Moggach.

Harrogate International Festival

1 Victoria Avenue, Harrogate, North
Yorkshire HG1 1EQ
☎01423 562303 Fax 01423 521264
Email info@harrogate-festival.org.uk
Website www.harrogate-festival.org.uk

Festival Director *William Culver-Dodds*
Festival Manager *Fiona Goh*

FOUNDED 1966. Annual two-week festival at
the end of July and beginning of August.
Events include international symphony orches-
tras, chamber concerts, ballet, celebrity recitals,
contemporary dance, opera, drama, jazz, comedy plus an international street theatre festival.

Hastings International Poetry Festival

'The Snoring Cat, 136 Harold Road,
Hastings, East Sussex TN35 5NN

Contact *Josephine Austin*

FOUNDED 1968. Annual weekend poetry festival held in November in the Marina Pavilion
in St Leonards-on-Sea. Runs the Hastings
National Poetry Competition; entry forms
available from the address above.

The Hay Festival

See **The Sunday Times Hay Festival**

Hebden Bridge Arts Festival

Tourist Information Centre, West End,
Hebden Bridge, West Yorkshire HX7 9EX
☎01422 842684 Fax 01422 846837
Email hbartsfestival@hotmail.com
Website www.hebdenbridge.co.uk/festival

Contact *Enid Stephenson*

FOUNDED 1994. Annual arts festival with
increasingly strong adult and children's litera-
ture events. Previous guest writers include
Roger McGough, Benjamin Zephaniah, Carol
Ann Duffy, Juliet Barker, Jacqueline Wilson,
Anthony Browne, Ian McMillan.

Hull Literature Festival

See **The Humber Mouth**

Humber Mouth – Hull Literature Festival

City Arts Unit, Central Library, Albion Street,
Kingston upon Hull HU1 3TF
☎01482 616875/6 Fax 01482 616827
Email humber.mouth@hullcc.gov.uk
Website www.humbermouth.org.uk

Contact *City Arts Unit*

FOUNDED 1992. Annual festival running in

November. Features an array of readings, performances and workshops by writers and artists from around the world and from the city.

Ilkley Literature Festival

The Manor House, Ilkley, West Yorkshire LS29 9DT
☎01943 601210   Fax 01943 817079
Email admin@ilkelyliteraturefestival.org.uk

Director *Dominic Gregory*

FOUNDED 1973. Major literature festival in the north with events running throughout the year. Large-scale festival in autumn each year. Telephone or e-mail to join free mailing list.

The International Festival of Mountaineering Literature

Bretton Hall Campus, West Bretton, Wakefield, West Yorkshire WF4 4LG
☎01924 830261   Fax 01924 832040
Email tgifford@bretton.ac.uk
Website www.terrygifford.co.uk

Director *Terry Gifford*

FOUNDED 1987. Annual one-day festival held at the end of November celebrating recent books, commissioning new writing, overviews of national literatures, debates of issues, discussion with Chair of Judges of the adjudication of the annual **Boardman Tasker Award** for the best mountaineering book of the year. Announces the winner of the festival writing competition run in conjunction with *High* magazine. Write to join free mailing list.

International Playwriting Festival

Warehouse Theatre, Dingwall Road, Croydon CR0 2NF
☎020 8681 1257   Fax 020 8688 6699
Email warehous@dircon.co.uk
Website www.warehousetheatre.co.uk

Acting Festival Administrator *Carolyn Braby*

FOUNDED 1985. Annual competition for full-length unperformed plays, judged by a panel of theatre professionals. Finalists given rehearsed readings during the festival week in November. Entries welcome from all parts of the world. Scripts plus two s.a.e.s (one script-sized) should reach the theatre by the end of June, accompanied by an entry form (available from the theatre). Previous winners produced at the theatre include: Kevin Hood *Beached*; Ellen Fox *Conversations with George Sandburgh After a Solo Flight Across the Atlantic*; Guy Jenkin *Fighting for the Dunghill*; James Martin Charlton *Fat Souls*; Peter Moffat *Iona Rain*; Dino Mahoney *YoYo*;

Simon Smith *Fat Janet is Dead*; Dominic McHale *The Resurrectionists*; Philip Edwards *51 Peg*; Roumen Shomov *The Dove*. 'Shares plays with our partner festival in Italy, the Premio Candoni Arta Terme.

Isle of Man Literature Festival

Isle of Man Arts Council, 10 Villa Marina Arcade, Douglas, Isle of Man IM1 2HN
☎01624 611316   Fax 01624 615423
Email maddrell@artscounciliom.freeserve.co.uk

Contact *Arts Development Manager*

FOUNDED 1997. Annual festival of literature, poetry and music. The 2001 Festival takes place from 11th to 14th October when the guests will include Jenny Joseph, Liz Lochhead, Sheridan Morley and Barb Junger.

Kent Literature Festival

The Metropole Arts Centre, The Leas, Folkestone, Kent CT20 2LS
☎01303 255070

Festival Director *Ann Fearey*

FOUNDED 1980. Annual week-long festival held at the end of September which aims to bring the best in modern writing to a large audience. Visiting authors and dramatic presentations are a regular feature along with readings, workshops and talks. Also runs the **Kent Short Story Competition**.

King's Lynn, The Fiction Festival

19 Tuesday Market Place, King's Lynn, Norfolk PE30 1JW
☎01553 691661 (office hours) or 761919
Fax 01553 691779

Contact *Anthony Ellis*

FOUNDED 1989. Annual weekend festival held in March. Over the weekend there are readings and discussions, attended by guest writers of which there are usually eight. Guests at the 2001 festival included Beryl Bainbridge, William Riviere, Ahdat Soueif, Liz Jensen, Matt Thorne, Geoff Dyer, Candida Clark.

King's Lynn, The Poetry Festival

19 Tuesday Market Place, King's Lynn, Norfolk PE30 1JW
☎01553 691661 (office hours) or 761919
Fax 01553 691779

Contact *Anthony Ellis*

FOUNDED 1985. Annual weekend festival held at the end of September (28th to 30th in 2001), with guest poets (usually eight). Previous guests have included Carol Ann Duffy, Paul Durcan,

Gavin Ewart, Peter Porter, Stephen Spender. Events include readings and discussion panels and the presentation of the King's Lynn Award; current Laureate is Pauline Stainer.

Lancaster LitFest
Sun Street Studios, 23–29 Sun Street, Lancaster LA11 1EW
☎01524 62166   Fax 01524 841216
Email info@lancslitfest.demon.co.uk
Website www.folly.co.uk/litfest

FOUNDED 1978. Regional Literature Development Agency, organising workshops, readings, residencies, publications. Year-round programme of literature-based events and annual festival in October featuring a wide range of writers from the UK and overseas. Organises annual poetry competition with winners receiving cash prizes and anthology publication.

Ledbury Poetry Festival
Town Council Offices, Church Lane, Ledbury, Herefordshire HR8 1DH
☎01531 634156
Email info@poetry-festival.com
Website www.poetry-festival.com

Contact *Charles Bennett*

FOUNDED 1997. Annual ten-day festival held in July. Includes readings, discussions, workshops, exhibitions, music and walks. There are also writers in residence at local schools and residential homes, a national poetry competition and the Town Party. Past guests have included Andrew Motion, Benjamin Zephaniah, Simon Armitage, Roger McGough, John Hegley and Germaine Greer. Full programme available in May.

Leicester Literature Festival
See **Words Out**

Lichfield International Arts Festival
7 The Close, Lichfield, Staffordshire WS13 7LD
☎01543 306270   Fax 01543 306274
Email lichfieldfest@lichfield-arts.org.uk
Website www.lichfieldfestival.org

Festival Director *Paul Spicer*

FOUNDED 1982. Annual July festival with events taking place in the 13th century Cathedral, the Civic Hall, Guildhall and Hawksyard Priory as well as various country churches and outdoor venues. Mainly music but also includes poetry reading events and poetry reading competition for schools; talks and lectures. Lichfield is the birthplace of Samuel Johnson and Johnson-

related events feature strongly in the festival programme.

City of London Festival
230 Bishopsgate, London EC2M 4HW
☎020 7377 0540   Fax 020 7377 1972
Email admin@colf.org
Website www.colf.org

Director *Michael MacLeod*

FOUNDED 1962. Annual three-week festival held in June and July. Features over fifty classical and popular music events alongside poetry and prose readings, street theatre and open-air extravaganzas, in some of the most outstanding performance spaces in the world.

London Festival of Literature
See **The Word**

London New Play Festival
40/7 Altenburg Gardens, London SW11 1JW
☎07050 641959   Fax 07050 642929
Email info@lnpf.co.uk
Website www.lnpf.co.uk

Artistic Director *Phil Setren*
Producer *Chris Cooke*
Literary Managers *Julia Parr, Ash Kotak*

FOUNDED 1989. Annual festival of new plays held in venues around London each September, centring on a short play platform season held in the West End in association with Really Useful Theatres. LNPF specialises in developing and producing new plays, normally working with early career playwrights. As well as the annual festival, LNPF stages education and production programmes throughout the year. Full information can be found on the website. Script submissions should be sent to *Julia Parr* at the address above.

Lowdham Book Festival
See **Nottinghamshire Readers and Writers Festivals**

Ludlow Festival
Castle Square, Ludlow, Shropshire SY8 1AY
☎01584 875070 (Admin)/872150 (Box Office)   Fax 01584 877673
Email info@ludlowfestival.co.uk
Website www.ludlowfestival.co.uk

Contact *Festival Administrator*

FOUNDED 1959. Annual two-week festival held in the last week of June and first week of July with an open-air Shakespeare production held at Ludlow Castle and a varied programme of events including recitals, opera, dance, popular and classical concerts, literary and historical lectures.

Manchester Festival of Writing

Manchester Central Library, St Peter's Square, Manchester M2 5PD
☎0161 234 1981
Email janem@libraries.manchester.gov.uk

Contact *Jane Mathieson*

FOUNDED 1990. An annual event organised by Manchester Libraries and Commonword community publishers. It consists of a short programme of practical writing workshops on specific themes/genres run by well-known writers. Attendance at all workshops is free to Manchester residents.

Manchester Poetry Festival

2nd Floor, Enterprise House, 15 Whitworth Street West, Manchester M1 5WG
☎0161 907 0031 Fax 0161 907 0032
Email mpf@dial.pipex.com

Contact *Richard Michael*

Held in the autumn (4th to 13th October in 2001), the Festival aims to bring the world's best poets to Manchester and promote Manchester poets to the rest of the world. Includes workshops and events for children.

Mere Literary Festival

Lawrence's, Old Hollow, Mere, Wiltshire BA12 6EG
☎01747 860475 Fax 01747 861211

Contact *Adrienne Howell*

FOUNDED 1997. Annual festival held in the second week of October in aid of registered charity, The Mere & District Linkscheme. Events include readings, quiz, workshop, writer's lunch and talks. Finale is adjudication of the festival's writing competition (see entry under **Prizes**) and presentation of awards.

Mole Valley Literature Festival

See **Wordswork**

National Eisteddfod of Wales

40 Parc Ty Glas, Llanishen, Cardiff CF14 5WU
☎029 2076 3777 Fax 029 2076 3737
Website www.eisteddfod.org.uk

The National Eisteddfod, held in August, is the largest arts festival in Wales, attracting over 170,000 visitors during the week-long celebration of more than 800 years of tradition. Competitions, bardic ceremonies and concerts.

National Student Drama Festival

See **University of Hull** under **Writers' Courses**

Norfolk and Norwich Festival

42–58 St George's Street, Norwich, Norfolk NR3 1AB
☎01603 614921 Fax 01603 632303
Email info@nnfest.demon.co.uk
Website www.nnfest.demon.co.uk

Festival Director *Peter Bolton*

FOUNDED 1772, this performing arts festival is the second oldest in the UK. Held annually in May, the festival includes talks by writers along with poetry and storytelling events.

North East Lincolnshire Literature Festival

Arts Development, North East Lincolnshire Council, Knoll Street, Cleethorpes, Lincolnshire DN35 8LN
☎01472 323007 Fax 01472 323005

Festival Programmer *Lynne Conlan*

FOUNDED 1997. Annual themed festival held in February/March. Reflecting the heritage of the area, the festival aims to make literature accessible to all ages and abilities through a varied and unusual programme. In 2001 the Festival was entitled 'Celebrations in Words and Visions'. Guests included Ian McMillan and events featured poetry readings, workshops and children's events.

Northern Children's Book Festival

Consett Library, Victoria Road, Consett DH8 5AT
☎01207 503606

Secretary *Carol Attewell* (at address above)

FOUNDED 1984. Annual two-week festival during November. Events in schools and libraries for children in the North East region. One Saturday during the festival sees the staging of a large book event hosted by one of the local authorities involved. Publications include books on holding your own book week such as: *Celebrating the North East*; *Getting the Show On the Road* and *Read On, Write On*.

Nottinghamshire Readers and Writers Festivals

Mansfield Library, Westgate, Mansfield, Nottinghamshire NG18 1NH
☎01623 647229 Fax 01623 629276

Contact *Ross Bradshaw*

FOUNDED 1999. Umbrella heading covering a

series of festivals including the Southwell Poetry Festival (guests have included Amanda Dalton, Brian Patten, U.A. Fanthorpe, Wendy Cope) and the annual Lowdham Book Festival. The latter, jointly organised by The Bookcase in Lowdham, is a week-long community and countrywide festival with lectures, readings and plays. Guests have included Ian McMillan, Alan Sillitoe and a theatrical production of *Captain Corelli's Mandolin*. Free mailing list available which includes a copy of *County Lit* magazine.

Off the Page Literature Festival
County Library Support Services, Glaisdale Parkway, Nottingham NG8 4GP
☎0115 985 4242 Fax 0115 928 6400

Contact *Pam Middleton*

Author visits aimed at making authors accessible to readers. In 2001 the series takes place at Nottingham Central Library in November. Programme available from late summer/early autumn.

Off the Shelf Literature Festival
Central Library, Surrey Street, Sheffield S1 1XZ
☎0114 273 4716/4400
Fax 0114 273 5009
Email off-the-shelf@pop3.poptel.org.uk
Website www.ots.aybara.com

Festival Organisers *Maria de Souza, Susan Walker*

FOUNDED 1992. Annual two-week festival held during the last fortnight in October. Lively and diverse mix of readings, workshops, children's events, storytelling and competitions. Previous guests have included Bill Bryson, Irvine Welsh, Benjamin Zephaniah, Terry Pratchett, Michael Palin, Carol Ann Duffy and Louis de Bernières.

Oxford Literary Festival
301 Woodstock Road, Oxford OX2 7NY
☎01865 514149 Fax 01865 514804
Email oxford.literary.festival@ntlworld.com

Directors *Sally Dunsmore, Angela Prysor-Jones*

FOUNDED 1997. Annual four-day festival held two weekends prior to Easter. Authors speaking about their books, covering a wide variety of writing: fiction, poetry, biography, travel, food, gardening, children's art. Previous guests have included William Boyd, Andrew Motion, Candia McWilliam, Beryl Bainbridge, Sophie Grigson, Jamie McKendrick, Bernard O'Donoghue, Philip Pullman and Korky Paul.

The Round Festival
c/o Word And Action (Dorset), 75 High Street, Wimborne, Dorset BH21 1HF
☎01202 883197 Fax 01202 881061

Contact *Anne Jennings*

FOUNDED 1990. International festival of theatre-in-the-round held in July offering a variety of workshops and performances celebrating and exploring the form. Programme includes performances and playreading (including new plays) in the round.

Royal Court Young Writers Programme
The Site, Royal Court Theatre, Sloane Square, London SW1W 8AS
☎020 7565 5050 Fax 020 7565 5001
Email ywp@royalcourttheatre.com
Website www.royalcourttheatre.com

Associate Director *Ola Animashawun*

Open to young people up to the age of 25. The YWP focuses on the process of playwriting by running a series of writers groups throughout the year at its base in Sloane Square. Additionally the YWP welcomes unsolicited scripts from all young writers from across the country. 'We are always looking for scripts for development and possible production (not film scripts).'

Rye Festival
PO Box 33, Rye, East Sussex TN31 7YB
☎01797 224982

Artistic Director *David Willison*

FOUNDED 1972. Annual two-week September event, plus short winter series. Variety of events with strong emphasis on literature (nominated by the *Independent on Sunday* as one of ten best British festivals), classical and modern music, visual arts, workshops and masterclasses. Write or phone to join free mailing list.

Salisbury Festival
Festival Office, 75 New Street, Salisbury, Wiltshire SP1 2PH
☎01722 332241 Fax 01722 410552

Director *Trevor Davies*

FOUNDED 1972. Annual festival held at the end of May/beginning of June, including classical music, theatre, jazz, exhibitions.

Scottish Young Playwrights Festival
Scottish Youth Theatre, 3rd Floor, Forsyth House, 111 Union Street, Glasgow G1 3TA
☎0141 221 5127 Fax 0141 221 9123

Email admin@scottishyouththeatre.freeserve.
co.uk

Website www.scottishyouththeatre.freeserve.
co.uk

Artistic Director *Mary McCluskey*

The Scottish Young Playwrights project operates throughout Scotland. In every region an experienced theatre practitioner runs regular young writers' workshops aimed at developing the best possible scripts from initial ideas. A representative selection of scripts is then selected to form a showcase. The festival is mounted in conjunction with the Royal Scottish Academy of Music and Drama. Scripts will be workshopped, revised and developed culminating in an evening presentation. Scripts are welcome throughout the year from young people aged 15–25 who are native Scots and/or resident in Scotland; synopses of unfinished scripts also considered. No restriction on style, content or intended media, but work must be original and unperformed. Further details from address above.

Southwell Poetry Festival
See **Nottinghamshire Readers and Writers Festivals**

Stoke Newington Festival
Room 15, Old Town Hall, Stoke Newington Church Street, London N16 0JR
☎020 8356 6410
Email fiona@stokenewingtonfestival.co.uk
Website www.stokenewingtonfestival.co.uk

Programme Producer *Fiona Fieber*

FOUNDED 1993. Annual month-long multi-arts festival held in June. Launched with a large one-day Street Festival which attracts some 50,000 people. This includes Poetry Street, a cul-de-sac dedicated to all things poetry with readings, performances and discussions. Other literature events are programmed throughout the festival. Previous guests have included Michael Rosen, John Mortimer, Ian Sinclair, Sue Gee, Peter Daniels, Mike Phillips, Charlie Higson and Patience Agbabi.

Stratford-upon-Avon Poetry Festival
The Shakespeare Centre, Henley Street, Stratford-upon-Avon, Warwickshire CV37 6QW
☎01789 204016 Fax 01789 296083
Email director@shakespeare.org.uk

Festival Director *Roger Pringle*

FOUNDED 1953. Annual festival held on Sunday evenings during July and August. Readings by poets and professional actors.

The Sunday Times Hay Festival
Festival Office, Hay-on-Wye HR3 5BX
☎01497 821217 Fax 01497 821066
Website www.hayfestival.co.uk

Festival Director *Peter Florence*

FOUNDED 1988. Annual May festival sponsored by *The Sunday Times*. Guests have included Paul McCartney, Bill Clinton, Salman Rushdie, Toni Morrison, Stephen Fry, Joseph Heller, Carlos Fuentes, Maya Angelou, Amos Oz, Arthur Miller.

Swansea Festivals
Dylan Thomas Centre, Somerset Place, Swansea SA1 1RR
☎01792 463980 Fax 01792 463993
Email dylan.thomas@cableol.uk
Website www.dylanthomas.org

Contact *David Woolley*

Wordplay (2nd to 7th October): seventh annual festival of literature and arts for young people. The Dylan Thomas Celebration (27th October to 9th November) is two weeks of performances, talks, lectures, films, music, poetry, exhibitions and celebrity guests.

Swindon Festival of Literature
Lower Shaw Farm, Shaw, Swindon, Wiltshire SN5 9PJ
☎01793 771080 Fax 01793 771080
Email swindonlitfest@lsfarm.globalnet.co.uk
Website www.swindonlink.com

Festival Director *Matt Holland*

FOUNDED 1994. Annual festival held in May, starting with 'Dawn Chorus' at sunrise on May Day and includes a wide range of authors, speakers, discussions, performances and workshops, plus the Clive Brain Memorial Lecture and the Swindon Poetry Slam.

Warwick & Leamington Festival
Warwick Arts Society, Northgate, Warwick CV34 4JL
☎01926 410747 Fax 01926 407606
Email admin@warwickarts.org.uk
Website www.welcome.to/warwickarts.org.uk

Festival Director *Richard Phillips*

FOUNDED 1980. Annual festival lasting 12 days in the first half of July. Basically a chamber and early music festival, with some open-air, large-scale concerts in Warwick Castle, the Festival also promotes plays by Shakespeare in historical settings. Large-scale education programme. Interested in increasing its literary content, both in performances and workshops.

Ways with Words
Droridge Farm, Dartington, Totnes, Devon TQ9 6JQ
☎01803 867373 Fax 01803 863688
Email admin@wayswithwords.co.uk
Website www.wayswithwords.co.uk
Festival Director *Kay Dunbar*

Ways with Words runs a major literature festival at Dartington Hall in south Devon for ten days in July each year. Features over 200 writers giving lectures, readings, interviews, discussions, performances, masterclasses and workshops.

Also, Words by the Water, a Cumbrian literature festival held in Keswick. The 2001 festival runs from 30th October to 4th November and features guests such as Brian Keenan, John Hegley, Jackie Kay, Roy Hattersley, Melvyn Bragg and George Alagiah. Ways With Words organises literary weekends in Southwold, Bury St Edmunds (Suffolk), plus writing, reading and painting courses in Italy.

Wellington Literary Festival
Civic Offices, Larkin Way, Tan Bank, Wellington, Telford, Shropshire TF1 1LX
☎01952 222935 Fax 01952 222936
Email WellTownCl@aol.com
Contact *Derrick Drew*

FOUNDED 1997. Annual festival held throughout October. Events include story telling, writers' forum, 'Pints and Poetry', children's poetry competition, story competition, theatre review and guest speakers.

Wells Festival of Literature
Tower House, St Andrew Street, Wells, Somerset BA5 2UN
☎01749 673385 Fax 01749 673385
Website www.somersite.co.uk/wellsfest.htm
Contact *Pamela Egan*

FOUNDED 1992. Annual weekend-plus festival held at the end of October. Main venue is the historic, moated Bishop's Palace. A wide range of speakers caters for different tastes in reading; previous guests: Douglas Hurd, Eric Newby, Elizabeth Jennings, P.D. James, Simon Jenkins, Barbara Trapido, Joan Aiken. Short story and poetry competitions are run in conjunction with the Festival.

Wessex Poetry Festival
38 Hod View, Stourpaine, Blandford Forum, Dorset DT11 8TN
☎01258 456803
Festival Director *David Caddy*

FOUNDED 1995. Annual international poetry festival held at the end of October, organised by the East Street Poets. Previous guests have included Irina Ratushinskaya, Michele Roberts, Iain Sinclair, Jon Silkin, Ketaki Kushari Dyson, Jim Burns, Jay Ramsay, Edwin Morgan, Pansy Maurer-Alvarez, Julian Bell.

The Word – The London Festival of Literature
245 St John Street, London EC1V 4NB
☎020 7837 2555 Fax 020 7278 0480
Email admin@theword.org.uk
Website www.theword.org.uk
Director *Peter Florence*

FOUNDED 1999. Annual ten-day autumn carnival celebration of the written and spoken word, featuring the best contemporary writing in every medium. Campaign and programme of competitions, conversations, debates, lectures, masterclasses, readings, receptions, workshops featuring writers and performance artists. Guest writers have included: Margaret Atwood, Chinua Achebe, Joseph Heller, Shirley Hughes, Hanif Kureishi, Doris Lessing, Armistead Maupin, Ian McEwan, Terry Pratchett, Edward Said, Wole Soyinka, Derek Walcott and Benjamin Zephaniah.

Wordplay
See **Swansea Festivals**

Words by the Water
See **Ways with Words**

Words Out – Leicester Literature Festival
Leicester City Council, Arts and Leisure, Block A, New Walk Centre, Welford Place, Leicester LE1 6ZG
☎0116 252 7347
Literature Development Officer *Sarah Butler*

Biannual festival held in October. A mixture of author events, workshops, profiles of community arts and spotlights on local writing held in a range of community/library/arts venues around the city.

Wordswork – Mole Valley Literature Festival

Mole Valley Leisure Services, Pippbrook, Dorking, Surrey RH4 1SJ
☎01273 478943   Fax 01273 478943
Email jo@koenig48.freeserve.co.uk

Literature Development Worker *Jo König*

A festival which celebrates literary talent both past and present throughout the Mole Valley. Includes a programme of readings, workshops, exhibitions, storytelling, performance poetry, children's and young people's events. Dedicated to encouraging, promoting and developing literature in its broadest sense. Initiates sustainable literary projects for all the community.

York Children's Festival of the Arts

15 Knowle Avenue, Burley, Leeds, West Yorkshire LS4 2PQ
☎0113 368 2439
Email caroline.wylie@virgin.net

Festival Director *Caroline Wylie*

Two-day festival of the arts – 29th/30th September 2001. Held in York for children aged 3–12 years. Brochure/booking form available August 2001.

European Publishers

Austria

Springer-Verlag KG
PO Box 89, A–1200 Vienna
☎00 43 1 3302415 Fax 00 43 1 3302426
FOUNDED 1924. *Publishes* anthropology, architecture, art, business, chemistry, computer science, communications, electronics, economics, education, interior design, environmental studies, engineering, law, maths, dentistry, medicine, nursing, philosophy, physics, psychology, technology and general science.

Verlag Carl Ueberreuter GmbH
Postfach 306, A–1091 Vienna
☎00 43 1 404440 Fax 00 43 1 404445
Website www.ueberreuter.de
FOUNDED 1548. *Publishes* fiction and general non-fiction: art, government, history, economics, political science, general science, health and nutrition, science fiction, fantasy, music and dance.

Paul Zsolnay Verlag GmbH
Postfach 142, A–1041 Vienna
☎00 43 1 50576610 Fax 00 43 1 505766110
FOUNDED 1923. *Publishes* biography, fiction, general non-fiction, history, poetry.

Belgium

Brepols Publishers NV
Begijnhof 67, 2300 Turnhout
☎00 32 14 448020 Fax 00 32 14 428919
FOUNDED 1796. *Publishes* academic monographs and collections in the humanities.

Facet NV
Willem Linnigstr 13, 2060 Antwerp
☎00 32 3 2274028 Fax 00 32 3 2273792
FOUNDED 1986. *Publishes* children's books.

Uitgeverij Lannoo NV
Kasteelstr 97, B-8700 Tielt
☎00 32 51 424211 Fax 00 32 51 401152
Website www.lannoo.com
FOUNDED 1909. *Publishes* general non-fiction, art, architecture and interior design, cookery, biography, economics, gardening, health, history, management, nutrition, photography, self-help, poetry, government, political science, religion, travel.

Standaard Uitgeverij
Belgiëlei 147a, 2018 Antwerp
☎00 32 3 2395900 Fax 00 32 3 2308550
FOUNDED 1919. *Publishes* education, fiction, humour.

Denmark

Forlaget Apostrof ApS
Postboks 2580, DK–2100 Copenhagen O
☎00 45 39 208420 Fax 00 45 39 208453
Website www.apostrof.dk
FOUNDED 1980. *Publishes* psychology and psychiatry.

Aschehoug Dansk Forlag A/S
PO Box 2179, DK–1017 Copenhagen K
☎00 45 33 305522 Fax 00 45 33 305822
Website www.aschehoug.dk
FOUNDED 1977. Part of the Egmont Group. *Publishes* fiction, biography, cookery, health, how-to, maritime and nutrition.

Borgens Forlag A/S
Valbygardsvej 33, DK–2500 Valby
☎00 45 36 153615 Fax 00 45 36 153616
Website www.borgens.dk
FOUNDED 1948. *Publishes* fiction, literature, literary criticism, general non-fiction, art, crafts, education, environmental studies, essays, games, gay and lesbian, hobbies, health, nutrition, music, dance, philosophy, poetry, psychology, psychiatry, religion.

Egmont Lademann A/S
Gerdasgade 37, DK–2500 Valby
☎00 45 36 156600 Fax 00 45 36 441162
Website www.egmont.com
FOUNDED 1954. *Publishes* general illustrated non-fiction.

Egmont Wangel AS
Gerdasgade 37, DK–1795 Valby
☎00 45 36 156600 Fax 00 45 36 441162
Website www.egmont.com

FOUNDED 1946. *Publishes* fiction and management.

Forum Publishers
Snaregade 4, DK–1205 Copenhagen K
☎00 45 33 147714 Fax 00 45 33 147791
FOUNDED 1940. *Publishes* fiction and mysteries.

GEC Gads Forlags Aktieselskab
Vimmelskaftet 32, DK–1161 Copenhagen K
☎00 45 33 150558 Fax 00 45 33 110800
FOUNDED 1855. *Publishes* general non-fiction, biological sciences, cookery, crafts, games, economics, education, English as a second language, environmental studies, gardening, history, mathematics, natural history, physics, plants, travel.

Gyldendalske Boghandel-Nordisk Forlag A/S
Klareboderne 3, DK–1001 Copenhagen K
☎00 45 33 755555 Fax 00 45 33 755533
Website www.gyldendal.dk
FOUNDED 1770. *Publishes* fiction, art, biography, dance, dentistry, education, history, how-to, medicine, music, poetry, nursing, philosophy, psychology, psychiatry, general and social sciences, sociology.

Hekla Forlag
Valbygaardsvej 33, DK–2500 Valby
☎00 45 36 153615 Fax 00 45 36 153616
FOUNDED 1979. *Publishes* general fiction and non-fiction.

Høst & Søns Publishers Ltd
PO Box 2212, DK–1018 Copenhagen
☎00 45 33 382888 Fax 00 45 33 382898
FOUNDED 1836. *Publishes* fiction, crafts, environmental studies, games, hobbies, regional interests, travel.

Lindhardt og Ringhof
Frederiksborggade 1, DK–1360 Copenhagen K
☎00 45 33 695000 Fax 00 45 33 695001
FOUNDED 1971. *Publishes* fiction and general non-fiction.

Munksgaard, International Publishers & Booksellers Ltd
PO Box 2148, DK–1016 Copenhagen K
☎00 45 77 127030 Fax 00 45 77 129387
Website www.munksgaard.dk
FOUNDED 1917. *Publishes* dentistry, medicine, nursing, psychology, psychiatry, general science.

Nyt Nordisk Forlag Arnold Busck A/S
Købmagergade 49, DK–1150 Copenhagen K
☎00 45 33 733575 Fax 00 45 33 733576
Website www.nytnordiskforlag.dk
FOUNDED 1896. *Publishes* fiction, art, biography, dance, dentistry, history, how-to, music, philosophy, religion, medicine, nursing, psychology, psychiatry, general and social sciences, sociology.

Politikens Forlag A/S
Vestergade 26, DK–1456 Copenhagen K
☎00 45 33 470707 Fax 00 45 33 470708
FOUNDED 1946. *Publishes* general non-fiction, art, crafts, dance, history, games, hobbies, how-to, music, natural history, sport, travel.

Samlerens Forlag A/S
Snaregade 4/1, DK–1205 Copenhagen K
☎00 45 33 131023 Fax 00 45 33 144314
FOUNDED 1942. *Publishes* essays, fiction, government, history, literature, literary criticism, political science.

Det Schønbergske Forlag
Landemaerket 5, DK–1119 Copenhagen K
☎00 45 33 733585 Fax 00 45 33 733586
FOUNDED 1857. *Publishes* art, biography, fiction, history, humour, philosophy, poetry, psychology, psychiatry, travel

Spektrum Forlagsaktieselskab
Snaregade 4, DK–1205 Copenhagen K
☎00 45 33 147714 Fax 00 45 33 147791
FOUNDED 1990. *Publishes* general non-fiction.

Tiderne Skifter Forlag A/S
Pilestraede 51/5, DK–1001 Copenhagen K
☎00 45 33 325772 Fax 00 45 33 144205
FOUNDED 1979. *Publishes* fiction, literature and literary criticism, essays, ethnicity, photography, behavioural sciences.

Finland
Gummerus Publishers
PO Box 749, SF–00101 Helsinki
☎00 358 9 584301 Fax 00 358 9 58430200
FOUNDED 1872. *Publishes* fiction, general non-fiction and textbooks.

Karisto Oy
PO Box 102, SF–13101 Hämeenlinna
☎00 358 3 6161551 Fax 00 358 3 6161565

FOUNDED 1900. *Publishes* fiction and general non-fiction.

Kirjayhtymä Oy
Urho Kekkosen Katu 4–6E, SF–00100 Helsinki
☎00 358 9 6937641 Fax 00 358 9 69376366
Website www.kirjayhtyma.fi
FOUNDED 1958. *Publishes* fiction and general non-fiction.

Otava Publishing Co.
PO Box 134, SF–00121 Helsinki
☎00 358 9 19961 Fax 00 358 9 643136
Website www.otava.fi
FOUNDED 1890. *Publishes* fiction, general non-fiction, how-to.

Werner Söderström Osakeyhtiö (WSOY)
PO Box 222, SF–00121 Helsinki
☎00 358 9 61681 Fax 00 358 9 6168467
FOUNDED 1878. *Publishes* fiction, general non-fiction, education.

Tammi Publishers
PO Box 410, SF–00101 Helsinki
☎00 358 9 6937621 Fax 00 358 9 69376266
Website www.tammi.net
FOUNDED 1943. *Publishes* fiction, general non-fiction.

France

Editions Arthaud SA
26 rue Racine, F–75006 Paris Cedex 06
☎00 33 1 4051 3008 Fax 00 33 1 4325 0118
FOUNDED 1890. Imprint of **Flammarion SA**. *Publishes* art, history, literature, literary criticism, essays, sport, travel.

Editions Belfond
12 avenue d'Italie, F–75627 Paris
☎00 33 1 4416 0500 Fax 00 33 1 4416 0505
FOUNDED 1963. *Publishes* fiction, literature, literary criticism, essays, mysteries, romance, poetry, general non-fiction, art, biography, dance, health, history, how-to, music, nutrition.

Editions Bordas
21 rue du Montparnasse BP50, F–75006 Paris Cedex 06
☎00 33 1 4439 4400 Fax 00 33 1 4439 4343
FOUNDED 1946. *Publishes* education and general non-fiction.

Editions Calmann-Lévy SA
3 rue Auber, F–75009 Paris
☎00 33 1 4742 3833 Fax 00 33 1 4742 7781
FOUNDED 1836. *Publishes* fiction, science fiction, fantasy, biography, history, humour, economics, philosophy, psychology, psychiatry, social sciences, sociology, sport.

Editions Denoël Sàrl
9 rue du Cherche-Midi, F–75006 Paris
☎00 33 1 4439 7373 Fax 00 33 1 4439 7390
FOUNDED 1932. *Publishes* art, economics, fiction, science fiction, fantasy, government, history, philosophy, political science, psychology, psychiatry.

Librairie Arthème Fayard
75 rue des Saints-Pères, F-75278 Paris Cedex 06
☎00 33 1 4549 8200 Fax 00 33 1 4222 4017
FOUNDED 1854. *Publishes* biography, fiction, history, dance, music, philosophy, religion, social sciences, sociology, general science, technology.

Flammarion SA
26 rue Racine, F–75006 Paris Cedex 06
☎00 33 1 4051 3008 Fax 00 33 1 4325 0118
FOUNDED 1875. *Publishes* general fiction and non-fiction, art, architecture, gardening, plants, interior design, literature, literary criticism, essays, medicine, nursing, dentistry, wine and spirits.

Editions Gallimard
5 rue Sébastien-Bottin, F–75341 Paris Cedex 07
☎00 33 1 4954 4200 Fax 00 33 1 4954 1616
FOUNDED 1911. *Publishes* fiction, poetry, art, biography, dance, history, music, philosophy.

Société des Editions Grasset et Fasquelle
61 rue des Saints-Pères, F–75006 Paris
☎00 33 1 4439 2200 Fax 00 33 1 4222 6418
FOUNDED 1907. *Publishes* fiction and general non-fiction, essays, literature, literary criticism, philosophy.

Hachette Livre
43 quai de Grenelle, F–75905 Paris Cedex 15
☎00 33 1 4392 3000 Fax 00 33 1 4392 3030
FOUNDED 1826. *Publishes* fiction and general non-fiction, architecture and interior design, art, economics, education, general engineering, government, history, language and linguistics, political science, philosophy, general science, self-help, social sciences, sociology, sport, travel.

Editions Robert Laffont, Nil, Fixot, Seghers, Julliard
24 ave Marceau, F–75008 Paris Cedex 08
☎00 33 1 5367 1400 Fax 00 33 1 5367 1414
Website www.laffont.fr
FOUNDED 1941. *Publishes* fiction and non-fiction; literature, literary criticism, essays, poetry, philosophy, self-help, general science, psychology.

Librairie Larousse
21 rue de Montparnasse, F–75298 Paris Cedex 06
☎00 33 1 4439 4400 Fax 00 33 1 4439 4343
FOUNDED 1852. *Publishes* general and social sciences, sociology, language arts, linguistics, technology.

Editions Jean-Claude Lattès
17 rue Jacob, F–75006 Paris
☎00 33 1 4441 7400 Fax 00 33 1 4325 3047
FOUNDED 1968. *Publishes* fiction and general non-fiction.

Les Editions Magnard Sàrl
20 rue Berbier-du-Mets, F–75647 Paris Cedex 13
☎00 33 1 4408 8585 Fax 00 33 1 4408 4979
FOUNDED 1933. *Publishes* education.

Michelin et Cie (Services de Tourisme)
46 ave de Breteuil, F–75324 Paris Cedex 07
☎00 33 1 4566 1234 Fax 00 33 1 4566 1163
FOUNDED 1900. *Publishes* travel.

Les Editions de Minuit SA
7 rue Bernard-Palissy, F–75006 Paris
☎00 33 1 4439 3920
Fax 00 33 1 4544 8236
FOUNDED 1942. *Publishes* fiction, essays, literature, literary criticism, philosophy, social science, sociology.

Fernand Nathan
9 rue Méchain, F–75676 Paris Cedex 14
☎00 33 1 4587 5000 Fax 00 33 1 4331 2169
FOUNDED 1881. *Publishes* education, history, philosophy, psychology, psychiatry, general and social sciences, sociology.

Presses de la Cité
12 ave d'Italie, F–75627 Paris Cedex 13
☎00 33 1 4416 0500 Fax 00 33 1 4416 0505
FOUNDED 1947. Imprint of **Editions Belfond**.

Publishes fiction and general non-fiction, science fiction, fantasy, biography, mysteries.

Presses Universitaires de France (PUF)
12 rue Jean-de-Beauvais, F–75005 Paris 06
☎00 33 1 4441 3939 Fax 00 33 1 4354 7887
Website www.puf.com
FOUNDED 1921. *Publishes* art, biography, dance, dentistry, government, general engineering, geography, geology, history, law, medicine, music, nursing, philosophy, psychology, psychiatry, religion, political science, social science, sociology.

Editions du Seuil
27 rue Jacob, F–75261 Paris Cedex 06
☎00 33 1 4046 5050 Fax 00 33 1 4329 0829
FOUNDED 1935. *Publishes* fiction, literature, literary criticism, essays, poetry, art, biography, dance, government, history, how-to, music, photography, philosophy, psychology, psychiatry, religion, general and social sciences, sociology.

Les Editions de la Table Ronde
7 rue Corneille, F–75006 Paris
☎00 33 1 4046 7070 Fax 00 33 1 4046 7101
FOUNDED 1944. *Publishes* fiction and general non-fiction, biography, history, psychology, psychiatry, religion.

Librairie Vuibert
20 rue Babier-du-Mets, F–75647 Paris Cedex 13
☎00 33 1 4408 4900 Fax 00 33 1 4408 4929
FOUNDED 1877. *Publishes* biological and earth sciences, chemistry, chemical engineering, economics, law, mathematics, physics.

Germany
Verlag C.H. Beck (OHG)
Postfach 400340, 80703 Munich
☎00 49 89 381890 Fax 00 49 89 38189398
FOUNDED 1763. *Publishes* general non-fiction, anthropology, archaeology, art, dance, economics, essays, history, language, law, linguistics, literature, literary criticism, music, philosophy, social sciences, sociology, theology.

C. Bertelsmann Verlag GmbH
Postfach 800360, 81603 Munich 80
☎00 49 89 431890 Fax 00 49 89 43189440
FOUNDED 1835. *Publishes* fiction and general

non-fiction, art, biography, government and political science.

Carlsen Verlag GmbH
Postfach 500380, 22703 Hamburg
☎00 49 40 3910090 Fax 00 49 40 39100962
FOUNDED 1953. *Publishes* humour – picture books and comics.

Deutscher Taschenbuch Verlag GmbH & Co. KG (dtv)
Postfach 400422, 80704 Munich
☎00 49 89 38167-0 Fax 00 49 89 346428
Website www.dtv.de
FOUNDED 1961. *Publishes* fiction and general non-fiction; art, astronomy, biography, child care and development, cookery, computer science, dance, education, government, history, how-to, music, poetry, psychiatry, psychology, philosophy, political science, religion, medicine, dentistry, nursing, social sciences, literature, literary criticism, essays, humour, travel.

Econ-Verlag GmbH
Postfach 151329, 80048 Munich
☎00 49 211 43596 Fax 00 49 211 4359768
FOUNDED 1950. *Publishes* general non-fiction and fiction, economics, general science.

Falken-Verlag GmbH
Postfach 1120, 65521 Niederhausen
☎00 49 6127 7020 Fax 00 49 6127 702133
FOUNDED 1923. *Publishes* crafts, cookery, education, games, gardening, health, history, hobbies, how-to, humour, nutrition, photography, sport.

S Fischer Verlag GmbH
Postfach 700355, 60553 Frankfurt am Main
☎00 49 69 60620 Fax 00 49 69 6062214
FOUNDED 1886. Part of the **Holtzbrinck Group**. *Publishes* fiction, general non-fiction, essays, literature, literary criticism.

Carl Hanser Verlag
Postfach 860420, 81631 Munich
☎00 49 89 998300 Fax 00 49 89 9834809
Email info@hanser.de
Website www.hanser.de
Managing Director, Non-Fiction *Wolfgang Beisler*
Managing Director, Fiction *Michael Krüger*
FOUNDED in 1928 in Munich. *Publishes* international and German contemporary literature; classics, anthropology, non-fiction on social

sciences and the arts; children's and juveniles; specialist books on engineering, natural science, plastics, computers and computer science, economics and management, dentistry. *Subsidiaries* **Paul Zsolnay Verlag**, Vienna; Sanssouci Verlag, Zurich; Verlag Nagel & Kimche, Zurich; Fachbuchverlag Leipzig, Leipzig; Hanser Gardner Publications, Cincinatti.

Wilhelm Heyne Verlag
Paul-Heyse-Str. 28, 80336 Munich
☎00 49 89 5148-0 Fax 00 49 89 5148-13
Email verlag@heyne.de
Website www.heyne.de
FOUNDED 1934. Owned by **Springer-Verlag**. *Publishes* fiction, mystery, romance, humour, science fiction, fantasy, astrology, biography, cookery, film, history, how-to, occult, psychology, psychiatry, video.

Hoffmann und Campe Verlag
Postfach 130444, 20139 Hamburg
☎00 49 40 441880 Fax 00 49 40 44188-290
FOUNDED 1781. *Publishes* fiction and general non-fiction; art, biography, dance, history, music, poetry, philosophy, psychology, psychiatry, general science, social sciences, sociology.

Verlagsgruppe Georg von Holtzbrinck GmbH
Gänsheidestrasse 26, 70184 Stuttgart
☎00 49 711 21500 Fax 00 49 711 2150269
Email info@holtzbrinck.com
Website www.holtzbrinck.com
FOUNDED 1948. One of the world's largest publishing groups with 12 book publishing houses and 40 imprints. Also publishes the newspapers, *Handelsblatt* and *Die Zeit*.

Hüthig Fachverlage GmbH
Im Weiher 10, 69121 Heidelberg
☎00 49 89 6221489 Fax 00 49 89 6221489279
Email info@huethig.de
Hüthig Fachverlage is Germany's fourth largest professional publisher.

Ernst Klett Verlag GmbH
Postfach 106016, 70049 Stuttgart
☎00 49 711 66720 Fax 00 49 711 6672-2000
FOUNDED 1897. *Publishes* education, career development, geography, geology.

Gustav Lübbe Verlag GmbH
Postfach 200180, 51431 Bergisch Gladbach
☎00 49 2202 1210 Fax 00 49 2202 121928
FOUNDED 1963. *Publishes* fiction and general

non-fiction, archaeology, biography, history, how-to.

Mosaik Verlag GmbH
Postfach 800360, 81673 Munich 80
☎00 49 89 431890 Fax 00 49 89 43189743
Publishes animals, antiques, architecture and interior design, child care and development, cookery, crafts, economics, finance, career development, film, gardening, games, hobbies, health, house and home, human relations, nutrition, pets, self-help, sport, video, wine and spirits, women's studies.

Pestalozzi–Verlag Graphische Gesellschaft mbH
Am Pestalozziring 14, 91051 Erlangen
☎00 49 9131 60600 Fax 00 49 9131 773090
FOUNDED 1844. *Publishes* crafts, games, hobbies.

Propylän Verlag, Zweigniederlassung Berlin der Ullstein Buchverlage
Charlottenstr 13, 10969 Berlin
☎00 49 30 25913500
Fax 00 49 30 25913533
FOUNDED 1903. *Publishes* fiction and general non-fiction, romance, mysteries, architecture and interior design, art, biography, dance, film, video, education, essays, ethnology, geography, geology, government, health, history, how-to, humour, literature, literary criticism, maritime, military science, music, nutrition, poetry, political science, general science, social sciences, sociology, travel.

Rowohlt Taschenbuch Verlag GmbH
Postfach 1349, 21462 Reinbeck
☎00 49 40 72720 Fax 00 49 40 7272319
Website www.rowohlt.de
FOUNDED 1953. *Publishes* fiction and general non-fiction; archaeology, art, computer science, crafts, education, essays, games and hobbies, government, history, literature, literary criticism, philosophy, psychology, psychiatry, religion, general science, social sciences, sociology.

Springer-Verlag GmbH & Co KG
Postfach 311340, 10643 Berlin
☎00 49 30 827870 Fax 00 49 30 8214091
Website www.springer.de
FOUNDED 1842. *Publishes* agriculture, architecture and interior design, astronomy, behavioural

sciences, business, biological sciences, chemical engineering, chemistry, civil engineering, computer science, dentistry, economics, finance, geography, geology, health, nutrition, library and information sciences, management, marketing, mechanical engineering, electronics, electrical engineering, general engineering, earth sciences, environmental studies, law, mathematics, medicine, nursing, psychology, psychiatry, physics, general science, technology.

Suhrkamp Verlag
Postfach 101945, 60019 Frankfurt am Main
☎00 49 69 756010 Fax 00 49 69 75601522
Website www.suhrkamp.de
FOUNDED 1950. *Publishes* fiction, poetry, biography, philosophy, psychology, psychiatry, general science.

Taschen Verlag GmbH
Hohenzollernring 53, 50672 Cologne
☎00 49 221 201800 Fax 00 49 221 2018042
Website www.taschen.com
FOUNDED 1980. *Publishes* photography, art, architecture and interior design.

K. Thienemanns Verlag
Blumenstr 36, 70182 Stuttgart
☎00 49 711 210550 Fax 00 49 711 2105539
FOUNDED 1849. *Publishes* fiction and general non-fiction.

WEKA Firmengruppe GmbH & Co KG
Postfach 1209, 86425 Kissing
☎00 49 8233 230 Fax 00 49 8233 23195
FOUNDED 1973. Germany's largest professional publisher. *Publishes* architecture and interior design, business, career development, civil engineering, general engineering, how-to, electrical engineering, outdoor recreation, communications, management, mechanical engineering, medicine, nursing and dentistry, law, technology, environmental studies, behavioural sciences.

Italy

Adelphi Edizioni SpA
Via S. Giovanni sul Muro 14, 20121 Milan
☎00 39 2 72000975 Fax 00 39 2 89010337
FOUNDED 1962. *Publishes* fiction, art, biography, dance, music, philosophy, psychology, psychiatry, religion, general science.

Bompiana–RCS Libri
Via Mecenate 91, 20138 Milan
☎00 39 2 50951 Fax 00 39 2 5065361
Website www.rcslibri.it
FOUNDED 1929. *Publishes* fiction and general non-fiction, art, drama, theatre and general science.

Bulzoni Editore SRL (Le Edizioni Universitarie d'Italia)
Via Dei Liburni 14, 00185 Rome
☎00 39 6 4455207 Fax 00 39 6 4450355
FOUNDED 1969. *Publishes* fiction, literature, literary criticism, essays, art, drama, general engineering, film, law, language, linguistics, philosophy, general science, social sciences, sociology, theatre, video.

Nuova Casa Editrice Licinio Cappelli GEM srl
Via Farini 14, 40124 Bologna
☎00 39 51 239060 Fax 00 39 51 239286
Website www.cappellieditore.com
FOUNDED 1851. *Publishes* fiction, art, biography, drama, film, government, history, music and dance, medicine, nursing, dentistry, philosophy, poetry, political science, psychology, psychiatry, religion, general science, social sciences, sociology, theatre, video.

Garzanti Editore
Via Newton 18A, 20148 Milan
☎00 39 2 487941 Fax 00 39 2 48794292
FOUNDED 1861. *Publishes* fiction, literature, literary criticism, essays, art, biography, history, poetry, government, political science.

Giunti Publishing Group
Via Bolognese 165, 50139 Florence
☎00 39 55 66791 Fax 00 39 55 6679298
FOUNDED 1840. *Publishes* fiction, literature, literary criticism, essays, art, chemistry, chemical engineering, education, history, how-to, language arts, linguistics, mathematics, psychology, psychiatry, general science. Italian publishers of National Geographical Society books.

Gremese Editore SRL
Via Agnelli 88, 00151 Rome
☎00 39 6 65740507 Fax 00 39 6 65740509
FOUNDED 1978. *Publishes* fiction and non-fiction; art, astrology, cookery, crafts, dance, drama, environmental studies, fashion, games, hobbies, essays, literature, literary criticism, music, occult, parapsychology, photography, sport, travel, theatre, film, video, television, radio.

Longanesi & C
Corso Italia 13, 20122 Milan
☎00 39 2 8692640 Fax 00 39 2 72000306
Website www.longanesi.it
FOUNDED 1946. *Publishes* fiction, art, biography, dance, history, how-to, medicine, nursing, dentistry, music, philosophy, psychology, psychiatry, religion, general and social sciences, sociology.

Arnoldo Mondadori Editore SpA
Via Mondadori, 20090 Segrate (Milan)
☎00 39 2 75421 Fax 00 39 2 75422302
Website www.mondadori.com
FOUNDED 1907. *Publishes* fiction, mystery, romance, art, biography, dance, dentistry, history, how-to, medicine, music, poetry, philosophy, psychology, psychiatry, religion, nursing, general science, education.

Società Editrice Il Mulino
Str Maggiore 37, 40125 Bologna
☎00 39 51 256011 Fax 00 39 51 256034
Website www.mulino.it
FOUNDED 1954. *Publishes* dance, drama, economics, government, history, law, language, linguistics, music, philosophy, political science, psychology, psychiatry, social sciences, sociology, theatre.

Gruppo Ugo Mursia Editore SpA
Via Tadino 29, 20124 Milan
☎00 39 2 29403030 Fax 00 39 2 29400165
FOUNDED 1922. *Publishes* fiction, poetry, art, biography, education, history, maritime, philosophy, religion, sport, general and social sciences, sociology.

RCS Libri SpA
Via Mecenate 91, 20138 Milan
☎00 39 2 50951 Fax 00 39 2 5065361
Website www.rcslibri.it
FOUNDED 1945. *Publishes* art, crafts, dance, business, games, hobbies, history, music, medicine, nursing, dentistry, outdoor recreation, general science.

Societa Editrice Internazionale – SEI
Corso Regina Margherita 176, 10152 Turin
☎00 39 11 52271 Fax 00 39 11 5211320
FOUNDED 1908. *Publishes* literature, literary

criticism, essays, education, geography, geology, history, mathematics, philosophy, physics, religion, psychology, psychiatry.

Sonzogno
Via Mecenate 91, 20138 Milan
☎00 39 2 50951 Fax 00 39 2 5065361
Website www.rcslibri.it
FOUNDED 1818. *Publishes* fiction, mysteries, and general non-fiction.

Sperling e Kupfer Editori SpA
Durazzo 4, 20134 Milan
☎00 39 2 217211 Fax 00 39 2 21721277
FOUNDED 1899. *Publishes* fiction and general non-fiction, biography, economics, health, how-to, management, nutrition, general science, sport, travel.

Sugarco Edizioni SRL
Via Fermi 9, 21040 Carnago (Varese)
☎00 39 331 985511 Fax 00 39 331 985385
FOUNDED 1956. *Publishes* fiction, biography, history, how-to, philosophy.

Todariana Editrice
Via Gardone 29, 20139 Milan
☎00 39 2 56812953 Fax 00 39 2 55213405
FOUNDED 1967. *Publishes* fiction, poetry, science fiction, fantasy, literature, literary criticism, essays, language arts, linguistics, psychology, psychiatry, social sciences, sociology, travel.

The Netherlands

Addison-Wesley Publishers BV
Concertgebouwplein 25, 1071 LM Amsterdam
☎00 31 20 671 7296 Fax 00 31 20 664 5334
FOUNDED 1942. Part of Pearson Education. *Publishes* education, business, computer science, economics, management, technology.

A.W. Bruna Uitgevers BV
Postbus 40203, 3504 AA Utrecht
☎00 31 30 247 0411 Fax 00 31 30 241 0018
FOUNDED 1868. *Publishes* fiction and general non-fiction; computer science, history, philosophy, psychology, psychiatry, general and social science, sociology.

Uitgeverij BZZTÔH
Laan van Meerdervoort 10, 2517 AJ Gravenhage
☎00 31 70 363 2934 Fax 00 31 70 363 1932
FOUNDED 1970. *Publishes* fiction, mysteries,

general non-fiction, animals, astrology, biography, cookery, dance, humour, music, occult, pets, religion (Buddhist), romance, travel.

Elsevier Science BV
Sara Burgehartst. 25, 1055 KV Amsterdam
☎00 31 20 586 2911 Fax 00 31 20 485 2457
FOUNDED 1946. Parent company – Reed Elsevier. *Publishes* sciences (all fields), medicine, nursing, dentistry, economics, engineering (computer, chemical and general), mathematics, physics, technology.

Uitgeversmaatschappij J. H. Kok BV
PO Box 5019, 8260 GA Kampen
☎00 31 38 339 2555 Fax 00 31 38 332 7331
FOUNDED 1894. *Publishes* fiction, poetry, history, religion, general and social sciences, sociology.

M & P Publishing House
Postbus 170, 3990 DD Houten
☎00 31 30 637 7736 Fax 00 31 30 637 7764
FOUNDED 1974. *Publishes* general non-fiction.

J.M. Meulenhoff & Co BV
Postbus 100, 1017 BV Amsterdam
☎00 31 20 553 3500 Fax 00 31 20 625 8511
FOUNDED 1895. *Publishes* international co-productions, fiction and general non-fiction. Specialises in Dutch and translated literature.

Uitgeverij Het Spectrum BV
Postbus 2073, 3500 GB Utrecht
☎00 31 30 265 0650 Fax 00 31 30 262 0850
FOUNDED 1935. *Publishes* science fiction, fantasy, literature, literary criticism, essays, mystery, criminology, general non-fiction, computer science, history, astrology, occult, management, environmental studies, travel.

Time-Life Books BV
O. Heldringstr. 5, 1066 AZ Amsterdam
☎00 31 20 487 4348 Fax 00 31 20 487 4295
Publishes art, archaeology, astronomy, cookery, gardening, plants, history, how-to, health and nutrition, house and home.

Unieboek BV
Postbus 97, 3990 DB Houten
☎00 31 30 637 7660 Fax 00 31 30 637 7600
FOUNDED 1891. *Publishes* fiction, general non-fiction, architecture and interior design, government, political science, literature, literary criticism, essays, archaeology, cookery, history.

Uniepers BV
Postbus 69, 1390 AB Abcoude
☎00 31 29 428 5111 Fax 00 31 29 428 3013
FOUNDED 1961. *Publishes* (mostly in co-editions) antiques, anthropology, archaeology, architecture and interior design, art, culture, dance, history, music, natural history.

Wolters Kluwer Nederlands
Postbus 23, 7400 GA Deventer
☎00 31 57 064 8111 Fax 00 31 57 064 1709
FOUNDED 1889. *Publishes* education, medical, technical encyclopedias, trade books and journals, law and taxation, periodicals.

Norway

H. Aschehoug & Co (W. Nygaard) A/S
Postboks 363, 0102 Sentrum, Oslo
☎00 47 22 400400 Fax 00 47 22 206395
FOUNDED 1872. *Publishes* fiction and general non-fiction, general and social science, sociology.

J.W. Cappelens Forlag A/S
Postboks 350, 0101 Sentrum, Oslo
☎00 47 22 365000 Fax 00 47 22 365040
FOUNDED 1829. *Publishes* fiction, general non-fiction, religion.

N.W. Damm og Søn A/S
Postboks 1755, Vika, 0122 Oslo
☎00 47 22 471000 Fax 00 47 22 360874
FOUNDED 1845. *Publishes* fiction and general non-fiction.

Egmont Hjemmets Bokforlag
Postboks 1755, Vika, 0055 Oslo
☎00 47 22 471000 Fax 00 47 22 471098
FOUNDED 1969. *Publishes* fiction and general non-fiction.

Ex Libris Forlag A/S
Postboks 2130, Grünerløkka, 0505 Oslo
☎00 47 22 809500 Fax 00 47 22 385160
FOUNDED 1982. *Publishes* cookery, health, nutrition, humour, human relations, publishing and book trade reference.

Gyldendal Norsk Forlag
Tor Brauti
Postboks 6860, 0130 St Olaf, Oslo
☎00 47 22 034100 Fax 00 47 22 034105

FOUNDED 1925. *Publishes* fiction, science fiction, fantasy, art, dance, biography, government, political science, history, how-to, music, social sciences, sociology, poetry, philosophy, psychology, psychiatry, religion.

NKS-Forlaget
Postboks 5853, 0308 Oslo
☎00 47 22 596000 Fax 00 47 22 596300
Website www.nks.no
FOUNDED 1971. *Publishes* accountancy, childcare and development, English as a second language, health, nutrition, mathematics, natural history, general and social sciences, sociology.

Tiden Norsk Forlag
PO Box 8813, Youngstorget, 0028 Oslo
☎00 47 22 007100 Fax 00 46 22 426458
FOUNDED 1933. *Publishes* fiction, general non-fiction; essays, literature, literary criticism, science fiction, fantasy, management.

Portugal

Bertrand Editora Lda
Rua Anchieta 29–1, 1200 Lisbon
☎00 351 1 3468286 Fax 00 351 1 3479728
FOUNDED 1727. *Publishes* art, essays, literature, literary criticism, social sciences, sociology.

Editorial Caminho SARL
Al Santo Antonio dos Capuchos 6B,
1100 Lisbon
☎00 351 1 3152683 Fax 00 351 1 534346
FOUNDED 1977. *Publishes* fiction, government, political science.

Livraria Civilizacão (Américo Fraga Lamares & Ca Lda)
Rua Alberto Aires de Gouveia 27, 4000 Porto
☎00 351 2 226006577
FOUNDED 1921. *Publishes* fiction, art, economics, history, social and political science, government, sociology.

Publicações Dom Quixote Lda
Avenida Cintura do Porto de Lisboa,
Urbanizaçao da Matinha, lote A, 2C,
1900 Lisbon
☎00 351 1 8610430 Fax 00 351 1 8610435
FOUNDED 1965. Part of Grupo Planeta. *Publishes* fiction, poetry, education, history, philosophy, general and social sciences, sociology.

Publicações Europa-America Lda

Apdo 8, Estrada Lisbon-Sintra Km 14,
2726 Mem Martins Cedex
☎00 351 1 9211461 Fax 00 351 1 9217940

FOUNDED 1945. *Publishes* fiction, poetry, art, biography, dance, education, general engineering, history, how-to, music, philosophy, medicine, nursing, dentistry, psychology, psychiatry, general and social sciences, sociology, technology.

Gradiva–Publicações Lda

Rua Almeida e Sousa 21–r/c Esq,
1300 Lisbon
☎00 351 1 3974067 Fax 00 351 1 3974068
Website www.gravida.pt

FOUNDED 1981. *Publishes* fiction, literature, literary criticism, essays, science fiction, fantasy, romance, anthropology, astronomy, archaeology, behavioural and biological science, communications, computer science, crafts, education, games, hobbies, economics, general engineering, geography, geology, natural history, history, humour, environmental studies, human relations, management, philosophy, general science, psychology, psychiatry, sociology.

Livros Horizonte Lda

Rua Chagas 17 - 1 Dto, 1200 Lisbon
☎00 351 1 3466917 Fax 00 351 1 3326921

FOUNDED 1953. *Publishes* art, education, history, psychology, psychiatry, social sciences, sociology.

Editorial Verbo SA

Rua Carlos Testa 1–2, 1000 Lisbon
☎00 351 1 3562121 Fax 00 351 1 3865396

FOUNDED 1959. *Publishes* education, history, general science.

Spain

Alhambra–Longman

Nunez de Balboa 120, 28006 Madrid
☎00 349 1 590 3432 Fax 00 349 1 590 3448

FOUNDED 1942. *Publishes* art, education, history, language arts, linguistics, medicine, nursing, dentistry, general science, psychology, psychiatry, philosophy.

Alianza Editorial SA

Juan Ignacio Luca de Tena 15, 28027 Madrid
☎00 349 1 393 8888 Fax 00 349 1 320 7480

FOUNDED 1965. *Publishes* fiction, poetry, art, history, mathematics, dance, music, philoso-

phy, government, political and social sciences, sociology, general science.

Ediciones Anaya SA

Juan Ignacio Luca de Tena 15, 28027 Madrid
☎00 349 1 393 8800 Fax 00 349 1 742 6631

FOUNDED 1959. *Publishes* education.

Editorial Don Quijote

Compãs del Porvenir 6, 41013 Seville
☎00 349 5 423 5080

FOUNDED 1981. *Publishes* fiction, literature, literary criticism, poetry, essays, drama, theatre, history.

EDHASA (Editora y Distribuidora Hispano – Americana SA)

Av Diagonal 519–521, 08029 Barcelona
☎00 349 3 494 9720 Fax 00 349 3 419 4584

FOUNDED 1946. *Publishes* fiction, literature, literary criticism, essays, history.

Editorial Espasa-Calpe SA

Apdo 547, Carreterade Irún Km 12, 200,
28049 Madrid
☎00 349 1 358 9689 Fax 00 349 1 358 8679

FOUNDED 1925. *Publishes* fiction, science fiction, fantasy, English as a second language, general non-fiction, art, child care and development, cookery, biography, essays, history, literature, literary criticism, self-help, social sciences, sociology.

Grijalbo Mondadori SA

Arago 385, 08013 Barcelona
☎00 349 3 476 7110 Fax 00 349 3 476 7119
Website www.grijalbo.com

FOUNDED 1942. *Publishes* fiction, general non-fiction, architecture, interior design, gardening, humour, literature, literary criticism, essays, poetry, human relations.

Grupo CEAC SA

Arago 472, 08013 Barcelona
☎00 349 3 307 5004 Fax 00 349 3 266 0067
Website www.ceacedit.com

Publishes education, technology, science fiction, fantasy.

Edicíones Hiperión SL

Calle Salustiano Olózaga 14, 28001 Madrid
☎00 349 1 557 6015 Fax 00 349 1 435 8690

FOUNDED 1976. *Publishes* literature, literary criticism, essays, poetry, religion (Islamic and Jewish).

Editorial Luis Vives (Edelvives)
C/Xaudaró 25, 28034 Madrid
☎00 349 1 334 4890 Fax 00 349 1 334 4892
FOUNDED 1890. *Publishes* education.

Editorial Molino
Calabria 166 baixos, 08015 Barcelona
☎00 349 3 226 0625 Fax 00 349 3 226 6998
Website www.editorialmolino.es
FOUNDED 1933. *Publishes* education, sport, fiction.

Editorial Planeta SA
Córcega 273–279, 08008 Barcelona
☎00 349 3 228 5800 Fax 00 349 3 217 7140
Website www.planeta.es
FOUNDED 1949. *Publishes* fiction and general non-fiction.

Plaza y Janés Editores SA
Traversera de Gracia 47–49, 08021 Barcelona
☎00 349 3 366 0300 Fax 00 349 3 366 0107
FOUNDED 1959. *Publishes* fiction and general non-fiction, biography, history.

Editorial Seix Barral SA
Provença 260, 4a planta, 08008 Barcelona
☎00 349 3 496 7003 Fax 00 349 3 496 7004
Website www.seix-barral.es
FOUNDED 1911. Part of Grupo Planeta. Foreign language publisher of literature.

Tusquets Editores
Cesare Cantù 8, 08017 Barcelona
☎00 349 3 253 0400 Fax 00 349 3 417 6703
FOUNDED 1969. *Publishes* fiction, biography, literature, essays, literary criticism, general science.

Ediciones Versal SA
Calabria 108, 08015 Barcelona
☎00 349 3 325 7404 Fax 00 349 3 423 6898
FOUNDED 1984. *Publishes* general non-fiction, biography, literature, literary criticism, essays.

Sweden

Albert Bonniers Förlag AB
Box 3159, S-103 63 Stockholm
☎00 46 8 6968000 Fax 00 46 8 6968361
FOUNDED 1837. *Publishes* fiction and general non-fiction.

Bokförlaget Bra Böcker AB
Södra Vägen, S-26380 Höganäs
☎00 46 42 339000 Fax 00 46 42 330504

FOUNDED 1965. *Publishes* fiction, geography, geology, history.

Brombergs Bokförlag AB
Box 12886, S-112 98 Stockholm
☎00 46 8 56262080 Fax 00 46 8 56262085
FOUNDED 1973. *Publishes* fiction, general non-fiction, government, political science, general science.

Bokförlaget Forum AB
PO Box 70321, S-107 23 Stockholm
☎00 46 8 6968440 Fax 00 46 8 6968367
FOUNDED 1944. *Publishes* fiction and general non-fiction.

Natur och Kultur/LTs Förlag
Box 27264, S-102 53 Stockholm
☎00 46 8 4538600 Fax 00 46 8 4538790
Website www.nok.se/lt
FOUNDED 1922. *Publishes* agriculture, cookery, craft, games, hobbies, house and home, gardening, pets, photography, general science, economics.

Norstedts Förlag AB
Box 2052, S-103 12 Stockholm
☎00 46 8 7893000 Fax 00 46 8 7893038
Website www.norstedt.se
FOUNDED 1823. *Publishes* fiction and general non-fiction.

AB Rabén och Sjögren Bokförlag
PO Box 2052, S-103 12 Stockholm
☎00 46 8 7893000 Fax 00 46 8 7893052
Website www.raben.se
FOUNDED 1942. *Publishes* general non-fiction.

Richters Egmont AB
Ostra Förstadsgatan 46, 205 75 Malmö
☎00 46 40 380600 Fax 00 46 40 933708
FOUNDED 1942. *Publishes* fiction.

B. Wählströms Bokförlag AB
Box 30022, S-104 25 Stockholm
☎00 46 8 6198600 Fax 00 46 8 6189761
Website www.wahlstroms.se
FOUNDED 1911. *Publishes* fiction and general non-fiction.

Switzerland

Arche Verlag AG, Raabe und Vitali
Postfach 112, CH-8030 Zurich
☎00 41 1 2522410 Fax 00 41 1 2611115
FOUNDED 1944. *Publishes* literature and literary

criticism, essays, biography, fiction, poetry, music, dance, travel.

Artemis Verlags AG

Munstergasse 9, CH-8001 Zurich
☎00 41 1 2521100 Fax 00 41 1 2624792

FOUNDED 1943. *Publishes* art, architecture and interior design, biography, history, philosophy, political science, government, travel.

Diogenes Verlag AG

Sprecherstr 8, CH-8032 Zurich
☎00 41 1 2528111 Fax 00 41 1 2528407

FOUNDED 1952. *Publishes* fiction, essays, literature, literary criticism, mysteries, art, drama, theatre, philosophy.

Langenscheidt AG Zürich-Zug

Postfach 326, CH-8021 Zurich
☎00 41 1 2115000 Fax 00 41 1 2122149

Part of Langenscheidt Group, Germany. *Publishes* language arts and linguistics.

Larousse (Suisse) SA

c/o Acces-Direct, 3 Route du Grand-Mont, CH-1052 Le Mont-sur-Lausanne
☎00 41 21 335336

Publishes dictionaries, reference and textbooks. Part of **Librairie Larousse**, France.

Neptun-Verlag

Postfach 307, CH-8280 Kreuzlingen
☎00 41 72 727262 Fax 00 41 72 642023

FOUNDED 1946. *Publishes* history and travel.

Orell Füssli Verlag

Nuschelerstrasse 22, CH-8022 Zurich
☎00 41 1 2113630 Fax 00 41 1 4667412
Website www.orell-fuessli-verlag.ch

FOUNDED 1519. *Publishes* art, biography, economics, education, geography, geology, history, how-to.

Editions Payot Lausanne

18 ave de la Gare, CP 529,
CH-1001 Lausanne
☎00 41 21 3290264 Fax 00 41 21 3290266

FOUNDED 1875. *Publishes* general non-fiction, anthropology, archaeology, architecture and interior design, dance, education, history, law, medicine, nursing, dentistry, music, philosophy, literature, literary criticism, essays, general science, social sciences and sociology.

Sauerländer AG

Laurenzenvorstadt 89, CH-5001 Aarau
☎00 41 64 8268626 Fax 00 41 64 8245780
Website www.sauerlaender.ch

FOUNDED 1807. *Publishes* education and general non-fiction.

Scherz Verlag AG

Theaterplatz 4–6, CH-3000 Berne 7
☎00 41 31 3277117 Fax 00 41 31 3277171
Website www.scherzverlag.ch

FOUNDED 1939. *Publishes* fiction and general non-fiction; biography, history, psychology, psychiatry, philosophy, parapsychology.

European Television Companies

Austria

ORF (Österreichisher Rundfunk)
Würzburggasse 30, A–1136 Vienna
☎00 43 1 87 8780 Fax 00 43 1 87 8783766
Website www.orf.at

Belgium

Radio-Télévision Belge de la Communauté Française (RTBF)
Boulevard Auguste Reyers 52, B–1044 Brussels
☎00 32 2 737 2111 Fax 00 32 2 737 2556
Website www.rtbf.be

Vlaamse Radio en Televisieomroep (VRT)
Reyerslaan 52, B–1043 Brussels
☎00 32 2 741 3111 Fax 00 32 2 739 9351
Email info@vrt.be
Website www.vrt.be

Vlaamse Televisie Maatschappij (VTM) (cable)
Medialaan 1, B–1800 Vilvoorde
☎00 32 2 255 3211 Fax 00 32 2 252 5141
Email info@vtm.be
Website www.vtm.be

Denmark

Danmarks Radio–TV
TV Byen, DK–2860 Søborg
☎00 45 35 20 3040 Fax 00 45 35 20 2644
Email dr@dr.dk
Website www.dr.dk

TV Danmark
Langebrogade 6A, DK–1411 Copenhagen K, Denmark
☎00 45 32 69 9600 Fax 00 45 32 69 9699
Email info@tvdanmark.dk
Website www.tvdanmark.dk

TV–2 Danmark
Rugaardsvej 25, DK–5100 Odense C
☎00 45 65 91 9191 Fax 00 45 65 91 3322
Website www.tv2.dk

Finland

MTV3 Finland
Ilmalantori 2, SF–00240 Helsinki
☎00 358 9 15001 Fax 00 358 9 1500707
Website www.mtv3.fi

Yleisradio Oy (YLE)
PO Box 90, FIN–00024 Yleisradio
☎00 358 9 14801 Fax 00 358 9 14803216
Email fbc@yle.fi
Website www.yle.fi

France

Canal + (pay TV)
85–89 quai André Citroën, 75015 Paris
☎00 33 1 44 25 10 00
Fax 00 33 1 44 25 12 34
Website www.cplus.fr

La Cinquième
10–14 rue Horace-Vernet, 92136 Issey Les Moulineaux
☎00 33 1 41 46 55 55 Fax 00 33 1 41 46 55 18
Website www.lacinquieme.fr

France Télévision (France 2/ France 3)
7 Esplanade Henri de France, 75907 Paris Cedex 15
☎00 33 1 56 22 42 42(France 2)/
00 33 1 56 22 30 30 (France 3)
Website www.france2.fr *and* www.france3.fr

M6 (Métropole Télévision)
89 ave Charles de Gaulle, 92575 Neuilly-sur-Seine
☎00 33 1 41 92 66 66 Fax 00 33 1 41 92 66 10
Website www.m6.fr

RFO (Radio Télévision Française d'Outre-mer)
5 ave du Recteur Poincaré, 75782 Paris Cedex 16
☎00 33 1 42 15 71 00 Fax 00 33 1 42 15 74 37
Email rfo@rfo.fr
Website www.rfo.fr

La Sept/Arte (cable & satellite)
8 rue Marceau, 92785 Issy les Moulineaux
Cedex 9
☎00 33 1 55 00 77 77
Fax 00 33 1 55 00 77 00
Website www.arte–tv.com

TF1 (Télévision Française 1)
1 quai du Pont du Jour, 92656 Boulogne
☎00 33 1 41 41 12 34
Fax 00 33 1 41 41 28 40
Website www.tf1.fr

Germany
ARD – Das Erste
ARD Büro, Bertramstr 8, 60320 Frankfurt am
Main
☎00 49 69 59 0607   Fax 00 49 69 15 52075
Website www.ard.de

ZDF (Zweites Deutsches Fernsehen)
Postfach 4040, 55100 Mainz
☎00 49 61 31/701   Fax 00 49 61 31 702157
Email info@zdf.de
Website www.zdf.de

Republic of Ireland
Radio Telefís Éireann (RTE – RTE 1)
Donnybrook, Dublin 4
☎00 353 1 208 3111
Fax 00 353 1 208 3080
Website www.rte.ie

Teilefís na Gaelige
Baile na hAbhann, Co. na Gaillimhe
☎00 353 91 505050   Fax 00 353 91 505021
Website www.tg4.ie

Italy
RAI (RadioTelevisione Italiana)
Viale Mazzini 14, 00195 Rome
☎00 39 06 38781   Fax 00 39 06 3226070
Website www.rai.it

Tele piu' (pay TV)
Via Piranesi 44/a, 20137 Milan
☎00 39 02 700 271
Fax 00 39 02 700 27201
Website www.telepiu.it

The Netherlands
AVRO (Algemene Omroep Vereniging)
Postbus 2, 1200 JA Hilversum
☎00 31 35 671 79 11
Fax 00 31 35 671 74 39
Website www.omroep.nl/avro

IKON
Postbus 10009, 1201 DA Hilversum
☎00 31 35 672 72 72
Fax 00 31 35 621 51 00
Email ikon@ikon.nl
Website www.omroep.nl/ikon

NCRV (Nederlandse Christelijke Radio Vereniging)
Postbus 25000, 1202 HB Hilversum
☎00 31 35 671 99 11
Fax 00 31 35 671 92 85
Website www.ncrv.nl

NOS (Nederlandse Omroep Stichting)
Postbus 26600, 1202 JT Hilversum
☎00 31 35 677 92 22   Fax 00 31 35 624 20 23
Website www.omroep.nl/nos/noshome/
index.html

NPS (Nederlandse Programma Stichting)
Postbus 29000, 1202 MA Hilversum
☎00 31 35 677 9333   Fax 00 31 35 677 4959
Email publiek@nps.nl
Website www.omroep.nl/nps

TROS (Televisie en Radio Omroep Stichting)
Postbus 28450, 1202 LL Hilversum
☎00 31 35 671 57 15   Fax 00 31 35 671 52 36
Website www.omroep.nl/tros

VARA
Postbus 175, 1200 AD Hilversum
☎00 31 35 671 19 11   Fax 00 31 35 671 13 33
Email vara@vara.nl
Website www.omroep.nl/vara

VPRO
Postbus 11, 1200 JC Hilversum
☎00 31 35 671 29 11   Fax 00 31 35 671 22 54
Email info@vpro.nl
Website www.vpro.nl

Norway

NRK (Norsk Rikskringkasting)
N–0340 Oslo
☎00 47 23 04 7000   Fax 00 47 23 04 7575
Email info@nrk.no
Website www.nrk.no

TVNorge
Sagveien 17, N–0459 Oslo 4
☎00 47 22 38 7800   Fax 00 47 22 35 1000
Website www.tvnorge.no

TV2
Postboks 7222, N–5020 Bergen
☎00 47 55 90 8070   Fax 00 47 55 90 8090
Website www.tv2.no

Portugal

Radiotelevisão Portuguesa (RTP)
Avenida 5 de Outubro 197, 1050–054 Lisbon
☎00 351 21 794 7000
Email rtp@rtp.pt
Website www.rtp.pt

TVI (Televisão Independente)
Rua Mário Castelhano 40, Queluz de Baixo,
2749–502 Barcarena
☎00 351 21 434 7500
Fax 00 351 21 434 7654
Website www.tvi.pt

Spain

RTVE (RadioTelevision Española)
Edificio Prado del Rey, E–28223 Madrid
☎00 349 1 581 7238   Fax 00 349 1 581 7239
Website www.rtve.es

TVE (Televisión Española, SA)
C/ Alcalde Saénz de Baranda 92, 28036
Madrid
☎00 349 1 346 4000   Fax 00 349 1 346 8533
Website www.tve.es

Sweden

Sveriges Television AB – SVT
S–105 15 Stockholm
☎00 46 8 784 0000   Fax 00 46 8 784 1500
Website www.svt.se

TV4
Tegeluddsvägen 5, S–11579 Stockholm
☎00 46 8 459 4000   Fax 00 46 8 459 4444
Website www.tv4.se

Switzerland

RTR (Radio e Television Rumantscha) (Romansch language TV)
Via dal Teater 1, CH–7002 Cuira
☎00 41 81 255 7575   Fax 00 41 81 255 7500

RTSI (Radiotelevisione svizzera di lingua Italiana) (Italian language TV)
Casella postale, CH–6903 Lugarno
☎00 41 91 803 51 11   Fax 00 41 91 803 5355
Email info@rtsi
Website www.rtsi.ch

SF DRS (Schweizer Fernsehen) (German language TV)
Fernsehenstrasse 1–4, CH–8052 Zurich
☎00 41 1 305 66 11   Fax 00 41 1 305 56 60
Email sfdrs@sfdrs
Website www.sfdrs.ch

SRG SSR idée suisse (Swiss Broadcasting Corp.)
Giacomettistr 3, CH–3000 Berne15
☎00 41 31 350 91 11   Fax 00 41 31 350 92 56
Website www.srg-ssr.ch

TSR (Télévision Suisse Romande)
Quai Ernest Ansermet 20,
CH–1211 Geneva 8
☎00 41 22 708 99 11
Fax 00 41 22 708 98 00

US Publishers

International Reply Coupons (IRCs)
For return postage, send IRCs, available from post offices. Letters, 60 pence;
mss according to weight.

ABC–CLIO
PO Box 1911, Santa Barbara CA 93116–1911
☎001 805 968 1911 Fax 001 805 685 9685
Email library@abc-clio.com
Website www.abc-clio.com
Vice-President/Publisher *Rolf A Janke*

FOUNDED 1953. *Publishes* academic and reference, focusing on history and social studies;
books and multimedia. No unsolicited mss;
synopses and ideas welcome.

    Royalties paid annually. *UK subsidiary* **ABC-
Clio Ltd**, Oxford.

Abingdon Press
201 Eighth Avenue South, Box 801, Nashville
TN 37202–0801
☎001 615 749 6404 Fax 001 615 749 6512
Website www.umph.org
Editorial Director *Harriett Jane Olson*

Publishes non-fiction: religious (lay and professional), children's religious and academic texts.
Over 100 titles a year. Approach in writing only
with synopsis and samples; ms submission guidelines available on the website. IRCs essential.

Harry N. Abrams, Inc.
100 Fifth Avenue, New York NY 10011
☎001 212 206 7715 Fax 001 212 645 8437
Editor-in-Chief *Eric Himmel*

FOUNDED 1950. *Publishes* illustrated books: art,
architecture, nature, entertainment and children's. No fiction. Submit completed mss (no
dot matrix), together with sample illustrations.

Academy Chicago Publishers
363 W. Erie Street, Chicago IL 60610
☎001 312 751 7300 Fax 001 312 751 7306
Email academy363@aol.com
Website www.academychicago.com
President/Senior Editor *Anita Miller*

FOUNDED 1975. *Publishes* quality mainstream
fiction; non-fiction: history, books for women.
No romance, children's, young adult, religious,
sexist or avant-garde. Send first three consecutive chapters with synopsis only, accompanied
by IRCs.

Royalties paid twice-yearly. *Distributed* in the
UK and Europe by Gazelle, Lancaster.

Access Press
See **HarperCollins Publishers, Inc.**

Ace/Putnam
See **Penguin Putnam Inc.**

Adams Media Corporation
260 Center Street, Holbrook MA 02343
☎001 781 767 8100 Fax 001 781 767 0994
Website www.adamsmedia.com
**Director of Series and Single Title
  Publishing** *Gary M. Krebs*

FOUNDED 1980. *Publishes* general non-fiction:
careers, business, personal finance, relationships, parenting, self-improvement, reference,
cooking and fitness. Send query letter with
IRCs.

Addison-Wesley
1185 Avenue of the Americas, New York,
NY 10036
☎001 212 782 3352 Fax 001 212 782 3313
Website www.awl.com
Acquisitons Editor (Education) *Aurora
  Martinez*

One of the world's largest educational publishers of books, multimedia and learning programmes. A division of Pearson Education.
Imprints **Addison-Wesley**; **Longman**;
Benjamin Cummings; **Allyn & Bacon**.

University of Alabama Press
Box 870380, Tuscaloosa AL 35487–0380
☎001 205 348 5180 Fax 001 205 348 9201
Director *Nicole Mitchell*

FOUNDED 1945. *Publishes* American history,
southern history and culture, American religious
history; Latin American history, American/
southeastern archaeology, mesoamerican archaeology, thenohistory, American literature and
criticism, rhetoric and communication, literary
journalism, African-American studies, Native
American studies, women's studies, Judaic

studies, public administration, theatre, natural history and environmental studies, regional studies of Alabama and the Southern states. Submissions are not invited in poetry, fiction or drama. About 50 titles a year.

Aladdin Books
See **Simon & Schuster Children's Publishing**

University of Alaska Press
PO Box 756240, University of Alaska, Fairbanks AK 99775–6240
☎001 907 474 5831 Fax 001 907 474 5502
Email fypress@uaf.edu
Website www.uaf.edu/uapress
Director *Claus. M. Naske*
Senior Editor *Carla Helfferich*
Acquisitions *Pam Odom*

Traces its origins back to 1927 but was relatively dormant until the early 1980s. *Publishes* scholarly works about Alaska and the North Pacific rim, with a special emphasis on circumpolar regions. 5–10 titles a year. No fiction or poetry.

DIVISIONS
Ramuson Library Historical Translation Series *Marvin Falk*; **Oral Biography Series** *William Schneider*; **Monograph Series** *Carla Helfferich*; **Classic Reprint Series** *Terrence Cole*; **Lanternlight Library** Informal non-fiction covering Northern interest. Unsolicited mss, synopses and ideas welcome.

Allen Lane The Penguin Press
See **Penguin Putnam Inc.**

Allyn & Bacon
See **Addison-Wesley**

AMACOM Books
1601 Broadway, New York NY 10019–7406
☎001 212 586 8100 Fax 001 212 903 8083
Email hkennedy@amanet.org
Website www.amanet.org
President & Publisher *Harold V. Kennedy*

FOUNDED 1972. Owned by American Management Association. *Publishes* business books only, including general management, business communications, sales and marketing, finance, computers and information systems, human resource management and training, career/personal growth skills, research development, project management and manufacturing, quality/customer service titles. 65–70 titles a year. Proposals welcome.
Royalties paid twice-yearly.

Amistad
See **HarperCollins Publishers, Inc.**

Anvil
See **Krieger Publishing Co.**

Archway Paperbacks
See **Pocket Books**

University of Arizona Press
355 S. Euclid Avenue, Ste. 103, Tucson AZ 85719
☎001 520 621 1441 Fax 001 520 621 8899
Website www.uapress.arizona.edu
Director *Christine Szuter*

FOUNDED 1959. *Publishes* academic non-fiction, particularly with a regional/cultural link, plus Native-American and Hispanic literature. About 50 titles a year.

University of Arkansas Press
McIlroy House, 201 Ozark Avenue, Fayetteville AR 72701
☎001 501 575 3246 Fax 001 501 575 6044
Website www.uapress.com
Director *Lawrence J. Malley*

FOUNDED 1980. *Publishes* scholarly monographs, poetry and general trade including biography, etc. Particularly interested at present in scholarly works in history, politics and literary criticism. About 30 titles a year.
Royalties paid annually.

Aspect
See **Warner Books Inc.**

Atheneum Books for Young Readers
See **Simon & Schuster Children's Publishing**

Atlantic Monthly Press
See **Grove/Atlantic Inc.**

AUP (Associated University Presses)
AUP New Jersey titles are handled in the UK by **Golden Cockerel Press** (see entry under **UK Publishers**).

Avery Publishing Group, Inc.
375 Hudson Street, New York NY 10014
☎001 212 366 2000 Fax 001 212 366 2666
Website www.penguinputnam.com
President *Rudy Shur*

FOUNDED 1976. Imprint of **Penguin Putnam**

Inc. *Publishes* professional and trade books, specialising in childbirth education, health, self-help, nutrition, psychiatry, how-to, government; college textbooks in history, science, mathematics, military science and history, technology and social science. About 50 titles a year. No unsolicited mss; synopses and ideas welcome if accompanied by s.a.e.

Royalties paid twice-yearly.

Avon Books
10 East 53rd Street, New York NY 10022
☎001 212 207 7000 Fax 001 212 207 7203
Website www.harpercollins.com

Senior Vice President/Publisher *Lou Aronica*

FOUNDED 1941. An imprint of **HarperCollins Publishers, Inc.** *Publishes* hardcover; trade and mass-market paperback reprints and originals including fiction, non-fiction, adult, juvenile and young adult. 500 titles a year. Submit query letter and sample chapter.

Baker Book House
PO Box 6287, Grand Rapids MI 49516–6287
☎001 616 676 9185 Fax 001 616 676 9573
Website www.bakerbooks.com

President *Dwight Baker*
Director of Publications *Don Stephenson*

FOUNDED 1939. Began life as a used-book store and began publishing in earnest in the 1950s, primarily serving the evangelical Christian market. About 165 titles a year. Additional information for authors on website.

DIVISIONS/IMPRINTS

Baker Books *Publishes* religious non-fiction and fiction, Bible reference, professional (pastors and church leaders) books, children's books. About 80 titles a year. Proposals welcome (request guidelines, specifying non-fiction, fiction, professional or children's).

Baker Academic *Jim Kinney Publishes* college/seminary textbooks, religious reference books, biblical studies monographs. About 30 titles a year. Proposals welcome (guidelines available on request). No unsolicited mss. **Fleming H. Revell** *Lonnie Hull Du Pont* FOUNDED 1870. A family-owned business until 1978, Revell was one of the first Christian publishers to take the step into secular publishing. Joined Baker Book House in 1992. *Publishes* adult fiction and non-fiction for evangelical Christians. About 45 titles a year. Synopses and ideas welcome. **Brazos Press** *Rodney Clapp Publishes* academic and trade books in theology, biblical studies, ethics, cultural criticism and spirituality (trade editions only). About 15 titles a year. No unsolicited mss.

Chosen Books *Jane Campbell* FOUNDED 1971; joined Baker Book House in 1992. *Publishes* charismatic adult non-fiction for evangelical Christians. About 10 titles a year. Synopses or ideas welcome.

Royalties paid twice-yearly.

Ballantine Publishing Group
1540 Broadway, 11th Floor, New York NY 10036 Fax 001 212 782 8439
Website www.randomhouse.com

President/Publisher *Gina Centrello*

FOUNDED 1952. A division of **Random House, Inc.** since 1973. *Publishes* fiction and non-fiction, science fiction.

DIVISIONS/IMPRINTS **Ballantine Books**; **Del Rey**; **Fawcett Books**; **Ivy**; **Library of Contemporary Thought**; **One World**; **Wellspring**. No unsolicited mss.

Banner Books
See **University Press of Mississippi**

Bantam Dell Publishing Group
1540 Broadway, New York NY 10036
☎001 212 782 9000 Fax 001 212 302 7985

President/Publisher *Irwyn Applebaum*

FOUNDED 1945. The largest mass market paperback publisher in the USA. A division of **Random House, Inc.** *Publishes* general commercial fiction and non-fiction, young readers and children's.

DIVISIONS/IMPRINTS **Bantam Hardcover**; **Bantam Classics**; **Bantam Mass Market**; **Bantam Trade Paperback**; **Delacorte Press**; **Dell**; **Delta**; **Dial Press**; **DTP**; **Island**.

Barron's Educational Series, Inc.
250 Wireless Boulevard, Hauppauge NY 11788–3917
☎001 516 434 3311 Fax 001 516 434 3723
Email info@barronseduc.com
Website www.barronseduc.com

President *Manuel H. Barron*
Managing Editor *Mark Miele*
Acquisitions Editor *Wayne Barr*

FOUNDED 1942. *Publishes* adult non-fiction, children's fiction and non-fiction, test preparation materials and language materials, cookbooks, pets, hobbies, sport, photography, health, business, law, computers, travel, business, art and painting. No adult fiction. 150 titles a year. Unsolicited mss, synopses and ideas for books welcome.

Royalties paid twice-yearly.

Beacon Press

25 Beacon Street, Boston MA 02108
☎001 617 742 2110   Fax 001 617 723 3097
Website www.beacon.org

Director *Helene Atwan*

FOUNDED 1854. *Publishes* general non-fiction. About 85 titles a year. Does not accept unsolicited mss. For further information, refer to website page.

Belknap Press

See **Harvard University Press**

Berkley Books

See **Penguin Putnam Inc.**

H. & R. Block

See **Simon & Schuster Trade Division**

BlueHen Books

See **Penguin Putnam Inc.**

Boulevard

See **Penguin Putnam Inc.**

Boyds Mills Press

815 Church Street, Honesdale PA 18431
☎001 570 253 1164   Fax 001 570 253 0179
Website www.boydsmillspress.com

Publisher *Kent Brown Jr*
Manuscript Coordinator *Beth Troop*

A subsidiary of Highlights for Children, Inc. FOUNDED 1990 as a publisher of children's trade books. *Publishes* children's fiction, non-fiction and poetry. About 50 titles a year. Unsolicited mss, synopses and ideas for books welcome. No romance or fantasy novels.
Royalties paid twice-yearly.

Bradford Books

See **The MIT Press**

Brassey's, Inc.

22841 Quicksilver Drive, Dulles VA 20166
☎001 703 661 1562   Fax 001 703 661 1547
Email djacobs@bookintl.com

Publisher *Don McKeon*
Senior Assistant Editor *Donald Jacobs*

FOUNDED 1983. *Publishes* non-fiction titles on topics of history (especially military history), world and US affairs, US foreign policy, defence, intelligence, biography, transport (especially automobiles) and sports. About 80 titles a year. No unsolicited mss; synopses and ideas welcome.
Royalties paid annually.

Brazos Press

See **Baker Book House**

Broadway Books

See **Doubleday Broadway Publishing Group**

University of California Press

2120 Berkeley Way, Berkeley CA 94720
☎001 510 642 4247   Fax 001 510 643 7127

Director *James H. Clark*

Publishes scholarly and scientific non-fiction; some fiction and poetry in translation. Preliminary letter with outline preferred.

Carolrhoda Books, Inc.

241 First Avenue North, Minneapolis MN 55401
☎001 612 332 3344   Fax 001 612 332 7615

Editor-in-Chief *Mary M. Rodgers*

FOUNDED 1969. *Publishes* children's: nature, biography, history, beginners' readers, world cultures, photo essays and historical fiction. Please send s.a.e. for author guidelines, making sure guideline requests are clearly marked on the envelope or they will be returned. 'We are *only* accepting submissions twice a year – from March 1–31 and October 1–31. Submissions postmarked with other dates will be returned unopened. Also, only submissions with s.a.e. will receive a response.'

Chapman & Hall

See **Kluwer Academic Publishers**

Charlesbridge Publishing

85 Main Street, Watertown MA 02472
☎001 617 926 0329   Fax 001 617 926 5720
Email books@charlesbridge.com
Website www.charlesbridge.com

Chairman *Brent Farmer*
Managing Editor, School Division *Elena Dworkin Wright*
Senior Editor, Trade Division *Dominic Barth*

FOUNDED 1980 as an educational publisher focusing on teaching reading and math processes. *Publishes* children's educational programmes, non-fiction picture books and fiction for 3- to 12-year-olds. Also publishes mathematical stories, *Maths Adventures*, in picture-book format. Complete mss or proposals welcome with self-addressed envelope and IRCs. Unsolicited mss are accepted but must be exclusive submissions. Responses are sent within three months.

University of Chicago Press
5801 South Ellis Avenue, Fourth Floor,
Chicago IL 60637
☎001 773 702 7700   Fax 001 773 702 9756
Email general@press.uchicago.edu
Website www.press.uchicago.edu

FOUNDED 1891. *Publishes* academic non-fiction
only.

Children's Press
See **Grolier Publishing**

Chosen Books
See **Baker Book House**

Chronicle Books LLC
85 Second Street, Sixth Floor, San Francisco
CA 94105
☎001 415 537 3730   Fax 001 415 537 4440
Website www.chroniclebooks.com

President/Publisher *Jack Jensen*

FOUNDED 1966. *Publishes* illustrated and non-
illustrated adult trade and children's books as
well as stationery and gift items. About 200
titles a year. Query or submit outline/synopsis
and sample chapters and artwork. Guidelines
for ms submissions on the website.
Royalties paid twice-yearly.

Clarkson Potter
See **Crown Publishing Group**

Cliff Street Books
See **HarperCollins Publishers, Inc.**

Contemporary Books
4255 West Touhy Avenue, Lincolnwood
IL 60712–1975
☎001 847 679 5500   Fax 001 847 679 2494

Vice-President/Publisher *John Nolan*

FOUNDED 1947. *Publishes* general adult non-
fiction. About 400 titles a year. Submissions
require s.a.e./IRCs for response.

Copper Beech Books
See **The Millbrook Press, Inc.**

Crown Publishing Group
299 Park Avenue, New York NY 10171
☎001 212 572 2600   Fax 001 212 572 6161
Website www.randomhouse.com

President/Publisher *Chip Gibson*

FOUNDED 1933. Division of **Random House,
Inc.** *Publishes* popular trade fiction and non-
fiction.

IMPRINTS **Clarkson Potter** *Lauren Shakely*;
Harmony; **Three Rivers Press** *Linda
Loewenthal*; **Crown** *Steve Ross*.

Benjamin Cummings
See **Addison-Wesley**

Currency
See **Doubleday Broadway Publishing
Group**

DAW Books, Inc.
375 Hudson Street, 3rd Floor, New York
NY 10014–3658
☎001 212 366 2096/Submissions: 366 2095
Fax 001 212 366 2090
Email daw@penguinputnam.com
Website www.dawbooks.com

Publishers *Elizabeth R. Wollheim, Sheila E.
Gilbert*
Submissions Editor *Peter Stampfel*

FOUNDED 1971 by Donald and Elsie Wollheim
as the first mass-market publisher devoted to science fiction and fantasy. *Publishes* science fic-
tion/fantasy, and some horror. No short stories,
anthology ideas or non-fiction. Unsolicited mss,
synopses and ideas for books welcome. About 36
titles a year.
Royalties paid twice-yearly.

Dearborn Financial Publishing, Inc.
155 N. Wacker Drive, Chicago IL 60606–1719
☎001 312 836 4400   Fax 001 312 836 1021
Website www.dearborn.com

President *Eric Cantor*

FOUNDED 1967. A niche publisher serving the
financial services industries. *Publishes* real estate,
insurance, financial planning, securities, com-
modities, investments, banking, professional
education, motivation and reference titles,
investment reference and how-to books for the
consumer (personal finance, real estate) and
small business owner. About 150 titles a year.

DIVISIONS/IMPRINTS   **Trade/Professional**
Cynthia Zigmund; **Securities Training** *Marcia
Burak*; **Insurance** *Dan Trombley*; **Textbook:
Real Estate Education Company** *Roy Lipner*.
Unsolicited mss, synopses and ideas welcome.
Royalties paid twice-yearly.

Del Rey
See **Ballantine Publishing Group**

Delacorte Press
See **Bantam Dell Publishing Group**

Dell
See **Bantam Dell Publishing Group**

Delta
See **Bantam Dell Publishing Group**

Dial Books for Young Readers
345 Hudson Street, New York NY
10014–3657
☎001 212 366 2800

Queries *Submissions Coordinator*

FOUNDED 1961. A division of Penguin Putnam
Books for Young Readers. *Publishes* children's
books, including picture books, beginning
readers, fiction and non-fiction for middle
grade and young adults. 50 titles a year.

IMPRINTS Hardcover only: **Dial Books for
Young Readers**; **Dial Easy-to-Read**. No
unsolicited mss accepted; query letters with
return postage only.

Royalties paid twice-yearly.

Dial Press
See **Bantam Dell Publishing Group**

Doubleday Broadway Publishing Group
1540 Broadway, New York NY 10036
☎001 212 782 9000   Fax 001 212 302 7985
Website www.randomhouse.com

President & Publisher *Stephen Rubin*

The Doubleday Broadway Publishing Group, a
division of **Random House, Inc.** was formed
by a merger of Doubleday and Broadway Books
in 1999. *Publishes* fiction and non-fiction.

DIVISION/IMPRINTS **Broadway Books**;
Currency; **Doubleday**; **Doubleday Religious
Publishing**; **Doubleday/Image**; **Harlem
Moon**; **Nan A. Talese**. No unsolicited material.

Lisa Drew Books
See **Simon & Schuster Trade Division**

DTP
See **Bantam Dell Publishing Group**

Thomas Dunne Books
See **St Martin's Press LLC**

Sanford J. Durst Publications
11 Clinton Avenue, Rockville Centre, New
York NY 11570
☎001 516 766 4444   Fax 001 516 766 4520

Owner *Sanford J. Durst*

FOUNDED 1975. *Publishes* non-fiction: numis-
matic and related, philatelic, legal and art. Also
children's books. About 12 titles a year.

Royalties paid twice-yearly.

Dushkin/McGraw-Hill
See **The McGraw-Hill Companies, Inc.**

Dutton/Dutton's Children's Books
See **Penguin Putnam Inc.**

The Ecco Press
See **HarperCollins Publishers, Inc.**

Edge Books
See **Henry Holt & Company Inc.**

William B. Eerdmans Publishing Co.
255 Jefferson Avenue SE, Grand Rapids
MI 49503
☎001 616 459 4591   Fax 001 616 459 6540
Email sales@eerdmans.com
Website www.eerdmans.com

President *William B. Eerdmans Jr*
Vice President/Editor-in-Chief *Jon Pott*

FOUNDED 1911 as a theological and reference
publisher. Gradually began publishing in other
genres with authors like C.S. Lewis, Dorothy
Sayers and Malcolm Muggeridge on its lists.
Publishes religious: theology, biblical studies,
ethical and social concern, social criticism and
children's, religious history, religion and literature. 120 titles in 2000.

DIVISIONS **Children's** *Judy Zylstra*; **Other** *Jon
Pott*. Unsolicited mss, synopses and ideas welcome.

Royalties paid twice-yearly.

Eos
See **HarperCollins Publishers, Inc.**

M. Evans & Co., Inc.
216 East 49th Street, New York NY 10017
☎001 212 688 2810   Fax 001 212 486 4544
Email mevans@sprynet.com

President *George C. de Kay*

FOUNDED 1954 as a packager. Began publishing in 1962. Best known for its popular psychology and health books, with titles like *Dr
Atkins' New Diet Revolution*, *This is How Love
Works*, *Bragging Rights* and *Robert Crayhan's
Nutrition Made Simple*. *Publishes* general non-
fiction and fiction. About 30 titles a year. No
unsolicited mss; query first. Synopses and ideas
welcome.

Royalties paid twice-yearly.

Everyman's Library
See **Random House, Inc.**

Faber & Faber, Inc.
19 Union Square West, New York
NY 10003
☎001 212 741 6900 Fax 001 212 633 9385
Editor *Denise Oswald*

FOUNDED 1976. An affiliate of **Farrar, Straus & Giroux, Inc.** *Publishes* primarily non-fiction books for adults with a focus on film, theatre, music, and literary and cultural criticism. Unsolicited mss accepted; please query first and include IRCs with letter.
Royalties paid twice-yearly.

Facts On File, Inc.
11 Penn Plaza, New York NY 10001
☎001 212 967 8800 Fax 001 212 967 9196
President *Mark McDonnell*
Publisher *Laurie E. Likoff*

Started life in the early 1940s with News Digest subscription series to libraries. Began publishing on specific subjects with the Checkmark Books series and developed its current reference and trade book programme in the 1970s. *Publishes* general trade, young adult trade and academic reference for the school and library markets. *Specialises* in single subject encyclopedias. About 135 titles a year. No fiction, cookery or popular non-fiction.

DIVISIONS

General Reference *Laurie Likoff*; **Academic Reference** *Owen Lancer*; **Adult Trade** *James Chambers*; **Young Adult & US History** *Nicole Bowen*; **Electronic Publishing** *James Housley*; **Literary Studies** *Anne Savarese*. Unsolicited synopses and ideas welcome; no mss. Send query letter in the first instance.
Royalties paid twice-yearly.

Farrar, Straus & Giroux, Inc.
19 Union Square West, New York NY 10003
☎001 212 741 6900

FOUNDED 1946. *Publishes* general fiction, non-fiction, juveniles. No unsolicited material.

Fawcett Books
See **Ballantine Publishing Group**

Fireside
See **Simon & Schuster Trade Division**

Fodor's Travel Publications
See **Random House, Inc.**

Phyllis Fogelman Books
See **Penguin Putnam Inc.**

Forge
See **St Martin's Press LLC**

The Free Press
See **Simon & Schuster Trade Division**

Samuel French, Inc.
45 West 25th Street, New York
NY 10010–2751
☎001 212 206 8990 Fax 001 212 206 1429
Email samuelfrench@earthlink.net
Website www.samuelfrench.com
Senior Editor *Lawrence Harbison*

FOUNDED 1830. *Publishes* plays in paperback: Broadway and off-Broadway hits, light comedies, mysteries, one-act plays and plays for young audiences. Unsolicited mss welcome. No synopses.
Royalties paid annually (books); twice-yearly (amateur productions); monthly (professional productions). *Overseas associates* in London, Toronto, Sydney and Johannesburg.

The Globe Pequot Press
PO Box 480, Guildford CT 06437
☎001 203 458 4500 Fax 001 203 458 4604
President *Linda Kennedy*
Associate Publisher *Michael K. Urban*

Publishes regional and international travel, how-to, regional and outdoor recreation. Also publishes the *Insiders'* guides. About 250 titles a year. Unsolicited mss, synopses and ideas welcome, particularly for travel and outdoor recreation books.
Royalties paid 'occasionally'.

Great Source Education Group
See **Houghton Mifflin Co.**

Griffin
See **St Martin's Press LLC**

Grolier Publishing
90 Sherman Turnpike, Danbury CT 06816
☎001 203 797 3500 Fax 001 203 797 3197
Website www.grolier.com
President *Joseph Tessitore*

FOUNDED 1895. Acquired by **Scholastic, Inc.** in 2000. *Publishes* juvenile non-fiction, encyclopedias, speciality reference sets, children's fiction and picture books. Aout 600 titles a year.
DIVISIONS/IMPRINTS **Children's Press**;

Grolier Educational; Grolier Interactive; Grolier Reference; Orchard Books.

Grosset & Dunlap/Grosset Putnam
See **Penguin Putnam Inc.**

Grove/Atlantic Inc.
841 Broadway, New York NY 10003–4793
☎001 212 614 7850 Fax 001 212 614 7886
President/Publisher *Morgan Entrekin*
Managing Editor *Michael Hornburg*
FOUNDED 1952. *Publishes* general fiction and non-fiction. IMPRINTS **Atlantic Monthly Press**; **Grove Press**.

Gulliver Books
See **Harcourt Children's Books Division**

Harcourt Children's Books Division
525 B Street, Suite 1900, San Diego CA 92101–4495
☎001 619 231 6616 Fax 001 619 699 6777
Website www.harcourt.com
Vice President/Publisher *Louise Pelan*

A division of Harcourt Inc. *Publishes* fiction, poetry and non-fiction covering a wide range of subjects: biography, environment and ecology, history, travel, science and current affairs for children and young adults. About 175 titles a year.
IMPRINTS **Gulliver Books**; **Harcourt Children's Books**; **Harcourt Paperbacks**; **Odyssey Paperbacks** Novels; **Red Wagon Books** For ages 6 months to 3 years; **Voyager Paperbacks** Picture books; **Silver Whistle**. No unsolicited mss.

Harlem Moon
See **Doubleday Broadway Publishing Group**

Harlequin Historicals
See **Silhouette Books**

Harmony
See **Crown Publishing Group**

HarperCollins Publishers, Inc.
10 East 53rd Street, New York NY 10022
☎001 212 207 7000 Fax 001 212 207 6968
Website www.harpercollins.com
President/Chief Executive Officer *Jane Friedman*
FOUNDED 1817. Owned by News Corporation. *Publishes* general and literary fiction, general non-fiction, business, children's, reference and religious books. No unsolicited material.
DIVISIONS/IMPRINTS
Adult Trade; **HarperCollins/HarperCollins Children's Books**; **HarperBusiness**; **Harper-Resource** (reference); **HarperEntertainment**; **HarperAudio**; **Avon Books** (see entry); **Amistad**; **Access Press**; **Eos**; **Cliff Street Books**; **Perennial**; **Quill**; **Regan Books**; **The Ecco Press**; **William Morrow**.
SUBSIDIARY **Zondervan Publishing House** (see entry).

Harvard University Press
79 Garden Street, Cambridge MA 02138–1499
☎001 617 495 2600 Fax 001 617 495 5898
Editor-in-Chief *Aida D. Donald*

FOUNDED 1913. *Publishes* scholarly non-fiction only: general interest, literature, science and behaviour, social science, history, humanities, psychology, political science, sociology, economics, law, business, classics, religion, cultural studies, philosophy, history of science, history of nature, African-American studies. Free book catalogue available. IMPRINT **Belknap Press**.

Hill Street Press
191 E. Broad Street, Suite 209, Athens GA 30601–2848
☎001 706 613 7200 Fax 001 706 613 7204
Email info@hillstreetpress.com
Senior Editor *Patrick Allen*

FOUNDED 1998. *Publishes* books on the American South – fiction and non-fiction: literary history/criticism, memoirs, history, current issues, cookery. No poetry, erotica, romance, children's or young adults. 20 titles in 2000. Unsolicited material welcome; approach in writing in the first instance.
Royalties paid twice-yearly.

Hippocrene Books, Inc.
171 Madison Avenue, New York NY 10016
☎001 212 685 4371 Fax 001 212 779 9338
Website www.hippocrenebooks.com
President/Editorial Director *George Blagowidow*

FOUNDED 1971. *Publishes* general non-fiction and reference books. Particularly strong on foreign language dictionaries, language studies, military history and international cookbooks. No fiction. Send brief summary, table of contents and one chapter for appraisal. S.a.e. essential for response. For manuscript return include sufficient postage cover (IRCs).

Holiday House, Inc.
425 Madison Avenue, New York NY 10017
☎001 212 688 0085 Fax 001 212 421 6134
Vice President/Editor-in-Chief *Regina Griffin*

Publishes children's general fiction and non-fiction (pre-school to secondary). About 50 titles a year. Send query letters only. IRCs for reply must be included.

Henry Holt & Company Inc.
115 West 18th Street, New York NY 10011
☎001 212 886 9200 Fax 001 212 633 0748
Website www.henryholt.com
President/Publisher *John Sterling*
Executive Editor, Adult Trade *David Sobel*
Executive Editor, Books for Young Readers *Nina Ignatowicz*

FOUNDED in 1866, Henry Holt is one of the oldest publishers in the United States. Part of Holtzbrinck Publishing Holdings. *Publishes* fiction, by both American and international authors, biographies, and books on history and politics, ecology and psychology. 230 titles a year. DIVISIONS/IMPRINTS **Adult Trade**; **Books for Young Readers**; **Edge Books**; **John Macrae Books** *John Macrae*; **Bill Martin Jr Books**; **Metropolitan Books** *Sara Bershtel*; **Owl Books**; **Red Feather Books**.

Houghton Mifflin Co.
222 Berkeley Street, Boston
MA 02116–3764
☎001 617 351 5000 Fax 001 617 351 1125
Website www.hmco.com
Contact *Submissions Editor*

FOUNDED 1832. *Publishes* literary fiction and general non-fiction, including autobiography, biography and history. Also school and college textbooks; children's fiction and non-fiction. Average 100 titles a year. Queries only for adult material; synopses, outline and sample chapters for children's non-fiction; complete mss for children's fiction. IRCs required with all submissions/queries.

DIVISIONS/SUBSIDIARIES **Houghton Mifflin College Division**; **Houghton Mifflin School Division**; **Houghton Mifflin Trade & Reference Division**; **Great Source Education Group**; **McDougal Littell Inc.**; **The Riverside Publishing Co.**; **Sunburst Technology** (multimedia and video).

HP Books
See **Penguin Putnam Inc.**

Hudson River Editions
See **Simon & Schuster Trade Division**

University of Illinois Press
1325 South Oak Street, Champaign
IL 61820–6903
☎001 217 333 0950 Fax 001 217 244 8082
Email uipress@uillinois.edu
Website www.press.uillinois.edu
Editorial Director *Willis Regier*

Publishes non-fiction, scholarly and general, with special interest in Americana, women's studies, African–American studies, American music and regional books. About 140–150 titles a year.

Image
See **Doubleday Broadway Publishing Group**

Indiana University Press
601 North Morton Street, Bloomington
IN 47404–3797
☎001 812 855 8817 Fax 001 812 855 8507
Email iupress@indiana.edu
Website www.indiana.edu/~iupress
Director *Peter-John Leone*

Publishes scholarly non-fiction in the following subject areas: African studies, anthropology, Asian studies, Afro-American studies, environment and ecology, film, folklore, history, Jewish studies, literary criticism, medical ethics, Middle East studies, military, music, paleontology, philanthropy, philosophy, politics, religion, semiotics, Russian and East European studies, Victorian studies, women's studies. Query in writing in first instance.

University of Iowa Press
Kuhl House, 119 West Park Road, Iowa City
IA 52242
☎001 319 335 2000 Fax 001 319 335 2055
Website www.uiowa.edu/~uipress
Director *Holly Carver*

FOUNDED 1969 as a small scholarly press publishing about five books a year. Now publishing about 35 a year in a variety of scholarly fields, plus local interest, short stories, creative non-fiction and poetry. No unsolicited mss; query first. Unsolicited ideas and synopses welcome.
Royalties paid annually.

Iowa State University Press
2121 South State Avenue, Ames IA 50010
☎001 515 292 0140 Fax 001 515 292 3348
Email vanhouten@isupress.com

Website www.isupress.com

Publishing Director *Gretchen Van Houten*

FOUNDED 1934 as an offshoot of the university's journalism department. Now a **Blackwell Science Ltd** company. *Publishes* reference books and textbooks, agriculture, aviation, food science, dietetics, journalism, and veterinary medicine. No fiction, trade books or poetry.

Royalties paid annually.

Island
See **Bantam Dell Publishing Group**

Ivy
See **Ballantine Publishing Group**

Jove
See **Penguin Putnam Inc.**

University Press of Kansas
2501 West 15th Street, Lawrence KS 66049–3905
☎001 785 864 4154 Fax 001 785 864 4586
Email mail@newpress.upress.ukans.edu
Website www.kansaspress.ku.edu

Director *Fred M. Woodward*

FOUNDED 1946. Became the publishing arm for all six state universities in Kansas in 1976. *Publishes* scholarly books in American history studies, legal studies, presidential studies, social and political philosophy, political science, military history and environmental. About 50 titles a year. Proposals welcome.

Royalties paid annually.

Jean Karl Books
See **Simon & Schuster Children's Publishing**

Kent State University Press
Kent OH 44242–0001
☎001 330 672 7913 Fax 001 330 672 3104

Director *John T. Hubbell*
Editor-in-Chief *Joanna Hildebrand Craig*

FOUNDED 1965. *Publishes* scholarly works in history and biography, literary studies and general non-fiction with an emphasis on American studies. 25–30 titles a year. Queries welcome; no mss.

Royalties paid annually.

Kluwer Academic Publishers
101 Philip Drive, Norwell MA 02061
☎001 781 871 6600 Fax 001 781 871 6528
Email kluwer@wkap.com
Website www.wkap.nl

President *Jeff Smith*
Managing Editor *Claire Stanton*

FOUNDED 1946. *Publishes* scholarly scientific books and journals. Over 300 titles a year. Queries only.

IMPRINTS **Kluwer Academic Publishers/ Plenum Publishers**; **Chapman & Hall** Science and technology.

Knopf Publishing Group
See **Random House, Inc.**

Krieger Publishing Co.
PO Box 9542, Melbourne FL 32902–9542
☎001 321 724 9542 Fax 001 321 951 3671
Email info@krieger-pub.com
Website www.web4u.com/krieger-publishing

Chairman *Robert E. Krieger*
President *Donald E. Krieger*
Vice-President *Maxine D. Krieger*

FOUNDED 1970. *Publishes* science, education, geology, ecology, social sciences, humanities, history, mathematics, psychology, chemistry, space science, technology and engineering.

IMPRINTS/SERIES **Anvil**; **Exploring Community History**; **Open Forum**; **Orbit**; **Professional Practices**; **Public History**. Unsolicited mss welcome. Not interested in synopses/ideas or trade type titles.

Royalties paid yearly.

Lanternlight Library
See **University of Alaska Press**

Lehigh University Press
See **Golden Cockerel Press** under **UK Publishers**

Lerner Publications Co. (A division of Lerner Publishing Group)
241 First Avenue North, Minneapolis MN 55401
☎001 612 332 3344 Fax 001 612 332 7615
Website www.lernerbooks.com

Submissions Editor *Jennifer Zimian*

Publishes primarily non-fiction for readers of all grade levels. List includes titles encompassing nature, geography, natural and physical science, current events, ancient and modern history, world art, special interest, sports, world cultures and numerous biography series. Some young adult and middle grade fiction. No alphabet, puzzle, song or text books, religious subject matter or plays. Submissions are accepted in the months of March and October *only*. Work received in any other month will be returned unopened. S.a.e. required for authors who wish to have their material returned. Please allow two to six months for a response. No phone calls.

Library of Contemporary Thought
See **Ballantine Publishing Group**

Little Simon
See **Simon & Schuster Children's Publishing**

Little, Brown and Company
Adult Trade Division: 1271 Avenue of the Americas, New York NY 10020
☎001 212 522 8700
Website www.twbookmark.com
CHILDREN'S BOOKS DIVISION: 3 Center Plaza, Boston, MA 02108–2084
☎001 617 227 0730
Subsidiary of Time Warner Trade Publishing. FOUNDED 1837. *Publishes* fiction, non-fiction and children's. DIVISIONS
   Adult Trade *Michael Pietsch*, VP/Editor-in-Chief. **Children's Books** *Maria Modugno*, VP/Editorial Director. No unsolicited mss.

Living Language
See **Random House, Inc.**

Llewellyn Publications
PO Box 64383, St Paul MN 55164–0383
☎001 612 291 1970 Fax 001 612 291 1908
Email nancym@llewellyn.com
Website www.llewellyn.com
President/Publisher *Carl L. Weschcke*
Acquisitions Manager *Nancy J. Mostad*

Division of Llewellyn Worldwide Ltd. FOUNDED 1901. *Publishes* self-help and how-to: astrology, alternative health, tantra, Fortean studies, tarot, yoga, Santeria, dream studies, metaphysics, magic, witchcraft, herbalism, shamanism, organic gardening, women's spirituality, graphology, palmistry, parapsychology. Also fiction with an authentic magical or metaphysical theme. About 100 titles a year. Unsolicited mss welcome; proposals preferred. IRCs essential in all cases.

Longman
See **Addison-Wesley**

Louisiana State University Press
Baton Rouge LA 70893
☎001 225 578 6295 Fax 001 225 578 6461

Director *L.E. Phillabaum*
Publishes non-fiction: Southern history, American history, Southern literary criticism, American literary criticism, biography, political science, music (jazz) and Latin American studies. About 80 titles a year. Send IRCs for mss guidelines.

Love Inspired
See **Silhouette Books**

The Lyons Press Inc.
123 West 18th Street, Sixth Floor, New York NY 10011
☎001 212 620 9580 Fax 001 212 929 1836
Website www.lyonspress.com
President/Publisher *Tony Lyons*
Managing Editor *Richard Rothschild*
FOUNDED 1978. *Publishes* general fiction and non-fiction; outdoor, natural history, sports, gardening and angling titles, plus cookery, woodwork and art. About 120 titles a year. No unsolicited mss; synopses and ideas welcome.
   Royalties paid twice-yearly.

McDougal Littell Inc.
See **Houghton Mifflin Co.**

Margaret K. McElderry Books
See **Simon & Schuster Children's Publishing**

McFarland & Company, Inc., Publishers
PO Box 611, Jefferson NC 28640
☎001 336 246 4460 Fax 001 336 246 5018
Email info@mcfarlandpub.com
Website www.mcfarlandpub.com
President/Editor-in-Chief *Robert Franklin*
Vice President *Rhonda Herman*
Senior Editor *Steve Wilson*
Editor *Virginia Tobiassen*
FOUNDED 1979. A library reference and upper-end speciality market press publishing scholarly books in many fields: international studies, performing arts, popular culture, sports, automotive history, women's studies, music and fine arts, chess, history and librarianship. *Specialises* in general reference. Especially strong in cinema studies. No fiction, poetry, children's, New Age or inspirational/devotional works. About 170 titles a year. No unsolicited mss; send query letter first. Synopses and ideas welcome.
   Royalties paid annually.

The McGraw-Hill Companies, Inc.

1221 Avenue of the Americas, New York NY 10020

☎001 212 512 2000

Website www.mcgraw-hill.com

President/CEO *Harold McGraw, III*

Contact *Submissions Editor*

FOUNDED 1873. US parent of the UK-based **McGraw-Hill Publishing Company**. *Publishes* a wide range of educational, professional, business, science, engineering and computing books.

DIVISIONS **Educational & Professional Publishing Group**; **Science, Technology & Medical Group**; **Electronic Publishing**; **Computer Book Group**; **School**; **Higher Education**; **Dushkin/McGraw-Hill**; **McGraw-Hill International Marine Publishing**; **McGraw-Hill/Irwin**; **Osborne/McGraw-Hill**; **Ragged Mountain Press**.

John Macrae Books

See **Henry Holt & Company Inc.**

Magic Attic Press

See **The Millbrook Press, Inc.**

Bill Martin Jr Books

See **Henry Holt & Company Inc.**

University of Massachusetts Press

PO Box 429, Amherst MA 01004–0429

☎001 413 545 2217 Fax 001 413 545 1226

Website www.umass.edu/umpress

Director *Bruce Wilcox*

Senior Editor *Clark Dougan*

FOUNDED 1964. *Publishes* scholarly, general interest, African-American, ethnic, women's and gender studies, cultural criticism, architecture and environmental design, literary criticism, poetry, philosophy, biography, history. Unsolicited mss considered but query letter preferred in the first instance. Synopses and ideas welcome. 40 titles a year.

Royalties paid annually.

Mentor

See **Penguin Putnam Inc.**

Meridian

See **Penguin Putnam Inc.**

Metropolitan Books

See **Henry Holt & Company Inc.**

The Millbrook Press, Inc.

2 Old New Milford Road, PO Box 335, Brookfield CT 06804

☎001 203 740 2220 Fax 001 203 775 5643

Website www.millbrookpress.com

School/Library Publisher *Jean Reynolds*

Publisher (Roaring Brook Press) *Simon Boughton*

Managing Editor *Colleen Seibert*

FOUNDED 1989. *Publishes* mainly non-fiction, children's and young adult, for trade, school and public library. About 150 titles a year.

IMPRINTS **Copper Beech Books**; **Twenty-First Century Books**; **Magic Attic Press**; **Roaring Brook Press**.

Royalties paid twice-yearly.

Minotaur

See **St Martin's Press LLC**

Minstrel Books

See **Pocket Books**

University Press of Mississippi

3825 Ridgewood Road, Jackson MS 39211–6492

☎001 601 432 6205 Fax 001 601 432 6217

Email press@ihl.state.ms.us

Website www.upress.state.ms.us

Director *Seetha Srinivasan*

Editor-in-Chief *Craig Gill*

FOUNDED 1970. Non-profit book publisher partially supported by the eight State universities. *Publishes* scholarly and trade titles in literature, history, American culture, Southern culture, African-American, women's studies, popular culture, folklife, ethnic, performance, art and photography, and other liberal arts. About 60 titles a year.

IMPRINTS **Muscadine Books** *Craig Gill* Regional trade titles. **Banner Books** Paperback reprints of significant fiction and non-fiction. Send letter of enquiry, prospectus, table of contents and sample chapter prior to submission of full mss.

Royalties paid annually. *Represented* worldwide. UK representatives: **Roundhouse Publishing Group**.

University of Missouri Press

2910 LeMone Boulevard, Columbia MO 65201

☎001 573 882 7641 Fax 001 573 884 4498

Website www.system.missouri.edu/upress

Director *Beverly Jarrett*

FOUNDED 1958. *Publishes* academic: history,

literary criticism, intellectual history and related humanities disciplines and short stories – usually four volumes a year. Best approach is by letter. Send one short story for consideration, and synopses for academic work. About 55 titles a year.

The MIT Press
5 Cambridge Ctr., Cambridge MA 02142
☎001 617 253 5646 Fax 001 617 258 6779
Website www.mitpress.org

Editor-in-Chief *Laurence Cohen*

FOUNDED 1961. *Publishes* scholarly and professional, technologically sophisticated books, including computer science and artificial intelligence, economics, finance, architecture, cognitive science, neuroscience, environmental studies, linguistics and philosophy. IMPRINT **Bradford Books**.

The Modern Library
See **Random House, Inc.**

Monograph Series
See **University of Alaska Press**

William Morrow
See **HarperCollins Publishers, Inc.**

MTV Books
See **Pocket Books**

Muscadine Books
See **University Press of Mississippi**

Mysterious Press
See **Warner Books Inc.**

NAL
See **Penguin Putnam, Inc.**

University of Nevada Press
MS 166, Reno NV 89557–0076
☎001 775 784 6573 Fax 001 775 784 6200

Director *Ronald Latimer*
Editor-in-Chief *Margaret Dalrymple*

FOUNDED 1960. *Publishes* scholarly and popular books; serious fiction, Native American studies, natural history, Western Americana, Basque studies and regional studies. About 40 titles a year including reprints. Unsolicited material welcome if it fits in with areas published, or offers a 'new and exciting' direction.
Royalties paid twice-yearly.

University Press of New England
23 South Main Street, Hanover NH
03755–2055
☎001 603 643 7100 Fax 001 603 643 1540
Website www.upne.com

Director & Acquisitions Editor *Richard Abel*
Editorial Director *Philip Pochoda*

FOUNDED 1970. A scholarly book publisher sponsored by five institutions of higher education in the region: Brandeis, Dartmouth, Middlebury, Tufts and the University of New Hampshire. *Publishes* general and scholarly non-fiction and Hardscrabble Books fiction of New England. About 80 titles a year. Unsolicited material welcome.
Royalties paid annually. *Overseas associates:* UK – University Presses Marketing; Europe – Premier Book Marketing.

University of New Mexico Press
1720 Lomas Boulevard NE, Albuquerque
NM 87131–1591
☎001 505 277 2346 Fax 001 505 277 9270
Website www.unmpress.com

Director *Elizabeth C. Hadas*
Editor *Larry Durwood Ball*

FOUNDED 1929. *Publishes* scholarly and regional books. No fiction, how-to, children's, humour, self-help, technical or textbooks.

University of North Texas Press
PO Box 311336, Denton TX 76203–1336
☎001 940 565 2142 Fax 001 940 565 4590
Email rchrisman@unt.edu
Website www.unt.edu/untpress

Director *Ronald Chrisman*

FOUNDED 1987. *Publishes* folklore, regional interest, contemporary, social issues, Texas history, military history, women's issues, multicultural. Publishes the Vassar Miller Poetry Prize winner each year. About 18 titles a year. No unsolicited mss. Approach by letter in the first instance. Synopses and ideas welcome.
Royalties paid annually.

W.W. Norton & Company, Inc.
500 Fifth Avenue, New York NY 10110–0017
☎001 212 354 5500 Fax 001 212 869 0856
Website www.wwnorton.com

Vice-President/Managing Editor *Nancy K. Palmquist*

FOUNDED 1923. *Publishes* fiction and non-fiction, college textbooks and professional books. About 300 titles a year.

Odyssey Paperbacks
See **Harcourt Children's Books Division**

University of Oklahoma Press
1005 Asp Avenue, Norman OK 73019–6051
☎001 405 325 2000 Fax 001 405 325 4000
Website www.ou.edu/oupress
Director *John N. Drayton*
FOUNDED 1928. *Publishes* general scholarly non-fiction only: American Indian studies, history of American West, classical studies, literary theory and criticism, anthropology, archaeology, natural history, political science and women's studies. About 100 titles a year.

One World
See **Ballantine Publishing Group**

Onyx
See **Penguin Putnam Inc.**

Open Forum
See **Krieger Publishing Co.**

Orbit
See **Krieger Publishing Co.**

Orchard Books
See **Grolier Publishing**

Osborne/McGraw Hill
See **The McGraw-Hill Companies, Inc.**

Owl Books
See **Henry Holt & Company Inc.**

Palgrave
See **St Martin's Press LLC**

Pantheon
See **Random House, Inc.**

Paper Star
See **Penguin Putnam Inc**

Paragon House
2700 University Avenue, Suite 200, St Paul MN 55114–1016
☎001 651 644 3087 Fax 001 651 644 0997
Email paragon@paragonhouse.com
Website www.paragonhouse.com
Executive Director *Dr Gordon L. Anderson*
FOUNDED 1982. *Publishes* non-fiction: reference and academic. Subjects include history, religion, philosophy, spirituality, Jewish interest, political science, international relations, psychology.
Royalties paid twice-yearly.

Pelican Publishing Company
Box 3110, Gretna LA 70054–3110
☎001 504 368 1175
Website www.pelicanpub.com
Editor-in-Chief *Nina Kooij*
Publishes general non-fiction: popular history, cookbooks, travel, art, business, children's, editorial cartoon, architecture, golf, Scottish interest, collectibles guides and motivational. About 100 titles a year. Initial enquiries required for all submissions.

Pelion Press
See **The Rosen Publishing Group, Inc.**

Penguin Putnam Inc.
375 Hudson Street, New York NY 10014
☎001 212 366 2000 Fax 001 212 366 2666
Email online@penguinputnam.com
Website www.penguinputnam.com
Chairman, The Penguin Group *David Wan*
President/CEO *Phyllis Grann*
Penguin Putnam is a division of the Penguin Group, which is owned by Pearson plc. The Group is the second-largest trade book publisher in the world. *Publishes* fiction and non-fiction in hardback and paperback; adult and children's. About 2500 titles a year. No unsolicited mss.

PENGUIN GROUP IMPRINTS Hardback: **Dutton**; **Viking**; **Viking Studio**; **Allen Lane The Penguin Press**; **DAW Books, Inc.** (see entry); Paperback: **Penguin**; **Plume**; **Signet/Signet Classics**; **Onyx**; **Roc**; **Topaz**; **Mentor**; **Meridian**; **Arkana**. CHILDREN'S DIVISION: **Dial Books for Young Readers** (see entry); **Dutton's Children's Books**; **Viking Children's Books**; **Puffin**; **Grosset & Dunlap**; **NAL**; **Phyllis Fogelman Books**; **Frederick Warne**.

PUTNAM BERKLEY IMPRINTS Hardback: **G.P. Putnam's Sons** (see entry); **Riverhead Books**; **BlueHen Books**; **Jeremy P. Tarcher**; **Avery** (see entry); **Grosset/Putnam**; **Ace/Putnam**; **Boulevard**; **Putnam**; **Price Stern Sloan**; Paperbacks: **Berkley Books**; **Jove**; **Perigee**; **Prime Crime**; **HP Books**; Children's Division: **Philomel**; **Grosset & Dunlap**; **Paper Star**; **Planet Dexter**.
Royalties paid twice-yearly.

University of Pennsylvania Press
4200 Pine Street, Philadelphia PA 19104–4011
☎001 215 898 6261 Fax 001 215 898 0404
Website www.upenn.edu/pennpress
Director *Eric Halpern*

FOUNDED 1890. *Publishes* serious non-fiction: scholarly, reference, professional, textbooks and semi-popular trade. No original fiction or poetry. About 75 titles a year. No unsolicited mss but synopses and ideas for books welcome.

Royalties paid annually.

Perennial
See **HarperCollins Publishers, Inc.**

Perigee
See **Penguin Putnam Inc.**

Philomel
See **Penguin Putnam Inc.**

Picador USA
See **St Martin's Press LLC**

Planet Dexter
See **Penguin Putnam Inc.**

Players Press
PO Box 1132, Studio City CA 91614-0132
☎001 818 789 4980
CEO *William-Alan Landes*

FOUNDED 1965 as a publisher of plays; now publishes across the entire range of performing arts: plays, musicals, theatre, film, cinema, television, costume, puppetry, plus technical theatre and cinema material. No unsolicited mss; synopses/ideas welcome. Send query letter.

Royalties paid twice-yearly. *Overseas subsidiaries* in Canada, Australia and the UK.

Plenum Publishers
See **Kluwer Academic Publishers**

Plume
See **Penguin Putnam Inc.**

Pocket Books
1230 Avenue of the Americas, New York NY 10020
☎001 212 698 1260 Fax 001 212 698 1253
President/Publisher *Judith Curr*

FOUNDED 1939. A division of Simon & Schuster Consumer Group. *Publishes* trade paperbacks and hardcovers; mass-market, reprints and originals. IMPRINTS **Archway Paperbacks**; **Minstrel Books**; **Pocket Books/Pocket Star Books/ Pocket Pulse**; **Washington Square Press**; **MTV Books**.

PowerKids Press
See **The Rosen Publishing Group, Inc.**

Price Stern Sloan
See **Penguin Putnam Inc.**

Prime Crime
See **Penguin Putnam Inc.**

Princeton Review
See **Random House, Inc.**

Professional Practices
See **Krieger Publishing Co.**

Public History
See **Krieger Publishing Co.**

Puffin
See **Penguin Putnam Inc**

G.P. Putnam's Sons (Children's)
345 Hudson Street, New York NY 10014
☎001 212 366 2000
Website www.penguinputnam.com
President/Publisher *Nancy Paulsen*
Senior Editor *Kathy Dawson*

A children's book imprint of Penguin Putnam Books for Young Readers, a member of **Penguin Putnam Inc.** *Publishes* picture books, middle-grade fiction and young adult fiction.

Quill
See **HarperCollins Publishers, Inc.**

Ragged Mountain Press
See **The McGraw-Hill Companies, Inc.**

Rand McNally
PO Box 7600, Chicago IL 60680
☎001 847 329 8100 Fax 001 847 673 0539
Website www.randmcnally.com
President/CEO *Richard Davis*

FOUNDED 1856. *Publishes* world atlases and maps, road atlases of North America and Europe, city and state maps of the United States and Canada, educational wall maps, atlases and globes, plus children's products. Includes electronic multimedia products.

Random House, Inc.
299 Park Avenue, New York NY 10170
☎001 212 751 2600 Fax 001 212 726 0600
Website www.randomhouse.com
Chairman/Chief Executive Officer *Peter Olson*

FOUNDED 1925. The world's largest English-language general trade book publisher. A division of the Bertelsmann Book Group AG, one of the foremost media companies in the world. The reach of Random House, Inc. is global with subsidiaries and affiliated companies in Canada, the UK, Australia, New Zealand and South Africa. Through Random House International, the books published by the imprints of Random House, Inc. are sold in virtually every country in the world. Submissions via agents preferred.

DIVISIONS/IMPRINTS
Random House Adult Books; **Ballantine Publishing Group** (see entry); **Bantam Dell Publishing Group** (see entry); **Crown Publishing Group** (see entry); **Doubleday Broadway Publishing Group** (see entry). **Knopf Publishing Group** (including **Everyman's Library**, **Knopf**, **Pantheon/ Schocken** and **Vintage Anchor**) FOUNDED 1915. Fiction and non-fiction. **Random House Audio Publishing Group**; **Random House Children's Books** (including **Random House Books for Young Readers**, **Knopf Books for Young Readers**, **Bantam**, **Crown Books for Young Readers**, **Delacorte Press** and **Doubleday Books for Young Readers**); **Random House Large Print Publishing**; **Random House Value Publishing**; **Random House New Media**; **Fodor's Travel Publications**; **Living Language**; **Princeton Review**; **Random House Reference & Information Publishing**; **Times Books** (see entry); **Villard**; **The Modern Library**.
Royalties paid twice-yearly.

Rawson Associates
See **Simon & Schuster Trade Division**

Reader's Digest Association Inc
Reader's Digest Road, Pleasantville, NY 10570–7000
☎001 914 238 1000 Fax 001 914 238 4559
Website www.readersdigest.com
Chairman/CEO *Thomas Ryder*

Publishes cooking, DIY, health, gardening, children's books; videos and magazines.

Red Feather Books
See **Henry Holt & Company Inc.**

Red Wagon Books
See **Harcourt Children's Books Division**

Regan Books
See **HarperCollins Publishers, Inc.**

Fleming H. Revell
See **Baker Book House**

Riverhead Books
See **Penguin Putnam Inc.**

The Riverside Publishing Co.
See **Houghton Mifflin Co.**

Roaring Brook Press
See **The Millbrook Press, Inc.**

Roc
See **Penguin Putnam Inc.**

The Rosen Publishing Group, Inc.
29 East 21st Street, New York NY 10010
☎001 212 777 3017 Fax 001 212 777 0277
President *Roger Rosen*
Associate Editor, PowerKids Press *Gina Strazzabosco-Hayn*
Editorial Director *Erin Hovanec*

FOUNDED 1950. *Publishes* non-fiction books (supplementary to the curriculum, reference and self-help) for a young adult audience. Reading levels are years 7–12, 4–6 (books for teens with literacy problems), and 5–9. Areas of interest include careers, self-esteem, sexuality, personal safety, science, sport, African studies, Holocaust studies and a wide variety of other multicultural titles. About 180 titles a year.
IMPRINTS **Pelion Press** Music titles; **PowerKids Press** Non-fiction books for Reception up to Year 4 that are supplementary to the curriculum. Subjects include conflict resolution, character building, health, safety, drug abuse prevention, history, self-help, religion and multicultural titles. 144 titles a year. For all imprints, write with outline and sample chapters.

Rutgers University Press
100 Joyce Kilmer Avenue, Piscataway NJ 08854–8099
☎001 732 445 7762 Fax 001 732 445 7039
Website rutgerspress.rutgers.edu
Director *Marlie Wasserman*
Editor-in-Chief *Leslie Mitchner*

FOUNDED 1936. *Publishes* scholarly books, regional, social sciences and humanities. Unsolicited mss, synopses and ideas for books welcome. No original fiction or poetry. About 90 titles a year.
Royalties paid annually.

St Martin's Press LLC
175 Fifth Avenue, New York NY 10010
☎001 212 674 5151 Fax 001 212 420 9314
Email inquiries@stmartins.com

Website www.stmartins.com

CEO (Holtzbrinck) *John Sargent*
President/Publisher (Trade Division)
Sally Richardson

FOUNDED 1952. A subsidiary of **Macmillan Publishers** (UK), St Martin's Press made its name and fortune by importing raw talent from the UK to the States and has continued to buy heavily in the UK. *Publishes* general fiction, especially mysteries and crime; and adult non-fiction: history, self-help, political science, travel, biography, scholarly, popular reference, college textbooks. All submissions via legitimate literary agents only.

IMPRINTS **Picador USA**; **Griffin** (Trade paperbacks); **St Martin's Paperbacks** (Mass market); **Thomas Dunne Books**; **Minotaur**; **Palgrave**; **Tor**; **Truman Talley Books**; **Forge**.

Scarecrow Press Inc.

4720 Boston Way, Lanham MD 20706
☎001 301 459 3366 Fax 001 301 459 2118
Website www.scarecrowpress.com

Editorial Director/Associate Publisher
Shirley Lambert

FOUNDED 1950 as a short-run publisher of library reference books. Acquired by **University Press of America, Inc.** in 1995 which is now part of Rowman and Littlefield Publishers, Inc. *Publishes* reference, scholarly and monographs (all levels) for libraries. Reference books in all areas except sciences, specialising in the performing arts, music, cinema and library science. About 165 titles a year. Unsolicited mss welcome but material will not be returned unless requested and accompanied by return postage. Unsolicited synopses and ideas for books welcome.

Royalties paid annually.

Schocken

See **Random House, Inc.**

Scholastic, Inc.

555 Broadway, New York NY 10012–3999
☎001 212 343 6100 Fax 001 212 343 6390
Website www.scholastic.com

Executive Vice President *Barbara Marcus*
Senior Vice-President/Publisher *Jean Feiwel*

FOUNDED 1920. The world's largest publisher and distributor of children's books in the English language. Acquired Grolier from the French Lagardere Group in April 2000. *Publishes* picture books and fiction for middle grade (8–12-year-olds) and young adults: family, friendship, humour, fantasy, mystery and school stories. Also non-fiction: biography, reference and multicultural subjects. About 500 titles a year. Does not accept unsolicited mss or queries unless the author is represented by an agent or has been published previously in book form.

Anne Schwartz Books

See **Simon & Schuster Children's Publishing**

Scott Foresman

1900 E Lake Avenue, Glenview
IL 60025–2086
☎001 847 729 3000 Fax 001 847 486 3999

President *Paul McFall*

FOUNDED 1896. *Publishes* elementary education materials. No unsolicited material.

Scribner

See **Simon & Schuster Trade Division**

Signet/Signet Classics

See **Penguin Putnam Inc.**

Silhouette Books

300 East 42nd Street, New York NY 10017
☎001 212 682 6080 Fax 001 212 682 4539

Editorial Director *Tara Gavin*

FOUNDED 1979 as an imprint of Simon & Schuster and was acquired by a wholly owned subsidiary of Toronto-based Harlequin Enterprises Ltd in 1984. *Publishes* category, contemporary romance fiction and historical romance fiction only. Over 360 titles a year across a number of imprints.

IMPRINTS
Silhouette Romance *Mary Theresa Hussey*; **Silhouette Desire** *Joan Marlow Golan*; **Silhouette Special Edition** *Karen Taylor Richman*; **Silhouette Intimate Moments** *Leslie Wainger*; **Harlequin Historicals** *Tracy Farrell*; **Steeple Hill** *Tracy Farrell*. Imprint, launched in 1997, **Love Inspired** publishes a line of inspirational contemporary romances with stories designed to 'lift readers' spirits and gladden their hearts'. No unsolicited mss. Submit query letter in the first instance or write for detailed submission guidelines/tip sheets.

Royalties paid twice-yearly. *Overseas associates* worldwide.

Silver Whistle

See **Harcourt Children's Books Division**

Simon & Schuster Children's Publishing

1230 Avenue of the Americas, New York
NY 10020
☎001 212 698 2112
President/Publisher *Kristina Peterson*

A division of the Simon & Schuster Consumer Group. *Publishes* pre-school to young adult, picture books, hardcover and paperback fiction, non-fiction, trade, library and mass-market titles. About 480 titles a year.

IMPRINTS
Aladdin Books *Ellen Krieger* Picture books, paperback fiction and non-fiction reprints and originals, and limited series for ages pre-school to young adult; **Atheneum Books for Young Readers** *Jonathan Lanman* Picture books, hardcover fiction and non-fiction books across all genres for ages three to young adult. Two lines within this imprint are **Jean Karl Books** quality fantasy-fiction and **Anne Schwartz Books** distinct picture books and high-quality fiction; **Little Simon** *Alison Weir* Mass-market novelty books (pop-ups, board books, colouring & activity) and merchandise (book and audiocassette) for ages birth through eight; **Margaret K. McElderry Books** *Margaret K. McElderry* Picture books, hardcover fiction and non-fiction trade books for children ages three to young adult; **Simon & Schuster Books for Young Readers** *Stephanie Owens Lurie* Picture books, hardcover fiction and non-fiction for children ages three to young adult. **Simon Spotlight** *Jennifer Koch* New imprint devoted exclusively to children's media tie-ins and licensed properties.

For submissions to all imprints: send envelope (US size 10) for guidelines, attention: *Manuscript Submissions Guidelines.*

Simon & Schuster Trade Division (Division of Simon & Schuster, Inc)

1230 Avenue of the Americas, New York
NY 10020
☎001 212 698 7000 Fax 001 212 698 7007
Website www.simonsays.com
President/Publisher *Carolyn K. Reidy*

Publishes fiction and non-fiction.

DIVISIONS
The Free Press *William Shinker* VP & Publisher; **Fireside/Touchstone** *Mark Gompertz* VP & Publisher, *Trish Todd* VP & Editor-in-Chief; **Scribner** *Susan Moldow* VP & Publisher, *Nan Graham* VP & Editor-in-Chief; **Simon and Schuster** *David Rosenthal* VP & Publisher, *Michael V. Korda* Senior VP &

Editor-in-Chief; **Trade Paperbacks** *Mark Gompertz* VP & Publisher, *Trish Todd* VP & Editor-in-Chief.

IMPRINTS
H. & R. Block; **Lisa Drew Books**; **Fireside**; **The Free Press**; **Free Press Paperbacks**; **Hudson River Editions**; **Rawson Associates**; **Scribner**; **Scribner Classics**; **Scribner Paperback Fiction**; **S&S Libros eñ Espanol**; **Simon & Schuster**; **Touchstone**. No unsolicited mss.

Royalties paid twice-yearly.

Simon Spotlight
See **Simon & Schuster Children's Publishing**

Southern Illinois University Press

PO Box 3697, Carbondale IL 62902–3697
☎001 618 453 2281 Fax 001 618 453 1221
Email jstetter@siu.edu
Director *John F. Stetter*
Acquisitions *Karl Kageff* (kageff@siu.ed)

FOUNDED 1956. *Publishes* scholarly and general interest non-fiction books and educational materials. 50 titles a year.
Royalties paid annually.

Stackpole Books

5067 Ritter Road, Mechanicsburg PA 17055
☎001 717 796 0411 Fax 001 717 796 0412
Email sales@stackpolebooks.com
Website www.stackpolebooks.com
President *David Ritter*
Vice President/Editorial Director *Judith Schnell*

FOUNDED 1933. *Publishes* outdoor sports, fishing, nature, photography, military reference, history, PA Books. 80 titles in 2001.
Royalties paid twice-yearly.

Stanford University Press

Stanford CA 94305-2235
☎001 650 723 9434 Fax 001 650 725 3457
Website www.sup.org
ManagingDirector *Geoffrey Burn*

Publishes non-fiction: scholarly works in all areas of the humanities, social sciences, history and literature, also professional lists in business, economics and law. About 120 titles a year. No unsolicited mss; query in writing first.

Steeple Hill
See **Silhouette Books**

Sterling Publishing Co. Inc.
387 Park Avenue South, 5th Floor, New York NY 10016–8810
☎001 212 532 7160 Fax 001 212 213 2495
Website www.sterlingpub.com
President *Lincoln Boehm*
Executive Vice-President *Charles Nurnberg*
Editorial Director *John Woodside*
FOUNDED 1949. *Publishes* non-fiction: reference and information books, science, nature, arts and crafts, architecture, home improvement, history, photography, children's humour, complementary health, wine and food, social sciences, sports, music, psychology, New Age, occult, woodworking, pets, hobbies, gardening, puzzles and games.

Sunburst Technology
See **Houghton Mifflin Co.**

Susquehanna University Press
See **Golden Cockerel Press** under **UK Publishers**

Syracuse University Press
621 Skytop Road, Suite 110, Syracuse NY 13244–5290
☎001 315 443 5534 Fax 001 315 443 5545
Acting Director *John Fruehwirth*
FOUNDED 1943. *Publishes* scholarly books in the following areas: contemporary Middle East studies, international affairs, Irish studies, Iroquois studies, women and religion, Jewish studies, peace studies, medieval studies, religion and politics, television, geography. About 70 titles a year. Also co-publishes with a number of organisations such as the American University of Beirut. No unsolicited mss. Send query letter with IRCs.
Royalties paid annually.

Nan A. Talese
See **Doubleday Broadway Publishing Group**

Jeremy P. Tarcher
See **Penguin Putnam Inc**

Temple University Press
1601 N. Broad Street, 083–42, Philadelphia PA 19122–6099
☎001 215 204 8787 Fax 001 215 204 4719
Email tempress@astro.ocis.temple.edu
Website www.temple.edu/tempress
Editor-in-Chief *Janet M. Francendese*
FOUNDED 1969. *Publishes* scholarly non-fiction: American history, Latin American studies, gay and lesbian studies, ethnic studies, Asian American studies, anthropology, law, cultural studies, sociology, women's studies, health care and disability, public policy, labour studies, urban studies, American studies and African American studies, ethnomusicology, Latino studies, geography, communication, political science, film, media and television studies, music, education, religion, animals and culture, baseball history. About 60 titles a year. Authors generally academics. Letter of inquiry with brief outline. Include fax/e-mail address.

University of Tennessee Press
110 Conference Center Bldg., Knoxville TN 37996
☎001 865 974 3321 Fax 001 865 974 3724
Website sunsite.utk.edu/utpress
Managing Editor *Stan Ivester*
FOUNDED in 1940. *Publishes* scholarly and regional non-fiction.
Royalties paid annually.

University of Texas Press
PO Box 7819, Austin TX 78713-7819
☎001 512 471 7233/Editorial: 471 4278
Fax 001 512 232 7178
Website www.utexas.edu/utpress/
Director *Joanna Hitchcock*
Assistant Director/Editor-in-Chief *Theresa J. May*
Publishes scholarly and regional non-fiction: anthropology, Old and New World archaeology, art, architecture, classics, environmental studies, film and media studies, geography, language studies, literary modernism; Latin American/Latino/Mexican American/Middle Eastern/Native American studies, natural history and ornithology, regional books (Texas and the southwest), women's studies. Unsolicited material welcome in above subject areas only. About 90 titles a year and 12 journals.
Royalties paid annually.

Three Rivers Press
See **Crown Publishing Group**

Times Books
201 East 50th Street, New York NY 10022
☎001 212 572 2170 Fax 001 212 940 7464
Vice-President/Publisher *Carie Freimuth*
FOUNDED 1959. A division of **Random House, Inc.** *Publishes* general non-fiction and consumer reference. Unsolicited mss not considered. Letter essential.

Topaz
See **Penguin Putnam Inc.**

Tor
See **St Martin's Press LLC**

Touchstone
See **Simon & Schuster Trade Division**

Truman Talley Books
See **St Martin's Press LLC**

Twenty-First Century Books
See **The Millbrook Press, Inc.**

Tyndale House Publishers, Inc.
PO Box 80, Wheaton IL 60189
☎001 630 668 8310 Fax 001 630 668 3245
President *Mark D. Taylor*
FOUNDED 1962. Non-denominational religious publisher of around 200 titles a year for the evangelical Christian market. Books cover a wide range of categories from home and family to inspirational, theology, doctrine, Bibles, general reference and fiction. Also produces video material, calendars and audio books for the same market. No poetry. No unsolicited mss. Synopses and ideas considered. Send query letter summarising contents of books and length. Include a brief biography, detailed outline and sample chapters. IRCs essential for response or return of material. No audio cassettes, disks or video tapes in lieu of mss. Response time around 12–16 weeks. No phone calls or e-mail submissions. Send s.a.e. for submission guidelines.
Royalties paid annually.

University Press of America, Inc.
4720 Boston Way, Lanham MD 20706
☎001 301 459 3366 Fax 001 301 459 2118
Website www.univpress.com
President/Publisher *James E. Lyons*
FOUNDED 1974. *Publishes* scholarly monographs, college and graduate level textbooks. No children's, elementary or high school. About 450 titles a year. Submit outline or request proposal questionnaire.
Royalties paid annually.

Viking/Viking Children's Books
See **Penguin Putnam Inc**

Villard
See **Random House, Inc.**

Vintage Anchor
See **Random House, Inc.**

Voyager Paperbacks
See **Harcourt Children's Books Division**

J. Weston Walch, Publisher
321 Valley Street, PO Box 658, Portland ME 04104-0658
☎001 207 772 2846 Fax 001 207 772 3105
Website www.walch.com
President *John Thoreson*
Editor-in-Chief *Susan Blair*
FOUNDED 1927. *Publishes* supplementary educational materials for middle and secondary schools across a wide range of subjects, including English/language arts, literacy, special needs, mathematics, social studies, science and school-to-career. Always interested in ideas from secondary school teachers who develop materials in the classroom. Proposal letters, synopses and ideas welcome.
Royalties

Walk Worthy Press
See **Warner Books Inc.**

Walker & Co.
435 Hudson Street, New York NY 10014
☎001 212 727 8300 Fax 001 212 727 0984
Contact *Submissions Editor*
FOUNDED 1959. *Publishes* mystery, children's and non-fiction. Please contact the following editors in advance before sending any material to be sure of their interest, then follow up as instructed: **Mystery** *Michael Seidman* 65–70,000 words. Send first three chapters and two-page synopsis. **Trade Non-fiction** *George Gibson* Permission and documentation must be available with mss. Submit prospectus first, with sample chapters and marketing analysis. **Books for Young Readers** *Emily Easton* Fiction and non-fiction for all ages. Query before sending non-fiction proposals. Especially interested in young science and picture books, historical and contemporary fiction for middle grades and young adults. BFYR will consider unsolicited submissions.

Frederick Warne
See **Penguin Putnam Inc**

Warner Books Inc.
1271 Avenue of the Americas, New York NY 10020
☎001 212 522 7200 Fax 001 212 522 7991
Senior Vice-President/Publisher *Jamie Raab*
Associate Publisher *Les Pockell*

FOUNDED 1961. A subsidiary of Time Warner Trade Publishing. *Publishes* fiction and non-fiction, audio books. About 250 titles a year.

IMPRINTS **Aspect** *Betsy Mitchell*; **Mysterious Press** *Sarah Ann Freed*; **Time Warner Audio Books**; **Warner Vision**; **Walk Worthy Press**. No unsolicited mss. Query or submit outline with sample chapters and letter.

Washington Square Press
See **Pocket Books**

Washington State University Press
PO Box 645910, Pullman WA 99164-5910
☎001 509 335 3518   Fax 001 509 335 8568
Email wsupress@wsu.edu
Website www.wsu.edu/wsupress
Director *Thomas H. Sanders*
FOUNDED 1928. Revitalised in 1984 to publish hardcover originals, trade paperbacks and reprints. *Publishes* mainly on the history, pre-history, culture, politics and natural history of the Northwest United States (Washington, Idaho, Oregon, Montana, Alaska) and British Columbia, but works that focus on national topics or other regions may also be considered if they have a Northwest connection. 8–10 titles a year. Unsolicited mss and queries welcome.
Royalties paid annually.

Franklin Watts (A division of Scholastic, Inc.)
90 Sherman Turnpike, Danbury CT 06816
☎001 203 797 3500   Fax 001 203 797 6986
Vice President/Publisher *John W. Selfridge*
FOUNDED 1942 and acquired by **Scholastic** in 2000. *Publishes* non-fiction: curriculum-based material for ages 5–18 across a wide range of subjects, including history, social sciences, natural and physical sciences, health and medicine,

biography. Over 100 titles a year. No unsolicited mss. Synopses and ideas considered. Address samples to 'Submissions' and include IRCs if response required. Be prepared for a three-month turnaround.
Royalties paid twice-yearly.

Wellspring
See **Ballantine Publishing Group**

John Wiley & Sons, Inc.
605 Third Avenue, New York NY 10158
☎001 212 850 6000   Fax 001 212 850 6088
Website www.wiley.com
Chief Executive Officer *William J. Pesce*
FOUNDED 1807. Acquired a major stake in Oxford-based business publisher Capstone Publishing Ltd in 2000. *Publishes* professional and trade print and electronic products in the following fields: culinary arts and hospitality, architecture/design, business, accounting, psychology, non-profit institution management, computers, engineering and general interest. Educational products: the sciences, mathematics, engineering, accounting, business, teacher education, modern languages, religion. Scientific, technical and medical publishers of journals, encyclopedias, available in print and electronic media. Unsolicited mss not accepted.

Zondervan Publishing House
5300 Patterson Avenue SE, Grand Rapids MI 49530
☎001 616 698 6900   Fax 001 616 698 3421
President/Chief Executive *Bruce E. Ryskamp*
FOUNDED 1931. Subsidiary of **HarperCollins Publishers, Inc.** *Publishes* Protestant religion, Bibles, books, audio & video, computer software, calendars and speciality items.

US Agents

★ = Members of the **Association of Authors' Representatives, Inc.**

Adler & Robin Books, Inc.
3000 Connecticut Avenue, NW, Suite 317,
Washington DC 20008
☎001 202 986 9275 Fax 001 202 986 9485
Email dmorris@morrisbelt.com
President *Bill Adler Jr*
Senior Agents *Laura Belt, Djana Pearson*
 Morris
Editor *Tracy Quinn*

FOUNDED 1988. *Handles* computer books and
non-fiction. Unsolicited synopses and queries
welcome with s.a.e. Electronic submissions
accepted. No reading fee. *Commission* Home
15%; UK 20%.

AMG/Renaissance
9465 Wilshire Boulevard, Beverly Hills
CA 90212
☎001 310 860 8000 Fax 001 310 860 8100
President *Joel Gotler*
Literary Associates *Alan Nevins, Irv Schwartz,*
 Judi Farkas, Michael Prevett, Lisa Hamilton

FOUNDED 1934. Fiction and non-fiction; film
and TV rights. No unsolicited mss. Send query
letter with IRCs in the first instance. No reading fee. *Commission* Home 10–15%.

Marcia Amsterdam Agency
41 West 82nd Street, New York
NY 10024–5613
☎001 212 873 4945
Contact *Marcia Amsterdam*

FOUNDED 1969. *Specialises* in mainstream fiction, horror, suspense, humour, young adult,
TV and film scripts. No poetry, books for the
8–10 age group or how-to. No unsolicited
mss. First approach by letter only and enclose
IRCs. No reading fee for outlines and synopses. *Commission* Home 15%; Dramatic 10%;
Foreign 20%.

Bart Andrews & Associates Inc
7510 Sunset Boulevard, Suite 100, Los
Angeles CA 90046–3418
☎001 310 271 9916
Contact *Bart Andrews*

FOUNDED 1982. General non-fiction: show
business, biography and autobiography, film

books, trivia, TV and nostalgia. No scripts. No
fiction, poetry, children's or science. No books
of less than major commercial potential.
Specialises in working with celebrities on autobiographies. No unsolicited mss. 'Send a brilliant letter (with IRCs for response) extolling
your manuscript's virtues. Sell me!' No reading
fee. *Commission* Home & Translation 15%.
Overseas associates **Abner Stein**, UK.

Malaga Baldi Literary Agency
204 84th Street, Suite 3C, New York
NY 10024
☎001 212 579 5075 Fax 001 212 579 5078
Email MBALDI@aol.com
Contact *Malaga Baldi*

FOUNDED 1986. *Handles* quality fiction and non-
fiction. No scripts. No westerns, men's adventure, science fiction/fantasy, romance, how-to,
young adult or children's. Writers of fiction
should send query letter describing the novel
plus IRCs. Allow ten weeks *minimum* for
response. For non-fiction, approach in writing
with a proposal, table of contents and two sample
chapters. No reading fee. *Commission* 15%.
Overseas associates **Abner Stein**, UK; Japan Uni.

The Balkin Agency, Inc.★
PO Box 222, Amherst MA 01004
☎001 413 548 9835 Fax 001 413 548 9836
Email balkin@crocker.com
Contact *Richard Balkin*

FOUNDED 1973. *Handles* adult non-fiction
only. No reading fee for outlines and synopses.
Commission Home 15%; Foreign 20%.

Meredith Bernstein
Literary Agency, Inc.★
2112 Broadway, Suite 503A, New York
NY 10023
☎001 212 799 1007 Fax 001 212 799 1145
Contacts *Meredith Bernstein, Elizabeth Cavanaugh*

FOUNDED 1981. *Handles* fiction (women's and
men's), mysteries, romance, and non-fiction
(women's issues, personal memoirs, parenting,
psychology, business, spirituality, science, travel,
fashion, inspiration and humour). 'Always interested in new ideas, voices and other original

projects. We are looking for mainstream fiction, psychological suspense, medical thrillers, love stories (but not romances).' Not taking on any unpublished romance writers at present. *Commission* Home & Dramatic 15%; Translation 20%. *Overseas associates* **Abner Stein**, UK; Lennart Sane, Holland, Scandinavia and Spanish language; Thomas Schluck, Germany; Bardon Chinese Media Agency; William Miller, Japan; Frederique Porretta, France; Agenzia Letteraria, Italy.

Reid Boates Literary Agency
PO Box 328, Pittstown NJ 08867-0328
☎001 908 730 8523 Fax 001 908 730 8931
Contact *Reid Boates*

FOUNDED 1985. *Handles* general fiction and non-fiction. No scripts. No science fiction, fantasy, romance, western, gothic, personal memoirs, children's or young adult. Enquire by letter with IRCs in first instance. No reading fee. *Commission* Home & Dramatic 15%; Translation 20%. *Overseas associates* worldwide.

Georges Borchardt, Inc.★
136 East 57th Street, New York NY 10022
☎001 212 753 5785 Fax 001 212 838 6518

FOUNDED 1967. Works mostly with established/published authors. *Specialises* in fiction, biography, and general non-fiction of unusual interest. Unsolicited mss not read. *Commission* Home, UK, Dramatic 15%; Translation 20%. *UK associates* **Sheil Land Associates Ltd** (Richard Scott Simon), London.

Brandt & Brandt Literary Agents, Inc.★
1501 Broadway, New York NY 10036
☎001 212 840 5760 Fax 001 212 840 5776
Contacts *Carl D. Brandt, Gail Hochman, Marianne Merola, Charles Schlessiger*

FOUNDED 1914. *Handles* non-fiction and fiction. No poetry or children's books. No unsolicited mss. Approach by letter describing background and ambitions. No reading fee. *Commission* Home & Dramatic 15%; Foreign 20%. *UK associates* **A.M. Heath & Co. Ltd**.

Pema Browne Ltd, Illustration and Literary Agents
HCR Box 104B, Neversink NY 12765
☎001 845 985 2936/2062
Fax 001 845 985 7635
Email ppbltd@catskill.net
Website www.geocities.com/pemabrowneltd

Contacts *Pema Browne, Perry Browne*

FOUNDED 1966. ('Pema rhymes with Emma.') *Handles* mass-market mainstream and hardcover fiction: romance, business, children's picture books and young adult; non-fiction: how-to and reference. No unsolicited mss; send query letter with IRCs. No fax or e-mail queries. Also handles illustrators' work. *Commission* Home 15%; Translation 20%; Dramatic 10%; Overseas authors 20%.

Sheree Bykofsky Associates, Inc.★
16 West 36th Street, 13th Floor, New York NY 10018
☎001 212 244 4144
Contact *Sheree Bykofsky*

FOUNDED 1985. *Handles* adult fiction and non-fiction. No scripts. No children's, young adult, horror, science fiction, romance, westerns, occult or supernatural. No unsolicited mss. Send query letter first with brief synopsis or outline and writing sample (1–3 pp) for fiction. IRCs essential for reply or return of material. No phone calls. No reading fee. *Commission* Home 15%; UK (including sub-agent's fee) 25%.

Maria Carvainis Agency, Inc.
1350 Avenue of the Americas, Suite 2905, New York NY 10019
☎001 212 245 6365 Fax 001 212 245 7196
Email mca@mariacarvainisagency.com
Contacts *Maria Carvainis, Frances Kuffel*

FOUNDED 1977. *Handles* fiction: literary and mainstream, contemporary women's, mystery, suspense, fantasy, historical, children's and young adult novels; non-fiction: business, finance, women's issues, political and film biography, medicine, psychology and popular science. No film scripts unless from writers with established credits. No science fiction. No unsolicited mss; they will be returned unread. Queries only, with IRCs for response. No reading fee. *Commission* Domestic & Dramatic 15%; Translation 20%.

Martha Casselman, Literary Agent
PO Box 342, Calistoga CA 94515
☎001 707 942 4341
Contact *Martha Casselman*

FOUNDED 1979. *Handles* all types of non-fiction. No fiction at present. Main interests: food/cookery, biography, current affairs, popular sociology. No scripts, textbooks, poetry, coming-of-age fiction or science fiction. Especially interested in cookery with an appeal to the American market for possible co-publication in UK. Send queries and brief summary, with return postage. No mss. If you do not wish return of material, please state so. Also include, where applicable, any material on previous publications, reviews, brief biography. No proposals via fax. No reading fee. *Commission* Home 15%.

The Catalog Literary Agency
PO Box 2964, Vancouver WA 98668
☎001 360 694 8531
Contact *Douglas Storey*

FOUNDED 1986. *Handles* popular, professional and textbook material in all subjects, especially business, health, money, science, technology, computers, electronics and women's interests; also how-to, self-help, mainstream fiction and children's non-fiction. No genre fiction. No scripts, articles, screenplays, plays, poetry or short stories. No reading fee. No unsolicited mss. Query with an outline and sample chapters, and include IRCs. *Commission* 15%.

Linda Chester & Associates★
Rockefeller Center, 630 Fifth Avenue, New York NY 10111
☎001 212 218 3350 Fax 001 212 218 3343
Contact *Joanna Pulcini, Associate*

FOUNDED 1978. *Handles* literary and commercial fiction and non-fiction in all subjects. No scripts, children's or textbooks. No unsolicited mss. No reading fee for solicited material. *Commission* Home & Dramatic 15%; Translation 25%.

Clausen, Mays & Tahan Literary Agency
249 West 34th Street, Suite 605, New York NY 10001
☎001 212 239 4343 Fax 001 212 239 5248
Email cmtassist@aol.com
Contacts *Stedman Mays, Mary M. Tahan*

Handles non-fiction work such as memoirs, biography, true crime, true stories, how-to, psychology, spirituality, relationships, style, health/nutrition, fashion/beauty, women's issues, humour and cookbooks. Some fiction. Send query letter only. Include IRCs. *UK associates* **David Grossman Literary Agency Ltd**.

Hy Cohen Literary Agency Ltd
66 Brookfield, Montclair NJ 07043
☎001 973 783 9494 Fax 001 973 783 9867
Email cogency@home.com
President *Hy Cohen*

FOUNDED 1975. Fiction and non-fiction. No

scripts. Unsolicited mss welcome, but synopsis with sample 100 pp preferred. IRCs essential. No reading fee. *Commission* Home & Dramatic 10%; Foreign 20%. *Overseas associates* **Abner Stein**, UK.

Frances Collin Literary Agent★
PO Box 33, Wayne PA 19087–0033
☎001 610 254 0555 Fax 001 610 254 5029
Contact *Frances Collin*

FOUNDED 1948. Successor to Marie Rodell. *Handles* general fiction and non-fiction. No scripts. No unsolicited mss. Send query letter only, with IRCs for reply, for the attention of *Marsha Kear*. No reading fee. Rarely accepts non-professional writers or writers not represented in the UK. *Overseas associates* worldwide.

Don Congdon Associates, Inc.★
156 Fifth Avenue, Suite 625, New York NY 10010–7002
☎001 212 645 1229 Fax 001 212 727 2688
Contacts *Don Congdon, Michael Congdon, Susan Ramer*

FOUNDED 1983. *Handles* fiction and non-fiction. No academic, technical, romantic fiction, or scripts. No unsolicited mss. Approach by letter in the first instance. No reading fee. *Commission* Home 10%; UK & Translation 19%. *Overseas associates* worldwide.

Richard Curtis Associates, Inc.
171 East 74th Street, Second Floor, New York NY 10021
☎001 212 772 7363 Fax 001 212 772 7393
Email shackworth@curtisagency.com
Website www.curtisagency.com
Contact *Richard Curtis*

FOUNDED 1969. *Handles* genre and mainstream fiction, plus commercial non-fiction. No children's books or scripts.

Curtis Brown Ltd★
10 Astor Place, New York NY 10003
☎001 212 473 5400
Book Rights *Laura Blake Peterson, Ellen Geiger, Peter L. Ginsberg, Emilie Jacobson, Ginger Knowlton, Marilyn E. Marlow, Maureen Walters, Mitchell Walters*
Film, TV, Audio Rights *Timothy Knowlton, Edwin Wintle*
Translation *Dave Barbor*

FOUNDED 1914. *Handles* general fiction and non-fiction. Also some scripts for film, TV and theatre. No unsolicited mss; queries only, with

IRCs for reply. No reading fee. *Overseas associates* Representatives in all major foreign countries.

Joan Daves Agency
21 West 26th Street, New York
NY 10010-1003
☎001 212 685 2663 Fax 001 212 685 1781
Director *Jennifer Lyons*
FOUNDED 1952. Literary fiction and non-fiction. No romance or textbooks. No scripts. Send query letter in the first instance. 'A detailed synopsis seems valuable only for non-fiction work. Material submitted should specify the author's background, publishing credits and similar pertinent information.' No reading fee. *Commission* Home 15%; Dramatic 15%; Foreign 20%.

Sandra Dijkstra Literary Agency*
PMB 515, 1155 Camino Del Mar, Del Mar
CA 92104-3115
☎001 858 755 3115 Fax 001 858 792 1494
Contact *Sandra Zane*
FOUNDED 1981. *Handles* quality and commercial non-fiction and fiction, including some genre fiction. No scripts. No westerns, contemporary romance or poetry. Willing to look at children's projects. *Specialises* in quality fiction, mystery/thrillers, narrative non-fiction, psychology, self-help, science, health, business, memoirs, biography. 'Dedicated to promoting new and original voices and ideas.' For fiction: send brief synopsis (one page) and first 50 pages; for non-fiction: send proposal with overview, chapter outline, author biog. and two sample chapters. All submissions should be accompanied by IRCs. No reading fee. *Commission* Home 15%; Translation 20%. *Overseas associates* **Abner Stein**, UK; Ursula Bender, Agence Hoffman, Germany; Monica Heyum, Scandinavia; Luigi Bernabo, Italy; M. Casanovas, Spain; Caroline Van Gelderen, Netherlands; M. Kling (La Nouvelle Agence), France; William Miller, The English Agency, Japan.

Jane Dystel Literary Management*
One Union Square West, Suite 904,
New York NY 10003
☎001 212 627 9100 Fax 001 212 627 9313
Website www.dystel.com
Contacts *Jane Dystel, Miriam Goderich, Todd Keithley, Jo Fagan, Stacey Glick, Tracey Gardner, Michael Bourret*
FOUNDED 1991. *Handles* non-fiction and fiction. *Specialises* in politics, history, biography,

cookbooks, current affairs, celebrities, commercial and literary fiction. No reading fee.

Educational Design Services, Inc.
PO Box 253, Wantagh NY 11793
☎001 718 539 4107/516 221 0995
Email linder.eds@juno.com *or*
eselzer@nyc.rr.com
President *Bertram Linder*
Vice President *Edwin Selzer*
FOUNDED 1979. *Specialises* in educational material and textbooks for sale to school markets. IRCs must accompany submissions. *Commission* Home 15%; Foreign 25%.

Elek International Rights Agents (a subsidiary of The Content Company, Inc.)
5111 JFK Boulevard East, West New York
NJ 07093
☎001 201 588 0323 Fax 001 201 558 0307
Email info@theliteraryagency.com
Website www.theliteraryagency.com
Contact *Lauren Mactas*
FOUNDED 1979. *Handles* adult non-fiction and children's picture books. No scripts, fiction, psychology, New Age, poetry, short stories or autobiography. No unsolicited mss; send letter of enquiry with IRCs for reply; include résumé, credentials, brief synopsis. No reading fee. *Commission* Home 15%; Dramatic & Foreign 20%.

Ann Elmo Agency, Inc.*
60 East 42nd Street, New York NY 10165
☎001 212 661 2880/1 Fax 001 212 661 2883
Contacts *Lettie Lee, Mari Cronin, Andree Abecassis*
FOUNDED in the 1940s. *Handles* literary and romantic fiction, mysteries and mainstream; also non-fiction in all subjects, including biography and self-help. Some children's (8–12-year-olds). Query letter with outline of project in the first instance. No reading fee. *Commission* Home 15–20%. *Overseas associates* **John Johnson Ltd**, UK.

ForthWrite Literary Agency & Speakers Bureau
23852 W. Pacific Coast Highway, Suite 701,
Malibu CA 90265
☎001 310 456 5698 Fax 001 310 456 6589
Website www.forthwriteliterary.com
Contact *Wendy L. Keller*

FOUNDED 1988. *Specialises* in non-fiction: biography, business (marketing, finance, management and sales), alternative health, cookery, gardening, nature, popular psychology, history, self-help, home and health, crafts, computer, how-to, animal care by experts known in the field. Handles electronic, foreign (translation and distribution) and resale rights for previously published books. Send query letter with IRCs. No reading fee. *Commission* Foreign 20%.

Robert A. Freedman Dramatic Agency, Inc.★

Suite 2310, 1501 Broadway, New York NY 10036
☎001 212 840 5760

President *Robert A. Freedman*
Vice President *Selma Luttinger*

FOUNDED 1928 as Brandt & Brandt Dramatic Department, Inc. Took its present name in 1984. Works mostly with established authors. *Specialises* in plays, film and TV scripts. Unsolicited mss not read. *Commission* Dramatic 10%.

Max Gartenberg, Literary Agent

521 Fifth Avenue, Suite 1700, New York NY 10175
☎001 212 292 4354 Fax 001 973 535 5033
Email gartenbook@hotmail.com

Contact *Max Gartenberg*

FOUNDED 1954. Works mostly with established/published authors. *Specialises* in non-fiction and trade fiction. Query first. *Commission* Home & Dramatic 10%; 15% on initial sale, 10% thereafter; Foreign 15/20%.

Gelfman Schneider Literary Agents, Inc.★

250 West 57th Street, Suite 2515, New York NY 10107
☎001 212 245 1993 Fax 001 212 245 8678

Contacts *Deborah Schneider, Jane Gelfman*

FOUNDED 1919 (London), 1980 (New York). Formerly John Farquharson Ltd. Works mostly with established/published authors. *Specialises* in general trade fiction and non-fiction. No poetry, short stories or screenplays. No reading fee for outlines. Submissions must be accompanied by IRCs. *Commission* Home 15%; Dramatic 15%; Foreign 20%. *Overseas associates* **Curtis Brown Group Ltd**, UK.

The Sebastian Gibson Agency

PO Box 13350, Palm Desert CA 92255–3350
☎001 760 322 2446 Fax 001 760 322 3857

Contact *Sebastian Gibson*

FOUNDED 1994. *Handles* all categories of fiction; psychological thrillers, historical novels, mysteries/suspense, action/adventure, crime/police, medical dramas. Also non-fiction written by celebrities, cookbooks or photography, children's and juvenile books. No poetry, textbooks, essays, short stories, child development, how-to, gardening, erotic, autobiography, drug recovery, religious books or scripts. 'We are constantly seeking something fresh and new with novel plot lines or a story told in a way that has never been told before. Grab our imagination and you may grab the imagination of a publisher as well.' No reading fee. Send query letter, synopsis and first three chapters with IRCs. No phone calls, faxes or e-mail. *Commission* Home 10%; Overseas & Translation 20%; Film & Ancilliary Rights 15%.

Sanford J. Greenburger Associates, Inc.★

15th Floor, 55 Fifth Avenue, New York NY 10003
☎001 212 206 5600 Fax 001 212 463 8718
Website www.greenburger.com

Contacts *Heide Lange, Faith Hamlin, Beth Vesel, Theresa Park, Elyse Cheney, Daniel Mandel*

Handles fiction and non-fiction. No unsolicited mss. First approach with query letter, sample chapter and synopsis. No reading fee.

The Charlotte Gusay Literary Agency

10532 Blythe Avenue, Los Angeles CA 90064
☎001 310 559 0831 Fax 001 310 559 2639

Contact *Charlotte Gusay*

FOUNDED 1988. *Handles* fiction, both literary and commercial, plus non-fiction: children's and adult humour, parenting, gardening, women's and men's issues, feminism, psychology, memoirs, biography, travel. No science fiction, horror, short pieces or collections of stories. No unsolicited mss; send query letter first, then if your material is requested, send succinct outline and first three sample chapters for fiction, or proposal for non-fiction. No response without IRCs. No reading fee. *Commission* Home 15%; Dramatic 10%; Translation & Foreign 25%.

Joy Harris Literary Agency, Inc.*

156 Fifth Avenue, Suite 617, New York
NY 10010
☎001 212 924 6269 Fax 001 212 924 6609
Email gen.office@jhlitagent.com

Contacts *Joy Harris, Stephanie Abou, Leslie
Daniels, Alexia Paul*

Handles adult non-fiction and fiction. No
unsolicited mss. Query letter in the first
instance. No reading fee. *Commission* Home &
Dramatic 15%; Foreign 20%. *Overseas associates*
Michael Meller, Germany; **Abner Stein**, UK;
Roberto Santachiara, Italy; various Japanese
agencies; **Andrew Nurnberg Associates**, rest
of the territories.

John Hawkins & Associates, Inc.*

71 West 23rd Street, Suite 1600, New York
NY 10010
☎001 212 807 7040 Fax 001 212 807 9555
Email JHA@JHAliterary.com

Contacts *John Hawkins, William Reiss*

FOUNDED 1893. *Handles* film and TV rights.
No unsolicited mss; send queries with 1–3-
page outline and one-page c.v. IRCs necessary
for response. No reading fee. *Commission*
Apply for rates.

The Jeff Herman Agency, LLC

332 Bleecker Street, Suite 6–31, New York
NY 10014
☎001 212 941 0540 Fax 001 212 941 0614
Email jeff@jeffherman.com
Website www.jeffherman.com

Contact *Jeffrey H. Herman*

Handles all areas of non-fiction, textbooks and
reference. No scripts. No unsolicited mss.
Query letter with IRCs in the first instance.
No reading fee. Jeff Herman publishes a useful
reference guide to the book trade called *The
Writer's Guide to Book Editors, Publishers &
Literary Agents* (Prima). *Commission* Home 15%;
Translation 10%.

Susan Herner Rights Agency, Inc.

PO Box 303, Scarsdale NY 10583
☎001 914 725 8967 Fax 001 914 725 8969

Contacts *Susan N. Herner, Sue P. Yuen*

FOUNDED 1987. Adult fiction and non-fiction
in all areas. No children's books. *Handles* film
and TV rights and software. Send query letter
with outline and sample chapters. No reading
fee. *Commission* Home 15%; Dramatic &
Translation 20%.

Frederick Hill Bonnie Nadell Inc.

1842 Union Street, San Francisco CA 94123
☎001 415 921 2910 Fax 001 415 921 2802

Contacts *Fred Hill, Bonnie Nadell, Irene Moore*

FOUNDED 1979. General fiction and non-fiction.
No scripts. Send query letter detailing past pub-
lishing history if any. IRCs required. *Commission*
Home & Dramatic 15%; Foreign 20%. *Overseas
associates* **Mary Clemmey Literary Agency**,
UK.

IMG Literary

825 Seventh Avenue, New York NY 10019
☎001 212 489 5400 Fax 001 212 246 1118

Contact *Mark Reiter (Vice President)*

FOUNDED 1986. A wholly-owned subsidary of
IMG, The Mark McCormack Group of
Companies. *Handles* non-fiction and fiction.
No science fiction, fantasy, poetry or photography. No scripts. Query first. Submissions
should include brief synopsis (typed), sample
chapters (50 pp maximum), publishing history,
etc. *Commission* Home & Dramatic 15%;
Foreign 20%. *Overseas associates* worldwide.

Janklow & Nesbit Associates

445 Park Avenue, New York NY 10022
☎001 212 421 1700
Fax 001 212 980 3671/355 1403
Email Postmaster@janklow.com

Partners *Morton L. Janklow, Lynn Nesbit*
Senior Vice-President *Anne Sibbald*
Agents *Tina Bennett, Luke Janklow, Richard
Morris, Eric Simonoff*

FOUNDED 1989. *Handles* fiction and non-
fiction; commercial and literary. No unsolicited mss. See also **Janklow & Nesbit (UK)
Ltd** under **UK Agents**.

Kidde, Hoyt & Picard*

333 East 51st Street, New York NY 10022
☎001 212 755 9461/9465
Fax 001 212 223 2501

Chief Associate *Katharine Kidde*
Associate *Laura Langlie*

FOUNDED 1981. *Specialises* in mainstream and
literary fiction, mysteries, romantic fiction (historical and contemporary), and quality non-
fiction in humanities and social sciences (biography, history, current affairs, the arts). No
reading fee. Query first, include s.a.e. *Commission* 15%.

Kirchoff/Wohlberg, Inc.★
866 United Nations Plaza, Suite 525, New York NY 10017
☎001 212 644 2020 Fax 001 212 223 4387

Authors' Representative *Elizabeth Pulitzer-Voges*

FOUNDED 1930. *Handles* books for children and young adults, specialising in children's picture books. No adult material. No scripts for TV, radio, film or theatre. Send letter of enquiry with synopsis or outline and IRCs for reply or return. No reading fee.

Paul Kohner, Inc.
9300 Wilshire Boulevard, Suite 555, Beverly Hills CA 90212
☎001 310 550 1060 Fax 001 310 276 1083

Contacts *Pearl Wexler, Stephen Moore, Deborah Obad*

FOUNDED 1938. *Handles* a broad range of books for subsidiary rights sales to film and TV. Few direct placements with publishers as film and TV scripts are the major part of the business. *Specialises* in true crime, biography and history. Non-fiction preferred to fiction for the TV market but anything 'we feel has strong potential' will be considered. No short stories, poetry, science fiction or gothic. Unsolicited material will be returned unread, if accompanied by s.a.e. Approach via a third-party reference or send query letter with professional résumé. No reading fee. *Commission* Home & Dramatic 10%; Publishing 15%.

Barbara S. Kouts, Literary Agent★
PO Box 560, Bellport NY 11713
☎001 516 286 1278 Fax 001 516 286 1538

Contact *Barbara S. Kouts*

FOUNDED 1980. *Handles* fiction, non-fiction and children's. No romance, science fiction or scripts. No unsolicited mss. Query letter in the first instance. No reading fee. *Commission* Home 15%; Foreign 20%.

Peter Lampack Agency, Inc.
551 Fifth Avenue, Suite 1613, New York NY 10176
☎001 212 687 9106 Fax 001 212 687 9109

Contact *Loren Soeiro*

FOUNDED in 1977. *Handles* commercial fiction: male action and adventure, contemporary relationships, historical, mysteries and suspense, literary fiction; also non-fiction from recognised experts in a given field, plus biographies, autobi-ographies. Also handles theatrical, motion picture, and TV rights from book properties. No original scripts or screenplays, series or episodic material. Best approach by letter in first instance. No reply without s.a.e. 'We will respond within three weeks and invite the submission of manuscripts which we would like to examine.' No reading fee. No unsolicited mss. *Commission* Home & Dramatic 15%; Translation & UK 20%.

The Lazear Agency, Inc.
800 Washington Avenue N., Suite 660, Minneapolis MN 55401
☎001 612 332 8640 Fax 001 612 332 4648

Contacts *Christi Cardenas, Jonathon Lazear, Wendy Lazear, Anne Blackstone, Tanya Cromey, Laura Brinkmeier, John Peter Larson*

FOUNDED 1984. *Handles* fiction: mysteries, suspense, young adult, commercial and literary; also commercial and serious non-fiction of all types; and children's books. No poetry or stage plays. Approach by letter, with description of mss, short autobiography and IRCs. No reading fee. *Commission* Home & Dramatic 15%; Translation 20%.

Ellen Levine, Literary Agency, Inc.★
Suite 1801, 15 East 26th Street, New York NY 10010-1505
☎001 212 899 0620 Fax 001 212 725 4501

Contacts *Diana Finch, Elizabeth Kaplan, Louise Quayle, Ellen Levine*

FOUNDED 1980. *Handles* all types of books. No scripts. No unsolicited mss, nor any other material unless requested. No telephone calls. First approach by letter; send US postage or IRCs for reply, otherwise material not returned. No reading fee. *Commission* Home 15%; Foreign 20%. *UK Associates* **A.M. Heath & Co. Ltd** .

Literary & Creative Artists Inc.★
3543 Albemarle Street NW, Washington DC 20008–4213
☎001 202 362 4688 Fax 001 202 362 8875
Website www.lcadc.com

Contacts *Muriel G. Nellis, Jane F. Roberts, Leslie Toussaint*

FOUNDED 1981. *Specialises* in a broad range of general non-fiction. No poetry, pornography, academic or educational textbooks. No unsolicited mss; query letter in the first instance. Include IRCs for response. No reading fee. *Commission* Home 15%; Dramatic 20%; Translation 20–25%.

Sterling Lord Literistic, Inc.
65 Bleecker Street, New York NY 10012
☎001 212 780 6050 Fax 001 212 780 6095
Contacts *Peter Matson, Sterling Lord*
FOUNDED 1979. *Handles* all genres, fiction and non-fiction, plus scripts for TV and film. No unsolicited mss. Prefers letter outlining all non-fiction. No reading fee. *Commission* Home 15%; UK & Translation 20%.

Richard P. McDonough, Literary Agent
34 Pinewood, Irvine CA 92604
☎001 949 654 5480 Fax 001 949 654 5481
Email cestmoi@msn.com
Contact *Richard P. McDonough*
FOUNDED 1986. General non-fiction and literary fiction. No genre fiction. No unsolicited mss; query first and include IRCs. No reading fee. *Commission* 15%.

McIntosh & Otis, Inc.★
353 Lexington Avenue, New York NY 10016
☎001 212 687 7400 Fax 001 212 687 6894
President *Eugene H. Winick*
Adult Books *Sam Pinkus, Elizabeth Winick, Barbara Kennedy*
Children's *Dorothy Markinko, Tracey Adams*
Motion Picture/Television *Evva Pryor*
FOUNDED 1928. Adult and juvenile literary fiction and non-fiction. No textbooks or scripts. No unsolicited mss. Query letter indicating nature of the work plus details of background. IRCs for response. No reading fee. *Commission* Home & Dramatic 15%; Foreign 20%. *UK Associates* **A.M. Heath & Co. Ltd**, UK.

The Evan Marshall Agency★
6 Tristam Place, Pine Brook NJ 07058–9445
☎001 973 882 1122 Fax 001 973 882 3099
Email evanmarshall@TheNovelist.com
Website www.TheNovelist.com
Contact *Evan Marshall*
FOUNDED 1987. *Handles* general adult fiction. No unsolicited mss; send query letter first. *Commission* Home 15%; UK & Translation 20%.

Mews Books Ltd
c/o Sidney B. Kramer, 20 Bluewater Hill, Westport CT 06880
☎001 203 227 1836 Fax 001 203 227 1144
Email mewsbooks@aol.com (initial contact only; submission by regular mail)
Contacts *Sidney B. Kramer, Fran Pollak*

FOUNDED 1970. *Handles* adult fiction and non-fiction, children's, pre-school and young adult. No scripts, short stories or novellas (unless by established authors). *Specialises* in cookery, medical, health and nutrition, scientific non-fiction, children's and young adult. Unsolicited material welcome. Presentation must be professional and should include summary of plot/characters, one or two sample chapters, personal credentials and brief on target market, all suitable for forwarding to a publisher. No reading fee. If material is accepted, agency asks $350 circulation fee (4–5 publishers), which will be applied against commissions (waived for published authors). Charges for photocopying, postage expenses, telephone calls and other direct costs. Principal agent is an attorney and former publisher (a founder of Bantam Books). Offers consultation service through which writers can get advice on a contract or on publishing problems. *Commission* Home 15%; Film & Translation 20%. *Overseas associates* **Abner Stein**, UK.

Maureen Moran Agency
PO Box 20191, Parkwest Station, New York NY 10025
☎001 212 222 3838 Fax 001 212 531 3464
Email maureenm@erols.com
Contact *Maureen Moran*
Formerly Donald MacCampbell, Inc. *Handles* novels only. No scripts, non-fiction, science fiction, westerns or suspense. *Specialises* in romance. No unsolicited mss; approach by letter. No reading fee. *Commission* US Book Sales 10%; First Novels US 15%.

Howard Morhaim Literary Agency★
841 Broadway, Suite 604, New York NY 10003
☎001 212 529 4433 Fax 001 212 995 1112
Contact *Howard Morhaim*
FOUNDED 1979. *Handles* general adult fiction and non-fiction. No scripts. No children's or young adult material, poetry or religious. No unsolicited mss. Send query letter with synopsis and sample chapters for fiction; query letter with outline or proposal for non-fiction. No reading fee. *Commission* Home 15%; UK & Translation 20%. *Overseas associates* worldwide.

Henry Morrison, Inc.
PO Box 235, Bedford Hills NY 10507
☎001 914 666 3500 Fax 001 914 241 7846
Contact *Henry Morrison*
FOUNDED 1965. *Handles* general fiction, crime

and science fiction, and non-fiction. No scripts unless by established writers. Unsolicited material welcome; but send query letter with outline (1–5 pp) in the first instance. No reading fee. *Commission* Home 15%; UK & Translation 25%.

Ruth Nathan Agency
53 East 34th Street, New York NY 10016
☎001 212 481 1185 Fax 001 212 481 1185

FOUNDED 1984. *Specialises* in illustrated books, fine art & decorative arts, historical fiction with emphasis on Middle Ages, true crime, showbiz. Query first. No unsolicited mss. No reading fee. *Commission* 15%.

B.K. Nelson Literary Agency
1500 So. Palm Canyon Drive #7 & 9, Palm Springs CA 92264
☎001 760 318 2773 Fax 001 760 318 2774
Website www.bknelson.com
President *Bonita K. Nelson*
Vice President *Leonard 'Chip' Ashbach*
Editorial Director *John W. Benson*

FOUNDED 1979. *Specialises* in novels, business, self-help, how-to, political, autobiography, celebrity biography. Major motion picture and TV documentary success. No unsolicited mss. Letter of inquiry. Reading fee charged. *Commission* 20%. Lecture Bureau for Authors founded 1994; Foreign Rights Catalogue established 1995; BK Nelson Infomercial Marketing Co. 1996, primarily for authors and endorsements, and BKNelson, Inc. for motion picture production in 1998. Signatory to Writers Guild of America, West (WGAW).

New England Publishing Associates, Inc.★
Box 5, Chester CT 06412
☎001 860 345 7323 Fax 001 860 345 3660
Email nepa@nepa.com
Website www.nepa.com
Contacts *Elizabeth Frost-Knappman, Edward W. Knappman, Kris Schiavi, Ron Formica*

FOUNDED 1983. *Handles* non-fiction and (clients only) fiction. *Specialises* in current affairs, history, science, women's studies, reference, psychology, politics, biography, true crime and literature. No textbooks or anthologies. No scripts. Unsolicited mss considered but query letter or phone call preferred first. No reading fee. *Commission* Home 15%. *Overseas associates* throughout Europe and Japan; Scott-Ferris, UK. Dramatic rights: Artists Management Group, Los Angeles.

Richard Parks Agency★
138 East 16th Street, Suite 5B, New York NY 10003
☎001 212 254 9067
Contact *Richard Parks*

FOUNDED 1989. *Handles* general trade fiction and non-fiction: literary novels, mysteries and thrillers, commercial fiction, science fiction, biography, pop culture, psychology, self-help, parenting, medical, cooking, gardening, etc. No scripts. No technical or academic. No unsolicited mss. Fiction read by referral only. No reading fee. *Commission* Home 15%; UK & Translation 20%. *Overseas associates* **The Marsh Agency**; **Barbara Levy Literary Agency**.

James Peter Associates, Inc.★
PO Box 670, Tenafly NJ 07670
☎001 201 568 0760 Fax 001 201 568 2959
Contact *Bert Holtje*

FOUNDED 1971. Non-fiction only. 'Many of our authors are historians, psychologists, physicians – all are writing trade books for general readers.' No scripts. No fiction or children's books. *Specialises* in history, popular culture, business, health, biography and politics. No unsolicited mss. Send query letter first with brief project outline, samples and biographical information. No reading fee. *Commission* 15%.

Alison J. Picard Literary Agent
PO Box 2000, Cotuit MA 02635
☎001 508 477 7192 Fax 001 508 477 7192 (notify before faxing)
Email ajpicard@aol.com
Contact *Alison Picard*

FOUNDED 1985. *Handles* mainstream and literary fiction, contemporary and historical romance, children's and young adult, mysteries and thrillers; plus non-fiction. No short stories or poetry. Rarely any science fiction and fantasy. Particularly interested in expanding non-fiction titles. Approach with written query. No reading fee. *Commission* 15%. *Overseas associates* **A.M. Heath & Co. Ltd**, UK.

Pinder Lane & Garon-Brooke Associates Ltd★
159 West 53rd Street, Suite 14–E, New York NY 10019
☎001 212 489 0880 Fax 001 212 489 7104
Owner Agents *Dick Duane, Robert Thixton*
Consulting Agent *Nancy Coffey*

FOUNDED 1951. Fiction and non-fiction. No category romance, westerns or mysteries. No unsolicited mss. First approach by query letter. No reading fee. *Commission* Home 15%; Dramatic 10–15%; Foreign 30%. *Overseas associates* **Abner Stein**, UK; Translation: Bernard Kurman.

PMA Literary & Film Management, Inc.
PO Box 1817, Old Chelsea Sta., New York NY 10011
☎001 212 929 1222   Fax 001 212 206 0238
Email pmalitfilm@aol.com
Website www.pmalitfilm.com
President *Peter Miller*
Vice President *Delin Cormeny*
Associate *Elaine Gartner*
FOUNDED 1976. Commercial fiction, non-fiction and screenplays. *Specialises* in books with motion picture and television potential, and in true crime. No poetry, pornography, non-commercial or academic. No unsolicited mss. Approach by letter with one-page synopsis. *Commission* Home 15%; Dramatic 10–15%; Foreign 20–25%.

Susan Ann Protter Literary Agent★
110 West 40th Street, Suite 1408, New York NY 10018
☎001 212 840 0480
Contact *Susan Ann Protter*
FOUNDED 1971. *Handles* general fiction, mysteries, thrillers, science fiction and fantasy; non-fiction: history, general reference, biography, true crime, science, health and parenting. No romance, poetry, westerns, religious, children's or sport manuals. No scripts. First approach with letter, including IRCs. No reading fee. *Commission* Home & Dramatic 15%; Foreign 25%. *Overseas associates* **Abner Stein**, UK; agents in all major markets.

Quicksilver Books, Literary Agents
50 Wilson Street, Hartsdale NY 10530
☎001 914 946 8748
President *Bob Silverstein*
FOUNDED 1973. *Handles* literary fiction and mainstream commercial fiction: blockbuster, suspense, thriller, contemporary, mystery and historical; and general non-fiction, including self-help, psychology, holistic healing, ecology, environmental, biography, fact crime, New Age, health, nutrition, enlightened wisdom and spirituality. No scripts, science fiction and fantasy,

pornographic, children's or romance. UK material being submitted must have universal appeal for the US market. Unsolicited material welcome but must be accompanied by IRCs for response, together with biographical details, covering letter, etc. No reading fee. *Commission* Home & Dramatic 15%; Translation 20%.

Helen Rees Literary Agency★
123 N. Washington Street, 5th Floor, Boston MA 02114
☎001 617 723 5232 ext 233
Fax 001 617 723 5211
Email wwhelen@aol.com *or* joanmaz@aol.com *or* brifkind@mediaone.com
Contact *Joan Mazmanian*
Associates *Barbara Rifkind, Ann Collette*
FOUNDED 1982. *Specialises* in books on health and business; also handles biography, autobiography and history; quality fiction. No scholarly, academic or technical books. No scripts, science fiction, children's, poetry, photography, short stories, cooking. No unsolicited mss. Send query letter with IRCs. No reading fee. *Commission* Home 15%; Foreign 20%.

Rights Unlimited, Inc.★
101 West 55th Street, Suite 2D, New York NY 10019
☎001 212 246 0900   Fax 001 212 246 2114
Email bkurman@rightsunlimited.com
Contact *Bernard Kurman*
FOUNDED 1985. *Handles* adult fiction, non-fiction. No scripts, poetry, short stories, educational or literary works. Unsolicited mss welcome; query letter with synopsis preferred in the first instance. No reading fee. *Commission* Home 15%; Translation 20%.

Rosenstone/Wender★
3 East 48th Street, 4th Floor, New York NY 10017
☎001 212 832 8330   Fax 001 212 759 4524
Contacts *Phyllis Wender, Susan Perlman Cohen, Sonia E. Pabley*
FOUNDED 1981. *Handles* fiction, non-fiction, children's, and scripts for film, TV and theatre. No material for radio. No unsolicited mss. Send letter outlining the project, credits, etc. No reading fee. *Commission* Home 15%; Dramatic 10%; Foreign 20%. *Overseas associates* La Nouvelle Agence, France; Andrew Nurnberg, Netherlands; The English Agency, Japan; Mohrbooks, Germany; Ole Licht, Scandinavia.

Jane Rotrosen Agency LLC★

318 East 51st Street, New York NY 10022
☎001 212 593 4330
Fax 001 212 935 6985

Contacts *Meg Ruley, Andrea Cirillo, Ruth Kagle, Stephanie Tade, Annelise Robey*

Handles commercial fiction: romance, horror, mysteries, thrillers and fantasy and popular non-fiction. No scripts, educational, professional or belles lettres. No unsolicited mss; send query letter in the first instance. No reading fee. *Commission* Home 15%; UK & Translation 20%. *Overseas associates* worldwide and film agents on the West Coast.

Victoria Sanders
& Associates LLC★

241 Avenue of the Americas, Suite 11H, New York NY 10014
☎001 212 633 8811   Fax 001 212 633 0525

Contacts *Victoria Sanders, Diane Dickensheid*

FOUNDED 1993. *Handles* general trade fiction and non-fiction, plus ancillary film and television rights. *Commission* Home & Dramatic 15%; Translation 20%.

Sandum & Associates

144 East 84th Street, New York NY 10028
☎001 212 737 2011

Contact *Howard E. Sandum*

FOUNDED 1987. *Handles* all categories of general adult non-fiction, plus occasional fiction. No scripts. No children's, poetry or short stories. No unsolicited mss. Third-party referral preferred but direct approach by letter, with synopsis, brief biography and IRCs, is accepted. No reading fee. *Commission* Home & Dramatic 15%; Translation & Foreign 20%. *Overseas associates* Scott Ferris Associates.

Jack Scagnetti
Talent & Literary Agency

5118 Vineland Avenue, Suite 102, North Hollywood CA 91601
☎001 818 762 3871

Contact *Jack Scagnetti*

FOUNDED 1974. Works mostly with established/published authors. *Handles* non-fiction, fiction, film and TV scripts. No reading fees. *Commission* Home & Dramatic 10% (scripts), 15% (books); Foreign 15%.

Schiavone Literary Agency, Inc.

236 Trails End, West Palm Beach FL 33413–2135
☎001 561 966 9294   Fax 001 561 966 9294
Email profschia@aol.com
Website www.freeyellow.com/members8/schiavone/index.html

Branch office (June/July/Aug. only): 3671 Henry Hudson Pkwy., Suite 11H, Bronx, NY 10463 ☎/Fax 001 718 543 5093
President *James Schiavone*

FOUNDED 1997. *Handles* fiction and non-fiction (all genres). *Specialises* in biography, autobiography, celebrity memoirs. No poetry. No unsolicited mss; send query with brief biog-sketch, synopsis, outline and sample chapters (enclose IRCs). No reading fee. *Commission* Home 15%; Foreign & Translation 20%. *Overseas associates* in Europe.

Susan Schulman,
A Literary Agency★

454 West 44th Street, New York NY 10036
☎001 212 713 1633/4/5
Fax 001 212 581 8830
Email schulman@aol.com
Website www.susan.schulman.com

Submissions Editor (Books) *Christine Maren*
Submissions Editor (Plays) *Brian Leifert*

FOUNDED 1979. *Specialises* in non-fiction of all types but particularly in health and psychology-based self-help for men, women and families. Other interests include business, the social sciences, biography, language and health. Fiction interests include contemporary fiction, including women's, mysteries, historical and thrillers 'with a cutting edge'. Always looking for 'something original and fresh'. No unsolicited mss. Query first, including outline and three sample chapters with IRCs. No reading fee. Represents properties for film and television, and works with agents in appropriate territories for translation rights. *Commission* Home & Dramatic 15%; Translation 20%. *Overseas associates* Plays: **Rosica Colin Ltd** and **The Agency Ltd**, UK; Children's books: Marilyn Malin, UK, Commercial fiction: **MBA Literary Agents**, UK.

Shapiro-Lichtman – Talent Agency

8827 Beverly Boulevard, Los Angeles CA 90048
☎001 310 859 8877   Fax 001 310 859 7153

FOUNDED 1969. Works mostly with established/published authors. *Handles* film and TV scripts.

Unsolicited mss will not be read. *Commission* Home & Dramatic 10%; Foreign 20%.

The Shepard Agency
Premier National Bank Building, Suite 3, 1525 Rt. 22, Brewster NY 10509
☎001 914 279 2900/3236
Fax 001 914 279 3239
Email shepardagcy@mindspring.com
Website home.mindspring.com/~shepardagcy

Contacts *Jean Shepard, Lance Shepard*

FOUNDED 1987. *Handles* non-fiction: business, food, self-help and travel; some fiction: adult, children's and young adult and the occasional script. No pornography. *Specialises* in business. Send query letter, table of contents, sample chapters and IRCs for response. No reading fee. *Commission* Home & Dramatic 15%; Translation 20%.

Lee Shore Agency Ltd
The Sterling Building, 440 Friday Road, Pittsburgh PA 15209
☎001 412 821 0440 Fax 001 412 821 6099
Email LeeShore1@aol.com
Website www.leeshoreagency.com

Contacts *Jennifer Piemme, Danielle Chiotti*

FOUNDED 1988. *Handles* non-fiction, including textbooks, and mass-market fiction: horror, romance, mystery, westerns, science fiction. Also some young adult and, more recently, screenplays. *Specialises* in New Age, self-help, how-to and quality fiction. No children's. No unsolicited mss. Send IRCs for guidelines before submitting work. Reading fee charged. *Commission* Home 15%; Dramatic 20%.

Bobbe Siegel Literary Agency
41 West 83rd Street, New York NY 10024
☎001 212 877 4985 Fax 001 212 877 4985

Contact *Bobbe Siegel*

FOUNDED 1975. Works mostly with established/published authors. *Specialises* in literary fiction, detective, suspense, historical, fantasy, biography, how-to, women's interest, fitness, health, beauty, sports, pop psychology. No scripts. No cookbooks, crafts, children's, short stories or humour. First approach with letter including IRCs for response. Will not accept queries via fax. No reading fee. Critiques given if the writer is taken on for representation. *Commission* Home 15%; Dramatic & Foreign 20%. (Foreign/Dramatic split 50/50 with sub-agent.) Also handles foreign rights for many US agents. *Overseas associates* in various countries, including **John Pawsey** in the UK.

Michael Snell Literary Agency
PO Box 1206, Truro MA 02666–1206
☎001 508 349 3718

President *Michael Snell*
Vice President *Patricia Smith*

FOUNDED 1980. Adult non-fiction, especially science, business and women's issues. *Specialises* in business and computer books (professional and reference to popular trade how-to); general how-to and self-help on all topics, from diet and exercise to parenting, relationships, health, sex, psychology and personal finance, plus literary and suspense fiction. No unsolicited mss. Send outline and sample chapter with return postage for reply. No reading fee for outlines. Brochure available on how to write a book proposal. Author of *From Book Idea to Bestseller*, published by Prima. Rewriting, developmental editing, collaborating and ghostwriting services available on a fee basis. Send IRCs. *Commission* Home 15%.

Southern Writers
Magee Building, 3004 Jackson Street, Suite A, Alexandria LA 71301–4745
☎001 318 445 6550 Fax 001 318 445 6650

President *Emilie Griffin*

FOUNDED 1979. *Handles* fiction and non-fiction of general interest. No scripts, short stories, poetry, autobiography or articles. No unsolicited mss. Approach in writing with query. Reading fee charged to authors unpublished in the field. *Commission* Home 15%; Dramatic & Translation 20%.

The Spieler Agency
154 West 57th Street, Room 135, New York NY 10019
☎001 212 757 4439 Fax 001 212 333 2019
Email SpielerLit@aol.com

The Spieler Agency/West, 1328 Sixth Street, #3, Berkeley, CA 94710
☎001 510 528 2616 Fax 001 510 528 8117

Contacts *Joseph Spieler, John Thornton, Lisa M. Ross, Dierdre Mullane, Ada Muellner* (New York); *Victoria Shoemaker* (Berkeley)

FOUNDED 1980. *Handles* literary fiction and non-fiction. No how-to or genre romance. *Specialises* in history, science, ecology, social issues and business. No scripts. Approach in writing with IRCs. No reading fee. *Commission* Home 15%; Translation 20%. *Overseas associates* **Abner Stein**; **The Marsh Agency**, UK.

Philip G. Spitzer Literary Agency★
50 Talmage Farm Lane, East Hampton NY 11937
☎001 516 329 3650 Fax 001 516 329 3651
Contact *Philip Spitzer*

FOUNDED 1969. Works mostly with established/published authors. *Specialises* in general non-fiction and fiction – thrillers. No reading fee for outlines. *Commission* Home & Dramatic 15%; Foreign 20%.

Lyle Steele & Co. Ltd
Literary Agents
511 East 73rd Street, Suite 6, New York NY 10021
☎001 212 288 2981
President *Lyle Steele*

FOUNDED 1985. *Handles* general non-fiction and category fiction. Also North American rights to titles published by major English publishers. No scripts unless derived from books already being handled. No romance. No unsolicited mss: query with IRCs in first instance. No reading fee. *Commission* 10%. *Overseas associates* worldwide.

Gloria Stern Agency (Hollywood)
12535 Chandler Boulevard, Suite 3, North Hollywood CA 91607
☎001 818 508 6296 Fax 001 818 508 6296
Contact *Gloria Stern*

FOUNDED 1984. *Handles* film scripts, genre (romance, detective, thriller and sci-fi) and mainstream fiction; electronic media. Accepts interactive material, games and electronic data. 'No books containing gratuitous violence.' Approach with letter, biography and synopsis. Reading fee charged by the hour. *Commission* Home 15%; Offshore 20%.

Gunther Stuhlmann
Author's Representative
PO Box 276, Becket MA 01223
☎001 413 623 5170
Contacts *Gunther Stuhlmann, Barbara Ward*

FOUNDED 1954. *Handles* literary fiction, biography and serious non-fiction. No film/TV scripts unless from established clients. No short stories, detective, romance, adventure, poetry, technical or computers. Query first with IRCs, including sample chapters and synopsis of project. '*We take on few new clients.*' No reading fee. *Commission* Home 10%; Foreign 15%; Translation 20%.

2M Communications Ltd
121 West 27th Street, Suite 601, New York NY 10001
☎001 212 741 1509 Fax 001 212 691 4460
Contact *Madeleine Morel*

FOUNDED 1982. *Handles* non-fiction only: everything from pop psychology and health to cookery books, biographies and pop culture. No scripts. No fiction, children's, computers or science. No unsolicited mss; send letter with sample pages and IRCs. No reading fee. *Commission* Home & Dramatic 15%; Translation 20%. *Overseas associates* Thomas Schluck Agency, Germany; Asano Agency, Japan; EAIS, France; Living Literary Agency, Italy; Nueva Agencia Literaria Internacional, Spain.

Van der Leun & Associates
32 Gramercy Park South #11L, New York City NY 10003
☎001 212 982 6165
Contact *Patricia Van der Leun*

FOUNDED 1984. *Handles* fiction and non-fiction. No scripts. No science fiction, fantasy or romance. *Specialises* in art and architecture, science, biography and fiction. No unsolicited mss; query first, with letter and short biography. No reading fee. *Commission* 15%. *Overseas associates* **Abner Stein**, UK; Michelle Lapautre, France; English Agency, Japan; Carmen Balcells, Spain; Lucia Riff, South America; Susanna Zevi, Italy.

Wales Literary Agency, Inc.★
PO Box 9428, Seattle WA 98109–0428
☎001 206 284 7114 Fax 001 206 284 0190
Email waleslit@aol.com
Contacts *Elizabeth Wales, Adrienne Reed*

FOUNDED 1988. *Handles* quality fiction and non-fiction. No genre fiction, westerns, romance, science fiction or horror. Special interest in 'Pacific Rim', West Coast, and Pacific Northwest stories. No unsolicited mss; send query letter with publication list and writing sample. No reading fee. No e-mail queries longer than one page. *Commission* Home 15%; Dramatic & Translation 20%.

John A. Ware Literary Agency
392 Central Park West, New York NY 10025
☎001 212 866 4733 Fax 001 212 866 4734
Contact *John Ware*

FOUNDED 1978. *Specialises* in non-fiction: biography, history, current affairs, investigative journalism, science, inside looks at phenomena, medicine and psychology (academic credentials required). Also handles literary fiction, mysteries/thrillers, sport, oral history, Americana and folklore. Unsolicited mss not read. Send query letter first with IRCs to cover return postage. No reading fee. *Commission* Home & Dramatic 15%; Foreign 20%.

Waterside Productions, Inc.
2191 San Elijo Avenue, Cardiff by the Sea CA 92007–839
☎001 760 632 9190 Fax 001 760 632 9295
Email bgladstone@compuserve.com
Contact *William Gladstone*
FOUNDED 1982. *Handles* general non-fiction: computers and technology, psychology, science, business, sports. All types of multimedia. No unsolicited mss; send query letter. No reading fee. *Commission* Home 15%; Dramatic 20%; Translation 25%. *Overseas associates* Serafina Clarke, UK; Asano Agency, Japan; Ulla Lohren, Sweden; Ruth Liepman, Germany; Vera Le Marie, EAIS, France; Bardon Chinese Media Agency, China; Grandi & Vitali, Italy; DRT, Korea; Mercedes Casanovas, Spain.

Watkins Loomis Agency, Inc.
133 East 35th Street, Suite 1, New York NY 10016
☎001 212 532 0080 Fax 001 212 889 0506
Contact *Katherine Fausset*
FOUNDED 1904. *Handles* fiction and non-fiction. No scripts for film, radio, TV or theatre. No science fiction, fantasy or horror. No reading fee. No unsolicited mss. Approach in writing with enquiry or proposal and s.a.e. *Commission* Home 15%; UK & Translation 20%. *Overseas associates* **Abner Stein**; **The Marsh Agency**, UK.

Wecksler–Incomco
170 West End Avenue, New York NY 10023
☎001 212 787 2239 Fax 001 212 496 7035
Contacts *Sally Wecksler, Joann Amparan-Close*
FOUNDED 1971. *Handles* literary fiction and non-fiction: business, reference, biography, performing arts and heavily illustrated books; also some children's books. Send queries only. No unsolicited mss. No submissions by fax or e-mail; hard copy only. No reading fee. Foreign rights. *Commission* Home 15%; Translation & UK 20%.

Cherry Weiner Literary Agency
28 Kipling Way, Manalapan NJ 07726
☎001 732 446 2096 Fax 001 732 792 0506
Email Cherry8486@aol.com
Contact *Cherry Weiner*
FOUNDED 1977. *Handles* all types of genre fiction: science fiction and fantasy, mainstream, romance, mystery, westerns. No scripts, non-fiction or unsolicited mss, no submissions except through referral. No reading fee. *Commission* 15%. *Overseas associates* **Abner Stein**, UK; Thomas Schluck, Germany; Borderline Literary Agency, Italy; International Editors Inc., Spain; Prava Prevodi Agency (Eastern Europe), Serbia; Elaine Benisti Agency, France; Nucihan Kesim Literary Agency, Turkey; English Agency (Japan) Ltd; Alex Korzhenevski Agency, Russia; Renaissance Media – movie agent. Also dealing with various e-book publishers.

Wieser & Wieser, Inc.
25 East 21st Street, New York NY 10010
☎001 212 260 0860
Contacts *Olga B. Wieser, Jake Elwell*
FOUNDED 1976. Works mostly with established/published authors. *Specialises* in literary and mainstream fiction, serious and popular historical fiction, and general non-fiction: business, finance, aviation, sports, travel and popular medicine. No poetry, children's, science fiction or religious. No unsolicited mss. First approach by letter with IRCs. No reading fee for outlines. *Commission* Home & Dramatic 15%; Foreign 20%.

Ann Wright Representatives
165 West 46th Street, Suite 1105, New York NY 10036–2501
☎001 212 764 6770 Fax 001 212 764 5125
Contact *Dan Wright*
FOUNDED 1961. *Specialises* in material with strong film potentical. *Handles* screenplays and novels, drama and fiction. No academic, scientific or scholarly. Approach by letter; no reply without IRCs. Include outline and credits only. 'Has reputation for encouraging new writers.' No reading fee. Signatory to the Writers Guild of America Agreement. *Commission* Literary 10–20%; Screenplays 10% of gross.

Writers House, LLC.★
21 West 26th Street, New York NY 10010
☎001 212 685 2400 Fax 001 212 685 1781
Contacts *Albert Zuckerman, Amy Berkower, Merrilee Heifetz, Susan Cohen, Susan Ginsburg, Fran Lebowitz, Karen Solem, Robin Rue, Simon Lipskar, Steven Malk, Jennifer Lyons*
FOUNDED 1974. *Handles* all types of fiction, including children's and young adult, plus

narrative non-fiction: history, biography, popular science, pop and rock culture. *Specialises* in popular fiction, women's novels, thrillers and children's. Represents novelisation rights for film producers such as New Line Cinema. No scripts. No professional or scholarly. For consideration of unsolicited mss, send letter of enquiry, 'explaining why your book is wonderful, briefly what it's about and outlining your writing background'. No reading fee. *Commission* Home & Dramatic 15%; Foreign 20%. Albert Zuckerman is author of *Writing the Blockbuster Novel*, published by Little, Brown & Co. and Warner Paperbacks.

US Media Contacts in the UK

ABC News Intercontinental Inc.
3 Queen Caroline Street, Mail Code 2303, London W6 9PE
☎020 8222 5000 Fax 020 8222 5020

Bureau Chief & Director of News Coverage, Europe, Middle East & Africa *Rex Granum*

Alaska Journal of Commerce
16 Cavaye Place, London SW10 9PT
☎0702 092 4480 Fax 0702 092 4482

Bureau Chief *Robert Gould*

The Associated Press
12 Norwich Street, London EC4A 1BP
☎020 7353 1515 Fax 020 7353 8118

Chief of Bureau/Managing Director, AP Ltd *Myron L. Belkind*

The Baltimore Sun
11 Kensington Court Place, London W8 5BJ
☎020 7460 2200 Fax 020 7460 2211

Bureau Chief *Bill Glauber*

Bloomberg Business News
City Gate House, 39–45 Finsbury Square, London EC2A 1PQ
☎020 7330 7500 Fax 020 7392 6666

London Bureau Chief *Ed Roussel*

Boston Globe
5 Milton Close, London N2 0QH
☎020 8458 7026 Fax 020 8458 7026

Bureau Chief *Kevin Cullen*

Bridge News
Winchmore House, 15 Fetter Lane, London EC4A 1BW
☎020 7842 4141

Managing Editor, Western Europe *Timothy Penn*

Business Week
1 Albemarle Street, London W1S 4DT
☎020 7491 8985 Fax 020 7409 7152

Bureau Chief *Stanley Reed*

Cable News Network Inc. (CNN)
CNN House, 19–22 Rathbone Place, London W1P 1DF
☎020 7637 6800 Fax 020 7637 6868

Bureau Chief *Thomas Mintier*

CBC Television and Radio
43/51 Great Titchfield Street, London W1P 8DD
☎020 7412 9200 Fax 020 7637 1892

London Bureau Manager *Ann Macmillan*

CBS News
68 Knightsbridge, London SW1X 7LL
☎020 7581 4801 Fax 020 7581 4431

Vice President/Bureau Chief *John Paxson*

Chicago Tribune Press Service
169 Piccadilly, London W1J 9EH
☎020 7499 8769 Fax 020 7499 8781

Chief European Correspondent *Ray Moseley*

CNBC
3 Shortlands, Hammersmith, London W6 8HX
☎020 8600 6380 Fax 020 8600 6390

Bureau Chief *Karen Nye*

Cox Newspapers
PO Box 75, East Horsley, Surrey KT24 6WA
☎01372 452279 Fax 01372 450530

Correspondent *Bert Roughton Jnr*

Dallas Morning News
18 Rusthall Avenue, London W4 1BP
☎020 8742 0495 Fax 020 8747 3275

European Bureau Chief *Gregory Katz*

Dow Jones Newswires
10 Fleet Place, Limeburner Lane, London EC4M 7QN
☎020 7842 9360

Editor (Europe, Middle East, Africa) *Jan Boucek*

Fairchild Publications of New York
20 Shorts Gardens, London WC2H 9AU
☎020 7240 0420 Fax 020 7240 0290

Bureau Chief *James Fallon*

Forbes Magazine
10 Rotherwick Road, London NW11 7DA
☎020 8455 0463 Fax 020 8455 0512
European Bureau Chief *Richard C. Morais*

Fox News Channel
6 Centaurs Business Park, Grant Way,
Isleworth, Middlesex TW7 5QD
☎020 7805 7143 Fax 020 7805 7140
Producer/Bureau Chief *Paul Tyson*

The Globe and Mail
43–51 Great Titchfield Street, London
W1W 7DA
☎020 7323 0449 Fax 020 7323 0428
European Correspondent *Alan Freeman*

International Herald Tribune
40 Marsh Wall, London E14 9TP
☎020 7510 5718 Fax 020 7987 3470
London Correspondent *Tom Buerkle*
(See entry under **National Newspapers**)

Los Angeles Times
150 Brompton Road, London SW3 1HX
☎020 7823 7315 Fax 020 7823 7308
Bureau Chief *Marjorie Miller*

Market News International
167 Fleet Street, 8th Floor, London EC4A 2EA
☎020 7353 4462 Fax 020 7353 9122
Deputy Bureau Chief *Ralph Johnston*

National Public Radio
Room G-10 East Wing, Bush House, Strand,
London WC2B 4PH
☎020 7557 1089 Fax 020 7379 6486
Bureau Chief *Julie McCarthy*

NBC News Worldwide Inc.
4th Floor, 3 Shortlands, Hammersmith,
London W6 8HX
☎020 8600 6600 Fax 020 8600 6601
Bureau Chief *Chris Hampson*

The New York Times
66 Buckingham Gate, London SW1E 6AU
☎020 7799 5050 Fax 020 7799 2962
Chief Correspondent *William Hoge*

Newsweek
18 Park Street, London W1K 2HQ
☎020 7629 8361 Fax 020 7408 1403
Bureau Chief *Stryker McGuire*

People Magazine
Brettenham House, Lancaster Place, London
WC2E 7TL
☎020 7322 1134 Fax 020 7322 1125
Bureau Chief *Brian Alexander*

Philadelphia Inquirer
2 Cranley Mews, London SW7 3BX
☎020 7460 6800 Fax 020 7460 6800
Bureau Chief *Andrea Gerlin*

Reader's Digest Association Ltd
11 Westferry Circus, Canary Wharf, London
E14 4HE
☎020 7715 8046 Fax 020 7715 8716
Editor-in-Chief, British Edition *Russell
Twisk*
(See entries under **UK Publishers** and
Magazines)

Time Magazine
Brettenham House, Lancaster Place, London
WC2E 7TL
☎020 7499 4080 Fax 020 7322 1230
Bureau Chief *Jef McAllister*
(See entry under **Magazines**)

USA Today
69 New Oxford Street, London
WC1A 1DG
☎020 7559 5859 Fax 020 7559 5895
Chief of European Correspondents *David
Lynch*

Voice of America
International Press Centre, 76 Shoe Lane,
London EC4A 3JB
☎020 7410 0960 Fax 020 7410 0966
Bureau Chief/Senior Editor *Gary Edquist*

Wall Street Journal
10 Fleet Place, Limeburner Lane, London
EC4M 7RB
☎020 7842 9200 Fax 020 7842 9201
London Bureau Chief *James R. Hagerty*

Washington Post
18 Park Street, London W1Y 4HH
☎020 7629 8958 Fax 020 7629 8950
Bureau Chief *T.R. Reid*

Commonwealth Publishers

Australia

ACER Press
19 Prospect Hill Road, Camberwell,
Victoria 3124
☎00 61 3 9277 5555 Fax 00 61 3 9277 5678
FOUNDED 1930. *Publishes* Education, human
relations, psychology, psychiatry.

Allen & Unwin Pty Ltd
PO Box 8500, St Leonards, Sydney,
NSW 1590
☎00 61 2 8425 0100 Fax 00 61 2 9906 2218
Website www.allen.unwin.com.au
FOUNDED 1976. *Publishes* general non-fiction,
art, Asian studies, business, cookery, earth sciences, economics, education, fiction, gay and
lesbian, government, political science, health
and nutrition, history, industrial relations, literature, literary criticism, essays, general science.

Edward Arnold (Australia) Pty Ltd
PO Box 885, Kew, Victoria 3101
☎00 61 3 859 9011 Fax 00 61 3 859 9141
FOUNDED 1966. Part of Hodder & Stoughton
(Australia) Pty Ltd. *Publishes* general nonfiction: accountancy, Asian studies, career development, computer science, cookery, geography, geology, government, political science,
health and nutrition, law, mathematics, psychology and psychiatry, technology.

Blackwell Science Pty Ltd
PO Box 378, South Carlton, Victoria 3053
☎00 61 3 9347 0300 Fax 00 61 3 9347 5552
FOUNDED 1971. Part of **Blackwell Science
Ltd**, UK. *Publishes* general science, medicine,
nursing, dentistry, engineering, computer science, mathematics, physical sciences, physics,
psychology, psychiatry.

Butterworths Australia Ltd
Reed Elsevier Building, Tower 2, 475–495
Victoria Avenue, Chatswood, NSW 2067113
☎00 61 2 9422 2222 Fax 00 61 2 9422 2444
FOUNDED 1910. A division of Reed
International Books Australia Pty Ltd. *Publishes*
accountancy, business and law.

Currency Press Pty Ltd
PO Box 2287, Strawberry Hills, NSW 2012
☎00 61 2 9332 1300 Fax 00 61 2 9319 3649
Website www.currency.com.au
FOUNDED 1971. Performing arts publisher –
drama, theatre, music, dance, film and video.

Dangaroo Press
PO Box 93, New Lambton, NSW 2305
☎00 61 4 954 5938 Fax 00 61 4 954 6531
FOUNDED 1978. *Publishes* general non-fiction,
art, literature, literary criticism, essays, poetry,
social sciences, women's studies.

E.J. Dwyer (Australia) Pty Ltd
Locked Bag 71, Alexandria, NSW 2015
☎00 61 2 9550 2355 Fax 00 61 2 9519 3218
FOUNDED 1904. *Publishes* self-help, marketing,
social sciences, sociology, religion, theology.

Harcourt Australia Pty Ltd
Locked Bag 16, St Peters, NSW 2044
☎00 61 2 9517 8999 Fax 00 61 2 9517 2249
FOUNDED 1972. *Publishes* business, education,
general science, medicine, nursing, dentistry,
psychology, psychiatry, veterinary science,
social sciences, mathematics.

HarperCollins Publishers (Australia) Pty Ltd
PO Box 321, Pymble, NSW 2073
☎00 61 2 9952 5000 Fax 00 61 2 9952 5600
Owner *HarperCollins Publishers Group*
FOUNDED 1872. *Publishes* fiction and general
non-fiction, biography, children's, gardening,
humour, government, political science,
regional interests, literature, literary criticism,
essays, women's studies. DIVISIONS **General
Illustrated Non-fiction** *Alison Presley*;
Children's *Brian Cook*; **Mass Market Non-
fiction** *Carolyn Walsh*.

Hodder Headline Australia
Level 22, 201 Kent Street, Sydney, NSW 2000
☎00 61 2 8248 0800 Fax 00 61 2 8248 0810
Owner *Hodder Headline (UK)*
FOUNDED 1958. *Publishes* general non-fiction
and fiction (adult and children's), education.

Hyland House Publishing Pty Ltd

PO Box 122, Flemington, Victoria 3031

☎00 61 3 9376 4461

FOUNDED 1976. *Publishes* general non-fiction, Asian studies, cookery, animals, pets, essays, fiction, gardening, literature, literary criticism.

Thomas C. Lothian Pty Ltd

11 Munro Street, Port Melbourne, Victoria 3207

☎00 61 3 9645 1544 Fax 00 61 3 9646 4882

FOUNDED 1888. *Publishes* general non-fiction: business, health and nutrition, New Age, self-help.

Macmillan Education Australia Pty Ltd

107 Moray Street, Melbourne, Victoria 3205

☎00 61 3 9646 6100 Fax 00 61 3 9646 5946

FOUNDED 1896. *Publishes* accountancy, economics, education, geography, geology, government, political science, history, management, mathematics, physics, general science, social sciences, sociology.

McGraw-Hill Book Company Australia Pty Ltd

PO Box 239, Roseville, NSW 2069

☎00 61 2 9415 9899 Fax 00 61 2 9417 8872

Website www.mcgraw-hill.com.au

Owner *McGraw-Hill Inc. (USA)*

FOUNDED 1964. *Publishes* accountancy, education, health and nutrition, advertising, aeronautics, aviation, anthropology, architecture and interior design, art, chemistry, child care and development, computer science, criminology, economics, electronics, electrical engineering, general engineering, English as a second language, environmental studies, film and video, geography, geology, journalism, industrial relations, language arts, linguistics, management, maritime, mathematics, mechanical engineering, medicine, nursing, dentistry, philosophy, photography, physics, psychology, psychiatry, sport, social sciences and sociology.

Melbourne University Press

PO Box 278, Carlton, South Victoria 3053

☎00 61 3 9347 3455 Fax 00 61 3 9349 2527

FOUNDED 1922. *Publishes* general non-fiction, biography, essays, history, literature, literary criticism, natural history, psychology, psychiatry, travel.

Openbook Publishers

GPO Box 1368J, Adelaide, SA 5001

☎00 61 8 8223 4568 Fax 00 61 8 8223 4552

Website www.openbooks.com.au

FOUNDED 1913. *Publishes* religious and educational books.

Pan Macmillan Pty Ltd

PO Box 124, Chippendale, NSW 2008

☎00 61 2 9261 5611 Fax 00 61 2 9261 5047

Website www.macmillan.com.au

Owner *Macmillan Publishers Ltd (UK)*

FOUNDED 1983. *Publishes* essays, fiction, literature, literary criticism.

Pearson Education

LMB 507, Frenchs Forest, NSW 1640

☎00 61 3 9454 2200 Fax 00 61 3 9453 0089

Website www.awl.com.au

Formerly Addison Wesley Longman. Australia's largest educational publisher.

Penguin Books Australia Ltd

PO Box 157, Ringwood, Victoria 3134

☎00 61 3 9871 2400 Fax 00 61 3 9870 9618

FOUNDED 1946. *Publishes* general non-fiction and fiction; biography, cookery, humour, literature, literary criticism, essays, science fiction, fantasy, self-help, travel.

University of Queensland Press

PO Box 6042, St Lucia, Queensland 4067

☎00 61 7 3365 2127 Fax 00 61 7 3365 7579

Website www.uqp.uq.edu.au

FOUNDED 1948. *Publishes* Aboriginal studies, general non-fiction and fiction, literature, literary criticism, essays, poetry, biography, history, sport, travel.

Random House Australia Pty Ltd

20 Alfred Street, First Floor, Milsons Point, NSW 2061

☎00 61 2 9954 9966 Fax 00 61 2 9954 4562

Email random@randomhouse.com.au

Website www.randomhouse.com.au

Publishes fiction and non-fiction.

Reader's Digest (Australia) Pty Ltd

PO Box 4353, Sydney, NSW 2001

☎00 61 2 9690 6935 Fax 00 61 2 9690 6390

FOUNDED 1946. Associate company of **Reader's Digest Association, Inc.** (USA). Educational publisher.

Reed Educational & Professional Publishing Australia
22 Salmon Street, Port Melbourne,
Victoria 3207
☎00 61 3 9646 6677 Fax 00 61 3 9646 6925
FOUNDED 1982. *Publishes* art, chemistry, chemical engineering, environmental studies, geography, geology, health and nutrition, history, mathematics, physics.

Scholastic Australia Pty Limited
PO Box 579, Gosford, NSW 2250
☎00 61 2 4328 3555 Fax 00 61 2 4329 1106
Owner *Scholastic, Inc. (USA)*
FOUNDED 1968. Educational publisher.

Science Press
Fitzroy & Chapel Streets, Marrickville,
NSW 2204
☎00 61 2 9516 1122 Fax 00 61 2 9550 1915
FOUNDED 1945. Educational publisher.

Simon & Schuster Australia Pty Ltd
PO Box 507, East Roseville, NSW 2069
☎00 61 2 9417 3255 Fax 00 61 2 9417 3188
FOUNDED 1987. Part of **Simon & Schuster Inc.**, USA. *Publishes* general non-fiction.

Transworld Publishers Pty Ltd
Private Bag 12, Neutral Bay, NSW 2089
☎00 61 2 9908 4366 Fax 00 61 2 9953 8563
Owner *Bertelsmann AG (Germany)*
FOUNDED 1980. *Publishes* non-fiction and fiction – romance, science fiction, fantasy, humour, health and nutrition, self-help.

University of Western Australia Press
The University of Western Australia,
Nedlands, WA 6009
☎00 61 8 9380 3182 Fax 00 61 8 9380 1027
FOUNDED 1954. *Publishes* general non-fiction, essays, literature, literary criticism, history, social sciences, sociology, natural history, autobiography.

John Wiley & Sons Ltd
PO Box 1226, Milton, Queensland 4064
☎00 61 7 3859 9755 Fax 00 61 7 3859 9715
Email brisbane@johnwiley.com.au
Website www.johnwiley.com.au
Owner *John Wiley & Sons Inc. (USA)*
FOUNDED 1954. *Publishes* general non-fiction and education books.

Canada

Arnold Publishing Ltd
11016 127th Street, Edmonton, Alberta
T5M 0T2
☎001 780 454 7477 Fax 001 780 454 7463
Email info@arnold.ca
Website www.arnold.ca
FOUNDED 1967. Educational textbooks and CD-ROMS.

Butterworths Canada Ltd
75 Clegg Road, Markham, Ontario L6G 1A1
☎001 905 479 2665 Fax 001 905 479 2826
Website www.butterworths.ca
FOUNDED 1912. Division of Reed Elsevier plc. *Publishes* law books, CD-ROMs, journals, newsletters, law reports and newspapers.

Canadian Scholars' Press, Inc
180 Bloor Street W, Suite 1202, Toronto,
Ontario M5S 2V6
☎001 416 929 2774 Fax 001 416 929 1926
Email info@cspi.org
Website www.cspi.org
FOUNDED 1987. *Publishes* scholarly books in English and French.

CGG Books Canada, Inc.
99 Yorkville Avenue, Suite 400, Toronto,
Ontario M5R 3K5
☎001 416 963 8830 Fax 001 416 923 4821
FOUNDED 1905. Formerly Macmillan Canada. *Publishes* fiction and non-fiction.

Fenn Publishing Co Ltd
34 Nixon Road, Bolton, Ontario L7E 1W2
☎001 905 951 6600 Fax 001 905 951 6601
Website www.hbfenn.com
FOUNDED 1977. *Publishes* fiction and non-fiction, children's.

Fitzhenry & Whiteside Limited
195 Allstate Parkway, Markham,
Ontario L3R 4T8
☎001 905 477 9700 Fax 001 905 477 9179
Email godwit@fitzhenry.ca
Website www.fitzhenry.ca
FOUNDED 1966. *Publishes* reference and children's books; educational material.

Golden Books Publishing (Canada) Inc
73 Water Street N., No 501, Cambridge,
Ontario N1R 5X2
☎001 519 623 3590 Fax 001 519 623 3598

Website www.goldenbooks.com
FOUNDED 1942. *Publishes* (in English and French) juvenile and adult books, Bibles.

Harcourt Canada Ltd
55 Horner Avenue, Toronto, Ontario M8Z 4X6
☎001 416 255 4491 Fax 001 416 255 4046
Website www.harcourtcanada.com
FOUNDED 1922. *Publishes* educational material.

HarperCollins Publishers Limited
55 Avenue Road, Suite 2900, Hazelton Lanes,
Toronto, Ontario M5R 3L2
☎001 416 975 9334 Fax 001 416 975 9884
Website www.harpercanada.com
FOUNDED 1989. *Publishes* fiction and non-fiction, children's and religious.

Irwin Publishing
325 Humber College Blvd., Toronto, Ontario
M9W 7C3
☎001 416 798 0424 Fax 001 416 798 1384
Email irwin@irwin-pub.com
Website www.irwin-pub.com
FOUNDED 1945. *Publishes* (in English and French) education.

McClelland & Stewart Ltd
481 University Avenue, Suite 900, Toronto,
Ontario M5G 2E9
☎001 416 598 1114 Fax 001 416 598 7764
Website www.mcclelland.com
FOUNDED 1906. *Publishes* fiction and non-fiction, poetry.

McGill–Queen's University Press
3430 McTavish Street, Montreal, Quebec
H3A 1X9
☎001 514 398 3750 Fax 001 514 398 4333
Email mqup@mqup.mcgill.ca
Website www.mcgill.ca/mqupress
FOUNDED 1969. *Publishes* (in English and French) scholarly and non-fiction.

McGraw-Hill Ryerson Ltd
300 Water Street, Whitby, Ontario L1N 9B6
☎001 905 430 5000 Fax 001 905 430 5020
Website www.mcgrawhill.ca
FOUNDED 1944. Subsidiary of the McGraw-Hill Companies. *Publishes* education, professional and general trade.

Nelson Thomson Learning
1120 Birchmount Road, Scarborough,
Ontario M1K 5G4
☎001 416 752 9100 Fax 001 416 752 9646

Website www.nelson.com
FOUNDED 1914. Division of Thomson Canada Ltd. *Publishes* educational, professional and reference.

New Star Books Ltd
107–3477 Commercial Street, Vancouver,
BC V5N 4E8
☎001 604 738 9429 Fax 001 604 738 9332
Email info@newstarbooks.com
Website www.newstarbooks.com
FOUNDED 1974. *Publishes* social issues and current affairs, fiction, literature, history, international politics, labour, feminist, gay and lesbian studies.

Pearson Education
PO Box 680, Don Mills, Ontario M3C 2T8
☎001 416 447 5101 Fax 001 416 443 0948
Website www.pearsoned.com
FOUNDED 1966. Formerly Addison Wesley Longman Canada. Fourth-largest educational publisher in Canada. Acquired HarperCollins' educational list in 1997. Publishes in English and French.

Penguin Books Canada Ltd
10 Alcorn Avenue, Suite 300, Toronto,
Ontario M4V 3B2
☎001 416 925 2249 Fax 001 416 925 0068
Website www.penguin.ca
FOUNDED 1974. Division of the Pearson Group. *Publishes* fiction and non-fiction books and audio cassettes.

Prentice Hall Canada
1870 Birchmount Road, Scarborough,
Ontario M1P 2J7
☎001 416 293 3621 Fax 001 416 299 2529
Website www.phcanada.com
FOUNDED 1960. *Publishes* education, textbooks, reference and non-fiction.

Random House of Canada
2775 Matheson Blvd. East, Mississauga,
Ontario L4W 4P7
☎001 905 624 0672 Fax 001 905 624 6217
Website www.randomhouse.com
FOUNDED 1944. *Publishes* fiction and non-fiction and children's.

Scholastic Canada Ltd
175 Hillmount Road, Markham, Ontario
L6C 1Z7
☎001 905 887 7323 Fax 001 905 883 4113
Website www.scholastic.ca

FOUNDED 1957. *Publishes* (in English and French) children's books and educational material.

Tundra Books Inc
481 University Avenue, Suite 802, Toronto, Ontario M5G 2E9
☎001 416 598 4786 Fax 001 416 598 0247
FOUNDED 1967. Division of **McClelland & Stewart Ltd**. *Publishes* (in English and French) children's illustrated books.

John Wiley & Sons Canada Ltd
22 Worcester Road, Etobicoke, Ontario M9W 1L1
☎001 416 236 4433 Fax 001 416 236 4447
Website www.wiley.com
FOUNDED 1968. Subsidary of **John Wiley & Sons Inc.**, USA. *Publishes* professional, reference and textbooks.

India

Affiliated East West Press Pvt Ltd
104 Nirmal Tower, 26 Barakhamba Road, New Delhi 110 001
☎00 91 11 331 5398 Fax 00 91 11 326 0538
FOUNDED 1962. *Publishes* Aeronautics, aviation, agriculture, anthropology, biological sciences, chemistry, engineering (chemical, civil, electrical, mechanical), computer science, economics, electronics, mathematics, microcomputers, physical sciences, physics, general science, veterinary science, women's studies.

Arnold Heinman Publishers (India) Pvt Ltd
AB-9, 1st Floor, Safdarjang Enclave, New Delhi 110 029
☎00 91 11 688 3422 Fax 00 91 11 687 7571
Associate company of **Edward Arnold (Publishers) Ltd**, UK. *Publishes* fiction, poetry, essays, literature, literary criticism, art, general engineering, government, political science, philosophy, religion, medicine, nursing, dentistry, social sciences and sociology.

S. Chand & Co Ltd
PO Box 5733, New Delhi 110 055
☎00 91 11 777 208011 Fax 00 91 11 777 7446
FOUNDED 1917. *Publishes* art, business, economics, government, political science, medicine, nursing, dentistry, philosophy, general science, technology.

Current Books
Round West, Trichur 680 001
☎00 91 487 335642 Fax 00 91 487 335660
FOUNDED 1952. *Publishes* fiction and general non-fiction.

General Book Depot
PO Box 1220, 1691 Nai Sarak, Delhi 110 006
☎00 91 11 326 3695
Fax 00 91 11 294 0861
FOUNDED 1936. *Publishes* general nonfiction; business, career development, how-to, English as a second language, language arts, linguistics, self-help, travel.

HarperCollins Publishers India Pty Ltd
7/61 Ansari Road, Daryaganj, New Delhi 110 002
☎00 91 11 327 8586 Fax 00 91 11 327 7294
FOUNDED 1991. *Publishes* fiction, poetry, biography and education.

Hind Pocket Books Private Ltd
18–19 Dilshad Garden Road, Delhi 110 095
☎00 91 11 202 046 Fax 00 91 11 228 332
FOUNDED 1958. *Publishes* fiction and general non-fiction; biography, how-to and self-help.

Jaico Publishing House
121–125 Mahatma Gandhi Road, Mumbai 400 023
☎00 91 22 267 6702 Fax 00 91 22 204 1673
FOUNDED 1945. *Publishes* biography, languages, linguistics, nutrition, cookery, law, criminology, astrology, occult, philosophy, religion, general engineering, economics, humour, history, government, political science, psychology, psychiatry.

Macmillan India Ltd
315/316 Raheja Chambers, 12 Museum Road, Bangalore 560 052
☎00 91 80 558 6563
Fax 00 91 80 558 8713
Email macmillan@aindia.com
Website www.macmillan–india.com
FOUNDED 1903. *Publishes* fiction, engineering (chemical and general), science (computer and general), history, philosophy, chemistry, medicine, nursing and dentistry, psychiatry, psychology, biological sciences, mathematics, social sciences, sociology, government, political science, management.

Munshiram Manoharlal Publishers Pvt Ltd

PO Box 5715, New Delhi 110 055
☎00 91 11 777 3650 Fax 00 91 11 751 2745

FOUNDED 1952. *Publishes* art, architecture and interior design, anthropology, archaeology, astrology, occult, religion (Buddhist, Hindu, Islamic), philosophy, history, language arts and linguistics, music, dance, drama, theatre, Asian studies.

National Book Trust India

H–5, Green Park, New Delhi 110 016
☎00 91 11 664 9962 Fax 00 91 11 685 1795

FOUNDED 1957. *Publishes* human relations and foreign countries.

National Publishing House

23 Daryaganj, New Delhi 110 002
☎00 91 11 327 4161

FOUNDED 1950. *Publishes* human relations, foreign countries.

Orient Longman Ltd

3–6–272 Himayat Nagar, Hyderabad 500 029
☎00 91 40 322 4294 Fax 00 91 40 322 2900

FOUNDED 1948. *Publishes* fiction and general non-fiction; business, biography, biological sciences, chemistry, chemical and electrical engineering, child care and development, civil engineering, computer and general science, cookery, crafts, games, hobbies, economics, education, electronics, English as a second language, environmental studies, genealogy, geography, geology, government, political science, history, literature, literary criticism, essays, management, mathematics, medicine, nursing and dentistry, philosophy, physics, religion (Hindu), social sciences, sociology, travel, women's studies.

Oxford University Press

PO Box 7035, New Delhi 110 002
☎00 91 11 202 1029 Fax 00 91 11 373 2312

FOUNDED 1912. *Publishes* business, biography, developing countries, economics, history, literature, literary criticism, essays, philosophy, religion (Hindu), sociology, natural history, politics, cultural studies, gender studies, ecology, science and medicine.

Rajpal & Sons

Madarasa Road, Kashmere Gate, Delhi 110 006
☎00 91 11 296 3904 Fax 00 91 11 296 7791

FOUNDED 1891. *Publishes* fiction, literature, literary criticism, essays, dictionaries, human relations, general science.

Scholastic India (Pvt) Ltd

29 Udyog Vihar, Phase-1,
Gurgaon 122 016 (Haryana)
☎00 91 12 634 3409
Fax 00 91 12 634 6825
Email scholasticindia@vsnl.com

FOUNDED 1997. Owned by **Scholastic, Inc.**, USA. Educational publishers.

Tata McGraw-Hill Publishing Co Ltd

4/12 Asaf Ali Road, 3rd Floor,
New Delhi 110 002
☎00 91 11 278 251 Fax 00 91 11 327 8253

FOUNDED 1970. Parent company **The McGraw Hill Companies**, USA. *Publishes* general engineering and science, business, social sciences, sociology and management.

Vidyarthi Mithram Press

Baker Road, Kottayam 686 001
☎00 91 481 563 281 Fax 00 91 481 562 616

FOUNDED 1928. *Publishes* child care and development, cookery, drama and theatre, economics, biography, biological sciences, chemistry and chemical engineering, computer science.

A.H. Wheeler & Co Ltd

411 Surya Kiran Building, 19 K G Marg,
New Delhi 110 001
☎00 91 11 331 2629 Fax 00 91 11 335 7798

FOUNDED 1879. *Publishes* computer science, behavioural sciences, accountancy, advertising, business, career development, civil engineering, communications.

New Zealand

Butterworths of New Zealand Ltd

PO Box 472, Wellington 1
☎00 64 4 385 1479 Fax 00 64 4 385 1598
Website www.butterworths.co.nz

FOUNDED 1914. *Publishes* accountancy, business, law and taxation.

Canterbury University Press

University of Canterbury, Private Bag 4800,
Christchurch
☎00 64 3 348 2009 Fax 00 64 3 364 2999
Email mail@cup.canterbury.ac.nz

FOUNDED 1960. *Publishes* general non-fiction; biography, biological sciences, history, natural history.

The Caxton Press
PO Box 25088, Christchurch
☎00 64 3 366 8516 Fax 00 64 3 365 7840

FOUNDED 1935. *Publishes* general non-fiction; biography, gardening and plants.

HarperCollins Publishers (New Zealand) Ltd
PO Box 1, Auckland
☎00 64 9 443 9400 Fax 00 64 9 443 9403
Website www.harpercollins.co.nz

FOUNDED 1888. *Publishes* fiction, art, humour, natural history, biography, gardening, sport, travel, self-help.

Hodder Moa Beckett Publishers Ltd
PO Box 3858, Auckland
☎00 64 9 444 3640 Fax 00 64 9 444 3646

FOUNDED 1971. Owned by **Hodder Headline**, UK. *Publishes* fiction and general non-fiction, biography.

University of Otago Press
PO Box 56, Dunedin
☎00 64 3 479 8807 Fax 00 64 3 479 8385
Email university.press@otago.ac.nz
Website www.otago.ac.nz

FOUNDED 1958. *Publishes* fiction, essays, literature, literary criticism, history, education, biography, anthropology, natural history, environmental studies, government and political science.

Pearson Education New Zealand
Private Bag 102908, North Shore Mail Centre, Glenfield, Auckland 10
☎00 64 9 444 4968 Fax 00 64 9 444 4957

FOUNDED 1968. Formerly Addison Wesley Longman New Zealand. Educational publishers.

Reed Publishing (NZ) Ltd
Private Bag 34901, Birkenhead, Auckland 10
☎00 64 9 480 4950 Fax 00 64 9 419 4999
Website www.reed.co.nz

FOUNDED 1988. *Publishes* fiction and general non-fiction, biography, cookery, history, natural history, regional interests, travel.

Southern Press Ltd
PO Box 50134, Porirua
☎00 64 4 233 1899 Fax 00 64 4 239 9835

FOUNDED 1971. *Publishes* aviation, aeronautics, maritime, transport, technology, mechanical and civil engineering, archaeology.

Tandem Press
1 Rugby Road, Birkenhead, Auckland 10
☎00 64 9 480 1452 Fax 00 64 9 480 1455

FOUNDED 1990. *Publishes* fiction and general non-fiction; cookery, business, alternative, ethnicity, health and nutrition, photography, psychology, psychiatry, self-help, women's studies.

Victoria University Press
PO Box 600, Wellington
☎00 64 4 496 6580 Fax 00 64 4 471 1701
Website www.vup.vuw.ac.nz

FOUNDED 1979. *Publishes* government, political science, essays, poetry, literature, literary criticism, drama, theatre, history, social sciences and sociology, anthropology, language and linguistics, law, architecture and interior design.

Viking Sevenseas NZ Ltd
PO Box 152, Paraparaumu, Wellington
☎00 64 4 297 1990 Fax 00 64 4 297 2040

FOUNDED 1963. *Publishes* general non-fiction; astrology, occult, health and nutrition, medicine, nursing and dentistry, ethnicity.

South Africa

Butterworths South Africa
PO Box 792, Durban 4000
☎00 27 31 294247 Fax 00 27 31 286350

Owned by Butterworths UK. *Publishes* general science, medicine, nursing and dentistry, economics, education, law.

Flesch Financial Publications (Pty) Ltd
PO Box 3473, Cape Town 8000
☎00 27 21 461 7472 Fax 00 27 21 461 3758

FOUNDED 1966. *Publishes* aviation, aeronautics, maritime, animals, pets, business.

Heinemann Publishers (Pty) Ltd
PO Box 781940, Sandown 21461, Johannesburg
☎00 27 11 322 8600 Fax 00 27 11 322 8715

FOUNDED 1986. Parent company: **Reed Educational & Professional Publishing**, UK. *Publishes* economics, education, English as a second language, mathematics, mechanical engineering.

Maskew Miller Longman (Pty) Ltd
PO Box 396, Cape Town 8000
☎00 27 21 531 7750 Fax 00 27 21 531 0716

FOUNDED 1893. *Publishes* education, language arts and linguistics, essays, literature, literary criticism.

University of Natal Press
PB X01, Scottsville, Pietermaritzburg 3209
☎00 27 331 260 5226 Fax 00 27 331 260 5599
Email books@press.unp.ac.za

FOUNDED 1947. *Publishes* essays, literature and literary criticism, natural history, history, women's studies.

Oxford University Press Southern Africa
PO Box 12119, N1 City 7463
☎00 27 21 595 4400 Fax 00 27 21 595 4430
Email oxford@oup.co.za

FOUNDED 1915. Academic publishers. Parent company: **Oxford University Press**, UK.

Ravan Press (Pty) Ltd
PO Box 145, Randburg, Johannesburg 2125
☎00 27 11 789 7636 Fax 00 27 11 789 7653

FOUNDED 1972. Part of Hodder & Stoughton Educational South Africa. *Publishes* fiction and general non-fiction; anthropology, biography, business, economics, education, environmental studies, ethnicity, government, political science, history, labour and industrial relations, management, music, dance, social studies and sociology, women's studies.

Shuter & Shooter (Pty) Ltd
PO Box 618, Ferndale 2160
☎00 27 11 792 8363 Fax 00 27 11 792 7024

FOUNDED 1925. *Publishes* general non-fiction; biography, history, ethnicity, general science, technology, social sciences and sociology.

Struik Publishers (Pty) Ltd
PO Box 1144, Cape Town 8000
☎00 27 21 517128 Fax 00 27 21 4624379

FOUNDED 1962. *Publishes* child care and development, cookery, gardening, environmental studies, natural history.

Witwatersrand University Press
PO Wits, Johannesburg 2050
☎00 27 11 484 5907 Fax 00 27 11 484 5971
Website www.wirs.ac.za/wup.html

FOUNDED 1922. *Publishes* essays, literature and literary criticism, drama, theatre, history, business, anthropology, archaeology, natural history, religion (Jewish), medicine, nursing and dentistry.

Professional Associations and Societies

Academi (Yr Academi Gymreig)

3rd Floor, Mount Stuart House, Mount Stuart Square, Cardiff CF10 5FQ
☎029 2047 2266 Fax 029 2049 2930
Email post@academi.org
Website www.academi.org

North West Wales office: Tŷ Newydd, Llanystumdwy, Cricieth, Gwynedd LL52 0LW
☎01766 522817 Fax 01766 523095
Email academi.gog@dial.pipex.com

West Wales office: Dylan Thomas Centre, Somerset Place, Swansea SA1 1RR
☎01792 463980 Fax 01792 463993
Email academi.dylan.thomas@business.ntl.com

North East Wales office: Yr Hen Garchar, 46 Clwyd Street, Ruthin, Denbighshire LL15 1HP
☎01824 708218 Fax 01824 708202 Email academi@denbighshire.gov.uk

Chief Executive *Peter Finch*

Academi is the trading name of Yr Academi Gymreig, the national society of Welsh writers. The Society exists to promote the literature of Wales. Yr Academi Gymreig was FOUNDED in 1959 as an association of Welsh language writers. An English language section was established in 1968. Membership, for those who have made a significant contribution to the literature of Wales, is by invitation. Membership currently stands at 400. The Academi runs courses, competitions (including the **Cardiff International Poetry Competition**), conferences, tours by authors, festivals and represents the interests of Welsh writers and Welsh writing both inside Wales and beyond. Its publications include *Taliesin*, a quarterly literary journal in the Welsh language, *The Oxford Companion to the Literature of Wales*, *The Welsh Academy English-Welsh Dictionary*, and a variety of translated works.

In 1998 the Academi won the franchise from the Arts Council of Wales to run the Welsh National Literature Promotion Agency. The new, much enlarged organisation now administers a variety of schemes including Writers on Tour, Writers Residencies and a number of literature development projects. It promotes an annual literary festival alternating between North and South Wales, runs its own programme of literary activity and publishes *A470*, a bi-monthly literature information magazine. The Academi is also in receipt of a lottery grant to publish the first Welsh National Encyclopedia. This is expected to be ready towards the end of 2003.

Those with an interest in literature in Wales can become an associate of the Academi (which carries a range of benefits). Rates are £15 p.a. (waged); £7.50 (unwaged).

ALCS

See **Authors' Licensing & Collecting Society**

Alliance of Literary Societies

22 Belmont Crescent, Havant, Hampshire PO9 3PU
☎023 9247 5855 Fax 08700 560330
Email rosemary@sndc.demon.co.uk
Website www.sndc.demon.co.uk/als.htm

Honorary Secretary *Mrs Rosemary Culley*

FOUNDED 1974. Aims to help and support its 80+ member societies and, when necessary, to act as a pressure group. Produces a handbook which holds useful information that is deemed important for the successful running of a literary society. It also contains details of the member societies and events to publicise them to the ALS members and the wider public.

Arts & Business (A&B)

Nutmeg House, 60 Gainsford Street, Butlers Wharf, London SE1 2NY
☎020 7378 8143 Fax 020 7407 7527
Email head.office@AandB.org.uk
Website www.AandB.org.uk

Arts & Business (formerly the Association for Business Sponsorship of the Arts) exists to promote and encourage partnerships between the private sector and the arts, to their mutual benefit and to that of the community at large. It provides a wide range of services to over 350 business members as well as to 700 arts organisations and museums through the Development Forum. To enable individual business people to share their skills with the arts, Arts & Business manages the Arthur Andersen Skills Bank and the NatWest Board Bank programmes. On behalf of the Department for Culture, Media and Sport, it manages the Arts & Business New Partners Programme, an incentive programme for new and established sponsors of the arts. Increasingly, Arts & Business is working with forward-looking businesses to determine the future of business/ arts partnerships. With the support of its President, HRH The Prince of Wales, it is exploring and developing new ways for business, the arts and society to interact. Runs its programmes from London and through a network of offices nationwide.

Arvon Foundation
See under **Writers' Courses, Circles and Workshops**

Association for Business Sponsorship of the Arts (ABSA)
See **Arts & Business**

Association for Scottish Literary Studies
c/o Department of Scottish History, 9 University Gardens, University of Glasgow, Glasgow G12 8QH
☎0141 330 5309 Fax 0141 330 5309
Email d.jones@scothist.arts.gla.ac.uk
Website www.asls.org.uk
Contact *Duncan Jones*
Subscription £33 (Individual); £61 (Institutional)

FOUNDED 1970. ASLS is an educational charity promoting the languages and literature of Scotland. *Publishes* works of Scottish literature; essays, monographs and journals; and *Scotnotes*, a series of comprehensive study guides to major Scottish writers. Also produces *New Writing Scotland*, an annual anthology of contemporary poetry and prose in English, Gaelic and Scots (see entry under **Magazines**).

Association of American Correspondents in London
Brettenham House, Lancaster Place, London WC2E 7Tl
☎020 7499 4080 Fax 020 7322 1230
Contact *Elizabeth Lea*
Subscription £90 (Organisations)

FOUNDED 1919 to serve the professional interests of its member organisations, promote social cooperation among them, and maintain the ethical standards of the profession. (An extra £30 is charged for each department of an organisation which requires separate listing in the Association's handbook.)

Association of American Publishers, Inc
71 Fifth Avenue, 2nd Floor, New York, NY 10003–3004, USA
☎001 212 255 0200 Fax 001 212 255 7007
Website www.publishers.org
Also at: 50 f Street, NW, Washington, DC 20001–1564
☎001 202 347 3375 Fax 001 202 347 3690
Contact *Tom McKee*

FOUNDED 1970. For information about subscription rates and membership, contact the Association's website.

Association of Authors' Agents
c/o Curtis Brown Group Ltd, 4th Floor, Haymarket House, 28/29 Haymarket, London SW1Y 4SP
☎020 7396 6600 Fax 020 7396 0110/1
Email jlloyd@curtisbrown.co.uk
Website www.agentsassoc.co.uk
President *Jonathan Lloyd*
Membership £50 p.a.

FOUNDED 1974. Membership voluntary. The AAA maintains a code of practice, provides a forum for discussion, and represents its members in issues affecting the profession. For a full list of members visit the AAA website.

Association of Authors' Representatives
PO Box 237201, Ansonia Station, New York, NY 10023, USA
☎001 212 252 3695
Email aarinc@mindspring.com
Website www.aar-online.org
Administrative Secretary *Leslie Carroll*

FOUNDED in 1991 through the merger of the Society of Authors' Representatives and the Independent Literary Agents Association. Membership of this US organisation is restricted to agents of at least two years' operation. Provides information, education and support for its members and works to protect their best interests.

Association of British Editors
See **Society of Editors**

Association of British Science Writers (ABSW)
23 Savile Row, London W1X 2NB
☎020 7439 1205 Fax 020 7973 3051
Email absw@absw.org.uk
Website www.absw.org.uk

Administrator *Barbara Drillsma*
Membership £35 p.a.; £30 (Associate);
£5 (Student)

ABSW has played a central role in improving the standards of science journalism in the UK over the last 40 years. It seeks to improve standards by means of networking, lectures and organised visits to institutional laboratories and industrial research centres and puts members in touch with major projects in the field and with experts worldwide. A member of the European Union of Science Journalists' Associations, ABSW is able to offer heavily subsidised places on visits to research centres in most other European countries and hosts reciprocal visits to Britain by European journalists. Membership is open to those who are considered to be *bona fide* science writers/editors who earn a substantial part of their income by promoting public interest in and understanding of science.

ABSW runs the administration and judging of the **Glaxo Science Writers' Awards** for outstanding science journalism in newspapers, journals and broadcasting and, with the Wellcome Trust, awards bursaries for science undergraduates taking a science communication course.

Association of Canadian Publishers

110 Eglinton Avenue West, Suite 401,
Toronto, Ontario M4R 1A3, Canada
☎001 416 487 6116 Fax 001 416 487 8815
Email info@canbook.org
Website www.publishers.ca

Executive Director *Monique M. Smith*

FOUNDED 1971. ACP represents over 140 Canadian-owned book publishers countrywide from the literary, general trade, scholarly and education sectors. Aims to encourage the writing, publishing, distribution and promotion of Canadian books and to support the development of a 'strong, independent and vibrant Canadian-owned publishing industry'. The organisation's website has information on getting published and links to many of their member publishers' websites.

Association of Christian Writers

73 Lodge Hill Road, Farnham, Surrey
GU10 3RB
☎01252 715746 Fax 01252 715746
Email admin@christianwriters.org.uk
Website www.christianwriters.org.uk

Administrator *Mr W.G. Crawford*
Subscription Single: £17 (£15 Direct Debit);
Joint Husband/Wife: £20 (£18 DD);
Overseas: £23 (£21 DD on UK a/c)

FOUNDED in 1971 'to inspire and equip men and women to use their talents and skills with integrity to devise, write and market excellent material which comes from a Christian worldview. In this way we seek to be an influence for good and for God in this generation.' *Publishes* a quarterly magazine. Runs three training events each year, biennial conference, competitions, postal workshops, area groups, prayer support and manuscript criticism. Charity No. 1069839.

Association of Freelance Editors, Proofreaders & Indexers (Ireland)

Skeagh, Skibbereen, Co. Cork, Republic of Ireland
☎00 353 28 38259 Fax 00 353 28 38004
Email gloria@redbarn-publishing.ie

Contact *Gloria Greenwood*
Subscription £15 p.a.

The organisation was established in Ireland to protect the interests of its members and to provide information to publishers on freelancers working in the relevant fields. Membership is restricted to freelancers with experience and/or references ('but we do not test or evaluate the skills of members'). New category of membership – Associate Member – available for trainees in proofreading/editing who are taking the Book House Training Centre correspondence courses in Proofreading and Copy-editing.

Association of Freelance Journalists

2 Glen Cottage, Brick Hill Lane, Beveley,
Ketley, Telford, Shropshire TF2 6SB
Email afj_UK@Yahoo.com
Website members.tripod.com/~media_2/
afj.html

Official Patron *Dr Carl Chinn, PhD*
Founding President *Martin Scholes*
Subscription £30 p.a.

Offers membership to all who work in the field of journalism but especially local correspondents, stringers, freelance journalists, news photographers, those at the beginning of their careers or long established. Also welcomes those who make a modest income writing for the specialist press or who self-publish; who have written for a hobby but now wish to make a career of their writing. Members receive a regular newsletters, a laminated press card, a free postal/e-mail advice service, the opportunity to network with other members (through the newsletter and a special Internet service) and editors who contact the AFJ. There are discounts on products and services, including the AFJ writing course.

Association of Freelance Writers

Sevendale House, 7 Dale Street, Manchester
M1 1JB
☎0161 228 2362, ext 210
Fax 0161 228 3533
Email fmn@writersbureau.com

Contact *Angela Cox*
Subscription £29 p.a.

FOUNDED in 1995 to help and advise new and
established freelance writers. Members receive
a copy of *Freelance Market News* each month
which gives news, views and the latest advice
and guidelines about publications at home and
abroad. Other benefits include one free
appraisal of prose or poetry each year, reduced
entry to **The Writers Bureau** writing competition, reduced fees for writing seminars and
discounts on books for writers.

Association of Golf Writers

106 Byng Drive, Potters Bar, Hertfordshire
EN6 1UJ
☎01707 654112 Fax 01707 654112

Honorary Secretary *Mark Garrod*

FOUNDED 1938. Aims to cooperate with golf-
ing bodies to ensure best possible working conditions.

Association of Illustrators

81 Leonard Street, London EC2A 4QS
☎020 7613 4328 Fax 020 7613 4417

Contact *Harriet Booth*

FOUNDED 1973 to promote illustration and illustrators' rights, and encourage professional standards. The AOI is a non-profit-making trade
association dedicated to its members, to protecting their interests and promoting their work.
Talks, seminars, a newsletter, regional groups,
legal and portfolio advice as well as a number of
related publications such as *Rights, The Illustrator's
Guide to Professional Practice* and *Survive, The
Illustrator's Guide to a Professional Career*.

Association of Independent Libraries

Leeds Library, 18 Commercial Street, Leeds,
West Yorkshire LS1 6AL
☎0113 245 3071

Chairman *Geoffrey Forster*

Established to 'further the advancement, conser-
vation and restoration of a little-known but
important living portion of our cultural heritage'.
Members include the **London Library, Devon
& Exeter Institution, Linen Hall Library** and
Plymouth Proprietary Library.

Association of Learned and Professional Society Publishers

South House, The Street, Clapham,
Worthing, West Sussex BN13 3UU
☎01903 871686 Fax 01903 871457
Email sec-gen@alpsp.org
Website www.alpsp.org

Secretary-General *Sally Morris*
Member Services Administrator *Lesley Ogg*
Editor, Learned Publishing *Michele
Benjamin*

FOUNDED in 1972 to serve, represent and
strengthen the community of not-for-profit
publishers and those who work with them to
disseminate academic and professional information. 'ALPSP believes that this is a time of
unprecedented change in the publishing environment and intends to play an active part in
shaping the future of academic and professional
communication, demonstrating the essential
role that its member publishers have to play.'

Association of Scottish Motoring Writers

c/o Scottish and Universal Newspapers, 5/15
Bank Street, Airdrie ML6 6AF
☎01236 748048 Fax 01236 748098

Secretary *John Murdoch*
Subscription £45 (Full); £25 (Associate)

FOUNDED 1961. Aims to co-ordinate the activities of, and provide shared facilities for, motoring writers resident in Scotland. Membership is
by invitation only.

Australian Copyright Council

245 Chalmers Street, Redfern, NSW 2016,
Australia
☎00 61 29318 1788 Fax 00 61 29698 3536
Email info@copyright.org.au
Website www.copyright.org.au

Contact *Customer Service*

FOUNDED 1968. The Council's activities and
services include a range of publications, organising and speaking about copyright at seminars,
research, consultancies and free legal advice.
Aims include assistance for copyright owners to
exercise their rights effectively, raising awareness about the importance of copyright, and
seeing changes to the law of copyright.

Australian Society of Authors

PO Box 1566, Strawberry Hills, NSW 2012,
Australia
☎00 61 2 9318 0877 Fax 00 61 2 9318 0530
Email asa@asauthors.org

Website www.asauthors.org

Executive Director *José Borghino*

FOUNDED 1963. The ASA aims to promote and protect the professional interests of Australian authors. Provides contract advice and assists authors on industry standards and practices. *Publishes Australian Author* magazine.

Author-Publisher Network

SKS, St Aldhelm, 20 Paul Street, Frome, Somerset BA11 1DX

☎01373 451777

Website www.author.co.uk

Administrator *Vicky Knowles*

Newsletter Editor *David Bosworth*

Subscription £15 (p.a.)

FOUNDED 1993. The association aims to provide an active forum for writers publishing their own work. An information network of ideas and opportunities for self-publishers. Explores the business and technology of writing and publishing. Regular newsletter (*Write to Publish!*), supplements, seminars and workshops, etc.

Authors North

c/o The Society of Authors, 84 Drayton Gardens, London SW10 9SB

☎020 7373 6642

Secretary *Colin Shelbourn*

A group within the **Society of Authors** which organises meetings for members living in the north of England.

Authors' Club

40 Dover Street, London W1S 4NP

☎020 7499 8581 Fax 020 7409 0913

Secretary *Mrs Ann de La Grange*

FOUNDED in 1891 by Sir Walter Besant, the Authors' Club welcomes as members writers, agents, publishers, critics, journalists, academics and anyone involved with literature. Administers the **Authors' Club Best First Novel Award** and **Sir Banister Fletcher Award**, and organises regular talks and dinners with well-known guest speakers. Membership fee: apply to secretary.

Authors' Licensing & Collecting Society Limited (ALCS)

Marlborough Court, 14–18 Holborn, London EC1N 2LE

☎020 7395 0600 Fax 020 7395 0660

Email alcs@alcs.co.uk

Website www.alcs.co.uk

Chief Executive *Dafydd Wyn Phillips*

Subscription £7.50 incl. VAT (UK; free to members of **Society of Authors**, **Writers' Guild**, **NUJ**, **BAJ** and **CIOJ**); £7.50 (EU residents); £10 (Overseas)

FOUNDED 1977. The UK collecting society for all writers and their successors, ALCS is a non-profit organisation whose principle purpose is to ensure that hard-to-collect revenues due to writers are efficiently collected and speedily distributed. Established to give assistance to writers in their battle to make a better living through the protection and exploitation of collective rights, ALCS has distributed some £65m. to writers since its creation. On joining, members give ALCS a mandate to administer on their behalf those rights which the law determines must be received or which are best handled collectively. Chief among these are: photocopying, cable retransmission (including the fees for BBC Prime and BBC World Service programming), rental and lending rights (but not British Public Lending Right), off-air recording, electronic rights, the performing right and public reception of broadcasts. The society is a prime resource and a leading authority on copyright matters and writers' collective interests. It maintains a watching brief on all matters affecting copyright both in Britain and abroad, making representations to UK government authorities and the EU. Consult the ALCS website or contact the office for application forms and further information.

BACB

See **British Association of Communicators in Business**

BAFTA (British Academy of Film and Television Arts)

195 Piccadilly, London W1J 9LN

☎020 7734 0022 Fax 020 7437 0473

Website www.bafta.org

Subscription £165 p.a. (Over 30); £80 p.a. (Under 30); £85 p.a. (Country); £75 p.a. (Overseas); £50 (Initial entry fee); £90 (Guest card)

FOUNDED 1947. Membership limited to 'those who have made a significant contribution to the industry' over a minimum period of three years. Best known for its annual awards ceremonies, now held separately for film, television, craft, children's programmes and interactive entertainment, the Academy runs a full programme of screenings, seminars, masterclasses, debates, lectures, etc. It also actively supports training and educational projects.

Also, BAFTA Scotland, BAFTA Wales,

BAFTA North, BAFTA LA, BAFTA East Coast (USA) run separate programmes and, in the case of Scotland, Wales and the North, hold their own awards.

BAPLA (British Association of Picture Libraries and Agencies)

18 Vine Hill, London EC1R 5DZ
☎020 7713 1780 Fax 020 7713 1211
Email enquiries@bapla.org.uk
Website www.bapla.org.uk

Represents the interests of the British picture library industry. Works on UK and world-wide levels on such issues as copyright and technology. Offers researchers free telephone referrals from its database and through its website. With access to 350 million images through its membership, BAPLA is a good place to start. *Publishes* a *Directory*, the definitive guide to UK picture libraries and the quarterly magazine, *Light Box*.

BFC
See **British Film Commission**

The Bibliographical Society
c/o The Wellcome Library, 183 Euston Road, London NW1 2BE
☎020 7611 7244 Fax 020 7611 8703
Email jm93@dial.pipex.com

President *M.M. Foot*
Honorary Secretary *D. Pearson*
Subscription £33 p.a.

Aims to promote and encourage the study and research of historical, analytical, descriptive and textual bibliography, and the history of printing, publishing, bookselling, bookbinding and collecting; to hold meetings at which papers are read and discussed; to print and publish works concerned with bibliography; to form a bibliographical library. Awards grants and bursaries for bibliographical research. *Publishes* a quarterly magazine called *The Library*.

Book Packagers Association
8 St John's Road, Saxmundham, Suffolk IP17 1BE
☎01728 604204 Fax 01728 604029

Treasurer *Charles Perkins*
Subscription £150 p.a.; £75 (Associate); £100 (Overseas)

Aims to provide members with a forum for the exchange of information, to improve the image of packaging and to represent the interests of members. Activities include meetings, semi-

nars, the provision of standard contracts and a stand at the London Book Fair.

Book Trust
Book House, 45 East Hill, London SW18 2QZ
☎020 8516 2977 Fax 020 8516 2978
Website www.booktrust.org.uk

Executive Director *Chris Meade*
Subscription £25 p.a.; £28 (Overseas)

FOUNDED 1925. Book Trust, the independent educational charity promoting books and reading, includes Young Book Trust (formerly Children's Book Foundation). The Trust offers a book information service (free to the public); administers many literary prizes (including the **Booker**); carries out surveys, *publishes* useful reference books and resource materials; houses a children's book reference collection, and promotes children's books through activities like Children's Book Week.

Booksellers Association of the UK & Ireland Ltd
Minster House, 272 Vauxhall Bridge Road, London SW1V 1BA
☎020 7834 5477 Fax 020 7834 8812
Email mail@booksellers.org.uk
Website www.booksellers.org.uk

Chief Executive *Tim Godfray*

FOUNDED 1895. The BA helps 3300 independent, chain and multiple members to sell more books, reduce costs and improve efficiency. It represents members' interests to the UK Government, European Commission, publishers, authors and others in the trade as well as offering marketing assistance, running training courses, conferences, seminars and exhibitions. Together with **The Publishers Association**, coordinates World Book Day. *Publishes* directories, catalogues, surveys and various other publications connected with the book trade and administers the **Whitbread Book Awards** and the **Samuel Johnson Prize for Non-fiction**.

British Academy of Composers and Songwriters
2nd Floor, British Music House, 25–27 Berners Street, London W1T 3LR
☎020 7636 2929 Fax 020 7636 2212
Email info@britishacademy.com
Website www.britishacademy.com

Head of Membership *Jason Bandy*

The Academy represents the interests of music writers of all genres, providing advice on professional and artistic matters. *Publishes* quarterly magazine, *The Works*. Administers the annual Ivor Novello Awards.

British Academy of Film and Television Arts
See **BAFTA**

British Association of Communicators in Business (BACB)
42 Borough High Street, London SE1 1XW
☎020 7378 7139 Fax 020 7387 7140
Email enquiries@bacb.org
Website www.bacb.org

Secretary General *Kathie Jones*

FOUNDED 1949. The Association aims to be the 'market leader for those involved in corporate media management and practice by providing professional, authoritative, dynamic, supportive and innovative services'.

British Association of Journalists
88 Fleet Street, London EC4Y 1PJ
☎020 7353 3003 Fax 020 7353 2310

General Secretary *Steve Turner*
Subscription National newspaper staff, national broadcasting staff, national news agency staff: £12.50 a month. Other seniors, including magazine journalists, PRs and freelances who earn the majority of their income from journalism: £7.50 a month. Journalists under 24: £5 a month. Trainee journalists: Free.

FOUNDED 1992. Aims to protect and promote the industrial and professional interests of journalists.

British Association of Picture Libraries and Agencies
See **BAPLA**

British Centre for Literary Translation
University of East Anglia, Norwich, Norfolk NR4 7TJ
☎01603 592134/592785 Fax 01603 592737
Email c.fuller@uea.ac.uk
Website www.literarytranslation.com

Contact *Catherine Fuller*

FOUNDED 1989. Aims to promote literary translation and the status of the literary translator by working in the UK and overseas with translator associations and centres (e.g. European network of Translation Centres), cultural policy-makers, teachers and researchers of literary translation, Regional Arts Boards, publishers and the media, libraries and schools. PhD programme in literary translation. Coordinates activities, mostly in collaboration with other organisations, include a summer school, conferences (e.g. British Council seminars on literary translation) and seminars, workshops and readings. With European and other funding, BCLT runs a translator-in-residence programme for translators to spend one calendar month in Norwich. *Publishes* proceedings and reports of its activities where possible and a newsletter; websites in conjunction with the **British Council** and Grinzane Cavour Foundation (www.readersonline-europa.com).

British Copyright Council
Copyright House, 29–33 Berners Street, London W1T 3AB
☎01986 788230 Fax 01986 788847
Email copyright@bcc2.demon.co.uk

Contact *Janet Ibbotson*

Works for the national and international acceptance of copyright and acts as a lobby/watchdog organisation on behalf of creators, publishers and performers on copyright and associated matters. Publications include *Guide to the Law of Copyright and Rights in Performances in the UK*; *Photocopying from Books and Journals*. An umbrella organisation which does not deal with individual enquiries.

The British Council
10 Spring Gardens, London SW1A 2BN
☎020 7930 8466/7389 4268 (Press Office)
Fax 020 7839 6347
Website www.britishcouncil.org

Head of Literature *Dr Alastair Niven*

The British Council promotes Britain abroad. It provides access to British ideas, expertise and experience in education, the English language, literature and the arts, science and technology and governance. Works in 110 countries running a mix of offices, libraries, resource centres and English teaching operations.

British Equestrian Writers' Association
Priory House, Station Road, Swavesey, Cambridge CB4 5QJ
☎01954 232084 Fax 01954 231362

Contact *Gillian Newsum*
Subscription £15

FOUNDED 1973. Aims to further the interests of

equestrian sport and improve, wherever possible, the working conditions of the equestrian press. Membership is by invitation of the committee. Candidates for membership must be nominated and seconded by full members and receive a majority vote of the committee.

British Film Commission (BFC)
10 Little Portland Street, London W1W 7JG
☎020 7861 7860 Fax 020 7861 7864
Email info@bfc.co.uk
Website www.bfc.co.uk

FOUNDED in 1991, the British Film Council is now part of a division of the Film Council. Its remit is to promote the UK as an international production centre by encouraging the use of British artists and technicians, technical services, facilities and locations, and to provide wide-ranging support to those filming and contemplating filming in the UK.

British Film Institute
21 Stephen Street, London W1T 1LN
☎020 7255 1444 Fax 020 7436 0439
Website www.bfi.org.uk

Chair *Joan Bakewell, CBE*
Director *Jon Teckman*
24-hour *bfi* events line: 0870 240 4050

'The *bfi* offers opportunities to experience, enjoy and discover more about the world of film and television.' Its three main departments are: *bfi* Education, comprising the *bfi* National Library, *bfi* Publishing, *Sight and Sound* magazine and *bfi* Education Projects, which encourages life-long learning about the moving image; *bfi* Exhibition, which runs the National Film Theatre on London's South Bank and the annual London Film Festival, and supports local cinemas and film festivals UK-wide; and *bfi* Collections, which preserves the UK's moving image heritage and promotes access to it through a variety of means, including film, video and DVD releases and touring exhibitions. The *bfi* also runs the *bfi* London IMAX Cinema at Waterloo, featuring the UK's largest screen.

British Guild of Beer Writers
15 Sollershott West, Letchworth,
Hertfordshire SG6 3PU
☎01462 685844 Fax 01462 685783
Email bsb@tccnet.co.uk

Secretary *Barry Bremner*
Subscription £30 p.a.

FOUNDED 1988. Aims to improve standards in beer writing and at the same time extend public knowledge of beers and brewing. *Publishes* a directory of members with details of their publications and their particular areas of interest; this is then circulated to newspapers, magazines, trade press and broadcasting organisations. Also *publishes* a monthly newsletter, the *BGBW Newsletter*. As part of the plan to improve writing standards and to achieve a higher profile for beer, the Guild offers annual awards, The Gold and Silver Tankard Awards, to writers and broadcasters judged to have made the most valuable contribution towards this end in their work. Meetings are held regularly.

British Guild of Travel Writers
The Manse, 183 Wells Road, Malvern Wells,
Worcestershire WR14 4HE
☎01684 565731

Chairman *Martin Roberts*
Honorary Secretary *Mary Johns*
Subscription £100 p.a.

The professional association of travel writers, broadcasters, photographers and editors which aims to serve its members' professional interests by acting as a forum for debate, discussion and 'networking'. The Guild *publishes* an annual Year Book giving full details of all its members, holds monthly meetings and has a monthly newsletter. Members are required to earn the majority of their income from travel reporting.

British Science Fiction Association
1 Long Row Close, Everdon, Daventry,
Northants NN11 3BE
☎01327 361661
Email bsfa@enterprise.net

Membership Secretary *Paul Billinger*
Subscription £21 p.a. (reduction for
  Unwaged)

FOUNDED originally in 1958 by a group of authors, readers, publishers and booksellers interested in science fiction. With a worldwide membership, the Association aims to promote the reading, writing and publishing of science fiction and to encourage SF fans to maintain contact with each other. Also offers postal writers workshop, a magazine chain and an information service. *Publishes Matrix* bi-monthly newsletter with comment and opinions, news of conventions, etc. Contributions from members welcomed; *Vector* bi-monthly critical journal – reviews of books and magazines; *Focus* biannual magazine with articles, original fiction and letters column. For further information, contact the Membership Secretary at the above address or via e-mail.

British Society of Comedy Writers
61 Parry Road, Ashmore Park,
Wolverhampton, West Midlands WV11 2PS
☎01902 722729 Fax 01902 722729
Email comedy@bscw.co.uk
Website www.bscw.co.uk

Contact *Ken Rock*

FOUNDED 1999. The Society aims to develop
good practice and professionalism among comedy writers while bringing together the best
creative professionals, and working to standards
of excellence agreed with the light entertainment industry. Offers a network of industry
contacts and a range of products, services and
training initiatives including specialised workshops, an annual international conference,
script assessment service and opportunities to
visit international festivals.

British Society of Magazine Editors (BSME)
137 Hale Lane, Edgware, Middlesex HA8 9QP
☎020 8906 4664 Fax 020 8959 2137
Email bsme@cix.co.uk

Contact *Gill Branston*

Holds regular industry forums and events as
well as an annual awards dinner.

Broadcasting Press Guild
Tiverton, The Ridge, Woking, Surrey
GU22 7EQ
☎01483 764895 Fax 01483 765882

Membership Secretary *Richard Last*
Subscription £15 p.a.

FOUNDED 1973 to promote the professional
interests of journalists specialising in writing or
broadcasting about the media. Organises
monthly lunches addressed by leading industry
figures, and annual TV and radio awards.
Membership by invitation.

BSME
See **British Society of Magazine Editors**

Bureau of Freelance Photographers
Focus House, 497 Green Lanes, London
N13 4BP
☎020 8882 3315 Fax 020 8886 5174
Email info@thebfp,com

Membership Secretary *Kelly Wood*
Subscription £45 p.a. (UK);
   £60 p.a. (Overseas)

FOUNDED 1965. Assists members in selling their
pictures through monthly *Market Newsletter*, and
offers advisory, legal assistance and other services.

Campaign for Press and Broadcasting Freedom
8 Cynthia Street, London N1 9JF
☎020 7278 4430 Fax 020 7837 8868
Email freepress@cpbf.org.co.uk
Website www.cpbf.org.co.uk

Subscription £15 p.a. (concessions available);
   £25 p.a. (Institutions/ Organisations)

Broadly based pressure group working for more
accountable and accessible media in Britain.
Advises on right of reply and takes up the issue of
the portrayal of minorities. Members receive *Free
Press* (bi-monthly), discounts on publications and
news of campaign progress.

Canadian Authors Association
National Office: Box 419, 320 South Shores
Road, Campbellford, ON K0L 1L0, Canada
☎001 705 653 0323 Fax 001 705 653 0593
Email canauth@redden.on.ca
Website www.CanAuthors.org

Administrator *Alec McEachern*

FOUNDED 1921. The CAA 'has expanded from
a group of published authors concerned with
protection of their own property to one that
now includes those not yet published who
want protection of what they might eventually
produce and who need help producing it.' The
Association has branches across the country
providing support to local members in the
form of advice, local contests, publications and
writers' circles. *Publishes National Newsline*
(quarterly) and *The Canadian Writer's Guide*.

Canadian Publishers' Council
250 Merton Street, Suite 203, Toronto,
Ontario M4S 1B1, Canada
☎001 416 322 7011 Fax 001 416 322 6999
Email pubadmin@pubcouncil.ca
Website www.pubcouncil.ca

Executive Director, External Relations
   Jacqueline Hushion

FOUNDED 1910. Trade association of English-
language publishers which represents the
domestic and international interests of member
companies.

The Caravan Writers' Guild
13 Grovelands Avenue, Hitchin, Hertfordshire
SG4 0QT
☎01462 432877 Fax 01462 632548
Email douglas.king@ntlworld.com

Membership Secretary *D. King*
Subscription £5 Joining fee plus £20 p.a.;
   Associates: £12.50

Guild for writers active in the specialist fields of caravan and camping journalism.

Careers Writers' Association

16 Caewal Road, Llandaff, Cardiff CF5 2BT
☎029 2056 3444   Fax 029 3056 6363
Email anne.goodman@cimaglobal.com
Membership Secretary *Anne Goodman*

FOUNDED 1979. An association of professional careers writers whose work meets its high standards of accuracy and impartiality. It provides a network for members to exchange information and experience and holds meetings on topics of interest to its members. Forges links with organisations that share related interests and maintains regular contact with national education and training bodies, government agencies and publishers. 'The association can provide a list of its members to organisations that require high standards of careers writing.'

Centreprise Literature Development Project

136–138 Kingsland High Street, London E8 2NS
☎020 7254 9362, exts. 211 & 214
Fax 020 7923 1951
Website www.centrepriseuk.freeserve.co.uk
Contacts *Catherine Johnson, Eva Lewin*

FOUNDED 1971. 'Centreprise has been at the forefront of community writing and publishing for nearly 30 years', making writing accessible to all the community. Although no longer a publisher it continues to nuture new writers with its New Writing and Black Literature Development Projects. CLDP offers creative writing courses, book discussion groups, and advice and information for writers. Offers links to other readers, writers and writers' organisations; produces *Calabash*, a twice-yearly free newsletter for Black and Asian writers.

Chartered Institute of Journalists

2 Dock Offices, Surrey Quays Road, London SE16 2XU
☎020 7252 1187   Fax 020 7232 2302
Email memberservices@ioj.co.uk
Website www.ioj.co.uk
General Secretary *Christopher Underwood*
Subscription £170 p.a./£15 (monthly)

FOUNDED 1884. The Institute is concerned with professional journalistic standards and with safeguarding the freedom of the media. It is open to writers, broadcasters and journalists (including self-employed) in all media. Affiliate membership

(£115) is available to part-time or occasional practitioners and to overseas journalists who can join the Institute's International Division. Members also belong to the IOJ (TU), an independent trade union which protects, advises and represents them in their employment or freelance work; negotiates on their behalf and provides legal assistance and support. The IOJ (TU) is a certificated independent trade union which represents members' interests in the workplace, and is also a constituent member of the National Council in the Training of Journalists, the Independent Unions Training Council and the **British Copyright Council**.

Children's Book Circle

c/o HarperCollins Publishers Ltd, 77–85 Fulham Palace Road, London W6 8JB
☎020 8741 7070   Fax 020 8307 4440
Membership Secretary *Jo Williamson*

The Children's Book Circle provides a discussion forum for anybody involved with children's books. Monthly meetings are addressed by a panel of invited speakers and topics focus on current and controversial issues. Administers the **Eleanor Farjeon Award**.

Children's Book Foundation

See **Book Trust**

Circle of Wine Writers

29 Rowan Road, London W6 7DT
☎020 8741 9589
Membership £45 p.a.

FOUNDED 1962. Open to all *bona fide* authors, broadcasters, journalists and photographers currently being published, as well as lecturers and tutors, all of whom are professionally engaged in communicating about wines and spirits. Aims to improve the standard of writing, broadcasting and lecturing about wines, spirits and beers; to contribute to the growing knowledge and interest in wine; to promote wines and spirits of quality and to comment adversely on faulty products or dubious practices; to establish and maintain good relations with the news media and the wine trade; to provide members with a strong voice with which to promote their views; to provide a programme of workshops, meetings, talks and tastings.

Cleveland Arts

Third Floor, Melrose House, Melrose Street, Middlesbrough TS1 2HZ
☎01642 264651   Fax 01642 264955

Website www.clevelandarts.org

Contact *Programme Manager (Literature)*

Not one of the Regional Arts Boards, Cleveland Arts is an independent arts development agency working in the areas of Middlesbrough, Stockton on Tees, Hartlepool and Redcar & Cleveland. The company works in partnership with local authorities, public agencies, the business sector, schools, colleges, individuals and organisations to coordinate, promote and develop the arts – crafts, film, video, photography, music, drama, dance, literature, public arts, disability, Black arts, community arts. The Word Foundation is the literature development unit which promotes writing classes, reading promotions, poetry readings and residencies, issues a free newsletter and assists local publishers and writers.

Clé, The Irish Book Publishers' Association

43/44 Temple Bar, Dublin 2, Republic of Ireland

☎00 353 1 6706393   Fax 00 353 1 6706642

Email cle@iol.ie *or* cleadmin@iol.ie

Website www.publishingireland.com

President *Sara Wilbourne*

Executive Director *Orla Martin*

FOUNDED 1970 to promote Irish publishing, protect members' interests and train the industry.

Comedy Writers' Association UK

Wisteria Cottage, Coombe Meadow, Bovey Tracey, Newton Abbot, Devon TQ13 9EZ

☎01626 833227

Email loyd@justtheone.freeserve.co.uk

Website www.cwauk.co.uk

Honorary President *Ken Dodd*

Chairman *Ann Baldwin*

Membership Secretary *Rob Loyd*

FOUNDED 1981 to assist and promote the work of comedy writers, the Association has grown to become the largest group of independent comedy writers in the UK. Holds annual and one-day seminars. Members receive a monthly newsletter and regular market opportunities.

Comhairle nan Leabhraichean/ The Gaelic Books Council

22 Mansfield Street, Glasgow G11 5QP

☎0141 337 6211   Fax 0141 353 0515

Email fios@gaelicbooks.net

Website www.gaelicbooks.net

Chairman *Donalda MacKinnon*

Director *Ian MacDonald*

FOUNDED 1968 and now a charitable company with its own bookshop. Encourages and promotes Gaelic publishing by giving grants to publishers and writers; providing editorial and word-processing services; retailing Gaelic books; producing a catalogue of all Gaelic books in print and answering enquiries about them; mounting occasional literary evenings and training courses.

Commercial Radio Companies Association

77 Shaftesbury Avenue, London W1D 5DU

☎020 7306 2603   Fax 020 7470 0062

Email info@crca.co.uk

Chairman *Lord Eatwell*

Chief Executive *Paul Brown*

Operations Director *Rachell Fox*

Public Affairs Manager *Nick Irvine*

The CRCA is the trade body for the independent radio stations. It represents members' interests to Government, the **Radio Authority**, trade unions, copyright organisations and other bodies.

Copyright Advice and Anti-Piracy Hotline

Clivemont House, 54 Clivemont Road, Maidenhead, Berkshire SL6 7BZ

☎0845 603 4567   Fax 01628 760350

Email contact@copyright-info.org

Website www.copyright-info.org

Copyright Line Administrator *Jo Holcroft*

FOUNDED 1999 to offer advice and information to anyone who wants to use film, music and software copyrights. The Hotline also helps the public and law enforcement agencies to identify and report piracy, and the intellectual property industries to monitor infringements and co-ordinate their responses. (See also the **Federation Against Copyright Theft (FACT) Limited**.)

The Copyright Licensing Agency Ltd

90 Tottenham Court Road, London W1T 4LP

☎020 7631 5555   Fax 020 7631 5500

Email cla@cla.co.uk

Website www.cla.co.uk

Chief Executive *Peter Shepherd*

FOUNDED 1982 by the **Authors' Licensing and Collecting Society (ALCS)** and the **Publishers Licensing Society Ltd (PLS)**, the CLA administers collectively photocopying and other copying rights that it is uneconomic for writers and publishers to administer for themselves. The Agency issues collective and transactional licences, and the fees it collects, after the deduction of its operating costs, are distributed at regular intervals to authors and publishers via their respective societies (i.e. ALCS or PLS). Since 1986, CLA has distributed approximately £83 million.

Council for British Archaeology

Bowes Morrell House, 111 Walmgate, York YO1 9WA
☎01904 671417 Fax 01904 671384
Email info@britarch.ac.uk
Website www.britarch.ac.uk
Information Officer *Mike Heyworth*

FOUNDED 1944 to represent and promote archaeology at all levels. Its aims are to improve the public's awareness in and understanding of Britain's past; to carry out research; to survey, guide and promote the teaching of archaeology at all levels of education; to publish a wide range of academic, educational, general and bibliographical works (see **CBA Publishing** under **UK Publishers**).

Council of Academic and Professional Publishers

See **The Publishers Association**

Crime Writers' Association (CWA)

PO Box 6939, Kings Heath, Birmingham B14 7LT
Email judith.cutler@virgin.net
Website www.thecwa.co.uk
Secretary *Judith Cutler*
Membership £45

Full membership is limited to professional crime writers, but publishers, literary agents, booksellers, etc. who specialise in crime, are eligible for Associate membership. The Association has regional chapters throughout the country, including Scotland. Meetings are held regularly in central London, with informative talks frequently given by police, scenes of crime officers, lawyers, etc., and a weekend conference is held annually in different parts of the country. Produces a monthly newsletter for members called *Red Herrings* and presents various annual awards (see **Prizes**).

The Critics' Circle

c/o Catherine Cooper, 69 Marylebone Lane, London W1V 2PH
☎020 7224 1410
President *Jane Edwardes*

Honorary General Secretary *Charles Hedges*
Subscription £18 p.a.

Membership by invitation only. Aims to uphold and promote the art of criticism (and the commercial rates of pay thereof) and preserve the interests of its members: professionals involved in criticism of film, drama, music and dance.

Cyngor Llyfrau Cymru

See **Welsh Books Council**

Department for Culture, Media and Sport

2–4 Cockspur Street, London SW1Y 5DH
☎020 7211 6000 Fax 020 7211 6270
Email toby.sargent@culture.gsi.gov.uk
Head of News *Toby Sargent*

The Department for Culture, Media and Sport has responsibilities for Government policies relating to the arts, museums and galleries, public libraries, sport, broadcasting, Press standards, the built heritage, the film and music industries, tourism and the National Lottery. It funds the **Arts Council**, national museums and galleries, the **British Library**, the Public Lending Right and the Royal Commission on Historical Manuscripts. It is responsible within Government for the public library service in England, and for library and information matters generally, where they are not the responsibility of other departments.

Directory & Database Publishers Association

PO Box 23034, London W6 0RJ
☎020 8846 9707
Website www.directory-publisher.co.uk
Contact *Rosemary Pettit*
Subscription £120 – £1200 p.a.

FOUNDED 1970 to promote the interests of *bona fide* directory and database publishers and protect the public from disreputable and fraudulent practices. The objectives of the Association are to maintain a code of professional practice to safeguard public interest; to raise the standard and status of directory publishing throughout the UK; to promote business directories as a medium for advertising; to protect the legal and statutory interests of directory publishers; to foster bonds of common interest among responsible directory publishers and to provide for the exchange of technical, commercial and management information between members. Meetings, seminars, conference, newsletter, awards, exhibitions.

Drama Association of Wales

The Old Library Building, Singleton Road,
Splott, Cardiff CF24 2ET
☎029 2045 2200 Fax 029 2045 2277
Email aled.daw@virgin.net

Contact *Teresa Hennessy*

Runs a large playscript lending library; holds an annual playwriting competition (see entry under **Prizes**); offers a script-reading service (£10 per script) which usually takes three months from receipt of play to issue of reports. From plays submitted to the reading service, selected scripts are considered for publication of a short run (250–750 copies). Writers receive a percentage of the cover price on sales and a percentage of the performance fee.

Edinburgh Bibliographical Society

Edinburgh University Library, George Square,
Edinburgh EH8 9LJ
☎0131 650 6823 Fax 0131 650 6863
Email p.freshwater@ed.ac.uk *or*
john@jvhoward.globalnet.co.uk

Honorary Treasurer *Peter B. Freshwater*
Acting Honorary Secretary *John V. Howard*
Subscription £10; £15 (Institution); £5
(Students)

FOUNDED 1890. Organises lectures on bibliographical topics and visits to libraries. *Publishes* an occasional journal called *Transactions*, which is free to members, and other occasional publications.

Educational Publishers Council

See **The Publishers Association**

Educational Television and Media Association ETmA

See **Learning on Screen**

Electronic Publishers' Forum

See **The Publishers Association**

The English Association

University of Leicester, University Road,
Leicester LE1 7RH
☎0116 252 3982 Fax 0116 252 2301
Email engassoc@le.ac.uk
Website www.le.ac.uk/engassoc/

Chief Executive *Helen Lucas*

FOUNDED 1906 to promote understanding and appreciation of the English language and its literatures. Activities include sponsoring a number of publications and organising lectures and conferences for teachers, plus annual sixth-form conferences. Publications include *Year's Work in Critical and Cultural Theory, English, Use of English, English 4–11, Essays and Studies* and *Year's Work in English Studies*.

Federation Against Copyright Theft (FACT) Limited

Unit 7, Victory Business Centre, Worton
Road, Isleworth, Middlesex TW7 6DB
☎020 8568 6646 Fax 020 8560 6364
Email davidlowe@fact-uk.co.uk

Director General *David Lowe*

FOUNDED in 1999, FACT is an investigative organisation funded by its members to combat counterfeiting piracy and misuse of their products. It assists all law enforcement authorities and will undertake private criminal prosecutions wherever possible. Membership is made up of major companies in the British and American film, video and television industries.

Federation of Entertainment Unions

1 Highfield, Twyford, Nr Winchester,
Hampshire SO21 1QR
☎01962 713134 Fax 01962 713134
Email harris@interalpha.co.uk

Secretary *Steve Harris*

Plenary meetings six times annually and meetings of the Film and Electronic Media Committee six times annually on alternate months. Additionally, there are Training & European Committees. Represents the following unions: British Actors' Equity Association; Broadcasting Entertainment Cinematograph and Theatre Union; Musicians' Union; AEEU; **National Union of Journalists**; **The Writers' Guild of Great Britain**.

The Federation of Worker Writers and Community Publishers (FWWCP)

67 The Boulevard, Stoke on Trent ST6 6BD
☎01782 822327 Fax 01782 822327
Email fwwcp@cwcom.net
Website www.fwwcp.mcmail.com

Administrator/Coordinator *Tim Diggles*

The FWWCP is a federation of writing groups committed to writing and publishing based on working-class experience and creativity. The FWWCP is the membership's collective national voice and has for some time been given funding by the **Arts Council**. Founded in 1976, it comprises around 60 member groups, each one with its own identity, reflecting its community and membership. They represent over 5000 people who regularly (often weekly) meet to offer constructive criticism, produce books and tapes, perform and share skills, offering creative and critical support. There are writers' workshops of long standing; adult literacy organisations; groups working mainly in oral and local history; groups and local networks of writers who come together to publish, train or perform; groups with a specific remit to further the aims of a section of the community such as the homeless or disabled. Although diverse in nature, member organisations share the aim to make writing and publishing accessible to people and encourage them to take an active, cooperative and democratic role in writing, performing and publishing. The main activities include training days and weekends to learn and share skills, a quarterly magazine, a quarterly broadsheet of members' writing, a major annual festival of writing and networking between member organisations. The FWWCP has published a number of anthologies and is willing to work with other organisations on publishing projects. Membership is open only to groups but individuals will be put in touch with groups which can help them, and become friends of the Federation. Contact the address above for an information leaflet.

Fellowship of Authors and Artists
PO Box 16554, London SE1 5ZS
☎020 7237 6356 Fax 020 7237 6356
Email fellowship@compassion-in-business.co.uk
Website www.author-fellowship.co.uk

Contact *Graham Irwin*

FOUNDED in 2000 to promote and encourage the use of writing and all art forms as a means of therapy and self healing; to provide a valuable resource and meeting point for all interested parties including, but not limited to, writers, artists, counsellors and healers; to publish as web pages or e-books any suitable works that may help to support or promote the aims of the fellowship.

Film Council
10 Little Portland Street, London W1W 7JG
☎020 7861 7861 Fax 020 7861 7862
Email info@filmcouncil.org.uk
Website www.filmcouncil.org.uk

A recently formed strategic agency responsible for developing the film industry in the UK. By helping those already in the business of filmmaking through its funding and training initiatives and also those wishing to become part of the film-making process and film culture in the UK, the Council aims to create a sustainable film industry for the future.

Foreign Press Association in London
11 Carlton House Terrace, London SW1Y 5AJ
☎020 7930 0445 Fax 020 7925 0469
Email secretariat@foreign-press.org.uk
Website www.foreign-press.org.uk

Contacts *Davina Crole, Catherine Flury*
Membership (incl. VAT) £128 p.a. (Full); £119 (Associate Journalists); £178 (Associate Non-Journalists)

FOUNDED 1888. Non-profit-making service association for foreign correspondents based in London, providing a variety of press-related services.

The Gaelic Books Council
See **Comhairle nan Leabhraichean**

The Garden Writers' Guild
c/o Institute of Horticulture, 14/15 Belgrave Square, London SW1X 8PS
☎020 7245 6943
Email gwg@horticulture.org.uk
Website www.gardenwriters.co.uk

Contact *Angela Clarke*
Subscription £30; (£25 to Institute of Horticulture members); £40 (Associate members)

FOUNDED 1990. Aims to raise the quality of gardening communication, to help members operate efficiently and profitably, to improve liaison between garden communicators and the horticultural industry. Administers an annual awards scheme. Operates a mailing service and organises press briefing days.

General Practitioner Writers' Association
West Carnliath, Strathtay, Perthshire PH9 0PG
☎01887 840380

Contact *Professor F.M. Hull (President)*
Subscription £30 p.a.; £40 (Joint)

FOUNDED in 1986 and expanding rapidly in membership and influence. Exists to promote and improve professional and lay writing activities within and for general practice. Open to doctors and other health professionals especially those working in the field of general practice; also to professional journalists writing on anything pertaining to general practice. Keen to develop input from interested parties who work mainly outside the profession. Regular workshops held around Britain. *Publishes* a twice-yearly journal (*The GP Writer*), anthologies and books from members, and a register of members and their writing interests.

Guild of Agricultural Journalists

Charmwood, 47 Court Meadow, Rotherfield, East Sussex TN6 3LQ
☎01892 853187   Fax 01892 853551
Email don.gomery@farmline.com
Website www.gaj.org.uk
Honorary General Secretary *Don Gomery*
Subscription £40 p.a.

FOUNDED 1944 to promote a high professional standard among journalists who specialise in agriculture, horticulture and allied subjects. Represents members' interests with representative bodies in the industry; provides a forum through meetings and social activities for members to meet eminent people in the industry; maintains contact with associations of agricultural journalists overseas; promotes schemes for the education of members and for the provision of suitable entrants into agricultural journalism.

Guild of Editors

See **Society of Editors**

The Guild of Food Writers

48 Crabtree Lane, London SW6 6LW
☎020 7610 1180   Fax 020 7610 0299
Email gfw@gfw.co.uk
Administrator *Christina Thomas*
Subscription £70

FOUNDED 1985. The objects of the Guild include: 'to bring together professional food writers including journalists, broadcasters and authors, to print and issue an annual list of members, to extend the range of members' knowledge and experience by arranging discussions, tastings and visits, and to encourage the development of new writers by every means including competitions and awards. The Guild aims to contribute to the growth of public interest in, and knowledge of, the subject of food and to campaign for improvements in the quality of food.'

Guild of Motoring Writers

30 The Cravens, Smallfield, Surrey RH6 9QS
☎01342 843294   Fax 01342 844093
Email sharon@scott-fairweather.freeserve.co.uk

Website www.newspress.co.uk/guild
General Secretary *Sharon Scott-Fairweather*
FOUNDED 1944. Represents members' interests and provides a forum for members to exchange information.

Horror Writers Association

UK Contact: 24 Pearl Road, Walthamstow, London E17 4QZ
Email hwa@horror.org
Website www.horror.org
US Contact: HWA Membership, PO Box 50577, Palo Alto, CA 94303, USA
☎001 650 322 4610
Contact (UK) *Jo Fletcher*

FOUNDED 1987. World-wide organisation of writers and publishers dedicated to promoting the interests of writers of horror and dark fantasy. *Publishes* a bi-monthly newsletter, issues e-mail bulletins, gives access to lists of horror agents, reviewers and bookstores; and keys to the 'Members Only' area of the HWA website. Presents the annual **Bram Stoker Awards** (see entry under **Prizes**).

HTML Writers Guild

Email membership-questions@hwg.org
Website www.hwg.org

FOUNDED in 1994 by a small group of HTML writers, the Guild is an international organisation for Internet designers with over 115,000 members world-wide and is open to anyone with an interest in the craft of web design. Provides extensive resources through the Guild website and mailing lists. Online classes to support members' efforts from the professional designer to the hobbyist designing a homepage. Various levels of membership available.

HWA

See **Horror Writers Association**

Independent Publishers Guild

PO Box 93, Royston, Hertfordshire SG8 5GH   Fax 01763 246293
Email sheila@ipg.uk.com
Website www.ipg.com
Secretary *Sheila Bounford*
Subscription £75 p.a.

FOUNDED 1962. Membership open to independent publishers, packagers and suppliers, i.e. professionals in allied fields. Regular meetings, conferences, seminars, mailings and a quarterly bulletin.

Independent Television Association

See **ITV Network Ltd**

Independent Television Commission (ITC)

33 Foley Street, London W1P 7LB
☎020 7255 3000 Fax 020 7306 7800
Website www.itc.org.uk

Chief Executive *Patricia Hodgson*

The ITC issues licences and regulates commercial television in the UK; maintains standards of the programmes which appear plus advertising and technical quality. Complaints against the service are investigated by the Commission which frequently publishes its findings and it is empowered to impose penalties on licensees that do not comply with their licence conditions.

Independent Theatre Council

12 The Leathermarket, Weston Street, London SE1 3ER
☎020 7403 1727 Fax 020 7403 1745
Email s.jones@itc-arts.org
Website www.itc-arts.org

Contact *Charlotte Jones*

The management association and representative body for small/middle-scale theatres (up to around 450 seats) and touring theatre companies. Negotiates contracts and has established standard agreements with Equity on behalf of all professionals working in the theatre. Negotiations with the WGGB for a contractual agreement covering rights and fee structure for playwrights were concluded in 1991. Terms and conditions were renegotiated and updated in September 1998. Copies of the minimum terms agreement can be obtained from the **Writers' Guild**. *Publishes* a booklet, *A Practical Guide for Writers and Companies* (£3.50 plus p&p), giving guidance to writers on how to submit scripts to theatres and guidance to theatres on how to deal with them.

Institute of Copywriting

Honeycombe House, Bagley, Wedmore BS28 4TD
☎01934 713563 Fax 01934 713492
Email copy@inst.org
Website www.inst.org/copy

Secretary *Lynn Hall*

FOUNDED 1991 to promote copywriters and copywriting (writing publicity material). Maintains a code of practice. Membership is open to students as well as experienced practitioners. Runs training courses (see entry under **Writers' Courses**). Has a list of approved copywriters. Answers queries relating to copywriting. Contact the Institute for a free booklet.

Institute of Linguists

Saxon House, 48 Southwark Street, London SE1 1UN
☎020 7940 3100 Fax 020 7940 3101
Email info@iol.org.uk
Website www.iol.org.uk

Chief Executive Officer *Henry Pavlovich*
Marketing Manager *Stephen Eden*

FOUNDED 1910. Professional association for translators, interpreters and trainers; examining body for languages at degree level and above for vocational purposes; the National Register of Public Service Interpreters is managed by NRPSI, an IoL subsidiary. Subscription rates on application. The Institute's limited company, Language Services Ltd, provides customised assessments of language-oriented requirements, skills, etc.

Institute of Translation and Interpreting (ITI)

377 City Road, London EC1V 1ND
☎020 7713 7600 Fax 020 7713 7650
Email info@iti.org.uk
Website www.iti.org.uk

FOUNDED 1986. The ITI is a professional association of translators and interpreters aiming to promote the highest standards in translating and interpreting. It has strong corporate membership and runs professional development courses and conferences, sometimes in conjunction with its language, regional and subject network. Membership is open to those with a genuine and proven involvement in translation and interpreting (including students). ITI's *Directory of Members*, its bi-monthly *Bulletin* and other publications are available from the Secretariat. The Secretariat offers a free referral service whereby enquirers can be given the names of suitable members for any interpreting/translating assignment. ITI is a full and active member of FIT (International Federation of Translators).

International Association of Puzzle Writers

42 Brigstocke Terrace, Ryde, Isle of Wight PO33 2PD
☎01983 811688
Email drsims@lineone.net

Contact *Dr Jeremy Sims*
Membership fee £25 p.a.

FOUNDED 1996 for writers of brainteasing puzzles, crosswords and word games, and for designers of games in general. Enquiries from publishers seeking material welcome. Aims to provide support and information and to promote the art of puzzle writing and games design to publishers, games manufacturers and the general public. *Publishes* bi-monthly newsletter – contributions welcome. Members must have e-mail. For further information, send s.a.e. to the address above.

Irish Book Publishers' Association
See **Clé**

Irish Copyright Licensing Agency Ltd
Irish Writers' Centre, 19 Parnell Square, Dublin 1, Republic of Ireland
☎00 353 1 872 9202 Fax 00 353 1 872 2035
Email icla@esatlink.com

Executive Director *Orla O'Sullivan*

FOUNDED 1992 by writers and publishers in Ireland to provide a scheme through which rights holders can give permission, and users of copyright material can obtain permission, to copy.

Irish Playwrights and Screenwriters Guild
Irish Writers' Centre, 19 Parnell Square, Dublin 1, Republic of Ireland
☎00 353 1 872 1302 Fax 00 353 1 872 6282
Email moffats@indigo.ie
Website www.writerscentre.ie/IPSG.html

Contact *Sean Moffatt*
Subscription IR£25

FOUNDED in 1969 to safeguard the rights of scriptwriters for radio, stage and screen.

Irish Translators' Association
Irish Writers' Centre, 19 Parnell Square, Dublin 1, Republic of Ireland
☎00 353 1 285 9137 Fax 00 353 1 872 6282
Email translation@eircom.net
Website homepage.eircom.net/~translation

Honorary Secretary *Miriam Lee*
Subscription IR£20 p.a. (Ordinary); IR£10 (Students, Unwaged, Pensioners, Members of affiliated organisations); IR£60 (Corporate); IR£40 (Professional – membership by application to Professional Membership Committee only)

FOUNDED 1986. The Association is for all translators: technical, commercial, literary and cultural, both written and spoken. It is also for those with an interest in translation such as teachers and students. Provides legal advice to members, issues a register of translators and *publishes* a quarterly newsletter, *Translation Ireland*.

Irish Writers' Union
Irish Writers' Centre, 19 Parnell Square, Dublin 1, Republic of Ireland
☎00 353 1 872 1302 Fax 00 353 1 872 6282

Secretary *Helen Brennan*
Chair *Tony Hickey*
Subscription £30 p.a.

FOUNDED 1986 to promote the interests and protect the rights of writers in Ireland.

ISBN & SAN Agency
Woolmead House, Bear Lane, Farnham, Surrey GU9 7LG
☎01252 742590 Fax 01252 742526
Email isbn@whitaker.co.uk
Website www.whitaker.co.uk/isbn.htm

ISBNs are product numbers used by all sections of the book trade for ordering and listing purposes. While ISBNs have no links to copyright and carry no form of legal protection for the book, they will enable your books to be listed on bibliographic databases and may therefore help sales. The UK Standard Book Numbering Agency is the national ISBN agency, responsible for assigning ISBN prefixes to publishers based in the UK or Republic of Ireland. Its services include advising publishers on the correct implementation of the ISBN system and maintaining a database of publishers and their prefixes, as well as providing technical advice and assistance to publishers and the booktrade on all aspects of ISBN usage. Applications for ISBNs for new publishers, help with calculating ISBNs and additional prefixes are all available from the Agency.

Isle of Man Authors
24 Laurys Avenue, Ramsey, Isle of Man IM8 2HE
☎01624 815634

Secretary *Mrs Beryl Sandwell*
Subscription £5 p.a.

An association of writers living on the Isle of Man, which has links with the **Society of Authors**.

ITC

See **Independent Television Commission**

ITI

See **Institute of Translation and Interpreting**

ITV Network Ltd.

200 Gray's Inn Road, London WC1X 8HF
☎020 7843 8000 Fax 020 7843 8158
Website www.itv.co.uk

Director of Programmes *David Liddiment*

The ITV Network Ltd., wholly owned by the ITV companies, independently commissions and schedules the television programmes which are shown across the ITV network. As a successor to the Independent Television Association, it also provides a range of services to the ITV companies where a common approach is required.

IVCA (International Visual Communication Association)

19 Pepper Street, Glengall Bridge, London E14 9RP
☎020 7512 0571 Fax 020 7512 0591
Email info@ivca.org
Website www.ivca.org

Chief Executive *Wayne Drew*

The IVCA is a professional association representing the interests of the users and suppliers of visual communications. In particular it pursues the interests of producers, commissioners and manufacturers involved in the non-broadcast and independent facilities industries and also business event companies. It represents all sizes of company and freelance individuals, offering information and advice services, publications, a professional network, special interest groups, a magazine and a variety of events including the UK's Film and Video Communications Festival.

Learning on Screen (The Society for Screen Based Learning)

9 Bridge Street, Tadcaster, North Yorkshire LS24 9AW
☎01937 530520 Fax 01937 530520
Email josie.key@learningonscreen.u-net.com
Website www.learningonscreen.org.uk

Administrator *Josie Key*

Learning on Screen is the new identity of the Educational Television and Media Association (ETmA). The Society for Screen Based Learning provides support and assistance to those involved in any form of screen-based learning. New members always welcome. Annual conference and production awards.

The Library Association

7 Ridgmount Street, London WC1E 7AE
☎020 7255 0500 Fax 020 7255 0501
Email info@la-hq.org.uk
Website www.la-hq.org.uk

Chief Executive *Bob McKee*

The professional body for librarians and information managers, with 25,000 individual and institutional members. **Library Association Publishing** produces 30–35 new titles each year and has over 250 in print. The *LA Record* is the monthly magazine for members. Further information from Information Services, The Library Association.

The Media Society

56 Roseneath Road, London SW11 6AQ
Contact *Peter Dannheisser*
Subscription £35 p.a.; £10 Entry fee
FOUNDED 1973. A registered charity which aims to provide a forum for the exchange of knowledge and opinion between those in public and political life, the professions, industry and education. Meetings (about 10 a year) usually take the form of luncheons and dinners in London with invited speakers. The society also acts as a 'think tank' and submits evidence and observations to royal commissions, select committees and review bodies.

Medical Journalists' Association

101 Cambridge Gardens, London W10 6JE
☎020 8968 1614 Fax 020 8968 7910

Chairman *John Illman*
Honorary Secretary *Sue Lowell*
Subscription £30 p.a.

FOUNDED 1967. Aims to improve the quality and practice of medical and health journalism and to improve relationships and understanding between medical and health journalists and the health and medical professions. Regular meetings with senior figures in medicine and medico politics; teach-ins on particular subjects to help journalists with background information; weekend symposium for members with people who have newsworthy stories in the field; awards for medical journalists offered by various commercial sponsors, plus MJA's own award financed by members. *Publishes* a detailed directory of members and freelances and two-monthly newsletter.

Medical Writers' Group & Medical Awards

The Society of Authors, 84 Drayton Gardens, London SW10 9SB
☎020 7373 6642 Fax 020 7373 5768
Email authorsoc@writers.org.uk

Contact *Dorothy Sym*

FOUNDED 1980. A specialist group within the **Society of Authors** offering advice and help to authors of medical books. Administers Medical Prizes.

Mystery Writers of America, Inc.

17 East 47th Street, 6th Floor, New York, NY 10017, USA
☎001 212 888 8171 Fax 001 212 888 8107
Email mwa_org@earthlink.net
Website www.mysterywriters.org

Admin Director *Mary Beth Becker*

Subscription $80 (US); $60 (Corresponding members)

FOUNDED 1945. Aims to promote and protect the interests of writers of the mystery genre in all media; to educate and inform its membership on matters relating to their profession; to uphold a standard of excellence and raise the profile of this literary form to the world at large. Holds an annual banquet at which the 'Edgars' are awarded (named after Edgar Allen Poe).

National Association for Literature Development

PO Box 140, Ilkley, West Yorkshire LS29 6RH
☎01943 872546
Email steve@nald.org
Website www.nald.org

Coordinator *Steve Dearden*

NALD exists to enable literature professionals to talk to each other, develop their professional skills and make the case for increased investment in their work. Offers individual, organisational or corporate membership.

National Association of Writers Groups

The Arts Centre, Biddick Lane, Washington, Tyne & Wear NE38 2AB
☎0191 416 9751 Fax 0191 431 1263

Contact *Brian Lister*

FOUNDED 1995 with the object of furthering the interests of writers' groups throughout the UK. A registered charity, No: 1059047, NAWG is strictly non-sectarian and non-political. *Publishes* a bi-monthly newsletter, distributed to member groups; gives free entry to competitions for group anthologies, poetry, short stories, articles, novels and sketches; holds an annual open festival of writing with 40 workshops, seminars, individual surgeries led by professional, high-profile writers. Membership is open to all writers' groups – there are no restrictions or qualifications required for joining; 120 groups are affiliated to-date.

National Association of Writers in Education

PO Box 1, Sheriff Hutton, York YO60 7YU
☎01653 618429
Email paul@nawe.co.uk
Website www.nawe.co.uk

Contact *Paul Munden*

Subscription £20 p.a. (Individual); £10 (Student); £60 (Institution)

FOUNDED 1991. Aims to promote the contribution of living writers to education and to encourage both the practice and the critical appreciation of creative writing. Has over 500 members. Organises national conferences and training courses. A directory of over 1200 writers who work in schools, colleges and the community is available online. *Publishes* a magazine, *Writing in Education*, issued free to members three times per year.

National Campaign for the Arts

Pegasus House, 37–43 Sackville Street, London W1S 3EH
☎020 7333 0375 Fax 020 7333 0660
Email nca@artscampaign.org.uk

Director *Victoria Todd*

FOUNDED 1984 to represent the cultural sector in Britain and to make sure that the problems facing the arts are properly put to Government, at local and national level. The NCA is an independent body relying on finance from its members. Involved in all issues which affect the arts: public finance, education, broadcasting and media affairs, the fight against censorship, the rights of artists, the place of the arts on the public agenda and structures for supporting culture. Membership open to all arts organisations and to individuals. Literature subscriptions available.

National Literacy Trust

Swire House, 59 Buckingham Gate, London SW1E 6AJ
☎020 7828 2435 Fax 020 7931 9986
Email contact@literacytrust.org.uk
Website www.literacytrust.org.uk *and* www.rif.org.uk

Director *Neil McClelland*

FOUNDED 1993. A registered charity (No: 1015539) which aims to make 'an independent, strategic contribution to the creation of a society in which all can enjoy the appropriate skills, confidence and pleasures of literacy to support their educational, economic, social and cultural goals.' Maintains an extensive website with literacy issues, research news and database detailing literacy practice nationwide; promotes and facilitates literacy partnerships; organises an annual conference, courses and training events; *publishes* quarterly magazine, *Literacy Today* (the Educational Publishing Company, subscription £18). Organised and implemented the National Year of Reading 1998–99 and is coordinating the National Reading Campaign. It also incorporates Reading Is Fundamental, UK, which provides books free to children.

National Union of Journalists

Acorn House, 314 Gray's Inn Road, London WC1X 8DP
☎020 7278 7916 Fax 020 7837 8143
Email acorn.house@nuj.org.uk
Website www.gn.apc.org/media/

General Secretary *John Foster*
Subscription £163 p.a. (Freelance) or 1% of annual income if lower; or 0.5% if income less than £12,000 p.a.

Represents journalists in all sectors of publishing, print and broadcast. Responsible for wages and conditions agreements which apply across the industry. Provides advice and representation for its members, as well as administering unemployment and other benefits. *Publishes* various guides and magazines: *Freelance Directory, Fees Guide, The Journalist* and *The Freelance*.

New Playwrights Trust

See **Writernet**

New Producers Alliance (NPA)

9 Bourlet Close, London W1W 7BP
☎020 7580 2480 Fax 020 7580 2484
Email queries@npa.org.uk
Website www.newproducer.co.uk

FOUNDED 1993; current membership of over 1000. Aims to encourage the production of commercial feature films for an international audience and to educate and inform film producers, writers and directors. The NPA is an independent networking organisation providing members with access to contacts, free legal advice and general help regarding film produc-

tion. *Publishes* a monthly newsletter and organises meetings, workshops and seminars. The NPA also actively lobbies for better access to funds for first- and second-time film makers. The NPA does not produce films so please do not send scripts or treatments.

The New SF Alliance (NSFA)

c/o BBR Magazine, PO Box 625, Sheffield, South Yorkshire S1 3GY
Website www.bbr-online.com/writers
Contact *Chris Reed*

FOUNDED 1989. Committed to supporting the work of new writers and artists by promoting independent and small press publications worldwide. 'Helps with finding the right market for your material by providing a mail-order service which allows you to sample magazines, and various publications including *Zene* magazine and *Scavenger's Newsletter* which feature the latest market news and tips.'

New Writing North

7/8 Trinity Chare, Quayside, Newcastle upon Tyne NE1 3DF
☎0191 232 9991 Fax 0191 230 1883
Email subtext.nwn@virgin.net
Website www.newwritingnorth.com

Director *Claire Malcolm*
Administrator *John McGagh*

New Writing North is the literature development agency for the **Northern Arts** region and offers many useful services to writers, organising events, readings and courses. NWN produces writing guides and has a website with literary news, events and opportunities. Administers the Northern Playwriting Panel (aiding new drama) and the Northern Writers' Awards, which include tailored development packages (mentoring and financial help). NWN has strong links with the post of Northern Literary Fellow – Ian Duhig is the present incumbent. NWN also programmes the **Durham Literature Festival**.

The Newspaper Society

Bloomsbury House, 74–77 Great Russell Street, London WC1B 3DA
☎020 7636 7014 Fax 020 7631 5119
Email ns@newspapersoc.org.uk
Website www.newspapersoc.org.uk

Director *David Newell*

FOUNDED in 1836, the Newspaper Society is the voice of Britain's regional and local newspapers. It represents and promotes the interests of over 1300 regional daily and weekly, paid for and free, titles. The range of activities and services provided by the Society can be split into two broad areas: marketing and lobbying. Holds a series of conferences and seminars each year and runs the annual Local Newspaper Week.

NPA
See **New Producers Alliance**

NSFA
See **The New SF Alliance**

Outdoor Writers' Guild
PO Box 520, Bamber Bridge, Preston, Lancashire PR5 8LF
☎01772 696732 Fax 01772 696732
Secretary *Terry Marsh*
Subscription £45 p.a.

FOUNDED 1980 to promote, encourage and assist the development and maintenance of professional standards among those involved in all aspects of outdoor journalism. Membership is not limited to writers but includes other outstanding professional media practitioners in the outdoor world such as broadcasters, photographers, filmmakers, editors, publishers and illustrators. *Publishes* a quarterly journal, *Bootprint*, and an annual *Directory* (£30; free to members) as well as guidelines, codes of practice and advice notes. Presents five Awards for Excellence plus other awards in recognition of achievement.

PACT (Producers Alliance for Cinema and Television)
45 Mortimer Street, London W1W 8HJ
☎020 7331 6000 Fax 020 7331 6700
Email enquiries@pact.co.uk
Website www.pact.co.uk
Chief Executive *John McVay*
Membership Officer *David Alan Mills*

FOUNDED 1991. PACT is the trade association of the UK independent television and feature film production sector and is a key contact point for foreign producers seeking British co-production, co-finance partners and distributors. Works for producers in the industry at every level and operates a members' regional network throughout the UK with a divisional office in Scotland. Membership services include: a dedicated industrial relations unit; discounted legal advice; a varied calendar of events; business advice; representation at international film and television markets; a comprehensive research programme; various publications: a monthly magazine, an annual members' directory; affiliation with European and international producers' organisations; extensive information and production advice. Lobbies actively with broadcasters, financiers and governments to ensure that the producer's voice is heard and understood in Britain and Europe on all matters affecting the film and television industry.

PEN
152–156 Kentish Town Road, London NW1 9QB
☎020 7267 9444 Fax 020 7267 9304
Email enquiries@pen.org.uk
Website www.pen.org.uk
Director *Diana Reich*
Membership £40 (London/Overseas); £35 (members living over 50 miles from London)

English PEN is part of International PEN, a worldwide association of published writers which fights for freedom of expression and speaks out for writers who are imprisoned or harassed for having criticised their governments, or for publishing other unpopular views. FOUNDED in London in 1921, International PEN now consists of over 130 centres in almost 100 countries. PEN originally stood for poets, essayists and novelists, but membership is now also open to published playwrights, editors, translators and journalists. A programme of talks and discussions is supplemented by a twice-yearly mailing and annual congress at one of the centre countries.

Performing Right Society
29–33 Berners Street, London W1T 3AB
☎020 7580 5544 Fax 020 7306 4455
Email info@prs.co.uk
Website www.prs.co.uk

Collects and distributes royalties arising from the performance and broadcast of copyright music on behalf of its composer, lyricist and music publisher members and members of affiliated societies worldwide.

Periodical Publishers Association (PPA)
Queens House, 28 Kingsway, London WC2B 6JR
☎020 7404 4166 Fax 020 7404 4167
Email info1@ppa.co.uk
Website www.ppa.co.uk

FOUNDED 1913 to promote and protect the interests of magazine publishers in the UK.

The Personal Managers' Association Ltd

1 Summer Road, East Molesey, Surrey KT8 9LX
☎020 8398 9796 Fax 020 8398 9796
Email info@thepma.com
Co-chairs *Marc Berlin, Tim Corrie*
Secretary *Angela Adler*
Subscription £250 p.a.

An association of artists' and dramatists' agents (membership not open to individuals). Monthly meetings for exchange of information and discussion. Maintains a code of conduct and acts as a lobby when necessary. Applicants screened. A high proportion of play agents are members of the PMA.

The Picture Research Association

Head Office: 2 Culver Drive, Oxted, Surrey RH8 9HP
☎01883 730123 Fax 01883 730144
Email pra@lippmann.co.uk
Website www.picture-research.org.uk
Chair *Charlotte Lippmann*
Subscription Members: £45 (Introductory); £50 (Full); £55 (Associate).
  Magazine only: £25

FOUNDED 1977 as the Society of Picture Researchers & Editors. The Picture Research Association is a professional body for picture researchers, managers, picture editors and all those involved in the research, management and supply of visual material to all forms of the media. The Association's main aims are to promote the interests and specific skills of its members internationally; to promote and maintain professional standards; to bring together those involved in the research and publication of visual material; to provide a forum for the exchange of information and to provide guidance to its members. Free advisory service for members, regular meetings, quarterly magazine, monthly newsletter and Freelance Register.

Player–Playwrights

9 Hillfield Park, London N10 3QT
☎020 8883 0371
Email P-P@dial.pipex.com
President *Olwen Wymark*
Contact *Peter Thompson* (at the address above)
Subscription £10 (Joining fee); £6 p.a.
  thereafter, plus £1.50 per attendance

FOUNDED 1948. A society giving opportunity for writers new to stage, radio and television, as well as others finding difficulty in achieving results, to work with writers established in those media. At weekly meetings (7.45 pm–10.00 pm, Mondays, upstairs at the Horse and Groom, 128 Great Portland Street, London W1), members' scripts are read or performed by actor members and afterwards assessed and dissected in general discussion. Newcomers and new acting members are always welcome.

PLS
See **Publishers Licensing Society Ltd**

PMA
See **The Personal Managers' Association Ltd**

Poetry Book Society
See **Organisations of Interest to Poets**

Poetry Ireland
See **Organisations of Interest to Poets**

The Poetry Society
See **Organisations of Interest to Poets**

Press Complaints Commission

1 Salisbury Square, London EC4Y 8JB
☎020 7353 1248 Fax 020 7353 8355
Email pcc@pcc.org.uk
Website www.pcc.org.uk
Director *Guy Black*
Information Officer *Tonia Milton*

FOUNDED in 1991 to deal with complaints from members of the public about the editorial content of newspapers and magazines. Administers the editors' Code of Practice covering such areas as accuracy, privacy, harrassment and intrusion into grief. Publications available: *Code of Practice* and *How to Complain*.

Private Libraries Association

16 Brampton Grove, Kenton, Harrow, Middlesex HA3 8LG
☎020 8907 6802 Fax 020 8907 6802
Email Frank@plantage.demon.co.uk
Honorary Secretary *Frank Broomhead*
Membership £25 p.a.

FOUNDED 1956. An international society of book collectors. The Association's objectives are to promote and encourage the awareness of the benefits of book ownership, and the study of books, their production, and ownership; to publish works concerned with this, particularly those which are not commercially profitable, to hold meetings at which papers on cognate subjects can be read and discussed. Lectures and exhibitions are open to non-members.

Producers Alliance for Cinema and Television
See **PACT**

The Publishers Association
1 Kingsway, London WC2B 6XD
☎020 7565 7474 Fax 020 7836 4543
Email mail@publishers.org.uk
Website www.publishers.org.uk
Chief Executive *Ronnie Williams, OBE*

The national UK trade association for books, learned journals, and electronic publications, with around 200 member companies in the industry. Very much a trade body representing the industry to Government and the European Commission, and providing services to publishers. *Publishes* the *Directory of Publishing* in association with **Continuum**. Also home of the Educational Publishers Council (school books), PA's International Division (BDCI), the Council of Academic and Professional Publishers, and the Electronic Publishers' Forum.

Publishers' Association of South Africa
PO Box 22640, Fish Hoek 7974, South Africa
☎00 27 21 7827677 Fax 00 27 21 7827679
Email pasa@publishsa.co.za
Website www.publishsa.co.za

FOUNDED in 1992 to represent publishing in South Africa, a small but key industry sector. With a membership of over 120 companies, the Association includes commercial organisations, university presses, one-person privately-owned publishers as well as importers and distributors.

Publishers Licensing Society Ltd
5 Dryden Street, Covent Garden, London WC2E 9NB
☎020 7829 8486 Fax 020 7829 8488
Email pls@dial.pipex.com
Website www.pls.org.uk
Chief Executive *Jens Bammel*
Manager *Caroline Elmslie*

FOUNDED in 1981, the PLS obtains mandates from publishers which grant PLS the authority to license photocopying of pages from published works. Some licences for digitisation of printed works are available. PLS aims to maximise revenue from licences for mandating

publishers and to expand the range and repertoire of mandated publishers available to licence holders. It supports the **Copyright Licensing Agency (CLA)** in its efforts to increase the number of legitimate users through the issuing of licences and vigorously pursues any infringements of copyright works belonging to rights' holders.

Publishers Publicity Circle
65 Airedale Avenue, London W4 2NN
☎020 8994 1881
Email ppc-@lineone.net
Contact *Heather White*

Enables book publicists from both publishing houses and freelance PR agencies to meet and share information regularly. Meetings, held monthly in central London, provide a forum for press journalists, television and radio researchers and producers to meet publicists collectively. A directory of the PPC membership is published each year and distributed to over 2500 media contacts.

Radio Authority
Holbrook House, 14 Great Queen Street, London WC2B 5DG
☎020 7430 2724 Fax 020 7405 7062
Email info@radioauthority.org.uk
Website www.radioauthority.org.uk

The Radio Authority plans frequencies, awards licences, regulates programming and advertising, and plays an active role in the discussion and formulation of policies which affect the Independent Radio industry and its listeners. The Authority also licenses digital radio services. The national commercial digital radio service was launched on 15 November 1999. The number of Independent Radio stations, now over 250, continues to increase with new licences being advertised on a regular basis.

Romance Writers of America
3707 FM 1960 W, Suite 555, Houston, TX 77068, USA
☎001 281 440 6885 Fax 001 281 440 7510
Email info@rwanational.com
Website www.rwanational.com
Communications Assistant *Nicole Kennedy*
Subscriptions $75 p.a. plus $25 joining fee

FOUNDED 1980. RWA, a non-profit association with more than 8400 members worldwide, provides a service to authors at all stages of their careers as well as to the romance publishing industry and its readers. Anyone pursuing a career in romantic fiction may join RWA. Holds an annual conference, and provides contests for both published and unpublished writers through the RITA Awards and Golden Hearts Awards.

The Romantic Novelists' Association

48 Southampton Road, Fareham, Hampshire PO16 7DY
☎01329 822196 Fax 01329 825248
Website www.rna-uk.org

Contact *Karen King*
Subscription Full & Associate: £28 p.a.; £33 (Overseas, non-EU); New Writers: £78; £83 (Overseas, non-EU)

Membership is open to published writers of romantic fiction (modern or historical), or those who have had two or more full-length serials published. Associate membership is open to publishers, editors, literary agents, booksellers, librarians and others having a close connection with novel writing and publishing. Membership, in the New Writers' Scheme, is available to writers who have not yet had a full-length novel published. New Writers must submit a manuscript each year. The mss receive a report from experienced published members and the reading fee is included in the subscription of £78. Meetings are held in London and the regions with interesting guest speakers. The *RNA News* is published quarterly and issued free to members. The Association makes two annual awards: **The Major Award** for the Romantic Novel of the Year, and **The New Writers Award** for the best published novel by a new writer.

Royal Festival Hall Literature & Talks

Performing Arts Department, Royal Festival Hall, London SE1 8XX
☎020 7921 0906 Fax 020 7928 2049
Email shoare@rfh.org.uk
Website www.sbc.org.uk

Head of Literature *Ruth Borthwick*

The Royal Festival Hall presents a year-round literature programme covering all aspects of writing. Regular series range from New Voices to Fiction International and there is a biennial Poetry International Festival. Literature events are now programmed in the Voice Box, Purcell Room and Queen Elizabeth Hall. To join the free mailing list, phone 020 7921 0971 or e-mail: Literature&Talks@rfh.org.uk

Royal Society of Literature

Somerset House, Strand, London WC2R 1LA
☎020 7845 4676 Fax 020 7845 4679
Email info@rslit.org
Website www.rslit.org

President *Lord Jenkins of Hillhead*
Subscription £30 p.a.

FOUNDED 1820. Membership by application to the Secretary. Fellowships are conferred by the Society on the proposal of two Fellows. Membership benefits include lectures, discussion meetings, poetry readings and two annual joint meetings with the Royal Society. Lecturers have included Margaret Drabble, Sebastian Faulks, Richard Holmes, Doris Lessing and Andrew Motion. Presents the **W.H. Heinemann Award**, the **Winifred Holtby Prize** and the **V.S. Pritchett Memorial Prize**.

Royal Television Society

Holborn Hall, 100 Gray's Inn Road, London WC1X 8AL
☎020 7430 1000 Fax 020 7430 0924
Email info@rts.org.uk
Website www.rts.org.uk

Subscription £65 p.a.

FOUNDED 1927. Covers all disciplines involved in the television industry. Provides a forum for debate and conferences on technical, social and cultural aspects of the medium. Presents various awards including journalism, programmes, technology, design and commercials. *Publishes Television Magazine* nine times a year for members and subscribers.

Science Fiction Foundation

Membership Secretary: D28, Department of Arts and Media, Buckinghamshire Chilterns University College, High Wycombe, Buckinghamshire HP11 2JZ
Email ambutler@enterprise.net
Website www.sf-foundation.org
Contact *Andrew M. Butler*

The SFF is a national academic body for the furtherance of science fiction studies. *Publishes* a thrice-yearly magazine, *Foundation* (see entry under **Magazines**), which features academic articles and reviews of new fiction. It also has a reference library (see entry under **Libraries**), housed at Liverpool University.

Scottish Book Trust

The Scottish Book Centre, 137 Dundee Street, Edinburgh EH11 1BG
☎0131 229 3663 Fax 0131 228 4293
Email scottish.book.trust@dial.pipex.com

Website www.scottishbooktrust.com

Contact *Lindsey Fraser*

FOUNDED 1956. Scottish Book Trust works with schools, libraries, writers, artists, publishers, bookshops and individuals to promote the pleasures of reading to people of all ages. It provides a book information service which draws on the children's reference library (a copy of every children's book published in the previous twelve months) and a range of press cuttings on Scottish literary themes. Scottish Book Trust administers **The Fidler Award** and the Blue Peter Book Awards; and *publishes* guides to Scottish books and writers, both adult and children's. It administers the *Writers in Scotland* scheme, coordinates National Poetry Day in Scotland and produces a range of posters and literary guides.

Scottish Daily Newspaper Society

48 Palmerston Place, Edinburgh EH12 5DE
☎0131 220 4353 Fax 0131 220 4344
Email info@sdns.org.uk

Director *Mr J.B. Raeburn*

FOUNDED 1915. Trade association representing publishers of Scottish daily and Sunday newspapers.

Scottish Library Association

Scottish Centre for Information & Library Services, 1 John Street, Hamilton, Strathclyde ML3 7EU
☎01698 458888 Fax 01698 458899
Email sla@liberator.amlibs.co.uk
Website www.slainte.org.uk

Director *Robert Craig*

FOUNDED 1908 to bring together everyone engaged in or interested in library work in Scotland. The Association has over 2300 members, covering all aspects of library and information work. Its main aims are the promotion of library services and the qualifications and status of librarians.

Scottish Newspaper Publishers Association

48 Palmerston Place, Edinburgh EH12 5DE
☎0131 220 4353 Fax 0131 220 4344
Email info@snpa.org.uk
Website www.snpa.org.uk

Director *Mr J.B. Raeburn*

FOUNDED around 1905. The representative body for the publishers of paid-for weekly and associated free newspapers in Scotland. Represents the interests of the industry to

Government, public and other bodies and provides a range of services including marketing of *The Scottish Weekly Press*, industrial relations, and education and training. It is an active supporter of the Press Complaints Commission.

Scottish Print Employers Federation

48 Palmerston Place, Edinburgh EH12 5DE
☎0131 220 4353 Fax 0131 220 4344
Email info@spef.org.uk
Website www.spef.org.uk

Director *Mr J.B. Raeburn*

FOUNDED 1910. Employers' organisation and trade association for the Scottish printing industry. Represents the interests of the industry to Government, public and other bodies and provides a range of services including industrial relations, education, training and commercial activities. Negotiates a national wages and conditions agreement with the Graphical, Paper and Media Union. The Federation is a member of Intergraf, the international confederation for employers' associations in the printing industry. In this capacity its views are channelled on the increasing number of matters affecting print businesses emanating from the European Union.

Scottish Publishers Association

Scottish Book Centre, 137 Dundee Street, Edinburgh EH11 1BG
☎0131 228 6866 Fax 0131 228 3220
Email enquiries@scottishbooks.org
Website www.scottishbooks.org

Director *Lorraine Fannin*
Marketing Manager *Alison Rae*
Promotions & Training Manager *Allan Shanks*
Administrator *Carol Lothian*

The Association represents over 80 Scottish publishers, from multinationals to small presses, in a number of capacities, but primarily in the cooperative promotion and marketing of their books. The SPA also acts as an information and advice centre for both the trade and general public. *Publishes* seasonal catalogues, membership lists, the annual *Directory of Publishing in Scotland* and regular newsletters. Represents members at international book fairs; runs an extensive training programme in publishing skills; carries out market research; and encourages export initiatives. Also provides administrative back-up for the Scottish Book Marketing Group, a cooperative venture with Scottish booksellers.

Society for Children's Book Writers & Illustrators

134 Glasgow Road, Perth PH2 0LW
British Isles Regional Advisor *Natascha Biebow*
Assistant Regional Advisor *Elizabeth Wein*

FOUNDED in 1968 by a group of Los Angeles-based writers, the Society acts as a network for the exchange of knowledge between writers, illustrators, editors, publishers, agents and others involved with literature for young people. With a membership of over 10,000 worldwide, it is the largest organisation of its kind in the world. Holds an annual national conference plus a number of regional ones, *publishes* a bi-monthly newsletter and awards grants for works in progress. The Golden Kite Award, which is presented annually, is for best fiction and non-fiction books. For membership enquiries, contact *Elizabeth Wein* at the address above.

The Society for Screen Based Learning

See **Learning on Screen**

The Society of Authors

84 Drayton Gardens, London SW10 9SB
☎020 7373 6642 Fax 020 7373 5768
Email authorsoc@writers.org.uk
Website www.writers.org.uk/society
General Secretary *Mark Le Fanu*
Subscription £70/75 p.a.

FOUNDED 1884. The Society of Authors is an independent trade union with some 7000 members. It advises on negotiations with publishers, broadcasting organisations, theatre managers and film companies; assists with complaints and takes action for breach of contract, copyright infringement, etc. Together with the **Writers' Guild**, the Society has played a major role in advancing the Minimum Terms Agreement for authors. Among the Society's publications are *The Author* (a quarterly journal) and the *Quick Guides* series to various aspects of writing (all free of charge to members). Other services include vetting of contracts, emergency funds for writers, and various special discounts. There are groups within the Society for scriptwriters, children's writers and illustrators, educational writers, medical writers and translators. Authors under 35 or over 65, not earning a significant income from their writing, may apply for lower subscription rates. Contact the Society for a free booklet and a copy of *The Author*.

The Society of Authors in Scotland

Bonnyton House, Arbirlot, Angus DD11 2PY
☎01241 874131 Fax 01241 874131
Email info@eileenramsay.co.uk
Website www.writersorg.co.uk
Secretary *Eileen Ramsay*

The Scottish branch of the **Society of Authors**, which organises business meetings, social and bookshop events throughout Scotland.

Society of Civil Service Authors

17 The Green, Corby Glen, Grantham, Lincolnshire NG33 4NP
Membership Secretary *Mrs Joan Hykin*
Subscription £15 p.a.

FOUNDED 1935. Aims to encourage authorship by present and past members of the Civil Service and to provide opportunities for social and cultural relationships between civil and public servants who are authors or who aspire to be authors. Annual competitions, open to members only, are held for short stories, poetry, sonnets, travel articles, humour, etc. Members receive *The Civil Service Author*, a quarterly magazine. Occasional meetings in London, poetry weekend outside London.

Society of Editors

University Centre, Granta Place, Mill Lane, Cambridge CB2 1RU
☎01223 304080 Fax 01223 304090
Email society@ukeditors.com
Website www.ukeditors.com
Executive Director *Bob Satchwell*

Formed by a merger of the Association of British Editors and the Guild of Editors, the Society of Editors has nearly 500 members in national, regional and local newspapers, broadcasting, new media, journalism education and media law. Campaigns for media freedom and self-regulation. For further information contact *Bob Satchwell* at the address above or on pager number 07625 155366.

Society of Freelance Editors and Proofreaders (SFEP)

Mermaid House, 1 Mermaid Court, London SE1 1HR
☎020 7403 5141 Fax 020 7407 1193
Email admin@sfep.org.uk
Website www.sfep.org.uk
Chair *Naomi Laredo*
Vice-chair *Adrian Sumner*

Secretary *Katie Lewis*

Subscription £65 p.a. (Individuals) plus £25 joining fee; Corporate membership available

FOUNDED 1988 in response to the growing number of freelance editors and their increasing importance to the publishing industry. Aims to promote high editorial standards by disseminating information through advice and training, and to achieve recognition of the professional status of its members. The Society also supports moves towards recognised standards of training and accreditation for editors and proofreaders.

Society of Indexers

Globe Centre, Penistone Road, Sheffield, South Yorkshire S6 3AE
☎0114 281 3060 Fax 0114 281 3061
Email admin@socind.demon.co.uk
Website www.socind.demon.co.uk

Secretary *Liza Weinkove*
Administrator *Wendy Burrow*
Subscription £50 p.a.; £75 (Institutions)

FOUNDED 1957. *Publishes The Indexer* (biannual, April and October) and a quarterly newsletter. Issues an annual list of members and *Indexers Available (IA)*, which lists members and their subject expertise. In addition, the Society runs an open-learning course entitled *Training in Indexing* and recommends rates of pay (currently £15–20 per hour).

Society of Picture Researchers & Editors

See **The Picture Research Association**

Society of Women Writers and Journalists

110 Whitehall Road, London E4 6DW
☎020 8529 0886
Email swwriters@aol.com

Honorary Secretary *Jean Hawkes*
Subscription £30 (Town); £25 (Country); £20 (Overseas). £10 Joining fee

FOUNDED 1894. The first of its kind to be run as an association of women engaged in journalism. Aims to encourage literary achievement, uphold professional standards, and establish social contacts with other writers. Lectures given at monthly lunchtime meetings. Offers advice to members and has regular seminars, etc. *Publishes* a society journal, *The Woman Writer*.

Society of Young Publishers

Endeavour House, 189 Shaftesbury Avenue, London WC2H 8JT
Email thesyp@thesyp.demon.co.uk
Website www.thesyp.demon.co.uk
Subscription £25 p.a.; £15 (Student/unwaged)

Provides facilities whereby members can increase their knowledge and widen their experience of all aspects of publishing, and holds regular social events. Open to those in related occupations, with associate membership available for over-35s. *Publishes* a monthly newsletter called *Inprint* and holds meetings on the last Wednesday of each month at the **Publishers Association**. Please enclose an s.a.e. when writing to the Society.

The South and Mid-Wales Association of Writers (SAMWAW)

c/o I.M.C. Consulting Group, Denham House, Lambourne Crescent, Cardiff CF14 5ZW
☎029 2076 1170 Fax 029 2076 1304
Email info@imcconsultinggroup.co.uk
Subscription £7 (Single); £12 (Joint)

FOUNDED 1971 to foster the art and craft of writing in all its forms. Provides a common meeting ground for writers, critics, editors, adjudicators from all over the UK and abroad. Organises an annual residential weekend conference and a day seminar in May and October respectively. Holds competitions, two for members only and two which are open to the public, in addition to **The Mathew Prichard Award for Short Story Writing** (see entry under **Prizes**).

Spoken Word Publishing Association (SWPA)

c/o Penguin Books Ltd, 80 Strand, London WC2R 0RL
☎020 7010 3000 Fax 020 7010 6060
Email audio@penguin.co.uk
Website www.swpa.org.uk

Chairman *Anna Archer*
Secretary *Connie Bristow-Stagg*

FOUNDED 1994. SWPA is the UK trade association for the spoken word industry with membership open to all those involved in the publishing of spoken word audio. *Publishes SWPA Resources Directory* available from the address above.

Sports Writers' Association of Great Britain

c/o Sport England External Affairs, 16 Upper Woburn Place, London WC1H 0QP
☎020 7273 1789 Fax 020 7383 0273

Subscription £23.50 p.a. incl. VAT (London); £11.75 (Regional)

FOUNDED 1948 to promote and maintain a high professional standard among journalists who specialise in sport in all its branches and to serve members' interests. *Publishes* a quarterly bulletin for members and promotes jointly with Sport England the annual British Sports Journalism Awards and the Sports Photographer of the Year award.

SWPA

See **Spoken Word Publishing Association**

Theatre Writers' Union

See **The Writers' Guild of Great Britain**

The Translators Association

84 Drayton Gardens, London SW10 9SB
☎020 7373 6642 Fax 020 7373 5768
Email authorsoc@writers.org.uk

Secretary *Dorothy Sym*

FOUNDED 1958 as a subsidiary group within the **Society of Authors** to deal exclusively with the special problems of literary translators into the English language. Benefits to members include free legal and general advice and assistance on all business matters relating to translators' work, including the vetting of contracts and advice on rates of remuneration. Membership is normally confined to translators who have had their work published in volume or serial form or produced in this country for stage, television or radio. The Association administers several prizes for translators of published work (see **Prizes**) and maintains a database to enable members' details to be supplied to publishers who are seeking a translator for a particular work.

Voice of the Listener and Viewer (VLV)

101 Kings Drive, Gravesend, Kent DA12 5BQ
☎01474 352835 Fax 01474 351112
Email vlv@btinternet.com

VLV represents the citizen and consumer interest in broadcasting. It is an independent, non-profit-making society working to ensure independence, quality and diversity in broadcasting. VLV is the only consumer body speaking for listeners and viewers on the full range of broadcasting issues. VLV is funded by its members and is free from sectarian, commercial and political affiliations. Holds public lectures, seminars and conferences, and has frequent contact with MPs, civil servants, the BBC and independent broadcasters, regulators, academics and other consumer groups. Produces a quarterly news bulletin and regular briefings on broadcasting issues. Holds its own archive and those of the former Broadcasting Research Unit (1980–90) and BACTV (British Action for Children's Television). Maintains a panel of speakers and the VLV Forum for Children's Broadcasting, and acts as secretariat for the European Alliance of Listeners' and Viewers' Associations (EURALVA). VLV has responded to all parliamentary and public enquiries on broadcasting since 1984 and to all consultation documents issued by the ITC and Radio Authority since 1990. The VLV does not handle complaints.

W.A.T.C.H.

See **Writers, Artists and their Copyright Holders**

Welsh Academy

See **Academi**

Welsh Books Council (Cyngor Llyfrau Cymru)

Castell Brychan, Aberystwyth, Ceredigion SY23 2JB
☎01970 624151 Fax 01970 625385
Email castellbrychan@cllc.org.uk
Website www.cllc.org.uk *and* www.gwales.com

Director *Gwerfyl Pierce Jones*
Head of Editorial Department *Dewi Morris Jones*

FOUNDED 1961 to stimulate interest in Welsh literature and to support authors. The Council distributes the government grant for Welsh language publications and promotes and fosters all aspects of both Welsh and Welsh-interest book production. Its Editorial, Design, Marketing and Children's Books departments and wholesale distribution centre offer central services to publishers in Wales. Writers in Welsh and English are welcome to approach the Editorial Department for advice on how to get their manuscripts published.

Welsh National Literature Promotion Agency

See **Academi**

Welsh Union of Writers

13 Tyn–y–Coed Road, Pentyrch, Cardiff
CF15 9NP
Website www.wuw.freeuk.com
Secretary *Jean Henderson*
Subscription £15 p.a. (Full); £5 (Associate);
£5 Joining fee (waived if standing order
agreed)

FOUNDED 1982. Independent union. Full
membership by application to persons born or
working in Wales with at least one publication
in a quality journal or other outlet. Associate
membership now available for other interested
supporters. Lobbies for writing in Wales, represents members in disputes; annual conference
and occasional events, publications and magazine, *Cursor* (Welsh literature in English).

Women in Publishing

c/o The Publishers Association, 1 Kingsway,
3rd Floor, London WC2B 6XF
Website www.cyberiacafe.net/wip/
Contact *Information Officer*
Membership £25 p.a. (Waged); £15
(Unwaged/Student); £30 (if paid for by
company)

Aims to promote the status of women working
within the publishing industry and related
trades, to encourage networking, and to provide training for career and personal development. Meetings (with panels of speakers) held
on the second Wednesday of the month at the
Publishers Association at 6.30 pm. Monthly
newsletter *WiPlash* and *Women in Publishing
Directory*.

Women Writers Network (WWN)

23 Prospect Road, London NW2 2JU
☎020 7794 5861
Membership Secretary *Cathy Smith*
Subscription £35 p.a. (Full); £25 p.a.
(Overseas); £20 p.a. ('Newsletter only' UK
membership)

FOUNDED 1985. Provides a forum for the
exchange of information, support, career and
networking opportunities for working women
writers. Meetings, seminars, excursions,
newsletter and directory. Full membership
includes free admission to monthly meetings, a
directory of members and a monthly newsletter. Details from the Membership Secretary at
the address above.

Word Arena, Leeds

Central Library, Calverley Street, Leeds, West
Yorkshire LS1 3TB
☎0113 224 3887 Fax 0113 247 8287
Email sean.burn@leeds.gov.uk
Manager *Sean Burn*

Leeds Word Arena is funded by Leeds City
Council as the Literature Development
Agency for the city. Provides a year-round
programme of projects supporting reader and
writer development, including residencies,
commissions, events as well as support, advice
and advocacy for Leeds-based writers, readers
and publishers. Runs an annual literary festival,
City Voice, (see entry under **Festivals**) in the
first two weeks of June.

Writernet

Cabin V, Clarendon Buildings, 25 Horsell
Road, Highbury, London N5 1XL
☎020 7609 7474 Fax 020 7609 7557
Email writernet@npt.easynet.co.uk
Website www.writernet.org.uk
Executive Director *Jonathan Meth*
Subscription (information on rates available
by post or on website)

Writernet (formerly the New Playwrights
Trust) is the national research and development
organisation for writing for all forms of live and
recorded performance. *Publishes* a range of
information pertinent to writers on all aspects
of development and production in the form of
pamphlets, and a six-weekly journal which also
includes articles and interviews on aesthetic
and practical issues. Writernet also runs a
script-reading service and a link service
between writers and producers, organises seminars and conducts research projects. The latter
includes research into the use of bilingual techniques in playwriting (*Two Tongues*), documentation of training programmes for writers
(*Going Black Under the Skin*) and an investigation of the relationship between live art and
writing (*Writing Live*).

The Writers' Guild of Great Britain

430 Edgware Road, London W2 1EH
☎020 7723 8074 Fax 020 7706 2413
Email admin@writersguild.org.uk
Website www.writers.org.uk/guild
General Secretary *Bernie Corbett*
Assistant General Secretaries *Jacob
Ecclestone, Anne Hogben*

Annual subscription 1% of that part of the author's income earned in the areas in which the Guild operates, with a basic subscription of £100 and a maximum of £950

FOUNDED 1959. The Writers' Guild is the writers' trade union, affiliated to the TUC. It represents writers in film, radio, television, theatre and publishing. The Guild has negotiated agreements on which writers' contracts are based with the BBC, Independent Television companies, and **PACT** (the Producers' Alliance for Cinema and Television). Those agreements are regularly renegotiated, both in terms of finance and conditions. In 1997, the Guild membership joined with that of the Theatre Writers' Union to create a new, more powerful union.

In 1979, together with the Theatre Writers' Union, the Guild negotiated the first ever industrial agreement for theatre writers, the TNC Agreement, which covers the **Royal National Theatre**, the **Royal Shakespeare Company**, and the **Royal Court**. Further agreements have been negotiated with the Theatrical Management Association which covers regional theatre and the **Independent Theatre Council**, the organisation which covers small theatres and the Fringe.

The Guild initiated a campaign over ten years ago which achieved the first ever publishing agreement for writers with the publisher W.H. Allen. Jointly with the **Society of Authors**, that campaign has continued and most years see new agreements with more publishers. Perhaps the most important breakthrough came with **Penguin** on 20 July 1990. The Guild now also has agreements covering **HarperCollins**, **Random House Group**, **Transworld** and others.

The Guild regularly provides individual help and advice to members on contracts, conditions of work, and matters which affect a member's life as a professional writer. Members are given the opportunity of meeting at craft meetings, which are held on a regular basis throughout the year. Writers can apply for Full Membership if they have one piece of written work for which payment has been received under a contract with terms not less than those negotiated by the Guild. Writers who do not qualify for Full Membership can apply for Candidate Membership. This is open to all those who wish to be involved in writing but have not yet had work published. The subscription fee for this is £50.

Writers, Artists and their Copyright Holders (W.A.T.C.H.)

The Library, The University of Reading, PO Box 223, Whiteknights, Reading, Berkshire RG6 6AE

☎0118 931 8783 Fax 0118 931 6636

Website www.watch-file.com

Contact *Dr David Sutton*

FOUNDED 1994. Provides an online database of information about the copyright holders of literary authors and artists. The database is available free of charge on the Internet and the Web. W.A.T.C.H. is the successor project to the Location Register of English Literary Manuscripts and Letters, and continues to deal with location register enquiries.

Yachting Journalists' Association

3 Friars Lane, Maldon, Essex CM9 6AG

☎01621 855943/0776 896 2936 (mobile)

Fax 01621 852212

Email Yjauk@cs.com

Website www.yja.co.uk

Honorary Secretary *Peter Cook*

Subscription £30 p.a.

To further the interest of yachting, sail and power, and to provide support and assistance to journalists in the field; current membership is just over 260 with 23 from overseas. A handbook, listing details of members and subscribing PR organisations, press facility recommendations, forthcoming events and other useful information, is published annually at a cost to non-members and non-advertisers of £10. Information for inclusion should be submitted by the end of August. The YJA organises the Yachtsman of the Year and Young Sailor of the Year Awards, that form part of the British Nautical Awards, presented annually at the beginning of January on the first Friday of the London International Boat Show.

Yr Academi Gymreig

See **Academi**

Keeping it in the Family

The latest instalment in the copyright saga

The communication revolution has made the protection of copyright ever more problematic. Unscrupulous media barons are having a field day. In the Far East it is reckoned that over 90 per cent of all videocassettes sold are pirated. Unauthorised printing of books in China, Russia and a motley of smaller nations is said to be depriving British publishers and their authors of £200 million a year. As for the photocopier, it is now responsible for some 300 billion pages of illegally reproduced material. Then there is the all-pervasive Internet which makes unauthorised duplication a doddle.

If there is any comfort, creators have legislation on their side. The Copyright Directive approved by the European Parliament in February extends ordinary copyright protection to new, digital media such as the Internet, digital television, cellular phones and other personal digital devices. There was a nasty moment when it looked as if the broadcasting companies had secured an amendment which would have allowed them to re-use or sell archive material without getting permission from writers or actors. But a swift counter-attack, led by the Writers' Guild, put paid to that little ruse. The Directive will be assimilated into national law over the next two years, bringing Europe into line with the US where the Digital Millennium Copyright Act has been in force for three years. How effective all this will be remains an open question. Much depends on developing an effective policing system. Reports are already filtering through the technological grapevine of new metering systems which will allow publishers to monitor and record the use of its information on the Internet and other networks. In early 1997, the World Intellectual Property Organisation, the UN's agency responsible for administering copyright conventions, required member states to outlaw devices aimed at bypassing technical measures to prevent unauthorised copying.

Meanwhile, there is much that the individual writer can do to guard against the free use of what is, or what might turn out to be, a valuable property with an earning capacity over 70 years. The starting point is the small print of a contract. Any publisher who offers a deal that is dependent on exclusive rights must be regarded with suspicion. It is likely that he has no intention of paying the author a single penny beyond a basic fee or royalty. This is what happens to contributors to academic and specialist journals who are invariably asked to assign their copyright as a condition of publication. Even those who make a living out of writing and are skilled in the devious ways of publishing can lose out simply by ignoring the subsidiary clauses of a contract or, if reading them, by not realising the long term implications.

Once surrendered, copyright cannot be retrieved. As Nicola Solomon, a lawyer specialising in copyright law, warns, 'an assignment of copyright is binding ... it is not contingent on an agreed fee or royalties being paid. If a publisher fails to pay, your only remedy ... is to sue for the unpaid debt but you will not be able to regain copyright.'

There may well be occasions when the surrender of copyright is justified. A writer who works to order, adapting material provided for a company training course, say, or a sponsored history to be used as a promotional tool, would be pushing his luck to argue for more than a set fee.

On occasion, it is not altogether clear who it is that has first claim to copyright. The most obvious example is the journalist – say, a columnist whose by-line appears twice weekly in a national newspaper. If he is on the payroll, with all the rights and responsibilities of an employee, then copyright on his articles is assumed to belong to his employer – 'unless otherwise agreed'. In other words, if the journalist is a self-assertive type who is ready to bargain with his editor he may well emerge with a contract which secures his copyright beyond the first printing. A scribe with less muscle might prefer to rely on his editor's sense of decency in handing over a share of any supplementary fees. As a general rule, those who commission work invariably demand exclusive copyright, including syndication rights. This applies to freelancers who, technically speaking, are entitled to copyright, as well as to regular employees. The journalists' unions urge members to resist but the need to make a living in a highly competitive market weakens the resolve of all but the star turns.

Film and television

In late 1992 the European Commission's Rental and Lending Directive declared the 'author' of a film to have the right to '"equitable" remuneration'. But who is the 'author'? Under British law, he is generally assumed to be the producer, an interpretation which naturally offends writers and directors. The European Community, on the other hand, takes its lead from France where the primary author of a film is the director and others, including the scriptwriter, can be named as co-authors. Producers have tried to frustrate the change, threatening expensive legal action but in late 1996, Parliament gave the go-ahead for scriptwriters and authors whose work has been filmed or broadcast to receive payments for the rental of their works. Checking who owes what to whom is made easier by signing up with the **Authors' Licensing and Collecting Society** which acts as a collecting agency on behalf of its members.

Problems remain, however. Lending is horrendously difficult to control. It has been known for years that the loss of income attributed to domestic sound and video recorders runs into billions. With the advance of technology, the problem is bound to worsen. Before long we will have video on demand, an almost limitless choice of programming available to any home at a push of the remote control. Imagine what that will do to undermine copyright.

Extent of copyright

In most books a copyright notice appears on one of the front pages. In its simplest form this is the symbol © followed by the name of the copyright owner and the year of first publication. The assertion of copyright may be emphasised by the phrase 'All rights reserved', and in case there are any lingering doubts the reader may be warned that 'No part of this publication may be reproduced or transmitted in any form or by any means without permission'.

But this is to overstate the case. In principle, a quotation of a 'substantial' extract from a copyright work or any quotation of copyright material, however short, for an anthology must be approved by the publishers of the original work.

But there is no fixed rule on what constitutes a substantial extract. In any case, even a lengthy quotation from a copyright work may not be an infringement if it is 'fair dealing . . . for purposes of criticism or review'. Much depends on the standing of the writer being quoted. If he is a world famous author he or his heirs are liable to take a tougher line than, say, the copyright holder of an esoteric work of limited circulation. The families of literary giants are notoriously stingy. In granting permission to quote they are liable to charge hefty fees or, if the applicant is at all suspect – a biographer who is liable to do the dirt on a revered memory, for example – to refuse to cooperate in any way. For this, if for no other reason, an author who needs permission to quote should deal with the matter at an early stage. Last minute requests just before a book goes to press can lead to crisis if fees are too high or if permission is refused.

A contract must specify the territory permissions will cover. The difference between British Commonwealth and the World can be a yawning gap in costs. Some publishers have a standard letter for clearing permissions, which may help to speed up negotiations. But rights departments are notoriously slow in responding to requests from individuals who are unclear as to what they want or who give the impression of writing in on spec.

Difficulties can arise when the identity of a copyright holder is unclear. The publisher of the relevant book may have gone out of business or been absorbed into a conglomerate, leaving no records of the original imprint. Detective work can be yet more convoluted when it comes to unpublished works. When copyright holders are hard to trace, the likeliest source of help is the **Writers, Artists and their Copyright Holders** project, otherwise known as WATCH. A joint enterprise of the universities of Texas and Reading, WATCH has created a database of English language authors whose papers are housed in archives and manuscript repositories. The database is available free of charge on the Internet.

If, despite best efforts, a copyright owner cannot be found, there are two options; either to cut the extract or to press ahead with publication in the hope that if the copyright holder does find out he will not object or will not demand an outrageous fee. The risk can be minimised by open acknowledgement that every effort to satisfy the law has been made.

Anthology and quotation rates

Prose The rate suggested by the **Society of Authors** and the **Publishers Association** is £120–£146 per 1,000 words for world rights. The rate for the UK and Commonwealth or the USA alone is usually half of the world rate. For an individual country, one quarter of the world rate. Where an extract is complete in itself (e.g. a chapter or short story) publishers sometimes charge an additional fee at half the rate applicable for 1,000 words. This scale generally covers one edition only. An additional fee may be payable if the material is used in a reset or offset edition or in a new format or new binding (e.g. a paperback edition) and will certainly be required if the publisher of an anthology sub-licenses publication rights to another publisher.

Fees vary according to the importance of the author quoted, the proportion of the original work that the user intends to quote and its value to the author/publisher requesting permission. The expected size of the print-run should also be taken into consideration. Fees for quotations in scholarly works with print-runs of under 1,000 copies are usually charged at half the normal rate.

Poetry The World rate for anthology publication is a minimum fee of £90–£120 for the first 10 lines; thereafter £2.10–£2.30 per line for the next 20 lines and £1.30–£1.50 a line subsequently but the rates for established poets may well be significantly higher. The rate for the UK and Commonwealth or the USA alone is usually half of the world rate.

Moral rights

With the 1988 Copyright Designs and Patents Act, the European concept of 'moral rights' was introduced into British law. The most basic is the right of paternity which entitles authors to be credited as the creators of their work. However, paternity must be asserted in writing and is not retrospective. No right of paternity attaches to authors of computer programs or to writers who create works as part of their employment or journalists or as contributors to a 'collective work' such as an encyclopaedia, dictionary or year book.

A second moral right is that of integrity. In theory, this opens the way to forceful objections to any 'derogatory treatment' if derogatory amounts to 'distortion or mutilation . . . or is otherwise prejudicial to the honour or reputation of the author'. Miscorrection of grammar by an illiterate editor does not qualify. In the absence of test cases it seems that a book would have to be savaged beyond recognition for an injunction to be granted. Those most likely to have their right of integrity infringed are film directors (specifically mentioned in the 1988 Act) and visual artists who might, for example, suffer the attentions of an airbrusher. For those in the writing trade, the Society of Authors urges 'locking the stable door before the horse bolts, by ensuring that your contract does not permit the publishers to make significant editorial changes without your agreement.' Though, with the virtual abandonment of hard copy in favour of disks, changes can be introduced without the author noticing – until it is too late.

Moral rights may 'be waived by written agreement or with the consent of the author'. There are cases where concession is justified, for example, a ghost writer who chooses to be anonymous may reasonably be expected to waive moral rights.

Titles and trademarks

Technically, there is no copyright in a title. But where a title is inseparable from the work of a particular author, proceedings for 'passing off' are likely to be successful. Everything depends on the nature of the rival works, the methods by which they are exploited and the extent to which the title is essentially distinctive.

The risks of causing offence multiply when a unique image is involved. Mickey Mouse, Thomas the Tank Engine, and the *Mr Men* characters created by Roger Hargreaves (60 million books sold to date) are examples of registered trademarks that protect against literary and other predators. The interesting feature of trademarks is that unlike copyright, they go on forever. The Coca-Cola and Kodak marks, for example, are well over 100 years old.

In theory it should be easier to preserve copyright in fictional characters than on titles. But in broadcasting, a frequent source of dispute is the lifting of characters from one series to another when there are two or more writers involved. Sometimes royalties are paid; other times, not. Production companies are liable to take possession of fictional characters unless their originators make a fuss.

The singularity of letters

The copyright status of a letter is something of a curiosity. The actual document belongs to the recipient, but the copyright remains with the writer and after death, to the writer's estate. This has caused difficulty for some biographers who have assumed that it is the owners of letters who are empowered to give permission to quote from them. This only applies if the writer has assigned copyright. Even then, the way may not be smooth. Witness the frustration of Eric Jacobs, the biographer of Sir Kingsley Amis, who found himself unable to quote from letters written by the novelist because the Bodleian Library, which has the bulk of the Amis papers, would not concede any part of the copyright Sir Kingsley has invested in them. The matter was resolved only when the letter writer himself requested permission to quote from his own correspondence.

Copyright in lectures and speeches

Even if a speaker talks without notes, copyright exists in a lecture as soon as it is recorded (in writing or otherwise) but not until then. The copyright belongs to the person who spoke the words, whether or not the recording was made by, or with the permission of, the speaker. There is one important exception: when a record of spoken words is made to report current events.

Copyright on ideas

Writers trying to sell ideas should start on the assumption that it is almost impossible to stake an exclusive claim. So much unsolicited material comes the way of publishers and script departments, the duplication of ideas is inevitable.

Frequent complaints of plagiarism have led publishers and production companies to point out the risks whenever they acknowledge an unsolicited synopsis or script, warning correspondents, 'it is often the case that we are currently considering or have already considered ideas that may be similar to your own'.

In America the studios are now so worried about being sued that any writer offering an idea or script must sign a document waiving rights.

A writer who is nervous of the attention of rivals is best advised to maintain a certain reticence in dealings with the media. He should resist the urge to give out all his best ideas at an expensive lunch or in a brainstorming session with an ever-so-friendly producer. It is flattering to be invited to hold forth but the experience can be costly unless there is an up-front fee.

At the same time, remember that there is no such thing as an entirely original plot. To succeed in an action for infringement of copyright on an idea or on the bare bones of a plot, the copying of 'a combination or series of dramatic events' must be very close indeed. Proceedings have failed because incidents common to two works have been stock incidents or revolving around stock characters common to many works.

A few years ago a Californian judge threw out a $100 million copyright infringement suit filed by two New Zealand playwrights against the producers of *The Full Monty*. The playwrights claimed the film closely resembled their 10 year-old play, *Ladies Night*. The late Hughie Green unsuccessfully fought a court battle to stop New Zealand producers making a show he claimed was a version of *Opportunity Knocks*. Since little of his original idea was ever committed to paper his claim was too difficult to prove.

For any queries on British copyright contact: The Copyright Directorate, The Patent Office, Harmsworth House, 13-15 Bouverie Street, London EC4Y 8DP (☎020 7596 6513/ 6566; fax 020 7596 6526; email copyright@patent.gov.uk; website www.patent.gov.uk).

*The WATCH website is at www.watch-file.com (See entry under **Professional Associations and Societies**)*

Copyright information may be sent to Dr David Sutton, director of research projects in the University of Reading Library at d.c.sutton@reading.ac.uk or the Library, University of Reading, PO Box 223, Whiteknights, Reading RG6 6AE.

Literary Societies

Most literary societies exist on a shoestring budget; it is a good idea to enclose an A5 s.a.e. with all correspondence needing a reply.

Margery Allingham Society

2B Higham Green, Winchelsea, East Sussex TN36 4HB
☎01797 222363 Fax 01797 222363
Website www.geocities.com/margeryallingham
Contact *Mrs Pamela Bruxner*
Subscription £10 p.a.

FOUNDED 1988 to promote interest in and study of the works of Margery Allingham. The Society *publishes* two issues of the newsletter, *The Bottle Street Gazette*, per year. Contributions welcome. Two social events a year. Open membership.

Jane Austen Society

22 Belmont Grove, Bedhampton, Havant, Hampshire PO9 3PU
☎023 9247 5855
Email rosemary@sndc.demon.co.uk
Website www.janeaustensociety.org.uk
Membership Secretary *Mrs Rosemary Culley*
Subscription UK: £5 (Student); £10 (Annual); £15 (Joint); £30 (Corporate); £150 (Life); Overseas: £12 (Annual); £18 (Joint); £33 (Corporate); £180 (Life)

FOUNDED 1940 to promote interest in and enjoyment of Jane Austen's novels and letters. The society has branches in Bath & Bristol, Midlands, London, Oxford, Kent and Hampshire. There are independent Societies in North America and Australia.

The Baskerville Hounds

6 Bramham Moor, Hill Head, Fareham, Hampshire PO14 3RU
☎01329 667325
Chairman *Philip Weller*
Subscription £6 p.a.

FOUNDED 1989. An international Sherlock Holmes society specialising solely in studies of *The Hound of the Baskervilles* and its Dartmoor associations. *Publishes* an annual journal and specialist monographs. It also organises many social functions, usually on Dartmoor. Open membership.

The B.B. Society

8 Park Road, Solihull, West Midlands B91 3SU
☎0121 704 1002
Chairman *Tom O'Reilly*
Secretary *Bryan Holden* (at address above)
Subscription £10 (Individual); £17.50 (Family); £50 (Corporate); £5 (Unwaged)

FOUNDED in 2000 to bring together the fans of the country writer B.B. (Denys) Watkins-Pitchford. The Society holds regular meetings, events and *publishes* newsletters and a journal.

The Beckford Society

15 Healey Street, London NW1 8SR
☎020 7267 7750 Fax 01985 213239
Email Sidney.Blackmore@btinternet.com
Secretary *Sidney Blackmore*
Subscription £10 (min.) p.a.

FOUNDED 1995 to promote an interest in the life and works of William Beckford (1760–1844) and his circle. Encourages Beckford studies and scholarship through exhibitions, lectures and publications, including an annual journal, *The Beckford Journal*, and occasional newsletters.

Thomas Lovell Beddoes Society

11 Laund Nook, Belper, Derbyshire DE56 1GY
☎01773 828066 Fax 01773 828066
Email john@beddoes.demon.co.uk
Website
www.nortexinfo.net/McDaniel/tlb.htm
Chairman *John Lovell Beddoes*
Secretary *Judith Higgens*

Formed to research the life, times and work of poet Thomas Lovell Beddoes (1803–1849), encourage relevant publications, further the reading and appreciation of his works by a wider public and liaise with other groups and organisations. *Publishes* an annual newsletter.

Arnold Bennett Society

106 Scotia Road, Burslem, Stoke on Trent ST6 4ET
☎01782 816311
Secretary *Mrs Jean Potter*

Subscription £7 (Single); £9 (Family) plus £2 for membership outside the EEC

Aims to promote interest in the life and works of 'Five Towns' author Arnold Bennett and other North Staffordshire writers. Annual dinner. Regular functions in and around Burslem plus annual seminar in London. Three newsletters a year. Open membership.

E.F. Benson Society

The Old Coach House, High Street, Rye, East Sussex TN31 7JF
☎01797 223114

Secretary *Allan Downend*
Subscription £7.50 (UK/Europe); £12.50 (Overseas)

FOUNDED 1985 to promote the life and work of E.F. Benson and the Benson family. Organises social and literary events, exhibitions, talks and Benson interest walks in Rye. *Publishes* a quarterly newsletter and annual journal, *The Dodo*, postcards and reprints of E.F. Benson articles and short stories in a series called 'Bensoniana'. Holds an archive which includes the Seckersen Collection (transcriptions of the Benson collection at the Bodleian Library in Oxford).

E.F. Benson/The Tilling Society

5 Friars Bank, Guestling, Hastings, East Sussex TN35 4EJ Fax 01424 813237

Contact *Cynthia Reavell*
Subscription Full starting membership (members receive all back newsletters) £28 (UK); £32 (Overseas); or Annual Membership (members receive only current year's newsletters) £8 (UK); £10 (Overseas).

FOUNDED 1982 for the exchange of news, information and speculation about E.F. Benson, his works and, in particular, his *Mapp & Lucia* novels. Readings, talks and substantial biannual newsletter. Annual get-together in Rye/'Tilling'. Acts as a clearing house for every sort of news and activity concerning E.F. Benson.

The Betjeman Society

35 Eaton Court, Boxgrove Avenue, Guildford, Surrey GU1 1XH
☎01483 560882

Honorary Secretary *John Heald*
Subscription £7 (Individual); £9 (Family); £3 (Student); £2 extra each category for Overseas members

Aims to promote the study and appreciation of the work and life of Sir John Betjeman. Annual programme includes poetry readings, lectures, discussions, visits to places associated with Betjeman, and various social events. Meetings are held in London and other centres. Regular newsletter and annual journal, *The Betjemanian*.

The Bewick Society

1A Crossroads, Medomsley, Consett, Co. Durham DH8 6RL
Membership Secretary *June Holmes*
Subscription £7 p.a.

FOUNDED 1988 to promote an interest in the life and work of Thomas Bewick, wood-engraver and naturalist (1753–1828). Organises related events and meetings, and is associated with the Bewick birthplace museum.

Birmingham Central Literary Association

23 Arden Grove, Ladywood, Birmingham B16 8HG
☎0121 454 9335
Email bakerbrum@netscapeonline.co.uk

Contact *The Secretary*

Holds fortnightly meetings in central Birmingham to discuss the lives and work of authors and poets. Holds an annual dinner to celebrate Shakespeare's birthday.

The George Borrow Society

60 Upper Marsh Road, Warminster, Wiltshire BA12 9PN
Email borrow@mskillman.freeserve.co.uk
Website www.clough5.fsnet.co.uk/gb.html

President *Sir Angus Fraser, KCB TD*
Membership Secretary *Michael Skillman*
Honorary Treasurer *David Pattinson*
Chairman/Editor *George Borrow Bulletin:*
   Dr Ann M. Ridler, St Mary's Cottage, 61 Thame Road, Warborough, Wallingford, Oxford OX10 7EA
   ☎01865 858379 Fax 01865 858575
   Email 113250.1724@compuserve.com
Subscription £12.50 p.a.

FOUNDED 1991 to promote knowledge of the life and works of George Borrow (1803–81), traveller, linguist and writer. The Society holds biennial conferences (with published proceedings) and informal intermediate gatherings, all at places associated with Borrow. *Publishes* the *George Borrow Bulletin* twice yearly, a newsletter containing scholarly articles, publications relating to Borrow, reports of past events and news of forthcoming events. Member of the **Alliance of Literary**

Societies and corporate associate member of the Centre of East Anglian Studies (CEAS) at the University of East Anglia, Norwich (Borrow's home city for many years).

Elinor Brent-Dyer
See **Friends of the Chalet School**

British Fantasy Society
201 Reddish Road, South Reddish,
Stockport, Cheshire SK5 7HR
☎0161 476 5368 (after 6pm)
Email faliol@yahoo.com
Website www.herebedragons.co.uk/bfs

President *Ramsey Campbell*
Chairman *Gary Couzens*
Secretary *Robert Parkinson*
Subscription from £20 p.a. (apply to Secretary.)

FOUNDED 1971 for devotees of fantasy, horror and related fields in literature, art and the cinema. *Publishes* a regular newsletter with information and reviews of new books and films, plus related fiction and non-fiction magazines. Annual conference at which the **British Fantasy Awards** are presented. These awards are voted on by the membership and are not an open competition.

The Brontë Society
Brontë Parsonage Museum, Haworth,
Keighley, West Yorkshire BD22 8DR
☎01535 642323   Fax 01535 647131
Email bronte@bronte.prestel.co.uk
Website www.bronte.org.uk

Contact *Membership Secretary*
Subscription £20 p.a. (UK/Europe);
£7.50 (Student); £5 (Junior – up to age 14); £30 (Overseas); Joint subscriptions and life membership also available

FOUNDED 1893. Aims and activities include the preservation of manuscripts and other objects related to or connected with the Brontë family, and the maintenance and development of the museum and library at Haworth. The society holds regular meetings, lectures and exhibitions; and *publishes* information relating to the family, a biannual society journal *Transactions* and a biannual *Gazette*. Freelance contributions for either publication should be sent to the Publications Secretary at the address above.

The Rupert Brooke Society
The Orchard, 45/47 Mill Way, Grantchester,
Cambridge CB3 9ND
☎01223 845788   Fax 01223 842331
Email rbs@callan.co.uk

Contact *Robin Callan*
Subscription £7.50 (UK); £10.50 (Overseas)

FOUNDED in 1999 to foster an interest in the work of Rupert Brooke, help preserve places associated with him and to increase the knowledge and appreciation of the village of Grantchester. Members receive a newsletter with information about events, new books and information on activities.

The Browning Society
163 Wembley Hill Road, Wembley Park,
Middlesex HA9 8EL
☎020 8904 8401

Honorary Secretary *Ralph Ensz*
Subscription £15 p.a.

FOUNDED 1969 to promote an interest in the lives and poetry of Robert and Elizabeth Barrett Browning. Meetings are arranged in the London area, one of which occurs in December at Westminster Abbey to commemorate Robert Browning's death.

The John Buchan Society
Main Street, Kings Newton, Melbourne,
Derbyshire DE73 1BX
☎01332 865315
Email moonfleet@greenmantle63.freeserve. co.uk

Secretary *Kenneth Hillier*
Subscription £10 (Full/Overseas);
£4 (Associate); £6 (Junior);
£20 (Corporate); £90 (Life)

To perpetuate the memory of John Buchan and to promote a wider understanding of his life and works. Holds regular meetings and social gatherings, *publishes* a journal, and liaises with the John Buchan Centre at Broughton in the Scottish borders.

The Burns Federation
Dean Castle Country Park Dower House,
Kilmarnock, Strathclyde KA3 1XB
☎01563 572469   Fax 01563 572469
Email robertburnsfederation@kilmarnock26. freeserve.co.uk

Chief Executive *Shirley Bell*
Subscription £20 p.a.(Individual);
£25 (Family); £40 (Club subscription)

FOUNDED 1885 to encourage interest in the life and work of Robert Burns and keep alive the old Scottish Tongue. The Society's interests go beyond Burns himself in its commitment to the development of Scottish literature, music and arts in general. *Publishes* the quarterly *Burns Chronicle/Burnsian*.

The Byron Society
Byron House, 6 Gertrude Street, London
SW10 0JN
☎020 7352 5112
Honorary Director, Byron Society
 Mrs Elma Dangerfield OBE
Subscription £20 p.a.

Also: Newstead Abbey Byron Society,
Newstead Abbey, Newstead Abbey Park,
Nottingham NG15 8GE
☎01623 797392
Honorary Secretary *Mrs Maureen Crisp*
FOUNDED 1876; revived in 1971. Aims to promote knowledge and discussion of Lord Byron's life and works, and those of his contemporaries, through lectures, readings, concerts, performances and international conferences. *Publishes* annually in April *The Byron Journal*, a scholarly journal – £5 plus £1.75 postage.

Randolph Caldecott Society
Clatterwick House, Little Leigh, Northwich,
Cheshire CW8 4RJ
☎01606 891303 (day)/781731 (evening)
Honorary Secretary *Kenneth N. Oultram*
Subscription £7–£10 p.a.

FOUNDED 1983 to promote the life and work of artist/book illustrator Randolph Caldecott. Meetings held in the spring and autumn in Caldecott's birthplace, Chester. Guest speakers, outings, newsletter, exchanges with the society's American counterpart. (Caldecott died and was buried in St Augustine, Florida.) A medal in his memory is awarded annually in the US for children's book illustration.

The Carlyle Society, Edinburgh
Dept of English Literature, The University of Edinburgh, David Hume Tower, George Square, Edinburgh EH8 9JX
Fax 0131 650 6898
Email ian.campbell@ed.ac.uk
Contact *The President*
Subscription £2 p.a.; £10 (Life); $20 (US)
FOUNDED 1929 to examine the lives of Thomas Carlyle and his wife Jane, their writings, contemporaries, and influences. Meetings are held about six times a year and occasional papers are published annually. Enquiries should be addressed to the President of the Society at the address above or to the Secretary at 16a Blackford Road, Edinburgh EH9 2DS.

Lewis Carroll Society
69 Cromwell Road, Hertford, Hertfordshire
SG13 7DP
☎01992 584530
Email alanwhite@tesco.net
Website aznet.co.uk/lcs
Secretary *Alan White*
Subscription Individual: £13 (UK); £15 (Europe); £17 (Outside Europe); £10 (Retired rate); £2 (Additional family members); Institutions: £26 (UK); £28 (Europe); £30 (Outside Europe)
FOUNDED 1969 to bring together people with an interest in Charles Dodgson and promote research into his life and works. *Publishes* biannual journal *The Carrollian*, featuring scholarly articles and reviews; a newsletter (*Bandersnatch*) which reports on Carrollian events and the Society's activities; and *The Lewis Carroll Review*, a book reviewing journal. Regular meetings held in London with lectures, talks, outings, etc.

Lewis Carroll Society (Daresbury)
Clatterwick House, Little Leigh, Northwich,
Cheshire CW8 4RJ
☎01606 891303 (day)/781731 (evening)
Honorary Secretary *Kenneth N. Oultram*
Subscription £5 p.a.
FOUNDED 1970. To promote the life and work of Charles Dodgson, author of the world-famous *Alice's Adventures*. Holds regular meetings in the spring and autumn in Carroll's birthplace, Daresbury, in Cheshire. Guest speakers, theatre visits and a newsletter. Appoints annually a 10-year-old 'Alice' who is available for public engagements.

Friends of the Chalet School
4 Rock Terrace, Coleford, Bath, Somerset
BA3 5NF
☎01373 812705   Fax 01373 813517
Email focs@rockterrace.co.uk
Website www.rockterrace.demon.co.uk/FOCS
Contacts *Ann Mackie-Hunter, Clarissa Cridland*
Subscription £7.50 p.a.; £6 (Under-18);
 Outside UK: details on application
FOUNDED 1989 to promote the works of Elinor Brent-Dyer. The society has members worldwide; *publishes* four magazines a year and runs a lending library.

The Raymond Chandler Society
6 Barkers Road, Nether Edge, Sheffield S7 1SE
☎0114 255 6302   Fax 0114 255 6302
Email william.adamson@zsp.uni-ulm.de

UK Contact *Simon Beckett*
Subscription £15 p.a. (£7 concessions)

Although based in Germany, the Society has an international membership. Its foremost concerns are with Raymond Chandler's works and his influence and reception within a historical and contemporary context, but it is also concerned with the genre of the 'crime novel' in general. Presents the 'Marlowe' awards (see entry under **Prizes**). *Publishes* the *Chandler Yearbook*, a scholarly publication containing reviews and articles on crime writing in both English and German. The Society attends international conferences such as 'Dead on Deansgate' and 'Bouchercon', and organises the Chandler Symposium, usually held in Ulm, Germany in July.

The Chesterton Society UK

11 Lawrence Leys, Bloxham, Near Banbury, Oxfordshire OX15 4NU
☎01295 720869/07747 786428 (mobile)
Honorary Secretary *Robert Hughes, KHS*
Subscription £12.50 p.a.

FOUNDED 1964 to promote the ideas and writings of G.K. Chesterton.

The Children's Books History Society

25 Field Way, Hoddesdon, Hertfordshire EN11 0QN
☎01992 464885 Fax 01992 464885
Email cbhs@abcgarrett.demon.co.uk
Membership Secretary *Mrs Pat Garrett*
Subscription £10 p.a. (UK/Europe); write for Overseas subscription details

ESTABLISHED 1969. Aims to promote an appreciation of children's books and to study their history, bibliography and literary content. The Society holds approximately six meetings per year in London and a summer meeting to a collection, or to a location with a children's book connection. Three substantial newsletters issued annually, also an occasional paper. The Society constitutes the British branch of the Friends of the Osborne and Lillian H. Smith Collections in Toronto, Canada, and also liaises with the **Library Association**. In 1990, the Society established its biennial Harvey Darton Award for a book, published in English, which extends our knowledge of some aspect of British children's literature of the past. 1998 joint-winners: John Goldthwaite *The Natural History of Make-Believe* and Peter Newbolt *G. A. Henty 1832–1902*. (No award given in 2000.)

The John Clare Society

The Stables, 1a West Street, Helpston, Peterborough PE6 7DU
☎01733 252678 Fax 01733 252678
Website vzone.virgin.net/linda.curry/jclaresociety.htm *or* english.ntu.ac.uk/clare/clare.html
Honorary Secretary *Peter Moyse*
Subscription £9.50 (Individual); £12.50 (Joint); £7.50 (Fully Retired); £9.50 (Joint Retired); £10 (Group/Library); £3 (Student, Full-time); £12.50 sterling draft/$25 (Overseas)

FOUNDED 1981 to promote a wider appreciation of the life and works of the poet John Clare (1793–1864). Organises an annual festival in Helpston in July; arranges exhibitions, poetry readings and conferences; and *publishes* an annual society journal and quarterly newsletter.

William Cobbett Society

Johnsons Farm, Sheet, Petersfield, Hampshire GU32 2BY
☎01730 262060
Chairman *Molly Townsend*
Subscription £8 p.a.

Also: Boynell House, Outlands Lane, Curdridge, Southampton SO30 2HR
☎01489 782453
Contact *David Chun*

FOUNDED in 1976 to bring together those with an interest in the life and works of William Cobbett (1763–1835) and to extend the interest to a wider public. Society activities include an annual Memorial Lecture; publication of an annual journal (*Cobbett's New Register*) containing articles on various aspects of his life and times; an annual expedition retracing routes taken by Cobbett on his Rural Rides in the 1820s; visits to his birthplace and his tomb in Farnham, Surrey. In association with the Society the Museum of Farnham, holds bound volumes of Cobbett's *Political Register*, a large collection of Cobbett's works, books about Cobbett, and has various Cobbett artefacts on display.

The Friends of Coleridge

87 Richmond Road, Montpelier, Bristol BS6 5EP
☎0117 942 6366
Email 113223.2774@compuserve.com
Membership Secretary *Shirley Watters*
Editor (Coleridge Bulletin) *Graham Davidson*
Subscription £10 (UK); £15 or £20 (Overseas)

FOUNDED in 1987 to advance knowledge about the life, work and times of Samuel Taylor Coleridge and his circle, and to support his Nether Stowey Cottage, with the National Trust, as a centre of Coleridge interest. Holds study weekends and a biennial international academic conference. *Publishes* the *Coleridge Bulletin* biannually. Short academic articles on Coleridge-related topics may be sent to the editor at the address above.

Wilkie Collins Society

47 Hereford Road, Acton, London W3 9JW
Email paul@wilkiecollins.org
Website www.wilkiecollins.org
Chairman *Andrew Gasson*
Membership Secretary *Paul Lewis* (at address above)
Subscription £10 (UK/Europe); £16 (RoW – remittance must be made in UK sterling)

FOUNDED 1980 to provide information on and promote interest in the life and works of Wilkie Collins, one of the first English novelists to deal with the detection of crime. *The Woman in White* appeared in 1860 and *The Moonstone* in 1868. *Publishes* newsletters, reprints of Collins' work and an annual academic journal.

The Arthur Conan Doyle Society

PO Box 1360, Ashcroft, British Columbia, Canada V0K 1A0
☎001 250 453 2045 Fax 001 250 453 2075
Email ashtree@ash-tree.bc.ca
Website www.ash-tree.bc.ca/acdsocy.html
Joint Organisers *Christopher Roden, Barbara Roden*
Membership Contact *R. Dixon-Smith*, 59 Stonefield, Bar Hill, Cambridge CB3 8TE
Subscription £16 (UK); £16 (Overseas); Family rates available

FOUNDED 1989 to promote the study and discussion of the life and works of Sir Arthur Conan Doyle. Occasional meetings, functions and visits. *Publishes* a biannual journal together with reprints of Conan Doyle's writings.

Joseph Conrad Society (UK)

c/o P.O.S.K., 238–246 King Street, Hammersmith, London W6 0RF
Fax 020 8240 4365
Email AllanSimmons@compuserve.com
Website www.ucrysj.ac.uk/conrad
Secretary *Hugh Epstein*
Treasurer/Editor (The Conradian) *Allan Simmons*

Subscription £15 p.a. (Individual); £20 p.a. (Institutions)

FOUNDED in 1973 to promote the study of the works and life of Joseph Conrad (1857–1924). A scholarly society, supported by the Polish Library at the Polish Cultural Association where a substantial library of Conrad texts and criticism is held in the Study Centre. *Publishes* a journal of Conrad studies – *The Conradian* – biannually and holds an annual International Conference in the first week of July.

The Rhys Davies Trust

10 Heol Don, Whitchurch, Cardiff CF14 2AU
☎029 2062 3359 Fax 029 2052 9202
Contact *Dr Meic Stephens*

FOUNDED 1990 to perpetuate the literary reputation of the Welsh prose writer, Rhys Davies (1901–78), and to foster Welsh writing in English. Organises competitions in association with other bodies such as **The Welsh Academy**, puts up plaques on buildings associated with Welsh writers, offers grant-aid for book production, etc.

The Walter de la Mare Society

Flat 15, Trinity Court, Vicarage Road, Twickenham, Middlesex TW2 5TY
☎020 8898 6563
Website www.bluetree.co.uk/wdlmsociety
Honorary President *John Bayley, CBE*
Honorary Secretary & Treasurer *Julie de la Mare*
Subscription £15 p.a.

FOUNDED in 1997 to honour the memory of Walter de la Mare; to promote the study and deepen the appreciation of his works; to widen the readership of his works; to facilitate research by making available the widest range of contacts and information about de la Mare; and to encourage and facilitate new Walter de la Mare publications. Produces a regular newsletter and organises events.

The Dickens Fellowship

48 Doughty Street, London WC1N 2LX
☎020 7405 2127 Fax 020 7831 5175
Email arwilliams33@compuserve.com
Website www.dickens.fellowship.btinternet.co.uk
Joint Honorary General Secretaries *Mrs Thelma Grove, Dr Tony Williams*
Subscription £5 (First year); £8.50 (Renewal)

FOUNDED 1902. The Society's particular aims

and objectives are: to bring together lovers of Charles Dickens; to spread the message of Dickens, his love of humanity ('the keynote of all his work'); to remedy social injustice for the poor and oppressed; to assist in the preservation of material and buildings associated with Dickens. Annual conference. *Publishes* journal called *The Dickensian* (available at special rate to members) and organises a full programme of lectures, discussions, visits and conducted walks throughout the year. Branches worldwide.

Early English Text Society
Christ Church, Oxford OX1 1DP
Fax 01865 286581
Executive Secretary *R.F.S. Hamer*
(at address above)
Editorial Secretary *Dr H.L. Spencer*
(at Exeter College, Oxford OX1 3DP)
Membership Secretary *Dr W.E.J. Collier*
(at Buffers Cottage, Station Road, Hope, Derbyshire S33 2RR)
Subscription £15 p.a. (UK); $30 (US); $35 (Canada)

FOUNDED 1864. Concerned with the publication of early English texts. Members receive annual publications (one or two a year) or may select titles from the backlist in lieu.

The George Eliot Fellowship
71 Stepping Stones Road, Coventry, Warwickshire CV5 8JT
☎024 7659 2231
Contact *Mrs Kathleen Adams*
Subscription £10 p.a.; £100 (Life); Concessions for pensioners

FOUNDED 1930. Exists to honour George Eliot and promote interest in her life and works. Readings, memorial lecture, birthday luncheon and functions. Issues a quarterly newsletter and an annual journal. Awards an annual prize for a George Eliot essay.

The John Meade Falkner Society
Main Street, Kings Newton, Melbourne, Derbyshire DE73 1BX
☎01332 865315
Email moonfleet@greenmantle63.freeserve.co.uk
Secretary *Kenneth Hillier*
Subscription £5

FOUNDED in 1999 to promote the appreciation and study of John Meade Falkner's life, times and works. Produces three newsletters a year and an annual journal.

Folly (Fans of Light Literature for the Young)
21 Warwick Road, Pokesdown, Bournemouth, Dorset BH7 6JW
☎01202 432562   Fax 01202 460059
Email folly@sims.abel.co.uk
Contact *Mrs Sue Sims*
Subscription £7.50 p.a. (UK); £9 (Europe); £11 (Worldwide)

FOUNDED 1990 to promote interest in a wide variety of children's authors – with a bias towards writers of girls' books and school stories. *Publishes* three magazines a year.

The Franco-Midland Hardware Company
6 Bramham Moor, Hill Head, Fareham, Hampshire PO14 3RU
☎01329 667325
Email franco.midland@btinternet.com
Website www.btinternet.com/~sherlock.fmhc
Chairman *Philip Weller*
Subscription £15 p.a.

FOUNDED 1989. 'The world's leading Sherlock Holmes correspondence study group and the most active Holmesian society in Britain.' *Publishes* annual journal, a biannual news magazine and an individual case study as a subscription package. Also publishes at least two specialist monographs a year. It provides certificated self-study courses and organises monthly functions at Holmes-associated locations. Open membership.

The Friends of Shandy Hall (The Laurence Sterne Trust)
Shandy Hall, Coxwold, York YO61 4AD
☎01347 868465   Fax 01347 868465
Website www.shandy-hall.org.uk
Honorary Secretary *Mrs J. Monkman*
Subscription £7 (Annual); £70 (Life)

Promotes interest in the works of Laurence Sterne and aims to preserve the house in which they were created (open to the public). *Publishes* annual journal, *The Shandean*. An Annual Memorial Lecture is delivered at Shandy Hall each summer.

The Gaskell Society
Far Yew Tree House, Over Tabley, Knutsford, Cheshire WA16 0HN
☎01565 634668
Email JoanLeach@aol.com
Website www.gaskellsociety.cwc.net
Honorary Secretary *Joan Leach*

Subscription £12 p.a.; £16 (Corporate & Overseas)

FOUNDED 1985 to promote and encourage the study and appreciation of the life and works of Elizabeth Cleghorn Gaskell. Meetings held in Knutsford, Manchester, Bath and London; residential study weekends and visits; annual journal and biannual newsletter. On alternate years holds either a residential weekend conference or overseas visit.

The Ghost Story Society
PO Box 1360, Ashcroft, British Columbia, Canada V0K 1A0
☎001 250 453 2045   Fax 001 250 453 2075
Email ashtree@ash-tree.bc.ca
Website www.ash-tree.bc.ca/gss.html
Joint Organisers *Barbara Roden, Christopher Roden*
Subscription UK: £14.50 (Surface mail)/ £16 (Airmail); $25 (US); $31 (Canadian)

FOUNDED 1988. Devoted mainly to supernatural fiction in the literary tradition of M.R. James, Walter de la Mare, Algernon Blackwood, E.F. Benson, A.N.L. Munby, R.H. Malden, etc. *Publishes* a thrice-yearly journal, *All Hallows*, which includes new fiction in the genre and non-fiction of relevance to the genre.

Graham Greene Birthplace Trust
Rhenigidale, Ivy House Lane, Berkhamsted, Hertfordshire HP4 2PP
☎01442 865158
Email secretary@grahamgreenebt.org
Website www.grahamgreenebt.org
Secretary *Ken Sherwood*
Subscription £7.50 (UK, £18 for 3 years); £9 (Europe, £22); £12 (RoW, £30)

FOUNDED on 2 October 1997, the 93rd anniversary of Graham Greene's birth, to promote the appreciation and study of his works. *Publishes* a quarterly newsletter and occasional papers. Organises the Graham Greene Festival.

Rider Haggard Society
27 Deneholm, Whitley Bay, Tyne & Wear NE25 9AU
☎0191 252 4516   Fax 0191 252 4516
Email RBallen544@cs.com
Contact *Roger Allen*
Subscription £9 p.a. (UK); £10 (Overseas)

FOUNDED 1985 to promote appreciation of the life and works of Sir Henry Rider Haggard, English novelist, 1856–1925. News/books exchange, and meetings every two years.

James Hanley Network
Old School House, George Green Road, George Green, Wexham, Buckinghamshire SL3 6BJ
☎01753 578632
Email gostick@altavista.net
Website www.jameshanley.mcmail.com/index.htm
Network Coordinator *Chris Gostick*

An informal international association FOUNDED in 1997 for all those interested in exploring and publicising the works and contribution to literature of the novelist and dramatist James Hanley (1901–1985). *Publishes* an annual newsletter and more formal publications. Occasional conferences are planned for the future. All enquiries welcome.

The Thomas Hardy Society
PO Box 1438, Dorchester, Dorset DT1 1YH
☎01305 251501   Fax 01305 251501
Honorary Secretary *Mrs Olive Blackburn*
Subscription £12 (Individual); £16 (Corporate); £15 (Individual Overseas); £20 (Corporate Overseas)

FOUNDED 1967 to promote the reading and study of the works and life of Thomas Hardy. Thrice-yearly journal, events and a biennial conference.

The Henty Society
Old Foxes, Kelshall, Royston, Hertfordshire SG8 9SE
☎01763 287208
Honorary Secretary *Mrs Ann J. King*
Subscription £13 p.a. (UK); £16 (Overseas)

FOUNDED 1977 to study the life and work of George Alfred Henty, and to publish research, bibliographical data and lesser-known works, namely short stories. Organises conferences and social gatherings in the UK and Canada, and *publishes* quarterly bulletins to members. Published in 1996: *G.A. Henty (1832–1902) a Bibliographical Study* by Peter Newbolt.

James Hilton Society
49 Beckingthorpe Drive, Bottesford, Nottingham NG13 0DN
Honorary Secretary *J.R. Hammond*
Subscription £10 (UK/EU); £7 Concessions

FOUNDED 2000 to promote interest in the life and work of novelist and scriptwriter James Hilton (1900–1954). *Publishes The James Hilton*

Newsletter (quarterly) and organises meetings and conferences.

Sherlock Holmes Society (Northern Musgraves)

Fairbank, Beck Lane, Bingley, West Yorkshire
BD16 4DN
☎01274 563426

Contacts *John Hall, Anne Jordan*
Subscription £17 p.a. (UK)

FOUNDED 1987 to promote enjoyment and study of Sir Arthur Conan Doyle's Sherlock Holmes through publications and meetings. One of the largest Sherlock Holmes societies in Great Britain. Honorary members include Bert Coules, Richard Lancelyn Green, Edward Hardwicke, Michael Williams, Clive Merrison and Douglas Wilmer. Past honorary members: Dame Jean Conan Doyle, Peter Cushing and Jeremy Brett. Open membership. Lectures, presentations and consultation on matters relating to Holmes and Conan Doyle available.

Sherlock Holmes

See **The Franco–Midland Hardware Company**

Hopkins Society

35 Manor Park, Gloddaeth Avenue,
Llandudno LL30 2SE
☎01492 878334
Email carolinemay@hopkinsoc.freeserve.co.uk
Website www.hopkinsoc.freeserve.co.uk

Contact *Ambrose Boothby*
Subscription £7 p.a. (UK); £10 (Overseas)

FOUNDED 1990 to celebrate the life and work of Gerard Manley Hopkins; to inform members of any publications, courses or events about the poet. Holds an annual lecture on Hopkins in the spring; produces two newsletters a year; sponsors and organises educational projects based on Hopkins' life and works.

Housman Society

80 New Road, Bromsgrove, Worcestershire
B60 2LA
☎01527 874136   Fax 01527 837274
Email jimpage@btinternet.com
Website www.knowledge.co.uk/housman/

Contact *Jim Page*
Subscription £10 (UK); £12.50 (Overseas)

FOUNDED 1973 to promote knowledge and appreciation of the lives and work of A.E. Housman and other members of his family, and to promote the cause of literature and poetry.

Sponsors a lecture at the **Sunday Times Hay Festival** each year under the title of 'The Name and Nature of Poetry'. *Publishes* an annual journal and biannual newsletter.

W.W. Jacobs Appreciation Society

3 Roman Road, Southwick, West Sussex
BN42 4TP
☎01273 871017   Fax 01273 871017

Contact *A.R. James*

FOUNDED 1988 to encourage and promote the enjoyment of the works of W.W. Jacobs, and stimulate research into his life and works. No subscription charge. Biography, bibliography, directories of plays and films are available for purchase, including *W.W. Jacobs*, a biography published in 1999, price £12, post paid.

Richard Jefferies Society

Eidsvoll, Bedwells Heath, Boars Hill, Oxford
OX1 5JE
☎01865 735678

Honorary Secretary *Lady Phyllis Treitel*
Membership Secretary *Mrs Margaret Evans*
Subscription £7 p.a. (Individual); £8 (Joint);
   Life membership for those over 50

FOUNDED 1950 to promote understanding of the work of Richard Jefferies, nature/country writer, novelist and mystic (1848–87). Produces newsletters, reports and an annual journal; organises talks, discussions and readings. Library and archives. Assists in maintaining the museum in Jefferies' birthplace at Coate near Swindon. Membership applications should be sent to *Margaret Evans*, 23 Hardwell Close, Grove, Nr Wantage, Oxon OX12 0BN.

Jerome K. Jerome Society

c/o Fraser Wood, Mayo and Pinson,
15/16 Lichfield Street, Walsall, West Midlands
WS1 1TS
☎01922 629000   Fax 01922 721065
Email tonygray@fraserwood.demon.co.uk

Honorary Secretary *Tony Gray*
Subscription £7 p.a. (Ordinary);
   £25 (Corporate); £6 (Joint);
   £2.50 (Under 21/Over 65)

FOUNDED 1984 to stimulate interest in Jerome K. Jerome's life and works (1859–1927). One of the Society's principal activities is the support of a small museum in the author's birthplace, Walsall. Meetings, lectures, events and a twice-yearly newsletter *Idle Thoughts*. Annual dinner in Walsall near Jerome's birth date (2nd May).

The Captain W.E. Johns Appreciation Society

Nottingham meeting: Wendover, Windy Harbour Lane, Bromley Cross, Bolton, Lancashire BL7 9AP
☎01204 306051
Email Biggles.uk@LineOne.net
Website website.lineone.net/~biggles.uk

Contacts *Mrs A. Thompson* (Nottingham), *Joy Tilley* (Hertford ☎01785 240299)

Hertford meeting: 8 Holmes Close, Castlefields, Stafford ST16 1AR

Society for the appreciation of W.E. Johns, creator of Biggles. Meets twice a year in Nottingham and Hertford. See contacts above.

Johnson Society

Johnson Birthplace Museum, Breadmarket Street, Lichfield, Staffordshire WS13 6LG
☎01543 264972

Hon. General Secretary *Mrs Norma Hooper*
Subscription £7.50 p.a.; £10 (Joint)

FOUNDED 1910 to encourage the study of the life, works and times of Samuel Johnson (1709–1784) and his contemporaries. The Society is committed to the preservation of the Johnson Birthplace Museum and Johnson memorials.

Johnson Society of London

255 Baring Road, Grove Park, London SE12 0BQ
☎020 8851 0173
Email JSL@nbbl.demon.co.uk
Website www.nbbl.demon.co.uk/index.html

President *Mary, Viscountess Eccles, PhD, DLitt*
Honorary Secretary *Mrs Z.E. O'Donnell*
Subscription £10 p.a.; £12.50 (Joint)

FOUNDED 1928 to promote the knowledge and appreciation of Dr Samuel Johnson and his works. *Publishes* an annual journal, *New Rambler* and occasional newsletter. Regular meetings from October to April in the Vestry Hall of St Edmund the King, Lombard Street in London on the second Saturday of each month, and a commemoration ceremony around the anniversary of Johnson's death (December) held in Westminster Abbey.

The Just William Society

18 Colthill Crescent, Milltimber, Aberdeen AB131 0EG
☎01224 732513

Secretary *Charles Wilson*
Treasurer *Phil Woolley*
Subscription £7 p.a. (UK); £10 (Overseas);

£5 (Juvenile/Student); £15 (Family)

FOUNDED 1994 to further knowledge of Richmal Crompton's *William* and *Jimmy* books. An annual 'William' meeting is held in April. The Honorary President of the Society is Richmal Crompton's niece, Richmal Ashbee.

The Keats–Shelley Memorial Association (Inc)

(Registered office): 1 Satchwell Walk, Royal Priors, Leamington Spa, Warwickshire CV32 4QE
☎01926 427400 Fax 01926 335133

Contact *Honorary Secretary*
Subscription £10 p.a.

FOUNDED 1903 to promote appreciation of the works of Keats and Shelley, and their circle. One of the Society's main tasks is the preservation of 26 Piazza di Spagna in Rome as a memorial to the British Romantic poets in Italy, particularly Keats and Shelley. *Publishes* an annual review of Romantic Studies called the *Keats-Shelley Review*, arranges events and lectures for Friends and promotes bursaries and competitive writing on Romantic Studies. The Review is edited by *Angus Graham-Campbell*, c/o Eton College, Windsor, Berkshire SL4 6EA.

The Kenny/Naughton Society

Aghamore, Ballyhaunis, Co Mayo, Republic of Ireland
Email paulwdrogers@hotmail.com

Chairman *Paul W.D. Rogers*
Patron *Mrs Erna Naughton*

FOUNDED in 1993 to commemorate two writers who had links with Aghamore: P.D. Kenny (1862–1944), who wrote under the pseudonym 'Pat' and Bill Naughton (1910–1992), best known as the author of *Alfie*. Holds an annual school over the October bank holiday weekend which includes lectures, drama, debate and competition (the **Bill Naughton Short Story Competition** – see entry under **Prizes**).

Kent & Sussex Poetry Society

23 Arundel Road, Tunbridge Wells, Kent TN1 1TB
☎01892 530438 Fax 01892 522502
Email walter.scape@which.net

Honorary Secretary *Joyce Walter*
Subscription £10 p.a. (Full);
£6 (Concessionary – country members living farther afield, senior citizens, under-16s, unemployed)

FOUNDED 1946 to promote the enjoyment of

poetry. Monthly meetings are held in Tunbridge Wells, including readings by major poets, a monthly workshop and an annual writing retreat week. *Publishes* an annual folio of members' work based on Members' Competition, adjudicated and commented upon by a major poet, and runs an Open Poetry Competition (see entry under **Prizes**) annually.

The Kilvert Society
The Old Forge, Kinnersley, Hereford HR3 6QB
☎01544 327426
Secretary *Mr M. Sharp*
Subscription £6 p.a.; £60 (Life)
FOUNDED 1948 to foster an interest in the Diary, the diarist and the countryside he loved. *Publishes* three journals each year; during the summer holds three weekends of walks, commemoration services and talks.

The Kipling Society
6 Clifton Road, London W9 1SS
☎020 7286 0194 Fax 020 7286 0194
Email kipling@fastmedia.demon.co.uk
Website www.kipling.org.uk
Honorary Secretary *Mrs Sharad Keskar*
Subscription £20 p.a.
FOUNDED 1927. The Society's main activities are: maintaining a specialised library in London; answering enquiries from the public (schools, publishers, writers and the media); arranging a regular programme of lectures, especially in London and in Sussex, and an annual luncheon with guest speaker; maintaining a small museum and reference at The Grange, in Rottingdean near Brighton; issuing a quarterly journal. (For the Kipling mailbox discussion list, e-mail: Rudyard-Kipling@jiscmail.ac.uk) This is a literary society for all who enjoy the prose and verse of Kipling (1865–1936) and are interested in his life and times. Please contact the Secretary by letter, telephone, fax or e-mail for further information (brownleaf@btinternet. com).

The Kitley Trust
Toadstone Cottage, Edge View, Litton, Derbyshire SK17 8QU
☎01298 871564
Email stottie2@waitrose.com
Contact *Rosie Ford*
FOUNDED 1990 by a teacher in Sheffield to promote the art of creative writing, in memory of her mother, Jessie Kitley. Activities include: biannual poetry competitions; a 'Get Poetry' day (distribution of children's poems in shop-

ping malls); annual sponsorship of a writer for a school; campaigns; organising conferences for writers and teachers of writing. Funds are provided by donations and profits (if any) from competitions.

Charles Lamb Society
BM Elia, London WC1N 3XX
Subscription £12 p.a. (Single); £18 (Joint & Corporate); US$28 (Overseas Personal); US$42 (Overseas Corporate)
FOUNDED 1935 to promote the study of the life, works and times of English essayist Charles Lamb (1775–1834). Holds regular bi-monthly meetings and lectures in London and organises society events over the summer. Annual luncheon in February. *Publishes* a quarterly bulletin, *The Charles Lamb Bulletin*. Contributions of Elian interest are welcomed by the editor *Rick Tomlinson* at 669 South Monroe Street, Decatur, Illinois 62522–3225, USA (Email kublakhan@poboxes.com). Membership applications should be sent to the box number address above. The Society's library is housed in the **Guildhall Library**, Aldermanbury, London EC2P 2EJ. Requests to consult printed sources must be made 48 hours in advance by letter to the Principal Reference Librarian, in person at the Printed Books Enquiry Desk or by telephone (020 7332 1868/1870). Member of the **Alliance of Literary Societies**. Registered Charity No: 803222.

Lancashire Authors' Association
Heatherslade, 5 Quakerfields, Westhoughton, Bolton, Lancashire BL5 2BJ
☎01942 791390
Email eholt@cwctv.net
General Secretary *Eric Holt*
Subscription £9 p.a.; £12 (Joint); £1 (Junior)
FOUNDED 1909 for writers and lovers of Lancashire literature and history. Aims to foster and stimulate interest in Lancashire history and literature as well as in the preservation of the Lancashire dialect. Meets four times a year on Saturday at various locations. *Publishes* a quarterly journal called *The Record*, which is issued free to members, and holds eight annual competitions (open to members only) for both verse and prose. Comprehensive library with access for research to members.

The Philip Larkin Society
c/o Department of English, The University of Hull, Hull HU6 7RX
☎01482 465637 Fax 01482 465641

Email j.booth@english.hull.ac.uk
Website www.philiplarkin.com
Contact *Dr James Booth*
Subscription £18 (Full rate); £12
(Unwaged/Senior Citizen); £8 (Student)

FOUNDED in 1995 to promote awareness of the
life and work of Philip Larkin (1922–1985) and
his literary contemporaries; to bring together
all those who admire Larkin's work as a poet,
writer and librarian; to bring about publications
on all things Larkinesque. Organises a programme of events ranging from lectures to
rambles exploring the countryside of Larkin's
schooldays and *publishes* a biannual newsletter,
About Larkin.

The D.H. Lawrence Society

24 Briarwood Avenue, Nottingham
NG3 6JQ
☎0115 950 3008
Secretary *Ron Faulks*
Subscription £11; £10 (Concession);
£13 (European); £16 (RoW)

FOUNDED 1974 to increase knowledge and the
appreciation of the life and works of D.H.
Lawrence. Monthly meetings, addressed by
guest speakers, are held in the library at
Eastwood (birthplace of DHL). Organises visits
to places of interest in the surrounding countryside, supports the activities of the D.H.
Lawrence Centre at Nottingham University,
and has close links with DHL Societies worldwide. *Publishes* two newsletters and one journal
each year, free to members.

The T.E. Lawrence Society

PO Box 728, Oxford OX2 6YP
Website www.telawrencesociety.org
Contact *Gigi Horsfield*
Subscription £15 (UK); £20 (Overseas)

FOUNDED 1985 as a non-profit making, educational, registered charity to advance awareness
of the life and work of Thomas Edward
Lawrence and to promote research into his life
and work. *Publishes* four newsletters and two
journals per year. A biennial symposium is
held, usually in Oxford, to bring members
together to share both academic and social
interests. The Society encourages the formation of regional groups of which, currently,
there are seven: three in England (Northwest,
London, Dorset), one in Europe (Netherlands),
two in the USA (Eastern and Western States)
and one in Japan.

The Leamington Literary Society

52 Newbold Terrace East, Leamington Spa,
Warwickshire CV32 4EZ
☎01926 425733
Honorary Secretary *Mrs Margaret Watkins*
Subscription £10 p.a.

FOUNDED 1912 to promote the study and
appreciation of literature and the arts. Holds
regular meetings every second Tuesday of the
month (except August) at the Royal Pump
Rooms, Leamington Spa. The Society has
published various books of local interest.

Lewes Monday Literary Club

c/o 12 Little East Street, Lewes, East Sussex
BN7 2NU
☎01273 472658
Email cm@aubrey1626.freeserve.co.uk
Contact *Mrs Christine Mason*
Subscription £15 p.a.; £3 (Guest, per
meeting)

FOUNDED in 1948 for the promotion and enjoyment of literature. Seven meetings are held during the winter on the last Monday of each month
(from October to April) at the White Hart Hotel
in Lewes. The Club attracts speakers of the highest quality and a balance between all forms of literature is aimed for. Guests are welcome to
attend meetings.

Wyndham Lewis Society

18 Coltsfoot Road, Ware, Hertfordshire
SG12 7NW
Email swo1@ntlworld.com
Contact *Sam Brown*
Subscription £10 p.a. (UK/Europe); £12 p.a.
(Institutions); US$25 (Rest of World); US$30
(Institutions, RoW) – all cheques payable to
the Wyndham Lewis Society

FOUNDED 1974 to promote recognition of the
value of Lewis's works and encourage scholarly
research on the man, his painting and his writing.
Publishes inaccessible Lewis writings; the annual
society journal (*The Wyndham Lewis Annual*),
newsletter and reproduces Lewis's paintings.

The Friends of Arthur Machen

Clemendy Cottage, 14 New Market Street,
Usk, Gwent NP5 1AT
☎01291 672869
Email gvbrangham@hotmail.com
Website www.machensoc.demon.co.uk/
welcome.htm
Contact *Godfrey Brangham*
Subscription £15 p.a. (UK); £18 (US)

FOUNDED 1998. (Formerly the Arthur Machen Society.) Promotes a wider readership of Arthur Machen and a greater understanding of his life and work. Members receive hardback journals (*Faunus*) and newsletters (*Machenalia*). 'While stocks last, new members also receive a hardback book, *Precious Balms*.'

The Marlowe Society
7 Rushworth House, Rushworth Close, Cheltenham, Gloucestershire GL51 0JR
☎01242 579472   Fax 01242 579472
Email marsoct@ntlworld.com
Website www.marlowe-society.org
Membership Secretary *Frieda Barker*
Treasurer *Peter Barker*
Subscription £12 p.a. (Individual);
£7 p.a. (Pensioners/Student/Unwaged);
£15 p.a. (Overseas); £200 (Group);
£100 (Individual Life Membership)

FOUNDED 1955. Holds meetings, lectures and discussions, stimulates research into Marlowe's life and works, encourages production of his plays and *publishes* a biannual newsletter. Currently promoting a memorial to the playwright and poet in Poets' Corner in Westminster Abbey.

The John Masefield Society
The Frith, Ledbury, Herefordshire HR8 1LW
☎01531 631647   Fax 01531 631647
Email petercarter@btinternet.com
Website www.my.genie.co.uk/masefield

Chairman *Peter Carter*
Subscription £5 p.a. (Individual); £8 (Family, Institutions, Libraries)' £10 (Overseas); £2.50 (Junior, Student)

FOUNDED in 1992 to stimulate the appreciation of and interest in the life and works of John Masefield (Poet Laureate 1930–1967). The Society is based in Ledbury, the Herefordshire market town of his birth and holds various public events in addition to publishing a journal and occasional papers.

William Morris Society
Kelmscott House, 26 Upper Mall, Hammersmith, London W6 9TA
☎020 8741 3735   Fax 020 8748 5207
Email william.morris@care4free.net
Website www.ccny.cuny.edu/wmorris/morris.html

Contact *Helen Elleteson*
Subscription £15 p.a.

FOUNDED 1953 to promote interest in the life, work and ideas of William Morris (1834–1896), English poet and craftsman.

The Neil Munro Society
8 Briar Road, Kirkintilloch, Glasgow G66 3SA
☎0141 776 4280
Email brian@bdosborne.fsnet.co.uk
Secretary *Brian D. Osborne*
Subscription £8 (Annual); £9 (Family); £5 (Unwaged); £15 (Institutional)

FOUNDED in 1996 to encourage interest in the works of Neil Munro (1863–1930), the Scottish novelist, short story writer, poet and journalist. An annual programme of meetings is held in Glasgow and Munro's home-town of Inveraray. *Publishes ParaGraphs*, a twice-yearly magazine, sponsors reprints of Munro's work and is developing a Munro archive.

Bill Naughton
See **The Kenny/Naughton Society**

Violet Needham Society
c/o 19 Ashburnham Place, London SE10 8TZ
☎020 8692 4562
Honorary Secretary *R.H.A. Cheffins*
Subscription £6 p.a. (UK & Europe); £9 (RoW)

FOUNDED 1985 to celebrate the work of children's author Violet Needham and stimulate critical awareness of her work. *Publishes* thrice-yearly *Souvenir*, the Society journal with an accompanying newsletter; organises meetings and excursions to places associated with the author and her books. The journal includes articles about other children's writers of the 1940s and '50s and on ruritanian fiction. Contributions welcome.

The Edith Nesbit Society
73 Brookehowse Road, London SE6 3TH
Website www.imagix.dial.pipex.com
Chairman *Nicholas Reed*
Secretary *Margaret McCarthy*
Subscription £6 p.a.; £8 (Joint); £75 (Life)

FOUNDED in 1996 to celebrate the life and work of Edith Nesbit (1858–1924), best known as the author of *The Railway Children*. The Society's activities include a regular newsletter, booklets, talks and visits to relevant places.

The Wilfred Owen Association
17 Belmont, Shrewsbury, Shropshire SY1 1TE
☎01743 235904
Website www.wilfred.owen.mcmail.com
Chairman *Helen McPhail*

Subscription Adults £4 (£6 Overseas); £2 (Senior Citizens/Students/Unemployed); £10 (Groups/Institutions)

FOUNDED 1989 to commemorate the life and works of Wilfred Owen by promoting readings, visits, talks and performances relating to Owen and his work, and supporting appropriate academic and creative projects. Membership is international with 600 members. *Publishes* a newsletter twice a year. Speakers are available for schools or clubs, etc.

The Elsie Jeanette Oxenham Appreciation Society

32 Tadfield Road, Romsey, Hampshire SO51 5AJ
☎01794 517149 Fax 01794 517149
Email abbey@bufobooks.demon.co.uk
Websites: ds.dial.pipex.com/ct/ejo.html *and* www.bufobooks.demon.co.uk/abbeylnk.htm

Contact *Ms Ruth Allen* (Editor, The Abbey Chronicle)
Subscription £6 p.a.; enquire for Overseas rates

FOUNDED 1989 to promote the works of Elsie J. Oxenham. Publishes a newsletter for members, *The Abbey Chronicle*, three times a year.

Thomas Paine Society

43 Eugene Gardens, Nottingham NG2 3LF
☎0115 986 0010
President *The Rt. Hon. Michael Foot*
Honorary Secretary/Treasurer
R.W.Morrell, MBE (at address above)
Subscription (Minimum) £12 p.a. (UK); $25 (Overseas); £5 (Unwaged/Pensioners/Students)

FOUNDED 1963 to promote the life and work of Thomas Paine, and continues to expound his ideals. Meetings, newsletters, lectures and research assistance. Membership badge. The Society has members worldwide and keeps in touch with American and French Thomas Paine associations. *Publishes* magazine, *Bulletin*, twice yearly (Editor: *R.W. Morrell*) and holds occasional exhibitions and talks on Paine's life.

Mervyn Peake Society

2 Mount Park Road, Ealing, London W5 2RP
Contact *Frank Surry*
FOUNDED 1975 to promote a wider understanding of Mervyn Peake's achievements as novelist, poet, painter and illustrator. Membership is open to all, irrespective of native language or country

of residence. *Publishes The Mervyn Peake Review* annually and the *MPS Newsletter* quarterly.

The John Polidori Literary Society

PO Box 6078, Nottingham NG16 4HX
Founder & President *Franklin Bishop*
Subscription £50 p.a.

FOUNDED 1990 to promote and encourage appreciation of the life and works of John William Polidori MD (1795–1821) – novelist, poet, tragedian, philosopher, diarist, essayist, reviewer, traveller and one of the youngest students to obtain a medical degree (at the age of 19). He was one-time intimate of the leading figures in the Romantic movement and travelling companion and private physician to Lord Byron. He was a pivotal figure in the infamous Villa Diodati ghost story sessions in which he assisted Mary Shelley in the creation of her *Frankenstein* tale. Polidori introduced into literature the enduring icon of the vampire portrayed as an aristocratic, handsome seducer with his seminal work *The Vampyre – A Tale*, published in 1819. Polidori was honoured in 1998 by the erection of a City of Westminster Plaque at his birthplace – 38 Great Pulteney Street, Westminster, London – officially unveiled by the Italian ambassador. The Society issues unique publications of the rare works of Polidori. International membership in Italy, USA, Canada and Spain.

The Beatrix Potter Society

Administration Office, Resources for Business, South Park Road, Macclesfield SK11 6SH
☎01625 267880 Fax 01625 267879
Email bps@resources.demon.co.uk
Subscription UK: £15 p.a. (Individual); £20 (Institution); Overseas: £20 (Individual); £25 (Institution)

FOUNDED 1980 to promote the study and appreciation of the life and works of Beatrix Potter (1866–1943). Potter was not only the author of *The Tale of Peter Rabbit* and other classics of children's literature; she was also a landscape and natural history artist, diarist, farmer and conservationist, and was responsible for the preservation of large areas of the Lake District through her gifts to the National Trust. The Society upholds and protects the integrity of the inimitable and unique work of Potter, her aims and bequests; holds regular talks and meetings in London with visits to places connected with Beatrix Potter. Biennial International Study Conferences are held in the UK and occasionally in the USA. The Society has an active publishing programme.

The Powys Society

The Old School House, George Green Road,
George Green, Wexham, Buckinghamshire
SL3 6BJ
☎01753 578632
Email gostick@altavista.net
Website www.powys-society.telinco.co.uk
Honorary Secretary *Chris Gostick*
Subscription £13.50 (UK); £16 (Overseas);
£6 (Students)

The Society (with a membership of 350) aims
to promote public education and recognition
of the writings, thought and contribution to
the arts of the Powys family; particularly of
John Cowper, Theodore and Llewelyn, but
also of the other members of the family and
their close associates. The Society holds two
major collections of Powys published works,
letters, manuscripts and memorabilia. *Publishes*
the *Powys Society Newsletter* in April, June and
November and *The Powys Journal* in August.
Organises an annual conference as well as lectures and meetings in Powys places.

The Queen's English Society

Membership Secretary: Fernwood,
Nightingales, West Chiltington, Pulborough,
West Sussex RH20 2QT
☎01798 813001
Website www.queens-english-society.co.uk
Hon. Membership Secretary *David Ellis*
Subscription £10 p.a. (Ordinary);
£12 (Family/Corporate); £100 (Life
member); reduced rates available for
students and long-term unemployed

FOUNDED in 1972 to promote and uphold the
use of good English and to encourage the enjoyment of the language. Holds regular meetings to
which speakers are invited, an annual luncheon
and *publishes* a quarterly journal, *Quest*, for which
original articles are welcome.

The Arthur Ransome Society Ltd

Abbot Hall Art Gallery & Museum, Kendal,
Cumbria LA6 5AL
☎01539 722464 Fax 01539 722494
Email tarsinfo@arthur-ransome.org
Website www.arthur-ransome.org/ar
Trustee Chairman *Roger Wardale*
Company Secretary *Bill Janes*
Subscription UK: £5 (Junior);
£10 (Student); £15 (Adult); £20 (Family);
£40 (Corporate); Overseas: £5 (Junior);
£10 (Student); £20 (Adult); £25 (Family)
Payable in local currency in US, Canada &
Australia

FOUNDED in 1990 to celebrate the life and to
promote the works and ideas of Arthur
Ransome, author of *Swallows and Amazons*
titles for children, biographer of Oscar Wilde,
works on the Russian Revolution and extensive articles on fishing. TARS seeks to encourage children and adults to engage in adventurous pursuits, to educate the public about
Ransome and his works, and to sponsor
research into his literary works and life.

The Followers of Rupert

31 Whiteley, Windsor, Berkshire SL4 5PJ
☎01753 865562
Email followersofrupert@hotmail.com
Membership Secretary *Mrs Shirley Reeves*
Subscription UK: £12; £14 (Joint); Europe,
airmail: £13 (Individual); £15 (Joint);
RoW, airmail: £15 (Individual); £17
(Joint)

FOUNDED in 1983. The Society caters for the
growing interest in the Rupert Bear stories,
past, present and future. *Publishes* the *Nutwood
Newsletter* quarterly which gives up-to-date
news of Rupert and information on Society
activities. A national get-together of members
– the Followers Annual – is held during the
autumn.

The Ruskin Society

49 Hallam Street, London W1W 6JP
☎020 7580 1894
Honorary Secretary *Dr Cynthia. J. Gamble*
Honorary Treasurer *The Hon. Mrs Catherine
Edwards*
Subscription £10 p.a. (payable on January 1st)

FOUNDED in 1997 to encourage a wider understanding of John Ruskin and his contemporaries. Organises lectures and events which seek
not only to explain to the public at large the
nature of Ruskin's theories but also to place
these in a modern context.

The Ruskin Society of London

351 Woodstock Road, Oxford OX2 7NX
☎01865 310987/515962 Fax 01865 240448
Honorary Secretary *Miss O.E. Forbes-Madden*
Subscription £10 p.a.

FOUNDED 1986 to promote interest in John
Ruskin (1819–1900) and his contemporaries. All
aspects of Ruskinia are introduced. Functions are
held in London. *Publishes* the annual *Ruskin
Gazette*, a journal concerned with Ruskin's
influence.

The Malcolm Saville Society

10 Bilford Road, Worcester WR3 8QA
Email mystery@witchend.demon.co.uk
General Secretary *Mark O'Hanlon*
Subscription £7.50 p.a. (UK); £12
  (Overseas)

FOUNDED in 1994 to remember and promote interest in the work of the popular children's author. Regular social activities, booksearch, library, contact directory and three magazines per year.

The Dorothy L. Sayers Society

Rose Cottage, Malthouse Lane,
Hurstpierpoint, West Sussex BN6 9JY
☎01273 833444 Fax 01273 835988
Website www.sayers.org.uk

Contact *Christopher Dean*
Subscription £14 p.a.; US$28 p.a.

FOUNDED 1976 to promote the study of the life, works and thoughts of Dorothy Sayers; to encourage the performance of her plays and publication of her books and books about her; to preserve original material and provide assistance to researchers. Acts as a forum and information centre, providing material for study purposes which would otherwise be unavailable. Annual seminars and other meetings. Co-founder of the Dorothy L. Sayers Centre in Witham. *Publishes* bi-monthly bulletin, annual proceedings and other papers.

The Bernard Shaw Information & Research Service

Yearnshaw House, 5 Singret Place, Cowley,
Uxbridge, Middlesex UB8 2NU
Email admin@georgebernardshaw.com
Website www.georgebernardshaw.com
President *Diane S. Uttley*

ESTABLISHED in 1997 by writer and Shaw specialist Diane S. Uttley who was custodian of and lived in the writer's home, Shaw's Corner, from 1989 to 1997. The service is used by enthusiasts and academics; literary, theatrical and biographical.

The Shaw Society

51 Farmfield Road, Downham, Bromley,
Kent BR1 4NF
☎020 8697 3619 Fax 020 8697 3619
Email anthnyellis@aol.com

Honorary Secretary *Ms Barbara Smoker*
Subscription £12 p.a. (Individual); £18
  (Joint)

FOUNDED 1941 to promote interest in the life and works of G. Bernard Shaw. Meetings are held on the last Friday of every month (except July, August and December) at Conway Hall, Red Lion Square, London WC1 (6.30 pm for 7 pm) at which speakers are invited to talk on some aspect of Shaw's life or works. Monthly playreadings are held on the first Friday of each month (except August). A 'Birthday Tribute' is held at Shaw's Corner, Ayot St Lawrence in Hertfordshire, on the weekend nearest to Shaw's birthday (26th July). *Publishes* a quarterly newsletter and a magazine, *The Shavian*, which appears approximately every nine months. (No payment for contributors.)

The Robert Southey Society

1 Lewis Terrace, Abergarwed, Neath
A11 4DL
☎01639 711480

Contact *Robert King*
Subscription £10 p.a.

FOUNDED 1990 to promote the work of Robert Southey. *Publishes* an annual newsletter and arranges talks on his life and work. Open membership.

The Laurence Sterne Trust

See **The Friends of Shandy Hall**

Robert Louis Stevenson Club

37 Lauder Road, Edinburgh EH9 1UE
☎0131 667 6256 Fax 0131 662 0353
Email mbeanconferences@compuserve.com

Contact *Margaret Bean, MA*
Subscription £15 p.a. (Individual); £20 p.a.
  (Overseas); £20 (Dual); £100 (Life)

FOUNDED in 1920 to foster interest in Robert Louis Stevenson's life and works. The Club organises an annual lunch and other events. *Publishes RLS Club News* three times a year.

The Bram Stoker Society

Regent House, Trinity College, Dublin 2,
Republic of Ireland
Fax 00 353 1 671 9003 (attn: David Lass)
Email dlass@tcd.ie

Honorary Secretary *David Lass*
Honorary Treasurer *Dr Albert Power* (43
  Castle Court, Killiney Hill Road, Killiney,
  Co. Dublin)
Subscription £10 p.a. (UK/Europe); $20 (US/
  RoW)

FOUNDED 1980. Aims to promote the study and appreciation of Bram Stoker's works, including his place in the Gothic horror tradition, and his influence on later writers in the areas of cinema, music and theatre. *Publishes* a quarterly newsletter, an annual journal of scholarly articles and organises a regular programme of activities with its affiliated body, The Bram Stoker Club of Trinity College Dublin. These include screenings, annual memorial lectures and the annual summer school held in July. Subscription payments by cheque or postal order (made out to Bram Stoker Society) should be sent to the Hon. Treasurer.

The R.S. Surtees Society
Manor Farm House, Nunney, Near Frome, Somerset BA11 4NJ
☎01373 836937   Fax 01373 836574
Website www.clique.co.uk/r.s.surteessociety
Contact *Orders and Membership Secretary*
Subscription £10
FOUNDED 1979 to republish the works of R.S. Surtees and others.

The Tennyson Society
Central Library, Free School Lane, Lincoln LN2 1EZ
☎01522 552862   Fax 01522 552858
Email kathleenjefferson@lincolnshire.gov.uk
Honorary Secretary *Miss K. Jefferson*
Subscription £8 p.a. (Individual);
   £10 (Family); £15 (Corporate); £125 (Life)
FOUNDED 1960. An international society with membership worldwide. Exists to promote the study and understanding of the life and work of Alfred, Lord Tennyson. The Society is concerned with the work of the Tennyson Research Centre, 'probably the most significant collection of mss, family papers and books in the world'. *Publishes* annually the *Tennyson Research Bulletin*, which contains articles and critical reviews; and organises lectures, visits and seminars. Annual memorial service at Somersby in Lincolnshire.

The Angela Thirkell Society
54 Belmont Park, London SE13 5BN
☎020 8244 9339
Email penny.aldred@tesco.net
Website www.sndc.demon.co.uk/als.htm
Honorary Secretary *Mrs. P. Aldred*
Subscription £7 p.a.
FOUNDED in 1980 to honour the memory of Angela Thirkell as a writer and to make her works available to new generations. *Publishes* an annual journal, holds an AGM in early October and a spring meeting which usually

takes the form of a visit to a location associated with Thirkell. Has a flourishing North American branch which has frequent contact with the UK parent society.

The Dylan Thomas Society of Great Britain
5 Church Park, Mumbles, Swansea SA3 4DE
☎01792 520080
Contact *Mrs Eryl Jenkins*
Subscription £5 (Individual); £8 (2 adults from same household)
FOUNDED 1977 to foster an understanding of the work of Dylan Thomas and to extend members' awareness of other 20th century writers, especially Welsh writers in English. Meetings take place monthly, mainly in Swansea.

The Edward Thomas Fellowship
Butlers Cottage, Halswell House, Goathurst, Bridgwater, Somerset TA5 2DH
☎01278 662856
Secretary *Richard Emeny*
Subscription £7 p.a. (Single); £10 p.a. (Joint)
FOUNDED 1980 to perpetuate and promote the memory of Edward Thomas and to encourage an appreciation of his life and work. The Fellowship holds a commemorative birthday walk on the Sunday nearest the poet's birthday, 3 March; issues newsletters and holds various events.

The Tolkien Society
65 Wentworth Crescent, Ash Vale, Surrey GU12 5LF   Fax 0870 0525569
Email membership@tolkiensociety.org
Website www.tolkiensociety.org
Membership Secretary *Trevor Reynolds*
Subscription £20 p.a. (UK); £22 (Overseas)
An international organisation which aims to encourage and further interest in the life and works of the late Professor J.R.R. Tolkien, CBE, author of *The Hobbit* and *Lord of the Rings*. Current membership stands at 620. *Publishes* *Mallorn* annually and *Amon Hen* bi-monthly.

The Trollope Society
9A North Street, Clapham, London SW4 0HN
☎020 7720 6789   Fax 020 7978 1815
Contacts *John Letts, Phyllis Eden*
FOUNDED 1987 to study and promote Anthony Trollope's works. *Publishes* the complete works of Trollope's novels and travel books.

Edgar Wallace Society

Kohlbergsgracht 40, 6462 CD Kerkrade, The Netherlands
☎00 31 455 67 0070 Fax 00 31 455 67 0060
Organiser *K.J. Hinz*
Subscription £15 p.a.; £10 (Senior Citizen/Student); Overseas: £20; £15 (Senior Citizen/Student)

FOUNDED 1969 by Wallace's daughter, Penelope, to bring together all who have an interest in Edgar Wallace. Members receive a brief biography of Edgar by Penelope Wallace, with a complete list of all published book titles. A quarterly newsletter, *Crimson Circle*, is published in February, May, August and November.

The Walmsley Society

April Cottage, No 1 Brand Road, Hampden Park, Eastbourne, East Sussex BN22 9PX
☎01323 506447
Email walmsley@haughshw.demon.co.uk
Honorary Secretary *Fred Lane*
Subscription £8 p.a.; £10 (Family); £7 (Students/Senior Citizens); £15 (Overseas, £25 for 2 years)

FOUNDED 1985 to promote interest in the art and writings of Ulric and Leo Walmsley. Two annual meetings – one held in Robin Hood's Bay on the East Yorkshire coast, spiritual home of the author Leo Walmsley. The Society also seeks to foster appreciation of the work of his father Ulric Walmsley. *Publishes* a journal twice-yearly and newsletters, and is involved in other publications which benefit the aims of the Society.

Sylvia Townsend Warner Society

2 Vicarage Lane, Dorchester, Dorset DT1 1LH
☎01305 266028
Email tartarus@pavilion.co.uk
Contact *Eileen Johnson*
Website www.freepages.pavilion.net/users/tartarus/warner1.htm
Subscription £10 p.a.; $20 (Overseas)

FOUNDED in 2000 to promote a wider readership and better understanding of the writings of Sylvia Townsend Warner.

Mary Webb Society

8 The Knowe, Willaston, Neston, Cheshire CH64 1TA
☎0151 327 5843
Email suehigginbotham@yahoo.co.uk
Website www.mary-webb.epoet.co.uk
Secretary *Sue Higginbotham*

Subscription £8 p.a. (Individual); £11 p.a. (Joint/Overseas)

FOUNDED 1972. Attracts members from the UK and overseas who are devotees of the literature of Mary Webb and of the beautiful Shropshire countryside of her novels. *Publishes* annual journal in September, organises summer schools in various locations related to the authoress's life and works. Archives; lectures; tours arranged for individuals and groups.

H.G. Wells Society

49 Beckingthorpe Drive, Bottesford, Nottingham NG13 0DN
Website www.rdg.ac.uk/~lhsjamse/wells/wells.htm
Honorary Secretary *J.R. Hammond*
Subscription £16 (UK/EU); £19 (Overseas); £20 (Corporate); £10 (Concessions)

FOUNDED 1960 to promote an interest in and appreciation of the life, work and thought of Herbert George Wells. *Publishes The Wellsian* (annual) and *The H.G. Wells Newsletter* (three issues yearly). Organises meetings and conferences.

West Country Writers' Association

Malvern View, Garway Hill, Hereford HR2 8EZ
☎01981 580495
Email annedouble@hotmail.com
Website www.westcountrywriters.co.uk
President *Christopher Fry*
Honorary Secretary *Mrs Anne Double*
Subscription £10 p.a.

FOUNDED 1951 in the interest of published authors with an interest in the West Country. Meets to discuss news and views and to listen to talks. Conference and newsletters.

The Oscar Wilde Society

100 Peacock Street, Gravesend, Kent DA12 1EQ
☎01474 535978
Email vanessa@salome.co.uk
Honorary Secretary *Vanessa Harris*

FOUNDED 1990 to promote knowledge, appreciation and study of the life, personality and works of the writer and wit Oscar Wilde. Activities include meetings, lectures, readings and exhibitions, and visits to locations associated with Wilde. Members receive a journal, *The Wildean*, twice-yearly and a newsletter, *Intentions* (six per year).

The Charles Williams Society
3 The Rise, Islip, Kidlington, Oxfordshire
OX5 2TG
Email rsturch@compuserve.com
Website www.geocities.com/charles_wm-soc
Contact *Honorary Secretary*

FOUNDED 1975 to promote interest in, and provide a means for the exchange of views and information on the life and work of Charles Walter Stansby Williams (1886–1945).

The Henry Williamson Society
16 Doran Drive, Redhill, Surrey RH1 6AX
☎01737 763228
Email mm@misterman.freeserve.co.uk
Website www.hwsoc.org.uk
Membership Secretary *Mrs Margaret Murphy*
Subscription £12 p.a.; £15 (Family);
£5 (Students)

FOUNDED 1980 to encourage, by all appropriate means, a wider readership and deeper understanding of the literary heritage left by the 20th-century English writer Henry Williamson (1895–1977). *Publishes* annual journal.

The P.G. Wodehouse Society (UK)
16 Herbert Street, Plaistow, London
E13 8BE
Website www.eclipse.co.uk/wodehouse
Membership Secretary *Helen Murphy*
Subscription £15 p.a.

Relaunched in May 1997 to advance the genius of P.G. Wodehouse. Publications include the *Wooster Source* quarterly journal and the *By The Way* newsletter. Regular national and international group meetings. Members in most countries throughout the world. Society patrons include Rt. Hon. Tony Blair MP and Stephen Fry. Wodehouse's grandson, Sir Edward Cazelet, is on the committee.

The Parson Woodforde Society
22 Gaynor Close, Wymondham, Norfolk
NR18 0EA
☎01953 604124
Email mabrayne@supanet.com
Website www.cix.co.uk~kcm/pwsoc.htm
Membership Secretary *Mrs Ann Elliott*
Subscription £12.50 (UK); £25 (Overseas)

FOUNDED 1968. Aims to extend and develop knowledge of James Woodforde's life and the society in which he lived and to provide the opportunity for fellow enthusiasts to meet together in places associated with the diarist.

Publishes a quarterly journal and newsletter. The Society is producing a complete edition of the diary of James Woodforde. To date, eleven volumes of diary material have been published covering the period 1759–1787.

The Virginia Woolf Society of Great Britain
Fairhaven, Charnleys Lane, Banks, Southport
PR9 8HJ
Email snclarke@talk21.com
Website orlando.jp.org/vwsgb/
Contact *Stuart N. Clarke*
Subscription £12 p.a.; £15 (Overseas)

FOUNDED 1998 to promote interest in the life and work of Virginia Woolf, author, essayist and diarist. The Society's activities include trips away, walks, reading groups and talks. *Publishes* a literary journal, *Virginia Woolf Bulletin*, three times a year.

WW2 HMSO PPBKS Society
3 Roman Road, Southwick, West Sussex
BN42 4TP
☎01273 871017   Fax 01273 871017
Contact *A.R. James*

FOUNDED 1994 to encourage collectors and to promote research into HMSO's World War II series of paperbacks. Most of them were written by well-known authors, though, in many cases anonymously. No subscription charge. Available for purchase: Collectors' Guide (£5); Bibliography (£3); Handbook, *Informing the People* (£10).

The Yeats Society Sligo
Yeats Memorial Building, Douglas Hyde Bridge, Sligo, Republic of Ireland
☎00 353 71 42693   Fax 00 353 71 42780
Email info@yeats-sligo.com
Website www.yeats-sligo.com
President *E.J. Wylie-Warren*
Subscription £15 (Single); £25 (Couple);
£100 (Corporate)

FOUNDED in 1958 to promote the heritage of W.B. Yeats and the Yeats family. Attractions include continuous updated Yeats exhibitions for public viewing, annual Yeats International Summer School in August and Yeats Winter School in January. The Yeats Summer Festival is held each August and lectures are held in the winter and spring, sponsored by the Institute of Technology, Sligo. *Publishes* a newsletter and organises year-round events/programmes in arts, culture, education for writers' groups, poetry/drama groups, etc.

Yorkshire Dialect Society

51 Stepney Avenue, Scarborough, North Yorkshire YO12 5BW

Secretary *Michael Park*
Subscription £7 p.a.

FOUNDED 1897 to promote interest in and preserve a record of the Yorkshire dialect. *Publishes* dialect verse and prose writing. Two journals to members annually. Details of publications available from YDS, Rosebank Cottage, Main Street, Great Heck, West Yorkshire DN14 0BQ.

Francis Brett Young Society

92 Gower Road, Halesowen, West Midlands B62 9BT
☎0121 422 8969

Honorary Secretary *Mrs Jean Hadley*
Subscription £7 p.a. (Individuals); £10 (Couples sharing a journal); £5 (Students); £7 (Organisations/ Overseas); £70 (Life); £100 (Joint, Life)

FOUNDED 1979. Aims to provide a forum for those interested in the life and works of English novelist Francis Brett Young and to collate research on him. Promotes lectures, exhibitions and readings; *publishes* a regular newsletter.

Arts Councils and Regional Arts Boards

The Arts Council of England
14 Great Peter Street, London SW1P 3NQ
☎020 7333 0100/Minicom: 020 7973 6564
Fax 020 7973 6590
Email enquiries@artscouncil.org.uk
Website www.artscouncil.org.uk
Chairman *Gerry Robinson*
Chief Executive *Peter Hewitt*

The national policy body for the arts in England, developing, sustaining and championing the arts. It distributes public money from government and from the National Lottery to artists and arts organisations both directly and through the ten Regional Arts Boards. It works independently and at arm's length from government. Information about Arts Council funding programmes is available on the website, by e-mail or by contacting the enquiry line on 020 7973 6517. Information about funding available from the Regional Arts Boards can be found on the website (www.arts.org.uk) or by contacting your Regional Arts Board.

The Irish Arts Council/ An Chomhairle Ealaíon
70 Merrion Square, Dublin 2
☎00 353 1 6180200 Fax 00 353 1 6761302
Email info@artscouncil.ie
Website www.artscouncil.ie
Literature Officer *Sinead MacAodha*

Has programmes under six headings to assist in the area of literature and book promotion: a) Writers; b) Literary Organisations; c) Publishers; d) Literary Magazines; e) Participation Programmes; f) Literary Events and Festivals. It also awards a number of annual bursaries (see **Arts Council Literature Bursaries, Ireland** under **Bursaries, Fellowships and Grants**).

The Arts Council of Northern Ireland
MacNeice House, 77 Malone Road, Belfast BT9 6AQ
☎028 9038 5200 Fax 028 9066 1715
Website www.artscouncil-ni.org
Literature Arts Officer *John Brown*

Funds book production by established publishers, programmes of readings, literary festivals, writers-in-residence schemes and literary magazines and periodicals. Occasional schools programmes and anthologies of children's writing are produced. Annual awards and bursaries for writers are available. Holds information also on various groups associated with local arts, workshops and courses.

Scottish Arts Council
12 Manor Place, Edinburgh EH3 7DD
☎0131 226 6051 Fax 0131 225 9833
Email administrator@scottisharts.org.uk
Website www.sac.org.uk
Chairman *Magnus Linklater*
Director *Tessa Jackson*
Literature Director *Jenny Brown*
Literature Officer *Gavin Wallace*
Literature Secretary *Catherine Allan*

Principal channel for government funding of the arts in Scotland. The Scottish Arts Council (SAC) is funded by the Scottish Executive. It aims to develop and improve the knowledge, understanding and practice of the arts, and to increase their accessibility throughout Scotland. It offers around 1300 grants a year to artists and arts organisations concerned with the visual arts, dance and mime, drama, literature, music, festivals and traditional, ethnic and community arts. It is also a distributor of National Lottery funds to the arts in Scotland. SAC's support for Scottish-based writers with a track record of publication includes bursaries, writing and translation fellowships and book awards (see entries under **Bursaries, Fellowships and Grants** and **Prizes**). Information offered includes lists of literary awards, literary magazines, agents and publishers.

The Arts Council of Wales
Museum Place, Cardiff CF10 3NX
☎029 2037 6500 Fax 029 2022 1447
Website www.ccc-acw.org.uk
Senior Literature Officer *Tony Bianchi*
Senior Officer: Dance and Drama *Anna Holmes*

Funds literary magazines and book production; *Writers on Tour* and bursary schemes; **Welsh**

Academy, Welsh Books Council, Hay-on-Wye Literature Festival and Tŷ Newydd Writers' Centre at Cricieth; also children's literature, annual awards and translation projects. The Council aims to develop theatrical experience among Wales-based writers through a variety of schemes – in particular, by funding writers on year-long attachments.

English Regional Arts Boards

5 City Road, Winchester, Hampshire SO23 8SD
☎01962 851063 Fax 01962 842033
Email info@erab.org.uk
Website www.arts.org.uk
Administrator *Carolyn Nixson*

English Regional Arts Boards is the representative body for the 10 Regional Arts Boards (RABs) in England. Its Winchester secretariat provides project management, services and information for the members, and acts on their behalf in appropriate circumstances. Scotland, Northern Ireland and Wales have their own Arts Councils. RABs are support and development agencies for the arts in the regions. Policies are developed in response to regional demand, and to assist new initiatives in areas of perceived need; they may vary from region to region. The RABs are now responsible for the distribution of Arts Council Lottery funding for capital and revenue projects under £100,000.

SUPPORT FOR WRITERS

All the Regional Arts Boards offer support for professional creative writers through a range of grants, awards, advice, information and contacts. Interested writers should contact the Board in whose region they live or access the RAB pages on the website.

At the time of writing the current system of RABs is under review and anyone experiencing problems getting in touch with their RAB is advised to contact the Arts Council of England.

East England Arts

Cherry Hinton Hall, Cambridge CB1 8DW
☎01223 215355 Fax 01223 248075
Email info@eearts.co.uk
Website www.arts.org.uk
Literature Officer *Emma Drew*
Drama Officer *Alan Orme*
Cinema & Broadcast Media Officer
   Martin Ayres

Covers Bedfordshire, Cambridgeshire, Essex, Hertfordshire, Norfolk and Suffolk. Policy emphasises quality and access. Support is given to publishers and literature promoters based in the EAB region, also to projects which develop audiences for literature performances and publishing, including electronic media. Bursaries are offered annually to individual published writers. Supplies lists of literary groups, workshops, local writing courses and writers working in the educational sector. Also provides advice on applying for National Lottery funds.

East Midlands Arts

Mountfields House, Epinal Way, Loughborough, Leicestershire LE11 0QE
☎01509 218292 Fax 01509 262214
Email info@em-arts.co.uk
Literature Officer *Sue Stewart*
Drama Officer *Helen Flach*

Covers Leicestershire, Rutland, Lincolnshire, Nottinghamshire, Derbyshire (excluding the High Peak district) and Northamptonshire. A comprehensive information service for regional writers includes an extensive *Writers' Information Pack*, with details of local groups, workshops, residential writing retreats, publishers and publishing information, regional magazines which offer a market for work, advice on approaching the media, on unions, courses and grants. Also available is a directory of writers, primarily to aid people wishing to organise workshops, readings or writer's attachments. Writers' awards are granted for work on a specific project – local history and biography are ineligible for support. Writing for the theatre can come under the aegis of both Literature and Drama. A list of writers' groups is available, plus *Foreword*, the literature newsletter.

London Arts

2 Pear Tree Court, London EC1R 0DS
☎020 7608 6100 Fax 020 7670 4100
Email kate.mervyn-jones@lonab.co.uk
Website www.arts.org.uk/londonarts
Literature Administrator *Kate Mervyn-Jones*

The London Arts Board is the Regional Arts Board for the Capital, covering the 32 boroughs and the City of London. Grants are available to support a variety of literature projects, focusing on three main areas: live literature, including storytelling; support for small presses and literary magazines in the publishing of new or underrepresented creative writing; bursaries for writers who have published one book and are working on their second work of fiction or poetry. There are two deadlines each year for applications. Please contact the Literature

Unit for more information and an application form.

North West Arts Board

Manchester House, 22 Bridge Street,
Manchester M3 3AB
☎0161 834 6644   Fax 0161 834 6969
Email info@nwarts.co.uk

Arts Officer – Literature *Bronwen Williams*
(Email bwilliams@nwarts.co.uk)
Arts Officer – Drama *Ian Tabbron* (Email
itabbron@nwarts.co.uk)

NWAB covers Cheshire, Greater Manchester, Merseyside, Lancashire and the High Peak district of Derbyshire. Offers financial assistance to a great variety of organisations and individuals through a number of schemes, including Writers' Bursaries, Residencies and Placements and the Live Writing scheme. NWAB publishes a directory of local writers' groups, a directory of writers and a range of information covering topics such as performance and publishing. For further details please contact the Literature or Drama Department.

Northern Arts Board

Central Square, Forth Street, Newcastle upon Tyne NE1 3PJ
☎0191 255 8500   Fax 0191 230 1020
Email info@northernarts.org.uk
Website www.arts.org.uk

Head of Film, Media and Literature *Mark Robinson*
Literature Officer *Chrissie Glazebrook*

Covers Cumbria, Durham, Northumberland, Teesside and Tyne and Wear, and was the first regional arts association in the country to be set up by local authorities. It supports both organisations and writers and aims to stimulate public interest in artistic events. The Northern Writers Awards scheme is operated through **New Writing North** (see entry under **Professional Associations and Societies**). Northern Arts also has a film/TV script development fund operated through the Northern Production Fund. Northern Arts makes drama awards to producers. Also funds writers' residencies, and has a fund for publications. Contact list of regional groups available.

South East Arts

Union House, Eridge Road, Tunbridge Wells, Kent TN4 8HF
☎01892 507200   Fax 01892 549383
Email info@seab.co.
Website www.arts.org.uk

Literature Officer *Suzy Joinson*
Drama Officer *Judith Hibberd*

Covers Kent, Surrey, East Sussex, West Sussex, Brighton and Hove and Medway (excluding the London boroughs). Grant schemes accessible to all art forms in the areas of new work, presentation of work and venue development. Awards for individuals include training bursaries and writers' awards schemes. The literature programme aims to raise the profile of contemporary literature in the region and encourage creative writing and reading development projects. Priorities include live literature, writers and readers in residence and training bursaries for writers resident in the region. A regular feature on literature appears in the *Arts News* newsletter.

South West Arts

Bradninch Place, Gandy Street, Exeter, Devon EX4 3LS
☎01392 218188   Fax 01392 413554
Email info@swa.co.uk
Website www.swa.co.uk

Director of Visual Arts and Media
   David Drake
Visual Arts and Media Administrators
   Sara Williams, Kate Offord, Maria Tilbury

Covers Cornwall, Devon, Dorset (excluding Bournemouth, Christchurch and Poole), Gloucestershire, Somerset and the unitary authorities of Bristol, Bath and North East Somerset, South Gloucestershire, North Somerset, Torbay and Plymouth. The central theme running through the Board's aims are 'promoting quality and developing audiences for new work'. Specific policies aim to support the development and promotion of new writing and performance work in all areas of contemporary literature and published arts. There is direct investment in small presses and magazine publishers, literary festivals, writer residencies and training, and marketing bursaries for individual writers. There is also a commitment to supporting the development of new writing in the performing arts, and critical writing within the visual arts and media department.

Southern Arts

13 St Clement Street, Winchester, Hampshire SO23 9DQ
☎01962 855099   Fax 0870 242 1257
Email info@southernarts.co.uk

Literature Officer *Keiren Phelan*
Film, Video & Broadcasting Officer
   Jane Gerson

Theatre Officer *Nic Young*

Covers Berkshire, Buckinghamshire, Hampshire, the Isle of Wight, Oxfordshire, Wiltshire and South East Dorset. The Literature Department funds festivals, magazines, publications and residencies. Development funds are available for programming and events, support for individual artists, writers working in education and the community, and new commissions.

West Midlands Arts

82 Granville Street, Birmingham B1 2LH
☎0121 631 3121 Fax 0121 643 7239
Website www.arts.org.uk/directory/regions/
west-mid

Literature Officer *Adrian Johnson*

There are special criteria across the art forms, so contact the Information Office for details of *Creative Ambition Awards* for writers (six application dates throughout the year) and other arts lottery schemes, as well as for the *Reading (Correspondence Mss Advice) Service*. There are contact lists of writers, storytellers, writing groups, etc. WMA supports the regional publication, *Raw Edge Magazine*: contact PO Box 4867, Birmingham B3 3HD, the Virtual Literature Centre for the West Midlands (and beyond) called 'Lit-net' (www.lit-net.org) and

the major storytelling and poetry festivals in Shropshire and Ledbury respectively.

Yorkshire Arts

21 Bond Street, Dewsbury, West Yorkshire
WF13 1AY
☎01924 455555 Fax 01924 466522
Email <firstname.surname>@yarts.co.uk
Website www.arts.org.uk

Literature Officer *Jane Stubbs*
Drama Officer *David Bown*
Literature & Audience Development
  Administrator *Sophie Moxon*

'Libraries, publishing houses, local authorities and the education service all make major contributions to the support of literature. Recognising the resources these agencies command, Yorkshire Arts actively seeks ways of acting in partnership with them, while at the same time retaining its particular responsibility for the living writer and the promotion of activities currently outside the scope of these agencies.' Funding goes to a range of independent publishers, festivals and literature development agencies. Yorkshire Arts also offers a range of development funds to support the individual writer and the promotion and distribution of literature. Holds lists of writers' groups throughout the region and *publishes Write Angles*, a bi-monthly newsletter. Contact *Sophie Moxon* for further information.

With a Little Help from the Experts

Writing can be taught but it all depends on who is doing the teaching.

Teaching people to write is a boom industry. It extends all the way from the postgraduate degree in creative writing pioneered by Malcolm Bradbury and Angus Wilson at the University of East Anglia to correspondence courses of dubious provenance pitched at would-be contributors to *Cat Lovers' Weekly*. In between are the writing holidays in rural retreats, adult education courses run by local authorities, and seminars given by transatlantic gurus. Throw in the proliferation of writers' circles and you have an awful lot of aspiring authors.

The question is what do they gain from their efforts? Heavyweight opinion says not much. There is no objective formula for a prize-winning novel or for any other literary masterpiece. The art of stringing together the best possible words in the best possible order reduces to an individual gift for dovetailing with a particular market. What makes one writer in a thousand click with his readers is lost in the mysteries of cultural evolution.

In other words, those who can, do. There is a story of the American writer Sinclair Lewis appearing, after a few drinks, at a university seminar for incipient authors. 'Hands up, all those who want to be writers,' he shouted. A forest of hands waved back at him. 'Then why the hell aren't you at home writing?' he demanded, and staggered from the room.

He had a point. There is no substitute for hard graft or, as Jack London put it, 'You can't wait for inspiration. You have to go after it with a club.'

Yet there are basics of narrative and dialogue that must be learned. The feel for English that makes it an art form follows on an appreciation of the language and the richness of its potential. Artists, composers and actors have their own colleges where they benefit from the experience of their mentors and the stimulation of their peers. Why not writers?

At which point I must come clean and confess that I am an active supporter of the National Academy of Writing, a project now in its second year of planning. Led by Melvyn Bragg and Ian Chapman, one-time chairman and CEO of Collins, and a galaxy of eminent authors, the NAW has found a home in Birmingham where it will offer a one-year course for budding professional writers and for those whose careers are dependent on communication skills. A new centre of writing excellence may help to engender the next generation of novelists and playwrights but, just as usefully, it could break with tradition by teaching future business leaders to express their ideas clearly and succinctly.

But if there are so many others in the business, what need can there be for one more institution, however prestigious? The short answer is that across the board quality is at a premium. Even where the intentions are good, as in most university courses in creative writing, the confusion of aims or, indeed, the absence of any clear objective leads to student frustration.

Take this for a not untypical misunderstanding of what creative writing is all about. Declaring that feedback was the most important feature of her creative writing course, a Sheffield University lecturer cited a middle-aged student who wanted to write a novel about a man watching a blackbird polluted by industrial waste. 'Man meets poisoned animal.' His tutor thought it might, at best, make a short story but encouraged him to develop his theme. It took six months for him to find that he was wrong - the idea was a non-starter. This example was offered as a benefit of the course: it set the student off on the path of self-discovery.

In six months? Does anyone have that amount of time to waste?

A Royal Society of Literature conference on creative writing, inspired by Hilary Mantel, brought in a profusion of testimonies, few of them complimentary to course organisers. A third of the responses came from retired people, many of whom still felt the disappointment of a childhood education stifled under a dead weight of rote learning. But writing courses were not the antidote they were looking for. Hilary Mantel was appalled by the arrogance of some of the tutors who wrote in. They seemed to think of themselves as therapists guiding their patients to self-realisation: the writing course as a substitute for the psychiatrist's couch. One correspondent sadly conceded, 'Over the years, I might well have produced more if I had spent time actually writing instead of just talking about it.'

Muddled thinking is abetted by muddled organisation. Michèle Roche recalls her year at Manchester:

> The day of registration finally came. It was badly organised. This was an ill omen but one I missed at the time. We were aged between 22 and 67, and were 14 in number – which made for a big circle in the longer than it is wide Writing Centre, where all the classes and workshops were held. It was not a room particularly conducive to thought or imagination, being rather untidy much of the time, with chairs left scattered from one class to the next. We met over nine months for two sessions a week, each lasting a couple of hours: one a workshop, the other a lecture or seminar on the thirty or so novels we had to read. Two novels were discovered to be out of print.

The chance to meet established writers was welcomed as was the experience of blunt criticism and realising 'the simple premise that writing can be a perilous and pernicious profession'. But at a fee of £2,300, it was hardly value for money.

'All the sweating over applications, the trials and the treats. I can't say I got all I was hoping for and expecting. It was certainly preferable to struggling alone.

This said, after fifteen years away from academia, it wasn't long before I was thinking to myself: Christ, what's academia like? Can we get real here, please, someone?'

Most students wind up with a piece of paper saying that they are qualified (to do what?) but there is rarely any follow up. Though publication is the objective, it is seldom achieved. As P.D. James has commented, 'In any other faculty, the teachers would be sacked.'

But if the success rate at university level is depressingly low, further down the academic scale it is virtually nil.

Anyone can set up as a teacher in creative writing. A small ad in a literary magazine will do the trick. And trick is the word. The skill of these so-called 'educational' institutions is to present modest achievements ('I was paid £19.99 for my article on hill climbing in the Cairngorms') as major triumphs. Satisfied customers are those who are pleased to see their names in print. They would even pay for the privilege; indeed they probably do pay to the extent of failing to earn enough to cover the course fees.

Not long ago, those who had signed up for a particular writing school (payment in advance) were a little perturbed when their assignments were returned 'addressee has gone away'. The self-styled director of studies has not been heard of since. It is as well to cast a severely critical eye over the promotional material before parting with money.

The heavyweight brochure put out by the Writers Bureau, based in Manchester, is awash with glowing testimonials from former students including one from Jon Eagle who is pictured holding aloft his first novel. The caption has him in euphoric mood: 'I was paid £25,000 (yes, twenty five thousand) for my first novel *Red*.' Convincing? Well, yes, except no publisher is mentioned. In fact, *Red* is put out by Minerva Press, which advertises openly as a vanity publisher. Their authors are expected to finance the costs of publication. Now, maybe, on this occasion Minerva had a rush of blood and decided to take a punt. But is it fair to suggest that other aspiring authors will be just as lucky?

It is also worth checking the credentials of the teachers. For sheer chutzpah, it is hard to beat the self-promotion of the American maestros who fly in periodically to share their know-how. There is one who claims to be a 'multi millionaire' novelist who has written seven bestsellers and to have been a creative consultant on some extremely well known movies. Not to worry that in fact he has only one book still in print and does not appear on the credits of any of the movies. Or maybe you do worry and save your money.

The creative-writing scene is not entirely black, however. There are good reports of those courses which limit themselves to a specific study, such as those run by the National Film and Television School and the various schools of journalism. Prospective novelists favour the MA course at the University of East Anglia. Helen Cross was lucky enough to have Andrew Motion as her tutor. 'He was like a good parent, instilling confidence by talking about what would happen *when* I met my editor, *when* I had an agent. There was always the assumption that I would achieve these things.' And she did. Having found an agent and a publisher, Helen is work-ing on her second novel.

Even distance learning has its fans when it is run by the National Extension College in Cambridge or the Open College of the Arts, linked to the University of Glamorgan.

But overall, the 5,000 or so students who sign on each year for one course or another in creative writing are poorly served. The universities in particular need to be clearer as to what they are offering. At the moment they try to satisfy var-ious and often conflicting aspirations. The student who is looking to write as a therapeutic exercise has nothing in common with the fledgling professional. Inevitably, both wind up disappointed.

With honourable exceptions such as East Anglia which takes in only fifty cre-ative writing students a year, the feeling of let down is accentuated by the lack of practical advice on subjects such as making an approach to publishers and agents, understanding contracts and coping with rejection.

A National Academy of Writing on a level with the Royal Academy of Dramatic Art and the Royal College of Music will help to redefine the teaching of writing and set standards which will expose the inadequacy of much that passes as career training. Supporters of the NAW believe that there is demand for an independent centre of excellence offering a new type of writing course, cov-ering a range of genres and skills. As the first teaching institution in the world to be set up by writers for writers, it could just work. Holders of the cultural purse strings, please note.

Writers' Courses, Circles and Workshops

UK

ENGLAND

Berkshire

University of Reading

Department of Continuing Education, London Road, Reading, Berkshire RG1 5AQ
☎0118 931 8347
Email Cont-Ed@reading.ac.uk
Website www.reading.ac.uk/ContEd

An expanding programme of creative writing courses, including *Life into Fiction; Poetry Workshop; Getting Started; Writers Helping Writers* (with **Southern Arts**' help, the course includes visits from well-known writers); *Writing Fiction; Becoming Independent; Publishing Poetry*; *Adventures in Writing* and *Scriptwriting*. There is also a support group for teachers of creative writing, a public lecture by a writer and a reading by students of their work, and various Saturday workshops. Tutors include the science fiction writer Brian Stableford, novelist Leslie Wilson and poets Jane Draycott, Elizabeth James and Susan Utting. Fees vary depending on the length of course. Concessions available.

Buckinghamshire

Missenden Abbey Continuing Education

Chilterns Consortium, The Misbourne Centre, Great Missenden, Buckinghamshire HP16 0BN
☎01494 862904 Fax 01494 890087
Email conedchil@buckscc.gov.uk
Website www.aredu.org.uk/missendenabbey

Residential and non-residential weekend workshops and summer school. Programmes have included *Writing Magazine Articles and Getting Them Published; Writing for Television and Radio; A Creative Approach to Non-Fiction Writing; Writing Poetry*. Missenden Abbey is a member of the Adult Residential Colleges Association.

National Film & Television School

Beaconsfield Studios, Station Road, Beaconsfield, Buckinghamshire HP9 1LG
☎01494 671234 Fax 01494 674042
Email admin@nftsfilm-tv.ac.uk
Website www.nftsfilm-tv.ac.uk

Intensive, one-year, full-time screenwriting course for people with established writing skills but little or no experience of writing for the screen. One-year, part-time course for people with some screenwriting experience who are ready to focus on feature script development. Completion of both courses, plus short dissertation, is required for the award of an MA. Courses develop an understanding of the practical stages involved in the making of film and television drama. Range of work covers comedy, TV series and serials, short-film, adaptation and narrative. The ability to collaborate successfully is developed through exercises and projects shared with students in other specialisations. 'We encourage the formation of working partnerships which will continue after graduation.'

Cambridgeshire

National Extension College

Michael Young Centre, Purbeck Road, Cambridge CB2 2HN
☎01223 450200 Fax 01223 313586
Website www.nec.ac.uk

Runs a number of home-study courses on writing. Courses include: *Essential Editing; Creative Writing; Writing for Money; Copywriting; Essential Desktop Publishing; Essential Design.* Contact the NEC for copy of the *Guide to Courses* which includes details of fees.

PMA Training

PMA House, Free Church Passage, St Ives, Cambridgeshire PE27 5AY
☎01480 300653 Fax 01480 496022
Email training@pma-group.com
Website www.pma-group.co.uk

One-/two-/three-day editorial, PR, design and publishing courses held in central London. High-powered, intensive courses run by Fleet Street journalists and magazine editors. Courses include: *News-Writing; Writing and Surviving as a Freelance; Feature Writing; Investigative Reporting; Basic Writing Skills.* Fees range from £150 to £600 plus VAT. Special rates for freelances.

Cheshire

The College of Technical Authorship – Distance Learning Course

The College of Technical Authorship, PO Box 7, Cheadle, Cheshire SK8 3BY
☎0161 437 4235   Fax 0161 437 4235
Email crossley@coltecha.u-net.com
Website www.coltecha.com

Contact *John Crossley*, DipDistEd, DipM, MCIM, FISTC, LCGI

Distance learning courses for City & Guilds Tech 536, Part 1, Technical Communication Techniques, and Part 2, Technical Authorship. Individual tuition by correspondence and fax; includes some practical work done at home. A member of the British Association for Open Learning.

Cornwall

Brackenside House

Polperro, Cornwall PL13 2RU
☎01503 273074   Fax 01503 273148
Email DavidMHinds@AfterStroke.fsbusiness.co.uk
Website www.AfterStroke.fsbusiness.co.uk

A series of weekend and mid-week residential courses in the historic Cornish village of Polperro, facilitated by David M. Hinds, author of *After Stroke*. The course, which is supported by senior academic staff, advises writers how to get their first book published and follows up the progress of individual writers. All-inclusive residential fees range from £350 to £850.

Falmouth College of Art

Woodlane, Falmouth, Cornwall TR11 4RH
☎01326 11077
Website www.falmouth.ac.uk/bloc

Contact *Admissions Secretary*

Postgraduate professional writing programme. An intensive vocational writing course with online features for screenwriting and fiction. Intended for writers wishing to develop their portfolio and gain work as freelancers or in the commercial world. The course commences in October.

Cumbria

Higham Hall College

Bassenthwaite Lake, Cockermouth, Cumbria CA13 9SH
☎01768 776276   Fax 01768 776013
Email admin@higham-hall.org.uk
Website www.higham-hall.org.uk

Winter and summer residential courses. Programme has included *Creative Writing*. Brochure available.

Derbyshire

Real Writers

PO Box 170, Chesterfield, Derbyshire S40 1FE
☎01246 238492   Fax 01246 238492
Email realwrtrs@aol.com
Website www.turtledesign.com/RealWriters/

Correspondence service with personal tuition from working writers. In addition to the support and appraisal service, runs an annual short story competition. Send s.a.e. for details.

University of Derby

Student Information Centre, Kedleston Road, Derby DE22 1GB
☎01332 622236   Fax 01332 622754
Email J.Bains@derby.ac.uk (prospectus requests only)
Website www.derby.ac.uk

Contact *Graham Parker*

With upwards of 300 students, *Experience of Writing* runs 21 modules as part of the undergraduate degree programme. These include: *Storytelling, Poetry, Playwriting, Writing for TV and Radio, Screenwriting, The Short Story, Journalism, Writing for Children.* The courses are all led by practising writers.

Writers' Summer School, Swanwick

The Hayes, Swanwick, Derbyshire
Email contact@wss.org.uk
Website www.wss.org.uk
Secretary *Jean Sutton*

A week-long summer school of informal talks and discussion groups, forums, panels, quizzes, competitions, and 'a lot of fun'. Open to everyone, from absolute beginners to published authors. Held in August from Saturday to Friday morning. Cost (2001) from £220, all inclusive. Contact the Secretary, at PO Box 5532, Heanor, Derbyshire DE75 7YF (☎01983 406759).

Devon

Arvon Foundation

Totleigh Barton, Sheepwash, Beaworthy,
Devon EX21 5NS
☎01409 231338 Fax 01409 231144
Email t-barton@arvonfoundation.org
Website www.arvonfoundation.org

Lumb Bank, Heptonstall, Hebden Bridge,
West Yorkshire HX7 6DF
☎01422 843714 Fax 01422 843714
Email l-bank@arvonfoundation.org

Moniack Mhor, Teavarran, Kiltarlity, Beauly,
Inverness-shire IV4 7HT
☎01463 741675
Email m-mhor@arvonfoundation.org

President *Terry Hands*
Chairman *Sir Robin Chichester-Clark*
National Director *David Pease*

FOUNDED 1968. Offers people of any age (over
16) and any background the opportunity to live
and work with professional writers. Four-and-a-
half-day residential courses are held throughout
the year at Arvon's three centres, covering
poetry, fiction, drama, writing for children,
songwriting and the performing arts. Bursaries
towards the cost of course fees are available for
those on low incomes, the unemployed, students
and pensioners. Runs a biennial poetry competition (see entry under **Prizes**).

Dartington College of Arts

Totnes, Devon TQ9 6EJ
☎01803 862224 Fax 01803 863569
Email registry@dartington.ac.uk
Website www.dartington.ac.uk

BA(Hons) course in *Performance Writing*:
exploratory approach to writing as it relates to
performance. The course is part of a performance arts programme which encourages
interdisciplinary work with arts management,
music, theatre, visual performance. The programme includes a range of elective modules in
digital media and emerging art forms which are
available to all students. Contact Subject
Director, Performance Writing: *Rick Allsopp*.

Exeter Phoenix

Bradninch Place, Gandy Street, Exeter,
Devon EX4 3LS
☎01392 667080 Fax 01392 667599
Website www.exeterphoenix.org.uk

Exeter Phoenix has regular literature events,
focusing on readings by living poets and other
writers and is often linked to aspects of a wider
performance programme. Tutors in a wide range
of writing skills run classes and workshops, listed
in the brochure of Phoenix activities.

University of Exeter

Exeter, Devon EX4 4QW
☎01392 264580

Contact *Dr Dee Heddon* (Drama Department,
Thornlea, New North Road, Exeter
EX4 4LA)

BA(Hons) in *Drama* with a third-year option in
Playwriting. MPhil and PhD in *Performance
Practice* (including *Playwriting*).

Dorset

Bournemouth University

Bournemouth Media School, Poole House,
Talbot Campus, Fern Barrow, Poole, Dorset
BH12 5BB
☎01202 595553 Fax 01202 595530

Contact *Katrina King, Programme Administrator*

Three-year, full-time BA(Hons) course in
Scriptwriting for Film and Television.

Essex

National Council for the Training of Journalists

Latton Bush Centre, Southern Way, Harlow,
Essex CM18 7BL
☎01279 430009 Fax 01279 438008
Email info@nctj.com
Website www.nctj.com

For details of journalism courses, both full-time
and via distance learning, please write to the
NCTJ enclosing a large s.a.e. or visit the website.

Gloucestershire

Chrysalis – The Poet In You

5 Oxford Terrace, Uplands, Stroud,
Gloucestershire GL5 1TW
☎01453 759436/01822 841081
Email ramsay@chrysalis37.fsnet.co.uk *or*
roselle.angwin@internet-today.co.uk

Offers postal courses, workshops (including 'The
Sacred Space of the Word'), one-to-one sessions,
and individual therapy related to the participant's
creative process. The course consists of Part 1,
'for those who feel drawn to reading more
poetry as well as wanting to start to write their
own', and Part 2, 'a more advanced course
designed for those who are already writing and
who want to go more deeply into its process and

technique'. Brochure and workshop dates available from the address above.

Hampshire
Highbury College, Portsmouth
Dovercourt Road, Cosham, Portsmouth, Hampshire PO6 2SA
☎023 9238 3131 Fax 023 9237 8382
Website www.highbury.ac.uk
Contact *Secretary* (☎023 9231 3287)

Courses include: one-year *Pre-entry Magazine Journalism*, run under the auspices of the Periodicals Training Council; 20-week *Pre-entry Newspaper Journalism* course, run under the auspices of the National Council for Training of Journalists; one-year Postgraduate Diploma in *Broadcasting Journalism*, run under the auspices of the Broadcast Journalism Training Council.

King Alfred's College
Winchester, Hampshire SO22 4NR
☎01962 841515 Fax 01962 842280
Website www.wkac.ac.uk

Three-year degree course in *Drama, Theatre and Television Studies*, including *Writing for Devised Community Theatre* and *Writing for Television Documentary*. Contact the Admissions Office (☎01962 827262).

MA course in *Theatre for Development* – one year, full-time course with major project overseas or in the UK. MA course in *Writing for Children* available on either a one- or two-year basis. Enquiries: Admissions Officer (☎01962 827235).

University of Southampton New College
The Avenue, Southampton SO17 1BG
☎023 8059 7261 Fax 023 8059 7271
Email vah@soton.ac.uk

Creative writing courses and writers' workshops. Courses are held in local/regional centres.

Hertfordshire
West Herts College
School of Media Communications, Hempstead Road, Watford, Hertfordshire WD1 3EZ
☎01923 812654
Email gaym@westherts.ac.uk
Contact *Admissions*

The 25-week postgraduate course in *Journalism,*

Radio and Advertising: Writing and Practice covers two options: *Writing for Print* and *Writing for Radio*. The college also offers a postgraduate diploma in *Publishing* with an option in *Multimedia Publishing*.

Kent
North West Kent College
Miskin Road, Dartford, Kent DA1 2LU
☎01322 629436 Fax 01322 629468
Website www.nwkent.ac.uk
Contact *Neil Nixon, Head of School, Media & Communications*

Two-year, full-time course that explores writing from a number of angles, teaching essential skills, market and academic aspects of the subject. Successful students progress to work or the University of Greenwich, the latter option allowing them to gain a BA(Hons) in Humanities from a further year of study. Staff include scriptwriters, novelists and a book publishers. Students produce their own creative work, compiling a portfolio in the final year under guidance from staff.

University of Kent at Canterbury
Unit for Regional Learning, Keynes College, Canterbury, Kent CT2 7NP
☎01227 823507 Fax 01227 458745
Email part-time@ukc.ac.uk
Website www.ukc.ac.uk/registry/URL
Contact *Information Office*

Certificate course in *Practical Writing* and *Imaginative Writing*. 20-week course in *Creative Writing*.

Lancashire
Alston Hall College
Alston Lane, Longridge, Preston, Lancashire PR3 3BP
☎01772 784661 Fax 01772 785835
Email alston.hall@ed.lancscc.gov.uk
Website www.alstonhall.u-net.com

Holds regular day-long creative writing workshops, also weekend residential courses. Brochure available.

Edge Hill College of Higher Education
St Helen's Road, Ormskirk, Lancashire L39 4QP
☎01695 575171
Email shepparr@edgehill.ac.uk

Contact *Dr R. Sheppard*

Offers a two-year, part-time MA in *Writing Studies*. Combines advanced-level writers' workshops with closely related courses in the poetics of writing and contemporary writing in English. There is also provision for MPhil- and PhD-level research in writing and poetics. A full range of creative writing courses is available at undergraduate level, in poetry and fiction writing which may be taken as part of a modular BA.

Lancaster University

Department of Creative Writing, Lonsdale College, Bailrigg, Lancaster LA1 4YN
☎01524 594169 Fax 01524 843934
Email L.Anderson@lancaster.ac.uk

Contact *Linda Anderson*

Offers practical graduate and undergraduate courses in writing fiction, poetry and scripts. All based on group workshops – students' work-in-progress is circulated and discussed. Distance learning MA now available. Visiting writers have included: Carol Ann Duffy, Kazuo Ishiguro, Bernard MacLaverty, David Pownall.

The Written Word

43 Green Lane, Beaumont, Lancaster LA1 2ES
☎01524 35215 Fax 01524 35215
Email steve@ashton01.freeserve.co.uk

Contact *Steve Ashton*

Postal course in all categories of short and full-length non-fiction work, with an emphasis on writing magazine feature articles and getting them published. Personal tuition from a working professional with 15 years' experience. £195 fee includes comprehensive course book plus detailed guidance and feedback on eight realistic assignments. Also, script evaluation service (£45 for articles, £95 for three chapters plus the synopsis of a book). Send for information leaflet.

Leicestershire

Leicester Adult Education College, Writing School

2 Wellington Street, Leicester LE1 6HL
☎0116 233 4343 Fax 0116 233 4344
Email admin@leicester-adult-ed.ac.uk
Website www.leicester-adult-ed.ac.uk

Contact *Valerie Moore*

Offers a wide range of creative writing and journalism courses throughout the year. The programme offers a mix of critical workshops and short craft courses. Specialises in support-ing new and more experienced writers through to publication and has strong links with local media. Occasional masterclasses and talks. Visiting writers have included Melvyn Bragg, Simon Brett, John Harvey, Roy Hattersley, Susan Hill, Rose Impey, Graham Joyce, Deric Longden, Simon Armitage and Andrew Motion.

Greater London

Blaze the Trail

2nd Floor, 241 High Street, London E17 7BH
☎020 8520 4569
Email training@coralmedia.co.uk
Website www.blaze-the-trail.com

ScriptCity at Blaze the Trail provides creative and professional training in screenwriting and story editing skills for writers, readers and script editors. *New Perspectives*: a 12-month intensive script development programme in association with professional editors and incorporating workshops and masterclasses; *Do the Write Thing*: for writers new to the screen; *Reading Room*: professional development for script readers; *Final Edition*: foundation and advanced training for script editors and producers; also one-on-one creative surgeries with professionals. Please call course coordinator for full details.

The Central School of Speech and Drama

Embassy Theatre, Eton Avenue, London NW3 3HY
☎020 7722 8183 Fax 020 7722 4132

Contact *Nick Wood*, Writing and Dramaturgy Tutor

MA in *Advanced Theatre Practice*. One-year, full-time course aimed at providing a grounding in principal areas of professional theatre practice – *Writing, Dramaturgy, Directing, Performance, Puppetry* and *Design*, with an emphasis on collaboration between the various strands. 'The Writing and Dramaturgy strands are particularly suitable for those wishing to work in a lively and stimulating atmosphere creating, with other practitioners, new work for the theatre.' Prospectus available.

The City Literary Institute

Humanities Dept, Stukeley Street, London WC2B 5LJ
☎020 7430 0542 Fax 020 7405 3347
Email humanities@citylit.ac.uk

The Writing School offers a wide range of courses from *Ways Into Creative Writing* and

Writing for Children to *Playwriting* and *Writing Short Stories*. The creative writing classes may be one-day Saturday classes, weekly sessions over one or more terms, or one-week intensive workshops. The Department offers information and advice during term time.

City University
Northampton Square, London EC1V 0HB
☎020 7477 8268 Fax 020 7477 8256
Website www.city.ac.uk/conted/cfa.htm

Contact *Courses for Adults*

Creative writing classes include: *Writer's Workshop; Wordshop* (poetry); *Writing Comedy; Playwright's Workshop; Writing Freelance Articles for Newspapers; Women Writers' Workshop; Creative Writing; Fiction Short and Long; Feature Journalism; Writing for Children.*

The Complete Creative Writing Course at the Groucho Club
☎020 7249 3711 Fax 020 7249 3711
Email maggie.h@blueyonder.co.uk
Website www.creative-writing.cwc.net

Contact *Maggie Hamand*

Courses of ten two-hour sessions held at the Groucho Club in London's Soho, starting in January, April and September, Monday or Saturday afternoons, 2.30 pm – 4.30 pm. Beginners and advanced courses offered. Each week looks at a different aspect of fiction writing and includes stimulating exercises, discussion and weekly homework. The tutors are novelists Maggie Hamand and Henrietta Soames. £195 for whole course.

The Drill Hall
16 Chenies Street, London WC1B 7EX
☎020 7307 5061 Fax 020 7307 5062
Email admin@drillhall.co.uk

Holds a number of writing classes and workshops. Regular tutors include Carol Burns and Peter Carty.

LNPF Writing School
See **London New Play Festival** under **Festivals**

London College of Printing
Elephant & Castle, London SE1 6SB
☎020 7514 6562
Website www.lcptraining.co.uk

Intensive courses in journalism. Short courses run by DALI (Developments at the London Institute) at the Elephant & Castle address above:

Guide to Magazine Writing/News Writing/Feature Writing/Freelance Journalism/Proof Reading/ Subbing on the Screen; Sub-editing. Also offers two-day specialist journalism courses in food writing, travel writing, writing for the music press, sports journalism and fashion writing, plus scriptwriting and documentary making. For individuals and companies 'tailor-made training' services can be provided. Prospectus and information leaflets available; telephone 020 7514 6770 or access the website where course bookings can be made securely online.

London School of Journalism
22 Upbrook Mews, London W2 3HG
☎020 7706 3790 Fax 020 7706 3780
Email info@lsjournalism.com
Website www.home-study.com

Contact *Student Administration Office*

Correspondence courses with an individual and personal approach. Students remain with the same tutor throughout their course. Options include: *Short Story Writing; Writing for Children; Poetry; Freelance Journalism; Improve Your English; Cartooning; Thriller Writing; English for Business; Journalism and Newswriting.* Fees vary but range from £215 for *Enjoying English Literature* to £395 for *Journalism and Newswriting.*

Middlesex University
School of Humanities, White Hart Lane, London N17 8HR
☎020 8411 5000 Fax 020 8411 6652
Email admissions@mdx.ac.uk
Website www.mdx.ac.uk

The UK's longest established writing degree now offers a Single or Joint Honours programme in *Writing & Media* (full- or part-time). This undergraduate modular programme gives an opportunity to explore journalism, poetry, prose fiction and dramatic writing for a wide range of genres and audiences. Option for work experience in the media and publishing. (Contact Admissions or *Maggie Butt*, Programme Leader.)

MA in *Writing* (full-time, part-time; day and evening classes) includes a specialist strand in Asian and Black British writing, approaches to the short story and novel; lectures and workshops from established writers. (Contact *Sue Gee* ☎020 8411 5941; e-mail: s.gee@mdx.ac.uk)

University of Surrey Roehampton
School of Arts, Roehampton Lane, London SW15 5PU
☎020 8392 3230 Fax 020 8392 3289
Email g.white@roehampton.ac.uk

Website www.roehampton.ac.uk

Contact *Graham White*

Three-year BA(Hons) programmes in *Drama and Theatre Studies* and *Film and Television Studies* include courses on writing for stage and screen.

University of Westminster

Harrow Campus, Watford Road, Harrow, Middlesex HA1 3TP
☎020 7911 5903 Fax 020 7911 5955
Email harrow-admissions@wmin.ac.uk
Website www.wmin.ac.uk

Part-time (evening) MAs available in *Journalism; Film and TV; Photography*.

Greater Manchester

Manchester Metropolitan University – The Writing School

Department of English, Geoffrey Manton Building, Rosamond Street West, off Oxford Road, Manchester M15 6LL
☎0161 247 1732/1 Fax 0161 247 6345

Course Convenor *Michael Schmidt*

Closely associated with **Carcanet Press Ltd** and *PN Review*, The Writing School offers two principal 'routes' for students to follow: *Poetry* and *The Novel*. A key feature of the programme is regular readings, lectures, workshops and masterclasses by writers, publishers, producers, booksellers, librarians and agents. Tutors include Simon Armitage, Carol Ann Duffy, Sophie Hannah, Jacqueline Roy and Jeffrey Wainwright.

University of Manchester

Department of English & American Studies, Arts Building, Oxford Road, Manchester M13 9PL
☎0161 275 3144 Fax 0161 275 3256
Email novel@man.ac.uk

Offers a one-year MA in *Novel Writing*.

University of Salford

Postgraduate Admissions, Dept. of Media & Performance, Adelphi Building, Peru Street, Salford, Greater Manchester M3 6EQ
☎0161 295 6027
Website www.salford.ac.uk

MA in *Television and Radio Scriptwriting*. Two-year, part-time course taught by professional writers and producers. Also offers a number of masterclasses with leading figures in the radio and television industry.

Password Training Ltd

23 New Mount Street, Manchester M4 4DE
☎0161 953 4071 Fax 0161 953 4001

Contact *Claire Turner*

Password Training provides training for publishers, writers' groups and individual writers in Internet publishing, planning, production, design, marketing, costing and distribution. Clients have included the Federation of Worker Writers and Community Publishers, The Arts Council, Regional Arts Boards, Yorkshire Art Circus and Corridor Community Press.

The Writers Bureau

Sevendale House, 7 Dale Street, Manchester M1 1JB
☎0161 228 2362 Fax 0161 236 9440
Email advisory@writersbureau.com
Website www.writersbureau.com

Comprehensive home-study writing course with personal tuition service from professional writers (fee: £249). Fiction, non-fiction, articles, short stories, novels, TV, radio and drama all covered in detail. Trial period, guarantee and no time limits. ODLQC accredited. Quote Ref. EH20. Free enquiry line: 0800 856 2008

The Writers Bureau College of Journalism

Address etc. as The Writers Bureau above

Home-study course covering all aspects of journalism. Real-life assignments assessed by qualified tutors with the emphasis on getting into print and enjoying the financial rewards. Comprises 28 modules and three handbooks with special introductory offers. Ref: EHJ20. Free enquiry line: 0800 298 7008.

The Writers College

Address etc. as The Writers Bureau above

The Art of Writing Poetry Course from The Writers Bureau sister college. A home-study course with a more 'recreational' emphasis. The 60,000-word course has 17 modules and lets you complete six written assignments for tutorial evaluation. Fees: £99. Quote Ref. EHP20. Free enquiry line: 0800 856 2008.

Merseyside

University of Liverpool

Centre for Continuing Education, 19 Abercromby Square, Liverpool L69 7ZG
☎0151 794 6900/6952 (24 hours)
Fax 0151 794 2544

Website www.merseyworld.com/cce

Head of Creative Arts *Keith Birch*

Courses include: *Introduction to Creative Writing; The Short Story and the Novel; Introduction to Writing Poetry; Introduction to Scripting for Radio and Television; Introduction to Writing Journalism; Science Fiction and Fantasy; Travel Writing; Songwriting; Popular Music Journalism; Theatre Playwrights Workshop; Scripting Situation Comedy; Scriptwriting: Film and Television.* Most courses are run in the evening over 10 or 20 weeks but there are some linked Saturday and weekday courses on offer. Students have the option of accreditation towards a university award in Creative Writing. Some of the above courses are also part of the university's part-time Flexible Degree pathway (Comb. Hons., Arts). No pre-entry qualifications required. Fees vary with concessions for the unwaged and those in receipt of benefit.

Norfolk

University of East Anglia

School of English & American Studies, Norwich, Norfolk NR4 7TJ
☎01603 593262 Fax 01603 593799
Email l.faith@uea.ac.uk
Website www.uea.ac.uk/eas

UEA has a history of concern with contemporary literary culture. Among its MA programmes is one in *Creative Writing*, Stream 1: Prose Fiction; Stream 2: Poetry; Stream 3: Scriptwriting.

Nottinghamshire

The Nottingham Trent University

Humanities Faculty Office (Post Graduate Studies), Clifton Lane, Nottingham NG11 8NS
☎0115 848 6335 Fax 0115 848 6339
Email jennifer.shaw@ntu.ac.uk
Website human.ntu.ac.uk/pg/courses/
  writing.html

Postgraduate Administrator *Jennifer Shaw*

MA in *Writing*. Hands-on and workshop-based, the course concentrates primarily on the practice and production of writing. A choice of options from *Fiction*, *Poetry* and *Life-Writing* (which includes *Feature* and *Travel Writing*). Assignments and a dissertation of your writing to complete for award of degree. No formal

exams. Staff are all established writers. Current visiting professors: Peter Porter, Michele Roberts and Miranda Seymour. Also a full programme of visiting speakers. Study either full-time (three evenings per week) or part-time (two evenings per week over two years). Further details and application forms from the Postgraduate Administrator.

Somerset

Bath Spa University College

Newton Park, Bath BA2 9BN
☎01225 875875 Fax 01225 875444
Email enquiries@bathspa.ac.uk
Website www.bathspa.ac.uk

Admissions Officer *Clare Brandram Jones*

Postgraduate Diploma/MA in *Creative Writing*. A course for creative writers wanting to develop their work. Teaching is by published writers in the novel, poetry, short stories and scriptwriting. In recent years, several students from this course have received contracts from publishers for novels, awards for poetry and short stories and have had work produced on BBC Radio.

Institute of Copywriting

Honeycombe House, Bagley, Wedmore, Somerset BS28 4TD
☎01934 713563 Fax 01934 713492
Email copy@inst.org
Website www.institute.org/copy

Comprehensive home-study course covering all aspects of copywriting, including advice on becoming a self-employed copywriter. Each student has a personal tutor who is an experienced copywriter and who provides detailed feedback on the student's assignments.

University of Bristol

Department of English, 3/5 Woodland Road, Bristol BS8 1TB
☎0117 954 6969 Fax 0117 928 8860
Email rowena.fowler@bris.ac.uk
Website www.bris.ac.uk/Depts/English/
  ce_creat.html

Courses: *Women and Writing*, for women who write or would like to begin to write (poetry, fiction, non-fiction, journals) and various other writing courses for the general public. *Certificate in Creative Writing* and *Certificate in Creative Writing for Therapeutic Purposes.* Detailed brochure available.

Staffordshire

Keele University

The Centre for Continuing and Professional Education, Keele University, (Freepost ST1666), Newcastle under Lyme, Staffordshire ST5 5BG
☎01782 583436

Weekend courses on literature and creative writing. The 2001 programme included fiction writing and writing for children. Also runs study days where major novelists or poets read and discuss their work.

Surrey

Royal Holloway

University of London, Egham Hill, Egham, Surrey TW20 0EX
☎01784 443922   Fax 01784 431018
Email drama@rhul.ac.uk
Contacts *Dan Rebellato, David Wiles*

Three-year BA course in *Theatre Studies* during which playwriting can be studied as an option in the second or third year. MA Theatre (Playwriting), a one- or two-year (full- or part-time) postgraduate degree.

University of Surrey

School of Educational Studies, University of Surrey, Guildford, Surrey GU2 5XH
☎01483 876172   Fax 01483 876171
Email r.curtis@surrey.ac.uk

The Open Access Continuing Education programme includes several *Creative Writing* courses, held at the University, the Guildford Institute and throughout the county. The courses carry credits and can build to a university award. For details, contact the Enrolment Secretary or *Lynda Strudwick, BEd, MSc*, Lecturer and Subject Leader in Creative Writing.

Sussex

University College Chichester

Bishop Otter Campus, College Lane, Chichester, West Sussex PO19 4PE
☎01243 816000   Fax 01243 816080
Email s.norgate@ucc.ac.uk

Contact *Stephanie Norgate,* Route Leader, MA in Creative Writing (☎01243 816296)

Postgraduate   Certificate/Diploma/MA   in *Creative Writing.*

The Earnley Concourse

Earnley, Chichester, West Sussex PO20 7JL
☎01243 670392   Fax 01243 670832
Email info@earnley.co.uk
Website www.earnley.co.uk

Offers a range of residential and non-residential courses throughout the year. Previous programme has included *Writing for Publication; You Can Sell What You Write.* Brochure available.

University of Sussex

Centre for Continuing Education, Education Development Building, Falmer, Brighton, East Sussex BN1 9RG
☎01273 678537   Fax 01273 678848
Email y.d.barnes@sussex.ac.uk
Website www.sussex.ac.uk
Contact (for all courses) *Yvonne Barnes*

Postgraduate Diploma in *Dramatic Writing*: the student is treated as a commissioned writer working in theatre, TV, radio or film with professional directors and actors. Includes workshops, masterclasses and a residential weekend. One-year, part-time. Convenor: *Richard Crane.* Certificate in *Creative Writing*: short fiction, novel and poetry for imaginative writers. One-year, part-time. Convenor: *Richard Crane.* Postgraduate Diploma in *Creative Writing and Personal Development*: for writers working in care services and self exploration. Convenor: *Celia Hunt.*

Tyne & Wear

University of Newcastle upon Tyne

Centre for Lifelong Learning, Newcastle upon Tyne NE1 7RU
☎0191 222 5680   Fax 0191 222 7090
Website www.ncl.ac.uk/lifelonglearning

Writing-related courses include: *Writing From the Inside Out; Writing Workshops.* Contact the Secretary, Adult Education Programme.

Warwickshire

University of Warwick

Open Studies, Continuing Education Department, Coventry, Warwickshire CV4 7AL
☎024 7652 3831
Email k.rainsley@warwick.ac.uk *or* l.downs@warwick.ac.uk

Creative writing courses held at the university

or in regional centres. Subjects include: *Starting to Write; Prose and Poetry Writing; Writing for Radio; Screenwriting for Beginners.* A one-year certificate in *Creative Writing* is available.

West Midlands

Sandwell College

Smethwick Campus, Crocketts Lane,
Smethwick B66 3BU
☎0121 556 6000
Contact *Tony Martin*

Creative writing courses held afternoons/evenings, from September to July. General courses covering short stories, poetry, autobiography, etc. Also women's writing courses.

University of Birmingham

School for Professional and Continuing Education, Selly Oak, Birmingham B29 6LL
☎0121 414 5607/5932 Fax 0121 414 5619
Email PACE@bham.ac.uk

Certificate of Higher Education in *Creative Writing* – two years, part-time in Birmingham, Shrewsbury and Worcester. Day and weekend classes, including theory and practice of writing in a wide range of literary genres, held at locations throughout Birmingham, the West Midlands, Herefordshire, Worcestershire and Shropshire. Course brochures are available from the address above. Please specify which course you are interested in. Students who can demonstrate qualifications/writing skills equivalent to Certificate Level, may apply to join the Diploma of Creative Writing.

The University also offers an MPhil in *Playwriting Studies* established by playwright David Edgar in 1989. Contact *April Di Angelis*, Course Director at the Department of Drama and Theatre Arts (☎0121 414 5790).

Wiltshire

Marlborough College Summer School

Marlborough, Wiltshire SN8 1PA
☎01672 892388/9 Fax 01672 892476
Email summer.school@marlboroughcollege.
   wilts.sch.uk
Website www.marlboroughcollege.org

Summer School with literature and creative writing included in its programme. Caters for residential and day students. Brochure available giving full details and prices.

Yorkshire

Arvon Foundation (Yorkshire)

See under **Devon**

Hull College

Queen's Gardens, Hull, East Yorkshire
HU1 3DG
☎01482 329943 Fax 01482 219079
Contact *Julia Billaney*

Offers part-time day/evening writing courses in *Novel Writing* and *Short Story Writing*, at Hull College, Park Street Centre. Courses begin each academic term. Writers are encouraged to contribute stories for a collection.

University of Hull

Scarborough Campus, Filey Road,
Scarborough, North Yorkshire YO11 3AZ
☎01723 362392 Fax 01723 370815
Website www.hull.ac.uk

BA Single Honours in *Theatre Studies* incorporates *Writing for Performance* and *Writing for Theatre*. Works closely with the Stephen Joseph Theatre and its artistic director Alan Ayckbourn. The theatre sustains a policy for staging new writers. (See entry under **Theatre Producers**.) The campus hosts the annual National Student Drama Festival which includes the International Student Playscript Competition (details from The National Information Centre for Student Drama; e-mail: nsdf@hull.ac.uk).

University of Leeds

Springfield Mount, Leeds, West Yorkshire
LS2 9JT
Email r.k.o'rourke@leeds.ac.uk
Contact *Rebecca O'Rourke*

Also at: Adult Education Centre, 37 Harrow Road, Middlesbrough, Cleveland, TS5 5NT
☎01642 814987

Creative writing courses held throughout Cleveland, North and West Yorkshire in the autumn, spring and summer terms. These are held weekly and as non-residential summer schools. Courses carry undergraduate credit, are part-time and offered in a range of subjects, at beginners, intermediate and advanced levels. Professional development courses for writers and writing development workers which carry post-graduate credit are also offered.

The Northern Film School

Leeds Metropolitan University, 2 Queen Square, Leeds, West Yorkshire LS2 8AF
☎0113 283 1900 Fax 0113 283 1901

Email nfs@lmu.ac.uk
Website www.lmu.ac.uk/hen/aad/nfs

Contact *Alby James*

The NFS offers a Postgraduate Diploma/MA course in *Fiction Screenwriting*. Full-time or part-time. Currently, graduates working on *The Bill, Family Affairs, Coronation Street*, three features and other professional projects.

Open College of the Arts

Unit 1B, Redbrook Business Park, Wilthorpe Road, Barnsley, South Yorkshire S75 1JN
☎01226 730495 Fax 01226 730838
Email open.arts@ukonline.co.uk
Website www.oca-uk.com

The OCA correspondence course, *Starting to Write*, offers help and stimulus from experienced writers/tutors. Emphasis is on personal development rather than commercial genre. Subsequent levels available include specialist poetry, fiction and autobiographical writing courses. OCA's *Creative Reading* course helps student writers understand how readers interact with their writing.

OCA writing courses are accredited to the University of Glamorgan. Prospectus and guide to courses available on request.

Sheffield Hallam University

School of Cultural Studies, Sheffield Hallam University, Collegiate Crescent, Sheffield S10 2BP
☎0114 225 4408 Fax 0114 225 4363
Email d.kelly@shu.ac.uk
Website www.shu.ac.uk/schools/cs/english/
english.htm

Offers MA in *Creative Writing* (one-year, full-time; also part-time).

University College Bretton Hall

School of English, Faculty of Arts, University College Bretton Hall, West Bretton, Wakefield, West Yorkshire WF4 4LG
☎01924 830261 Fax 01924 832006
Email rwatson@bretton.ac.uk

Contact *Rob Watson*

Offers one-year full-time/two-year part-time MA course in *Creative Writing* designed for competent though not necessarily published writers.

University of Sheffield

Division of Adult Continuing Education, 196–198 West Street, Sheffield S1 4ET
☎0114 222 7000 Fax 0114 222 7001

Certificate in *Creative Writing* (Degree Level 1)

and a wide range of courses, from foundation level to specialist writing areas, open to all members of the public. 'We encourages a community of writers with our own magazine, visits to readings, our own readings, links to city writing events, etc.' Courses in poetry, prose, journalism, scriptwriting, comedy, travel writing, writing using ICT/Web, writing for children. Brochures and information available from the address above.

IRELAND

Dingle Writing Courses Ltd

Ballintlea, Ventry, Co. Kerry, Republic of Ireland
☎00 353 66 9159052 Fax 00 353 66 9159052
Email dinglewc@iol.ie
Website www.iol.ie/~dinglewc

Directors *Abigail Joffe, Nicholas McLachlan*

A summer and autumn programme of weekend and five-day residential courses for beginners and experienced writers alike. Tutored by professional writers the courses take place in 'an inspirational setting overlooking Inch strand'. The programme includes poetry, fiction, starting to write and writing for theatre as well as special themed courses.

Past tutors have included Jennifer Johnston, Paul Durcan, Mary O'Malley, Leland Bardwell and Graham Mort. Writing courses for schools are also available. Brochures and further information available from the directors at the address above.

University of Dublin (Trinity College)

Graduate Studies Office, Arts Building, Trinity College, Dublin 2, Republic of Ireland
☎00 353 1 608 1166 Fax 00 353 1 671 2821
Email gradinfo@tcd.ie
Website www.tcd.ie/owc

Contact *Admissions*

Offers an MPhil *Creative Writing* course. A one-year, full-time course intended for students who are seriously committed to writing, are practising, or prospective authors.

Queen's University of Belfast

Institute of Lifelong Learning, Belfast BT7 1NN
☎028 9027 3323 Fax 028 9023 6909
Email ice@qub.ac.uk
Website www.qub.ac.uk/ice

Courses have included *Creative Writing; Writing*

for Profit and Pleasure; *Scriptwriting* and *Creative Writing for Beginners*.

University of Ulster
Short Course & Professional Development Unit, Room 17C21, University of Ulster, Belfast BT37 0QB
☎028 9036 5131 Fax 028 9036 6060
Contact *Administrative Officer*

Creative writing course/workshop, usually held in the autumn and spring terms. Concessions available.

SCOTLAND

University of Aberdeen
Key Learning Opportunities, Regent Building, Regent Walk, Aberdeen AB24 3FX
☎01224 272449 Fax 01224 272478
Email evening-classes@abdn.ac.uk

Creative writing evening class held weekly, taught by published author. Participants may join at any time.

Arvon Foundation (Inverness-shire)
See under **Devon**

University of Dundee
Continuing Education, Nethergate, Dundee DD1 4HN
☎01382 344128 Fax 01382 221057
Email k.mackle@dundee.ac.uk
Website www.dundee.ac.uk/education

Various creative writing courses held at the University and elsewhere in Dundee, Perthshire and Angus. Detailed course brochure available.

Edinburgh University
Office of Lifelong Learning, 11 Buccleuch Place, Edinburgh EH8 9LW
☎0131 650 4400 Fax 0131 667 6097
Email cce@ed.ac.uk
Website www.cce.ed.ac.uk

Several writing-orientated courses and summer schools. Beginners welcome. Intensive two-week course in *Playwriting* is held in July, culminating in a rehearsed reading by professional actors and recorded on video for participants to take away. Tuition in word-processing and use of computer room. Course brochure available.

University of Glasgow
Department of Adult and Continuing Education, 59 Oakfield Avenue, Glasgow G12 8LW
☎0141 330 4032/4394 (Brochure/Enquiries)
Fax 0141 330 3525
Email enquiry@ace.gla.ac.uk
Website www.gla.ac.uk/Acad/AdultEd

Runs writers' workshops and courses at all levels; all friendly and informal. Daytime and evening meetings. Tutors are all experienced published writers in various fields.

University of St Andrews
School of English, The University, St Andrews, Fife KY16 9AL
☎01334 462666 Fax 01334 462655
Email english@st-andrews.ac.uk
Website www.st-andrews.ac.uk

Offers postgraduate study in *Creative Writing*. Candidates choose two topics from: *Fiction: The Novel; Craft and Technique in Poetry* and all take the *Short Story* module. In September students submit a dissertation of original writing – prose fiction of 15,000 words or a collection of around 30 short poems. Taught by John Burnside, Robert Crawford, Douglas Dunn and Kathleen Jamie.

7:84 Summer School
See **7:84 Theatre Company Scotland** under **Theatre Producers**

WALES

Tŷ Newydd Writers' Centre
Llanystumdwy, Cricieth, Gwynedd LL52 0LW
☎01766 522811 Fax 01766 523095
Email tynewydd@dial.pipex.com

Residential writers' centre set up by the Taliesin Trust with the support of the **Arts Council of Wales** to encourage and promote writing in both English and Welsh. Most courses run from Monday evening to Saturday morning. Each course has two tutors and takes a maximum of 16 participants. The centre offers a wide range of specific courses for writers at all levels of experience. Early booking essential. Fee: £310 (single)/£340 (twin-bedded) inclusive. People on low incomes may be eligible for a grant or bursary. Course leaflet available. (See also **Organisations of Interest to Poets**.)

University of Glamorgan
Treforest, Pontypridd CF37 1DL
☎01443 482551
Website www.glam.ac.uk

MPhil in *Writing* – a two-year part-time Masters

degree for writers of fiction and poets. ESTABLISHED 1993. Contact: *Professor Tony Curtis* at the School of Humanities and Social Sciences.

Also, MA in *Scriptwriting (Theatre, TV or Radio)* – a two-year part-time Masters degree for scriptwriters. Contact: *Dr Richard J. Hand.*

University of Wales, Aberystwyth

Department of English, Hugh Owen Building, Aberystwyth, Ceredigion SY23 3DY
☎01970 622534 Fax 01970 622530
Website www.aber.ac.uk

BA *Writing and English*, a three-year course taught in part by practising writers, including novelist Patricia Duncker and poet Tiffany Atkinson. Also offers an MA in *Writing* with modules in narratology and poetry, writing and publication.

University of Wales, Bangor

Department of English, College Road, Bangor LL57 2DG
☎01248 382102 Fax 01248 382102
Email els029@bangor.ac.uk

MA *Creative Studies (Creative Writing)* degree programme offers writers the chance to develop their work. Also MA *Creative Studies (Film)* and MA *Creative Studies (Media and Journalism)*. The Development Centre for the Creative and Performing Arts at the University of Wales, Bangor, is the location of the UK national database on creative writing education and the well-known UK research programme: Creative Writing in Universities and Colleges.

Europe

GREECE

Creative Writing in Corfu

Poetry Greece, Triklino, Corfu 49100, Greece
☎00 30 661 58468 Fax 00 30 661 58468
Email poetrygreece@hotmail.com
Website
users.otenet.gr/~wendyhol/poetry_greece

A variety of writing and related courses held on the island of Corfu from April to October. For details of courses and fees, contact *Wendy Holborow* by post or e-mail.

Circles and Workshops

Writers' Circles Handbook

Oldacre, Horderns Park Road, Chapel-en-le-Frith, High Peak SK23 9SY
☎01298 812305
Email jillie@cix.co.uk
Website www.cix.co.uk/~oldacre/

New handbook for writers' circles, with invaluable information, articles and a comprehensive list of all known circles and groups meeting in the UK. Some overseas entries too. Regular updates available after initial purchase. Contact *Jill Dick* at the address above for further details and post-free price.

Annual Writers' Conference Winchester

'Chinook', Southdown Road, Winchester, Hampshire SO21 2BY
☎01962 712307
Email WriterConf@aol.com
Website www.gmp.co.uk/writers/conference
Conference Director *Barbara Large, MBE, FRSA*

Having grown over the past 20 years from a creative writing workshop, this event now attracts international authors, playwrights, poets, agents and editors who give workshops, mini courses, editor appointments, lectures and seminars to help writers harness their creativity and develop technical skills. Plenary address: P.D. James, OBE. 15 writing competitions are attached to the conference. All first-place winners are published in *The Best of* series annually. The 2002 Conference will be held over the weekend of 28–30 June at King Alfred's University College, Winchester, with workshops from 1–5 July. The Bookfair offers delegates a wide choice of exhibits including Internet author services, publishers, booksellers, printers and trade associations.

Ayr Writers' Club

Meeting place: Wallace Tower, High Street, Ayr
Contact *May Stevenson* (☎01292 2637900)
FOUNDED in 1970, this well-established writers'

club is strong on encouraging its members towards achieving success in various genres and many of them have bben published. Meetings are held every Wednesday from September to April at 7.30 pm. These take the form of club nights and workshops at which published authors are invited to speak once a month. A library of books on the mechanics of writing is available free to members.

Carmarthern Writers' Circle
Lower Carfan, Tavernspite, Whitland, Pembrokeshire SA34 0NP
☎01994 240441

Contact *Jenny White*

FOUNDED 1989. The Circle meets on the second Monday of every month upstairs at the Queen's Hotel in Carmarthen. Both beginners and experienced writers are welcome. Activities include workshops and 'poets and pints' evenings. More information available from address above.

Children's Novel Writers' Folio
See **Short Story Writers' Folio**

Chiltern Writers' Group
151 Chartridge Lane, Chesham, Buckinghamshire HP5 2SE
Email anything@chilwriters.scripterz.org
Website www.chilwriters.scripterz.org

Invites writers, publishers, editors and agents to speak at its monthly meetings at Wendover Public Library. Regular newsletter and competitions. Annual subscription: £15; concessions: £10. Non-members meeting: £3.

Concordant Poets Folios
17 Stone Close, Braintree, Essex CM7 1LJ
☎01376 342095
Email whogg@onetel.net.uk

An independent postal workshop for poets which at present consists of two folios of eight members each. The purpose of the folios being to submit work for appreciation and criticism by folio members. Send s.a.e. for details.

The Cotswold Writers' Circle
Dar-es-Salaam, Beeches Park, Hampton Fields, Minchinhampton, Gloucestershire GL6 9BA
☎01453 882912

Patron *Elizabeth Webster*
Honorary Treasurer *Charles Hooker*

The Circle meets fortnightly during the day (10.30 am to 12.30 pm) in Cirencester. Circle activities include organising an International

Open Writing Competition – closing date 31 January 2002; details from the address above (enclose s.a.e.). Publishes an anthology to include winning entries of the Competition. Arranges writing workshops conducted by well-known authors. Contact the Treasurer for further details.

Cumbrian Literary Group
'Calgarth', The Brow, Flimby, Maryport, Cumbria CA15 8TD
☎01900 813444

President *George Bott*
Secretary *Joyce E. Fisher*

FOUNDED in 1946 to provide a meeting place for readers and writers in Cumbria. The Group meets once a month (April to November), usually in Windermere. Invites speakers to meetings and holds annual competitions for poetry and prose. *Publishes* a magazine, *Bookshelf.* Subscription: £8 p.a. For further details contact the Secretary at the address above.

'Sean Dorman' Manuscript Society
Cherry Trees, Crosemere Road, Cockshutt, Ellesmere, Shropshire SY12 0JP
☎01939 270293

Director *Mary Driver*

FOUNDED 1957. The Society provides mutual help among writers and aspiring writers in England, Wales and Scotland. By means of circulating manuscript parcels, members receive constructive criticism of their own work and read and comment on the work of others. Each 'Circulator' has up to nine participants and members' contributions may be in any medium: short stories, chapters of a novel, poetry, magazine articles, etc. Members may join two such circulators if they wish. Each circulator has a technical section and a letters section in which friendly communication between members is encouraged, and all are of a general nature apart from one, specialising in mss for the Christian market. Full details and application forms available on receipt of s.a.e. Subscription: £6.50 p.a.

East Anglian Writers
52 Riverside Road, Norwich, Norfolk NR1 1SR
☎01603 629088 Fax 01603 629088
Email Anthony.vivis@tesco.net

Contact *Anthony Vivis (Chair)*

A group of over 80 professional writers living in Norfolk and Suffolk. Affiliated to the **Society of Authors**. Informal pub meetings, occasional speakers' evenings and contact point for professional writers new to the area.

Equinoxe Screenwriting Workshops

Association Equinoxe, 4 Square du Roule, 75008 Paris, France
☎00 33 1 5353 4488 Fax 00 33 1 5353 4489
Email equinoxef@aol.com

Contact *Claire Dubert*

FOUNDED 1993, with Jeanne Moreau as president, to promote screenwriting and to establish a link between European and American film production. In association with Canal+, Sony Pictures Entertainment, Fondation Daniel Langlais and Media Programme of the European Union, Château Beychevelle, Equinoxe supports young writers of all nationalities by creating a screenwriting community capable of appealing to an international audience. Open to selected professional screenwriters able to speak either English or French fluently. To-date, Equinoxe has helped 153 European and American authors to perfect and promote scripts. 50 of these have been brought to the screen and several are in production.

Euroscript

Suffolk House, 1–8 Whitfield Place, London W1P 5SF
☎020 7387 5880 Fax 020 7387 5880
Email euroscript@netmatters.co.uk
Website www.euroscript.co.uk

Euroscript, a MEDIA programme of the EU to advance European scriptwriting, is a distance training project working in EU languages. It develops screenplays, reads, selects and promotes scripts, writers and writer/producer teams. Also runs workshops and supports writers' groups. Two story competitions per year: deadlines 30 April and 31 October. Write or access the website for further information.

Finchley Writers' Group

124 Friern Park, London, N12 9PN

Contact *Rosalyn Rappaport* (☎020 8446 3690) or *John Burns* (at the address above)

Encourages people who are writing with a view to being published. Members include aspiring and established authors. The Group meets every Tuesday at 7.30 pm upstairs at the Tally Ho! pub in north Finchley in London.

Gay Authors Workshop

BM Box 5700, London WC1N 3XX
☎020 8520 5223

Contact *Kathryn Byrd*

Established 1978 to encourage and support lesbian/gay writers. Regular meetings and a newsletter. The publishing arm – Paradise Press – considers high quality fiction from GAW members only.

Historical Novel Folio

17 Purbeck Heights, Mount Road, Parkstone, Poole, Dorset BH14 0QP
☎01202 741897

Contact *Doris Myall-Harris*

An independent postal workshop – single folio dealing with any period before World War II. Send s.a.e. for details.

The International Inkwell

See entry under **Miscellany**

Kops and Ryan Advanced Playwriting Workshops

41B Canfield Gardens, London NW6 3JL
☎020 7624 2940/7263 8740

Tutors *Bernard Kops, Tom Ryan*

Three ten-week terms per year beginning in September. Students may join course any term. Workshops on Tuesday, 7 pm–10 pm or Thursday, 7 pm–10 pm, or Saturday, 2 pm–5 pm. Small groups. Focuses on structure, character, language, meaning and style through written and improvised exercises; readings of scenes from students' current work; and readings of full-length plays. Two actors attend each session. Also, instruction in film technique and private tutorials. Call for details.

London Writer Circle

27 Braycourt Avenue, Walton-on-Thames, Surrey KT12 2AZ
☎01932 269635
Email wendy.stickler@org.uk

Contact *Wendy Hughes (Editor & Membership Secretary)*

FOUNDED 1924. Aims to help and encourage writers of all grades. Monthly evening meetings with well-known speakers on aspects of literature and journalism, and workshops for short story writing, poetry and feature writing. Occasional social events and quarterly magazine. Subscription: £20 (London); £10 (Country); £6 (Overseas).

NWP (North West Playwrights)

18 St Margaret's Chambers, 5 Newton Street, Manchester M1 1HL

☎0161 237 1978   Fax 0161 237 1978
Email newplaysnw@hotmail.com
Website www.newplaysnw.com

FOUNDED 1982. Award-winning organisation whose aim is to develop and promote new theatre writing. Operates a script-reading service, classes and script development scheme and *The Lowdown* newsletter. Services available to writers in the region only. Also disburses grants to support commissions, residencies, etc.

QueenSpark Books

See entry under **Small Presses**

Screenwriters' Workshop

Suffolk House, 1–8 Whitfield Place, London W1T 5JU
☎020 7387 5511
Email screenoffice@cwcom.net
Website www.lsw.org.uk

ESTABLISHED 1983. Formerly London Screenwriters Workshop, the SW is open to writers from all over Britain and Europe. The Workshop is an educational charity whose aim is to help writers into the film and TV industries. Many high-profile members. Offers a rolling programme of tuition, networking and events including guest speakers and showcasing opportunities. Membership: £35 p.a. Runs *Feedback* – a script-reading service with reduced rates for SW members – contact *K. Way* (☎020 8520 9103).

Scribo

1/31 Hamilton Road, Boscombe, Bournemouth, Dorset BH1 4EQ
☎01202 302533

Contact *K. & P. Sylvester*

Scribo (established for more than 20 years) is a postal workshop for novelists. Mss criticism foilos cover fantasy/sci-fi, crime/thrillers, mainstream, women's fiction, literary. Forums offer information, discussion on all topics relating to writing and literature. No annual subscription. £5 joining fee only. Full details from the address above; enclose s.a.e., please.

Short Story Writers' Folio/ Children's Novel Writers' Folio

5 Park Road, Brading, Sandown, Isle of Wight PO36 0HU
☎01983 407697
Email dawn.wortley-nott@lineone.net

Contact *Mrs Dawn Wortley-Nott*

Postal workshops – members receive constructive criticism of their work and read and offer advice on fellow members' contributions. Send an s.a.e. for further details.

Society of Sussex Authors

Bookends, Lewes Road, Horsted Keynes, Haywards Heath, West Sussex RH17 7DP
☎01825 790755   Fax 01825 790755
Email michael@bookends.claranet.com

Contact *Michael Legat*

FOUNDED 1968 to promote the interests of its members and of literature, particularly within the Sussex area. Regular meetings and exchange of information; plus social events. Membership restricted to writers who live in Sussex and who have had at least one book commercially published, or other writings used professionally. Meetings are held six times a year in Lewes. Annual subscription: £10.

South Eastern Writers' Association

114 Church Road, Harold Wood, Romford, Essex RM3 0SD
☎01708 703479
Email GrandeCoppy@aol.com

President *Marion Hough*
Secretary *Janice Grande*

FOUNDED 1989 to bring together experienced and novice writers, in an informal atmosphere. Non-profit-making, the Association holds an annual residential weekend each spring at Bulphan, Essex. Free workshops and discussion groups included in the overall cost. Previous guest speakers: Simon Brett, Bernard Cornwell, Maureen Lipman, Deric Longden, Terry Pratchett, Jack Rosenthal. Contact the Secretary at the address above.

South Manchester Writer's Workshop

c/o Didsbury Methodist Church Hall, Sandhurst Road, Didsbury, Manchester M20
☎0161 431 4717
Email Philcave@aol.com
Website www.manchester-writers.freeserve.co.uk

Contact *Philip Caveney*

The Workshop, which has been running for around 20 years, provides a lively and informative forum where writers at all levels of their craft can meet to read and discuss their work. Meetings held every Tuesday, 7.30 pm–9.30 pm. The first session is free and thereafter a small charge (currently £1.50) is made. Write or access the website for more details.

Southport Writers' Circle

40 Pilkington Road, Southport, Merseyside
PR8 6PD

Contact *Marjorie Harriman*

Meets 51 weeks of the year for the reading and discussion of mss. Organises an annual international poetry competition (see entry under **Prizes**) and hosts a one-day writers' seminar on the first Saturday in October each year which includes a literary competition for those who attend.

Southwest Scriptwriters

☎0117 909 5522 Fax 0117 907 3816
Website www.southwest-scriptwriters.co.uk

Secretary *John Colborn*

FOUNDED 1994 to offer encouragement and advice to those writing for stage, screen, radio and TV in the region. The group, which attracts professional writers, enthusiasts and students, meets regularly at the Theatre Royal, Bristol to read aloud and provide critical feedback on members' work, discuss writing technique and exchange market information. Lucy Catherine, writer-in-residence at the Bristol Old Vic, acts as Honorary President. Subscription: £5 p.a.

Speakeasy – Milton Keynes Writers' Group

46 Wealdstone Place, Springfield, Milton Keynes MK6 3JG
☎01908 663860
Email speakeasy@ukgateway.net

Contact *Martin Brocklebank*

Invites lovers of the written and spoken word to their monthly meetings on the first Friday of each month, 8 pm. Full and varied programme including Local Writers Nights where work can be read and performed, Guest Nights where writers, poets and journalists are invited to speak. Mini-workshops and information nights are also in the programme. Invite entries to their Open Creative Writing Competitions. Phone, e-mail or send s.a.e. for details to address above.

Sussex Playwrights' Club

2 Brunswick Mews, Hove, East Sussex
BN3 1HD
☎01273 730106
Website www.newventure.org.uk

Secretary *Dennis Evans*

FOUNDED 1935. Aims to encourage the writing of plays for stage, radio and TV by giving monthly dramatic readings of members' work by experienced actors, mainly from local drama groups. Gives constructive, critical suggestions as to how work might be improved, and suggests possible marketing. Membership is not confined to writers but to all who are interested in theatre in all its forms, and all members are invited to take part in discussions. Guests are always welcome at a nominal £1. Meetings held at New Venture Theatre, Bedford Place, Brighton, East Sussex. Subscription: £5 p.a. Contact the Secretary for details or visit the 'features' page on the website.

Ver Poets

Haycroft, 61–63 Chiswell Green Lane, St Albans, Hertfordshire AL2 3AL
☎01727 867005

Chairman *Ray Badman*

Editor/Organiser *May Badman*

FOUNDED 1966 to promote poetry and to help poets. With postal and local members, holds meetings in St Albans; runs a poetry bookstall for members' books and publications from other groups; publishes members' work in anthologies and organises poetry competitions, including the annual **Ver Poets Open** competition. Gives help and advice whenever they are sought and makes information available to members about other poetry groups, events and opportunities for publication. Membership: £12.50 p.a.; £15 or US$30 (Overseas).

Word Broccoli Writing Workshops

Bruach Mhor, Fionnphort, Isle of Mull
PA66 6BL
☎01681 700757
Email wordbroc@lineone.net
Website website.lineone.net/~wordbroc

Owner/Facilitator *Carla Lamont*

Residential writing holidays set in castles and cottages on the Hebridean Isles of Iona and Mull. Emphasis is on the 'white heat' of creative energy and generating fresh material, rather than the more technical aspects of writing. Writing pilgrimages to stone circles, ancient ruins and sacred sites incorporated into each workshop.

Workers' Educational Association

National Office: Temple House, 17 Victoria Park Square, London E2 9PB
☎020 8983 1515 Fax 020 8983 4840
Email nationaloffice@wea.org.uk
Website www.wea.org.uk

FOUNDED in 1903, the WEA is a voluntary body with members drawn from all walks of life. It runs writing courses and workshops throughout the country and all courses are open to everyone. Branches in most towns and many villages, with 13 district offices in England and one in Scotland. Contact your district WEA office for courses in your region. All correspondence should be addressed to the District Secretary.

Cheshire, Merseyside & West Lancashire: 7/8 Bluecoat Chambers, School Lane, Liverpool L1 3BX (☎0151 709 8023)

Eastern: Botolph House, 17 Botolph Lane, Cambridge CB2 3RE (☎01223 350978)

East Midlands: 39 Mapperley Road, Mapperley Park, Nottingham NG3 5AQ (☎0115 962 8400)

London: 4 Luke Street, London EC2A 4NT (☎020 7388 7261)

Northern: 51 Grainger Street, Newcastle upon Tyne NE1 5JE (☎0191 232 3957)

North Western: 4th Floor, Crawford House, University Precinct Centre, Oxford Road, Manchester M13 9GH (☎0161 273 7652)

South Eastern: 57 Riverside 2, Sir Thomas Longley Road, Rochester, Kent ME2 4BH (☎01634 730101)

South Western: Sandon Court, The Millfields, 1 Craigie Drive, Plymouth, Devon PL1 3JB (☎01752 664989)

Thames & Solent: 6 Brewer Street, Oxford OX1 1QN (☎01865 246270)

Western: 40 Morse Road, Redfield, Bristol BS5 9LB (☎0117 935 1764)

West Mercia: 78–80 Sherlock Street, Birmingham B5 6LT (☎0121 666 6101)

Yorkshire North: 6 Woodhouse Square, Leeds, W. Yorkshire LS3 1AD (☎0113 245 3304)

Yorkshire South: Chantry Buildings, 6–20 Corporation Street, Rotherham S60 1NG (☎01709 837001)

Scottish Association: Riddle's Court, 322 Lawnmarket, Edinburgh EH1 2PG (☎0131 226 3456)

Writers in Oxford

6 Princes Street, Oxford OX4 1DD
☎01865 791202
Email admin@ita.org.uk
Membership Secretary *Brian Levison*

FOUNDED 1992. Open to published authors, playwrights, poets and journalists. Linked to the **Society of Authors** but organised locally. Arranges a programme of meetings, seminars and social functions. Publishes newsletter, *The Oxford Writer*. Subscription: £15 p.a.

The Writers' Workshop

Cowfields Farm, Rotherfield Greys, Henley-on-Thames, Oxfordshire RG9 4PX
☎01491 628819 Fax 01491 628581

The Writers' Workshop runs regular daytime sessions on aspects of creative writing together with talks from guest speakers. Published writers and beginners are equally welcome.

Yorkshire Playwrights

3 Trinity Road, Scarborough, North Yorkshire YO11 2TD
☎01723 367449 Fax 01723 367449
Email ScarTam@aol.com
Website www.yorkshireplaywrights.com
Administrator *Ian Watson*

FOUNDED 1989 out of an initiative by Jude Kelly and William Weston of the **West Yorkshire Playhouse**. A group of professional writers of plays for stage, TV and radio whose aims are to encourage the writing and performance of new plays in Yorkshire. Open to any writers living in Yorkshire who are members, preferably, of the **Writers' Guild**, or the **Society of Authors**. Contact the Administrator for an information sheet.

The Perils of Libel

*David Hooper gives advice on how to avoid
an expensive court appearance*

Libel remains a perilous business for writers even though the balance has swung
some way in favour of those defending libel actions in the last few years.
Claimants do not have to prove actual damage to their reputation and defamatory words are assumed to be false. The burden of proving that the defamatory
words are true lies upon the author. Repetition of words that are defamatory is
not of itself a defence and the notoriety of a potential libel claimant is no guarantee he will not sue. These factors will be relevant to assessing the risk of a libel
claim and should a claim be made, would be relevant to the level of damages.

The main area of risk in libel is in non-fiction. The best working test is
whether the tendency of the words used is to diminish the reputation of the
claimant. If you were in the claimant's position, could you validly object to what
was written about you? There is unfortunately no substitute for careful research
and checking. Some errors pass into mythology. A British police officer called
Morton collected damages on no less than three occasions from W.H. Allen,
Secker & Warburg and Weidenfeld & Nicolson for the repetition of the canard
that he was responsible for the shooting in cold blood of Abram Stern head of
the Stern gang in Palestine.

The issue is what readers would reasonably conclude that the words meant.
The fact that the author did not intend to libel the claimant is not a defence.
The reader is in any event unlikely to know what the author's intention was and
would form his own view on the interpretation of the words on the page. The
fact that a libel was the result of an honest mistake rather than deliberate would
be relevant to the amount of damages awarded. Unhappily experience shows
that libel is, particularly in the area of publishing, the product of mistake rather
than the product of a failed exposé. Publishers are in any event increasingly
reluctant to run the risk of publishing investigative books. Cases involving the
exposure of the wrongdoing of footballers, policemen or doctors normally
involve newspapers or television companies. Writers need therefore to check
the accuracy of what they write. They do well, for example, not to confuse the
Chancellor of Glasgow University, Sir Alec Cairncross with his brother a sus-
pected member of the Cambridge spy ring. Nor is it wise to suggest that a
Nigerian-born singer had said that 'it was time to support apartheid' when in
reality she had said nothing more sinister than 'it was time to support a party'.

The writer should focus on all people who might bring a claim. Often controversial books successfully avoid an action from the principal target only to
invite a claim from some minor character over a relatively trivial indiscretion.

Claims can come from unlikely sources. Recently, a Russian businessman Grigori Loutchansky successfully sued *The Times* over a report linking him with money laundering even though the paper may have felt such a claim was unlikely as he was banned from this country because his presence was deemed undesirable by the Home Secretary and he had served a lengthy prison sentence for dishonesty in the USSR. Unfortunately, the libel laws in this country have attracted a number of libel tourists wishing to impress on the world their spotless reputation. Writers should bear in mind that the libel laws in the United States are unfavourable to plaintiffs with the result that people like Dr Armand Hammer sued the English edition of a hostile biography in this country whereas he had decided not to bring a claim in the USA.

If a claim for libel is notified, advice should be sought. An outraged response can raise the level of damages. Section 2 of the Defamation Act 1996 has significantly amended the defence of offer of amends which enables a swift and less expensive resolution of a claim where a mistake has been made. It involves an admission of liability and, if the parties cannot agree, an assessment of damages by the judge but it can stop the greed of the claimant in its tracks. Writers need to discover whether they are covered by the publisher's insurance and, if so, what excess attaches to any claim. Increasingly libel insurance only cuts in after the claim has cost five figures – scant consolation for the author who is likely to have warranted in the publishing contract that the book is free from libel. Very often publishers will not enforce that indemnity in the absence of serious blameworthy conduct on the part of the writer but again that is little consolation as publishers will not commit themselves in advance to their probable reaction to a libel claim. It is important therefore to consider whether the book should be read for libel and, if so, whether it is necessary to have it all read or simply part of it.

Many publishing contracts are silent on the question of who pays for the libel reading. Writers who try to modify the standard form indemnity given to publishers normally face a thankless task, but it is worth considering whether there is scope for agreeing that the writer's liability should be modified in respect of potential defamations of which the publisher is aware where the writer has complied with all the requirements of the lawyer reading the book for libel. Practical steps which can be taken include considering whether a particular passage should be sent to the person written about. If it can be shown that the person consented to what was written, that is a defence to a claim for libel. The problem, however, is that normally such persons will not give consent.

Libel actions cannot be brought on behalf of those who are dead. The death of a plaintiff in the course of a libel action, as happened with Robert Maxwell's claim against Faber, brings the claim to an immediate halt, but each side is left bearing their own legal costs. Writers are sometimes well advised to consult a helpful volume called *Who was Who*.

Another defence is justification which involves the author proving that what was written was true. If what was written was fair comment on a matter of public interest based on facts which were substantially true the writer will have a defence. By virtue of the Human Rights Act 1998 the English courts will increasingly take note of the decisions made under Article 10 of the European Convention of Human Rights which upholds the freedom of speech and which has a greater tendency to rule that criticisms made of a claimant were matters of comment rather than allegations of fact which have to be justified.

One of the most promising developments has been the expansion of the defence of qualified privilege in the libel action brought by the former Irish Prime Minister Albert Reynolds against the *Sunday Times*. If the writer can prove that on a matter of public interest there was a duty to inform the public who had a corresponding interest in receiving that information, there will be a defence which does not require proving that the particular allegation was true. The Court will, however, look very carefully at the research carried out, the language used and the attempt to put both sides of the matter.

Qualified privilege was the issue in the Loutchansky case where the newspaper argued that it required the protection of qualified privilege to write about the alleged activities of Loutchansky which were by their nature very difficult to prove. The judge concluded, however, that the paper had made insufficient attempts to contact Loutchansky and should not have published until it had done so. The most helpful development for writers is the recognition by the courts of the importance of freedom of speech. The press has to discharge vital functions as a bloodhound as well as a watchdog and any lingering doubts should be resolved in favour of publication. One law lord, Lord Hoffmann has observed that freedom of speech is a trump card.

Writers of fiction face fewer libel problems. However, their use of auto-biographical material can lead to some of their characters being identifiable. The inadvertent use of the name of a real peer has led to a novel being pulped. Directories should, where possible, be consulted to ensure there are no similarly named people in a comparable occupation, and names chosen at random. Care should be taken to see on whom characters are based and whether any of the surrounding events actually happened. Often there is much to be said for a carefully worded disclaimer of reference to living individuals. Compton Mackenzie used to pick names from old telephone directories. Unfortunately, even when this expedient was used by the novelist Paul Watkins in his book *Stand up before your God*, a randomly chosen name of a villainous character was by ill-fortune the name of one of his contemporaries at Eton College. Damages had to be paid as checks in the school directories could have avoided this error.

Writers of fiction will benefit from the defence of accidental defamation under Section 2 of the Defamation Act which will limit damages and costs but, even so, failure to make these checks can be expensive. Derek Jameson's experiences in accidentally changing the name of a sergeant who had been convicted of treason to spare that man's family's feelings to a randomly chosen name which turned out to be that of a journalist showed that the road to libel could be paved with good intentions.

The growth of faction and the introduction of living people into works of fiction do increase the risk of libel claims by blurring the distinction between fact and imagination. A roman-à-clef can present significant libel problems and it was perhaps not surprising that recently a publisher could not be found for a novel featuring unattractive characteristics of a person described as the wife of a Labour Prime Minister who as 'a young chap with a phoney smile' was felt not to be sufficiently unrecognisable.

Changes introduced by the Defamation Act 1996 and procedural changes regarding the conduct of libel actions to make them less tortuous and expensive and to require each side to disclose the strengths and weaknesses of their cases at an earlier stage certainly are an improvement. Libel nevertheless remains a very costly pitfall even if the damages awarded are much less. Damages are now capped at £150,000 for the most serious libels, but on top of that there are the legal costs. Most cases settle for a fraction of that. There are fast-track procedures where libel damages will be capped at £10,000. This is little consolation to writers as these changes together with the willingness of lawyers to bring libel claims on a conditional fee basis – that is to say the lawyer does not get paid unless he wins the case – serve only to encourage the bringing of smaller, but nevertheless expensive, claims. Things are improving but at present the only certainty about libel is its expense.

David Hooper is media partner of Pinsent Curtis Biddle and author of Reputations under Fire, *published by Little Brown (2001).*

Miscellany

Arjay Research
20 Rookery View, Little Thurrock, Grays,
Essex RM17 6AS
☎01375 372199 Fax 01375 372199
Email RogWJ@aol.com

Contact *Roger W. Jordan*

All aspects of international merchant shipping
and naval research undertaken by former shipping archivist and editor. Extensive maritime
library and comprehensive databases on *inter
alia* ships wrecked/lost and passenger and cruise
ships. Terms by arrangement.

Authors' Research Services
32 Oak Village, London NW5 4QN
☎020 7284 4316 Fax 020 7284 4316
Email rmwindserv@aol.com

Contact *Richard Wright*

Research and document supply service, particularly to authors, academics and others without
easy access to London libraries and sources of
information. Also indexing of books and journals. Rates negotiable.

Combrógos
10 Heol Don, Whitchurch, Cardiff CF14 2AU
☎029 2062 3359 Fax 029 2052 9202
Email meic@heoldon.fsnet.co.uk

Contact *Dr Meic Stephens*

FOUNDED 1990. Arts and media research, editorial services, specialising in books about Wales or
by Welsh authors. 'Encyclopaedic knowledge of
Welsh history, language, literature and culture.'

CopyPlus of Monmouth
Hadnock Road, Monmouth NP5 3NQ
☎01600 772600 Fax 01600 712896
Email info@copyplus.demon.co.uk

Contact *Anne King/Welfast Media and
    Publications Ltd*

Advice and technical assistance to poets, writers
and organisations that wish to self-publish.
Specialises in bespoke publications with print
runs as low as 25 copies.

Jacqueline Edwards
104 Earlsdon Avenue South, Coventry,
Warwickshire CV5 6DQ

Contact *Jacqueline Edwards, MA, LLB(Hons)*

Historical research – family, local and 19th and
20th century legal history. Covers Warwickshire,
Gloucestershire,   Wiltshire,   Worcestershire,
Cambridgeshire and the Public Record Office,
Kew London.

International Booksearch Service
8 Old James Street, London SE15 3TS
☎020 7639 8900/07713 612752
Email scfordham@talk21.com
Website www.scfordham.com

Contact *S.C. Fordham*

FOUNDED 1992. International book search service for out-of-print books. A free service with
no obligation to buy the book when found.
Experienced in finding books for authors,
researchers, TV and film companies, newspapers, magazines, etc.

The International Inkwell, a writers' retreat
Cafe du Livre, Rue de la Mairie,
11170 Montolieu, Aude France
☎00 33 468 248117
Email cafedulivre@aol.com
Website www.cafedulivre.com

Also: London address: 96 Edith Grove,
Chelsea, London SW10 0NH
☎020 7460 1441 Fax 020 7352 3951

Contact *Lucia Stuart*

Set in the French medieval village of
Montolieu, which boasts 14 bookshops to a
population of 800, The International Inkwell
rents rooms for writers. Open from June to
September, groups are welcome for writing
courses, reading weeks or forums. For further
details contact *Lucia Stuart* at the address in
France from May to September or the London
address from November to April.

Murder Files
81 Churchfields Drive, Bovey Tracey, Devon
TQ13 9QU
☎01626 833487 Fax 01626 835797
Email enquiry@murderfiles.com
Website www.murderfiles.com

Contact *Paul Williams*

FOUNDED 1994. Crime writer and researcher
specialising in UK murders. Holds information

on thousands of well-known and less well-known murders dating from 1400 to the present day. Copies of press cuttings available from 1920 onwards. Details of executions, particularly at the Tyburn and Newgate. Information on British hangmen. Specialist in British police murders since 1700. Service available to general enquirers, writers, researchers, TV, radio, video, etc.

Netcontent
42 Brigstocke Terrace, Ryde, Isle of Wight PO33 2PD
☎0870 741 5802 Fax 0870 163 9835
Email netcontent@healthguider.com
Contacts *Dr Jeremy Sims, Dr Sean Radford*

FOUNDED 1999. Develops content for both paper-based and web-based publishers. Currently has access to over 200 writers. Provides content for magazines, newspapers and websites across a broad range of subjects including quizzes, puzzles, crosswords, health, travel, entertainment and information technology.

Ormrod Research Services
Weeping Birch, Burwash, East Sussex TN19 7HG
☎01435 882541 Fax 01435 882541
Contact *Richard Ormrod*

ESTABLISHED 1982. Comprehensive research service: literary, historical, academic, biographical, commercial. Verbal quotations available.

Roger Palmer Limited, Media Contracts
Antonia House, 262 Holloway Road, London N7 6NE
☎020 7609 4828 Fax 020 7609 4878
Email contracts@rogerpalmerltd.co.uk
Website www.rogerpalmerltd.co.uk
Contact *Peter Palmer*

ESTABLISHED 1993. Drafts, advises on and negotiates all media contracts (on a regular or *ad hoc* basis) for publishers, literary and merchandising agents, authors, packagers, charities and others. Manages and operates clients' complete contracts functions, undertakes contractual audits, devises contracts and permissions systems, advises on copyright and related issues and provides training and seminars on an individual or group basis. Extensive private client list, with special rates for members of the **Society of Authors** and the **Writers' Guild**.

Patent Research
Dachsteinstr. 12a, D–81825 Munich, Germany
☎00 49 89 430 7833
Contact *Gerhard Everwyn*

All world, historical patents for researchers, authors, archives, museums and publishers. Rates on application.

Teral Research Services
45 Forest View Road, Moordown, Bournemouth, Dorset BH9 3BH
☎01202 516834 Fax 01202 516834
Contact *Terry C. Treadwell*

All aspects of research undertaken but specialises in all military, aviation, naval and defence subjects, both past and present. Extensive book and photographic library, including a leading collection of World War One aviation photographs. Terms by arrangement.

Melanie Wilson
Ten Steps, Church Street, Seagrave LE12 7LT
☎01509 812806 Fax 01509 812334
Email MelanieWilson@bigfoot.com
Contact *Melanie Wilson*

Comprehensive research service for books, magazines, newspapers, documentaries, films, radio, education, TV drama. Includes free worldwide booksearch service and groundwork for factual basis for all media presentations, particularly in historical research, costume and textiles, crafts, food and cooking, weapons and uniforms, traditional storytelling, past technology, living history displays and exhibitions.

Press Cuttings Agencies

BMC News

89½ Worship Street, London EC2A 2BF
☎020 7377 1742 Fax 020 7377 6103
Website www.bmc.com

Television, radio, national and European press monitoring agency. Cuttings from national and all major European press available seven days a week, with early morning delivery. Also monitoring of all news and current affairs programmes – national, international and satellite. Retrospective research service and free telephone notification. Sponsorship evaluation from all media sources.

Clipserver

Newserve House, Singer Street, London EC2A 4BQ
☎020 7959 1200 Fax 020 7959 1201
Email info@clipserver.com
Website www.clipserver.com

Contact *Gary Forrest*

Offers an overnight national and international press monitoring service with same day, early morning delivery. Also coverage of European and regional papers, and weekly/monthly business/trade magazines. Rates on application.

Durrants Press Cuttings Ltd

Discovery House, 28–42 Banner Street, London EC1Y 8QE
☎020 7674 0200 Fax 020 7674 0222
Email contact@durrants.co.uk
Website www.durrants.co.uk

Wide coverage of all print media sectors; foreign press in association with agencies abroad; current affairs and news programmes from UK broadcast media. High speed, early morning press cuttings from the national press. Overnight delivery via courier to most areas or first-class mail. Well pre-

sented, laser printed, A4 cuttings. Rates on application.

International Press–Cutting Bureau

224–236 Walworth Road, London SE17 1JE
☎020 7708 2113 Fax 020 7701 4489
Email ipcb2000@aol.com

Contact *Robert Podro*

Covers national, provincial, trade, technical and magazine press. Cuttings are normally sent twice weekly by first-class post and there are no additional service charges or reading fees. Subscriptions for 100 and 250 cuttings are valid for six months. 100 cuttings, £250; £500 (plus VAT).

Romeike Media Intelligence

Hale House, 290–296 Green Lanes, London N13 5TP
☎0800 289543 Fax 020 8882 6716
Email info@romeike.com
Website www.romeike.com

Contact *Mary Michael*

Monitors national and international dailies and Sundays, provincial papers, consumer magazines, trade and technical journals, teletext services as well as national radio and TV networks. Back research, advertising checking and Internet monitoring are also available.

We Find It (Press Clippings)

103 South Parade, Belfast BT7 2GN
☎028 9064 6008 Fax 028 9064 6008

Contact *Avril Forsythe*

Specialises in Northern Ireland press and magazines, both national and provincial. Rates on application.

Bursaries, Fellowships and Grants

Amazon.co.uk Writers' Bursaries

Amazon.co.uk., Patriot Court, 1–9 The
Grove, Slough, Berkshire SL1 1QP
☎020 8636 9200 Fax 020 8636 9400
Website www.amazon.co.uk

Contact *Rachel Holmes*

FOUNDED 2000. Annual scheme 'to mark
Amazon.co.uk.'s commitment to literature'.
Entrants must have published one previous
novel or volume of short stories in the past two
years. Recommendations by publishers only.
2000 winners: James Flint, Justina Robson.

Award £2500 plus three-month sabbatical
post.

Aosdána

An Chomhairle Ealaíon (The Irish Arts
Council), 70 Merrion Square, Dublin 2,
Republic of Ireland
☎00 353 1 6180200 Fax 00 353 1 6761302
Email aosdana@artscouncil.ie
Website www.artscouncil.ie/aosdana

Aosdána is an affiliation of creative artists
engaged in literature, music and the visual arts,
and consists of not more than 200 artists who
have gained a reputation for achievement and
distinction. Membership is by competitive
sponsored selection and is open to Irish citizens
or residents only. Members are eligible to
receive an annuity for a five-year term to assist
them in pursuing their art full-time.

Arts Council Literature Bursaries, Ireland

An Chomhairle Ealaíon (The Irish Arts
Council), 70 Merrion Square, Dublin 2,
Republic of Ireland
☎00 353 1 6180200 Fax 00 353 1 6761302
Email info@artscouncil.ie
Website www.artscouncil.ie

Literature Officer *Sinéad Mac Aodha*

Bursaries in literature awarded to creative writers of fiction, poetry and drama in Irish and
English to enable development or completion
of, specific projects. A limited number of bursaries may also be given to non-fiction projects
of a contemporary nature. Open to Irish citizens or residents only.

Awards €5000–10,500/IR£3937–8269 p.a.
(€13,000–20,500/IR£10,238–16,145 (for two-
year bursaries).

Arts Council Theatre Writing Bursaries

Arts Council of England, 14 Great Peter
Street, London SW1P 3NQ
☎020 7973 6431 Fax 020 7973 6983
Email jemima.lee@artscouncil.org.uk
Website www.artscouncil.org.uk

Contact *Theatre Writing Section*

Intended to provide experienced playwrights
with an opportunity to research and develop a
play for the theatre independently of financial
pressures and free from the need to write for a
particular market. Bursaries are also available
for theatre translation projects. Writers must be
resident in England. Writers resident in Wales,
Scotland or Northern Ireland should approach
their own Arts Council.

Award £5500.

Arts Council Theatre Writing Commission Award

Arts Council of England, 14 Great Peter
Street, London SW1P 3NQ
☎020 7973 6431 Fax 020 7973 6983
Email jemima.lee@artscouncil.org.uk
Website www.artscouncil.org.uk

Contact *Theatre Writing Section*

Theatre companies and groups based in
England can apply for a grant of up to half the
cost of paying a writer (resident anywhere in
the UK) a commission or fee to write a new
play, to secure the rights to an unperformed
play or to rewrite an unperformed play. The
theatre company or organisation is expected to
find at least half the cost of the fee from their
own resources. Commissions are also available
for theatre translation projects. Further details
available from the theatre writing section.

The Authors' Contingency Fund

The Society of Authors, 84 Drayton Gardens,
London SW10 9SB
☎020 7373 6642 Fax 020 7373 5768

This fund makes modest grants to published

authors who find themselves in sudden financial difficulties. Contact the **Society of Authors** for an information sheet and application form.

The Authors' Foundation

The Society of Authors, 84 Drayton Gardens, London SW10 9SB
☎020 7373 6642 Fax 020 7373 5768

Grants to writers whose publisher's advance is insufficient to cover the costs of research involved. Application by letter to The Authors' Foundation giving details, in confidence, of the advance and royalties, together with the reasons for needing additional funding. Grants are sometimes given even if there is no commitment by a publisher, so long as the applicant has had a book published and the new work will almost certainly be published. About £80,000 is distributed each year. Contact the **Society of Authors** for an information sheet. Final entry dates: 30 April and 31 October.

The K. Blundell Trust

The Society of Authors, 84 Drayton Gardens, London SW10 9SB
☎020 7373 6642 Fax 020 7373 5768

Grants to writers whose publisher's advance is insufficient to cover the costs of research. Author must be under 40, has to submit a copy of his/her previous book and the work must 'contribute to the greater understanding of existing social and economic organisation'. Application by letter. Contact the **Society of Authors** for an information sheet. Final entry dates: 30 April and 31 October.

Alfred Bradley Bursary Award

c/o BBC Radio Drama, Room 1119, New Broadcasting House, Oxford Road, Manchester M60 1SJ
☎0161 244 4252 Fax 0161 244 4248

Contact *Coordinator*

ESTABLISHED 1992. Biennial award in commemoration of the life and work of the distinguished radio producer Alfred Bradley. Aims to encourage and develop new radio writing talent in the BBC North region. There is a change of focus for each award, e.g. previous years have targeted comedy drama, verse drama, etc. Entrants must live or work in the North region. The award is given to help writers to pursue a career in writing for radio. The next award will be lauched in spring 2002, with a deadline for scripts in autumn 2002. Previous winners: Lee Hall, Mandy Precious, Peter Straughan, Pam Leeson.

Award Up to £6000 over two years and a BBC Radio Drama commission, the opportunity to develop further ideas with Radio Drama.

British Academy Small Personal Research Grants

10 Carlton House Terrace, London SW1Y 5AH
☎020 7969 5200 Fax 020 7969 5300
Website www.britac.ac.uk

Contact *Assistant Secretary, Research Grants*

Quarterly award to further original creative research at postdoctoral level in the humanities and social sciences. Entrants must no longer be registered for postgraduate study, and must be resident in the UK. Final entry dates: end of September, November, February and April.

Award £5000 (maximum).

Cholmondeley Awards

The Society of Authors, 84 Drayton Gardens, London SW10 9SB
☎020 7373 6642 Fax 020 7373 5768

FOUNDED 1965 by the late Dowager Marchioness of Cholmondeley. Annual honorary awards to recognise the achievement and distinction of individual poets. 2000 winners: Alistair Elliot, Michael Hamburger, Adrian Henri, Carole Satyamurti.

Award £8000 (total).

The Economist/ Richard Casement Internship

The Economist, 25 St James's Street, London SW1A 1HG
☎020 7830 7000
Website www.economist.com

Contact *Science Editor (re. Casement Internship)*

For an aspiring journalist under 25 to spend three months in the summer writing for *The Economist* about science and technology. Applicants should write a letter of introduction along with an article of approximately 600 words suitable for inclusion in the Science and Technology Section. Competition details normally announced in the magazine late January or early February and 4–5 weeks allowed for application.

European Jewish Publication Society

PO Box 19948, London N3 3ZJ
☎020 8346 1668 Fax 020 8346 1776
Email cs@ejps.org.uk
Website www.ejps.org.uk

Contact *Dr Colin Shindler*

ESTABLISHED in 1995 to help fund the publication of books of European Jewish interest which would otherwise remain unpublished. Helps with the marketing, distribution and promotion of such books. Publishers who may be interested in publishing works of Jewish interest should approach the Society with a proposal and manuscript in the first instance. Books which have been supported include: *The Vanished Shtetl* Stanislav Brunstein; *Tidings from Zion* Jennifer Glynn; *Botchki* David Zagier; *Just One More Dance* Ernest Levy. Also supports the publication of poetry, and translations from and into other European languages.

Grant £3000 (maximum).

Fulbright Awards

The Fulbright Commission, Fulbright House, 62 Doughty Street, London WC1N 2JZ
☎020 7404 6880 Fax 020 7404 6834
Website www.fulbright.co.uk

Contact *British Programme Manager*

The Fulbright Commission has a number of scholarships given at postgraduate level and above, open to any field (science and the arts) of study/research to be undertaken in the USA. Length of award is typically an academic year. Application deadline for postgraduate awards is usually late October/early November of preceding year of study; and mid-March/early April for distinguished scholar awards. Further details and application forms are available on the Commission's website. Alternatively, send A4 envelope with sufficient postage for 100g with a covering letter explaining which level of award is of interest.

Fulton Fellowship

David Fulton (Publishers) Ltd, Ormond House, 26/27 Boswell Street, London WC1N 3JD
☎020 7405 5606 Fax 020 7831 4840
Email david.fulton@fultonbooks.co.uk
Website www.fultonbooks.co.uk

Chairman and Publisher *David Fulton*
Managing Director *David Hill*

The Fulton Fellowship in Special Education was ESTABLISHED in 1995 and is administered by the Centre for Special Education, University College, Worcester. The Fellowship, worth £2000, has been extended to offer schools as well as individual teachers the chance to share work their staff have done or are doing collaboratively through written publication to a wider audience. 2000 Fellow: Mordaunt School, Southampton.

Tony Godwin Memorial Trust

c/o Laurence Pollinger Limited, 9 Staple Inn, London WC1V 7QH
☎020 7404 0342 Fax 020 7242 5737
Email info@tgmt.org.uk
Website www.tgmt.org.uk

Contact *Lesley Hadcroft*
Chairman *Iain Brown* (020 7627 4244)

Biennial award established to commemorate the life of Tony Godwin, a prominent publisher in the 1960s/70s. Open to all young people (under 35 years old) who are UK nationals and working, or intending to work, in publishing. The award provides the recipient with the means to spend at least one month as the guest of an American publishing house in order to learn about international publishing. The recipient is expected to submit a report upon return to the UK. Next award: 2002; final entry date: 31 December 2001. Previous winners: George Lucas (Hodder), Clive Priddle (Fourth Estate), Richard Scrivener (Penguin), Lisa Shakespeare (Weidenfeld & Nicolson), Fiona Stewart (HarperCollins).

Award Bursary of approx. US$5000.

Eric Gregory Trust Fund

The Society of Authors, 84 Drayton Gardens, London SW10 9SB
☎020 7373 6642 Fax 020 7373 5768

Annual awards of varying amounts are made for the encouragement of poets under the age of 30 on the basis of a submitted collection. Open only to British-born subjects resident in the UK. Final entry date: 31 October. Contact the **Society of Authors** for further information. 2000 winners: Eleanor Margolies, Antony Rowland, Antony Dunn, Karen Goodwin, Clare Pollard.

Award £24,000 (total).

The Guardian Research Fellowship

Nuffield College, Oxford OX1 1NF
☎01865 278520 Fax 01865 278676

Contact *Warden's Secretary*

One-year fellowship endowed by the Scott Trust, owner of *The Guardian*, to give someone working in the media the chance to put their experience into a new perspective, publish the outcome and give a *Guardian* lecture. Applications welcomed from journalists and management members, in newspapers, periodicals or broadcasting. Research or study proposals should be directly related to experience of working in the media. Accommodation and meals in college will be provided and a stipend. Advertised biennially in November.

Hawthornden Castle Fellowship

Hawthornden Castle, The International Retreat for Writers, Lasswade, Midlothian EH18 1EG
☎0131 440 2180

Contact *The Administrator*

ESTABLISHED 1982 to provide a peaceful setting where published writers can work without disturbance. The Retreat houses five writers at a time, who are known as Hawthornden Fellows. Writers from any part of the world may apply for the fellowships. No monetary assistance is given, nor any contribution to travelling expenses, but once arrived at Hawthornden, the writer is the guest of the Retreat. Applications on forms provided must be made by the end of September for the following calendar year. Previous winners include: Les Murray, Alasdair Gray, Helen Vendler, Olive Senior, Hilary Spurling.

Francis Head Bequest

The Society of Authors, 84 Drayton Gardens, London SW10 9SB
☎020 7373 6642 Fax 020 7373 5768

Provides grants to published British authors over the age of 35 who need financial help during a period of illness, disablement or temporary financial crisis. Contact the **Society of Authors** for an information sheet and application form.

Ralph Lewis Award

University of Sussex Library, Brighton, East Sussex BN1 9QL
☎01273 678158 Fax 01273 678441
Email p.a.ringshaw@sussex.ac.uk

ESTABLISHED 1985. Occasional award set up by Ralph Lewis, a Brighton author and art collector who left money to fund awards for promising manuscripts which would not otherwise be published. The award is given in the form of a grant to a UK-based publisher in respect of an agreed three-year programme of publication of literary works by new authors or by established authors using new styles or forms. No direct applications from writers. Previous winners: **Peterloo Poets** (1989–91); **Serpent's Tail** (1992–94); **Stride Publications** (1997–99).

Macaulay Fellowship

An Chomhairle Ealaíon (The Irish Arts Council), 70 Merrion Square, Dublin 2, Republic of Ireland
☎00 353 1 6180200 Fax 00 353 1 6761302

Email info@artscouncil.ie
Website www.artscouncil.ie
Literature Officer *Sinéad Mac Aodha*

To further the liberal education of a young creative artist. Candidates for this triennial award must be under 30 on 30 June, or 35 in exceptional circumstances, and must be Irish citizens or residents. The Fellowship is offered on rotation between Music, Visual Arts and Literature (Music in 2001).
Award €5000/IR£3937.

The John Masefield Memorial Trust

The Society of Authors, 84 Drayton Gardens, London SW10 9SB
☎020 7373 6642 Fax 020 7373 5768

This trust makes occasional grants to professional poets (or their immediate dependants) who are faced with sudden financial problems. Contact the **Society of Authors** for an information sheet and application form.

Somerset Maugham Trust Fund

The Society of Authors, 84 Drayton Gardens, London SW10 9SB
☎020 7373 6642 Fax 020 7373 5768

Annual awards designed to encourage writers under the age of 35 to travel. Given on the basis of a published work of fiction, non-fiction or poetry. Open only to British-born subjects resident in the UK. Final entry date: 20 December. 2000 winners: Bella Bathurst *The Lighthouse Stevensons*; Sarah Waters *Affinity*.
Awards £12,000 (total).

The Airey Neave Trust

40 Charles Street, London W1J 5EF
☎020 7495 0554 Fax 020 7491 1118

Contact *Hannah Scott*

INITIATED 1989. Annual research fellowships for up to three years – towards a book or paper – for serious research connected with national and international law, and human freedom. Must be attached to a particular university in Britain. Interested applicants should come forward with ideas, preferably before March in any year.

Newspaper Press Fund

Dickens House, 35 Wathen Road, Dorking, Surrey RH4 1JY
☎01306 887511 Fax 01306 888212

Director/Secretary *David Ilott*

Aims to relieve distress among journalists and

their dependants. Limited help available to non-member journalists. Continuous and/or occasional financial grants; also retirement homes for eligible beneficiaries. Further information and subscription details available from the Secretary or via the Reuter Foundation website on: www.foundation.reuters.com/npf

Northern Arts Literary Fellowship
Northern Arts, Central Square, Forth Street, Newcastle upon Tyne NE1 3PJ
☎0191 255 8500 Fax 0191 230 1020

Contact *Film, Media & Literature Department*

A competitive fellowship in association with the Universities of Durham and Newcastle upon Tyne. Contact Northern Arts for details.

Northern Playwriting Panel
See **New Writing North** under **Professional Associations and Societies**

Northern Writers' Awards
See **New Writing North** under **Professional Associations and Societies**

The PAWS (Public Awareness of Science) Drama Script Fund
The PAWS Office, OMNI Communications, Chancel House, Neasden Lane, London NW10 2TU
☎020 8214 1543 Fax 020 8214 1544
Email pawsomni@globalnet.co.uk

Contacts *Barrie Whatley, Andrew Millington*

ESTABLISHED 1994. Annual award aimed at encouraging television scriptwriters to include science and engineering scenarios in their work. Grants (currently £2000) are given to selected writers to develop their script ideas into full treatments; prizes are awarded for the best of these treatments. The PAWS Fund holds meetings enabling writers to meet scientists and engineers and also offers a contacts service to put writers in 'one-to-one' contact with specialists who can help them develop their ideas. See also **The PAWS Midas Prize** under **Prizes**.

Pearson Playwrights' Scheme
3 Burlington Gardens, London W1X 1LE

Administrator *Jack Andrews*

Awards four bursaries to playwrights annually, each worth £5000. Applicants must be sponsored by a theatre which then submits the play for consideration by a panel. Each award allows the playwright a twelve-month attachment. Applications invited via theatres in October each year. For up-to-date information, contact *Jack Andrews* (☎020 8943 8176).

The Margaret Rhondda Award
The Society of Authors, 84 Drayton Gardens, London SW10 9SB
☎020 7373 6642 Fax 020 7373 5768

Competitive award given to a woman writer as a grant-in-aid towards the expenses of a research project in journalism. Contact the **Society of Authors** for an information sheet. Triennial (next award: 2005). Final entry date: 20 December 2004. 1999 winner: Sue Branford.
Award approx. £1000.

The Royal Literary Fund
3 Johnson's Court, off Fleet Street, London EC4A 3EA
☎020 7353 7150 Fax 020 7353 1350
Email egunnrlf@globalnet.co.uk

Secretary *Eileen Gunn*

Grants and pensions are awarded to published authors in financial need, or to their dependants. Examples of author's works are needed for assessment by Committee. Write for further details and application form.

Scottish Arts Council Book Awards
Scottish Arts Council, 12 Manor Place, Edinburgh EH3 7DD
☎0131 226 6051 Fax 0131 225 9833
Email gavin.wallace@scottisharts.org.uk
Website www.sac.org.uk

Contact *Gavin Wallace, Literature Officer*

Four awards of £1000 each are made in both spring and autumn. Preference is given to literary fiction and verse, but literary non-fiction is also considered. Authors should be Scottish or resident in Scotland, but books of Scottish interest by other authors are eligible for consideration. Applications from publishers only.

Scottish Arts Council Creative Scotland Awards
Scottish Arts Council, 12 Manor Place, Edinburgh EH3 7DD
☎0131 240 2443/ Help Desk: 0131 240 2443/4 Fax 0131 225 9833
Email administrator@scottisharts.org.uk
Website www.sac.org.uk

This scheme provides awards of £25,000 each

to established artists based in Scotland working in any medium, including writing and who have already made an important contribution in their field. The aim of this is to provide them with a major opportunity to experiment, to refresh their skills and to realise imaginative ideas. Closing date: October 2001; awards announced 25 January 2002.

Scottish Arts Council Writers' Bursaries

Scottish Arts Council, 12 Manor Place, Edinburgh EH3 7DD
☎0131 226 6051 Fax 0131 225 9833
Email jenny.brown@scottisharts.org.uk
Website www.sac.org.uk

Contact *Jenny Brown, Literature Director*

A limited number of bursaries – of between £3000 and £10,000 – are offered to enable professional writers, including writers for children, to devote more time to writing. Priority is given to writers of fiction and verse, but writers of literary non-fiction are also considered. Application normally open only to writers who have been living and working in Scotland for at least two years.

Laurence Stern Fellowship

Department of Journalism, City University, Northampton Square, London EC1V 0HB
☎020 7040 8224 Fax 020 7040 8594
Website www.city.ac.uk/journalism

Contact *Bob Jones*

FOUNDED 1980. Awarded to a young journalist experienced enough to work on national stories. It gives them the chance to work on the national desk of the *Washington Post*. Benjamin Bradlee, the *Post*'s Vice-President-at-Large, selects from a shortlist drawn up in March/April. 2001 winner: Glenda Cooper. Full details available on the website.

Tom-Gallon Trust

The Society of Authors, 84 Drayton Gardens, London SW10 9SB
☎020 7373 6642 Fax 020 7373 5768

A biennial award made on the basis of a submitted story to fiction writers of limited means who have had at least one short story accepted for publication. Contact the **Society of Authors** for an information sheet. Final entry date 20 September 2002.
Award £1000.

The Betty Trask Awards

The Society of Authors, 84 Drayton Gardens, London SW10 9SB
☎020 7373 6642 Fax 020 7373 5768

These annual awards are for authors who are under 35 and Commonwealth citizens, awarded on the strength of a first novel (published or unpublished) of a traditional or romantic nature. The awards must be used for a period or periods of foreign travel. Final entry date: 31 January. Contact the **Society of Authors** for an information sheet. 2000 winners: Jonathan Tulloch *The Season Ticket*; Julia Leigh *The Hunter*; Susan Elderkin *Sunset Over Chocolate Mountains*; Galaxy Craze *By the Shore*; Nicholas Griffin *The Requiem Shark*.
Award £25,000 (total).

The Travelling Scholarships

The Society of Authors, 84 Drayton Gardens, London SW10 9SB
☎020 7373 6642 Fax 020 7373 5768

Annual honorary grants to established British writers. 2000 winners: Robert Edric, Georgina Hammick, Grace Ingoldby, Walter Perrie.
Award £6000 (total).

UEA Writing Fellowship

University of East Anglia, University Plain, Norwich, Norfolk NR4 7TJ
☎01603 592734 Fax 01603 593522

Director of Personnel & Registry Services
J.R.L. Beck

ESTABLISHED 1971. Awarded to a writer of established reputation in prose fiction and poetry for a period of six months, January to end June. The duties of the Fellowship are discussed at an interview. It is assumed that one activity will be the pursuit of the Fellow's own writing. In addition the Fellow will be expected to (a) offer an undergraduate creative writing workshop in the School of English and American Studies during the Spring semester; (b) make contact with groups around the county in association with **East England Arts**. Office space and some limited secretarial assistance will be provided, and some additional funds will be available to help the Fellow with the activities described above. Applications for the fellowship should be lodged with the Director of Personnel & Registry Services in the autumn; candidates should submit two examples of recent work. Previous winner: Roger Garfitt.
Award £7500 plus free flat on campus.

Prizes

ABSW/Glaxo Science Writers' Awards

Association of British Science Writers, 23 Savile Row, London W1X 2NB
☎020 7439 1205 Fax 020 7973 3051

ABSW Administrator *Barbara Drillsma*

A series of annual awards for outstanding science journalism in newspapers, journals and broadcasting.

J.R. Ackerley Prize

English Centre of International PEN, 152–156 Kentish Town Road, London NW1 9QB
☎020 7267 9444 Fax 020 7267 9304
Email enquiries@pen.org.uk
Website www.pen.org.uk

Commemorating the novelist/autobiographer J.R. Ackerley, this prize is awarded for a literary autobiography, written in English and published in the year preceding the award. Entry restricted to nominations from the Ackerley Trustees only ('please do not submit books'). 2000 winner: Mark Frankland *Child of My Time.*

Acorn–Rukeyser Chapbook Contest

Mekler & Deahl, Publishers, 237 Prospect Street South, Hamilton, Ontario, Canada L8M 2Z6
☎001 905 312 1779 Fax 001 905 312 8285
Email james@meklerdeahl.com
Website www.meklerdeahl.com

Contacts *James Deahl, Gilda Mekler*

ESTABLISHED in 1996, this annual award is named after the poets Milton Acorn and Muriel Rukeyser in order to honour their achievements as populist poets. Poets may enter as many as 30 poems for a fee of £5. Final entry date: 31 October. Contact the above address for a copy of the rules or access the website.

Prizes 1st and 2nd, US$100 and publication of the manuscript.

Aldeburgh Poetry Festival Prize

Reading Room Yard, The Street, Brockdish, Diss, Norfolk IP21 4JZ
☎01379 668345 Fax 01379 668844

Contact *Naomi Jaffa*

ESTABLISHED 1989 by the Aldeburgh Poetry Trust. Sponsored by the Aldeburgh Bookshop for the best first collection published in Britain or the Republic of Ireland in the preceding twelve months. Open to any first collection of poetry of at least 40pp. Final entry date: 1 October. Previous winners include: Donald Atkinson, Susan Wicks, Gwyneth Lewis, Glyn Wright, Robin Robertson, Tamar Yoseloff, Colette Bryce.

Prize £500, plus an invitation to read at the following year's festival.

Alexander Prize

Royal Historical Society, University College London, Gower Street, London WC1E 6BT
☎020 7387 7532 Fax 020 7387 7532

Contact *Executive Secretary*

Awarded for a historical essay of not more than 8000 words. Competitors may choose their own subject for the essay. Closing date: 1 November.

Prize £250 or a silver medal.

An Duais don bhFilíocht i nGaeilge

An Chomhairle Ealaíon (The Irish Arts Council), 70 Merrion Square, Dublin 2, Republic of Ireland
☎00 353 1 6180200 Fax 00 353 1 6761302
Email info@artscouncil.ie
Website www.artscouncil.ie

Literature Officer *Sinéad Mac Aodha*

Triennial award for the best book of Irish poetry. Works must have been published in the Irish language in the preceding three years. Next award in 2004.

Prize €4000/IR£3150.

Hans Christian Andersen Awards

IBBY, Nonnenweg 12, Postfach, CH-4003 Basel, Switzerland
☎00 41 61 272 2917 Fax 00 41 61 272 2757
Email ibby@eye.ch
Website www.ibby.org

Executive Director *Leena Maissen*

The highest international prizes for children's literature: The Hans Christian Andersen Award for Writing ESTABLISHED 1956; The Hans Christian Andersen Award for Illustration ESTABLISHED

1966. Candidates are nominated by National Sections of IBBY (The International Board on Books for Young People). Biennial prizes are awarded, in even-numbered years, to an author and an illustrator whose body of work has made a lasting contribution to children's literature. 2000 winners: Award for Writing: Ana Maria Machado (Brazil); Award for Illustration: Anthony Browne (UK).

Award Gold medals.

Angus Book Award
Angus Council Cultural Services, County Buildings, Forfar DD8 3WF
☎01307 461460 Fax 01307 462590

Contact *Norman Atkinson (Director of Cultural Services)*

ESTABLISHED 1995. Designed to try to help teenagers develop an interest in and enthusiasm for reading. Eligible books are read and voted on by third-year schoolchildren in all eight Angus secondary schools. 2000 winner: Tim Bowler *Shadows*.

Prize £250 cheque, plus trophy in the form of a replica Pictish stone.

Annual Theatre Book Prize
See **The Society for Theatre Research Annual Theatre Book Prize**

Arts Council Children's Award
Arts Council of England, 14 Great Peter Street, London SW1P 3NQ
☎020 7973 6431 Fax 020 7973 6983
Email jemima.lee@artscouncil.org.uk
Website www.artscouncil.org.uk

Contact *Theatre Writing Section*

A new annual award for playwrights who write for children. The plays, which must have been produced professionally between 1 July 2001 and 30 June 2002, should be suitable for children up to the age of 12 and be at least 45 minutes long. The playwright must be resident in England. Closing date for entries: 4 July 2002. Contact the Theatre Writing Section for full details and application form.

Award £6000.

Arvon Foundation International Poetry Competition
11 Westbourne Crescent, London W2 3DB
☎020 7262 2788 Fax 020 7262 4004
Email london@arvonfoundation.org
Website www.arvonfoundation.org

Contact *National Administration*

ESTABLISHED 1980. Biennial competition (next in 2002) for poems written in English and not previously broadcast or published. There are no restrictions on the number of lines, themes, age of entrants or nationality. No limit to the number of entries. Entry fee: £5 per poem. Previous winners: Paul Farley *Laws of Gravity*; Don Paterson *A Private Bottling*.

Prize (1st) £5000 and £5000 worth of other prizes sponsored by Duncan Lawrie Limited.

Asher Prize
See **Medical Book Awards**

Authors' Club First Novel Award
Authors' Club, 40 Dover Street, London W1S 4NP
☎020 7499 8581 Fax 020 7409 0913

Contact *Mrs Ann de La Grange*

ESTABLISHED 1954. This award is made for the most promising work published in Britain by a British author, and is presented at a dinner held at the Authors' Club in April. Entries for the award are accepted from publishers by the end of November of the year in question and must be full-length – short stories are not eligible. 2001 winner: Brian Clarke *The Stream*.

Award £750 (sponsored by the Folio Society).

BAAL Book Prize
BAAL Publications Secretary, Department of English Studies, University of Stirling, Stirling FK9 4LA
☎01786 467974 Fax 01786 466210
Email j.l.delin@stir.ac.uk

Contact *Dr Judy Delin*

Annual award made by the British Association for Applied Linguistics to an outstanding book in the field of applied linguistics. Final entry at the end of Oct/Nov. Nominations from publishers only. Previous winners: Susan Berk-Seligson *The Bilingual Courtroom*; Joshua A. Fishman *Reversing Language Shift*; Deborah Cameron *Verbal Hygiene*; Marco Jacquemet *Credibility in Court*; Ana Celia Zentella *Growing Up Bilingual*; Colin Baker and Sylvia Prys Jones *Encyclopedia of Bilingualism and Bilingual Education*.

Barclays Bank Prize
See **Lakeland Book of the Year Awards**

Verity Bargate Award
The Soho Theatre Company, 21 Dean Street, London W1D 3NE
☎020 7287 5060 Fax 020 7287 5061
Email writers@sohotheatre.com

Contact *Jo Ingham, Literary Officer*

The award was set up to commemorate the late Verity Bargate, founder and director of the **Soho Theatre Company**. This national award is presented biennially for a new and unperformed play (next in 2002). To go on the mailing list, please send s.a.e. to Sara Murray or e-mail. Previous winners include: Shan Khan, Fraser Grace, Lyndon Morgans, Adrian Pagan, Diane Samuels, Judy Upton and Toby Whithouse.

The Herb Barrett Award

Mekler & Deahl, Publishers, 237 Prospect Street South, Hamilton, Ontario, Canada L8M 2Z6
☎001 905 312 1779 Fax 001 905 312 8285
Email james@meklerdeahl.com
Website www.meklerdeahl.com
Contact *James Deahl*

ESTABLISHED in 1996, this annual award is named in honour of Herb Barrett, founder of the Hamilton Chapter of the Canadian Poetry Association. Poets may enter up to 10 haiku for a fee of £5. Final entry date: 30 November. Contact the address above for a copy of the rules or access the website.

Prize (US) $200, $150 and $100; anthology publication for the winners and all other worthy entries.

BBC Wildlife Magazine Awards for Nature Writing

PO Box 229, Bristol BS99 7JN
☎0117 973 8402 Fax 0117 946 7075
Email nina.epton@bbc.co.uk
Contact *Nina Epton*

Annual competition for professional and amateur writers. Entries (no longer than 1000 words) should be based on personal observations of, or thoughts about, nature – general or specific. The entry form appears in the magazine; closing date varies.

Prizes Winner: £500 plus publication in the magazine; runners-up: cash prizes plus publication; two young writers' awards.

BBC Wildlife Magazine Poet of the Year Awards

PO Box 229, Bristol BS99 7JN
☎0117 973 8402 Fax 0117 946 7075
Email nina.epton@bbc.co.uk
Contact *Nina Epton*

Annual award for a poem, the subject of which must be the natural world and/or our relationship with it. Entrants may submit one poem only of no more than 50 lines with the entry

form which appears in the magazine. New category for limericks with wildlife or environmental theme. Closing date for entries varies from year to year.

Prizes Poet of the Year: £500, publication in the magazine, plus reading of the poem on Radio 4's *Poetry Please*; runners-up: cash prizes plus publication in the magazine; four young poets awards. Winning limerick: £100.

David Berry Prize

Royal Historical Society, University College London, Gower Street, London WC1E 6BT
☎020 7387 7532 Fax 020 7387 7532
Contact *Executive Secretary*

Annual award for an essay of not more than 10,000 words on Scottish history. Closing date: 31 October.

Prize £250.

Besterman/McColvin Medal

See **The Library Association Besterman/McColvin Medal**

The Biographers' Club Prize

17 Sutherland Street, London SW1V 4JU
☎020 7828 1274 Fax 020 7828 7608
Email lownie@globalnet.co.uk
Website www.andrewlownie.co.uk
Contact *Andrew Lownie*

ESTABLISHED 1999 by literary agent, biographer and founder of the Biographers' Club, Andrew Lownie, to finance and encourage first-time writers researching a biography. Open to previously un-commissioned writers producing a proposal of 15–20 pp, broken down by chapter with a note of author's credentials, the market for the book, sources used and competing/comparable books. 2000 winner: Adrienne Gavin.

Prize £1000.

Birdwatch Bird Book of the Year

c/o Birdwatch Magazine, 3D/F Leroy House, 436 Essex Road, Islington, London N1 3QP
☎020 7704 9495
Contact *Dominic Mitchell*

ESTABLISHED in 1992 to acknowledge excellence in ornithological publishing – an increasingly large market with a high turnover. Annual award. Entries, from publishers, must offer an original and comprehensive treatment of their particular ornithological subject matter and must have a broad appeal to British-based readers. 2000 winner: *Collins Bird Guide* Killian Mullarney, Lars Svensson, Dan Zetterstrom, Peter Grant.

James Tait Black Memorial Prizes

University of Edinburgh, David Hume Tower, George Square, Edinburgh EH8 9JX
☎0131 650 3619 Fax 0131 650 6898

Contact *Department of English Literature*

ESTABLISHED in 1918 in memory of a partner of the publishing firm of **A.&C. Black Ltd**. Two prizes, one for biography and one for fiction. Closing date for submissions: 30 September. Each prize is awarded for a book published in Britain in the previous twelve months. Prize winners are announced in December each year. 2000 winners: Martin Amis *Experience*; Zadie Smith *White Teeth*. *Prizes* £3000 each.

The Robert Bloomfield Memorial Awards for Rustic Poetry

Hilton House (Publishers), Hilton House, 39 Long John Hill, Norwich, Norfolk NR1 2JP
☎01603 660224

Contact *Michael K. Moore*

Annual competition to publicise the works of the Suffolk poet and to promote descriptive poetry with a rural theme, drawing attention to the wonders of nature in the British and Irish countryside and emphasising the necessity for protecting the environment and wildlife. Entry forms available from 2 January on receipt of s.a.e. or two IRCs. Closing date: 30 September. Previous winners: Lynne Wycherley, Anna Wigley. Cash *prizes* £100; £50; £25. All winners, runners-up and commended poets receive complimentary copy of awards booklet containing their winning poems. The three main winners are also published in *Advance! – Poetry Quarterly*

Boardman Tasker Award

14 Pine Lodge, Dairyground Road, Bramhall, Stockport, Cheshire SK7 2HS
☎0161 439 4624 Fax 0161 439 4624

Contact *Dorothy Boardman*

ESTABLISHED 1983, this award is given for a work of fiction, non-fiction or poetry, whose central theme is concerned with the mountain environment and which can be said to have made an outstanding contribution to mountain literature. Authors of any nationality are eligible, but the book must have been published or distributed in the UK for the first time between 1 November 2000 and 31 October 2001. Entries from publishers only. 2000 winner: Peter and Leni Gillman *The Wildest Dream*. *Prize* £2000 (at Trustees' discretion).

Bollinger Everyman Wodehouse Prize

Everyman Publishers, Gloucester Mansions, 140A Shaftesbury Avenue, London WC2H 8HD
☎020 7539 7608 Fax 020 7379 4060
Email becke@everyman.uk.com
Website www.everyman.uk.com

Contact *Becke Parker*

ESTABLISHED in 2000 by David Campbell, publisher of Everyman's Library, and the **Sunday Times Hay Festival** to celebrate comic writing in memory of P.G. Wodehouse. Books are nominated by readers of the *Sunday Times* and visitors to www.bol.com. 2000 winner: Howard Jacobson *The Mighty Waltzer*.

Booker Prize for Fiction

Book Trust, Book House, 45 East Hill, London SW18 2QZ
☎020 8516 2973 Fax 020 8516 2978
Email sandra@booktrust.org.uk
Website www.booktrust.org.uk

Contact *Sandra Vince*

The leading British literary prize, set up in 1968 by Booker McConnell Ltd, with the intention of rewarding merit, raising the stature of the author in the eyes of the public and increasing the sale of the books. The announcement of the winner has been televised live since 1981, and all books on the shortlist experience a substantial increase in sales. Eligible novels must be written in English by a citizen of Britain, the Commonwealth, the Republic of Ireland or South Africa, and must be published in the UK for the first time between 1 October and 30 September of the year of the prize. Self-published books are no longer accepted. Entries are accepted from UK publishers who may each submit not more than two novels within the appropriate scheduled publication dates. The judges may also ask for certain other eligible novels to be submitted to them. Annual award. 2000 winner: Margaret Atwood, *The Blind Assassin*. Previous winners include: J.M. Coetzee *Disgrace*; Ian McEwan *Amsterdam*; Arundhati Roy *God of Small Things*; Graham Swift *Last Orders*; Pat Barker *The Ghost Road*; James Kelman *How Late It Was, How Late*. *Prize* £20,000 winner; £1000, shortlist.

The Books for Children Award

BCA, Greater London House, Hampstead Road, London NW1 7TZ
☎020 7760 6500 Fax 020 7760 6829

Contact *Books for Children Editor*

ESTABLISHED 1979. Formerly known as the BFC Mother Goose Award. Annual award open to writers and illustrators of a first children's work published in the UK. Previous winner: Niamh Sharkey *The Gigantic Turnip* and *Tales of Wisdom and Wonder*.
Prize £1000.

Author of the Year Award
Booksellers Association Ltd
Booksellers Association Ltd, 272 Vauxhall Bridge Road, London SW1V 1BA
☎020 7834 5477 Fax 020 7834 8812
Email denise.bayat@booksellers.org.uk
Website www.booksellers.org.uk
Contact *Denise Bayat*

Founded as part of the BA Annual Conference to involve authors more closely in the event. Authors must be British or Irish. Not an award open to entry but voted on by the BA's membership. 2001 winner: Philip Pullman.
Award £1000 plus trophy.

Border Television Prize
See **Lakeland Book of the Year Awards**

The Harry Bowling Prize
c/o MBA Literary Agents, 62 Grafton Way, London W1T 5DW
☎020 7387 2076 Fax 020 7387 2042
Email laura@mbalit.co.uk
Contact *Laura Longrigg*

ESTABLISHED in 2000 in honour of Harry Bowling, 'the King of Cockney sagas' who died in 1999. Biennial award, sponsored by **Headline Book Publishing**, aimed at encouraging new, unpublished fiction. Open to anyone who has not had an adult novel published in any genre, including under a pseudonym. Entries must be set in London and in the storytelling tradition of Harry Bowling but not necessarily confined to any particular fiction genre, past or present. Final entry date: 31 March 2002. Entry forms from MBA Literary Agents (enclose s.a.e.). Entry fee charged. 2000 winner: P.J.P. Granger *Not All Tarts Are Apple*.

The BP Natural World Book Prize
Book Trust, Book House, 45 East Hill, London SW18 2QZ
☎020 8516 2973 Fax 020 8516 2978
Email sandra@booktrust.org.uk
Website www.booktrust.org.uk
Contact *Sandra Vince*

ESTABLISHED in 1996 as an amalgamation of the Natural World Book Prize (the magazine of the Wildlife Trusts) and the BP Conservation Book Prize. Award for a book on creative conservation of the environment. Entries from UK publishers only. 2000 winner: Brian Clarke *The Stream*.
Prizes (1st) £5000; Runner-up: £1000.

The Branford Boase Award
18 Grosvenor Road, Portswood, Southampton, Hampshire SO17 1RT
☎023 8055 5057
Email locol@compuserve.com
Website www.henriettabranford.co.uk
Administrator *Lois Beeson*

ESTABLISHED in 2000 in memory of children's novelist, Henrietta Branford and editor and publisher, Wendy Boase. To be awarded annually to encourage and celebrate the most promising novel by a new writer of children's books, while at the same time highlighting the importance of the editor in nurturing new talent. 2000 winners: Katherine Roberts *SongQuest* (book); Barry Cunningham, **The Chicken House** (editor).
Award £1000.

The Bridport Prize
Bridport Arts Centre, South Street, Bridport, Dorset DT6 3NR
☎01308 459444 Fax 01308 459166
Website www.bridportprize.org.uk
Contact *Competition Secretary*

Annual competition for poetry and short story writing. Unpublished work only, written in English. Winning stories are read by a literary agent (**A.M. Heath**), the winning poems are put forward to *Poetry Review* and the **Forward Prize**, and an anthology of winning entries is published. Final entry date: 30 June. Send s.a.e. for entry forms.
Prizes £3000, £1000 & £500 in each category, plus various supplementary prizes.

Katharine Briggs Folklore Award
The Folklore Society, The Warburg Institute, Woburn Square, London WC1H 0AB
☎020 7862 8564
Contact *The Convenor*

ESTABLISHED 1982. An annual award in November for the book, published in Britain and Ireland between 1 June and 30 May in the previous calendar year, which has made the most distinguished non-fiction contribution to folklore studies. Intended to encourage serious research in the field which Katharine Briggs did so much to establish. The term folklore studies is interpreted broadly to include all aspects of traditional and popular culture, narrative, belief, custom and folk arts.

Prize £50, plus engraved goblet.

British Book Awards

Publishing News, 39 Store Street, London WC1E 7DB
☎020 7692 2900 Fax 020 7419 2111
Email mailbox@publishingnews.co.uk
Website www.publishingnews.co.uk

ESTABLISHED 1988. Viewed by the book trade as the one to win, 'The Nibbies' are presented annually in February. The awards are made in various categories. Each winner receives the prestigious Nibbie and the awards are presented to those who have made the most impact in the book trade during the previous year. Winners have included: J.K. Rowling, Spike Milligan, Louis de Bernières, Alan Bennett, Salman Rushdie, Dava Sobel, Sebastian Faulks, Books etc., Waterstone's, Ottakar's, and the publishers **Transworld**, **Bloomsbury**, **Little, Brown** and **Random House**. For further information contact: Merric Davidson, 12 Priors Heath, Goudhurst, Cranbrook, Kent TN17 2RE (☎/Fax 01580 212041).

British Comparative Literature Association/British Centre for Literary Translation Competition

School of Language, Linguistics and Translation Studies, University of East Anglia, Norwich, Norfolk NR4 7TJ
Email J.Boase-Beier@uea.ac.uk or transcomp@uea.ac.uk
Website www.bcla.org
Competition Organiser Dr Jean Boase-Beier

ESTABLISHED 1983. Annual competition open to unpublished literary translations from all languages. Maximum submission: 25 pages.

Prizes £350 (1st); £200 (2nd); £100 (3rd); plus publication for all winning entries in the Association's annual journal Comparative Criticism (**Cambridge University Press**). Other entries may receive commendations.

British Fantasy Awards

201 Reddish Road, South Reddish, Stockport, Cheshire SK5 7HR
☎0161 476 5368 (after 6.00 pm)
Email faliol@yahoo.com
Website www.herebedragons.co.uk/bfs
Secretary Robert Parkinson

Awarded by the **British Fantasy Society** by members at its annual conference for Best Novel and Best Short Story categories, among others. Not an open competition. Previous winners include: Ramsey Campbell, Dan Simmonds, Michael Marshall Smith, Thomas Ligotti.

British Press Awards

Press Gazette, Quantum House, 19 Scarbrook Road, Croydon, Surrey CR9 1LX
☎020 8565 4200 Fax 020 8565 4395
Email pged@qpp.co.uk

'The Oscars of British journalism.' Open to all British morning and Sunday newspapers sold nationally and news agencies. March event. Run by Press Gazette.

British Science Fiction (Association) Award

The Bungalow, 27 Lower Evingar Road, Whitchurch, Hampshire RG28 7BX
☎01256 893253
Email awards@sandman.enterprise-plc
Award Administrator Chris Hill

ESTABLISHED 1966. The BSFA awards a trophy each year in three categories – novel, short fiction and artwork – published in the preceding year. 2000 winners: Mary Gentle Ash: A Secret History (novel); Peter F. Hamilton The Suspect Genome (short fiction); Dominic Harman Hideaway (artwork).

British Sports Journalism Awards

See **Sports Writers' Association of Great Britain** under **Professional Associations and Societies**

James Cameron Award

City University, Department of Journalism, Northampton Square, London EC1V 0HB
☎020 7477 8221 Fax 020 7477 8594
Contact The Administrator

Annual award for journalism to a reporter of any nationality, working for the British media, whose work is judged to have contributed most during the year to the continuance of the Cameron tradition. Administered by the City University Department of Journalism. 2000 winner: Jon Swain, Sunday Times.

Canadian Poetry Association Annual Poetry Contest

Box 22571, St George Postal Outlet, 264 Bloor Street West, Toronto, Ontario, Canada M5S 1V8
Website www.mirror.org/cpa

Annual contest open to members and non-members of the CPA worldwide. Submission fee: $5 per poem. All winning poems are published on the British Columbia Chapter CPA website.

Six cash *Prizes* and publication in *Poetmata*.

The Canongate Prize

Canongate Books, 14 High Street, Edinburgh EH1 1TE
☎0131 557 5111 Fax 0131 557 5211
Email info@canongate.co.uk
Website www.canongate-prize.com

ESTABLISHED in 1999 by **Canongate Books** and Waterstone's to stimulate innovative new prose writing. The theme of the competition for 2000 was 'Sin'. Submissions must be previously unpublished. All styles and genres (e.g. short story, reportage, essay or sketch) may be submitted; the length between 2000 and 5000 words. Closing date and theme for 2002 will be announced at the Edinburgh International Book Festival. Leaflet available from the address above or access the website for further details.

Prizes 15 winners receive £2000 each plus publication in the Canongate Prize anthology.

Cardiff International Poetry Competition

PO Box 438, Cardiff CF10 5YA
☎029 2047 2266 Fax 029 2049 2930
Email post@academi.org
Website www.academi.org

Contact *Peter Finch*

ESTABLISHED 1986. An annual competition for unpublished poems in English of up to 50 lines. Closing date in June.

Prize £5000 (total) .

Carey Award

Society of Indexers, Globe Centre, Penistone Road, Sheffield, South Yorkshire S6 3AE
☎0114 281 3060 Fax 0114 281 3061
Email admin@socind.demon.co.uk
Website www.socind.demon.co.uk

Secretary *Liza Weinkove*

A private award made by the Society to a member who has given outstanding services to indexing. The recipient is selected by Council with no recommendations considered from elsewhere.

Carnegie Medal

See **The Library Association Carnegie Medal**

The Raymond Chandler Society's 'Marlowe' Award for Best International Crime Novel

Heidenheimerstr. 106, 89075 Ulm, Germany
☎0114 255 6302 (UK contact)
Fax 0114 255 6302
Email william.adamson@zsp.uni-ulm.de

Contact *Simon Beckett* (UK), *Dr William R. Adamson* (Germany)

ESTABLISHED 1991. Annual award to the best English language crime novel. Awards also for best German language crime novel and best German language crime short story. Entry details from UK contact number. Submissions direct to the Society. Previous international 'Marlowe' winners include: Sara Paretsky, Minette Walters, Michael Connelly, Liza Cody, George P. Pelecanos.

Sid Chaplin Short Story Competition

Shildon Town Council, Civic Centre Square, Shildon, Co Durham DL4 1AH
☎01388 772563 Fax 01388 775227

Contact *Mrs J.M. Stafford*

ESTABLISHED 1986. Annual themed short story competition (2000 subject was 'The Family'). Maximum 3000 words; £2 entrance fee (juniors free). All stories must be unpublished and not broadcast and/or performed. Application forms available from September 2001. Closing date: 31 December.

Prizes £300 (1st); £150 (2nd); £75 (3rd); £50 (Junior).

Children's Book Award

The Federation of Children's Book Groups, The Old Malt House, Aldbourne, Wiltshire SN8 2DW
☎01672 540629 Fax 01672 541280

Coordinator *Marianne Adey*

ESTABLISHED 1980. Awarded annually for best book of fiction suitable for children. Unique in that it is judged by the children themselves. 2000 winner: Michael Morpurgo *Kensuke's Kingdom*.

Award A silver and oak sculpture made by Graham Stewart and Tim Stead, plus portfolio of letters, drawings and comments from the children who took part in the judging; category winners receive silver bowls designed by the same artists and portfolios.

Children's Book Circle
Eleanor Farjeon Award
See **Eleanor Farjeon Award**

The Children's Laureate
18 Grosvenor Road, Portswood,
Southampton, Hampshire SO17 1RT
☎023 8055 5057
Email locol@compuserve.com
Website www.waterstones.co.uk

Administrator *Lois Beeson*

ESTABLISHED 1998. Sponsored by Waterstone's, the Laureate is awarded biennially to an eminent British writer or illustrator of children's books both in celebration of a lifetime's achievement and to highlight the role of children's book creators in making the readers of the future. 2001 winner: Anne Fine.
Award Medal and £10,000.

Arthur C. Clarke
Award for Science Fiction
60 Bournemouth Road, Folkestone, Kent
CT19 5AZ
☎01303 252939 Fax 01303 252939
Email clarke@appomattox.demon.co.uk

Administrator *Paul Kincaid*

ESTABLISHED 1986. The Arthur C. Clarke Award is given annually to the best science fiction novel with first UK publication in the previous calendar year. Both hardcover and paperback books qualify. Made possible by a generous donation from Arthur C. Clarke, this award is selected by a rotating panel of judges nominated by the **British Science Fiction Association**, the **Science Fiction Foundation** and the Science Museum. 2000 winner: Bruce Sterling *Distraction*.
Award £2001 plus trophy.

The Cló Iar-Chonnachta
Literary Award
Cló Iar-Chonnachta Teo, Indreabhán,
Conamara, Co. Galway, Republic of Ireland
☎00 353 91 593307 Fax 00 353 91 593362
Website www.cic.ie

Editor *Róisín Ní Mhianànn*

An annual prize for a newly written and unpublished work in the Irish language. Awarded in 2000 for the best novel and in 2001 for best collection of short stories or long play. 2000 winner: Siobhàn Ní Shúilleabháin for her novel, *Aistríu*.
Prize IR£5000.

David Cohen
British Literature Prize
Arts Council of Great Britain, 14 Great Peter Street, London SW1P 3NQ
☎020 7333 0100 Fax 020 7973 6520
Website www.artscouncil.org.uk

Literature Director *Gary McKeone*
Literature Assistant *Hilary Davidson*

ESTABLISHED 1993. One of the most distinguished literary prizes in Britain, the British Literature Prize, launched by the Arts Council, is awarded biennially. Anyone is eligible to suggest candidates and the award recognises writers who use the English language and who are British citizens, encompassing dramatists as well as novelists, poets and essayists. The prize is for a lifetime's achievement rather than a single play or book and is donated by the David Cohen Family Charitable Trust. Set up in 1980 by David Cohen, GP and son of a property developer, the Trust has helped composers, choreographers, dancers, poets, playwrights and actors. The Council is providing a further £10,000 to enable the winner to commission new work, with the dual aim of encouraging young writers and readers. 2000 winner: Doris Lessing. Previous winners: William Trevor, Dame Muriel Spark, Harold Pinter, V.S. Naipaul.
Award £30,000, plus £10,000 towards new work.

The Commonwealth Writers Prize
Book Trust, Book House, 45 East Hill,
London SW18 2QZ
☎020 8516 2973 Fax 020 8516 2978
Email sandra@booktrust.org.uk
Website www.booktrust.org.uk

Contact *Sandra Vince*

ESTABLISHED 1987. An annual award to reward and encourage the upsurge of new Commonwealth fiction. Any work of prose or fiction is eligible, i.e. a novel or collection of short stories. No drama or poetry. The work must be written in English by a citizen of the Commonwealth and be first published in the year before its entry for the prize. Entries must be submitted by the publisher to the region of the writer's Commonwealth citizenship. The four regions are: Africa, Eurasia, S.E. Asia and South Pacific, Caribbean and Canada. 2001 winners: Peter Carey *True History of the Kelly Gang* (Best Book); Zadie Smith *White Teeth* (Best First Book).
Prizes £10,000 for Best Book; £3000 for Best First Book; 8 prizes of £1000 for each best and first best book in four regions.

The Thomas Cook/Daily Telegraph Travel Book Award

Thomas Cook Publishing, PO Box 227, Peterborough PE3 6PU
☎01733 503566 Fax 01733 503596
Email joan.lee@thomascook.com

Contact *Joan Lee, Publishing*

ESTABLISHED in 1980 by The Thomas Cook Group. Annual award given to the author of the book, published (in the English language) in the previous year, which most inspires the reader to want to travel. Submissions by publishers only. 2000 winner: Jason Elliot *An Unexpected Light.*
Award £10,000.

The Duff Cooper Prize

54 St Maur Road, London SW6 4DP
☎020 7736 3729 Fax 020 7731 7638

Contact *Artemis Cooper*

An annual award for a literary work of biography, history, politics or poetry, published by a recognised publisher (member of the **Publishers Association**) during the previous 12 months. The book must be submitted by the publisher, not the author. Financed by the interest from a trust fund commemorating Duff Cooper, first Viscount Norwich (1890–1954). 2000 winner: Robert Skidelsky *John Maynard Keynes.*
Prize £3000.

Rose Mary Crawshay Prize

The British Academy, 10 Carlton House Terrace, London SW1Y 5AX
☎020 7969 5200 Fax 020 7969 5300
Website www.britac.ac.uk

Contact *British Academy Secretary*

ESTABLISHED 1888 by Rose Mary Crawshay, this prize is given for a historical or critical work by a woman of any nationality on English literature, with particular preference for a work on Keats, Byron or Shelley. The work must have been published in the preceding three years.
Prizes Normally two of approximately £500 each.

Crime Writers' Association (Cartier Diamond Dagger)

PO Box 6939, Kings Heath, Birmingham B14 7LT
Contact *The Secretary*

An annual award for a lifetime's oustanding contribution to the genre. 2001 winner: Lionel Davidson.

Crime Writers' Association (The CWA Ellis Peters Historical Dagger)

PO Box 6939, Kings Heath, Birmingham B14 7LT
Contact *The Secretary*

ESTABLISHED 1999. Annual award for the best historical crime novel. Nominations from publishers only. 2000 winner: Gillian Linscott *Absent Friends.*
Award Dagger, plus cheque.

Crime Writers' Association (The Macallan Gold Dagger for Non-Fiction)

PO Box 6939, Kings Heath, Birmingham B14 7LT
Contact *The Secretary*

Annual award for the best non-fiction crime book published during the year. Nominations from publishers only. 2000 winner: Edward Bunker *Mr Blue.*
Award Dagger, plus cheque (sum varies).

Crime Writers' Association (The Macallan Gold and Silver Daggers for Fiction)

PO Box 6939, Kings Heath, Birmingham B14 7LT
Contact *The Secretary*

Two annual awards for the best crime fiction published during the year. Nominations for Gold Dagger from publishers only. 2000 winners: Jonathan Lethem *Motherless Brooklyn* (Gold); Donna Leon *Friends in High Places* (Silver).
Award Dagger, plus cheque (sum varies).

Crime Writers' Association (The Macallan Short Story Dagger)

PO Box 6939, Kings Heath, Birmingham B14 7LT
Contact *The Secretary*

ESTABLISHED 1993. An award for a published crime story. Publishers should submit three copies of the story by 30 September. 2000 winner: Denise Mina *Helena and the Babies.*
Prize Dagger, plus cheque.

Crime Writers' Association (The Creasey Dagger for Best First Crime Novel)

PO Box 6939, Kings Heath, Birmingham B14 7LT
Contact *The Secretary*

ESTABLISHED 1973 following the death of crime writer John Creasey, founder of the **Crime Writers' Association**. This award, sponsored by **Chivers Press**, is given annually for the best crime novel by an author who has not previously published a full-length work of fiction. Nominations from publishers only. 2000 winner: Boston Teran *God is a Bullet*.
Award Dagger, plus cheque.

Curtis Brown Prize
Curtis Brown Group Ltd, Haymarket House, 28/29 Haymarket, London SW1Y 4SP
☎020 7396 6600 Fax 020 7396 0110
Email cb@curtisbrown.co.uk

Contact *Giles Gordon*
(GilesG@CurtisBrown.co.uk)

ESTABLISHED 1998. Annual prize for the best novel, in the opinion of Curtis Brown, written by a student on the MA in Novel Writing programme run by the University of Manchester. Open to all those not currently represented by a literary agent or under contract to a publisher.
Prize £1000. (Curtis Brown reserves the right to offer to act as literary agent to the winner.)

Harvey Darton Award
See **The Children's Books History Society** under **Literary Societies**

Hunter Davies Prize
See **Lakeland Book of the Year Awards**

Isaac & Tamara Deutscher Memorial Prize
SOAS, University of Sussex, Falmer, Brighton, East Sussex BN1 9RH
☎01273 606755
Email J.P.Rosenberg@Sussex.ac.uk

Secretary *Professor Justin Rosenberg*

An annual award in recognition of, and as an encouragement to, outstanding research in or about the Marxist tradition. Made to the author of an essay or full-scale work published or in manuscript. Final entry date: 1 May.
Award £250.

George Devine Award
17A South Villas, London NW1 9BS
☎020 7267 9793

Contact *Christine Smith*

Annual award for a promising new playwright writing for the stage in memory of George Devine, artistic director of the **Royal Court Theatre**, who died in 1965. The play, which can be of any length, does not need to have been produced. Send two copies of the script, plus outline of work, to Christine Smith by the end of March. Information leaflet available.
Prize £10,000.

Denis Devlin Memorial Award for Poetry
An Chomhairle Ealaíon (The Irish Arts Council), 70 Merrion Square, Dublin 2, Republic of Ireland
☎00 353 1 6180200 Fax 00 353 1 6761302
Email info@artscouncil.ie
Website www.artscouncil.ie

Literature Officer *Sinéad Mac Aodha*

Triennial award for the best book of poetry in English by an Irish poet, published in the preceding three years. Next award 2004.
Award €2500/IR£1968.

Drama Association of Wales Playwriting Competition
The Old Library, Singleton Road, Splott, Cardiff CF24 2ET
☎029 2045 2200 Fax 029 2045 2277
Email aled.daw@virgin.net

Contact *Teresa Hennessy*

Annual competition held to promote the writing of one-act plays in English and Welsh of between 20 and 45 minutes' playing time. The theme of the competition is changed each year (the 2001 title was *Rites of Passage*). Application forms from the address above.
Prizes awarded for Best Play for an All Female Cast; Best Play in the Welsh Language; Best Play for a Children's/Youth Cast; Best Author Under 25; Best Adult Play; Best Overall Play.

Eccles Prize
Columbia Business School, 834 Uris Hall, 3022 Broadway, New York NY 10027, USA
☎001 212 854 2747 Fax 001 212 854 3050

Contact *Office of Public Affairs*

ESTABLISHED 1986 by Spencer F. Eccles in commemoration of his uncle, George S. Eccles, a 1922 graduate of the Business School. Annual award for excellence in economic writing. One of the US's most prestigious book prizes. Books must have a business theme and be written for a general audience. Previous winners: Ron Chernow *The Warburgs*; Jagdish Bhagwati *A Stream of Windows: Unsettling Reflections on Trade, Immigration and Democracy*.

The T.S. Eliot Prize

The Poetry Book Society, Book House,
45 East Hill, London SW18 2QZ
☎020 8870 8403/8874 6361
Fax 020 8877 1615
Email info@poetrybooks.co.uk
Website www.poetrybooks.co.uk
Contact *Clare Brown, Director*

ESTABLISHED 1993. Annual award named after
T.S. Eliot, one of the founders of the **Poetry
Book Society**. Open to books of new poetry
published in the UK and Republic of Ireland
during the year and over 32 pages in length. At
least 75 per cent of the collection must be pre-
viously unpublished in book form. Final entry
date is in August. Previous winners: Michael
Longley *The Weather in Japan*; Ciaran Carson
First Language; Paul Muldoon *The Annals of
Chile*; Mark Doty *My Alexandria*; Les Murray
Subhuman Redneck Poems; Don Paterson *God's
Gift to Women*; Ted Hughes *Birthday Letters*;
Hugo Williams *Billy's Rain*.
Award £10,000.

The Encore Award

The Society of Authors, 84 Drayton Gardens,
London SW10 9SB
☎020 7373 6642 Fax 020 7373 5768
ESTABLISHED 1990. Awarded for the best sec-
ond published novel or novels of the year.
Final entry date: 30 November. Details from
the **Society of Authors**. 2000 winner: John
Burnside *The Mercy Boys*; Claire Messud *The
Last Life*; Matt Thorne *Eight Minutes Idle*; Phil
Whitaker *Triangulation*.
Prize £10,000 (total).

Envoi Poetry Competition

Envoi, 44 Rudyard Road, Biddulph Moor,
Stoke on Trent, Staffordshire ST8 7JN
☎01782 517892
Contact *Roger Elkin*

Run by *Envoi* poetry magazine. Competitions
are featured regularly, with prizes of £300, plus
three annual subscriptions to *Envoi*. Winning
poems along with full adjudication report are
published. Send s.a.e. to Competition
Secretary, 17 Millcroft, Bishops Stortford,
Hertfordshire CM23 2BP.

Euroscript

See entry under **Writers' Courses, Circles
and Workshops**

Geoffrey Faber Memorial Prize

Faber & Faber Ltd, 3 Queen Square, London
WC1N 3AU
☎020 7465 0045 Fax 020 7465 0034
ESTABLISHED 1963 as a memorial to the founder
and first chairman of **Faber & Faber**, this prize
is awarded in alternate years for the volume of
verse and the volume of prose fiction published
in the UK in the preceding two years, which is
judged to be of greatest literary merit. Authors
must be under 40 at the time of publication and
citizens of the UK, Commonwealth, Republic
of Ireland or South Africa. 2000 winner:
Kathleen Jamie *Jizzen*. *Prize* £1000.

Eleanor Farjeon Award

c/o Children's Book Circle, Transworld
Publishers Ltd., 61–63 Uxbridge Road,
London W5 5SA
☎020 8231 6768 Fax 020 8231 6737
Contact *Alexandra Antscherl*

This award, named in memory of the much-
loved children's writer, is for distinguished services to children's books either in this country or
overseas, and may be given to a librarian,
teacher, publisher, bookseller, author, artist,
reviewer, television producer, etc. Nominations
from members of the **Children's Book Circle**.
Sponsored by **Scholastic**. 2000 winner: *Julia
Eccleshare*. *Award* £750.

The Fidler Award

c/o Scottish Book Trust, The Scottish Book
Centre, 137 Dundee Street, Edinburgh
EH11 1BG
☎0131 229 3663 Fax 0131 228 4293
Email scottish.book.trust@dial.pipex.com
Website www.scottishbooktrust.com

Sponsored by Hodder Children's Books for an
unpublished novel for children aged 8–12, to
encourage authors new to writing for this age
group. The award is administered by **Scottish
Book Trust**. Authors should not previously
have had a novel published for this age group.
Final entry date: end December. Previous winners: Theresa   Breslin   *Simon's   Challenge*;
Catherine McPhail *Run Zan Run*; Thomas Bloor
The Memory Prisoner; Gill Vickery *The Ivy Crown*.
Award Publication, £1000 advance and
trophy.

Fish (Publishing) Short Story Prize

Fish Publishing, Durrus, Bantry, Co. Cork,
Republic of Ireland
☎00 353 27 61246
Email info@fishpublishing.com

Website www.fishpublishing.com

Contacts *Clem Cairns, Jula Walton*

ESTABLISHED 1994. Annual international award which aims to discover, encourage and publish exciting new literary talent. Stories of 5000 words maximum which have not been published previously may be entered. An entry fee of £8 is charged for the first entry and £5 per subsequent entry. (£5 for pensioners, unemployed and full-time students.) Closing date: 30 November. Previous winners: Gina Oschner *From the Bering Strait*; Kathy Hughes *Five O'Clock Shadow*. Honorary Patrons: Roddy Doyle, Dermot Healy and Frank McCourt.

Prize £1000; the best 15 stories are published in an anthology.

Sir Banister Fletcher Award

Authors' Club, 40 Dover Street, London W1S 4NP

☎020 7499 8581 Fax 020 7409 0913

Contact *Mrs Ann de La Grange*

This award was created by Sir Bannister Fletcher, President of the **Authors' Club** for many years, and is presented annually. The prize alternates between books on architecture and the fine arts. In 2002 the prize will be awarded for the best book on the fine arts published during the previous two years. Submissions to Mrs Ann de La Grange at the Authors' Club. Previous winners: David Alan Brown *Leonardo da Vinci*; Richard Weston *Alvar Aalto*; Dr Megan Aldrich *Gothic Revival*; Professor Thomas Markus *Building and Power*; John Onians *Bearers of Meaning: Classical Orders in Antiquity*; Sir Michael Levey *Gianbattista Tiepolo: his life and art*; John Allan *Berthold Lubetkin – Architecture and The Tradition of Progress*.

Award Sir Banister Fletcher Salver.

The John Florio Prize

See **The Translators Association Awards**

The Forward Prizes for Poetry

Colman Getty PR, 17 & 18 Margaret Street, London W1W 8RP

☎020 7631 2666 Fax 020 7631 2699

Email pr@colmangettypr.co.uk

Contact *Truda Spruyt*

ESTABLISHED 1992. Three awards: the Forward Prize for Best Collection, the Waterstone's Prize for Best First Collection and the Tolman Cunard Prize for Best Single Poem which is not already part of an anthology or collection. All entries must be published in the UK or Eire and submitted by poetry publishers (collec-tions) or newspaper and magazine editors (single poems). Individual entries of poets' own work are not accepted. 2000 winners: Michael Donaghy, Andrew Waterhouse, Tessa Biddington.

Prizes £10,000 for best collection; £5000 for best first collection; £1000 for best single poem.

The Frogmore Poetry Prize

42 Morehall Avenue, Folkestone, Kent CT19 4EF

Website www.frogmorepress.co.uk

Contact *Jeremy Page*

ESTABLISHED 1987. Awarded annually and sponsored by the Frogmore Foundation. The winning poem, runners-up and short-listed entries are all published in the magazine. Previous winners: David Satherley, Caroline Price, Bill Headdon, John Latham, Diane Brown, Tobias Hill, Mario Petrucci, Gina Wilson, Ross Cogan, Joan Benner, Ann Alexander.

Prize The winner receives 200 guineas and a life subscription to the biannual literary magazine, *The Frogmore Papers*.

Martha Gellhorn Trust Prize

Rutherfords, Herbert Road, Salcombe, Devon TQ8 8HN

Annual prize for journalism in honour of one of the twentieth century's greatest reporters. Open for journalism published in English, giving 'the view from the ground – a human story that penetrates the established version of events and illuminates an urgent issue buried by prevailing fashions of what makes news.' The subject matter can involve the UK or abroad. The first award was won in 2000 by Nick Davies for his 'Schools in Crisis'series published in *The Guardian*.

Prize 5000.

The Gladstone History Book Prize

Royal Historical Society, University College London, Gower Street, London WC1E 6BT

☎020 7387 7532 Fax 020 7387 7532

Contact *Executive Secretary*

ESTABLISHED 1998. Annual award for the best new work on any historical subject which is not primarily related to British history, published in the UK in the preceding calendar year. The book must be the author's first (solely written) history book and be an original and scholarly work of historical research. Closing date: 31 December. Previous winner:

Frances Stonor Saunders *Who Paid the Piper? The CIA and the Cultural Cold War.*
   Prize £1000.

Glaxo Science Writers' Awards
See **ABSW/Glaxo Science Writers' Awards**

Glenfiddich Food & Drink Awards
4 Bedford Square, London WC1B 3RA
☎020 7255 1100   Fax 020 7631 0602

Known as the 'Cooker Bookers' or the 'Oscars' of the gastronomic world, the awards aim to recognise excellence in writing, publishing and broadcasting on the subjects of food and drink. There are 12 category winners from work published or broadcast in the UK and the Republic of Ireland. 2001 winners: Drink Book: *Essential Winetasting* Michael Schuster; Food Writer: Rose Prince for work in the *Daily Express*; Magazine Cookery Writer: Elisabeth Luard for work in *Waitrose Food Illustrated*; Television Programme: *Rick Stein's Seafood Lover's Guide*, BBC2; Radio Programme: *The Food Programme* presented by Andrew Jefford for BBC Radio 4; Visual Work: Jason Lowe for work in *The Independent Magazine* and Paul Slater for work in *The Times Magazine*; Drink Writer: Arthur Taylor for work in *What's Brewing*; Food Book: *marie claire Flavours* Donna Hay; Newspaper Cookery Writer: Hugo Arnold for work in *The Business FT Weekend Magazine*; Regional Writer: David Adlard for work in *Eastern Daily Press Norfolk Magazine*; Restaurant Critic: Jay Rayner for work in *Life: The Observer Magazine*; Wine Writer: Michael Broadbent for work in *Decanter*; Special Award: The Royal Society of Arts 'Focus on Food' Campaign; 2001 Glenfiddich Trophy Winner: Rick Stein.
   Award Overall winner (chosen from the category winners) £3000, plus the Glenfiddich Trophy (which is held for one year); category winners £1000 each, plus a case of Glenfiddich Single Malt Scotch Whisky.

Golden Kite Award
See **Society for Children's Book Writers & Illustrators** under **Professional Associations and Societies**

Golden PEN Award for Lifetime Distinguished Services to Literature
English Centre of International PEN, 152–156 Kentish Town Road, London NW1 9QB
☎020 7267 9444   Fax 020 7267 9304
Email enquiries@pen.org.uk

Website www.pen.org.uk
Awarded to a senior writer, with a distinguished body of work over many years, who has made a significant and constructive impact on fellow writers, the reading public and the literary world. Nominations by members of English PEN only.

The Phillip Good Memorial Prize
QWF Magazine, PO Box 1768, Rugby CV21 4ZA
Email jo.good@ntlworld.com
Website www.qwfmagazine.co.uk
Contact *Competition Secretary*

ESTABLISHED in 1997, the competition is run by *QWF Magazine* and a percentage of the entry fee goes to charity. The prize commemorates the memory of Phillip Good (late husband of *QWF* editor, Jo Good) and is for short stories of less than 5000 words in any style or genre (except children's). Open entry. Entrants may request in-depth critique of their stories for an extra fee. For entry forms send s.a.e. to the address above. Closing date: 21 August.
   Prizes (total) at least £525 plus free subscription to *QWF Magazine*; also book prizes and publication for winning authors.

Edgar Graham Book Prize
c/o Development Studies, School of Oriental and African Studies, Thornhaugh Street, Russell Square, London WC1H 0XG
☎020 7898 4485   Fax 020 7898 4519
Contact *Professor Henry Bernstein*

ESTABLISHED 1984. Biennial award in memory of Edgar Graham. Aims to encourage research work in Third World agricultural and industrial development. Open to published works of original scholarship on agricultural and/or industrial development in Asia and/or Africa. No edited volumes. Next award 2002.
   Prize £1500.

Kate Greenaway Medal
See **The Library Association Kate Greenaway Medal**

The Griffin Poetry Prize for Excellence in Poetry
6610 Edwards Boulevard, Mississauga, Ontario, Canada L5T 2V6
☎001 905 565 5993   Fax 001 905 564 3645
Email info@griffinpoetryprize.com
Website www.griffinpoetryprize.com
Contact *Ruth Smith*

Annual   award   ESTABLISHED   in   2000   by

Toronto-based industrialist and philanthropist, Scott Griffin, for individual poetry collections. Trustees include Margaret Atwood and Michael Ondaatje. Submissions from publishers only, to a maximum of three books per publisher.

Prizes A total of Canadian $80,000, divided into two categories: International and Canadian.

The Guardian Children's Fiction Award

The Guardian, 119 Farringdon Road, London EC1R 3ER
☎020 7239 9694 Fax 020 7713 4366

Children's Book Editor *Julia Eccleshare*

ESTABLISHED 1967. Annual award for an outstanding work of fiction for children aged seven and over by a British or Commonwealth author, first published in the UK in the preceding year, excluding picture books. Final entry date: 1 June. No application form necessary. 2000 winner: Jacqueline Wilson *The Illustrated Mum*.

Award £1500.

The Guardian First Book Award

The Guardian, 119 Farringdon Road, London EC1R 3ER
☎020 7239 9694 Fax 020 7713 4366

Contact *Literary Editor*

ESTABLISHED 1999. Annual award for first time authors published in English in the UK. All genres of writing eligible, apart from academic, guidebooks, children's, educational, manuals, reprints and TV, radio and film tie-ins. 2000 winner: Zadie Smith *White Teeth*.

Award £10,000, plus *Guardian/Observer* advertising package and £1000 endowment of books to UK school of winner's choice.

Guild of Food Writers Awards

48 Crabtree Lane, London SW6 6LW
☎020 7610 1180 Fax 020 7610 0299
Email awards@gfw.co.uk
Website www.gfw.co.uk

Contact *Christina Thomas*

ESTABLISHED 1985. Annual awards in recognition of outstanding achievement in all areas in which food writers work and have influence. Entry is not restricted to members of the Guild. Entry form available from the address above. 2000 winners: Special Award for a lifetime achievement in food writing: Arabella Boxer and Alan Davidson; Michael Smith Award: Laura Mason and Catherine Brown *The Traditional Foods of Britain* and Gary Rhodes

New British Classics; Jeremy Round Award: Sara Jayne-Stanes *Chocolate: The Definitive Guide*; Food Book of the Year: Alan Davidson *Oxford Companion to Food*; Cookery Book of the Year: Paul Gayler *A Passion for Vegetables* and Dan Lepard and Richard Whittington *Baking with Passion*; Recipe Writer of the Year: Kate McBain; Food Journalist of the Year: Clarissa Hyman; Cookery Journalist of the Year: Katie Stewart; Food Broadcast of the Year: Jamie Oliver *The Naked Chef*.

Gwobr Llyfr y Flwyddyn

See **Arts Council of Wales Book of the Year Awards**

James W. Hackett Award

See **The British Haiku Society** under **Organisations of Interest to Poets**

Hastings National Poetry Competition

See **Hastings International Poetry Festival** under **Festivals**

W.H. Heinemann Award

Royal Society of Literature, Somerset House, Strand, London WC2R 1LA
☎020 7845 4676 Fax 020 7845 4679
Email info@rslit.org
Website www.rslit.org

ESTABLISHED 1945. Works of any kind of literature may be submitted by publishers under this award, which aims to encourage genuine contributions to literature. Books must be written in the English language and have been published in the previous year; translations are not eligible for consideration nor are single poems, nor collections of pieces by more than one author, nor may individuals put forward their own work. Preference tends to be given to publications which are unlikely to command large sales: poetry, biography, criticism, philosophy, history. Publishers must contact the Secretary for details of how to submit works. Final entry date: 15 December. Up to three awards may be given. Previous winner: Anthony Sampson *Mandela*.

Prize £5000.

Felicia Hemans Prize for Lyrical Poetry

University of Liverpool, PO Box 147, Liverpool, Merseyside L69 3BX
☎0151 794 2458 Fax 0151 794 2454
Email wilderc@liv.ac.uk

Contact *The Registrar*

ESTABLISHED 1899. Annual award for published or unpublished verse. Open to past or present members and students of the University of Liverpool. One poem per entrant only. Closing date 1 May.

Prize £30.

Heywood Hill Literary Prize

10 Curzon Street, London W1J 5HH
☎020 7629 0647

Contact *John Saumarez Smith*

ESTABLISHED 1995 by the Duke of Devonshire to reward a lifetime's contribution to the enjoyment of books. Three judges chosen annually. No applications are necessary for this award. 2000 winner: Charles Causley.

Prize £12,500.

William Hill Sports Book of the Year

Greenside House, Station Road, Wood Green, London N22 7TP
☎020 8918 3731 Fax 020 8918 3728

Contact *Graham Sharpe*

ESTABLISHED 1989. Annual award introduced by Graham Sharpe of bookmakers William Hill. Sponsored by William Hill and thus dubbed the 'bookie' prize, it is the first, and only, Sports Book of the Year award. Final entry date: September. 2000 winner: Lance Armstrong with Sally Jenkins *It's Not About the Bike*.

Prize (reviewed annually) £12,000 package including £10,000 cash, hand-bound copy, £1000 free bet. Runners-up prizes.

Hilton House Poet of the Year/ Open/Spiritual Competitions

Hilton House (Publishers), Hilton House, 39 Long John Hill, Norwich, Norfolk NR1 2JP
☎01603 660224

Contact *Michael K. Moore*

ESTABLISHED 1995. Annual awards to promote interest in poetry and to encourage high standards. Unpublished poems only, of up to 40 lines; no limit to number of entries. Entrants must apply for rules and entry forms. Final entry dates: 31 March (Poet of the Year); 31 August (Open); 30 November (Spiritual). Previous winners: Andrew Farmer, Allister Fraser MBE, Paul Hampton, Pippa McCathy, Dame Stella Browning.

Cash prizes £100; £50; £25. All winners, runners-up and commended poets receive a complimentary copy of awards booklet containing their winning poems. The three main winners are also published in *Advance! – Poetry Quarterly*.

Calvin & Rose G. Hoffman Prize

King's School, Canterbury, Kent CT1 2ES
☎01227 595501

Contact *The Headmaster*

Annual award for distinguished publication on Christopher Marlowe, established by the late Calvin Hoffman, author of *The Man Who was Shakespeare* (1955) as a memorial to himself and his wife. For unpublished works of at least 5000 words written in English for their scholarly contribution to the study of Christopher Marlowe and his relationship to William Shakespeare. Final entry date: 1 September. 1999 winner: Prof. Ken Cartwright. (Prize not awarded in 2000.)

Winifred Holtby Prize

Royal Society of Literature, Somerset House, Strand, London WC2R 1LA
☎020 7845 4676 Fax 020 7845 4679
Email info@rslit.org
Website www.rslit.org

ESTABLISHED 1966 by Vera Brittain who gave a sum of money to the RSL to provide an annual prize in honour of Winifred Holtby who died at the age of 37. Administered by the **Royal Society of Literature**. The prize is for the best regional novel of the year written in the English language. The writer must be of British or Irish nationality, or a citizen of the Commonwealth. Translations, unless made by the author himself of his own work, are not eligible for consideration. If in any year it is considered that no regional novel is of sufficient merit the prize money may be awarded to an author, qualified as aforesaid, of a literary work of non-fiction or poetry, concerning a regional subject. Publishers are invited to submit works published during the current year and must contact the Secretary for details. Final entry date: 15 December. Previous winners: Eden Robinson *Traplines*; Andrew O'Hagan *Our Fathers*; Giles Foden *The Last King of Scotland*.

Prize £1000.

L. Ron Hubbard's Writers of the Future Contest

PO Box 218, East Grinstead, West Sussex RH19 4GH

Contest Administrator *Andrea Grant-Webb*

ESTABLISHED 1984 by L. Ron Hubbard to encourage new and amateur writers of science fiction, fantasy and horror. Quarterly awards with an annual grand prize. Entrants must submit a short story of up to 10,000 words, or a novelette less than 17,000 words, which must not have been published previously. The contest is open only to those who have not been published professionally. Previous winners: Roge Gregory, Malcolm Twigg, Janet Martin, Alan Smale, Janet Stephenson. Send s.a.e. for entry form.

Prizes £640 (1st), £480 (2nd) and £320 (3rd) each quarter; Annual Grand Prize: £2500. All winners are awarded a trip to the annual L. Ron Hubbard Achievement Awards which include a series of professional writers' workshops, and are published in the *L. Ron Hubbard Presents Writers of the Future* anthology.

The Richard Imison Memorial Award

The Society of Authors, 84 Drayton Gardens, London SW10 9SB
☎020 7373 6642 Fax 020 7373 5768

Contact *The Secretary, The Broadcasting Committee*

Annual award established 'to perpetuate the memory of Richard Imison, to acknowledge the encouragement he gave to writers working in the medium of radio, and in memory of the support and friendship he invariably offered writers in general, and radio writers in particular'. Administered by the **Society of Authors** and generally sponsored by the Peggy Ramsay Foundation, the purpose is 'to encourage new talent and high standards in writing for radio by selecting the radio drama by a writer new to radio which, in the opinion of the judges, is the best of those submitted.' An adaptation for radio of a piece originally written for the stage, television or film is not eligible. Any radio drama first transmitted in the UK between 1 January and 31 December by a writer or writers new to radio, is eligible, provided the work is an original piece for radio and it is the first dramatic work by the writer(s) that has been broadcast. Submission may be made by any party to the production in the form of two copies of an audio cassette (not-returnable) accompanied by a nomination form. 2000 winner: Peter Morgan *A Matter of Interpretation*.
Prize £1500.

The Independent Foreign Fiction Prize

The Independent, Independent House, 191 Marsh Wall, London E14 9RS
☎020 7005 2000 Fax 020 7005 2999

Website www.independent.co.uk
Awarded for translated fiction by living authors published in Britain in the year preceding the award. 2001 winner: *The Alphonse Courrier Affair* by Marta Morazzoni; translated by Emma Rose.
Prize £10,000 shared equally between author and translator.

The International IMPAC Dublin Literary Award

Dublin City Public Libraries, Administrative Headquarters, Cumberland House, Fenian Street, Dublin 2 Republic of Ireland
☎00 353 1 6644800 Fax 00 353 1 6761628
Email dubaward@iol.ie
Website www.impacdublinaward.ie

ESTABLISHED 1995. Sponsored by Dublin Corporation and a US-based productivity improvement firm, IMPAC, this prize is awarded for a work of fiction written and published in the English language or written in a language other than English and published in English translation. Initial nominations are made by municipal public libraries in major and capital cities worldwide, each library putting forward up to three books to the international panel of judges in Dublin. 2001 winner: Alistair MacLeod *No Great Mischief*.
Prize IR£100,000 (if the winning book is in English translation, the prize is shared IR£75,000 to the author and IR£25,000 to the translator).

International Reading Association Literacy Award

International Reading Association, 800 Barksdale Road, PO Box 8139, Newark, Delaware 19714-8139, USA
☎001 302 731 1600 Fax 001 302 731 1057

Executive Director *Alan E. Farstrup*

The International Reading Association is a non-profit education organisation devoted to improving reading instruction and promoting literacy worldwide. In addition to the US $15,000 award presented each year on International Literacy Day (September 8), the organisation gives more than 25 awards in recognition of achievement in reading research, writing for children, media coverage of literacy, and literacy instruction.

International Student Playscript Competition

See **University of Hull** under **Writers' Courses, Circles and Workshops**

Irish Times Irish Literature Prizes

The Irish Times Ltd, 10–16 D'Olier Street,
Dublin 2, Republic of Ireland
☎00 353 1 679 2022 Fax 00 353 1 670 9383
Administrator, Book Prizes *Gerard
Cavanagh*

ESTABLISHED 1989. Biennial prizes awarded in
four different categories: fiction (a novel,
novella or collection of short stories), non-fiction prose (history, biography, autobiography,
criticism, politics, sociological interest, travel,
current affairs and belles-lettres), poetry (collection or a long poem or a sequence of poems,
or a revised/updated edition of a previously
published selection/collection) and for a work
in the Irish language (fiction, poetry or non-
fiction). The author must have been born in
Ireland or be an Irish citizen, but may live in
any part of the world. Books are nominated by
literary editors and critics, and are then called
in from publishers. Next awards to be
announced in autumn 2001. Previous winners:
Paddy Devlin *Straight Left* (non-fiction);
Kathleen Ferguson *A Maid's Tale* (fiction);
Robert Greacen *Collected Poems*; Brian Keenan
An Evil Cradling; John MacKenna *The Fallen
and Other Stories*.
Prizes IR£7500 (International Fiction
Prize); IR£5000 each of the remaining categories.

Jewish Quarterly Literary Prizes

PO Box 2078, London W1A 1JR
☎020 7629 5004 Fax 020 7629 5110
Contact *Gerald Don*

Formerly the H.H. Wingate Prize. Annual
awards (one for fiction and one for non-fiction) for works which best stimulate an interest
in and awareness of themes of Jewish interest.
Books must have been published in the UK in
the year of the award and be written in English
by an author resident in Britain, the
Commonwealth, Israel, Republic of Ireland or
South Africa. 2001 winners: Mona Yahia *When
the Grey Beetles Took Over Baghdad* (fiction);
Mark Roseman *The Past in Hiding* (non-fiction).
Prizes Fiction: £4000; Non-fiction: £3000.

The Samuel Johnson Prize for Non-fiction

The Booksellers Association, Minster House,
272 Vauxhall Bridge Road, London
SW1V 1BA
☎020 7834 5477 Fax 020 7834 8812
Email 100437.2261@compuserve.com

Contact *Gill Cronin*

ESTABLISHED 1998. Annual prize sponsored by
an anonymous retired British businessman to
reward the best of non-fiction. Eligible categories include the arts, autobiography, biography, business, commerce, current affairs, history,
natural history, popular science, religion, sport
and travel. Entries submitted by publishers only.
2000 winner: David Cairns *Berlioz*.
Prize £30,000; £2500 to each shortlisted
author.

Mary Vaughan Jones Award

Cyngor Llyfrau Cymru (Welsh Books
Council), Castell Brychan, Aberystwyth,
Dyfed SY23 2JB
☎01970 624151 Fax 01970 625385
Email castellbrychan@cllc.org.uk
Website www.wbc.org.uk

Contact *The Administrator*

Triennial award for distinguished services in
the field of children's literature in Wales over a
considerable period of time. 2000 winner:
J. Selwyn Lloyd.
Award Silver trophy.

Keats–Shelley Prize

Keats–Shelley Memorial Association,
117 Cheyne Walk, London SW10 0ES
☎020 7352 2180 Fax 020 7352 6705
Website www.demon.co.uk.heritage/
 Keats.House.Rome

Contact *Harriet Cullen*

ESTABLISHED 1998. Annual award to promote
the study and appreciation of Keats and
Shelley, especially in the universities, and of
creative writing inspired by the younger
Romantic poets. Two categories: essay and
poem; open to all ages and nationalities.
Previous winners: Sarah Wootton, Rukmini
Maria Callimachi, James Burton, Cate Parish.
Prize £3000 distributed between the win-
ners of the two categories.

The Keeley-Sherrard Translation Award

Poetry Greece, Triklino, Corfu 49100, Greece
☎00 30 661 58468 Fax 00 30 661 58468
Email poetrygreece@hotmail.com
Website
users.otenet.gr/~wendyhol/poetry_greece/

Contact *Wendy Holborow*

Annual award in memory of the late Philip
Sherrard who worked closely with Edmund
Keeley translating many Greek poets into

English. The award is for Greek poetry translated into English. Potential translators should contact Poetry Greece for further information.

The Petra Kenney Poetry Competition

PO Box 32, Filey, Yorkshire YO14 9YG
Email morgan@petrapoetrycompetition.co.uk
Website www.petrapoetrycompetition.co.uk
Contact *Secretary*

ESTABLISHED 1995. Annual poetry award. Original, unpublished poems up to 80 lines on any theme. Closing date: 1 December. Entry fee: £3 per poem. Send s.a.e. for rules and entry form. 1999 winners: Matt Robinson, Tim Bowling, Judith Barrington, Brian Bartlett, Mark Cochrane, Diana Syder.

Prizes £1000 (1st); £500 (2nd); £250 (3rd) and three highly commended prizes of £125 each; plus publication in *Writers' Forum* and inscribed Royal Brierley Crystal Vase to each winner.

Kent & Sussex Poetry Society Open Competition

13 Ruscombe Close, Southborough,
Tunbridge Wells, Kent TN4 0SG
☎01892 543862
Chairman *Clive R. Eastwood*

Annual competition. Entry fee: £3 per poem, maximum 40 lines.

Prizes £1000 (total).

Kent Short Story Competition

Kent Literature Festival, The Metropole Arts Centre, The Leas, Folkestone, Kent CT20 2LS
☎01303 255070
Contact *Ann Fearey*

ESTABLISHED 1992. For a short story of up to 3000 words by anyone over the age of 16. Sponsored by Midland Bank and supported by Saga and Shepway District Council. Send s.a.e. for entry forms, available from March.

Prizes £350 (1st); £175 (2nd); £100 (3rd).

Kraszna-Krausz Book Awards

122 Fawnbrake Avenue, London SE24 0BZ
☎020 7738 6701 Fax 020 7738 6701
Email k-k@dial.pipex.com
Website www.k-k.org.uk
Administrator *Andrea Livingstone*

ESTABLISHED 1985. Annual award to encourage and recognise oustanding achievements in the publishing and writing of books on the art, practice, history and technology of photography and the moving image (film, television, video and related screen media). Books in any language, published worldwide, are eligible. Entries must be submitted by publishers only. Prizes for books on still photography alternate annually with those for books on the moving image (2001: moving image). 2000 winners: Boris Mikhailov *Case History*; Sidney F. Ray *Scientific Photography and Applied Imaging*.

Prizes £5000 in each of the main categories; £1000 special commendations.

Lakeland Book of the Year Awards

Cumbria Tourist Board, Ashleigh, Holly Road, Windermere, Cumbria LA23 2AQ
☎015394 44444 Fax 015394 44041
Email mail@cumbria-tourist-board.co.uk
Contact *Annette Vidler*

Six annual awards set up by Cumbrian author Hunter Davies and the Cumbria Tourist Board. The **Hunter Davies Prize** was established in 1984 and is awarded for the book which best helps visitors or residents enjoy a greater love or understanding of any aspect of life in Cumbria and the Lake District. In 1993 three awards were established with funding from the private sector: the **Tullie House Prize**, for a book on environmental or social issues; the **Barclays Bank Prize**, for the best researched book on any aspect of Cumbrian life, its people or culture; and the **Border Television Prize**, for the book which best illustrates the beauty and character of Cumbria. A further two prizes were established in 1999: the **Ron Sands Prize**, for the best book on a cultural theme; and the **Titus Wilson Prize**, for the best book on people. Final entry date mid-March. 2000 winners: Hunter Davies Prize/Titus Wilson Prize: Harry Griffin *Coniston Tigers, Seventy Years of Mountain Adventure*; Barclays Bank Prize: Gordon L. Routledge *Gretna's Secret War*; Border Television Prize: Roger Robson *Cumberland and Westmorland Wresting*; Ron Sands Prize: Robert Woof and Stephen Hebron *Romantic Icons*; Tullie House Prize: Ian Tyler *Thirlmere Mines and The Drowning of the Valley*.

Prize £100 and certificate.

Lancashire County Library Children's Book of the Year Award

Lancashire County Library Headquarters, County Hall, PO Box 61, Preston, Lancashire PR1 8RJ
☎01772 264040 Fax 01772 264043
Manager, Young People's Service *Jean Wolstenholme*

ESTABLISHED 1986. Annual award, presented in June for a work of original fiction suitable for 12–14-year-olds. The winner is chosen by 13–14-year-old secondary school pupils in Lancashire. Books must have been published between 1 September and 31 August in the year of the award and authors must be UK residents. Final entry date: 1 September each year. 2000 joint winners: Melvyn Burgess *Bloodtide* and Malcolm Rose *Plague*.

Prize £500 plus engraved glass decanter.

Lannan Literary Award

Lannan Foundation, 313 Read Street, Santa Fe, New Mexico 87501, USA
☎001 505 954 5149
Website www.lannan.org

ESTABLISHED 1989. Annual awards to honour both established and emerging writers whose work is of exceptional quality. Candidates for the awards are recommended to the Lannan Foundation by a network of writers, literary scholars, publishers and editors. Applications for the awards are *not* accepted. The Lifetime Achievement award is accompanied by $100,000; eight Literary Awards, in Poetry, Fiction and Non-fiction, are accompanied by $75,000. 2000 winners: Evan S. Connell (Lifetime Achievement); Herbert Morris, Jay Wright (Poetry); Robert Coover, David Maloud, Cynthia Ozick, Leslie Marmon Silko (Fiction); Bill McKibben, Carl Safina (Non-fiction).

Legend Writing Award for Short Fiction

Hastings Writers' Group, 39 Emmanuel Road, Hastings, East Sussex TN34 3LB

Contact *Legend Coordinator*

ESTABLISHED 2001. Annual award to encourage writers of short fiction (2000 words) resident in the UK who have not previously had a novel or book of short stories commercially published. Final entry date: 31 August. Entry fee: £4. Please send s.a.e. for rules and entry form (essential). The competition is organised by Hastings Writers' Group and sponsored by its patron, author David Gemmell, who also selects the prize-winning entries.

Prizes £500 (1st); £250 (2nd); £100 (3rd); plus two runners-up prizes of £25.

The Library Association Besterman/McColvin Medal

7 Ridgmount Street, London WC1E 7AE
☎020 7255 0650 Fax 020 7255 0501

Annual award for an outstanding reference work first published in the UK during the preceding year. Consists of two categories: printed and electronic. Works eligible for consideration include: encyclopedias, general and special dictionaries; annuals, yearbooks and directories; handbooks and compendia of data; atlases. Nominations are invited from members of **The Library Association**, publishers and others.

Award Medal and cash prize for each category.

The Library Association Carnegie Medal

7 Ridgmount Street, London WC1E 7AE
☎020 7255 0650 Fax 020 7255 0501

ESTABLISHED 1936. Presented for an outstanding book for children written in English and first published in the UK during the preceding year. Fiction, non–fiction and poetry are all eligible. 1999 winner: Aidan Chambers *Postcards From No-Man's Land*.

Award Medal.

The Library Association Kate Greenaway Medal

7 Ridgmount Street, London WC1E 7AE
☎020 7255 0650 Fax 020 7255 0501

ESTABLISHED 1955. Presented annually for the most distinguished work in the illustration of children's books first published in the UK during the preceding year. 1999 winner: Helen Oxenbury *Alice's Adventures in Wonderland*.

Award Medal. The Colin Mears Award (£5000 cash) is given annually to the winner of the Kate Greenaway Medal.

The Library Association Walford Award

7 Ridgmount Street, London WC1E 7AE
☎020 7255 0650 Fax 020 7255 0501

Awarded to an individual who has made a sustained and continual contribution to British bibliography over a period of years. The nominee need not be resident in the UK. The award is named after Dr A.J. Walford, a bibliograper of international repute. Previous winners include: Prof. Stanley Wells, Prof. J.D. Pearson and Prof. R.C. Alston

Award Cash prize and certificate.

The Library Association Wheatley Medal

7 Ridgmount Street, London WC1E 7AE
☎020 7255 0650 Fax 020 7255 0501

ESTABLISHED 1962. Annual award for an outstanding index first published in the UK during the preceding three years. Whole work must have originated in the UK and recommendations for the award are invited from members of **The Library Association**, the **Society of Indexers**, publishers and others. Previous winners include: Elizabeth Moys *British Tax Encyclopedia*; Paul Nash *The World of Environment 1972–1992*; Richard Raper *The Works of Charles Darwin*.

Award Medal and cash prize.

Literary Review Grand Poetry Competition

See *Literary Review* under **Magazines**

The London Writers Competition

Room 224a, The Town Hall, Wandsworth High Street, London SW18 2PU
☎020 8871 8711 Fax 020 8871 8712
Email arts@wandsworth.gov.uk
Website www.wandsworth.gov.uk

Contact *Wandsworth Arts Office*

Arranged by Wandsworth Borough Council in association with Waterstone's. Annual competition, open to all writers of 16 or over who live, work or study in the Greater London area. Work must not have been published previously. There are three sections: poetry, short story and play.

Prizes £1000 for each section, with a first prize of £600. Poetry and story winners are published and the winning play is produced in a London venue.

Longman-*History Today* Book of the Year Award

c/o History Today, 20 Old Compton Street, London W1D 4TW
☎020 7534 8000

Contacts *Peter Furtado, Marion Soldan*

ESTABLISHED 1993. Annual award set up as joint initiative between the magazine *History Today* and the publisher Longman (**Pearson Education**) to mark the past links between the two organisations, to encourage new writers, and to promote a wider public understanding of, and enthusiasm for, the study and publication of history. Submissions are made by publishers only. 2001 winner: David Armitage *The Ideological Origins of the British Empire*. *Prize* £1000 (see *History Today* from July 2001).

Sir William Lyons Award

The Guild of Motoring Writers, 30 The Cravens, Smallfield, Surrey RH6 9QS
☎01342 843294 Fax 01342 844093
Email sharon@scott-

fairweather.freeserve.co.uk

Contact *Sharon Scott-Fairweather*

An annual competitive award to encourage young people in automotive journalism and to foster interests in motoring and the motor industry. Entrance by two essays and interview with Awards Committee. Applicants must be British, aged 17–23 and resident in UK. Final entry date: 31 August. Presentation date in December.

Award £1000 plus trophy.

The Macallan/Scotland on Sunday Short Story Competition

Scotland on Sunday, 108 Holyrood Road, Edinburgh EH8 8AS
☎0131 620 8341 Fax 0131 620 8334

Contact *Rachel Dodd*

ESTABLISHED 1990. Annual competition to recognise the best in new Scottish writing. Stories are accepted from those who were born or are living in Scotland, or from Scots living abroad. Up to three stories per applicant permitted. Maximum 3000 words per story. Final entry date in March. The top 20 entries are published in a book in conjunction with the **Scottish Arts Council**. Previous winners: David Strachan, Alan Spence, Ali Smith, Chris Dolan, Michael Faber, Anne Donovan.

Prizes £6000 (1st); £2000 (2nd); four runners-up receive £500 each. Winning story is published in *Scotland on Sunday* and four of six shortlisted will be broadcast on BBC Radio Scotland.

McColvin Medal

See **The Library Association Besterman/McColvin Medal**

W.J.M. Mackenzie Book Prize

Political Studies Association, Department of Politics, University of Newcastle, Newcastle upon Tyne NE1 7RU
☎0191 222 8021 Fax 0191 222 5069

PSA Executive Director *Jack Arthurs*

ESTABLISHED 1987. Annual award to best work of political science published in the UK during the previous year. Submissions from publishers only. Final entry date: end of October. 1999 winner: Dr John Barry *Rethinking Green Politics*.

McKitterick Prize

Society of Authors, 84 Drayton Gardens, London SW10 9SB
☎020 7373 6642 Fax 020 7373 5768

Contact *Awards Secretary*

Annual award for a full-length novel in the English language, first published in the UK or unpublished. Open to writers over 40 who have not had any novel published other than the one submitted (excluding works for children). Closing date: 20 December. 2000 winner: Chris Dolan *Ascension Day*.

Prize £4000.

Enid McLeod Prize

Franco-British Society, Room 623, Linen Hall, 162–168 Regent Street, London W1R 5TB
☎020 7734 0815 Fax 020 7734 0815
Executive Secretary *Lady Strabolgi*

ESTABLISHED 1982. Annual award to the author of the work of literature published in the UK which, in the opinion of the judges, has contributed most to Franco-British understanding. Any full-length work written in English by a citizen of the UK, Commonwealth, Republic of Ireland, Pakistan, Bangladesh and South Africa. No English translation of a book written originally in any other language will be considered. Nominations from publishers for books published between 1 January and 31 December of the year of the prize. 1999 winner: Reverend Canon Ian Dunlop *Louis XIV*.

Prize Cheque.

Macmillan Prize for a Children's Picture Book

Macmillan Children's Books, 20 New Wharf Road, London N1 9RR
☎020 7843 6250 Fax 020 7843 2651
Contact *Marketing Dept., Macmillan Children's Books*

Set up in order to stimulate new work from young illustrators in art schools, and to help them start their professional lives. Fiction or non-fiction. **Macmillan** have the option to publish any of the prize winners.

Prizes £1000 (1st); £500 (2nd); £250 (3rd).

Macmillan Silver PEN Award

The English Centre of International PEN, 152–156 Kentish Town Road, London NW1 9QB
☎020 7267 9444 Fax 020 7267 9304
Email enquiries@pen.org.uk
Website www.pen.org.uk

Sponsored by **Macmillan Publishers**. An annual award for a volume of short stories written in English by a British author and published in the UK in the year preceding the prize. Nominations by the PEN Executive Committee

only. Please do not submit books. 2000 winner: Cressida Connolly *The Happiest Days*.

Prize £500, plus silver pen.

The Mail on Sunday Novel Competition

Postal box address changes each year (see below)

Annual award ESTABLISHED 1983. Judges look for a story/character that springs to life in the 'tantalising opening 50–150 words of a novel'. Details of the competition, including the postal box address, are published in *The Mail on Sunday* in July/August. 2000 winner: Madelein Burton.

Awards (1st) £400 book tokens and a writing course at the **Arvon Foundation**; (2nd) £300 tokens; (3rd) £200 tokens; three further prizes of £150 tokens each.

The Mail on Sunday/John Llewellyn Rhys Prize

Book Trust, Book House, 45 East Hill, London SW18 2QZ
☎020 8516 2973 Fax 020 8516 2978
Email sandra@booktrust.org.uk
Website www.booktrust.org.uk

Contact *Sandra Vince*

ESTABLISHED 1942. An annual young writer's award for a memorable work of any kind. Entrants must be under the age of 35 at the time of publication; books must have been published in the UK in the year of the award. The author must be a citizen of Britain or the Commonwealth, writing in English. 2000 winner: David Mitchell *Ghostwritten*.

Prize £5000 (1st); £500 for shortlisted entries.

Marsh Award for Children's Literature in Translation

National Centre for Research in Children's Literature, University of Surrey Roehampton, Digby Stuart College, Roehampton Lane, London SW15 5PH
☎020 8392 3008 Fax 020 8392 3819
Contact *Dr Gillian Lathey*

ESTABLISHED 1995 and sponsored by the Marsh Christian Trust, the award aims to encourage translation of foreign children's books into English. It is a biennial award (next award: 2003), open to British translators of books for 4–16-year-olds, published in the UK by a British publisher. Any category will be considered with the exception of encyclopedias and reference books. No electronic books. First winner: Anthea Bell *A Dog's Life* by Christine Nostlinger. 2001 winner: Betsy Rosenberg for her translation of *Duel* by David Grossman.

Prize £750.

Marsh Biography Award

The English-Speaking Union, Dartmouth House, 37 Charles Street, London W1J 5ED
☎020 7529 1565 Fax 020 7495 6108
Email ann_ferrier@esu.org
Website www.esu.org

Contact *Ann Ferrier-Ilic*

A biennial award for the most significant biography published over a two-year period by a British publisher. Next award October 2001. 1999 winner: Richard Holmes *Coleridge: Darker Reflections*. Previous winners: Jim Ring *Erskine Childers*; Selina Hastings *Evelyn Waugh*; Patrick Marnham *The Man Who Wasn't Maigret*; Hugh and Mirabel Cecil *Clever Hearts*.

Award A year's membership of the ESU and £4000, plus a silver inkwell presented at a dinner.

Kurt Maschler Award

Book Trust, Book House, 45 East Hill, London SW18 2QZ
☎020 8516 2973 Fax 020 8516 2978
Email sandra@booktrust.org.uk
Website www.booktrust.org.uk

Contact *Sandra Vince*

ESTABLISHED 1982. Annual award for 'a work of imagination in the children's field in which text and illustration are of excellence and so presented that each enhances, yet balances the other'. Books published in the current year in the UK by a British author and/or artist, or by someone resident for ten years, are eligible. 1999 winner: Helen Oxenbury's *Lewis Carrol's Alice's Adventures in Wonderland*. (No award in 2000.)

Award £1000 plus bronze Emil trophy.

Colin Mears Award

See **Library Association Kate Greenaway Medal**

Medical Book Awards

The Society of Authors, 84 Drayton Gardens, London SW10 9SB
☎020 7373 6642 Fax 020 7373 5768

Contact *Dorothy Wright*

Annual awards sponsored by the Royal Society of Medicine. Nine categories for medical texts published in the twelve months preceding the

deadline. Contact the **Society of Authors** for entry details. Closing date: 30 April.

Prizes £6500 (total).

Mere Literary Festival Open Competition

'Lawrences', Old Hollow, Mere, Wiltshire BA12 6EG
☎01747 860475

Contact *Mrs Adrienne Howell (Events Organiser)*

Annual open competition which alternates between short stories and poetry. The winners are announced at the Mere Literary Festival during the second week of October. The 2002 competition is for short stories with a closing date for entries in July. For further details, including entry fees and form, contact the address above from 1 March with s.a.e.

Cash prizes.

Meyer-Whitworth Award

Arts Council of England, 14 Great Peter Street, London SW1P 3NQ
☎020 7973 6431 Fax 020 7973 6983
Email jemima.lee@artscouncil.org.uk
Website www.artscouncil.org.uk

Contact *Theatre Writing Section*

In 1908 the movement for a National Theatre joined forces with that to create a memorial to William Shakespeare. The result was the Shakespeare Memorial National Theatre Committee, the embodiment of the campaign for a National Theatre. This award was established to commemorate all those who worked with the SMNT. The Award, endowed by residual funds of the SMNT and now transferred to the Royal National Theatre Foundation, is intended to help further the careers of UK playwrights who are not yet established, and to draw contemporary theatre writers to the public's attention. The award is given to the writer whose play most nearly satisfies the following criteria: a play which embodies Geoffrey Whitworth's dictum that 'drama is important in so far as it reveals the truth about the relationships of human beings with each other and the world at large'; a play which shows promise of a developing new talent; a play in which the writing is of individual quality. Nominations are from professional theatre companies. Plays must have been written in the English language and produced professionally in the UK in the 12 months preceding the award. *Candidates will have had no more than two of their plays professionally produced.*

No writer who has won the award previously may reapply and no play that has been submitted previously for the award is eligible. Closing date: 31 August 2002.

Award £8000.

Milton Acorn Prize for Poetry

Poetry Forever, PO Box 68018, Hamilton, Ontario, Canada L8M 3M7

☎001 905 312 1779 Fax 001 905 312 8285

ESTABLISHED 1998. Open to poets worldwide who write in English. All types of poetry welcome; maximum 30 lines. Entry fee: £1.50 per poem (cheques payable to Poetry Forever). All profits from the contest will be used to fund publication of full-size collections by Milton Acorn, 'the People's Poet' (1923–86). Also runs the Orion Prize for Poetry to fund publication of work by Ottawa poet Marty Flomen (1942–97) and the Tidepool Prize for Poetry for work by Hamilton poet Herb Barrett (1912–95).

Cash prizes.

MIND Book of the Year

Granta House, 15–19 Broadway, London E15 4BQ

☎020 8519 2122 Fax 020 8522 1725

Email publication@mind.org.uk

Website www.mind.org.uk

ESTABLISHED 1981. Annual award, in memory of Sir Allen Lane, for the author of a book published in the current year (fiction or non-fiction), which furthers public understanding of mental health problems. 2000 winners: Herb A. Kutchins and Stuart A. Kirk *Making us Crazy: DSM – The Psychiatric Bible and the Creation of Mental Disorders.*

The Mitchell Prize for Art History/The Eric Mitchell Prize

c/o The Burlington Magazine, 14–16 Duke's Road, London WC1H 4SZ

☎020 7388 8157 Fax 020 7388 1230

Executive Director *Caroline Elam*

ESTABLISHED 1977 by art collector, philanthropist and businessman, Jan Mitchell, to draw attention to exceptional achievements in the history of art. Consists of two prizes: The Mitchell Prize, given for an outstanding and original contribution to the study and understanding of visual arts, and The Eric Mitchell Prize, given for the outstanding exhibition catalogue of the year. The prizes are awarded to authors of books in English that have been published in the previous 12 months. Books are submitted by publishers before the end of February. Previous winners: The Mitchell Prize: *Nicolas Poussin* Elizabeth Cropper and Charles Dempsey; The Eric Mitchell Prize: *The Triumph of Vulcan* Suzanne Brown Butters.

Prizes $10,000 (Mitchell Prize); $10,000 (Eric Mitchell Prize)

Scott Moncrieff Prize

See **The Translators Association Awards**

The Montagu of Beaulieu Trophy

Guild of Motoring Writers, 30 The Cravens, Smallfield, Surrey RH6 9QS

☎01342 843294 Fax 01342 844093

Email sharon@scott-fairweather.freeserve.co.uk

Contact *Sharon Scott-Fairweather*

First presented by Lord Montagu on the occasion of the opening of the National Motor Museum at Beaulieu in 1972. Awarded annually to a member of the **Guild of Motoring Writers** who, in the opinion of the nominated jury, has made the greatest contribution to recording in the English language the history of motoring or motor cycling in a published book or article, film, television or radio script, or research manuscript available to the public.

Prize Trophy.

Brian Moore Short Story Award

Creative Writers' Network, 15 Church Street, Belfast BT1 1ER

☎028 9031 2361 Fax 028 9043 4669

Email mmooney.cwn@virgin.net

Website www.creativewriters.org.uk

Contact *The Development Officer*

ESTABLISHED 1996. Annual competition to encourage short fiction in Northern Ireland. Open to writers born or resident outside Northern Ireland. Final entry date in September; full details available from May. 'Entries of a more adventurous or experimental nature are especially welcome.' In 2000 three winners shared a prize fund of £1000.

Mother Goose Award

See **The Books for Children Award**

Shiva Naipaul Memorial Prize

The Spectator, 56 Doughty Street, London WC1N 2LL

☎020 7405 1706 Fax 020 7242 0603

Email emma@spectator.co.uk

Contact *Emma Bagnall*

ESTABLISHED 1985. Annual prize given to an English language writer of any nationality under the age of 35 for an essay of not more than 4000 words describing a culture alien to the writer. Final entry date is 30 April. 2000 winner: Mary Wakefield.

Prize £3000.

NASEN Special Educational Needs Book Awards

The Educational Publishers Council, The Publishers Association, 1 Kingsway, London WC2B 6XD
☎020 7565 7474 Fax 020 7836 4543
Email mail@publishers.org.uk
Website www.publishers.org.uk

ESTABLISHED 1992. Organised by the National Association for Special Education Needs (NASEN) and the Educational Publishers Council. Two awards: The Children's Book Award, for the book that most successfully provides a positive image of children with special needs; The Academic Book Award celebrates the work of authors and editors who have made an outstanding contribution to the theory and practice of special education. Books must have been published in the UK within the year preceding the award. 2000 winners: Jeanne Willis and Tony Ross *Susan Laughs* (Children's); Clare Sainsbury *The Martian in the Playground* (Academic). *Prize* £500.

National Poetry Competition (in association with BT)

The Poetry Society, 22 Betterton Street, London WC2H 9BX
☎020 7420 9880 Fax 020 7240 4818
Email info@poetrysoc.com
Website www.poetrysoc.com

Contact *Competition Organiser (WH)*

One of Britain's major open poetry competitions. Closing date: 31 October. Poems on any theme, up to 40 lines. For rules and entry form send s.a.e. to the competition organiser at the address above or enter the competition via the website.

Prizes £5000 (1st); £1000 (2nd); £500 (3rd); plus 10 commendations of £50 and six additional prizes courtesy of BT.

Bill Naughton Short Story Competition

Box No. 2001, Aghamore, Ballyhaunis, Co. Mayo, Republic of Ireland

Organised by the **Kenny/Naughton Society** (see entry under **Literary Societies**). Stories may be on any topic and no more than 2500

words in length. All work must be unpublished; typed scripts only with no name or address appearing on the work. Entry fee: £3 per story (£1.50 unwaged); three stories may be submitted for the price of two. Closing date: 1 September 2001.

Prizes £150 (1st); £100 (2nd); £50 (3rd). Best stories published in a collection entitled *Splinters*.

Nestlé Smarties Book Prize

Book Trust, Book House, 45 East Hill, London SW18 2QZ
☎020 8516 2973 Fax 020 8516 2978
Email sandra@booktrust.org.uk
Website www.booktrust.org.uk

Contact *Sandra Vince*

ESTABLISHED 1985 to encourage high standards and stimulate interest in books for children, this prize is given for a children's book (fiction), written in English by a citizen of the UK or an author resident in the UK, and published in the UK in the year ending 31 October. There are three age-group categories: 5 and under, 6–8 and 9–11. 2000 winners: *Max* Bob Graham (5 and under); *Lizzie Zipmouth* Jacqueline Wilson (6–8 and Kids' Clubs Network Special Award); *The Wind Singer* William Nicholson (9–11).

Prizes in each category: £2500 (gold); £1000 (silver); £500 (bronze).

The New Writer Prose & Poetry Prizes

The New Writer, PO Box 60, Cranbrook, Kent TN17 2ZR
☎01580 212626 Fax 01580 212041
Email admin@thenewwriter.com
Website www.thenewwriter.com

Contact *Merric Davidson*

ESTABLISHED 1997. Annual award founded by *The New Writer* poetry editor and poet, Abi Hughes-Edwards. Open to all poets writing in the English language for an original, previously unpublished poem or collection of six to ten poems. Also open to writers of short stories and novellas/serials, features, articles, essays and interviews. Final entry date: 30 November. Previous winners: Mark Granier, Ros Barber, Celia de Fréine, John Hilton.

Prizes (total) £3000 plus publication in collection.

No Love Lost Poetry Anthology Contest

See **SEEDS International Poetry Chapbook Anthology Contest**

Nobel Prize

The Nobel Foundation, PO Box 5232,
102 45 Stockholm, Sweden
☎00 46 8 663 0920 Fax 00 46 8 660 3847
Website www.nobel.se

Contact *Information Section*

Awarded yearly for outstanding achievement in physics, chemistry, physiology or medicine, literature and peace. FOUNDED by Alfred Nobel, a chemist who proved his creative ability by inventing dynamite. In general, individuals cannot nominate someone for a Nobel Prize. The rules vary from prize to prize but the following are eligible to do so for Literature: members of the Swedish Academy and of other academies, institutions and societies similar to it in constitution and purpose; professors of literature and of linguistics at universities or colleges; Nobel Laureates in Literature; presidents of authors' organisations which are representative of the literary production in their respective countries. British winners of the literature prize, first granted in 1901, include Rudyard Kipling, John Galsworthy and Winston Churchill. Recent winners: Seamus Heaney; Camilio Jose Cela (Spain); Octavio Paz (Mexico); Nadine Gordimer (South Africa); Derek Walcott (St Lucia); Toni Morrison (USA); Kenzaburo Oe (Japan); Wislawa Szymborska (Poland); Dario Fo (Italy); José Saramago (Portugal); Günter Grass (Germany). Nobel Laureate in Literature 2000: Gao Xingjian (France). *Prize* 2000: SEK9,000,000 (approx. £900,000), increasing each year to cover inflation.

The Noma Award for Publishing Africa

PO Box 128, Witney, Oxfordshire OX8 5XU
☎01993 775235 Fax 01993 709265
Email maryljay@aol.com

Contact *Mary Jay, Secretary to the Managing Committee*

ESTABLISHED 1979. Annual award, founded by the late Shoichi Noma, President of Kodansha Ltd, Tokyo, to encourage the publication of works by African writers and scholars within Africa. The award is for an outstanding book, published in Africa by an African writer, in three categories: scholarly and academic; literature and creative writing; children's books. Entries, by publishers only, by 28 February for a title published in the previous year. Maximum number of three entries. Previous winners: Kitia Touré *Destins Parallèles*; A. Adu Boahen *Mfantsipim and the Making of Ghana: A Centenary History 1876–1976*; Peter Adwok Nyaba *The Politics of Liberation in South Sudan; An Insider's View*; Djibril Samb *L'intérpretation des rêves dans la région Sénégambienne. Suivi de la clef des songes de la Sénégambie, de l'Egypte pharaonique et de la tradition islamique*; Kimari Njogu and Rocha Chimerah *uFundishaji wa Fasihi. Nadharia na Mbinu*.
Prize US$10,000 and presentation plaque.

C.B. Oldman Prize

Aberdeen University Library, Queen Mother Library, Meston Walk, Aberdeen AB24 3UE
☎01224 272592 Fax 01224 487048
Email r.turbet@abdn.ac.uk

Contact *Richard Turbet*

ESTABLISHED 1989 by the International Association of Music Libraries, UK Branch. Annual award for best book of music bibliography, librarianship or reference published the year before last (i.e. books published in 1999 considered for the 2001 prize). Previous winners: Michael Twyman, Andrew Ashbee, Michael Talbot, Donald Clarke, John Parkinson, John Wagstaff, Stanley Sadie, William Waterhouse, Richard Turbet, John Gillaspie.
Prize £150.

Open Window Poetry Anthology Contest

See **SEEDS International Poetry Chapbook Anthology Contest**

Orange Prize for Fiction

Book Trust, 45 East Hill, London SW18 2QZ
☎020 8516 2973 Fax 020 8516 2978
Email sandra@booktrust.org.uk
Website www.booktrust.org.uk

Contact *Sandra Vince*

ESTABLISHED 1996. Annual award founded by a group of senior women in publishing to 'create the opportunity for more women to be rewarded for their work and to be better known by the reading public'. Awarded for a full-length novel written in English by a woman of any nationality, and published in the UK between 1 April and 31 March of the following year. 2000 winner: Linda Grant *When I Lived in Modern Times*.
Prize £30,000 and a work of art (a limited edition bronze figurine to be known as 'The Bessie' in acknowledgement of anonymous prize endowment).

Orion Prize for Poetry

See **Milton Acorn Prize for Poetry**

The Orwell Prize

Specialist Conferences Ltd, 21 The Lodge,
Kensington Park Gardens, London W11 3HA
☎020 7727 9732

Contact *Maxine Vlieland*

Jointly ESTABLISHED in 1993 by the George
Orwell Memorial Fund and the *Political Quarterly*
to encourage and reward writing in the spirit of
Orwell's 'What I have most wanted to do ... is to
make political writing into an art'. Two categories: book or pamphlet; newspaper and/or
articles, features, columns, or sustained reportage
on a theme. Submissions by editors, publishers or
authors. Previous winners: David Aaronovitch
(journalism); Michael Ignatieff (book).

Prizes £1000 for each category.

Outposts Poetry Competition

Outposts, 22 Whitewell Road, Frome,
Somerset BA11 4EL
☎01373 466653

Contact *Roland John*

Annual competition for an unpublished poem of
not more than 60 lines run by **Hippopotamus
Press**.

Prizes £500 (1st), £200 (2nd), £100 (3rd).

The Wilfred Owen Award for Poetry

17 Belmont, Shrewsbury, Shropshire SY1 1TE
☎01743 235904 Fax 01743 235904
Website www.wilfred.owen.mcmail.com

Contact *Helen McPhail*

Biennial award ESTABLISHED in 1988 by the
Wilfred Owen Association. Given to a poet
whose poetry reflects the spirit of Owen's
work in its thinking, expression and inspiration. Applications are not sought; the decision
is made by the Association's committee.
Previous winner: Seamus Heaney.

Award A silver and gunmetal work of art,
suitably decorated and engraved.

OWG Awards for Excellence

Outdoor Writers' Guild, PO Box 520,
Bamber Bridge, Preston, Lancashire PR5 8LF
☎01772 696732 Fax 01772 696732

Contact *Terry Marsh*

ESTABLISHED 1980. Annual award by the
Outdoor Writers' Guild to raise the standard of outdoor writing, journalism and broadcasting. Winning categories include guidebook, outdoor book, feature (one-off), feature
(regular), photography. Open to OWG members only. Final entry date: March.

Catherine Pakenham Award

The Sunday Telegraph, 1 Canada Square,
Canary Wharf, London E14 5DT
☎020 7538 6257 Fax 020 7513 2512

Contact *Charlotte Ibarra*

ESTABLISHED in 1970, the award is designed to
ecourage women journalists as they embark on
their careers. Open to women aged 18–25 who
have had at least one piece of work published,
however small. 2000 winner: Laura Barton.

Award £1000 and a writing commission
with one of the Telegraph publications; three
runner-up prizes of £200 each.

The Parker Romantic Novel of the Year

2 Broad Oak Lane, Wigginton, York
YO32 3SB
☎01904 765035

Award Organiser *Joan Emery*

ESTABLISHED 1960. Formerly known as the
Romantic Novelists' Association Major
Award. Sponsorship for the 2001 award is by
Parker Pen. Annual award for the best romantic novel of the year, open to non-members as
well as members of the **Romantic Novelists'
Association**. Novels must be published
between specified dates. Authors must be based
in the UK unless members of the RNA. 2001
winner: Cathy Kelly *Someone Like You*.
Contact the Organiser for entry form.

Award £5000.

The PAWS (Public Awareness of Science) Midas Prize

The PAWS Office, OMNI Communications,
Chancel House, Neasden Lane, London
NW10 2TU
☎020 8214 1543 Fax 020 8214 1544
Email pawsomni@globalnet.co.uk

Contacts *Barrie Whatley, Andrew Millington*

ESTABLISHED 1998. Annual prize awarded to
the writer and producer of the best television
drama, first transmitted in the year up to the
end of October, that bears in a significant way
on science or engineering. The drama may be a
single play or an episode of a series, serial or
soap. It need not necessarily be centred on a
science or engineering theme, although clearly
it can be. The context and quality of the drama
and the audience size all weigh alongside the
science in making the Award. To enter a programme or suggest that a programme should be
entered, contact the PAWS office above.

Prize £5000.

PEN Awards

See **J.R. Ackerley Prize**; **Golden PEN Award for Lifetime Distinguished Services to Literature**; **Macmillan Silver PEN Award**; **The Stern Silver PEN Non-Fiction Award**

Peterloo Poets Open Poetry Competition

The Old Chapel, Sand Lane, Calstock, Cornwall PL18 9QX
☎01822 833473

Contact *Harry Chambers*

ESTABLISHED 1986. Annual competition for unpublished English language poems of not more than 40 lines. Final entry date: 1 March. Send s.a.e. for rules and entry form. Previous winners: John Watts, Jem Poster, David Craig, Rodney Pybus, Debjani Chatterjee, Donald Atkinson, Romesh Gunesekera, Anna Crowe, Carol Ann Duffy, Mimi Khalvati, John Lyons, M.R. Peacocke, Alison Pryde, Carol Shergold, Maureen Wilkinson, Chris Woods.

Prizes £2000 (1st); £1000 (2nd); £500 (3rd); £100 (4th); plus 10 prizes of £50; 15–19 age group: 5 prizes of £100.

Pets on Parade Short Story Competition

Bridlington and District RSPCA, 42 Quay Road, Bridlington, East Yorkshire YO16 2AP
Competition Organiser *Viv Stamford*

Annual short story competition. The 20 winning stories are published in book form which is sold to raise funds to help animals. For further details send s.a.e. to the address above.

Prize £100 (1st).

Poetry Business Competition

The Studio, Byram Arcade, Westgate, Huddersfield, West Yorkshire HD1 1ND
☎01484 434840   Fax 01484 426566
Email edit@poetrybusiness.co.uk
Website www.poetrybusiness.co.uk

Contact *The Competition Administrator*

ESTABLISHED 1986. Annual award which aims to discover and publish new writers. Entrants should submit a manuscript of poems. Winners will have their work published by the **Poetry Business** under the Smith/Doorstop imprint. Final entry date: end of October. Previous winners include: Pauline Stainer, Michael Laskey, Mimi Khalvati, David Morley, Julia Casterton, Liz Cashdan, Moniza Alvi, Selima Hill. Send s.a.e. for full details.

Prizes Publication of full collection; runners-up have pamphlets; 20 complimentary copies. Also cash prize (£1000) to be shared equally between all winners.

Poetry Life Poetry Competition

1 Blue Ball Corner, Water Lane, Winchester, Hampshire SO23 0ER
Email adrian.abishop@virgin.net
Website freespace.virgin.net/poetry.life/
Contact *Adrian Bishop*

ESTABLISHED 1993. Open competition for original poems in any style which have not been published in a book. Maximum length of 80 lines. Entry fee of £3 per poem. Send s.a.e. for details.

Prizes £500 (1st); £100 (2nd); £50 each (3rd & 4th).

The Poetry Society's National Poetry Competition

See **National Poetry Competition**

Peter Pook Humorous Novel Competition

See **Emissary Publishing** under **UK Publishers**

The Portico Prize

The Portico Library, 57 Mosley Street, Manchester M2 3HY
☎0161 236 6785   Fax 0161 236 6803

Contact *Miss Emma Marigliano*

ESTABLISHED 1985. Administered by the Portico Library in Manchester. Biennial award for a work of fiction or non-fiction published between the two closing dates. Set wholly or mainly in the North-West of England, including Cumbria and the High Peak District of Derbyshire. Next award: June 2002. Previous winners include: John Stalker *Stalker*; Alan Hankinson *Coleridge Walks the Fells*; Jenny Uglow *Elizabeth Gaskell: A Habit of Stories*.

Prize £3000.

The Dennis Potter Screenwriting Award

BBC Broadcasting House, Whiteladies Road, Bristol BS8 2LR
☎0117 974 7586
Email BBC2Awards@bbc.co.uk

Editor *Jeremy Howe*

Annual award ESTABLISHED in 1995 in memory of the late television playwright to 'nurture and encourage the work of new writers of talent and personal vision'. The winning drama is screened as part of the BBC2 Awards programme in November. Submissions should be made through a BBC TV drama producer or an independent production company. For further information contact the editor.

The Premio Valle Inclán
See **The Translators Association Awards**

The Mathew Prichard Award for Short Story Writing
Competition Secretary, 2 Rhododendron Close, The Greenways, Cyn Coed, Cardiff CF23 7HS

Competition Organiser *Philip Beynon*
Competition Secretary *Marjorie Williams*

ESTABLISHED 1996 to provide sponsorship and promote Wales and its writers. Competition open to all writers in English; the final entry date is 1 March each year.
   Prizes A total of £2000.

V.S. Pritchett Memorial Prize
Royal Society of Literature, Somerset House, Strand, London WC2R 1LA
☎020 7845 4676 Fax 020 7845 4679
Email info@rslit.org
Website www.rslit.org

ESTABLISHED 1999. Awarded for a previously unpublished short story of between 2000 and 5000 words. For entry forms please contact the Secretary from February onwards. Closing date for entries: 30 April.

Pulitzer Prizes
The Pulitzer Prize Board, 709 Journalism, Columbia University, New York NY 10027, USA
☎001 212 854 3841/2
Website www.pulitzer.org

Awards for journalism in US newspapers, and for published literature, drama and music by American nationals. Deadlines: 1 February (journalism); 1 March (music); 1 March (drama); 1 July for books published between 1 Jan–30 June, and 1 Nov for books published between 1 July–31 Dec (literature). Previous winners include: Michael Chabon *The Amazing Adventures of Kavalier & Clay*; Joseph J. Ellis *Founding Brothers: The Revolutionary Generation*; David Levering Lewis *W.E.B. Du Bois: The Fight for Equality and the American Century, 1919–1963*; Stephen Dunn *Different Hours*; Herbert P. Bix *Hirohito and the Making of Modern Japan*.

The *Real* Writers/The Book Pl@ce Short Story Awards
PO Box 170, Chesterfield, Derbyshire S40 1FE
☎01246 238492 Fax 01246 238492
Email realwrtrs@aol.com
Website www.turtledesign.com/RealWriters/

Formerly the *Real* Writers Short Story Competition, ESTABLISHED 1994. Sponsored by www.thebookplace.com Closing date: 20 September. Entry fee: £5. Optional critiques. S.a.e. to the address above for entry forms, etc.
   Prizes (1st) £2500 plus 10 regional awards.

Trevor Reese Memorial Prize
Institute of Commonwealth Studies, University of London, 28 Russell Square, London WC1B 5DS
☎020 7862 8844 Fax 020 7862 8820

Contact *Events & Publicity Officer*

ESTABLISHED 1979 with the proceeds of contributions to a memorial fund to Dr Trevor Reese, Reader in Commonwealth Studies at the Institute and a distinguished scholar of imperial history (d.1976). Biennial award (next award 2002) for a scholarly work, usually by a single author, in the field of Imperial and Commonwealth History published in the preceding two academic years. All correspondence relating to the prize should be marked 'Trevor Reese Memorial Prize'.
   Prize £1000.

Regional Press Awards
Press Gazette, Quantum House, 19 Scarbrook Road, Croydon, Surrey CR9 1LX
☎020 8565 4463 Fax 020 8565 4462
Email pged@qpp.co.uk

Comprehensive range of journalist and newspaper awards for the regional press. Five newspapers of the year, by circulation and frequency, and a full list of journalism categories. Open to all regional journalists, whether freelance or staff. July event. Run by the *Press Gazette*.

Renault UK Journalist of the Year Award
Guild of Motoring Writers, 30 The Cravens, Smallfield, Surrey RH6 9QS
☎01342 843294 Fax 01342 844093
Email sharon@scott-fairweather.freeserve.co.uk

Contact *Sharon Scott-Fairweather*

Originally the Pierre Dreyfus Award and

ESTABLISHED 1977. Awarded annually by Renault UK Ltd in honour of Pierre Dreyfus, president director general of Renault 1955–75, to the member of the **Guild of Motoring Writers** who is judged to have made the most outstanding journalistic effort during the year.
Prize (1st) £1500, plus trophy.

John Llewellyn Rhys Prize
See **The Mail on Sunday/John Llewellyn Rhys Prize**

Romantic Novelists' Association Major Award
See **The Parker Romantic Novel of the Year**

Rooney Prize for Irish Literature
Rooney Prize, Strathin, Templecarrig, Delgany, Co. Wicklow, Republic of Ireland
☎00 353 1 287 4769 Fax 00 353 1 287 2595
Email rooney-prize@ireland.com

Contacts *Jim Sherwin, Thelma Cloake*

ESTABLISHED 1976. Annual award to encourage young Irish writing to develop and continue. Authors must be Irish, under 40 and published. A non-competitive award with no application procedure.
Prize IR£6000.

Royal Economic Society Prize
c/o University of York, York YO10 5DD
☎01904 433575 Fax 01904 433575

Contact *Professor Mike Wickens*

Annual award for the best article published in *The Economic Journal*. Open to members of the Royal Economic Society only. Previous winners: Professors Kip Viscusi, Daniel Friedman and Darren Acemoglu.
Prize £3000.

Royal Society of Literature Awards
See **Winifred Holtby Memorial Prize** and **W.H. Heinemann Prize**

Runciman Award
The Anglo–Hellenic League, c/o The Hellenic Centre, 16–18 Paddington Street, London W1U 5AS
☎020 7486 9410 Fax 020 7486 4254

Contact *The Administrator*

ESTABLISHED 1985. Annual award, sponsored by the National Bank of Greece. Founded by the Anglo–Hellenic League to promote Anglo–Greek understanding and friendship, for a work wholly or mainly about some aspect of Greece or the Hellenic scene, which has been published in its first English edition in the UK during the previous year and listed in Whitaker's Books in Print. Named after the late Sir Steven Runciman, former chairman of the Anglo–Hellenic League. The Award may be given for a work of fiction, drama or non-fiction; concerned academically or non-academically with the history of any period; biography or autobiography, the arts, archaeology; a guide book or a translation from the Greek of any period. Final entry date in February; award presented in May/June. 2000 winner: Professor John Luce *Celebrating Homer's Landscapes* .
Awards of at least £2000.

Sagittarius Prize
Society of Authors, 84 Drayton Gardens, London SW10 9SB
☎020 7373 6642 Fax 020 7373 5768

ESTABLISHED 1990. For first published novel by an author over the age of 60. Final entry date: 20 December. Full details available from the **Society of Authors**. 2000 winner: David Crackanthorpe *Stolen Marches*.
Prize £2000.

Sainsbury's Baby Book Award
Book Trust, Book House, 45 East Hill, London SW18 2QZ
☎020 8516 2973 Fax 020 8516 2978
Email sandra@booktrust.org.uk
Website www.booktrust.org.uk

Contact *Sandra Vince*

ESTABLISHED 1999. Annual award, set up by **Book Trust** with sponsorship from Sainsbury's, for the best book for a baby under one year old, published in the UK. 2000 winner: Alex Ayliffe *Boo Barney*.
Prize £2000 and trophy to the winner; certificate and trophy to the winning publisher.

The Saltire Literary Awards
Saltire Society, 9 Fountain Close, 22 High Street, Edinburgh EH1 1TF
☎0131 556 1836 Fax 0131 557 1675

Administrator *Kathleen Munro*

ESTABLISHED 1982. Annual awards, one for Book of the Year, the other for Best First Book by an author publishing for the first time. Open to any author of Scottish descent or living in Scotland, or to anyone who has written a book which deals with either the work and life of a Scot or with a Scottish problem, event or situation. Nominations are invited from editors of leading newspapers, magazines and periodicals. Previous winners: Saltire Scottish Book of the Year: Ronald Frame *The Lantern Bearers*; The Post Office/Saltire Best First Book: Douglas Galbraith *The Rising Sun*.

Prizes £5000 (Scottish Book); £1500 (First Book).

Sandburg-Livesay Anthology Contest

Mekler & Deahl, Publishers, 237 Prospect Street South, Hamilton, Ontario, Canada L8M 2Z6

☎001 905 312 1779 Fax 001 905 312 8285
Email james@meklerdeahl.com
Website www.meklerdeahl.com

Contacts *James Deahl, Gilda Mekler*

FOUNDED 1996. Annual award named after the poets Carl Sandburg and Dorothy Livesay to honour their achievement as populist poets. Up to ten poems may be entered for a fee of £6. A copy of the rules is available from the above address or from the website. Final entry date: 31 October. *Prizes* US$250 (1st); US$150 (2nd); US$100 (3rd); anthology publication for the winners and all other worthy entries.

Ron Sands Prize

See **Lakeland Book of the Year Awards**

The Biennial Sasakawa Prize

British Haiku Society, Sinodun, Shalford, Braintree, Essex CM7 5HN
☎01371 851097 Fax 01371 851097
Website www.BritishHaikuSociety.org

Contact *David Cobb*

ESTABLISHED 1999. Biennial prize (next in 2003) for original contributions in the field of haikai (haiku and related genres). Open to entrants domiciled in either the UK or Japan. Closing date: 31 December 2003. Entry details available from the British Haiku Society at the address above or on the website.

Prize £2500, partly in the form of a return air ticket to Japan (or to the UK for a Japanese winner).

Schlegel-Tieck Prize

See **The Translators Association Awards**

Scottish Arts Council Children's Book Awards

Scottish Arts Council, 12 Manor Place, Edinburgh EH3 7DD
☎0131 226 6051 Fax 0131 225 9833
Email jenny.brown@scottisharts.org.uk

Website www.sac.org.uk

Literature Director *Jenny Brown*

A number of awards are given annually (spring) to authors of published books in recognition of high standards in children's fiction or non-fiction from new or established writers. Awards are made in three categories: picture books for children, books aimed at 6–9 years, and books aimed at 10+ years. Authors should be Scottish or resident in Scotland, or books must be of Scottish interest. Applications from publishers only. 2000 winners: Debi Gliori *Mr Bear's New Baby*; Judith O'Neill *Whirlwind*; Julie Bertagna *Soundtrack*; Margaret Ryan and (illus.) Priscilla Lamont *The Queen's Birthday Hat*; Richard Brassey and Stewart Ross *The Story of Scotland*.

Award £1000 each.

Scottish Book of the Year

See **The Saltire Literary Awards**

Scottish Historical Book of the Year

The Saltire Society, 9 Fountain Close, 22 High Street, Edinburgh EH1 1TF
☎0131 556 1836 Fax 0131 557 1675
Email saltire@saltire.org.uk
Website www.saltire-society.demon.co.uk

Administrator *Kathleen Munro*

ESTABLISHED 1965. Annual award in memory of the late Dr Agnes Mure Mackenzie for a published work of distinguished Scottish historical research of scholarly importance (including intellectual history and the history of science). Editions of texts are not eligible. Nominations are invited and should be sent to the Administrator. Previous winner: Eric Richards *Patrick Sellar and the Highland Clearances, Homicide, Eviction and the Price of Progress*.

Prize Bound and inscribed copy of the winning publication.

SCSE Book Prizes

Institute of Education, University of London, 20 Bedford Way, London WC1H 0AL
☎020 7612 6003 Fax 020 7612 6330

Contact *Professor G. Grace (Chair of Book Prize Committee)*

Annual awards given by the Standing Conference on Studies in Education for the best books on Education published during the preceding year. Nomination by members of the Standing Conference and publishers or by individual authors based in the UK.

Prizes £1000, £750 and £300.

SEEDS International Poetry Chapbook Anthology Contest

Hidden Brook Press, 412–701 King Street West, Toronto, Ontario, Canada M5V 2W7
☎001 416 504 3966 Fax 001 801 751 1837
Email writers@hiddenbrookpress.com
Website www.HiddenBrookPress.com

Biannual international poetry competition. Electronic and hard copy submissions are required. Send three poems, of any style, theme or length, with name, address, phone number and e-mail address on the back of each sheet. Send three poems with fee (US$14 for submissions outside of Canada) and follow this with submission by e-mail (no attachments). Closing dates: 1 May and 1 October. Cash *Prizes*; all prize winners are published in the *SEEDS International Poetry Chapbook Anthology* and on the website.

(Also runs two further international anthology contests: No Love Lost and The Open Window. See website for details.)

Bernard Shaw Translation Prize

See **The Translators Association Awards**

Signal Poetry for Children Award

Thimble Press, Lockwood, Station Road, South Woodchester, Stroud, Gloucestershire GL5 5EQ
☎01453 755566/872208 Fax 01453 878599
Contact *Nancy Chambers*

This award is given annually for particular excellence in one of the following areas: single-poet collections published for children; poetry anthologies published for children; the body of work of a contemporary poet; critical or educational activity promoting poetry for children. All books for children published in Britain are eligible regardless of the original country of publication. Unpublished work is not eligible. Previous winners include: Helen Dunmore *Secrets*; Roger McGough *Bad, Bad Cats*.

Award Substantial article-citation in each May issue of the journal *Signal*; certificate designed by Michael Harvey.

André Simon Memorial Fund Book Awards

5 Sion Hill Place, Bath BA1 5SJ
☎01225 336305 Fax 01225 421862
Email tessa@tantraweb.co.uk
Contact *Tessa Hayward*

ESTABLISHED 1978. Three awards given annually for the best book on drink, best on food

and special commendation in either. 2000 winners: Michael Schuster *Essential Winetasting*; Nigel Slater *Appetite*; Sue Shephard *Pickled, Potted and Canned* (special commendation).

Awards £2000 (best books); £1000 (special commendation); £200 to shortlisted books.

WHSmith Book Awards

WHSmith PLC, Nations House, 103 Wigmore Street, London W1U 1WH
☎020 7514 9623 Fax 020 7514 9635
Email elizabeth.walker@group-whsmith.co.uk
Website www.whsmith.co.uk
Contact *Elizabeth Walker, Awards Manager*

A newly-established Award voted for by the public (presented for the first time on 26 April 2001) celebrating excellence in published works across a broad spectrum of subjects. The eight new public-voting categories are: Biography/Autobiography; Children's Book of the Year; Fiction; Travel Writing; Business; General Knowledge; New Talent; Home & Leisure. A panel of judges for each category selects its own short list with the general public voting for the winners in WHSmith stores or via the internet at www.whsmith.co.uk/awards

The ninth category incorporates the long-standing WHSmith Literary Award.

WHSmith's Thumping Good Read Award

WHSmith PLC, Greenbridge Road, Swindon, Wiltshire SN3 3LD
☎01793 616161 Fax 01793 562590
Contact *Award Administrator*

ESTABLISHED 1992 to promote new writers of popular fiction. Books must have been published in the twelve months preceding the award. Submissions, made by publishers, are judged by a panel of customers to be the most un-put-down-able from a shortlist of six. 2000 winner: Boris Starling *Storm*.

Award £5000.

The Society for Theatre Research Annual Theatre Book Prize

c/o The Theatre Museum, 1e Tavistock Street, London WC2E 7PA
Email e.cottis@btinternet.com
Website www.str.org.uk

ESTABLISHED 1997. Annual award for books, in English, of original research into any aspect of the history and technique of the British Theatre. Not restricted to authors of British nationality nor books solely from British publishers. Books

must be first published in English (no translations) during the calendar year. Play texts and those treating drama as literature are not eligible. Publishers submit books directly to the independent judges and should contact the Book Prize Administrator for further details. 2000 winner: Nicholas de Jongh *Politics, Prudery and Perversions: The Censoring of the English Stage 1901–1968.*
Award £400.

Sony Radio Awards

Alan Zafer & Associates, 47–48 Chagford Street, London NW1 6EB
☎020 7723 0106   Fax 020 7724 6163
Email secretariat@radioawards.org
Website www.radioawards.org

Contact *The Secretariat*

ESTABLISHED 1981 by the **Society of Authors**. Sponsored by Sony and presented in association with the Radio Academy. Annual awards to recognise excellence in radio broadcasting. Entries must have been broadcast in the UK between 1 January and 31 December in the year preceding the award. The categories for the awards are reviewed each year.

Southport Writers' Circle Poetry Competition

46 Sandon Road, Southport, Merseyside PR8 4QH

Contact *Mrs Hilary Tinsley*

For previously unpublished work. Entry fee: £2 per poem. Any subject, any form; maximum 40 lines. Closing date: end April. Poems must be entered under a pseudonym, accompanied by a sealed envelope marked with the pseudonym and title of poem, containing s.a.e. Entries must be typed on A4 paper and be accompanied by the appropriate fee payable to Southport Writers' Circle. No application form is required. Envelopes should be marked 'Poetry Competition'. Postal enquiries only. No calls.
Prizes £250 (1st); £50 (2nd); £25 (3rd); additional £25 Humour Prize.

Spoken Word Awards

The Spoken Word Publishing Association, BBC Spoken Word, Room A1047 Woodlands, 80 Wood Lane, London W12 0TT
☎020 8433 2708
Email Connie.Bristow-Stagg@bbc.co.uk

Contact *Connie Bristow-Stagg*

Hosted by the **Spoken Word Publishing Association**, the Awards are for excellence in the spoken word industry and recognise the valuable work of all those involved with the production of audio books. There are 22 categories of award, consisting of 14 Consumer Awards (including Drama, Biography, Poetry, Children's and Comedy), four Trade Awards (including Best Retailer and Best Media Coverage) and four Performance Awards (Male and Female Performer of the Year, Publisher of the Year and Spoken Word Audio of the Year).
Prizes Glass trophy for the 'Gold' awards; certificates for Silver and Bronze.

The Stern Silver PEN Non-Fiction Award

English Centre of International PEN, 152–156 Kentish Town Road, London NW1 9QB
☎020 7267 9444   Fax 020 7267 9304
Email enquiries@pen.org.uk
Website www.pen.org.uk

ESTABLISHED 1986 and sponsored, from 1997, by the family of James Stern in memory of their father. An annual award for an outstanding work of non-fiction written in English and published in England in the year preceding the prize. Nominations by the PEN Executive Committee only. Please do not submit books. 2000 winner: Andrew Roberts *Salisbury; Victorian Titan.*
Prize £1000, plus silver pen.

Bram Stoker Awards for Superior Achievement

Horror Writers Association, PO Box 50577, Palo Alto, CA 94303, USA
☎001 650 322 4610
Email hwa@horror.org
Website www.horror.org

Contact *Nancy Etchemendy*

FOUNDED 1988 and named in honour of Bram Stoker, author of *Dracula*. Presented annually by the **Horror Writers Association** (HWA) for works of horror first published in the English language. Works are eligible during their first year of publication. HWA members recommend works for consideration in twelve categories: novel, first novel, short fiction, long fiction, fiction collection, anthology, non-fiction, illustrated narrative, screenplay, work for young readers, poetry, and other media. In addition, Lifetime Achievement Stokers are occasionally presented to individuals whose entire body of work has substantially influenced horror.

The Strokestown Poetry Prize

Strokestown Poetry Festival, Strokestown, Co. Roscommon, Republic of Ireland
☎00 353 78 33759
Email twiggezvous@eircom.net

Website www.strokestownpoetryprize.com
Contacts *M. Harpur, Pat Compton*

Annual competition ESTABLISHED in 1999 by Strokestown Community Development Association to reward excellence in poetry. A centrepiece of the Strokestown Poetry Festival held the first weekend in May. Final entry date: mid-February. Maximum length: 70 lines. All short-listed poets are expected to attend the festival and read their poem.

Prizes £3000; £1000; £500; and nine runner-up prizes of £50 each. Also prizes totalling £2000 for a poem in Irish (max. 50 lines); and £300 for a political satire in verse.

Sunday Times **Award for Small Publishers**

Independent Publishers Guild, PO Box 93, Royston, Hertfordshire SG8 5GH
Fax 01763 246293
Email sheila@ipg.uk.com
Contact *Sheila Bounford*

ESTABLISHED 1988, the first winner was **Fourth Estate**. Open to any publisher producing between five and forty titles a year, which must primarily be original titles, not reprints. Entrants are invited to submit their catalogues for the last twelve months, together with two representative titles. Award presented at the London Book Fair. 2001 winner: **Hambledon and London**. Previous winners include: **Carcanet Press**; **Profile Books**; **Nick Hern Books**; **Tarquin Publications**; **Ellipsis**; **Bradt Publications**.

Sunday Times **Writer of the Year Award**

The Sunday Times, 1 Pennington Street, London E1 9XW
☎020 7782 5770 Fax 020 7782 5798

ESTABLISHED 1987. Annual award to fiction and non-fiction writers. The panel consists of *Sunday Times* journalists and critics. Previous winners: Anthony Burgess, Seamus Heaney, Stephen Hawking, Ruth Rendell, Muriel Spark, William Trevor, Martin Amis, Margaret Atwood, Ted Hughes, Harold Pinter, Tom Wolfe, Robert Hughes. No applications; prize at the discretion of the Literary Editor.

Sunday Times **Young Writer of the Year Award**

The Society of Authors, 84 Drayton Gardens, London SW10 9SB
☎020 7373 6642 Fax 020 7373 5768
Contact *Awards Secretary*

ESTABLISHED 1991. Annual award given on the strength of the promise shown by a full-length published work of fiction, non-fiction, poetry or drama. Entrants must be British citizens, resident in Britain and under the age of 35. The panel consists of *Sunday Times* journalists and critics. Closing date: 20 December. The work must be by one author, in the English language, and published in Britain. Applications by publishers via the **Society of Authors**. 2000 winner: Sarah Waters *Affinity*.

Tabla Poetry Competition

Department of English, University of Bristol, 3–5 Woodland Road, Bristol BS8 1TB
Fax 0117 928 8860
Email stephen.james@bristol.ac.uk
Website www.bris.ac.uk/tabla
Contact *Stephen James*

ESTABLISHED 1991. Annual award for poems of any length which have not been published or broadcast. Minimum age of entrants must be 16. Final entry date: 31 May. No poems by e-mail, please. Winning and other selected entries are published, alongside leading names, in the annual *Tabla Book of New Verse*. Previous winners: Philip Gross, Henry Shukman.

Prizes £500 (1st); £200 (2nd); 3 runners-up, £100 each.

Reginald Taylor and Lord Fletcher Essay Prize

Journal of the British Archaeological Association, Institute of Archaelogy, 36 Beaumont Street, Oxford OX1 2PG
Contact *Dr Martin Henig*

A biennial prize, in memory of the late E. Reginald Taylor and of Lord Fletcher, for the best unpublished essay, not exceeding 7500 words, on a subject of archaeological, art history or antiquarian interest within the period from the Roman era to AD 1830. The essay should show *original* research on its chosen subject, and the author will be invited to read the essay before the Association. The essay may be published in the journal of the Association if approved by the Editorial Committee. Closing date for entries is 1 June 2002. All enquiries by post please. No phone calls. Send s.a.e. for details.

Prize £300 and a medal.

The Teixeira Gomes Prize
See **The Translators Association Awards**

Tidepool Prize for Poetry
See **Milton Acorn Prize for Poetry**

The Times Educational Supplement Book Awards

Times Educational Supplement, Admiral House, 66–68 East Smithfield, London E1W 1BX

☎020 7782 3000 Fax 020 7782 3200
Email friday@tes.co.uk
Website www.tes.co.uk

Contact *Awards Administrator*

ESTABLISHED 1973. The Awards are under review at present.

The Tir Na N-Og Award

Cyngor Llyfrau Cymru (Welsh Books Council), Castell Brychan, Aberystwyth, Dyfed SY23 2JB

☎01970 624151 Fax 01970 625385
Email castellbrychan@cllc.org.uk
Website www.wbc.org.uk

An annual award given to the best original book published for children in the year prior to the announcement. There are three categories: Best Welsh Fiction; Best Welsh Non-fiction; Best English Book with an authentic Welsh background.

Awards £1000 (each category).

TLS/Blackwells Poetry Competition

Times Literary Supplement, Admiral House, 66–68 East Smithfield, London E1W 1BX

☎020 7782 3000
Website www.the-tls.co.uk

Contact *Mick Imlah (Poetry Editor, TLS)*

ESTABLISHED 1997. Annual open competition. Final entry date: 30 November. 1999 winner: Matthew Francis.

Prizes £2000; three runners-up £500 each.

Tolman Cunard Prize

See **The Forward Prizes for Poetry**

Marten Toonder Award

An Chomhairle Ealaíon (The Irish Arts Council), 70 Merrion Square, Dublin 2, Republic of Ireland

☎00 353 1 6180200 Fax 00 353 1 6761302
Email info@artscouncil.ie
Website www.artscouncil.ie

Music Officer *Maura Eaton*

The award, made possible by Dutch artist Marten Toonder, honours established artists in music, literature and the visual arts. In 2001 the award was made for literature; in 2002 it will be for visual art and music in 2003. Applicants should enclose a detailed c.v. as well as an excerpt or copy of their work. The standard application form for individuals should be used and is available on request.

Award €10,000/IR£7875.

The Translators Association Awards

The Translators Association, 84 Drayton Gardens, London SW10 9SB

☎020 7373 6642 Fax 020 7373 5768

Contact *Dorothy Sym*

Various awards for published translations into English from Dutch and Flemish (The Vondel Translation Prize), French (Scott Moncrieff Prize), German (Schlegel-Tieck Prize), Italian (The John Florio Prize), Portuguese (The Teixeira Gomes Prize), Spanish (The Premio Velle Inclán), Swedish (Bernard Shaw Translation Prize) and Japanese (Sasakawa Prize). Contact the **Translators Association** for full details.

The Betty Trask Prize

See entry under **Bursaries, Fellowships and Grants**

Travelex Travel Writers' Awards

Ingrams, 120–122 Seymour Place, London W1H 1EL

☎020 7339 7777 Fax 020 7339 7878

ESTABLISHED in 1993 to reward excellence in UK travel journalism. An overall winner is selected from the eight category winners. These cover national daily newspaper, national Sunday newspaper, regional newspaper, trade press, consumer magazine, radio, television and guidebook. 2000 winner: Tony Wheeler (founder of **Loney Planet**).

Prizes £1000 and special crystal trophy; £500 and crystal trophy for each category winner.

The Trewithen Poetry Prize

Chy-an-Dour, Trewithen Moor, Stithians, Truro, Cornwall TR3 7DU

Contact *Competition Secretary*

ESTABLISHED 1995 in order to promote poetry with a rural theme. Entry forms available from the address above (enclose s.a.e.). Closing date: 31 October. Entry fee of £3 for first poem, £1.75 for subsequent entries. Previous winners include: Elizabeth Rapp, David Smart, Ann Drysdale, Roger Elkin.

Prizes (total) £800 plus publication in *The Trewithen Chapbook*.

Tullie House Prize
See **Lakeland Book of the Year Awards**

UNESCO Prize for Children's and Young People's Literature in the Service of Tolerance
Division of Arts and Cultural Enterprise, UNESCO, 1 rue Miollis, 75732–Paris Cedex 15, France
☎00 33 1 45 68 43 40
Fax 00 33 1 45 68 55 95
Email m.bulos@unesco.org
Website www.unesco.org/culture/toleranceliterature
Contact *Ms Maha Bulos*

The UNESCO Prize is awarded every two years in recognition of works for the young that 'best embody the concepts and ideals of tolerance and peace, and promote mutual understanding based on respect for other people and cultures'. The works may be novels, collections of short stories or illustrated picture books, and fall within two categories: for children up to the age of 12 and for young people aged 13 to 18. Submissions by publishers only. The International Jury will select the 2003 winners in December 2002.
Prizes US$8000 in each category.

The V.B. Poetry Prize
20 Clifton House, Club Row, London E2 7HB
Email LOOKLEARN@aol.com
Website www.looklearn.com
Contact *Nicholas Morgan*

Annual open competition for original single unpublished poems, any style, maximum length 40 lines. Entry fee: £3 for first two poems, £1.50 for each additional poem. Closing date: 30 June 2002. Send s.a.e. for full details and entry form.
Prizes £400 (1st), £150 (2nd), £50 (3rd). Winning poems will be published on the Look and Learn Productions' website.

Ver Poets Open Competition
Haycroft, 61–63 Chiswell Green Lane, St Albans, Hertfordshire AL2 3AL
☎01727 867005
Contact *May Badman*

Various competitions are organised by **Ver Poets**, the main one being the annual Open for unpublished poems of no more than 30 lines written in English. Entry fee: £3 per poem. Entries must be made under a pseudonym, with name and address on form or separate sheet. Two copies of poems typed on A4 white paper. *Vision On*, the anthology of winning and selected poems, and the adjudicators' report are normally available from mid-June. Final entry date: 30 April. Back numbers of the anthology are available for £3, post-free.
Prizes £500 (1st); £300 (2nd); two runner-up prizes of £100.

Vogue Talent Contest
Vogue, Vogue House, Hanover Square, London W1S 1JU
☎020 7499 9080 Fax 020 7408 0559
Contact *Frances Bentley*

ESTABLISHED 1951. Annual award for young writers and journalists (under 25 on 1 January in the year of the contest). Final entry date is in April. Entrants must write three pieces of journalism on given subjects.
Prizes £1000, plus a month's paid work experience with *Vogue*; £500 (2nd).

The Vondel Translation Prize
See **The Translators Association Awards**

Wadsworth Prize for Business History
Business Archives Council, 101 Whitechapel High Street, London E1 7RE
☎020 7247 0024 Fax 020 7422 0026
Chairman *Mrs Lenore Symons*

ESTABLISHED 1978. Annual award for the best book published on British business history. 2000 winner: David Kynaston *The City of London; Vol. 3: Illusions of Gold 1914–1945*.
Prize £500.

Arts Council of Wales Book of the Year Awards
Arts Council of Wales, Museum Place, Cardiff CF10 3NX
☎029 2037 6500 Fax 029 2022 1447
Email information@ccc–acw.org.uk
Contact *Tony Bianchi*

Annual non-competitive prizes awarded for works of exceptional literary merit written by Welsh authors (by birth or residence), published in Welsh or English during the previous calendar year. There is one major prize in English, the Book of the Year Award, and one major prize in Welsh, Gwobr Llyfr y Flwyddyn. Shortlists of three titles in each language are announced in April; winners announced in May. 2000 winners:

Sheenagh Pugh *Stonelight*; Gwyneth Lewis *Y Llofrudd Iaith*.

Prizes £3000 (each); £1000 to each of four runners-up.

Walford Award
See **The Library Association Walford Award**

Waterstone's Prize
See **The Forward Prizes for Poetry**

The David Watt Prize
Rio Tinto plc, 6 St James's Square, London SW1Y 4LD
☎020 7930 2399 Fax 020 7930 3249
Email davidwattprize@riotinto.com

Contact *The Administrator*

INITIATED in 1987 to commemorate the life and work of David Watt. Annual award, open to writers currently engaged in writing for English language newspapers and journals, on international and national affairs. The winners are judged as having made 'outstanding contributions towards the greater understanding of national, international or global issues'. Entries must have been published during the year preceding the award. Final entry date 31 March. The 2000 winner was Edward Said for 'Unoccupied Territory', published in the *London Review of Books*.

Prize £7500.

The Harri Webb Prize
10 Heol Don, Whitchurch, Cardiff CF14 2AU
☎029 2062 3359 Fax 029 2052 9202
Email meic@heoldon.fsnet.co.uk

Contact *Dr Meic Stephens*

ESTABLISHED 1995. Annual award to commemorate the Welsh poet, Harri Webb (1920–94), for a single poem in any of the categories in which he wrote: ballad, satire, song, polemic or a first collection of poems. The poems are chosen by three adjudicators; no submissions. 1999 winner: Grahame Davies.

Prizes £100/£200.

The Weidenfeld Translation Prize
New College, Oxford OX1 3BW
☎01865 279525 Fax 01865 279590
Email karen.leeder@new.ox.ac.uk

Contact *The Fellows' Secretary*

ESTABLISHED in 1996 by publisher Lord Weidenfeld to encourage good translation into English. Annual award to the translator(s) of a work of fiction, poetry or drama written in any living European language. Submissions from publishers only. For further information, contact Dr David Constantine at the Queen's College address above. 2000 winner: Margaret Jull Costa for her translation of *All the Names* by José Saramago.

Prize £1000.

The Wellcome Trust Prize
Consultation and Education Dept., The Wellcome Trust, 210 Euston Road, London NW1 2BE
☎020 7611 7221 Fax 020 7611 8269
Email r.birse@wellcome.ac.uk
Website www.wellcome.ac.uk

Contact *Ruth Birse*

ESTABLISHED 1997. Biennial award for a book that 'will educate, captivate and inspire the non-specialist lay reader', to be written by a professional life scientist who is unpublished and resident in the UK or Ireland. Contact the Wellcome Trust for rules and guidelines or visit the website. The winning book will be published by **Weidenfeld & Nicolson**. Previous winners: Dr Guy Brown, Professor Chris McManus.

Prize £25,000 (in four instalments, depending on progress of the book).

Wellington Town Council Award
Civic Offices, Tan Bank, Wellington, Telford, Shropshire TF1 1LX
☎01952 222935 Fax 01952 222936

Contacts *Martin Scholes, Derrick Drew*

ESTABLISHED 1995. Annual short story competition to promote the ancient town of Wellington, now part of the Wellington annual literary festival. Open to all for a minimum fee of £2.50; prizes are sponsored so all entry fee monies go to charity. 2000 winners: K. Howard (Overall winner); J.S. Turner (Best Shropshire Entry); J. Beeton (Best Story for Children).

Prizes Trophies and money.

Wheatley Medal
See **The Library Association Wheatley Medal**

Whitbread Book Awards
The Booksellers Association, Minster House, 272 Vauxhall Bridge Road, London SW1V 1BA
☎020 7834 5477 Fax 020 7834 8812
Email denise.bayat@booksellers.co.uk

Website www.whitbread-bookawards.co.uk

Contact *Denise Bayat*

ESTABLISHED 1971. The awards celebrate and promote the best contemporary British writing. They are judged in two stages and offer a total of £40,000 prize money. The awards are open to Novel, First Novel, Biography, and Poetry, each judged by a panel of three judges. The winner of each award receives £3500. Three adult judges and two young judges select a shortlist of four books from which the Whitbread Children's Book of the Year is chosen, the winner receiving £3500. The Whitbread Book of the Year (£22,500) is chosen from winners of the Novel, First Novel, Biography and Poetry Awards. Writers must have lived in Britain and Ireland for three or more years. Submissions received from publishers only. Closing date: early July. Sponsored by Whitbread PLC. 2000 winners: Jamila Gavin *Coram Boy* (children's); Matthew Kneale *English Passengers* (novel and overall winner); Zadie Smith *White Teeth* (first novel); Lorna Sage *Bad Blood – A Memoir* (biography); John Burnside *The Asylum Dance* (poetry).

Whitfield Prize

Royal Historical Society, University College London, Gower Street, London WC1E 6BT
☎020 7387 7532 Fax 020 7387 7532

Contact *Executive Secretary*

ESTABLISHED 1977. An annual award for the best new work within a field of British history, published in the UK in the preceding calendar year. The book must be the author's first (solely written) history book and be an original and scholarly work of historical research. Final entry date: 31 December. 1999 winner: John Walter *Understanding Popular Violence in the English Revolution: The Colchester Plunderers.*
Prize £1000.

John Whiting Award

Arts Council of England, 14 Great Peter Street, London SW1P 3NQ
☎020 7973 6431 Fax 020 7973 6983
Email jemima.lee@artscouncil.org.uk
Website www.artscouncil.org.uk

Contact *Theatre Writing Section*

FOUNDED 1965. Annual award to commemorate the life and work of the playwright John Whiting (*The Devils, A Penny for a Song*). Any writer who has received during 2001 and 2002: (a) an award through the **Arts Council's**

Theatre Writing Schemes; (b) a commission from a theatre company in receipt of an annual or revenue subsidy from either the Arts Council or a Regional Arts Board; or (c) a première production by a theatre company in receipt of annual subsidy is eligible to apply. The play must have been written during 2000 and/or 2001. Awarded to the writer whose play most nearly satisfies the following criteria: a play in which the writing is of special quality; a play of relevance and importance to contemporary life; a play of potential value to the British theatre. No writer who has won the award previously may reapply and no play that has been submitted for the award previously is eligible. Closing date for entries: 9 January 2003.
Prize £6000.

Alfred and Mary Wilkins Memorial Poetry Competition and Lecture

Birmingham & Midland Institute, 9 Margaret Street, Birmingham B3 3BS
☎0121 236 3591 Fax 0121 212 4577

Administrator *Mr P.A. Fisher*

Alternating competition and lecture. The next competition, to be held in 2002, is for an unpublished poem, not exceeding 40 lines, written in English by an author over the age of 15. The poem should not have been entered for any other poetry competition. The 2001 lecture, to be held on 8th October, will be made by Tobias Hill. Details from the address above.
Prizes (total) £2000.

Titus Wilson Prize
See **Lakeland Book of the Year Awards**

H.H. Wingate Prize
See **Jewish Quarterly Literary Prizes**

Wolf Web
PO Box 136, Norwich, Norfolk NR3 3NJ
☎01603 440944 Fax 01603 440940

Contact *Tricia Frances*

Sayana Wolf Trust publishes *Wolf Web Quarterly* and runs one poetry competiton annually. Unpublished poems only on the theme of 'wolf'. All profits go to the work of The Sayana Wolf Trust who fund personal development, educational and community projects for British and North American children and adults. For more details, write to the above address (no replies without s.a.e.).
Prizes One-year's membership to Wolf Web.

Wolfson History Prizes

Wolfson Foundation, 8 Queen Anne Street, London W1G 9LD
☎020 7323 5730 Fax 020 7323 3241

Contact *Executive Secretary*

The Wolfson History Prize, ESTABLISHED in 1972, is awarded annually to promote and encourage standards of excellence in the writing of history for the general reading public. 1999 winners: Lord Briggs, for his distinguished contribution to the writing of history; Andrew Roberts *Salisbury: Victorian Titan*; Joanna Bourke *An Intimate History of Killing*.
Prizes vary each year.

The David T.K. Wong Short Story Prize

International PEN, 9/10 Charterhouse Buildings, Goswell Road, London EC1M 7AT
☎020 7253 4308 Fax 020 7253 5711
Email intpen@dircon.co.uk
Website www.oneworld.org/internatpen

Contact *Gilly Vincent*

ESTABLISHED 2000. An international, biannual prize to promote literary excellence in the form of the short story written in English. Unpublished stories (6000 words maximum) are welcome from writers worldwide, as long as their entries are submitted via their local PEN Centre and incorporate one or more of International PEN's ideals as set out in its Charter. Writers in those few countries without a PEN Centre can be directed to the nearest appropriate centre by International PEN.
Prize £7500 (1st).

World Wide Writers Award

PO Box 3229, Bournemouth, Dorset BH1 1ZS
☎01202 716043 Fax 01202 740995
Email writintl@globalnet.co.uk
Website www.users.globalnet.co.uk/~wrtintl

Contacts *John Jenkins, Mary Hogarth*

ESTABLISHED 1997. Quarterly and annual competitions for original, unpublished short stories of between 2500 and 5000 words. Entries are published in *World Wide Writers* magazine. Entry fee: £10 (£6 for subscribers to *World Wide Writers*). Entry fee includes back issue of the magazine. Closing dates: end of January, March, June and September. Previous winners: Sally Zigmond, Shirley Nunes, Judi Moore, Gerald Phillipson, Brian Dixon, L. Morgana Braveraven. Annual *prize* £3000 and medal.

The Writers Bureau Poetry and Short Story Competition

The Writers Bureau, Sevendale House, 7 Dale Street, Manchester M1 1JB
☎0161 228 2362 Fax 0161 228 3533
Email compent@writersbureau.com
Website www.writersbureau.com

Competition Secretary *Angela Cox*

ESTABLISHED 1994. Annual award. Poems should be no longer than 40 lines and short stories no more than 2000 words. £4 entry fee. Closing date: 31 July 2002.
Prizes in each category: £1000 (1st); £400 (2nd); £200 (3rd); £100 (4th); £50 x 6.

Yorkshire Post Book of the Year Award

The Rectory, Ripley, Near Harrogate, North Yorkshire HG3 3AY
☎01423 772217 Fax 01423 772217

Contact *Margaret Brown*

An annual award for the book (either fiction or non-fiction) which, in the opinion of the judges, is the best work published in the preceding year. Closing date: 31 December. Previous winner: John Ehrman *The Younger Pitt, Vol. III: The Consuming Struggle*.
Prize £1200.

Young Science Writer Award

The Daily Telegraph, 1 Canada Square, Canary Wharf, London E14 5DT
☎020 7538 6960/Hotline: 020 7704 5315
Email enquiries@science-writer.co.uk
Website www.science-writer.co.uk

Contact *Amelia Watson-Steele*

ESTABLISHED 1987, this award is designed to bridge the gap between science and writing, challenging the writer to come up with a piece of no more than 700 words that is friendly, informative and, above all, understandable. Sponsored by BASF, the award is open to two age groups: 16–19 and 20–28.
Award Winners and runners-up receive cash prizes and have the opportunity to have their pieces published on the science pages of *The Daily Telegraph*. The winner in each category also gets an all expenses paid trip to the USA for the meeting of the American Association for the Advancement of Science and an invitation to meet Britain's most distinguished scientists at the British Association's Festival of Science. Visit the website, telephone the hotline number or e-mail for further information.

More for Less – Writers' Earnings from Lending and Copying

A campaign led by the Society of Authors for more government money to be put into Public Lending Right has born fruit with the announcement of a £2 million boost. This takes the fund, which recompenses authors for library borrowings, to £7 million, the equivalent in real terms of its value in 1979 before inflation and state parsimony worked their wicked ways. As from April 2002, around 18,000 authors will receive a welcome, if still modest, supplement to their royalty income.

The bad news is that fewer books are being taken out from libraries. Three years ago the total was over 500 million. Now it is down to 460 million. Jim Parker, the PLR registrar, expects the decline to level out as 'there is so much good work being done in attracting people to libraries'. But the number of registered authors who receive nothing at all from PLR (around 12,000 this year) because their book loans fail to show up in the library samplings, looks set to increase.

There are other aggrieved writers who fail to qualify for PLR for one or other of their activities. When, for example, will talking books be ranked with conventional volumes? But a short step forward is promised with the extension of the scheme to authors resident in other European countries. The first PLR payments to expats will be made in February 2002.

There is mixed news too from the Authors' Licensing & Collecting Society, which distributes fees to writers whose work has been copied, broadcast or recorded. On the plus side ALCS has started collecting fees for authors of journal articles. Other recent initiatives include a scheme allowing authors 'equitable remuneration' for the rental of videos and other recordings of their work, an agreement with the Newspaper Licensing Agency to receive on behalf of freelance journalists a share of revenues from the photocopying of newspapers and a licensing deal on the creation, storage and use of digital versions of printed works.

But last year's £7.57 million distribution was a disappointing £2 million or so down on 1999. This was blamed on a less than expected overseas income and the introduction of a new computer system. More serious is the threat of a reduction in copying fees brought by the Committee of Vice Chancellors who are arguing for a 90 per cent reduction in the agreed page rate on which the fee level is based. The case is not likely to be decided before the end of the year. But even if ALCS is triumphant it will be a costly business. No less than £1 million has been set aside for the legal battle.

Membership of the ALCS is via one of the writers' organisations. For example, a member of the Society of Authors or Writers' Guild automatically belongs to ALCS and will profit accordingly. On the other hand, it is as well to register items of work as they become available to the public. Not all media promoters hand over fees willingly. Every bit of additional information gathered by the ALCS helps it to become more effective as a policing as well as a collecting agency.

PLR application forms and details can be obtained from the Registrar of Public Lending Right at Richard House, Sorbonne Close, Stockton-on-Tees TS17 6DA. ☎01642 604699; fax 01642 615641; email authorservices@plr.uk.com website www.plr.uk.com

The Authors' Licensing & Collecting Society Ltd (ALCS), is at Marlborough Court, 14–18 Holborn, London EC1N 2LE. ☎020 7395 0600; fax 020 7395 0660; email alcs@alcs.co.uk website www.alcs.co.uk

Library Services

Aberdeen Central Library

Rosemount Viaduct, Aberdeen AB25 1GW
☎01224 652500 Fax 01224 641985
Email centlib@arts-rec.aberdeen.net.uk

Open 9.00 am to 7.00 pm Monday to
Thursday; 9.00 am to 5.00 pm Friday
(Reference & Local Studies: 9.00 am to
8.00 pm); 9.00 am to 5.00 pm Saturday.
Branch library opening times vary

Open access
General reference and loans. Books, pamphlets, periodicals and newspapers; videos, CDs
and cassettes; arts equipment lending service;
DTP, Internet and WP for public access; photographs of the Aberdeen area; census records,
maps; online database, patents and standards.
The library offers special services to housebound
readers. Non-resident administrative fee for
audiovisual and lending services.

Armitt Library

Ambleside, Cumbria LA22 9BL
☎015394 31212 Fax 015394 31313

Open 10.00 am to 12.30 pm and 1.30 pm to
4.00 pm Monday to Friday

Free access (To view original material please
give prior notice)
A small but unique reference library of rare
books, manuscripts, pictures, antiquarian prints
and museum items, mainly about the Lake
District. It includes early guidebooks and topographical works, books and papers relating to
Ruskin, H. Martineau, Charlotte Mason and
others; fine art including work by W. Green,
J.B. Pyne, John Harden, K. Schwitters, and
Victorian photographs by Herbert Bell; also a
major collection of Beatrix Potter's scientific
watercolour drawings and microscope studies.
Museum and Exhibition open seven days per
week from 10.00 am to 5.00 pm. Entry charge.

The Athenaeum, Liverpool

Church Alley, Liverpool L1 3DD
☎0151 709 7770 Fax 0151 709 0418
Email library@athena.force9.net
Website www.athena.force9.co.uk

Open 9.00 am to 4.00 pm Monday to Friday

Access To club members; researchers by
application only

General collection, with books dating from
the 15th century, now concentrated mainly on
local history with a long run of Liverpool
directories and guides. *Special collections*
Liverpool playbills; William Roscoe; Blanco
White; Robert Gladstone; 18th-century plays;
19th-century economic pamphlets; the Norris
books; Bibles; Yorkshire and other genealogy.
Some original drawings, portraits, topographical material and local maps.

Bank of England Information Centre

Threadneedle Street, London EC2R 8AH
☎020 7601 4715 Fax 020 7601 4356
Email informationcentre@bankofengland.co.uk
Website www.bankofengland.co.uk

Open 9.30 am to 5.30 pm Monday to Friday

Access For research workers by prior arrangement only, when material is not readily available elsewhere
50,000 volumes of books and periodicals.
2000 periodicals taken. UK and overseas coverage of banking, finance and economics.
Special collections Central bank reports; UK
17th–19th-century economic tracts; Government reports in the field of banking.

Barbican Library

Barbican Centre, London EC2Y 8DS
☎020 7638 0569 Fax 020 7638 2249
Email barbicanlib@corpoflondon.gov.uk

Open 9.30 am to 5.30 pm Monday,
Wednesday, Thursday, Friday; 9.30 am to
7.30 pm Tuesday; 9.30 am to 12.30 pm
Saturday

Open access
Situated on Level 2 of the Barbican Centre,
this is the Corporation of London's largest lending library. Limited study facilities are available.
In addition to a large general lending department, the library seeks to reflect the Centre's
emphasis on the arts and includes strong collections (including videos and CD-ROMs), on
painting, sculpture, theatre, cinema and ballet, as
well as a large music library with books, scores
and CDs (sound recording loans available at a
small charge). Also houses the City's main
children's library and has special collections on

finance, natural resources, conservation, social-ism and the history of London. Service available for housebound readers. A literature events pro-gramme is organised by the Library which sup-plements and provides cross-arts planning oppor-tunities with the Barbican Centre artistic programme.

Barnsley Public Library

Central Library, Shambles Street, Barnsley, South Yorkshire S70 2JF
☎01226 773930 Fax 01226 773955
Email Librarian@Barnsley.ac.uk
Website bmbc-online/internet-site/educat/libraries/index.html

Open Lending & Reference: 9.30 am to 7.00 pm Monday and Wednesday; 9.30 am to 5.30 pm Tuesday and Friday; 9.30 am to 4.00 pm Saturday. Please telephone to check hours of other departments.

Open access
General library, lending and reference. Archive collection of family history and local firms; local studies: coal mining, local authors, Yorkshire and Barnsley; European Business Information Unit; large junior library. (Specialist departments are closed on certain weekday evenings and Saturday afternoons.)

BBC Written Archives Centre

Peppard Road, Caversham Park, Reading, Berkshire RG4 8TZ
☎0118 946 9280/1/2 Fax 0118 946 1145
Email wac.enquiries@bbc.co.uk
Website www.bbc.co.uk/thenandnow

Contact *Jacqueline Kavanagh*

Open 9.30 am to 5.30 pm Monday to Friday

Access For reference, by appointment only on Wednesday to Friday.

Holds the written records of the BBC, including internal papers from 1922 to 1979 and published material to date. 20th century biography, social history, popular culture and broadcasting. Charges for certain services.

Bedford Central Library

Harpur Street, Bedford MK40 1PG
☎01234 350931/270102 (Reference Library)
Fax 01234 342163
Website www.bcclgis.gov.uk

Open 9.30 am to 7.00 pm Monday and Wednesday; 9.30 am to 5.30 pm Tuesday, Thursday, Friday; 9.30 am to 5.00 pm Saturday

Open access

Lending library with a wide range of stock, including books, music (CDs and cassettes), audio books and videos; reference and infor-mation library, children's library, local history library, Internet facilities and gallery.

Belfast Public Libraries: Central Library

Royal Avenue, Belfast BT1 1EA
☎028 9050 9150 Fax 028 9033 2819
Email info@libraries.belfast-elb.gov.uk

Open 9.30 am to 8.00 pm Monday and Thursday; 9.30 am to 5.30 pm Tuesday, Wednesday, Friday; 9.30 am to 1.00 pm Saturday

Open access To lending libraries; reference libraries by application only

Over two million volumes for lending and reference. *Special collections* United Nations/UNESCO depository; complete British Patent Collection; Northern Ireland Newspaper Library; British and Irish government publica-tions. The Central Library offers the following reference departments: General Reference; Irish and Local Studies; Business and Law; Electronic Information Services; Fine Arts, Language and Literature; Music and Recorded Sound. The lending library, supported by twenty branch libraries and two mobile libraries, offers special services to hospitals, prisons and housebound readers.

BFI National Library

21 Stephen Street, London W1T 1LN
☎020 7255 1444 Fax 020 7436 2338
Email library@bfi.org.uk
Website www.bfi.org.uk

Open 10.30 am to 5.30 pm Monday and Friday; 10.30 am to 8.00 pm Tuesday and Thursday; 1.00 pm to 8.00 pm Wednesday; Telephone Enquiry Service operates from 10.00 am to 5.00 pm

Access For reference only; annual and limited day membership available

The world's largest collection of information on film and television including periodicals, cuttings, scripts, related documentation, per-sonal papers. Information available through SIFT (Summary of Information on Film and Television).

Birmingham and Midland Institute

9 Margaret Street, Birmingham B3 3BS
☎0121 236 3591 Fax 0121 212 4577

Administrator & General Secretary *Philip Fisher*

Access For research, to students (loans restricted to members)

ESTABLISHED 1854. Later merged with the Birmingham Library which was founded in 1779. The Library specialises in the humanities, with approximately 100,000 volumes in stock. Founder member of the **Association of Independent Libraries**. Meeting-place of many affiliated societies devoted to poetry and literature.

Birmingham Library Services

Central Library, Chamberlain Square,
Birmingham B3 3HQ
☎0121 303 4511
Website www.birmingham.gov.uk

Open 9.00 am to 8.00 pm Monday to Friday;
9.00 am to 5.00 pm Saturday

Over a million volumes. *Research collections* include the Shakespeare Library; War Poetry Collection; Parker Collection of Children's Books and Games; Johnson Collection; Milton Collection; Cervantes Collections; Early and Fine Printing Collection (including the William Ridler Collection of Fine Printing); Joseph Priestley Collection; Loudon Collection; Railway Collection; Wingate Bett Transport Ticket Collection; Labour, Trade Union and Co-operative Collections. Photographic Archives: Sir John Benjamin Stone; Francis Bedford; Francis Frith; Warwickshire Photographic Survey; Boulton and Watt Archive; Charles Parker Archive; Birmingham Repertory Theatre Archive and Sir Barry Jackson Library; Local Studies (Birmingham); Patents Collection; Song Sheets Collection; Oberammergau Festival Collection.

Book Data Ltd

Globe House, 1 Chertsey Road,
Twickenham, Middlesex TW1 1LR
☎020 8843 8620 Fax 020 8843 8744
Email sales@bookdata.co.uk
Website www.bookdata.co.uk

Contact *Sales Department*

FOUNDED 1987. Leading supplier of content-rich bibliographic information about English-language books to booksellers and libraries in the UK and worldwide, bringing together information about books and other published media from around the world – the UK and Europe, USA, Australia, New Zealand, Southern Africa and other countries. Its services comprise full bibliographic details, plus descriptive summaries, tables of contents, extensive subject-related information and market rights details. Book Data's customer base extends to over 100 countries worldwide and includes major players in the field – including retail bookchains, Internet bookshop sites. Its products and services are used extensively by booksellers and libraries alike – from a range of bibliographic products (on CD-ROM or online), to more custom-built solutions to fit customers' internal systems or individual requirements. Also offers web hosting and design services for publishers.

Bradford Central Library

Princes Way, Bradford, West Yorkshire
BD1 1NN
☎01274 753600 Fax 01274 395108
Email public.libraries@bradford.gov.uk

Open 9.00 am to 7.30 pm Monday to Friday;
9.00 am to 5.00 pm Saturday

Open access
Wide range of books and media loan services. Comprehensive reference and information services, including major local history collections and specialised business information service. Bradford Libraries run *Reader2Reader*, a groundbreaking, reader-centred literature development project (www.Reader2Reader.com)

Brighton Central Library

Vantage Point, New England Street, Brighton,
East Sussex BN1 2GW
☎01273 290800 Fax 01273 296951

Local Studies Library: Church Street,
Brighton BN1 2UE

Open 10.00 am to 7.00 pm Monday to Friday (closed Wednesday); 10.00 am to 4.00 pm Saturday

Access Limited stock on open access; all material for reference use only

FOUNDED 1869, the library has a large stock covering most subjects. Specialisations include art and antiques, history of Brighton and Sussex, family history, local illustrations, TSO, business and large bequests of antiquarian books and ecclesiastical history.

Bristol Central Library

College Green, Bristol BS1 5TL
☎0117 903 7200 Fax 0117 922 1081
Website www.bristol-city.gov.uk *or*
www.digitalbristol.org

Open 9.30 am to 7.30 pm Monday, Tuesday and Thursday; 9.30 am to 5.00 pm Wednesday, Friday and Saturday; 1.00 pm to 4.00 pm Sunday

Open access
Lending, reference, art, music, commerce and local studies are particularly strong.

British Architectural Library

Royal Institute of British Architects, 66 Portland Place, London W1B 1AD
☎020 7580 5533 Fax 020 7631 1802
Email bal@inst.riba.org
Website www.architecture.com

Members' Information Line (50p per min.): 0906 302 0444; Public Information Line (50p per min.): 0906 302 0400

Open 1.30 pm to 5.00 pm Monday; 10.00 am to 7.00 pm Tuesday and Thursday; 10.00 am to 5.00 pm Wednesday and Friday; 10.00 am to 1.30 pm Saturday

Access Free to RIBA members; non-members must buy a day ticket (£10/£5 concessions, but on Tuesdays and Thursdays between 5.00 pm–7.00 pm and Saturdays £5/£2.50); subscriber membership available (write for details); loans available to RIBA and library members only

Collection of books, drawings, manuscripts, photographs and periodicals. All aspects of architecture, current and historical. Material both technical and aesthetic, covering related fields including: interior design, landscape architecture, topography, the construction industry and applied arts. Brochure available; queries by telephone, letter or in person. Charge for research (min. charge £30).

The British Library

Admission to St Pancras Reading Rooms

The British Library does not provide access to all those who request admission to use its research facilities but operates an admissions policy which grants access to those who need to use the collection because they cannot find the material they require in other libraries.

Admission is by interview and applicants are required to demonstrate that they need access to the reading rooms because: (a) material they need to consult is not available elsewhere; (b) their work or studies require the facilities of a large research library; (c) they need access to the Library's public records.

For further information, contact the Reader Admissions Office, The British Library, 96 Euston Road, London NW1 2DB Email reader-admissions@bl.uk ☎020 7412 7677 Fax 020 7412 7794

British Library Business Information Service (BIS)

96 Euston Road, London NW1 2DB
Email business-information@bl.uk
Website www.bl.uk
Free enquiry service ☎020 7412 7977
Fax 020 7412 7453
Priced enquiry service: ☎020 7412 7457
Fax 020 7412 7453

Open 10.00 am to 8.00 pm Monday; 9.30 am to 8.00 pm Tuesday to Thursday; 9.30 am to 5.00 pm Friday and Saturday; closed for public holidays

Access Pass required for access

BIS holds the most comprehensive collection of business information literature in the UK. This includes market research reports and journals, directories, company annual reports, trade and business journals, house journals, trade literature and CD-ROM services.

British Library Early Printed Collections

96 Euston Road, London NW1 2DB
☎020 7412 7676 Fax 020 7412 7577
Email rare-books@bl.uk
Website www.bl.uk

Open 10.00 am to 8.00 pm Monday; 9.30 am to 8.00 pm Tuesday to Thursday; 9.30 am to 5.00 pm Friday and Saturday; closed for public holidays

Access By British Library reader's pass

General enquiries about reader services and advance reservations: ☎020 7412 7676 Fax 020 7412 7609 Email reader-services-enquiries@bl.uk

The Early Printed Collections Department, which is an integral part of British Library Reader Services and Collection Development, selects, acquires, researches and provides access to material in the humanities collections printed in the British Isles to 1914 and in Western European languages before 1851. The collections are available in the Rare Books and Music Reading Room at St Pancras which also functions as the focus for the British Library's extensive collection of humanities microforms. Further information about Early Printed Collections can be found at the British Library website.

British Library Humanities Reading Room

96 Euston Road, London NW1 2DB
☎020 7412 7676 Fax 020 7412 7609
Email reader-services-enquiries@bl.uk

Website www.bl.uk

Open 10.00 am to 8.00 pm Monday; 9.30 am to 8.00 pm Tuesday, Wednesday, Thursday; 9.30 am to 5.00 pm Friday and Saturday; closed for public holidays

Access By British Library reader's pass

This reading room is the focus for the Library's modern collections service in the humanities. It is on two levels, Humanities 1 and Humanities 2 and provides access to the Library's comprehensive collections of books and periodicals in all subjects in the humanities and social sciences and in all languages apart from Oriental. These collections are not available for browsing at the shelf. Material is held in closed access storage and needs to be identified and ordered from store using an online catalogue. A selective open access collection on most humanities subjects can be found in Humanities 1 whilst in Humanities 2 there are open access reference works relating to periodicals and theses, to recorded sound and to librarianship and information science.

To access British Library catalogues, go to the website at blpc.bl.uk

British Library Manuscript Collections

96 Euston Road, London NW1 2DB
☎020 7412 7513 Fax 020 7412 7745
Email mss@bl.uk
Website www.bl.uk

Open 10.00 am to 5.00 pm Monday; 9.30 am to 5.00 pm Tuesday to Saturday; closed for public holidays

Access Reading facilities only, by British Library reader's pass; a written letter of recommendation and advance notice is required for certain categories of material

Two useful publications, *Index of Manuscripts in the British Library,* Cambridge 1984–6, 10 vols, and *The British Library: Guide to the Catalogues and Indexes of the Department of Manuscripts* by M.A.E. Nickson, help to guide the researcher through this vast collection of manuscripts dating from Ancient Greece to the present day. Approximately 300,000 mss, charters, papyri and seals are housed here.

For information on British Library collections and services and to access British Library catalogues, including the Manuscripts online catalogue, visit the website.

British Library Map Library

96 Euston Road, London NW1 2DB
☎020 7412 7702 Fax 020 7412 7780
Email maps@bl.uk

Website www.bl.uk/collections/maps

Open 10.00 am to 5.00 pm Monday; 9.30 am to 5.00 pm Tuesday to Saturday; closed for public holidays

Access By British Library reader's pass

A collection of two million maps, charts and globes with particular reference to the history of British cartography. Maps for all parts of the world in a wide range of scales and dates, including the most comprehensive collection of Ordnance Survey maps and plans. *Special collections* King George III Topographical Collection and Maritime Collection, and the Crace Collection of maps and plans of London.

For information on British Library collections and services, visit the website.

To access main British Library catalogues, go to the website at blpc.bl.uk (NB Map Library catalogue on CD-ROM; not yet available online.)

British Library Music Collections

96 Euston Road, London NW1 2DB
☎020 7412 7772 Fax 020 7412 7751
Email music-collections@bl.uk
Website www.bl.uk

Open 10.00 am to 8.00 pm Monday; 9.30 am to 8.00 pm Tuesday to Thursday; 9.30 am to 5.00 pm Friday and Saturday; closed for public holidays

Access By British Library reader's pass

Special collections The Royal Music Library (containing almost all Handel's surviving autograph scores) and the Paul Hirsch Music Library. Also a large collection (about one and a quarter million items) of printed music and about 100,000 items of manuscript music, both British and foreign.

The British Library website contains details of collections and services, and provides access to the catalogues.

British Library National Sound Archive

96 Euston Road, London NW1 2DB
☎020 7412 7440 Fax 020 7412 7441
Email nsa@bl.uk
Website cadensa.bl.uk

Open 10.00 am to 8.00 pm Monday; 9.30 am to 8.00 pm Tuesday to Thursday; 9.30 am to 5.00 pm Friday and Saturday; closed for public holidays

Listening service (by appointment)

Northern Listening Service:
British Library Document Supply Centre,

Boston Spa, West Yorkshire: 9.15 am to 4.30 pm Monday to Friday

Open access

An archive of over 1,000,000 discs and more than 185,000 tape recordings, including all types of music, oral history, drama, wildlife, selected BBC broadcasts and BBC Sound Archive material. Produces a thrice-yearly newsletter, *Playback*.

For information on British Library National Sound Archive collections and services, visit the website.

British Library Newspaper Library

Colindale Avenue, London NW9 5HE
☎020 7412 7353 Fax 020 7412 7379
Email newspaper@bl.uk
Website www.bl.uk/collections/newspaper

Open 10.00 am to 4.45 pm Monday to Saturday (last newspaper issue 4.15 pm); closed for public holidays

Access By British Library reader's pass or Newspaper Library pass (available from and valid only for Colindale)

Major collections of English provincial, Scottish, Welsh, Irish, Commonwealth and selected overseas foreign newspapers from *c*.1700 are housed here. Some earlier holdings are also available. London newspapers from 1801 and many weekly and fortnightly periodicals are also in stock. (London newspapers pre-dating 1801 are housed at the new library building in St Pancras – 96 Euston Road, NW1 2DB – though many are available at Colindale Avenue on microfilm.) Readers are advised to check availability of material in advance.

For information on British Library Newspaper Library collections and services, visit the website.

British Library Oriental and India Office Collections

96 Euston Road, London NW1 2DB
☎020 7412 7873 Fax 020 7412 7641
Email oioc-enquiries@bl.uk
Website www.bl.uk

Open 10.00 am to 5.00 pm Monday; 9.30 am to 5.00 pm Tuesday to Saturday; closed for public holidays

Access By British Library reader's pass (identification required)

A comprehensive collection of printed volumes and manuscripts in the languages of North Africa, the Near and Middle East and all of Asia, plus records of the East India Company and British government in India until 1947.

Also prints, drawings and paintings by British artists of India.

For information on British Library collections and services, visit the website.

To access British Library catalogues, go to the website at blpc.bl.uk

British Library Science, Technology and Business

96 Euston Road, London NW1 2DB
☎020 7412 7494/7496 (General Enquiries)
Fax 020 7412 7495
Email scitech@bl.uk
Website www.bl.uk
British/EPO patent equiries: 020 7412 7919
Business enquiries: 020 7412 7454/7977
(Business quick enquiry line available 9.00 am to 5.00 pm Monday to Friday)

Open 10.00 am to 8.00 pm Monday; 9.30 am to 8.00 pm Tuesday to Thursday; 9.30 am to 5.00 pm Friday and Saturday; closed for public holidays

Engineering, business information on companies, markets and products, physical science and technologies. British, European and Patent Co-operation Treaty patents and trade marks.

For information on British Library collections and services, visit the website.

To access British Library catalogues go to the website at blpc.bl.uk

British Library Social Policy Information Service

96 Euston Road, London NW1 2DB
☎020 7412 7536 Fax 020 7412 7761
Website www.bl.uk/services/stb/spis.html

Open 10.00 am to 8.00 pm Monday; 9.30 am to 8.00 pm Tuesday to Thursday; 9.30 am to 5.00 pm Friday and Saturday; closed for public holidays

Access By British Library reader's pass

Provides an information service on social policy, public administration, and current and international affairs, and access to current and historical official publications from all countries and intergovernmental bodies, including House of Commons sessional papers, UK legislation, UK electoral registers, up-to-date reference books on official publications and on the social sciences, a major collection of statistics and a browsing collection of recent social science books and periodicals. Also offers a priced research service providing literature surveys, current awareness and topic briefings for clients on demand.

To access British Library catalogues, go to the website at blpc.bl.uk

British Museum Department of Ethnography Library

6 Burlington Gardens, London W1S 3EX
☎020 7323 8031 Fax 020 7323 8013

Open 10.00 am to 4.45 pm Monday to Friday

Access By ticket-holders only. Tickets are given to scholars and postgraduate students, with special privileges accorded to Fellows of the Royal Anthropological Institute. Reference tickets are issued to *bona fide* researchers provided that the material is not available elsewhere. Undergraduates are admitted only if engaged in a research project

In 1976 the important library of the Royal Anthropological Institute (RAI) was donated to the Department of Ethnography Library and the RAI continues to support the library with donations of books and periodicals.

The collection consists of books (120,000), periodicals (1000 current titles), congress reports, newsletters, maps, microforms, manuscripts. It covers every aspect of anthropology: cultural anthropology (notably material culture and the arts), archaeology, biological anthropology and linguistics, together with such related fields as history, sociology, description and travel. Geographically the collection's scope is worldwide. Particular strengths are in British Commonwealth, Eastern Europe and the Americas. Mesoamerica is well represented as the library holds the Sir John Eric Thompson (1898–1970) collection.

British Psychological Society Library

c/o Psychology Library, University of London, Senate House, Malet Street, London WC1E 7HU
☎020 7862 8451/8461 Fax 020 7862 8480
Email enquiries@ull.ac.uk

Open Term-time: 9.00 am to 9.00 pm Monday to Thursday; 9.00 am to 6.30 pm Friday; 9.30 am to 5.30 pm Saturday (Holidays: 9.00 am to 6.00 pm Monday to Friday; 9.30 am to 5.30 pm Saturday)

Access Members only; Non-members £7 day ticket

Reference library, containing the British Psychological Society collection of periodicals – over 140 current titles housed alongside the University of London's collection of books and journals. Largely for academic research. General queries referred to **Swiss Cottage Library** in London which has a good psychology collection.

Bromley Central Library

London Borough of Bromley - Leisure & Community Services, High Street, Bromley, Kent BR1 1EX
☎020 8460 9955 Fax 020 8313 9975
Email reference.library@bromley.gov.uk
Website www.bromley.gov.uk

Open 9.30 am to 6.00 pm Monday, Wednesday, Friday; 9.30 am to 8.00 pm Tuesday and Thursday; 9.30 am to 5.00 pm Saturday

Open access

A large selection of fiction and non-fiction books for loan, both adult and children's. Also DVDs, videos, CDs, cassettes, language courses, open learning packs for hire. Other facilities include a business information service (email bis@bromley.gov.uk), CD-ROM, computer hire, Internet, local studies library, 'Upfront' teenage section, large reference library with photocopying, fax, microfiche and film facilities and specialist 'Healthpoint', 'Signpost' – online community information and 'Careerpoint' sections. *Specialist collections* include: H.G. Wells, Walter de la Mare, Crystal Palace, The Harlow Bequest, and the history and geography of Asia, America, Australasia and the Polar regions.

CAA Library and Information Centre

Aviation House, Gatwick Airport, West Sussex RH6 0YR
☎01293 573725 Fax 01293 573181
Website www.srg.caa.co.uk

Open 9.30 am to 4.30 pm Monday to Friday; 10.00 am to 4.30 pm first Wednesday of the month

Open access

Books, periodicals and reports on air transport, air traffic control, electronics, radar and computing.

Cambridge Central Library (Reference Library & Information Service)

7 Lion Yard, Cambridge CB2 3QD
☎01223 712000 Fax 01223 712018
Email cambridge.central.library@camcnty. gov.uk
Website www.cambridgeshire.gov.uk/library/ ver1/cam.htm

Open 9.00 am to 7.00 pm Monday to Friday; 9.00 am to 5.30 pm Saturday

Open access

Large stock of books, periodicals, newspapers, maps, plus comprehensive collection of directories and annuals covering UK, Europe and the world. Microfilm and fiche reading and printing services. Online access to news and business databases. News databases on CD-ROM; Internet access. Monochrome and colour photocopiers.

Camomile Street Library
12–20 Camomile Street, London
EC3A 7EX
☎020 7247 8895 Fax 020 7377 2972
Open 9.30 am to 5.30 pm Monday to Friday

Open access
Corporation of London lending library. Wide range of fiction and non-fiction books and language courses on cassette, foreign fiction, paperbacks, maps and guides for travel at home and abroad, children's books, a selection of large print, and collections of music CDs and of videos.

Cardiff Central Library
Frederick Street, St David's Link, Cardiff
CF10 2DU
☎029 2038 2116 Fax 029 2087 1599
Email robboddy@hotmail.com
Open 9.00 am to 6.00 pm Monday, Tuesday, Wednesday, Friday; 9.00 am to 7.00 pm Thursday; 9.00 am to 5.30 pm Saturday

General lending library with the following departments: leisure, music, children's, local studies, information, science and humanities.

Carmarthen Public Library
St Peter's Street, Carmarthen SA31 1LN
☎01267 224830 Fax 01267 221839
Open 9.30 am to 7.00 pm Monday, Tuesday, Wednesday, Friday; 9.30 am to 5.00 pm Thursday and Saturday

Open access
Comprehensive range of fiction, non-fiction, children's books and reference works in English and in Welsh. Large local history library. Free Internet access and CD-ROM facilities. Large Print books, books on tape, CDs, cassettes, and videos available for loan.

Catholic Central Library
Lancing Street, London NW1 1ND
☎020 7383 4333 Fax 020 7388 6675
Email librarian@catholic-library.org.uk

Website www.catholic-library.org.uk
Open 10.30 am to 5.00 pm Monday, Tuesday, Thursday, Friday; 10.30 am to 7.00 pm Wednesday

Open access For reference (non-members must sign in; loans restricted to members)
Contains books, many not readily available elsewhere, on theology, religions worldwide, scripture and the history of churches of all denominations.

The Centre for the Study of Cartoons and Caricature
See entry under **Picture Libraries**

City Business Library
1 Brewers Hall Garden, off Aldermanbury Square, London EC2V 5BX
☎020 7332 1812 Fax 020 7332 1847
☎0171 480 7638 (recorded information)
Open 9.30 am to 5.00 pm Monday to Friday

Open access
Local authority public reference library run by the Corporation of London. Books, pamphlets, periodicals and newspapers of current business interest, mostly financial. Aims to satisfy the day-to-day information needs of the City's business community, and in so doing has become one of the leading public resource centres in Britain in its field. Strong collection of directories for both the UK and overseas, plus companies information, market research sources, management, law, banking, insurance, statistics and investment. No academic journals or textbooks.

Commonwealth Institute
Commonwealth Resource Centre, Kensington High Street, London W8 6NQ
☎020 7603 4535 Fax 020 7603 2807
Email crc@commonwealth.org.uk
Website www.commonwealth.org.uk
Open 10.00 am to 4.00 pm Monday to Saturday

Open Access to the public. Loan service available on an annual subscription basis
The Commonwealth Literature collection includes fiction, poems, drama and critical writings. *Special collection* Books and periodicals on the 54 Commonwealth countries. Also a collection of directories and reference books on the Commonwealth and information on arts, geography, history and literature, cultural organisations and bibliography.

Commonwealth Secretariat Library
Marlborough House, Pall Mall, London
SW1Y 5HX
☎020 7747 6164/5/6/7 Fax 020 7747 6168
Email library@commonwealth.int
Website www.thecommonwealth.org
Open 9.15 am to 5.00 pm Monday to Friday
Access For reference only, by appointment
Extensive reference source concerned with economy, development, trade, production and industry of Commonwealth countries; also human resources including women, youth, health, management and education.

Corporation of London Libraries
See **Barbican Library; Camomile Street Library; City Business Library; Guildhall**

Coventry Central Library
Smithford Way, Coventry, Warwickshire
CV1 1FY
☎024 7683 2314/2395 (Minicom)
Fax 024 7683 2440
Email covinfo@discover.co.uk
Website www.coventry.gov.uk/accent.htm
Open 9.00 am to 8.00 pm Monday, Tuesday, Thursday; 9.30 am to 8.00 pm Wednesday; 9.00 am to 5.00 pm Friday; 9.00 am to 4.30 pm Saturday
Open access
Located in the middle of the city's main shopping centre. Approximately 120,000 items (books, cassettes, CDs and DVDs) for loan; plus reference collection of business information and local history. *Special collections* Cycling and motor industries; George Eliot; Angela Brazil; Tom Mann Collection (trade union and labour studies); local newspapers on microfilm from 1740 onwards. Over 300 periodicals taken. 'Peoplelink' community information database available.

Derby Central Library
Wardwick, Derby DE1 1HS
☎01332 255398 Fax 01332 369570
Website www.derby.gov.uk/libraries
Open 10.00 am to 7.00 pm Monday, Tuesday, Thursday, Friday; 10.00 am to 1.00 pm Wednesday and Saturday
LOCAL STUDIES LIBRARY
25B Irongate, Derby DE1 3GL
☎01332 255393 Fax 01332 255381
Open 10.00 am to 7.00 pm Monday and Tuesday; 10.00 am to 5.00 pm Wednesday,

Thursday, Friday; 10.00 am to 1.00 pm
Saturday
Open access
General library for lending, information and Children's Services. The Central Library also houses specialist private libraries: Derbyshire Archaeological Society; Derby Philatelic Society. The Local Studies Library houses the largest multimedia collection of resources in existence relating to Derby and Derbyshire. The collection includes mss deeds, family papers, business records including the Derby Canal Company, Derby Board of Guardians and the Derby China Factory. Both libraries offer Internet access for a small charge.

Devon & Exeter Institution Library
7 Cathedral Close, Exeter, Devon EX1 1EZ
☎01392 251017
Email M.Midgley@exeter.ac.uk
Website www.ex.ac.uk/library/devonex.html
Open 9.00 am to 5.00 pm Monday to Friday
Access Members only (Temporary membership available)
FOUNDED 1813. Under the administration of Exeter University Library. Contains over 36,000 volumes, including long runs of 19th-century journals, theology, history, topography, early science, biography and literature. A large and growing collection of books, journals, newspapers, prints and maps relating to the South West.

Doncaster Libraries and Information Services
Central Library, Waterdale, Doncaster, South Yorkshire DN1 3JE
☎01302 734305 Fax 01302 369749
Email Reference.Library@doncaster.gov.uk
Open 9.30 am to 6.00 pm Monday; 9.00 am to 6.00 pm Tuesday to Friday; 9.00 am to 4.00 pm Saturday
Open access
Books, cassettes, CDs, videos, picture loans. Reading aids unit for people with visual handicap; activities for children during school holidays, including visits by authors, etc. Occasional funding available to support literature activities. Also reference library.

Dorchester Library (part of Dorset County Library)
Colliton Park, Dorchester, Dorset DT1 1XJ
☎01305 224440 (lending)/224448 (reference)

Fax 01305 266120

Open 10.00 am to 7.00 pm Monday; 9.30 am to 7.00 pm Tuesday, Wednesday, Friday; 9.30 am to 5.00 pm Thursday; 9.00 am to 4.00 pm Saturday

Open access

General lending and reference library, including Local Studies Collection, special collections on Thomas Hardy, the Powys Family and William Barnes. Periodicals, children's library, CD-ROMs, free Internet access. Video lending service.

Dundee Central Library

The Wellgate, Dundee DD1 1DB
☎01382 434318 Fax 01382 434642

Open Lending Departments: 9.30 am to 7.00 pm Monday, Tuesday, Thursday, Friday; 10.00 am to 7.00 pm Wednesday; 9.30 am to 5.00 pm Saturday.

General Reference Department: 9.30 am to 9.00 pm Monday, Tuesday, Thursday, Friday; 10.00 am to 9.00 pm Wednesday; 9.30 am to 5.00 pm Saturday.

Local History Department: 9.30 am to 5.00 pm Monday, Tuesday, Friday, Saturday; 10.00 am to 7.00 pm Wednesday; 9.30 am to 7.00 pm Thursday.

Access Reference services available to all; lending services to those who live, work, study or were educated within Dundee City

Adult lending, reference and children's services. Art, music, audio and video lending services. Internet access. Schools service (Agency). Housebound and mobile services. *Special collections*: The Wighton Collection of National Music; The Wilson Photographic Collection; The Lamb Collection.

English Nature

Northminster House, Peterborough, Cambridgeshire PE1 1UA
☎01733 455000 Fax 01733 568834
Email enquiries@english-nature.org.uk
Website www.english-nature.org.uk

Open 8.30 am to 5.00 pm Monday to Thursday; 8.30 am to 4.30 pm Friday

Access To *bona fide* students only. Telephone library for appointment on 01733 455094

Information on nature conservation, nature reserves, SSSIs, planning, legislation, etc. English Nature is the government-funded body whose purpose is to promote the conservation of England's wildlife and natural features.

Equal Opportunities Commission

Arndale House, Arndale Centre, Manchester M4 3EQ
☎0161 833 9244 Fax 0161 838 8312
Email info@eoc.org.uk
Website www.eoc.org.uk

The Library at the EOC is not open to the public. The Customer Contact Point is available to deal with/pass on calls or mail publications.

Essex County Council Libraries

County Library Headquarters, Goldlay Gardens, Chelmsford, Essex CM2 0EW
☎01245 284981 Fax 01245 492780
Email essexlib@essexcc.gov.uk
Website www.essexcc.gov.uk

Essex County Council Libraries has 74 static libraries throughout Essex as well as 13 mobile libraries and three special-needs mobiles. Services to the public include books, newspapers, periodicals, CDs, cassettes, videos, pictures, CD-ROM and Internet access as well as postal cassettes for the blind and subtitled videos. Specialist subjects and collections are listed below at the relevant library.

Chelmsford Library

PO Box 882, Market Road, Chelmsford, Essex CM1 1LH
☎01245 492758 Fax 01245 492536

Open 9.00 am to 7.00 pm Monday, Tuesday, Thursday, Friday; 10.00 am to 7.00 pm Wednesday; 9.00 am to 5.00 pm Saturday

Science and technology, business information and social sciences.

Colchester Library

Trinity Square, Colchester, Essex CO1 1JB
☎01206 245900 Fax 01206 245901

Open 9.00 am to 7.30 pm Monday, Tuesday, Friday; 10.00 am to 7.30 pm Wednesday; 9.00 am to 5.00 pm Thursday and Saturday

Local studies, music scores and education. Harsnett collection (early theological works 16th/17th-century); Castle collection (18th-century subscription library); Cunnington collection; Margaret Lazell collection; Taylor collection.

Harlow Library

The High, Harlow, Essex CM20 1HA
☎01279 413772 Fax 01279 424612

Open 9.00 am to 7.00 pm Monday, Tuesday, Thursday, Friday; 10.00 am to 7.00 pm Wednesday; 9.00 am to 5.00 pm Saturday

Fiction, language and literature. Sir John Newson Memorial collection; Maurice Hughes Memorial collection.

Loughton Library
Traps Hill, Loughton, Essex IG10 1HD
☎020 8502 0181 Fax 020 8508 5041

Open 9.30 am to 7.00 pm Monday and Friday; 10.00 am to 7.00 pm Tuesday and Wednesday; 9.30 am to 1.30 pm Thursday; 9.00 am to 5.00 pm Saturday

National Jazz Foundation Archive.

Saffron Walden Library
2 King Street, Saffron Walden, Essex CB10 1ES
☎01799 523178 Fax 01799 513642

Open 9.00 am to 7.00 pm Monday, Tuesday, Thursday, Friday; 9.00 am to 5.00 pm Saturday; 1.00 pm to 4.00 pm Sunday (closed Wednesday)

Victorian studies collection.

Witham Library
18 Newland Street, Witham, Essex CM8 2AQ
☎01376 519625 Fax 01376 501913

Open 9.00 am to 7.00 pm Monday, Tuesday, Thursday, Friday; 9.00 am to 5.00 pm Saturday (closed Wednesday)

Drama. Dorothy L. Sayers and Maskell collections.

The Fawcett Library
See **The Women's Library**

Foreign and Commonwealth Office Library
King Charles Street, London SW1A 2AH
☎020 7270 3925 Fax 020 7270 3270
Website www.fco.gov.uk

Access By appointment only
An extensive stock of books, pamphlets and other reference material on all aspects of historical, socio-economic and political subjects relating to countries covered by the Foreign and Commonwealth Office. Particularly strong on colonial history, early works on travel, and photograph collections, mainly of Commonwealth countries and former colonies, c. 1850s–1960s.

Forestry Commission Library
Forest Research Station, Alice Holt Lodge, Wrecclesham, Farnham, Surrey
GU10 4LH
☎01420 22255 Fax 01420 23653
Email library@forestry.gsi.gov.uk
Website www.forestry.gov.uk/forest_research

Open 9.00 am to 5.00 pm Monday to Thursday; 9.00 am to 4.30 pm Friday

Access By appointment for personal visits
Approximately 20,000 books on forestry and arboriculture, plus 500 current journals. CD-ROMS include TREECD (1939 onwards). Offers a Research Advisory Service for advice and enquiries on forestry (☎01402 23000) with a charge for consultations and diagnosis of tree problems exceeding ten minutes.

French Institute Library
17 Queensberry Place, London SW7 2DT
☎020 7838 2144 Fax 020 7838 2145
Email library@ambafrance.org.uk

Open 12.00 noon to 7.00 pm Tuesday to Friday; 12 noon to 6.00 pm Saturday; Children's Library: 12 noon to 6.00 pm Tuesday to Saturday

Open access For reference and consultation (loans restricted to members)
A collection of over 40,000 volumes mainly centred on French cultural interests with special emphasis on language, literature and history. Books in French and English. Collection of videos, periodicals, CDs (French music), CD-ROMs; Children's library (8000 books); also a special collection about 'France Libre'. Inter-library loans; quick information service; Internet access. Group visits on request.

John Frost Newspapers
22b Rosemary Avenue, Enfield, Middlesex
EN2 0SS
☎020 8366 1392/0946 Fax 020 8366 1379
Email andrew@johnfrostnewspapers.com
Website www.johnfrostnewspapers.co.uk

Contacts *Andrew Frost, John Frost*

A collection of 80,000 original newspapers (1630 to the present day) and 200,000 press cuttings available, on loan, for research and rostrum/stills work (TV documentaries, book and magazine publishers and audiovisual presentations). Historic events, politics, sports, royalty, crime, wars, personalities, etc., plus many in-depth files.

Gloucestershire County Library Arts & Museums Service
Quayside House, Shire Hall, Gloucester
GL1 2HY
☎01452 425020 Fax 01452 425042
Email gclams@gloscc.gov.uk
Website www.gloscc.gov.uk

Open access

The service includes 39 local libraries and six mobile libraries. The website (GlosNet) includes library opening hours, mobile library route schedules; the library catalogue; and a book renewal/reservations facility.

Goethe-Institut Library

50 Princes Gate, Exhibition Road, London SW7 2PH
☎020 7596 4040 Fax 020 7594 0230
Email Library@London.goethe.org
Website www.goethe.de/london

Librarian *Gerlinde Buck*

Open 12.00 am to 8.00 pm Monday to Thursday; 11.00 am to 5.00 pm Saturday

Library specialising in German literature and books/audiovisual material on German culture and history: 25,000 books (4800 of them in English), 140 periodicals, 14 newspapers, 2800 audiovisual media (including 1000 videos), selected press clippings on German affairs from the German and UK press, information service, photocopier, video facility. Also German language teaching material for teachers and students of German.

Greater London Record Office

See **London Metropolitan Archives**

Guildford Institute of the University of Surrey Library

Ward Street, Guildford, Surrey GU1 4LH
☎01483 562142
Email c.miles@surrey.ac.uk

Librarian *Clare Miles*

Open 10.00 am to 3.00 pm Tuesday to Friday

Open access To members only but open to enquirers for research purposes

FOUNDED 1834. Some 12,000 volumes of which 7500 were printed before the First World War. The remaining stock consists of recently published works of fiction, biography and travel. Newspapers and periodicals also available. *Special collections* include an almost complete run of the *Illustrated London News* from 1843–1906, a collection of Victorian scrapbooks, and about 400 photos and other pictures relating to the Institute's history and the town of Guildford. Publishes Library newsletter twice-yearly.

Guildhall Library

Aldermanbury, London EC2P 2EJ
☎See below Fax 020 7600 3384
Website www.corpoflondon.gov.uk

Access For reference (but much of the material is kept in storage areas and is supplied to readers on request; proof of identity is required for consultation of certain categories of stock)

Part of the Corporation of London libraries. Seeks to provide a basic general reference service but its major strength, acknowledged worldwide, is in its historical collections. The library is divided into three sections, each with its own catalogues and enquiry desks. These are: Printed Books; Manuscripts; the Print & Maps Room.

PRINTED BOOKS
Open 9.30 am to 5 pm Monday to Saturday NB closes on Saturdays preceding Bank Holidays; check for details ☎020 7332 1868/1870

Strong on all aspects of London history, with wide holdings of English history, topography and genealogy, including local directories, poll books and parish register transcripts. Also good collections of English statutes, law reports, parliamentary debates and journals, and House of Commons papers. Home of several important collections deposited by London institutions: the Marine collection of the Corporation of Lloyd's, the Stock Exchange's historical files of reports and prospectuses, the Clockmakers' Company library and museum (currently under refurbishment; call for further information), the Gardeners' Company, Fletchers' Company, the Institute of Masters of Wine, International Wine and Food Society and Gresham College.

MANUSCRIPTS
Open 9.30 am to 4.45 pm Monday to Saturday (no requests for records after 4.30 pm) NB closes on Saturdays preceding Bank Holidays; check for details ☎020 7332 1863 Email manuscripts.guildhall@ corpoflondon.gov.uk Website ihr.sas.ac.uk/gh/

The official repository for historical records relating to the City of London (except those of the Corporation of London itself, which are housed at the Corporation Records Office). Records date from the 11th century to the present day. They include archives of most of the City's parishes, wards and livery companies, and of many individuals, families, estates, schools, societies and other institutions, notably the Diocese of London and St Paul's Cathedral, as well as the largest collection of business archives in any public repository in the UK. Although mainly of City interest, holdings include material for the London area as a whole and beyond.

PRINT & MAPS ROOM

Open 9.30 am to 5.00 pm Monday to Friday
☎ 020 7332 1839 Email print&maps@
corpoflondon.gov.uk
Website collage.nhil.com

An unrivalled collection of prints and drawings relating to London and the adjacent counties. The emphasis is on topography, but there are strong collections of portraits and satirical prints. The map collection includes maps of the capital from the mid-16th century to the present day and various classes of Ordnance Survey maps. Other material includes photographs, theatre bills and programmes, trade cards, book plates and playing cards as well as a sizeable collection of Old Master prints. Over 30,000 items have been digitally imaged on Collage, including topographical prints, some maps, a small number of photographs and all the Guildhall art collection.

Free, *limited* enquiry service available. Also a fee-based service for in-depth research – ☎020 7332 1854 Fax 020 7600 3384 E-mail search.guildhall@corpoflondon.gov.uk Website www.cityoflondon.gov.uk/search_guildhall

Guille–Alles Library

Market Street, St Peter Port, Guernsey, Channel Islands GY1 1HB
☎01481 720392 Fax 01481 712425
Email gsylib@cionlne.com

Open 9.00 am to 5.00 pm Monday, Thursday, Friday, Saturday; 10.00 am to 5.00 pm Tuesday; 9.00 am to 8.00 pm Wednesday

Open access For residents; payment of returnable deposit by visitors. Music CD collection: £10 for two-year subscription

Lending, reference and information services. Public Internet service.

Herefordshire Libraries and Information Service

Shirehall, Hereford HR1 2HY
☎01432 359830 Fax 01432 260744

Open Opening hours vary in the libraries across the county

Access Information and reference services open to anyone; loans to members only (membership criteria: resident, being educated, working, or an elector in the county or neighbouring authorities; temporary membership to visitors. Proof of identity and address required)

Information service, reference and lending libraries. Non-fiction and fiction for all age groups, including normal and large print, spoken

word cassettes, sound recordings (CD and cassette), videos, maps, local history, CD-ROMs for reference at Hereford and Leominster Libraries. *Special collections* Cidermaking; Beekeeping; Alfred Watkins; John Masefield; Pilley.

University of Hertfordshire Library

College Lane, Hatfield, Hertfordshire
AL10 9AB
☎01707 284678 Fax 01707 284666
Website www.herts.ac.uk/lis

Open See website for term-time and vacation opening hours

Access For reference use of printed collections

Volumes and journals in science technology and social science, including law, across all five of the university's campuses. There are four other site libraries: at the Business School at Hertford, at the Watford campus near Radlett (education and humanities), at the Art & Design building in Hatfield and at the Law School in St Albans.

Highgate Literary and Scientific Institution Library

11 South Grove, London N6 6BS
☎020 8340 3343 Fax 020 8340 5632
Email admin@hlsi.demon.co.uk

Open 10.00 am to 5.00 pm Tuesday to Friday; 10.00 am to 4.00 pm Saturday (closed Sunday and Monday)

Annual membership £42 (individual); £68 (household)

25,000 volumes of general fiction and non-fiction, with a children's section and extensive local archives. *Special collections* on local history, London, and local poets Samuel Taylor Coleridge and John Betjeman.

Highland Libraries, The Highland Council, Cultural and Leisure Services

Library Support Unit, 31a Harbour Road, Inverness IV1 1UA
☎01463 235713 Fax 01463 236986
Email libraries@highland.gov.uk
Website www.highland.gov.uk

Open Library opening hours vary to suit local needs. Contact Administration and support services for details (8.00 am to 6.00 pm Monday to Friday)

Open access

Comprehensive range of lending and reference stock: books, pamphlets, periodicals, newspapers, compact discs, audio and video cassettes, maps, census records, genealogical records, photographs, educational materials, etc. Highland Libraries provides the public library service throughout the Highlands with a network of 41 static and 12 mobile libraries.

Holborn Library

32–38 Theobalds Road, London WC1X 8PA
☎020 7974 6345/6

Open 10.00 am to 7.00 pm Monday and Thursday; 10.00 am to 6.00 pm Tuesday and Friday; 10.00 am to 5.00 pm Saturday (closed all day Wednesday)

Open access
London Borough of Camden public library. Includes a law collection and the London Borough of Camden Local Studies and Archive Centre.

Sherlock Holmes Collection (Westminster)

Marylebone Library, Marylebone Road, London NW1 5PS
☎020 7641 1206 Fax 020 7641 1019
Email c.cooke@dial.pipex.com
Website www.westminster.gov.uk/el/libarch/services/special/sherlock.html

Open 9.30 am to 8.00 pm Monday, Tuesday, Thursday, Friday; 10.00 am to 8.00 pm Wednesday; Closed Saturday and Sunday (unless by prior arrangement)

Telephone for access By appointment only
Located in Westminster's Marylebone Library. An extensive collection of material from all over the world, covering Sherlock Holmes and Sir Arthur Conan Doyle. Books, pamphlets, journals, newspaper cuttings and photos, much of which is otherwise unavailable in this country. Some background material.

Imperial College Central Library

See **Science Museum Library**

Imperial War Museum

Department of Printed Books, Lambeth Road, London SE1 6HZ
☎020 7416 5000 Fax 020 7416 5374
Email books@iwm.org.uk
Website www.iwm.org.uk

Open 10.00 am to 5.00 pm Monday to Saturday (restricted service Saturday; closed on Bank Holiday Saturdays and last two full weeks of November for annual stock check)

Access For reference (but at least 24 hours' notice must be given for intended visits)

A large collection of material on 20th-century life with detailed coverage of the two world wars and other conflicts. Books, pamphlets and periodicals, including many produced for short periods in unlikely wartime settings; also maps, biographies and privately printed memoirs, and foreign language material. Additional research material available in the following departments: Art, Documents, Exhibits and Firearms, Film, Sound Records, Photographs. Active publishing programme based on reprints of rare books held in library. Catalogue available.

Instituto Cervantes

102 Eaton Square, London SW1W 9AN
☎020 7235 0324 Fax 020 7235 0329
Email biblon@cervantes.es
Website www.cervantes.es

Open 12.00 pm to 6.30 pm Monday to Thursday; 9.30 am to 1.30 pm Saturday (closed Friday)

Open access For reference and lending
Spanish literature, history, art, philosophy. The library houses a collection of books, periodicals, videos, slides, tapes, CDs, cassettes, films and CD-ROMs specialising entirely in Spain and Latin America.

Italian Institute Library

39 Belgrave Square, London SW1X 8NX
☎020 7235 1461 Fax 020 7235 4618
Email maria.dangelo@italcultur.org.uk
Website www.italcultur.org.uk

Open 10.00 am to 1.00 pm and 2.00 pm to 5.00 pm Monday, Tuesday, Wednesday, Friday (Thursday till 8.00 pm)

Open access For reference
A collection of over 21,000 volumes relating to all aspects of Italian culture. Texts are mostly in Italian, with some in English.

Jersey Library

Halkett Place, St Helier, Jersey JE2 4WH
☎01534 59991 (lending)/59992 (reference)
Fax 01534 69444
Email piano@itl.net
Website www.jsylib.gov.je *and*
www.itl.net/vc/europe/jersey/education/library/index.html

Open 9.30 am to 5.30 pm Monday, Wednesday, Thursday, Friday; 9.30 am to 7.30 pm Tuesday; 9.30 am to 4.00 pm Saturday

Open access
Books, periodicals, newspapers, CDs, cassettes, CD-ROMs, videos, microfilm, specialised

local studies collection, public Internet access. Branch Library at Les Quennevais School, St Brelade. Mobile library service.

Kent County Central Library
Kent County Council Arts & Libraries, Springfield, Maidstone, Kent ME14 2LH
☎01622 696511 Fax 01622 753338

Open 9.30 am to 5.30 pm Monday, Wednesday, Friday; 9.30 am to 6.00 pm Tuesday; 9.30 am to 7.00 pm Thursday; 10.00 am to 5.00 pm Saturday

Open access
50,000 volumes available on the floor of the library plus 250,000 volumes of non-fiction, mostly academic, available on request to staff. English literature, poetry, classical literature, drama (including play sets), music (including music sets). Strong, too, in sociology, art history, business information and government publications. Loans to all who live or work in Kent; those who do not may consult stock for reference or arrange loans via their own local library service.

Lansdowne Library
Meyrick Road, Bournemouth, Dorset BH1 3DJ
☎01202 555532 Fax 01202 291781
Email reference.library@bournemouth.gov.uk

Open 10.00 am to 7.00 pm Monday; 9.30 am to 7.00 pm Tuesday, Thursday, Friday; 9.30 am to 5.00 pm Wednesday; 9.00 am to 1.00 pm Saturday

Open access
Main library for Bournemouth with separate lending, music and reference departments, the latter including Bournemouth Local Studies Collection. Collection of government publications; children's section, periodicals.

The Law Society
113 Chancery Lane, London WC2A 1PL
☎0870 606 2500
Website www.lawsociety.org.uk

Open 9.00 am to 5.00 pm with out-of-hours answerphone back-up

Access Library restricted to solicitors/members
Provides all information about solicitors, the legal profession in general, law reform issues, etc.

Leeds Central Library
Calverley Street, Leeds, West Yorkshire LS1 3AB
☎0113 247 8274 Fax 0113 247 8426
Website www.leeds.gov.uk/libraries

Open 9.00 am to 8.00 pm Monday and Wednesday; 9.00 am to 5.30 pm Tuesday and Friday; 9.30 am to 5.30 pm Thursday; 10.00 am to 5.00 pm Saturday

Open access to lending libraries; Reference material on request
Lending Library covering all subjects. Telephone number as above.
Music Library contains scores, books, video and audio. ☎0113 247 8273
Business & Research Library Company information, market research, statistics, directories, journals and computer-based information. Extensive files of newspapers and periodicals plus all government publications since 1960. *Special collections* include military history, Judaic, early gardening books, and mountaineering. ☎0113 247 8426/8282 E-mail information.for.business@leeds.gov.uk *and* research.and.studies@leeds.gov.uk
Art Library (in Art Gallery) has a major collection of material on fine and applied arts. ☎0113 247 8247
Local Studies Library contains an extensive collection on Leeds and Yorkshire, including maps, books, pamphlets, local newspapers, illustrations and playbills. Census returns for the whole of Yorkshire also available. International Genealogical Index and parish registers. ☎0113 247 8290 E-mail local.studies @leeds.gov.uk
Leeds City Libraries has an extensive network of 65 branch and mobile libraries.

Leeds Library
18 Commercial Street, Leeds, West Yorkshire LS1 6AL
☎0113 245 3071 Fax 0113 243 8218

Open 9.00 am to 5.00 pm Monday to Friday

Access To members; research use upon application to the librarian
FOUNDED 1768. Contains over 120,000 books and periodicals from the 15th century to the present day. *Special collections* include Reformation pamphlets, Civil War tracts, Victorian and Edwardian children's books and fiction, European language material, spiritualism and psychical research, plus local material.

Lincoln Central Library
Free School Lane, Lincoln LN2 1EZ
☎01522 510800 Fax 01522 535882
Email lincoln.library@lincolnshire.gov.uk
Website www.lincolnshire.gov.uk

Open 9.30 am to 7.00 pm Monday to Friday; 9.30 am to 4.00 pm Saturday

Open access to the library; appointment required for the Tennyson Research Centre

Lending and reference library. Special collections include Lincolnshire local history (printed and published material, photographs, maps, directories and census data) and the Tennyson Research Centre (contact *Susan Gates*).

Linen Hall Library
17 Donegall Square North, Belfast BT1 5GB
☎028 9032 1707   Fax 028 9043 8586
Email info@linenhall.com
Librarian *John Gray*
Open 9.30 am to 5.30 pm Monday to Friday;
   9.30 am to 4.00 pm Saturday

Open access For reference (loans restricted to members)

FOUNDED 1788. Contains about 200,000 books. Major Irish and local studies collections, including the Northern Ireland Political Collection relating to the current troubles (c. 140,000 items).

Literary & Philosophical Society of Newcastle upon Tyne
23 Westgate Road, Newcastle upon Tyne
NE1 1SE
☎0191 232 0192   Fax 0191 261 4494
Librarian *Kay Easson*
Open 9.30 am to 7.00 pm Monday,
   Wednesday, Thursday, Friday; 9.30 am to
   8.00 pm Tuesday; 9.30 am to 1.00 pm
   Saturday

Access Members; research facilities for *bona fide* scholars on application to the Librarian

200-year-old library of 140,000 volumes, periodicals (including 130 current titles), classical music on vinyl recordings and CD, plus a collection of scores. A programme of lectures and recitals provided. Recent publications include: *The Reverend William Turner: Dissent and Reform in Georgian Newcastle upon Tyne* Stephen Harbottle; *History of the Literary and Philosophical Society of Newcastle upon Tyne, Vol. 2 (1896–1989)* Charles Parish; *Bicentenary Lectures 1993* ed. John Philipson.

Liverpool City Libraries
William Brown Street, Liverpool LE3 8EW
☎0151 233 5829   Fax 0151 233 5886
Email refbt.central.library@liverpool.gov.uk
Website www.liverpool.gov.uk
Open 9.00 am to 7.30 pm Monday to
   Thursday; 9.00 am to 5.00 pm Friday;
   10.00 am to 5.00 pm Saturday; 12.00 pm to
   4.00 pm Sunday

Open access
   Humanities Reference Library A total stock in excess of 120,000 volumes and 24,000 maps, plus book plates, prints and autographed letters. *Special collections* Walter Crane and Edward Lear illustrations, Kelmscott Press, Audubon.
   Business and Technology Reference Library Extensive stock dealing with all aspects of science, commerce and technology, including British and European standards and patents and trade directories.
   Audio Visual Library Extensive stock relating to all aspects of music. Includes 128,000 volumes and music scores, 18,500 records, and over 3000 cassettes and CDs.
   Record Office and Local History Department Printed and audiovisual material relating to Liverpool, Merseyside, Lancashire and Cheshire, together with archive material mainly on Liverpool. Some restrictions on access, with 30-year rule applying to archives.

The London Institute – London College of Printing: Library and Learning Resources
Elephant and Castle, London SE1 6SB
☎020 7514 6527   Fax 020 7514 6597
Website www.linst.ac.uk/library
Access By arrangement

Library and Learning Resources operates from the two sites of the college at: Elephant & Castle and Back Hill (Clerkenwell). Books, periodicals, slides, CD-ROMs, videos and computer software on all aspects of the art of the book, printing, management, film/photography, graphic arts, plus retailing. *Special collections* Private Press books and the history and development of printing and books.

The London Library
14 St James's Square, London SW1Y 4LG
☎020 7930 7705   Fax 020 7766 4766
Email membership@londonlibrary.co.uk
Website www.londonlibrary.co.uk
Librarian *Mr A.S. Bell*
Open 9.30 am to 5.30 pm Monday, Friday,
   Saturday; 9.30 am to 7.30 pm Tuesday,
   Wednesday, Thursday

Access For members only (£150 p.a., 2000)

With over a million books and 8400 members, The London Library 'is the most distinguished private library in the world; probably the largest, certainly the best loved'. Founded in 1841, it is a registered charity and wholly independent of public funding. Its permanent collection embraces most European languages as well as English. Its subject range is predominantly within the humanities, with emphasis on literature, history, fine and applied art, architecture, bibliography, philosophy, religion, and topography and travel. Some 6000–7000 titles are added yearly. Most of the stock is on open shelves to which members have free access. Members may take out up to 10 volumes; 15 if they live more than 20 miles from the Library. The comfortable Reading Room has an annexe for users of personal computers. There are photocopiers, CD-ROM workstations, free access to the Internet, and the Library also offers a postal loans service.

Prospective members are required to submit a refereed application form in advance of admission, but there is at present no waiting list for membership. The London Library Trust may make grants to those who are unable to afford the full annual fee; details on application.

London Metropolitan Archives
40 Northampton Road, London
EC1R 0HB
☎020 7332 3820 Fax 020 7833 9136
Email ask.lma@corpoflondon.gov.uk
Website www.cityoflondon.gov.uk
Minicom 020 7278 8703

Open 9.30 am to 4.45 pm Monday, Wednesday, Friday; 9.30 pm to 7.30 pm Tuesday and Thursday

Access For reference only
Formerly, the Greater London Record Office Library. Covers all aspects of the life and development of London, specialising in the history and organisation of local government in general, and London in particular. Books on London history and topography, covering many subjects. Also London directories dating back to 1677, plus other source material including Acts of Parliament, Hansard reports, statistical returns, atlases, yearbooks and periodicals.

Lord Louis Library
Orchard Street, Newport, Isle of Wight
PO30 1LL
☎01983 527655/823800 (Reference Library)
Fax 01983 825972
Email reflib@llouis.demon.co.uk

Open 9.30 am to 5.30 pm Monday to Wednesday and Friday; 9.00 am to 8.00 pm Thursday; 9.00 am to 5.00 pm Saturday

Open access
General adult and junior fiction and non-fiction collections; local history collection and

periodicals. Also the county's main reference library.

Manchester Central Library
St Peters Square, Manchester M2 5PD
☎0161 234 1900 Fax 0161 234 1963
Email mclib@libraries.manchester.gov.uk
Website www.manchester.gov.uk/mccdlt/index.htm

Open 10.00 am to 8.00 pm Monday to Thursday; 10.00 am to 5.00 pm Friday and Saturday; Commercial and European Units: 10.00 am to 6.00 pm Monday to Thursday; 10.00 am to 5.00 pm Friday and Saturday

Open access
One of the country's leading reference libraries with extensive collections covering all subjects. Departments include: Commercial, European, Technical, Social Sciences, Arts, Music, Local Studies, Chinese, General Readers, Language & Literature. Large lending stock and VIP (visually impaired) service available.

Marylebone Library (Westminster)
See **Sherlock Holmes Collection**

Ministry of Agriculture, Fisheries and Food
Nobel House, 17 Smith Square, London
SW1P 3JR
☎020 7238 3000 Fax 020 7238 6591
MAFF Helpline 0645 335577 (local call rate) – general contact point which can provide information on the work of MAFF, either directly or by referring callers to appropriate contacts. Available 9.00 am to 5.00 pm Monday to Friday (excluding Bank Holidays)

Open 9.30 am to 5.00 pm Monday to Friday

Access For reference (but at least 24 hours notice must be given for intended visits)
Large stock of volumes on temperate agriculture.

The Mitchell Library
North Street, Glasgow G3 7DN
☎0141 287 2999 Fax 0141 287 2815
Website www.libarch.glasgow.gov.uk

Open 9.00 am to 8.00 pm Monday to Thursday; 9.00 am to 5.00 pm Friday and Saturday

Open access
One of Europe's largest public reference libraries with stock of over 1,200,000 volumes. It subscribes to 48 newspapers and more than 2000 periodicals. There are collections in

microform, records, tapes and videos, as well as CD-ROMs, electronic databases, illustrations, photographs, postcards, etc.

The library contains a number of special collections, e.g. the Robert Burns Collection (5000 vols), the Scottish Poetry Collection (12,000 items) and the Scottish Drama Collection (1650 items).

Morrab Library

Morrab House, Morrab Gardens, Penzance, Cornwall TR18 4DA
☎01736 364474

Librarian *Annabelle Read*

Open 10.00 am to 4.00 pm Tuesday to Friday; 10.00 am to 1.00 pm Saturday

Access Non-members may use the library for a small daily fee, but may not borrow books

Formerly known as the Penzance Library. An independent subscription lending library of over 60,000 volumes covering virtually all subjects except modern science and technology, with large collections on history, literature and religion. There is a comprehensive Cornish collection of books, newspapers and manuscripts including the Borlase letters; a West Cornwall photographic archive; many runs of 18th- and 19th-century periodicals; a collection of over 2000 books published before 1800.

National Library of Scotland

George IV Bridge, Edinburgh EH1 1EW
☎0131 226 4531 Fax 0131 622 4803
Email enquiries@nls.uk
Website www.nls.uk

Open Main Reading Room: 9.30 am to 8.30 pm Monday, Tuesday, Thursday, Friday; 10.00 am to 8.30 pm Wednesday; 9.30 am to 1.00 pm Saturday. Map Library: 9.30 am to 5.00 pm Monday, Tuesday, Thursday, Friday; 10.00 am to 5.00 pm Wednesday; 9.30 am to 1.00 pm Saturday. Scottish Science Library: 9.30 am to 5.00 pm Monday, Tuesday, Thursday, Friday; 10.00 am to 8.30 pm Wednesday.

Access To all reading rooms, for research not easily done elsewhere, by reader's ticket

Collection of over seven million volumes. The library receives all British and Irish publications. Large stock of newspapers and periodicals. Many special collections, including early Scottish books, theology, polar studies, baking, phrenology and liturgies. Also large collections of maps, music and manuscripts including personal archives of notable Scottish persons.

National Library of Wales

Aberystwyth, Ceredigion SY23 3BU
☎01970 632800 Fax 01970 615709
Website www.llgc.org.uk

Open 9.30 am to 6.00 pm Monday to Friday; 9.30 am to 5.00 pm Saturday (closed Bank Holidays and first week of October)

Access To reading rooms by reader's ticket, available on application. Open acess to regular exhibition programme and to permanent exhibition 'The Treasures of the Nation'

Collection of over four million books and including large collections of periodicals, maps, manuscripts and audiovisual material. Particular emphasis on humanities in printed foreign material, and on Wales and other Celtic areas in all collections.

National Meteorological Library and Archive

London Road, Bracknell, Berkshire RG12 2SZ
☎01344 854841 Fax 01344 854840
Email metlib@metoffice.com
Website www.metoffice.com

Open Library & Archive: 8.30 am to 4.30 pm Monday to Friday; Archive closed between 1.00 pm and 2.00 pm

Access By Visitor's Pass available from the reception desk; advance notice of a planned visit is appreciated

The major repository of most of the important literature on the subjects of meteorology, climatology and related sciences from the 16th century to the present day. The Library houses a collection of books, journals, articles and scientific papers, plus published climatological data from many parts of the world. The Technical Archive (The Scott Building, Sterling Centre, Eastern Road, Bracknell, Berks RG12 2PW, ☎01344 855960; Fax 01344 855961) holds the document collection of meteorological data and charts from England, Wales and British overseas bases, including ships' weather logs. Records from Scotland are stored in Edinburgh and those from Northern Ireland in Belfast.

The Natural History Museum Library

Cromwell Road, London SW7 5BD
☎020 7942 5460 Fax 020 7942 5559
Email library@nhm.ac.uk
Website www.nhm.ac.uk/library/index.html

Open 10.00 am to 4.30 pm Monday to Friday

Access To *bona fide* researchers, by reader's ticket on presentation of identification (telephone first to make an appointment)

The library is in five sections: general; botany; zoology; entomology; earth sciences. The sub-department of ornithology is housed at the Zoological Museum, Akeman Street, Tring, Herts HP23 6AP (Tel 01442 834181). Resources available include books, journals, maps, manuscripts, drawings and photographs covering all aspects of natural history, including palaeontology and mineralogy, from the 14th century to the present day. Also archives and historical collection on the museum itself.

Newcastle upon Tyne City Library
Princess Square, Newcastle upon Tyne NE99 1DX
☎0191 277 4100   Fax 0191 277 4168
Email city.information@newcastle.gov.uk *or* city.reference.library@newcastle.gov.uk *or* business.information.gateway@newcastle.gov.uk *or* local.studies@newcastle.gov.uk

Open 9.30 am to 8.00 pm Monday and Thursday; 9.30 am to 5.00 pm Tuesday, Wednesday, Friday; 9.00 am to 5.00 pm Saturday

Open access
Extensive local studies collection, including newspapers, illustrations and genealogy. Also business, science, humanities and arts, open learning resource centre, marketing advice centre. Patents advice centre.

Norfolk Library & Information Service
Norfolk and Norwich Central Library, Bethel Street, Norwich, Norfolk NR1 3AD
Website www.norfolk.gov.uk/council/departments/lis/libhome.htm

Open Lending Library, Reference and Information Service and Norfolk Studies: 10.00 am to 8.00 pm Monday to Friday; 9.00 am to 5.00 pm Saturday

Open access
Reference and lending library with wide range of stock for loan, including books, recorded music, music scores, plays and videos. Houses the 2nd Air Division Memorial Library and has a strong Local Studies Library. Extensive range of reference stock including business information. Online database and CD-ROM services. Public fax and colour photocopying, access to the Internet. Information brokerage provides in-depth research services.

Northamptonshire Libraries & Information Service
Library HQ, PO Box 216, John Dryden House, 8–10 The Lakes, Northampton NN4 7DD
☎01604 237959   Fax 01604 237937
Email nrowland@northamtonshire.gov.uk

Since 1991, the Libraries and Information Service have run two to three programmes of literary events for adults each year. Programmes so far have included visiting authors, poetry readings, workshops and other events and activities. The programmes are supported by regular touring fiction displays, writers' advice sessions and dedicated notice boards in libraries across the county.

Northumberland Central Library
The Willows, Morpeth, Northumberland NE61 1TA
☎01670 534518/534514   Fax 01670 534513

Open 10.00 am to 8.00 pm Monday, Tuesday, Wednesday, Friday; 9.30 am to 12.30 pm Saturday (closed Thursday)

Open access
Books, periodicals, newspapers, cassettes, CDs, videos, microcomputers, CD-ROMs, Internet access, prints, microforms, vocal scores, playsets, community resource equipment. *Special collections* **Northern Poetry Library**: 15,000 volumes of modern poetry (see entry under **Organisations of Interest to Poets**); Cinema: comprehensive collection of about 5000 volumes covering all aspects of the cinema; Family History.

Nottingham Central Library
Angel Row, Nottingham NG1 6HP
☎0115 915 2828   Fax 0115 915 2850
Email arts@notlib.demon.co.uk

Open 9.30 am to 7.00 pm Monday to Friday; 9.00 am to 1.00 pm Saturday

Open access
General public lending library: business information, online information, the arts, local studies, religion, community languages, literature. Videos, periodicals, spoken word, recorded music, CD-ROM service – textual information on CD-ROM on public access machines. Internet on public access. *Special collection* D.H. Lawrence. Extensive back-up reserve stocks. Drama and music sets for loan to groups. Art gallery – contemporary exhibitions; coffee shop.

Nottingham Subscription Library Ltd

Bromley House, Angel Row, Nottingham
NG1 6HL
☎0115 947 3134
Librarian *Julia Wilson*
Open 9.30 am to 5.00 pm Monday to Friday;
also first Saturday of each month from
10.00 am to 12.30 pm
Access For members only
FOUNDED 1816. Collection of 30,000 books
including local history, topography, biography,
travel and fiction.

Office for National Statistics, National Statistics Information and Library Service

1Drummond Gate, London SW1V 2QQ
☎0845 601 3034/Minicom: 01633 812399
Fax 01633 652747
Email info@statistics.gov.uk
Website www.statistics.gov.uk
Open 9.00 am to 5.00 pm; no appointment
required
Also: National Statistics Information and
Library Service, Government Buildings,
Cardiff Road, Newport NP9 1XG
Open as above
Wide range of government statistical publications and access to government Internet-
based data. Census statistical data from 1801;
population and health data from 1837; government social survey reports from 1941; recent
international statistical data (UN, Eurostat,
etc.); monograph and periodical collections of
statistical methodology. The library in south
Wales holds a wide range of government economic and statistical publications.

Orkney Library

Laing Street, Kirkwall, Orkney KW15 1NW
☎01856 873166 Fax 01856 875260
Email orkey.library@ork.gov.uk
Open 9.00 am to 8.00 pm Monday to Friday;
9.00 am to 5.00 pm Saturday.
Archives: 9.00 am to 1.00 pm and 2.00 pm
to 4.45 pm Monday to Friday
Open access
Local studies collection. Archive includes
sound and photographic departments.

Oxford Central Library

Westgate, Oxford OX1 1DJ
☎01865 815549 Fax 01865 721694
Website www.oxfordshire.gov.uk

Open Call 01865 815509 for details
General lending and reference library including the Centre for Oxfordshire Studies. Also
periodicals, audio visual materials, music library,
children's library and Business Information
Point.

PA News Library

292 Vauxhall Bridge Road, London
SW1V 1AE
☎020 7963 7012 Fax 020 7963 7065
Website www.pa.press.net
Open 8.00 am to 8.00 pm Monday to Friday;
9.00 am to 5.00 pm Saturday and Sunday
Open access
PA News, the 24-hour national news and
information group, offers public access to its
press cutting archive. Covering a wide range of
subjects, the library includes over 14 million cuttings dating back to 1928. Personal callers welcome or research undertaken by in-house staff.

Penzance Library

See **Morrab Library**

City of Plymouth Library and Information Services

Central Library, Drake Circus, Plymouth,
Devon PL4 8AL
Website www.plymouth.gov.uk/star/
library.htm
Open access

CENTRAL LIBRARY LENDING DEPARTMENTS:
Lending ☎01752 305912
Children's Department ☎01752 305916
Music & Drama Department ☎01752
305914 Email music@plymouth.gov.uk
Open 9.30 am to 7.00 pm Monday and
Friday; 9.30 am to 5.30 pm Tuesday,
Wednesday, Thursday; 9.30 am to 4.00 pm
Saturday

The Lending departments offer books on all
subjects; language courses on cassette and foreign language books; the Holcenberg Jewish
Collection; books on music and musicians,
drama and theatre; music parts and sets of
music parts; play sets; DVDs, videos; song
index; cassettes and CDs.

CENTRAL LIBRARY REFERENCE
DEPARTMENTS:
Reference ☎ 01752 305907/8
Email ref@plymouth.gov.uk
Business Information ☎01752 305906
Email keyinfo@plymouth.gov.uk
Local Studies & Naval History Department

☎01752 305909 Email localstudies@plymouth.
gov.uk

Open 9.00 am to 7.00 pm Monday to Friday;
9.00 am to 4.00 pm Saturday

The Reference departments include an extensive collection of Ordnance Survey maps and town guides; community and census information; marketing and statistical information; Patents and British Standards; books on every aspect of Plymouth; naval history; Mormon Index on microfilm; Baring Gould manuscript of 'Folk Songs of the West'.

Plymouth Proprietary Library
Alton Terrace, 111 North Hill, Plymouth,
Devon PL4 8JY
☎01752 660515

Librarian *John R. Smith*
Open Monday to Saturday from 9.30 am
(closing time varies)

Access To members; visitors by appointment
only
FOUNDED 1810. The library contains approximately 17,000 volumes of mainly 20th-century work. Member of the **Association of Independent Libraries**.

The Poetry Library
See entry under **Organisations of Interest to Poets**

Polish Library
238–246 King Street, London W6 0RF
☎020 8741 0474   Fax 020 8741 7724

Open 10.00 am to 8.00 pm Monday and
Wednesday; 10.00 am to 5.00 pm Friday;
10.00 am to 1.00 pm Saturday (library
closed Tuesday and Thursday)

Access For reference to all interested in Polish affairs; limited loans to members and *bona fide* scholars only through inter-library loans

Books, pamphlets, periodicals, maps, music, photographs on all aspects of Polish history and culture. *Special collections* Emigré publications; Joseph Conrad and related works; Polish underground publications; bookplates.

Poole Central Library
Dolphin Centre, Poole, Dorset BH15 1QE
☎01202 262421   Fax 01202 262442
Email poolelendlib@hotmail.com

Open 10.00 am to 7.00 pm Monday; 9.30 am
to 7.00 pm Tuesday to Friday; 9.00 am to
1.00 pm Saturday

Open access

General lending and reference library, including Healthpoint health information centre, business information, children's library, periodicals and newspapers.

Press Association Library
See **PA News Library**

Harry Price Library of Magical Literature
University of London Library, Senate House,
Malet Street, London WC1E 7HU
☎020 7862 8470   Fax 020 7862 8480
Website www.ull.ac.uk

Open 9.30 am to 6.00 pm Monday to Friday;
9.30 am to 1.00 pm, 2.00 pm to 5.15 pm
Saturday (by prior appointment only);
Monday evenings in term time (by prior
appointment only)

Restricted access For reference only, restricted to members of the University and *bona fide* researchers (apply in writing); items must be requested from, and consulted in, the Special Collections Reading Room

Over 14,000 volumes and pamphlets on psychic phenomena and pseudo-phenomena; books relating to spiritualism and its history, to hypnotism, telepathy, astrology, conjuring and quackery.

Public Record Office
Ruskin Avenue, Kew, Richmond, Surrey
TW9 4DU
☎020 8876 3444   Fax 020 8878 8905
Email enquiry@pro.gov.uk
Website www.pro.gov.uk

Also at: The Family Record Centre,
1 Myddleton Street, London EC1R 1UW

Open 9.00 am to 5.00 pm Monday,
Wednesday, Friday; 10.00 am to 7.00 pm
Tuesday; 9.00 am to 7.00 pm Thursday;
9.30 am to 5.00 pm Saturday

Access For reference, by reader's ticket, available free of charge on production of proof of identity (UK citizens: banker's card or driving licence; non-UK: passport or national identity card. Telephone for further information)

Over 168 kilometres of shelving house the national repository of records of central Government in the UK and law courts of England and Wales, which extend in time from the 11th–20th century. Medieval records and the records of the State Paper Office from the early 16th–late 18th century, plus the records of the Privy Council Office and the Lord

Chamberlain's and Lord Steward's departments. Modern government department records, together with those of the Copyright Office dating mostly from the late 18th century. Under the Public Records Act, records are normally only open to inspection when they are 30 years old.

Reading Central Library

Abbey Square, Reading, Berkshire RG1 3BQ
☎0118 901 5955 Fax 0118 901 5954
Email reading.borough.libraries@reading.gov.uk
Website www.reading.gov.uk

Open 9.30 am to 5.30 pm Monday and
Friday; 9.30 am to 7.00 pm Tuesday and
Thursday; 9.30 am to 5.00 pm Wednesday
and Saturday

Open access
Lending library; reference library; local studies library, bringing together every aspect of the local environment and human activity in Berkshire; business library; music and drama library. Special collections: Mary Russell Mitford; local illustrations.

Public meeting room available.

Religious Society of Friends Library

Friends House, 173 Euston Road, London
NW1 2BJ
☎020 7663 1135 Fax 020 7663 1001
Email library@quaker.org.uk
Website www.quaker.org.uk

Open 1.00 pm to 5.00 pm Monday, Tuesday,
Thursday, Friday; 10.00 am to 5.00 pm
Wednesday

Open access A letter of introduction from someone in good standing is required for researchers who are not members of the Society

Quaker history, thought and activities from the 17th century onwards. Supporting collections on peace, anti-slavery and other subjects in which Quakers have maintained long-standing interest. Also archives and manuscripts relating to the Society of Friends.

Richmond Central Reference Library

Old Town Hall, Whittaker Avenue,
Richmond, Surrey TW9 1TP
☎020 8940 5529 Fax 020 8940 6899
Email reference.services@richmond.gov.uk
Website www.richmond.gov.uk

Open 10.00 am to 6.00 pm Monday,
Thursday, Friday (Tuesday till 1.00 pm;

Wednesday till 8.00 pm and Saturday till 5.00 pm)

Open access
General reference library serving the needs of local residents and organisations. Internet access and online databases for public use.

Royal Anthropological Institute Library

See **British Museum Department of Ethnography Library**

Royal Geographical Society Library (with the Institute of British Geographers)

1 Kensington Gore, London SW7 2AR
☎020 7591 3040 Fax 020 7591 3001
Email library@rgs.org
Website www.rgs.org

Open 11.00 am to 5.00 pm Monday to Friday

Access to the library and reading rooms restricted to use by Fellows and members. Visitors strictly by appointment. There is a charge of £10 per person per day, with a reduction of £5 for those who are unwaged or in full-time education

Books and periodicals on geography, topography, cartography, voyages and travels. The Map Room houses map and chart sheets, atlases and RGS-sponsored expedition reports. Photographs on travel and exploration are housed in the picture library, for which an appointment is necessary. (See entry under **Picture Libraries**.)

Royal Society Library

6 Carlton House Terrace, London SW1Y 5AG
☎020 7451 2606 Fax 020 7930 2170
Website www.royalsoc.ac.uk

Open 10.00 am to 5.00 pm Monday to Friday

Access For research only, to *bona fide* researchers; contact the Library in advance of first visit

History of science, scientists' biographies, science policy reports, and publications of international scientific unions and national academies from all over the world.

RSA (Royal Society for the Encouragement of Arts, Manufactures & Commerce)

8 John Adam Street, London WC2N 6EZ
☎020 7930 5115 Fax 020 7839 5805
Email library@rsa-uk.demon.co.uk
Website www.rsa.org.uk

Open Library: 8.30 am to 8.00 pm every weekday. Archive material by appointment

Access to Fellows of RSA; by application and appointment to non-Fellows (Contact *Julie Cranage* Library Services Coordinator, ☎020 7451 6874 or e-mail julie.cranage@rsa-uk. demon.co.uk)

Archives of the Society since 1754. A collection of approximately 10,000 volumes; international exhibition material.

Royal Society of Medicine Library

1 Wimpole Street, London W1G 0AE
☎020 7290 2940 Fax 020 7290 2939
Email library@rsm.ac.uk
Website www.rsm.ac.uk

Director of Information Services *Ian Snowley*
Head of Customer Services *Sheron Burton*
Open 9.00 am to 8.30 pm Monday to Friday;
10.00 am to 5.00 pm Saturday

Access For reference only, on introduction by Fellow of the Society (temporary membership is available to non-members; £10 per day; £25 per week; £75 per month)

Books and periodicals on general medicine, biochemistry and biomedical science. Extensive historical material and portrait collection.

St Bride Printing Library

Bride Lane, London EC4Y 8EE
☎020 7353 4660 Fax 020 7583 7073
Email stbride@corpoflondon.gov.uk
Open 9.30 am to 5.30 pm Monday to Friday
Open access

Corporation of London public reference library. Appointments advisable for consultation of special collections. Every aspect of printing and related matters: publishing and bookselling, newspapers and magazines, graphic design, calligraphy and type, papermaking and bookbinding. One of the world's largest specialist collections in its field, with over 40,000 volumes, over 3000 periodicals (200 current titles), and extensive collection of drawings, manuscripts, prospectuses, patents and materials for printing and typefounding. Noted for its comprehensive holdings of historical and early technical literature.

Science Fiction Foundation Research Library

Liverpool University Library, PO Box 123,
Liverpool L69 3DA
☎0151 794 3142 Fax 0151 794 2681
Email asawyer@liverpool.ac.uk

Website www.liv.ac.uk/~sawyer/
sffchome.html
Contact *Andy Sawyer*
Access For research, by appointment only (telephone first)

This is the largest collection outside the US of science fiction and related material – including autobiographies and critical works. *Special collection* Runs of 'pulp' magazines dating back to the 1920s. Foreign-language material (including a large Russian collection), and the papers of the Flat Earth Society. The collection also features a growing range of archive and manuscript material, including the Eric Frank Russell archive. The University of Liverpool also holds the Olaf Stapledon and John Wyndham archives.

Science Museum Library

Imperial College Road, London SW7 5NH
☎020 7942 4242 Fax 020 7942 4243
Email smlinfo@nmsi.ac.uk
Website www.nmsi.ac.uk/library

Open 9.30 am to 9.00 pm Monday to Friday (closes 5.30 pm outside academic terms); 9.30 am to 5.30 pm Saturday

Open access Reference only; no loans

National reference library for the history and public understanding of science and technology, with a large collection of source material. Operates jointly with Imperial College Central Library.

Scottish Poetry Library

See entry under **Organisations of Interest to Poets**

Sheffield Libraries, Archives and Information

Central Library, Surrey Street, Sheffield S1 1XZ
☎0114 273 4711 Fax 0114 273 5009

Sheffield Archives
52 Shoreham Street, Sheffield S1 4SP
☎0114 203 9395 Fax 0114 203 9398
Email sheffield.archives@dial.pipex.com

Open 10.00 am to 5.30 pm Monday; 9.30 am to 5.30 pm Tuesday to Thursday; 9.30 am to 1.00 pm and 2.00 pm to 5.00 pm Saturday (documents should be ordered by 5.00 pm Thursday for Saturday); closed Friday

Access By reader's pass

Holds documents relating to Sheffield and South Yorkshire, dating from the 12th century to the present day, including records of the City Council, churches, businesses, landed estates, families and individuals, institutions and societies.

Arts and Social Sciences Reference Service
☎0114 273 4747/8

Open 10.00 am to 8.00 pm Monday; 9.30 am to 5.30 pm Tuesday and Friday; 9.30 am to 8.00 pm Wednesday; 9.30 am to 4.30 pm Saturday (closed Thursday)

Access For reference only
A comprehensive collection of books, periodicals and newspapers covering all aspects of arts (excluding music) and social sciences.

Music and Video Service
☎0114 273 4733

Open as for Arts and Social Sciences above

Access For reference (loans to ticket holders only)
An extensive range of books, CDs, cassettes, scores, etc. related to music. Also a video cassette and DVD loan service.

Local Studies Service
☎0114 273 4753

Open as for Arts & Social Sciences above (except Wednesday 9.30 am to 5.30 pm)

Access For reference
Extensive material covering all aspects of Sheffield and its population, including maps, photos and videos.

Business, Science and Technology Reference Services
☎0114 273 4736/7 or 273 4742

Open as for Arts & Social Sciences above

Access For reference only
Extensive coverage of science and technology as well as commerce and commercial law. British patents and British and European standards with emphasis on metals. Hosts the World Metal Index. The business section holds a large stock of business and trade directories, plus overseas telephone directories and reference works with business emphasis.

Sheffield Information Service
☎0114 273 4760/1 or 273 4712
Fax 0114 275 7111
Email nd54@dial.pipex.com
Website dis.shef.ac.uk/help_yourself

Open 10.00 am to 5.30 pm Monday; 9.30 am to 5.30 pm Tuesday, Wednesday, Friday; 9.30 am to 4.30 pm Saturday (closed Thursday)

Full local information service covering all aspects of the Sheffield community and a generalist advice service on a sessional basis.

Children's and Young People's Library Service
☎0114 273 4734

Open 10.30 am to 5.00 pm Monday and Friday; 1.00 pm to 5.00 pm Tuesday and Wednesday; 9.30 am to 4.30 pm Saturday (closed Thursday)

Books, spoken word sets, videos; under-five play area; teenage reference section; readings and promotions; storytime sessions.

Sports Library
☎0114 273 5929
Email sports.library@dial.pipex.com

Open 10.00 am to 1.00 pm and 2.00 pm to 6.00 pm Monday and Wednesday; 10.00 pm to 1.00 pm and 2.00 pm to 4.30 pm Tuesday and Friday (closed Thursday and Saturday)

Information on all aspects of sport and physical recreation including sports medicine, physiology, nutrition, coaching, recreation management, sports history. Special collection on mountaineering.

Shetland Library
Lower Hillhead, Lerwick, Shetland ZE1 0EL
☎01595 693868 Fax 01595 694430
Email info@shetland-library.gov.uk
Website www.shetland-library.gov.uk

Open 10.00 am to 7.00 pm Monday, Wednesday, Friday; 10.00 am to 5.00 pm Tuesday, Thursday, Saturday

General lending and reference library; extensive local interest collection including complete set of *The Shetland Times, The Shetland News* and other local newspapers on microfilm and many old and rare books; audio collection including talking books/newspapers. Junior room for children. Disabled access and Housebound Readers Service (delivery to reader's home). Mobile library services to rural areas. Open Learning Service. Same day photocopying service. Publishing programme of books in dialect, history, literature.

Shoe Lane Library
Hill House, Little New Street, London EC4A 3JR
☎020 7583 7178
Email shoelane@corpoflondon.gov.uk
Website www.corpoflondon.gov.uk

Open 9.30 am to 5.30 pm Monday, Wednesday, Thursday, Friday; 9.30 am to 6.30 pm Tuesday

Open access

Corporation of London general lending library, with a comprehensive stock of 50,000 volumes, most of which are on display.

Shrewsbury Library

Castlegates, Shrewsbury, Shropshire SY1 2AS
☎01743 255300 Fax 01743 255309
Email shrewsbury.library@shropshire-cc.gov.uk
Website www.shropshire-cc.gov.uk/library.nsf

Open 9.30 am to 5.00 pm Monday and Wednesday; 9.30 am to 1.00 pm Thursday; 9.30 am to 7.30 pm Tuesday and Friday; 9.30 am to 4.00 pm Saturday

Open access

The largest public lending library in Shropshire. Books, cassettes, CDs, talking books, videos, language courses. Open Learning, homework and study centre with public use computers for word processing, CD-ROMs and Internet access. Strong music, literature and art book collection. Reference and local studies provision in adjacent buildings.

Spanish Institute Library

See **Instituto Cervantes**

Suffolk County Council Libraries & Heritage

St Andrew House, County Hall, St Helens Street, Ipswich, Suffolk IP4 1LJ
☎01473 584564 Fax 01473 584549
Email (general enquiries) infolink@libher. suffolkcc.gov.uk
Website www.suffolkcc.gov.uk/libraries_ and_heritage/

Open Details on application to St Andrew House above. Major libraries open six days a week

Access A single user registration card gives access to the lending service of 42 libraries across the county

Full range of lending and reference services. Free public access to the Internet and multimedia CD-ROMs in all libraries. Catalogue with self-service facilities for registered borrowers available on the website. *Special collections* include Suffolk Archives and Local History Collection; Benjamin Britten Collection; Edward Fitzgerald Collection; Seckford Collection and Racing Collection (Newmarket). The Suffolk Infolink service gives details of local groups and societies and is available in libraries throughout the county.

Sunderland City Library and Arts Centre

28–30 Fawcett Street, Sunderland, Tyne & Wear SR1 1RE
☎0191 514 1235 Fax 0191 514 8444

Open 9.30 am to 7.30 pm Monday and Wednesday; 9.30 am to 5.00 pm Tuesday, Thursday, Friday; 9.30 am to 4.00 pm Saturday

The city's main library for lending and reference services. Local studies and children's sections, plus Sound and Vision department (CDs, cassettes, videos, CD-ROMs, talking books). The City of Sunderland also maintains community libraries of varying size, offering a range of services, plus mobile libraries. A Books on Wheels service is available to housebound readers; the Schools Library Service serves teachers and schools. Two writers' groups meet at the City Library and Arts Centre: Janus Writers, every Wednesday, 1.30 pm to 3.30 pm. Tuesday Writers, every Tuesday, 7.30 pm to 9.30 pm.

Swansea Central Reference Library

Alexandra Road, Swansea SA1 5DX
☎01792 516753/516757 Fax 01792 615759
Email central.library@swansea.gov.uk
Website www.swansea.gov.uk/culture/ libraries/libraryIntro.htm

Open 9.00 am to 7.00 pm Monday, Tuesday, Wednesday, Friday; 9.00 am to 5.00 pm Thursday and Saturday. The library has a lending service but hours tend to be shorter – check in advance (☎01792 516750/1)

Access For reference only (Local Studies closed access: items must be requested on forms provided)

General reference material (approx. 100,000 volumes); also British standards, statutes, company information, maps, European Community information. Local studies: comprehensive collections on Wales; Swansea & Gower; Dylan Thomas. Local maps, periodicals, illustrations, local newspapers from 1804. B&w and colour photocopying facilities, access to the Internet and microfilm/microfiche copying facility.

Swiss Cottage Central Library

88 Avenue Road, London NW3 3HA
☎020 7974 6522

Open 10.00 am to 7.00 pm Monday and Thursday; 10.00 am to 6.00 pm Tuesday, Wednesday, Friday; 10.00 am to 5.00 pm Saturday

Open access

Over 300,000 volumes in the lending and reference libraries and 300 periodicals (200 current titles). Home of the London Borough of Camden's Information and Reference Services.

Theatre Museum Library & Archive

1e Tavistock Street, London WC2E 7PR
☎020 7943 4700 Fax 020 7943 4777
Website theatremuseum.org

Open 10.30 am to 4.30 pm Tuesday to Friday

Access By appointment only

The Theatre Museum was founded as a separate department of the Victoria & Albert Museum in 1974 and moved to its own building in Covent Garden in 1987. The museum (open Tuesday to Sunday 10.00 am to 6.00 pm) houses permanent displays, temporary exhibitions, a studio theatre, and organises a programme of special events, performances, lectures, guided visits and workshops. The library houses the UK's largest performing arts research collections, including books, photographs, designs, engravings, programmes, press cuttings, etc. All the performing arts are covered but strengths are in the areas of theatre, dance, musical theatre and stage design. The Theatre Museum has acquired much of the British Theatre Association's library and is providing reference access to its collections of play texts and critical works.

Thurrock Council Leisure, Libraries & Cultural Services Department

Grays Library, Orsett Road, Grays, Essex RM17 5DX
☎01375 383611 Fax 01375 370806
Virtual Enquiry Desk: acairns@thurrock.gov.uk

Open 9.00 am to 7.00 pm Monday, Tuesday, Thursday; 9.00 am to 5.00 pm Wednesday, Friday, Saturday; branch library opening times vary

Open access

General library lending and reference through nine libraries and a mobile library. Services include books, magazines, newspapers, audiocassettes, CDs, videos, pictures and language courses. Large collection of Thurrock materials. Internet and word processing.

Truro Library

Union Place, Pydar Street, Truro, Cornwall TR1 1EP
☎01872 279205 (lending)/272702 (reference)

Open 9.30 am to 5.00 pm Monday to Thursday; 9.30 am to 7.00 pm Friday; 9.00 am to 4.00 pm Saturday

Books, cassettes, CDs and videos for loan through branch or mobile networks. Reference collection. *Special collections* on local studies.

United Nations Information Centre

Millbank Tower (21st Floor), 21–24 Millbank, London SW1P 4QH
☎020 7630 1981 Fax 020 7976 6478
Email info@uniclondon.org
Website www.unitednations.org.uk

Open Library: 9.30 am to 1.00 pm and 2.00 pm to 5.30 pm Monday to Thursday

Open access By appointment only

A full stock of official publications and documentation from the United Nations.

Western Isles Libraries

Public Library, 19 Cromwell Street, Stornoway, Isle of Lewis HS1 2DA
☎01851 703064 Fax 01851 708676

Open 10.00 am to 5.00 pm Monday to Thursday; 10.00 am to 7.00 pm Friday; 10.00 am to 5.00 pm Saturday

Open access

General public library stock, plus local history and Gaelic collections including maps, printed music, cassettes and CDs; census records and Council minutes; music collection (cassettes). Branch libraries on the isles of Barra, Benbecula, Harris and Lewis.

City of Westminster Archives Centre

10 St Ann's Street, London SW1P 2DE
☎020 7641 5180 Fax 020 7641 5179
Website www.westminster.gov.uk

Open 9.30 am to 7.00 pm Tuesday, Thursday, Friday; 9.30 am to 9.00 pm Wesdnesday; 9.30 am to 5.00 pm Saturday (closed Monday)

Access For reference

Comprehensive coverage of the history of Westminster and selective coverage of general London history. 22,000 books, together with a large stock of maps, prints, photographs, theatre programmes and archives.

Westminster Music Library

Victoria Library, 160 Buckingham Palace
Road, London SW1W 9UD
☎020 7641 4292 Fax 020 7641 4281
Email westmuslib@dial.pipex.com
Website www.earl.org.uk/music/westminster/
composers

Open 11.00 pm to 7.00 pm Monday to
Friday; 10 am to 5.00 pm Saturday

Open access

Located at Victoria Library, this is the largest
public music library in the South of England,
with extensive coverage of all aspects of music,
including books, periodicals and printed scores.
No recorded material, notated only. Lending
library includes a small collection of CDs and
videos.

Westminster Reference Library

35 St Martin's Street, London WC2H 7HP
☎020 7641 4636 Fax 020 7641 4606
Email westreflib@dial.pipex.com
Website www.westminster.gov.uk/el/libarch/
index.html
General Reference & Performing Arts:
☎020 7641 4636
Art & Design: ☎020 7641 4638
Business and Official Publications: ☎020
7641 4634

Open 10.00 am to 8.00 pm Monday to
Friday; 10.00 am to 5.00 pm Saturday

Access For reference only

A general reference library with emphasis on
the following: Art & Design – fine and decorative arts, architecture, graphics and design;
Performing Arts – theatre, cinema, radio, television and dance; Official Publications – major
collection of HMSO publications from 1947,
plus parliamentary papers dating back to 1906;
Business – UK directories, trade directories,
company and market data; Official EU
Depository Library – carries official EU material;
Periodicals – long files of many titles. One working day's notice is required for some government
documents, some monographs and most older
periodicals.

The Wiener Library

4 Devonshire Street, London W1W 5BH
☎020 7636 7247 Fax 020 7436 6428
Email lib@wl.u-net.com
Website wienerlibrary.co.uk

Open 10.00 am to 5.30 pm Monday to Friday

Access By letter of introduction (readers need-

ing to use the Library for any length of time
should become members)

Private library – one of the leading research
centres on European history since the First
World War, with special reference to the era of
totalitarianism and to Jewish affairs. Founded
by Dr Alfred Wiener in Amsterdam in 1933, it
holds material that is not available elsewhere.
Books, periodicals, press archives, documents,
pamphlets, leaflets and brochures. Much of the
material can be consulted on microfilm.

Vaughan Williams Memorial Library

English Folk Dance and Song Society, Cecil
Sharp House, 2 Regent's Park Road, London
NW1 7AY
☎020 7485 2206 ext. 18/19
Fax 020 7284 0523
Email library@efdss.org
Website www.efdss.org

Open 9.30 am to 5.30 pm Tuesday to Friday;
10.00 am to 4.00 pm 1st & 3rd Saturday
(sometimes closed between 1.00 pm and
2.00 pm)

Access For reference to the general public, on
payment of a daily fee; members may borrow
books and use the library free of charge

A multimedia collection: books, periodicals,
manuscripts, tapes, records, CDs, films, videos.
Mostly British traditional culture and how this
has developed around the world. Some foreign
language material, and some books in English
about foreign cultures. Also, the history of the
English Folk Dance and Song Society.

Dr Williams's Library

14 Gordon Square, London WC1H 0AR
☎020 7387 3727 Fax 020 7388 1142

Open 10.00 am to 5.00 pm Monday,
Wednesday, Friday; 10.00 am to 6.30 pm
Tuesday and Thursday

Open access to reading room (loans restricted
to subscribers). Visitors required to supply
identification

Annual subscription £10; ministers of
religion and certain students £5

Primarily a library of theology, religion and
ecclesiastical history. Also philosophy, history
(English and Byzantine). Particularly important
for the study of English Nonconformity.
Trustees of Dr William's Library manage the
Congregational Library on behalf of the
Memorial Hall Trustees.

Wolverhampton Central Library

Snow Hill, Wolverhampton WV1 3AX
☎01902 552025 (lending)/552026 (reference)
Fax 01902 552024
Email wolverhampton.libraries@dial.pipex.com
Website www.wolverhampton.gov.uk

Open 9.00 am to 7.00 pm Monday to
Thursday; 9.00 am to 5.00 pm Friday and
Saturday

Archives & Local Studies Collection

42–50 Snow Hill, Wolverhampton WV2 4AB
☎01902 552480

Open 10.00 am to 5.00 pm Monday,
Tuesday, Friday, 1st and 3rd Saturday of
each month; 10.00 am to 7.00 pm
Wednesday; closed Thursday

General lending and reference libraries, plus
children's library and audiovisual library holding cassettes, CDs, videos and music scores.
Internet access.

The Women's Library

London Guildhall University, Calcutta House,
Old Castle Street, London E1 7NT
☎020 7320 1189 Fax 020 7320 1188
Email fawcett@lgu.ac.uk
Website www.lgu.ac.uk/fawcett

Open See final paragraph below

The Women's Library, national research library
for women's history, is the UK's oldest and most
comprehensive research library on all aspects of
women in society, with both historical and contemporary coverage. The Library includes materials on feminism, work, education, health, the
family, law, arts, sciences, technology, language,
sexuality, fashion and the home. The main
emphasis is on Britain but many other countries
are represented, especially the Commonwealth
and the Third World. Established in 1926 as the
library of the London Society of Women's
Service (formerly Suffrage), a non-militant
organisation led by Millicent Fawcett. In 1953
the Society was renamed after her and the library
became the Fawcett Library.

Collections include: women's suffrage,
work, education; women and the church, the
law, sport, art, music; abortion, prostitution.
Mostly British materials but some American,
Commonwealth and European works. Books,
journals, pamphlets, archives, photographs,
posters, postcards, audiovisual materials, artefacts, scrapbooks, albums and press cuttings
dating mainly from the 19th century although
some materials date from the 17th century.

The Library will close in its present premises
in April 2001 and re-open in October 2001.
Intending readers are advised to check with the
Library by telephone, e-mail, fax, letter, via the
website or in person, about detailed opening
arrangements nearer the time. The new building will include a reading room, exhibition
space, café, education areas and a conference
room, and will be the cultural and research
centre for anyone interested in women's lives
and achievements.

Worcestershire Libraries and Information Service

Cultural Services, County Hall, Spetchley
Road, Worcester WR5 2NP
☎01905 766231 Fax 01905 766244
Website www.worcestershire.gov.uk/libraries

Open Opening hours vary in the 22 libraries
and mobile libraries covering the county; all
full-time libraries open at least one evening
a week until 7.00 pm or 8.00 pm, and on
Saturday until 1 pm; 8 largest libraries open
until 4.00 pm on Saturday; part-time
libraries vary

Access Information and reference services open
to anyone; loans to members only (membership
criteria: resident, being educated, working, or an
elector in the county or neighbouring authorities; temporary membership to visitors. Proof of
identity and address required. No charge for
membership or for borrowing books.)

Information service, and reference and lending libraries. Non-fiction and fiction for all age
groups, including normal and large print, spoken
word cassettes, sound recordings (CD, cassette),
videos, maps, local history, CD-ROMs for reference at main libraries, free public Internet access
in all libraries. *Special collections* Carpets and
Textiles; Needles & Needlemaking; Stuart
Period; A.E. Housman.

York Central Library

Museum Street, York YO1 7DS
☎01904 655631 Fax 01904 611025

Lending Library

Open 9.30 am to 8.00 pm Monday, Tuesday,
Friday; 9.30 am to 5.30 pm Wednesday and
Thursday; 9.30 am to 4.00 pm Saturday

General lending library including videos, CDs,
music cassettes, audio books, children's story-
tapes language courses and printed music.
Photocopying and fax facilities.

Reference Library

Open 9.00 am to 8.00 pm Monday, Tuesday,
Wednesday, Friday; 9.00 am to 5.30 pm
Thursday; 9.00 am to 4.00 pm Saturday

General reference library; organisations database; local studies library for York and surrounding area; business information service; microfilm/fiche readers for national and local newspapers; census returns and family history resource; general reference collection. Maintains strong links with other local history resource centres, namely the Borthwick Institute, York City Archive and York Minster Library. CD-ROM and Internet facilities. Room 18: IT resource centre available to the public. In addition, 14 branch libraries and one mobile, serving the City of York Council area.

Young Book Trust Children's Reference Library

Book House, 45 East Hill, London SW18 2QZ
☎020 8516 2985 Fax 020 8516 2978
Email ed@booktrust.org.uk
Website www.booktrust.org.uk

Contact *Mr E. Zaghini*

Open 9.00 am to 5.00 pm Monday to Friday (by appointment only)

Access For reference only

A comprehensive collection of children's literature, related books and periodicals. Aims to hold most of all children's titles published within the last two years. An information service covers all aspects of children's literature, including profiles of authors and illustrators. Reading room facilities.

Zoological Society Library

Regent's Park, London NW1 4RY
☎020 7449 6293 Fax 020 7586 5743
Email library@zsl.org
Website www.zsl.org

Open 9.30 am to 5.30 pm Monday to Friday

Access To members and staff; non-members by application and on payment of fee

160,000 volumes on zoology including 5000 journals (1300 current) and a wide range of books on animals and particular habitats. Slide collection available and many historic zoological prints.

Picture Libraries

A–Z Botanical Collection Ltd
192 Goswell Road, London EC1V 7DT
☎020 7253 0991 Fax 020 7253 0992
Email azbotanical@yahoo.com
Website www.a-z.picture-library.com

Contact *James Wakefield*

300,000 transparencies, specialising in plants and related subjects.

Acme
See **Popperfoto**

Action Plus
54–58 Tanner Street, London SE1 3PH
☎020 7403 1558 Fax 020 7403 1526
Email info@actionplus.co.uk

Specialist sports and action library with a vast comprehensive collection of small-format colour and b&w images covering all aspects of over 300 professional and amateur sports from around the world. As well as personalities, events, venues, etc, also covers themes such as success, celebration, dejection, teamwork, effort and exhaustion. Offers same-day despatch of pictures or alternatively, clients with modem or ISDN links can receive digital images direct.

Lesley & Roy Adkins Picture Library
Ten Acre Wood, Whitestone, Exeter, Devon EX4 2HW
☎01392 811357 Fax 01382 811435
Email mail@adkinsarchaology.com
Website www.adkinsarchaeology.com

Colour coverage of archaeology, heritage and related subjects in the UK, Europe, Egypt and Turkey. Subjects include towns, villages, housing, landscape and countryside, churches, temples, castles, monasteries, art and architecture, gravestones and tombs, inscriptions and antiquarian views. No service charge if pictures are used.

The Advertising Archive Limited
45 Lyndale Avenue, London NW2 2QB
☎020 7435 6540 Fax 020 7794 6584
Email suzanne@advertisingarchives.co.uk
Website www.advertisingarchives.co.uk

Contacts *Suzanne Viner, Larry Viner*

With over one million images, the largest collection of British and American press ads and magazine cover illustrations in Europe. Material from 1870 to the present day. Visitors by appointment. Research undertaken; rapid service, competitive rates. Exclusive UK agents for *Saturday Evening Post* cover illustrations including artwork of Norman Rockwell and Josef Leyendecker.

AKG London Ltd, The Arts and History Picture Library
5 Melbray Mews, 158 Hurlingham Road, London SW6 3NS
☎020 7610 6103 Fax 020 7610 6125
Email enquiries@akg-london.co.uk
Website www.akg-london.co.uk

Contact *Julia Engelhardt*

Collection of 200,000 images with direct access to ten million (100,000 available via ISDN as high resolution scans) kept in the Berlin AKG Library. *Specialises* in art, archaeology, history, topography, music, personalities and film.

Bryan & Cherry Alexander Photography
Higher Cottage, Manston, Sturminster Newton, Dorset DT10 1EZ
☎01258 473006 Fax 01258 473333
Email alexander@arcticphoto.co.uk
Website www.arcticphoto.co.uk

Contact *Cherry Alexander*

Arctic and Antarctic specialists; indigenous peoples, wildlife and science in polar regions; Norway, Iceland, Siberia and Alaska.

Allsport (UK) Ltd
3 Greenlea Park, Prince George's Road, London SW19 2JD
☎020 8685 1010 Fax 020 8648 5240
Email lmartin@allsport.co.uk
Website www.allsport.com

Contact *Lee Martin*

A large specialist library with six million colour transparencies, covering 140 different sports and top sports personalities. Represented in 27 countries worldwide. Digital wiring facilities through Macintosh picture desk. Online digital archive access available via ISDN and Internet.

Alvey & Towers

Enterprise House, Ashby Road, Coalville, Leicestershire LE67 3LA
☎01530 450011 Fax 01530 450011
Email alveytower@aol.com
Website www.alveyandtowers.com

Contact *Emma Rowen*

Houses two separate collections; one covering the modern railway industry and all related supporting industries, the other features a more general 'lifestyle' collection with the emphasis on people and day-to-day living plus a substantial selection of transport images.

Andes Press Agency

26 Padbury Court, London E2 7EH
☎020 7613 5417 Fax 020 7739 3159
Email photos@andespress.demon.co.uk

Contacts *Val Baker, Carlos Reyes*

80,000 colour transparencies and 300,000 b&w, specialising in social documentary, world religions, Latin America and Britain.

Heather Angel/Natural Visions

Highways, 6 Vicarage Hill, Farnham, Surrey GU9 8HJ
☎01252 716700 Fax 01252 727464
Email hangel@naturalvisions.co.uk
Website www.naturalvisions.co.uk

Contact *Valerie West*

Constantly expanding worldwide natural history, wildlife and landscapes: polar regions, tropical rainforest flora and fauna, all species of plants and animals in natural habitats from Africa, Asia (notably China and Malaysia), Australasia, South America and USA, urban wildlife, pollution, biodiversity, global warming. Also worldwide gardens and cultivated flowers. Transparencies only loaned to publishers after contract exchanged with author.

Ansel Adams

See **Corbis Images**

Aquarius Library

PO Box 5, Hastings, East Sussex TN34 1HR
☎01424 721196 Fax 01424 717704
Email aquarius.lib@clara.net

Contact *David Corkill*

Over one million images specialising in cinema past and present, television, pop music, ballet,
opera, theatre, etc. The library includes various American showbiz collections. Film stills date back to the beginning of the century. Interested in film stills, the older the better. Current material is supplied by own suppliers.

Aquila Wildlife Images

PO Box 1, Studley, Warwickshire B80 7JG
☎01527 852357 Fax 01527 857507
Email interbirdnet@birder.co.uk
Website www.birder.co.uk

Natural history library specialising in birds, British and European wildlife, North America, Africa and Australia, environmental subjects, farming, habitats and related subjects, domestic animals and pets.

Architectural Association Photo Library

36 Bedford Square, London WC1B 3ES
☎020 7887 4078 Fax 020 7414 0782
Email photolib@aaschool.ac.uk
Website www.aaschool.ac.uk

Contacts *Valerie Bennett, Sarah Farmer, Sarah Franklin*

100,000 35mm transparencies on architecture, historical and contemporary. Archive of large-format b&w negatives from the 1920s and 1930s.

Ardea London Ltd

35 Brodrick Road, London SW17 7DX
☎020 8672 2067 Fax 020 8672 8787
Email ardea@ardea.co.uk
Website www.ardea.co.uk

Specialist natural history photographic library supplying images of animals, birds, plants, fish, reptiles and amphibians in their natural habitat worldwide and domestic pets. Coverage includes landscapes, conservation and environmental images.

Art Directors & Trip Photo Library

57 Burdon Lane, Cheam, Surrey SM2 7BY
☎020 8642 3593/8661 7104
Fax 020 8395 7230
Email images@artdirectors.co.uk
Website www.artdirectors.co.uk

Contacts *Helene Rogers, Bob Turner*

Englarged newly-merged library with over 750,000 images. Extensive coverage of all countries, lifestyles, religion, peoples, etc. Backgrounds a speciality. Catalogues available free to professionals.

art71

PO Box One, Newtown, Powys SY16 2WP
☎01686 621421   Fax 01686 621421
Email photo@art71.com
Website www.art71.com/photo

Contact *Mike Slater*

Specialist collection of photo-art images, abstract colour and form; close-up nature photography. Available as transparencies and also supplied as prints, including framed prints of any size.

Artbank Illustration Library

8 Woodcroft Avenue, London NW7 2AG
☎020 8906 2288   Fax 020 8906 2289
Email info@artbank.com
Website www.artbank.com

Illustration and art library holding thousands of images by many renowned contemporary illustrators. Large-format transparencies and digital files. Catalogue available on faxed request. Represents a diverse group of UK and American illustrators for commissioned work. Portfolios and stock images available for viewing online.

Aspect Picture Library Ltd

40 Rostrevor Road, London SW6 5AD
☎020 7736 1998/7731 7362
Fax 020 7731 7362
Email Aspect.Ldn@btinternet.com
Website www.aspect-picture-library.co.uk

Colour and b&w worldwide coverage of countries, events, industry and travel, with large files on art, namely paintings, space, China and the Middle East.

Atlantic Syndication Partners

See **Solo Syndication Ltd**

Australia Pictures

28 Sheen Common Drive, Richmond TW10 5BN
☎020 7602 1989   Fax 020 7602 1989

Contact *John Miles*

Collection of 4000 transparencies covering all aspects of Australia: Aboriginal people, paintings, Ayers Rock, Kakadu, Tasmania, underwater, reefs, Arnhem Land, Sydney. Also Africa, Middle East and Asia.

Aviation Images – Mark Wagner

42B Queens Road, London SW19 8LR
☎020 8944 5225   Fax 020 8944 5335
Email mark.wagner@aviation-images.com
Website www.aviation-images.com

Contact *Mark Wagner*

500,000+ aviation images, civil and military, technical and generic. Mark Wagner is the photographer for *Flight International* magazine. Member of **BAPLA** and RAeS.

Aviation Photographs International

15 Downs View Road, Swindon, Wiltshire SN3 1NS
☎01793 497179   Fax 01793 434030

The 250,000 photographs comprise a comprehensive coverage of army, naval and airforce hardware ranging from early pistols to the latest ships. Extensive coverage of military and civil aviation includes modern together with many air-to-air views of vintage/warbird types. Collections available on disk. Commissions undertaken for additional photography and research.

Aviation Picture Library

116 The Avenue, St Stephens, West Ealing, London W13 8JX
☎020 8566 7712   Fax 020 8566 7714
Email avpix@aol.com

Contacts *Austin John Brown, Chris Savill*

Specialists in the aviation field but also a general library which includes travel, architecture, transport, landscapes and skyscapes. *Special collections*: aircraft and all aspects of the aviation industry, including the archival collection of John Stroud; aerial obliques of Europe, USA, Caribbean and West Africa; architectural and town planning. Commissions undertaken on the ground and in the air.

Axel Poignant Archive

115 Bedford Court Mansions, Bedford Avenue, London WC1B 3AG
☎020 7636 2555   Fax 020 7636 2555
Email Rpoignant@aol.com

Contact *Roslyn Poignant*

Anthropological and ethnographic subjects, especially Australia and the South Pacific. Also Scandinavia (early history and mythology), Sicily and England.

Barnaby's Picture Library

See **Mary Evans Picture Library**

Barnardos Photographic and Film Archive

Tanners Lane, Barkingside, Ilford, Essex IG6 1QG
☎020 8550 8822   Fax 020 8550 0429
Email john.kirkham@barnardos.org.uk
Website www.barnardos.org.uk

Contact *John Kirkham*

Specialises in social history (1874 to present day), child care, education, war years, emigration/ migration. Half a million prints, slides, negatives. Images are mainly b&w, colour since late 1940s/early '50s. Archive of 200 films dating back to 1905. Visitors by appointment Monday to Friday, 9.30 am to 4.30 pm.

Colin Baxter Photography Limited

Woodlands Industrial Estate, Grantown-on-Spey PH26 3NA
☎01479 873999 Fax 01479 873888
Email colin.baxter@zetnet.co.uk
Contacts *Colin B. Kirkwood* (Marketing),
Mike Rensner (Editorial)

Over 50,000 images specialising in Scotland. Also the Lake District, Yorkshire, France, Iceland and a special collection on Charles Rennie Mackintosh's work. *Publishes* books, calendars, postcards and greetings cards on landscape, cityscape and natural history containing images which are primarily, but not exclusively, Colin Baxter's. Also publishers of the *Worldlife Library* of natural history books.

BBC Natural History Unit Picture Library

Broadcasting House, Whiteladies Road, Bristol BS8 2LR
☎0117 974 6720 Fax 0117 923 8166
Email nhu.picture.library@bbc.co.uk
Website www.bbcwild.com
Contact *Helen Gilks*

A collection of 120,000 transparencies of wildlife from around the world, especially animal portraits and behaviour. Other subjects covered include plants, landscapes, environmental issues and photos relating to the making of the Natural History Unit's films. Wildlife sound recordings and film footage also available.

The Photographic Library Beamish, The North of England Open Air Museum

The North of England Open Air Museum, Beamish, County Durham DH9 0RG
☎0191 370 4000 Fax 0191 370 4001
Email museum@beamish.org.uk
Website www.beamish.org.uk
Keeper of Resource Collections *Jim Lawson*

Comprehensive collection; images relate to the North East of England and cover agricultural, industrial, topography, advertising and shop scenes, people at work and play. Also on laser disk for rapid searching. Visitors by appointment weekdays.

Francis Bedford

See **Birmingham Library Services** under **Library Services**

Ivan J. Belcher Colour Picture Library

57 Gibson Close, Abingdon, Oxfordshire OX14 1XS
☎01235 521524 Fax 01235 521524

Extensive colour picture library specialising in top-quality medium-format transparencies depicting the British scene. Particular emphasis on tourist, holiday and heritage locations, including famous cities, towns, picturesque harbours, rivers, canals, castles, cottages, rural scenes and traditions photographed throughout the seasons. Mainly of recent origin, and constantly updated.

Andrew Besley PhotoLibrary

'Trenerth Barton', Fraddam, Near Hayle, Cornwall TR27 5EP
☎01736 850086 Fax 01736 850086
Email bes.pix@btinternet.com
Website www.andrewbesley-photolibrary.co.uk
Contact *Andrew Besley*

Specialist library of 20,000 images of West Country faces, places and moods.

Bettmann Archive

See **Corbis Images**

BFI Stills, Posters and Designs

British Film Institute, 21 Stephen Street, London W1T 1LN
☎020 7957 4797 Fax 020 7323 9260
Website ww.bfi.org.uk

Holds images from more than 60,000 films and TV programmes on seven million b&w prints and over 500,000 colour transparencies. A further 20,000 files hold portraits of film and TV personalities and cover related general subjects such as studios, equipment, awards. Also holds original posters and set and costume designs. Visitors welcome by appointment only (from 11.00 am to 4.00 pm, Tuesday to Thursday).

Blackwoods Picture Library

See **Geoslides Photography**

Anthony Blake Photo Library

20 Blades Court, Deodar Road, Putney, London SW15 5AL
☎020 8877 1123 Fax 020 8877 9787

Email info@abpl.co.uk
Website ww.abpl.co.uk

'Europe's premier source' of food and wine related images. From the farm and the vineyard to the plate and the bottle. Cooking and kitchens, top chefs and restaurants, country trades and markets, worldwide travel with an extensive Italian section. Many recipes available to accompany transparencies. Free brochure available.

Peter Boardman Collection
See **Chris Bonnington Picture Library**

Boats & Boating Features (Keith Pritchard)
9 High Street, Southwell, Portland, Dorset DT5 2EH
☎01305 861006   Fax 0870 132 4192
Email boats@btinternet.com

Contact *Keith Pritchard*

International marine photojournalist – photographs, features and news on up-market speedboats, classic sail, eco-tourism, '999' craft, ethnic fishing. Images of more than 300 kinds of craft.

Chris Bonington Picture Library
Badger Hill, Nether Row, Hesket
Newmarket, Wigton, Cumbria CA7 8LA
☎016974 78286   Fax 016974 78238
Email frances@bonington.com
Website www.bonington.com

Contact *Frances Daltrey*

Based on the personal collection of climber and author Chris Bonington and his extensive travels and mountaineering achievements; also work by Doug Scott and other climbers, including the Peter Boardman and Joe Tasker Collections. Full coverage of the world's mountains, from British hills to Everest, depicting expedition planning and management stages, the approach march showing inhabitants of the area, flora and fauna, local architecture and climbing action shots on some of the world's highest mountains.

Boulton and Watt Archive
See **Birmingham Library Services** under **Library Services**

The Bridgeman Art Library
17–19 Garway Road, London W2 4PH
☎020 7727 4065   Fax 020 7792 8509
Email info@bridgeman.co.uk
Website Catalogue: www.bridgeman.co.uk

Head of Marketing *Vivien Wheeler*

Fine art photo archive acting as an agent to more than 1000 museums, galleries and picture owners around the world. Large-format colour transparencies of private collections, artists, paintings, sculptures, prints, manuscripts, antiquities and the decorative arts. The Library is currently expanding at the rate of 500 new images each week and has offices in Paris and New York. Collections represented by the library include the British Library, the National Galleries of Scotland, the National Library of Australia, and the National Gallery of South Africa. Fully searchable catalogue online and printed catalogue available.

British Library Reproductions
British Library, 96 Euston Road, London NW1 2DB
☎020 7412 7614   Fax 020 7412 7771
Email bl-repro@bl.uk
Website www.bl.uk

Twelve million books and approximately five million other items available for photography, microfilming or photocopying by Library staff. Specialist subjects include illuminated manuscripts, stamps, music, maps, botanical and zoological illustration, portraits of historical figures, history of India and South East Asia. All copies should be ordered as far in advance as possible.

However, for photographs for commercial reproduction a picture library service is available which enables orders to be processed more quickly. The picture library has a small but unique collection of colour and b&w images mainly covering royalty, religion, medieval life and world maps plus a selection of natural history. Customers are welcome to visit the collection.

Brooklands Museum Picture Library
Brooklands Museum, Brooklands Road, Weybridge, Surrey KT13 0QN
☎01932 857381   Fax 01932 855465

Contacts *John Pulford* (Curator of Collections), *Julian Temple* (Curator of Aviation)

About 40,000 b&w and colour prints and slides. Subjects include: Brooklands Motor Racing 1907–1939; British aviation and aerospace 1908–present day – particularly BAC, Hawker, Sopwith and Vickers aircraft built at Brooklands.

Hamish Brown
Scottish Photographic
26 Kirkcaldy Road, Burntisland, Fife KY3 9HQ
☎01592 873546

Contact *Hamish M. Brown*

Colour and b&w coverage of most topics and areas of Scotland (sites, historic, buildings, landscape, mountains), also travel and mountains abroad, Ireland and Morocco. Commissions undertaken.

Camera Press
21 Queen Elizabeth Street, London SE1 2PD
☎020 7378 1300 Fax 020 7278 5126

Quality studio images of celebrities, photofeatures, news, personality portraits, humour, royals, fashion and beauty.

Camera Ways Ltd Picture Library
Court View, Stonebridge Green Road,
Egerton, Ashford, Kent TN27 9AN
☎01233 756454
Email derek@cameraways.co.uk

Contacts *Derek, Caryl*

Founded by award-winning film-maker and photographer, Derek Budd, the digital scanned library specialises in rural activities and natural history. It contains 35mm and 6x4.5mm, colour and b&w images as well as 16mm film and video footage on Beta SP and digital Betacam formats. Coverage includes: wildlife habitats, flora and fauna of Britain and Europe, traditional country crafts and people, village scenes, landscapes, gardens, coastal and aquatic life, dinosaurs, aerial surveys, storm damage and M.O.D. reserves. Commissions undertaken in all aspects of commercial multi-media photography, 16mm film, broadcast and corporate video production.

Capital Pictures
49–51 Central Street, London EC1V 8AB
☎020 7253 1122 Fax 020 7253 1414
Email sales@capitalpictures.com
Website www.capitalpictures.com

Contact *Phil Loftus*

500,000 images. *Specialises* in photographs of famous people from the worlds of showbusiness, rock and pop, television, politics, royalty and film stills.

The Casement Collection
Erin Lodge, Jigs Lane South, Warfield,
Berkshire RG42 3DR
☎01344 302067 Fax 01344 303158
Email jackcasement@btinternet.com

Website www.jackcasement.btinternet.co.uk

Colour and b&w travel library, particularly strong on North America and the Gulf. Not just beaches and palm trees. Based on Jack Casement's collection. Digitised images available.

The Centre for the Study of
Cartoons and Caricature
The Templeman Library, University of Kent at Canterbury, Canterbury, Kent CT2 7NU
☎01227 823127 Fax 01227 823127
Email N.P.Hiley@ukc.ac.uk *or*
J.M.Newton@ukc.ac.uk
Website library.ukc.ac.uk/cartoons/

Contacts *Dr Nicholas Hiley, Jane Newton*

A national research archive of over 85,000 20th century cartoons and caricatures, supported by a library of books, papers, journals, catalogues and assorted ephemera. A computer database provides quick and easy catalogued access. A source for exhibitions and displays as well as a picture library service. *Specialises* in historical, political and social cartoons from British newspapers.

Cephas Picture Library
Hurst House, 157 Walton Road, East
Molesey, Surrey KT8 0DX
☎020 8979 8647 Fax 020 8224 8095
Email pictures@cephas.co.uk
Website www.cephas.co.uk

The wine industry and vineyards of the world is the subject on which Cephas has made its reputation. 100,000 images, mainly original 6x7" make this the most comprehensive and up-to-date archive in Britain. Almost all wine-producing countries and all aspects of the industry are covered in depth. Spirits, beer and cider also included. A major food and drink collection now also exists, through preparation and cooking, to eating and drinking.

Giles Chapman Library
3A Peacock Yard, Iliffe Street, London
SE17 3LH
☎020 7708 5818 Fax 020 7703 8209

Contact *Giles Chapman*

Around 100,000 colour and b&w images of cars and motoring, from 1945 to the present day. No research fees.

Christel Clear Marine Photography
Roselea, Church Lane, Awbridge, Near
Romsey, Hampshire SO51 0HN
☎01794 341081 Fax 01794 340890
Email christel.clear@btinternet.com

Website www.christelclear.com

Contacts *Nigel Dowden, Christel Dowden*

Over 70,000 images on 35mm and 645 transparency: yachting and boating from Grand Prix sailing to small dinghies, cruising locations and harbours. Recent additions include angling, fly fishing and travel. Visitors by appointment.

Christian Aid Photo Section

PO Box 100, London SE1 7RT
☎020 7523 2235 Fax 020 7960 2706

Pictures are mainly from Africa, Asia and Latin America, relating to small-scale, community-based programmes. Mostly development themes: agriculture, health, education, urban and rural life.

Christie's Images Ltd

1 Langley Lane, London SW8 1TJ
☎020 7582 1282 Fax 020 7582 5632
Email imageslondon@christies.com
Website www.christiesimages.com

Contact *Emma Strouts*

The UK's largest fine art photo library. 150,000 images of fine and decorative art. An extensive list of subjects is covered through paintings, drawings and prints of all periods as well as silver, ceramics, jewellery, sculpture, textiles and many other decorative and collectable items. Staff will search files and database to locate specific requests or supply a selection for consideration. Visits by appointment. Search fee.

Chrysalis Picture Library

64 Brewery Road, London N7 9NT
☎020 7700 7799 Fax 020 7619 0757
Email Tforshaw@chrysalisbooks.co.uk

Contact *Terry Forshaw*

750,000 photographs and illustrations, colour and b&w, on military, history, transport, cookery, crafts, natural history, space and travel.

The Cinema Museum

The Master's House, Old Lambeth Workhouse, off Renfrew Road, London SE11 4TH
☎020 7840 2200 Fax 020 7840 2299
Email martin@cinemamuseum.org.uk

Colour and b&w coverage (including stills) of the motion picture industry throughout its history, including the Ronald Grant Archive. Smaller collections on theatre, variety, television and popular music.

John Cleare/Mountain Camera

Hill Cottage, Fonthill Gifford, Salisbury, Wiltshire SP3 6QW
☎01747 820320 Fax 01747 820320
Email cleare@btinternet.com
Website www.mountaincamera.com

Colour and b&w coverage of mountains and wild places, climbing, ski-touring, trekking, expeditions, wilderness travel, landscapes, people and geographical features from all continents. *Specialises* in the Himalaya, Andes, Antarctic, Alps and the British countryside, and a range of topics from reindeer in Lapland to camels in Australia, from whitewater rafting in Utah to ski-mountaineering in China. Commissions and consultancy work undertaken. Researchers welcome by appointment. Member of **BAPLA** and the **OWG**.

Michael Cole Camerawork

The Coach House, 27 The Avenue, Beckenham, Kent BR3 2DP
☎020 8658 6120 Fax 020 8658 6120
Website www.tennisphotos.com

Contacts *Michael Cole, Derrick Bentley*

Probably the largest and most comprehensive collection of tennis pictures in the world. Over 50 years' coverage of the Wimbledon Championships. M.C.C. incorporates the tennis archives of Le Roye Productions, established in 1945.

Collections

13 Woodberry Crescent, London N10 1PJ
☎020 8883 0083 Fax 020 8883 9215
Email collections@btinternet.com

Contact *Brian Shuel*

Extensive coverage of the British and Ireland from the Shetlands to the Channel Islands, and Connemara to East Anglia, including people, traditional customs, workers, religions and pastimes, as well as places both well known and obscure, and an extensive collection of 'things'. Includes the landscapes of Fay Godwin. Visitors are welcome but please make an appointment.

Concannon Golf History Library

See **Phil Sheldon Golf Picture Library**

Corbis Images

12 Regents Wharf, All Saints Street, London N1 9RL
☎020 7843 4444 Fax 020 7278 1408
Email info@uk.corbis.com
Website www.corbis.com

Contact *Anna Calvert*

A unique and comprehensive resource containing more than 65 million images, with over 2.1 million of them available online. The images come from professional photographers, museums, cultural institutions and public and private collections worldwide, including images from the Bettmann Archive, Ansel Adams, Lynn Goldsmith, the Turnley Collection and Hulton Deutsch. Subjects include history, travel, celebrities, events, science, world art and cultures. Free catalogues are available or register for a free password to search, save and order online.

Sylvia Cordaiy Photo Library

45 Rotherstone, Devizes, Wiltshire SN10 2DD
☎01380 728327 Fax 01380 728328
Email sylviacordaiy@compuserve.com
Website www.sylvia-cordaiy.com

Over 150 countries on file from the obscure to main stock images – Africa, North, Central and South America, Asia, Atlantic, Indian and Pacific Ocean islands, Australasia, Europe, polar regions. Covers travel, architecture, ancient civilisations, people worldwide, environment, wildlife, natural history, Antarctica, domestic pets, livestock, marine biology, veterinary treatment, equestrian, ornithology, flowers. UK files cover cities, towns villages, coastal and rural scenes, London. Transport, railways, shipping and aircraft (military and civilian). Aerial photography. Backgrounds and abstracts. Also the Paul Kaye B/W archive.

Country Collections

Unit 9, Ditton Priors Trading Estate, Bridgnorth, Shropshire WV16 6SS
☎01746 712533/861330
Contact *Robert Foster*

Small select collection of colour transparencies specialising in sundials, Celtic culture, villages, churches and ancient monuments. Assignments undertaken.

Country Images Picture Library

27 Camwood, Bamber Bridge, Preston, Lancashire PR5 8LA
☎01772 321243 Fax 0870 137 8888
Email terrymarsh@countrymatters.demon.co.uk
Contact *Terry Marsh*

35mm and 645 colour coverage of landscapes and countryside features generally throughout the UK (Cumbria, North Yorkshire, Lancashire, southern Scotland, Isle of Skye, Wales, Cornwall), France (French Alps, French Pyrenees, Provence) and Australia. Commissions undertaken.

Country Life Picture Library

King's Reach Tower, Stamford Street, London SE1 9LS
☎020 7261 6337 Fax 020 7261 6216
Email camilla_costello@ipcmedia.com
Website www.countrylifelibrary.co.uk
Contact *Camilla Costello*

Over 150,000 b&w negatives dating back to 1897, and 15,000 colour transparencies. Country houses, stately homes, churches and town houses in Britain and abroad, interiors of architectural interest (ceilings, fireplaces, furniture, paintings, sculpture), and exteriors showing many landscaped gardens, sporting and social events, crafts, people and animals. Visitors by appointment. Open Tuesday to Friday.

Philip Craven
Worldwide Photo-Library

Surrey Studios, 21 Nork Way, Nork, Banstead, Surrey SM7 1PB
☎01252 627233 Fax 01252 812399
Contact *Eve Horan*

Extensive coverage of British scenes, cities, villages, English countryside, gardens, historic buildings and wildlife. Worldwide travel and wildlife subjects on medium- and large-format transparencies.

CTC Picture Library

CTC Ltd, Longfield, Midhurst Road, Fernhurst, Haslemere, Surrey GU27 3HA
☎01428 661441 Fax 01428 641071
Email ctcreate@globalnet.co.uk
Website www.crightonthomascreative.com
Contact *Neil Crighton*

One of the biggest specialist libraries in the UK with 250,000 slides covering world and UK agriculture, horticulture, and environmental subjects. Also a small section on travel.

Cumbria Picture Library

See **Eric Whitehead Photography**

Sue Cunningham Photographic

56 Chatham Road, Kingston upon Thames, Surrey KT1 3AA
☎020 8541 3024 Fax 020 8541 5388
Email pictures@scphotographic.com
Website www.scphotographic.com

Extensive coverage of many geographical areas: South America (especially Brazil), Eastern Europe from the Baltic to the Balkans, various African countries, Western Europe including the UK. Colour and b&w. Member of **BAPLA**.

Dalton–Watson Collection
See **The Ludvigsen Library Limited**

James Davis Travel Photography
65 Brighton Road, Shoreham, West Sussex BN43 6RE
☎01273 452252 Fax 01273 440116
Email eyeubiquitous@msn.com

Travel collection: people, places, emotive scenes and tourism. Constantly updated by James Davis and a team of photographers, both at home and abroad. Same-day service available.

The Defence Picture Library
Sherwell House, 54 Staddiscombe Road, Plymouth, Devon PL9 9NB
☎01752 401800 Fax 01752 402800
Email picdesk@defencepictures.com
Website www.defencepictures.com

Contacts *David Reynolds, Jessica Kelly, James Rowlands, Andrew Chittock*

Leading source of military photography covering all areas of the UK Armed Forces, supported by a research agency of facts and figures. More than 500,000 images with a significant number on CD-ROM. Campaigns in Aden, the Falklands, Ulster, the Gulf and Kosovo. Specialist collections include the Chinese Armed Forces, US Special Forces, as well as military units of Italy, Spain and France. Visitors welcome by appointment.

Douglas Dickins Photo Library
2 Wessex Gardens, Golders Green, London NW11 9RT
☎020 8455 6221

Sole Proprietor *Douglas Dickins, FRPS*

Worldwide colour and b&w coverage, specialising in Asia, particularly India, Indonesia and Japan. Meeting educational requirements on landscape, archaeology, arts, history, religions, customs, people and folklore.

CM Dixon
The Orchard, Marley Lane, Kingston, Canterbury, Kent CT4 6JH
☎01227 830075 Fax 01227 831135

Colour coverage of ancient civilisations, archaeology and art, ethnology, mythology, world religion, museum objects, geography, geology, meteorology, landscapes, people and places from many countries including most of Europe, former USSR, Ethiopia, Iceland, Jordan, Morocco, Sri Lanka, Tunisia, Turkey, Egypt, Uzbekistan.

Dominic Photography
4B Moore Park Road, London SW6 2JT
☎020 7381 0007 Fax 020 7381 0008

Contacts *Zoë Dominic, Catherine Ashmore*

Colour and b&w coverage of the entertainment world from 1957 onwards: dance, opera, theatre, ballet, musicals and personalities.

E&E Picture Library – Ecclesiastical and Eccentricities
Beggars Roost, Woolpack Hill, Brabourne Lees, Near Ashford, Kent TN25 6RR
☎01303 812608 Fax 01303 812608
Email isobel@picture-library.freeserve.co.uk
Website www.picture-library.freeserve.co.uk

Contact *Isobel Sinden*

Specialises in religions, Biblelands (including Iraq, Iran, Israel and Turkey), death and burial, curiosities and oddities, ceremony, clergy, festivals. Also weather, wind and water.

Patrick Eagar Photography
5 Ennerdale Road, Kew Gardens, Surrey TW9 3PG
☎020 8940 9269 Fax 020 8332 1229
Email patrickeager@compuserve.com
Website www.patrickeager.com

Colour and b&w coverage of cricket from 1965. Test matches, overseas tours and all aspects of the sport. Also a constantly expanding wine library (colour) of vineyards, grapes, cellars and winemakers of France, Italy, Germany, Lebanon, Australia, New Zealand, South Africa (and England). Digital photograph transmission by ISDN and modem.

Ecoscene
The Oasts, Headley Lane, Passfield, Liphook, Hampshire GU30 7RX
☎01428 751056 Fax 01428 751057
Email sally@ecoscene.com
Website www.ecoscene.com

Contact *Sally Morgan*

Expanding colour library of over 80,000 transparencies specialising in all aspects of the environment: pollution, conservation, recycling, restoration, natural history, habitats, education, landscapes, industry and agriculture. All parts of the globe are covered. Specialist collections of Antarctica, Australia, North America. Sally Morgan, who runs the library, is a professional ecologist and expert source of information on all environmental topics. Photographic and writing commissions undertaken. Images delivered by post, on CD-ROM, by e-mail and ISDN.

Edifice
14 Doughty Street, London WC1N 2PL
☎020 7242 0740 Fax 020 7267 3632
Email info@edificephoto.com
Website www.edificephoto.com
Contacts *Philippa Lewis, Gillian Darley*

Colour coverage of architecture, buildings of all possible descriptions, gardens, urban and rural landscape. *Specialises* in details of ornament, period style and material. British Isles, USA, Africa, Europe and Japan all covered. Detailed list available, visits by appointment.

Edinburgh Photographic Library
14 Garscube Terrace, Edinburgh EH12 6BQ
☎0131 337 7615 Fax 0131 337 0303
Email epl@mercat.co.uk
Website www.mercat.co.uk
Contact *James Young*

15,000 transparencies of Scotland: cities, towns and villages, castles, bridges, scenery, mountains, lochs, activities, wildlife, traditional industries. Visitors by appointment only.

Education Photos
April Cottage, Warners Lane, Albury Heath, Guildford, Surrey GU5 9DE
☎01483 203846 Fax 01483 203846
Email johnwalmsley@educationphotos.co.uk
Website www.educationphotos.co.uk

Formerly the John Walmsley Photo Library. Specialist library of learning/training/working subjects. Comprehensive coverage of learning environments such as playgroups, schools, colleges and universities. Images reflect a multi-racial Britain. Commissions undertaken. Subject list available on request.

English Heritage Photo Library
23 Savile Row, London W1S 2ET
☎020 7973 3338/9 Fax 020 7973 3027
Email celia.sterne@english-heritage.org.uk
Contact *Celia Sterne*

Images of English castles, abbeys, houses, gardens, Roman remains, ancient monuments, battlefields, industrial and post-war buildings, interiors, paintings, artifacts, architectural details, conservation, archaeology.

Mary Evans Picture Library
59 Tranquil Vale, Blackheath, London SE3 0BS
☎020 8318 0034 Fax 020 8852 7211
Email lib@mepl.co.uk
Website www.mepl.co.uk

Collection of historical illustrations documenting social, political, cultural, technical, geographical and biographical themes from ancient times to the recent past (up to mid-20th century). Photographs, prints and ephemera backed by large book and magazine collection. Many special collections including Sigmund Freud, the **Women's Library** (women's rights), the paranormal, the Meledin Collection (20th-century Russian history) and individual photographers such as Roger Mayne and Grace Robertson. Recently acquired the Weimar Archive and Barnaby's Picture Library. Brochure sent on request. Compilers of the *Picture Researcher's Handbook* by Pira International.

Exile Images
1 Mill Row, West Hill Road, Brighton, East Sussex BN1 3SU
☎01273 208741 Fax 01273 382782
Email pics@exileimages.co.uk
Website www.exileimages.co.uk
Contact *Howard Davies*

Over 15,000 b&w and colour 35mm slides of refugees, asylum seekers, conflict, third world development and daily life, UK protests, travel. CD-ROM available via the website to picture editors and researchers.

Express Newspapers Syndication
Ludgate House, 245 Blackfriars Road, London SE1 9UX
☎020 7922 7884 Fax 020 7922 7871
Email syndication@express.co.uk
Manager *Adam Williams*

Two million images updated daily, with strong collections on personalities, royalty, showbiz, sport, fashion, nostalgia and events. Also includes the *OK! Magazine* collection. Electronic transmission available. Daily news and feature service.

Eye Ubiquitous
65 Brighton Road, Shoreham, East Sussex BN43 6RE
☎01273 440113 Fax 01273 440116
Email eyeubiquitous@msn.com
Contact *Paul Seheult*

General stock specialising in social documentary worldwide, including the work of Tim Page, and now incorporating the **James Davis Travel** library (see entry).

Famous Pictures & Features Agency
13 Harwood Road, London SW6 4QP
☎020 7731 9333 Fax 020 7731 9330
Email info@famous.uk.com
Website www.famous.uk.com

Pictures and features agency with a growing library of interviews and colour transparencies dating back to 1985. Portrait, party and concert shots of rock and pop stars plus international entertainers, film and TV celebrities. The library is supplied by a team of photographers and journalists from the UK and around the world, keeping it up-to-date on a daily basis.

ffotograff
10 Kyveilog Street, Pontcanna, Cardiff CF11 9JA
☎029 2023 6879 Fax 029 2022 9326
Email ffotograff@easynet.co.uk

Contact *Patricia Aithie*

Library and agency specialising in travel, exploration, the arts, architecture, traditional culture, archaeology and landscape. Based in Wales but specialising in the Middle and Far East; Africia, Central and South America; Yemen and Wales are unusually strong aspects of the library. Churches and cathedrals of Britain and Crusader castles.

Financial Times Pictures
1 Southwark Bridge, London SE1 9HL
☎020 7873 3671 Fax 020 7873 4606
Email richard.pigden@ft.com

Photographs from around the world ranging from personalities in business, politics and the arts, people at work and other human interests and activities. '*FT* Graphics are outstanding in their ability to make complex issues comprehensible.' Delivery via modem, ISDN or e-mail.

Fine Art Photographic Library Ltd
2A Milner Street, London SW3 2PU
☎020 7589 3127 Fax 020 7584 1944
Email info@fineartphotolibrary.com

Contact *Linda Hammerbeck*

Over 20,000 large-format transparencies, with a specialist collection of 19th-century paintings. CD-ROM available.

Firepix International
68 Arkles Lane, Anfield, Liverpool, Merseyside L4 2SP
☎0151 260 0111/0777 5930419 (mobile)
Fax 0151 250 0111
Email info@firepix.com
Website www.firepix.com

Contact *Tony Myers*

The UK's only fire photo library. 23,000 images of fire-related subjects, firefighters, fire equipment manufacturers. Website contains 15 cate-

gories from industrial fire, domestic, digital images and abstract flame. Member of **BAPLA**.

Fogden Wildlife Photographs
Basement, 10 Bellevue, Bristol BS8 1DA
☎0117 923 8849 Fax 0117 923 8543
Email susan.fogden@virgin.net
Website www.fogdenphotos.com

Contact *Susan Fogden*

Natural history collection, with special reference to rain forests and deserts. Emphasis on quality rather than quantity; growing collection of around 10,000 images.

Food Features
Farnham Forge, 5 Upper Church Lane, Farnham, Surrey GU9 7PW
☎01252 735240 Fax 01252 735242
Email frontdesk@foodpix.co.uk
Website www.foodpix.co.uk

Contacts *Steve Moss, Alex Barker*

Specialised high-quality food and drink photography, features and tested recipes. Clients' specific requirements can be incorporated into regular shooting schedules.

Christine Foord Colour Picture Library
155B City Way, Rochester, Kent ME1 2BE
☎01634 847348 Fax 01634 847348

Specialist library with over 1000 species of British and European wild flowers, plus garden flowers, trees, indoor plants, pests and diseases, mosses, lichen, cacti and the majority of larger British insects.

Forest Life Picture Library
231 Corstorphine Road, Edinburgh EH12 7AT
☎0131 314 6411 Fax 0131 314 6285
Email n.campbell@forestry.gsi.gov.uk

Contacts *Douglas Green, Neill Campbell*

The official image bank of the Forestry Commission, the library provides a single source for all aspects of forest and woodland management. The comprehensive subject list includes tree species, scenic landscapes, employment, wildlife, flora and fauna, conservation, sport and leisure.

Werner Forman Archive Ltd
36 Camden Square, London NW1 9XA
☎020 7267 1034 Fax 020 7267 6026
Email wfa@btinternet.com

Website www.btinternet.com/~wfa

Colour and b&w coverage of ancient civilisations, oriental and primitive societies around the world. A number of rare collections. Subject lists available.

Format Photographers
19 Arlington Way, London EC1R 1UY
☎020 7833 0292 Fax 020 7833 0381
Email format@formatphotogs.demon.co.uk
Website www.formatphotographers.co.uk
Contact *Maggie Murray*

Over 100,000 documentary images in colour and b&w covering education, health, disability and women's issues in the UK and abroad.

Formula One Pictures
29 Merlin Close, Waltham Abbey, Essex EN9 3NG
☎01992 787800 Fax 01992 714366
Email jt@f1pictures.com
Website www.f1pictures.com
Contacts *John Townsend, Erika Townsend*

500,000 35mm colour slides, b&w and colour negatives of all aspects of Formula One grand prix racing including driver profiles and portraits.

Robert Forsythe Picture Library
16 Lime Grove, Prudhoe, Northumberland NE42 6PR
☎01661 834511 Fax 01661 834511
Email robert@forsythe.demon.co.uk
Website www.forsythe.demon.co.uk
Contacts *Robert Forsythe, Fiona Forsythe*

25,000 transparencies of industrial and transport heritage; plus a unique collection of 50,000 items of related publicity ephemera from 1945. Image finding service available. Robert Forsythe is a transport/industrial heritage historian and consultant. Nationwide coverage, particularly strong on Northern Britain. A bibliography of published material is available.

Fortean Picture Library
Henblas, Mwrog Street, Ruthin LL15 1LG
☎01824 707278 Fax 01824 705324
Email janet.bord@forteanpix.demon.co.uk
Website www.forteanpix.demon.co.uk
Contact *Janet Bord*

30,000 colour and 45,000 b&w images: mysteries and strange phenomena worldwide, including ghosts, UFOs, witchcraft and mon-

sters; also antiquities, folklore and mythology. Subject list available.

The Fotomas Index
12 Pickhurst Rise, West Wickham, Kent BR4 0AL
☎020 8776 2772 Fax 020 8776 2236/2772
Contact *John Freeman*

General historical collection, mostly pre-1900. Subjects include London, topography, art, satirical, social and political history. Large portrait section.

The Francis Frith Collection
Frith's Barn, Teffont, Salisbury, Wiltshire SP3 5QP
☎01722 716376 Fax 01722 716881
Email john_buck@francisfrith.co.uk
Website www.francisfrith.co.uk
Contact *John Buck*

Publishers of *Frith's Photographic Memories* series of illustrated local books, all featuring nostalgic photographs from the archive, founded by Frith in 1860. The archive now contains over 360,000 images of 7000 British towns.

John Frost Newspapers
See entry under **Library Services**

Andrew N. Gagg's Photo Flora
Town House Two, Fordbank Court, Henwick Road, Worcester WR2 5PF
☎01905 748515
Email a.n.gagg@ntlworld.com
Website homepage.ntlworld.com/a.n.gagg/ photo/photoflora.html

Specialist in British and European wild plants, flowers, ferns, grasses, trees, shrubs, etc. with colour coverage of most British and many European species (rare and common) and habitats; also travel in India, Sri Lanka, Nepal, Egypt, China, Mexico, Thailand, Tibet, Vietnam and Cambodia.

Galaxy Picture Library
1 Milverton Drive, Ickenham, Uxbridge, Middlesex UB10 8PP
☎01895 637463 Fax 01895 623277
Email robin@galaxypix.com
Website www.galaxypix.com
Contact *Robin Scagell*

Specialises in astronomy, space, telescopes, observatories, the sky, clouds and sunsets. Composites of foregrounds, stars, moon and planets prepared to commission. Editorial service available.

Garden and Wildlife Matters Photo Library

'Marlham', Henley's Down, Battle, East Sussex TN33 9BN
☎01424 830566 Fax 01424 830224
Email gardens@ftech.co.uk
Website web.ftech.net/~gardens

Contact *Dr John Feltwell*

Collection of 110,000 6x4″ and 35mm images. General gardening techniques and design; cottage gardens and USA designer gardens. 9000 species of garden plants and over 1000 species of trees. Flowers, wild and house plants, trees and crops. Environmental, ecological and conservation pictures, including sea, air, noise and freshwater pollution, SE Asian and Central and South American rainforests; Eastern Europe, Mediterranean. Recycling, agriculture, forestry, horticulture and oblique aerial habitat shots from Europe and USA. High-quality images required. Digital images supplied worldwide by ISDN.

The Garden Picture Library

Unit 12, Ransome's Dock, 35 Parkgate Road, London SW11 4NP
☎020 7228 4332 Fax 020 7924 3267
Email info@gardenpicture.com
Website www.gardenpicture.com

Contact *Lorraine Shill, Picture Research Manager*

'Our inspirational images of gardens, plants and gardening offer plenty of scope for writers looking for original ideas to write about.' Special collections include al fresco food, floral graphics and the still life photography of Linda Burgess. From individual stock photos to complete features, photographers submit material from the UK, Europe, USA and Australia on 35mm and medium formats. In-house picture research can be undertaken on request or review 10,000 images on 'The Collection' page of the website. Visitors to the library are welcome by appointment and copies of promotional literature are available on request.

Ed Geldard Photo Collection

9 Sunderland Bridge Village, Durham DH6 5HB
☎0191 378 2592

Contact *Ed Geldard*

Approximately 20,000 colour transparencies and b&w negs, all by Ed Geldard, specialising in mountain landscapes: particularly the mountain regions of the Lake District; and the Yorkshire limestone areas, from valley to summit. Commissions undertaken. Books published: *The Lake District*; *Wainwright's Tour of the Lake District*; *Wainwright in the Limestone Dales* .

Genesis Space Photo Library

Greenbanks, Robins Hill, Raleigh, Bideford, Devon EX39 3PA
☎01237 471960 Fax 01237 472060
Email tim@spaceport.co.uk
Website www.spaceport.co.uk

Contact *Tim Furniss*

Contemporary and historical colour and b&w spaceflight collection including rockets, spacecraft, spacemen, Earth, moon and planets. Stock list available on request.

Geo Aerial Photography

4 Christian Fields, London SW16 3JZ
☎020 8764 6292/0115 981 9418
Fax 020 8764 6292/0115 981 5474/9418
Email geo.aerial@geo-group.demon.co.uk

Contact *Kelly White*

Established 1990 and now a growing collection of aerial oblique photographs from the UK, Scandinavia, Asia and Africa – landscapes, buildings, industrial sites, etc. Commissions undertaken.

GeoScience Features

6 Orchard Drive, Wye, Kent TN25 5AU
☎01233 812707 Fax 01233 812707
Email gsf@geoscience.demon.co.uk
Website www.geoscience.demon.co.uk

Fully computerised and comprehensive library containing the world's principal source of volcanic phenomena. Extensive collections, providing scientific detail with technical quality, of rocks, minerals, fossils, microsections of botanical and animal tissues, animals, biology, birds, botany, chemistry, earth science, ecology, environment, geology, geography, habitats, landscapes, macro/microbiology, peoples, sky, weather, wildlife and zoology. Over 300,000 original colour transparencies in medium- and 35mm-format. Subject lists and CD-ROM catalogue available on application. Incorporates the RIDA photolibrary.

Geoslides Photography

4 Christian Fields, London SW16 3JZ
☎020 8764 6292/0115 981 9418
Fax 020 8764 6292/0115 981 9418
Email geoslides@geo-group.demon.co.uk

Contact *John Douglas*

Established in 1968. Landscape and human interest subjects from the Arctic, Antarctica, Scandinavia, UK, Africa (south of Sahara),

Middle East, Asia (south and southeast); also Australia, via Blackwoods Picture Library. Also specialist collections of images from British India (the Raj) and Boer War.

Getty Images
101 Bayham Street, London NW1 0AG
☎020 7544 3333 Fax 020 7544 3334
Email info@getty-images.com
Website www.gettyone.com
Contact *Sales Dept.*

Various collections including Hulton Getty, The Image Bank and Tony Stone Images. With over 15 million images, Getty Images is the largest picture resource in Europe with images from ancient history through the early years of photography up to the present day. As well as many old newspaper archives, the extensive contemporary collections cover lifestyles, travel, science, business.

Lynn Goldsmith
See **Corbis Images**

Martin and Dorothy Grace
40 Clipstone Avenue, Mapperley, Nottingham NG3 5JZ
☎0115 920 8248 Fax 0115 962 6802
Email graces@lineone.net

Colour coverage of Britain's natural history, specialising in trees, shrubs and wild flowers. Also ferns, birds and butterflies, habitats, landscapes, ecology.

Ronald Grant Archive
See **The Cinema Museum**

Sally and Richard Greenhill
357 Liverpool Road, London N1 1NL
☎020 7607 8549 Fax 020 7607 7151
Email sr.greenhill@virgin.net
Website www.shadow.org.uk/photolibrary
Photo Librarian *Denise Lalonde*

Social documentary photography in colour and b&w of working lives: pregnancy and birth, child development, education, work, old people, medical, urban. Also Modern China, 1971 to the present; most London statues. Some material from Borneo, USA, India, Israel, Philippines and Sri Lanka.

V.K. Guy Ltd
Silver Birches, Troutbeck, Windermere, Cumbria LA23 1PN
☎015394 33519 Fax 015394 32971
Email vic@v.k.guy.co.uk

Website www.vk.guy.co.uk
Contacts *Vic Guy, Pauline Guy, Mike Guy, Paul Guy, Nicola Guy*

British landscapes and architectural heritage. 20,000 5x4″ transparencies, suitable for tourism brochures, calendars, etc. Colour catalogue available.

Angela Hampton 'Family Life Picture Library'
Holly Tree House, The Street, Walberton, Arundel, West Sussex BN18 0PH
☎01243 555952 Fax 01243 555952
Contact *Angela Hampton*

Over 50,000 transparencies on all aspects of contemporary lifestyle, including pregnancy, childbirth, babies, children, parenting, behaviour, education, medical, holidays, pets, family life, relationships, teenagers, women and men's health, over-50s and retirement. Also comprehensive stock on domestic and farm animal life. Isle of Wight travel pictures in 35mm. Commissions undertaken. Offers fully illustrated text packages on most subjects and welcomes ideas for collaboration from writers with proven, successful background.

Tom Hanley
61 Stephendale Road, London SW6 2LT
☎020 7731 3525
Fax 020 7736 8831/7731 3525
Email Tomhanley31@hotmail.com
Website www.Fleetwoodowen.com

Colour and b&w coverage of London, England, Europe, Canada, India, the Philippines, Brazil, China, Japan, Korea, Taiwan, the Seychelles, Cayman Islands, USA. Also pop artists of the '60s, First World War trenches, removal of London Bridge to America, and much more. Current preoccupation with Greece, Turkey, Spain and Egypt, ancient and modern.

Robert Harding Picture Library
58–59 Great Marlborough Street, London W1F 7JY
☎020 7478 4000 Fax 020 7631 1070
Email info@robertharding.com
Website www.robertharding.com

A leading source of stock photography with over two million colour images covering a wide range of subjects – worldwide travel and culture, geography and landscapes, people and lifestyle, architecture, business and industry, medicine, sports, food and drink. Can supply images as transparencies, on CD or ISDN. Visitors welcome; telephone or visit the website.

Dennis Hardley Photography, Scottish Photo Library

Rosslynn, Benderloch, Oban, Argyll
PA37 1ST
☎01631 720434 Fax 01631 720434
Email dennishardley@sol.co.uk
Website www.scottishphotographic.com *or*
www.englishphotographic.com

Contacts *Dennis Hardley, Tony Hardley*
ESTABLISHED 1974. About 30,000 images (6x7, 6x9 format colour transparences) of Scotland: castles, historic, scenic landscapes, islands, transport, etc. Also English views – Liverpool, Chester, Bath, Weston Super Mare, Sussex, Somerset and Cambridge.

Jim Henderson Photographer & Publisher

Crooktree, Kincardine O'Neil, Aboyne, Aberdeenshire AB34 4JD
☎01339 882149 Fax 01339 882149
Email JHende7868@aol.com
Website www.jimhendersonphotography.com

Contact *Jim Henderson, AMPA, ARPS*
Scenic and general activity coverage of the north east Scotland/Grampian region and Highlands for tourist, holiday and activity illustration. Specialist collection of over 150 Aurora Borealis displays from 1989–2000 in Grampian and co-author of *The Aurora* (pub. 1997). Large collection of recent images of Egypt: Cairo through to Abu-Simbel. Commissions undertaken.

Heritage and Natural History Photographic Library

37 Plainwood Close, Summersdale, Chichester, West Sussex PO19 4YB
☎01243 533822 Fax 01243 533822

Contact *Dr John B. Free*
Specialises in insects (particularly bees and bee-keeping), tropical and temperate agriculture and crops, archaeology and history worldwide.

John Heseltine Picture Library

Mill Studio, Frogmarsh Mill, South Woodchester, Gloucestershire GL5 5ET
☎01453 873792 Fax 01453 873793
Email Johnhes@aol.com
Website www.heseltine.co.uk

Contact *John Heseltine*
Over 150,000 colour transparencies of landscapes, architecture, food and travel with particular emphasis on Italy and the UK.

Christopher Hill Photographic Library

17 Clarence Street, Belfast BT2 8DY
☎028 9024 5038 Fax 028 9023 1942
Email ChrisHillPhotographic@btclick.com
Website www.scenic-ireland.com

Contact *Christopher Hill*
A comprehensive collection of landscapes of Northern Ireland, from Belfast to the Giant's Causeway, updated daily. Images of farming, food and industry. 'We will endeavour to supply images overnight.'

Hobbs Golf Collection

5 Winston Way, New Ridley, Stocksfield, Northumberland NE43 7RF
☎01661 842933 Fax 01661 842933
Email hobbs.golf@btinternet.com

Contact *Michael Hobbs*
Specialist golf collection: players, courses, art, memorabilia and historical topics (1300–present). 40,000+ images – mainly 35mm colour transparencies and b&w prints. Commissions undertaken. Author of 30 golf books.

David Hoffman Photo Library

21 Norman Grove, London E3 5EG
☎020 8981 5041 Fax 020 8980 2041
Email info@hoffmanphotos.com
Website www.hoffmanphotos.com

Contact *David Hoffman*
Commissioned photography and stock library with a strong emphasis on social issues built up from 35mm journalistic and documentary work dating from the late 1970s. Files on drugs and drug use, policing, disorder, riots, youth, protest, homelessness, housing, environmental demonstrations and events, waste disposal, alternative energy, industry and pollution. Wide range of images especially from UK and Europe but also USA, Canada, Venezuela and Thailand. General files on topical issues and current affairs plus specialist files from leisure cycling to local authority services.

Holt Studios International Ltd

The Courtyard, 24 High Street, Hungerford, Berkshire RG17 0NF
☎01488 683523 Fax 01488 683511
Email library@holt-studios.co.uk
Website www.holt-studios.co.uk

Director *Nigel Cattlin*
Specialist photo library covering world agriculture, horticulture, gardens and gardening from

pictorial and technical aspects. Worldwide assignments undertaken.

Bill Hopkins Collection
See **The Special Photographers Library**

Houghton's Horses/ Kit Houghton Photography
Radlet Cottage, Spaxton, Bridgwater, Somerset TA5 1DE
☎01278 671362 Fax 01278 671739
Email kit@enterprise.net
Website www.houghtonshorses.com
Contacts *Kit Houghton, Debbie Cook*

Specialist equestrian library of over 200,000 transparencies on all aspects of the horse world, with images ranging from the romantic to the practical, step-by-step instructional and competition pictures in all equestrian disciplines worldwide. Online picture delivery with ISDN facility.

Houses and Interiors
192 Goswell Road, London EC1V 7DT
☎020 7253 0991 Fax 020 7253 0992
Email housesandinteriors@yahoo.com
Manager *Anna Bedewell*

Stylish house interiors and exteriors, home dossiers, renovations, architectural details, interior design, gardens, houseplants and cookery. Also step-by-step photographic sequences of DIY subjects and gardening techniques. Large format and 35mm. Member of **BAPLA**.

Chris Howes/Wild Places Photography
51 Timbers Square, Cardiff CF24 3SH
☎029 2048 6557 Fax 029 2048 6557
Email photos@wildplaces.co.uk
Contacts *Chris Howes, Judith Calford*

Expanding collection of over 50,000 colour transparencies and b&w prints covering travel, topography and natural history worldwide, plus action sports such as climbing. *Specialist areas* include caves, caving and mines (with historical coverage using engravings and early photographs), wildlife, landscapes and the environment, including pollution and conservation. Europe (including Britain), USA, Africa and Australia are all well represented within the collection. Commissions undertaken.

Hulton Deutsch
See **Corbis Images**

Hulton Getty
See **Getty Images**

Huntley Film Archive
78 Mildmay Park, Islington, London N1 4PR
☎020 7923 0990 Fax 020 7241 4929
Email films@huntleyarchives.com
Website www.huntleyarchives.com
Contact *Amanda Huntley*

Originally a private collection, the library is now a comprehensive archive of rare and vintage documentary film dating from 1895. 30,000–35,000 films on all subjects of a documentary nature, plus 50,000 feature film stills. Hollywood and the British film studios plus a television archive of rare stills and films. On-line catalogue available.

Jacqui Hurst
66 Richford Street, Hammersmith, London W6 7HP
☎020 8743 2315/07970 781336 (mobile)
Fax 020 8743 2315
Email jacquih@dircon.co.uk
Contact *Jacqui Hurst*

A specialist library of traditional and contemporary designers and crafts, regional food producers and markets. The photos form illustrated essays of how something is made and finish with a still life of the completed object. The collection is always being extended and a list is available on request. Commissions undertaken.

Hutchison Picture Library
118B Holland Park Avenue, London W11 4UA
☎020 7229 2743 Fax 020 7792 0259
Email library@hutchisonpic.demon.co.uk
Website www.hutchisonpictures.co.uk

Worldwide contemporary images from the straight-forward to the esoteric and quirky. With over half a million documentary colour photographs on file and more than 200 photographers continually adding new work, this is an ever-growing resource covering people, places, customs and faiths, agriculture, industry and transport. *Special collections* include the environment and climate, family life (including pregnancy and birth), ethnic minorities worldwide (including Disappearing World archive), conventional and alternative medicine, and music around the world. Search service available.

Illustrated London News Picture Library
20 Upper Ground, London SE1 9PF
☎020 7805 5585 Fax 020 7805 5905
Email iln.pictures@ilng.co.uk

Website www.ilng.co.uk

Engravings, photographs and illustrations from 1842 to the present day, taken from magazines published by Illustrated Newspapers: *Illustrated London News; Graphic; Sphere; Tatler; Sketch; Illustrated Sporting and Dramatic News; Illustrated War News 1914–18; Bystander; Britannia & Eve.* Social history, London, Industrial Revolution, wars, travel. CD-ROM available. Visitors by appointment.

The Image Bank
See **Getty Images**

Images Colour Library/ Landscape Only
Ramillies House, 1–2 Ramillies Street, London W1F 7LN
☎020 7734 7344 Fax 020 7287 3933

15/17 High Court Lane, The Calls, Leeds, West Yorkshire LS2 7EU
Tel 0113 243 3389
Fax 0113 242 5605

A general contemporary library specialising in top-quality advertising, editorial and travel photography. Catalogues available. Visitors welcome. Also holds the Landscape Only collection featuring the work of top photographers Charlie Waite, Nick Meers, Joe Cornish and many others.

Images of Africa Photobank
11 The Windings, Lichfield, Staffordshire WS13 7EX
☎01543 262898 Fax 01543 417154
Email info@imagesofafrica.co.uk
Website www.imagesofafrica.co.uk

Contact *Jacquie Shipton*
Owner *David Keith Jones, FRPS*

Over 135,000 images covering the following African countries: Botswana, Chad, Egypt, Ethiopia, Kenya, Lesotho, Madagasca, Malawi, Namibia, Rwanda, South Africa, Swaziland, Tanzania, Uganda, Zaire, Zambia, Zanzibar and Zimbabwe. 'Probably the best collection of photographs of Kenya in Europe.' Wide range of topics covered. Particularly strong on African wildlife with over 80 species of mammals including many sequences showing action and behaviour. Popular animals like lions and elephants are covered in encyclopædic detail. Other strengths include National Parks and reserves, natural beauty, tourism facilities, traditional and modern people. Most work is by David Keith Jones, FRPS; several other photographers are represented.

Images of India
See **Link Picture Library**

Imperial War Museum Photograph Archive
All Saints Annexe, Austral Street, London SE1 4SL
☎020 7416 5333 Fax 020 7416 5355
Email photos@iwm.org.uk
Website www.iwm.org.uk

A national archive of over six million photographs illustrating all aspects of 20th century conflict. Emphasis on the two world wars but includes material from other conflicts involving Britain and the Commonwealth. Majority of material is b&w, although holdings of colour material increases with more recent conflicts. Visitors welcome by appointment, Monday to Friday, 10.00 am. to 5.00 pm.

Infoterra
Arthur Street, Barwell, Leicestershire LE9 8GZ
☎01455 849227 Fax 01455 841785

Contact *Joanne Burchnall*

Leading supplier of earth observation data, including satellite imagery, aerial photography and airborne remote sensing.

International Photobank
Loscombe Barn Farmhouse, West Knighton, Dorchester, Dorset DT2 8LS
☎01305 854145 Fax 01305 853065
Email peter@internationalphotobank.co.uk
Website www.internationalphotobank.co.uk

Over 360,000 transparencies, mostly medium-format. Colour coverage of travel subjects: places, people, folklore, events. Assignments undertaken for guide books and brochure photography.

The Isle of Wight Photo Library
The Old Rectory, Calbourne, Isle of Wight PO30 4JE
☎01983 531247 Fax 01983 531253
Email oliver@mathews.photography.com
Website www.mathews-photography.com

Contact *The Librarian*

Stock material represents all that is best on the Isle of Wight – landscapes, seascapes, architecture, gardens, boats.

Robbie Jack Photography
45 Church Road, Hanwell, London W7 3BD
☎020 8567 9616 Fax 020 8567 9616
Email rjackphoto@aol.com

Contact *Robbie Jack*

Built up over the last 18 years, the library contains over 300,000 colour transparencies of the performing arts – theatre, dance, opera and music. Includes West End shows, the RSC and Royal National Theatre productions, English National Opera and Royal Opera. The dance section contains images of the Royal Ballet, English National Ballet, the Rambert Dance Company, plus many foreign companies. Also holds the largest selection of colour material from the Edinburgh International Festival. Researchers are welcome to visit by appointment.

Jayawardene Travel Photo Library

7A Napier Road, Wembley, Middlesex HA0 4UA
☎020 8902 3588 Fax 020 8902 7114
Email rjayawarde@aol.com
Website members.aol.com/rjayawarde

Contact *Rohith Jayawardene*

170,000 colour transparencies of travel and travel-related subjects, covering countries worldwide. Most places have been photographed in depth, with more than 600 images per destination. Shot in 35mm and medium format and regularly updated. Commissions undertaken. Contributing photographers welcome (please telephone first) – minimum initial submission: 200 transparencies.

Trevor Jones Thoroughbred Photography

The Hornbeams, 2 The Street, Worlington, Suffolk IP28 8RU
☎01638 713944 Fax 01638 713945
Email trevorjones@thorobredphoto.co.uk

Contacts *Trevor Jones, Gill Jones*

Extensive library of high-quality colour transparencies depicting all aspects of thoroughbred horse racing dating from 1987. Major group races, English classics, studs, stallions, mares and foals, early morning scenes, personalities, jockeys, trainers and prominent owners. Also international work: USA Breeders Cup, Arc de Triomphe, French Classics, Irish Derby, Dubai racing scene, Japan Cup and Hokkaido stud farms; and more unusual scenes such as racing on the sands at low tide, Ireland, and on the frozen lake at St Moritz. Visitors by appointment.

Katz Pictures

Zetland House, 5–25 Scrutton Street, London EC2A 4HJ
☎020 7377 5888 Fax 020 7613 1274

Email katzpictures@katzpictures.com
Contact *Alyson Whalley*

Contains an extensive collection of colour and b&w material covering a multitude of subjects from around the world – business, environment, industry, lifestyles, politics plus celebrity portraits from the entertainment world. Also Hollywood portraits and film stills dating back to the twenties.

David King Collection

90 St Pauls Road, London N1 2QP
☎020 7226 0149 Fax 020 7354 8264

Contact *David King*

250,000 b&w original and copy photographs and colour transparencies of historical and present-day images. Russian history and the Soviet Union from 1900 to the fall of Khrushchev; the lives of Lenin, Trotsky and Stalin; the Tzars, Russo-Japanese War, 1917 Revolution, World War I, Red Army, the Great Purges, Great Patriotic War, etc. Special collections on China, Eastern Europe, the Weimar Republic, John Heartfield, American labour struggles, Spanish Civil War. Open to qualified researchers by appointment, Monday to Friday, 10.00 am to 6.00 pm. Staff will undertake research; negotiable fee for long projects. David King's latest photographic book, *The Commissar Vanishes*, documents the falsification of photographs and art in Stalin's Russia.

The Kobal Collection

4th Floor, 184 Drummond Street, London NW1 3HP
☎020 7383 0011 Fax 020 7383 0044

Colour and b&w coverage of Hollywood films: portraits, stills, publicity shots, posters, ephemera. Visitors by appointment.

Kos Picture Source Ltd

7 Spice Court, Ivory Square, Plantation Wharf, London SW11 3UE
☎020 7801 0044 Fax 020 7801 0055
Email images@kospictures.com
Website www.kospictures.com

Specialists in water-related images including international yacht racing and cruising, classic boats and superyachts, and extensive range of watersports. Also worldwide travel including seascapes, beach scenes, underwater photography and the weather.

Ed Lacey Collection

See **Phil Sheldon Golf Picture Library**

Landscape Only
See **Images Colour Library**

Frank Lane Picture Agency Ltd
Pages Green House, Wetheringsett,
Stowmarket, Suffolk IP14 5QA
☎01728 860789 Fax 01728 860222
Email pictures@flpa-images.co.uk
Website www.flpa-images.co.uk

Colour and b&w coverage of natural history,
environment, pets and weather. Represents
Sunset from France, Foto Natura from Holland,
Minden Pictures from the US and works closely
with Eric and David Hosking, plus 270 freelance
photographers.

Last Resort Picture Library
Manvers Studios, 12 Ollerton Road, Tuxford,
Newark, Nottinghamshire NG22 0LF
☎01777 870166 Fax 01777 871739
Email LRPL@dmimaging.co.uk
Website www.dmimaging.co.uk

Contact *Jo Makin*

Images of agriculture, architecture, education,
social issues landscape, industry, food, people at
work, computing and new technology. Images
cover a wide variety of areas rather than specialising, ranging from the everyday to the obscure.

LAT Photographic
Somerset House, Somerset Road, Teddington
TW11 8RU
☎020 8251 3000 Fax 020 8251 3001
Email digital@latphoto.co.uk
Website www.latphoto.co.uk

Motor sport collection of over nine million
images dating from 1895 to the present day.

André Laubier Picture Library
4 St James Park, Bath BA1 2SS
☎01225 420688 Fax 01225 420688

An extensive library of photographs from 1935
to the present day in 35mm- and medium-
format. Main subjects are: archaeology and architecture, art and artists (wood carving, sculptures,
contemporary glass), botany, historical buildings,
sites and events, landscapes, nature, leisure sports,
events, experimental artwork and photography,
people and travel. Substantial stock of many
other subjects including: birds, buildings and
cities, folklore, food and drink, gardens, transport. Special collection: Images d'Europe
(Austria, Britain, France, Greece, S.W. Ireland,

Italy, Spain, Turkey, Norway and former
Yugoslavia). Private collection: World War II to
D-Day. List available on request. Photo assign-
ments, artwork, design, and line drawings under-
taken. Correspondence welcome in English,
French or German.

Lebrecht Music Collection
58b Carlton Hill, London NW8 0ES
☎020 7625 5341/7372 8233
Fax 020 7625 5341
Email pictures@lebrecht.co.uk
Website www.lebrecht.co.uk

Contact *Elbie Lebrecht*

50,000 prints and transparencies covering classical music, from antiquity to 21st century mini-
malists. Instruments, opera singers, concert halls
and opera houses, composers and musicians.

The Erich Lessing Archive of Fine Art & Culture
c/o AKG London Ltd, The Arts and History
Picture Library, 5 Melbray Mews,
158 Hurlingham Road, London SW6 3NS
☎020 7610 6103 Fax 020 7610 6125
Email enquiries@akg-london.co.uk
Website www.akg-london.co.uk

Archive of large-format transparencies depicting the contents of many of the world's finest
art galleries as well as ancient archaeological
and biblical sites. High resolution scans available via ISDN. Mac and PC-compatible CD-
ROMs. Represented by **AKG London Ltd**.

Life File Ltd
76 Streathbourne Road, London SW17 8QY
☎020 8767 8832 Fax 020 8672 8879
Email simontaylor@attglobal.net

Contact *Simon Taylor*

300,000 images of people and places, lifestyles,
industry, environmental issues, natural history
and customs, from Afghanistan to Zimbabwe.
Stocks most of the major tourist destinations
throughout the world, including the UK.

Lindley Library, Royal Horticultural Society
80 Vincent Square, London SW1P 2PE
☎020 7821 3603 Fax 020 7828 3022

Contact *Jennifer Vine*

18,000 original drawings and approx. 8000
books with hand-coloured plates of botanical
illustrations. Appointment is absolutely essential;
all photography is done by own photographer.

Link Picture Library

33 Greyhound Road, London W6 8NH
☎020 7381 2261/2433 Fax 020 7385 6244
Email lib@linkpics.demon.co.uk
Website www.linkphotographers.com

Contact *Orde Eliason*

100,000 images of South Africa, India, China, Vietnam and Israel. A more general collection of colour transparencies from 100 countries worldwide. Link Picture Library and its partner, Images of India, has an international network and can source material not in its file from Japan, USA, Holland, Scandinavia, Germany and South Africa. Original photographic commissions undertaken.

London Aerial Photo Library

PO Box 25, Ashwellthorpe, Norwich, Norfolk NR16 1HL
☎01508 488320 Fax 01508 488282
Email aerialphotos@btinternet.com
Website www.londonaerial.co.uk

Contact *Sandy Stockwell*

80,000 colour negatives of aerial photographs covering most of Britain, with particular emphasis on London and surrounding counties. No search fee. Photocopies of library prints are supplied free of charge to enquirers. Welcomes enquiries in respect of either general subjects or specific sites and buildings.

The London Film Archive

78 Mildmay Park, Islington, London N1 4PR
☎020 7923 4074 Fax 020 7241 4929
Email info@londonfilmarchive.org
Website www.londonfilmarchive.org

Contact *Robert Dewar*

Archive which concentrates on all aspects of commercial, political and social life in the City and suburbs of London. The collection is primarily a film collection but also has stills, glass plate negatives, posters, advertising and documents of London interest.

London Metropolitan Archives

40 Northampton Road, London EC1R 0HB
☎020 7332 3820 Fax 020 7833 9136
Email ask.lma@corpoflondon.gov.uk
Website www.cityoflondon.gov.uk

Contact *The Senior Librarian*

Approximately 500,000 images of London, mostly topographical and architectural. Subjects include education, local authority housing, transport, the Thames, parks, churches, hospitals, war damage, pubs, theatres and cinemas. Also major redevelopments like the South Bank, the City, Covent Garden and Docklands.

London's Transport Museum Photographic Library

39 Wellington Street, London WC2E 7BB
☎020 7379 6344 Fax 020 7565 7252
Website www.ltmuseum.co.uk

Contacts *Hugh Robertson, Simon Murphy, Martin Harrison-Putnam*

Around 100,000 b&w images from the 1860s and 10,000 colour images from c.1975. *Specialist collections* Poster archive, Underground construction, corporate design and architecture, street scenes, London Transport during the war. Collection available for viewing by appointment on Monday and Tuesday. No loans system but prints and transparences can be purchased. Digital images available on CD-ROM.

Lonely Planet Images

See **Lonely Planet Publications** under **UK Publishers**

Ludvigsen Library Limited

73 Collier Street, London N1 9BE
☎020 7837 1700 Fax 020 7837 1776
Email library@ludvigsen.com
Website www.ludvigsen.com

Contact *Karl Ludvigsen*

Extensive information research facilities for writers and publishers. Approximately 400,000 images (both b&w and many colour transparencies) of automobiles and motorsport, from 1920s through 1980s. Glass plate negatives from the early 1900s; Formula One, Le Mans, motor car shows, vintage, antique and classic cars from all countries. Includes the Dalton–Watson Collection and noted photographers such as John Dugdale, Edward Eves, Peter Keen, Max le Grand, Karl Ludvigsen, Rodolfo Mailander, Ove Nielsen, Stanley Rosenthall and others.

MacQuitty International Photographic Collection

7 Elm Lodge, River Gardens, Stevenage Road, London SW6 6NZ
☎020 7385 5606 Fax 020 7385 5606
Email miranda.macquitty@btinternet.com

Contact *Dr Miranda MacQuitty*

Colour and b&w collection on aspects of life in over 70 countries: dancing, music, religion, death, archaeology, buildings, transport, food, drink, nature. Visitors by appointment.

Magnum Photos Ltd
Moreland Buildings, 2nd Floor, 5 Old Street, London EC1V 9HL
☎020 7490 1771 Fax 020 7608 0020
Email magnum@magnumphotos.co.uk
Website www.magnumphotos.com
Head of Library *Hamish Crooks*

FOUNDED 1947 by Cartier Bresson, George Rodger, Robert Capa and David 'Chim' Seymour. Represents over 50 of the world's leading photo-journalists. Coverage of all major world events from the Spanish Civil War to present day. Also a large collection of personalities.

The Raymond Mander & Joe Mitchenson Theatre Collection
c/o Salvation Army Headquarters, PO Box 249, 101 Queen Victoria Street, London EC4P 4EP
☎020 7236 0182 Fax 020 7236 0184
Email richard@mander-and-mitchenson.co.uk
Website www.mander-and-mitchenson.co.uk

Contact *Richard Mangan*

Enormous collection covering all aspects of the theatre: plays, actors, dramatists, music hall, theatres, singers, composers, etc. Visitors welcome by appointment. (The collection will be moving to King Charles Court in the Royal Naval College, Greenwich in September 2001, joining forces with the library of Trinity College of Music to form The Jerwood Library of the Performing Arts.)

S&O Mathews Photography
The Old Rectory, Calbourne, Isle of Wight PO30 4JE
☎01983 531247 Fax 01983 531253
Email oliver@mathews-photography.com
Website www.mathews-photography.com

Library of colour transparencies of gardens, plants and landscapes.

Institution of Mechanical Engineers
1 Birdcage Walk, London SW1H 9JJ
☎020 7973 1265 Fax 020 7222 4557
Email k_moore@imeche.org.uk
Website www.imeche.org.uk
Senior Librarian & Archivist *Keith Moore*

Historical and contemporary images on mechanical engineering. Open 9.15 am to 5.30 pm, Mon. to Fri. Telephone for appointment.

Medimage
32 Brooklyn Road, Coventry CV1 4JT
☎024 7666 8562 Fax 024 7666 8562
Email chambersking@ntlworld.com
Contacts *Anthony King, Catherine King*

Medium format colour transparencies of Mediterranean countries (also some from the Czech Republic) covering a wide range of subjects – agriculture, archaeology, architecture, arts, crafts, education, festivals, flora, geography, history, industry, landscapes, markets, recreation, seascapes, sports and transport. The collection is added to on a regular basis and photographic commissions are undertaken. No search fees. Pictures by other photographers are not accepted.

Meledin Collection
See **Mary Evans Picture Library**

Lee Miller Archives
Farley Farm House, Chiddingly, Near Lewes, East Sussex BN8 6HW
☎01825 872691 Fax 01825 872733
Email archives@leemiller.co.uk
Website www.leemiller.co.uk

The work of Lee Miller (1907–77). As a photojournalist she covered the war in Europe from early in 1944 to VE Day with further reporting from the Balkans. Collection includes photographic portraits of prominent Surrealist artists: Ernst, Eluard, Miró, Picasso, Penrose, Carrington, Tanning, and others. Surrealist and contemporary art, poets and writers, fashion, the Middle East, Egypt, the Balkans in the 1930s, London during the Blitz, war in Europe and the liberation of Dachau and Buchenwald.

Mirror Syndication International
22nd Floor, 1 Canada Square, Canary Wharf, London E14 5AP
☎020 7293 3700 Fax 020 7293 2712
Email desk@mirpix.com
Website www.mirrorpix.com
Managing Director *John Churchill*

Major photo library specialising in current affairs, personalities, royalty, sport, pop and glamour, plus extensive British and world travel pictures. Major motion picture archive up to 1965. Agents for Mirror Group Newspapers. Syndicator of photos and text for news/features.

Monitor Picture Library
The Forge, Roydon, Harlow, Essex CM19 5HH
☎01279 792700 Fax 01279 792600

Website www.monitorpicturelibrary.com

Colour and b&w coverage of leading international personalities. Politics, entertainment, royals, judicial, commerce, religion, trade unions, well-known buildings. Also an archive library dating back to 1840, and a specialist file on Lotus cars. Syndication to international, national and local media.

Moroccan Scapes

Seend Park, Seend, Wiltshire SN12 6NZ
☎01380 828533 Fax 01380 828630
Email chris@morocco-travel.com

Contact *Chris Lawrence*

Specialist collection of Moroccan material: scenery, towns, people, markets and places, plus the Atlas Mountains. Over 16,000 images.

Motoring Picture Library

National Motor Museum, Beaulieu,
Hampshire SO42 7ZN
☎01590 614656 Fax 01590 612655
Email motoring.pictures@beaulieu.co.uk

Contact *Jonathan Day*

Three-quarters of a million b&w images, plus 80,000 colour transparencies covering all forms of motoring history from the 1880s to the present day. Commissions undertaken. Own studio.

Mountain Camera

See **John Cleare**

Moving Image Communications

61 Great Titchfield Street, London W1W 7PP
☎020 7580 3300 Fax 020 7580 2242
Email mail@milibrary.com
Website www.milibrary.com

Contact *Kevin Smalley*

Over 11,350 hours of quality archive and contemporary footage, including: RSPB Film Library; TVAM Archive 1983–92, Leo & Mandy Dickinson Action & Adventure Sports Archive, The Lonely Planet (TV travel series); Shark Bay Films (tropical and sub-aqua); British Tourist Authority – BTA (1930 to present day); TIDA Public Information Films (BTA's predecessory); Buff Films (aviation archive/NATO planes and ships); Drummer Films (travel classics, 1950–70); British Airways; Universal Newsreels (1950s-60s); Medical Technology; The Freud Archive (1930–39); Natural World; Stockshots (time-lapse, cityscapes, land and seascapes, chroma-key); Space Exploration (NASA); WPA Film Library (America's most extensive film library).

Museum of Antiquities Picture Library

University and Society of Antiquaries of Newcastle upon Tyne, Newcastle upon Tyne NE1 7RU
☎0191 222 7846 Fax 0191 222 8561
Email m.o.antiquities@ncl.ac.uk
Website www.ncl.ac.uk/antiquities

Contact *Lindsay Allason-Jones*

25,000 images, mostly b&w, of special collections including: Hadrian's Wall Archive (b&ws taken over the last 100 years); Gertrude Bell Archive (during her travels in the Near East, 1900–26); and aerial photographs of archaeological sites in the North of England. Visitors welcome by appointment.

Museum of London Picture Library

150 London Wall, London EC2Y 5HN
☎020 7814 5604 Fax 020 7600 1058
Email picturelib@museumoflondon.org.uk

The Picture Library tells the story of London from its earliest settlers to the present day. Suffragettes: photographs and memorabilia; Museum Objects: gallery and reserve collections – Prehistoric, Roman, Saxon, Medieval, Tudor, Stuart, Georgian, Victorian, London Now; Photographs: social history of the capital – working life, East End, inter-war years, the Blitz, post-war; Prints and Caricatures: political and social satire, architecture; Paintings: dating from the 17th century, portraits, landscapes, cityscapes.

National Galleries of Scotland Picture Library

The Dean Gallery, Belford Road, Edinburgh EH4 3DS
☎0131 624 6258/6260 Fax 0131 623 7135
Email picture.library@natgalscot.ac.uk

Contact *Deborah Hunter*

Over 30,000 b&w and several thousand images in colour of works of art from the Renaissance to present day. Specialist subjects cover fine art (painting, sculpture, drawing), portraits, Scottish, historical, still life, photography and landscape. Colour leaflet, scale of charges and application forms available on request.

National Maritime Museum Picture Library

Greenwich, London SE10 9NF
☎020 8312 6631/6704 Fax 020 8312 6533
Email picturelibrary@nmm.ac.uk
Website www.nmm.ac.uk

Contacts *David Taylor, Eleanor Heron*

Over three million maritime-related images and artefacts, including oil paintings from the 16th century to present day, prints and drawings, historic photographs, plans of ships built in the UK since the beginning of the 18th century, models, rare maps and charts, instruments, etc. Over 50,000 items in the collection are now photographed and with the Historic Photographs Collection form the basis of the stock.

National Meteorological Library and Archive

See entry under **Library Services**

National Monuments Record

National Monuments Record Centre, Kemble Drive, Swindon, Wiltshire SN2 2GZ
☎01793 414600 Fax 01793 414606
Email nmrinfo@english-heritage.org.uk
Website www.english-heritage.org.uk

The National Monuments Record is the first stop for photographs and information on England's heritage. Over 12 million photographs, documents and drawings are held. English architecture from the first days of photography to the present, air photographs covering every inch of England from the first days of flying to the present, and archaeological sites. The record is now the public archive of English Heritage and includes the material gathered by the Royal Commission on the Historical Monuments of England in its 90-year history. The London office specialises in the architecture of the capital city – for more information e-mail (nmrlondon@english-heritage.org.uk) or phone 020 7208 8200.

National Portrait Gallery Picture Library

St Martin's Place, London WC2H 0HE
☎020 7312 2473/4/5/6 Fax 020 7312 2464
Email picturelibrary@npg.org.uk
Website www.npg.org.uk

Contact *Tom Morgan*

Access to over 900,000 portraits of famous British men and women dating from the middle ages to the present. Images can be searched, viewed and ordered on the website.

National Railway Museum Picture Library

Leeman Road, York YO26 4XJ
☎01904 621261 Fax 01904 611112
Email nrm@nmsi.ac.uk
Website www.nrm.org.uk

1.5 million images, mainly b&w, covering every aspect of railways from 1850s to the present day. Visitors by appointment.

The National Trust Photo Library

36 Queen Anne's Gate, London SW1H 9AS
☎020 7447 6788/9 Fax 020 7447 6767
Email photolibrary@ntrust.org.uk
Website www.nationaltrust.org.uk/photolibrary

Contact *Ed Gibbons*

Collection of mixed-format transparencies covering landscape and coastline throughout England, Wales and Northern Ireland; also architecture, interiors, gardens, paintings and conservation, plus a new collection of wildlife photographs. Award-winning brochure available on request. Profits from the picture library are reinvested in continuing the work of the Trust.

Natural History Museum Picture Library

Cromwell Road, London SW7 5BD
☎020 7942 5401/5324 Fax 020 7942 5443
Email nhmpl@nhm.ac.uk
Website www.nhm.ac.uk/images

Contacts *Lodvina Mascarenhas, Hillary Smith*

Pictures from the Museum's collections, including dinosaurs, man's evolution, extinct species and fossil remains. Also of gems, minerals, birds and animals, plants and insect specimens, plus historical artworks depicting the natural world.

Natural History Photographic Agency

See **NHPA**

Natural Science Photos

33 Woodland Drive, Watford, Hertfordshire WD17 3BY
☎01923 245265 Fax 01923 246067

Colour coverage of natural history subjects worldwide. The work of some 150 photographers, it includes angling, animals, birds, reptiles, amphibia, fish, insects and other invertebrates, habitats, plants, fungi, geography, weather, scenics, horticulture, agriculture, farm animals and registered dog breeds. Researched by experienced scientists Peter and Sondra Ward. Visits by appointment. Commissions undertaken.

Nature Photographers Ltd

West Wit, New Road, Little London, Tadley, Hampshire RG26 5EU
☎01256 850661 Fax 01256 851157
Email naturephotographers@cwcom.net

Website www.naturephotographers.cwc.net

Contact *Dr Paul Sterry*

Over 150,000 images on worldwide natural history and environmental subjects. The library is run by a trained biologist and experienced author on his subject.

Peter Newark's Pictures

3 Barton Buildings, Queen Square, Bath
BA1 2JR
☎01225 334213 Fax 01225 480554

Over one million images covering world history from ancient times to the present day. Includes an extensive military collection of photographs, paintings and illustrations. Also a special collection on American history covering Colonial times, exploration, social, political and the Wild West and Native-Americans in particular. Subject list available. Telephone, fax or write for further information.

NHPA (Natural History Photographic Agency)

Little Tye, 57 High Street, Ardingly, West Sussex RH17 6TB
☎01444 892514 Fax 01444 892168
Email nhpa@nhpa.co.uk
Website www.nhpa.co.uk

Library Manager *Tim Harris*

Extensive coverage on all aspects of natural history – animals, plants, landscapes, environmental issues, gardens and pets. 150 photographers worldwide provide a steady input of high-quality transparencies. Specialist files include the unique high-speed photography of Stephen Dalton, extensive coverage of African and American wildlife, also rainforests, marine life and the polar regions. UK agents for the ANT collection of Australasian material. Loans are generally made direct to publishers; individual writers must request material via their publisher.

Odhams Periodicals Library

See **Popperfoto**

Only Horses Picture Agency

27 Greenway Gardens, Greenford, Middlesex
UB6 9TU
☎020 8578 9047 Fax 020 8575 7244
Email onlyhorsespics@aol.com
Website www.onlyhorsespictures.com

Colour and b&w coverage of all aspects of the horse. Foaling, retirement, racing, show jumping, eventing, veterinary, polo, breeds, personalities.

Oxford Picture Library

15 Curtis Yard, North Hinksey Lane, Oxford
OX2 0LX
☎01865 723404 Fax 01865 725294
Email chris.andrews@virgin.net
Website www.cap-ox.co.uk

Contacts *Annabel Webb, Chris Andrews, Angus Palmer*

Specialist collection on Oxford: the city, university and colleges, events, people, spires and shires; the Cotswolds, architecture and landscape from Stratford-upon-Avon to Bath; the Thames and Chilterns, including Henley on Thames and Windsor; Channel Islands, especially Guernsey and Sark. Aerial views of all areas specified above. General collection includes wildlife, trees, plants, clouds, sun, sky, water and teddy bears. Commissions undertaken.

Oxford Scientific Films Photo Library

Lower Road, Long Hanborough, Oxfordshire
OX8 8LL
☎01993 881881 Fax 01993 882808
Email photo.library@osf.uk.com
Website www.osf.uk.com

Head of Film & Photo Library *Suzanne Aitzetmuller*

Account Managers *Nick Jessop, Rebecca Warren, Ruth Blair*

Collection of 300,000 colour transparencies of wildlife and natural science images supplied by over 300 photographers worldwide, covering all aspects of wildlife plus landscapes, weather, seasons, plants, environment, anthropology, habitats, industry, space, creative textures and backgrounds, and geology. Macro and micro photography. UK agents for Animals Animals, USA, Okapia, Germany and Dinodia, India. Research by experienced researchers for specialist and creative briefs. Visits welcome, by appointment.

PA News Photo Library

PA News Centre, 292 Vauxhall Bridge Road, London SW1V 1AE
☎020 7963 7990 Fax 020 7963 7066
Email paphotos@pa.press.net
Website www.paphotos.com

PA News, the 24-hour national news and information group, offers public access to its photographic archives. Photographs, dating from 1890 to the present day, cover everything from news and sport to entertainment and royalty, with around 50 new pictures added daily.

PAL (Performing Arts Library)

First Floor, Production House, 25 Hackney Road, London E2 7NX
☎020 7749 4850 Fax 020 7749 4858
Email performingartspics@pobox.com
Website www.PerformingArtsLibrary.co.uk

Continually updated specialist image collection covering classical music, opera, theatre, musicals, instruments, festivals, venues, circus, ballet and contemporary dance. Almost one million images from late 19th century onwards. Please phone, fax or e-mail to make a selection.

Hugh Palmer

Knapp House, Shenington, Near Banbury, Oxfordshire OX15 6NE
☎01295 670433 Fax 01295 670709
Email hupalmer@msn.com
Website www.hughpalmer.com

Extensive coverage of gardens from Britain and Europe, as well as rural landscapes and architecture. Medium-format transparencies from numerous specialist commissions for books and magazines.

Panos Pictures

1 Chapel Court, Borough High Street, London SE1 1HH
☎020 7234 0010 Fax 020 7357 0094
Email pics@panos.co.uk
Website www.panos.co.uk

Documentary colour and b&w library specialising in Third World and Eastern Europe, with emphasis on environment and development issues. Leaflet available. Fifty per cent of all profits from this library go to the Panos Institute to further its work in international sustainable development.

Papilio Natural History & Travel Library

The Oasts, Headley Lane, Passfield, Liphook, Hampshire GU30 7RX
☎01428 751056 Fax 01428 751057
Email library@papiliophotos.com
Website www.papiliophotos.com

Contacts *Robert Pickett, Vicki Coombs*

Over 100,000 colour transparencies of natural history, including birds, animals, insects, flowers, plants, fungi and landscapes; plus travel worldwide including people, places and cultures. Commissions undertaken. Colour catalogue and digital slide show on disk available; call for further information. Visits by appointment only.

Charles Parker Archive

See **Birmingham Library Services** under **Library Services**

Ann & Bury Peerless Picture Library

St David's, 22 King's Avenue, Minnis Bay, Birchington-on-Sea, Kent CT7 9QL
☎01843 841428 Fax 01843 848321

Contacts *Ann or Bury Peerless*

Specialist collection on world religions: Hinduism, Buddhism, Jainism, Christianity, Islam, Sikhism. Geographical areas covered: India, Afghanistan (Bamiyan Valley of the Buddhas), Pakistan, Bangladesh, Sri Lanka, Cambodia (Angkor), Java (Borobudur), Bali, Thailand, Russia, Republic of China, Spain, Poland, Uzbekistan (Samarkand and Bukhara), Vietnam. 10,000 35mm colour transparencies.

Performing Arts Library

See **PAL**

Photo Resources

The Orchard, Marley Lane, Kingston, Canterbury, Kent CT4 6JH
☎01227 830075 Fax 01227 831135

Colour and b&w coverage of archaeology, art, ancient art, ethnology, mythology, world religion, museum objects.

Photofusion

17A Electric Lane, London SW9 8LA
☎020 7738 5774 Fax 020 7738 5509
Email library@photofusion.org
Website www.photofusion.org

Contact *Liz Somerville*

Colour and b&w coverage of contemporary social issues including babies and children, disability, education, the elderly, environment, family, health, housing, homelessness, people and work. Brochure available.

The Photolibrary Wales

Bro-nant, Church Road, Pentyrch, Cardiff CF15 9QG
☎029 2089 0311 Fax 029 2089 2650
Email info@photolibrarywales.com
Website www.photolibrarywales.com

Contacts *Steve Benbow, Kate Benbow*

Over 60,000 colour transparences covering all areas and subjects of Wales. Represents the work of 140 photographers, living and working in Wales.

Photos Horticultural

PO Box 105, Ipswich, Suffolk IP1 4PR
☎01473 257329 Fax 01473 233974
Email library@photos.keme.co.uk
Website www.photos-horticultural.co.uk

Wide coverage of gardens and all aspects of gardening from library established in 1968. Now incorporates the Kenneth Scowen Collection. 'Extensive travelling ensures the best material from around the world is on file.'.

PictureBank Photo Library Ltd

Parman House, 30–36 Fife Road, Kingston upon Thames, Surrey KT1 1SY
☎020 8547 2344 Fax 020 8974 5652
Website www.picturebank.co.uk

Over 400,000 colour transparencies covering people (girls, couples, families, children), travel and scenic (UK and world), moods (sunsets, seascapes, deserts, etc.), industry and technology, environments and general. Commissions undertaken. Visitors welcome. Member of **BAPLA**. New material on medium/large format welcome.

Pictures Colour Library

10 James Whatman Court, Turkey Mill, Ashford Road, Maidstone, Kent ME14 5SS
☎01622 609809 Fax 01622 609806
Email Researcher@PicturesColourLibrary.co.uk
Website www.picturescolourlibrary.co.uk

Travel and travel-related images depicting lifestyles and cultures, people and places, attitudes and environments from around the world, including a comprehensive section on Great Britain.

H.G. Ponting

See **Popperfoto**

Popperfoto

The Old Mill, Overstone Farm, Overstone, Northampton NN6 0AB
☎01604 670670 Fax 01604 670635
Email popperfoto@msn.com
Website www.popperfoto.com

Home to over 14 million images, covering 150 years of photographic history. Renowned for its archival material, a world-famous sports library and stock photography. Popperfoto's credit line includes Reuters, Bob Thomas Sports Photography, UPI, Acme, INP, Planet, Paul Popper, Exclusive News Agency, Victory Archive, Odhams Periodicals Library, Illustrated, Harris Picture Agency, and H.G. Ponting which

holds the Scott 1910–1912 Antarctic expedition. Colour from 1940, b&w from 1870 to the present. Major subjects covered worldwide include events, personalities, wars, royalty, sport, politics, transport, crime, history and social conditions. Material available on the same day to clients throughout the world. Mac-desk available. Researchers welcome by appointment. Free catalogue available.

PPL Photo Agency Ltd

Bookers Yard, The Street, Walberton, Arundel, West Sussex BN18 0PF
☎01243 555561 Fax 01243 555562
Email ppl@mistral.co.uk
Website www.pplmedia.com

Contacts *Barry Pickthall, Richard Johnson*

Two million pictures of sailing and boating, watersports, travel, water and coastal scenes. British Steel Multimedia Library – all aspects of steel and steel making. Construction, science and technology, transport, mining and industry.

Premaphotos Wildlife

Amberstone, 1 Kirland Road, Bodmin, Cornwall PL30 5JQ
☎01208 78258 Fax 01208 72302
Email authors@premaphotos.co.uk
Website www.premaphotos.co.uk

Contact *Jean Preston-Mafham*, Library Manager

Natural history worldwide. Subjects include flowering and non-flowering plants, fungi, slime moulds, fruits and seeds, galls, leaf mines, seashore life, mammals, birds, reptiles, amphibians, insects, spiders, habitats, scenery and cultivated cacti. Commissions undertaken. Visitors welcome. 'Make sure your name is on our mailing list to receive regular, colourful mailers.'

Professional Sport UK Ltd

18–19 Shaftesbury Quay, Hertford, Hertfordshire SG14 1SF
☎01992 505000 Fax 01992 505020
Email pictures@prosport.co.uk
Website www.prosport.co.uk

Photographic coverage of tennis, soccer, athletics, golf, cricket, rugby, winter sports and many minor sports. Major international events including the Olympic Games, World Cup soccer and all Grand Slam tennis events. Also news and feature material supplied worldwide. Computerised library with in-house processing and studio facilities; photo transmission services available for editorial and advertising.

Public Record Office Image Library

Ruskin Avenue, Kew, Richmond, Surrey TW9 4DU
☎020 8392 5225 Fax 020 8392 5266
Email image-library@pro.gov.uk

Contacts *Paul Johnson, Hugh Alexander*

British and colonial history from the Domesday Book to the 1960s, shown in photography, maps, illuminations, posters, advertisements, textiles and original manuscripts. Approximately 30,000 5x4″ and 35mm colour transparencies and b&w negatives. Open: 9.00 am to 5.30 pm, Monday to Friday.

Punch Cartoon Library

Trevor House, 100 Brompton Road, London SW3 1ER
☎020 7225 6710 Fax 020 7225 6712
Email punch.library@harrods.com

Owner *Liberty Publishing*

Gives access to the 500,000 cartoons published in *Punch* magazine between 1841–1992. The library has a 500+ subject listing and can search on any topic. Social history, politics, fashion, fads, famous people and more by the world's most famous cartoonists, including Tenniel, du Maurier, Pont, Fougasse, E.H. Shepard and Emett.

PWA International Ltd

City Gate House, 399–425 Eastern Avenue, Gants Hill, Ilford, Essex IG2 6LR
☎020 8518 2057 Fax 020 8518 2241
Email pwaint@dircon.co.uk

Contact *Terry Allen*

Leading comprehensive library of story illustrations comprising work by some of the UK's best-known illustrators, including book covers and magazines. Also over half a million images of beauty, cookery and craft.

Railfotos

Millbrook House Ltd., Unit 1, Oldbury Business Centre, Pound Road, Oldbury, West Midlands B68 8NA
☎0121 544 2970 Fax 0121 253 6836 (quote Millbrook House)

One of the largest specialist libraries dealing comprehensively with railway subjects worldwide. Colour and b&w dating from the turn of the century to present day. Up-to-date material on UK, South America and Far East. Visitors by appointment.

Redferns Music Picture Library

7 Bramley Road, London W10 6SZ
☎020 7792 9914 Fax 020 7792 0921
Email info@redferns.com
Website www.redferns.com

Music picture library covering every aspect of popular music from 1920's jazz to present day. Over 12,000 artists on file plus other subjects including musical instruments, recording studios, crowd scenes, festivals, etc. Brochure available.

Remote Source

See **Royal Geographical Society Picture Library**

Retna Pictures Ltd

Ground Floor, 53–56 Great Sutton Street, London EC1V 0DG
☎020 7608 4800 Fax 020 7608 4805
Email london@retna.com
Website www.retna.com

Colour and b&w coverage of international rock and pop performers, actors, actresses, entertainers and celebrities. Also a general stock library covering a wide range of subjects, including travel, people, sport and leisure, flora and fauna, and the environment.

Retrograph Nostalgia Archive Ltd

164 Kensington Park Road, London W11 2ER
☎020 7727 9378 Fax 020 7229 3395
Email retropix1@aol.com
Website www.Retrograph.com

Contact *Jilliana Ranicar-Breese*

'Number One for nostalgia!' A vast archive of commercial and decorative art (1860–1960). Worldwide labels and packaging for food, wine, chocolate, soap, perfume, cigars and cigarettes; fine art and commercial art journals, fashion and lifestyle magazines, posters, Victorian greetings cards, scraps, Christmas cards, Edwardian postcards, wallpaper and giftwrap sample books, music sheets, folios of decorative design and ornament – Art Nouveau and Deco; hotel, airline and shipping labels; memorabilia, tourism, leisure, food and drink, transport and entertainment. Lasers for book dummies, packaging, mock-ups, film/TV action props. Colour brochure on request. Picture research service. Design consultancy service. Victorian-style montages conceived, designed and styled (RetroMontages).

Rex Features Ltd

18 Vine Hill, London EC1R 5DZ
☎020 7278 7294 Fax 020 7696 0974
Email library@rexfeatures.com
Website www.rexfeatures.com

Contact *Glen Marks*, Library Sales Manager

Extensive picture library established in the 1950s. Daily coverage of news, politics, personalities, show business, glamour, humour, art, medicine, science, landscapes, royalty, etc.

Royal Air Force Museum

Grahame Park Way, Hendon, London NW9 5LL
☎020 8205 2266 Fax 020 8200 1751
Email christine.gregory@rafmuseum.org.uk

Contact *Christine Gregory*

About a quarter of a million images, mostly b&w, with around 1500 colour in all formats, on the history of aviation. Particularly strong on the activities of the Royal Air Force from the 1870s to 1970s. Researchers are requested to enquire in writing only.

The Royal Collection

Windsor Castle, Windsor, Berks SL4 1NJ
☎01753 868286 Fax 01753 620046
Email photoservices@royalcollection.org.uk

Contact *Shruti Patel*

Photographic material of items in the Royal Collection, particularly oil paintings, drawings and watercolours, works of art, and interiors and exteriors of royal residences. 35,000 colour transparencies plus 25,000 b&w negatives.

Royal Geographical Society Picture Library

1 Kensington Gore, London SW7 2AR
☎020 7591 3060 Fax 020 7591 3061
Website www.rgs.org/picturelibrary

Contact *Joanna Scadden*

A strong source of geographical and historical images, both archival and modern, showing the world through the eyes of photographers and explorers dating from the 1830s to the present day. The Remote Source Collection provides up-to-date transparencies from around the world, highlighting aspects of cultural activity, environmental phenomena, anthropology, architectural design, travel, mountaineering and exploration. Offers a professional and comprehensive service for both commercial and academic use.

The Royal Photographic Society Picture Library

The Octagon, Milsom Street, Bath BA1 1DN
☎01225 462841 Fax 01225 469880
Email sam@collection.rps.org
Website www.rps.org/piclib.html

Contact *Samantha Johnson*

History of photography, with an emphasis on pictorial photography as an art rather than a documentary record. Photographic processes and cameras, landscape, portraiture, architecture, India, Victorian and Edwardian life.

RSPB Images

St Mark's House, Shepherdess Walk, London N1 7LH
☎020 7871 7951 Fax 020 7871 7704
Email rspb@sevenww.co.uk
Website www.rspb-images.com

Contact *Kirstin Davidson*

Colour and b&w images of birds, butterflies, moths, mammals, reptiles and their habitats. Also colour images of all RSPB reserves. Growing selection of various habitats. Over 52,000 slides available digitally or in any desired format.

RSPCA Photolibrary

RSPCA Trading Limited, Wilberforce Way, Southwater, Horsham, West Sussex RH13 7WN
☎0870 754 0150 Fax 0870 753 0048
Email pictures@rspcaphotolibrary.com
Website www.rspcaphotolibrary.com

Photolibrary Manager *Andrew Forsyth*

Over 70,000 colour transparencies and over 5000 b&w/colour prints. A comprehensive collection of natural history images whose subjects include mammals, birds, domestic and farm animals, amphibians, insects and the environment, as well as a unique photographic record of the RSPCA's work. Also includes the Wild Images collections. Catalogue available. No search fees.

Russia and and Eastern Images

'Sonning', Cheapside Lane, Denham, Uxbridge, Middlesex UB9 5AE
☎01895 833508 Fax 01895 831957
Email easteuropix@btinternet.com

Architecture, cities, landscapes, people and travel images of Russia and the former Soviet Union. Considerable background knowledge available and Russian language spoken.

Peter Sanders Photography

24 Meades Lane, Chesham, Buckinghamshire HP5 1ND
☎01494 773674/771372   Fax 01494 773674
Email photos@petersanders.com
Website www.petersanders.com

Contacts *Peter Sanders, Hafsa Garwatuk*

Specialises in the world of Islam in all its aspects from culture, arts, industry, lifestyles, celebrations, etc. Areas included are north, east and west Africa, the Middle East (including Saudi Arabia), China, Asia, Europe and USA. A continually expanding library.

Science & Society Picture Library

Science Museum, Exhibition Road, London SW7 2DD
☎020 7942 4400   Fax 020 7942 4401
Email piclib@nmsi.ac.uk
Website www.nmsi.ac.uk/piclib/

Contacts *Angela Murphy, Venita Paul*

25,000 reference prints and 100,000 colour transparencies, incorporating many from collections at the Science Museum, the National Railway Museum and the National Museum of Photography Film and Television. Collections illustrate the history of science, industry, technology, medicine, transport and the media. Plus three archives documenting British society in the twentieth century.

Science Photo Library

327–329 Harrow Road, London W9 3RB
☎020 7432 1100   Fax 020 7286 8668
Email info@sciencephoto.com
Website www.sciencephoto.com

Specialises in pictures of science, medicine, technology, earth, space and nature. 130,000 images in the collection.

Kenneth Scowen Collection

See **Photos Horticultural**

Seaco Picture Library

Sea Containers House, 20 Upper Ground, London SE1 9PF
☎020 7805 5831   Fax 020 7805 5807
Email seaco.pictures@seacontainers.com

Contact *Maureen Elliott*

Approx. 250,000 images of containerisation, shipping, fast ferries, manufacturing, fruit farming, ports, hotels and leisure.

Mick Sharp Photography

Eithinog, Waun, Penisarwaun, Caernarfon, Gwynedd LL55 3PW
☎01286 872425   Fax 01286 872425
Email mick.jean@virgin.net

Contacts *Mick Sharp, Jean Williamson*

Colour transparencies (6x4.5cm and 35mm) and black & white prints (5x4″ and 6x4.5cm negatives) of subjects connected with archaeology, ancient monuments, buildings, churches, countryside, environment, history, landscape, past cultures and topography from Britain and abroad. Photographs by Mick Sharp and Jean Williamson, plus access to other specialist collections on related subjects. Commissions undertaken.

Phil Sheldon Golf Picture Library

40 Manor Road, Barnet, Hertfordshire EN5 2JQ
☎020 8440 1986   Fax 020 8440 9348
Email GolfSnap@aol.com

An expanding collection of over 500,000 quality images of the 'world of golf'. In-depth worldwide tournament coverage including every Major championship & Ryder Cup since 1976. Instruction, portraits, trophies and over 300 golf courses from around the world. Also the Dale Concannon collection covering the period 1870 to 1940, the classic 1960s collection by photographer Sidney Harris and the Ed Lacey Collection.

Skishoot–Offshoot

Hall Place, Upper Woodcott, Whitchurch, Hampshire RG28 7PY
☎01635 255527   Fax 01635 255528
Email skishoot@surfersparadise.net
Website www.skishoot.net

Contacts *Jane Blount, Kate Parker*

Skishoot ski and snowboarding picture library has 300,000 images. Offshoot travel library specialises in France.

The Skyscan Photolibrary

Oak House, Toddington, Cheltenham, Gloucestershire GL54 5BY
☎01242 621357   Fax 01242 621343
Email info@skyscan.co.uk
Website www.skyscan.co.uk

As well as the Skyscan Photolibrary collection of unique balloon's-eye views of Britain, the library now includes the work of photographers from across the aviation spectrum; air to ground, aviation, aerial sports – 'in fact, anything aerial!'. Links have been built with photographers across the world; photographs can be handled on an agency basis and held in house, or as a brokerage where the collection stays with the photographer; terms 50/50 for both. Commissioned photography undertaken. Enquiries welcome.

SMG Newspapers Ltd
200 Renfield Street, Glasgow G2 3PR
☎0141 302 7364 Fax 0141 302 7383

Over six million images: b&w and colour photographs from *c*.1900 from the *Herald* (Glasgow) and *Evening Times*. Current affairs, Scotland, Glasgow, Clydeside shipbuilding and engineering, personalities, World Wars I and II, sport.

Snookerimages
(Eric Whitehead Photography)
PO Box 33, Kendal, Cumbria LA9 4SU
☎015394 48894 Fax 015394 48294
Email eric@snookerimages.co.uk
Website www.snookerimages.co.uk

Over 20,000 images of snooker from 1982 to the present day. The agency covers local news events, PR and commercial material.

SOA Photo Library
Lovells Farm, Dark Lane, Stoke St Gregory, Taunton, Devon TA3 6EU
☎0870 333 6062 Fax 0870 333 6082
Email info@soaphotoagency.com
Website www.soaphotoagency.com

Contact *Sabine Oppenlander*

85,000 colour slides, 15,000 b&w photos covering *Stern* productions, sports, travel & geographic, advertising, social subjects. Representatives of Voller Ernst, Interfoto, Picture Press, Look and many freelance photographers. Free catalogues available.

Solo Syndication Ltd (trading as Atlantic Syndication Partners)
17–18 Haywards Place, Clerkenwell, London EC1R 0EQ
☎020 7566 0360 Fax 020 7566 0388

Syndication Director *Trevor York*
Sales *Danny Howell, Nick York*
Online transmissions *Geoff Malyon* (☎020 7566 0370)

Three million images from the archives of the *Daily Mail, Mail on Sunday, Evening Standard* and *Evening News*. Hard prints or Mac-to-mac delivery. 24-hour service.

Sotheby's Picture Library
34-35 New Bond Street, London W1A 2AA
☎020 7293 5383 Fax 020 7293 5062
Email piclib.london@sothebys.com

Contacts *Sue Daly, David Johnson*

The library mainly consists of over 50,000 selected transparencies of pictures sold at Sotheby's. Images from the 15th to the 20th century. Oils, drawings, watercolours, prints and decorative items. 'Happy to do searches or, alternatively, visitors are welcome by appointment.'

South American Pictures
48 Station Road, Woodbridge, Suffolk IP12 4AT
☎01394 383963/380423 Fax 01394 380176
Email morrison@south-american-pic.com
Website www.south-american-pic.com

Contact *Marion Morrison*

Colour and b&w images of South/Central America, Cuba, Mexico, New Mexico (USA), Dominican Republic and Haiti, including archaeology and the Amazon. There is an archival section, with pictures and documents from most countries. Now with 40 contributing photographers.

The Special Photographers Library
21 Kensington Park Road, London W11 2EU
☎020 7221 3489 Fax 020 7792 9112
Email info@specialphotographers.com
Website www.specialphotographers.com

Contacts *Chris Kewbank*

Represents over 100 contemporary fine art photographers who are unusual in style, technique or subject matter. Also has exclusive access to the Bill Hopkins Collection – an archive of thousands of vintage pictures dating back to the early 20th century.

Frank Spooner Pictures Ltd
Unit B7, Hatton Square, 16–16A Baldwin's Gardens, London EC1N 7US
☎020 7632 5800 Fax 020 7632 5828
Email fsp/pix@compuserve.com

Subjects include current affairs, show business, fashion, politics, travel, adventure, sport, personalities, films, animals and the Middle East. Represented in more than 30 countries and handles UK distribution of Gamma Presse Images and Roger-Viollet of Paris. Commissions undertaken.

The Still Moving Picture Co.
157 Broughton Road, Edinburgh EH7 4JJ
☎0131 557 9697 Fax 0131 557 9699
Email info@stillmovingpictures.com
Website www.stillmovingpictures.com

Contacts *John Hutchinson, Sue Hall*

Over 100,000 colour images of Scotland and sport. (Fully digitised service via www.stilldigital.co.uk) Scottish agents for **Allsport (UK) Ltd**.

Still Pictures' Whole Earth Photolibrary
199 Shooters Hill Road, Blackheath, London SE3 8UL
☎020 8858 8307 Fax 020 8858 2049
Email info@stillpictures.com
Website www.stillpictures.com

Contacts *Theresa de Salis, Mark Edwards*

FOUNDED 1970, the library is a leading source of pictures illustrating the human impact on the environment, Third World development issues, industrial ecology, nature and wildlife, endangered species and habitats. 400,000 colour medium-format transparencies, 100,000 b&w prints. Over 400 leading photographers from around the world supply the library with stock pictures. Write, phone or fax for Still Pictures' Environment and Third World catalogue and Still Pictures' Nature and Wildlife catalogue.

Stockfile
5 High Street, Sunningdale, Berkshire SL5 0LX
☎01344 872249 Fax 01344 872263
Email info@stockfile.co.uk
Website www.stockfile.co.uk

Contacts *Jill Behr, Steven Behr*

Specialist cycling- and skiing-based collection covering most aspects of these activities, with emphasis on mountain biking. Expanding adventure sports section.

Stockscotland Photo Library
Croft Roy, Crammond Brae, Tain, Ross-shire IV19 1JG
☎01862 892298 Fax 01862 892298
Email info@stockscotland.com
Website www.stockscotland.com

Contact *Hugh Webster*

150,000 colour transparencies of Scotland. Not just a travel library; images cover industry, agriculture, fisheries and many other subjects. Submissions from photographers welcome. Commissions undertaken. Call for CD catalogue.

Sir John Benjamin Stone
See **Birmingham Library Services** under **Library Services**

Tony Stone Images
See **Getty Images**

Jessica Strang Photo Library
504 Brody House, Strype Street, Spitalfields, London E1 7LQ
☎020 7247 8982 Fax 020 7247 8982
Email Jessica.Strang@virgin.net

Contact *Jessica Strang*

Approximately 60,000 transparencies covering architecture, interiors (contemporary), gardens, 'obsessive and not just small but tiny, or from almost no space at all', men, women, couples and animals in architecture, and vanishing London details. Recycled ideas for the home.

Joe Tasker Collection
See **Chris Bonnington Picture Library**

Tate Enterprises Picture Library
Tate Gallery Publishing Ltd, Millbank, London SW1P 4RG
☎020 7887 8867 Fax 020 7887 8905
Email picture.library@tate.org.uk
Website www.tate.org.uk

Contact *Chris Webster*

Approximately 8000 images of British art from the 16th century; international 20th century painting and sculpture. Artists include William Blake, William Hogarth, J.M.W. Turner, Dante Gabriel Rossetti, Barbara Hepworth, Henry Moore, Stanley Spencer, Pablo Picasso, Mark Rothko, Salvador Dali, Lucien Freud and David Hockney. Colour transparencies of more than half the works in the main collection are available for hire. For a fee, new photography is available depending on the location and condition of the art work. B&w prints of nearly all the works in the collection can be purchased. Colour slides and prints can be made on request providing a colour transparency exists. Picture researchers must make an appointment to visit the library. All applications must be made by fax or letter.

Telegraph Colour Library
101 Bayham Street, London NW1 0AG
☎020 7859 8900
Website www.tcl-images.co.uk

Part of **Getty Images**. Leading stock photography agency covering a wide subject range: business, sport, people, industry, animals, medical, nature, space, travel and graphics. Free catalogue available. Same-day service to UK clients.

Bob Thomas Sports Photography
See **Popperfoto**

Patrick Thurston Photography
The Gallery, 12 High Street, Chesterton, Cambridge CB4 1NG
☎01223 352547/368109 Fax 01223 366274
Email patrickthurston@hotmail.com

Colour photography of Britain: scenery, people, museums, churches, coastline. Also various countries abroad. Commissions undertaken.

Rick Tomlinson
Marine Photo Library
18 Hamble Yacht Services, Port Hamble, Hamble, Southampton, Hampshire SO31 4NN
☎023 8045 8450 Fax 023 8045 8350
Email ricktom@compuserve.com
Website www.rick-tomlinson.com

Contacts *Rick Tomlinson, Julie Birchall*

ESTABLISHED 1985. *Specialises* in marine subjects. 60,000 35mm transparencies of yachting, racing, cruising, Whitbread Round the World Race, Tall Ships, RNLI Lifeboats, Antarctica, wildlife and locations.

Topham Picturepoint
PO Box 33, Edenbridge, Kent TN8 5PB
☎01342 850313 Fax 01342 850244
Email admin@topfoto.co.uk
Website www.topfoto.co.uk

Contact *Alan Smith*

Eight million contemporary and historical images, ideal for advertisers, publishers and the travel trade. Delivery online.

B.M. Totterdell Photography
Constable Cottage, Burlings Lane, Knockholt, Kent TN14 7PE
☎01959 532001 Fax 01959 532001
Email btrial@btinternet.com

Contact *Barbara Totterdell*

Specialist volleyball library covering all aspects of the sport.

Tessa Traeger Library
7 Rossetti Studios, 72 Flood Street, London SW3 5TF
☎020 7352 3641 Fax 020 7352 4846

Food, gardens, travel and artists.

Travel Ink
Photo & Feature Library
The Old Coach House, 14 High Street, Goring on Thames, Nr Reading, Berkshire RG8 9AR
☎01491 873011 Fax 01491 875558
Email info@travel-ink.co.uk
Website www.travel-ink.co.uk

Contact *Abbie Enock*

Around 100,000 colour images covering about 130 countries (including the UK). Close links with other specialist libraries mean most topics can be accessed. Subjects include travel, tourism, lifestyles, business, industry, transport, children, religion, history, activities. Specialist collections on Hong Kong (including construction of the Tsing Ma bridge), Greece, North Wales, Germany, the Cotswolds, France, and many others.

Peter Trenchard's Image Store Ltd
The Studio, West Hill, St Helier, Jersey, Channel Islands JE2 3HB
☎01534 769933 Fax 01534 789191

Contact *Peter Trenchard, FBIPP, AMPA, PPA*

Slide library of the Channel Islands – mainly tourist and financial-related. Commissions undertaken.

Tropical Birds Photo Library
PO Box 100, Mansfield, Nottinghamshire NG20 9NZ
☎01623 846430 Fax 01623 846430

Contact *Rosemary Low*

Transparencies (35mm) of parrots and other tropical birds, and tropical butterflies. Also colour and b&w prints and large format transparencies of parrots. Specialises in parrots: more than 250 species.

Tropix Photo Library
156 Meols Parade, Meols, Wirral CH47 6AN
☎0151 632 1698 Fax 0151 632 1698
Email tropixphoto@talk21.com
Website www.merseyworld.com/tropix/

Contact *Veronica Birley*

Specialists on the developing world and travel. Assignment photography UK and overseas. 'New collections welcome. Must be 35mm or larger colour transparencies, top professional quality only, taken 2000 or later. See website for detailed submission guidelines. Always e-mail Tropix in the first instance so we can advise whether your stock is currently required.'

True North Picture Source
26 New Road, Hebden Bridge, West
Yorkshire HX7 8EF
☎01422 845532 Fax 01422 845532
Email john@trunorth.demon.co.uk
Website www.trunorth.demon.co.uk

Contact *John Morrison*

30,000 transparencies on 35mm and 6x4.5cm
format on the life and landscape of the north of
England, photographed by John Morrison.

Turnley Collection
See **Corbis Images**

Ulster Museum (National Museums and Galleries of Northern Ireland)
Botanic Gardens, Belfast BT9 5AB
☎028 9038 3000 ext 3113 Fax 028 9038 3103
Email patricia.mclean.um@nics.gov.uk

Contact *Mrs Pat McLean*

Specialist subjects: art – fine and decorative,
late 17th–20th century, particularly Irish art,
archaeology, ethnography, treasures from the
Armada shipwrecks, geology, botany, zoology,
local history and industrial archaeology.
Commissions welcome for objects not already
photographed.

Universal Pictorial Press & Agency Ltd
29–31 Saffron Hill, London EC1N 8SW
☎020 7421 6000 Fax 020 7421 6006

News Editor *Peter Dare*

Photo archive dates back to 1944 and contains
approximately four million pictures. Colour and
b&w coverage of news, royalty, politics, sport,
arts, and many other subjects. Commissions
undertaken for press and public relations. Fully
interactive digital photo archive in addition to
bulletin board accessible via ISDN or modem.
Full digital scanning, retouching and transmission
facilities.

UPI
See **Popperfoto**

V&A Picture Library
Victoria and Albert Museum, South
Kensington, London SW7 2RL
☎020 7942 2487/2483 Fax 020 7942 2482
Email picture.library@vam.ac.uk

70,000 colour and half a million b&w photos of
decorative and applied arts, including ceramics,
ivories, furniture, costumes, textiles, stage, musical instruments, toys, Indian, Far Eastern, Islamic
objects, sculpture, painting and prints, from
medieval to present day.

Valley Green
Barn Ley, Valley Lane, Buxhall, Stowmarket,
Suffolk IP14 3EB
☎01449 736090 Fax 01449 736090
Email pics@valleygreen.co.uk

Contacts *Joseph Barrere, Colette Barrere*

'Profusion of perennials – all correctly labelled'.
Over 10,000 hardy plant transparencies in stock,
plus watercolours and line drawings available.
Commissions undertaken as well as creative
copywriting.

Victory Archive
See **Popperfoto**

Vin Mag Archives Ltd
203–213 Mare Street, London E8 3QE
☎020 8533 7588 Fax 020 8533 7283
Email piclib.vintage@ndirect.co.uk
Website www.vinmag.com

Formerly the Vintage Magazine Company. A
large collection of movie stills and posters,
photographs, illustrations and advertisements
covering music, glamour, social history, theatre
posters, ephemera, postcards.

John Walmsley Photo Library
See **Education Photos**

Christopher Ware Pictures
65 Trinity Street, Barry, Glamorgan CF62 7EX
☎01446 732816/07802 865999 (mobile) Fax
01446 413471
Email crware@ntlworld.com
Website www.soundandvision–wales.co.uk

Contact *Christopher Ware*

Large collection of images (b&w and colour) of
S.E. Wales, including Barry docks and the Steam
Graveyard, railways, Vale of Glamorgan landscapes, civil and military aircraft over the last 40
years. Images available on CD-ROM or via e-
mail. Digital post-production. Commissions.
Other photographers' work not accepted.

Warwickshire Photographic Survey
See **Birmingham Library Services** under
Library Services

Waterways Photo Library

39 Manor Court Road, Hanwell, London
W7 3EJ
☎020 8840 1659 Fax 020 8567 0605
Email watphot39@aol.com

Contact *Derek Pratt*

A specialist photo library on all aspects of
Britain's inland waterways. Top-quality 35mm-
and medium-format colour transparencies, plus a
large collection of b&w. Rivers and canals,
bridges, locks, aqueducts, tunnels and waterside
buildings. Town and countryside scenes, canal
art, waterway holidays, boating, fishing, wind-
mills, watermills, watersports and wildlife.

Philip Way Photography

2 Green Moor Link, Winchmore Hill,
London N21 2ND
☎020 8360 3034

Contact *Philip Way*

Over 5000 images of St Paul's Cathedral – historical exteriors, interiors and events
(1686–2001).

Weimar Archive

See **Mary Evans Picture Library**

Wellcome Photo Library

210 Euston Road, London NW1 2BE
☎020 7611 8348 Fax 020 7611 8577
Email photolib@wellcome.ac.uk
Website www.wellcome.ac.uk

Contacts *Sonya Brown, Julie Dorrington*

Approximately 180,000 images on the history
of medicine and human culture worldwide,
including modern clinical medicine, healthcare, family life and biomedica.

Eric Whitehead Photography

PO Box 33, Kendal, Cumbria LA9 4SU
☎015394 48894 Fax 015394 48284
Email eric@ewphotography.com
Website www.ewphotography.com

Incorporates the Cumbria Picture Library. The
agency covers local news events, PR and commercial material, also leading library of snooker
images (see **Snookerimages**).

Wild Images

See **RSPCA Photolibrary**

Wilderness Photographic Library

Mill Barn, Broad Raine, Sedbergh, Cumbria
LA10 5ED
☎015396 20196 Fax 015396 21293

Contact *John Noble*

Striking colour images from around the world,
from polar wastes to the Himalayas and Amazon
jungle. Subjects: mountains, Arctic, deserts, ice-
bergs, wildlife, rainforests, glaciers, geysers,
exploration, caves, rivers, eco-tourism, people
and cultures, canyons, seascapes, marine life,
weather, volcanoes, mountaineering, skiing,
geology, conservation, adventure sports, national
parks.

David Williams Picture Library

50 Burlington Avenue, Glasgow G12 0LH
☎0141 339 7823 Fax 0141 337 3031

Colour coverage of Scotland and Iceland.
Smaller collections of the Faroes, France,
Spain, Portugal, Czech Republic, Hungary and
various other European countries; also Western
USA. Landscapes, historical sites, buildings,
geology and physical geography. Medium format and 35mm. Catalogue available. Commissions undertaken.

The Neil Williams Classical Collection

22 Avon, Hockley, Tamworth, Staffordshire
B77 5QA
☎01827 286086 Fax 01827 286086
Email TNWcc@aol.com
Website members.aol.com/TNWCC/
TNWCC.htm

Contact *Neil Williams, BA(Hons), Dip Mus.*

Archive specialising in classical music
ephemera, particularly portraits of composers,
musicians, conductors and opera singers comprising of old and sometimes very rare photographs, postcards, antique prints, cigarette
cards, stamps, First Day Covers, concert programmes, Victorian newspapers, etc. Also
modern photos of composer references such as
museums, statues, busts, paintings, monuments,
memorials and graves. Other subjects covered
include ballet, musical instruments, concert
halls, opera houses, 'music in art', manuscripts,
opera scenes, music–caricatures, bands, orches-
tras and other music groups.

Vaughan Williams Memorial Library

English Folk Dance and Song Society, Cecil
Sharp House, 2 Regent's Park Road, London
NW1 7AY
☎020 7485 2206 ext. 18/19
Fax 020 7284 0523
Email library@efdss.org
Website www.efdss.org

Mainly b&w coverage of traditional/folk music, dance and customs worldwide, focusing on Britain and other English-speaking nations. Photographs date from the late 19th century to the 1990s.

The Wilson Photographic Collection

See **Dundee Central Library** under **Library Services**

Windrush Photos, Wildlife and Countryside Picture Agency

99 Noah's Ark, Kemsing, Sevenoaks, Kent
TN15 6PD
☎01732 763486 Fax 01732 763285

Contact *David Tipling*

Specialists in birds (worldwide) and British wildlife. Photographic and features commissions are regularly undertaken for publications in the UK and overseas. The agency acts as ornithological consultants for all aspects of the media. Offers expert captioning service. **BAPLA** member.

Woodfall Wild Images

17 Bull Lane, Denbigh, Denbighshire
LL16 3SN
☎01745 815903 Fax 01745 814581
Email WWImages@btinternet.com
Website www.woodfall.com

Contact *Theresa Black*

Specialist environmental, conservation, landscape and wildlife photographic library. A constantly expanding collection of images reflecting the natural world and man's effect upon it, both positively and negatively. New pictures of the Arctic, sharks and whales. Please call for a brochure, stock cards or prospective photographer notes. New specialist panoramic coverage available including world city scapes.

World Pictures

85a Great Portland Street, London
W1W 7LT
☎020 7437 2121/7436 0440
Fax 020 7439 1307
Email Worldpictures@btinternet.com
Website www.worldpictures.co.uk

Contacts *David Brenes, Carlo Irek*

600,000 colour transparencies of travel and emotive material.

WWF UK Photolibrary

Panda House, Weyside Park, Catteshall Lane, Godalming, Surrey GU7 1XR
☎01483 412336 Fax 01483 861360

Contact *Patricia Patton*

Specialist library covering natural history, endangered species, conservation, environment, forests, habitats, habitat destruction, and pollution in the UK and abroad. 25,000 colour slides (35mm).

Yemen Pictures

28 Sheen Common Drive, Richmond
TW10 5BN
☎020 7602 1989 Fax 020 7602 1989

Large collection (4000 transparencies) covering all aspects of Yemen – culture, people, architecture, dance, qat, music. Also Africa, Australia, Middle East, and Asia.

York Archaeological Trust Picture Library

Cromwell House, 13 Ogleforth, York
YO1 7FG
☎01904 663000 Fax 01904 663024
Email enquiries@yorkarchaeology.co.uk
Website www.yorkarchaeology.co.uk

Specialist library of rediscovered artifacts, historic buildings and excavations, presented by the creators of the highly acclaimed Jorvik Viking Centre. The main emphasis is on the Roman, Anglo-Saxon and Viking periods.

The John Robert Young Collection

61 De Montfort Road, Lewes, East Sussex
BN7 1SS
☎01273 475216 Fax 01273 475216

Contact *Jennifer Barrett*

50,000 transparencies and monochrome prints on religion, travel and military subjects. Major portfolios: religious communities; the French Foreign Legion; the Spanish Legion; the Royal Marines; the People's Liberation Army (China).

Balancing the Books –
Tax and the Writer

'No man in the country is under the smallest obligation, moral or other, to arrange his affairs as to enable the Inland Revenue to put the largest possible shovel in his stores.

The Inland Revenue is not slow, and quite rightly, to take every advantage which is open to it ... for the purpose of depleting the taxpayer's pockets. And the taxpayer is, in like manner, entitled to be astute to prevent as far as he honestly can the depletion of his means by the Inland Revenue.'

Lord Clyde, *Ayrshire Pullman v Inland Revenue Commissioners, 1929*

Income Tax

What is a professional writer for tax purposes?

Writers are professionals while they are writing regularly with the intention of making a profit; or while they are gathering material, researching or otherwise preparing a publication.

A professional freelance writer is taxed under Case II of Schedule D of the *Income and Corporation Taxes Act 1988*. The taxable income is the amount receivable, either directly or by an agent, on his behalf, less expenses wholly and exclusively laid out for the purpose of the profession. If expenses exceed income, the loss can either be set against other income of the same or preceding years or carried forward and set against future income from writing. If tax has been paid on that other income, a repayment can be obtained, or the sum can be offset against other tax liabilities. Special loss relief can apply in the opening years of the profession. Losses made in the first four years can be set against income of up to three earlier years.

Where a writer receives very occasional payments for isolated articles, it may not be possible to establish that these are profits arising from carrying on a continuing profession. In such circumstances these 'isolated transactions' may be assessed under Case VI of Schedule D of the *Income and Corporation Taxes Act 1988*. Again, expenses may be deducted in arriving at the taxable income but, if expenses exceed income, the loss can only be set against the profits from future isolated transactions, or other income assessable under Case VI.

In the tax year 1996/97 a new tax system came into effect called Self Assessment. Under Self Assessment the onus is on the individual to declare income and expenses correctly. Each writer therefore has to decide whether profits arise from a professional or occasional activity. The consequences of getting it wrong can be expensive by way of interest, penalties and surcharges on additional tax subsequently found to be due. If in any doubt the writer should seek professional advice.

Income

A writer's income includes fees, advances, royalties, commissions, sale of copyrights, reimbursed expenses, etc., from any source anywhere in the world whether or not brought to the UK (non UK resident or domiciled writers should seek professional advice).

Agents

It should be borne in mind that the agent stands in the shoes of the principal. It is not always realised that when the agent receives royalties, fees, advances, etc. on behalf of the author those receipts became the property of the author on the date of their receipt by the agent. This applies for Income Tax and Value Added Tax purposes.

Expenses

A writer can normally claim the following expenses:

(a) Secretarial, typing, proofreading, research. Where payment for these is made to the author's wife or husband they should be recorded and entered in the spouse's tax return as earned income which is subject to the usual personal allowances. If payments reach relevant levels, PAYE should be operated.

(b) Telephone, faxes, Internet costs, computer software, postage, stationery, printing, equipment maintenance, insurance, dictation tapes, batteries, any equipment or office requisites used for the profession.

(c) Periodicals, books (including presentation copies and reference books) and other publications necessary for the profession, but amounts received from the sale of books should be deducted.

(d) Hotels, fares, car running expenses (including repairs, petrol, oil, garaging, parking, cleaning, insurance, road fund tax, depreciation), hire of cars or taxis in connection with:

(i)   business discussions with agents, publishers, co–authors, collaborators, researchers, illustrators, etc.

(ii) travel at home and abroad to collect background material.

As an alternative to keeping details of full car running costs, a mileage rate can be claimed for business use. This rate depends on the engine size and varies from year to year. This is known as the Fixed Profit Car Scheme and is available to writers whose turnover does not exceed the VAT registration limit, currently £54,000.

(e) Publishing and advertising expenses, including costs of proof corrections, indexing, photographs, etc.

(f) Subscriptions to societies and associations, press cutting agencies, libraries, etc., incurred wholly for the purpose of the profession.

(g) Rent, council tax and water rates, etc., the proportion being determined by the ratio of the number of rooms used exclusively for the profession, to the total number of rooms in the residence. But see note on *Capital Gains Tax* below.

(h) Lighting, heating and cleaning. A carefully calculated figure of the business use of these costs can be claimed as a proportion of the total.

(i) Agent's commission, accountancy charges and legal charges incurred wholly in the course of the profession including cost of defending libel actions, damages in so far as they are not covered by insurance, and libel insurance premiums. However, where in a libel case damages are awarded to punish the author for having acted maliciously the action becomes quasi–criminal and costs and damages may not be allowed.

(j) TV and video rental (which may be apportioned for private use), and cinema or theatre tickets, if wholly for the purpose of the profession.

(k) Capital allowances for business equipment. These are now divided into three categories:

   (i) Computer equipment including printers, scanners, cabling, etc. For any such equipment purchased subsequent to 1 April 2000 there is a First Year Allowance of 100%. Prior to that the First Year Allowance was 40% of the cost of the equipment purchased after 1 July 1998 and 50% on equipment purchased after 1 July 1997. For equipment purchased prior to 1 April 2000, after the first year there is an annual Writing Down Allowance of 25% of the reducing balance.

   (ii) On motor cars the allowance is 25% in the first year and 25% of the reducing balance in each successive year limited to £3000 each year.

   (iii) For all other business equipment, e.g. TV, radio, hi-fi sets, tape and video recorders, Dictaphones, office furniture, photographic equipment, etc. there is a First Year Allowance of 40%. After the first year there is an annual Writing Down Allowance of 25% of the reducing balance. The allowances for all the three categories mentioned above will be reduced to exclude personal (non-professional) use where necessary.

(l) Lease rent. The cost of lease rent of equipment is allowable; also on cars, subject to restrictions for private use, and for expensive cars.

(m) Other expenses incurred wholly and exclusively for professional purposes. (Entertaining expenses are not allowable in any circumstances.)

NB It essential to keep detailed records. Diary entries of appointments, notes of fares and receipted bills are much more convincing to the Inland Revenue who are very reluctant to accept estimates. **The Self Assessment regime makes it a legal requirement for proper accounting records to be kept. These records must be sufficient to support the figures declared in the tax return.**

In addition to the above, tax relief is available on:

(a)   Premiums to pension schemes such as the *Society of Authors Retirement Benefits Scheme*. Depending on age, up to 40% of net earned income can be paid into a personal pension plan.
(b)   Covenants to charities. (Deeds executed prior to 6 April 2000.)
(c)   Gift Aid payments to charities. Any amount. (Prior to 6 April 2000, single payments of £250 or more.)

Capital Gains Tax

The exemption from Capital Gains Tax which applies to an individual's main residence does not apply to any part of that residence which is used exclusively for business purposes. The effect of this is that the appropriate proportion of any increase in value of the residence since 31 March 1982 can be taxed when the residence is sold, subject to adjustment for inflation to March 1998 and subsequent length of ownership, at the individual's highest rate of tax.

Writers who own their houses should bear this in mind before claiming expenses for the use of a room for writing purposes. Arguments in favour of making such claims are that they afford some relief now, while Capital Gains Tax in its present form may not stay for ever. Also, where a new house is bought in place of an old one, the gain made on the sale of the first study may be set off against the cost of the study in the new house, thus postponing the tax payment until the final sale. For this relief to apply, each house must have a study and the author must continue his profession throughout. On death there is an exemption of the total Capital Gains of the estate.

Alternatively, writers can claim that their use is non-exclusive and restrict their claim to the cost of extra lighting, heating and cleaning to avoid any Capital Gains Tax liability.

Can a writer average out his income over a number of years for tax purposes?

The Budget in March 2001 introduced measures which will enable writers to average their profits (made wholly or mainly from creative works) over two or more consecutive years. If the profits of the lower year are less than 70% of the profits of the higher year or the profits of one year (but not both) are nil, the author will be able to claim to have the profits averaged. Where the profits of the lower year are more than 70% but less than 75% of the profits of the higher year a pro-rata adjustment is made to both years to reduce the difference between them.

The first years that can be averaged are 2000/1 and 2001/2. These new provisions will be of much greater relevance to the circumstances of many more authors than the previous ones. These (under Section 534 of the Income and Corporation Taxes Act 1988) enabled a writer, in certain circumstances, to spread over two or three fiscal years lump sum payments whenever received and royalties received during two years from the date of first publication or performance of work. These old rules now only apply to sums received before 6 April 2001.

It is also possible to average out income within the terms of publishers' contracts, but professional advice should be taken before signature. Where a husband and wife collaborate as writers, advice should be taken as to whether a formal partnership agreement should be made or whether the publishing agreement should be in joint names.

Is a lump sum paid for an outright sale of the copyright or is part of the copyright exempt from tax?

No. All the money received from the marketing of literary work, by whatever means, is taxable. Some writers, in spite of clear judicial decisions to the contrary, still seem to think that an outright sale of, for instance, the film rights in a book is not subject to tax.

Remaindering

To avoid remaindering authors can usually purchase copies of their own books from the publishers. Monies received from sales are subject to income tax but the cost of books sold should be deducted because tax is only payable on the profit made.

Is there any relief where old copyrights are sold?

Section 535 of the *Income and Corporation Taxes Act 1988* gives relief where not less than ten years after the first publication of the work the author of a literary, dramatic, musical or artistic work assigns the copyright therein wholly or partially, or grants any interest in the copyright by licence, and:

(a) the consideration for the assignment or grant consists wholly or partially of a lump sum payment, the whole amount of which would, but for this section, be included in computing the amount of his/her profits or gains for a single year of assessment, and

(b) the copyright or interest is not assigned or granted for a period of less than two years.

In such cases, the amount received may be spread forward in equal yearly instalments for a maximum of six years, or, where the copyright or interest is assigned or granted for a period of less than six years, for the number of whole years in that period. A 'lump sum payment' is defined to include a non-returnable advance on account of royalties.

It should be noted that a claim may not be made under this section in respect of a payment if a prior claim has been made under Section 534 of the *Income and Corporation Taxes Act 1988* (see section on spreading lump sum payments over two or three years) or vice versa. Relief under Sections 534 and 535 was withdrawn from partnerships some years ago and is withdrawn altogether for sums received after 5 April 2001.

Are royalties payable on publication of a book abroad subject to both foreign tax as well as UK tax?

Where there is a Double Taxation Agreement between the country concerned and the UK, then on the completion of certain formalities no tax is deductible at source by the foreign payer, but such income is taxable in the UK in the ordinary way. When there is no Double Taxation Agreement, credit will be given against UK tax for overseas tax paid. A complete list of countries with which the UK has conventions for the avoidance of double taxation may be obtained from FICO, Inland Revenue, St John's House, Merton Road, Bootle, Merseyside L69 9BB, or a local tax office.

Residence abroad

Writers residing abroad will, of course, be subject to the tax laws ruling in their country of residence, and as a general rule royalty income paid from the United Kingdom can be exempted from deduction of UK tax at source, providing the author is carrying on his profession abroad. A writer who is intending to go and live abroad should make early application for future royalties to be paid without deduction of tax to FICO, address as above. In certain circumstances writers resident in the Irish Republic are exempt from Irish Income Tax on their authorship earnings.

Are grants or prizes taxable?

The law is uncertain. Some Arts Council grants are now deemed to be taxable, whereas most prizes and awards are not, though it depends on the conditions in each case. When submitting the Self Assessment annual returns, such items should be excluded, but reference made to them in the 'Additional Information' box on the self-employment (or partnership) pages.

What is the item 'Class 4 N.I.C.' which appears on my Self Assessment return?

All taxpayers who are self-employed pay an additional national insurance contribution if their earned income exceeds a figure which varies each year. This contribution is described as Class 4 and is calculated when preparing the return. It is additional to the self-employed Class 2 contribution but confers no additional benefits and is a form of levy. It applies to men aged under 65 and women under 60.

Value Added Tax

Value Added Tax (VAT) is a tax currently levied at 17.5% on:

- (a)   the total value of taxable goods and services supplied to consumers,
- (b)   the importation of goods into the UK,
- (c)   certain services or goods from abroad if a taxable person receives them in the UK for the purpose of their business.

Who is taxable?

A writer resident in the UK whose turnover from writing and any other business, craft or art on a self-employed basis is greater than £54,000 annually, before deducting agent's commission, must register with HM Customs & Excise as a taxable person. Turnover includes fees, royalties, advances, commissions, sale of copyright, reimbursed expenses, etc. A business is required to register:

- at the end of any month if the value of taxable supplies in the past twelve months has exceeded the annual threshold; or
- if there are reasonable grounds for believing that the value of taxable supplies in the next twelve months will exceed the annual threshold.

Penalties will be claimed in the case of late registration. A writer whose turnover is below these limits is exempt from the requirements to register for VAT but may apply for voluntary registration and this will be allowed at the discretion of HM Customs & Excise.

A taxable person collects VAT on outputs (turnover) and deducts VAT paid on inputs (taxable expenses) and where VAT collected exceeds VAT paid, must remit the difference to HM Customs & Excise. In the event that input exceeds output, the difference will be refunded by HM Customs & Excise.

Outputs (Turnover)

A writer's outputs are taxable services supplied to publishers, broadcasting organisations, theatre managements, film companies, educational institutions, etc. A taxable writer must invoice, i.e. collect from, all the persons (either individuals or organisations) in the UK for whom supplies have been made, for fees, royalties or other considerations plus VAT. An unregistered writer cannot and must not invoice for VAT. A taxable writer is not obliged to collect VAT on royalties or other fees paid by publishers or others overseas. In practice, agents usually collect VAT for the registered author.

Remit to Customs

The taxable writer adds up the VAT which has been paid on taxable inputs, deducts it from the VAT received and remits the balance to Customs. Business with HM Customs is conducted through the local VAT offices of HM Customs which are listed in local telephone directories, except for VAT returns which are sent direct to the Customs & Excise VAT Central Unit, Alexander House, 21 Victoria Avenue, Southend on Sea, Essex SS99 1AA.

Accounting

A taxable writer is obliged to account to HM Customs & Excise at quarterly intervals. Returns must be completed and sent to VAT Central Unit by the dates shown on the return. Penalties can be charged if the returns are late.

It is possible to account for the VAT liability under the Cash Accounting Scheme (leaflet 731), whereby the author accounts for the output tax when the invoice is paid or royalties, etc., are received. The same applies to the input tax,

Inputs

Taxable at the standard rate if supplier is registered	Taxable at the zero or special rate	Not liable to VAT
Rent of certain commercial premises	Books (zero)	Rent of non-commercial premises
Advertisements in newspapers, magazines, journals and periodicals	Coach, rail and air travel (zero)	Postage
Agent's commission (unless it relates to monies from overseas)	Agent's commission (on monies from overseas)	Services supplied by unregistered persons
Accountant's and solicitor's fees for business matters	Domestic gas and electricity (5%)	Subscriptions to the Society of Authors, PEN, NUJ, etc.
Agency services (typing, copying, etc.)		Insurance
Word processors, typewriters and stationery		
Artists' materials		
Photographic equipment		
Tape recorders and tapes		
Hotel accommodation		*Outside the scope of VAT*
Taxi fares		
Motorcar expenses		PLR (Public Lending Right)
Telephone		Profit shares
Theatres and concerts		Investment income
NB This list is not exhaustive		

but as most purchases are probably on a 'cash basis', this will not make a considerable difference to the author's input tax. This scheme is only applicable to those with a taxable turnover of less than £600,000 and, therefore, is available to the majority of authors. The advantage of this scheme is that the author does not have to account for VAT before receiving payments, thereby relieving the author of a cash flow problem.

It is also possible to pay VAT by nine estimated direct debits, with a final balance at the end of the year (see leaflet 732). This annual accounting method also means that only one VAT return is submitted.

Registration
A writer will be given a VAT registration number which must be quoted on all VAT correspondence. It is the responsibility of those registered to inform those to whom they make supplies of their registration number. The taxable turnover

limit which determines whether a person who is registered for VAT may apply for cancellation of registration is £52,000.

Voluntary registration

A writer whose turnover is below the limits may apply to register. If the writer is paying a relatively large amount of VAT on taxable inputs – agent's commission, accountant's fees, equipment, materials, or agency services, etc. – it may make a significant improvement in the net income to be able to offset the VAT on these inputs. A writer who pays relatively little VAT may find it easier, and no more expensive, to remain unregistered.

Fees and royalties

A taxable writer must notify those to whom he makes supplies of the VAT Registration Number at the first opportunity. One method of accounting for and paying VAT on fees and royalties is the use of multiple stationery for 'self-billing', one copy of the royalty statement being used by the author as the VAT invoice. A second method is for the recipient of taxable outputs to pay fees, including authors' royalties, without VAT. The taxable writer then renders a tax invoice for the VAT element and a second payment, of the VAT element, will be made. This scheme is cumbersome but will involve only taxable authors. Fees and royalties from abroad will count as payments of the exported services and will accordingly be zero-rated.

Agents and accountants

A writer is responsible to HM Customs for making VAT returns and payments. Neither an agent nor an accountant nor a solicitor can remove the responsibility, although they can be helpful in preparing and keeping VAT returns and accounts. Their professional fees or commission will, except in rare cases where the adviser or agent is himself unregistered, be taxable at the standard rate and will represent some of a writer's taxable inputs.

Income Tax – Schedule D

An unregistered writer can claim some of the VAT paid on taxable inputs as a business expense allowable against income tax. However, certain taxable inputs fall into categories which cannot be claimed under the income tax regulations. A taxable writer, who has already claimed VAT on inputs, cannot charge it as a business expense for the purposes of income tax.

Certain services from abroad

A taxable author who resides in the United Kingdom and who receives certain services from abroad must account for VAT on those services at the appropriate tax rate on the sum paid for them. Examples of the type of services concerned include: services of lawyers, accountants, consultants, provision of information and copyright permissions.

Inheritance Tax

Inheritance Tax was introduced in 1984 to replace Capital Transfer Tax, which had in turn replaced Estate Duty, the first of the death taxes of recent times. Paradoxically, Inheritance Tax has reintroduced a number of principles present under the old Estate Duty.

The general principle now is that all assets owned at death are chargeable to tax (currently 40%) except the first £242,000 of the estate and any assets passed to a surviving spouse or a charity. Gifts made more than seven years before death are exempt, but those made within this period are taxed on a sliding scale. No tax is payable at the time of making the gift.

In addition, each individual may currently make gifts of up to £3000 in any year and these will be considered to be exempt. A further exemption covers any number of annual gifts not exceeding £250 to any one person.

If the £3000 is not fully utilised in one year, any unused balance can be carried forward to the following year (but no later). Gifts out of income, which do not reduce one's living standards, are also exempt if they are part of normal expenditure.

At death all assets are valued; they will include any property, investments, life policies, furniture and personal possessions, bank balances and, in the case of authors, the value of copyrights. All, with the sole exception of copyrights, are capable (as assets) of accurate valuation and, if necessary, can be turned into cash. The valuation of copyright is, of course, complicated and frequently gives rise to difficulty. Except where they are bequeathed to the owner's husband or wife, very real problems can be left behind by the author.

Experience has shown that a figure based on two to three years' past royalties may be proposed by the Inland Revenue in their valuation of copyright. However, this may not be reasonable and may require negotiation. If a book is running out of print or if, as in the case of educational books, it may need revision at the next reprint, these factors must be taken into account. In many cases the fact that the author is no longer alive and able to make personal appearances, or provide publicity, or write further works, will result in lower or slower sales. Obviously, this is an area in which help can be given by the publishers, and in particular one needs to know what their future intentions are, what stocks of the books remain, and what likelihood there will be of reprinting.

There is a further relief available to authors who have established that they have been carrying on a business, normally assessable under Case II of Schedule D, for at least two years prior to death. It has been possible to establish that copyrights are treated as business property and in these circumstances, Inheritance Tax 'business property relief' is available. This relief at present is 100% so that the tax saving can be quite substantial. The Inland Revenue may wish to be assured that the business is continuing and consideration should therefore be given to the appointment, in the author's will, of a literary executor who should be a qualified business person or, in certain circumstances, the formation of partnership between the author and spouse, or other relative, to ensure that it is established the business is continuing after the author's death.

If the author has sufficient income, consideration should be given to building up a fund to cover future Inheritance Tax liabilities. One of a number of ways would be to take out a whole life assurance policy which is assigned to the children, or other beneficiaries, the premiums on which are within the annual exemption of £3000. The capital sum payable on the death of the assured is exempt from inheritance tax.

Anyone wondering how best to order his affairs for tax purposes should consult an accountant with specialised knowledge in this field. Experience shows that a good accountant is well worth his fee which, incidentally, so far as it relates to professional matters, is an allowable expense.

The information contained in this section has been prepared by Ian Spring of Moore Stephens, Chartered Accountants, who will be pleased to answer questions on tax problems. Please write to Ian Spring, c/o The Writer's Handbook, 34 Ufton Road, London N1 5BX.

Company Index

Subject Index

Drama/Plays: Libraries

Drama/Plays: Magazines

Drama/Plays: National & Regional TV & Radio

Drama/Plays: Poetry Magazines

Drama/Plays: Prizes

Drama/Plays: Professional Associations

Drama/Plays: Publishers (Commonwealth)

Drama/Plays: Publishers (European)

Drama/Plays: Publishers (Irish)

Drama/Plays: Publishers (UK)

Drama/Plays: Publishers (US)

Fiction: Audio Books

Fiction: Book Clubs

Fiction: Bursaries, Fellowships & Grants

Fiction: Electronic Publishers

Fiction: Festivals

Fiction: Magazines

Fiction: Poetry Magazines

Fiction: Poetry Presses

Fiction: Prizes